THE BRITISH BOXING BOARD OF CONTROL
BOXING
YEARBOOK
2007

EDITED BY
BARRY J. HUGMAN

MAINSTREAM
PUBLISHING

EDINBURGH AND LONDON

First published in Great Britain in 2006 by
MAINSTREAM PUBLISHING COMPANY (EDINBURGH) LTD
7 Albany Street
Edinburgh EH1 3UG

ISBN 978 1 84596 096 4 (from Jan 2007)
ISBN 1 84596 096 3

A catalogue record for this book is available
from the British Library

Typeset and designed by Typecast (Artwork & Design)

Printed and bound in Great Britain by
William Clowes Ltd, Beccles, Suffolk

Contents

TARA BOXING PROMOTIONS & MANAGEMENT

Doughty's Gym, Princess Road, Shaw, Oldham OL2 7AZ
Tel/Fax: 01706-845753 (Office)
Mobile: 07932-085865
Tel: 01706-846762 (Gym)

Trainers: JACK DOUGHTY & GARY FORD
Matchmaker: RICHARD POXON
MC: MICHAEL PASS

<u>BOXERS</u>
Choi Tseveenpurev - WBF World Featherweight Champion
Charles Shepherd - Former British, Commonwealth & IBO World
S.Featherweight Champion
Darren Stubbs - L. Heavyweight
Shinny Bayaar - Flyweight
Wayne Shepherd - Middleweight
Gary Dixon - S. Middleweight

Acknowledgements

Now in its 23rd year, this publication has always been very much a team effort, with many of the original members still participating, and I would like to take time out and thank all those who have helped to hopefully establish the *British Boxing Yearbook* as the '*Wisden*' of British boxing.

As in previous years, I am indebted to the BBBoC's General Secretary, Simon Block, along with Lynne Conway, Helen Oakley, Donna Streeter and newcomer Sarah Aldridge, for their help and support in placing information at my disposal and being of assistance when required. Simon's assistant, Robert Smith, who is also the Southern Area Secretary and a former pro fighter of note, was again extremely helpful, as was John Carey.

On a business front, I would like to thank the BBBoC for their support and Bernard Hart, the Managing Director of the Lonsdale International Sporting Club, for his efforts in helping to organise the annual British Boxing Board of Control Awards Dinner where the book will be officially launched. The Awards Luncheon/Dinner has been an ongoing function since 1984, when it was established by myself and the Board to coincide with the launch of the first *Yearbook* and Bernard, ably backed up by Kymberley and Chas Taylor, helps to make sure that the standard remains top class. At the same time, I would like to thank all of those who advertised within these pages for their support.

Ron Olver has been with the *Yearbook* from day one. Once again, despite it being another difficult year and suffering continued ill-health, Ron has produced the Directory of Ex-Boxers' Associations with the help of his daughter, Pat. A former Assistant Editor of both *Boxing News* and *Boxing World*, he is also well known as the British correspondent of *The Ring*; the author of *The Professionals*; for producing the boxing section within *Encyclopedia Britannica*; his work on *Boxing*, Foyles' library service; and as the former co-editor of the *Boxing News Annual*. His honorary work, which included being the Chairman of the BBBoC Charity Grants' Committee; the Vice-President of many ex-boxers' associations; the Public Relations Officer of the London Ex-Boxers' Association; membership of the Commonwealth Boxing Council as New Zealand's representative; and the International Hall of Fame has, in recent years, seen him honoured by the Boxing Writers' Club, the BBBoC, and the Commonwealth Boxing Council. He has been further honoured by the Boxing Writers' Club, who have made him an Honorary Life Member. It was due to Ron's promptings that the ex-boxers' associations came into being as we now know them, and he will always be remembered by the *Boxing News'* readership as the man responsible for the 'Old Timers' page, now in its 38th year.

Members of the *Yearbook* 'team' who wrote articles for this year's edition and who have recently been published, or are in the process of publishing their own books are: John Jarrett (who is currently working on a biography about the 'Toy Bulldog', Mickey Walker); Bob Lonkhurst (having published *Fen Tiger: The Success of Dave 'Boy' Green*, which was his fourth biography in seven years, Bob took time out to catch up with his life. Now refreshed, he is once again thinking seriously of producing a book on Eric Boon as a natural follow up to the Green story); Ralph Oates (as a boxing quizbook specialist, Ralph is hopeful that his latest project, the *Muhammad Ali Quizbook*, will be on sale this coming April. He is also working on another book that will be titled *Aspects of Heavyweight Boxing*); Tracey Pollard (continues to work on a book about the life and times of Brian London, the former British heavyweight champion); Keith Robinson (is soon to publish *Lanky Bob: The Life, Times and Contemporaries of Bob Fitzsimmons*); Bert Blewett (the former editor of South Africa's *Boxing World* magazine for 27 years and the author of *The A-Z of World Boxing*, Bert is currently working on another publication) and Wynford Jones (has recently published the *Class of the '60s*, which covers the Eddie Thomas stable of fighters during that period).

Yet again, Wynford, a Class 'A' referee and a big supporter of boxing, came to my aid when travelling to the Board's offices on a regular basis in order to collate vital data required for this publication. Other members of the *Yearbook* 'team' are Bob Yalen, who has covered boxing with ABC across the world and looks after the World Title Bouts' section; Harold Alderman, an unsung hero who has spent over 40 years researching the early days of boxing through to modern times, has extended the Early Gloved Championship Boxing section to take on board records of some of the men who practiced their trade in the period prior to 1909; Chris Kempson, who produces 'Highlights from the Amateur Season', is our man in the world of amateur boxing; Eric Armit, the Chairman of the Commonwealth Boxing Council and a leading authority on boxers' records throughout the world, is responsible for the 'A-Z of Current World Champions'; and Derek O'Dell, a former amateur boxer and Chairman of Croydon EBA, produces the 'Obituaries" section.

Regarding photographs, as in previous years the great majority were produced by Les Clark (Les also puts together 'A Boxing Quiz with a Few Below the Belt' within these pages), who has possibly the largest library of both action and poses from British rings over the last 20 years or more. If anyone requires a copy of a photo that has appeared in the *Yearbook* credited to Les, or requires a list, he can be reached at 352 Trelawney Avenue, Langley, Berks SL3 7TS. Other photos were supplied by my good friend Philip Sharkey. More help came in the shape of Larry Braysher, a well-known collector, who supplied several photos for the 'Obituaries" and 'Early Gloved Championship Boxing' sections and the 'Bunny Johnson: Britain's First Black Heavyweight Champion' article.

Also, additional input came from Neil Blackburn (who yet again provided information to make the 'Obituaries" section as complete as possible); Mrs Enza Jacoponi, the Secretary of the European Boxing Union (EBU Championship data covering the past 12 months); Simon Block (Commonwealth and British Championship data); Patrick Myler (Irish amateur boxing); Malcolm Collins (Welsh amateur boxing); Moira, John McKay and Brian Donald (Scottish amateur boxing); Peter Foley, Dave Cockell, Saphire Lee, Jenny Peake, Dave Norman and Harry Pritchard (English Amateur Boxing); Mary from the National Association of Clubs for Young People and Robert Smith, John Jarrett, Brian McAllister, Ken Morton and Les Potts (Area title data). Last but not least on the boxing information front, I must mention John Sheppard, of BoxRec.Com, who kindly delivered the current British-based boxers' records in the correct order for me to start my audit.

Finally, my thanks go to Jean Bastin, who continued to produce a high standard of typesetting and design, and my wife, Jennifer, who looks after the proof reading.

EVANS-WATERMAN PROMOTIONS LTD
Licensed to the British Boxing Board of Control
88 WINDSOR ROAD, MAIDENHEAD, BERKS SL6 2DJ
Tel: 01628 623640   Fax: 01628 684633
Mobile: 07768 954643
e-mail: boxevans@yahoo.co.uk

CURRENT LIST

HEAVYWEIGHTS			WELTERWEIGHT		
Roman Greenberg	–	22-0-0	Spiros Ioannidis	–	Debut
Jacklord Jacobs	–	5-3-5			
Luke Simpkin	–	9-24-3	**LIGHT-WELTERWEIGHTS**		
			Shane Watson	–	5-0-0
LIGHT-HEAVYWEIGHTS			Ruben Giles	–	1-0-0
Shpetim Hoti	–	2-9-2			
Nick Okoth	–	3-10-2	**LIGHTWEIGHTS**		
			Gareth Couch	–	7-0-0
SUPER-MIDDLEWEIGHT			Chill John	–	8-7-0
Matthew Barr	–	13-4-0	David Mulholland	–	1-0-0
MIDDLEWEIGHT			**SUPER-FEATHERWEIGHT**		
Geard Ajetovic	–	11-1-0	Henry Castle	–	11-3-0
LIGHT-MIDDLEWEIGHTS			**SUPER-BANTAMWEIGHT**		
Anthony Young	–	1-1-0	Eilon Kedem	–	2-0-1
John-Paul Temple	–	4-10-1			
George Katsimpas	–	2-0-0			

WEST LONDON'S FASTEST RISING STABLE
Trainers: Dave Laxen - Darren Whitman

Introduction

by Barry J. Hugman

It gives me great pleasure to welcome you to the 23rd edition of the *British Boxing Yearbook*. The format hasn't changed too much over the years, certainly not since the 1993 edition, as myself and the team continue to monitor and update the current goings on, while also continuing to research the past and pass on our findings.

Beginning with the modern era, once again we have decided to stay with the way we produce Active British Based-Boxers: Complete Records. The decision to have one alphabet, instead of separating champions, being taken on the grounds that because there are so many champions these days – British, Commonwealth, European, IBF, WBA, WBC, WBO, and more recently WBU, IBO, WBF, etc, etc, and a whole host of Inter-Continental and International titles – it would cause confusion rather than what was really intended. If you wish to quickly locate whether or not a boxer fought during the past season (1 July 2005 to 30 June 2006) then the Boxers' Record Index at the back of the book is the place to look. Also, as in the very first edition, we chart the promotions in Britain throughout the season, thus enabling one to refer to the exact venue within a boxer's record.

Regarding our records, if a fighter is counted out standing up we have continued to show it as a stoppage rather than that of a kayo or technical kayo, as in fights where the referee dispenses with the count. Thus fights are recorded as count outs (the count being tolled with the fighter still on the canvas), retirements (where a fighter is retired on his stool) and referee stopped contest. Of course, other types of decisions would take in draws, no contests, and no decisions. In these days of health and safety fears, more and more boxers are being counted out either standing up or when initially floored, especially when a referee feels that the man on the receiving end is unable to defend himself adequately or requires immediate medical attention. One of the reasons that we have yet to discriminate between cut-eye stoppages and other types of endings, is because a fighter who is stopped because of cuts is often on his way to a defeat in the first place. Thus, if you want to get a true reflection on the fight it is probably better to consult the trade paper, *Boxing News*, rather than rely on a referee's decision to tell you all you want to know; the recorded result merely being a guide.

Continuing the trend, there are always new articles to match the old favourites. Regular features such as Home and Away with British Boxers (John Jarrett), World Title Bouts During the Season (Bob Yalen), A-Z of Current World Champions (Eric Armit), Highlights from the Amateur Season (Chris Kempson), Directory of Ex-Boxers' Associations (Ron Olver), Obituaries (Derek O'Dell) and two regular quizzes (Ralph Oates and Les Clark), etc, being supported this year with interesting articles such as Jack Lindsay: A Lifetime in Boxing (Bob Lonkhurst); Gary De'Roux: A Man on a Mission (Ralph Oates); Colin Jones: The Gorseinon Gravedigger (Wynford Jones); Bunny Johnson: Britain's First Black Heavyweight Champion (Tracey Pollard); The Oliver Family and Finchley & District ABC (Keith R. Robinson); and Boxing's Biggest Success Story (Bert Blewett).

Elsewhere, hopefully, you will find all you want to know about British Area, English, Celtic, British, Commonwealth, European and world title bouts that took place in 2005-2006, along with the amateur championships that were held in England, Scotland, Wales and Ireland, as well as being able to access details on champions from the past, both amateur and professional. This year, I have taken the decision to drop the amateur international tournaments as they have virtually got lost these days among a welter of multi-nationals, which space, unfortunately, does not allow us to cover.

Historically, what was started several years ago under the heading of Early Gloved Championship Boxing, has now been extended to presenting records of some of the leading fighters of the pre-1909 days. Much of this work was due to Harold Alderman painstakingly piecing together results for the pre-Lonsdale Belt and named-weight division period. There are still many who believe as gospel much of what was reported down the ages by 'respected' men such as Nat Fleischer, the owner of The *Ring Magazine* and the *Ring Record Book*, and then copied by numerous historians who failed to grasp what the sport was really like before the First World War. Basically, boxing prior to the period in question was a shambles, following bare fists with an assortment of driving gloves, knuckle gloves, and two-ounce gloves, etc, until it arrived at what we recognise today. There were no commissions, newspapermen becoming all-powerful by naming their own champions at all kinds of weights, and in much of America the sport was illegal, no-decision contests rescuing it from being abolished. If you thought today was dire, then boxing prior to that period was almost impossible in all divisions bar the heavyweights. Because travel was difficult and news travelled slowly, fighters were able to move from town to town proclaiming themselves to be the best and 'ringers' constantly prevailed. With today's research being aided by access to early newspapers, and the use of computers, it is becoming clear that men like Fleischer 'took' the best fighters of the day and then 'fitted' them into the named-weight divisions we now know so well. If that is still as clear as mud, then turn to the pages in question.

Abbreviations and Definitions used in the record sections of the Yearbook:
PTS (Points), CO (Count Out), RSC (Referee Stopped Contest), RTD (Retired), DIS (Disqualification), NC (No Contest), ND (No Decision).

7

British Boxing Board of Control Ltd: Structure

(Members of the Commonwealth Boxing Council and European Boxing Union)

PRESIDENT	Lord Brooks of Tremorfa DL
CHAIRMAN	Charles Giles
VICE CHAIRMAN	John Handelaar
GENERAL SECRETARY	Simon Block

ADMINISTRATIVE STEWARDS
Baroness Golding*
Sir Geoffrey Inkin OBE
John Rees QC
Dave Roden
Andrew Vanzie*
Billy Walker*
John Williamson

REPRESENTATIVE STEWARDS
Tony Behan
Geoff Boulter
Michael Collier*
Bernard Connolly
Ken Honniball
Alec Kirby*
Kevin Leafe*
Reginald Long*
Phil Lundgren
Ron Pavett
Fred Potter
Brian Renney*
Derry Treanor*

STEWARDS OF APPEAL*
Robin Simpson QC
Geoffrey Finn
William Tudor John
Robert Kidby
Prof. Andrew Lees
Timothy Langdale QC
John Mathew QC
Colin Ross-Munro QC
Peter Richards FRCS
Nicholas Valios QC

HONORARY STEWARDS*
Sir Henry Cooper OBE, KSG
Mary Peters DBE
Leonard Read QPM
Bill Sheeran

HONORARY MEDICAL CONSULTANT*
Dr Roger C. Evans FRCP

HONORARY PARLIAMENTARY CONSULTANT*
Jimmy Wray MP
Ian Stewart MP

LEGAL CONSULTANT
Michael Boyce DL

MARKETING CONSULTANT
Nicky Piper MBE

HEAD OFFICE
The Old Library
Trinity Street
Cardiff CF10 1BH
Tel: 02920 367000
Fax: 02920 367019
E-mail: sblock@bbbofc.com
Website: www.bbbofc.com

* Not directors of the company

AREA COUNCILS - AREA SECRETARIES

AREA NO 1 (SCOTLAND)
Brian McAllister
11 Woodside Crescent, Glasgow G3 7UL
Telephone 0141 3320392. Fax 0141 3312029
E-Mail bmacallister@mcallisters-ca.com

AREA NO 2 (NORTHERN IRELAND)
John Campbell
8 Mount Eden Park, Belfast, Northern Ireland BT9 6RA
Telephone 02890 683310. Fax 02890 683310
Mobile 07715 044061

AREA NO 3 (WALES)
Robert Smith
The Old Library, Trinity Street, Cardiff CF10 1BH
Telephone 02920 367000
Fax 02920 367019
E-Mail rsmith@bbbofc.com

AREA NO 4 (NORTHERN)
(Northumberland, Cumbria, Durham, Cleveland, Tyne and Wear, North Yorkshire [north of a line drawn from Whitby to Northallerton to Richmond, including these towns].)
John Jarrett
5 Beechwood Avenue, Gosforth, Newcastle upon Tyne NE3 5DH
Telephone/Fax 01912 856556
E-Mail john.jarrett5@btopenworld.com

AREA NO 5 (CENTRAL)
(North Yorkshire [with the exception of the part included in the Northern Area - see above], Lancashire, West and South Yorkshire, Greater Manchester, Merseyside and Cheshire, Isle of Man, North Humberside.)
Richard Jones
1 Churchfields, Croft, Warrington, Cheshire WA3 7JR
Telephone/Fax 01925 768132
E-Mail r.m.jones@mmu.ac.uk

AREA NO 6 (SOUTHERN)
(Bedfordshire, Berkshire, Buckinghamshire, Cambridgeshire, Channel Islands, Isle of Wight, Essex, Hampshire, Kent, Hertfordshire, Greater London, Norfolk, Suffolk, Oxfordshire, East and West Sussex.)
Robert W. Smith
The Old Library, Trinity Street, Cardiff CF10 1BH
Telephone 02920 367000. Fax: 02920 367019
E-Mail rsmith@bbbofc.com

AREA NO 7 (WESTERN)
(Cornwall, Devon, Somerset, Dorset, Wiltshire, Avon, Gloucestershire.)
Robert Smith
The Old Library, Trinity Street, Cardiff CF10 1BH
Telephone 02920 367000
Fax 02920 367019
E-Mail rsmith@bbbofc.com

AREA NO 8 (MIDLANDS)
(Derbyshire, Nottinghamshire, Lincolnshire, Salop, Staffordshire, Herefordshire and Worcestershire, Warwickshire, West Midlands, Leicestershire, South Humberside, Northamptonshire.)
Les Potts
1 Sunnyside Villas, Gnosall, Staffordshire
Telephone 01785 823641. Mobile 07973 533835
E-Mail lezpotts@hotmail.com

Foreword

by Simon Block *(General Secretary, British Boxing Board of Control)*

Despite the fantastic success of both Ricky Hatton and Clinton Woods over the last 12 months, for many Joe Calzaghe's emphatic win over Jeff Lacy in March will be the outstanding single performance of the year. In last year's 'Foreword' I commented on the need for Joe to take part in a career-defining contest and this seems to have been the one.

Many of us believed that Joe could win the contest, but I think very few will have thought that he would have done so in quite the overwhelming manner that he did. The much vaunted power and skill of Lacy really played no part in the contest and I believe he should have been pulled out of the contest by his corner two or three rounds before the end. He had shown nothing in all the previous rounds to suggest that he was going to find the big one to turn the contest around. It is not losing that ends a boxer's career it is hard contests such as this one. Promoter Frank Warren's tough job now will be to match Joe again in a contest against a meaningful opponent with a negotiated purse that makes it economically possible. Although boxing politics may negate the possibility of domestic showdowns against either Clinton Woods or Carl Froch, we cannot rule out either possibility within the next 12 months.

On the home front I was sorry that the clash of young prospects, John Murray and Kevin Mitchell, did not take place. That contest was proposed by the Board as a final eliminator for the British super-featherweight championship, but even without it this has been an excellent year in terms of the quality of some of the main event contests that have taken place. It is pleasing to see that so many over the last 12 months were for what I always call 'Real Titles' such as British, Commonwealth and European, along with those of the four main world sanctioning organisations, and there was even one non-title contest, Earl v Romanov, a rare event for headline television contests these days, that was among those considered to be included in the category of 'Contest of the Year'. As Secretary to the Board's Awards Committee I can testify that in all the years I have been doing the job this has been the hardest year of all, not merely to decide on a winner of that category but which of the exciting contests that have taken place we were going to have to leave off the list of nominees. It was also pleasing to see that not one promoter dominated all the contests under consideration and contests promoted by Barry Hearn, Frank Warren, Hennessy Sports, Frank Maloney and Paul Boyce were all under consideration.

The contest that perhaps should have been the 'Contest of the Year' was the December 2005 Commonwealth heavyweight championship clash between Danny Williams and Audley Harrison. In terms of appeal beforehand this was like the great old days of Wembley and the Albert Hall, the Excel Arena in East London being sold out, and I had great difficulty in purchasing some tickets myself. The fact that ITV recorded eight million viewers represented a massive public interest in an age when multiplicity of channel choice means that sport will only rarely attract double figure million viewers, as was the norm in decades gone by for major events. The tournament itself turned out to be an excellent one with good undercard contests and a very good atmosphere among the capacity crowd, the only letdown being the contest itself, something both Audley and Danny have had to acknowledge. Danny did rehabilitate himself in a winning crowd-pleasing punch-up against Matt Skelton in February 2006, but was disappointing when losing to Skelton in the return. Audley, after suffering a further loss in America, is now picking up the pieces of his career with the much respected trainer, Buddy McGirt, endeavouring to help him achieve his undoubted potential.

The injuries sustained by Valery Odin as a result of his contest in Hartlepool at the end of April 2006 and the very slow recovery progress that he has thus far made underlines to us all the dangers of this sport. It also reminds us of the need to constantly strive to minimise any unnecessary risk. To this end a Sub-Committee sat in June 2006 to consider what further progress can be made and although at this stage this merely involves tweaking some of the controls already in place there is a resolve to constantly monitor the situation to ensure best practice in the interests of the boxers.

In last year's 'Foreword' I paid tribute to my dear friend and supporter Bob Graham who died shortly before publication of the Yearbook, but it was only a matter of days later that I lost another dear friend in Dr Oswald 'Ossie' Ross, who was a key element of the Board's medical controls over the previous couple of decades and who was of immense help to me in my career. The Board and the sport of boxing can ill afford to lose people of such quality who contribute so much for no financial reward.

Once again I am grateful to my staff at the Board's Head Office for helping me through another year and who, for most of the year, work under extreme pressure doing so efficiently and courteously. Thanks must go to the army of volunteer Inspectors, Area Secretaries, Area Medical Officers and Council Members who assist without any payment in the Board's work and I am always grateful to my bosses, the Stewards of the Board, who continue to employ me and who are also all volunteers.

Editor Barry Hugman has not been too well of late but he and his team have still been able to produce this excellent annual record, which only goes to show that you cannot keep a good man down for long.

10

British Boxing Board of Control Awards

Now in its 23rd year, the BBBoC Awards Ceremony will be held in London later this year and will once again be co-hosted by the Lonsdale International Sporting Club's Bernard Hart. The winners of these prestigious statuettes, designed in the form of a boxer, are selected by a well-informed panel of judges who make a judgement on the season as a whole at an annual meeting.

British Boxer of the Year: The outstanding British Boxer at any weight. 1984: Barrry McGuigan. 1985: Barry McGuigan. 1986: Dennis Andries. 1987: Lloyd Honeyghan. 1988: Lloyd Honeyghan. 1989: Dennis Andries. 1990: Dennis Andries. 1991: Dave McAuley. 1992: Colin McMillan. 1993: Lennox Lewis. 1994: Steve Robinson. 1995: Nigel Benn. 1996: Prince Naseem Hamed. 1997: Robin Reid. 1998: Carl Thompson. 1999: Billy Schwer. 2000: Glenn Catley. 2001: Joe Calzaghe. 2002: Lennox Lewis. 2003: Ricky Hatton. 2004: Scott Harrison. 2005: Ricky Hatton.

British Contest of the Year: Although a fight that took place in Europe won the 1984 Award, since that date, the Award, presented to both participants, has applied to the best all-action contest featuring a British boxer in a British ring. 1984: Jimmy Cable v Said Skouma. 1985: Barry McGuigan v Eusebio Pedroza. 1986: Mark Kaylor v Errol Christie. 1987: Dave McAuley v Fidel Bassa. 1988: Tom Collins v Mark Kaylor. 1989: Michael Watson v Nigel Benn. 1990: Orlando Canizales v Billy Hardy. 1991: Chris Eubank v Nigel Benn. 1992: Dennis Andries v Jeff Harding. 1993: Andy Till v Wally Swift Jnr. 1994: Steve Robinson v Paul Hodkinson. 1995: Steve Collins v Chris Eubank. 1996: P. J. Gallagher v Charles Shepherd. 1997: Spencer Oliver v Patrick Mullings. 1998: Carl Thompson v Chris Eubank. 1999: Shea Neary v Naas Scheepers. 2000: Simon Ramoni v Patrick Mullings. 2001: Colin Dunne v Billy Schwer. 2002: Ezra Sellers v Carl Thompson. 2003: David Barnes v Jimmy Vincent. 2004: Michael Gomez v Alex Arthur. 2005: Jamie Moore v Michael Jones.

Overseas Boxer of the Year: For the best performance by an overseas boxer in a British ring. 1984: Buster Drayton. 1985: Don Curry. 1986: Azumah Nelson. 1987: Maurice Blocker. 1988: Fidel Bassa. 1989: Brian Mitchell. 1990: Mike McCallum. 1991: Donovan Boucher. 1992: Jeff Harding. 1993: Crisanto Espana. 1994: Juan Molina. 1995: Mike McCallum. 1996: Jacob Matlala. 1997: Ronald Wright. 1998: Tim Austin. 1999: Vitali Klitschko. 2000: Keith Holmes. 2001: Harry Simon. 2002: Jacob Matlala. 2003: Manuel Medina. 2004: In-Jin Chi. 2005: Joshua Okine.

Special Award: Covers a wide spectrum, and is an appreciation for services to boxing. 1984: Doctor Adrian Whiteson. 1985: Harry Gibbs. 1986: Ray Clarke. 1987: Hon. Colin Moynihan. 1988: Tom Powell. 1989: Winston Burnett. 1990: Frank Bruno. 1991: Muhammad Ali. 1992: Doctor Oswald Ross. 1993: Phil Martin. 1994: Ron Olver. 1995: Gary Davidson. 1996: Reg Gutteridge and Harry Carpenter. 1997: Miguel Matthews and Pete Buckley. 1998: Mickey Duff and Tommy Miller. 1999: Jim Evans and Jack Lindsay. 2000: Henry Cooper. 2001: John Morris and Leonard 'Nipper' Read. 2002: Roy Francis and Richie Woodhall. 2003: Michael Watson. 2004: Dennie Mancini and Bob Paget. 2005: Barry McGuigan.

Sportsmanship Award: This Award recognises boxers who set a fine example, both in and out of the ring. 1986: Frank Bruno. 1987: Terry Marsh. 1988: Pat Cowdell. 1989: Horace Notice. 1990: Rocky Kelly. 1991: Wally Swift Jnr. 1992: Duke McKenzie. 1993: Nicky Piper. 1994: Francis Ampofo. 1995: Paul Wesley. 1996: Frank Bruno. 1997: Lennox Lewis. 1998: Johnny Williams. 1999: Brian Coleman. 2000: Michael Ayers and Wayne Rigby. 2001: Billy Schwer. 2002: Mickey Cantwell. 2003: Francis Ampofo. 2004: Dale Robinson and Jason Booth. 2005: Ricky Hatton and Kostya Tszyu.

Ricky Hatton, the proud winner of the 2005 British 'Boxer of the Year' award, poses with Charles Giles, the Chairman of the BBBoC   Les Clark

12

Boxing's Biggest Success Story

by Bert Blewett

History will record that black empowerment was boxing's biggest success story of the 20th century. At the dawn of the year 1900 only one black man – featherweight George Dixon – held a world title and he lost it to Terry McGovern nine days later!

Today only a handful of whites can truthfully call themselves world champions, and this despite the fact that the number of weight divisions in the sport has increased from eight to 17. Moreover, it was only in the second half of the 20th century that blacks – boxers, promoters, trainers, managers and officials – began to get the breaks that enabled them to compete on even terms with whites. It might be hard for many to imagine the hardships that blacks faced at the dawn of the 20th century, but you need only read the American and Australian press before and after the world heavyweight title fight between Jack Johnson and Tommy Burns in Sydney in December 1908 to detect the racist tone.

Jack London's emotional report from ringside for the *New York Herald* did little to placate white resentment, but the Australian media was even more irresponsible. *Fairplay*, an Australian weekly, called Johnson a "huge primordial ape", while the *Bulletin's* cartoons likened the black American to a shaven-headed reptile.

It was this kind of naked racism that encouraged many to search for a white heavyweight capable of beating Johnson. With hindsight we now know that it was London who was largely to blame for the start of the deplorable White Hope Era in boxing. The famous author ended his report on the Johnson-Burns fight with an appeal to former champion Jim Jeffries. "But one thing remains," he wrote, "Jeffries must emerge from his alfalfa farm and remove that smile from Johnson's face. Jeff, it's up to you". "Nix, nothing doing," Jeffries replied but despite his reluctance, 18 months later he was persuaded to return to the ring in a futile attempt to regain the title. Johnson knocked him out in the 15th round.

The White Hope Era ended in April 1915 when Jess Willard knocked out Johnson in the 26th round in Havana, Cuba to become the new world champion. "Now mebbe de'll let me alone", Johnson said afterwards. Fat chance! For the next 20 years Johnson was blamed for having made it virtually impossible for another black man to challenge for the heavyweight championship of the world. Worth mentioning that it wasn't only in the United States that Johnson's outrageous lifestyle – his fancy clothes, his expensive cigarette holders, his white wives and his luxurious motor cars – caused widespread resentment. A proposed title fight between Johnson and Bombardier Billy Wells at Earl's Court in London in September 1911 was cancelled when the church, the police, the Home Office and almost everyone else objected.

It took a quietly-spoken, modest heavyweight nicknamed the 'Brown Bomber' to finally break most of the racial barriers. And this despite the fact that Joe Louis also often dated white women like Hollywood stars Lana Turner and Sonia Heine. The big difference was that Louis' sex life was a well-kept secret.

Against all odds, Louis was given a title shot at Jim Braddock in 1937 and when Joe won on a knockout in the eighth round, the so-called 'gentlemen's agreement' between white boxing men (designed to keep another black from winning the richest prize in sport) was broken for ever. And yet when Louis first met Mike Jacobs in 1934, the American promoter warned him not to make the same mistakes as Johnson. "He told me then there was a colour line – at that time a gentlemen's agreement – and that there wouldn't be another coloured champion", Louis recalled years later.

It explained why Harry Wills, a talented black heavyweight, never got the chance to challenge Jack Dempsey for the title in the 1920s, even though promoter Tex Rickard went as far as to have tickets printed for the fight. And it explained why even those who did acknowledge Louis's greatness in the early days of his career, invariably apologised for Joe's race with the familiar words "…even though coloured".

It took political dictators like Benito Mussolini and Adolf Hitler to swing the balance of public opinion in Louis' favour in the 1930s. Louis even got an endorsement from the US president, Franklin D. Roosevelt, who met with the 'Brown Bomber' before his rematch with Max Schmeling in 1938 and after feeling Joe's biceps, told him: "We're depending on those muscles for America". Louis knocked out Schmeling in the first round. "To be honest, on that night nobody would have beaten Louis", Schmeling told me years later. "They poisoned his mind against me and he fought like an animal. I never had a chance".

When Louis retired as undefeated champion in 1949 an editorial in *Life* magazine credited him with having opened the doors not only for other black sportsmen but also for entertainers and for the appointment of Dr Ralph Bunche as the United Nations mediator in what was then called Palestine.

"How important was Joe"? Dick Edwards, a veteran black sportswriter for the *New Age Press*, asked in 1987. "If Joe hadn't won that title, I don't know if we'd have ever gotten out of the jailhouse".

Even so, boxing remained segregated in some of the southern states of America until the late 1940s, which was about the time that the colour bar in British boxing was also lifted. Dick Turpin celebrated the belated change in the rules by beating Vince Hawkins over 15 rounds at the Aston Villa football ground on 28 June 1948 to win the British middleweight title.

On the other hand, it wasn't until December 1973 that the first mixed fight officially took place in South Africa, Pierre Fourie challenging Bob Foster before a segregated audience in Johannesburg for the light heavyweight championship of the world. Despite white fears, the promotion was a great success and once again the sport of boxing had taken the lead in breaking down racial barriers.

An age where black is beautiful had finally dawned and long before the end of the 20th century Don King had proved that he was arguably the greatest promoter in the history of the sport; Bobby Lee and Larry Hazzard became top administrators, and boxers like Joe Frazier, Larry Holmes, Sugar Ray Leonard, Mike Tyson, Marvin Hagler and Thomas Hearns became household names worldwide. King's induction into the International Boxing Hall of Fame in 2001 was marred by bad press in the United States, but nor was the American media alone in showing their dislike of the man who single-handedly has revolutionised world boxing.

Both the FBI and the IRS had done their damndest to nail King in the past. In fact, the first time I met King in his New York offices in 1983 he welcomed me warmly, made sure I had everything I needed and then apologised for having to rush off to court. "Everyone wants to sue me", he said. "From boxing bums to the FBI. I tell them all to join the queue".

King has never attempted to hide his past but he claims he was rehabilitated in prison and his police record was wiped clean when he was given a pardon by Ohio governor, James Rhodes. Even so, few in the American media are prepared to accept him without reservation as the 'world's greatest boxing promoter'.

The world sanctioning bodies have shown no such reservations and between them the World Boxing Association, the World Boxing Council and the International Boxing Federation have named King the 'Promoter of the Century' and the 'Greatest Promoter of All Time'.

Last but not least there was Cassius Marcellus Clay, who changed his name to Muhammad Ali and called himself 'The Greatest'. Well, he certainly got that right! Ali was unquestionably the standout sports star of the 20th century: a man who not only had a profound influence on boxing but whose handsome face became the most recognisable in sport.

Ali brought qualities to the ring that no other heavyweight champion ever had. Most of the old champions relied almost entirely on their physical prowess to win fights. Ali added another dimension: the mental edge. He had a waspish tongue and he used it to browbeat one opponent after another.

In many, respects Ali was a product of his time – the Swinging '60s – when all the old values were being questioned and when young people were determined to make their voices heard. A heavyweight champion who claimed that he could "float like butterfly and sting like a bee" was new to boxing and not everyone was convinced that he really belonged. And when he told reporters at the height of the Vietnam War that "I ain't got no quarrel with them Viet Congs", the establishment was quick to ostracize him (in an earlier age he would probably have been burnt at the stake). Politicians labelled him a 'traitor' and the boxing controlling bodies stripped him of his world title. To his credit, Ali stood by his convictions even though it cost him three of the best years of his boxing life.

Ali's contribution to black empowerment in boxing should never be underestimated, although it was largely boxers like Joe Louis and Sugar Ray Robinson who paved the way for the subsequent success of the black man in the sport. Even so, few will deny that Ali's name has since been cast in stone and that only time is likely to erode it.

Two of the great black fighters who benefitted from exposure afforded them were Sugar Ray Leonard (left) and Marvin Hagler. The pair are seen acknowledging each other, prior to Hagler losing his WBC middleweight title to Leonard on points over 12 rounds in Las Vegas on 6 April 1987, in what would be the loser's last fight   Tom Casino

Bunny Johnson: Britain's First Black Heavyweight Champion

by Tracey Pollard

It all began with table tennis and led to Bunny Johnson becoming the first black British heavyweight champion, the Commonwealth champion at the same weight and the undefeated British light-heavyweight champion. He also had the added distinction of being the only man to win the titles in that order, rather than moving up in weight.

It was Colin's fault. As a young boy in Jamaica Bunny played a lot of table tennis. "Table tennis was very popular", he recalls, "All you really needed was a table or something remarkably like a table. But this lad, Colin, kept beating me so, as usual, I went to my favourite place, the library, and learnt all about backhands and so on". On subsequent trips to the library, Bunny started to hang around the sports section and he was fascinated by a story in a book by someone called Nat Fleischer. It was all about a boxer who, against all the odds, became the first black heavyweight champion of the world. Plus he was called Johnson! Bunny was captivated. Jack Johnson became his inspiration.

This was by no means an epiphany though, and it would be some time before he decided to become a boxer. Fitzroy Dexter Johnson, nicknamed 'Bunny' by his family, was an avid reader and also studied books on law. By the time he came to England as a 16-year-old youngster he was torn between becoming a lawyer or a boxer. In the end, to his mother's disappointment, boxing seemed to offer a more immediate escape from life in a factory so that was that. Bunny joined Kyrle Hall amateur boxing club, which was next to Birmingham University. "I told everyone that I was going to be a boxer. When I found a gym I was so excited and I said that I was going to train and be the first black heavyweight champion of Great Britain. When I look back I can't believe I said that as I hadn't had a single fight!" He taught himself everything he could from books on boxing and studied the more experienced members of the gym and always remembers the date of his first fight because it was in the same month in 1964 when Ali beat Liston for the world title. Bunny confidently entered the ring for the first time, armed with all the knowledge he had acquired from hours of fervent study and his conviction in his destiny. His destiny suffered a minor setback when he lost, but he wasn't unduly disheartened though, being just keen to get back in the gym.

Bunny remembers watching the boxing on telly with his dad. "Dad was always bent over the TV trying to get a picture. One of the first fights I remember seeing was a film of the fight between Brian London and Dick Richardson". Now, this was probably not the ideal choice of fight to educate a youngster in the art of the noble sport, but it inspired the teenage Bunny as he recently recalled in Brian's presence: "I was really impressed, and one of the things I learned was how to throw a left jab", 'And a head', added Brian wryly.

Bunny had 36 amateur fights and won 30 of them, but his only interest was in becoming a pro. As an amateur the opponent he was most impressed with was Zbigniew Pietrzykowski, who had been defeated for the gold medal by Cassius Clay in the Rome Olympics in 1960. "He was the very best I fought as an amateur. I was doing reasonably well, but I could feel the difference in class, especially in the way he avoided my punches. I didn't really feel that way about any of my professional opponents, although there was one time that I felt I was seriously stepping up in class and that was when I sparred with Henry Cooper. I'd had about 20 fights and was so excited. It was only sparring but it was such a step up".

Bunny entered the professional ranks eager to pursue his goal, but he wasn't naive and knew it wouldn't be easy. "Jack Johnson was the original rebel, but I read that after he lost his title it was another 20 years before another black man got a shot. I knew I'd have to box for a few years before I got my shot so I just got on with it. I've seen in the *Yearbook* that Barry Hugman mentions when the colour bar came into British boxing and I've read about the Earl of Lonsdale and how he arranged for Johnson to box at the National Sporting Club. Apparently Johnson reneged on the deal and Lonsdale swore that no other black man would ever box at the NSC and as I understood it, you could only receive the belt if you defended it at the Club. When I came over in 1963 they had a semi-colour bar. Randolph Turpin had no trouble because he was born here, but people like me had to wait ten years to fight for the Commonwealth title. I think I was the first to overcome that. I'm not sure and I've always wondered if that was all true".

Bunny signed up with George Biddles. "He was the local man soaking up all the local talent". Bunny had to travel to Bristol for his first fight, but he got off to a good start with a second-round stoppage win over Peter Thomas. Two more early finishes followed and there would be two more before his first defeat after ten wins, but despite his success he was already becoming disillusioned with his chosen career. He had been fighting twice a month and after defeating the unfortunate Lloyd Walford twice in the same month he faced Guinea Roger for the second time in November of 1968. Bunny had beaten him on points three months earlier, but this time Roger managed to stop him in the seventh round. "The pay was rubbish and there was one fight that I didn't want. We sparred in this little six by six foot ring upstairs in a Swadlincote pub and every time I got in the ring with Jack Bodell it was a war! Jack was not particularly skilled, but he was very physical and he used brute force to overpower me. I was thinking that I'd had enough, but I came back to the gym and Biddles immediately said he'd got a fight for me. I said I didn't want it I hadn't trained, but he insisted it was an easy fight and on TV so I was persuaded. I got badly beaten by Roger Tighe".

Tighe stopped Bunny in the sixth round at the Cafe Royal in London, but he followed that second stoppage with victories over Peter Boddington and Hans Jorgen Jacobsen.

Bunny celebrates another victory

He defeated Boddington on points and, in his first fight abroad, stopped Jacobsen in the second round of their contest in Denmark. But he was unsettled and it was around this time that he decided a change was in order. "I began to take stock. Biddles had his mind set on what he wanted me to do and wouldn't listen so, like all northern fighters, I decided that things would be better in London". Bunny signed with Al Phillips for two years or so and would travel down two or three weeks before a fight to train in the BBBoC gym on Haversock Hill.

His next dozen fights included two defeats. The first came once again at the hands of Roger Tighe, this time on points over ten rounds, while the other was against Eddie Avoth, again on points. His victories included two wins over Eddie's brother, Dennis, and five stoppages, three in the first round over Billy Wynter, Terry Daly and Guinea Roger. He also had early stoppages over Maxie Smith and Rocky Campbell, but had to go the distance with Billy Aird, Dick Hall and Jerry Judge. He would meet Aird three times and would always have to stay until the final bell. Billy gave him the only draw of his 55-fight career.

The fight with Jerry Judge was a tough one over ten rounds. "Jerry looked like a hillbilly", Bunny remembers, "but that guy could punch! He was a dangerous fighter". But his next fight three weeks later would be tougher still when he encountered the man who he would meet three times in the most memorable fights of his career. In this first meeting in Wolverhampton in April of '71, Richard Dunn got the verdict after eight hard rounds. Bunny also lost the decision in his next fight when Dennis Avoth managed to avenge the defeat he suffered on points over ten rounds less than a year earlier. This time he earned the verdict over eight. The loss to Avoth would be his last for the next 21 fights as he coasted up the rankings. Along the way he met many of his old adversaries and overturned earlier defeats, stopping 12 of his opponents and fighting in two eliminators before challenging for the British heavyweight title.

Bunny stopped Eddie Avoth in their second meeting, the referee intervening during the third round and, after two defeats to Roger Tighe, he finally got the better of him third time around. He then met Guinea Roger again in October of '72 and for a fifth time on 30 April '73, but Roger was unable to repeat his victory of '68, making a total of four wins in five for Bunny, the final being a sixth-round stoppage. Bunny would enter his next fight as holder of a very special title – British citizen. In May, after ten years in the country, he qualified for British citizenship. Meanwhile, he continued to supplement his income by sparring. "I sparred with Joe Bugner, Jack Bodell, Carl Gizzi and others, but what I really wanted was to fight these guys". He never did get to fight them but he was now a top-rated heavyweight in a talented division. It was decided that there would be a series of eliminators among the top heavyweights, and when John Conteh dropped out of the heavyweight rankings Bunny was substituted. It had been a long wait but now he would get his chance.

His first eliminator for the title was against Les Stevens from Reading. They were fighting for the right to meet Bradford's Richard Dunn in a final eliminator for the title held by Danny McAlinden. With 32 wins in 38 fights and undefeated in his last ten, Bunny was favourite against the former ABA champion who had only one loss (on a cut eye) in 18 outings. "Stevens was a fine boxer", recalls Bunny, "that is one of the fights that I look back on and remember enjoying. They said, 'Stevens will get him with his jab', so I thought, right, I'll show them *my* jab. I think I should get some credit for *my* jab! And I did". *Boxing News* reported that Stevens, 22, was given a boxing lesson for the first four rounds. Johnson, looking cool and relaxed, sniped with left jabs and whipped in flashy hooks and combinations… Stevens was trying to out-jab Bunny from long range and coming off second best up to the finish. He defeated Stevens on points, winning seven of the ten rounds with one even, but it was unusual for Bunny to enjoy a fight. "I didn't particularly like boxing, I still don't. I enjoyed the competition aspect of it and I used to enjoy watching it to learn. Sugar Ray Robinson was the greatest in the world, effortless with rapid-fire punches. He was as near to perfection as can be. I wasn't what you would call a natural-born fighter, not like, say, Nigel Benn. I saw a fight recently, a really tight fight, where both fighters enjoyed it so much that they were slapping gloves at the end of every round. I wasn't like that and honed it on being technical. My friend, Frankie Lucas, another middleweight like Benn, loved it. If you said here's a fight, he'd say, 'Yeah, come on'. I just wasn't a natural like that".

His lack of fighting instinct certainly didn't hold him back. Before he got his final eliminator with Dunn he had to face a dangerous American, Morrie Jackson, who had recently demolished McAlinden within three rounds. That defeat cost 'Dangerous' Danny his £40,000 European title challenge against Joe Bugner. Bunny already had experience of dangerous Americans, having outpunched the tricky Dick Hall who had beaten Bugner. He swiftly disposed of this next transatlantic obstacle, stopping Jackson in the fifth round. Now nothing stood between Bunny and his return to Dunn. It was at this time that Bunny joined the stable of George Francis, who had no doubt that Bunny could defeat Dunn. "I could see Bunny's potential", he later said, "he was a far better boxer than Dunn, much faster, well able to put his whole weight into a punch". The two boxers would later meet for a third time and asked which fights are the most memorable of his career, Bunny says either of these last two with Dunn. He looks back on the first. "This was a final eliminator to achieve my dream. It was tough, hard. He came to win and I came to win. I gave away nearly 23lbs, but I knew that if I lost that I wouldn't achieve my dream".

The fight at Belle Vue in Manchester on 11th October 1973 was expected to be a real battle between the heavier, hard-hitting Dunn and the skilful, classy Johnson. Bunny had two clear points wins over the tough Billy Aird, while Dunn's verdict over Aird was considered controversial. Dunn had that earlier victory over Bunny, but it was apparent that this was a different Bunny than the one who had been so obviously off his game at the time. The fight nearly didn't happen when the day before Bunny was struck down with a heavy cold and he and George Francis had to consider the risk of going into an important 12-round fight against a much heavier opponent. They decided to take the risk and what a risk it was!

Bunny's face was a bloody mess at the end of the fight, his lip split and bleeding badly, with a nasty cut over his eye. But Dunn too, bore the scars of a hard-fought championship. Dunn swung huge lefts and rocked Bunny early, but mostly he deftly slipped out of harm's way and demonstrated his own power, stunning Dunn in the third round and putting him down twice in the fifth. The Bradford man managed to survive and come back in the sixth and the seventh round was described as possibly the most exciting round seen anywhere in Britain that year. Dunn was decked for the third time by a right uppercut but, on rising at 'eight', he rushed at Bunny and caught him flush on the chin. Bunny hung on desperately as Dunn whaled into him and the referee had to separate them as the bell went unheard. One of Dunn's heavy lefts dropped Bunny in the next round but he managed to get back to his feet at 'nine' and return fire. In the ninth he sustained that split lip and looked a beaten man, but in the tenth he caught an exhausted Dunn with a right followed by a left. Dunn went down and failed to beat the count, although he claimed he had been thumbed in the eye.

Bunny became the first immigrant to challenge for the British heavyweight title under the ten-year residential rule. "We want a quick crack at McAlinden", said Francis, "Bunny's won the final eliminator and I'm not having the sort of situation where he has to wait around for a title fight". Bunny would be ready to fight by December according to Francis, but it would actually be January when the fight took place – January 1975 that is! First Danny had to cancel because he broke his thumb early in a fight with Pat Duncan. He doggedly fought on to the final bell, but had to cancel his planned title defences. Then he had to cancel again when he got flu. It was disappointing for both fighters, especially McAlinden who had been dogged by cancellations during his career and had only fought four times in two years. Meanwhile, Bunny had another three fights while he waited for his title shot. Three victories, two by early kayo over Roy Wallace and Koli Vailea and one on points over Oliver Wright. Then he was forced to cancel the title fight when he caught a virus himself. Finally the date was set and both fighters were fit and ready. Another war was expected, but this time Bunny was expected to be on the losing side. "I think Terry (Lawless) will have turned out another winner", wrote John Jarrett for *Boxing News*, "and I pick Danny McAlinden to stop Johnson, possibly in the late rounds of a bitter battle".

The war failed to materialise and became more of a gentleman's disagreement. Bunny boxed cleverly and efficiently, while McAlinden seemed to be suffering from the months of setbacks and inactivity. Danny salvaged a couple of rounds midway through the fight, but Bunny had control, always being out of range and popping Danny with left jabs that turned his legs to jelly. Bunny was down twice during the fight, once from a slip and again in the ninth when he fell to the canvas with euphoria as McAlinden was counted out.

In the dressing room the first black British heavyweight champion set his sights on his next title, the European crown held by Joe Bugner. "I want Bugner now, I know I can beat him". George Francis had his eye on a bigger bauble, Ali's world title. "Muhammad Ali has been talking about fighting in Jamaica. Why doesn't he fight a home-town boy like Bunny?" Asked how he thought Lord Lonsdale would have felt about Bunny wearing his belt, Bunny replied: "I'm sure Lord Lonsdale would have been proud of the way I boxed tonight. The fight went just the way I planned it". However, it was more likely that his Lordship would have been spinning in his grave, but Bunny was living his dream.

Bunny didn't take any time off and was back in action the following month. He fought in February, March, May and June, and racked up wins against Pedro Agosto (pts), Angel Oquendo (rsc), Obie English (rsc) and the American, Ray Anderson, a former world light-heavyweight challenger (pts). Next came his first defence of the title and it would be a rubber match with the man he had beaten to get his shot, Richard Dunn. Bradford paratrooper, Dunn, had recently signed with George Biddles who had been in the opposite corner when the two fighters met for the first time. "I was in Johnson's corner in 1971 when Richard beat him on points at Wolverhampton and I'm very confident Dunn will beat him again. This time I reckon Richard will finish Johnson inside the distance". George said that he had every respect for Bunny and felt that they had parted amicably and Bunny believed Jack Bodell was getting all George's time and attention, but he felt that Dunn would have the advantage of size and reach.

The other George was equally confident. Francis said: "It was a great fight last time, but just a bit too hard. We don't aim to make it so hard now". He also said that: "we're not worried about Dunn being a southpaw". Another member of the Francis stable, John Conteh, often jokes about his habit of saying 'We'. John says he remembers lying on the canvas thinking 'We've been knocked out'. "Don't get the idea we're underestimating Dunn – we know he's a very capable fighter – but Bunny's very confident he can beat him and so am I". So, George No. 1 thinks that Dunn will finish it inside the distance and George No. 2 thinks that it won't be such a hard fight this time. Maybe they forgot to tell their fighters the plan.

Boxing News also felt that Dunn's extra stone and a half would decide the fight and be too much for Bunny over 15 rounds. George Francis naturally disagreed, but conceded that Bunny was light for a heavyweight. "Look, Bunny could do light-heavyweight tomorrow no trouble, but he's made his name as a heavy so we're sticking to that for a moment. As a matter of fact, I've been offered a world light-heavyweight title fight for Bunny. Victor Galindez for the WBA championship. There's a very good chance that will come off in Jamaica in December if we get past Dunn". Considering that Bunny had waited and fought for ten long years to become a British citizen and British champion, George seemed very keen to get him a fight in Jamaica. (It never happened with Bunny, but George did get there with Bunny Sterling).

First, of course, he had to get past Dunn. Bunny was

Bunny (left) and Danny McAlinden at the weigh-in prior to their British and Commonwealth heavyweight title fight at the Grosvenor House in London on 13 January 1975. Bunny took the Irishman's titles following a ninth-round kayo victory

favourite to win, despite conceding weight, height and reach. He was considered too classy for Dunn, who would never be able to outbox him and was even unlikely to outpunch him. Surprisingly, Bunny had a better record for punching and taking punches. He had a higher knock-out percentage and had only been knocked out twice in his 49 fights, whereas Dunn had been counted out five times in 38 contests. This time though, nobody would be kissing canvas and the crowd at the Empire Pool, Wembley would not be treated to the same thriller as last time. Twice they resorted to a slow hand clap and in the ninth round the referee warned both fighters to get stuck in. Bunny boxed with accuracy and caution, while Dunn showed unusual restraint and used his size and weight in the clinches. From the ninth Dunn began to overpower and overwhelm Bunny, pinning him in the corner in the 12th and piling on the pressure. Bunny didn't look to have recovered in the next round, but Dunn was also tiring. Both managed to land good shots, but in the 14th Bunny reasserted himself. He staggered Dunn with a right to the jaw, but he was drained now and Dunn came back in the last round, his wild ungainly punches landing heavily. Referee, Roland Dakin, scored the fight 149-145$\frac{1}{2}$ to Dunn. Like Bunny, he had fought long and hard to reach the top and now perhaps the part time paratrooper could give up his day job as a scaffolder. Dunn said the fight had not been easy and it wasn't even easy to say so, because one of Bunny's uppercuts had cut his tongue!

In his biography, George Francis explains why he thinks Bunny lost the fight. "Bunny had been commuting up and down the M1 to train with me, but he was getting weary of the journey and when he opened a nightclub in Birmingham he decided to do most of his training there. I wasn't happy but let Bunny talk me into it and when Bunny came to London the Saturday before the fight we went for our usual run and he was struggling on the return stretch. He was in terrible shape and I wanted him to pull out, but he adamantly refused. It cost him the fight with Ali that Dunn got instead".

Bunny was expected to move down to light-heavy, but he wasn't going to give up his title that easily. He wanted a rematch but he had to re-enter the race with another eliminator. He got his chance the following March and bided his time with a few minutes boxing in New Zealand. Well, he went to Auckland to fight Young Sekona, but that lasted less than two of the intended ten and, with that win tucked under the space where his belt used to be, it was back home to fight an eliminator with his old foe, Billy Aird. Bunny couldn't understand this. "I had only just lost the title and normally in that situation an eliminator would not be necessary. I shouldn't have needed one. I didn't think it was fair".

Nobody had ever done Billy any favours, that's for sure. Most people felt that he had deserved the verdict over Dunn when they fought in '73 and most agreed that he beat Bernd August when their match was judged a draw. Now those two were to split a £28,000 purse for their European title fight in April, while Billy was looking at a share of £1,140, Jack Solomon's winning bid for the eliminator. Both fighters were disgusted but felt unable to refuse and miss their chance, particularly Billy, who believed this was probably his last chance. "Bunny has beaten me twice already", he said, "but the first time I was only having my eighth fight and the second time I took the job on less than a week's notice. I've got a lot of respect for him but it's going to be my turn now". Bunny weighed 12 stone, 12lbs in the run-up to the fight and was still planning to fight Victor Galindez after two or three light-heavyweight fights, but this fight was seen as giving the winner a direct shot at Dunn, a return Bunny was considered favourite to win.

At least Bunny gave less weight away this time at 13-2 to Aird's 13-11, but he still ended the fight looking the more tired of the two. He had every right to look tired as it had been a rough ten rounds with some less-than-Queensberry tactics on both sides. Harry Mullan, at ringside, thought that Bunny won clearly, albeit not as clearly as George Francis believed. Not surprisingly, Billy was sure he had won. "Look at me, I'm not marked and I'm fresh enough to go another ten rounds, no bother". Bunny was certainly marked. The welts on his shoulder were caused by Billy biting him he said. "Sure I bit him", Billy confessed cheerfully to Mullan and cited a few of the old tricks he said Bunny had used on him. "He tried to butt me a couple of times so I bit him to even things up". That's okay then, surely the Board would think that was reasonable. Bunny did. "The guy just can't help it, it's his style", he said. "He's the same every time I've boxed him. Aird is always a hard man to beat but, even if I didn't give my best tonight, I know I did more than enough to win". The two men stood with their arms around each other's shoulders as they waited for the verdict and both looked like they's been sucker-punched when Roland Dakin announced a draw. Then they both shrugged and left, agreeing that they would be glad to do it again but definitely not for the paltry sum they earned that night. Looking back, Bunny remembers how disappointed he was that night. "It was a close fight but I felt I did enough to win. To give it a draw was terrible", Billy recalls. "We had three close encounters which could have gone either way but that's boxing. Dunn had beaten me as an amateur and as a pro, I boxed him out of sight but he got it". It had also been Ronald Dakin who gave Dunn that disputed verdict in '73. "The thing is" Billy added with his scouse twang, "Bunny had such long arms. How can someone so short out-jab him? He had the longest arms you've ever seen".

The draw meant that Bunny's next scheduled fight and career-best pay day could still go ahead against America's Duane Bobick, rated number five in the world, on the undercard of Dunn v Ali in Munich. A loss would have cost him the somewhat better wages of £10,000, which is one of the reasons that George Francis had lodged an official complaint with the Board of Control. Bunny describes the fight, his last at heavyweight, against an opponent over 29lb heavier: "He was a big guy, too heavy. I outboxed him but I remember his trainer shouting all the time. He kept saying, 'Sit on him, sit on him', meaning cut him off. Then I got cut inside my mouth and I was bleeding badly so George pulled me out. I was talking to Micky Duff the next day and he said. 'What are you, about 12-7, why don't you campaign at light-heavyweight?' I'm not particularly tall, but I was long-armed and big-boned. I wasn't really a heavyweight and it was always hard getting the weight. At 21, 22 even Conteh weighed heavier than me". Stablemate, Conteh, now held the WBC world title at light-heavy.

He suffered an eight-round stoppage in the Bobick fight which he made up for in his next fight with a seventh-round kayo over Peter Brisland in London. Within just three months he was fighting an eliminator for the British light-heavyweight title, his opponent being Manchester's Phil Martin, a fighter he had encountered before. "When I first went to Manchester as the champion, I had to do an exhibition bout and they selected Phil to get in with me. I don't know if he was trying to make a name for himself, but instead of the usual routine, he opened up straight away. When we met for the fight he seemed really cocky. He probably thought I was getting on a bit and they probably told him I'd struggle to make the weight". Bunny was 29 when they fought at the Gala Baths in West Bromwich. He had originally been supposed to fight Martin in September, but Brisland had stepped in when Martin suffered a cut eye in sparring. It was Phil's second shot at the title, having lost a controversial decision to Tim Wood for the vacant title. His impressive amateur career had included just 15 losses in 127 bouts, one of those a points defeat by John Conteh. His manager, Tommy Miller, said: "I'm not convinced that Bunny can be strong at light-heavy. Phil will be chasing him all the way, staying right on top of him and shoving him around. Phil is younger and stronger than Bunny and he's ambitious". He was actually only younger by two years, but Miller seized upon every advantage and was quick to complain about the appointment of James Brimmell as referee. Brimmell had refereed the Tim Wood fight.

Bunny's strategy was to allow Martin to tire himself, which he did eventually, after gaining a lot of ground in the middle rounds. George Francis was apoplectic in the corner. "I was going mad with him in the corner. I had to call him a cissy at the end of the eighth to get him going. He took a big risk waiting for the other fellow to tire, but you can't argue with success. Bunny turned out to be right in his estimate of the fight. I had to apologise for the names I called him". In the ninth, Bunny stepped it up and stopped a flagging Martin in the tenth. "It was much stiffer than I thought it would be", said Bunny, who weighed exactly the same as his opponent, 12st 5¼lb. "Martin was very strong. My plan was always to contest and contain until the latter part of the fight when my punches usually come much better. Tonight I felt good enough to be world champion". Recently Bunny spoke of his other motivation during the fight: "When you see defeat staring you in the face it can be a frightening thing. Phil Martin gave me a good fight and I felt fear – fear of losing. George said: 'You're losing the fight' and somehow I was able to turn it on. Anyone who thinks that was an easy fight has no idea". The fight nearly didn't happen when fire broke out above the ring during an earlier support bout. Referee, John Coyle, stood in the ring and fired an extinguisher at the lighting rig above, dousing the flames – and the pressmen at ringside!

This time Bunny went straight from his first eliminator into the title fight, a decision by the Board that raised a few eyebrows as others were waiting in the wings to challenge the champion, Tim Wood. Both men had dropped down to light-heavy, although Wood naturally lacked experience compared to Bunny's 55 fights. Bunny had been sparring with Conteh, while Wood, strangely enough, had been sparring with Phil Martin, which must have been a bitter pill for Phil to swallow. Wood felt he had the greater stamina and workrate but he was fully aware of Bunny's power. Despite the fact that he was usually much lighter than his opponents, 26 of Bunny's 46 wins had come by stoppage, sometimes against men over a stone heavier. "Johnson can take your head off if he catches you right so I know what I have to do to beat him. I'm not kidding myself that it's going to be easy but I know I can do it".

In complete contrast to the Martin fight, Bunny rushed straight into action and 103 seconds and a right to the jaw later it was all over with Wood flat out on his back. This time no-one would argue with referee, Roland Dakin. "I expected to knock him out", said Bunny, "and it was partly planned that it would be in the first round". He knew that Wood was a slow starter and Wood knew that Bunny could take his head off so it's hardly surprising that Tim looked tense and drawn when he entered the ring. He looked even more drawn as he was helped back to his corner, still dazed. "It wasn't the best punch Bunny has thrown", said a clinical George Francis: "Wood still had some life in him, but when Bunny knocked out Young Sekona in New Zealand the poor guy was out for about eight minutes".

Bunny's former manager, George Biddles, at ringside to comment for local radio, was equally unsurprised. "It was a predictable result, Bunny is in my opinion the hardest puncher at any weight in the United Kingdom. I've seen him knock over big heavyweights when he's been wearing 16 ounce gloves in the gym". So, now Bunny, the first immigrant British heavyweight champion had become the first immigrant British light-heavyweight champion and, although three other fighters had won both titles, none had won them in reverse order. Jack Peterson, Len Harvey and Don Cockell had all won the light-heavyweight title first, (although Harvey regained the title at light-heavy five years after winning the heavyweight title). Now all he had to do was to keep it.

His first defence was made against Harry White almost before Tim Wood managed to lift his head from the canvas, but the Board would only sanction a ten rounder. In the event, White, also from the West Indies, lasted nine. Bunny was streets ahead when he dropped White, who only just managed to beat the count and was unable to offer any resistance against Bunny's ensuing onslaught before being rescued by the ref. Bunny then fought Terry Mintus and scored his fifth straight win inside the distance since dropping to light-heavy, again in the first round. He'd certainly have to do something similar to win his next fight as he was challenging for the vacant European title – in Italy!

"We know what goes on out there", said George Francis: "The only way to be sure of winning is to do what

Frankie Lucas did last week". Bunny's stablemate had knocked out Angelo Jacopucci, who Francis felt was favoured by the ref when he fought Bunny Sterling the year before. He also claimed the referee actually altered his score card when Sterling fought Elio Calcabrini for the European title. Johnson was to fight Aldo Traversaro in Genoa and it was generally accepted that he was unlikely to win a distance fight. Early in the fight it didn't look like he'd have to, but in no time it became apparent that there was little likelihood of him ending the fight early. After a promising start Bunny faded completely until, during a third standing count in the tenth round, the referee rightly decided he needed saving. "The fellow couldn't believe his luck", said Francis: "The normal Bunny would have taken him apart. Bunny had done everything right, having trained well, loved well and worked well but it wasn't his night. I've never seen you looking so lethargic", George said to Bunny who sat with his head in his hands. Now questions were asked, even by Bunny himself, about whether he should continue at the grand old age of 30. Quite surprising really, on recent form and after one bad night. Up to this fight Bunny had avenged five of his eight losses and had only been on the floor three times in his last 43 contests. The natural light-heavy had won the British heavyweight title by repeatedly demolishing far heavier men. Now he held the light-heavyweight title. Was it really time to hang up his gloves? Not yet. Bunny, as it turned out, still had some good wins left in him, including two successful title defences.

Back home, Bunny's next fight did nothing to restore his confidence. David Conteh stopped him in three rounds when they met in Islington in February of '78. It would be seven months before he returned to the ring, amid suggestions that he was making a mistake and should retire. He chose to ignore them and travelled over to Paris to face the French prospect, Sylvain Watbled. It looked like he'd made a big mistake when he was floored in the opening round by a heavy left hook but he survived, came back and proceeded to outbox Watbled. He dropped the strong Frenchman in the fourth with a short right and finished him with a corker of a left in the sixth. Watbled fell flat on his face, struggled to rise and fell back, unconscious. "It was exactly the sort of punch that he knocked out Young Sekona with", said George Francis. "Maybe this win will show the people who keep saying I'm finished", said Bunny.

Bunny had yet to defend his title, won over 18 months earlier. After several cancellations he was set to fight Rab Affleck, but Affleck pulled out and was substituted by novice, Dennis Andries. Bunny was winning comfortably until the last rounds when his stamina seemed to fail him. He was floored in the ninth round finished the fight with a cut eye and bleeding from his mouth. Andries came close to stopping him, but Bunny had done enough to win comfortably on points. It did nothing to silence his critics though and his next fight gave them even more ammunition when he lost a points decision over six rounds to Mustapha Wassaja in Denmark. They claimed that Bunny was constantly struggling to make the weight and were right but this was nothing new for Bunny. He spent the first half of his career trying to beef up for every fight and the second

half trying to get down to light-heavy. "Looking back, some of those fights must have looked very comical. At times I seemed dwarfed by the other guy". Now, he realises that he was a cruiserweight. Unfortunately, they hadn't been invented yet. Affleck must have been feeling pretty confident when they finally met over two years after Bunny became champion.

The Scotsman also had the advantage of home turf as the fight would be at St Andrew's Sporting Club in Glasgow shortly after Bunny's 32nd birthday. He also had the advantage of height and youth at just 26. Affleck had advantages, but Bunny had so much more. Bunny described as having probably the hardest pound for pound left hook in the British game at that time. It was a punch he had worked hard to develop as an amateur. Having been proud of his right, but his old trainer had told him that all good pro's have a left hook so he tried to develop his. "It became my favourite punch and I achieved more knockouts with my left than my right, even though I am right handed". Affleck had also knocked a few over, having recently met head on with that left of Sylvain Watbled's in the opening round, he didn't get up – for over a minute. Affleck started confidently and rocked Bunny in the first and second rounds, but then Bunny got into his stride and in the fourth he unleashed classy combinations, the second of which saw Affleck slide to the canvas, apparently unconscious. "He hit me hard enough to let me know he was a puncher", said Bunny, "but I wasn't hurt at any time" and, in response to his critics he told Francis, "Pass me my crutch so I can get to the shower".

For his next fight Bunny faced one of the top five light-heavyweights in the world. The fight was a little unusual in that his unbeaten American opponent was serving 30-40 in a New Jersey prison. James Scott was serving his time for armed robbery and parole violation at Rahway State Prison. (An almighty violation presumably as his original sentence was only 13-17 years!) His sentence was under appeal, but meanwhile he climbed the rankings with successive wins televised from inside the prison. Mickey Duff would later refuse to allow Lotte Mwale to box there, but Bunny said: "It's a boxing ring whether it's Madison Square Garden or a prison". The TV people paid Bunny $17,500 plus expenses and Scott received the same. "It was a little intimidating", Bunny said recently. "The only people rooting for me were the guards!", which may or may not be a comfort in a maximum security institution. Scott was escorted to the ring by guards, not because he was dangerous but to protect him from those clamouring for autographs. (I'm not making this stuff up!) In the ring though, Scott was dangerous. A non-stop puncher, unbeaten in ten as a free man, he had seen off another five from behind bars. Around 200 invited guests watched from ringside on seats around the outdoor ring, with a similar number of permanent guests watching from behind a wire fence. For six rounds Scott pounded Bunny with his relentless and powerful punches until he was retired on his stool at the end of the sixth. After defeating the British champion, Scott next stopped the Italian champ. By then he was ranked third in the world and planned to work his way through foreign champions until he got a shot at the world title. All this from behind bars. He also had a win over

Eddie Mustafa Muhammad, the leading WBA contender, and was without doubt a serious contender. He never did get to fight for the title though and suffered his second defeat in his 19th fight, on points to Dwight Muhammad Qawi in September '81. More importantly, his appeals failed and he was only recently released from Rahway.

Lotte Mwale, Bunny's stablemate and sparring partner, was his next opponent. The fight lasted the distance, largely because the world ranked Zambian knew from experience how to survive against Bunny, who proved that stamina and age were not a problem. He gave a classic Bunny performance and finished the stronger looking of the two. When the verdict was given in Lotte's favour the crowd booed, but there would be no dissent when the next fight ended the same way. Bunny returned to France for a rematch with Sylvain Watbled. This time the Frenchman was a clear winner even before he dropped Bunny late in the fight. Was this indicative of Bunny's decline since they last met a year before, or of Watbled's improvement? His third loss in a row certainly didn't bode well for his all-important belt-claiming title defence.

It was also a year since Bunny had last fought his challenger, Dennis Andries. Then he had been deemed lucky to have survived the closing rounds of their fight and now Andries was confident that the extra rounds would give him an advantage. His manager, Ernie Fossey, called him a 20-round fighter for his impressive stamina, although Andries, another of those pesky 26 year olds, claimed he wouldn't need the full 15 rounds as he could finish Bunny in 12. Of course, with retrospect, we now know the calibre of fighter that Andries would become so it is no surprise that he would be a handful. But Bunny had an incredible incentive – a burning desire to claim the Lonsdale Belt. "In boxing there are only a very small percentage lucky enough to gain full ownership of a belt and on Wednesday I get the chance to be amongst them". Critics were still calling for Bunny to retire and Andries was expected to make the decision for him and end his career.

As a stylist, Andries wasn't even in the same ballpark as Bunny and he only succeeded in extending the fight the full distance by constantly wrestling and brawling and smothering Bunny's skilful boxing. In the 12th he twice manhandled Bunny through the ropes, presumably in a desperate attempt to live up to his prediction. They crashed into the press benches and were lucky to avoid injury. The crowd booed frequently. Referee, James Brimmell, who had nearly been put down himself when Andries crashed into him in the seventh round, described it as the worst fight he had ever refereed or watched. "Johnson defended beautifully", wrote Harry Mullan, "rolling and swaying to make Andries miss repeatedly until finally Andries, in exasperation, clubbed him on top of the head". "It was a hell of a fight" says Bunny, "he was a young, strong man and it was a tough, hard fight but I wanted that belt so much. I was using my skills but he was using skills I didn't have. He would head-butt you in the groin, things like that!" Brimmell scored it as a close fight but gave Bunny the verdict. Mullan felt that Bunny was an absolutely overwhelming winner and said: "I felt desperately sorry for Johnson, a dignified and worthy champion who has graced British boxing for 12 years and who deserved to win his belt in a more edifying way". It still sounds like a career epitaph but there was yet another chapter of Bunny's career to be boxed. An ugly victory is still a victory and he was now the outright owner of a Lonsdale Belt. That 16-year-old Jamaican kid certainly knew what he was talking about.

Bunny had parted company with George Francis when his contract was up, partly because there would be a conflict of interest over Lotte Mwale. "Francis was a father-figure to us, we had a really good camp", says Bunny and with mock sadness added: "My career had peaked and I was getting old. 32, 33 is very old. Also, I was so well established by now that people came to me to offer my fights and I was confident I could handle my own affairs. John Conteh and Bunny Sterling had fought in Australia and said it was great out there so when I got a call from Australian promoter, Peter Foster, offering me a fight there with Tony Mundine, I jumped at it". He had one last fight in Europe, six rounds against John Odhiambo in Denmark. It would have been nice to pack his bags and leave on a win, but unfortunately he lost on points. At least his first fight in Oz would be more successful – eventually.

Bunny then found himself embroiled in a promotional saga. Foster was young and inexperienced but was very good at getting publicity, while Mundine's promoter, on the other hand, had plenty of experience and the first thing he did was to contact the BBBoC who said that Bunny had to return to Britain to get permission to fight. Bunny was incredulous. He had informed the Secretary of the Board that he was leaving and had simply been advised to be sure and leave time to get acclimatised. Bunny said: "the idea of going all that way back! Naturally I protested. Then suggestions started to appear in the press that I was going to take the money and run and not really compete. The Australian Commission refused to sanction the fight until the BBBoC gave clearance. I was training in Sydney and I thought, something's not right. They can't stop me from earning. Every man has the right to work". Bunny then enlisted the services of a solicitor in England and eventually the Board agreed that he could fight, but he had to have a warm-up contest before fighting Munroe. "After all that it would have been great to knock Mundine out in one round and go on to win the world title, but unfortunately that only happens in movies".

He would have to wait nine months for the Mundine fight, but he gave a V-sign of a performance against Mike Quarry, who received a standing count in the sixth round before being rescued by the ref in the seventh. Sadly, the Mundine fight at the idyllic sounding, Surfers Paradise in Queensland, was rather less satisfying and Bunny lost on a tenth-round stoppage. He redeemed himself two months later by knocking out Fetaki Namoa in the sixth round but, when he was stopped in the same round by Steve Aczel two months after that, it marked the end of his illustrious career.

The defeat was just one factor in his decision to retire, especially when he realised that his enthusiasm for constant training and the novelty of running to TV studios for interviews had worn off. Bunny also found the Australian press intrusive and unpleasant to deal with, in contrast to the polite British reporters with whom he had enjoyed a good relationship. He even became a journalist himself with his own sports column and must be unique in being the only boxer to write the preview for his own fight, which he did for the Quarry fight.

Bunny loved Australia and would stay there for seven years. "It was a marvellous country and I enjoyed my time there. Sydney was the most beautiful city in the world and I had a good time – except for the boxing!" Having made his decision, he wrote to the BBBoC and relinquished his title. "Even when I finished at 33 I thought it was a little early, but I had seen great fighters go on too long and I didn't want to do that. The older you get you don't realise that you just start getting hit more".

Bunny helped to form a cricket club in Sydney called 'The Sydney Windies', although his cricket skills were not immediately apparent. "I couldn't bat and I couldn't bowl. There were very few West Indians in Sydney at the time so we all got together. I tried to be an opening batsman but I was so slow and laborious. I had a lot of enthusiasm though! It's funny I was always the chairman, never the batsman. When I went back in 2001 I was pleased to see the club is still going. I have always liked to be involved in community enterprises".

Back in Birmingham in the early '90s Bunny started the St Theresa boxing club, inspired by another of his idols. "Archie Moore had started a club called the ACC, 'The Anybody Can Club', and that always stuck in my mind as a great idea. It was not just for boxing but all sports". For example, Bunny encouraged one lad who was good at football and got him a trial. He also worked with the amateur boxers and the club had several promotions around Birmingham before having to close through lack of local government support.

Bunny has been married three times and has six children, Marcia, Michelle, Javena, Jamaan, Joshua and Jessica. As it turned out, he has enjoyed careers in both boxing and the law as he is now a Police Station Adviser in criminal law. He lives in Birmingham with his wife, Maisie, and their children, Joshua and Jessica and his mother, now 86, lives nearby. He is President of the Midlands EBA and he is justifiably proud of his achievements and his Lonsdale Belt. "It is still a very prestigious belt, the most famous in the world as far as I am concerned". And as for young Colin, who started all this, he ended up in tears because Bunny did of course read his books and then proceeded to thrash him at table tennis.

Bunny with his most prized possession, the light-heavyweight Lonsdale Belt he won outright in 1980

Colin Jones: The Gorseinon Gravedigger

by Wynford Jones

Colin Jones was born in Gorseinon, Swansea on 21 March 1959. As a youngster he joined the Penyrheol Boxing Club where he came under the watchful guidance of Gareth Bevan, a man who was to become an ever-present figure in Colin's corner and a life-long friend.

Enjoying an extremely successful amateur career, Colin gained titles at schoolboy level before going on to win both the Welsh and ABA welterweight titles in 1976 and 1977 and was a Welsh international before representing Great Britain against the United States at Wembley on 16 June 1976. Colin stopped Ralph Fratto in the third round and the British team enjoyed a 6-5 victory. His team-mates included Charlie Magri, Pat Cowdell, Cornelius Boza-Edwards and Clinton McKenzie. The biggest name on the American team was undoubtedly that of Thomas Hearns, who was beaten by George Gilbody.

Colin then went on to represent Great Britain at the 1976 Olympic Games held in Montreal and was one of our youngest ever representatives. Unfortunately, he was eliminated, but gave the Romanian, Victor Silberman, a great contest. This was a memorable experience for the young Welshman, with gold medallists including Teofilo Stevenson at heavyweight, the brothers Leon and Michael Spinks at light-heavyweight and middleweight, respectively, Sugar Ray Leonard at light-welterweight, and Howard Davies at lightweight. After retaining his ABA title in 1977, Colin decided to turn professional and teamed up with Eddie Thomas, himself a former welterweight champion and at the time, one of the most successful managers in British boxing.

Colin's first pro contest took place at the Afan Lido, Aberavon on 3 October 1977, his opponent being Mike Copp. Even though the young Welshman began somewhat apprehensively, by the fifth round he had caught up with his opponent who was counted out. This was followed with a four-round win over Martin Bridges, thus bringing 1977 to a successful conclusion.

He began 1978 in fine style by stopping Alan Reid and Willie Turkington, both in the first round, but he was then matched with Tony Martey of Ghana in a contest which I had the good fortune to referee. Martey was a Commonwealth Games silver medallist at Christchurch, New Zealand in 1974 and on paper he looked more than capable of extending Colin. Before the third round had ended I felt sure that Colin had decided that here was an opponent he would not be able to knock out and what followed was a superb exhibition of boxing. Colin treated Martey with respect, and rightly so, since the Ghanaian always looked capable of landing big punches right up to the final bell. Jones took all eight rounds on my card, but going the distance for the first time provided him with valuable experience.

In his next contest his superiority was less clearly marked. He was matched with the Belgian, Frankie Decaesteckter, at Aberavon and was fully stretched, so much so that many thought him lucky to gain the six-round points decision. Wins over Horace McKenzie and Johnny Pincham further extended his unbeaten run, which was to continue through 1979 with victories over America's Sam Hailstock, Cornish-Italian Salvo Nuciforo, and a spectacular stoppage defeat of France's Alain Salmon. On this occasion at Aberavon, Colin showed the devastating power of his body punching.

With such an impressive record, it was clear that Wales was producing another welterweight of high calibre and he was soon matched with the tall Joey Mack of Birmingham in a final eliminator for the welterweight championship of Great Britain, which would take place at the Club Double Diamond in Caerphilly. Colin once again displayed his devastating punching power and referee Harry Gibbs stopped the embarrassingly one-sided contest in the tenth round after Mack had paid as many visits to the canvas.

The path to the title was now clear, but to remain active Colin accepted a contest against fellow-Welshman Billy Waith at the World Sporting Club. It was a pity that a contest such as this was taken out of Wales because on paper it could have been a great match, with the box-fighter against Waith, the defensive master boxer who displayed his skills in rings all over the world. During the 1970s, Waith was probably the best boxer in Britain not to win a title. As it turned out, the contest was a disappointment and Waith was counted out in the sixth round. It was the first time in a long and distinguished career that he had suffered this indignity and there were howls of protest following the contest regarding alleged low blows and a blow which landed at the base of the spine. Having been in the ring with Billy several times, I noticed he used to turn his body in a defensive movement and against a puncher like Colin he would have been contributing to his own downfall.

Following an announcement that Colin should meet Kirkland Laing for the British title, agreement could not be reached and the contest went to purse offers. Eddie Thomas wanted the contest for Wales, but he was out-bid by the London team of Mike Barrett and Mickey Duff who had reputedly secured the contest with a bid of around £15,000. This was to be the first time that a boxer managed by Thomas had appeared on a Barrett promotion since 1968, thus bringing to an end a feud which began following Howard Winstone's world title victory at the Royal Albert Hall in 1968.

The contest was set for 1 April 1980 and was to be held at the Wembley Conference Centre, perhaps the most luxurious boxing venue in Britain at that time. My diary account of the contest reads as follows: "Laing gave an impressive display of boxing skills. He kept moving and was able to outbox Jones at long range with his greater height and reach. It was not until the third round that Colin began to settle and to land one or two solid blows. As the

Colin lifted the British welterweight title when stopping Kirkland Laing in the ninth round at the Wembley Conference Centre on 1 April 1980

contest proceeded, Laing continued to build up an impressive points lead and by the end of the eighth round, a realistic assessment would have been six rounds to Laing, one to Jones and one even. Laing continued to hold the initiative in the ninth, but suddenly Colin got to his man and stayed with him, giving another display of superb punching power until the referee stepped between them. Roland Dakin thus raised the arm of Colin Jones, who, in his 14th contest, had captured the welterweight championship of Great Britain, the title held by his manager Eddie Thomas, some 30 years previously. There were many empty seats at the Conference Centre, but of those taken, a large proportion were occupied by Welshmen who had made the trip to London in the hope of recapturing the glories of days gone by and Colin gave them exactly what they wanted. He had now become a promoter's dream namely a boxer with a big punch.

He was back in action again on 3 June, knocking out Richard House in the first round at the Royal Albert Hall, before returning to home soil and stopping Peter Neal in the fifth round of a British title defence at Gowerton, just a short distance from where he lived. The National Eisteddfod of Wales was being held there in 1980 and Eddie Thomas hit on the idea of hiring the pavilion at the end of the week-long festival. It was a huge success and the singing and the support for Colin was incredible. I had the honour of conducting the National Anthem before the contest started and the sound of this will forever live in my mind. Eddie always spoke with passion about Merthyr's place in history and was always anxious to promote Merthyr musicians. Linking culture with sport he invited the Dowlais Male Choir to sing at this promotion and as the choir's Musical Director at that time I was responsible for the musical arrangements. The singing made quite an impression on referee Mike Jacobs who was handling his first British title fight and many of the choristers felt that Peter Neal must have been intimidated by their efforts!

In March 1981, Colin returned to the Wembley Conference Centre and stopped Mark Harris in nine rounds to win the vacant Commonwealth title and followed this in April with a return against Kirkland Laing at the Royal Albert Hall. Laing was an exceptionally talented boxer but something of an enigmatic character, so much so that after beating the legendary Roberto Duran he virtually disappeared for a year when most boxers would have wanted to profit handsomely from that result. This contest followed exactly the same pattern as their first meeting, with Laing well ahead on points before being given time to recover from low blows. The ninth round proved to be decisive yet again. Colin was stalking his man in his customary menacing manner and with devastating punches now getting through, referee John Coyle eventually had to step between them to stop the contest.

By his victory, Colin earned outright ownership of the Lonsdale Belt, an achievement which had eluded Eddie, but he was soon to taste defeat for the first time when he was disqualified in the third round against America's Curtis Ramsey at Sophia Gardens, Cardiff. He had dominated Ramsey from the first bell, but unfortunately had followed

up with a punch after flooring Ramsey and was disqualified by referee Adrian Morgan for the offence.

A couple of appearances at Wembley followed when he beat two Americans, Pete Seward and Gary Giron. Shortly afterwards, he knocked out Sakaria Ve in the second round, again at Wembley, to retain his Commonwealth title. He was then matched with Hans Henrik Palm for the European title, but shortly before the contest Colin was admitted to hospital with appendicitis. Having recovered well from surgery Colin went forward to meet Palm on 5 November 1982. Palm was stopped in the second round in Copenhagen and so, by becoming European champion, Colin emulated the achievements of his manager as a triple title holder.

Negotiations now started for a world title fight and, on 19 March 1983 he was matched with Milton McCrory at Reno for the vacant WBC title. I felt this was a golden opportunity for Colin and was sure that after seven rounds, McCrory would have little left to offer. This turned out to be the case with the six foot, three inch McCrory using his jab and dancing away with Colin stalking him hoping to land those wicked hooks to the body by cutting down the ring. Having spoken to Colin about this, he agreed that the opportunity was there but he was afraid to go all out at that point because of the problems he himself might have encountered had he failed to take McCrory out. The contest was refereed by Octavio Meyran, who some years later would be involved in another piece of boxing history when Buster Douglas knocked out Mike Tyson in Tokyo to become heavyweight champion of the world, and the result was a draw with one judge scoring 116-114 to Colin, another 116-113 for McCrory, while the Venezuelan judge saw it as a draw at 115 points apiece. The scoring reflects the closeness of the contest and a return was set for Las Vegas on 13 August thus ensuring another lucrative payday.

Unfortunately, Colin lost the rematch on points over 12 rounds, the contest taking place in the afternoon heat of the Dunes Hotel car park. Having used the famous Johnny Tocco gym during his build-up to the fight, Colin was in his customary peak condition when the first bell rang, but one has to question the wisdom and indeed the motive in staging a contest of such importance in furnace-like conditions. Colin did not make the best of starts and found himself on the canvas towards the end of the first. He gradually worked his way back into the contest and the fifth round was a good one for him, as indeed was the ninth when he had McCrory in all sorts of trouble. McCrory was dancing again in the tenth round but tired badly in the 12th and final round. The scoring of the contest makes interesting reading with one judge awarding the contest to McCrory by 115-114, and the second judge voting for Colin by 114-113. Everything now hinged on the scoring of the third judge who awarded it to McCrory by a ridiculously lopsided 115-111. In a close contest some rounds can be very difficult to score and it is under these circumstances that some judges tend to favour the home fighter, which certainly seems to have been the case here.

Milton McCrory, favoured by former champion Sugar Ray Leonard to win their first encounter, was now on top of the world and resisted talk of a third match. This left

Colin contemplating his future and in 1984 he beat Allan Braswell and Billy Parks in an attempt to re-establish himself. Then, on 19 January 1985 he was matched with Don Curry at the NEC, Birmingham for the WBA title. Curry was a formidable champion and shortly before the fight I watched a video with Eddie Thomas of Curry's win over the Italian, Nino la Rocca. Curry was such a compact fighter. Economical, yet so precise in his work, there were doubts about his ability to make the welterweight limit. Sadly, the contest was a huge disappointment for Colin, who never really got going. He sustained a gaping gash across the bridge of his nose and looked a sorry sight when the referee stopped the contest in the fourth round and the harsh reality dawned on him that he would not win a world title.

This was to be Colin's last contest and at the age of 25 retirement beckoned, while Curry failed to heed the warning signs of continuing to box at the welterweight limit and he looked a mere shell of his old self when he was destroyed by Lloyd Honeyghan,

As a young man, Colin had been employed as a gravedigger and journalists were quick to exploit this angle in the coverage of his career. After retiring, he worked in the motor trade for many years and enjoyed the wheeling and dealing that went with it, but he has also shown himself to be a superb analyst of the sport and has worked frequently on radio and television. Colin has covered all the world title contests involving boxers such as Steve Robinson, Robbie Regan and Joe Calzaghe for Radio Wales, while I have covered the same contests for Radio Cymru, the Welsh language service. We have travelled to many contests together and I am always fascinated by the stories of his years with Eddie Thomas. Eddie was in many ways quite old fashioned and he was also superstitious, but they were undoubtedly a formidable partnership and his respect and admiration for Eddie continues to shine through.

Frequently in demand as a speaker at sporting dinners, one function Colin tries not to miss is the annual dinner of the Boxing Writers' Club. As a past winner of their annual award for the best young boxer it is always a special night for him, but it was also special for Eddie and Colin has told me that he will always be there for those very reasons.

Colin Jones can look back on his career with pride. He was without equal in Britain and Europe and came so close to winning the world title against McCrory. He was a boxer of immense skill and power, while there was always a sense of menace in the way he would stalk an opponent, and his vicious hooks to the body proved too much for many of the fighters he faced. His appearance in the ring always gave rise to expectation and an air of excitement and he was undoubtedly one of the most devastating punchers of his era.

Colin (right) and Eddie Avoth, Wales' former British and Commonwealth light-heavyweight champion, meet up in more recent times

The Oliver Family and Finchley & District ABC

by K R Robinson

I visited ABC's Anchor Hall Gym in leafy, suburban New Barnet on Saturday mornings when the nursery classes were in full swing. A couple of dozen or more youngsters trained and received instruction under the practiced eye of Finchley stalwart, George Phillips, and his assistants. A crowd of family and friends of the lads and lassies bunched around the door and lined the walls. Clean, light and airy, the gym has a gallery of photographs of ancient and modern fistic greats dominated by Spencer 'The Omen' Oliver, the Club President and local hero. There are hundreds of boxing clubs scattered across the country and each has a tale to tell, a fighting hero, a dedicated benefactor, a charismatic trainer, or maybe a cast-iron team spirit which carries all before it. Finchley has claimed its fair share of newspaper space over recent years, but the strength of the club today reflects a club firmly rooted in the local community.

Finchley and Barnet have had connections with pugilism from bare-knuckle days. The commons were the venue for prize-fights and the 'Five Bells' public house on East End Road, Finchley became popular as a training resort and some notable ringmen prepared there. As favoured encampment sites for gypsies, the commons hosted many a romany fistic encounter. Barnet Fair traditionally attracted a boxing booth, which no doubt benefited from the gypsy presence.

What is now Finchley and District Amateur Boxing Club first came into being during the 1930s. From its earliest days the club suffered from a lack of facilities. An early member, Len Fowler, who joined the club in 1937, gained prominence after moving to Barnet where he became club captain. Through the dark days of the 1940s local men who boxed in good class such as Frank Williams and Frank Hunt did so with other clubs.

In the 1950s the club was based at Northside School Lodge, where training was supervised by Les Kirk, a former Navy professional boxer who also fought in the booths. Although training moved to Christ's College, Finchley Central, equipment remained stored at Northside between shows. With only the most basic of equipment and a single rope ring the club attracted many local youngsters and some few seniors from outside the area such as Mick Mold, Mick Mulley and Barry Hughes, though none stayed very long. The club's star during this period was Teddy McGovern, a middleweight, who turned professional in 1959. One senior member was Johnny Cummings who reached the semi-final of the North-West Divisional Championships at heavyweight. Another was Barry Hugman, the editor of the *Yearbook*, having often to train and fight as a bantamweight outside of the local area due to parental disapproval. Barry was down to represent Finchley at the North-West Divs in 1961, but suffered a broken hand a week or so earlier. Coming back the following year he failed to make the weight and on being offered a place with the featherweights, he sensibly declined on inspection of one of the strongest lists in the Divs, which included from memory Brian Anderson, Jimmy Anderson, Billy Schwer (senior) and Johnny Head.

Prince Merchant took over from Kirk as trainer in 1963, with his son Johnny and Mick Flavin as the club's leading lights. Future pro manager and trainer, Darkie Smith, succeeded Merchant and produced a strong junior team, with Angelo D'Amore and Bobby Frankham capturing National Association of Boys Clubs titles in 1981, Steve Griffith winning one in the following year when Terry Collins won a Junior ABA title. Darkie left the club in the early 1980s.

Charles Oliver (born Hackney 1920) divided his time between boxing as an amateur and fighting in boxing booths, a practice which seems not to have been unusual in the area. Charlie's sons – Patrick (born 1942), John (1944) and Jim (1950) – have been connected with Finchley ABC since the 1960s, while his grandsons – Danny (1971) and Spencer (1975) – had successful careers with the club before turning professional.

"I was an amateur and boxed in the clubs at Tufnel Park, Park Royal and down the Caledonian Road in the 1930s.

Charlie, with trophy, at home in pre-war days

They each had so many boys that they could raise a full team. Large firms like Standard Telephones also had their own boxing clubs and teams. My boxing club was Alexandra Palace – Finchley was just starting then at the 'Five Bells', East End Road. My father had died in 1925 from injuries received at Arras during the First War, leaving five children. I started in the booths when I was 16 or 17 to earn a few bob. They showed at Barnet Fair, Putney Heath and Wimbledon Common before going into their winter quarters. There were some good blokes in there and I remember Sam Minto from America, who was a nice fellow".

"I was in the Territorial Army and during the Munich crisis the police came and got me out to go to Waltham Abbey. When the war started a little while after that I went into the Middlesex Regiment and spent three and a half years in Northern Ireland, before going back into the booths. I was on Parkin's booth amongst others. They wanted me to travel with them, but I was on the buildings as a hod carrier and did some tree felling, before spending 20 years with the Water Board. It was a hard life coming home from work then going to the booth".

"Back in the booth after the war I met Stan Hawthorne, Paddy Roche and Les Haycox, who came from Nottingham and was a top class pro who fought Eric Boon. He got me some fights in the booths. Les worked at Covent Garden market and married a local girl. I had a fight with a green grocer from Finchley called Ernie Booth. I said 'Don't knock yourself out for the sake of ten bob', but he came out and smacked me in the face in the first before I gave him a good hiding and stopped him in the second. We became friends years later and he's still alive. I used to get about two pounds ten shillings a night from the booth and with nobbins it could be seven quid".

Charlie's eldest son Patrick had taken up judo, but he tried boxing when the club was at Christ's College. "I went down a few times to train and spar but I was already a judo brown belt so stayed with it. My brother John and I used to go with the old man to Barnet Fair. I remember him getting knocked down once when we were only kids. He looked up and his eyes were gone, but he always did alright".

"We later went down to Victoria Park as I wanted to take the wrestlers on. They put me up against 'The Bear', another bloke from the audience. He put his hand up and I did and they put the two young silly b......s in together! He was a local called Paul Makoski, a great big feller, who's dead now. His brother runs the Barnet club. I was trying to get him down, the ref was interfering and John was in my corner shouting 'Knock him out!'. It was a bit of a tussle and every time I got in I threw him down on the floor and the bloody ref was saying 'Get a strangle on him and put him out!' anyway he stopped it. I done my knee on the canvas and was off work for a fortnight!".

"The old man was there he said 'I'll have a go', but they wouldn't let him fight. He wanted to take the boxers on and would have done alright. He was 40/50 odd, but he was still fairly fit in those days and he always surprised me that even at that age he had the fitness in him. When he was tree felling he had magnificent shoulders. He had the moves and

fitness. The fair phoned me up later and wanted me to travel with them, but he wouldn't let me go. He said 'You ain't 'aving none of that'. We were in the dressing room at the back afterwards and there was a kid there about 18 or 19 who'd been punched to hell. That's what the old man was afraid of – he didn't want me going in like that. So I never did it, but I was a bit disappointed at the time".

Pat stayed with judo, becoming British Judo Council all-comers champion in 1970 after being runner up the previous year. He was a 2nd Dan and a Black Belt in all the Associations. As a contemporary of Brian Jacks and Dave Starbrook he was part of the Olympic squad, but had to drop out through injury. "It was a tough sport and I suffered damage to both shoulders and knees and falls can be very hard. Like boxing if you get the right one in it's all over. While at Andover with the Olympic squad we stayed in the TA Barracks. They've a wonderful school down there with swimming pools and everything. I joined the TA, did their physical training course there and became a PTI and got the crossed swords up". Pat later became a clockmaker and runs his own business.

Charlie's second son, John, was taken to Barnet Fair to see his dad in the booth. "I remember going up to the fair with my older brother, Pat. I was only nine or ten and Pat two years older. They wouldn't let us in so we went around the back and found a gap to look through. I couldn't see and Pat was winding me up saying 'he's got knocked out!' and I was shouting 'No! No!'. Who was you fighting Dad? The answer was Jackie Grimes".

John had a booth bout against Boswell St Louis, a classy Trinidadian welterweight of the 1950s. "Dad told me what it was all about. The old trick being two pairs of gloves, one set eight ounce and the other ten or 12. Dad said they'll ask you what you want – straight or a gee. Boswell came in and asked me if I wanted it straight or a gee. I said I'll have the gee for the money you're paying! Three quid I got. I was hitting him on the shoulders, but every now and again he'd let me know what it was all about – he'd let one go".

"The booths made their money from the local yobbos who used to go in to show off. They used to try and lay in to the booth boys but nearly always come unstuck. We used to watch them. There was Boswell and Sid Cain, a big heavyweight who'd come in as if he was drunk and fall on the floor. It was all a big wind-up. They done their six or eight rounds then went round with the hat. Another bloke who was on the circuit was Joe Somerville, who used to be on the booths as well and he'd take on anybody. Joe and Sid Cain – they used to get at it on the booth. Joe does marathons now".

Like John, Jimmy faced Boswell St Louis. "I boxed in the booth when I was 15. I was mad on boxing and boxed against Boswell, which was an honour for me. Behind the screen he said just put up a good show. Really it was just a sparring match, but I remember making his nose bleed. I was over the moon! I got ten bob for it, which was a lot of money for me then. We done three rounds. There were a lot of good fighters about then who would be champions now like Boswell".

Jimmy had been the first of Charlie's sons to get

Spencer seen here with his manager, Jess Harding, during his fighting days

Les Clark

involved in boxing. "I went to Finchley Boxing Club when it was at the school and I was about eight. When I went to secondary school I went into the schoolboy championships. At that time you didn't need to belong to a club you just entered the competition. I was aged 11, broke my hand in my first fight and lost. I joined the club after that and did quite a lot of schools boxing, going right through into the amateurs".

"None of us really trained in those days – they only opened the school on Tuesdays and Thursdays. It wasn't 'till the Board of Control opened their gym at the 'Load of Hay' in the 1960s that there were more opportunities. George Daly was down there – he was a character – and we used to see him every day, learning so much. Top fighters trained there and we met Floyd Patterson, George Chuvalo, Vicente Saldivar, Jose Legra, Jose Napoles, but not Muhammad Ali. When he came over to fight Cooper they closed the gym and charged a pound to get in. In those days a pound was a lot of money and I refused to pay".

John remembers meeting Marciano. "Rocky came in with George Parnassus, the big Californian promoter. Rocky was in a gold mohair suit – they say someone looks a million dollars – and Rocky looked a million dollars. I was awestruck. He shook hands like he was one of the boys".

"John went into the army for a couple of years when he was 16 or 17 and did a little bit in there. When he came out he joined Jimmy at Finchley and did well, winning a North-West Divisional welterweight title in 1968". John mixed in good company as an amateur and met ABA champs Peter Cragg, Peter Henderson and Alan Edwards; Service champs Mick Bowden and Colin O'Bray and London champ Howard Sharpe. "I boxed Terry Henderson and Brian Whelan, who boxed my head off. I couldn't get near him, he was that good. I also boxed Matty Payne, who was Eastern Counties light-middleweight champion back in the 1960s, and beat him".

"As an amateur I used to spar Bunny Sterling, who was managed by George Francis, but Bunny got so good that it got to the point that you couldn't spar him. I turned pro with George as 'John Charles', after my Dad, as I was in the Fire Service and they frowned on pro boxing. I did myself a favour as nobody knew who I was. Another trick from George – I was an unknown as such – was to get one over Mickey Duff, 'cos he didn't have a record of me! One time George said I got a fight for you against Dusty Smith. I said he's a mate of mine, but George said do you want the money or don't you? I'd boxed Dusty four times as an amateur and beat him that night. That was the last time I saw Dusty, who was managed by Sid Cain".

John had 12 fights, against men such as Ronnie Van Der Walt, Billy Brown, Johnny Shepherd, Les Pearson and Ricky Porter, winning the first ten before retiring. Jimmy retired too. "I more or less retired at the same time, but made a comeback with John training me. I had a few fights and did the North-West Divs. Lined up for a bout, I was crushed in an accident at work and had to retire again. John carried on training for a while after, then we sort of drifted away from it, but we still bought the *Boxing News* and read about it. Then Danny and Spencer started at the club. We lived just

up the road, but they came down on their own. I came down to watch them and they said will you help us?"

Danny and Spencer had sparred at home from an early age, Spencer said: "Dad had us sparring in the front room when I was six or seven years old. Danny was three years older than me and he used to knock s…t out of me all the time. I remember every time Dad came in my brother was there waiting to spar. This was before we came down to the gym and I used to think, here we go again, I'm gonna get another hiding, and that happened right through our careers really. Danny was older and always stronger than me, but it benefited me later on always sparring a stronger man".

Jimmy travelled with his boys to shows. "Before they got carded – medicalled – we used to take them round the little gym shows where they boxed without results. We took Spencer all over and he had about 20 of these bouts. He built up such a name and reputation that when he did get medicalled we couldn't get him a fight. On his 11th birthday we managed to get him a kid called Seamus Kenny from St Pancras, who'd had eight fights or something like that. Spencer took him on and won at Ruislip. I always found it hard to get him bouts on club shows and he always had to give a year in age or a couple of kilos in weight, whatever. It was always like that, but once he started winning titles he got fights that way".

Spencer won a National Schoolboy title, two Junior ABAs, got the England vest, boxed in representative matches and was in top class. "I never lost to a British kid from just before I started winning titles in 1990 to the finish of my career. I remember the first time I boxed abroad was when I was 11, being the youngest kid who ever boxed for Middlesex, and it was about my sixth fight. We drove to Germany. It took about 14 hours – you can fly to Vegas in less these days".

Jimmy recalled Spencer's successes. "Spencer only lost twice in international competition; once in the Commonwealth Games (against Robbie Peden of Australia) and in a multi-nations match (against Robert Kubate of Germany). He was one of the first boxers in Britain ever to compete with computer scoring. When Spence boxed Robert Ciba at the multi-nations tournament at Liverpool the England coach said: 'We're gonna let him fight but if it gets too awkward we'll pull him out!' Spencer beat him easy and he was world class".

"Danny lost ten of his first 13 fights. When he came back for his second season I overmatched him by mistake – reading the record wrong – against a kid from Harlow called Tyrone Linton Bonton, a big southpaw and a good kid. Danny, who was about 13 or 14 at the time, knocked him clean out. Bonton was unconscious before he hit the floor – it being one of the most spectacular of knockouts – and they didn't even count. The doctor jumped into the ring. That's when we realised that he could really punch".

"Danny was small but very strong. He went to Germany with Spence for Middlesex, scoring a knockout, and started winning titles, being Class 'B' & 'C' Boys Clubs champion, while gaining a best boxer award. He was also a London Junior and Senior finalist and a London rep, having about 80 bouts and winning 60-65. There were a lot of pro managers

Finchley ABC: A world away from earlier days

Ian Jackson

after him, but he suffered a set back when refused a licence by the Board because of a 'lazy eye'. However, George Francis put us in contact with Cornelius Boza-Edwards in Las Vegas, who said: 'bring Danny over'. So my brother John and I took him over there and set him up. He was there for three months with Boza-Edwards as trainer and manager and got top class sparring with Robert Wangila, Justin Juuko and Roger Mayweather. He was also friendly with Mike Tyson. He came home then went back and had two pro fights. He drew one against Jose Hernandez – a technical draw because he was floored in the first round – and won the second on a knockout against George Young. He got homesick, came home again – with his girlfriend here – and didn't go back".

Danny wasn't finished with the ring. "After a while I decided to try and get reinstated as an amateur, training with Spencer to get fit again, but when we started sparring I suddenly realised that I didn't have it any longer, having been a British champion as an amateur and a pro in the States. I'd done all I'd wanted to do, but win a world title and there's not many that do that. I worked with Spencer throughout his career and I'm now a trainer here at Finchley".

Spencer won the senior ABA bantamweight championship and a silver at the Commonwealth Games in 1994, then turned pro with Mike Jacobs and John Spensley before moving on to Jess Harding. He made rapid progress, gaining the European super-bantamweight championship from Bulgaria's Martin Krastev during May 1997.

After defending against Serge Poilblan, Vincenzo Belcastro and Fabrice Benichou, Spencer was matched against the Ukrainian, Sergei Devakov, on 2 May 1998 at the Royal Albert Hall. Devakov had failed to impress in two previous appearances in the UK and, though gym reports suggested that he might be stronger than expected, Spencer was a clear favourite. Going into the tenth the champion was ahead with two of the three ringside judges, despite having suffered a 'three' count in the first. Alfred Asaro, the referee, called the bout off after two minutes, 13 seconds of the round as Spencer crouched on the canvas after taking a heavy right hand. Following treatment in the ring, Spencer was removed to hospital where he underwent an operation to remove a blood clot.

Jimmy and Danny were in Vegas with John and the Finchley team when Spencer was injured. "We were all in Vegas at the time", said John. "I got Jimmy and Danny away on the aeroplane home and was left to hold the fort so to speak and I don't know how I did it. I've never seen the fight to this day and I don't think Jimmy has and I don't want to. It was just one of those things, that's right, I don't want to see it. What really happened was that he was European champion and committed to defend that title, but had really outgrown super-bantam and should have gone up to feather. He boiled down and we believe that's why he had his brain injury".

Spencer recalls: "I was only 21 when I won the European title and just turned 23 when my career ended, having had five European title fights in one year, including

33

two hard 12 rounders. I was committed to defend the title and fit voluntaries in between, but was out-growing super-bantam and had to boil down. When I won it I was comfortable, but was still growing, and in the two years before my career finished it was a nightmare to make the weight. If I'd had to make the weight on the day of the fight, I'd never had made super-bantam. On the day of the weigh in I was dead. Didn't eat or drink for three days before and training like a demon to get the weight off".

Jimmy explained how Spencer's corner man saved his life. "We had a trainer here at the time called Eddie Carter – he still comes in to workout – who is a top-class hospital nurse and he went with Spence as a pro as his cutsman. We were at the show when Chris Henry got knocked out and had a brain haemorrhage. Eddie was there and took over from the medics and saved him – though he's paralyzed in one arm. The Board of Control called him in and they started doing lectures. Eddie was in Spencer's corner and when it happened he saved his life, taking over straight away and putting him under an anaesthetic. He knew exactly what to do. Eddie Carter saved his life".

Spencer is still immersed in the world of boxing as Club President and as a resident ringside expert for Sky Sports. Besides work as a personal trainer he has a professional trainer's licence and has worked with Adrian Dodson and Wayne Llewelyn. He still enjoys gum work and often lends a hand at Finchley.

The magnificent Anchor Hall Gym in Bulmer Road, New Barnet is the result of many years of hard work in fund raising and delicate negotiation with local and national government, as well as other organizations. This all started in 1978 when word was received that the hall was for sale. Once the committee had decided to buy the building a Trust was formed which enabled grants and loans to be obtained to the value of £17,835, the remaining (almost) £10,000 coming from fundraising in the community. Having purchased the hall, much work was needed to bring it to a reasonable state of repair. As time passed the Trust was reformed and in 1993 it was estimated that urgent replacement of the roof would cost £24,000. Undaunted, the

committee decided on a complete refurbishment of the building and facilities, the works being finally completed in September 2003 at a cost of almost £200,000, of which Club fundraising contributed £40,000. The Anchor Hall now boasts two rings, a variety of big bags – quilted, angle and maize, floor to ceiling balls and a weights room dominated by a huge poster for Spencer's championship defence against Benichou, facilities beyond the wildest dreams of the club's earliest members.

The Club has been competing annually, in the US, against a Las Vegas select team for over ten years. Firstly against Nevada Partners Inc., a club formed after the riots of 1992 under gym manager, Richard Steele, the top flight referee. Then against Barry's Gym, the pride of former fighter Pat Barry and his wife Dawn. Though a ProAm gym, the Barrys insist that it is run for the kids and the good kids at that Pat said: "I don't want the bad kids; give me those kids that are at the point where they could go either way, the ones who are on the line. There is so much out there for the bad kids, but nothing for the good kids". The club motto is 'We teach the science, not the violence'. The Barrys run a tight ship, assisted by son-in-law and former Prince Nassem world title challenger, Augie Sanchez. Both were employed in law enforcement.

Jim remembers how the transatlantic links came about. "You read about the American kids being great and all that, but looking round the gyms they're no different to this gym. We talked about it and they said bring the boys over and it snowballed from there. One of the blokes who was a trainer here for a while was something to do with the airlines and tried to get us cheap flights. It fell through, but we raised some money, which we have to do separately from the club – and took a team to Vegas. We hitched up with Richard Steele, before going our separate ways and teaming up with Barry's Boxing. We get the satisfaction of taking the boys over but they don't seem to get that excited. I went to Jersey to box when I was a kid and I was over the moon. It was the first time I'd been in an aeroplane and it was unbelievable, but they travel the world now and some of our kids have been to India, Russia and Latvia".

"At our shows in Vegas we have a lot of celebrities. Julio Cesar Chavez, film star 'The Man in Black' – Will Smith, Wayne McCullough – he's an avid supporter and has never missed. The whole team went out to his house to watch him spar Kevin Kelley eight rounds – 98 degrees in his garage all suited up. Absolutely incredible to see them go like that. Two world champions – you can only see that in America. World champions Floyd Mayweather, Roger Mayweather, Boza-Edwards, 'The Body Snatcher' Mike McCallum, Diego Corrales they've all been there. Even Wayne Bobbit was training there to do some unlicenced fighting".

John rates Eddie Mustafa Muhammad. "Me and Eddie go back to the first time in 1996 and you know where Eddie's coming from. He's shouting, I'm shouting. We have a shouting match! There's a lot of respect out there, something you could only get in America. I don't think you get that here, not to that extent anyway. They do a lot of good things out there. The same with Mike Tyson. When

Charlie (left) and Spencer deep in discussion

Ian Jackson

Danny was there in the gym Mike came down to watch and spent all afternoon chatting, nice as pie. He was as nice a bloke as you could meet. It was at the time of the Michael Watson accident and he was really concerned about it. I said 'You're a world champion and you walk in here and sit down with us.' He said 'This is where I'm coming from man, we're all coming from the same place'. He was going to fight Holyfield but it never come off and that's when the trouble started. There was another fellow there shouting at Tyson called Kelcie Banks, recognised as one of America's greatest amateurs and an Olympic gold medallist. Both men came from the same area in the Bronx and all the banter going on was terrific. You can't buy that".

"Chavez was there and one of our boys boxed his nephew. They were about 12 or 13 then. Luke Calvert had had eight fights with six wins, Chavez had 26 with 24 wins, mostly knockouts. We didn't want it so we said no, but his father said he's come all this way and wants to fight. On a club show it would never happen. He done well though he lost on points. Last time we were out there we met young Chavez, who's now fighting as a pro. He said 'You're the guys from London.' They remember you from years back".

"There's a terrific atmosphere as they shout America, America, America or Mexico... – there's usually a majority of Hispanics in their team – and our guys are shouting too. There's also great rivalry. Back in 2003, Mehmet Mehmet outpointed Devon Lawson in a tough fight. The next year the Americans said 'We don't care who else you bring over as long as you bring Mehmet'. Lawson, a strong, tattooed ex con, was determined to get his revenge and had been training for months, but Mehmet still had his number and took the decision to the chants of his team mates, 'Mehmet is the Gov'nor!'. Devon showed his class in stopping at ringside to shake hands with Mehmet's family".

Due to good matchmaking every tournament is close and competitive. There are disputed decisions, but after ten years of friendly rivalry the crowd are remarkably unbiased and while the judges often favour American aggression over Finchley finesse the crowd are not slow to show their displeasure. The Finchley boys' families and friends, usually numbering around three hundred, attend as part of a travel package to give solid, good natured vocal support.

Finchley's biggest recent star is Novice and Senior ABA super-heavyweight champion and Four Nations silver medallist, Derek Chisora, who has tempted John Oliver into the pro ranks to continue as his trainer. Derek was born in February 1984 and didn't lace on a glove 'till he was 19, since when he's been guided by John who's very excited about his prospects. John said: "We're very close – on the 'phone all the time. I was very close to George Francis right up to his death and have the same relationship with Derek. George was a great teacher and I'm trying to pass that on. He's fast on his feet, can really box and he can punch. He's shown character in coming from behind to win and scored some heavy knockouts. I think he's got a big future".

Along with Chisora's championships, popular feather-weight, Mehmet Mehmet, won the North-West Divs title in 2004. However, over the years it has been through the schoolboy and junior ranks that the club has achieved its greatest successes. Danny Martin Oliver, a cousin to Spencer and Danny, was a junior ABA champion and recent winners include Joe Smyth (junior), three-times Schools champion, multi-nations gold medal winner, England rep and team captain; Ashley Sexton, three-times Schools champion, NABC & NACYP champion and Four Nations gold medal winner; Grant Skehill, Schools champion, and another recent pro signing; and a succession of competition winners, including Billy Moy and Rudi Rizzo, who won Golden Belts, and Schoolboy Golden Gloves champion, Joe Winson. Many youngsters gain invaluable experience travelling abroad for representative matches and to contest championships. Despite that, some Finchley stars have moved to other clubs, which is not unusual – John's son John turned out for Repton a few seasons ago.

Head trainer at the Saturday morning nursery session, George Phillips, is another with booth experience. Former professional champion, Sean Murphy, brings a wealth of experience to bear as twice ABA and Commonwealth champion, gold medallist in the Acropolis and Canada Cups and outright winner of a Lonsdale Belt. Sean's son Danny is also a Finchley Club member. Joe Smyth (senior), Sennan McNamarra, Danny and John Oliver, Pat Walsh, Johnny Shannon, Lee Tierney, Steve Conlon and Gary Foley make up the training establishment led by Jimmy Oliver. Pat Walsh doubles as a club trustee.

Even thriving amateur clubs, especially those that are active in international circles, are constantly strapped for cash. Finchley's gym and their regular trips to Las Vegas evidence the club's success in fundraising and the on-going commitment of members and officials. During 2005, Jimmy Oliver and Steve Holohan took part in a seven-day sponsored 200 mile trek in the Sahara Desert, braving temperatures of 105 degrees to raise cash for Vegas, and on one occasion John finished the London marathon the day before flying to Nevada. Spencer has run two London Marathons and joined Michael Watson in crossing the line after his epic London run. Pat Walsh, Gary Foley and Sennan McNamarra, along with committee men Dave Spicer, Chris McGovern and Arthur Geeves have also run the London Marathon.

After spending their lives in boxing the Oliver family now enjoy their involvement in the London Ex-Boxers Association, being regular attenders at the Association's monthly meetings.

Footnote: Whilst this article was coming together, the editor in trying to trace his old trainer, Les Kirk, discovered he had died in Godalming, Surrey on 24 March 1983, aged just 55. After giving up training the boys at Finchley ABC, Les had qualified as an osteopath and set up a successful surgery. He was survived by his wife, Richardene, whom I spoke to in order to write this tribute to him.

Born on 7 June 1927 in Barnet, Les turned to boxing while serving in the Navy prior to successfully being awarded a BBBoC pro license in February 1948. Managed by Jackie Hopwood, he started with a first-round kayo of Len Jones on 19 April 1948 at Leyton Baths before suffering his first defeat at the hands of George Smith in his seventh contest. Although the rest of his career was a bit up and down prior to him hanging up the gloves in May 1954, his finest win came in August 1951 when he scored a first-round knockout over Bernie Newcombe, then a hot prospect. Other men he beat included Don Desborough, Eric Stevens, Reg McMurdie, Jack Alpress, Terry Stannard, Ron King, Ken Bebington and Joe White, while he drew with Peter Glen and Morley Nightingale. He also tangled with Johnny Oldham, Bert Middleton, Tom Johnston, Bob Foster, Ron Kensington and Danny Gill, before bowing out at the hands of Les Morgan, a former ABA champion, having proved himself to be a hard-hitting left hooker who won 16, drew two and lost 13 of 31 contests. He also boxed on the booths.

I first met him when I was in and out of a very basic Finchley ABC during the late 1950s, but once I decided to give it a shot he was normally in my corner, where he gave me the utmost confidence in my ability, especially as a puncher. Hard hitting was his forte and he was a great believer in getting a contest over as quickly as possible; his last-minute advice to me always being "just go and knock him out". This is how I will always affectionately remember him. Rest in Peace, Les.

The Fighting Olivers: standing: left to right: Pat, John, Charlie and Jim. Front: left to right: Spencer and Danny

Ian Jackson

Jack Lindsay: A Lifetime in Boxing

by Bob Lonkhurst

It is often claimed that particular events during childhood can have a major impact on a person's life. That theory certainly appears to be accurate in respect of veteran boxing trainer, Jack Lindsay, who vividly remembers his introduction to the noble art. During the early hours of 30 August 1937, he sat with his parents at their home in Surbiton, Surrey listening to Bob Bowman's commentary of the intense battle between Tommy Farr and Joe Louis in New York. Jack was just five years old.

Although nobody in his family was actively involved in boxing, the excitement of that particular fight clearly had a tremendous impression upon him. From then onwards, whenever a major contest was broadcast he pleaded with his father to be allowed to stay up and listen. Another fight he recollects clearly was the British light-heavyweight championship encounter between Len Harvey and Jock McAvoy at Harringay on 7 April 1938.

As Jack grew up, his fascination about boxing developed and would eventually lead him into a lifetime involvement with the sport, firstly as a boxer and then for over 40 years as a coach in both amateur and professional sides of the sport. It is perhaps fitting that his life took that route because unbeknown to him until recent years, he is a distant relative of Tom Sayers, the formidable pugilist who was recognised as champion of England from 1849-1859. The discovery was made by a nephew of Jack's during research and creation of a family tree. It transpired that Sayers was Jack's great, great, great uncle from his mother's side of the family.

Jack was born at Kingston upon Thames on 30 July 1932 and had a sister and four brothers. The family lived at Surbiton until moving to Luton in 1942 just as the blitz was starting during the Second World War. It was there in a local field that he was first taught the rudiments of boxing by a serving British Army sergeant. Whenever he was home on leave, Sergeant Ellis showed Jack and a group of about nine boys how to jab, throw crosses and hooks, and generally defend themselves. He provided pairs of gloves, and the boys formed a ring as he put each one through his paces. Jack loved boxing and competed at school whenever he could, although during the war there was a black-out and regulations seriously restricted competition between schoolboys at night.

In 1946, he joined Vauxhall Motors ABC at Luton as a junior, boxing at nine stone, and remained there until called up for national service in 1950. On joining the Royal Air Force Jack was attached to Bomber Command and after completing three months basic training at RAF Melksham he was transferred to RAF Wyton in Cambridgeshire. At the earliest opportunity he volunteered for boxing training and within a few months entered the No 3 Group championships, staged at RAF Coningsby on 31 October 1951. He became the Group light-welterweight champion, winning all of his three contests by knockouts in the second round. Two weeks later, Lindsay represented No 3 Group against No 1 Group in the Command championships at Coningsby where he beat Aircraftsman Smith (RAF Bassingbourn) on points. Two team-mates from RAF Wyton were also victorious. The following week, 22 November 1951, Jack boxed for Bomber Command at RAF Benson. In a tough light-welterweight contest he was narrowly outpointed by Leading Aircraftsman John Hall.

After winning a Group championship in 1952, Jack again won a Bomber Command title at RAF Coningsby. Still boxing a light-welterweight he won his semi-final by a first round knockout and beat Aircraftsman Jones (RAF Waddington) on points in the final. That year he boxed for Bomber Command in representative matches against Northern Counties, Metropolitan Police and the United States Airforce, and was unbeaten. He also represented RAF Wyton at club shows in and around Cambridgeshire.

Although Jack spent much of his National Service time boxing and enjoying the perks that went with it, he was still up at 5am each morning and did his share of guard duty. He is appreciative of what the RAF did for him because apart from giving him a good grounding in team comradeship, it instilled discipline into him, something which is seriously lacking in many youngsters in modern times. He had great respect for officers and when he was demobbed in December 1952, as Airman First Class, his discharge papers described his conduct as excellent.

Back in civilian life Jack worked as a hod-carrier on building sites for a number of years. It was strength building and excellent training for boxing. He rejoined Vauxhall Motors ABC and boxed for the club from 1953 to 1956. On a massive club show staged in the factory canteen on 9 May 1953, he was outpointed by Don Flack (RAOC) at lightweight. Most of the contestants, active or former servicemen included such stars as Henry Cooper, who boxed Jack Harper (later known as London), Brian Harper (London), Dennis Hinson, Ron Barton, Percy Lewis, who boxed Alan Sillett, Bruce Wells against Dennis Booty and Frankie Jones versus George Dormer. Barton, Lewis and Wells were all full-time airmen attached to Bomber Command and based in Oxfordshire with the Queen's Flight. Jack knew them personally from boxing for Bomber Command during his national service.

In 1956, Lindsay joined Davis ABC, a well known gas stove manufacturing company at Luton. He remained with the club for several years. Although he was nearing the end of his boxing career, he moved clubs again, this time to Napier English Electric based at Crescent Road, before retiring a few months later having taken part in about 70 amateur contests with only a handful of defeats. Having no desire to turn professional, Jack had already become involved in coaching. He clearly had a talent for teaching others because the Bedfordshire, Hertfordshire and North Buckinghamshire ABA appointed him as assistant trainer to the association team to meet Essex ABA at Southend on 16 December 1961.

Whilst he was still with Napier Jack made frequent visits to nearby Hightown Youth Club, based at Charles Street. It had a boxing section run by a good Irish boxer, Dave Dowdall, who founded the club. The two quickly became friends and after a few discussions about boxing, Dave asked Jack to join him. At about that time Napier was due to close because English Electric wanted the premises back for redevelopment. The opportunity for Jack to move to Hightown Youth therefore came at the right moment. Lindsay and Dowdall worked well together and created good local interest. There came a time, however, when the local council decided to develop the site into a complex, but because of what they had achieved were keen for Jack and Dave to continue. Consequently, they were offered new council-owned premises at Chapel Langley. The building, constructed in 1912, was used partly as a junior school during the day and a youth club at night. It was known as Chapel Langley Youth Club, but the two trainers were given a free rein to set up and develop a boxing club within the premises.

Mostly at their own expense Lindsay and Dowdall set up a gym with all necessary training facilities. Within a month, however, Dowdall, a foreman with Vauxhall Motors, was transferred to a plant at Ellesmere Port. It was a major set-back to the plans, but possessing good organising skills and an abundance of determination Jack went it alone. Retaining the name of Hightown Youth ABC, he built a boxing club that would remain on the site for over 40 years.

At the time he started coaching at the club, Jack was employed by Vauxhall Motors. Because of the nature of his work with Hightown Youth, the council made him a youth leader and paid him on a monthly basis. Everything was done correctly because there was insurance in place against accidents and injury. A steady stream of youngsters joined the club as its reputation grew, including Noel McIvor, an established boxer who had been with Vauxhall Motors ABC as a schoolboy. Jack coached him as a senior amateur and he developed into a quality boxer. He won the 1970 London North-West Divisional lightweight title and boxed in the Irish championships the same year. He was also selected by the Ulster Council of the Irish ABA in a 20-man squad to prepare for final trials ahead of the Commonwealth Games at Edinburgh.

Other newcomers included Roy Commosioung and Henry Rhiney. An established member of the original Hightown Youth Club was Brian Whelan who turned

Jack (left), representing Bomber Command in 1952, is pictured here in action against John Drummond of the American Air Force

Jack (left) is seen here training Henry Rhiney for his British welterweight title fight against Pat Thomas in December 1976

professional in 1968, having been barred by the ABA for pushing a referee. Over the next few years McIvor, Rhiney and Commosioung also joined the paid ranks. Jack had built special relationships with these young men and their respect for him was such that all asked him to continue training them at Hightown while they fought for pay. Having coached them since they joined the club, Lindsay saw nothing wrong with this. He didn't foresee the likely reaction of the ABA who strongly objected to an amateur coach being involved with professionals. Once the ABA became aware of the situation, they advised him to attach himself to one body or the other – amateur or professional. He refused, and over a period of time there were some heated discussions. Eventually, Jack was banned from working in his boxer's corners, and finally, in 1975, he was banned from the amateur game. It was a situation which still angers him.

By sheer determination and his love of the sport, Lindsay had been able to train the professionals and still give the same amount of time to schoolboys and senior amateurs. His professionals were respected fighters. Brian Whelan lost only five of 19 contests between 1968 and 1970, and at one stage had an unbeaten run of nine. Noel McIvor won the Southern Area lightweight title in 1972, beating Alan Salter in two rounds. He lost it to Tommy

Dunn on points at Reading in December 1974 and the following year was stopped by Dunn in seven rounds when he attempted to regain it. Noel retired in 1976 with a credible record of 25 wins and four draws from 47 contests. Roy Commosioung, a Jamaican boxing out of Luton, was a genuine hard man with a great defence. Although he won only 18 of 47 professional contests between 1974 and 1978, he was stopped only once. That was by Charlie Cooper in a final eliminator for the Southern Area middleweight title in 1977.

Henry Rhiney was the first of Jack's real success stories. He turned professional in 1973 and progressed slowly although not dramatically. Then, in 1976, he won both the Southern Area and British welterweight championships in back-to-back contests against Mickey Ryce and Pat Thomas. He successfully defended the British title against Billy Waith in February 1978, before winning the European championship in dramatic style in December of the same year, knocking out Josef Pachler in ten rounds in Austria. That, however, was the peak of Henry's career and after losing his European title in five rounds to Dave 'Boy' Green, he was stopped in ten by Kirkland Laing in defence of his British title. After four more defeats, all on points, he retired in 1980 with a record of 32 victories and eight draws from 55 contests. At a press conference in London to announce Rhiney's European title defence against Green, the promoters wanted the two boxers to dress up in chefs' clothing and pose for the cameras carving a Christmas turkey. Although Dave was agreeable, Henry flatly refused. "I'm a fighter," he snapped, "not a clown". Despite pleas from the promoters, Henry wouldn't budge. Lindsay, however, was always a diplomat. Taking his boxer to one side, he said: "Look they are paying you more money for this fight than you've earned in your entire career. If they tell you to take your clothes off, you do it". Eventually Henry saw sense and conformed to the promoter's request. Green was still a massive attraction and to prevent Rhiney being lured to Denmark to defend his title, Mike Barrett and Mickey Duff paid him £26,000 for a London defence. Rhiney disappeared from the boxing scene following his retirement and now lives in Florida. The fact that he has remained in touch with Lindsay all these years speaks volumes for the respect he has for his old trainer. A hand painted portrait of himself sent from Florida is proudly displayed in Jack's house.

Over the years a steady stream of fighters were coached at Jack's gym, including professionals such as Monty Wright (Southern Area light-heavyweight champion and British title challenger), Everton Blake (Southern Area cruiserweight champion), Kevin McCarthy (Southern Area welterweight champion), Danny, Shane and Eddie Porter, Les Foster, Tim Hands, Renard Ashton, Norris Dennis, Alan Baptiste, Stuart Fishermac, Marco Fattore, Dave Fallon, Matthew Tait, Soni Thind, Kenric Edwards and Mark Tierney. Lindsay has also trained boxers for a number of managers. The first was Johnny Barclay from Tring who he first met when he was trying to find a manager for Brian Whelan in 1968. Other fighters managed by Mickey Duff, Terry Lawless and Dennie Mancini were coached by Jack from time to time. His gym was also used by other boxers on occasions for sparring. They included Joe Calzaghe, Colin Dunne, Tony Sibson, Carl Wright, Howard Eastman, Jonathan Thaxton, Colin Moorcroft, Graham Earl and Bobby Banghar. Andy Smith took Joe Bugner (junior), Des Morrison, and his son Robert Smith, now Assistant General Secretary of the British Boxing Board of Control. Robert was nearing the end of his professional career and sparred with Billy Schwer who was still an amateur.

Billy Schwer was a talented and successful amateur, who was originally a member of Luton Irish ABC where he was trained by his father. During the last two years of his amateur career, however, Lindsay was also involved in coaching him. In 1990 when Billy decided to turn professional, he asked Jack to train him. Lindsay suggested that before making a commitment, he looked around at other trainers. Two months later Billy and his father called at Jack's gym and told him they had signed a promotional deal with Mickey Duff. They wanted him to be Billy's trainer. This suited Jack who got on well with Duff, having trained a number of boxers for him over the years as well as others managed by Terry Lawless, Dennie Mancini and Terry Toole. Mancini, a highly respected cuts-man, would be part of Schwers' team.

Despite his involvement training boxers, Jack had also been self-employed as a boiler engineer since 1979 with a huge client list. It was a major asset being self-employed because it ensured that he was always available when required by the boxers. As Schwer progressed they spent more and more time in the gym to the extent that training him eventually became a full-time job.

Schwer's career has been well documented, but it is important to stress that his success was built on an abundance of determination and trust by all members of his team. He won British, Commonwealth and European lightweight championships and the IBO light-welterweight title. He also challenged unsuccessfully for the IBF, WBC and WBU lightweight titles. When he retired in 2001 he had lost just six of 45 contests and taken part in 17 championship bouts. As Billy was susceptible to cuts around the eyes, the part played by Dennie Mancini was crucial to his success. Lindsay is convinced that his skill probably prolonged Billy's career by several years. Jack has great affection for Mancini. "He was always generosity itself to me", he remarked. "He was one of the nicest people I knew in this business, and always paid me well for my services".

Schwer's promoters always valued Jack's opinion and he was frequently consulted when a particular opponent was being considered. Meetings took place at the Wardour Street offices of National Promotions, and there was only one occasion when he strongly objected to an opponent. That was in 1995 when plans were being made to match Schwer against David Tetteh of Ghana in a Commonwealth title defence. Very little was known about Tetteh in Britain other than he had been sparring Azumah Nelson. Short and stocky, with a record of one loss from eight bouts, he was an unknown quantity which concerned Jack, who anticipated that he could pose Billy problems he had never encountered before. Defeat would mean that plans to get a rematch with Rafael Ruelas and a proposed shot at the European title would be shot to pieces. Mickey Duff took Lindsay's concerns seriously and agreed to search for another opponent. Despite his efforts nobody could be found leaving no alternative for Schwer but to face Tetteh. Jack remained extremely apprehensive, and during the fight his worst fears became reality. After being badly hurt in round four, Billy was always fighting an uphill battle. Tetteh was squat and powerfully built. His crouching style meant he was always punching upwards particularly with damaging hooks. The end came after one minute, four seconds of the final round when the Luton man was badly marked about the eyes and, according to the referee, had no chance of winning.

Jack enjoyed every minute of the time he spent working with Schwer. One of the most amusing stories he tells relates to Billy's unsuccessful challenge for the IBF lightweight championship against Rafael Ruelas at Las Vegas in 1995. In the dressing room before the fight while Lindsay was taping Billy's hands, a group of American officials were hovering over them like hawks. At one point there was criticism over the style of taping, which infuriated Mickey Duff and Dennie Mancini. Although Jack was relaxed and quite happy to deal with the problem, Duff flew into a rage and there was an almighty row. After it had all calmed down, Mickey suddenly turned to the officials and said: "I'm sorry gentlemen, you will all have to leave, Billy Schwer wants to pray". With that he ushered the group out of the room and locked the door. Despite the tenseness of the pre-fight situation, Billy couldn't stop laughing. Jack was totally bemused, but it was quick thinking by Duff who wanted his boxer's hands prepared professionally with a minimum of interference from petty officials.

Schwer trained at Lindsay's gym at Chapel Langley from the day he turned professional. He spent so much time there it became like a second home, but in 1996 Bedfordshire County Council threatened to close it down following a recommendation to ban boxing in council premises. The proposal attracted considerable media interest. "It will be devastating for the lads if the boxing section of this youth club is shut down", Jack told local reporters. He explained in great detail how he built the gym with the help of hundreds of boys and their parents. "The boys paid £2 a night to train and spar, and the boxing section has never asked the Luton Area Youth Committee for money. On the contrary, they contributed to club funds". Lindsay explained how Henry Rhiney and Billy Schwer were given civic receptions when they became champions. "Everyone loved us, including the council", he remarked. "Now they want to close us down, claiming it is to save money. That's a bad joke – they have never funded us except for any part-time wages. I am under contract and they have offered me youth work elsewhere, so they can't save that much money anyway". There was considerable public support for the club and demands for it to stay open. In a close-run, and sometimes heated debate, the motion to close it was defeated by ten votes to nine. Jack carried on at the gym for a further six years, and although it eventually closed in 2002 it was because a surveyors report stated it was structurally in a bad state and beyond economical repair. It was an emotional situation because it was the end of an era. Yet everyone parted as good friends, with council members who ran the complex holding a farewell party for Jack. A plaque bearing the title 'THE LINDSAY ROOM' was attached to the wall of the old gym.

Away from boxing Jack is very knowledgeable about classical music and more particularly art, hobbies not generally associated with participants of such a demanding trade as boxing. Art came to him naturally many years ago. He has spent a lot of time at the National Gallery and over the years built up his own library of books about the subject. Yet as he explains: "I've always been more of a looker than a doer. I just love browsing around galleries and museums". That having been said, however, he still has an extensive display of his own paintings. Lindsay is great friends with modern day painter, Peter Deighan, who also lives at Luton.

Jack (right) celebrates with Billy Schwer, Billy Schwer (senior) and Mickey Duff (left) following Billy's successful defence of his British and Commonwealth lightweight titles against Howard Grant at Stevenage on 16 February 1994

Jack (left) discusses tactics with Billy Schwer at Wembley on 29 November 1999, prior to Billy's contest against Steve Johnston for the WBC lightweight championship

He went to him for art lessons for over a year between 1969 and 1970. Deighan has great interest in boxing and once painted a portrait of Billy Schwer. Amongst his other subjects are Muhammed Ali, John Major, the Beatles, and many of the world's leading golfers.

Jack has been married to Anne for 54 years and they have two sons, two daughters, 14 grandchildren and one great granddaughter. One son, Gregory, is a professional painter with studios at Wimbledon. He is also an extremely talented musician. His interest developed rapidly from the day he and Jack stopped to look in a music shop window. Gregory pointed to a flute and said he wanted it because he had played one at school. Although Jack had only £28 in his pocket at the time, his wages for his youth club work, he bought it. He maintains it was the best present he ever gave his son who played it at every possible opportunity. His skills developed dramatically and with passing of time he has had many auditions for big orchestras and put on waiting lists. When he left college, Gregory had the option of going to the Guildhall School of Music or an Art College. He opted for the latter and graduated with all the necessary qualifications to make a career of it. Jack advised him to centralise his skills on either art or music, and although he concentrated on art, he never gave up the music. He currently plays flute and piccolo, and is a regular member of a symphony orchestra and folk bands.

Jack Lindsay is respected throughout the boxing world, and over the years his contributions to the sport have been acknowledged by a variety of sources. In 1976, the *Luton News* presented him with a Certificate of Congratulation to mark his achievement in training Henry Rhiney to become British welterweight champion and in 1999 he received a special award from the British Boxing Board of Control for his services to boxing. He was very honoured, especially as previous recipients included Muhammed Ali, Mickey Duff, Harry Carpenter and Reg Gutteridge.

Locally, Jack has been regarded as a celebrity for many years, particularly through his involvement with Henry Rhiney and Billy Schwer. When Billy retired from boxing in 2001, Luton Town Council presented him with a sculptured figure of himself because he was generally regarded as one of the finest sportsmen ever to come from the town. They also acknowledged Jack's massive contribution and presented him with an identical trophy inscribed: "To Jack Lindsay for his efforts in training Billy Schwer". The retirement of Schwer followed by the closure of his gym meant that Jack became less involved in boxing. Despite the set-backs, however, he remains firmly in the sport and currently trains come-backing heavyweight, Matt Legg, and Kenroy Lambert. A documentary about Tom Sayers and the era in which he lived is currently being filmed and incorporates Jack as a trainer in modern times.

Lindsay is a trainer from the old school who benefited tremendously from his national service days. He has been a massive servant to the sport in Britain and is respected by everyone who knows him. Long may he continue.

Gary De'Roux: A Man on a Mission

by Ralph Oates

Anyone who has ever boxed at any level, be it professional or amateur, will know how hard it is to walk away from the sport. It gets into your blood, into your very soul and you just cannot shake it out of your system; it is really an addiction. The training which becomes part of your daily life is badly missed. Certainly you may well moan and groan a little when you have to go through your paces but when it's gone a vacant space opens up which is difficult to fill. To a degree everything becomes a little dull without that routine which once gave a real sense of purpose. Many boxers have, over the years, gone through this. The end of ones fighting life must of course come to a close one day and it's a situation which boxers do come to terms with eventually. Every fighter knows that a moment comes when he has heard the bell sound for the last time. The never-ending tick of the clock dictates to the body that it can no longer perform in the way it once did and the signs are often there to be seen. The trick is to identify them, since age is the opponent who will always win in the end. Many who do not like or indeed understand the sport will not be able to appreciate the passion a fighter gets for that square ring; the challenge on the night and the feeling that runs through the mind at the start of the round. The joy of victory and the despair of defeat is indeed a strange mix. Yet those who perform love it and when the fighting days are over many have to stay involved in some capacity or another and this is a good thing for both the fighter and the sport. Experience is a valuable commodity and is something which cannot be bought. Let's be honest, an ex-fighter is ideal to be in the corner of a young boxer who is just starting out on the pugilistic path for he really knows what it's all about – the various doubts which may be running through the mind of

Gary (right), seen here in his fighting days, connects with a right hander on his way to a points win over Gary King at Peterborough on 19 February 1987

his charge, the nerves which pulsate through his body before the first jab is even thrown. The urge the young fighter will have to just go out and throw punches without any thought must be tempered and in its place a scientific approach taught. This is not an easy task and it takes time and patience and calls for a man who is respected. Such a man is Gary De'Roux, a former British featherweight champion, who was without doubt a good-class fighter, a man who is boxing through and through. Gary is one who came back to the sport once his boxing days were over to train and thus give the benefit of his vast ring experience to younger boxers seeking to make their way in the sport. Just recently, Gary moved over from training amateurs to the professional code, which should see in the years which follow a number of potential champions emerge from The Phoenix Gym. Make no mistake, boxing is Gary's life. He really lives it and this can only be good for the game that a man of his calibre gives so much of his time to the noble art. The former British champions been there; he knows what the game is all about and is more than aware that talent is not enough alone to get a fighter to the top. A boxer, like all sportsmen, must do the necessary training and there is no short cut to any kind of championship. Having Gary in your corner is an ace card for any fighter. When fighting, Gary was always looking for ways to improve his own technique. He would also fight anyone, anywhere and at any time – indeed he fought in Italy twice and America once during his professional career. The man was a fighters' fighter, who always gave of his very best, win or lose. Gary knew that you could never learn enough. In life there is always a new lesson to absorb and in boxing you could say the same. A fighter cannot afford to rest on his or her laurels and even after a good victory they must seek to improve on each and every performance. Likewise, a defeat is not the end of the world. However, in some cases a defeat can have a psychological affect on a boxer which duly impedes his future performances. Fighters must be fit in both mind and body. A set back should be put in its correct context and every effort put in place to ensure that the fighter does not lose heart and thus his ambition by any defeat he may suffer. Gary is more than conversant with these facts. They say that knowledge is power and in boxing that is so very true. After hearing about his good work I contacted Gary on behalf of the *Yearbook* to ask about his career and his general views about the sport.

(*Ralph Oates*) In which year were you born?
(*Gary De'Roux*) 1962.
(*RO*) Where were you born?
(*GD*) Crossleys Hospital, Great Ancoats, Manchester, weighing in at 5lbs 4oz.
(*RO*) How old were you when you first started to box?
(*GD*) I was 21 years of age, when I started to go to the local amateur boxing club.
(*RO*) Have any other members of your family ever boxed?
(*GD*) Not that I know of. My father was a big boxing fan, and apparently, Wayne Llewelyn the heavyweight is distantly related.
(*RO*) What made you take up boxing?

(*GD*) I was always quite handy with my fists from a very early age. After I got married I wanted something constructive to do in the evenings following work, so I eventually went to the local amateur club and took up boxing as a hobby. I loved it from the first moment I had the gloves on. I could fight and get trophies, instead of the police turning up at my front door. Even better, as I improved they then started to pay me to fight once I became a professional.
(*RO*) Which club did you box for?
(*GD*) Focus ABC in Peterborough. However, I am sorry to say this club has now sadly closed down after surviving for more than 25 years. Hence the lack of boxing clubs in the area inspired me to create Phoenix ABC in 1988.
(*RO*) Who were your trainers at the Focus?
(*GD*) Terry Shufflebottom (head coach) and Raf Tuccillo who was the assistant coach.
(*RO*) Approximately how many amateur bouts did you have?
(*GD*) I had 20 bouts in two seasons.
(*RO*) Can you remember how many bouts you actually won and how many inside the distance?
(*GD*) In my first contest, I represented the Eastern Counties in a select squad in Jersey and won to my great delight in the first round by a knockout. In my very first season I won all my contests by stoppages. It was not until my sixth fight that I actually went the distance and thus lost points in a championship final. Unbelievably I had boxed a total of just six rounds before my championship bout. I won a total of 15 out of 20 contests in the amateurs, nine by knockout.
(*RO*) Did you attend many amateur shows after you retired from boxing?
(*GD*) Yes, since I ran the successful Phoenix amateur club in Peterborough for eight years, and got out to many amateur shows. My first national champion went on to box for England and, as an ABA coach, I found it very disappointing not to be involved. I decided from this point that it was time to move on and leave the amateur's to go into the professional side of boxing, knowing that the sport would be kept alive in Peterborough with the new clubs which have since started up. In fact I spent most weekends at amateur shows up and down the country, while I had my own club. I also spent time travelling in Cuba during 2005. This I must say was the ultimate amateur show for me, it being very difficult to compare British boxing with the Cuban boxing lifestyle and commitment. The trip was an experience I shall never forget. I feel I more than succeeded in the amateur game, having five champions from regional level upwards, but as an ex-professional, I never felt totally comfortable in the ABA environment.
(*RO*) In which stance did you box?
(*GD*) Orthodox.
(*RO*) Many boxers do not like fighting southpaws. How did you feel about meeting them in combat?
(*GD*) I regularly boxed southpaws and most of them didn't last the distance. My right hand-left hook usually took care of them.
(*RO*) Who was your most difficult opponent in the amateur ranks?

(GD) Alan Lesbirel from the Army. I won on points but he was a really clever, fit and tough lad who gave me all sorts of problems.

(RO) What was your proudest moment in the amateur ranks?

(GD) An international competition in Germany. I boxed against Perres and Dusgun, both bouts ending in a kayo in the first round and two wins to England in a competition against the host country, Germany. I can't remember if we won the tournament overall. It took place in 1985.

(RO) What was your biggest disappointment in the amateur ranks?

(GD) I can honestly say that there were no disappointments. I remember the amateurs as great fun and lots of good fights. I squeezed 20 fights into two seasons. I learnt as I went along in competition, the hard way. This is what made me tough physically and mentally.

(RO) What made you decide to turn professional?

(GD) I was a strong featherweight and it became very difficult to get matches.

(RO) In which year did you have your first professional contest?

(GD) In 1986 in Peterborough, my hometown. I boxed Tony Carter from Manchester and it was a second-round stoppage.

(RO) Who was your manager?

(GD) I never stuck with one manager and eventually I became self managed.

(RO) Who was your trainer?

(GD) I started off with my amateur trainer, Terry Shufflebottom. Terry took several of the Focus ABC lads into the professional ranks before Kevin Sanders took over. We all had early successful fights, but in the end we all went our separate ways. I have been able to work with some of the best trainers in the country such as Jimmy Tibbs, Dean Powell, Terry Toole and John Ingle, just to name a few. However, without doubt the most influential trainer for me was Brendan Ingle.

(RO) Who was your most difficult opponent in the professional ranks?

(GD) Henry Armstrong, who was an excellent box-fighter. I had a headache for three days after our first fight, which took place on 20 September 1989 in Stoke. This was a comeback for me since I had not fought since 26 November 1988. I lost the bout to Armstrong on points over eight rounds, but in a return contest, which took place in Oldham on 19 April 1990, I won by a nasty knockout in the eighth with only seconds to spare in the last round. To this day I don't think either one of us wants the decider. We both took a great deal out of each other and you can't have too many fights like those in your career. I really do have a great deal of respect and admiration for Henry, in fact, I still get nose bleeds when I think about our fights.

(RO) How many bouts did you have during your professional career?

(GD) I had 22 bouts, winning 13, drawing one and losing eight.

(RO) Do you believe that boxing instils discipline and respect to those who participate in the sport?

(GD) Whole-heartedly, and much more besides. I instil in the boxers I train the 3 D's, Determination, Dedication and Discipline.

(RO) How did you feel upon winning your first professional championship, which was the vacant Southern Area featherweight title?

(GD) Very happy since the title helped to boost my rating and my opponent, Alan McKay, who I defeated for the crown was a very good fighter. He had outpointed Steve Robinson over six rounds in his contest prior to mine and he also held a three-round stoppage win over Colin McMillan.

(RO) What would you say was your proudest moment when boxing in the professional ranks?

(GD) Winning the British featherweight title despite only two weeks prior notice. I knocked out the defending champion, Sean Murphy, in five rounds at Millwall on 5 March 1991. You really have to take your chances when you get them. Chance favours the prepared mind, body and soul. I have always believed this and it is inscribed on my gym wall to remind others. To not only beat Murphy, but to stop him was such an achievement for me and people still remember that fight today, he was a good rated fighter at the time. Sean won the vacant title by knocking out John Doherty in three rounds on 22 May 1990 and made a first defence against Johnny B. Good on 25 September 1990 by a knockout in two rounds. A win against me would have seen him win the Lonsdale Belt outright. Prior to our meeting in the ring, Sean had only lost one professional fight in a total of 20 and that was to Ray Minus on 1 July 1987, when stopped in round five while challenging for the Commonwealth bantamweight title in only his eighth bout. Let's not forget that after I defeated him he went on and attempted to regain the British featherweight crown from McMillan on 29 October 1991, being outpointed over 12 rounds. Then, on 27 February 1993, Murphy stopped Alan McKay in round nine to regain the British featherweight title which was vacant at the time. Sean even had a crack at the WBO version of the world featherweight title, being knocked out in round nine by the then holder, Steve Robinson, on 10 July 1993. Murphy later challenged Billy Schwer for the British and Commonwealth lightweight titles on 16 February 1994, being stopped in the third round. To win the British championship was unbelievable, but to win it in such a memorable fight against a man like Murphy was even better.

(RO) You lost your British title in your first defence against Colin McMillan. How did you rate him?

(GD) Colin was a splendid boxer, who of course went on to win the WBO version of the world featherweight title. I have no complaints about the defeat, Colin was a mover and I always had difficulty with that style. If he had stood and traded punches with me the outcome might well have been different. Colin was being groomed for great things. I could have ducked him for a time, but felt that a champion is supposed to be the best, thus my view was and still is if you are the best you meet the best and you do not avoid any challengers. I would do the same today if in the same position.

(RO) Were you ever superstitious in anyway before a contest?

(GD) Not really, but I have to confess that I carried a plait of hair from my wife and daughter tucked into my boxing boots during a contest.

(RO) What was your biggest disappointment in the professional ranks?

(GD) I always felt that I was avoided by the top names and it really took a long time to finally get a chance at the British featherweight title. My opportunity really should have come earlier than it did for both the Southern Area and British featherweight titles. This is where a good manager and promoter comes in handy.

(RO) Was there a boxer who you would have liked to have fought in the professional ranks and for one reason or another the bout was not made?

(GD) I would have fought anyone in the top ten, Robert Dickie, who held the British featherweight and British super-featherweight titles, Paul Hodkinson, who captured the WBC and European featherweight crowns, and John Davison, also a British featherweight king, were the top guys I would have liked to have fought.

(RO) Did you ever have any awkward moments during your boxing career?

(GD) The first sparring session I had with Prince Naseem Hamed. He was not well known to the general public at the time and did a switch, before hitting me out of nowhere. Remember, I was a former British champion and knew my way around, it was unbelievable.

(RO) How do you feel about female involvement in the sport?

(GD) Live and let live.

(RO) Who is your favourite old time fighter?

(GD) Former world heavyweight champion, Jack Johnson. Now that's what you call pressure, he must have been so tough mentally and physically.

(RO) How do you feel about title fights being held over the duration of 12 rounds rather than 15?

(GD) I personally would prefer 15 rounds. Those extra three rounds could make all the difference in a championship bout.

(RO) How do you feel boxers today compare with past boxers with regard to both their skill and technique?

(GD) It is all relative, there are many great fighters both old and new. How would past boxers compare under today's conditions and how would today's boxers compare under old timers' conditions. I'll wait for the time machine on that one.

(RO) Who is your favourite modern-day fighter?

(GD) I would have to say Floyd Mayweather.

(RO) Which is your favourite weight division?

(GD) None, in particular. A great fighter is a great fighter in any weight division.

(RO) Who do you feel was the greatest boxer to emerge from Britain?

(GD) Prince Naseem Hamed put us back on the international map. We have had many great fighters over the years, but no one really stands out for me as a world-wide boss yet.

(RO) Who in your opinion was the best heavyweight champion in the history of the sport?

(GD) Larry Holmes, who held the WBC and IBF versions of the title was a particular favourite of mine. Muhammad Ali is an obvious choice and Mike Tyson in the early years. However, I would say that, at this moment in time, Lennox Lewis has been the most all-round success story.

(RO) Which is your favourite world heavyweight title fight?

(GD) Any of Mike Tyson's early career title bouts.

(RO) How do you feel about boxers who continue to box even when middle aged?

(GD) Dangerous and sad.

(RO) What changes if any would you like to see in the sport?

(GD) No head guards and longer bandages in the amateurs. Credit given for technique, rather than workrate, similar to the Cuban regime. In the pros and amateurs, more ex-boxers should be encouraged back to the sport.

(RO) Out of all the boxers in recent years, who would you say was an excellent role model for the sport?

(GD) Lennox Lewis did everything just right. I just hope he does not make a comeback and ruin it.

(RO) What annoys you most in the sport?

(GD) Too much bureaucracy and not enough progression.

(RO) How do you feel about the vast number of world governing bodies in the sport at the moment?

(GD) They provide more opportunities for everyone.

(RO) How do you feel about there being so many weight divisions in the sport today?

(GD) Once again more opportunities for everyone.

(RO) What would you say to those who would like to ban boxing.

(GD) It is a natural force. Educate yourself and then make informed constructive criticisms. As my friend and mentor, Brendan Ingle, told me: "Boxing is dangerous if not taught properly, it could damage your health, but smoking, drinking and drugs will damage your health anyway". I personally would be happy to see boxing brought back into the schools.

(RO) There have been a number of films made about boxing over the years. Do you have a favourite?

(GD) I have lived, eaten, slept and breathed the real thing, I have seen nothing in films which comes even close.

(RO) What advice were you given when boxing?

(GD) Duck, bob and weave and keep your hands up when in range, is what I should have been told. But go out there and knock 'em out was mainly what I got. It was a good job I was a natural.

(RO) Looking at the domestic scene at the moment, who do you tip for the top?

(GD) Difficult to say really. I have a gym full of my own contenders to be thinking about and one who comes very much to mind from my gym is a young lad called Tariq Quaddus, who is just 16 years of age. I know it can be very risky to make predictions in this sport, but he really is special and I mean special. Tariq is extremely talented, hard working, fully focussed, and very eager to learn. However, in general looking outside of my gym, I would say that Amir

Khan seems to be doing the right things with the TV right now and is attracting attention, thus helping to put the game in the spotlight. It really is great to see boxing back on Terrestrial TV, which can only be good for all of us in the sport. I would like to also add that Kell Brook, Carl Froch, David Haye, Lee Haskins, Anthony Small and Nicki (The Nightmare) Smedley are all good and well worth watching.

(RO) How long have you been married?

(GD) I have been married for 23 years to the lovely Belfast girl, Linda.

(RO) I understand you have a daughter?

(GD) Yes. My princess, Sadie has had the gloves on since she was three years of age. A real Daddy's girl.

(RO) Do you discuss boxing much at home?

(GD) I certainly do. A good average would be 24/7.

(RO) Do you have a hobby?

(GD) Boxing, boxing and boxing, with some more boxing. If I am not training, I am on the telephone to other matchmakers, or organising a boxing show, or discussing the last show. Boxing is my life and my hobby, full stop.

(RO) Do you still keep fit?

(GD) I still run almost every day and eat a healthy diet. Having been running a successful sports and fitness consultancy for the last ten years, fitness is important. I also run a boxing gym in Peterborough for serious contenders.

(RO) Do you have a favourite sport apart from boxing?

(GD) I like football and athletics and appreciate most physical competitive sports.

(RO) What advice would you give to anyone embarking on a career in boxing?

(GD) Duck, bob and weave, keep your hands up when in range and get a good trainer, manager and promoter (This is not as easy as you would think).

(RO) Looking back at your professional career to date, would you do anything different if you had your time over?

(GD) No, I learned valuable lessons from everything I did. Most importantly, I never lost sight of my goals and dreams.

(RO) Have you ever been given any advice with regards to the training side of your career?

(GD) Yes. Brian Hughes of Manchester's advice has proven to be invaluable and I really do appreciate it.

(RO) What did you do when you retired from boxing?

(GD) I really didn't know what to do at first and taking a nine to five job had me climbing the walls. I had to rediscover what my life was all about, find out who my real friends were, and enjoy my young family. Eventually I moved on to be a much more balanced and rounded person. I then started an amateur club in Peterborough, as I wanted to get back to the grass roots of the sport I enjoyed. I found my skills as a boxing trainer, far out weighed my skills as a boxer and new goals and dreams have given me a renewed and exciting future in the sport, which I have come to be passionate about again.

(RO) You had your last professional contest against Hichem Dahmani on 17 December 1993 in Ascona, Italy, which resulted in a six-round stoppage. What prompted you to retire from the sport?

(GD) Dahmani was a good fighter and during the course of this bout I found that the fire I once had within me had gone

The short and the tall: Gary pictured with Felix Savon, the legendary Cuban heavyweight winner of three Olympic golds and six-time world champion

out and in its place was a cold empty wind. I knew then it was time to quit. I finished my career with Brendan Ingle, a man who taught me more in a short space of time than I had ever learnt previously in the early days of my career, and have every respect for Brendan. If I had teamed up with him earlier I could have gone a great deal further. However, I am not complaining I won the British featherweight title and that is something I hold in high esteem.

(RO) What are your ambitions for the future?

(GD) Amazingly, 15 years after I won the British featherweight title, and despite a large contingent of pro and amateur clubs in the area, no one from Peterborough has ever come close to the Lonsdale Belt, let alone gone any further. So my ambition is simple. It is to train Peterborough's next generation of boxing champions. My Phoenix Gym consists of the best ten boxers that I have seen and if I take on a new lad, the whole stable raise their game

to keep up. I go for quality, not quantity and really have no patience for time wasters. I will only ever have time for ten dedicated boxers and consequently they are always the best.

It was a pleasure talking to Gary, for here is a man who really serves boxing well. It is so very obvious to hear the enthusiasm in his voice when speaking about the sport and his plans for the future. It would, in all truth, be correct to say that the fight game is indeed lucky to have such a man. Gary is very contented with his life and family and works hard at the sport which he clearly loves. Any success that he achieves in the future will be fully deserved. The former British featherweight champion appears to be a man on a mission, a mission to seek out talent and thus cultivate it to a high standard. This can only be good for British boxing. On behalf of the *Yearbook*, I wish Gary, his wife Linda, and daughter Sadie, the very best for the future.

Gary seen here with his hot prospect, Tariq Quaddus, the former Golden Gloves and ABA Youth champion, who won a Four-Nations gold medal last season

Home and Away with British Boxers, 2005-2006

by John Jarrett

JULY

Big time boxing hit Bolton like a bombshell. In fact, they even had a bomb scare towards the end of the show, which fortunately turned out to be a hoax. Top of the bill on Frank Warren's first promotion for ITV in ten years was a fight for the British heavyweight title, champion Matt Skelton v former champ Danny Williams.

But make no mistake; the star on this show was local amateur hero, Amir Khan, the Olympic silver medallist making his professional debut. The sellout crowd of 7,000 had come to cheer boxing's new wonder boy, and he didn't let them down. Slated for four rounds, Khan had matters all wrapped up in just 109 seconds, his blazing fists dumping David Bailey twice before it was stopped. The bandwagon was rolling...

Danny Williams was to have been Matt Skelton's big fight. The banger from Bedford was undefeated in 16 bouts, all but one inside schedule, but this one would show he had the stuff to move forward. At 37, Matt didn't have time on his side. But late the previous night, Warren was told Danny Williams had pulled out of the fight!

Although he had passed the Board doctor at the afternoon weigh-in, the former champion claimed he was suffering 'flu symptoms and had been advised not to fight. So he didn't. (At the subsequent Board inquiry, Williams was fined £2,000) With 12 hours to go, matchmaker Dean Powell found Chesterfield's Mark Krence at work in his shop and offered the English champion the chance of a lifetime. He grabbed it with both hands. Mark lived the fairytale those 12 hours but late in the evening reality set in. He fought bravely against the odds but Skelton, almost two and a half stones heavier, was too much fighter and Krence, flagging in the seventh, was hurt by a left hook to the ribs and couldn't come out for the eighth. The dream had ended.

Chorley welterweight, Michael Jennings, took his dream to the Bolton Arena and made it come true with a stunning first-round knockout of Birmingham hard man, Jimmy Vincent, to win the British championship stripped from his stablemate, David Barnes. Vincent had lost a controversial verdict when challenging Barnes but he wasn't at the races this night as Jennings destroyed him with the final punch of the first round to stay unbeaten in 27 fights.

At the Nottingham Arena, Carl Froch sent his fans home happy as he retained his British and Commonwealth super-middleweight titles with a hard-earned decision over Matthew Barney. The Southampton spoiler is nobody's favourite opponent and Froch did well to stick to the game plan and come out a decisive winner over the former champion. Carl stayed unbeaten in 16 bouts, 12 inside.

Also on the Nottingham card, Junior Witter hung on to his European light-welterweight title with a unanimous decision over Andreas Kotelnik, a Ukrainian based in Germany, but it was a close run thing as the visitor came on strong from round six to give Witter enough trouble for two fights. Although Junior took his record to 32-1-2, it was not one of his better nights.

Salford's Jamie Moore regained the British light-middleweight title and made the Lonsdale Belt his own property when he stopped the champion, Michael Jones, in the sixth round of a thriller. This was the rubber, with Moore winning the first match and losing the return on a DQ for hitting on the break. In a blazing third round, the southpaw was decked twice, prior to getting up to rock Jones before the bell. He took control and Jones was a bloody mess in round five when he was dropped twice. Down again in the sixth, the referee had seen enough and Moore went home with the belt.

Veteran European super-featherweight champion, Boris Sinitsin, stepped into the lion's den at Edinburgh's Meadowbank Stadium to defend against British and Commonwealth titleholder, Alex Arthur. The local man called it right when he predicted: "He's 34. I don't think he'll live with my pace", Arthur was right on the money as the canny Russian gradually weakened and did well to survive a knockdown in the final round. At the bell, Alex was a triple champion.

Mixed fortunes for our boys overseas. In Nuremburg, former champion, Howard Eastman, suffered his third defeat in 43 fights when challenging Armenian puncher, Arthur Abraham, for his WBA Inter-Continental middleweight title. A pro for two years, Abraham took his unbeaten slate to 17-0 (15) and had too much for the 34-year-old Londoner. The decision was close but unanimous for the champion.

On the same show, Belfast's Brian Magee looked unlucky when losing a split decision to fellow southpaw Vitaly Tsypko of the Ukraine for the vacant European super-middleweight title. The Irishman outworked his rival and the crowd booed the decision when the scores were announced.

In Las Vegas, the Pocket Rocket, Belfast's Wayne McCullough, was stopped for the first time in his colourful career when his challenge to WBC super-bantamweight champion Oscar Larios was halted on the advice of the ringside physician after the tenth round. Youth was served and Wayne's admirers were hoping that the 35-year-old former WBC bantamweight champ would hang them up for good.

Tough Jane Couch from Bristol found things a bit too hot when she flew to California for a fight with Jessica Rakoczy on an open-air show at Leemore. Rakoczy, a Canadian fighting out of Vegas, was defending her IBA lightweight title with the new WBC bauble also in the pot, and she was a winner when it was stopped with two seconds left in the sixth round. In fairness to Jane, the bout was staged in blistering sunshine with the temperature an official 108 degrees and a staggering 124 under the ring lights. That's hot enough for two summers in Bristol!

AUGUST

Fighting in the other guy's backyard never did worry Robin Reid. In October 1996, he travelled to Milan and knocked out Italy's Vincenzo Nardiello in seven rounds to take the WBC super-middleweight title back home to Runcorn. Then, in December 2003, Robin journeyed to Nuremburg to challenge Sven Ottke for the WBA and IBF super-middleweight championships.

Nobody was beating the cagey German. Reid did, but at the final bell Ottke was the winner and still champion, thanks to the bumbling interference of the Belgian referee. Warned so many times for petty infringements, Robin complained: "I was almost afraid to hit him!"

Now the man from Cheshire was getting ready to fight Jeff Lacy for his IBF super-middleweight title in Lacy's sunny backyard, St Petersburg, Florida. The American was strong, a big puncher, and undefeated in 20 pro fights, and he was 28, Reid 34. But Robin had never been stopped in 43 fights (38-4-1) had never even been on the deck!

Well, 'Left Hook' Jeff Lacy changed all that. It was rough in there with both men guilty, but the American's power was the deciding factor. Robin was smashed to the canvas four times before being pulled out by long-time trainer, Brian Hughes, at the end of round seven. A jubilant Lacy was already talking up a fight with Joe Calzaghe, a fight manager Shelley Finkel had all but signed for, with the Americans ready to come to Wales if need be.

There was some joy for the Brits on the bill. Manchester super-featherweight, John Murray, took his unbeaten pro record to 13-0 as he romped to a six-rounds decision over Detroit's Johnny Walker, dumping the American with a left hook in the fifth round to seal a fine victory.

Standing an impressive 6`5" with an extraordinary reach of 86" and bouncing the scales around 18 stones, Audley Harrison is big enough to eat the entire heavyweight division, but the former Olympic champion prefers to nibble at the beef trust rather than take a hearty bite. After putting 18 pro fights in the book, 13 inside schedule, Harrison, at 33, should have been tackling a big steak, but he was still snacking!

Latest entrée on his plate was 36-year-old Robert Wiggins, a full-time dock worker from Rhode Island. Harrison's business manager claimed they had approached such as Shannon Briggs and Calvin Brock, but they settled for Wiggins. The fight was scheduled for ten rounds at the HP Pavilion in San Jose, California.

Audley made his usual cautious start, posing when he should have been punching. Dwarfing his opponent, he finally figured he had nothing to beat and in the fourth round turned loose a barrage of leather that convinced Wiggins it was time to head back to the docks.

A big man, Harrison talks big. "There's no doubt in my mind I'll be heavyweight champion of the world", he told reporters before the fight. "I have star quality". It was time he started performing like a star. With fights like this one,

Audley Harrison becomes a household name only in his own Las Vegas household.

Irish middleweight champion, Matthew Macklin, chalked up an impressive win on his American debut when he blasted his way to a three-rounds stoppage over journeyman, Leo Laudat, at Atlantic City, taking his pro log to 14-1 with 10 inside schedule. The crowd went wild as the Irishman unloaded heavy shots from both hands and although the American didn't go down, he did some funny things standing up and was relieved when the referee called it off and sent him to the showers. "You haven't seen the best of me yet", Macklin told reporters afterwards. Watch this boy!

Italy is a nice place for a holiday, not so good if you are boxing there. Trainer, Adam Booth, made the trip to Rimini with three pugilists; Cathy Brown, Peter McDonagh, and Brett James. Cathy, who likes to be known as 'The Bitch' although she's really a nice girl, was boxing a rematch with Stefania Bianchini, ten two-minute rounds for the inaugural WBC women's flyweight championship.

In their previous meeting, for the European title in 2003, the Italian girl won on a split decision. Bianchini won this one, too, but it was close after a so-so fight. My old friend Rinze Van Der Meer was at ringside and thought Brown deserved a draw at least. Booth was further upset at a new WBC ruling that stipulated both contestants wear headguards.

There was further disappointment when Adam's other two entries came in second. McDonagh, an Irishman from Galway via Bermondsey, was a former Southern Area lightweight champion and he was boxing well against Brunet Zamora when his left shoulder dislocated in the third round. Peter stuck it out and lost a close decision. One judge marked the fight a draw.

In another six-rounder, Camden welterweight, Brett James, like McDonagh a former Southern Area champion, acquitted himself well against Leonard Bundu but the judges saw it for Bundu. There was worse to come! Booth and his troupe returned to the dressing room to find they had been robbed of their money and mobile phones. Like I was saying, Italy is a nice place for a holiday!

Outside the ropes, cracks were appearing in the relationship between promoter Frank Warren and his star performer, Ricky Hatton. Ricky was talking to other promoters on the world scene who were chasing the world light-welterweight champion since his tremendous victory over Kostya Tszyu in Manchester. Money may be the root of all evil, but it's what professional boxing is all about.

SEPTEMBER

At long last the big one was all set, Joe Calzaghe versus Jeff 'Left Hook' Lacy, WBO super-middleweight champion versus International Boxing Federation titleholder, the unification battle signed for London 5 November. Bonfire night! Fireworks!

Well, forget it. The fireworks fizzled out this night at the International Arena in Cardiff where a packed house watched their poster boy walk through the 17th defence of his title against a blown up African middleweight named

Evans Ashira and blow his big chance with Lacy. And what always happens when you take a fight with Joe Soap, happened. A broken metacarpal in Joe's left hand put the Welshman on the shelf and brought an immediate reaction from the American's promoter, Gary Shaw, who announced that: "You will not see Jeff in England or Wales".

Even with a busted hand, Calzaghe was able to handle his challenger who survived a cut left eye early in the fight. It was terribly one-sided with Joe winning every round to stay unbeaten in 40 contests. But the one contest he dreamed of now appeared no more than a mirage on the horizon.

Star of the show that night in Cardiff was the Olympic hero, Amir Khan, who dazzled Coventry's game Baz Carey over four one-sided rounds. Carey finished with a bloody nose and a cut on his left eye, but did well to hear the final bell still standing on his feet. In winning his second professional bout, the boy from Bolton gave a brilliant performance that had ringsider Don King's hair standing on end! Okay, it's always like that, but he was impressed.

Gary Lockett was another impressive winner as he destroyed London's Allan Gray in two rounds of their middleweight encounter to take his pro log to 23-1. Southpaw Gray, stopped for the first time in a ten-year pro career taking in 27 fights, took the count from a blazing right and it was all over at 65 seconds of round two.

Clinton Woods goes from strength to strength. In hometown Sheffield, the IBF light-heavyweight champion retained his title with a fine victory over his tough challenger, Julio Gonzalez, the unanimous decision giving Woods his 38th win in 42 fights. The Mexican was a former WBO champion at the weight and brought a 38-2 resume to the ring, but the Yorkshireman tamed him in what was probably his finest performance. At 33, Clinton Woods is the goods!

For all British boxers the Lord Lonsdale Challenge Belt is the sport's most coveted prize, a trophy most can only dream about as they drop off to sleep after a tough night in the gym. For Plymouth's Scott Dann, his dream became a reality as he retained his British middleweight title against Wayne Elcock to make the belt his own property in front of his adoring fans at the Pavilions.

A power puncher, with 16 early wins in a 22-2 record, 'Dynamite' Dann had won eight fights in his hometown, all inside schedule, but he had to travel 12 rounds this night as the Birmingham man, a former WBU champion, boxed carefully enough to survive Dann's punches but not well enough to sway the judges, operating for the first time in British boxing. For Dann, the unanimous decision, and the belt.

Kevin Anderson won a thriller over Commonwealth welterweight champion, Joshua Okine, at Kirkaldy Ice Rink to take a split decision and the title. The southpaw

John 'Boy' Humphrey (left), the former Southern Area light-middleweight titleholder, became the Southern Area middleweight champion when outscoring Hussain Osman in a battle for the vacant title at York Hall, Bethnal Green   Les Clark

51

from Ghana had stopped David Barnes to win this title but the Scot stuck to his guns to come out a winner again, now 15-0.

In Manchester, British light-middleweight champion, Jamie Moore, turned back the gritty challenge of David Walker, who was floored at the end of round three then again in the fourth by which time trainer Robert McCracken had seen enough. He followed the towel into the ring and it was stopped. The fight left Walker pondering his future, while Moore looked for better and bigger things to happen. They will.

With a Saturday night crowd sitting in sunshine at the local football ground, local favourite Jon Thaxton made Vasile Dragomir wish he'd stayed home in Romania rather than journey to Norwich. The convincer came in round four, a blasting right to the jaw sending the visitor down for the full count as Thaxton retained his WBF lightweight title and took his record to 28-7, 15 early.

When you visit the Hilton Hotel in London's Mayfair, you don't expect treatment such as was handed to young Colin McNeil. But the Scot was not there as a guest, he was there as an opponent, at short notice, for Commonwealth light-middleweight champion, Ossie Duran. The man from Ghana had never lost to a British fighter in ten previous visits and he didn't lose this time, but the Fauldhouse southpaw made him go all the way to take a unanimous decision.

Bleeding from the nose and his left eye, Newmarket's John 'Boy' Humphrey won the Southern Area middleweight title in a hard match with Hussain Osman at York Hall. He had previously held the light-middle title in a 17-3 career. Southern Area welterweight champion, Ross 'The Boss' Minter, with father Alan looking on, kept his title when Bracknell's Sammy Smith was rescued by the referee in the third round after being dropped in the second.

The Central Area super-featherweight title was vacant when Carl Johanneson met Birkenhead's Peter Allen at Leeds. The local man was too much fighter for Allen and it was stopped in the eighth round as the towel came in from his corner. At the Dome in Doncaster, the local southpaw, Stefy Bull, claimed the vacant WBF Inter-Continental lightweight title with a ten-rounds decision over Carl Allen of Wolverhampton.

Heavyweight action at Kirkby in Ashfield saw a grim struggle between veteran Luke Simpkin and huge (21st) Carl Baker, with the Sheffield man retaining his British Masters belt on a close decision.

OCTOBER

Fight of the month, hell, fight of the year for me, was Michael Hunter's tremendous victory over Esham Pickering to add the Newark man's European and Commonwealth super-bantamweight titles to his British crown to become a triple champion in front of a jam-packed Borough Hall in hometown Hartlepool.

The Ingle fighter must have thought he was home and dry when he decked Hunter in the opening round, then again in round two. Anxious moments for the crowd with their favourite already four points down after two rounds.

But the word 'defeat' does not figure in the vocabulary of Michael Hunter, he'd never been beaten as a pro (22-0-1) and he wasn't going to lose this one.

From the third round he started to work his way back into the contest and Pickering knew he had a fight on his hands. He sold his titles dearly, but whatever he tried, Hunter just refused to buckle and he seemed to grow stronger as the rounds flew by. At the final bell he looked a winner and the judges confirmed it, 114-113, 114-112 for Hunter and a 113-113 draw. The old Borough Hall erupted as the crowd saluted their hero. Hartlepool belonged to Hunter this night!

The odds were stacked against Wales' Bradley Pryce going against British welterweight champion, Michael Jennings, for the title in Preston. Jennings was unbeaten in 27 fights, Pryce, having his first fight in ten months, had lost three of his last five bouts. So what happens? Bradley comes out punching and dumps the champion in a blazing first round.

Jennings gets up and he settles in after that and when they come up for the final round he looks a winner. But Pryce almost does it again with a sizzling right hand and once again Jennings is fighting for his life. He makes it to the bell and keeps his title and his unbeaten record. But he won't be looking for Bradley Pryce any time soon.

You could understand that Junior Witter was becoming somewhat jaded. He hadn't lost a fight in five years and the guy who beat him was Zab Judah, IBF champion who had gone on to become undisputed welterweight champ. The Bradford switch-hitter had won British, Commonwealth and European light-welterweight titles, was rated number

Junior Witter (left), defending his British, Commonwealth and European light-welterweight titles, has his challenger, Colin Lynes, going in this shot, but ultimately had to be satisfied with a points win at the York Hall, Bethnal Green

Les Clark

one by the WBC, and was looking for the big ones such as Mayweather and Gatti.

At York Hall in Bethnal Green he got Colin Lynes. The Hornchurch man was a decent opponent with a 26-1 pro record, but he looked in over his head and out of his class against the champion. He was, too, but luckily for Colin, Witter gave something less than a world-class performance although a clear winner. Admitting he couldn't get himself motivated for fights like these, Witter may never get the big one he craves. The man who once strung 15 stoppages together had been taken the distance for the third time in a row, and at 31 time was not on his side.

In a 34-fight pro career (27-7) Michael Sprott had collected Southern Area, British and Commonwealth, and WBF heavyweight titles, and now he was the European Union champion going back to Germany to fight big (6` 6" and 17stone) Italian, Paolo Vidoz, for the European title 'proper'. But the big Italian proved too big a problem for Sprott to solve without the aid of artillery and he came out on the wrong end of the decision.

Dublin fight fans are all excited over Bernard Dunne. The 'Dublin Dynamo' won the vacant IBC super-bantamweight title with a second-round stoppage of Pontefract's Sean Hughes. Sean likes to be called 'Short Fuse', but it was short fight this night at a sold out National Stadium with Dunne outpunching the Yorkshireman to take his record to 17-0. In another IBC title bout, Jim Rock kept his fans happy as he took the vacant middleweight belt with a unanimous decision over Wales' Alan Jones and take his pro log to 26-4.

Wembley's 21-year-old featherweight, Billy Corcoran, moved up a notch when he tackled the former British champion, Roy Rutherford, for his English super-featherweight belt. The Coventry man had been out for 16 months and at 32 was relying on experience. It wasn't enough at York Hall as Corcoran blazed his way to victory. Rutherford was dropped in the first round and bleeding from a cut over his right eye when his corner baled him out at the end of round four.

Winning his fourth fight after a two-year layoff, John 'Boy' Humphrey added the vacant British Masters middleweight title to his Southern Area belt in a gruelling decision victory over Turkish-Londoner, Gokhan Kazaz, on a stormy night at York Hall. The storm broke at the end of the ninth round as mindless spectators (I won't call them fans) started their own fight that threatened to bring the show to a premature halt. Kazaz finally took the mike to quiet his fans and the final round was fought. The Turk had been dropped in the second and finished with a lump over his right eye, while the winner took ten stitches in a badly-cut right eyebrow and suffered left-hand damage that put him back on the shelf. Boxing was the loser this night.

British fighters fared well in rings over the Atlantic. In Philadelphia, at middleweight, Matthew Macklin scored his second win in the States when he stopped Anthony Little in round two. The following night, at Gatineau, Quebec, Manchester lightweight, John Murray, kept his unbeaten record as he dismantled Tyrone Wiggins inside four rounds.

Thetford's Rocky Dean was not so fortunate in his first fight abroad. After a nightmare journey to Kharkov in the Ukraine, Rocky lost a gruelling fight with unbeaten Andrey Isaev for the WBF Inter-Continental featherweight title, being stopped in the 12th round.

Warming up for a European cruiserweight championship, David Haye turned his big punches loose on unfortunate Vincenzo Rossitto who didn't see out the second round.

Billy Corcoran (left) became the new English super-featherweight champion following a four-round retirement win over Roy Rutherford on the Witter v Lynes bill Les Clark

NOVEMBER

It was all change for Ricky Hatton. No Frank Warren. No 20,000 local fans jamming the MEN Arena in Manchester in his last big fight in Britain as he cast his eyes over the Atlantic. At the Hallam FM Arena in Sheffield, with new promoter, Fight Academy (Dennis Hobson, Robert Waterman, Jim Evans), Hatton was going after the WBA light-welterweight title belonging to an unlikely champion in Carlos Maussa.

It started badly. Just 20 seconds into the fight, a clash of heads left Hatton streaming blood from a bad cut over his left eye, and in round three he was cut on the right eye. The Columbian was awkwardly effective and gave Ricky problems that he eventually solved with a booming left hook in the eighth round. Now the IBF/WBA champion, Hatton was still undefeated in 40 fights, 30 inside.

At the Braehead Arena in Renfrew, the WBO featherweight champion, Scott Harrison, retained his title with a unanimous decision over his Australian challenger, Nedal Hussein, who survived a fifth-round knockdown to battle bravely to the final bell. Harrison was cut on his nose in the opener and bled from a scalp wound in the second that later took three stitches. But he was too strong and too busy for the man from Down Under.

After winning his British bantamweight title in a cracking fight with Dale Robinson, Martin Power had another fight on his hands when facing Ian Napa at York

Hall. The Hackney challenger boxed beautifully and even had the champion in trouble in the ninth round with some stunning rights to the head. There was a 'break' at half time when crowd trouble caused the fight to be halted but they were soon away again and at the final bell Power had it by a split decision, still undefeated at 18-0.

Three weeks later, Napa accepted a job against Damaen Kelly at Liverpool and lost again as the brilliant Irishman showed his class in taking the ten-rounds decision. He had trained for an IBF challenge in Sidney, but no money, no fight!

It was no Roman holiday for Johnny Nelson, at 38, coming off a 14-month layoff, putting his WBO cruiserweight title on the line for the 13th time against the rugged challenge of Vincenzo Cantatore. But the Sheffield stylist was up for the job. He was 'Johnny Cool' during the introductions, even doing the splits as he fixed the Italian with his steady gaze.

Nelson was too good for the local man but step out in the rain and you'll get wet. It was raining leather for Johnny in round nine as a big left hook took him off his feet. It was a good round for Cantatore and the timekeeper helped him, letting his clock run for four minutes, 20 seconds! But he couldn't repeat his success and the veteran champion survived another scare to come out the winner on a split decision.

On the Rome bill, Gary Lockett and Enzo Maccarinelli made it a British hat trick, beating Victor Kpadenou and Marco Heinichen, respectively. The Welsh middleweight had a solid workout against the West African over eight rounds, but Enzo, looking forward to a mandated challenge to Nelson, would have spent his time better at home in the gym hitting the bag. He stopped the chubby German inside 95 seconds of round one, the referee waving it off after the second knockdown.

On a Sunday afternoon at Shaw in Lancashire, a tough little Mongolian warrior named Choi Tseveenpurev won the vacant WBF International featherweight title with a storming tenth-round attack that forced the referee to save Alexei Volchan from further punishment. Choi, a local resident for five years, delighted his fans and also manager Jack Doughty, who was looking for bigger things for his protégé.

The championship dreams of Barking's Marc Callaghan received another setback when he was stopped in the opening round of a vacant Commonwealth featherweight title fight at Dagenham by Uganda's Jackson Asiku. A super-bantam really, Marc had lost to British champ, Michael Hunter, at that weight.

Another fighter matched out of his class was Walsall's super-featherweight, Steve Gethin, offered as the third victim to 18-year-old Olympic hero, Amir Khan, on the Renfrew show. Khan is a big lad, more a light-welter, and he was too big a problem for Steve, who was still trying to solve it when it was stopped in round three.

Nigel Wright is one of British boxing's best kept secrets. The southpaw from Crook in County Durham had won the English light-welterweight title and on the big Renfrew show he iced Paisley's Kevin McIntyre with a first-round blitz to win this final eliminator for the British championship. Only one defeat in 15 bouts, Nigel was looking for Junior Witter but the Bradford man will probably vacate. The British featherweight title was up for grabs when Andy Morris tackled John Simpson in his 13th fight. It was unlucky for Simpson as Morris turned in a classy performance to become a champion.

Sunderland-based Scot, Ryan Kerr, kept his unbeaten record (13-0) with a comprehensive points win over Simeon Cover at the Roker Hotel just around the coast and retained his English super-middleweight belt. However, manager Tommy Conroy thinks Ryan is not big enough for the division and is planning a move down to middleweight.

Irish middleweight, John Duddy, had a date with Canada's Byron Mackie at the Hammerstein Ballroom in New York City but they weren't dancing. They were having a fight and the bouncers let them get on with it. Mackie would have liked them to intervene as Duddy was bouncing him off the canvas. Byron was down four times and it was his corner team who eventually saved him in the fourth round.

Basingstoke's former British super-middleweight champion, Dean Francis, was now aiming at cruiserweight honours and the way he destroyed Hastings Rasani in six rounds on the Bristol show augured well for his chances.

DECEMBER

It was the big fellow's big chance, and he blew it. Big time! Audley Harrison was back in Britain, back on national television, back in a big fight that would show what he had learned in the American gyms and rings. Still boasting an undefeated record in 19 contests since winning Olympic gold in 2000, Harrison was matched with Danny Williams, the former British and Commonwealth champion, at a sold-out ExCel Arena in London.

Surprise, surprise! Yes, it was the same old Audley, cautious beyond reason, posing when he should have been punching, stepping back when he should have been pressing forward. After 12 dreary rounds, played out against a background of boos, catcalls, shouts of, "What a load of rubbish!" Williams was awarded a split decision because he wasn't quite as bad as Harrison.

A knockdown scored by Williams in the tenth round could have been the deciding factor in the result. It was a looping right hand to the side of the head that sent Harrison down heavily by the ropes. He beat the count, his first, and tucked up even more than before, but Williams failed to press his advantage for whatever reason and the contest ground on through the final two rounds to see Williams take the verdict and the vacant Commonwealth championship.

Danny has a few options but for Harrison it was not so much a case of back to the drawing board but find a new architect. At 34 time is not on his side and his chances of making it to even one version of the world title look dimmer than ever.

British champion, Matt Skelton, was on the show, defending his crown against John McDermott. It was a bad match and Skelton made the best of it, smashing his man to summary defeat in 79 seconds of the opening round. McDermott spent more time on the deck than on his feet, four times before it was called off.

There were some bright moments for the fans. There was another brilliant display by Bolton's Olympic hero, Amir Khan, as he destroyed Sheffield's game Daniel Thorpe inside two rounds to take his pro log to 4-0 (3). Kevin Mitchell went undefeated in 17 outings as he picked up his first title, the IBF Inter-Continental super-featherweight belt, with a sixth-round stoppage of the tough Frenchman, Mohammed Medjadi. The visitor did well to survive a second-round left hook that floored him, but he was bleeding from eyes and nose and under fire when it was ended. Ross Minter won the vacant English welterweight title with a fourth-round victory over Brett James. The son of former world champ Alan, Ross hit too hard and too often for the man from Camden Town and chalked up his 15th victory against one draw and one loss.

The crowd love a puncher and they will pay again to watch David Haye in action. But don't be late getting to your seat. At the Bracknell Leisure Centre, the 25-year-old Londoner used just one blasting right hand to finish off Alexander Gurov in 45 seconds to win the European cruiserweight championship. The tall Ukrainian southpaw had twice challenged for world titles, but he was never at the races in this one as David racked up his 15th victory, all inside schedule, against one defeat.

Is Carl Froch as good as he thinks he is? He had no trouble retaining his Commonwealth super-middleweight title against Ruben Groenwald at the Nottingham Ice Arena, the third man stopping it in round five, but at times his performance was sloppy and careless and with a more demanding opponent than the tough South African things might have been different. Froch moved to 17-0 (13) and may one day win a world championship, as he did in the amateurs. But he needs to stay focused!

Michael Sprott went to Austria for a fight. Nice place. Pity about the verdict. Fighting unbeaten Vladimir Virchis for the WBO Inter-Continental heavyweight belt, Sprott looked a winner but the judges couldn't see him. Winner, Virchis!

Jane Couch went to Paris for a fight. Great shopping. Pity about the fight. Mounting a challenge to Myriam Lamare for the WBA light-welterweight title, Jane was stopped in the third round when the American referee decided she was taking too many blows. The lovely Ms Couch was most upset as her record hit 26-8.

Honest, if you can't win a title today, you should hang your gloves up! There was a fight for something called the WBC Youth lightweight championship on the Froch bill at Nottingham and John Murray took the belt home with him after beating Nacho Mendoza, a Colombian fighting out of Spain. It was a tough one up to round seven when a clash of heads left Manchester's Murray with a lump on his left

David Haye watches as Alexander Gurov, the reigning European cruiserweight champion, is counted out after just 45 seconds of their title fight at Bracknell

Les Clark

forehead. It had to be stopped in round eight, and as Murray was ahead he was awarded the technical decision and the title.

At Coventry, Steve Bendall won the English middleweight championship when Donovan Smillie was sent to his corner in the fifth round with a cut on his right eyebrow. The local southpaw was headed for victory, quite literally, as heads bumped frequently and the winner himself came in for extensive embroidery, 14 stitches to stop both eyes bleeding.

Big Henry Akinwande is still in the title mix, even if it was only the IBF Inter-Continental title. The veteran won a decision over America's Ed Mahone in Leipzig, but it was not anything to write home about for either of them. In the closing rounds the referee, Howard Foster, worked as hard as the fighters in pulling them apart.

Still with the heavyweights, Southampton's Colin Kenna tossed a shock defeat into the more experienced Wayne Llewelyn at Portsmouth. Kenna sent his man crashing in round two with smashing right hands to the head. Wayne beat the count but the referee took one look at him and waved it over. Colin took the vacant Southern Area title, the icing on the cake.

Colin Kenna is seen bludgeoning Wayne Llewelyn to a second-round kayo defeat in their battle for the Southern Area heavyweight title at Portsmouth   Les Clark

JANUARY

Despite the fact that he had lost only one of his 20 fights, had won Midlands Area and English titles at light-welterweight, Young Muttley was nobody's poster boy. So nobody expected him to beat the British welterweight champion, Michael Jennings, in their fight at Nottingham. Muttley was pushing 30 and stepping up a division against the titleholder who hadn't lost in 28 fights. Jennings was hot, Muttley was not! Fast forward 12 rounds, final bell, collect the cards. Winner and new champion, Young Muttley!

It was a good fight and at the end one judge went for the champion, the other two for the challenger, and it was that way with those close to the ring, many thinking

Jennings had done enough to hang on to his belt, just as many being swayed by the storming finish put in by Muttley, going 12 rounds for the first time. This time, the sun shone on the boy from the Black Country.

The sun continued to shine on the poster boy from Bolton, Amir Khan, who moved effortlessly into the six-round class with a 75-seconds demolition job on Belarus' Vitali Martynov. A couple of left hooks and a bombing right floored the visitor. He got up, but the third man took one look in his eyes and sent him back to the dressing room. Barely 19, Khan has 'Champion' written all over him!

Liverpool's Derry Mathews claimed the vacant English featherweight title when Steve Chinnock pulled out at the end of round six with a damaged shoulder. Rugeley's Chinnock had won the Midlands title, but was always running second to the former ABA champion who moved to 15-0, 9 inside.

Manchester southpaw, David Barnes, won a Lonsdale Belt outright as undefeated British welterweight champion. Now under a new trainer, Anthony Farnell, David had France's Fabrice Colombel down three times for a fourth-round stoppage.

With just a dozen fights on his resume, Lenny Daws put himself on the page for a crack at the British light-welterweight title, recently vacated by Junior Witter. By forcing the ninth-round retirement of Colin Lynes at York Hall, Lenny earned a place in the championship ring with English titleholder, Nigel Wright. Lynes, from Hornchurch, had made Witter go the full route in a triple title fight four months previously and was a former IBO champ at the weight.

Daws had been lined up to box for the Commonwealth title against James Armah, but when the latter withdrew Lynes stepped in, looking for a way back. But it was not to

Without any kind of title on the line, Graham Earl (left) overcame the world-rated Yuri Romanov over 12 rounds at Dagenham   Les Clark

be. Colin was outworked by Daws and was running second when he was forced to retire after nine rounds, feeling sick and unable to breathe.

In a see-saw battle, former English light-middle titleholder, Matthew Thirlwall, won the final eliminator for the super-middle belt with a terrific ninth-round knockout over Donovan Smillie on the York Hall bill. Thirlwall almost ended matters in the fourth when he had Smillie on the deck, but the Bradford man rallied to have Matthew in trouble before a thunderous right left Donovan down and out. The crowd loved it!

Over in Dublin a sellout crowd packed the National Stadium to cheer their favourites on to victory as Peter McDonagh, Bernard Dunne, Brian Magee and Colin Kenna all posted wins. McDonagh, the London-based Irishman, forced Michael Gomez to quit after the former British super-featherweight champion and Lonsdale Belt winner had been decked in the sixth round. Gomez had fought well up to the knockdown, but walked to his corner after getting up. *No mas* comes to Dublin!

Unbeaten super-bantam, Bernard Dunne, racked up another fine win as the former British and European bantamweight champion, Noel Wilders, was waved to his corner after a sixth-round knockdown. The Dublin Dynamo, in taking his record to 19-0, was looking for European champ, Michael Hunter.

Belfast southpaw light-heavy, Brian Magee, racked up Belarus' Danill Prakapsou for a second-round stoppage to move to 25-2. Heavyweight Colin Kenna returned to the city of his birth to pound out an eighth-round decision over Swadlincote's Luke Simpkin and looked good doing it.

At the Goresbrook Leisure Centre in Dagenham, British and Commonwealth lightweight champion, Graham Earl, turned loose a brilliant performance to beat dangerous Yuri Romanov of Belarus over 12 rounds. In tackling the man rated number six by the WBC, the Luton lad risked his mandatory European contender status and many questioned the wisdom of the match.

But Graham outboxed and outpunched the London-based Romanov in a thrilling fight, telling reporters as he came out of the ring: "I said I'd deliver. I took a risk and made a statement". Romanov got the message.

British light-middleweight champion, Jamie Moore, celebrated joining the Maloney brothers by punching out a third-round stoppage over tough Ukrainian, Vladimir Borovski, who was floored twice before it was called off. After 23 wins in 26 fights, Moore was looking for something big.

There's no stopping Gary Woolcombe. The Welling light-middleweight chalked up his 19th straight win with a stunning stoppage over the Leeds' southpaw, Lee Murtagh, in the fourth round. Decked by a left hook, the Central

The Undefeated Gary Woolcombe (left) made it 19 out of 19 when he stopped Lee Murtagh, the Central Area light-middleweight champion, inside four rounds at Dagenham on the Earl v Romanov bill   Les Clark

Area champion beat the count but was still dazed and he was sent back to his stool by the referee.

He is still climbing through the ropes to give some up-and-coming kid a few lessons and earn a few bob in the process. Who else but Pete Buckley, 257 professional fights on his dance card and fighting on the annual Burns night show at Glasgow's St Andrew's Sporting club. Former Scottish international, David Appleby, passed his debut test, taking every round, but Pete enjoyed his haggis.

FEBRUARY

His big fight experience and boxing savvy took Danny Williams to a hard-earned split decision over Matt Skelton to retain his Commonwealth heavyweight title at London's ExCel Arena. The 32-year-old Williams was enjoying something of an Indian summer in his career as this fight followed on his humbling of Audley Harrison just before Christmas.

That fight was a stinker, but Williams-Skelton made up for it. The British champion, whose title was not at stake here, came late to boxing after a career in K1 fighting, and he is all strength and strong-arm stuff. It gave him a slight lead after half way but down the stretch the fundamental boxing of Williams, a former British and Commonwealth champion, got him home in front, taking his record to 35-4.

The decision was closer than it should have been. Skelton was fortunate not to be docked a point in at least two of the 12 rounds. In the very first round he bullied Danny to the ropes then went in with his head. In the seventh he leaned on Williams and almost pushed him out of the ring on three occasions. Rough game this boxing business! Skelton came out with a cut on his head and his first defeat in 19 fights.

This Amir Khan is going to take some beating. He went unbeaten in six fights with a three rounds thrashing of Jackson Williams. The Norwich boy was down in the second but saved by the bell. Round three saw the finish as Khan decked his man twice before the referee did the humane thing and stopped it.

Another young talent is Kevin Mitchell, still undefeated in 18 fights after retaining his IBF Inter-Continental super-featherweight championship with a unanimous decision over sturdy French champion, Youssouf Djibaba. The stocky little guy from over the Channel defied the efforts of Dagenham's 21-year-old Mitchell to send him home early.

The punch-happy punters of Plymouth packed the Pavilions to cheer their favourites on to Commonwealth title glory, as Scott Dann added to his British middleweight title and Lee Haskins claimed the vacant flyweight title

Scott Dann (right) won the vacant Commonwealth middleweight title when knocking out Canada's Larry Sharpe inside nine rounds at Plymouth

Les Clark

with a stunning second-round stoppage of Tanzania's Anthony Mathias.

Now 31, the Plymouth southpaw is ready to move on to a bigger stage. As British champion he had won the Lonsdale Belt outright and against fellow southpaw, Larry Sharpe from Canada, he didn't put a glove wrong in annexing the vacant Commonwealth bauble. Comfortably ahead going into the ninth round, Scott set his fans alight as he whipped home a terrific left uppercut to send Sharpe to his knees, blood pouring from his right eye. He didn't get up in time.

Bristol's Haskins, a southpaw, was all over his man, dropping him in round one with a straight left, and when a right and left sent him stumbling across the ring in round two the referee called it off. The visitor protested but he had thrown nothing back and Haskins was the new champion, still unbeaten in 14 fights, nine inside.

At York Hall in Bethnal Green, British and Commonwealth super-middleweight champion, Carl Froch, put the latter title on the line for Australia's Dale Westerman to shoot at. The Aussie missed, and was being beaten down when the referee intervened in round nine to save him further aggravation. Froch is undoubtedly talented but in taking his undefeated pro log to 18-0 he still left questions unanswered.

At the Goresbrook Leisure Centre in Dagenham, local man Nicky Cook retained his European featherweight championship with a unanimous decision over Yuri Voronin, a tough little southpaw from the Ukraine. The unbeaten Cook protected his WBC number one ranking in taking his record to 26-0, but emerged with a bad cut on his right eyebrow. Voronin also picked up a nasty gash to his right eye, both injuries the result of head clashes.

Basingstoke battler, Dean Francis, a former British super-middleweight champion, stepped up to cruiser to win the English title with a ten-rounds decision over Tommy Eastwood at Bristol's Whitchurch Sports Centre, but his ring future was again in doubt as his troublesome right shoulder gave out in the fourth round. Somehow Dean managed to hide the injury from the Epsom man and left-handed his way to a hard-earned victory, but at 32 he can't keep fighting with one hand!

Another fighter going through the pain barrier was Alex Arthur, defending his European, British and Commonwealth super-featherweight titles against fellow Scot, Ricky Burns, at Edinburgh's Meadowbank arena. The Coatbridge contender gave Arthur all the trouble he wanted in the early rounds but the champion finished strongly over the long haul, although in agony from pains in his calf muscles. The local hero came out with right-eye damage but his body punches took all the fight out of his young opponent.

Comebacks. At 37, Johnny Armour was fighting again, taking a six-twos decision over Delroy Spencer at the York Hall. The former WBU, European and Commonwealth bantamweight champion had half-a-stone on the Birmingham lad who did well against the Chatham veteran. At the ExCel Arena in London, the former English and British Masters champion, Alan Bosworth, was back under

new management (Ingles) to kick off his comeback campaign with a 24-seconds win over Jus Wallie. Too easy and too early to say how far the 38-year-old welter will go.

One career came to an end as Hartlepool stylist Alan Temple succumbed to the heavy shots of Jon Thaxton. Alan was floored twice early on, yet boxed his back through rounds three and four, only to hit the deck again in the fifth. He got up but was bleeding from the nose and his right eye and the referee waved it off. Alan was boxing's 'Nearly Man', meeting the best in a 16-20 fight career.

MARCH

On the eve of his 34th birthday, after defending his WBO super-middleweight championship 17 times in an eight-and-a-half year reign, after racking up 40 straight fights without defeat, Joe Calzaghe finally got the fight he wanted. It came in the early hours of a Sunday morning at the MEN Arena in Manchester, at a time when most of us were asleep, but the Welsh southpaw was wide awake.

He had to be. Coming at him from the opposite corner was the unbeaten American, Jeff 'Left Hook' Lacy, IBF and IBO champion at the weight, and this one was for all the marbles. For Calzaghe it was put up or shut up.

Well, Joe put up his gloves and he shut up the Americans, leaving them and many of us speechless with a flawless display from first bell to last, 12 rounds of a non-stop masterclass that left young Mr Lacy battered, bewildered, bloody and beltless. It was the kind of defeat that would send the young man back home to Florida thinking of a new career move, and it was the kind of victory that put Joe and his promoter, Frank Warren, firmly in the driving seat. Think super-middleweight, think Joe Calzaghe, super-champ!

Up on the North-East coast, Hartlepool idol, Michael Hunter, retained his European super-bantamweight title with an easy two rounds stoppage over Yersin Jailauov in the bedlam of the Borough Hall, the referee saving the man from Kazakhstan as he was hammered into the ropes. He could have gone on, but from my ringside seat not for much longer. Hunter is a fierce competitor which is why he is still champion of Britain, Europe, and the Commonwealth and still without defeat (24-0-1).

On the same bill, Hartlepool-born Steve Conway had friends and relatives cheering as he hammered out a unanimous decision over Mihaly Kotai to relieve the Hungarian of his IBO light-middleweight title. What a home-coming!

After winning a battle with the scales, European cruiserweight champion, David Haye, won his first title defence with an eighth-round stoppage of the unbeaten Dane, Lasse Johansen, a victim from their amateur days. The 6' 3" boxer from Bermondsey admitted he was actually 15st 5lbs when he climbed into the ring at London's York Hall and his future looms at heavyweight, which is okay by us. We don't have many big fellows with David's undoubted talents. 16 victories, all inside schedule, against one defeat. Good stats, good stuff.

That same night, over in Florida, Battersea's one-time 'Bomber', Howard Eastman, was left to consider his ring future after being punched to seventh-round defeat by Edison Miranda of Columbia. For the 35-year-old former British, European and Commonwealth middleweight champion, there were not many dates left on his card and the fans left the Hard Rock Arena in Hollywood talking about the unbeaten 'Panther' Miranda after the 25-year-old clawed his way to his 26th pro victory, 23 inside.

On the big Manchester bill, WBU cruiserweight champion, Enzo Maccarinelli, took a unanimous decision over British and Commonwealth titleholder Mark Hobson to retain his belt and show that he is more than just a big punch. Hobson felt the power of that punch when floored in the third round and Enzo reminded him of it for the rest of a gruelling fight. The Swansea man had won 17 of his 22 wins via the hammer in his fists, but showed he was no one-trick pony with this victory.

A week after Calzaghe and Maccarinelli strutted their stuff, two more Welsh fighters were in title action at Newport and gave inspired performances. Gary Lockett claimed the vacant WBU middleweight championship with a stunning right to the head of Gilbert Eastman and it was all over in 2.25, round one! To be fair to the Battersea resident, he was a substitute for Ryan Rhodes and was stepping up from light-middle, in fact he was the Southern Area champion.

Ghana's Commonwealth light-middleweight champion, Ossie Duran, had beaten eight British opponents in a row and was looking to make Bradley Pryce number nine, but the Newport man had other ideas. After a shaky start he outboxed and outpunched the African to take the decision and the title.

On a cold night in Kirkcaldy, Kevin Anderson retained his Commonwealth welterweight championship against the Glasgow challenger, Craig Dickson, the referee stopping it halfway through round seven. Both lads were unbeaten, the champion taking his record to 16-0 while Dickson slipped to 12-1-1.

The New York Irish turned out in force to see John Duddy fight Shelby Pudwill for the vacant WBC Continental Americas middleweight title. It was the day before St Patrick's Day and a sellout crowd of 5,000 were in The Theatre at Madison Square Garden and they went home happy after seeing Duddy blast out the man from South Dakota inside 1.31 of the opening round. Pudwill was down three times and the unbeaten Irishman never will lose against guys like this. A gym session with the big bag would have been more beneficial to John, now 16-0, 14 early.

In Detroit, another young Irishman in Andy Lee got his pro career off to a winning start with a six-rounds decision over Anthony Cannon who survived three counts to finish on his feet. Lee, a 2004 Olympian, pleased mentor Emanuel Steward in his corner. "Perfect", said the Kronk guru.

Two wins in Monte Carlo for our boys as Finchley's Roman Greenberg stopped Alexander Vassilev on cuts in round six of their fight for the vacant IBO Inter-Continental heavyweight belt, while Matthew Hatton was also a sixth-round winner over the hapless Alexander Abramenko at welter.

Former British and Commonwealth light-heavyweight champion, Neil Simpson, said goodbye to his Coventry fans with a first-round stoppage of Varuzhan Davytan.

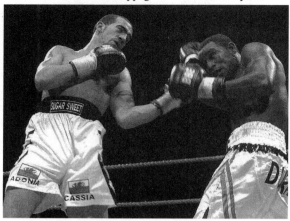

Bradley Pryce (left) upset the formbook at Newport somewhat when he outscored Ossie Duran to take the Ghanaian's Commonwealth light-middleweight title Les Clark

APRIL

Remember the Three Blind Mice? Well, they finally landed a job, working as judges for the European Boxing Union. This month there was a nice trip to Belfast to work the bantamweight title bout between Damaen Kelly and the champion, Simone Maludrottu of Italy, sitting in the three best seats in Andersonstown Leisure Centre.

The former British flyweight champion is one of the best pure boxers on the planet and he displayed his artistry throughout this 12 rounder to earn a comprehensive victory and another title. But wait a few minutes, they've just given the decision, and, believe it or not, the Italian is announced as the winner by a unanimous decision! Not even close! One judge has the champion SEVEN points clear.

Damaen Kelly and the crowd were stunned into silence, disbelief. Ringside critics had the Irishman winning nine rounds to three. Top boxing journalist, Bob Mee, said it for everyone when he wrote: "The three officials…must be asked to provide some justification for an interpretation that seemed at best eccentric, at worst prejudicial".

In Edinburgh, the hometown favourite, Alex Arthur, had better luck defending his European super-featherweight title against a lanky, awkward Belarussian named Sergei Gulyakevich. The visitor was a puncher by reputation, but it was the power in Arthur's fists that defined the contest and put the champion ahead on the scorecards when they had to be reckoned up after the fight was stopped in round seven with Sergei bleeding from a jagged cut over the left eye.

Heads had banged in the fight and in the sixth round the challenger was docked two points after blatantly bringing his head up under Arthur's chin. In the next exchange, heads clashed again and this time Gulyakevich was the injured party. Three minutes later it was all over.

Taking his record to 23-1, Arthur was hoping for a world title shot before Christmas.

On the Edinburgh card, Wythenshawe's British featherweight champion, Andy Morris, made a first defence against Rendall Munroe, taking a unanimous decision after a close fight. The Leicester southpaw was unbeaten in ten fights and was contesting a British championship which would have been unheard of years ago. But this was 2006 and Munroe gave the champion, himself undefeated in a mere 13 contests, a great scrap and the punters enjoyed it. So what's the big deal?

Michael Hunter once again thrilled the Hartlepool faithful with another defence of his European super-bantamweight title, this time against his mandatory challenger, a Spaniard named German Guartos. After seeing off Yersin Jailauov inside two rounds in March, Hunter forced Guartos to submit after three rounds, during which the man from Madrid took two counts. Still undefeated, Hunter moved to 25-0-1 and looks ready for bigger things.

A cloud hung over the Hartlepool show as Valery Odin was removed to hospital after becoming ill in his corner as the six rounder ended, leaving unbeaten Scottish light-heavyweight, Stevie McGuire, with his seventh pro win. Odin, Guadeloupe-born who fought out of London, was in intensive care for over a week before responding to treatment. His boxing career was over, but fortunately his life was not.

Out in California, Audley Harrison suffered his second straight defeat when blowing a decision to one-time prospect Dominick Guinn. It was the same old story with the former Olympic gold medallist, doing too little too late in a fight he was capable of winning. Yet, was he capable of winning? Why didn't he win it if he was able? Maybe the truth is Harrison isn't able to crack the game at the top level. After racking up 19 straight wins against assorted timber, felling 14 of them, Audley is not fighting as he should and, now 34, maybe he never will. He talked the talk okay, but he couldn't walk the walk.

Six years after taking an unknown Mongolian boxer into his home and into his gym at Shaw in Lancashire, promoter/manager Jack Doughty saw his protégé, Choi Tseveenpurev, win the vacant WBF featherweight title with a stoppage of Kenyan southpaw, David Kiilu. Choi was just too strong and powerful for the African who had been decked three times before the referee stopped it halfway through the third round.

Bristol's Lee Haskins retained his Commonwealth flyweight championship with a unanimous decision over veteran South African, Zolile Mbityi, but in taking his pro log to 15-0 (9) the 22-year-old local southpaw star learned a few lessons along the way. He had stopped Anthony Mathias, another African, inside two rounds last time out to take the title but this guy took him all the way and taught him a thing or two. Good!

On the Belfast show, Motherwell light-welterweight, Barry Morrison, met a tartar in Mihaita Mutu, a Romanian based in France. Barry had won 12 in a row but he didn't win this one as the visitor handed him a boxing lesson over eight rounds.

York Hall patrons had a double helping with shows on two days running. Steve Foster (junior) retained his WBU featherweight belt with a unanimous decision over Glasgow's John Simpson in a competitive bout, while the Scottish lightweight, Martin Watson, beat his southpaw rival, Ryan Barrett, over ten rounds of a British title eliminator. Also on the card was former heavyweight champion, Matt Skelton, bouncing back from his defeat by Danny Williams to rack up a fourth-round knockout over Armenia's Suren Kalachyan.

Next day, Tontcho Tontchev showed he still had something left as he blasted out Wales' Dean Phillips in 1.46 of round one. Phillips had gone 12 rounds in a Commonwealth lightweight title challenge, but he wasn't at the races with the Bulgarian who ended matters with an explosive left hook. It was bombs away in Glasgow as Darren Johnstone climbed off the deck to knock out another Welshman in Henry Jones in the fourth round to claim the British Masters super-featherweight title.

Steve Foster (right) made a successful defence of his WBU featherweight title when outpointing Scotland's John Simpson at Bethnal Green's York Hall   Les Clark

Despite carrying a badly damaged right hand for much of the fight, Martin Watson (right) eased his way comfortably past Ryan Barrett in a British lightweight title eliminator on the Foster v Simpson bill   Les Clark

MAY

It was a gamble that almost came unstuck. Ricky Hatton making his big-time debut in America, fight one of a three-fight deal with TV giant HBO, and stepping up to welterweight to challenge Luis Collazo for his WBA championship. The New York Puerto Rican, despite his 26-1 pro record, was regarded as a hand-picked opponent for Ricky's entry on the Stateside stage to ease the way to mega-fights with Floyd Mayweather, Shane Mosley, or even Oscar de la Hoya.

The gamble looked a racing cert in the opening minute of round one at the TD Banknorth Garden in Boston. A short left hook put Collazo on his backside for the mandatory count, but Hatton couldn't repeat the dose and had to dig deep in a rugged encounter that saw Collazo battle all the way and almost snatch victory with a storming final round.

The decision was unanimous for Hatton, but he finished with both eyes swollen and confessed to having had his toughest fight in his unbeaten run of 41. Trainer, Billy Graham, hadn't wanted the move to welterweight and his tiger admitted: "I felt strong but still believe I'm a light-welter", adding, "If I'm going to stay at welterweight, I have to grow into the weight".

Ricky's kid brother Matthew initiated a family double when he opened the show, outboxing and outpunching substitute Jose Medina, a Mexican fighting out of New Hampshire, over eight rounds at light-middleweight. It was Matthew's American debut, a solid win for the former undefeated Central Area welter and light-middleweight champion.

With Dennis Hobson (manager/promoter) in Boston on Hatton duty, Fight Academy's other world champ, IBF light-heavyweight titleholder Clinton Woods got on with the job at home, defending his crown against Australia's Jason DeLisle.

Clinton had beaten the man from Down Under in 2004 in an IBF eliminator, but he had to get off the deck to stop his rival in the final round, and DeLisle was determined to stick the champ on the floor again, this time for good. Trouble is, Woods has matured into a good all-round professional and turned in a brilliant performance to crush DeLisle inside six rounds for his second defence. Next job Clinton was looking forward to would be against an old foe, Glen Johnson, his mandatory challenger. After a narrow defeat and a draw, Woods could get third time lucky.

Kevin Mitchell retained his IBF Inter-Continental super-featherweight title for the second time on the York Hall bill with a two-rounds win over the Russian veteran, Kirkor Kirkorov. A left hook to the body dropped the visitor in round two and although he beat the count, he was pulled out in the interval claiming a damaged rib. It was another victory for Mitchell as he moved to 19-0, 13 inside. Jon Thaxton punched out a good win over unbeaten Argentina's Jorge Daniel Miranda, who did well to finish the course after a sixth-round knockdown. Sunderland heavyweight, David Dolan, Commonwealth Games super-heavy champion in 2002, got his pro debut out of the way with a four-rounds decision over France's Nabil Haciane.

Margate's Takaloo went into the lion's den when meeting local hard man, Eamonn Magee, in the King's Hall, Belfast. A former WBU light-middleweight champion, Takaloo was going for Magee's WBU welterweight title and at the end of 12 boring rounds he had it, but by then the fans couldn't care less. They did enjoy Amir Khan winning his first six rounder against a tough test in Hungary's Laszlo Komjathi. The Bolton boy took his log to 7-0 and is still on course. Danny Williams warmed up for his rematch with Matt Skelton with an easy win over Adnan Serin, a Turk based in Germany. Conceding three stones, Serin was down in the first and retired at the end of round three with a gashed left eye.

The Nottingham puncher, Carl Froch, retained his British and Commonwealth super-middleweight titles at York Hall with an impressive 11th-round knockout over Belfast southpaw Brian Magee, who fought back well after a shock knockdown in the opening round. It was Carl's 19th straight win, all but four ending early, and he was looking for a European title shot as he came out of the ring.

Boxing was back in the Bethnal Green venue four days later when the British bantamweight champion, Martin Power, gave Darlington's Isaac 'Argy' Ward a shot at his title. Both men were undefeated going in, Ward in 15 (2 draws), while the champion who was making his second defence, was on 18-0. It was a fight too far for Ward as Power dropped him in the first round and again in round eight when it was stopped.

The York Hall crowd had seen another North-East hopeful lose the big one when Nigel Wright suffered a unanimous points defeat to Lenny Daws, who claimed the vacant British light-welterweight title. Daws had beaten the lad from County Durham in the amateurs and he did it again here for his 14th straight victory. Wright, a southpaw, will come again and would love a rematch.

On the same bill, Salford's Lee Meager hammered out a sixth-round stoppage over his stablemate, Dave Stewart,

Defending his British bantamweight title against a game Isaac Ward at the York Hall, Bethnal Green, St Pancras' Martin Power (right) proved far too versatile for his rival, prior to recording an eighth-round stoppage win   Les Clark

to take the vacant British lightweight championship. The Scot was unbeaten in 19 bouts, but was always struggling and was down in the fourth before the ending came two rounds later. The new champion took his log to 20-1-1.

When they clashed in 2003, Lawrence Murphy upset the form book with a stunning first-round knockout of Wayne Elcock, but this time at the International Conference Centre in Birmingham, the local man took his revenge over the Scot with the Irish name, dropping him twice in round five for a stoppage. Scheduled for ten rounds, this was an eliminator for the British middleweight title.

JUNE

The crowds rolled up to the Aston Villa Leisure Centre in Birmingham hoping to see a good fight with British welterweight champion, Young Mutley, from nearby West Brom facing up to Scotland's Kevin Anderson, king of the Commonwealth. Both titles were on the line, winner take all, and by the half-way stage that winner looked home and dry. Anderson was bleeding from his right eyebrow and had been smashed to the deck in round two by a vicious left hook. He did well to get up.

Anderson did get up and by the eighth round had clawed his way back into the fight, and by now Mutley was looking jaded. In the tenth, he walked into a thudding left hook that took all the fight out of him, and as Anderson piled on the pressure the man from the Midlands was rescued by the referee. The Scot was a double champion, but his coronation was marred by some ugly crowd scenes as the local chapter of Yobs R Us spit out their dummies and ran riot for ten minutes.

They are not boxing fans, these people. They are mindless morons looking for trouble and if they can't find any they will make some. Two genuine warriors give their all in a sporting contest and these people couldn't care less. They should have a mark on their foreheads so that security can pick them out, and put them out! I've sat ringside at a couple of riots and they weren't pretty. They were pretty awful!

At the Barnsley Metrodome, Huddersfield's Mark Hobson had to dig deep to hang on to his British and Commonwealth cruiserweight titles against a determined challenge from John 'Buster' Keeton. Hoping for a third-time lucky bid for the titles, Keeton almost realised his dream in the second round when a big right hand brought the champion to his knees. Hobson got up but was badly shaken and shipped more punishment. But by round four he was in control and Buster was busted. It was stopped and Hobson had a Lonsdale Belt to take home, to keep!

Back in the York Hall ring just four weeks after turning back the challenge of Isaac Ward, the British bantamweight champion, Martin Power, could have been forgiven for thinking he had an easy job on his hands. Due to box dangerous Ian Napa, Power found himself facing a substitute in Tshifhiwa Munyai of South Africa with the vacant Commonwealth title in the pot.

Unbeaten in ten fights (1 draw) against prelim boys and none over six rounds, the African was a revelation. Tall, lanky, and dangerous, Munyai shocked Power and his fans by forcing a stoppage in the ninth round, handing the Londoner his first defeat in 20 contests to step on to the big stage. Just 21, Munyai is a mystery no longer. Ask Martin Power.

Another sensational performer from the African continent was Jackson Asiku, the Ugandan who took possession of the Commonwealth featherweight title with a first-round stoppage over Marc Callaghan. In his first defence at Liverpool, Asiku didn't hang about, sending the former British champion, Jamie McKeever, to the showers after just 2.35 of round one. In that short time, Asiku didn't put a punch wrong and Jamie was down twice before the referee saved him. Watch this space!

There were joyous scenes at Carmarthen as Scott Gammer, a 29-year-old heavyweight from Pembroke Dock, overpowered the English champion, Mark Krence, in the ninth round to win the vacant British title. Just over a year previously, Gammer had stopped Krence in eight rounds, this time Mark took him into the ninth before a big left hook sent him crashing. He beat the count, but Scott wouldn't leave him and the referee had to jump in and call a halt.

Amer Khan won a title at Manchester. This Amer (not that Amir) is a southpaw light-heavyweight from Sheffield and he had to survive a torrid eighth-round knockdown to take the decision and the vacant Central Area title over Darren 'Stubby' Stubbs.

Triple super-bantamweight champion, Michael Hunter, made the switch from his native Hartlepool to breezy Blackpool to defend his European title for the third time in four months. Coming from the opposite corner was the tough Frenchman, Tuncay Kaya, and he kept coming for the best part of nine rounds, until a thudding left hook to the stomach dropped him to his knees where he saw out the count. It had been tougher than expected for Hunter and he looked forward to the summer holidays.

In three overseas fights, British beef came out two to one. The big fellow, Audley Harrison, anxious to put his last two losing fights behind him, took a six-rounds walk-out bout at Atlantic City and knocked out Louisiana journeyman, Andrew Greeley, in three rounds. Harrison won a so-what? encounter that took his record to 20-2 (15).

In New York, the transplanted Irish middleweight, John Duddy, continued to build his fan base with a stoppage of tough Freddy Cuevas to retain his WBC Continental Americas title. Freddy's corner stopped it after seven rounds as Duddy moved to 17-0 with 15 inside. The New York Irish love him!

Steve Conway was not so fortunate in his trip to foreign climes, losing his IBO light-middleweight title to Attila Kovacs in the Hungarian town of Tiszaliget. The 12-rounds points defeat saw Steve, from Hartlepool via Dewsbury, drop to 34-7.

Bernard Dunne continued packing the National Stadium in Dublin as he upped his record to 21-0 with an eighth-round stoppage of David Martinez, the man from Albuquerque, sending out a message to European champion, Michael Hunter.

At Liverpool, Tony Dodson looked more like his old self as he dismantled Jamie Hearn in five rounds to win the vacant English super-middleweight title. The former British champion at the weight, Dodson had been sidelined by injuries and a car accident, but was up for this one and still has places to go.

Facts and Figures, 2005-2006

There were 632 (577 in 2004-2005) British-based boxers who were active between July 2005 and 30 June 2006, spread over 190 (177 in 2004-2005) promotions held in Britain, not including the Republic of Ireland, during the same period. Those who were either already holding licenses or had been re-licensed amounted to 483, while there were 128 (121 in 2004-2005) new professionals. There were also 17 men who started their careers elsewhere and four women.

Unbeaten During Season (Minimum Qualification: 6 Contests)

8: Michael Grant (1 draw). 7: Amir Khan, Mark Thompson. 6: Darren Barker, Jonjo Finnegan (1 draw), Mark Lloyd, Lee McAllister, Andrew Murray, John O'Donnell, Cello Renda, Nicki Smedley.

Longest Unbeaten Sequence (Minimum Qualifications: 10 Contests)

41: Joe Calzaghe, Ricky Hatton. 27: Michael Hunter (1 draw). 26: Nicky Cook. 23: Gavin Rees. 21: Steve Foster (1 draw), Johnny Nelson (1 draw), Gary Woolcombe. 20: Roman Greenberg, Enzo Maccarinelli. 19: Carl Froch, Kevin Mitchell. 18: Nadeem Sidique, Junior Witter. 17: Kevin Anderson, Scott Gammer (1 draw), Jose Olusegun. 16: Tony Doherty, Derry Matthews, John Murray, Paul Smith. 15: Matthew Hall, Lee Haskins, Ryan Kerr (2 draws), Lee McAllister. 14: Lenny Daws, Femi Fehintola, Andy Morris, Danny Smith (1 draw), Carl Wright (1 draw). 13: Paul Halpin (1 draw). 12: Peter Haymer (1 draw), Amer Khan. 11: Kell Brook, Darren McDermott (1 draw), John O'Donnell, Anthony Small. 10: Darren Barker, Steve Bell (2 draws), Scott Dann, John Fewkes, Gareth Hogg, Gary Lockett, Ross Minter (1 draw).

Most Wins During Season (Minimum Qualification: 6 Contests)

7: Michael Grant, Amir Khan, Mark Thompson. 6: Darren Barker, Mark Lloyd, Lee McAllister, Andrew Murray, John O'Donnell, Cello Renda, Nicki Smedley.

Most Contests During Season (Minimum Qualification: 10 Contests)

22: Billy Smith. 21: Pete Buckley, Ernie Smith. 17: Ben Hudson, Kristian Laight. 15: Peter Dunn, Daniel Thorpe. 14: David Kehoe. 13: Paul Bonson, Howard Clarke, Jason Nesbitt. 12: Duncan Cottier, Delroy Spencer. 11: Darren Gethin, Jimi Hendricks, Mark Phillips, Lance Verallo. 10: Tony Booth, Robert Burton, Neil Marston, Joe Mitchell, Silence Saheed, Karl Taylor.

Most Contests During Career (Minimum Qualification: 50 Contests)

270: Pete Buckley. 146: Tony Booth. 120: Ernie Smith. 116: Paul Bonson. 113: Karl Taylor. 105: Howard Clarke. 100: Arv Mittoo. 94: Ojay Abrahams. 87: Michael Pinnock. 84: Dave Hinds. 74: Carl Allen, Daniel Thorpe. 71: Jason Nesbitt. 70: David Kirk, Lee Williamson. 69: Peter Dunn. 62: Jason Collins. 59: Johnny Nelson. 52: Henry Akinwande.

Stop Press: Results for July/August 2006 (British-based fighters' results only)

Colorado Springs, Colorado, USA – 5 July

Jerome Ellis w rsc 5 Neil Sinclair.

Millenium Stadium, Cardiff – 7 July (Promoter: Warren)

Matt Skelton w pts 12 Danny Williams (Commonwealth Heavyweight Title), Enzo Maccarinelli w rsc 9 Marcelo Dominguez (WBO Interim Cruiserweight Title), Bradley Pryce w rsc 4 Hassan Matumla (Commonwealth L.Middleweight Title), Gary Lockett w pts 12 Ryan Rhodes (WBU Middleweight Title), Amir Khan w rsc 2 Colin Bain, Gavin Rees w pts 6 Martin Watson, Tony Doherty w co 1 Ihar Filonau, Ross Minter w pts 6 Duncan Cottier, Kevin Mitchell w rsc 2 Imad Ben Khalifa, Matthew Hall w rsc 1 Kevin Phelan, Barrie Jones w rsc 2 James Paisley, Kerry Hope w pts 4 Ryan Rowlinson, Nathan Cleverly w pts 4 Mark Phillips.

Lvov, Ukraine – 8 July

Roman Dzuman w pts 12 Eugenio Monteiro.

Alicante, Spain – 14 July

Garry Buckland w pts 4 Ubagel Soto, Laurent Gomis w rtd 1 Gatis Skuja.

Hamburg, Germany - 15 July

Ruslan Chagaev w rsc 8 Michael Sprott (WBA Inter-Continental Heavyweight Title. WBO Asian-Pacific Heavyweight Title).

The Leisure Centre, Altrincham - 21 July

David Haye w pts 12 Ismael Abdoul (European Cruiserweight Title), Jamie Moore w rsc 5 Mike Algoet, Anthony Small w pts 6 Vladimir Borovski, John Fewkes w rsc 5 Kristian Laight, Mark Thompson w rsc 3 Ernie Smith, Graeme Higginson w pts 4 James Brown, Alex Matvienko w pts 4 Simone Lucas, Danny Harding w pts 4 Neal McQuade, Stuart McFadyen w rsc 1 Neil Read, Brett Flounoy w co 1 Tommy Jones.

Goresbrook Leisure Centre, Dagenham – 23 July

Juliette Winter w pts 8 Shanee Martin (British Masters S.Flyweight Title), Ryan Barrett w pts 6 Baz Carey, Shon Davies w rsc 1 Richard Horton, Gary Ojuederie w pts 4 Carl Wright, Tommy Eastwood w pts 4 Tony Booth, Danny Goode w pts 4 Ben Hudson, Dean Marcantonio w pts 4 Rocky Muscus.

Diary of British Boxing Tournaments, 2005-2006

Tournaments are listed by date, town, venue and named promoter, as licensed by the BBBoC, and cover the period 1 July 2005 to 30 June 2006.

Code: SC = Sporting Club

Date	Town	Venue	Promoters
01.07.05	Fulham	Ibis Hotel	Merton
08.07.05	Altrincham	The Leisure Centre	Hearn
09.07.05	Nottingham	The Ice Arena	Hennessy
09.07.05	Bristol	Whitchurch Sports Centre	Sanigar
16.07.05	Chigwell	Prince Regent Hotel	Burns
16.07.05	Bolton	The Arena	Warren
23.07.05	Edinburgh	Meadowbank Arena	Warren
24.07.05	Leicester Square	The Equinox	Pyle/Feld
24.07.05	Sheffield	Octagon Centre	Hobson/Evans
02.09.05	Derby	Heritage Hotel	Shinfield
03.09.05	Norwich	Carrow Road Football Ground	Featherby
09.09.05	Sheffield	Hallam FM Arena	Hobson/Evans
10.09.05	Cardiff	International Arena	Warren
11.09.05	Kirkby in Ashfield	Festival Hall	Ashton
16.09.05	Plymouth	The Pavilions	Sanigar
16.09.05	Doncaster	The Dome	Rushton
16.09.05	Telford	Oakengates Theatre	Johnson
18.09.05	Bethnal Green	York Hall	Roe
19.09.05	Glasgow	Holiday Inn	T.Gilmour
21.09.05	Bradford	Hilton Hotel	Garber
23.09.05	Mayfair	Hilton Hotel	Warren
23.09.05	Manchester	George Carnall Leisure Centre	Hearn
24.09.05	Coventry	Leofric Hotel	Coventry SC
25.09.05	Southampton	The Guildhall	Bishop
25.09.05	Leeds	The Town Hall	Manners/J.Ingle
30.09.05	Kirkcaldy	The Ice Rink	T.Gilmour
30.09.05	Carmarthen	The Showground	Boyce
30.09.05	Burton	Meadowside Leisure Centre	Johnson
01.10.05	Wigan	The Arena	Dixon
06.10.05	Sunderland	Marriott Hotel	Conroy
06.10.05	Dudley	The Town Hall	Johnson
06.10.05	Longford	Heathrow Thistle Hotel	Carman
07.10.05	Bethnal Green	York Hall	Maloney
09.10.05	Hammersmith	The Palais	Pyle/Feld
10.10.05	Birmingham	Holiday Inn	Cowdell
14.10.05	Huddersfield	The Leisure Centre	Hobson/Evans
14.10.05	Motherwell	The Civic Centre	C.Gilmour
16.10.05	Peterborough	Werrington Sports Centre	Pauly
21.10.05	Bethnal Green	York Hall	Hearn/Hennessy
22.10.05	Mansfield	The Leisure Centre	Scriven
22.10.05	Coventry	Mercia Park Sports Centre	Cowdell
24.10.05	Glasgow	Holiday Inn	T.Gilmour
25.10.05	Preston	The Guildhall	Warren
28.10.05	Hartlepool	Borough Hall	Hearn
29.10.05	Aberdeen	Beach Ballroom	J.Ingle
30.10.05	Sheffield	Concord Sports Centre	Rhodes
30.10.05	Bethnal Green	York Hall	Maloney
03.11.05	Sunderland	Roker Hotel Marquee	Conroy

04.11.05	Glasgow	Holiday Inn	T.Gilmour
04.11.05	Bethnal Green	York Hall	Maloney
05.11.05	Renfrew	Braehead Arena	Warren
08.11.05	Leeds	Elland Road Conference & Exhibition Centre	Spratt
12.11.05	Bristol	Thistle Hotel	Hay
12.11.05	Sheffield	Grosvenor House Hotel	Hobson (senior)
12.11.05	Stoke	King's Hall	Carney
12.11.05	Glasgow	Thistle Hotel	Morrison
13.11.05	Leeds	The Town Hall	Manners
17.11.05	Bristol	Ashton Gate Conference Centre	Sanigar
17.11.05	Piccadilly	Café Royal	Helliet
18.11.05	Dagenham	Goresbrook Leisure Centre	Hearn
19.11.05	Southwark	Elephant & Castle Leisure Centre	D.V.Williams
20.11.05	Shaw	Tara Sports & Leisure Centre	Doughty
21.11.05	Glasgow	Holiday Inn	Gilmour
23.11.05	Mayfair	Hilton Hotel	Evans
24.11.05	Clydach	Manor Park Hotel	Boyce
25.11.05	Liverpool	Olympia	Hearn
25.11.05	Hull	KC Stadium Banqueting Suite	Hull & District SC
25.11.05	Walsall	The Town Hall	Johnson
26.11.05	Sheffield	Hallam FM Arena	Hobson/Evans
02.12.05	Nottingham	The Ice Arena	Hennessy
02.12.05	Coventry	Leofric Hotel	Coventry SC
02.12.05	Doncaster	The Dome	Rushton
04.12.05	Portsmouth	Mountbatten Centre	Bishop
04.12.05	Telford	Oakengates Theatre	Johnson
05.12.05	Leeds	Queen's Hotel	Walker
08.12.05	Derby	Heritage Hotel	Alton
08.12.05	Sunderland	Marriott Hotel	Conroy
09.12.05	Iver Heath	Pinewood Studios	Hearn
10.12.05	Canning Town	ExCel Arena	Warren
11.12.05	Norwich	Lava & Ignite Nightclub	Featherby
11.12.05	Chigwell	Prince Regent Hotel	Burns
12.12.05	Leicester	Ramada Jarvis Hotel	Griffin
12.12.05	Birmingham	Holiday Inn	Cowdell
12.12.05	Peterborough	Moat House Hotel	Pauly
14.12.05	Blackpool	Hilton Hotel	Dixon
15.12.05	Coventry	Mercia Park Sports Centre	Cowdell
15.12.05	Cleethorpes	Winter Gardens	Frater
16.12.05	Bracknell	The Leisure Centre	Hobson/Evans
18.12.05	Bolton	Reebok Stadium	Wood
19.12.05	Longford	Heathrow Thistle Hotel	Carman
20.01.06	Bethnal Green	York Hall	Hennessy
23.01.06	Glasgow	Holiday Inn	T.Gilmour
27.01.06	Dagenham	Goresbrook Leisure Centre	Maloney
28.01.06	Nottingham	The Ice Arena	Warren
02.02.06	Holborn	New Connaught Rooms	Helliet
10.02.06	Plymouth	The Pavilions	Sanigar
11.02.06	Bethnal Green	York Hall	Maloney
12.02.06	Manchester	George Carnall Leisure Centre	Wood
16.02.06	Dudley	The Town Hall	Johnson
17.02.06	Bethnal Green	York Hall	Hennessy
17.02.06	Sheffield	Concord Sports Centre	Rhodes
18.02.06	Stoke	King's Hall	Carney
18.02.06	Edinburgh	Meadowbank Stadium	Warren
20.02.06	Glasgow	Holiday Inn	T.Gilmour

23.02.06	Leeds	The Town Hall	Manners
24.02.06	Dagenham	Goresbrook Leisure Centre	Hearn/Harding
24.02.06	Birmingham	Centennial Centre	Rowson
24.02.06	Scarborough	The Spa	Pollard
25.02.06	Bristol	Whitchurch Sports Centre	Sanigar
25.02.06	Canning Town	ExCel Arena	Warren
27.02.06	Birmingham	Holiday Inn	Cowdell
28.02.06	Leeds	Elland Road Conference & Exhibition Centre	Spratt
02.03.06	Blackpool	Norbreck Castle Hotel	Dixon
03.03.06	Hartlepool	Borough Hall	Hearn
03.03.06	Doncaster	The Dome	Rushton
04.03.06	Manchester	MEN Arena	Warren
04.03.06	Coventry	Mercia Park Sports Centre	Hollier
05.03.06	Southampton	The Guildhall	Bishop
05.03.06	Sheffield	Octagon Centre	Hobson
09.03.06	Sunderland	Roker Hotel	Conroy
10.03.06	Walsall	Bescot Stadium Conference Centre	Rowson
11.03.06	Newport	The Sports Centre	Warren
13.03.06	Glasgow	Holiday Inn	T.Gilmour
17.03.06	Kirkcaldy	Fife Ice Arena	T.Gilmour
18.03.06	Coventry	Leofric Hotel	Coventry SC
20.03.06	Leeds	Queen's Hotel	Walker
23.03.06	The Strand	Savoy Hotel	Sanders
24.03.06	Bethnal Green	York Hall	Maloney
25.03.06	Burton	Meadowside Leisure Centre	Rowson
25.03.06	Irvine	Volunteer Rooms	T.Gilmour
30.03.06	Piccadilly	Café Royal	Helliet
30.03.06	Bloomsbury	Royal National Hotel	D.V.Williams
30.03.06	Peterborough	Holiday Inn	Pauly
31.03.06	Inverurie	Thainstone Centre	Bambrick/T.Gilmour
01.04.06	Bethnal Green	York Hall	Warren
02.04.06	Bethnal Green	York Hall	Maloney
02.04.06	Shaw	Tara Sports & Leisure Centre	Doughty
06.04.06	Piccadilly	Café Royal	Evans
07.04.06	Bristol	Whitchurch Sports Centre	Sanigar
07.04.06	Longford	Heathrow Thistle Hotel	Carman
13.04.06	Leeds	The Town Hall	Manners
14.04.06	Telford	Oakengates Theatre	Johnson
21.04.06	Belfast	Anderstown Leisure Centre	Hearn
21.04.06	Doncaster	The Dome	Rushton
22.04.06	Glasgow	Thistle Hotel	Morrison
23.04.06	Chester	The Racecourse	Goodall
24.04.06	Glasgow	Holiday Inn	T.Gilmour
24.04.06	Cleethorpes	Winter Gardens	Frater
28.04.06	Hartlepool	Borough Hall	Hearn
28.04.06	Manchester	Midland Hotel	I.Robinson
29.04.06	Edinburgh	Meadowbank Arena	Warren
06.05.06	Irvine	Magnum Centre	C.Gilmour
06.05.06	Birmingham	National Exhibition Centre Seni Arena	Ashton
06.05.06	Birmingham	International Conference Centre	Purchase
06.05.06	Blackpool	Norbreck Castle Hotel	Dixon
06.05.06	Stoke	King's Hall	Carney
09.05.06	Leeds	Elland Road Conference & Exhibition Centre	Spratt/Bateson
11.05.06	Sunderland	Roker Hotel	Conroy
12.05.06	Bethnal Green	York Hall	Hennessy
13.05.06	Sheffield	Ponds Forge Leisure Centre	Hobson/Evans

13.05.06	Bethnal Green	York Hall	Warren
13.05.06	Sutton in Ashfield	The Leisure Centre	Calow
14.05.06	Derby	Heritage Hotel	Shinfield
18.05.06	Walsall	The Town Hall	Johnson/Rowson
20.05.06	Belfast	King's Hall	Warren
20.05.06	Bristol	Thistle Hotel	Hay
21.05.06	Bristol	Jury's Hotel	Couch
21.05.06	Bethnal Green	York Hall	Helliet/Feld
22.05.06	Birmingham	Holiday Inn	Cowdell
26.05.06	Bethnal Green	York Hall	Maloney
26.05.06	Hull	KC Stadium Banqueting Suite	Hull & District SC
27.05.06	Glasgow	Thistle Hotel	Morrison
27.05.06	Aberdeen	Beach Ballroom	J.Ingle
28.05.06	Longford	Heathrow Park Hotel	Carman
28.05.06	Wakefield	Light Waves Leisure Centre	Rhodes
30.05.06	Bethnal Green	York Hall	Maloney
01.06.06	Barnsley	The Metrodome	Warren
01.06.06	Birmingham	Aston Villa Leisure Centre	Johnson/Hearn
03.06.06	Chigwell	Prince Regent Hotel	Burns
05.06.06	Glasgow	Holiday Inn	T.Gilmour
09.06.06	Doncaster	The Dome	Rushton
15.06.06	Peterborough	Holiday Inn	Pauly
16.06.06	Carmarthen	The Showground	Boyce
16.06.06	Liverpool	Everton Park Sports Centre	Hearn
18.06.06	Manchester	George Carnall Leisure Centre	Wood
22.06.06	Sheffield	Park Hotel	Hobson
23.06.06	Blackpool	Winter Gardens	Hearn
23.06.06	Birmingham	Centennial Centre	Purchase
29.06.06	Bethnal Green	York Hall	Maloney
29.06.06	Dudley	The Town Hall	Rowson

Active British-Based Boxers: Career Records

Shows the complete record for all British-based boxers who have been active between 1 July 2005 and 30 June 2006. Names in brackets are real names, where they differ from ring names, and the first place name given is the boxer's domicile. Boxers are either shown as being self-managed or with a named manager, the information being supplied by the BBBoC shortly before going to press. Also included are foreign-born fighters who made their pro debuts in Britain, along with others like Jadgar Abdulla (Denmark), Jackson Asiku (Uganda), Shinny Bayaar (Mongolia), Karl David (Poland), Varuzhan Davtyan (Armenia), Ruben Groenewald (South Africa), Davis Kamara (Sierra Leone), Istvan Kecskes (Hungary), Moses Kinyua (Kenya), Oscar Milkitas (Lithuania), Eugenio Monteiro (Portugal), Harry Ramogoadi (South Africa), Hastings Rasani (Zimbabwe), Yuri Romanov (Belarus), Sergei Rozhakmens (Latvia), Jed Syger (Turkey) and Choi Tseveenpurev (Mongolia), who, although starting their careers elsewhere, now hold BBBoC licenses.

Mick Abbott

Stoke. *Born* Stoke, 26 February 1973
Featherweight. Ht 5' 6"
Manager M. Carney
12.11.05 Neil Read W PTS 6 Stoke
18.02.06 Barrington Brown L PTS 6 Stoke
Career: 2 contests, won 1, lost 1.

Jadgar Abdulla

London. *Born* Denmark, 4 September, 1980
Featherweight. Ht. 5'5"
Manager F. Maloney
14.06.02 Frankie DeMilo W PTS 4 Copenhagen, Denmark
13.09.02 Jacob Mohlabi W PTS 6 Randers, Denmark
26.10.02 Karim Ketoun W PTS 6 Esbjerg, Denmark
29.11.02 Jean-Marie Codet W PTS 6 Copenhagen, Denmark
07.03.03 Jackie Gunguluza W PTS 6 Pandrup, Denmark
13.06.03 Anthony Martinez W CO 1 Aalborg, Denmark
24.10.03 Evangelio Perez W PTS 6 Copenhagen, Denmark
13.12.03 Robert Osiobe DREW 6 Copenhagen, Denmark
28.02.04 Robert Osiobe T DRAW 4 Aalborg, Denmark
12.11.04 Nordine Barmou W PTS 6 Copenhagen, Denmark
24.03.06 Buster Dennis DREW 4 Bethnal Green
Career: 11 contests, won 8, drew 3.

Ojay Abrahams

Watford. *Born* Lambeth, 17 December, 1964
L.Heavyweight. Former British Masters Middleweight Champion. Ht. 5'8½"
Manager Self
21.09.91 Gordon Webster W RSC 3 Tottenham
26.10.91 Mick Reid W RSC 5 Brentwood
26.11.91 John Corcoran W PTS 6 Bethnal Green
21.01.92 Dave Andrews DREW 6 Norwich
31.03.92 Marty Duke W RSC 2 Norwich
19.05.92 Michael Smyth L PTS 6 Cardiff
16.06.92 Ricky Mabbett W PTS 6 Dagenham
13.10.92 Vince Rose L RSC 3 Mayfair

30.01.93 Vince Rose DREW 6 Brentwood
19.05.93 Ricky Mabbett L RSC 4 Leicester
18.09.93 Ricky Mabbett L PTS 6 Leicester
09.12.93 Nick Appiah W PTS 6 Watford
24.01.94 Errol McDonald W RSC 2 Glasgow
09.02.94 Vince Rose W PTS 6 Brentwood
23.05.94 Spencer McCracken L PTS 6 Walsall
11.06.94 Darren Dyer W RSC 1 Bethnal Green
29.09.94 Gary Logan L PTS 10 Bethnal Green
(Southern Area Welterweight Title Challenge)
13.12.94 Geoff McCreesh L PTS 6 Potters Bar
11.02.95 Gary Murray L PTS 8 Hamanskraal, South Africa
17.07.95 Andreas Panayi L PTS 8 Mayfair
02.10.95 Larbi Mohammed L RTD 5 Mayfair
08.12.95 Jason Beard W CO 2 Bethnal Green
09.04.96 Kevin Thompson W RSC 3 Stevenage
07.05.96 Harry Dhami L RSC 5 Mayfair
(Vacant Southern Area Welterweight Title)
12.11.96 Spencer McCracken L PTS 8 Dudley
22.04.97 Paul King W RSC 4 Bethnal Green
29.05.97 Paul Ryan L RSC 3 Mayfair
30.06.97 Ahmet Dottuev L RSC 4 Bethnal Green
08.11.97 Anthony McFadden L PTS 8 Southwark
24.03.98 Leigh Wicks W PTS 6 Bethnal Green
28.04.98 Jim Webb L RSC 2 Belfast
10.09.98 Delroy Leslie L PTS 10 Acton
(Vacant Southern Area L. Middleweight Title)
19.12.98 Michael Jones L PTS 6 Liverpool
23.01.99 Wayne Alexander L DIS 1 Cheshunt
(Vacant Southern Area L. Middleweight Title)
01.05.99 Wayne Alexander L RSC 3 Crystal Palace
26.06.99 Geoff McCreesh L PTS 8 Millwall
05.10.99 Hussain Osman L PTS 4 Bloomsbury
23.10.99 Paul Samuels L PTS 8 Telford
18.01.00 Howard Eastman L RSC 2 Mansfield
23.03.00 Pedro Thompson DREW 6 Bloomsbury
08.04.00 Anthony Farnell L PTS 8 Bethnal Green
16.05.00 Ryan Rhodes L PTS 6 Warrington
23.05.00 Alexandru Andrei L PTS 6 Paris, France
04.07.00 Lester Jacobs L PTS 4 Tooting
21.09.00 Harry Butler W PTS 6 Bloomsbury
07.10.00 Kofi Jantuah L RTD 3 Doncaster
25.11.00 Donovan Smillie W RSC 2 Manchester
16.12.00 Marlon Hayes L RTD 6 Sheffield
15.01.01 Gordon Behan L DREW 6 Manchester
24.02.01 Ruben Groenewald L PTS 6 Bethnal Green
22.04.01 Harry Butler W PTS 6 Streatham

17.05.01 Lee Murtagh W RSC 2 Leeds
(Vacant British Masters L. Middleweight Title)
21.06.01 Charden Ansoula L PTS 4 Earls Court
28.07.01 Gary Logan L RSC 4 Wembley
10.12.01 Jimmy Vincent L PTS 10 Birmingham
(British Masters L. Middleweight Title Challenge)
28.01.02 Ian Cooper W PTS 6 Barnsley
16.03.02 John Humphrey L PTS 10 Bethnal Green
(Vacant Southern Area L.Middleweight Title)
13.04.02 Mihaly Kotai L PTS 6 Liverpool
20.04.02 Freeman Barr L PTS 8 Cardiff
10.05.02 Carl Froch L RSC 1 Bethnal Green
15.06.02 Sam Soliman L PTS 4 Tottenham
17.08.02 Wayne Elcock L PTS 4 Cardiff
17.09.02 David Starie L RSC 4 Bethnal Green
25.10.02 Gilbert Eastman L PTS 4 Bethnal Green
12.12.02 Allan Gray L PTS 10 Leicester Square
(Southern Area Middleweight Title Challenge. Vacant WBF International Middleweight Title)
05.03.03 David Walker L PTS 6 Bethnal Green
19.04.03 Geard Ajetovic L PTS 4 Liverpool
12.05.03 Jason Collins L PTS 10 Birmingham
(Vacant British Masters S.Middleweight Title)
05.07.03 Allan Foster L PTS 4 Brentwood
18.09.03 Steve Roache W CO 2 Mayfair
18.10.03 Michael Jones L PTS 6 Manchester
22.11.03 Jason McKay L PTS 4 Belfast
01.12.03 Omar Gumati L PTS 6 Leeds
10.02.04 Daniel Teasdale L PTS 6 Barnsley
23.02.04 Matt Galer L PTS 4 Nottingham
08.03.04 Hamed Jamali L PTS 8 Birmingham
02.04.04 Scott Dann L RSC 6 Plymouth
06.05.04 Daniel Teasdale L PTS 4 Barnsley
13.05.04 Conroy McIntosh L RSC 2 Bethnal Green
12.06.04 Matthew Macklin L PTS 4 Manchester
10.09.04 Paul Smith L PTS 4 Liverpool
29.10.04 Tom Cannon L PTS 4 Renfrew
12.11.04 Matthew Hall L RSC 1 Halifax
27.01.05 Eder Kurti L PTS 6 Piccadilly
27.05.05 Paul Buchanan L PTS 6 Spennymoor
04.06.05 Ricardo Samms L PTS 4 Manchester
18.06.05 Jon Ibbotson L PTS 4 Barnsley
25.10.05 Ricardo Samms L PTS 4 Preston
24.11.05 Jason McKay L PTS 4 Lurgan
04.03.06 Tony Quigley L PTS 4 Manchester
20.03.06 Danny Thornton L PTS 6 Leeds
01.04.06 Richard Horton L PTS 4 Bethnal Green
14.05.06 Rod Anderton L PTS 6 Derby
27.05.06 Andrew Facey L PTS 6 Aberdeen
Career: 94 contests, won 20, drew 4, lost 70.

Terry Adams

Birmingham. *Born* Birmingham, 1
November, 1978
Middleweight. Ht. 5'8½"
Manager Self

19.02.04	Neil Addis W CO 2 Dudley
15.04.04	Geraint Harvey W PTS 6 Dudley
08.07.04	Geraint Harvey W RSC 6 Birmingham
15.10.04	Jamie Coyle L RSC 5 Glasgow
13.02.05	Michael Lomax L RSC 1 Brentwood
07.04.05	Keith Jones W PTS 6 Birmingham
24.07.05	Gavin Smith W PTS 6 Sheffield
30.09.05	Matt Galer L PTS 10 Burton
	(Vacant Midlands Area L.Middleweight Title)
24.02.06	Gatis Skuja DREW 4 Birmingham
05.03.06	Danny Goode L PTS 8 Southampton
30.03.06	Cello Renda L PTS 4 Peterborough
06.05.06	Ernie Smith W PTS 6 Birmingham
28.05.06	Danny Reynolds L RSC 1 Wakefield

Career: 13 contests, won 6, drew 1, lost 6.

Geard Ajetovic

Liverpool. *Born* Beocin, Yugoslavia, 28
February, 1981
S.Middleweight. Ht. 5'8½"
Manager D. Hobson

19.04.03	Ojay Abrahams W PTS 4 Liverpool
17.05.03	Jason Samuels W PTS 4 Liverpool
26.09.03	Gary Beardsley W RSC 3 Reading
07.11.03	Joel Ani W RTD 1 Sheffield
06.02.04	Tomas da Silva W RSC 4 Sheffield
12.05.04	Dmitry Donetskiy W PTS 6 Reading
10.12.04	Conroy McIntosh W PTS 6 Sheffield
21.01.05	Dmitry Yanushevich W RSC 4 Brentford
24.07.05	Conroy McIntosh W PTS 6 Sheffield
14.10.05	Jason Collins W RSC 6 Huddersfield
26.11.05	Magid Ben Driss W PTS 8 Sheffield
18.03.06	Christophe Canclaux L PTS 8 Monte Carlo, Monaco
13.05.06	Manoocha Salari W RSC 4 Sheffield

Career: 13 contests, won 12, lost 1.

Geard Ajetovic   Les Clark

Henry Akinwande

Dulwich. *Born* London, 12 October, 1965
IBF Inter-Continental Heavyweight
Champion. Former Undefeated WBN &
WBC FeCarBox Heavyweight Champion.
Former Undefeated WBO, European &
Commonwealth Heavyweight Champion.
Ht. 6'7"
Manager Self

04.10.89	Carlton Headley W CO 1 Kensington
08.11.89	Dennis Bailey W RSC 2 Wembley
06.12.89	Paul Neilson W RSC 1 Wembley
10.01.90	John Fairbairn W RSC 1 Kensington
14.03.90	Warren Thompson W PTS 6 Kensington
09.05.90	Mike Robinson W CO 1 Wembley
10.10.90	Tracy Thomas W PTS 6 Kensington
12.12.90	Francois Yrius W RSC 1 Kensington
06.03.91	J. B. Williamson W RSC 2 Wembley
06.06.91	Ramon Voorn W PTS 8 Barking
28.06.91	Marshall Tillman W PTS 8 Nice, France
09.10.91	Gypsy John Fury W CO 3 Manchester
	(Elim. British Heavyweight Title)
06.12.91	Tim Bullock W CO 3 Dusseldorf, Germany
28.02.92	Young Joe Louis W RSC 3 Issy les Moulineaux, France
26.03.92	Tucker Richards W RSC 2 Telford
10.04.92	Lumbala Tshimba W PTS 8 Carquefou, France
05.06.92	Kimmuel Odum W DIS 6 Marseille, France
18.07.92	Steve Garber W RTD 2 Manchester
19.12.92	Axel Schulz DREW 12 Berlin, Germany
	(Vacant European Heavyweight Title)
18.03.93	Jimmy Thunder W PTS 12 Lewisham
	(Vacant Commonwealth Heavyweight Title)
01.05.93	Axel Schulz W PTS 12 Berlin, Germany
	(Vacant European Heavyweight Title)
06.11.93	Frankie Swindell W PTS 10 Sun City, South Africa
01.12.93	Biagio Chianese W RSC 4 Kensington
	(European Heavyweight Title Defence)
05.04.94	Johnny Nelson W PTS 10 Bethnal Green
23.07.94	Mario Schiesser W CO 7 Berlin, Germany
	(European Heavyweight Title Defence)
08.04.95	Calvin Jones W CO 2 Las Vegas, Nevada, USA
22.07.95	Stanley Wright W RSC 2 Millwall
16.12.95	Tony Tucker W PTS 10 Philadelphia, Pennsylvania, USA
27.01.96	Brian Sergeant W RSC 1 Phoenix, Arizona, USA
23.03.96	Gerard Jones W DIS 7 Miami, Florida, USA
29.06.96	Jeremy Williams W CO 3 Indio, California, USA
	(Vacant WBO Heavyweight Title)
09.11.96	Alexander Zolkin W RSC 10 Las Vegas, Nevada, USA
	(WBO Heavyweight Title Defence)
11.01.97	Scott Welch W PTS 12 Nashville, Tennessee, USA
	(WBO Heavyweight Title Defence)
12.07.97	Lennox Lewis L DIS 5 Stateline, Nevada, USA
	(WBC Heavyweight Title Challenge)
13.12.97	Orlin Norris W PTS 12 Pompano Beach, Florida, USA
	(Final Elim. WBA Heavyweight Title)
06.03.99	Reynaldo Minus W RSC 2 St Paul, Minnesota, USA
15.05.99	Najeed Shaheed W RSC 9 Miami, Florida, USA
22.02.00	Chris Serengo W RSC 1 Capetown, South Africa
25.05.00	Russull Chasteen W CO 5 Tunica, Mississippi, USA
08.12.00	Ken Craven W CO 1 Tallahassee, Florida, USA
	(Vacant WBC FeCarBox Heavyweight Title)
17.03.01	Peter McNeeley W CO 2 Tallahassee, Florida, USA
16.06.01	Maurice Harris W CO 1 Cincinnati, USA
17.11.01	Oliver McCall L CO 10 Las Vegas, Nevada, USA
08.03.02	Curt Paige W RSC 1 Kissimmee, Florida, USA
29.10.02	Sam Ubokane W RSC 7 Capetown, South Africa
10.12.02	Roman Sukhoterin W PTS 12 Constanta, Romania
	(WBN Inter-Continental Heavyweight Title Challenge)
31.05.03	Timo Hoffmann W PTS 12 Frankfurt, Germany
	(IBF Inter-Continental Heavyweight Title Challenge)
10.04.04	Anton Nel W RSC 10 Carabas, Nigeria
	(IBF Inter-Continental Heavyweight Title Defence)
14.05.05	Alex Vasiliev W PTS 8 Bayreuth, Germany
24.09.05	Tipton Walker W RSC 2 Atlantic City, New Jersey, USA
10.12.05	Ed Mahone W PTS 12 Leipzig, Germany
	(Vacant IBF Inter-Continental Heavyweight Title)
04.03.06	Cisse Salif W PTS 12 Oldenburg, Germany
	(IBF Inter-Continental Heavyweight Title Defence)

Career: 52 contests, won 49, drew 1, lost 2.

Omar Akram

Glasgow. *Born* Glasgow, 6 December, 1984
Featherweight. Ht. 5'7"
Manager A. Morrison

27.05.06	Graeme Higginson L RSC 2 Glasgow

Career: 1 contest, lost 1.

Mark Alexander

Hackney. *Born* Hackney, 18 November, 1975
Lightweight. Ht. 5'9¹/₂"
Manager Self

10.04.01	Steve Hanley W PTS 4 Wembley
31.07.01	Damien Dunnion W PTS 4 Bethnal Green
19.12.01	Dazzo Williams L PTS 6 Coventry
15.05.03	Buster Dennis W PTS 4 Mayfair
01.08.03	Arv Mittoo W PTS 4 Bethnal Green
25.09.03	Henry Castle L PTS 6 Bethnal Green
01.11.03	John Simpson L PTS 4 Glasgow
19.11.05	Graeme Higginson W PTS 4 Southwark
21.05.06	Steve Gethin W PTS 4 Bethnal Green

Career: 9 contests, won 6, lost 3.

Wayne Alexander

Croydon. *Born* Tooting, 17 July, 1973
WBU L.Middleweight Champion. Former
Undefeated British & European
L.Middleweight Champion. Former
Undefeated Southern Area L.Middleweight
Champion. Ht. 5'8¾"
Manager Self

10.11.95	Andrew Jervis W RTD 3 Derby
13.02.96	Paul Murray W PTS 4 Bethnal Green
11.05.96	Jim Webb W RSC 2 Bethnal Green
13.07.96	John Janes W RSC 3 Bethnal Green
05.06.97	Prince Kasi Kaihau W CO 4 Bristol
29.11.97	John Janes W RSC 1 Norwich
21.03.98	Darren Covill W RSC 2 Bethnal Green
09.05.98	Pedro Carragher W CO 2 Sheffield
14.07.98	Lindon Scarlett W RSC 5 Reading
05.12.98	Jimmy Vincent W RSC 3 Bristol
23.01.99	Ojay Abrahams W DIS 1 Cheshunt
	(Vacant Southern Area
	L. Middleweight Title)
01.05.99	Ojay Abrahams W RSC 3 Crystal
	Palace
07.08.99	George Richards W RSC 2 Dagenham
19.02.00	Paul Samuels W RSC 3 Dagenham
	(Vacant British L. Middleweight Title)
12.08.00	Paul Denton W RSC 1 Wembley
10.02.01	Harry Simon L RSC 5 Widnes
	(WBO L. Middleweight Title Challenge)
28.07.01	Viktor Fesetchko W PTS 8 Wembley
17.11.01	Joe Townsley W RSC 2 Glasgow
	(British L. Middleweight Title Defence)
19.01.02	Paolo Pizzamiglio W RSC 3 Bethnal
	Green
	(Vacant European L. Middleweight
	Title)
18.01.03	Viktor Fesetchko W PTS 6 Preston
06.12.03	Delroy Mellis L RSC 8 Cardiff
07.02.04	Howard Clarke W RSC 2 Bethnal
	Green
10.09.04	Takaloo W RSC 2 Bethnal Green
	(Vacant WBU L. Middleweight Title)
11.12.04	Delroy Mellis W PTS 10 Canning Town
04.06.05	Christian Bladt W CO 5 Manchester
04.03.06	Thomas McDonagh W PTS 12
	Manchester
	(WBU L.Middleweight Title Defence)

Career: 26 contests, won 24, lost 2.

Haider Ali   Les Clark

Haider Ali

Shadwell. *Born* Quetta, Pakistan, 12
November, 1979
Lightweight. Ht. 5'8½"
Manager E. Johnson

24.05.03	Buster Dennis W PTS 4 Bethnal Green
17.07.03	Jason Nesbitt W PTS 4 Dagenham
29.11.03	Jus Wallie W PTS 4 Renfrew
22.05.04	Steve Bell L PTS 6 Widnes
21.01.05	Jamie Arthur W RSC 3 Bridgend
17.06.05	Ricky Burns L PTS 8 Glasgow
25.11.05	Daniel Thorpe L RTD 4 Walsall
16.02.06	Kristian Laight W PTS 4 Dudley
25.03.06	Carl Allen DREW 4 Burton

Career: 9 contests, won 5, drew 1, lost 3.

Carl Allen

Wolverhampton. *Born* Wolverhampton, 20
November, 1969
L.Welterweight. Former Undefeated
Midlands Area S. Bantamweight
Champion. Ht. 5'7¼"
Manager P. Bowen

26.11.95	Gary Jenkinson W PTS 6 Birmingham
29.11.95	Jason Squire L PTS 6 Solihull
17.01.96	Andy Robinson L PTS 6 Solihull
13.02.96	Ervine Blake W RSC 5
	Wolverhampton
21.02.96	Ady Benton L PTS 6 Batley
29.02.96	Chris Jickells W PTS 6 Scunthorpe
27.03.96	Jason Squire DREW 6 Whitwick
26.04.96	Paul Griffin L RSC 3 Cardiff
30.05.96	Roger Brotherhood W RSC 5 Lincoln
26.09.96	Matthew Harris W PTS 10 Walsall
	(Midlands Area S. Bantamweight Title
	Challenge)
07.10.96	Emmanuel Clottey L RTD 3 Lewisham
21.11.96	Miguel Matthews W PTS 8 Solihull
30.11.96	Floyd Havard L RTD 3 Tylorstown
29.01.97	Pete Buckley W PTS 8 Stoke
11.02.97	David Morris DREW 8
	Wolverhampton
28.02.97	Ian McLeod L RTD 3 Kilmarnock
21.05.97	David Burke L PTS 4 Liverpool
30.06.97	Duke McKenzie L PTS 8 Bethnal
	Green
12.09.97	Brian Carr L PTS 8 Glasgow
04.10.97	Sergei Devakov L PTS 6 Muswell Hill
03.12.97	Chris Lyons W PTS 8 Stoke
21.05.98	Roy Rutherford L PTS 6 Solihull
09.06.98	Scott Harrison L RSC 6 Hull
30.11.98	Gary Hibbert L PTS 4 Manchester
09.12.98	Chris Jickells W RSC 3 Stoke
04.02.99	Mat Zegan L PTS 4 Lewisham
17.03.99	Craig Spacie W PTS 8 Stoke
08.05.99	Phillip Ndou L RSC 2 Bethnal Green
14.06.99	Pete Buckley W PTS 6 Birmingham
22.06.99	David Lowry L PTS 4 Ipswich
11.10.99	Lee Williamson L PTS 6 Birmingham
19.10.99	Tontcho Tontchev L CO 2 Bethnal
	Green
20.12.99	Nicky Cook L CO 3 Bethnal Green
08.02.00	Lee Williamson W PTS 8
	Wolverhampton
29.02.00	Bradley Pryce L PTS 4 Widnes
28.03.00	Lee Williamson W PTS 8
	Wolverhampton
16.05.00	Bradley Pryce L RSC 3 Warrington
24.06.00	Michael Gomez L CO 2 Widnes
10.10.00	Steve Hanley W PTS 8 Brierley Hill
05.02.01	Lee Meager DREW 6 Hull

12.03.01	Pete Buckley W PTS 6 Birmingham
27.03.01	Pete Buckley W PTS 8 Brierley Hill
15.09.01	Esham Pickering L PTS 6 Derby
17.11.01	Steve Conway L PTS 8 Dewsbury
08.12.01	Esham Pickering L PTS 8 Chesterfield
07.02.02	Mark Bowen L PTS 6 Stoke
20.04.02	Esham Pickering L PTS 6 Derby
21.07.02	Eddie Nevins L PTS 4 Salford
07.09.02	Colin Toohey DREW 6 Liverpool
26.10.02	Dazzo Williams W RSC 2 Maesteg
02.12.02	Esham Pickering L PTS 6 Leicester
28.01.03	Lee Meager L PTS 8 Nottingham
09.05.03	Jeff Thomas DREW 6 Doncaster
08.11.03	Baz Carey W RSC 2 Coventry
28.11.03	Carl Greaves L PTS 4 Derby
28.02.04	Michael Kelly L PTS 4 Bridgend
03.04.04	Andy Morris L PTS 4 Manchester
16.04.04	Dave Stewart L PTS 6 Bradford
17.06.04	Scott Lawton L PTS 10 Sheffield
	(Vacant Midlands Area Lightweight
	Title)
03.09.04	Gavin Rees L PTS 6 Newport
22.10.04	Craig Johnson L PTS 6 Mansfield
12.11.04	Billy Corcoran L RSC 5 Wembley
13.12.04	Jonathan Thaxton L RSC 1
	Birmingham
05.03.05	Ryan Barrett L PTS 4 Dagenham
15.05.05	Scott Lawton L PTS 6 Sheffield
18.06.05	Joe McCluskey L PTS 6 Coventry
16.09.05	Stefy Bull L PTS 10 Doncaster
	(Vacant WBF Inter-Continental
	Lightweight Title)
13.11.05	Carl Johanneson L RTD 2 Leeds
17.02.06	Dwayne Hill L PTS 6 Sheffield
25.02.06	Damian Owen L PTS 6 Bristol
10.03.06	Martin Gethin L PTS 4 Walsall
25.03.06	Haider Ali DREW 4 Burton
21.05.06	Andrew Murray L PTS 4 Bethnal
	Green
01.06.06	Tristan Davies L PTS 6 Birmingham

Career: 74 contests, won 18, drew 6, lost 50.

Mike Allen

Rhyl. *Born* St Asaph, 12 September, 1980
S. Middleweight. Ht. 5'10"
Manager T. Gilmour

08.11.03	Freddie Yemofio W RSC 4 Bridgend
28.02.04	Gary Ojuederie L RSC 1 Bridgend
01.05.04	William Webster W CO 2 Bridgend
16.06.06	Richard Turba L RSC 2 Liverpool

Career: 4 contests, won 2, lost 2.

Peter Allen

Birkenhead. *Born* Birkenhead, 13 August,
1978
S.Featherweight. Ht. 5'5½"
Manager T. Miller

30.04.98	Sean Grant L PTS 6 Pentre Halkyn
21.06.98	Garry Burrell W PTS 6 Liverpool
20.09.98	Simon Chambers L PTS 6 Sheffield
16.11.98	Stevie Kane W PTS 6 Glasgow
07.12.98	Simon Chambers L PTS 6 Bradford
28.02.99	Amjid Mahmood L PTS 6 Shaw
12.03.99	Marc Callaghan L PTS 4 Bethnal
	Green
15.09.99	Steve Brook L PTS 6 Harrogate
07.10.99	Nicky Wilders L PTS 6 Sunderland
18.10.99	Mark Hudson L PTS 6 Bradford
15.11.99	Craig Docherty L RSC 1 Glasgow
09.12.01	Jeff Thomas L PTS 6 Blackpool
01.03.02	Andrew Ferrans L PTS 8 Irvine

15.03.02	Ricky Burns L PTS 6 Glasgow	
17.04.02	Andrew Smith W PTS 6 Stoke	
24.06.02	Tasawar Khan L PTS 6 Bradford	
14.09.02	Carl Greaves L PTS 6 Newark	
08.10.02	Andrew Ferrans L PTS 8 Glasgow	
21.10.02	Tony McPake L PTS 6 Glasgow	
17.11.02	Choi Tseveenpurev L RSC 4 Shaw	
16.02.03	Darryn Walton L PTS 6 Salford	
31.05.03	Mally McIver L PTS 6 Barnsley	
29.08.03	Steve Mullin L PTS 6 Liverpool	
25.04.04	Craig Johnson L PTS 6 Nottingham	
08.05.04	Michael Graydon L PTS 6 Bristol	
30.05.04	Willie Valentine W PTS 4 Dublin	
10.09.04	Steve Mullin L PTS 4 Liverpool	
05.11.04	Damian Owen L RSC 1 Hereford	
04.03.05	Isaac Ward DREW 6 Hartlepool	
10.04.05	Lloyd Otte L PTS 6 Brentwood	
30.04.05	Eddie Nevins W PTS 6 Wigan	
25.09.05	Carl Johanneson L RTD 9 Leeds	
	(Vacant Central Area S.Featherweight	
	Title)	
16.06.06	David Appleby DREW 4 Liverpool	

Career: 33 contests, won 5, drew 2, lost 26.

Leigh Alliss

Stroud. *Born* Stroud, 11 September, 1975
Western Area L.Heavyweight Champion.
Ht. 5'9½"
Manager C. Sanigar

06.03.03	Ovill McKenzie L PTS 4 Bristol	
12.05.03	Mark Phillips W PTS 6 Southampton	
13.06.03	Egbui Ikeagbu W PTS 6 Bristol	
09.10.03	Mark Phillips W PTS 4 Bristol	
05.12.03	Dale Nixon W RSC 2 Bristol	
13.02.04	Hastings Rasani W PTS 6 Bristol	
08.05.04	Michael Pinnock W PTS 4 Bristol	
03.07.04	Karl Wheeler W PTS 4 Bristol	
01.10.04	Shane White W RSC 2 Bristol	
	(Vacant Western Area L.Heavyweight	
	Title)	
03.12.04	Valery Odin L RSC 5 Bristol	
29.04.05	Varuzhan Davtyan W PTS 4 Plymouth	
16.09.05	Neil Simpson W RSC 3 Plymouth	
17.11.05	Varuzhan Davtyan W PTS 4 Bristol	

07.04.06	Peter Haymer L RSC 9 Bristol	
	(English L.Heavyweight Title	
	Challenge)	

Career: 14 contests, won 11, lost 3.

Adnan Amar

Nottingham. *Born* Nottingham, 17
February, 1983
British Masters L.Middleweight Champion.
Ht. 5'9½"
Manager J. Ingle

11.06.01	Steve Hanley W PTS 4 Nottingham	
13.11.01	Duncan Armstrong W PTS 6 Leeds	
21.10.02	Jason Gonzales W PTS 6 Cleethorpes	
23.02.03	Arv Mittoo W PTS 6 Shrewsbury	
16.03.03	Gareth Wiltshaw W PTS 6 Nottingham	
16.04.03	Dave Cotterill W PTS 4 Nottingham	
28.04.03	Ernie Smith W PTS 6 Cleethorpes	
12.05.03	Pedro Thompson W RSC 4	
	Birmingham	
08.06.03	David Kirk W PTS 6 Nottingham	
06.09.03	Chris Duggan W PTS 4 Aberdeen	
23.02.04	Wayne Shepherd W RSC 5 Nottingham	
10.05.04	Ernie Smith W PTS 6 Birmingham	
04.06.04	Dean Hickman L RSC 8 Dudley	
	(Vacant Midlands Area L.Welterweight	
	Title)	
29.10.04	Daniel Thorpe W PTS 4 Worksop	
25.06.05	Ernie Smith W PTS 6 Melton	
	Mowbray	
28.01.06	Ben Hudson W PTS 4 Nottingham	
27.02.06	Simon Sherrington W RSC 6	
	Birmingham	
	(Vacant British Masters	
	L.Middleweight Title)	

Career: 17 contests, won 16, lost 1.

Jamie Ambler

Aberystwyth. *Born* Aberystwyth, 16
January 1985
S.Middleweight. Ht. 6'2½"
Manager N. Hodges

Jamie Ambler (right) scores with a right hand through Danny Goode's guard
Les Clark

12.11.05	Liam Stinchcombe W RTD 3 Bristol	
12.12.05	Jason Welborn L RSC 1 Birmingham	
10.02.06	Jon Harrison L PTS 4 Plymouth	
07.04.06	Danny Goode L PTS 4 Longford	
21.04.06	Scott Jordan L PTS 4 Belfast	

Career: 5 contests, won 1, lost 4.

James Ancliff

Fettercairn. *Born* Perth, 26 February, 1984
Featherweight. Ht. 5'5"
Manager A. Morrison/F. Warren

22.04.06	Mickey Coveney L PTS 6 Glasgow	

Career: 1 contest, lost 1.

Kevin Anderson

Buckhaven. *Born* Kirkcaldy, 26 April, 1980
British & Commonwealth Welterweight
Champion. Former Undefeated Celtic
Welterweight Champion. Ht. 5'8¾"
Manager T. Gilmour

12.04.03	Paul McIlwaine W RSC 2 Bethnal	
	Green	
19.04.03	Piotr Bartnicki W RSC 2 Liverpool	
17.05.03	Georges Dujardin W RSC 1 Liverpool	
05.07.03	Mohamed Bourhis W CO 2 Brentwood	
06.09.03	Sergei Starkov W PTS 6 Huddersfield	
01.11.03	Alban Mothie W PTS 8 Glasgow	
14.02.04	Andrei Napolskikh W PTS 8	
	Nottingham	
13.03.04	Lance Hall W RSC 1 Huddersfield	
22.04.04	Dmitri Yanushevich W RSC 2	
	Glasgow	
27.05.04	Danny Moir W RSC 1 Huddersfield	
15.10.04	Stephane Benito W RSC 6 Glasgow	
26.11.04	Tagir Rzaev W PTS 6 Altrincham	
31.01.05	Glenn McClarnon W RSC 4 Glasgow	
	(Vacant Celtic Welterweight Title)	
11.06.05	Vladimir Borovski W PTS 10	
	Kirkcaldy	
30.09.05	Joshua Okine W PTS 12 Kirkcaldy	
	(Commonwealth Welterweight Title	
	Challenge)	
17.03.06	Craig Dickson W RSC 7 Kirkcaldy	
	(Commonwealth Welterweight Title	
	Defence)	
01.06.06	Young Muttley W RSC 10 Birmingham	
	(British Welterweight Title Challenge.	
	Commonwealth Welterweight Title	
	Defence)	

Career: 17 contests, won 17.

Rod Anderton

Nottingham. *Born* Nottingham, 17 August,
1978
L.Heavyweight. Ht. 5'11¼"
Manager M. Shinfield

22.04.05	Michael Pinnock W PTS 6 Barnsley	
18.06.05	Nicki Taylor W RSC 4 Barnsley	
02.09.05	Paul Billington W RTD 1 Derby	
08.12.05	Gary Thompson W PTS 6 Derby	
28.01.06	Nick Okoth W PTS 4 Nottingham	
14.05.06	Ojay Abrahams W PTS 6 Derby	

Career: 6 contests, won 6.

Csaba Andras

Langport. *Born* Hungary, 9 September,
1979
Cruiserweight. Ht. 6'0¾"
Manager T. Woodward

25.02.05	Billy McClung L PTS 6 Irvine
12.06.05	Coleman Barrett L RSC 1 Leicester Square
17.11.05	Tommy Eastwood L PTS 4 Piccadilly
25.11.05	Tony Moran L PTS 4 Liverpool
16.12.05	Vadim Usenko L RSC 1 Bracknell
02.03.06	Richard Turba L RSC 3 Blackpool
24.04.06	Tyrone Wright L CO 2 Cleethorpes

Career: 7 contests, lost 7.

Steve Anning

Barry. *Born* Cardiff, 24 September, 1980
L.Middleweight. Ht. 5'6½"
Manager B. Coleman

02.04.06	Paul Porter DREW 4 Bethnal Green

01.06.06	Pietro Luigi Zara L PTS 6 Porto Torres, Italy

Career: 2 contests, drew 1, lost 1.

John Anthony

Doncaster. *Born* Doncaster, 16 October, 1974
Cruiserweight. Ht. 5'11½"
Manager D. Coldwell

22.04.05	Gary Thompson W PTS 4 Barnsley
18.06.05	Lee Mountford W RSC 5 Barnsley
04.11.05	Sandy Robb L PTS 6 Glasgow
12.02.06	Lee Kellett W RSC 1 Manchester
03.06.06	Andrew Lowe L PTS 6 Chigwell

Career: 5 contests, won 3, lost 2.

David Appleby

Edinburgh. *Born* Edinburgh, 7 February, 1986
L.Welterweight. Ht. 5'9½"
Manager T. Gilmour

23.01.06	Pete Buckley W PTS 6 Glasgow
17.03.06	Gavin Deacon W PTS 4 Kirkcaldy
16.06.06	Peter Allen DREW 4 Liverpool

Career: 3 contests, won 2, drew 1.

Paul Appleby

Edinburgh. *Born* Edinburgh, 22 July, 1987
Featherweight. Ht. 5'9"
Manager T. Gilmour

23.01.06	Graeme Higginson W RTD 3 Glasgow
17.03.06	Ian Reid W RSC 3 Kirkcaldy
28.04.06	Andy Davis W RSC 1 Hartlepool
01.06.06	Graeme Higginson W RSC 2 Birmingham

Career: 4 contests, won 4.

Paul Appleby   Les Clark

John Armour

Chatham. *Born* Chatham, 26 October, 1968
Featherweight. Former WBU Bantamweight Champion. Former Undefeated European & Commonwealth Bantamweight Champion. Ht. 5'4¾"
Manager Self

24.09.90	Lupe Castro W PTS 6 Lewisham
31.10.90	Juan Camero W RSC 4 Crystal Palace
21.01.91	Elijro Mejia W RSC 1 Crystal Palace
30.09.91	Pat Maher W CO 1 Kensington
29.10.91	Pete Buckley W PTS 6 Kensington
14.12.91	Gary Hickman W RSC 6 Bexleyheath
25.03.92	Miguel Matthews W PTS 6 Dagenham
30.04.92	Ndabe Dube W RSC 12 Kensington *(Vacant Commonwealth Bantamweight Title)*
17.10.92	Mauricio Bernal W PTS 8 Wembley
03.12.92	Albert Musankabala W RSC 5 Lewisham *(Commonwealth Bantamweight Title Defence)*
28.01.93	Ricky Romero W CO 1 Southwark
10.02.93	Morgan Mpande W PTS 12 Lewisham *(Commonwealth Bantamweight Title Defence)*

Kevin Anderson   Les Clark

09.06.93	Boualem Belkif W PTS 10 Lewisham
01.12.93	Karl Morling W CO 3 Kensington
14.01.94	Rufus Adebayo W RSC 7 Bethnal Green

(Commonwealth Bantamweight Title Defence)

23.09.94	Shaun Anderson W RSC 11 Bethnal Green

(Commonwealth Bantamweight Title Defence)

14.02.95	Tsitsi Sokutu W RSC 7 Bethnal Green

(Commonwealth Bantamweight Title Defence)

19.04.95	Antonio Picardi W RSC 8 Bethnal Green

(Vacant European Bantamweight Title)

19.05.95	Matthew Harris W RSC 3 Southwark
29.11.95	Redha Abbas W CO 5 Bethnal Green

(European Bantamweight Title Defence)

17.12.96	Lyndon Kershaw W RSC 8 Bethnal Green
29.01.97	Petrica Paraschiv W PTS 12 Bethnal Green

(Vacant Interim WBC International Bantamweight Title)

20.05.97	Anatoly Kvitko W RSC 8 Gillingham
28.11.97	Ervine Blake W PTS 10 Bethnal Green
12.12.98	Carlos Navarro L RSC 4 Southwark

(WBU S. Bantamweight Title Challenge)

19.06.99	Mohamed Ouzid W RSC 5 Dublin
25.07.00	Alexander Tiranov W PTS 8 Southwark
09.12.00	Francis Ampofo W PTS 12 Southwark

(Vacant WBU Bantamweight Title)

01.12.01	Ian Turner W PTS 8 Bethnal Green
11.05.02	Francis Ampofo W PTS 12 Dagenham

(WBU Bantamweight Title Defence)

21.09.02	Francis Ampofo W PTS 12 Brentwood

(WBU Bantamweight Title Defence)

05.07.03	Nathan Sting L RTD 11 Brentwood

(WBU Bantamweight Title Defence)

16.06.05	Tuncay Kaya L PTS 6 Dagenham
11.02.06	Delroy Spencer W PTS 6 Bethnal Green

Career: 34 contests, won 31, lost 3.

Prince Arron

Droylsden. *Born* Crumpsall, 27 December, 1987
L.Middleweight. Ht. 6'3"
Manager W. Barker

28.04.06	Tommy Jones W PTS 6 Manchester
18.06.06	Karl Taylor W PTS 6 Manchester

Career: 2 contests, won 2.

Alex Arthur

Edinburgh. *Born* Edinburgh, 26 June, 1978
European & Commonwealth
S.Featherweight Champion. Former
Undefeated British, WBO Inter-
Continental, WBA Inter-Continental & IBF
Inter-Continental S.Featherweight
Champion. Former British S.Featherweight
Champion. Ht. 5'9"
Manager F. Warren

25.11.00	Richmond Asante W RSC 1 Manchester
10.02.01	Eddie Nevins W RSC 1 Widnes

26.03.01	Woody Greenaway W RTD 2 Wembley
28.04.01	Dafydd Carlin W PTS 4 Cardiff
21.07.01	Rakhim Mingaleev W PTS 4 Sheffield
15.09.01	Dimitri Gorodetsky W RSC 1 Manchester
27.10.01	Alexei Slyautchin W RSC 1 Manchester
17.11.01	Laszlo Bognar W RSC 3 Glasgow
19.01.02	Vladimir Borov W RSC 2 Bethnal Green
11.03.02	Dariusz Snarski W RSC 10 Glasgow

(Vacant IBF Inter-Continental S.Featherweight Title)

08.06.02	Nikolai Eremeev W RTD 5 Renfrew

(Vacant WBO Inter-Continental S.Featherweight Title)

17.08.02	Pavel Potipko W CO 1 Cardiff
19.10.02	Steve Conway W CO 4 Renfrew

(Vacant British S. Featherweight Title)

14.12.02	Carl Greaves W RSC 6 Newcastle

(British S.Featherweight Title Defence)

22.03.03	Patrick Malinga W RSC 6 Renfrew

(Vacant WBA Inter-Continental S.Featherweight Title)

12.07.03	Willie Limond W RSC 8 Renfrew

(British S.Featherweight Title Defence)

25.10.03	Michael Gomez L RSC 5 Edinburgh

(British S.Featherweight Title Defence)

27.03.04	Michael Kizza W CO 1 Edinburgh

(Vacant IBF Inter-Continental S.Featherweight Title)

22.10.04	Eric Odumasi W RSC 6 Edinburgh

(IBF Inter-Continental S.Featherweight Title Defence)

03.12.04	Nazareno Ruiz W PTS 12 Edinburgh

(IBF Inter-Continental S.Featherweight Title Defence)

08.04.05	Craig Docherty W CO 9 Edinburgh

(Vacant British S.Featherweight Title. Commonwealth S.Featherweight Title Challenge)

23.07.05	Boris Sinitsin W PTS 12 Edinburgh

(European S.Featherweight Title Challenge)

18.02.06	Ricky Burns W PTS 12 Edinburgh

(British, Commonwealth & European S.Featherweight Title Defences)

29.04.06	Sergey Gulyakevich W TD 7 Edinburgh

(European S.Featherweight Title Defence)

Career: 24 contests, won 23, lost 1.

Jamie Arthur

Cwmbran. *Born* Aberdeen, 17 December, 1979
S.Featherweight. Ht. 5'9"
Manager F. Warren/F. Maloney

22.03.03	Daniel Thorpe W PTS 4 Renfrew
28.06.03	James Gorman W PTS 4 Cardiff
13.09.03	Dave Hinds W RTD 1 Newport
11.10.03	Dafydd Carlin W RSC 4 Portsmouth
15.11.03	Andrei Mircea W RSC 3 Bayreuth, Germany
06.12.03	Jus Wallie W PTS 6 Cardiff
27.03.04	Karl Taylor W PTS 6 Edinburgh
03.07.04	Frederic Bonifai W PTS 6 Newport
03.09.04	Buster Dennis W PTS 6 Newport
21.01.05	Haider Ali L RSC 3 Bridgend
23.07.05	Harry Ramogoadi L RSC 5 Edinburgh

Career: 11 contests, won 9, lost 2.

Ryan Ashworth

Scarborough. *Born* Stockton, 20 March, 1984
Middleweight. Ht. 5'8¹/₄"
Manager T. Gilmour/C. Aston

05.12.05	Omar Gumati W PTS 6 Leeds
24.02.06	Jak Hibbert L PTS 6 Scarborough
09.05.06	Peter Dunn W PTS 6 Leeds

Career: 3 contests, won 2, lost 1.

Jackson Asiku

Rugby. *Born* Kampala, Uganda, 21 October, 1978
Commonwealth Featherweight Champion.
Former Undefeated Australian, WBO Asia-
Pacific & ABU Featherweight Champion.
Ht. 5'6"
Manager D. Lutaaya

01.12.00	Danny Wilson W PTS 6 Morphettville, Australia
24.02.01	Hichem Blida W PTS 4 Melbourne, Australia
01.06.01	John Green W CO 3 Adelaide, Australia
13.07.01	Paul Griffin W RSC 5 Sydney, Australia
14.09.01	Selvio Glinoco W RSC 3 Adelaide, Australia
18.10.01	Arnel Barotillo W TD 6 Sydney, Australia

(Vacant Australian Featherweight Title)

01.03.02	Nacer Keddam W PTS 6 Adelaide, Australia
18.09.02	Serikzhan Yeshmangbetov W PTS 12 Sydney, Australia

(Vacant WBO Asia-Pacific Featherweight Title)

25.10.02	Nedal Hussein L PTS 10 Sydney, Australia
28.02.03	Mohammed Khalil Payal W CO 2 Broadbeach Waters, Australia
15.06.03	Patrick Key W RSC 3 Mile End, Australia
12.08.03	Moses Seran W CO 5 Jakarta, Indonesia
12.12.03	Gairy St Clair L PTS 8 Homebush Bay, Australia
26.02.04	Fahprakorb Rakkiatgym L PTS 12 Bangkok, Thailand

(IBF Pan-Pacific Featherweight Title)

30.03.04	Leed Shabu W PTS 10 Jakarta, Indonesia
24.09.04	Frankie De Milo W CO 6 Southport, Australia

(Vacant Australian Featherweight Title)

15.10.04	Patiphan Simalay W PTS 8 West Beach, Australia
11.03.05	Kridsana Pumroy W PTS 6 West Beach, Australia
18.06.05	Saulus Kaunda W CO 3 Kampala, Uganda

(ABU Featherweight Title Challenge)

01.10.05	Robert Oyan W PTS 8 Hobart, Tasmania, Australia
22.10.05	Frederic Gosset W PTS 6 Coventry
18.11.05	Marc Callaghan W RSC 1 Dagenham

(Vacant Commonwealth Featherweight Title)

16.06.06	Jamie McKeever W RSC 1 Liverpool

(Commonwealth Featherweight Title Defence)

Career: 23 contests, won 20, lost 3.

David Bailey

Pimlico. *Born* London, 23 August, 1980
L. Welterweight. Ht. 5'6¹/₂"
Manager Self

07.05.04	Dean Ward W PTS 6 Bethnal Green
25.06.04	Mickey Coveney L PTS 4 Bethnal Green
18.09.04	Craig Johnson W PTS 6 Newark
27.09.04	Rendall Munroe L PTS 6 Cleethorpes
21.01.05	David Pereira L PTS 6 Brentford
05.03.05	Mickey Bowden L PTS 6 Southwark
20.05.05	Warren Dunkley W PTS 4 Southwark
16.07.05	Amir Khan L RSC 1 Bolton

Career: 8 contests, won 3, lost 5.

Colin Bain

Glasgow. *Born* Hawick, 10 August, 1978
Lightweight. Ht. 5'8¹/₂"
Manager A. Morrison

14.03.03	Dafydd Carlin W PTS 6 Glasgow
16.05.03	Martin Hardcastle W PTS 6 Glasgow
12.07.03	Gareth Wiltshaw W PTS 4 Renfrew
25.10.03	Dave Hinds W PTS 4 Edinburgh
27.03.04	Dave Hinds W PTS 4 Edinburgh
23.04.04	Pete Buckley W PTS 6 Glasgow
19.06.04	Henry Jones W PTS 4 Renfrew
29.10.04	Pete Buckley W PTS 4 Renfrew
12.12.04	Ricky Burns L PTS 6 Glasgow
12.11.05	Gavin Deacon W PTS 6 Glasgow
27.05.06	Mark Bett DREW 6 Glasgow

Career: 11 contests, won 9, drew 1, lost 1.

Carl Baker

Sheffield. *Born* Sheffield, 3 January, 1982
British Masters Heavyweight Champion.
Ht. 6'4"
Manager J. Ingle

06.09.03	Dave Clarke W RSC 1 Aberdeen
15.09.03	Billy Wilson W RSC 2 Leeds
28.11.03	Slick Miller W CO 1 Hull
03.04.04	Paul King L PTS 6 Sheffield
17.09.04	Scott Gammer L PTS 4 Plymouth
04.03.05	Paul King W RSC 2 Rotherham
26.04.05	Luke Simpkin L RSC 4 Leeds
25.06.05	Scott Lansdowne W RSC 8 Melton Mowbray
	(Vacant British Masters Heavyweight Title)
11.09.05	Luke Simpkin W PTS 10 Kirkby in Ashfield
	(British Masters Heavyweight Title Defence)
13.05.06	David Ingleby W RSC 4 Sheffield

Career: 10 contests, won 7, lost 3.

Vince Baldassara

Clydebank. *Born* Clydebank, 6 November, 1978
Scottish Middleweight Champion. Ht. 5'11¹/₂"
Manager Self

14.03.03	George Telfer L PTS 4 Glasgow
28.02.04	Rob MacDonald W PTS 6 Manchester

08.10.04	Barrie Lee DREW 6 Glasgow
09.12.04	Eddie Haley W PTS 6 Sunderland
21.02.05	Cafu Santos W CO 2 Glasgow
08.04.05	Barrie Lee L PTS 4 Edinburgh
25.04.05	Ciaran Healy W RSC 4 Glasgow
20.05.05	Mark Wall W PTS 6 Glasgow
17.06.05	Jak Hibbert W RSC 1 Glasgow
12.11.05	Craig Lynch W PTS 10 Glasgow
	(Vacant Scottish Area Middleweight Title)
09.03.06	Ryan Kerr DREW 6 Sunderland

Career: 11 contests, won 7, drew 2, lost 2.

Aaron Balmer

Worthing. *Born* Hampstead, 4 October, 1981
L.Middleweight. Ht. 5'10"
Manager M. Alldis

30.10.05	Duncan Cottier W PTS 4 Bethnal Green

Career: 1 contest, won 1.

Aaron Balmer   Les Clark

Ted Bami (Minsende)

Brixton. *Born* Zaire, 2 March, 1978
Welterweight. Former WBF
L.Welterweight Champion. Ht. 5'7"
Manager Self

26.09.98	Des Sowden W RSC 1 Southwark
11.02.99	Gary Reid W RSC 2 Dudley
10.03.00	David Kehoe W PTS 4 Bethnal Green
08.09.00	Jacek Bielski L RSC 4 Hammersmith
29.03.01	Keith Jones W PTS 4 Hammersmith
05.05.01	Francis Barrett W PTS 6 Edmonton
31.07.01	Lance Crosby W PTS 6 Bethnal Green
19.03.02	Michael Smyth W CO 4 Slough
23.06.02	Keith Jones W RSC 4 Southwark
17.08.02	Bradley Pryce W RSC 6 Cardiff
26.10.02	Adam Zadworny W PTS 4 Maesteg
07.12.02	Sergei Starkov W PTS 4 Brentwood
08.03.03	Andrei Devyataykin W RSC 1 Bethnal Green
12.04.03	Laszlo Herczeg W RSC 9 Bethnal Green
	(Vacant WBF L.Welterweight Title)
26.07.03	Samuel Malinga L RSC 3 Plymouth
	(WBF L.Welterweight Title Defence)
09.10.03	Zoltan Surman W RSC 3 Bristol

31.01.04	Jozsef Matolcsi W PTS 6 Bethnal Green
08.05.04	Viktor Baranov W RSC 2 Dagenham
08.10.04	Rafal Jackiewicz W PTS 8 Brentwood
13.02.05	Ricardo Daniel Silva W CO 2 Brentwood
21.10.05	Silence Saheed W PTS 6 Bethnal Green
24.02.06	Maurycy Gojko W CO 4 Dagenham

Career: 22 contests, won 20, lost 2.

(Michal) Michael Banbula

Staines. *Born* Poland, 26 December, 1980
Cruiserweight. Ht. 5'11¹/₂"
Manager G. Carman

30.04.05	Gareth Lawrence L PTS 6 Dagenham
14.05.05	Tommy Tolan L PTS 4 Dublin
02.06.05	Cello Renda DREW 6 Peterborough
01.07.05	Gareth Lawrence L PTS 4 Fulham
16.07.05	Daniel Cadman L PTS 6 Chigwell
06.10.05	Danny McIntosh L PTS 6 Longford
22.10.05	Neil Tidman L PTS 6 Coventry
19.11.05	Danny Tombs L RSC 2 Southwark

Career: 8 contests, drew 1, lost 7.

Darren Barker

Barnet. *Born* Harrow, 19 May, 1982
Middleweight. Ht. 6'0¹/₂"
Manager T. Sims

24.09.04	Howard Clarke W PTS 6 Nottingham
12.11.04	David White W RSC 2 Wembley
26.03.05	Leigh Wicks W RTD 4 Hackney
10.04.05	Andrei Sherel W RSC 3 Brentwood
09.07.05	Ernie Smith W PTS 6 Nottingham
16.07.05	Dean Walker W PTS 6 Chigwell
02.12.05	John-Paul Temple W RSC 6 Nottingham
20.01.06	Richard Mazurek W PTS 8 Bethnal Green
17.02.06	Louis Mimoune W RSC 2 Bethanl Green
12.05.06	Danny Thornton W RSC 6 Bethnal Green

Career: 10 contests, won 10.

David Barnes (Smith)

Manchester. *Born* Manchester, 16 January, 1981
Welterweight. Former Undefeated British Welterweight Champion. Ht. 5'8¹/₂"
Manager Self

07.07.01	Trevor Smith W RSC 2 Manchester
15.09.01	Karl Taylor W PTS 4 Manchester
27.10.01	Mark Sawyers W RSC 2 Manchester
15.12.01	James Paisley W RTD 2 Wembley
09.02.02	David Kirk W RTD 1 Manchester
04.05.02	David Baptiste W CO 3 Bethnal Green
01.06.02	Dimitri Protkunas W RSC 1 Manchester
28.09.02	Sergei Starkov W PTS 6 Manchester
12.10.02	Rusian Ashirov W PTS 6 Bethnal Green
14.12.02	Rozalin Nasibulin W RSC 3 Newcastle
18.01.03	Brice Faradji W PTS 6 Preston
05.04.03	Viktor Fesetchko W PTS 8 Manchester
17.07.03	Jimmy Vincent W PTS 12 Dagenham
	(Vacant British Welterweight Title)
13.12.03	Kevin McIntyre W RTD 8 Manchester
	(British Welterweight Title Defence)

03.04.04	Glenn McClarnon W PTS 12 Manchester	

03.04.04 Glenn McClarnon W PTS 12
Manchester
(British Welterweight Title Defence)
12.11.04 James Hare W RSC 6 Halifax
(British Welterweight Title Defence)
28.01.05 Juho Tolppola W PTS 10 Renfrew
22.04.05 Ali Nuumbembe DREW 12 Barnsley
(Vacant WBO Inter-Continental Welterweight Title)
04.06.05 Joshua Okine L RSC 12 Manchester
(Commonwealth Welterweight Title Challenge)
28.01.06 Fabrice Colombel W RSC 4 Nottingham
04.03.06 Silence Saheed W PTS 4 Manchester
Career: 21 contests, won 19, drew 1, lost 1.

Matthew Barney

Southampton. *Born* Fareham, 25 June, 1974
S.Middleweight. Former Undefeated WBU
L.Heavyweight Champion. Former
Undefeated British, IBO Inter-Continental,
Southern Area & British Masters
S.Middleweight Champion. Ht. 5'10¾"
Manager C. Sanigar

04.06.98 Adam Cale W PTS 6 Barking
23.07.98 Adam Cale W PTS 6 Barking
02.10.98 Dennis Doyley W PTS 4 Cheshunt
22.10.98 Kevin Burton W PTS 6 Barking
07.12.98 Freddie Yemofio W PTS 4 Acton
17.03.99 Simon Andrews W RTD 4 Kensington
09.05.99 Gareth Hogg W PTS 4 Bracknell
20.05.99 Bobby Banghar W RSC 5 Kensington
(British Masters S. Middleweight Final)
05.06.99 Paul Bowen DREW 10 Cardiff
(Southern Area S. Middleweight Title Challenge)
20.08.99 Adam Cale W PTS 4 Bloomsbury
05.10.99 Delroy Leslie L PTS 10 Bloomsbury
(Vacant Southern Area Middleweight Title)
15.04.00 Mark Dawson W PTS 6 Bethnal Green
06.05.00 Jason Hart W PTS 10 Southwark
(Vacant Southern Area S. Middleweight Title)
30.09.00 Neil Linford L PTS 10 Peterborough
(Elim. British S. Middleweight Title)
02.02.01 Darren Covill W PTS 6 Portsmouth
16.03.01 Matt Mowatt W RSC 1 Portsmouth
(British Masters S. Middleweight Title Defence)
14.07.01 Robert Milewics W PTS 8 Wembley
20.10.01 Jon Penn W RSC 4 Portsmouth
26.01.02 Hussain Osman L RTD 9 Dagenham
(Vacant IBO Inter-Continental S.Middleweight Title. Southern Area S.Middleweight Title Defence)
08.04.02 Hussain Osman W PTS 12 Southampton
(IBO Inter-Continental & Southern Area S. Middleweight Title Challenges)
22.09.02 Paul Owen W CO 7 Southwark
(Vacant British Masters S.Middleweight Title)
20.10.02 Chris Nembhard W PTS 10 Southwark
(Southern Area S. Middleweight Title Defence)
29.03.03 Dean Francis W PTS 12 Wembley
(Vacant British S.Middleweight Title)
01.08.03 Charles Adamu L PTS 12 Bethnal Green

(Vacant Commonwealth S.Middleweight Title)
11.10.03 Tony Oakey W PTS 12 Portsmouth
(WBU L.Heavyweight Title Challenge)
10.09.04 Simeon Cover W PTS 4 Wembley
26.03.05 Thomas Ulrich L PTS 12 Riesa, Germany
(European L.Heavyweight Title Challenge)
09.07.05 Carl Froch L PTS 12 Nottingham
(British & Commonwealth S.Middleweight Title Challenges)
Career: 28 contests, won 21, drew 1, lost 6.

Matthew Barr

Walton. *Born* Kingston, 22 May, 1977
Middleweight. Ht. 5'11"
Manager Self

02.12.97 Keith Palmer L RSC 3 Windsor
23.02.98 Martin Cavey W RSC 1 Windsor
14.05.98 Gerard Lawrence L RSC 1 Acton
29.10.98 Sonny Thind W RSC 2 Bayswater
20.05.99 Paul Knights L RSC 1 Barking
31.10.99 Allan Gray W PTS 4 Raynes Park
25.02.00 John Humphrey W RSC 1 Newmarket
06.05.00 Ernie Smith W PTS 4 Southwark
22.10.00 Ernie Smith W PTS 4 Streatham
23.11.00 Harry Butler W PTS 4 Bayswater
23.11.01 John Humphrey L RSC 2 Bethnal Green
13.09.02 Brian Knudsen W PTS 6 Randers, Denmark
29.03.03 Lee Hodgson W RSC 1 Wembley
29.10.03 Jimi Hendricks W RSC 4 Leicester Square
27.11.03 Leigh Wicks W PTS 4 Longford
21.01.05 Gareth Lawrence W RSC 2 Brentford
16.12.05 Howard Clarke W PTS 4 Bracknell
Career: 17 contests, won 13, lost 4.

Coleman Barrett

Wembley. *Born* Galway, 10 November, 1982
Heavyweight. Ht. 6'1"
Manager R. McCracken

11.12.03 Marcus Lee W PTS 4 Bethnal Green
12.03.04 Dave Clarke W PTS 6 Nottingham
02.06.04 Terry Morrill W PTS 4 Nottingham
05.03.05 Valery Semishkur W PTS 6 Durres, Albania
12.06.05 Csaba Andras W RSC 1 Leicester Square
24.07.05 Tony Booth W PTS 4 Leicester Square
Career: 6 contests, won 6.

Ryan Barrett

Thamesmead. *Born* London, 27 December, 1982
Lightweight. Ht. 5'10"
Manager Self

13.06.02 Gareth Wiltshaw W PTS 4 Leicester Square
06.09.02 Jason Gonzales W PTS 4 Bethnal Green
12.12.02 Martin Turner W RSC 1 Leicester Square
08.03.03 David Vaughan DREW 4 Bethnal Green
04.10.03 Dafydd Carlin L PTS 4 Belfast
01.05.04 Marty Kayes W RSC 2 Gravesend

19.06.04 Kristian Laight W PTS 4 Muswell Hill
16.10.04 Daniel Thorpe W PTS 4 Dagenham
19.12.04 James Paisley W DIS 5 Bethnal Green
21.01.05 Peter McDonagh W PTS 8 Brentford
05.03.05 Carl Allen W PTS 4 Dagenham
23.03.05 Pete Buckley W PTS 6 Leicester Square
20.06.05 Anthony Christopher W RSC 1 Longford
01.04.06 Martin Watson L PTS 10 Bethnal Green
(Elim. British Lightweight Title)
Career: 14 contests, won 11, drew 1, lost 2.

(Alex) Sandy Bartlett

Inverness. *Born* Dingwall, 20 April, 1976
Featherweight. Ht. 5'7"
Manager T. Gilmour

15.03.04 Marty Kayes W PTS 6 Glasgow
19.04.04 Abdul Mougharbel L PTS 6 Glasgow
11.10.04 Abdul Mougharbel W PTS 6 Glasgow
05.11.04 Ricky Owen L RSC 2 Hereford
19.09.05 Neil Marston W PTS 6 Glasgow
04.11.05 Craig Bromley L RSC 2 Glasgow
20.02.06 Kevin Townsley L PTS 4 Glasgow
25.03.06 John Bothwell L RSC 2 Irvine
Career: 8 contests, won 3, lost 5.

Greg Barton

Southend. *Born* , Rochford, 4 April, 1982
Middleweight. Ht. 5'11½"
Manager A. Gower

26.02.06 Leon Owen L RSC 1 Dagenham
Career: 1 contest, lost 1.

(Shinebayer) Shinny Bayaar (Sukhbaatar)

Carlisle. *Born* Mongolia, 27 August, 1977
Flyweight. Ht. 5'5½"
Manager J. Doughty

30.07.99 Saohin Sorthanikul L RSC 4 Bangkok, Thailand
25.02.00 Yura Dima DREW 10 Erdene, Mongolia
28.06.00 Manny Melchor L PTS 12 Manila, Philippines
(WBC International M.Flyweight Title Challenge)
10.10.01 Damien Dunnion L PTS 8 Stoke
09.12.01 Delroy Spencer W PTS 4 Shaw
17.11.02 Anthony Hanna W PTS 6 Shaw
20.03.03 Sunkanmi Ogunbiyi L PTS 4 Queensway
08.06.03 Darren Cleary W RSC 2 Shaw
19.10.03 Delroy Spencer W PTS 6 Shaw
21.02.04 Reidar Walstad W RSC 1 Cardiff
31.10.04 Delroy Spencer W PTS 6 Shaw
11.12.04 Martin Power L PTS 10 Canning Town
20.11.05 Abdul Mougharbel W PTS 4 Shaw
02.04.06 Delroy Spencer W PTS 6 Shaw
Career: 14 contests, won 8, drew 1, lost 5.

Andy Bell (Langley)

Nottingham. *Born* Doncaster, 16 July, 1985
S.Featherweight. Ht. 5'8"
Manager M. Scriven

22.10.04 Steve Gethin W RSC 5 Mansfield
10.12.04 Dean Ward W PTS 6 Mansfield
06.03.05 Abdul Mougharbel W PTS 4 Mansfield

24.04.05 Wayne Bloy L PTS 4 Askern
13.05.06 Steve Gethin L RSC 2 Sutton in Ashfield
Career: 5 contests, won 3, lost 2.

Steve Bell

Manchester. *Born* Manchester, 11 June, 1975
L.Welterweight. Ht. 5'10"
Manager F. Warren

08.05.03 Jus Wallie DREW 4 Widnes
27.09.03 Jaz Virdee W RSC 1 Manchester
13.12.03 Fred Janes W PTS 4 Manchester
03.04.04 Pete Buckley W PTS 4 Manchester
22.05.04 Haider Ali W PTS 6 Widnes
01.10.04 Daniel Thorpe W PTS 6 Manchester
11.02.05 Henry Janes W RTD 3 Manchester
03.06.05 Buster Dennis DREW 6 Manchester
04.03.06 Pete Buckley W PTS 4 Manchester
01.04.06 Jason Nesbitt W PTS 6 Bethnal Green
Career: 10 contests, won 8, drew 2.

Steve Bell   Les Clark

Steven Bendall

Coventry. *Born* Coventry, 1 December, 1973
English Middleweight Champion. Former Undefeated IBO Inter-Continental & WBU Inter-Continental Middleweight Champion. Ht. 6'0"
Manager Self

15.05.97 Dennis Doyley W RSC 2 Reading
13.09.97 Gary Reyniers W PTS 4 Millwall
27.02.99 Israel Khumalo W PTS 4 Oldham
02.07.99 Darren Covill W RTD 3 Bristol
24.09.99 Sean Pritchard W PTS 6 Merthyr
03.12.99 Ian Toby W PTS 6 Peterborough
07.04.00 Des Sowden W RSC 3 Bristol
02.06.00 Simon Andrews W RSC 5 Ashford
08.09.00 Jason Barker W PTS 6 Bristol
03.11.00 Eddie Haley W RSC 1 Ebbw Vale
01.12.00 Peter Mitchell W PTS 8 Peterborough
22.08.01 Bert Bado W RSC 1 Hammanskraal, South Africa
29.09.01 Alan Gilbert W RTD 3 Southwark
08.12.01 Jason Collins W PTS 12 Dagenham
         (Vacant WBU Inter-Continental Middleweight Title)

02.03.02 Ahmet Dottouev W RTD 4 Brakpan, South Africa
         (WBU Inter-Continental Middleweight Title Defence)
26.04.02 Viktor Fesetchko W RSC 10 Coventry
         (Vacant IBO Inter-Continental Middleweight Title)
13.07.02 Phillip Bystrikov W RSC 5 Coventry
06.09.02 Tomas da Silva W RSC 8 Bethnal Green
24.01.03 Lee Blundell W RSC 2 Sheffield
         (IBO Inter-Continental Middleweight Title Defence)
26.04.03 Mike Algoet W PTS 12 Brentford
         (IBO Inter-Continental Middleweight Title Defence)
14.11.03 Kreshnik Qato W PTS 8 Bethnal Green
17.09.04 Scott Dann L RSC 6 Plymouth
         (Vacant British Middleweight Title)
18.06.05 Ismael Kerzazi W PTS 8 Coventry
22.10.05 Magid Ben Driss W PTS 6 Coventry
15.12.05 Donovan Smillie W RSC 5 Coventry
         (English Middleweight Title Challenge)
22.04.06 Sebastian Sylvester L RSC 3 Mannheim, Germany
         (European Middleweight Title Challenge)
Career: 26 contests, won 24, lost 2.

Billy Bessey

Portsmouth. *Born* Portsmouth, 8 January 1974
Heavyweight. Ht. 6'1"
Manager D. Garside

01.10.00 Paul Fiske W PTS 6 Hartlepool
26.02.01 Mark Hobson L PTS 4 Nottingham
06.05.01 Luke Simpkin W PTS 6 Hartlepool
04.06.01 Gary Williams W PTS 4 Hartlepool
21.11.04 Ebrima Secka W PTS 6 Bracknell
06.02.05 Paul King L PTS 6 Southampton
18.03.05 Martin Rogan L PTS 4 Belfast
04.12.05 Dave Clarke W PTS 6 Portsmouth
Career: 8 contests, won 5, lost 3.

Mark Bett

Larkhall. *Born* Lanark, 30 September, 1982
L. Welterweight. Ht. 5'7"
Manager A. Morrison

22.04.06 Marco Cittadini DREW 6 Glasgow
27.05.06 Colin Bain DREW 6 Glasgow
Career: 2 contests, drew 2.

Jim Betts

Scunthorpe. *Born* Tickhill, 6 October, 1977
Featherweight. Former Undefeated British Masters Flyweight Champion. Ht. 5'6½"
Manager Self

26.03.98 Des Gargano W PTS 6 Scunthorpe
13.05.98 David Jeffrey W RSC 3 Scunthorpe
05.06.98 Chris Price W PTS 6 Hull
11.09.98 Marty Chestnut W PTS 6 Newark
16.10.98 Marty Chestnut W PTS 6 Salford
28.11.98 Ola Dali W PTS 4 Sheffield
17.05.99 Dave Travers W RTD 4 Cleethorpes
17.07.99 Ross Cassidy W RSC 1 Doncaster
27.09.99 Graham McGrath W PTS 6 Cleethorpes
19.02.00 Chris Price W PTS 6 Newark
19.06.00 Chris Price W PTS 4 Burton
30.08.00 David Coldwell W RSC 2 Scunthorpe
         (Vacant British Masters Flyweight Title. Elim. British Flyweight Title)

26.02.01 Chris Emanuele L PTS 6 Nottingham
08.05.01 Sean Grant W RSC 3 Barnsley
11.06.01 Daniel Ring W PTS 6 Nottingham
15.09.01 Nicky Booth L RSC 7 Nottingham
         (British & Commonwealth Bantamweight Title Challenges)
18.03.02 Ian Turner W RTD 4 Crawley
18.05.02 Gareth Payne W PTS 6 Millwall
27.07.02 Colin Moffett W RSC 3 Nottingham
27.04.04 Jason Nesbitt W PTS 6 Leeds
19.12.04 Rocky Dean L PTS 8 Bethnal Green
19.02.05 Bernard Dunne L CO 5 Dublin
30.04.05 Mickey Coveney L CO 4 Dagenham
16.07.05 Steve Foster L RTD 5 Bolton
23.09.05 Jamie McKeever L RSC 4 Manchester
Career: 25 contests, won 18, lost 7.

Akaash Bhatia

Harrow. *Born* Loughborough, 1 May, 1983
Featherweight. Ht. 5'7"
Manager F. Maloney

30.05.06 Kristian Laight W PTS 4 Bethnal Green
29.06.06 Nikita Lukin W PTS 4 Bethnal Green
Career: 2 contests, won 2.

Akaash Bhatia   Les Clark

Paul Billington

Warrington. *Born* Billinge, 1 March, 1972
Cruiserweight. Ht. 5'10"
Manager J. Gill

14.09.02 Michael Monaghan L RSC 4 Newark
29.05.03 Karl Wheeler L PTS 6 Sunderland
21.09.03 Shane White DREW 6 Bristol
12.10.03 Danny Grainger L PTS 6 Sheffield
01.12.03 Mark Flatt W RSC 2 Bradford
21.12.03 Shane White L RSC 2 Bristol
22.04.04 Steve McGuire L RTD 3 Glasgow
08.07.04 Jonjo Finnegan L PTS 6 Birmingham
15.12.04 Jon Ibbotson L PTS 4 Sheffield
02.09.05 Rod Anderton L RTD 1 Derby
25.11.05 Jonjo Finnegan L PTS 6 Walsall
14.12.05 Richard Turba L PTS 6 Blackpool
Career: 12 contests, won 1, drew 1, lost 10.

Steven Birch

St Helens. *Born* Whiston, 25 September, 1981
Heavyweight. Ht. 6'0½"
Manager D. Hobson

09.09.05 Nick Okoth L PTS 4 Sheffield
Career: 1 contest, lost 1.

Steven Birch   Les Clark

Chris Black

Coatbridge. *Born* Bellshill, 19 November, 1979
L. Middleweight. Ht. 5'7¹/₂"
Manager A. Morrison/R. Bannan

22.10.04	Brian Coleman W PTS 4 Edinburgh
12.12.04	Jak Hibbert W RSC 2 Glasgow
28.01.05	Geraint Harvey W PTS 4 Renfrew
01.04.05	Tony Randell W PTS 6 Glasgow
17.06.05	Ciaran Healy DREW 4 Glasgow
22.04.06	Barrie Lee L PTS 10 Glasgow
	(Scottish L.Middleweight Title Challenge)

Career: 6 contests, won 4, drew 1, lost 1.

Wayne Bloy

Grimsby. *Born* Grimsby, 30 November, 1982
Bantamweight. Ht. 5'5"
Manager S. Fleet

14.06.04	Neil Read DREW 6 Cleethorpes
20.09.04	Gary Ford W PTS 6 Cleethorpes
24.04.05	Andy Bell W PTS 4 Askern
23.05.05	Neil Marston W PTS 6 Cleethorpes
24.02.06	Abdul Mougharbel W PTS 6 Scarborough

Career: 5 contests, won 4, drew 1.

Lee Blundell

Wigan. *Born* Wigan, 11 August, 1971
S. Middleweight. British Masters Middleweight Champion. Former Undefeated WBF Inter-Continental Middleweight Champion. Former Undefeated Central Area L. Middleweight Champion. Ht. 6'2"
Manager L. Veitch/J. Gill

25.04.94	Robert Harper W RSC 2 Bury
20.05.94	Freddie Yemofio W RSC 6 Acton
08.09.94	Gordon Blair DREW 6 Glasgow
07.12.94	Kesem Clayton W RTD 2 Stoke
18.02.95	Glenn Catley L RSC 6 Shepton Mallet
11.12.95	Martin Jolley W PTS 6 Morecambe
16.03.97	Martin Jolley W PTS 6 Shaw
08.05.97	Paul Jones L RSC 4 Mansfield
19.09.99	Dean Ashton W RSC 4 Shaw
28.10.99	Jason Collins DREW 6 Burnley
06.12.99	Danny Thornton W PTS 6 Bradford

05.03.00	Ian Toby W RTD 3 Shaw
21.05.00	Phil Epton W RSC 2 Shaw
30.11.00	Danny Thornton W RSC 8 Blackpool
	(Vacant Central Area L.Middleweight Title)
08.03.01	Paul Wesley W RSC 3 Blackpool
03.04.01	Spencer Fearon W PTS 6 Bethnal Green
26.07.01	Harry Butler W RSC 4 Blackpool
15.09.01	Anthony Farnell L RSC 2 Manchester
	(Vacant WBO Inter-Continental L.Middleweight Title)
09.12.01	Neil Bonner W RSC 3 Blackpool
16.03.02	Ryan Rhodes W RSC 3 Bethnal Green
	(Vacant WBF Inter-Continental Middleweight Title)
03.08.02	Alan Gilbert W RSC 6 Blackpool
	(WBF Inter-Continental Middleweight Title Defence)
26.10.02	Darren McInulty W RSC 1 Wigan
	(WBF Inter-Continental Middleweight Title Defence)
24.01.03	Steven Bendall L RSC 2 Sheffield
	(IBO Inter-Continental Middleweight Title Challenge)
19.12.04	Michael Pinnock W PTS 6 Bolton
06.03.05	Howard Clarke W PTS 6 Shaw
30.04.05	Simeon Cover W PTS 10 Wigan
	(Vacant British Masters Middleweight Title)
13.05.05	Michael Pinnock W PTS 4 Liverpool
02.03.06	Hamid Jamali W PTS 6 Blackpool
06.05.06	Conroy McIntosh W PTS 6 Blackpool

Career: 29 contests, won 23, drew 2, lost 4.

(Aivaras) Ivor Bonavic (Urbonavicius)

Canning Town. *Born* Jonava, Russia, 22 April, 1982
L.Middleweight. Ht. 5'8"
Manager Self

12.03.04	Chris Long L PTS 6 Millwall
08.05.04	Arek Malek L PTS 4 Dagenham
05.06.04	Gary Woolcombe L PTS 4 Bethnal Green
08.07.04	Robert Lloyd-Taylor L PTS 4 The Strand
30.09.04	Neil Jarmolinski DREW 4 Glasgow
08.10.04	Arek Malek W PTS 4 Brentwood
15.10.04	George McIlroy DREW 4 Glasgow
22.10.04	Colin McNeil L PTS 4 Edinburgh
29.10.04	George Telfer L PTS 4 Renfrew
24.11.04	Rocky Muscus W PTS 4 Mayfair
21.01.05	Robert Lloyd-Taylor L CO 2 Brentford
12.06.05	Francis Barrett W RSC 2 Leicester Square
09.07.05	Lenny Daws L PTS 6 Nottingham
16.07.05	Martin Concepcion W RSC 2 Bolton
25.09.05	Jay Morris W PTS 6 Southampton
05.11.05	Gary Young L RSC 8 Renfrew
04.12.05	Jay Morris L PTS 6 Portsmouth

Career: 17 contests, won 5, drew 2, lost 10.

Neil Bonner

Abergele. *Born* Enfield, 13 October, 1975
Middleweight. Ht. 5'9"
Manager Self

22.09.00	Drea Dread W RSC 4 Wrexham
03.11.00	James Lee L PTS 4 Ebbw Vale
04.02.01	Richard Inquieti W PTS 6 Queensferry
26.08.01	Colin McCash W RSC 1 Warrington

09.09.01	Peter Jackson L PTS 6 Hartlepool
21.10.01	Matt Scriven NC 1 Glasgow
09.12.01	Lee Blundell L RSC 3 Blackpool
08.03.02	Paul Buchanan L PTS 6 Ellesmere Port
19.04.02	Lee Murtagh L PTS 6 Darlington
11.05.02	Darrell Grafton L PTS 6 Chesterfield
08.06.02	Joe Townsley L PTS 6 Renfrew
06.10.02	Wayne Shepherd W PTS 6 Rhyl
01.11.02	Dean Cockburn L RSC 2 Preston
24.05.03	Dean Walker L PTS 6 Sheffield
07.04.06	Kevin Phelan L RSC 2 Longford

Career: 15 contests, won 4, lost 10, no contest 1.

Paul Bonson

Featherstone. *Born* Castleford, 18 October, 1971
Cruiserweight. Former Central Area L. Heavyweight Champion. Ht. 5'10"
Manager Self

04.10.96	Michael Pinnock W PTS 6 Wakefield
14.11.96	Michael Pinnock DREW 6 Sheffield
22.12.96	Pele Lawrence DREW 6 Salford
20.04.97	Shamus Casey W PTS 6 Leeds
26.06.97	Andy Manning L PTS 6 Sheffield
19.09.97	Mike Gormley W PTS 6 Salford
03.10.97	Rudi Marcussen L PTS 4 Copenhagen, Denmark
03.12.97	Alex Mason DREW 6 Stoke
14.12.97	Willie Quinn L RSC 4 Glasgow
15.01.98	Alex Mason L PTS 6 Solihull
13.02.98	Peter Mason L PTS 4 Seaham
23.02.98	Martin McDonough W PTS 6 Windsor
07.03.98	Michael Bowen L PTS 6 Reading
14.03.98	Alain Simon L PTS 6 Pont St Maxence, France
08.04.98	Tim Brown DREW 4 Liverpool
21.05.98	Mark Hobson L PTS 6 Bradford
21.06.98	Kenny Rainford L PTS 6 Liverpool
01.09.98	Roberto Dominguez L PTS 8 Vigo, Spain
23.10.98	Rob Galloway W PTS 6 Wakefield
16.11.98	Chris P. Bacon L PTS 8 Glasgow
11.12.98	Robert Zlotkowski L PTS 4 Prestwick
20.12.98	Glenn Williams L PTS 6 Salford
24.04.99	Kenny Gayle DREW 4 Peterborough
29.05.99	Dave Johnson L PTS 6 South Shields
19.06.99	Sebastiaan Rothmann L PTS 8 Dublin
12.07.99	Jim Twite L PTS 4 Coventry
07.08.99	Juan Perez Nelongo L PTS 8 Arona, Tenerife
11.09.99	Mark Hobson L PTS 4 Sheffield
02.10.99	Enzo Maccarinelli L PTS 4 Cardiff
16.10.99	Robert Zlotkowski L PTS 6 Bethnal Green
27.10.99	Peter McCormack W PTS 6 Birmingham
04.12.99	Glenn Williams W PTS 4 Manchester
11.12.99	Chris Davies L PTS 4 Merthyr
05.02.00	Paul Maskell L PTS 4 Bethnal Green
11.03.00	Tony Dodson L PTS 4 Kensington
26.03.00	Wayne Buck L PTS 8 Nottingham
29.04.00	Cathal O'Grady L PTS 4 Wembley
13.05.00	Mark Hobson L PTS 4 Barnsley
25.06.00	Andy Manning W PTS 10 Wakefield
	(Vacant Central L. Heavyweight Title)
08.09.00	Robert Milewicz L PTS 4 Hammersmith
21.10.00	Jon Penn L PTS 6 Sheffield
12.11.00	Glenn Williams L PTS 10 Manchester
	(Central Area L.Heavyweight Title Defence)
24.11.00	Alex Mason L PTS 6 Darlington

09.12.00	Mark Baker L PTS 6 Southwark	
23.01.01	Calvin Stonestreet W PTS 4 Crawley	
03.02.01	Tony Dodson L PTS 4 Manchester	
18.02.01	Butch Lesley L PTS 6 Southwark	
13.03.01	Konstantin Schvets L PTS 6 Plymouth	
07.04.01	Rob Hayes-Scott L PTS 4 Wembley	
26.04.01	Mike White L PTS 6 Gateshead	
17.05.01	Clint Johnson W PTS 6 Leeds	
24.05.01	Sven Hamer L PTS 4 Kensington	
04.06.01	Joe Gillon DREW 6 Glasgow	
11.06.01	Darren Chubbs L PTS 4 Nottingham	
21.06.01	Michael Pinnock W PTS 6 Sheffield	
27.07.01	Clinton Woods L PTS 6 Sheffield	
09.09.01	Eamonn Glennon W PTS 6 Hartlepool	
28.09.01	Elvis Michailenko L PTS 6 Millwall	
13.11.01	Tony Moran L PTS 6 Leeds	
23.11.01	Elvis Michailenko L PTS 6 Bethnal Green	
06.12.01	Shaun Bowes W RSC 5 Sunderland	
16.12.01	Tommy Eastwood L PTS 4 Southwark	
26.01.02	Dominic Negus L PTS 4 Bethnal Green	
10.02.02	Butch Lesley L PTS 4 Southwark	
25.02.02	Roman Greenberg L PTS 6 Slough	
15.03.02	Michael Thompson L PTS 6 Spennymoor	
22.03.02	Mark Smallwood L PTS 6 Coventry	
19.04.02	Michael Thompson L PTS 6 Darlington	
11.05.02	Mark Brookes L PTS 4 Chesterfield	
15.06.02	Peter Haymer L PTS 4 Tottenham	
23.06.02	Scott Lansdowne W PTS 4 Southwark	
13.07.02	Jason Brewster W PTS 6 Wolverhampton	
27.07.02	Albert Sosnowski L PTS 4 Nottingham	
08.09.02	Varuzhan Davtyan L PTS 4 Wolverhampton	
22.09.02	Neil Linford L PTS 6 Southwark	
29.09.02	Tony Dowling L PTS 6 Shrewsbury	
12.10.02	Andrew Lowe L PTS 4 Bethnal Green	
25.10.02	Carl Froch L PTS 6 Bethnal Green	
30.11.02	Robert Norton L PTS 6 Coventry	
14.12.02	Nathan King W PTS 4 Newcastle	
18.01.03	Enzo Maccarinelli L PTS 4 Preston	
08.02.03	Steven Spartacus L PTS 6 Norwich	
05.03.03	Marcus Lee W PTS 4 Bethnal Green	
18.03.03	Mark Krence L PTS 4 Reading	
28.03.03	Eric Teymour L PTS 6 Millwall	
19.04.03	Tony Moran L PTS 4 Liverpool	
12.05.03	Colin Kenna L PTS 6 Southampton	
10.06.03	Lee Swaby L PTS 4 Sheffield	
26.09.03	Garry Delaney L PTS 6 Reading	
06.10.03	Pinky Burton L PTS 6 Barnsley	
07.11.03	Carl Thompson L PTS 6 Sheffield	
14.11.03	Tony Booth L PTS 6 Hull	
01.12.03	David Ingleby W PTS 6 Leeds	
20.02.04	Colin Kenna L PTS 6 Southampton	
13.03.04	Neil Dawson L PTS 4 Huddersfield	
16.04.04	John Keeton L PTS 4 Bradford	
01.05.04	Carl Wright L PTS 6 Coventry	
26.11.04	Tony Booth L PTS 6 Hull	
06.12.04	Robert Norton L CO 6 Leicester	
	(Vacant British Masters Cruiserweight Title)	
06.02.05	Ovill McKenzie L PTS 4 Southampton	
30.04.05	Tony Moran L PTS 6 Wigan	
14.05.05	John Keeton L PTS 4 Aberdeen	
18.06.05	Neil Simpson L PTS 6 Coventry	
09.07.05	Dean Francis L PTS 6 Bristol	
24.07.05	Toks Owoh L PTS 4 Leicester Square	
03.09.05	Sam Sexton L PTS 6 Norwich	
23.09.05	Gyorgy Hidvegi L PTS 4 Manchester	
07.10.05	Junior MacDonald L PTS 4 Bethnal Green	
20.11.05	Darren Stubbs L PTS 6 Shaw	
10.12.05	Bruce Scott L PTS 4 Canning Town	

24.02.06	Gyorgy Hidvegi DREW 8 Dagenham	
05.03.06	Amer Khan L PTS 6 Sheffield	
23.03.06	Ovill McKenzie L PTS 6 The Strand	
30.03.06	Ovill McKenzie L RSC 3 Bloomsbury	
06.05.06	Billy McClung L PTS 6 Irvine	
09.06.06	Dean Cockburn L PTS 6 Doncaster	

Career: 116 contests, won 19, drew 7, lost 90.

Tony Booth

Hull. *Born* Hull, 30 January, 1970
Heavyweight. Former Undefeated British
Masters L. Heavyweight Champion.
Former Undefeated British Central Area
Cruiserweight Champion. Ht. 5'11¼"
Manager Self

08.03.90	Paul Lynch L PTS 6 Watford	
11.04.90	Mick Duncan W PTS 6 Dewsbury	
26.04.90	Colin Manners W PTS 6 Halifax	
16.05.90	Tommy Warde W PTS 6 Hull	
05.06.90	Gary Dyson W PTS 6 Liverpool	
05.09.90	Shaun McCrory L PTS 6 Stoke	
08.10.90	Bullit Andrews W RSC 3 Cleethorpes	
23.01.91	Darron Griffiths DREW 6 Stoke	
06.02.91	Shaun McCrory L PTS 6 Liverpool	
06.03.91	Billy Brough L PTS 6 Glasgow	
18.03.91	Billy Brough W PTS 6 Glasgow	
28.03.91	Neville Brown L PTS 6 Alfreton	
17.05.91	Glenn Campbell L RSC 2 Bury	
	(Central Area S. Middleweight Title Challenge)	
25.07.91	Paul Murray W PTS 6 Dudley	
01.08.91	Nick Manners DREW 8 Dewsbury	
11.09.91	Jim Peters L PTS 8 Hammersmith	
28.10.91	Eddie Smulders L RSC 6 Arnhem, Holland	
09.12.91	Steve Lewsam L PTS 8 Cleethorpes	
30.01.92	Serg Fame W PTS 6 Southampton	
12.02.92	Tenko Ernie W RSC 4 Wembley	
05.03.92	John Beckles W RSC 6 Battersea	
26.03.92	Dave Owens W PTS 6 Hull	
08.04.92	Michael Gale L PTS 8 Leeds	
13.05.92	Phil Soundy W PTS 6 Kensington	
02.06.92	Eddie Smulders L RSC 1 Rotterdam, Holland	
18.07.92	Maurice Core L PTS 6 Manchester	
07.09.92	James Cook L PTS 8 Bethnal Green	
30.10.92	Roy Richie DREW 6 Istrees, France	
18.11.92	Tony Wilson DREW 8 Solihull	
25.12.92	Francis Wanyama L PTS 6 Izegem, Belgium	
09.02.93	Tony Wilson W PTS 8 Wolverhampton	
01.05.93	Ralf Rocchigiani DREW 8 Berlin, Germany	
03.06.93	Victor Cordoba L PTS 8 Marseille, France	
23.06.93	Tony Behan W PTS 6 Gorleston	
01.07.93	Michael Gale L PTS 8 York	
17.09.93	Ole Klemetsen L PTS 8 Copenhagen, Denmark	
07.10.93	Denzil Browne DREW 8 York	
02.11.93	James Cook L PTS 8 Southwark	
12.11.93	Carlos Christie W PTS 6 Hull	
28.01.94	Francis Wanyama L RSC 2 Waregem, Belgium	
	(Vacant Commonwealth Cruiserweight Title)	
26.03.94	Torsten May L PTS 6 Dortmund, Germany	
21.07.94	Mark Prince L RSC 3 Battersea	
24.09.94	Johnny Held L PTS 8 Rotterdam, Holland	
07.10.94	Dirk Wallyn L PTS 6 Waregem, Belgium	

27.10.94	Dean Francis L CO 1 Bayswater	
23.01.95	Jan Lefeber L PTS 8 Rotterdam, Holland	
07.03.95	John Foreman L PTS 6 Edgbaston	
27.04.95	Art Stacey W PTS 10 Hull	
	(Vacant Central Area Cruiserweight Title)	
04.06.95	Montell Griffin L RSC 2 Bethnal Green	
06.07.95	Nigel Rafferty W RSC 7 Hull	
22.07.95	Mark Prince L RSC 2 Millwall	
06.09.95	Leif Keiski L PTS 8 Helsinki, Finland	
25.09.95	Neil Simpson W PTS 8 Cleethorpes	
06.10.95	Don Diego Poeder L RSC 2 Waregem, Belgium	
11.11.95	Bruce Scott L RSC 3 Halifax	
16.12.95	John Marceta L RSC 2 Cardiff	
20.01.96	Johnny Nelson L RSC 2 Mansfield	
15.03.96	Slick Miller W PTS 6 Hull	
27.03.96	Neil Simpson L PTS 6 Whitwick	
17.05.96	Mark Richardson W RSC 2 Hull	
13.07.96	Bruce Scott L PTS 8 Bethnal Green	
03.09.96	Paul Douglas L PTS 4 Belfast	
14.09.96	Kelly Oliver L RSC 2 Sheffield	
06.11.96	Martin Jolley W PTS 4 Hull	
22.11.96	Slick Miller W RSC 5 Hull	
11.12.96	Crawford Ashley L RSC 1 Southwark	
18.01.97	Kelly Oliver L RSC 4 Swadlincote	
27.02.97	Kevin Morton L PTS 6 Hull	
25.03.97	Nigel Rafferty DREW 8 Wolverhampton	
04.04.97	John Wilson L PTS 6 Glasgow	
16.04.97	Robert Norton L RSC 4 Bethnal Green	
15.05.97	Phill Day W PTS 4 Reading	
11.09.97	Steve Bristow L PTS 4 Widnes	
22.09.97	Martin Langtry W PTS 6 Cleethorpes	
04.10.97	Bruce Scott W PTS 8 Muswell Hill	
28.11.97	Martin Jolley W PTS 6 Hull	
15.12.97	Nigel Rafferty W PTS 6 Cleethorpes	
06.03.98	Peter Mason W RSC 3 Hull	
09.06.98	Crawford Ashley L RSC 6 Hull	
	(British L. Heavyweight Title Challenge. Vacant Commonwealth L. Heavyweight Title)	
18.07.98	Omar Sheika W PTS 8 Sheffield	
26.09.98	Toks Owoh L PTS 6 Norwich	
29.10.98	Nigel Rafferty W PTS 8 Bayswater	
14.12.98	Sven Hamer W PTS 6 Cleethorpes	
05.01.99	Ali Saidi W RSC 4 Epernay, France	
17.05.99	Darren Ashton W PTS 6 Cleethorpes	
12.07.99	Neil Simpson L PTS 10 Coventry	
	(Elim. British L. Heavyweight Title)	
27.09.99	Adam Cale W PTS 6 Cleethorpes	
16.10.99	Cathal O'Grady L CO 4 Belfast	
18.01.00	Michael Sprott L PTS 6 Mansfield	
12.02.00	Thomas Hansvoll L PTS 6 Sheffield	
29.02.00	John Keeton L RSC 2 Widnes	
09.04.00	Greg Scott-Briggs W PTS 10 Alfreton	
	(Vacant British Masters L. Heavyweight Title)	
15.05.00	Michael Pinnock W PTS 6 Cleethorpes	
19.06.00	Toks Owoh W PTS 6 Burton	
08.09.00	Dominic Negus W PTS 6 Bristol	
30.09.00	Robert Norton L RSC 3 Peterborough	
31.10.00	Firat Aslan L RSC 2 Hammersmith	
11.12.00	Mark Krence L PTS 6 Sheffield	
05.02.01	Denzil Browne L RSC 5 Hull	
	(Vacant Central Area Cruiserweight Title)	
01.04.01	Kenny Gayle DREW 4 Southwark	
10.04.01	Mark Baker L PTS 4 Wembley	
16.06.01	Butch Lesley L RSC 3 Dagenham	
09.09.01	Tommy Eastwood L PTS 4 Southwark	
22.09.01	Peter Haymer L PTS 4 Bethnal Green	

15.10.01	Colin Kenna L PTS 6 Southampton
01.11.01	Terry Morrill W RSC 7 Hull
24.11.01	Matt Legg L PTS 4 Bethnal Green
16.12.01	Blue Stevens L PTS 4 Southwark
19.01.02	John McDermott L RSC 1 Bethnal Green
20.04.02	Enzo Maccarinelli L PTS 4 Cardiff
28.04.02	Scott Lansdowne W RSC 4 Southwark
10.05.02	Paul Buttery L PTS 4 Preston
23.06.02	Neil Linford L RSC 5 Southwark
03.08.02	Mark Krence L PTS 4 Derby
17.08.02	Enzo Maccarinelli L RTD 2 Cardiff
23.09.02	Slick Miller W PTS 6 Cleethorpes
05.10.02	Phill Day W PTS 4 Coventry
19.10.02	James Zikic L PTS 4 Norwich
27.10.02	Hughie Doherty L PTS 4 Southwark
21.11.02	Jamie Warters W PTS 8 Hull
28.11.02	Roman Greenberg L PTS 4 Finchley
08.12.02	David Haye L RTD 2 Bethnal Green
30.01.03	Mohammed Benguesmia L RTD 4 Algiers, Algeria
05.04.03	Jason Callum L PTS 6 Coventry
17.05.03	Tony Moran L PTS 6 Liverpool
26.07.03	Kelly Oliver L PTS 4 Plymouth
26.09.03	Radcliffe Green W PTS 6 Millwall
14.11.03	Paul Bonson W PTS 6 Hull
14.02.04	Oneal Murray W PTS 8 Holborn
01.05.04	Elvis Michailenko L RTD 4 Gravesend
15.08.04	Bash Ali L RSC 4 Lagos, Nigeria (WBF Cruiserweight Title Challenge)
26.11.04	Paul Bonson W PTS 6 Hull
11.12.04	Hovik Keuchkerian L CO 1 Madrid, Spain
05.03.05	Junior MacDonald L PTS 4 Southwark
15.04.05	Johny Jensen L PTS 6 Copenhagen, Denmark
04.06.05	Martin Rogan L RSC 2 Manchester
24.07.05	Coleman Barrett L PTS 4 Leicester Square
10.09.05	Darren Morgan L PTS 4 Cardiff
24.09.05	Carl Wright L PTS 4 Coventry
06.10.05	Tommy Eastwood L PTS 4 Longford
25.11.05	Dave Clarke DREW 6 Hull
26.02.06	Ovill McKenzie L PTS 4 Dagenham
05.03.06	Jon Ibbotson L PTS 4 Sheffield
30.03.06	Ervis Jegeni L RSC 1 Piccadilly
13.05.06	Paul Souter L PTS 4 Bethnal Green
26.05.06	Lee Mountford W PTS 6 Hull

Career: 146 contests, won 46, drew 9, lost 91.

Tyan Booth

Sheffield. *Born* Nottingham, 20 March, 1983
Middleweight. Ht. 6'2½"
Manager J. Ingle

29.10.05	Jimi Hendricks W PTS 6 Aberdeen
08.11.05	Jimi Hendricks W PTS 6 Leeds
27.02.06	Jason Welborn W CO 4 Birmingham
06.05.06	Richard Turba W PTS 6 Blackpool
17.05.06	Alexis Callero L PTS 6 Lanzarote, Canary Islands, Spain

Career: 5 contests, won 4, lost 1.

Alan Bosworth

Northampton. *Born* Northampton, 31 December, 1967
L.Welterweight. Former Undefeated English Lightweight Champion. Former Undefeated British Masters L.Welterweight Champion. Ht. 5'7"
Manager Self

17.10.95	Simon Hamblett W RSC 2 Wolverhampton
29.10.95	Shaun Gledhill W PTS 6 Shaw
16.11.95	Brian Coleman W PTS 6 Evesham
23.11.95	David Thompson W RSC 4 Tynemouth
13.01.96	Jason Blanche W PTS 6 Halifax
31.01.96	Arv Mittoo W PTS 6 Stoke
16.02.96	John Docherty W PTS 6 Irvine
24.03.96	Scott Walker DREW 6 Shaw
16.05.96	Yifru Retta W PTS 6 Dunstable
07.03.97	Wayne Rigby L RSC 5 Northampton
09.09.97	Colin Dunne L RSC 8 Bethnal Green
31.10.98	Alan Temple L PTS 6 Basingstoke
26.02.99	Des Sowden W PTS 6 Longford
13.03.99	Paul Burke L PTS 6 Manchester
24.04.99	Jan Bergman L RSC 6 Munich, Germany
02.07.99	Keith Jones W PTS 6 Bristol
24.09.99	Woody Greenaway L PTS 6 Merthyr
03.12.99	Darren Underwood W CO 5 Peterborough
20.01.00	Brian Coleman W PTS 6 Piccadilly
24.03.00	Allan Vester L PTS 12 Aarhus, Denmark (IBF Inter-Continental L. Welterweight Title Challenge)
28.04.00	George Scott L PTS 8 Copenhagen, Denmark
02.06.00	Mohamed Helel W PTS 6 Ashford
25.07.00	Shea Neary L PTS 10 Southwark
01.12.00	David Kirk DREW 8 Peterborough
13.03.01	Eamonn Magee L RSC 5 Plymouth
23.06.01	Keith Jones W PTS 6 Peterborough
23.11.01	Daniel James W RSC 7 Bethnal Green (Elim. British L.Welterweight Title)
16.03.02	Junior Witter L RSC 3 Northampton (Vacant British L.Welterweight Title)
28.09.02	Eamonn Magee L RSC 5 Manchester
28.01.03	Oscar Hall L PTS 10 Nottingham (Elim. British L. Welterweight Title)
25.07.03	Gavin Down W RSC 5 Norwich (British Masters L.Welterweight Title Challenge. Elim. British L.Welterweight Title)
11.12.03	Stephen Smith W PTS 10 Bethnal Green (Vacant English L.Welterweight Title)
12.11.04	Francis Barrett L PTS 10 Wembley (European Union L.Welterweight Title Challenge)
27.05.05	Nigel Wright L PTS 10 Spennymoor (English L.Welterweight Title Challenge)
25.02.06	Jus Wallie W RSC 1 Canning Town
13.05.06	James Paisley W PTS 4 Bethnal Green

Career: 36 contests, won 19, drew 2, lost 15.

John Bothwell

Ballieston. *Born* Glasgow, 8 August, 1981
S. Featherweight. Ht. 5'5"
Manager T. Gilmour

17.10.03	Marty Kayes W PTS 6 Glasgow
30.10.03	Colin Moffett DREW 4 Belfast
07.12.03	Ian Reid W PTS 6 Glasgow
06.03.04	Fred Janes DREW 4 Renfrew
08.04.04	Chris Hooper L CO 2 Peterborough
28.05.04	Jason Nesbitt L RSC 3 Glasgow
01.04.05	Michael Crossan L PTS 6 Glasgow
20.05.05	Buster Dennis L RTD 4 Glasgow
14.10.05	Paul Griffin L RSC 1 Dublin
25.03.06	Sandy Bartlett W RSC 2 Irvine
05.06.06	Neil Marston W PTS 6 Glasgow

Career: 11 contests, won 4, drew 2, lost 5.

Omid Bourzo

Sheffield. *Born* Tehran, Iran, 1 September, 1979
Cruiserweight. Ht. 6'1"
Manager J. Ingle

11.10.04	Peter McCormack L PTS 6 Birmingham
09.04.05	Danny McIntosh L PTS 6 Norwich
24.04.05	Jonjo Finnegan W PTS 6 Derby
15.12.05	Neil Tidman L RSC 3 Coventry
22.05.06	Peter McCormack W PTS 6 Birmingham

Career: 5 contests, won 2, lost 3.

Paul Bowen

West Ham. *Born* Barking, 14 May, 1973
Cruiserweight. Former Undefeated Southern Area S. Middleweight Champion. Ht. 6'0"
Manager Self

13.02.96	Lee Bird W RSC 2 Bethnal Green
13.04.96	Pat Durkin W RSC 3 Wythenshawe
13.07.96	Mark Dawson W RSC 3 Bethnal Green
08.02.97	Darren Ashton W PTS 4 Millwall
29.11.97	Ian Toby W RSC 4 Norwich
17.01.98	Mark Dawson W PTS 4 Bristol
16.05.98	Eddie Knight W RSC 3 Bethnal Green
10.10.98	Enzo Giordano W RSC 10 Bethnal Green (Vacant Southern Area S. Middleweight Title)
27.02.99	Phil Epton W RSC 2 Oldham
05.06.99	Matthew Barney DREW 10 Cardiff (Southern Area S. Middleweight Title Defence)
25.07.00	Andy Manning W PTS 4 Southwark
18.11.00	Paul Wesley W PTS 4 Dagenham
03.04.01	Ruben Groenewald L PTS 6 Bethnal Green
18.03.02	Darren Ashton W PTS 6 Crawley
09.10.05	Gary Thompson W CO 1 Hammersmith

Career: 15 contests, won 13, drew 1, lost 1.

Ryan Brawley

Irvine. *Born* Irvine, 2 February, 1986
Lightweight. Ht. 5'10½"
Manager T. Gilmour

19.09.05	Pete Buckley W PTS 6 Glasgow
14.10.05	Lance Verallo W PTS 6 Motherwell
20.02.06	Gavin Deacon W PTS 4 Glasgow
25.03.06	Chris Long W PTS 8 Irvine
06.05.06	Dariusz Snarski W PTS 6 Irvine

Career: 5 contests, won 5.

Gordon Brennan

Dunfermline. *Born* Dunfermline, 1 August, 1982
L.Heavyweight. Ht. 5'11"
Manager T. Gilmour

31.03.06	Jimi Hendricks W PTS 6 Inverurie

Career: 1 contest, won 1.

Craig Bromley

Sheffield. *Born* Sheffield, 28 June, 1986
S.Featherweight. Ht. 5'5"
Manager J. Ingle

10.12.04	Darren Broomhall L PTS 6 Mansfield

19.12.04 Paddy Folan DREW 6 Bolton
13.02.05 Paddy Folan W PTS 6 Bradford
15.04.05 Neil Marston W RSC 1 Shrewsbury
24.07.05 Neil Read W PTS 4 Sheffield
16.09.05 Dave Hinds W PTS 4 Doncaster
14.10.05 Shaun Walton W PTS 4 Huddersfield
04.11.05 Sandy Bartlett W RSC 2 Glasgow
Career: 8 contests, won 6, drew 1, lost 1.

(Ezekiel) Kell Brook

Sheffield. *Born* Sheffield, 3 May, 1986
L. Welterweight. Ht. 5'9"
Manager F. Warren

17.09.04 Pete Buckley W PTS 6 Sheffield
29.10.04 Andy Cosnett W CO 1 Worksop
09.11.04 Lee Williamson W RSC 2 Leeds
10.12.04 Brian Coleman W RSC 4 Sheffield
19.12.04 Karl Taylor W PTS 6 Bolton
04.03.05 Lea Handley W PTS 6 Rotherham
15.05.05 Ernie Smith W PTS 6 Sheffield
09.07.05 Jonathan Whiteman W RSC 2 Nottingham
10.09.05 Ernie Smith W PTS 4 Cardiff
29.04.06 Ernie Smith W PTS 6 Edinburgh
01.06.06 Geraint Harvey W RSC 3 Barnsley
Career: 11 contests, won 11.

Casey Brooke

Great Wyrley. *Born* Birmingham, 8 July, 1971
L.Middleweight. Ht. 5'11"
Manager Self

06.06.00 Arv Mittoo L PTS 6 Brierley Hill
07.07.00 John Tiftik L RSC 2 Chigwell
10.10.00 Rene Grayel L PTS 6 Brierley Hill
28.11.00 Rene Grayel L PTS 6 Brierley Hill
03.02.01 Gary Harrison L PTS 6 Brighton
12.03.01 Tony Smith L PTS 6 Birmingham
26.09.03 Nathan Ward L RSC 1 Reading
26.10.03 Danny Cooper L PTS 6 Longford
30.11.03 Chris Brophy L PTS 6 Swansea
20.02.04 Tony Smith L PTS 6 Doncaster
30.03.04 Jay Morris L RSC 1 Southampton
24.04.05 Scott Conway L PTS 6 Derby
24.07.05 Jamal Morrison L PTS 4 Leicester Square
Career: 13 contests, lost 13.

Stuart Brookes

Mexborough. *Born* Mexborough, 31 August, 1982
Middleweight. Ht. 5'9"
Manager D. Hobson

15.05.05 Geraint Harvey W PTS 6 Sheffield
24.07.05 Tony Randell W PTS 6 Sheffield
09.09.05 Tony Randell W RSC 3 Sheffield
26.11.05 Howard Clarke W PTS 6 Sheffield
05.03.06 Magic Kidem W RSC 1 Sheffield
Career: 5 contests, won 5.

Chris Brophy

Swansea. *Born* Preston, 28 January, 1979
L.Middleweight. Ht. 5'10"
Manager N. Hodges

29.10.03 Aidan Mooney L RSC 5 Leicester Square
30.11.03 Casey Brooke W PTS 6 Swansea
21.12.03 Gary O'Connor L PTS 6 Bolton
21.02.04 Tony Doherty L RSC 2 Cardiff
02.04.04 Tommy Marshall DREW 6 Plymouth
26.04.04 Scott Haywood L RSC 5 Cleethorpes
05.06.04 Ashley Theophane L RSC 3 Bethnal Green
17.09.04 Tommy Marshall W PTS 6 Plymouth
21.11.04 Jay Morris L RSC 1 Bracknell
31.01.05 George McIlroy L RSC 6 Glasgow
16.09.05 Garry Buckland L PTS 4 Plymouth
24.10.05 Mike Reid L RSC 2 Glasgow
26.02.06 Freddie Luke L PTS 4 Dagenham
11.03.06 Stephen Burke L PTS 4 Newport
13.05.06 Grant Skehill L PTS 4 Bethnal Green
Career: 15 contests, won 2, drew 1, lost 12.

Barrington Brown

Nottingham. *Born* Nottingham, 11 May, 1982
S.Featherweight. Ht. 5'7"
Manager J. Gill/T. Harris

06.03.05 Paddy Folan W RSC 6 Shaw
30.09.05 Craig Morgan L PTS 6 Carmarthen
09.10.05 Vinesh Rungea W PTS 6 Hammersmith
18.02.06 Mick Abbott W PTS 6 Stoke
24.04.06 Kevin Townsley L PTS 6 Glasgow
30.05.06 Lloyd Otte W RSC 1 Bethnal Green
Career: 6 contests, won 4, lost 2.

Cathy Brown

Peckham. *Born* Leeds, 28 July, 1970
Flyweight. Former Undefeated Womens BF European Flyweight Champion. Ht. 5'2"
Manager Self

31.10.99 Veerle Braspenningsx W PTS 5 Raynes Park
05.02.00 Veerle Braspenningsx W RSC 6 Sint-Truiden, Belgium
01.07.00 Jan Wild W PTS 6 Southwark
(Vacant Womens BF European Flyweight Title)
31.10.00 Viktoria Vargal W RSC 3 Hammersmith
28.02.01 Marietta Ivanova W PTS 4 Kensington
26.04.01 Oksana Vasilieva L PTS 4 Kensington
16.06.01 Romona Gughie W RSC 3 Wembley
22.11.01 Audrey Guthrie W PTS 6 Mayfair
(Womens BF European Flyweight Title Defence)
13.12.01 Ilina Boneva W RSC 5 Leicester Square
13.03.02 Svetla Taskova W PTS 4 Mayfair
13.06.02 Alina Shaternikova L PTS 10 Leicester Square
(Vacant Womens BF Flyweight Title)
30.10.02 Monica Petrova W PTS 6 Leicester Square
20.03.03 Juliette Winter L PTS 4 Queensway
26.04.03 Regina Halmich L PTS 10 Schwerin, Germany
(Womens IBF Flyweight Title Challenge)
17.12.03 Stefania Bianchini L PTS 10 Bergamo, Italy
(Womens BF European Flyweight Title Challenge)
06.11.04 Bettina Csabi L PTS 10 Szentes, Hungary
(Womens BF/GBU Bantamweight Title Challenges)
02.12.04 Viktoria Varga W RSC 3 Crystal Palace
12.06.05 Svetla Taskova W RSC 6 Leicester Square
07.08.05 Stefania Bianchini L PTS 10 Rimini, Italy
(Vacant Womens IBF Interim Flyweight Title)
08.04.06 Julia Sahin L PTS 10 Kiel, Germany
(Vacant Womens IBF L.Flyweight Title)
Career: 20 contests, won 12, lost 8.

James Brown

Salford. *Born* Salford, 15 August, 1986
Lightweight. Ht. 5'10"
Manager S. Wood

18.06.06 Pete Buckley W PTS 6 Manchester
Career: 1 contest, won 1.

Paul Buchanan

West Denton. *Born* Newcastle, 23 October, 1981
Middleweight. Ht. 5'10"
Manager Self

31.01.01 Gary Jones W RTD 1 Piccadilly
26.04.01 Lee Woodruff W PTS 6 Gateshead
08.03.02 Neil Bonner W PTS 6 Ellesmere Port
25.03.02 Dean Cockburn W PTS 6 Sunderland

Stuart Brookes   Les Clark

Barrington Brown   Les Clark

06.03.04 Davey Jones W PTS 4 Renfrew
01.05.04 Gareth Lawrence W PTS 4 Gravesend
05.11.04 Jason McKay W PTS 6 Hereford
27.05.05 Ojay Abrahams W PTS 6 Spennymoor
25.11.05 Wayne Pinder DREW 6 Liverpool
Career: 9 contests, won 8, drew 1.

Garry Buckland

Cardiff. *Born* Cardiff, 12 June 1986
L.Welterweight. Ht. 5'7"
Manager B. Powell

05.03.05 Warren Dunkley W PTS 4 Dagenham
24.07.05 Danny Gwilym W RSC 2 Leicester
          Square
16.09.05 Chris Brophy W PTS 4 Plymouth
17.11.05 Bheki Moyo W RSC 3 Bristol
10.02.06 Anthony Christopher W RSC 4
          Plymouth
07.04.06 Judex Meemea W RSC 5 Bristol
Career: 6 contests, won 6.

Garry Buckland   Les Clark

Pete Buckley

Birmingham. *Born* Birmingham, 9 March,
1969
Welterweight. Former Undefeated
Midlands Area S. Featherweight Champion.
Former Midlands Area S. Bantamweight
Champion. Ht. 5'8"
Manager Self

04.10.89 Alan Baldwin DREW 6 Stafford
10.10.89 Ronnie Stephenson L PTS 6
          Wolverhampton
30.10.89 Robert Braddock W PTS 6 Birmingham
14.11.89 Neil Leitch W PTS 6 Evesham
22.11.89 Peter Judson W PTS 6 Stafford
11.12.89 Stevie Woods W PTS 6 Bradford
21.12.89 Wayne Taylor W PTS 6 Kings Heath
10.01.90 John O'Meara W PTS 6 Kensington
19.02.90 Ian McGirr L PTS 6 Birmingham
27.02.90 Miguel Matthews DREW 6 Evesham
14.03.90 Ronnie Stephenson DREW 6 Stoke
04.04.90 Ronnie Stephenson L PTS 8 Stafford
23.04.90 Ronnie Stephenson W PTS 6
          Birmingham
30.04.90 Chris Clarkson L PTS 8 Mayfair
17.05.90 Johnny Bredahl L PTS 6 Aars, Denmark
04.06.90 Ronnie Stephenson W PTS 8
          Birmingham
28.06.90 Robert Braddock W RSC 5
          Birmingham

01.10.90 Miguel Matthews W PTS 8
          Cleethorpes
09.10.90 Miguel Matthews L PTS 8
          Wolverhampton
17.10.90 Tony Smith W PTS 6 Stoke
29.10.90 Miguel Matthews W PTS 8
          Birmingham
21.11.90 Drew Docherty L PTS 8 Solihull
10.12.90 Neil Leitch W PTS 8 Birmingham
10.01.91 Duke McKenzie L RSC 5 Wandsworth
18.02.91 Jamie McBride L PTS 8 Glasgow
04.03.91 Brian Robb W RSC 7 Birmingham
26.03.91 Neil Leitch DREW 8 Wolverhampton
01.05.91 Mark Geraghty W PTS 8 Solihull
05.06.91 Brian Robb W PTS 10 Wolverhampton
          (Vacant Midlands Area
          S. Featherweight Title)
09.09.91 Mike Deveney L PTS 8 Glasgow
24.09.91 Mark Bates W RTD 5 Basildon
29.10.91 John Armour L PTS 6 Kensington
14.11.91 Mike Deveney L PTS 6 Edinburgh
28.11.91 Craig Dermody L PTS 6 Liverpool
19.12.91 Craig Dermody L PTS 6 Oldham
18.01.92 Alan McKay DREW 8 Kensington
20.02.92 Brian Robb W RSC 10 Oakengates
          (Midlands Area S. Featherweight Title
          Defence)
27.04.92 Drew Docherty L PTS 8 Glasgow
15.05.92 Ruben Condori L PTS 10 Augsburg,
          Germany
29.05.92 Donnie Hood L PTS 8 Glasgow
07.09.92 Duke McKenzie L RTD 3 Bethnal
          Green
12.11.92 Prince Naseem Hamed L PTS 6
          Liverpool
19.02.93 Harald Geier L PTS 12 Vienna, Austria
          (Vacant WBA Penta-Continental S.
          Bantamweight Title)
26.04.93 Bradley Stone L PTS 8 Lewisham
18.06.93 Eamonn McAuley L PTS 6 Belfast
01.07.93 Tony Silkstone L PTS 8 York
06.10.93 Jonjo Irwin L PTS 8 Solihull
25.10.93 Drew Docherty L PTS 8 Glasgow
06.11.93 Michael Alldis L PTS 8 Bethnal Green
30.11.93 Barry Jones L PTS 4 Cardiff
19.12.93 Shaun Anderson L PTS 6 Glasgow
22.01.94 Barry Jones L PTS 6 Cardiff
29.01.94 Prince Naseem Hamed L RSC 4
          Cardiff
10.03.94 Tony Falcone L PTS 4 Bristol
29.03.94 Conn McMullen W PTS 6 Bethnal
          Green
05.04.94 Mark Bowers L PTS 6 Bethnal Green
13.04.94 James Murray L PTS 6 Glasgow
06.05.94 Paul Lloyd L RTD 4 Liverpool
03.08.94 Greg Upton L PTS 6 Bristol
26.09.94 John Sillo L PTS 6 Liverpool
05.10.94 Matthew Harris L PTS 6
          Wolverhampton
07.11.94 Marlon Ward L PTS 4 Piccadilly
23.11.94 Justin Murphy L PTS 4 Piccadilly
29.11.94 Neil Swain L PTS 4 Cardiff
13.12.94 Michael Brodie L PTS 6 Potters Bar
20.12.94 Michael Alldis L PTS 6 Bethnal Green
10.02.95 Matthew Harris W RSC 6 Birmingham
          (Midlands Area S. Bantamweight Title
          Challenge)
23.02.95 Paul Ingle L PTS 8 Southwark
20.04.95 John Sillo L PTS 6 Liverpool
27.04.95 Paul Ingle L PTS 8 Bethnal Green
09.05.95 Ady Lewis L PTS 4 Basildon
23.05.95 Spencer Oliver L PTS 4 Potters Bar
01.07.95 Dean Pithie L PTS 4 Kensington
21.09.95 Patrick Mullings L PTS 6 Battersea

29.09.95 Marlon Ward L PTS 4 Bethnal Green
25.10.95 Matthew Harris L PTS 10 Telford
          (Midlands Area S. Bantamweight Title
          Defence)
08.11.95 Vince Feeney L PTS 8 Bethnal Green
28.11.95 Barry Jones L PTS 6 Cardiff
15.12.95 Patrick Mullings L PTS 4 Bethnal
          Green
05.02.96 Patrick Mullings L PTS 8 Bexleyheath
09.03.96 Paul Griffin L PTS 4 Millstreet
21.03.96 Colin McMillan L RSC 3 Southwark
14.05.96 Venkatesan Deverajan L PTS 4
          Dagenham
29.06.96 Matt Brown W RSC 1 Erith
03.09.96 Vince Feeney L PTS 4 Bethnal Green
28.09.96 Fabrice Benichou L PTS 8 Barking
09.10.96 Gary Marston DREW 8 Stoke
06.11.96 Neil Swain L PTS 4 Tylorstown
29.11.96 Alston Buchanan L PTS 8 Glasgow
22.12.96 Brian Carr L PTS 6 Glasgow
11.01.97 Scott Harrison L PTS 4 Bethnal Green
29.01.97 Carl Allen L PTS 8 Stoke
12.02.97 Ronnie McPhee L PTS 6 Glasgow
25.02.97 Dean Pithie L PTS 4 Sheffield
07.03.97 Jason Booth L PTS 6 Northampton
20.03.97 Thomas Bradley W PTS 6 Newark
08.04.97 Sergei Devakov L PTS 6 Bethnal
          Green
25.04.97 Matthew Harris L PTS 6 Cleethorpes
08.05.97 Gregorio Medina L RTD 2 Mansfield
13.06.97 Mike Deveney L PTS 6 Paisley
19.07.97 Richard Evatt L PTS 4 Wembley
30.08.97 Michael Brodie L PTS 8 Cheshunt
06.10.97 Brendan Bryce W PTS 6 Piccadilly
20.10.97 Kelton McKenzie L PTS 6 Leicester
20.11.97 Ervine Blake L PTS 8 Solihull
06.12.97 Danny Adams L PTS 4 Wembley
13.12.97 Gary Thornhill L PTS 6 Sheffield
31.01.98 Scott Harrison L PTS 4 Edmonton
05.03.98 Steve Conway L PTS 6 Leeds
18.03.98 Ervine Blake L PTS 8 Stoke
26.03.98 Graham McGrath W RTD 4 Solihull
11.04.98 Salim Medjkoune L PTS 6 Southwark
18.04.98 Tony Mulholland L PTS 4 Manchester
27.04.98 Alston Buchanan L PTS 8 Glasgow
11.05.98 Jason Squire W RTD 2 Leicester
21.05.98 Lee Armstrong L PTS 6 Bradford
06.06.98 Tony Mulholland L PTS 6 Liverpool
14.06.98 Lee Armstrong L PTS 6 Shaw
21.07.98 David Burke L PTS 6 Widnes
05.09.98 Michael Gomez L PTS 6 Telford
17.09.98 Brian Carr L PTS 6 Glasgow
03.10.98 Justin Murphy L PTS 6 Crawley
05.12.98 Lehlohonolo Ledwaba L PTS 8 Bristol
19.12.98 Acelino Freitas L RTD 3 Liverpool
09.02.99 Chris Jickells L PTS 6 Wolverhampton
16.02.99 Franny Hogg L PTS 6 Leeds
26.02.99 Richard Evatt L RSC 5 Coventry
17.04.99 Martin O'Malley L RSC 3 Dublin
29.05.99 Richie Wenton L PTS 6 Halifax
14.06.99 Carl Allen L PTS 6 Birmingham
26.06.99 Paul Halpin L PTS 4 Millwall
15.07.99 Salim Medjkoune L PTS 6
          Peterborough
07.08.99 Steve Murray L PTS 6 Dagenham
12.09.99 Kevin Gerowski L PTS 6 Nottingham
20.09.99 Mat Zegan L PTS 6 Peterborough
02.10.99 Jason Cook L PTS 4 Cardiff
09.10.99 Brian Carr L PTS 6 Manchester
19.10.99 Gary Steadman L PTS 4 Bethnal Green
27.10.99 Miguel Matthews W PTS 8
          Birmingham
20.11.99 Carl Greaves L PTS 10 Grantham
          (British Masters S. Featherweight Title
          Challenge)

11.12.99 Gary Thornhill L PTS 6 Liverpool
29.01.00 Bradley Pryce L PTS 4 Manchester
19.02.00 Gavin Rees L PTS 4 Dagenham
29.02.00 Tony Mulholland L PTS 4 Widnes
20.03.00 Carl Greaves L PTS 4 Mansfield
27.03.00 James Rooney L PTS 4 Barnsley
08.04.00 Delroy Pryce L PTS 4 Bethnal Green
17.04.00 Franny Hogg L PTS 8 Glasgow
11.05.00 Craig Spacie L PTS 4 Newark
25.05.00 Jimmy Phelan DREW 6 Hull
19.06.00 Delroy Pryce L PTS 4 Burton
01.07.00 Richard Evatt L PTS 4 Manchester
16.09.00 Lee Meager L PTS 4 Bethnal Green
23.09.00 Gavin Rees L PTS 4 Bethnal Green
02.10.00 Brian Carr L PTS 4 Glasgow
14.10.00 Gareth Jordan L PTS 4 Wembley
13.11.00 Kevin Lear L PTS 6 Bethnal Green
24.11.00 Lee Williamson L PTS 6 Hull
09.12.00 Leo O'Reilly L PTS 4 Southwark
15.01.01 Eddie Nevins L PTS 4 Manchester
23.01.01 David Burke L PTS 4 Crawley
31.01.01 Tony Montana L PTS 6 Piccadilly
19.02.01 Kevin England W PTS 6 Glasgow
12.03.01 Carl Allen L PTS 6 Birmingham
19.03.01 Duncan Armstrong L PTS 6 Glasgow
27.03.01 Carl Allen L PTS 8 Brierley Hill
05.05.01 Danny Hunt L PTS 4 Edmonton
09.06.01 Gary Thornhill L PTS 4 Bethnal Green
21.07.01 Scott Miller L PTS 4 Sheffield
28.07.01 Kevin Lear L PTS 4 Wembley
25.09.01 Ricky Eccleston L PTS 4 Liverpool
07.10.01 Nigel Senior L PTS 6 Wolverhampton
31.10.01 Woody Greenaway L PTS 6 Birmingham
16.11.01 Jimmy Beech L PTS 6 West Bromwich
01.12.01 Chill John L PTS 4 Bethnal Green
09.12.01 Nigel Senior W PTS 6 Shaw
26.01.02 Scott Lawton L PTS 4 Bethnal Green
09.02.02 Sam Gorman L PTS 6 Coventry
23.02.02 Alex Moon L PTS 4 Nottingham
04.03.02 Leo Turner L PTS 6 Bradford
11.03.02 Martin Watson L PTS 4 Glasgow
26.04.02 Scott Lawton L PTS 4 Coventry
10.05.02 Lee Meager L PTS 6 Bethnal Green
08.06.02 Bradley Pryce L RSC 1 Renfrew
20.07.02 Jeff Thomas L PTS 4 Bethnal Green
23.08.02 Ben Hudson DREW 4 Bethnal Green
06.09.02 Dave Stewart L PTS 6 Bethnal Green
14.09.02 Peter McDonagh L PTS 4 Bethnal Green
20.10.02 James Paisley L PTS 4 Southwark
12.11.02 Martin Hardcastle DREW 6 Leeds
29.11.02 Daniel Thorpe L PTS 6 Hull
09.12.02 Nicky Leech L PTS 6 Nottingham
16.12.02 Joel Viney L PTS 6 Cleethorpes
28.01.03 Billy Corcoran L PTS 6 Nottingham
08.02.03 Colin Toohey L PTS 6 Liverpool
15.02.03 Terry Fletcher L PTS 4 Wembley
22.02.03 Dean Lambert L PTS 4 Huddersfield
05.03.03 Billy Corcoran L PTS 6 Bethnal Green
18.03.03 Nathan Ward L PTS 4 Reading
05.04.03 Baz Carey L PTS 4 Manchester
15.05.03 Mike Harrington W PTS 4 Clevedon
27.05.03 Dave Stewart L PTS 6 Bethnal Green
07.06.03 Rimell Taylor DREW 6 Coventry
12.07.03 George Telfer L PTS 4 Renfrew
22.07.03 Chas Symonds L PTS 4 Bethnal Green
01.08.03 Jas Malik W PTS 4 Bethnal Green
06.09.03 John Murray L PTS 4 Huddersfield
13.09.03 Isaac Ward L PTS 6 Wakefield
25.09.03 Gary Woolcombe L PTS 6 Bethnal Green
06.10.03 Scott Haywood L PTS 6 Barnsley
20.10.03 Joel Viney W PTS 6 Bradford
29.10.03 David Kehoe L PTS 6 Leicester Square

07.11.03 Femi Fehintola L PTS 6 Sheffield
14.11.03 Dave Stewart L PTS 4 Bethnal Green
21.11.03 Henry Castle L PTS 4 Millwall
28.11.03 Lee Meager L PTS 4 Derby
13.12.03 Derry Matthews L PTS 4 Manchester
21.12.03 Daniel Thorpe L PTS 6 Bolton
16.01.04 Nadeem Siddique L PTS 4 Bradford
16.02.04 Scott Haywood L PTS 6 Scunthorpe
29.02.04 Gary O'Connor L PTS 6 Shaw
03.04.04 Steve Bell L PTS 4 Manchester
16.04.04 Isaac Ward L PTS 6 Hartlepool
23.04.04 Colin Bain L PTS 6 Glasgow
06.05.04 Amir Ali L PTS 4 Barnsley
13.05.04 Lee Beavis L PTS 4 Bethnal Green
04.06.04 Tristan Davies L PTS 6 Dudley
03.07.04 Barrie Jones L PTS 4 Newport
03.09.04 Stefy Bull L PTS 6 Doncaster
10.09.04 Tiger Matthews L PTS 4 Liverpool
17.09.04 Kell Brook L PTS 6 Sheffield
24.09.04 Ceri Hall L PTS 6 Dublin
11.10.04 Darren Johnstone L PTS 6 Glasgow
22.10.04 Jonathan Whiteman L PTS 6 Mansfield
29.10.04 Colin Bain L PTS 4 Renfrew
09.11.04 Tom Hogan L PTS 6 Leeds
21.11.04 Chris McDonagh L PTS 4 Bracknell
10.12.04 Craig Johnson L PTS 6 Mansfield
17.12.04 Steve Mullin L PTS 4 Liverpool
12.02.05 Jay Morris L PTS 6 Portsmouth
21.02.05 Stuart Green L PTS 6 Glasgow
05.03.05 Paul Buckley L PTS 6 Southwark
23.03.05 Ryan Barrett L PTS 6 Leicester Square
09.04.05 Nadeem Siddique L PTS 6 Norwich
25.04.05 Jimmy Gilhaney L PTS 6 Glasgow
14.05.05 James Gorman L PTS 6 Dublin
27.05.05 Alan Temple L PTS 4 Spennymoor
04.06.05 Patrick Hyland L PTS 4 Dublin
25.06.05 Sean Hughes DREW 6 Wakefield
24.07.05 Scott Lawton L PTS 6 Sheffield
03.09.05 Jackson Williams L PTS 6 Norwich
19.09.05 Ryan Brawley L PTS 6 Glasgow
14.10.05 Jimmy Gilhaney L PTS 6 Motherwell
23.11.05 Shane Watson L PTS 6 Mayfair
02.12.05 Billy Corcoran L PTS 4 Nottingham
14.12.05 Stephen Burke L PTS 4 Blackpool
23.01.06 David Appleby L PTS 6 Glasgow
02.02.06 Michael Grant L PTS 4 Holborn
18.02.06 Jimmy Doherty L PTS 6 Stoke
04.03.06 Steve Bell L PTS 4 Manchester
13.03.06 Gary McArthur L PTS 6 Glasgow
25.03.06 Brian Murphy L PTS 6 Irvine
02.04.06 Barry Downes L PTS 6 Shaw
13.04.06 Paul Newby L PTS 4 Leeds
28.04.06 Gary O'Connor L PTS 6 Manchester
06.05.06 Ian Clyde L PTS 6 Stoke
20.05.06 Stephen Haughian L PTS 4 Belfast
09.06.06 Wez Miller L PTS 6 Doncaster
18.06.06 James Brown L PTS 6 Manchester
29.06.06 Rob Hunt L PTS 6 Dudley
Career: 270 contests, won 31, drew 11, lost 228.

(Andrew) Stefy Bull (Bullcroft)

Doncaster. *Born* Doncaster, 10 May, 1977
WBF Inter-Continental Lightweight
Champion. Central Area Lightweight
Champion. Former Undefeated Central
Area Featherweight Champion. Ht. 5'10"
Manager J. Rushton

30.06.95 Andy Roberts W PTS 4 Doncaster
11.10.95 Michael Edwards W PTS 6 Stoke
18.10.95 Alan Hagan W RSC 1 Batley
28.11.95 Kevin Sheil W PTS 6 Wolverhampton
26.01.96 Robert Grubb W PTS 6 Doncaster

12.09.96 Benny Jones W PTS 6 Doncaster
15.10.96 Kevin Sheil DREW 6 Wolverhampton
24.10.96 Graham McGrath W PTS 6 Birmingham
17.12.96 Robert Braddock W RSC 4 Doncaster
 *(Vacant Central Area Featherweight
 Title)*
10.07.97 Carl Greaves W PTS 6 Doncaster
11.10.97 Dean Pithie L RSC 11 Sheffield
 *(Vacant WBO Inter-Continental
 S. Featherweight Title)*
19.03.98 Chris Lyons W RSC 4 Doncaster
08.04.98 Alex Moon L RSC 3 Liverpool
31.07.99 Jason Dee L RSC 4 Carlisle
09.05.03 Joel Viney W RTD 3 Doncaster
02.06.03 Jason Nesbitt W PTS 6 Cleethorpes
05.09.03 Dave Hinds W PTS 6 Doncaster
20.02.04 Anthony Christopher W PTS 6 Doncaster
07.05.04 Daniel Thorpe W PTS 10 Doncaster
 *(Central Area Lightweight Title
 Challenge)*
03.09.04 Pete Buckley W PTS 6 Doncaster
29.10.04 Haroon Din W RSC 2 Doncaster
 *(Central Area Lightweight Title
 Defence)*
04.02.05 Gwyn Wale W PTS 10 Doncaster
 *(Central Area Lightweight Title
 Defence)*
11.03.05 Jimmy Beech W PTS 4 Doncaster
20.05.05 Billy Smith W PTS 6 Doncaster
16.09.05 Carl Allen W PTS 10 Doncaster
 *(Vacant WBF Inter-Continental
 Lightweight Title)*
02.12.05 David Kehoe W PTS 6 Doncaster
03.03.06 Baz Carey W PTS 10 Doncaster
 *(WBF Inter-Continental Lightweight
 Title Defence)*
09.06.06 Scott Lawton L RSC 8 Doncaster
 (Vacant English Lightweight Title)
Career: 28 contests, won 23, drew 1, lost 4.

Craig Bunn

Manchester. *Born* Tameside,1 April, 1986
L.Middleweight. Ht. 6'1"
Manager S. Wood

18.12.05 Gary Round W PTS 6 Bolton
12.02.06 Howard Clarke W PTS 6 Manchester
18.06.06 Ryan Rowlinson W PTS 6 Manchester
Career: 3 contests, won 3.

Stephen Burke　　　　Les Clark

Stephen Burke

Liverpool. *Born* Liverpool, 18 March, 1979
Welterweight. Ht. 5'8"
Manager S. Vaughan

13.05.05 Imad Khamis W RSC 3 Liverpool
14.12.05 Pete Buckley W PTS 4 Blackpool
11.03.06 Chris Brophy W PTS 4 Newport
Career: 3 contests, won 3.

Paul Burns

Uddingston. *Born* Rutherglen, 5 January, 1983
L.Middleweight. Ht. 6'2"
Manager T. Gilmour

06.06.05 Terry Carruthers DREW 6 Glasgow
14.10.05 Surinder Sekhon W PTS 6 Motherwell
21.11.05 Malik Khan W RTD 2 Glasgow
13.03.06 David Kehoe W PTS 6 Glasgow
Career: 4 contests, won 3, drew 1.

Ricky Burns

Coatbridge. *Born* Bellshill, 13 April, 1983
S.Featherweight. Ht. 5'10"
Manager R. Bannan/A. Morrison

20.10.01 Woody Greenaway W PTS 4 Glasgow
15.03.02 Peter Allen W PTS 6 Glasgow
08.06.02 Gary Harrison W RSC 1 Renfrew
06.09.02 Ernie Smith W PTS 6 Glasgow
19.10.02 Neil Murray W RSC 2 Renfrew
08.12.02 No No Junior W PTS 8 Glasgow
08.10.04 Daniel Thorpe W PTS 6 Glasgow
29.10.04 Jeff Thomas W PTS 4 Renfrew
12.12.04 Colin Bain W PTS 6 Glasgow
25.02.05 Graham Earl W PTS 8 Wembley
08.04.05 Buster Dennis W PTS 6 Edinburgh
17.06.05 Haider Ali W PTS 8 Glasgow
23.07.05 Alan Temple W PTS 4 Edinburgh
18.02.06 Alex Arthur L PTS 12 Edinburgh
          *(British, Commonwealth & European
          S.Featherweight Title Challenges)*
01.04.06 Adolph Avadja W RSC 5 Bethnal
          Green
Career: 15 contests, won 14, lost 1.

Chris Burton

Darlington. *Born* Darlington, 27 February, 1981
Heavyweight. Ht. 6'5"
Manager D. Garside

02.06.05 David Ingleby W RSC 3 Yarm
03.03.06 Istvan Kecskes W PTS 4 Hartlepool
28.04.06 Istvan Kecskes W PTS 4 Hartlepool
23.06.06 Simon Goodwin W RSC 3 Blackpool
Career: 4 contests, won 4.

Robert Burton

Barnsley. *Born* Barnsley, 1 April, 1971
L.Heavyweight. Former Central Area
L.Middleweight Champion. Former Central
Area Welterweight Champion. Ht. 5'9"
Manager Self

05.02.01 Gavin Pearson W RSC 3 Bradford
23.02.01 Scott Millar W CO 5 Irvine
20.03.01 Peter Dunn W PTS 6 Leeds
08.05.01 Arv Mittoo W PTS 4 Barnsley
10.06.01 Martyn Bailey DREW 6 Ellesmere Port
08.10.01 Gavin Pearson W RSC 2 Barnsley
16.11.01 Martyn Bailey DREW 4 Preston
24.11.01 Peter Dunn L PTS 6 Wakefield

28.01.02 Peter Dunn W RSC 8 Barnsley
          *(Vacant Central Area Welterweight
          Title)*
23.08.02 David Walker L RSC 2 Bethnal Green
19.10.02 John Humphrey L RTD 4 Norwich
09.02.03 Donovan Smillie L PTS 6 Bradford
24.03.03 Andy Halder L PTS 6 Barnsley
31.05.03 David Keir W RSC 9 Barnsley
          *(Central Area Welterweight Title
          Defence)*
01.11.03 Scott Dixon L PTS 6 Glasgow
08.12.03 Jed Tytler W PTS 6 Barnsley
10.02.04 Paul Lomax W PTS 6 Barnsley
06.05.04 Matthew Hatton L PTS 10 Barnsley
          *(Central Area Welterweight Title
          Defence)*
08.06.04 Lee Murtagh W CO 3 Sheffield
          *(Vacant Central Area L.Middleweight
          Title)*
12.11.04 Matthew Hatton L PTS 10 Halifax
          *(Central Area L.Middleweight Title
          Defence)*
11.02.05 Paul Smith L CO 1 Manchester
22.04.05 John Marshall L RTD 4 Barnsley
23.07.05 Craig Lynch L PTS 4 Edinburgh
30.09.05 Jonjo Finnegan DREW 6 Burton
22.10.05 Richard Mazurek W PTS 6 Coventry
25.11.05 Matthew Hough L PTS 4 Walsall
12.12.05 Cello Renda L CO 1 Peterborough
11.03.06 Matthew Hall L CO 1 Newport
13.04.06 Donovan Smillie DREW 6 Leeds
29.04.06 Craig Lynch L PTS 4 Edinburgh

01.06.06 Ryan Rowlinson W PTS 4 Barnsley
22.06.06 Jon Ibbotson DREW 6 Sheffield
Career: 32 contests, won 12, drew 5, lost 15.

Danny Butler

Bristol. *Born* Bristol, 10 November, 1987
Middleweight. Ht. 5'10½"
Manager T. Woodward

25.02.06 Magic Kidem W PTS 6 Bristol
07.04.06 Tommy Jones W PTS 4 Bristol
21.05.06 Martin Sweeney W PTS 6 Bristol
Career: 3 contests, won 3.

Paul Butlin

Oakham. *Born* Oakham, 16 March, 1976
Heavyweight. Ht. 6'1½"
Manager Self

05.10.02 Dave Clarke W PTS 4 Coventry
16.11.02 Gary Williams W RSC 1 Coventry
09.12.02 Slick Miller W PTS 6 Nottingham
08.03.03 Dave Clarke W PTS 6 Coventry
19.04.03 Paul Buttery L RSC 3 Liverpool
27.04.04 Ebrima Secka W PTS 6 Leeds
26.09.04 Lee Mountford W PTS 6 Stoke
06.12.04 David Ingleby W CO 5 Leicester
30.04.05 David Ingleby L PTS 6 Coventry
25.06.05 Mal Rice W PTS 4 Melton Mowbray
22.10.05 Jason Callum W PTS 4 Coventry
18.03.06 David Ingleby W PTS 6 Coventry
Career: 12 contests, won 10, lost 2.

Ricky Burns   Les Clark

Daniel Cadman

Waltham Abbey. *Born* Harlow, 25 June, 1980
S.Middleweight. Ht. 5'10"
Manager Self

25.07.03	Leigh Wicks W PTS 4 Norwich
04.10.03	Patrick Cito W PTS 6 Muswell Hill
28.11.03	Harry Butler W PTS 4 Derby
30.01.04	Mike Duffield W RSC 1 Dagenham
02.06.04	Joel Ani W CO 2 Nottingham
12.11.04	Howard Clarke W PTS 6 Wembley
26.03.05	Lee Williamson W PTS 4 Hackney
10.04.05	Howard Clarke W PTS 4 Brentwood
16.07.05	Michael Banbula W PTS 6 Chigwell
02.12.05	Jason Collins W PTS 6 Nottingham
20.01.06	Magid Ben Driss L RSC 2 Bethnal Green
12.05.06	Paul David L RSC 6 Bethnal Green

Career: 12 contests, won 10, lost 2.

Marc Callaghan

Barking. *Born* Barking, 13 November, 1977
English S.Bantamweight Champion. Former Undefeated Southern Area S.Bantamweight Champion. Ht. 5'6"
Manager Self

08.09.98	Kevin Sheil W PTS 4 Bethnal Green
31.10.98	Nicky Wilders W RSC 1 Southend
12.01.99	Nicky Wilders W RTD 2 Bethnal Green
12.03.99	Peter Allen W PTS 4 Bethnal Green
25.05.99	Simon Chambers L RSC 1 Mayfair
16.10.99	Nigel Leake W PTS 4 Bethnal Green
20.12.99	Marc Smith W PTS 4 Bethnal Green
05.02.00	Steve Brook W RSC 2 Bethnal Green
01.04.00	John Barnes W PTS 4 Bethnal Green
19.08.00	Anthony Hanna W PTS 4 Brentwood
09.10.00	Jamie McKeever L PTS 6 Liverpool
04.11.00	Nigel Senior W RSC 4 Bethnal Green
03.03.01	Anthony Hanna W PTS 6 Wembley
26.05.01	Roy Rutherford L RSC 3 Bethnal Green
01.12.01	Nigel Senior L CO 1 Bethnal Green
26.01.02	Richmond Asante W PTS 4 Dagenham
18.03.02	Michael Hunter DREW 4 Crawley
11.05.02	Andrew Ferrans W PTS 6 Dagenham
21.09.02	Steve Gethin W PTS 6 Brentwood
07.12.02	Stevie Quinn L PTS 4 Brentwood
08.03.03	Dazzo Williams L PTS 8 Bethnal Green
05.07.03	Mark Payne L PTS 6 Brentwood
08.05.04	Baz Carey W PTS 6 Dagenham
27.05.04	Steve Gethin W PTS 6 Huddersfield
20.09.04	John Simpson L PTS 8 Glasgow
19.11.04	Michael Hunter L RSC 10 Hartlepool *(British S.Bantamweight Title Challenge)*
16.06.05	Ian Napa W PTS 10 Dagenham *(Vacant Southern Area S.Bantamweight Title)*
18.11.05	Jackson Asiku L RSC 1 Dagenham *(Vacant Commonwealth Featherweight Title)*
03.03.06	Sean Hughes W PTS 10 Hartlepool *(Vacant English S.Bantamweight Title)*

Career: 29 contests, won 18, drew 1, lost 10.

Jason Callum

Coventry. *Born* Coventry, 5 April, 1977
Heavyweight. Ht. 6'3"
Manager Self

05.04.03	Tony Booth W PTS 6 Coventry
15.11.03	Slick Miller W PTS 4 Coventry
01.05.04	David Ingleby W PTS 6 Coventry
06.12.04	Scott Lansdowne L CO 1 Leicester
22.10.05	Paul Butlin L PTS 4 Coventry
11.12.05	Sam Sexton L PTS 6 Norwich
17.03.06	Ian Millarvie L CO 3 Kirkcaldy

Career: 7 contests, won 3, lost 4.

Joe Calzaghe

Newbridge. *Born* Hammersmith, 23 March, 1972
WBO & IBF S.Middleweight Champion. Former Undefeated British S. Middleweight Champion. Ht. 5'11"
Manager F. Warren

01.10.93	Paul Hanlon W RSC 1 Cardiff
10.11.93	Stinger Mason W RSC 1 Watford
16.12.93	Spencer Alton W RSC 2 Newport
22.01.94	Martin Rosamond W RSC 1 Cardiff
01.03.94	Darren Littlewood W RSC 1 Dudley
04.06.94	Karl Barwise W RSC 1 Cardiff
01.10.94	Mark Dawson W RSC 1 Cardiff
30.11.94	Trevor Ambrose W RSC 2 Wolverhampton
14.02.95	Frank Minton W CO 1 Bethnal Green
22.02.95	Bobbi Joe Edwards W PTS 8 Telford
19.05.95	Robert Curry W RSC 1 Southwark
08.07.95	Tyrone Jackson W RSC 4 York
30.09.95	Nick Manners W RSC 4 Basildon
28.10.95	Stephen Wilson W RSC 8 Kensington *(Vacant British S. Middleweight Title)*
13.02.96	Guy Stanford W RSC 1 Cardiff
13.03.96	Anthony Brooks W RSC 2 Wembley
20.04.96	Mark Delaney W RSC 5 Brentwood *(British S. Middleweight Title Defence)*
04.05.96	Warren Stowe W RTD 2 Dagenham
15.05.96	Pat Lawlor W RSC 2 Cardiff
21.01.97	Carlos Christie W CO 2 Bristol
22.03.97	Tyler Hughes W CO 1 Wythenshawe
05.06.97	Luciano Torres W RSC 3 Bristol
11.10.97	Chris Eubank W PTS 12 Sheffield *(Vacant WBO S. Middleweight Title)*
24.01.98	Branco Sobot W RSC 3 Cardiff *(WBO S. Middleweight Title Defence)*
25.04.98	Juan Carlos Gimenez W RTD 9 Cardiff *(WBO S. Middleweight Title Defence)*
13.02.99	Robin Reid W PTS 12 Newcastle *(WBO S. Middleweight Title Defence)*
05.06.99	Rick Thornberry W PTS 12 Cardiff *(WBO S. Middleweight Title Defence)*
29.01.00	David Starie W PTS 12 Manchester *(WBO S, Middleweight Title Defence)*
12.08.00	Omar Sheika W RSC 5 Wembley *(WBO S.Middleweight Title Defence)*
16.12.00	Richie Woodhall W RSC 10 Sheffield *(WBO S. Middleweight Title Defence)*
28.04.01	Mario Veit W RSC 1 Cardiff *(WBO S. Middleweight Title Defence)*
13.10.01	Will McIntyre W RSC 4 Copenhagen, Denmark *(WBO S. Middleweight Title Defence)*
20.04.02	Charles Brewer W PTS 12 Cardiff *(WBO S. Middleweight Title Defence)*
17.08.02	Miguel Jimenez W PTS 12 Cardiff *(WBO S. Middleweight Title Defence)*
14.12.02	Tocker Pudwill W RSC 2 Newcastle *(WBO S. Middleweight Title Defence)*
28.06.03	Byron Mitchell W RSC 2 Cardiff *(WBO S.Middleweight Title Defence)*
21.02.04	Mger Mkrtchian W RSC 7 Cardiff *(WBO S.Middleweight Title Defence)*
22.10.04	Kabary Salem W PTS 12 Edinburgh *(WBO S.Middleweight Title Defence)*
07.05.05	Mario Veit W RSC 6 Braunschweig, Germany *(WBO S.Middleweight Title Defence)*
10.09.05	Evans Ashira W PTS 12 Cardiff *(WBO S.Middleweight Title Defence)*
04.03.06	Jeff Lacy W PTS 12 Manchester *(IBF S.Middleweight Title Challenge. WBO S.Middleweight Title Defence)*

Career: 41 contests, won 41.

Alex Carey

Sheffield. *Born* Trowbridge, 25 March, 1976
S.Middleweight. Ht. 5'10"
Manager I. Pauly

14.03.97	Pat Durkin W RSC 6 Hull
16.05.97	Kevin Burton L PTS 6 Hull
09.06.97	Carlton Williams DREW 6 Birmingham
16.10.05	Jimi Hendricks W PTS 6 Peterborough

Career: 4 contests, won 2, drew 1, lost 1.

(Barry) Baz Carey

Coventry. *Born* Coventry, 11 March, 1971
Welterweight. Ht. 5'4½"
Manager P. Carpenter

19.12.01	J.J. Moore L PTS 4 Coventry
18.01.02	J.J. Moore DREW 4 Coventry
25.02.02	Chris McDonagh L PTS 6 Slough
19.03.02	Ilias Miah W PTS 6 Slough
21.09.02	Jackson Williams L PTS 6 Norwich
10.10.02	Dean Scott W RSC 2 Stoke
19.10.02	Lee McAllister L PTS 4 Renfrew
21.11.02	Chris Hooper L RTD 3 Hull
22.03.03	Dave Hinds W PTS 6 Coventry
05.04.03	Pete Buckley W PTS 4 Manchester
12.05.03	Matthew Marshall L PTS 6 Southampton
07.06.03	Joel Viney W PTS 6 Coventry
26.07.03	Andrew Ferrans DREW 4 Plymouth
13.09.03	Paul McIlwaine W RTD 2 Coventry
12.10.03	Daniel Thorpe DREW 6 Sheffield
08.11.03	Carl Allen L RSC 2 Coventry
15.03.04	Andrew Ferrans L PTS 10 Glasgow *(Vacant British Masters S.Featherweight Title)*
17.04.04	Michael Kelly L PTS 4 Belfast
26.04.04	Rendall Munroe L PTS 6 Cleethorpes
08.05.04	Marc Callaghan L PTS 6 Dagenham
06.11.04	Daniel Thorpe L PTS 6 Coventry
20.11.04	Dave Hinds W RSC 4 Coventry
17.12.04	Kristian Laight W PTS 6 Coventry
30.04.05	Billy Smith W PTS 6 Coventry
26.05.05	Daniel Thorpe L PTS 6 Mayfair
10.09.05	Amir Khan L PTS 4 Cardiff
24.09.05	Billy Smith NC 5 Coventry
03.12.05	Billy Smith W PTS 6 Coventry
14.12.05	Jeff Thomas W PTS 6 Blackpool
03.03.06	Stefy Bull L PTS 10 Doncaster *(WBF Inter-Continental Lightweight Title Challenge)*
06.05.06	Scott Lawton L PTS 10 Stoke *(Midlands Area Lightweight Title Challenge)*
01.06.06	Martin Gethin L PTS 4 Birmingham

Career: 32 contests, won 11, drew 3, lost 17, no contest 1.

Terry Carruthers

Birmingham. *Born* Birmingham, 4
February, 1986
L. Welterweight. Ht. 5'8"
Manager Self

21.02.05	Andy Cosnett L PTS 6 Birmingham
06.03.05	Jonathan Whiteman DREW 6 Mansfield
25.04.05	Darren Gethin W RSC 3 Cleethorpes
16.05.05	Andy Cosnett DREW 6 Birmingham
06.06.05	Paul Burns DREW 6 Glasgow
26.06.05	Justin Murphy L RSC 1 Southampton
18.02.06	Danny Johnston W PTS 6 Stoke
11.03.06	Barrie Jones L RSC 1 Newport

Career: 8 contests, won 2, drew 3, lost 3.

Terry Carruthers   Les Clark

Henry Castle

Salisbury. *Born* Southampton, 7 February,
1979
Lightweight. Ht. 5'6³/₄"
Manager Self

29.01.01	Jason Nesbitt W CO 6 Peterborough
26.03.01	Eddie Nevins W RSC 2 Peterborough
23.11.01	Jimmy Beech W PTS 4 Bethnal Green
11.03.02	David Lowry W RSC 1 Glasgow
20.04.02	Jason Nesbitt W PTS 4 Cardiff
25.05.02	Jimmy Beech W PTS 4 Portsmouth
17.08.02	Joel Viney W RSC 1 Cardiff
23.11.02	John Mackay L RTD 8 Derby
29.03.03	Jus Wallie L RSC 2 Portsmouth
25.09.03	Mark Alexander W PTS 6 Bethnal Green
21.11.03	Pete Buckley W PTS 4 Millwall
20.02.04	Daleboy Rees W RSC 4 Bethnal Green
26.06.05	Karl Taylor W PTS 6 Southampton
04.12.05	Gareth Couch L PTS 6 Portsmouth

Career: 14 contests, won 11, lost 3.

Stephen Chinnock

Rugeley. *Born* Lichfield, 4 December, 1975
S.Featherweight. Midlands Area
Featherweight Champion. Ht. 5'10"
Manager Self

10.09.00	Neil Read W RSC 5 Walsall
06.11.00	Jason Nesbitt W PTS 6 Wolverhampton
27.11.00	Jason White W PTS 4 Birmingham
20.05.01	Gareth Wiltshaw W PTS 6 Wolverhampton

07.10.01	Kevin Gerowski W PTS 10 Wolverhampton
	(Vacant Midlands Area Featherweight Title)
18.01.02	John Mackay W PTS 4 Coventry
13.04.02	Neil Read W CO 3 Wolverhampton
	(Midlands Area Featherweight Title Defence)
08.09.02	Nigel Senior W PTS 6 Wolverhampton
17.05.03	Dazzo Williams L PTS 10 Liverpool
	(Elim. British Featherweight Title)
20.09.03	Mickey Bowden W PTS 8 Nottingham
14.02.04	Roy Rutherford L RSC 4 Nottingham
	(Vacant English S.Featherweight Title)
26.02.05	Andrew Ferrans L RTD 5 Burton
30.09.05	Lance Verallo W PTS 4 Burton
28.01.06	Derry Matthews L RTD 6 Nottingham
	(Vacant English Featherweight Title)

Career: 14 contests, won 10, lost 4.

Karl Chiverton

Mansfield. *Born* Sutton in Ashfield, 1
March, 1986
Middleweight. Ht. 5'9³/₄"
Manager S. Calow

18.09.04	Karl Taylor W PTS 6 Newark
10.12.04	Cafu Santos L RSC 4 Mansfield
13.05.06	Mark Wall W PTS 6 Sutton in Ashfield

Career: 3 contests, won 2, lost 1.

Anthony Christopher

Aberystwyth. *Born* Aberystwyth, 18
August, 1981
Welterweight. Ht. 5'8¹/₄"
Manager Self

23.09.01	Arv Mittoo DREW 6 Shaw
29.09.02	Ernie Smith W PTS 6 Shrewsbury
03.12.02	Ernie Smith L PTS 6 Shrewsbury
23.02.03	Dean Larter L PTS 6 Aberystwyth
20.02.04	Stefy Bull L PTS 6 Doncaster
06.03.04	Gary Young L CO 1 Renfrew
08.05.05	Dwayne Hill L PTS 6 Sheffield
20.06.05	Ryan Barrett L RSC 1 Longford
01.10.05	Jeff Thomas L PTS 6 Wigan
24.10.05	Jimmy Gilhaney L PTS 6 Glasgow
04.11.05	Peter McDonagh L PTS 4 Bethnal Green
12.12.05	Gary Coombes W RSC 2 Birmingham
10.02.06	Garry Buckland L RSC 4 Plymouth
07.04.06	Shane Watson L RSC 1 Longford
20.05.06	Jason Nesbitt L RSC 4 Bristol

Career: 15 contests, won 2, drew 1, lost 12.

Marco Cittadini

Glasgow. *Born* Glasgow, 12 September,
1977
L.Welterweight. Ht. 5'7³/₄"
Manager R. Bannan

17.06.05	Barrie Jones L RSC 2 Glasgow
22.04.06	Mark Bett DREW 6 Glasgow

Career: 2 contests, drew 1, lost 1.

Dave Clarke

Blackpool. *Born* Dover, 20 June, 1976
Heavyweight. Ht. 6'1"
Manager W. Barker

22.11.01	Roman Greenberg L RSC 5 Paddington
11.02.02	Colin Kenna L RSC 4 Southampton
15.03.02	Shaun Bowes L PTS 6 Spennymoor

24.03.02	Tommy Eastwood L PTS 6 Streatham
11.05.02	Ivan Botton L PTS 6 Newark
03.06.02	Tony Moran L PTS 6 Glasgow
25.06.02	Carl Wright L PTS 6 Rugby
20.07.02	Matt Legg L RSC 2 Bethnal Green
05.10.02	Paul Butlin L PTS 4 Coventry
12.10.02	Enzo Maccarinelli L RSC 2 Bethnal Green
20.11.02	Costi Marin W RSC 2 Leeds
30.11.02	Ahmad Cheleh W RSC 1 Liverpool
05.12.02	Roman Greenberg L RSC 1 Sheffield
08.01.03	Scott Gammer L PTS 4 Aberdare
08.03.03	Paul Butlin L PTS 6 Coventry
17.03.03	Costi Marin W PTS 6 Glasgow
24.03.03	Neil Dawson L PTS 4 Barnsley
13.04.03	Oneal Murray W PTS 4 Streatham
28.04.03	Shane Woollas L PTS 6 Cleethorpes
15.05.03	Matt Skelton L RSC 1 Mayfair
28.06.03	Scott Gammer L RSC 1 Cardiff
06.09.03	Carl Baker L RSC 1 Aberdeen
06.10.03	Neil Dawson L PTS 6 Barnsley
01.12.03	Lee Mountford L PTS 6 Bradford
24.01.04	Augustin N'Gou L PTS 6 Wembley
16.02.04	Chris Woollas L PTS 6 Scunthorpe
12.03.04	Coleman Barrett L PTS 6 Nottingham
25.04.04	Luke Simpkin L RSC 2 Nottingham
07.06.04	Dave McKenna L PTS 6 Glasgow
20.09.04	David Ingleby L RTD 5 Glasgow
04.06.05	Darren Morgan L RSC 1 Manchester
25.09.05	Lee Mountford L PTS 4 Leeds
25.11.05	Tony Booth DREW 6 Hull
04.12.05	Billy Bessey L PTS 6 Portsmouth

Career: 34 contests, won 4, drew 1, lost 29.

Howard Clarke

Warley. *Born* London, 23 September, 1967
S.Middleweight. Ht. 5'10"
Manager Self

15.10.91	Chris Mylan W PTS 4 Dudley
09.12.91	Claude Rossi W RSC 3 Brierley Hill
04.02.92	Julian Eavis W PTS 4 Alfreton
03.03.92	Dave Andrews W RSC 3 Cradley Heath
21.05.92	Richard O'Brien W CO 1 Cradley Heath
29.09.92	Paul King W PTS 6 Stoke
27.10.92	Gordon Blair L RSC 4 Cradley Heath
16.03.93	Paul King W PTS 6 Edgbaston
07.06.93	Dean Bramhald W RTD 2 Walsall
29.06.93	Paul King W PTS 6 Edgbaston
06.10.93	Julian Eavis L PTS 8 Solihull
30.11.93	Julian Eavis W PTS 8 Wolverhampton
08.02.94	Nigel Bradley W RTD 6 Wolverhampton
18.04.94	Andy Peach W PTS 6 Walsall
28.06.94	Dennis Berry L RSC 3 Edgbaston
12.10.94	Julian Eavis W PTS 8 Stoke
25.10.94	Andy Peach W RSC 3 Edgbaston
02.11.94	Julian Eavis W PTS 8 Birmingham
29.11.94	Julian Eavis W PTS 6 Cannock
07.12.94	Peter Reid W PTS 8 Stoke
25.01.95	Dennis Berry L PTS 8 Stoke
08.03.95	Andrew Jervis W PTS 6 Solihull
11.05.95	David Bain W RSC 1 Dudley
20.09.95	Michael Smyth DREW 6 Ystrad
02.10.95	Nigel Wenton L PTS 6 Mayfair
02.12.96	Martin Smith L PTS 8 Birmingham
29.01.97	Gary Beardsley W PTS 6 Stoke
11.02.97	Prince Kasi Kaihau L RSC 4 Wolverhampton
19.03.97	Mark Cichocki W PTS 6 Stoke
15.04.97	Prince Kasi Kaihau W PTS 6 Edgbaston

30.04.97	Allan Gray W PTS 8 Acton
22.05.97	Michael Alexander W RSC 3 Solihull
21.06.97	Paul Samuels L PTS 8 Cardiff
09.09.97	Harry Dhami L PTS 8 Bethnal Green
05.11.97	Andras Galfi W PTS 8 Tenerife
27.01.98	Mack Razor L PTS 8 Hammanskraal, South Africa
23.03.98	Lindon Scarlett DREW 6 Crystal Palace
18.07.98	Jason Papillion W PTS 8 Sheffield
13.03.99	Fernando Vargas L RSC 4 NYC, New York, USA*
	(IBF L. Middleweight Title Challenge)
05.11.99	Michael Rask L PTS 12 Aalberg, Denmark
	(WBA Inter-Continental L. Middleweight Title Challenge)
29.05.00	Anthony Farnell L PTS 12 Manchester
	(WBO Inter-Continental L. Middleweight Title Challenge)
12.08.00	Takaloo L PTS 12 Wembley
	(Vacant IBF Inter-Continental L.Middleweight Title)
04.11.00	Richard Williams L CO 4 Bethnal Green
16.12.00	Ryan Rhodes L PTS 6 Sheffield
03.02.01	Michael Jones L PTS 4 Manchester
26.02.01	Jawaid Khaliq L PTS 6 Nottingham
07.04.01	Gary Lockett L RSC 2 Wembley
06.05.01	Ian Cooper L PTS 6 Hartlepool
04.06.01	James Docherty L PTS 6 Hartlepool
14.07.01	Gary Lockett L CO 1 Wembley
15.09.01	Thomas McDonagh L PTS 6 Manchester
10.11.01	Ossie Duran L PTS 6 Wembley
26.11.01	Wayne Pinder L PTS 6 Manchester
16.12.01	Erik Teymour L PTS 6 Southwark
27.01.02	Paul Samuels L PTS 6 Streatham
03.02.02	Lee Murtagh NC 2 Shaw
20.04.01	Wayne Elcock L PTS 4 Cardiff
25.05.02	Ross Minter W RSC 2 Portsmouth
08.06.02	Alexander Vetoux L RSC 4 Renfrew
27.07.02	Mihaly Kotai L RSC 1 Nottingham
08.12.02	Matthew Tait L PTS 6 Bethnal Green
21.12.02	Matthew Thirlwall L PTS 6 Dagenham
25.01.03	Paul Samuels L PTS 6 Bridgend
08.02.03	Michael Jones L PTS 6 Liverpool
05.03.03	Gilbert Eastman L PTS 6 Bethnal Green
05.04.03	Paul Smith L PTS 4 Manchester
21.06.03	Wayne Pinder L PTS 4 Manchester
01.08.03	Arthur Shekhmurzov L PTS 6 Bethnal Green
17.10.03	Scott Dixon L PTS 6 Glasgow
25.10.03	Lawrence Murphy L PTS 6 Edinburgh
14.11.03	Sonny Pollard L PTS 6 Hull
07.02.04	Wayne Alexander L RSC 2 Bethnal Green
03.04.04	Paul Smith L PTS 4 Manchester
10.04.04	Wayne Pinder L PTS 4 Manchester
08.05.04	Allan Foster L PTS 4 Dagenham
04.06.04	Andrew Facey L PTS 6 Hull
17.06.04	Patrick J. Maxwell L RSC 1 Sheffield
24.09.04	Darren Barker L PTS 6 Nottingham
01.10.04	Matthew Hall L RSC 5 Manchester
12.11.04	Daniel Cadman L PTS 6 Wembley
20.11.04	Jason Collins L DIS 3 Coventry
10.12.04	Anthony Small L PTS 4 Sheffield
17.12.04	Paul Smith L CO 1 Liverpool
04.02.05	Jason Rushton L PTS 4 Doncaster
12.02.05	Gary Woolcombe L PTS 6 Portsmouth
20.02.05	Michael Monaghan L PTS 6 Sheffield
06.03.05	Lee Blundell L PTS 6 Shaw
23.03.05	Gareth Lawrence L PTS 6 Leicester Square
10.04.05	Daniel Cadman L PTS 4 Brentwood

21.04.05	Darren McDermott L RTD 1 Dudley
27.05.05	Andrew Buchanan L PTS 4 Spennymoor
16.06.05	Anthony Small L PTS 6 Mayfair
09.07.05	David Walker L PTS 4 Nottingham
03.09.05	Danny McIntosh L PTS 4 Norwich
25.09.05	Darren Rhodes L PTS 6 Leeds
16.10.05	Cello Renda L PTS 4 Peterborough
29.10.05	Andrew Facey L PTS 6 Aberdeen
08.11.05	Ady Clegg L PTS 6 Leeds
26.11.05	Stuart Brookes L PTS 6 Sheffield
03.12.05	Andy Halder L PTS 8 Coventry
16.12.05	Matthew Barr L PTS 4 Bracknell
12.02.06	Craig Bunn L PTS 6 Manchester
23.02.06	Danny Thornton L PTS 6 Leeds
02.04.06	Darren Stubbs L PTS 6 Shaw
23.06.06	Cello Renda L PTS 8 Birmingham

Career: 105 contests, won 27, drew 2, lost 75, no contest 1.

Darren Cleary

Salford. *Born* Salford, 28 February, 1980
Featherweight. Ht. 5'5"
Manager Self

27.05.01	Marty Kayes W PTS 4 Manchester
07.07.01	Marty Kayes W PTS 4 Manchester
18.03.02	Jamil Hussain DREW 4 Crawley
27.04.02	Jamil Hussain DREW 4 Huddersfield
11.05.02	Jimbo Rooney W PTS 4 Dagenham
08.07.02	Martin Power L PTS 4 Mayfair
21.12.02	Rocky Dean L PTS 4 Millwall
08.06.03	Shinny Bayaar L RSC 2 Shaw
17.07.03	Martin Power L PTS 6 Dagenham
26.02.04	Mark Moran L PTS 4 Widnes
22.05.04	Mark Moran DREW 4 Widnes
10.12.05	Matthew Marsh L PTS 4 Canning Town
04.03.06	Neil Marston W PTS 4 Manchester

Career: 13 contests, won 4, drew 3, lost 6.

(Adrian) Ady Clegg

Pontefract. *Born* Pontefract, 30 May, 1984
Middleweight. Ht. 5'10"
Manager K. Walker

13.09.03	Brian Coleman W PTS 6 Wakefield
06.10.03	Richard Inquieti W PTS 6 Barnsley
15.03.04	Richard Inquieti W PTS 6 Bradford
19.04.04	Keith Ellwood W CO 5 Glasgow
27.05.04	Jon Harrison L PTS 4 Huddersfield
08.11.05	Howard Clarke W PTS 6 Leeds
28.02.06	Mo W PTS 6 Leeds

Career: 7 contests, won 6, lost 1.

Nathan Cleverly

Cefn Forest. *Born* Caerphilly, 17 February, 1987
Middleweight. Ht. 6'1½"
Manager E. Calzaghe

23.07.05	Ernie Smith W PTS 4 Edinburgh
10.09.05	Darren Gethin W PTS 4 Cardiff
04.12.05	Lance Hall W RSC 3 Telford
04.03.06	Jon Foster W PTS 4 Manchester
01.06.06	Brendan Halford W PTS 4 Barnsley

Career: 5 contests, won 5.

Ian Clyde

Crewe. *Born* Ashington, 25 June, 1972
L.Welterweight. Ht. 6'0"
Manager M. Carney

06.05.06	Pete Buckley W PTS 6 Stoke
18.05.06	Rob Hunt L RSC 1 Walsall

Career: 2 contests, won 1, lost 1.

Dean Cockburn

Doncaster. *Born* Doncaster, 28 March, 1979
Central Area S.Middleweight Champion.
Ht. 5'9½"
Manager J. Rushton

17.09.01	Mark Chesters W RSC 4 Glasgow
17.11.01	Paul Wesley W PTS 4 Glasgow
25.03.02	Paul Buchanan L PTS 6 Sunderland
21.06.02	Darren Stubbs W RSC 1 Leeds
08.10.02	Jason McKay L PTS 4 Glasgow
21.10.02	Tom Cannon DREW 4 Glasgow
01.11.02	Neil Bonner W RSC 2 Preston
20.11.02	Harry Butler W PTS 6 Leeds
17.03.03	Barry Thorogood W PTS 4 Southampton
10.05.03	George Robshaw L PTS 6 Huddersfield
07.05.04	Simeon Cover W PTS 6 Doncaster
14.06.04	Terry Morrill W RTD 4 Cleethorpes
03.09.04	Dean Walker W PTS 10 Doncaster
	(Vacant Central Area S.Middleweight Title)
29.10.04	Lee Nicholson W RSC 2 Doncaster
13.12.04	Lee Nicholson W RSC 3 Cleethorpes
04.02.05	Jason Collins W RSC 8 Doncaster
	(Central Area S.Middleweight Title Defence)
11.03.05	Gary Thompson W RSC 4 Doncaster
20.05.05	Jason Collins W PTS 10 Doncaster
	(Central Area S.Middleweight Title Defence)
16.09.05	Simeon Cover L PTS 10 Doncaster
	(British Masters S.Middleweight Title Challenge)
09.06.06	Paul Bonson W PTS 6 Doncaster

Career: 20 contests, won 15, drew 1, lost 4.

Jason Collins

Walsall. *Born* Walsall, 5 December, 1972
S.Middleweight. Former Undefeated British Masters S. Middleweight Champion.
Ht. 5'9"
Manager B. Ingle

18.02.99	Biagio Falcone L PTS 6 Glasgow
17.03.99	Stuart Harper W RSC 2 Stoke
06.06.99	Jon Foster DREW 6 Nottingham
15.08.99	Matt Galer W PTS 6 Derby
28.10.99	Lee Blundell DREW 6 Burnley
20.11.99	Dennis Berry L PTS 6 Grantham
14.12.99	Jorge Araujo L PTS 6 Telde, Gran Canaria, Spain
15.01.00	Martin Jolley W RTD 1 Doncaster
18.02.00	Oscar Hall DREW 6 West Bromwich
27.02.00	Jawaid Khaliq L PTS 6 Leeds
05.03.00	Wayne Shepherd W PTS 6 Shaw
21.03.00	Sharden Ansoula W PTS 6 Telde, Gran Canaria
21.05.00	Neville Brown L RSC 2 Derby
08.07.00	Darren Rhodes DREW 6 Widnes
04.09.00	Darren Rhodes W PTS 4 Manchester
01.10.00	Juergen Braehmer L CO 1 Hamburg, Germany
13.11.00	Takaloo L RSC 2 Bethnal Green
16.12.00	Louis Swales DREW 4 Sheffield
27.01.01	Spencer Fearon W PTS 4 Bethnal Green
26.03.01	Patrick J. Maxwell W PTS 4 Wembley
20.04.01	Jim Rock L PTS 6 Dublin
08.06.01	Leigh Wicks W PTS 4 Hull
21.06.01	Lester Jacobs L CO 9 Earls Court
	(WBF Middleweight Title Challenge)
07.09.01	Delroy Mellis W DIS 5 Bethnal Green

22.09.01	Ian Cooper L PTS 10 Newcastle	
	(Vacant British Masters Middleweight	
	Title)	
27.10.01	Ryan Rhodes L PTS 4 Manchester	
17.11.01	Gerard Murphy L PTS 4 Glasgow	
08.12.01	Steven Bendall L PTS 12 Dagenham	
	(Vacant WBU Inter-Continental	
	Middleweight Title)	
12.02.02	Delroy Leslie L RSC 1 Bethnal Green	
18.03.02	Andrew Buchanan W PTS 4 Crawley	
01.06.02	Wayne Elcock L RSC 2 Manchester	
17.08.02	Jeff Lacy L CO 1 Cardiff	
21.09.02	Wayne Asker DREW 6 Norwich	
10.10.02	Mike Duffield W PTS 4 Piccadilly	
25.10.02	Matthew Thirlwall L RSC 5 Bethnal	
	Green	
23.11.02	Wayne Elcock L RSC 1 Derby	
24.02.03	Michael Monaghan L PTS 8	
	Birmingham	
20.03.03	Kreshnik Qato L PTS 4 Queensway	
29.03.03	Gary Lockett L CO 1 Portsmouth	
12.05.03	Ojay Abrahams W PTS 10 Birmingham	
	(Vacant British Masters	
	S.Middleweight Title)	
06.06.03	Danny Thornton L PTS 10 Hull	
	(Vacant Central Area Middleweight	
	Title)	
12.07.03	Lawrence Murphy L PTS 4 Renfrew	
25.07.03	Gilbert Eastman L RSC 1 Norwich	
06.10.03	Alan Jones L PTS 8 Birmingham	
28.11.03	Danny Thornton L PTS 10 Hull	
	(Central Area Middleweight Title	
	Challenge)	
25.04.04	Michael Monaghan L PTS 6	
	Nottingham	
10.05.04	Hamed Jamali L PTS 8 Birmingham	
30.05.04	Jonathan O'Brian NC 3 Dublin	
02.06.04	Alan Jones L PTS 6 Hereford	
17.09.04	Andrew Facey L PTS 4 Sheffield	
24.09.04	Matthew Thirlwall W PTS 6	
	Nottingham	
01.10.04	Paul Smith L RSC 1 Manchester	
20.11.04	Howard Clarke W DIS 3 Coventry	
03.12.04	Matthew Hall L PTS 6 Edinburgh	
04.02.05	Dean Cockburn L RSC 8 Doncaster	
	(Central Area S.Middleweight Title	
	Challenge)	
09.04.05	Danny Smith L PTS 6 Norwich	
20.05.05	Dean Cockburn L PTS 10 Doncaster	
	(Central Area S.Middleweight Title	
	Challenge)	
03.09.05	Andrew Facey L PTS 4 Norwich	
23.09.05	Wayne Pinder L PTS 6 Manchester	
01.10.05	Eugenio Monteiro L PTS 6 Wigan	
14.10.05	Geard Ajetovic L RSC 6 Huddersfield	
02.12.05	Daniel Cadman L PTS 6 Nottingham	

Career: 62 contests, won 15, drew 6, lost 40, no
contest 1.

Martin Concepcion

Leicester. *Born* Leicester, 11 August, 1981
Middleweight. Ht. 5'9"
Manager F. Maloney/F. Warren

06.12.03	Danny Gwilym W RSC 2 Cardiff
07.02.04	Jed Tytler W RSC 2 Bethnal Green
27.03.04	Joel Ani W RTD 3 Edinburgh
05.06.04	William Webster W RSC 1 Bethnal
	Green
30.07.04	Brian Coleman W RSC 1 Bethnal
	Green
10.09.04	Rob MacDonald W RSC 2 Bethnal
	Green
12.11.04	Andrew Butlin W RSC 1 Halifax

03.12.04	David Kirk W PTS 4 Edinburgh
11.12.04	Bertrand Souleyras W RSC 1 Canning
	Town
25.02.05	Craig Lynch W PTS 6 Wembley
03.06.05	Ernie Smith W PTS 4 Manchester
16.07.05	Ivor Bonavic L RSC 2 Bolton
28.01.06	Manoocha Salari L RSC 2 Nottingham

Career: 13 contests, won 11, lost 2.

Scott Conway

Derby. *Born* Derby, 27 October, 1979
L.Middleweight. Ht. 6'0"
Manager Self

27.09.04	Rocky Flanagan W RSC 2 Cleethorpes
16.12.04	Tony Randell L PTS 6 Cleethorpes
20.02.05	Sujad Elahi DREW 6 Sheffield
24.04.05	Casey Brooke W PTS 6 Derby
18.06.05	Joe Mitchell L RSC 5 Barnsley
02.09.05	Darren Gethin L RSC 1 Derby
08.12.05	Lance Verallo W PTS 6 Derby
25.03.06	Tye Williams DREW 4 Burton
14.05.06	Tye Williams L RSC 5 Derby

Career: 9 contests, won 3, drew 2, lost 4.

Steve Conway

Dewsbury. *Born* Hartlepool, 6 October,
1977
L.Middleweight. Former IBO
L.Middleweight Champion. Ht. 5'8"
Manager M. Marsden

21.02.96	Robert Grubb W PTS 6 Batley
24.04.96	Ervine Blake W PTS 6 Solihull
20.05.96	Chris Lyons W PTS 6 Cleethorpes
30.05.96	Ram Singh W PTS 6 Lincoln
03.02.97	Jason Squire W PTS 6 Leicester
11.04.97	Marc Smith W PTS 4 Barnsley
22.09.97	Arv Mittoo W PTS 6 Cleethorpes
09.10.97	Arv Mittoo W PTS 6 Leeds
01.11.97	Brian Carr L PTS 6 Glasgow
14.11.97	Brendan Bryce W PTS 6 Mere
04.12.97	Kid McAuley W RSC 5 Doncaster
15.12.97	Nicky Wilders W PTS 6 Cleethorpes
05.03.98	Pete Buckley W PTS 6 Leeds
25.04.98	Dean Phillips W PTS 6 Cardiff
09.05.98	Gary Flear W PTS 4 Sheffield
18.05.98	Brian Coleman W PTS 6 Cleethorpes
05.09.98	Benny Jones W PTS 4 Telford
19.12.98	Gary Thornhill L RSC 9 Liverpool
	(WBO Inter-Continental
	S. Featherweight Title Challenge)
04.06.99	Brian Coleman W PTS 6 Hull
27.09.99	Brian Coleman W PTS 6 Leeds
27.02.00	Chris Price W RTD 3 Leeds
21.03.00	Pedro Miranda L RSC 3 Telde, Gran
	Canaria
15.07.00	Arv Mittoo W PTS 6 Norwich
20.10.00	Junior Witter L RTD 4 Belfast
25.02.01	Ram Singh W RSC 2 Derby
02.06.01	Jimmy Phelan W PTS 7 Wakefield
18.08.01	Keith Jones W PTS 8 Dewsbury
17.11.01	Carl Allen W PTS 8 Dewsbury
27.04.02	Steve Robinson W PTS 8 Huddersfield
05.10.02	Rakheem Mingaleev W RSC 4
	Huddersfield
19.10.02	Alex Arthur L CO 4 Renfrew
	(Vacant British S. Featherweight Title)
05.07.03	Dariusz Snarski W RSC 4 Brentwood
05.10.03	Brian Coleman W PTS 6 Bradford
06.11.03	Yuri Romanov L PTS 8 Dagenham
23.11.03	Gareth Wiltshaw W RSC 5 Rotherham
16.04.04	Norman Dhalie W CO 3 Hartlepool

23.10.04	Ernie Smith W PTS 6 Wakefield
25.09.05	Lee Williamson W PTS 6 Leeds
02.12.05	Mihaly Kotai W PTS 10 Nottingham
03.03.06	Mihaly Kotai W PTS 12 Hartlepool
	(IBO L.Middleweight Title Challenge)
03.06.06	Attila Kovacs L PTS 12 Szolnok,
	Hungary
	(IBO L.Middleweight Title Defence)

Career: 41 contests, won 34, lost 7.

Jason Cook

Maesteg. *Born* Maesteg, 27 February, 1975
L.Welterweight. Former IBO Lightweight
Champion. Former Undefeated Welsh
L.Welterweight Champion. Former
Undefeated European Lightweight
Champion. Ht. 5'9"
Manager Self

11.10.96	Brian Robb W RSC 2 Mayfair
27.11.96	Andrew Reed W RSC 3 Bethnal Green
27.05.97	Marc Smith W PTS 4 Mayfair
31.10.97	Marc Smith W PTS 4 Mayfair
24.01.98	David Kirk W RSC 3 Cardiff
26.05.98	Trevor Smith L RSC 1 Mayfair
23.02.99	Darren Woodley W RSC 4 Cardiff
28.05.99	Dave Hinds W RSC 1 Liverpool
02.10.99	Pete Buckley W PTS 4 Cardiff
11.12.99	Woody Greenaway W RSC 1 Merthyr
	(Vacant Welsh L. Welterweight Title)
26.02.00	Harry Butler W PTS 6 Swansea
17.04.00	Andrei Sinepupov W RTD 3
	Birmingham
12.05.00	Keith Jones W PTS 10 Swansea
	(Welsh L. Welterweight Title Defence)
09.10.00	Assen Vasilev W PTS 6 Liverpool
17.02.01	Dariusz Snarski W PTS 8 Kolbrzeg,
	Poland
18.03.02	Nono Junior W RSC 1 Crawley
11.05.02	Andrei Devyataykin W PTS 6
	Dagenham
29.06.02	Viktor Baranov W PTS 6 Brentwood
03.08.02	Sandro Casamonica W RSC 3 San
	Mango D'Aquino, Italy
	(Vacant European Lightweight Title)
26.10.02	Nasser Lakrib W RSC 5 Maesteg
	(European Lightweight Title Defence)
25.01.03	Stefano Zoff W PTS 12 Bridgend
06.09.03	Vincent Howard W RTD 3 Huddersfield
08.11.03	Ariel Olveira W RSC 7 Bridgend
	(Vacant IBO Lightweight Title)
01.05.04	Kevin Bennett W PTS 12 Bridgend
	(IBO Lightweight Title Defence)
05.11.04	Aldo Rios L RSC 3 Hereford
	(IBO Lightweight Title Defence)
25.11.05	Gary Reid W DIS 2 Liverpool

Career: 26 contests, won 24, lost 2.

Lee Cook

Morden. *Born* London, 26 June, 1981
Lightweight. Ht. 5'8"
Manager D. Powell/F.Maloney

24.09.04	Jus Wallie W RSC 2 Bethnal Green
26.11.04	Willie Valentine W PTS 4 Bethnal
	Green
05.03.05	Billy Smith W PTS 4 Southwark
29.04.05	Eddie Anderson W RSC 2 Southwark
20.05.05	Ian Reid W PTS 4 Southwark
04.11.05	Buster Dennis DREW 4 Bethnal Green
11.02.06	David Kehoe W RTD 2 Bethnal Green
02.04.06	Rakhim Mingaleev W PTS 4 Bethnal
	Green

Career: 8 contests, won 7, drew 1.

Nicky Cook

Dagenham. *Born* Stepney, 13 September, 1979
Featherweight. Former Undefeated British, European & Commonwealth Featherweight Champion. Former Undefeated WBF Inter-Continental S. Featherweight Champion. Ht. 5'6½"
Manager J. Harding

11.12.98	Sean Grant W CO 1 Cheshunt
26.02.99	Graham McGrath W CO 2 Coventry
27.04.99	Vasil Paskelev W CO 1 Bethnal Green
25.05.99	Wilson Acuna W PTS 4 Mayfair
12.07.99	Igor Sakhatarov W PTS 4 Coventry
20.08.99	Vlado Varhegyi W PTS 4 Bloomsbury
27.11.99	John Barnes W PTS 6 Liverpool
20.12.99	Carl Allen W CO 3 Bethnal Green
10.03.00	Chris Jickells W RSC 1 Bethnal Green
27.05.00	Anthony Hanna W PTS 6 Mayfair
16.06.00	Salem Bouaita W PTS 6 Bloomsbury
04.11.00	Vladimir Borov W RSC 1 Bethnal Green
08.12.00	Rakhim Mingaleev W PTS 8 Crystal Palace
19.05.01	Foudil Madani W RSC 1 Wembley
28.11.01	Woody Greenaway W RSC 3 Bethnal Green
19.12.01	Marcelo Ackermann W RSC 3 Coventry
	(Vacant WBF Inter-Continental S.Featherweight Title)
20.04.02	Jackie Gunguluza W RTD 4 Wembley
	(WBF Inter-Continental S.Featherweight Title Defence)
10.07.02	Andrei Devyataykin W PTS 8 Wembley
05.10.02	Gary Thornhill W RSC 7 Liverpool
	(WBF Inter-Continental S.Featherweight Title Defence)
08.02.03	Mishek Kondwani W RSC 12 Brentford
	(Vacant Commonwealth Featherweight Title)
31.05.03	David Kiilu W CO 2 Bethnal Green
	(Commonwealth Featherweight Title Defence)
24.10.03	Anyetei Laryea W PTS 12 Bethnal Green
	(Commonwealth Featherweight Title)
20.03.04	Cyril Thomas W CO 9 Wembley
	(European Featherweight Title Challenge)
08.10.04	Johny Begue W PTS 12 Brentwood
	(European Featherweight Title Defence)
16.06.05	Dazzo Williams W CO 2 Dagenham
	(European & Commonwealth Featherweight Title Defences. British Featherweight Title Challenge)
24.02.06	Yuri Voronin W PTS 12 Dagenham
	(European Featherweight Title Defence)

Career: 26 contests, won 26.

Gary Coombes

Birmingham. *Born* Solihull, 10 August, 1978
L. Welterweight. Ht. 5'8"
Manager Self

15.04.04	Justin Hicks DREW 6 Dudley
10.05.04	Andy Cosnett W RSC 3 Birmingham
04.06.04	Kristian Laight DREW 6 Dudley
21.02.05	Lea Handley L PTS 6 Peterborough
07.04.05	Gavin Tait L RSC 3 Birmingham
24.07.05	Dwayne Hill L RSC 3 Sheffield
12.12.05	Anthony Christopher L RSC 2 Birmingham
28.02.06	Danny Reynolds L CO 1 Leeds

Career: 8 contests, won 1, drew 2, lost 5.

Billy Corcoran

Wembley. *Born* Galway, 18 November, 1980
English S.Featherweight Champion. Ht. 5'7¾"
Manager Self

23.08.02	Jason Nesbitt W PTS 4 Bethnal Green
25.10.02	Jason Nesbitt W RSC 2 Bethnal Green
21.12.02	Daniel Thorpe W CO 2 Dagenham
28.01.03	Pete Buckley W PTS 6 Nottingham
05.03.03	Pete Buckley W PTS 6 Bethnal Green
16.04.03	Mark Payne DREW 4 Nottingham
27.05.03	Jimmy Beech L PTS 6 Dagenham
04.10.03	Martin Hardcastle W PTS 6 Muswell Hill
28.11.03	Haroon Din W RSC 3 Derby
30.01.04	Rakhim Mingaleev W PTS 6 Dagenham
16.04.04	Anthony Hanna W PTS 4 Bradford
12.11.04	Carl Allen W RSC 5 Wembley
09.07.05	Steve Gethin W PTS 6 Nottingham
21.10.05	Roy Rutherford W RTD 4 Bethnal Green
	(English S.Featherweight Title Challenge)
02.12.05	Pete Buckley W PTS 4 Nottingham
20.01.06	Frederic Bonifai W PTS 8 Bethnal Green

Career: 16 contests, won 14, drew 1, lost 1.

Billy Corcoran   Les Clark

Dennis Corpe

Nottingham. *Born* Nottingham, 6 May, 1976
L.Middleweight. Ht. 5'9¾"
Manager D. Coldwell

22.10.04	Joe Mitchell L PTS 6 Mansfield
16.09.05	Mark Lloyd L PTS 6 Telford
01.10.05	Tiger Matthews L PTS 4 Wigan

Career: 3 contests, lost 3.

Duncan Cottier

Woodford. *Born* Isleworth, 10 October, 1977
Welterweight. Ht. 5'7½"
Manager M. Roe

05.03.05	Geraint Harvey W PTS 4 Dagenham
10.04.05	John O'Donnell L PTS 4 Brentwood
28.04.05	Stuart Phillips DREW 4 Clydach
13.05.05	David Burke L PTS 6 Liverpool
20.05.05	Colin McNeil L PTS 6 Glasgow
16.06.05	Robert Lloyd-Taylor L RSC 1 Mayfair
30.10.05	Aaron Balmer L PTS 4 Bethnal Green
19.11.05	Ashley Theophane L PTS 6 Southwark
04.12.05	Shane Watson L PTS 4 Portsmouth
19.12.05	Gilbert Eastman L RTD 3 Longford
28.01.06	Stephen Haughian L PTS 4 Dublin
18.02.06	Paul McCloskey L PTS 6 Edinburgh
26.02.06	Nathan Graham L PTS 4 Dagenham
05.03.06	Jay Morris W RSC 2 Southampton
30.03.06	Jamal Morrison DREW 4 Bloomsbury
06.04.06	Ben Hudson W PTS 4 Piccadilly
22.04.06	Paddy Pollock L PTS 6 Glasgow
12.05.06	John O'Donnell L RTD 3 Bethnal Green

Career: 18 contests, won 3, drew 2, lost 13.

Gareth Couch

High Wycombe. *Born* High Wycombe, 11 September, 1982
L.Welterweight. Ht. 5'7½"
Manager J. Evans

19.12.04	Oscar Milkitas W PTS 6 Bethnal Green
23.03.05	Ian Reid W RSC 6 Leicester Square
16.06.05	David Pereira W PTS 4 Mayfair
01.07.05	Silence Saheed W PTS 4 Fulham
23.11.05	Kyle Taylor W PTS 6 Mayfair
04.12.05	Henry Castle W PTS 6 Portsmouth
18.03.06	Martino Ciano W PTS 6 Monte Carlo, Monaco

Career: 7 contests, won 7.

Gareth Couch   Les Clark

Jane Couch

Fleetwood. *Born* Fleetwood, 12 August, 1968
Welterweight. Former Undefeated Womens IBF Welterweight Champion. Former Undefeated Womens BF Welterweight Champion. Former Undefeated Womens IBF Lightweight Champion. Former Womens BF L.Welterweight Champion. Ht. 5'7"
Manager T. Woodward

30.10.94	Kalpna Shah W RSC 2 Wigan
29.01.95	Fosteres Joseph W PTS 6 Fleetwood
18.04.95	Jane Johnson W RSC 4 Fleetwood
01.07.95	Julia Shirley W PTS 6 Fleetwood
24.05.96	Sandra Geiger W PTS 10 Copenhagen, Denmark
	(Womens IBF Welterweight Title Challenge)
01.03.97	Andrea Deshong W RSC 7 New Orleans, Louisiana, USA
	(Womens IBF Welterweight Title Defence)
24.08.97	Leah Mellinger W PTS 10 Ledyard, Connecticut, USA
	(Womens IBF Welterweight Title Defence)
24.10.97	Dora Webber L PTS 6 Lula, Mississippi, USA
10.01.98	Dora Webber L PTS 10 Atlantic City, New Jersey, USA
	(Vacant Womens BF L.Welterweight Title)
25.11.98	Simone Lukic W RSC 2 Streatham
20.02.99	Marisch Sjauw W PTS 10 Thornaby
	(Womens IBF Welterweight Title Defence. Vacant Womens BF Welterweight Title)
01.04.99	Heike Noller W PTS 8 Birmingham
31.10.99	Sharon Anyos W PTS 10 Raynes Park
	(Vacant Womens IBF Lightweight Title)
09.03.00	Michelle Straus W RSC 3 Bethnal Green
01.07.00	Galina Gumliska W RSC 6 Southwark
	(Womens IBF Lightweight Title Defence)
19.08.00	Liz Mueller L PTS 6 Mashantucket, Connecticut, USA
16.06.01	Viktoria Oleynikov W PTS 4 Wembley
31.07.01	Shakurah Witherspoon W PTS 4 Montego Bay, Jamaica
16.12.01	Tzanka Karova W RSC 3 Bristol
21.06.02	Sumya Anani L RSC 4 Waco, Texas, USA
	(Vacant Womens IBA L.Welterweight Title)
03.08.02	Borislava Goranova W PTS 6 Blackpool
08.12.02	Borislava Goranova W PTS 10 Bristol
	(Vacant Womens BF L.Welterweight Title)
26.02.03	Borislava Goranova W RSC 7 Bristol
15.05.03	Larisa Berezenko W PTS 8 Clevedon
21.06.03	Lucia Rijker L PTS 8 Los Angeles, California, USA
21.09.03	Brenda Bell-Drexel W PTS 10 Bristol
21.12.03	Brenda Bell-Drexel W PTS 8 Bristol
29.02.04	Borislava Goranova W PTS 6 Bristol
03.04.04	Nathalie Toro L PTS 10 Vise, Belgium
	(Vacant Womens European L.Welterweight Title)
12.06.04	Jaime Clampitt W PTS 10 Mashantucket, Connecticut, USA
	(Womens BF L.Welterweight Title Defence)
02.12.04	Larisa Berezenko W PTS 6 Bristol
21.07.05	Jessica Rakoczy L RSC 6 Lemoore, California, USA
	(Vacant Womens WBC Lightweight Title. Womens IBA Lightweight Title Challenge)
12.11.05	Oksana Chernikova W PTS 6 Bristol
05.12.05	Myriam Lamare L RSC 3 Paris, France
	(Vacant Womens IBF L.Welterweight Title)
25.02.06	Galina Gumliiska W RSC 3 Bristol
06.05.06	Viktoria Oleynik W PTS 6 Birmingham

Career: 36 contests, won 28, lost 8.

Mickey Coveney

West Ham. *Born* London, 26 November, 1981
Featherweight. Ht. 5'4"
Manager Self

12.06.00	Stevie Quinn W PTS 4 Belfast
30.11.00	Gareth Wiltshaw W PTS 4 Peterborough
24.02.01	Dazzo Williams L CO 1 Bethnal Green
03.06.01	Gareth Wiltshaw W PTS 4 Southwark
09.09.01	Richmond Asante W PTS 4 Southwark
28.11.01	Steve Gethin W PTS 4 Bethnal Green
24.03.02	Anthony Hanna W PTS 4 Streatham
25.06.04	David Bailey W PTS 4 Bethnal Green
05.03.05	Rocky Dean L PTS 10 Dagenham
	(Vacant Southern Area Featherweight Title)
30.04.05	Jim Betts W CO 4 Dagenham
23.09.05	Andy Morris L RSC 4 Mayfair
22.04.06	James Ancliff W PTS 6 Glasgow
01.06.06	Derry Matthews L PTS 8 Barnsley

Career: 13 contests, won 9, lost 4.

Simeon Cover

Worksop. *Born* Clapton, 12 March, 1978
S.Middleweight. Former British Masters
S.Middleweight Champion. Ht. 5'11"
Manager D. Ingle

28.03.01	Danny Smith L PTS 6 Piccadilly
18.08.01	Rob Stevenson W PTS 6 Dewsbury
24.09.01	Colin McCash L PTS 6 Cleethorpes
01.11.01	Rob Stevenson L PTS 6 Hull
16.11.01	Jon O'Brien L PTS 6 Dublin
24.11.01	Darren Rhodes L RSC 5 Wakefield
31.01.02	Shpetim Hoti W PTS 6 Piccadilly
13.04.02	Earl Ling L CO 4 Norwich
13.05.02	Roddy Doran DREW 8 Birmingham
02.06.02	Gary Dixon W PTS 6 Shaw
03.08.02	Mike Duffield W RSC 2 Derby
14.09.02	Ivan Botton L PTS 6 Newark
05.12.02	Mark Brookes L RSC 3 Sheffield
15.02.03	Peter Jackson W RSC 2 Wolverhampton
23.02.03	Roddy Doran L PTS 10 Shrewsbury
	(Vacant British Masters S.Middleweight Title)
22.03.03	Barry Connell L PTS 4 Renfrew
12.04.03	Danny Smith L CO 5 Norwich
08.06.03	Ivan Botton W PTS 6 Nottingham
25.07.03	Steven Spartacus L CO 3 Norwich
	(Vacant British Masters L.Heavyweight Title)
06.10.03	Hamed Jamali L PTS 6 Birmingham
17.10.03	Barry Connell L PTS 6 Glasgow
14.11.03	Terry Morrill W PTS 6 Hull
01.12.03	Clint Johnson L PTS 6 Leeds
15.12.03	Lee Nicholson W RSC 4 Cleethorpes
06.02.04	Mark Brookes L RSC 4 Sheffield
12.03.04	Hastings Rasani L CO 6 Irvine
07.05.04	Dean Cockburn L PTS 6 Doncaster
15.05.04	Gary Thompson W PTS 6 Aberdeen
04.06.04	Danny Norton L RSC 3 Dudley
10.09.04	Matthew Barney L PTS 4 Wembley
05.10.04	Andrew Flute W PTS 4 Dudley
04.11.04	Gary Thompson W PTS 6 Piccadilly
13.12.04	Hamed Jamali W PTS 10 Birmingham
	(Vacant British Masters S.Middleweight Title)
21.01.05	Jamie Hearn L PTS 4 Brentford
23.03.05	Jamie Hearn W CO 7 Leicester Square

	(Vacant British Masters S.Middleweight Title)
30.04.05	Lee Blundell L PTS 10 Wigan
	(Vacant British Masters Middleweight Title)
14.05.05	Danny Thornton DREW 6 Aberdeen
03.06.05	Paul Smith L PTS 6 Manchester
20.06.05	Ryan Walls L RSC 8 Longford
16.09.05	Dean Cockburn W PTS 10 Doncaster
	(British Masters S.Middleweight Title Defence)
25.09.05	Danny Thornton L PTS 6 Leeds
03.11.05	Ryan Kerr L PTS 10 Sunderland
	(English S.Middleweight Title Challenge)
02.02.06	Jimi Hendricks W PTS 4 Holborn
26.02.06	Gary Ojuederie L PTS 4 Dagenham
30.03.06	Joey Vegas L PTS 10 Piccadilly
	(British Masters S.Middleweight Title Defence)
01.06.06	Tony Quigley L PTS 4 Barnsley
16.06.06	Steve McGuire L PTS 6 Liverpool

Career: 47 contests, won 15, drew 2, lost 30.

Jamie Coyle

Bannockburn. *Born* Stirling, 24 August, 1976
L. Middleweight. Ht. 6'0"
Manager Self

02.06.03	Richard Inquieti W RSC 2 Glasgow
20.10.03	Jed Tytler W RSC 2 Glasgow
04.12.03	George Robshaw DREW 6 Huddersfield
28.02.04	Geraint Harvey W PTS 4 Bridgend
22.04.04	Peter Dunn W PTS 6 Glasgow
15.10.04	Terry Adams W RSC 5 Glasgow
17.12.04	Arv Mittoo W RSC 5 Huddersfield
25.04.05	Tony Montana W RSC 3 Glasgow
16.06.05	Michael Lomax L PTS 6 Dagenham
30.09.05	Arek Malek W PTS 6 Kirkcaldy
04.11.05	Arek Malek W PTS 6 Glasgow
17.03.06	Karl David L RSC 1 Kirkcaldy
23.06.06	Ben Hudson W PTS 6 Blackpool

Career: 13 contests, won 10, drew 1, lost 2.

Jamie Coyle   Les Clark

Matthew Crouch

Bristol. *Born* Bristol, 8 December, 1980
S.Middleweight. Ht. 5'8¾"
Manager T. Woodward

25.02.06	Simone Lucas L PTS 6 Bristol

Career: 1 contest, lost 1.

Scott Dann   Les Clark

Scott Dann

Plymouth. *Born* Plymouth, 23 July, 1974
British & Commonwealth Middleweight
Champion.
Former Undefeated English & IBO
Inter-Continental Middleweight Champion.
Ht. 5'10¹/₂"
Manager C. Sanigar

15.11.97	Jon Rees W RSC 1 Bristol
25.04.98	Israel Khumalo W RSC 3 Cardiff
30.05.98	Michael Alexander W PTS 4 Bristol
14.07.98	Richard Glaysher W RSC 1 Reading
24.10.98	James Donoghue W PTS 6 Bristol
27.02.00	James Donoghue W RSC 1 Plymouth
07.04.00	Martin Jolley W RSC 2 Bristol
08.09.00	Sean Pritchard W RSC 5 Bristol
06.10.00	Peter Mitchell W RSC 3 Maidstone
03.11.00	Anthony Ivory W PTS 8 Ebbw Vale
13.03.01	Jason Hart W RSC 2 Plymouth
12.05.01	Elvis Adonesi W CO 7 Plymouth
	(Vacant IBO Inter-Continental Middleweight Title)
13.09.01	Jon Penn L RSC 5 Sheffield
10.05.02	Mark Phillips W PTS 6 Bethnal Green
10.07.02	Mark Phillips W PTS 4 Wembley
29.11.02	Delroy Leslie W RSC 1 Liverpool
	(Final Elim. British Middleweight Title)
16.04.03	Howard Eastman L RSC 3 Nottingham
	(British, Commonwealth & European Middleweight Title Challenges)
26.07.03	Kreshkik Qato W RSC 2 Plymouth
09.10.03	Hussain Osman W PTS 8 Bristol
02.04.04	Ojay Abrahams W RSC 6 Plymouth
08.05.04	Danny Thornton W RSC 3 Bristol
	(Vacant English Middleweight Title)
17.09.04	Steven Bendall W RSC 6 Plymouth
	(Vacant British Middleweight Title)
04.02.05	Alan Jones W CO 3 Plymouth
	(British Middleweight Title Defence)
29.04.05	Andy Halder W CO 1 Plymouth
	(British Middleweight Title Defence)
16.09.05	Wayne Elcock W PTS 12 Plymouth
	(British Middleweight Title Defence)
10.02.06	Larry Sharpe W CO 9 Plymouth
	(Vacant Commonwealth Middleweight Title)
07.04.06	Yuri Tsarenko W PTS 8 Bristol

Career: 27 contests, won 25, lost 2.

James Davenport

Manchester. *Born* Salford, 8 January, 1977
Cruiserweight. Ht. 5'9"
Manager S. Foster

23.12.01	William Webster W RSC 5 Salford
17.02.02	Chris Steele W PTS 6 Salford
09.03.02	Martin Scotland W RSC 1 Manchester
28.05.02	Paul Lomax L CO 3 Liverpool
04.03.06	Mark Phillips W PTS 4 Manchester

Career: 5 contests, won 4, lost 1.

(David) Karl David (Kowalski)

Cardiff. *Born* Wroclaw, Poland, 16
November, 1978
Welterweight. Ht. 5'6"
Manager P. Boyce

18.05.01	Jozef Kubovsky W RSC 1 Warsaw, Poland
09.06.01	Mariusz Glowacki W RSC 1 Kolobrzeg, Poland
11.08.01	William Gdula W RSC 1 Jaworzno, Poland
10.11.01	Karoly Koos W RSC 4 Wloclawek, Poland
24.11.01	Grzegorz Lewandowski W PTS 4 Lodz, Poland
23.02.02	Vasile Herteg L PTS 6 Wloclawek, Poland
04.05.02	Marian Bunea W PTS 6 Wroclaw, Poland
24.05.02	Rafal Jackiewicz L CO 3 Plonsk, Poland
27.07.02	Cenk Ulug W PTS 6 Kolobrzeg, Poland
18.10.02	Dimitriu Razvan W PTS 6 Kozienice, Poland
21.02.03	Artur Drinaj L PTS 6 Radom, Poland
30.05.03	Marcen Gierke W PTS 6 Lublin, Poland
02.08.03	Abdelilah Benabbou W RSC 5 Wladyslawowo, Poland
14.11.03	Rastislav Kovac W RSC 1 Slupsk, Poland
06.12.03	Virgil Meleg W PTS 6 Tarnow, Poland
28.02.04	Zsolt Botos W PTS 6 Warsaw, Poland
04.06.04	Mircea Lurci W PTS 10 Warsaw, Poland
26.11.04	Virgil Meleg W PTS 6 Warsaw, Poland
10.12.04	Ondra Skala W RSC 4 Jaworzno, Poland
25.02.05	Slawomir Ziemlewicz DREW 8 Wloclawek, Poland
	(Vacant Polish L.Welterweight Title)
29.04.05	Luciano Abis L PTS 12 Cagliari, Italy
	(Vacant IBF Inter-Continental Welterweight Title)
30.09.05	Silence Saheed L PTS 6 Carmarthen
16.12.05	Robert Lloyd-Taylor L PTS 4 Bracknell
17.03.06	Jamie Coyle W RSC 1 Kirkcaldy
16.06.06	David Kehoe W RSC 1 Carmarthen

Career: 25 contests, won 18, drew 1, lost 6.

Paul David

Sheffield. *Born* Northampton, 2 September,
1984
Cruiserweight. Ht. 6'0¹/₂"
Manager J. Ingle

27.02.06	Peter McCormack W RTD 2 Birmingham
17.03.06	Steve McGuire L PTS 6 Kirkcaldy
25.03.06	Duane Reid W RSC 3 Burton
12.05.06	Daniel Cadman W RSC 6 Bethnal Green
23.06.06	Richard Turba W PTS 6 Blackpool

Career: 5 contests, won 4, lost 1.

John Davidson

Manchester. *Born* Manchester, 13 April,
1986
Lightweight. Ht. 5'8¹/₂"
Manager J. Trickett

26.11.04	Jason Nesbitt L RSC 1 Altrincham
01.10.05	Billy Smith L PTS 6 Wigan

Career: 2 contests, lost 2.

Dai Davies

Merthyr Tydfil. *Born* Merthyr Tydfil, 20
April, 1983
S. Featherweight. Ht. 5'6"
Manager D. Gardiner

08.07.04	Neil Marston W PTS 6 Birmingham
01.10.04	Riaz Durgahed W PTS 4 Bristol
02.12.04	Martin Lindsay L RSC 1 Crystal Palace
25.02.05	Matthew Marsh L PTS 4 Wembley
16.07.05	Derry Matthews L RSC 2 Bolton
12.12.05	Riaz Durgahed L PTS 6 Peterborough
13.04.06	Gary Sykes L CO 3 Leeds
09.06.06	Jamie McDonnell DREW 4 Doncaster
29.06.06	Jed Syger W PTS 6 Bethnal Green

Career: 9 contests, won 3, drew 1, lost 5.

Tristan Davies

Telford. *Born* Shrewsbury, 13 October, 1978
L.Welterweight. Ht. 5'10"
Manager E. Johnson

04.06.04	Pete Buckley W PTS 6 Dudley
05.10.04	Gavin Tait W PTS 6 Dudley
17.02.05	Stuart Phillips W PTS 6 Dudley
16.09.05	Karl Taylor W PTS 4 Telford
04.12.05	Jonathan Whiteman W PTS 4 Telford
14.04.06	Kristian Laight W PTS 6 Telford
01.06.06	Carl Allen W PTS 6 Birmingham

Career: 7 contests, won 7.

Andy Davis

Abercynon. *Born* Aberdare, 28 December,
1985
Featherweight. Ht. 5'7"
Manager B. Coleman

10.03.06	Shaun Walton W PTS 6 Walsall
28.04.06	Paul Appleby L RSC 1 Hartlepool

Career: 2 contests, won 1, lost 1.

Gary Davis (Harding)

St Helens. *Born* Liverpool, 17 October,
1982
Central Area & British Masters
S.Bantamweight Champion. Ht. 5'6"
Manager C. Sanigar

01.06.02 Steve Gethin L RSC 2 Manchester
05.10.02 Jason Thomas W RSC 5 Liverpool
29.11.02 Simon Chambers W RSC 2 Liverpool
15.11.04 Furhan Rafiq W PTS 6 Glasgow
18.09.05 Rocky Dean L RSC 4 Bethnal Green
24.02.06 Chris Hooper W RSC 1 Scarborough
(Vacant Central Area S.Bantamweight
Title. Vacant British Masters
S.Bantamweight Title)
Career: 6 contests, won 4, lost 2.

Gary Davis   Les Clark

Varuzhan Davtyan

Birmingham. *Born* Armenia, 11 August,
1972
Cruiserweight. Ht. 5'8¹/₂"
Manager Self

17.04.93 Teymuraz Kekelidze L CO 5 Tbilisi,
Georgia
09.03.02 Tony Dodson W PTS 6 Manchester
09.05.02 Rasmus Ojemaye W RSC 3 Leicester
Square
29.06.02 Elvis Michailenko L PTS 6 Brentwood
08.09.02 Paul Bonson W PTS 4 Wolverhampton
05.10.02 Mark Hobson L RSC 3 Huddersfield
30.11.02 Eric Teymour L PTS 6 Liverpool
14.12.02 Tomasz Adamek L RTD 4 Newcastle
05.03.03 Carl Froch L RSC 5 Bethnal Green
17.05.03 Jason McKay L PTS 6 Liverpool
24.05.03 Eric Teymour L PTS 4 Bethnal Green
28.06.03 Nathan King L PTS 4 Cardiff
26.07.03 Tony Dodson L RTD 3 Plymouth
20.09.03 Adrian Dodson W PTS 4 Nottingham
20.03.04 Andrew Lowe L PTS 6 Wembley
30.03.04 Jamie Hearn W PTS 4 Southampton
02.06.04 Steven Spartacus L RSC 1 Nottingham
28.10.04 Sam Price L PTS 6 Sunderland
08.12.04 Ryan Walls L PTS 4 Longford
17.12.04 Courtney Fry L RTD 2 Liverpool
12.02.05 Tony Oakey L RTD 5 Portsmouth
10.04.05 Andrew Lowe L PTS 6 Brentwood
29.04.05 Leigh Allis L PTS 4 Plymouth
03.06.05 Tony Quigley L PTS 4 Manchester
11.06.05 Steve McGuire L PTS 6 Kirkcaldy
23.09.05 Tony Dodson L PTS 4 Manchester
14.10.05 Brian Magee L RSC 2 Dublin
17.11.05 Leigh Alliss L PTS 4 Bristol
11.12.05 Steven Spartacus L RSC 1 Chigwell
18.03.06 Neil Simpson L RSC 1 Coventry
21.05.06 Peter Haymer L RSC 4 Bethnal Green
Career: 31 contests, won 5, lost 26.

Lenny Daws

Morden. *Born* Carshalton, 29 December,
1978
British L.Welterweight Champion. Former
Undefeated Southern Area L.Welterweight
Champion. Ht. 5'10¹/₂"
Manager Self

16.04.03 Danny Gwilym W RSC 2 Nottingham
27.05.03 Ben Hudson W RSC 2 Dagenham
25.07.03 Karl Taylor W RTD 2 Norwich
04.10.03 Ernie Smith W PTS 4 Muswell Hill
28.11.03 Tony Montana W PTS 6 Derby
11.12.03 Keith Jones W PTS 6 Bethnal Green
30.01.04 Denis Alekseev W CO 3 Dagenham
24.09.04 Ernie Smith W PTS 6 Nottingham
12.11.04 Keith Jones W PTS 8 Wembley
10.04.05 Silence Saheed W PTS 6 Brentwood
09.07.05 Ivor Bonavic W PTS 6 Nottingham
28.10.05 Oscar Hall W RTD 7 Hartlepool
(Elim. English L.Welterweight Title)
20.01.06 Colin Lynes W RTD 9 Bethnal Green
(Elim. British L.Welterweight Title.
Vacant Southern Area L.Welterweight
Title)
12.05.06 Nigel Wright W PTS 12 Bethnal Green
(Vacant British L.Welterweight Title)
Career: 14 contests, won 14.

Neil Dawson

Rotherham. *Born* Rotherham, 1 July, 1980
Cruiserweight. Ht. 6'4"
Manager C. Aston

12.11.02 Eamonn Glennon W PTS 6 Leeds
24.03.03 Dave Clarke W PTS 4 Barnsley
06.10.03 Dave Clarke W PTS 6 Barnsley
04.12.03 Wlodek Kopec W PTS 4 Huddersfield
13.03.04 Paul Bonson W PTS 4 Huddersfield
08.06.04 Greg Scott-Briggs W RSC 3 Sheffield
20.02.05 Gary Thompson W PTS 6 Sheffield
08.07.05 Tony Moran W RSC 4 Altrincham
Career: 8 contests, won 8.

Gavin Deacon

Northampton. *Born* Northampton, 5 June,
1982
L.Welterweight. Ht. 5'9¹/₄"
Manager J. Cox

12.11.05 Colin Bain L PTS 6 Glasgow
12.02.06 Danny Harding L PTS 6 Manchester
20.02.06 Ryan Brawley L PTS 4 Glasgow
03.03.06 Wez Miller L PTS 4 Doncaster
17.03.06 David Appleby L PTS 4 Kirkcaldy
Career: 5 contests, lost 5.

Rocky Dean

Thetford. *Born* Bury St Edmonds, 17 June,
1978
Southern Area Featherweight Champion.
Ht. 5'5"
Manager Self

14.10.99 Lennie Hodgkins W PTS 6
Bloomsbury
30.10.99 Lennie Hodgkins W PTS 6 Southwark
18.05.00 Danny Lawson W RSC 1 Bethnal Green
29.09.00 Anthony Hanna W PTS 4 Bethnal
Green
10.11.00 Chris Jickells L RSC 1 Mayfair
19.04.02 Peter Svendsen W PTS 6 Aarhus,
Denmark

19.10.02 Sean Grant W RSC 3 Norwich
21.12.02 Darren Cleary W PTS 4 Millwall
08.02.03 Steve Gethin DREW 4 Norwich
11.07.03 Isaac Ward DREW 4 Darlington
26.07.03 Michael Hunter L RSC 1 Plymouth
10.10.03 Isaac Ward L PTS 6 Darlington
06.11.03 Martin Power L PTS 6 Dagenham
07.12.03 Michael Crossan L PTS 6 Glasgow
24.09.04 Simon Wilson W PTS 4 Millwall
19.12.04 Jim Betts W PTS 8 Bethnal Green
05.03.05 Mickey Coveney W PTS 10 Dagenham
(Vacant Southern Area Featherweight
Title)
20.05.05 Andy Morris L PTS 10 Southwark
(Vacant English Featherweight Title)
18.09.05 Gary Davis W RSC 4 Bethnal Green
21.10.05 Andrey Isaev L RSC 12 Kharkov,
Ukraine
(Vacant WBF Inter-Continental
Featherweight Title)
26.02.06 Vinesh Rungea W PTS 6 Dagenham
Career: 21 contests, won 12, drew 2, lost 7.

Garry Delaney

West Ham. *Born* Newham, 12 August, 1970
Heavyweight. Former Undefeated Southern
Area & British Masters Cruiserweight
Champion. Former Commonwealth, WBO
Inter-Continental & Southern Area
L.Heavyweight Champion. Ht. 6'3"
Manager Self

02.10.91 Gus Mendes W RSC 1 Barking
23.10.91 Joe Frater W RSC 1 Bethnal Green
13.11.91 John Kaighin W PTS 6 Bethnal Green
11.12.91 Randy B. Powell W RSC 1 Basildon
11.02.92 Simon Harris DREW 8 Barking
12.05.92 John Williams W PTS 6 Crystal Palace
16.06.92 Nigel Rafferty W CO 5 Dagenham
15.09.92 Gil Lewis W CO 2 Crystal Palace
06.10.92 Simon McDougall W PTS 8 Antwerp,
Belgium
10.11.92 John Oxenham W CO 5 Dagenham
12.12.92 Simon McDougall W PTS 8 Muswell
Hill
30.01.93 Simon Collins W PTS 8 Brentwood
28.09.93 Glazz Campbell W CO 6 Bethnal
Green
(Southern Area L. Heavyweight Title
Challenge)
06.11.93 John Kaighin W CO 1 Bethnal Green
21.12.93 Ray Albert W RSC 3 Mayfair
(Vacant WBO Inter-Continental
L. Heavyweight Title)
11.01.94 Jim Murray W RSC 7 Bethnal Green
(WBO Inter-Continental
L. Heavyweight Title Defence)
09.04.94 Simon Harris W CO 6 Bethnal Green
(WBO Inter-Continental & Southern
Area L. Heavyweight Title Defences)
09.07.94 Sergio Merani W PTS 12 Earls Court
(WBO Inter-Continental
L. Heavyweight Title)
30.09.94 Arigoma Chiponda W CO 2 Bethnal
Green
(Vacant Commonwealth
L. Heavyweight Title)
18.03.95 Ernest Mateen W RTD 7 Millstreet
(Vacant WBO Inter-Continental
L. Heavyweight Title)
09.05.95 Noel Magee L RTD 7 Basildon
(Commonwealth L. Heavyweight Title
Defence)

06.02.96	Francis Wanyama W PTS 6 Basildon	
09.04.96	Joey Paladino W RSC 1 Stevenage	
07.02.97	John Kiser W PTS 6 Las Vegas, Nevada, USA	
04.03.97	Peter Oboh W DIS 8 Southwark	
27.09.97	Julius Francis L RSC 6 Belfast	
	(Vacant British Heavyweight Title. Commonwealth Heavyweight Title Challenge)	
05.06.98	Darron Griffiths W PTS 6 Southend	
23.01.99	John Keeton L PTS 12 Cheshunt	
	(Vacant WBO Inter-Continental Cruiserweight Title)	
01.05.99	Tim Brown W PTS 8 Crystal Palace	
04.09.99	Lee Swaby W PTS 8 Bethnal Green	
29.04.00	Jesper Kristiansen L RTD 10 Varde, Denmark	
	(Vacant WBO Inter-Continental Cruiserweight Title)	
06.10.00	Dominic Negus W PTS 10 Maidstone	
	(Southern Area Cruiserweight Title Challenge)	
10.03.01	Bruce Scott L RTD 3 Bethnal Green	
	(British Cruiserweight Title Challenge. Vacant Commonwealth Cruiserweight Title)	
15.06.01	Darren Ashton W RTD 4 Millwall	
	(Vacant British Masters Cruiserweight Title)	
14.07.01	Chris P. Bacon W RSC 10 Liverpool	
	(British Masters Cruiserweight Title Defence)	
20.10.01	Tony Dowling W RSC 6 Glasgow	
02.03.02	Sebastiaan Rothmann L PTS 12 Brakpan, South Africa	
	(WBU Cruiserweight Title Challenge)	
26.09.03	Paul Bonson W PTS 6 Reading	
21.02.04	Enzo Maccarinelli L RSC 8 Cardiff	
	(WBU Cruiserweight Title Challenge)	
12.11.04	Steffen Nielsen L PTS 6 Copenhagen, Denmark	
11.12.04	Konstantin Prizyuk L PTS 6 Madrid, Spain	
21.01.05	David Haye L RTD 3 Brentford	
19.04.05	Valery Chechenev L PTS 6 Bischofshofen, Austria	
10.05.05	Alexey Mazikin L PTS 4 Palma de Mallorca, Spain	
24.07.05	Micky Steeds L PTS 6 Leicester Square	

Career: 45 contests, won 31, drew 1, lost 13.

Tony Delaney

Mossley. *Born* Tameside, 29 July, 1983
L.Welterweight. Ht. 5'7¼"
Manager T. Jones

04.03.06	Jason Nesbitt W PTS 4 Manchester	

Career: 1 contest, won 1.

Graham Delehedy

Liverpool. *Born* Liverpool, 7 October, 1978
L.Middleweight. Ht. 5'8"
Manager T. Gilmour

17.05.03	Joel Ani W RSC 4 Liverpool	
27.10.03	Rocky Muscus W RSC 2 Glasgow	
01.12.03	Gary Cummings W RSC 1 Bradford	
27.05.04	Ernie Smith W RSC 3 Huddersfield	
08.10.04	David Kehoe W RSC 2 Brentwood	
26.11.04	Tony Montana W PTS 6 Altrincham	
30.04.05	Cafu Santos W RSC 1 Wigan	
23.09.05	Arek Malek W PTS 6 Manchester	
28.04.06	Taz Jones L CO 6 Hartlepool	

Career: 9 contests, won 8, lost 1.

(Dennis) Buster Dennis (Mwanze)

Canning Town. *Born* Mawokota, Uganda, 31 December, 1981
S.Featherweight. Ht. 5'0"
Manager Self

28.03.03	Vitali Makarov W RSC 2 Millwall	
03.04.03	Chris Hooper L RSC 1 Hull	
15.05.03	Mark Alexander L PTS 4 Mayfair	
24.05.03	Haider Ali L PTS 4 Bethnal Green	
21.11.03	Anthony Hanna W PTS 6 Millwall	
30.11.03	Daleboy Rees W PTS 6 Swansea	
20.02.04	Chris Hooper W RSC 2 Bethnal Green	
01.04.04	Kevin O'Hara L PTS 4 Bethnal Green	
19.06.04	Riaz Durgahed L PTS 4 Muswell Hill	
03.09.04	Jamie Arthur L PTS 6 Newport	
10.09.04	Derry Matthews L PTS 6 Liverpool	
26.11.04	Eddie Hyland L PTS 4 Altrincham	
13.12.04	Matt Teague W PTS 6 Cleethorpes	
11.02.05	Andy Morris L PTS 6 Manchester	
08.04.05	Ricky Burns L PTS 6 Edinburgh	
20.05.05	John Bothwell W RTD 4 Glasgow	
03.06.05	Steve Bell DREW 6 Manchester	
18.06.05	Musa Njue W RSC 7 Kampala, Uganda	
18.09.05	Paul Griffin W PTS 4 Bethnal Green	
04.11.05	Lee Cook DREW 4 Bethnal Green	
10.12.05	Steve Foster DREW 8 Canning Town	
24.03.06	Jadgar Abdulla DREW 4 Bethnal Green	

Career: 22 contests, won 8, drew 4, lost 10.

Reagan Denton

Sheffield. *Born* Sheffield, 26 June, 1978
Middleweight. Ht. 5'11"
Manager Self

15.05.99	Pedro Thompson W PTS 4 Sheffield	
15.11.99	Colin Vidler W PTS 4 Bethnal Green	
25.09.00	William Webster W PTS 4 Barnsley	
08.10.01	Martyn Bailey W PTS 4 Barnsley	

15.12.01	Darren Covill W PTS 4 Sheffield	
24.03.03	Dave Pearson W PTS 6 Barnsley	
06.10.03	Michael Pinnock W PTS 6 Barnsley	
23.11.03	Gary Dixon L PTS 4 Rotherham	
08.12.03	William Webster W RSC 6 Barnsley	
15.12.04	Leigh Wicks W PTS 6 Sheffield	
17.02.06	Tony Randell W PTS 6 Sheffield	

Career: 11 contests, won 10, lost 1.

Craig Dickson

Glasgow. *Born* Glasgow, 6 March, 1979
Welterweight. Ht. 5'11"
Manager T. Gilmour

21.10.02	Paul Rushton W RSC 2 Glasgow	
18.11.02	Ernie Smith W PTS 6 Glasgow	
17.02.03	Jon Hilton W RSC 2 Glasgow	
14.04.03	Richard Inquieti W PTS 4 Glasgow	
20.10.03	Danny Moir W RSC 3 Glasgow	
19.01.04	Dean Nicholas W RSC 5 Glasgow	
19.04.04	Ernie Smith W PTS 6 Glasgow	
30.09.04	Taz Jones DREW 6 Glasgow	
15.11.04	Tony Montana W PTS 8 Glasgow	
21.03.05	David Keir W RTD 3 Glasgow	
30.09.05	Vadzim Astapuk W RSC 4 Kirkcaldy	
21.11.05	David Kehoe W PTS 8 Glasgow	
20.02.06	Arek Malek W RSC 5 Glasgow	
17.03.06	Kevin Anderson L RSC 7 Kirkcaldy	
	(Commonwealth Welterweight Title Challenge)	
01.06.06	Darren Gethin L PTS 6 Birmingham	

Career: 15 contests, won 12, drew 1, lost 2.

Haroon Din

Sheffield. *Born* Middlesbrough, 21 May, 1978
Lightweight. Former Undefeated British Masters L.Welterweight Champion. Ht. 5'8"
Manager D. Coldwell

Following his unsuccessful Commonwealth title challenge, next time out Craig Dickson (left) was outscored by Darren Gethin
Les Clark

21.09.98 Les Frost L PTS 6 Cleethorpes
14.12.98 Les Frost L RSC 1 Cleethorpes
02.05.99 Amjid Mahmood W PTS 6 Shaw
20.05.00 Dave Travers W PTS 6 Leicester
24.06.00 Willie Limond L PTS 4 Glasgow
30.08.00 Leon Dobbs W CO 1 Scunthorpe
19.11.00 Carl Greaves L RSC 4 Chesterfield
24.09.01 Nigel Senior W PTS 6 Cleethorpes
17.12.01 Nigel Senior W PTS 6 Cleethorpes
31.01.02 Ilias Miah W RSC 3 Piccadilly
20.04.02 Gareth Wiltshaw W PTS 6 Derby
17.11.02 Gareth Wiltshaw W PTS 6 Bradford
05.04.03 Andy Morris L RSC 1 Manchester
28.11.03 Billy Corcoran L RSC 3 Derby
05.03.04 Jason Nesbitt W PTS 6 Darlington
14.05.04 Jackson Williams W RSC 5 Sunderland
(Vacant British Masters L.Welterweight Title)
29.10.04 Stefy Bull L RSC 2 Doncaster
(Central Area Lightweight Title Challenge)
03.11.05 Paul Holborn DREW 6 Sunderland
17.11.05 Sam Rukundo L RSC 3 Piccadilly
Career: 19 contests, won 10, drew 1, lost 8.

Terry Dixon
Harlesden. *Born* London, 29 July, 1966
Heavyweight. Ht. 5'11"
Manager Self

21.09.89 Dave Mowbray W RSC 1 Southampton
30.11.89 Brendan Dempsey W RSC 8 Barking
08.03.90 Cordwell Hylton W PTS 8 Watford
06.04.90 Prince Rodney W RSC 7 Stevenage
23.10.90 Dennis Bailey W PTS 6 Leicester
07.03.91 Carl Thompson L PTS 8 Basildon
22.04.91 Everton Blake L RSC 8 Mayfair
25.03.92 Mark Bowen W RTD 1 Kensington
27.04.92 Ian Bulloch W RSC 4 Mayfair
17.10.92 Darren McKenna L RSC 3 Wembley
04.10.93 Steve Yorath W RSC 4 Mayfair
03.08.94 Chemek Saleta L PTS 8 Bristol
09.05.02 Kevin Barrett DREW 4 Leicester Square
30.10.02 Leighton Morgan W RSC 1 Leicester Square
29.03.03 Mal Rice W PTS 4 Wembley
12.06.05 Slick Miller W RSC 2 Leicester Square
24.07.05 Mal Rice W PTS 4 Leicester Square
Career: 17 contests, won 12, drew 1, lost 4.

Craig Docherty
Glasgow. *Born* Glasgow, 27 September, 1979
S.Featherweight. Former Commonwealth S.Featherweight Champion. Ht. 5'7"
Manager T. Gilmour

16.11.98 Kevin Gerowski W PTS 6 Glasgow
22.02.99 Des Gargano W PTS 6 Glasgow
19.04.99 Paul Quarmby W RSC 4 Glasgow
07.06.99 Simon Chambers W PTS 6 Glasgow
20.09.99 John Barnes W PTS 6 Glasgow
15.11.99 Peter Allen W RSC 1 Glasgow
24.01.00 Lee Williamson W PTS 6 Glasgow
19.02.00 Steve Hanley W PTS 6 Prestwick
05.06.00 Sebastian Hart W PTS 4 Glasgow
23.10.00 Lee Armstrong DREW 8 Glasgow
22.01.01 Nigel Senior W RSC 4 Glasgow
20.03.01 Jamie McKeever W RSC 3 Glasgow
11.06.01 Rakhim Mingaleev W PTS 8 Nottingham
27.10.01 Michael Gomez L RSC 2 Manchester
(British S.Featherweight Title Challenge)

18.03.02 Joel Viney W CO 1 Glasgow
13.07.02 Dariusz Snarski W PTS 6 Coventry
25.01.03 Nikolai Eremeev W PTS 6 Bridgend
12.04.03 Dean Pithie W CO 8 Bethnal Green
(Commonwealth S. Featherweight Title Challenge)
01.11.03 Abdul Malik Jabir W PTS 12 Glasgow
(Commonwealth S.Featherweight Title Defence)
22.04.04 Kpakpo Allotey W RSC 6 Glasgow
(Commonwealth S.Featherweight Title Defence)
15.10.04 Boris Sinitsin L PTS 12 Glasgow
(European S.Featherweight Title Challenge)
08.04.05 Alex Arthur L CO 9 Edinburgh
(Vacant British S.Featherweight Title. Commonwealth S.Featherweight Title Defence)
30.09.05 John Mackay W RSC 7 Kirkcaldy
Career: 23 contests, won 19, drew 1, lost 3.

Tony Dodson
Liverpool. *Born* Liverpool, 2 July, 1980
English S.Middleweight Champion. Former Undefeated British S.Middleweight Champion. Former Undefeated Central Area S.Middleweight Champion. Former WBF Inter-Continental S.Middleweight Champion. Ht. 6'0½"
Manager Self

31.07.99 Michael McDermott W RTD 1 Carlisle
02.10.99 Sean Pritchard W RSC 3 Cardiff
22.01.00 Mark Dawson W PTS 4 Birmingham
11.03.00 Paul Bonson W PTS 4 Kensington
19.08.00 Jimmy Steel W RSC 3 Brentwood
09.09.00 Danny Southam W RSC 2 Manchester
09.10.00 Elvis Michailenko DREW 6 Liverpool
03.02.01 Paul Bonson W PTS 4 Manchester
25.09.01 Paul Wesley W PTS 6 Liverpool
13.10.01 Roman Divisek W CO 1 Budapest, Hungary
10.11.01 Valery Odin W RSC 4 Wembley
10.12.01 Jon Penn W RSC 2 Liverpool
(Vacant Central Area S.Middleweight Title)
23.02.02 Jason Hart W RSC 2 Nottingham
09.03.02 Varuzhan Davtyan L PTS 6 Manchester
13.04.02 Brian Barbosa W PTS 8 Liverpool
07.09.02 Mike Algoet W PTS 10 Liverpool
(Vacant WBF Inter-Continental S.Middleweight Title)
26.10.02 Albert Rybacki L RSC 9 Maesteg
(WBF Inter-Continental S.Middleweight Title Defence)
19.04.03 Pierre Moreno L RSC 9 Liverpool
(Vacant WBF Inter-Continental S.Middleweight Title)
26.07.03 Varuzhan Davtyan W RTD 3 Plymouth
22.11.03 Allan Foster W RSC 11 Belfast
(Vacant British S.Middleweight Title)
23.09.05 Varuzhan Davtyan W PTS 4 Manchester
25.11.05 Szabolcs Rimovszky W RSC 3 Liverpool
03.03.06 Dmitry Adamovich W PTS 4 Hartlepool
16.06.06 Jamie Hearn W RSC 4 Liverpool
(Vacant English S.Middleweight Title)
Career: 24 contests, won 20, drew 1, lost 3.

Tony Dodson　　　　　Les Clark

Jimmy Doherty
Stoke. *Born* Stafford, 15 August, 1985
Welterweight. Ht. 5'11"
Manager M. Carney

12.11.05 Surinder Sekhon W PTS 6 Stoke
18.02.06 Pete Buckley W PTS 6 Stoke
06.05.06 Jason Nesbitt W PTS 6 Stoke
Career: 3 contests, won 3.

Shaun Doherty
Bradford. *Born* Bradford, 15 November, 1982
S.Bantamweight. Ht. 5'7"
Manager C. Aston

23.11.05 Eylon Kedem DREW 6 Mayfair
24.02.06 Neil Marston L PTS 6 Birmingham
Career: 2 contests, drew 1, lost 1.

Tony Doherty
Pontypool. *Born* London, 8 April, 1983
Celtic Welterweight Champion. Ht. 5'8"
Manager F. Warren/B. Hughes

08.05.03 Karl Taylor W PTS 4 Widnes
28.06.03 Paul McIlwaine W RSC 1 Cardiff
13.09.03 Darren Covill W PTS 4 Newport
06.12.03 James Paisley W RSC 3 Cardiff
21.02.04 Chris Brophy W RSC 2 Cardiff
24.04.04 Keith Jones W PTS 6 Reading
22.05.04 Karl Taylor W RTD 2 Widnes
03.07.04 David Kirk W PTS 4 Newport
30.07.04 Ernie Smith W PTS 6 Bethnal Green
03.09.04 Keith Jones W PTS 6 Newport
10.09.04 Peter Dunn W RSC 2 Bethnal Green
19.11.04 Karl Taylor W RSC 2 Bethnal Green
21.01.05 Emmanuel Fleury W RSC 2 Bridgend
22.04.05 Belaid Yahiaoui W PTS 8 Barnsley
16.07.05 Ernie Smith NC 2 Bolton
10.09.05 Taz Jones W PTS 10 Cardiff
(Vacant Celtic Welterweight Title)
28.01.06 Ernie Smith W PTS 6 Nottingham
13.05.06 Andrzej Butowicz W PTS 6 Bethnal Green
Career: 18 contests, won 17, no contest 1.

Marko Doknic

Liverpool. *Born* Novi Sad, 1 February, 1982
L. Heavyweight. Ht. 6'0"
Manager J. Evans

17.11.05 Dan Guthrie L PTS 4 Bristol
Career: 1 contest, lost 1.

David Dolan

Sunderland. *Born* Sunderland, 7 October, 1979
Heavyweight. Ht. 6'2"
Manager D. Hobson

13.05.06 Nabil Haciani W PTS 4 Sheffield
Career: 1 contest, won 1.

Gavin Down

Bolsover. *Born* Chesterfield, 2 February, 1977
Welterweight. Former Undefeated Midlands Area L.Middleweight Champion. Former British Masters L.Welterweight Champion. Former Undefeated Midlands Area L.Welterweight Champion. Ht. 5'9"
Manager D. Ingle

21.09.98 Peter Lennon W RSC 1 Cleethorpes
27.11.98 Trevor Tacy L PTS 6 Nottingham
07.12.98 Brian Coleman W PTS 6 Manchester
26.02.99 Brian Gifford W PTS 6 West Bromwich
27.03.99 Lee Molyneux W PTS 4 Derby
15.05.99 Les Frost W RSC 1 Sheffield
27.06.99 Lee Molyneux W PTS 6 Alfreton
03.10.99 Ernie Smith W RSC 1 Chesterfield
28.11.99 Dave Gibson W PTS 6 Chesterfield
09.04.00 Sammy Smith W PTS 6 Alfreton
21.05.00 Arv Mittoo W PTS 6 Derby
19.06.00 Brian Coleman W PTS 4 Burton
13.08.00 Lee Bird W PTS 6 Nottingham
30.08.00 Ram Singh W PTS 6 Scunthorpe
04.11.00 Sebastian Hart W RSC 4 Derby
19.11.00 David Kirk W PTS 10 Chesterfield
(Vacant British Masters L.Welterweight Title)
11.12.00 Dave Gibson W RSC 5 Cleethorpes
25.02.01 Jay Mahoney W RSC 3 Alfreton
01.04.01 Steve Saville W RSC 3 Alfreton
(Vacant Midlands Area L.Welterweight Title)
16.06.01 Arv Mittoo W PTS 6 Derby
21.07.01 Tommy Peacock W RSC 1 Sheffield
15.09.01 Lee Williamson W PTS 6 Derby
08.12.01 Brian Coleman W RSC 1 Chesterfield
12.02.02 Bradley Pryce L RSC 9 Bethnal Green
(Vacant IBF Inter-Continental L.Welterweight Title)
11.05.02 Woody Greenaway W RSC 3 Chesterfield
05.10.02 Daniel Thorpe W RSC 2 Chesterfield
19.10.02 Daniel James W RTD 5 Norwich
28.01.03 Tony Montana W PTS 6 Nottingham
25.07.03 Alan Bosworth L RSC 5 Norwich
(British Masters L.Welterweight Title Defence. Elim. British L.Welterweight Title)
16.01.04 Paul Denton W RSC 4 Bradford
12.03.04 Jon Hilton W RTD 1 Nottingham
02.06.04 Francis Barrett L PTS 10 Nottingham
(Vacant European Union L.Welterweight Title)
05.10.04 Young Muttley L RSC 6 Dudley
(English L.Welterweight Title Challenge. Vacant WBF Inter-Continental L.Welterweight Title)

25.11.04 Steve Brumant W PTS 10 Birmingham
(Vacant Midlands Area L.Middleweight Title)
03.06.05 Michael Jennings L RSC 9 Manchester
(English Welterweight Title Challenge)
23.09.05 Ali Nuumbembe L RSC 3 Manchester
Career: 36 contests, won 29, lost 7.

Barry Downes

Rochdale. *Born* Rochdale, 10 December, 1984
Welterweight. Ht. 5'10½"
Manager C. Aston

20.11.05 Kristian Laight DREW 6 Shaw
02.04.06 Pete Buckley W PTS 6 Shaw
13.04.06 Sujad Elahi W RSC 3 Leeds
28.05.06 Ruben Giles L PTS 4 Longford
18.06.06 Johnny Hussey L PTS 6 Manchester
Career: 5 contests, won 2, drew 1, lost 2.

Barry Downes   Les Clark

Wayne Downing

West Bromwich. *Born* Sandwell, 30 December, 1979
L.Middleweight. Ht. 5'9"
Manager E. Johnson

16.02.06 Peter Dunn L PTS 4 Dudley
18.05.06 Malik Khan L RSC 3 Walsall
Career: 2 contests, lost 2.

Peter Dunn

Pontefract. *Born* Doncaster, 15 February, 1975
Middleweight. Ht. 5'8"
Manager Self

08.12.97 Leigh Daniels W PTS 6 Bradford
15.05.98 Peter Lennon W PTS 6 Nottingham
18.09.98 Jan Cree L RSC 5 Belfast
23.10.98 Bobby Lyndon W PTS 6 Wakefield
03.12.98 Craig Smith L RSC 3 Sunderland
17.03.99 Des Sowden W PTS 6 Kensington
15.05.99 Ray Wood DREW 4 Blackpool
29.05.99 Dean Nicholas L PTS 6 South Shields
01.10.99 Jon Honney L PTS 4 Bethnal Green
18.10.99 Jan Cree W PTS 6 Glasgow
26.11.99 Gavin Pearson DREW 6 Wakefield
18.02.00 John T. Kelly L PTS 6 Pentre Halkyn
11.03.00 Iain Eldridge L RSC 2 Kensington
18.09.00 Joe Miller L PTS 6 Glasgow
26.10.00 Ram Singh W PTS 6 Stoke
27.11.00 Young Muttley L RSC 3 Birmingham
22.02.01 Darren Spencer W PTS 6 Sunderland

03.03.01 Glenn McClarnon L PTS 4 Wembley
20.03.01 Robert Burton L PTS 6 Leeds
08.04.01 Martyn Bailey L PTS 6 Wrexham
17.05.01 Gavin Pearson L PTS 6 Leeds
25.09.01 Darren Spencer L PTS 4 Liverpool
06.10.01 Lee Byrne L RSC 4 Manchester
13.11.01 Richard Inquieti DREW 6 Leeds
24.11.01 Robert Burton W PTS 6 Wakefield
28.01.02 Robert Burton L RSC 8 Barnsley
(Vacant Central Area Welterweight Title)
23.03.02 Colin Lynes L PTS 4 Southwark
19.04.02 Oscar Hall L PTS 6 Darlington
28.05.02 Matt Scriven L PTS 8 Leeds
29.06.02 Darren Bruce L PTS 6 Brentwood
28.09.02 Surinder Sekhon L PTS 6 Wakefield
13.09.03 Wayne Shepherd W PTS 6 Wakefield
20.09.03 Michael Lomax L PTS 4 Nottingham
04.10.03 Andy Gibson L PTS 6 Belfast
25.10.03 Gary Young L PTS 6 Edinburgh
13.12.03 Michael Jennings L PTS 6 Manchester
19.02.04 Young Muttley L PTS 4 Dudley
26.02.04 Matthew Hatton L PTS 6 Widnes
06.03.04 Jason Rushton L PTS 6 Renfrew
10.04.04 Ali Nuumembe L PTS 6 Manchester
22.04.04 Jamie Coyle L PTS 6 Glasgow
06.05.04 Jason Rushton L PTS 4 Barnsley
19.06.04 Chris Saunders L PTS 4 Muswell Hill
03.07.04 Oscar Hall L PTS 6 Blackpool
10.09.04 Tony Doherty L RSC 2 Bethnal Green
09.10.04 Steve Russell W PTS 6 Norwich
23.10.04 Geraint Harvey L PTS 6 Wakefield
11.12.04 Gary Woolcombe L PTS 4 Canning Town
19.12.04 Freddie Luke L PTS 4 Bethnal Green
25.02.05 Chas Symonds L PTS 4 Wembley
07.04.05 Jonjo Finnegan L PTS 6 Birmingham
26.04.05 Tyrone McInerney L RSC 6 Leeds
03.06.05 Oscar Hall L PTS 6 Hull
19.06.05 Gary Woolcombe L RSC 6 Bethnal Green
21.09.05 Danny Moir L PTS 6 Bradford
30.09.05 Paul McInnes L PTS 6 Burton
10.10.05 Joe Mitchell L PTS 6 Birmingham
13.11.05 Khurram Hussain L PTS 4 Leeds
21.11.05 Muhsen Nasser L RSC 4 Glasgow
16.02.06 Wayne Downing W PTS 4 Dudley
23.02.06 Darren Rhodes L PTS 6 Leeds
05.03.06 Muhsen Nasser L PTS 4 Sheffield
30.03.06 Oscar Milkitas L PTS 6 Bloomsbury
14.04.06 Gary Round L PTS 4 Telford
21.04.06 Jason Rushton L PTS 6 Doncaster
29.04.06 Lee McAllister L PTS 6 Edinburgh
09.05.06 Ryan Ashworth L PTS 6 Leeds
18.05.06 Stuart Elwell L PTS 6 Walsall
29.06.06 Marcus Portman L PTS 6 Dudley
Career: 69 contests, won 11, drew 3, lost 55.

Riaz Durgahed

Bristol. *Born* Mauritius, 4 May, 1977
S.Featherweight. Ht. 5'6"
Manager C. Sanigar

29.02.04 Jason Thomas W RSC 1 Bristol
19.06.04 Buster Dennis W PTS 4 Muswell Hill
01.10.04 Dai Davies L PTS 4 Bristol
02.12.04 Lloyd Otte L PTS 6 Crystal Palace
08.04.05 Scott Flynn L PTS 4 Edinburgh
02.06.05 Jason Nesbitt W PTS 6 Peterborough
02.09.05 Rendall Munroe L PTS 6 Derby
16.10.05 Dave Hinds W PTS 6 Peterborough
18.11.05 Lloyd Otte DREW 4 Dagenham
12.12.05 Dai Davies W PTS 6 Peterborough
03.03.06 Jamie McKeever L PTS 6 Hartlepool
Career: 11 contests, won 5, drew 1, lost 5.

95

Graham Earl   Les Clark

Graham Earl

Luton. *Born* Luton, 26 August, 1978
Commonwealth Lightweight Champion.
Former Undefeated British Lightweight
Champion. Former Undefeated Southern
Area Lightweight Champion. Ht. 5'5¾"
Manager F. Warren

02.09.97	Mark O'Callaghan W RSC 2 Southwark
06.12.97	Mark McGowan W PTS 4 Wembley
11.04.98	Danny Lutaaya W RSC 2 Southwark
23.05.98	David Kirk W PTS 4 Bethnal Green
12.09.98	Brian Coleman W PTS 4 Bethnal Green
10.12.98	Marc Smith W RSC 1 Barking
16.01.99	Lee Williamson W RSC 4 Bethnal Green
08.05.99	Benny Jones W PTS 6 Bethnal Green
15.07.99	Simon Chambers W CO 6 Peterborough
04.03.00	Ivo Golakov W RSC 1 Peterborough
29.04.00	Marco Fattore W PTS 6 Wembley
21.10.00	Lee Williamson W RSC 3 Wembley
10.03.01	Brian Gentry W RSC 8 Bethnal Green
	(Vacant Southern Area Lightweight Title)
22.09.01	Liam Maltby W CO 1 Bethnal Green
	(Southern Area Lightweight Title Defence)
15.12.01	Mark Winters W PTS 10 Wembley
	(Elim. British Lightweight Title)
12.10.02	Chill John W PTS 10 Bethnal Green
	(Southern Area Lightweight Title Defence)
15.02.03	Steve Murray W RSC 2 Wembley
	(Southern Area Lightweight Title Defence. Final Elim. British Lightweight Title)
24.05.03	Nikolai Eremeev W PTS 8 Bethnal Green
17.07.03	Bobby Vanzie W PTS 12 Dagenham
	(British Lightweight Title Challenge)
11.10.03	Jon Honney W PTS 8 Portsmouth
05.06.04	Bobby Vanzie W PTS 12 Bethnal Green
	(Vacant British Lightweight Title)
30.07.04	Steve Murray W RSC 6 Bethnal Green
	(British Lightweight Title Defence)
25.02.05	Ricky Burns L PTS 8 Wembley
19.06.05	Kevin Bennett W RSC 9 Bethnal Green
	(Commonwealth Lightweight Title Challenge. British Lightweight Title Defence)
27.01.06	Yuri Romanov W PTS 12 Dagenham

Career: 25 contests, won 24, lost 1.

Gilbert Eastman

Battersea. *Born* Guyana, 16 November, 1972
L.Middleweight. Former Southern Area
L.Middleweight Champion. Ht. 5'10"
Manager G. Carman

22.04.96	Wayne Shepherd W PTS 4 Crystal Palace
09.07.96	Costas Katsantonis W RSC 1 Bethnal Green
11.01.97	Mike Watson W RSC 1 Bethnal Green
25.03.97	Danny Quacoe W RSC 3 Lewisham
30.08.97	Karl Taylor W PTS 4 Cheshunt
08.11.97	Ray Newby W PTS 6 Southwark
14.02.98	Cam Raeside W RSC 5 Southwark
21.04.98	Dennis Berry W RSC 6 Edmonton
23.05.98	Shaun O'Neill W RSC 1 Bethnal Green
12.09.98	Everald Williams W RTD 5 Bethnal Green
21.11.98	Lindon Scarlett W RTD 3 Southwark
06.03.99	Kofi Jantuah L RSC 11 Southwark
	(Commonwealth Welterweight Title Challenge)
25.10.02	Ojay Abrahams W PTS 4 Bethnal Green
21.12.02	Pedro Thompson W RSC 2 Dagenham
05.03.03	Howard Clarke W PTS 6 Bethnal Green
16.04.03	Andrew Facey L RSC 3 Nottingham
25.07.03	Jason Collins W RSC 1 Norwich
04.10.03	Spencer Fearon W RSC 4 Muswell Hill
	(Vacant Southern Area L.Middleweight Title)
28.11.03	Eugenio Monteiro L PTS 8 Derby
30.01.04	Craig Lynch W PTS 6 Dagenham
16.04.04	Delroy Mellis W RSC 5 Bradford
	(Southern Area L.Middleweight Title Defence)
24.09.04	Clive Johnson W PTS 6 Nottingham
19.12.05	Duncan Cottier W RTD 3 Longford
11.03.06	Gary Lockett L RSC 1 Newport
	(Vacant WBU Middleweight Title)
26.05.06	Gary Woolcombe L RSC 7 Bethnal Green
	(Southern Area L.Middleweight Title Defence)

Career: 25 contests, won 20, lost 5.

Howard Eastman

Battersea. *Born* New Amsterdam, Guyana,
8 December, 1970
Middleweight. Former Undefeated British,
Commonwealth, European, IBO Inter-
Continental, WBA Inter-Continental &
Southern Area Middleweight Champion.
Ht. 5'11"
Manager Self

06.03.94	John Rice W RSC 1 Southwark
14.03.94	Andy Peach W PTS 6 Mayfair
22.03.94	Steve Phillips W RSC 5 Bethnal Green
17.10.94	Barry Thorogood W RSC 6 Mayfair
06.03.95	Marty Duke W RSC 1 Mayfair
20.04.95	Stuart Dunn W RSC 2 Mayfair
23.06.95	Peter Vosper W RSC 1 Bethnal Green
16.10.95	Carlo Colarusso W RSC 1 Mayfair
29.11.95	Brendan Ryan W RSC 2 Bethnal Green
31.01.96	Paul Wesley W RSC 1 Birmingham
13.03.96	Steve Goodwin W RSC 5 Wembley
29.04.96	John Duckworth W RSC 5 Mayfair
11.12.96	Sven Hamer W RSC 10 Southwark
	(Vacant Southern Area Middleweight Title)
18.02.97	John Duckworth W CO 7 Cheshunt
25.03.97	Rachid Serdjane W RSC 7 Lewisham
14.02.98	Vitali Kopitko W PTS 8 Southwark
28.03.98	Terry Morrill W RTD 4 Hull
23.05.98	Darren Ashton W RSC 4 Bethnal Green
30.11.98	Steve Foster W RSC 7 Manchester
	(Vacant British Middleweight Title)
04.02.99	Jason Barker W RSC 6 Lewisham
06.03.99	Jon Penn W RSC 3 Southwark
	(Vacant IBO Inter-Continental S. Middleweight Title)
22.05.99	Roman Babaev W RSC 6 Belfast
	(WBA Inter-Continental Middleweight Title Challenge)
10.07.99	Teimouraz Kikelidze W RSC 6 Southwark
	(WBA Inter-Continental Middleweight Title Defence)
13.09.99	Derek Wormald W RSC 3 Bethnal Green
	(British Middleweight Title Defence)
13.11.99	Mike Algoet W RSC 8 Hull
	(WBA Inter-Continental Middleweight Title Defence)
18.01.00	Ojay Abrahams W RSC 2 Mansfield
04.03.00	Viktor Fesetchko W RTD 4 Peterborough
29.04.00	Anthony Ivory W RTD 6 Wembley
25.07.00	Ahmet Dottouev W RTD 5 Southwark
	(WBA Inter-Continental Middleweight Title Defence)
16.09.00	Sam Soliman W PTS 12 Bethnal Green
	(Commonwealth Middleweight Title Challenge)
05.02.01	Mark Baker W RTD 5 Hull
10.04.01	Robert McCracken W RSC 10 Wembley
	(British & Commonwealth Middleweight Title Defences. Vacant European Middleweight Title)
17.11.01	William Joppy L PTS 12 Las Vegas, Nevada, USA
	(Vacant WBA Interim Middleweight Title)
25.10.02	Chardan Ansoula W RSC 1 Bethnal Green
21.12.02	Hussain Osman W RTD 4 Dagenham
28.01.03	Christophe Tendil W RTD 4 Nottingham
	(Vacant European Middleweight Title)
05.03.03	Gary Beardsley W RSC 2 Bethnal Green
16.04.03	Scott Dann W RSC 3 Nottingham
	(British, Commonwealth & European Middleweight Title Defences)
25.07.03	Hacine Cherifi W RTD 8 Norwich
	(European Middleweight Title Defence)
30.01.04	Sergei Tatevosyan W PTS 12 Dagenham
	(European Middleweight Title Defence)
24.09.04	Jerry Elliott W PTS 10 Nottingham
19.02.05	Bernard Hopkins L PTS 12 Los Angeles, California, USA
	(WBC, WBA, IBF & WBO Middleweight Title Challenges)

16.07.05 Arthur Abraham L PTS 12 Nuremburg, Germany
(WBA Inter-Continental Middleweight Title Challenge)
24.03.06 Edison Miranda L RSC 7 Hollywood, Florida, USA
(Final Elim. IBF Middleweight Title)
Career: 44 contests, won 40, lost 4.

Tommy Eastwood

Epsom. *Born* Epsom, 16 May, 1979
Cruiserweight. Ht. 5'11½"
Manager Self

09.09.01 Tony Booth W PTS 4 Southwark
16.12.01 Paul Bonson W PTS 4 Southwark
12.02.02 Adam Cale W PTS 4 Bethnal Green
24.03.02 Dave Clarke W PTS 6 Streatham
23.06.02 Brodie Pearmaine W PTS 4 Southwark
24.01.03 Lee Swaby L PTS 6 Sheffield
26.11.03 Brian Gascoigne W RSC 2 Mayfair
10.09.04 Ovill McKenzie W PTS 8 Wembley
06.10.05 Tony Booth W PTS 4 Longford
17.11.05 Csaba Andras W PTS 4 Piccadilly
25.02.06 Dean Francis L PTS 10 Bristol
(Vacant English Cruiserweight Title)
28.05.06 Paul King W PTS 4 Longford
Career: 12 contests, won 10, lost 2.

Steve Ede

Gosport. *Born* Southampton, 22 June, 1976
S.Middleweight. Ht. 5'10"
Manager Self

06.02.05 Jed Tytler W RSC 4 Southampton
26.06.05 Mark Wall W PTS 6 Southampton
25.09.05 Rocky Muscus W PTS 6 Southampton
16.12.05 Lee Hodgson W PTS 4 Bracknell
05.03.06 Anthony Young W RSC 3 Southampton

26.05.06 Jake Guntert W RSC 2 Bethnal Green
Career: 6 contests, won 6.

Chris Edwards

Stoke. *Born* Stoke, 6 May, 1976
Bantamweight. Former Undefeated British Masters S.Bantamweight Champion. Ht. 5'3"
Manager M. Carney

03.04.98 Chris Thomas W RSC 2 Ebbw Vale
21.09.98 Russell Laing L PTS 6 Glasgow
26.02.99 Delroy Spencer L PTS 6 West Bromwich
17.04.99 Stevie Quinn L RSC 4 Dublin
19.10.99 Lee Georgiou L RSC 2 Bethnal Green
03.12.99 Daniel Ring L PTS 4 Peterborough
15.05.00 Paddy Folan L PTS 6 Bradford
07.10.00 Andy Roberts W PTS 4 Doncaster
27.11.00 Levi Pattison W PTS 4 Birmingham
16.03.01 Jamie Evans L PTS 6 Portsmouth
03.06.01 Darren Taylor DREW 6 Hanley
08.10.01 Levi Pattison L PTS 4 Barnsley
06.12.01 Neil Read W PTS 8 Stoke
10.10.02 Neil Read W PTS 6 Stoke
13.06.03 Lee Haskins L PTS 6 Bristol
23.04.04 Delroy Spencer DREW 6 Leicester
26.09.04 Neil Read W RSC 2 Stoke
(Vacant British Masters S.Bantamweight Title)
28.10.04 Colin Moffett L PTS 4 Belfast
12.11.05 Delroy Spencer W PTS 4 Stoke
18.02.06 Gary Ford L PTS 6 Stoke
10.03.06 Andrea Sarritzu L CO 4 Bergamo, Italy
06.05.06 Gary Sheil W PTS 6 Stoke
Career: 22 contests, won 8, drew 2, lost 12.

Lee Edwards

Sheffield. *Born* Huntingdon, 25 May, 1984
Middleweight. Ht. 5'11"
Manager G. Rhodes

08.05.05 Sergey Haritonov W PTS 6 Sheffield
24.07.05 Lee Williamson W PTS 6 Sheffield
30.10.05 Joe Mitchell L RSC 2 Sheffield
17.02.06 Malik Khan W RSC 6 Sheffield
Career: 4 contests, won 3, lost 1.

Sujad Elahi

Bradford. *Born* Bradford, 13 October, 1982
Welterweight. Ht. 5'11"
Manager G. Rhodes

23.09.04 David Pinkney L PTS 6 Gateshead
09.12.04 Gary Connolly W RSC 2 Sunderland
20.02.05 Scott Conway DREW 6 Sheffield
08.05.05 Lance Verallo W PTS 6 Sheffield
25.06.05 Andy Cosnett W CO 2 Wakefield
13.04.06 Barry Downes L RSC 3 Leeds
Career: 6 contests, won 3, drew 1, lost 2.

Wayne Elcock

Birmingham. *Born* Birmingham, 12 February, 1974
Middleweight. Former WBU Middleweight Champion. Ht. 5'9½"
Manager Self

02.12.99 William Webster W PTS 6 Peterborough
04.03.00 Sonny Pollard W RSC 3 Peterborough
07.07.01 Darren Rhodes W PTS 4 Manchester
09.10.01 Valery Odin W PTS 4 Cardiff
02.03.02 Charles Shodiya W RSC 1 Bethnal Green
20.04.02 Howard Clarke W PTS 4 Cardiff
01.06.02 Jason Collins W RSC 2 Manchester
17.08.02 Ojay Abrahams W PTS 4 Cardiff
23.11.02 Jason Collins W RSC 1 Derby
15.02.03 Yuri Tsarenko W PTS 10 Wembley
05.04.03 Anthony Farnell W PTS 12 Manchester
(WBU Middleweight Title Challenge)
29.11.03 Lawrence Murphy L CO 1 Renfrew
(WBU Middleweight Title Defence)
07.02.04 Farai Musiiwa W PTS 6 Bethnal Green
05.06.04 Michael Monaghan W PTS 4 Bethnal Green
07.04.05 Darren Rhodes W CO 1 Birmingham
16.09.05 Scott Dann L PTS 12 Plymouth
(British Middleweight Title Challenge)
06.05.06 Lawrence Murphy W RSC 5 Birmingham
(Elim. British Middleweight Title)
Career: 17 contests, won 15, lost 2.

Stuart Elwell

Darlaston. *Born* Walsall, 14 December, 1977
L.Middleweight. Midlands Area Welterweight Champion. Ht. 5'9"
Manager E. Johnson

06.11.00 Ernie Smith W PTS 6 Wolverhampton
28.01.01 Arv Mittoo W PTS 6 Wolverhampton
01.04.01 Richard Inquieti W PTS 6 Wolverhampton
06.10.05 Ernie Smith W PTS 6 Dudley
25.11.05 Ben Hudson W PTS 4 Walsall
10.03.06 David Kirk W PTS 10 Walsall
(Vacant Midlands Area Welterweight Title)
18.05.06 Peter Dunn W PTS 6 Walsall
23.06.06 Franny Jones W RSC 1 Blackpool
Career: 8 contests, won 8.

Steve Ede (left) fights it out with Anthony Young prior to scoring a third-round stoppage win
Les Clark

Andrew Facey

Sheffield. *Born* Wolverhampton, 20 May, 1972
S.Middleweight. English L.Middleweight Champion. Former Undefeated Central Area Middleweight Champion. Ht. 6'0"
Manager Self

06.12.99	Peter McCormack W CO 2 Birmingham	
09.06.00	Matthew Pepper W RSC 1 Hull	
04.11.00	Earl Ling W PTS 6 Derby	
11.12.00	Gary Jones W PTS 6 Cleethorpes	
10.02.01	Louis Swales W RSC 3 Widnes	
17.03.01	Darren Rhodes L PTS 4 Manchester	
24.03.01	Matthew Tait W PTS 4 Chigwell	
16.06.01	Earl Ling DREW 6 Derby	
09.12.01	Michael Pinnock W PTS 6 Shaw	
02.03.02	Darren Rhodes W RSC 6 Wakefield	

(Vacant Central Area Middleweight Title)

20.04.02	Darren Ashton W PTS 6 Derby
13.04.02	Leigh Wicks W PTS 6 Norwich
03.08.02	Damon Hague L CO 5 Derby

(Final Elim. WBF Middleweight Title)

25.10.02	William Webster W PTS 4 Cotgrave
16.04.03	Gilbert Eastman W RSC 3 Nottingham
06.11.03	Matthew Macklin W PTS 10 Dagenham

(Vacant English L.Middleweight Title)

22.11.03	Jamie Moore L RSC 7 Belfast

(British & Commonwealth L.Middleweight Title Challenges)

04.06.04	Howard Clarke W PTS 6 Hull
17.09.04	Jason Collins W PTS 4 Sheffield
03.09.05	Jason Collins W PTS 4 Norwich
29.10.05	Howard Clarke W PTS 6 Aberdeen
27.05.06	Ojay Abrahams W PTS 6 Aberdeen

Career: 22 contests, won 18, drew 1, lost 3.

Femi Fehintola

Bradford. *Born* Bradford, 1 July, 1982
Lightweight. Ht. 5'7"
Manager D. Hobson

26.09.03	John-Paul Ryan W PTS 6 Reading
07.11.03	Pete Buckley W PTS 6 Sheffield
10.12.03	Jason Nesbitt W PTS 6 Sheffield
06.02.04	Jason Nesbitt W PTS 6 Sheffield
20.04.04	Kristian Laight W PTS 6 Sheffield
17.06.04	Anthony Hanna W PTS 6 Sheffield
24.10.04	John-Paul Ryan W PTS 6 Sheffield
10.12.04	Philippe Meheust W PTS 6 Sheffield
04.03.05	Daniel Thorpe W PTS 6 Rotherham
24.07.05	Jason Nesbitt W PTS 6 Sheffield
14.10.05	Rakhim Mingaleev W PTS 8 Huddersfield
16.12.05	Frederic Gosset W PTS 8 Bracknell
18.03.06	Ivo Golakov W RSC 2 Monte Carlo, Monaco
13.05.06	Nikita Lukin W PTS 8 Sheffield

Career: 14 contests, won 14.

Andrew Ferrans

New Cumnock. *Born* Irvine, 4 February, 1981
S.Featherweight. Former Undefeated British Masters S.Featherweight Champion. Ht. 5'9"
Manager Self

19.02.00	Chris Lyons W PTS 6 Prestwick
03.03.00	Gary Groves W RSC 1 Irvine
20.03.00	John Barnes DREW 6 Glasgow
06.06.00	Duncan Armstrong W PTS 6 Motherwell
18.09.00	Steve Brook W PTS 6 Glasgow
20.11.00	Duncan Armstrong W PTS 6 Glasgow
23.02.01	Dave Cotterill L RSC 2 Irvine
30.04.01	Dave Cotterill W RSC 1 Glasgow
04.06.01	Jason Nesbitt W RSC 2 Glasgow
17.09.01	Gary Flear W PTS 8 Glasgow
10.12.01	Jamie McKeever L PTS 6 Liverpool
21.01.02	Joel Viney W PTS 8 Glasgow
01.03.02	Peter Allen W PTS 8 Irvine
13.04.02	Tony Mulholland L PTS 4 Liverpool
11.05.02	Marc Callaghan L PTS 6 Dagenham
23.09.02	Greg Edwards W RTD 4 Glasgow
08.10.02	Peter Allen W PTS 8 Glasgow
18.11.02	Joel Viney W PTS 6 Glasgow
30.11.02	Colin Toohey L PTS 6 Liverpool
28.02.03	Simon Chambers W RSC 7 Irvine
28.04.03	Craig Spacie L PTS 6 Nottingham
26.07.03	Baz Carey DREW 4 Plymouth
01.11.03	Anthony Hanna W PTS 4 Glasgow
19.01.04	Dariusz Snarski W PTS 6 Glasgow
15.03.04	Baz Carey W PTS 10 Glasgow

(Vacant British Masters S.Featherweight Title)

08.05.04	Carl Johanneson L RSC 6 Bristol

(WBF S.Featherweight Title Challenge)

26.02.05	Stephen Chinnock W RTD 5 Burton
24.10.05	Kristian Laight W PTS 8 Glasgow
23.02.06	Carl Johanneson L RSC 2 Leeds

(Final Elim. British S.Featherweight Title)

06.05.06	Sergii Tertii W PTS 6 Irvine

Career: 30 contests, won 20, drew 2, lost 8.

John Fewkes

Sheffield. *Born* Sheffield, 16 July, 1985
Central Area L.Welterweight Champion. Ht. 5'8"
Manager T. Gilmour/G. Rhodes

17.09.04	Mark Dane W RSC 2 Sheffield
24.10.04	Lea Handley W PTS 6 Sheffield
10.12.04	Jason Nesbitt W PTS 6 Sheffield
04.03.05	Jason Nesbitt W PTS 6 Rotherham
08.05.05	Chris Long W PTS 8 Sheffield
25.06.05	Billy Smith W PTS 6 Wakefield
24.07.05	Karl Taylor W PTS 6 Sheffield
09.09.05	Rakhim Mingaleev W PTS 4 Sheffield
30.10.05	Tony Montana W PTS 6 Sheffield
17.02.06	Tony Montana W PTS 10 Sheffield

(Central Area L.Welterweight Title Challenge)

Career: 10 contests, won 10.

(John Joseph) Jonjo Finnegan

Burton on Trent. *Born* Burton on Trent, 25 April, 1980
L.Heavyweight. Ht. 6'1"
Manager E. Johnson

08.07.04	Paul Billington W PTS 6 Birmingham
25.11.04	Nick Okoth DREW 6 Birmingham
26.02.05	Arv Mittoo W PTS 4 Burton
07.04.05	Peter Dunn W PTS 6 Birmingham
24.04.05	Omid Bourzo L PTS 6 Derby
30.09.05	Robert Burton DREW 4 Burton
25.11.05	Paul Billington W PTS 6 Walsall
28.01.06	Dave Pearson W PTS 4 Nottingham
25.03.06	Dave Pearson W PTS 8 Burton
13.05.06	Ernie Smith W PTS 6 Sutton in Ashfield
01.06.06	Mark Phillips W PTS 4 Birmingham

Career: 11 contests, won 8, drew 2, lost 1.

Jonjo Finnegan (left) is seen under attack from Mark Phillips before going on to win

Les Clark

Simon Fleck

Leicester. *Born* Leicester, 26 March, 1979
Middleweight. Ht. 6'0"
Manager M. Shinfield

22.10.05	Simone Lucas W RSC 5 Mansfield	
08.12.05	Tommy Jones W PTS 6 Derby	
02.03.06	Mark Thompson L CO 3 Blackpool	
24.04.06	Karl Taylor W PTS 6 Cleethorpes	

Career: 4 contests, won 3, lost 1.

Thomas Flynn

Darwin. *Born* Blackburn, 23 February, 1977
Middleweight. Ht. 5'11½"
Manager T. Schofield

22.06.06 Jak Hibbert L RSC 3 Sheffield

Career: 1 contest, lost 1.

Gary Ford

Oldham. *Born* Oldham, 27 July, 1973
S.Bantamweight. Ht. 5'1"
Manager J. Doughty

19.09.99	Paddy Folan W PTS 6 Shaw
05.03.00	Paddy Folan W PTS 6 Shaw
21.05.00	Andy Roberts DREW 6 Shaw
24.09.00	Nicky Booth L PTS 6 Shaw
18.03.01	Andrew Greenaway W RSC 1 Shaw
17.05.01	Levi Pattison L RSC 5 Leeds
20.09.04	Wayne Bloy L PTS 6 Cleethorpes
31.10.04	Neil Read W PTS 6 Shaw
06.06.05	Abdul Mougharbel L PTS 6 Glasgow
20.11.05	Tasif Khan DREW 6 Shaw
18.02.06	Chris Edwards W PTS 6 Stoke

Career: 11 contests, won 5, drew 2, lost 4.

Lee Fortt

Cardiff. *Born* Cardiff, 15 March, 1986
S.Bantamweight. Ht. 5'7¾"
Manager F. Maloney

30.10.05 Delroy Spencer W PTS 4 Bethnal
Green

Career: 1 contest, won 1.

Jon Foster

Oldham. *Born* Nottingham, 18 October, 1979
S.Middleweight. Ht. 6'1"
Manager M. Scriven

31.10.97	David Thompson W RSC 4 Ilkeston
26.11.97	Billy McDougall W RSC 2 Stoke
20.03.98	Phil Molyneux W PTS 6 Ilkeston
03.04.98	Harry Butler W PTS 6 Ebbw Vale
23.04.98	Hughie Davey L PTS 8 Newcastle
11.09.98	Brian Dunn W RTD 3 Cleethorpes
07.12.98	Darren Christie W RSC 6 Cleethorpes
06.06.99	Jason Collins DREW 6 Nottingham
20.09.99	Joe Townsley L PTS 6 Glasgow
11.12.99	Jacek Bielski L PTS 6 Merthyr
12.02.00	Zoltan Sarossy L RSC 1 Sheffield
06.06.00	James Docherty L PTS 6 Motherwell
24.09.00	Lee Murtagh L PTS 6 Shaw
25.04.05	Jed Tytler L RSC 2 Cleethorpes
28.01.06	Matthew Hall L RSC 3 Nottingham
04.03.06	Nathan Cleverly L PTS 4 Manchester
13.04.06	Brendan Halford L PTS 6 Leeds
14.05.06	Adie Whitmore L RSC 6 Derby

Career: 18 contests, won 6, drew 1, lost 11.

Steve Foster

Salford. *Born* Salford, 16 September, 1980
WBU Featherweight Champion. Former
Undefeated English Featherweight
Champion. Ht. 5'6"
Manager S.Foster/S.Wood/F.Warren

15.09.01	Andy Greenaway W PTS 4 Manchester
27.10.01	Gareth Wiltshaw W PTS 4 Manchester
02.03.02	Andy Greenaway W RSC 1 Bethnal Green
04.05.02	Gareth Wiltshaw W PTS 4 Bethnal Green
08.07.02	Ian Turner W RSC 1 Mayfair
20.07.02	Paddy Folan W CO 1 Bethnal Green
28.09.02	Jason White W RSC 3 Manchester
14.12.02	Sean Green W RSC 3 Newcastle
22.03.03	David McIntyre W PTS 4 Renfrew
24.05.03	Henry Janes W PTS 6 Bethnal Green
12.07.03	David McIntyre W RTD 3 Renfrew
18.09.03	Alexander Abramenko W RTD 4 Dagenham
06.11.03	Vladimir Borov W RSC 8 Dagenham
13.12.03	Steve Gethin W RTD 3 Manchester
26.02.04	Sean Hughes W RSC 6 Widnes *(Vacant English Featherweight Title)*
30.07.04	Jean-Marie Codet W PTS 8 Bethnal Green
01.10.04	Gary Thornhill W RSC 9 Manchester *(English Featherweight Title Defence)*
11.02.05	Livinson Ruiz W CO 10 Manchester *(Vacant WBU Featherweight Title)*
16.07.05	Jim Betts W RTD 5 Bolton
10.12.05	Buster Dennis DREW 8 Canning Town
01.04.06	John Simpson W PTS 12 Bethnal Green *(WBU Featherweight Title Defence)*

Career: 21 contests, won 20, drew 1.

Steve Foster   Les Clark

Dean Francis

Basingstoke. *Born* Basingstoke, 23 January, 1974
English Cruiserweight Champion. Former

Undefeated British, European & WBO
Inter-Continental S. Middleweight
Champion. Ht. 5'10½"
Manager Self

28.05.94	Darren Littlewood W PTS 4 Queensway
17.06.94	Martin Jolley W PTS 6 Plymouth
21.07.94	Horace Fleary W RSC 4 Tooting
02.09.94	Steve Osborne W RTD 4 Spitalfields
27.10.94	Tony Booth W CO 1 Bayswater
22.11.94	Darron Griffiths W RTD 1 Bristol
30.03.95	Paul Murray W RSC 2 Bethnal Green
25.05.95	Hunter Clay W RSC 8 Reading
16.06.95	Paul Murray W RTD 3 Southwark
20.10.95	Zafarou Ballogou L RSC 10 Ipswich *(WBC International S. Middleweight Title Challenge)*
16.12.95	Kid Milo W RSC 3 Cardiff
13.02.96	Mike Bonislawski W RSC 2 Bethnal Green
26.04.96	Neil Simpson W RSC 3 Cardiff
08.06.96	John Marceta W RSC 8 Newcastle
14.09.96	Larry Kenny W RSC 2 Sheffield
19.10.96	Rolando Torres W RSC 4 Bristol *(Vacant WBO Inter-Continental S. Middleweight Title)*
14.03.97	Cornelius Carr W RSC 7 Reading *(WBO Inter-Continental S. Middleweight Title Defence)*
15.05.97	Kit Munro W RSC 2 Reading *(WBO Inter-Continental S. Middleweight Title Defence)*
19.07.97	David Starie W RSC 6 Wembley *(British S. Middleweight Title Challenge)*
19.12.97	Frederic Seillier W RSC 9 Millwall *(Vacant European S. Middleweight Title)*
07.03.98	Mark Baker W RSC 12 Reading *(British & WBO Inter-Continental S. Middleweight Title Defences)*
22.08.98	Xolani Ngemntu W CO 2 Hammanskraal, South Africa *(WBO Inter-Continental S. Middleweight Title Defence)*
31.10.98	Undra White L RTD 4 Basingstoke *(Vacant IBO Inter-Continental S. Middleweight Title)*
20.04.02	Mondili Mbonambi W PTS 8 Wembley
29.03.03	Matthew Barney L PTS 12 Wembley *(Vacant British S. Middleweight Title)*
09.07.05	Paul Bonson W PTS 6 Bristol
12.11.05	Hastings Rasani W RSC 6 Bristol
25.02.06	Tommy Eastwood W PTS 10 Bristol *(Vacant English Cruiserweight Title)*

Career: 28 contests, won 25, lost 3.

Julius Francis

Woolwich. *Born* Peckham, 8 December, 1964
Heavyweight. Former Undefeated
Commonwealth Heavyweight Champion.
Former British Heavyweight Champion.
Former Undefeated Southern Area
Heavyweight Champion. Ht. 6'2"
Manager Self

23.05.93	Graham Arnold W RSC 5 Brockley
23.06.93	Joey Paladino W CO 4 Edmonton
24.07.93	Andre Tisdale W PTS 4 Atlantic City, New Jersey, USA

99

28.08.93 Don Sargent W RSC 2 Bismark, USA
01.12.93 John Keeton W PTS 4 Bethnal Green
27.04.94 Manny Burgo W PTS 4 Bethnal Green
25.05.94 John Ruiz L CO 4 Bristol
12.11.94 Conroy Nelson W RSC 4 Dublin
23.11.94 Gary Charlton W RSC 1 Piccadilly
23.02.05 Damien Caesar W RSC 8 Southwark
(Vacant Southern Area Heavyweight Title)
27.04.95 Keith Fletcher W PTS 10 Bethnal Green
(Southern Area Heavyweight Title Defence)
25.05.95 Steve Garber W PTS 8 Reading
01.07.95 Scott Welch L RSC 10 Kensington
(Southern Area Heavyweight Title Defence. Final Elim. British Heavyweight Title)
24.10.95 Neil Kirkwood W RSC 7 Southwark
30.11.95 Nikolai Kulpin L PTS 10 Saratov, Russia
05.02.96 Michael Murray L PTS 10 Bexleyheath
(Elim. British Heavyweight Title)
09.04.96 Damien Caesar W CO 1 Stevenage
(Vacant Southern Area Heavyweight Title)
07.05.96 Darren Fearn W PTS 8 Mayfair
09.07.96 Mike Holden W PTS 10 Bethnal Green
28.09.96 James Oyebola W RSC 5 Barking
(Southern Area Heavyweight Title Defence)
15.02.97 Zeljko Mavrovic L RSC 8 Vienna, Austria
(European Heavyweight Title Challenge)
30.06.97 Joseph Chingangu W PTS 12 Bethnal Green
(Vacant Commonwealth Heavyweight Title)
27.09.97 Garry Delaney W RSC 6 Belfast
(Commonwealth Heavyweight Title Defence. Vacant British Heavyweight Title)
28.02.98 Axel Schulz L PTS 12 Dortmund, Germany
18.04.98 Vitali Klitschko L RSC 2 Aachen, Germany
30.01.99 Pele Reid W RSC 3 Bethnal Green
(British & Commonwealth Heavyweight Title Defences)
03.04.99 Danny Williams W PTS 12 Kensington
(British & Commonwealth Heavyweight Title Defences)
26.06.99 Scott Welch W PTS 12 Millwall
(British & Commonwealth Heavyweight Title Defences)
29.01.00 Mike Tyson L RSC 2 Manchester
13.03.00 Mike Holden L PTS 12 Bethnal Green
(British Heavyweight Title Defence)
03.04.01 Mike Holden W PTS 12 Bethnal Green
(Final Elim. British Heavyweight Title)
28.07.01 Danny Williams L CO 4 Wembley
(British & Commonwealth Heavyweight Title Challenges)
10.05.02 Luke Simpkin DREW 6 Millwall
13.09.02 Steffen Nielsen W CO 6 Randers, Denmark
26.04.03 Sinan Samil Sam L RSC 7 Schwerin, Germany
(European Heavyweight Title Challenge)
13.06.03 Steffen Nielsen L PTS 10 Aalborg, Denmark
(Vacant European Union Heavyweight Title)

06.09.03 Vladimir Virchis L PTS 12 Kiev, Ukraine
(Vacant IBF Inter-Continental Interim Heavyweight Title)
18.10.03 Luan Krasniqi L PTS 8 Hamburg, Germany
27.11.03 Oleg Maskaev L RSC 2 Moscow, Russia
07.02.04 Matt Skelton L PTS 10 Bethnal Green
(English Heavyweight Title Challenge)
08.05.04 Audley Harrison L PTS 12 Bristol
(WBF Heavyweight Title Challenge)
31.07.04 Alexander Dimitrenko L PTS 8 Stuttgart, Germany
21.09.04 Taras Bidenko L PTS 10 Hamburg, Germany
10.12.04 Roman Greenberg L PTS 10 Sheffield
24.04.05 Micky Steeds L PTS 8 Leicester Square
26.06.05 Colin Kenna L PTS 4 Southampton
30.09.05 Scott Gammer L PTS 8 Carmarthen
21.05.06 Scott Lansdowne L PTS 4 Bethnal Green

Career: 48 contests, won 23, drew 1, lost 24.

Mark Franks (Whitemore)

Wakefield. *Born* Hannover, Germany, 29 September, 1975
L. Middleweight. Ht. 5'7¾"
Manager Self

06.12.04 Tommy Marshall L PTS 6 Leeds
18.04.05 Kaye Rehman DREW 6 Bradford
30.04.05 Rob MacDonald W RSC 6 Wigan
01.06.05 Geraint Harvey W PTS 6 Leeds
21.09.05 Malik Khan W RSC 1 Bradford
05.12.05 Simone Lucas W RSC 6 Leeds
20.03.06 Omar Gumati L RTD 4 Leeds

Career: 7 contests, won 4, drew 1, lost 2.

Carl Froch

Nottingham. *Born* Nottingham, 2 July, 1977
British & Commonwealth S.Middleweight Champion. Former Undefeated English S.Middleweight Champion. Ht. 6'4"
Manager Self

16.03.02 Michael Pinnock W RSC 4 Bethnal Green
10.05.02 Ojay Abrahams W RSC 1 Bethnal Green
23.08.02 Darren Covill W RSC 1 Bethnal Green
25.10.02 Paul Bonson W PTS 6 Bethnal Green
21.12.02 Mike Duffield W RSC 1 Dagenham
28.01.03 Valery Odin W RSC 6 Nottingham
05.03.03 Varuzhan Davtyan W RSC 5 Bethnal Green
16.04.03 Michael Monaghan W RSC 3 Nottingham
04.10.03 Vage Kocharyan W PTS 8 Muswell Hill
28.11.03 Alan Page W RSC 7 Derby
(Vacant English S.Middleweight Title. Elim. British S.Middleweight Title)
30.01.04 Dmitri Adamovich W RSC 2 Dagenham
12.03.04 Charles Adamu W PTS 12 Nottingham
(Commonwealth S.Middleweight Title Challenge)
02.06.04 Mark Woolnough W RSC 11 Nottingham
(Commonwealth S.Middleweight Title Defence)
24.09.04 Damon Hague W RSC 1 Nottingham

(Vacant British S.Middleweight Title. Commonwealth S.Middleweight Title Defence)
21.04.05 Henry Porras W RSC 8 Hollywood, California, USA
09.07.05 Matthew Barney W PTS 12 Nottingham
(British & Commonwealth S.Middleweight Title Defences)
02.12.05 Ruben Groenewald W RSC 5 Nottingham
(Commonwealth S.Middleweight Title Defence)
17.02.06 Dale Westerman W RSC 9 Bethnal Green
(Commonwealth S.Middleweight Title Defence)
26.05.06 Brian Magee W RSC 11 Bethnal Green
(British & Commonwealth S.Middleweight Title Defences)

Career: 19 contests, won 19.

Carl Froch   Les Clark

Courtney Fry

Wood Green. *Born* Enfield, 19 May, 1975
L. Heavyweight. Ht. 6'1½"
Manager C. Sanigar

29.03.03 Harry Butler W RSC 3 Wembley
31.05.03 Darren Ashton W PTS 4 Bethnal Green
24.10.03 Ovill McKenzie W PTS 4 Bethnal Green
20.03.04 Clint Johnson W RSC 2 Wembley
02.04.04 Paulie Silva W PTS 4 Plymouth
08.05.04 Radcliffe Green W PTS 6 Bristol
19.06.04 Valery Odin W PTS 8 Muswell Hill
17.12.04 Varuzhan Davtyan W RTD 2 Liverpool
13.05.05 Ovill McKenzie L PTS 4 Liverpool
07.04.06 Vasyl Kondor W PTS 6 Bristol

Career: 10 contests, won 9, lost 1.

G

Matt Galer

Burton. *Born* Burton, 15 December, 1973
Midlands Area L.Middleweight Champion.
Ht. 5'8"
Manager Self

30.09.97	Martin Cavey W CO 1 Edgbaston
18.11.97	Chris Pollock W PTS 6 Mansfield
16.03.98	Mike Duffield W PTS 6 Nottingham
14.05.98	Freddie Yemofio W RSC 4 Acton
14.10.98	Carlton Williams L PTS 6 Stoke
25.03.99	Gordon Behan L RSC 9 Edgbaston
	(Midlands Area Middleweight Title Challenge)
15.08.99	Jason Collins L PTS 6 Derby
13.11.01	Danny Thornton W RSC 4 Leeds
09.02.02	Anthony Farnell L RSC 3 Manchester
23.02.04	Ojay Abrahams W PTS 4 Nottingham
12.06.04	Gary Lockett L RSC 4 Manchester
24.09.04	Jim Rock L PTS 6 Dublin
26.02.05	Mark Phillips W PTS 6 Burton
30.09.05	Terry Adams W PTS 10 Burton
	(Vacant Midlands Area L.Middleweight Title)

Career: 14 contests, won 8, lost 6.

Scott Gammer

Pembroke Dock. *Born* Pembroke Dock, 24
October, 1976
British Heavyweight Champion. Ht. 6'2"
Manager P. Boyce

15.09.02	Leighton Morgan W RSC 1 Swansea
26.10.02	James Gilbert W RSC 1 Maesteg
08.01.03	Dave Clarke W PTS 4 Aberdare
25.01.03	Ahmad Cheleh W CO 1 Bridgend
28.06.03	Dave Clarke W RSC 1 Cardiff
13.09.03	Derek McCafferty W PTS 6 Newport
08.11.03	Mendauga Kulikauskas DREW 6 Bridgend
28.02.04	James Zikic W PTS 6 Bridgend
01.05.04	Paul Buttery W CO 1 Bridgend
02.06.04	Paul King W RSC 3 Hereford
17.09.04	Carl Baker W PTS 4 Plymouth
05.11.04	Roman Bugaj W RSC 2 Hereford
18.02.05	Micky Steeds W PTS 6 Brighton
15.05.05	Mark Krence W RSC 8 Sheffield
	(Elim. British Heavyweight Title)
30.09.05	Julius Francis W PTS 8 Carmarthen
10.12.05	Suren Kalachyan W PTS 6 Canning Town
16.06.06	Mark Krence W RSC 9 Carmarthen
	(Vacant British Heavyweight Title)

Career: 17 contests, won 16, drew 1.

Brian Gascoigne

Kirkby in Ashfield. *Born* Kirkby in
Ashfield, 4 June, 1970
Cruiserweight. Ht. 6'5"
Manager M. Scriven

23.11.98	Lennox Williams W RSC 3 Piccadilly
30.04.99	Shane Woollas DREW 6 Scunthorpe
03.10.99	Lee Swaby DREW 6 Chesterfield
06.12.99	Mark Hobson L RSC 3 Bradford
09.04.00	Nigel Rafferty W PTS 6 Alfreton

25.06.00	Danny Southam L RSC 4 Wakefield
04.12.00	Huggy Osman L PTS 6 Bradford
10.04.01	Kevin Barrett L RSC 1 Wembley
26.09.02	Adam Cale W PTS 4 Fulham
17.02.03	Tony Moran L RSC 1 Glasgow
31.05.03	Nate Joseph W RTD 1 Barnsley
02.06.03	Costi Marin W PTS 6 Glasgow
26.11.03	Tommy Eastwood L RSC 2 Mayfair
12.11.04	Simon Francis L RSC 1 Halifax
11.09.05	Gary Thompson DREW 6 Kirkby in Ashfield

Career: 15 contests, won 5, drew 3, lost 7.

Darren Gethin

Walsall. *Born* Walsall, 19 August, 1976
L.Middleweight. Ht. 5'8"
Manager E. Johnson

08.07.04	Joe Mitchell DREW 6 Birmingham
12.09.04	Joe Mitchell W PTS 6 Shrewsbury
12.11.04	Tyrone McInerney L PTS 4 Halifax
26.02.05	Tye Williams DREW 4 Burton
18.04.05	Joe Mitchell W PTS 6 Bradford
25.04.05	Terry Carruthers L RSC 3 Cleethorpes
02.06.05	Franny Jones L PTS 8 Yarm
02.09.05	Scott Conway W RSC 1 Derby
10.09.05	Nathan Cleverly L PTS 4 Cardiff
01.10.05	Johnny Hussey L PTS 6 Wigan
22.10.05	Joe McCluskey DREW 6 Coventry
12.02.06	Mark Thompson L PTS 4 Manchester
23.02.06	Khurram Hussain DREW 4 Leeds
03.03.06	Jason Rushton W PTS 6 Doncaster
24.04.06	Gary McArthur L PTS 6 Glasgow
09.05.06	Danny Reynolds DREW 4 Leeds
18.05.06	Lance Hall W PTS 6 Walsall
01.06.06	Craig Dickson W PTS 6 Birmingham

Career: 18 contests, won 6, drew 5, lost 7.

Martin Gethin

Walsall. *Born* Walsall, 16 November, 1983
L.Welterweight. Ht. 5'6"
Manager E. Johnson

18.11.04	Kristian Laight W RSC 4 Shrewsbury
15.04.05	Jason Nesbitt W PTS 6 Shrewsbury
06.10.05	John-Paul Ryan W RSC 2 Dudley
25.11.05	Michael Medor W PTS 4 Walsall
10.03.06	Carl Allen W PTS 4 Walsall
01.06.06	Baz Carey W PTS 4 Birmingham

Career: 6 contests, won 6.

Martin Gethin　　　　　Les Clark

Steve Gethin

Walsall. *Born* Walsall, 30 July, 1978
Lightweight. Ht. 5'9"
Manager Self

03.09.99	Ike Halls W RSC 3 West Bromwich
24.10.99	Ricky Bishop W RSC 4 Wolverhampton
22.01.00	Sebastian Hart L PTS 4 Birmingham
10.09.00	Nigel Senior DREW 6 Walsall
03.06.01	Richmond Asante L PTS 4 Southwark
28.11.01	Mickey Coveney L PTS 4 Bethnal Green
09.12.01	Gary Groves W PTS 6 Shaw
17.02.02	Gary Groves W PTS 6 Wolverhampton
01.06.02	Gary Davis W RSC 2 Manchester
21.09.02	Marc Callaghan L PTS 6 Brentwood
02.12.02	Neil Read W RTD 3 Leicester
14.12.02	Isaac Ward L PTS 4 Newcastle
08.02.03	Rocky Dean DREW 4 Norwich
15.02.03	Anthony Hanna W PTS 6 Wolverhampton
08.05.03	Derry Matthews L RSC 3 Widnes
07.09.03	Henry Janes L PTS 4 Shrewsbury
02.10.03	Mark Moran L PTS 4 Liverpool
20.10.03	John Simpson L PTS 8 Glasgow
30.10.03	Gareth Payne W PTS 6 Dudley
13.12.03	Steve Foster L RTD 3 Manchester
05.03.04	Isaac Ward L PTS 6 Darlington
27.05.04	Marc Callaghan L PTS 6 Huddersfield
30.07.04	Chris Hooper L PTS 4 Bethnal Green
08.10.04	Ian Napa L PTS 6 Brentwood
22.10.04	Andy Bell L RSC 5 Mansfield
17.12.04	Mark Moran L PTS 4 Liverpool
13.02.05	Patrick Hyland L PTS 4 Brentwood
24.04.05	Darren Broomhall W CO 5 Derby
09.07.05	Billy Corcoran L PTS 6 Nottingham
05.11.05	Amir Khan L RSC 3 Renfrew
24.03.06	Ian Wilson L PTS 4 Bethnal Green
06.05.06	Paul Newby L PTS 4 Birmingham
13.05.06	Andy Bell W RSC 2 Sutton in Ashfield
21.05.06	Mark Alexander L PTS 4 Bethnal Green

Career: 34 contests, won 10, drew 2, lost 22.

Alan Gilbert

Crawley. *Born* Bromley, 17 November,
1970
Middleweight. Ht. 5'11"
Manager Self

02.12.97	Martin Cavey W RSC 1 Windsor
06.01.98	Harry Butler W PTS 4 Brighton
23.02.98	Jon Harrison W PTS 6 Windsor
21.04.98	Paul Henry L PTS 4 Edmonton
08.08.98	Lee Murtagh L PTS 4 Scarborough
03.10.98	C. J. Jackson W RSC 3 Crawley
25.02.99	Justin Simmons W RSC 5 Kentish Town
01.05.99	Anthony Farnell L RSC 8 Crystal Palace
07.08.99	Wayne Shepherd DREW 8 Dagenham
	(Vacant British Masters L.Middleweight Title)
11.03.00	Michael Jones L RTD 3 Kensington
12.06.00	Jim Rock L PTS 6 Belfast
22.07.00	Delroy Mellis L RSC 3 Watford
	(Vacant Southern Area L.Middleweight Title)
23.01.01	Delroy Mellis L RSC 3 Crawley
	(Southern Area L. Middleweight Title Challenge)
29.09.01	Steven Bendall L RTD 3 Southwark
10.02.02	Allan Gray DREW 4 Southwark
28.04.02	Allan Gray L PTS 10 Southwark
	(Vacant Southern Area Middleweight Title)

03.08.02	Lee Blundell L RSC 6 Blackpool	

(IBF Inter-Continental Middleweight Title Challenge)

15.10.02	Dean Powell W PTS 4 Bethnal Green
28.04.03	Ben Ogden L RSC 1 Nottingham
20.06.03	Leigh Wicks W PTS 4 Gatwick
25.07.03	Ryan Rhodes L RSC 5 Norwich
21.02.04	Leigh Wicks W PTS 4 Brighton
17.04.04	Jason McKay L PTS 6 Belfast
13.05.04	Gokhan Kazaz L PTS 4 Bethnal Green
24.04.05	Ruben Groenewald L RSC 10 Leicester Square

(Vacant WBF Inter-Continental S.Middleweight Title)

19.06.05	Gokhan Kazaz L PTS 6 Bethnal Green
16.07.05	Ryan Rhodes L RSC 2 Bolton

Career: 27 contests, won 8, drew 2, lost 17.

Ruben Giles

Virginia Water. *Born* Woking, 1 April, 1987
L.Middleweight. Ht. 5'7½"
Manager J. Evans

28.05.06	Barry Downes W PTS 4 Longford

Career: 1 contest, won 1.

Jimmy Gilhaney

Newmains. *Born* Lanark, 8 April, 1982
Lightweight. Ht. 5'7"
Manager T. Gilmour

25.04.05	Pete Buckley W PTS 6 Glasgow
14.10.05	Pete Buckley W PTS 6 Motherwell
24.10.05	Anthony Christopher W PTS 6 Glasgow
20.02.06	Sergei Rozhakmens W PTS 6 Glasgow

Career: 4 contests, won 4.

Tom Glover

Maldon, Essex. *Born* Maldon, 21 June, 1981
L.Welterweight. Ht. 5'6½"
Manager F. Maloney

11.02.06	Billy Smith W PTS 4 Bethnal Green
24.03.06	Gavin Tait L PTS 4 Bethnal Green
03.06.06	Ben Hudson W PTS 4 Chigwell

Career: 3 contests, won 2, lost 1.

Wayne Goddard

Bordon. *Born* Portsmouth, 10 March, 1986
Welterweight. Ht. 5'8¾"
Manager F. Maloney

30.10.05	Ben Hudson W PTS 4 Bethnal Green
27.01.06	James Gorman W PTS 4 Dagenham
26.05.06	Omar Gumati W PTS 4 Bethnal Green

Career: 3 contests, won 3.

Michael Gomez (Armstrong)

Manchester. *Born* Dublin, 21 June, 1977
Lightweight. Former WBU S.Featherweight Champion. Former Undefeated WBO Inter-Continental & British S.Featherweight Champion. Former WBO Inter-Continental S.Featherweight Champion. Former Undefeated Central Area & IBF Inter-Continental Featherweight Champion. Ht. 5'5"
Manager F. Warren/T. Jones

10.06.95	Danny Ruegg W PTS 6 Manchester
15.09.95	Greg Upton L PTS 4 Mansfield
24.11.95	Danny Ruegg L PTS 4 Manchester
19.09.96	Martin Evans W RSC 1 Manchester
09.11.96	David Morris W PTS 4 Manchester
22.03.97	John Farrell W RSC 2 Wythenshawe
03.05.97	Chris Williams L PTS 4 Manchester
11.09.97	Wayne Jones W RSC 2 Widnes
18.04.98	Benny Jones W PTS 4 Manchester
16.05.98	Craig Spacie W RSC 3 Bethnal Green
05.09.98	Pete Buckley W PTS 6 Telford
14.11.98	David Jeffrey W RSC 1 Cheshunt
19.12.98	Kevin Sheil W RSC 4 Liverpool
13.02.99	Dave Hinds W PTS 6 Newcastle
27.02.99	Chris Jickells W RSC 5 Oldham

(Vacant Central Area Featherweight Title)

29.05.99	Nigel Leake W RSC 2 Halifax

(Vacant IBF Inter-Continental Featherweight Title)

07.08.99	William Alverzo W PTS 6 Atlantic City, New Jersey, USA
04.09.99	Gary Thornhill W RSC 2 Bethnal Green

(Vacant British S. Featherweight Title)

06.11.99	Jose Juan Manjarrez W PTS 12 Widnes

(WBO Inter-Continental S. Featherweight Title Defence)

11.12.99	Oscar Galindo W RSC 11 Liverpool

(WBO Inter-Continental S. Featherweight Title Defence)

29.01.00	Chris Jickells W RSC 4 Manchester
29.02.00	Dean Pithie W PTS 12 Widnes

(British S. Featherweight Title Defence)

24.06.00	Carl Allen W CO 2 Glasgow
08.07.00	Carl Greaves W CO 2 Widnes

(British S. Featherweight Title Defence)

19.10.00	Awel Abdulai W PTS 8 Harrisburg, USA
11.12.00	Ian McLeod W PTS 12 Widnes

(British S.Featherweight Title Defence)

10.02.01	Laszlo Bognar L RSC 9 Widnes

(WBO Inter-Continental S. Featherweight Title Defence)

07.07.01	Laszlo Bognar W RSC 3 Manchester

(WBO Inter-Continental S. Featherweight Title Challenge)

27.10.01	Craig Docherty W RSC 2 Manchester

(British S.Featherweight Title Defence)

01.06.02	Kevin Lear L RTD 8 Manchester

(Vacant WBU S. Featherweight Title)

28.09.02	Jimmy Beech W RSC 4 Manchester
18.01.03	Rakhim Mingaleev W RTD 4 Preston
05.04.03	Vladimir Borov W RSC 3 Manchester
25.10.03	Alex Arthur W RSC 5 Edinburgh

(British S.Featherweight Title Challenge)

03.04.04	Ben Odamattey W RSC 3 Manchester

(Vacant WBU S.Featherweight Title)

22.05.04	Justin Juuko W RSC 2 Widnes

(WBU S.Featherweight Title Defence)

01.10.04	Leva Kirakosyan W RTD 6 Manchester

(WBU S.Featherweight Title Defence)

11.02.05	Javier Osvaldo Alvarez L RSC 6 Manchester

(WBU S.Featherweight Title Defence)

28.01.06	Peter McDonagh L RSC 5 Dublin

(Vacant All-Ireland Lightweight Title)

Career: 39 contests, won 32, lost 7.

Danny Goode

New Milton. *Born* Wimbledon, 15 January, 1980
Middleweight. Ht. 5'8"
Manager M. Roe

16.10.04	Geraint Harvey W PTS 4 Dagenham
06.02.05	Neil Jarmolinski W PTS 4 Southampton
23.03.05	Tony Randell W PTS 6 Leicester Square
30.04.05	John-Paul Temple W PTS 4 Dagenham
26.06.05	John-Paul Temple W PTS 4 Southampton
18.09.05	Rocky Muscus W PTS 4 Bethnal Green
05.03.06	Terry Adams W PTS 8 Southampton
07.04.06	Jamie Ambler W PTS 4 Longford

Career: 8 contests, won 8.

Simon Goodwin

Cambridge. *Born* Cambridge, 13 January, 1979
Cruiserweight. Ht. 6'2"
Manager Self

28.07.03	Marcus Lee L PTS 4 Plymouth
06.12.04	Billy Wilson L PTS 6 Leeds
16.12.05	Matt Paice L PTS 4 Bracknell
23.06.06	Chris Burton L RSC 3 Blackpool

Career: 4 contests, lost 4.

James Gorman

Belfast. *Born* Belfast, 1 August, 1979
L.Welterweight. Ht. 5'8"
Manager Self

28.06.03	Jamie Arthur L PTS 4 Cardiff
11.10.03	Lee Beavis L PTS 4 Portsmouth
25.10.03	George Telfer L PTS 4 Edinburgh
22.11.03	Peter McDonagh W PTS 4 Belfast
28.02.04	Ceri Hall L PTS 6 Bridgend
01.04.04	Lee Beavis L RTD 2 Bethnal Green
24.09.04	Silence Saheed L PTS 6 Millwall
12.11.04	Jas Malik W RTD 2 Belfast
18.03.05	Stephen Haughian L PTS 4 Belfast
14.05.05	Pete Buckley W PTS 6 Dublin
24.06.05	Daniel Thorpe W PTS 6 Belfast
30.09.05	George Hillyard L RSC 1 Kirkcaldy
24.11.05	Stephen Haughian L PTS 6 Lurgan
27.01.06	Wayne Goddard L PTS 4 Dagenham

Career: 14 contests, won 4, lost 10.

Sam Gorman

Alfreton. *Born* Nuneaton, 19 October, 1981
L.Middleweight. Ht. 5'9"
Manager P. Carpenter

17.11.01	Shaune Danskin W RSC 3 Coventry
09.02.02	Pete Buckley W PTS 6 Coventry
22.03.02	Brian Coleman W PTS 6 Coventry
25.06.02	Pedro Thompson W PTS 6 Rugby
17.11.02	Wayne Shepherd L PTS 6 Shaw
18.03.06	Tony Randell L PTS 6 Coventry

Career: 6 contests, won 4, lost 2.

Nathan Graham

Aylesbury. *Born* Aylesbury, 21 September, 1982
Middleweight. Ht. 5'9"
Manager D. Williams

24.04.04	Tom Price W RSC 2 Reading
02.12.04	David Payne W RSC 3 Crystal Palace
26.03.05	Gatis Skuja W RSC 1 Hackney
19.11.05	Geraint Harvey W PTS 4 Southwark
26.02.06	Duncan Cottier W PTS 4 Dagenham

Career: 5 contests, won 5.

Danny Grainger

Chesterfield. *Born* Chesterfield, 1 September, 1979
Cruiserweight. Ht. 5'11"
Manager Self

05.10.02 Jamie Wilson W PTS 6 Chesterfield
21.10.02 Jamie Wilson W PTS 6 Cleethorpes
29.11.02 Gary Jones W PTS 6 Hull
08.06.03 Darren Stubbs W RSC 2 Shaw
12.10.03 Paul Billington W PTS 6 Sheffield
03.04.04 Terry Morrill W RSC 5 Sheffield
04.06.04 Patrick Cito W PTS 6 Hull
15.05.05 Hastings Rasani L RSC 5 Sheffield
05.03.06 Jimi Hendricks W PTS 6 Sheffield
Career: 9 contests, won 8, lost 1.

Michael Grant

Tottenham. *Born* London, 2 November, 1983
L.Welterweight. Ht. 5'7"
Manager C. Hall

24.07.05 David Kehoe W PTS 4 Leicester Square
16.09.05 Judex Meemea W RSC 3 Plymouth
09.10.05 Ali Wyatt DREW 4 Hammersmith
13.01.06 Patrik Prokopecz W PTS 4 Torrevieja, Spain
02.02.06 Pete Buckley W PTS 4 Holborn
30.03.06 Franck Aiello W PTS 4 Piccadilly
19.05.06 Lubos Priehradnik W PTS 6 Torrevieja, Spain
03.06.06 Ali Wyatt W PTS 4 Chigwell
Career: 8 contests, won 7, drew 1.

Michael Grant   Les Clark

Allan Gray

Putney. *Born* Roehampton, 4 August, 1971
Middleweight. Former Undefeated Southern Area Middleweight Champion. Former Undefeated WBF Inter-Continental Southern Area Middleweight Champion. Ht. 5'9"
Manager Self

19.05.95 Darren Covill W PTS 6 Southwark
23.06.95 Wayne Jones W PTS 6 Bethnal Green
27.09.95 Brian Coleman W PTS 6 Bethnal Green
28.10.95 John O. Johnson W PTS 6 Kensington
29.11.95 Justin Simmons L PTS 6 Bethnal Green

08.12.95 Mike Watson W PTS 8 Bethnal Green
15.03.96 Mike Watson DREW 6 Dunstable
29.04.96 Mike Watson W PTS 6 Mayfair
03.07.96 Jon Harrison W PTS 6 Wembley
24.10.96 Costas Katsantonis W PTS 6 Mayfair
29.01.97 Gary Hiscox W PTS 6 Bethnal Green
19.02.97 Costas Katsantonis W PTS 6 Acton
30.04.97 Howard Clarke L PTS 8 Acton
27.01.98 Peter Nightingale W PTS 6 Streatham
26.09.98 Harry Dhami L PTS 10 Southwark
(Southern Area Welterweight Title Challenge)
16.02.99 Lee Bird W PTS 6 Brentford
31.10.99 Matthew Barr L PTS 4 Raynes Park
15.04.00 Jim Rock L PTS 10 Bethnal Green
(Vacant All-Ireland L. Middleweight Title)
22.10.00 Delroy Mellis L RSC 6 Streatham
(Southern Area L.Middleweight Title Challenge)
28.10.01 Leigh Wicks W PTS 4 Southwark
16.12.01 Leigh Wicks W PTS 4 Southwark
10.02.02 Alan Gilbert DREW 4 Southwark
28.04.02 Alan Gilbert W PTS 10 Southwark
(Vacant Southern Area Middleweight Title)
12.12.02 Ojay Abrahams W PTS 10 Leicester Square
(Southern Area Middleweight Title Defence. Vacant WBF Inter-Continental Middleweight Title)
05.07.03 Dirk Dzemski L PTS 12 Dessau, Germany
(NBA Middleweight Title Challenge)
20.02.04 Matthew Tait W PTS 10 Bethnal Green
(Southern Area Middleweight Title Defence)
10.09.05 Gary Lockett L CO 2 Cardiff
12.05.06 Ben Hudson L PTS 4 Bethnal Green
Career: 28 contests, won 17, drew 2, lost 9.

Michael Graydon

Bristol. *Born* Bristol, 30 October, 1985
L.Welterweight. Ht. 5'9"
Manager C. Sanigar

13.02.04 Fred Janes DREW 6 Bristol
08.05.04 Peter Allen W PTS 6 Bristol
03.07.04 Henry Jones DREW 6 Bristol
01.10.04 Daleboy Rees W PTS 6 Bristol
07.04.06 Billy Smith L PTS 4 Bristol
Career: 5 contests, won 2, drew 2, lost 1.

(Roger) Radcliffe Green

Balham. *Born* Jamaica, 24 November, 1973
Cruiserweight. Ht. 5'9½"
Manager W. Fuller

26.03.01 Peter Haymer L PTS 4 Wembley
22.04.01 Adam Cale W CO 5 Streatham
03.06.01 Rob Hayes-Scott W RSC 4 Southwark
21.07.01 John Keeton L PTS 4 Sheffield
28.10.01 Michael Pinnock W PTS 4 Southwark
16.11.01 Darren Corbett L PTS 8 Dublin
10.02.02 Valery Odin L PTS 6 Southwark
20.04.02 Nathan King L PTS 6 Cardiff
04.05.02 Andrew Lowe L PTS 4 Bethnal Green
22.09.02 Mark Baker L PTS 6 Southwark
27.10.02 Neil Linford DREW 10 Southwark
(Vacant British Masters L.Heavyweight Title)
08.02.03 Eric Teymour L RTD 1 Norwich
29.03.03 Andrew Lowe L PTS 10 Wembley
(Vacant Southern Area L. Heavyweight Title)

26.09.03 Tony Booth L PTS 6 Millwall
07.11.03 Andrew Lowe L PTS 6 Sheffield
07.02.04 Bruce Scott L PTS 6 Bethnal Green
08.05.04 Courtney Fry L PTS 6 Bristol
15.12.04 Simon Francis L PTS 6 Sheffield
04.02.05 Gareth Hogg L PTS 4 Plymouth
20.02.05 Henry Smith L PTS 6 Bristol
08.04.05 Neil Hosking W RSC 2 Bristol
19.06.05 Junior MacDonald L RTD 1 Bethnal Green
25.11.05 Gyorgy Hidvegi L RTD 2 Liverpool
25.02.06 Darren Morgan L RSC 3 Canning Town
Career: 24 contests, won 4, drew 1, lost 19.

Stuart Green

Glenrothes. *Born* Kirkcaldy, 13 December, 1984
Lightweight. Ht. 5'6"
Manager T. Gilmour

17.11.03 Chris Long W PTS 6 Glasgow
12.03.04 Jason Nesbitt W PTS 8 Irvine
07.06.04 Gavin Tait W PTS 6 Glasgow
11.10.04 Paul Holborn L PTS 6 Glasgow
21.02.05 Pete Buckley W PTS 6 Glasgow
11.06.05 Dave Hinds W PTS 4 Plymouth
30.09.05 Fred Janes W PTS 4 Kirkcaldy
17.03.06 Adam Kelly W PTS 4 Kirkcaldy
21.04.06 Michael Kelly L PTS 6 Belfast
27.05.06 Lee McAllister L RSC 8 Aberdeen
(Vacant Scottish Area Lightweight Title)
Career: 10 contests, won 7, lost 3.

Roman Greenberg

Finchley. *Born* Russia, 18 May, 1982
IBO Inter-Continental Heavyweight Champion. Ht. 6'2½"
Manager J. Evans

22.11.01 Dave Clarke W RSC 5 Paddington
25.02.02 Paul Bonson W PTS 6 Slough
25.04.02 Jakarta Nakyru W RSC 4 Las Vegas, Nevada, USA
28.11.02 Tony Booth W PTS 4 Finchley
05.12.02 Dave Clarke W RSC 1 Sheffield
20.12.02 Derek McCafferty W PTS 4 Bracknell
24.01.03 Piotr Jurczyk W CO 1 Sheffield
04.03.03 Calvin Miller W RSC 2 Miami, Florida, USA
18.03.03 Gary Williams W RSC 1 Reading
15.05.03 Tracy Williams W RTD 2 Miami, Florida, USA
29.05.03 Troy Beets W RSC 3 Miami, Florida, USA
05.09.03 Luke Simpkin W RTD 4 Sheffield
18.09.03 Konstanin Prizyuk W RSC 1 Mayfair
26.11.03 Mendauga Kulikauskas W RSC 5 Mayfair
15.04.04 Jason Gethers W RSC 6 NYC, New York, USA
10.09.04 Vitaly Shkraba W PTS 6 Wembley
10.12.04 Julius Francis W PTS 10 Sheffield
28.01.05 Marcus McGee W RSC 4 NYC, New York, USA
11.06.05 Josh Gutcher W RSC 4 Las Vegas, Nevada, USA
20.07.05 Mamadou Sacko W PTS 8 Monte Carlo, Monaco
16.12.05 Kendrick Releford W PTS 10 Bracknell

18.03.06 Alex Vassilev W RSC 6 Monte Carlo, Monaco
(Vacant IBO Inter-Continental Heavyweight Title)
Career: 22 contests, won 22.

Derrick Grieve

Bradford. *Born* Darwen, 10 March, 1982
L.Middleweight. Ht. 5'10½"
Manager D. Coldwell

06.05.06 Danny Johnston L RSC 3 Stoke
Career: 1 contest, lost 1.

Ruben Groenewald

Beckton. *Born* Brakpan, South Africa, 13 October, 1977
S.Middleweight. Former Undefeated WBF Inter-Continental S.Middleweight Champion. Former Undefeated WBU Middleweight Champion. Former Undefeated British Masters S.Middleweight Champion. Former Undefeated All-African Middleweight Champion. Ht. 5'11"
Manager Self

27.03.96 Andries Gogome DREW 4 Johannesburg, South Africa
21.04.96 Clifford Smith W PTS 4 Thabong, South Africa
03.07.96 Michael Ramabele W PTS 4 Johannesburg, South Africa
11.08.96 Alpheus Phungula W PTS 4 Durban, South Africa
01.09.96 Andries Gogome L PTS 4 Johannesburg, South Africa
22.06.97 Edward Ramathape W RSC 2 Johannesburg, South Africa

25.11.97 David Ramantsi W RSC 1 Temba, South Africa
31.05.98 Roland Francis DREW 6 Durban, South Africa
24.06.98 Sipho Ndele W RSC 4 Johannesburg, South Africa
26.08.98 Boyisela Mashalele W PTS 6 Johannesburg, South Africa
14.10.98 Mondi Mbonambi W PTS 8 Secunda, South Africa
03.08.99 Sipho Sibeko DREW 6 Temba, South Africa
23.11.99 John Tshabalala W PTS 6 Temba, South Africa
10.03.00 Delroy Leslie L PTS 12 Bethnal Green
(Vacant Interim WBF Middleweight Title)
20.09.00 Elvis Adonisi W CO 10 Carnival City, South Africa
24.10.00 Cyprian Emeti W RSC 11 Carnival City, South Africa
(Vacant All-African L.Middleweight Title)
24.02.01 Ojay Abrahams W PTS 6 Bethnal Green
03.04.01 Paul Bowen W PTS 6 Bethnal Green
21.07.01 Terry Morrill W RSC 4 Sheffield
20.09.01 Harry Butler W PTS 4 Blackfriars
09.10.01 Leigh Wicks W PTS 6 Cardiff
10.02.02 Wayne Asker W PTS 10 Southwark
(Vacant British Masters S.Middleweight Title)
01.06.02 Anthony Farnell W PTS 12 Manchester
(Vacant WBU Middleweight Title)
28.09.02 Anthony Farnell L PTS 12 Manchester
(WBU Middleweight Title Defence)
23.10.04 Danilo Haussler L PTS 8 Berlin, Germany
24.04.05 Alan Gilbert W RSC 10 Leicester Square

(Vacant WBF Inter-Continental S.Middleweight Title)
02.12.05 Carl Froch L RSC 5 Nottingham
(Commonwealth S.Middleweight Title Challenge)
Career: 27 contests, won 19, drew 3, lost 5.

Omar Gumati

Chester. *Born* Chester, 18 May, 1984
Middleweight. Ht. 5'9"
Manager Self

07.05.03 Craig Goodman W PTS 6 Ellesmere Port
02.10.03 Danny Moir L PTS 6 Sunderland
01.12.03 Ojay Abrahams W PTS 6 Leeds
05.12.05 Ryan Ashworth L PTS 6 Leeds
15.12.05 Davey Jones L PTS 6 Cleethorpes
11.02.06 Paul Porter W RSC 3 Bethnal Green
09.03.06 Martin Marshall DREW 6 Sunderland
20.03.06 Mark Franks W RTD 4 Leeds
23.04.06 Joe Mitchell W PTS 4 Chester
26.05.06 Wayne Goddard L PTS 4 Bethnal Green
Career: 10 contests, won 5, drew 1, lost 4.

Jake Guntert

Abingdon. *Born* Oxford, 14 January, 1983
S.Middleweight. Ht. 5'10"
Manager F. Maloney

07.05.04 Lee Williamson W PTS 6 Bethnal Green
25.06.04 Mark Wall W CO 1 Bethnal Green
24.09.04 Neil Addis W PTS 6 Bethnal Green
26.11.04 Dean Powell W PTS 4 Bethnal Green
12.02.05 Leigh Wicks W PTS 4 Portsmouth
30.10.05 Tony Randell W PTS 4 Bethnal Green
26.05.06 Steve Ede L RSC 2 Bethnal Green
Career: 7 contests, won 6, lost 1.

Dan Guthrie

Yeovil. *Born* Taunton, 23 July, 1982
S.Middleweight. Ht. 6'2"
Manager C. Sanigar

03.12.04 Mark Phillips W RSC 1 Bristol
04.02.05 Egbui Ikeagwo DREW 4 Plymouth
08.04.05 Nick Okoth W RSC 2 Bristol
16.09.05 Paulie Silva L RSC 2 Plymouth
17.11.05 Marko Doknic W PTS 4 Bristol
10.02.06 David Payne W RSC 2 Plymouth
07.04.06 Hamid Jamali W RSC 3 Bristol
Career: 7 contests, won 5, drew 1, lost 1.

Danny Gwilym

Bristol. *Born* Bristol, 15 January, 1975
L.Middleweight. Ht. 5'7"
Manager Self

16.12.01 Wayne Wheeler L RSC 2 Bristol
11.02.02 James Lee L PTS 6 Southampton
12.07.02 Mo W PTS 6 Southampton
26.02.03 Wasim Hussain W PTS 6 Bristol
17.03.03 Danny Cooper L PTS 6 Southampton
16.04.03 Lenny Daws L RSC 2 Nottingham
26.09.03 Darren Covill W PTS 6 Millwall
12.10.03 Mo L PTS 6 Sheffield
06.12.03 Martin Concepcion L RSC 2 Cardiff
09.07.05 Arv Mittoo W RSC 4 Bristol
24.07.05 Garry Buckland L RSC 2 Leicester Square
12.11.05 Kristian Laight W PTS 6 Bristol
Career: 12 contests, won 5, lost 7.

Roman Greenberg (right) is pictured on his way to a ten-round points win over Kendrick Releford
Les Clark

Andy Halder

Coventry. *Born* Coventry, 22 August, 1973
S.Middleweight. Former Undefeated WBF
Inter-Continental Middleweight Champion.
Former Midlands Area Middleweight
Champion. Ht. 5'11"
Manager Self

13.07.02	Martin Scotland W PTS 4 Coventry
05.10.02	Andrei Ivanov W PTS 6 Coventry
25.10.02	Jon Hilton W PTS 6 Cotgrave
18.11.02	Andy Gibson L PTS 4 Glasgow
30.11.02	Conroy McIntosh W PTS 4 Coventry
24.01.03	Chris Steele W PTS 4 Sheffield
08.03.03	Conroy McIntosh W PTS 4 Coventry
24.03.03	Robert Burton W PTS 6 Barnsley
10.06.03	Patrick J. Maxwell L RSC 1 Sheffield
13.09.03	Lee Williamson W PTS 6 Coventry
08.11.03	Lee Williamson W PTS 6 Coventry
21.02.04	Michael Thomas W RSC 3 Brighton
10.07.04	Conroy McIntosh W PTS 10 Coventry
	(Vacant Midlands Area Middleweight
	Title)
12.09.04	Roddy Doran W PTS 10 Shrewsbury
	(Vacant WBF Inter-Continental
	Middleweight Title)
29.04.05	Scott Dann L CO 1 Plymouth
	(British Middleweight Title Challenge)
18.06.05	Roddy Doran W RTD 7 Coventry
	(WBF Inter-Continental
	Middleweight Title Defence)
06.10.05	Darren McDermott L RTD 5 Dudley
	(Midlands Area Middleweight Title
	Defence)
03.12.05	Howard Clarke W PTS 8 Coventry
28.02.06	Dimitri Sartison L CO 5 Stuttgart,
	Germany

Career: 19 contests, won 14, lost 5.

Brendan Halford

Huddersfield. *Born* Folkestone, 30 July,
1973
L.Middleweight. Ht. 5'8½"
Manager C. Aston

09.02.02	Wayne Shepherd W PTS 6 Coventry
08.12.05	Martin Marshall W RSC 5 Sunderland
13.04.06	Jon Foster W PTS 6 Leeds
01.06.06	Nathan Cleverly L PTS 4 Barnsley

Career: 4 contests, won 3, lost 1.

Ceri Hall

Loughor. *Born* Swansea, 25 March, 1980
Welterweight. Ht. 5'10"
Manager Self

15.09.02	Martin Turner W RSC 1 Swansea
10.04.03	Silence Saheed DREW 4 Clydach
08.11.03	Peter McDonagh W PTS 4 Bridgend
28.02.04	James Gorman W PTS 6 Bridgend
19.06.04	Chris Long W PTS 4 Muswell Hill
24.09.04	Pete Buckley W PTS 6 Dublin
25.11.04	Dean Hickman L PTS 4 Birmingham
19.02.05	Robbie Murray L PTS 8 Dublin
28.04.05	Jason Nesbitt W RTD 2 Clydach
30.09.05	David Kehoe W PTS 6 Carmarthen

24.11.05	Silence Saheed W PTS 6 Clydach
25.03.06	Giorgio Marinelli L PTS 10 Rome,
	Italy
	(Vacant European Union
	L.Welterweight Title)
16.06.06	Billy Smith W PTS 6 Carmarthen

Career: 13 contests, won 9, drew 1, lost 3.

Lance Hall

Birmingham. *Born* Sutton Coldfield, 16
March, 1976
Welterweight. Ht. 5'5"
Manager Self

22.09.03	Luke Teague L RSC 1 Cleethorpes
24.10.03	Jas Malik W RSC 1 Bethnal Green
08.11.03	Stuart Phillips L PTS 4 Bridgend
26.11.03	Nathan Ward W PTS 4 Mayfair
20.02.04	Ben Coward W RSC 2 Doncaster
13.03.04	Kevin Anderson L RSC 1 Huddersfield
12.05.04	Anthony Small L RSC 1 Reading
04.12.05	Nathan Cleverly L RSC 3 Telford
24.02.06	Billy Smith L PTS 6 Birmingham
30.03.06	Lea Handley DREW 6 Peterborough
06.05.06	Dave Wakefield L PTS 6 Birmingham
18.05.06	Darren Gethin L PTS 6 Walsall
23.06.06	Ali Wyatt L RSC 5 Birmingham

Career: 13 contests, won 3, drew 1, lost 9.

Matthew Hall

Manchester. *Born* Manchester, 5 July, 1984
Middleweight. Ht. 5'7¾"
Manager F. Warren/B. Hughes

28.09.02	Pedro Thompson W RSC 1 Manchester
14.12.02	Pedro Thompson W PTS 4 Newcastle
18.01.03	Clive Johnson W PTS 4 Preston
05.04.03	Brian Coleman W RSC 1 Manchester
08.05.03	Patrick Cito W PTS 4 Widnes
06.05.04	Craig Lynch W PTS 6 Barnsley
12.06.04	Isidro Gonzalez W RSC 3 Manchester
01.10.04	Howard Clarke W RSC 5 Manchester
12.11.04	Ojay Abrahams W RSC 1 Halifax
03.12.04	Jason Collins W PTS 6 Edinburgh
21.01.05	Leigh Wicks W PTS 4 Bridgend
11.02.05	Sylvestre Marianini W CO 1
	Manchester
04.06.05	Matt Scriven W RSC 2 Manchester
28.01.06	Jon Foster W RSC 3 Nottingham
11.03.06	Robert Burton W CO 1 Newport

Career: 15 contests, won 15.

Matthew Hall   Les Clark

(Michael) Oscar Hall

Darlington. *Born* Darlington, 8 November,
1974
Northern Area Welterweight Champion.
Ht. 5'9"
Manager Self

09.05.98	Trevor Smith W PTS 4 Sheffield
27.02.99	Lee Molyneux W PTS 4 Oldham
15.05.99	Chris Price W PTS 4 Sheffield
29.05.99	Brian Gifford W RSC 1 Halifax
04.06.99	Arv Mittoo W PTS 6 Hull
27.09.99	Dave Gibson W PTS 6 Leeds
11.12.99	Brian Coleman W PTS 6 Liverpool
18.02.00	Jason Collins DREW 6 West Bromwich
02.03.00	Ernie Smith W PTS 6 Birkenhead
09.06.00	Dave Gibson W PTS 6 Hull
19.06.00	Paul Denton W PTS 4 Burton
13.08.00	Lee Molyneux W PTS 6 Nottingham
04.11.00	Ram Singh W PTS 6 Derby
24.11.00	Dean Nicholas W PTS 6 Darlington
11.12.00	Ram Singh W CO 4 Cleethorpes
16.06.01	David Kirk W PTS 6 Derby
18.08.01	David White W PTS 6 Dewsbury
22.09.01	Dean Nicholas W DIS 9 Newcastle
	(Vacant Northern Area Welterweight
	Title)
17.11.01	Paul Lomax W PTS 4 Dewsbury
15.03.02	Stuart Rimmer W RSC 4 Spennymoor
19.04.02	Peter Dunn W PTS 6 Darlington
10.05.02	Arv Mittoo W PTS 4 Bethnal Green
28.01.03	Alan Bosworth W PTS 10 Nottingham
	(Elim. British L.Welterweight Title)
11.07.03	William Webster W PTS 8 Darlington
10.10.03	Gary Reid L RSC 2 Darlington
11.12.03	Francis Barrett L PTS 10 Bethnal
	Green
05.03.04	Karl Taylor W PTS 6 Darlington
16.04.04	Junior Witter L RSC 3 Bradford
04.06.04	Lee Williamson W PTS 6 Hull
03.07.04	Peter Dunn W PTS 6 Blackpool
21.04.05	Young Muttley L PTS 10 Dudley
	(English & WBF Inter-Continental
	L.Welterweight Title Challenges)
03.06.05	Peter Dunn W PTS 6 Hull
28.10.05	Lenny Daws L RTD 7 Hartlepool
	(Elim. English L.Welterweight Title)
26.05.06	Amaro Diallo L PTS 6 Ibiza, Spain

Career: 34 contests, won 27, drew 1, lost 6.

Paul Halpin

Brighton. *Born* Brighton, 4 August, 1974
S.Featherweight. Former Undefeated
Southern Area Featherweight Champion.
Ht. 5'5"
Manager Self

04.04.97	Graham McGrath W PTS 6 Brighton
20.05.97	David Jeffrey W PTS 6 Gillingham
11.07.97	Wayne Jones W RSC 5 Brighton
08.10.97	Greg Upton DREW 4 Poplar
27.02.98	Taffy Evans W RSC 3 Brighton
16.05.98	Chris Lyons W PTS 6 Chigwell
26.02.99	Justin Murphy W RSC 2 Bethnal Green
	(Vacant Southern Area Featherweight
	Title)
26.06.99	Pete Buckley W PTS 4 Millwall
15.11.99	Chris Jickells W PTS 6 Bethnal Green
19.06.00	Chris Jickells W RSC 4 Burton
12.08.00	Eddie Nevins W PTS 6 Wembley
02.03.02	Gary Reid W RSC 3 Bethnal Green
11.12.05	Karl Taylor W PTS 4 Chigwell

Career: 13 contests, won 12, drew 1.

Lea Handley

Peterborough. *Born* Peterborough, 29 June 1985
L. Welterweight. Ht. 5'9"
Manager I. Pauly

17.09.04	Matthew Marshall L RSC 6 Plymouth
16.10.04	Freddie Luke L PTS 4 Dagenham
24.10.04	John Fewkes L PTS 6 Sheffield
09.11.04	Tye Williams W RSC 1 Leeds
26.11.04	Nathan Ward L CO 2 Bethnal Green
21.01.05	Barrie Jones L PTS 4 Bridgend
21.02.05	Gary Coombes W PTS 6 Peterborough
04.03.05	Kell Brook L PTS 6 Rotherham
30.03.06	Lance Hall DREW 6 Peterborough
15.06.06	Judex Meemea L PTS 6 Peterborough

Career: 10 contests, won 2, drew 1, lost 7.

Danny Harding

Stockport. *Born* Stockport, 5 January, 1981
Lightweight. Ht. 5'8"
Manager S. Wood

12.02.06	Gavin Deacon W PTS 6 Manchester

Career: 1 contest, won 1.

James Hare

Robertown. *Born* Dewsbury, 16 July, 1976
Welterweight. Former WBF Welterweight Champion. Former Undefeated Commonwealth & European Union Welterweight Champion. Ht. 5'6"
Manager C. Aston

20.01.96	Brian Coleman W PTS 6 Mansfield
25.06.96	Mike Watson W PTS 4 Mansfield
13.07.96	Dennis Griffin W RSC 4 Bethnal Green
14.09.96	Paul Salmon W RSC 4 Sheffield
14.12.96	Jon Harrison W PTS 4 Sheffield
25.02.97	Kid McAuley W RSC 4 Sheffield
12.04.97	Andy Peach W RSC 1 Sheffield
13.12.97	Costas Katsantonis W RSC 3 Sheffield
09.05.98	Peter Nightingale W PTS 4 Sheffield
18.07.98	Karl Taylor W PTS 4 Sheffield
28.11.98	Peter Nightingale W PTS 6 Sheffield
15.05.99	Lee Williamson W RSC 2 Sheffield
23.10.99	Mark Winters DREW 6 Telford
23.10.00	Dean Nicholas W RSC 1 Glasgow
23.01.01	Mark Ramsey W PTS 6 Crawley
26.02.01	Paul Denton W PTS 4 Nottingham
08.05.01	Jessy Moreaux W RSC 3 Barnsley
26.05.01	John Humphrey W RSC 7 Bethnal Green
	(Elim. British Welterweight Title)
08.10.01	John Ameline W PTS 8 Barnsley
26.11.01	Paul Denton W RTD 4 Manchester
28.01.02	Monney Seka W PTS 10 Barnsley
	(Vacant European Union Welterweight Title)
27.04.02	Julian Holland W RSC 6 Huddersfield
	(Commonwealth Welterweight Title Challenge)
15.06.02	Abdel Mehidi W PTS 8 Leeds
05.10.02	Farai Musiiwa W RSC 8 Huddersfield
	(Commonwealth Welterweight Title Defence)
30.11.02	Earl Foskin W RSC 1 Liverpool
	(Commonwealth Welterweight Title Defence)
22.02.03	Frans Hantindi W RSC 1 Huddersfield
	(Commonwealth Welterweight Title Defence)
21.06.03	Roman Dzuman W PTS 12 Manchester
	(Vacant WBF Welterweight Title)
06.09.03	Jan Bergman W RSC 2 Huddersfield
	(WBF Welterweight Title Defence)
18.10.03	Jozsef Matolcsi W RSC 10 Manchester
	(WBF Welterweight Title Defence)
04.12.03	Cosme Rivera L RSC 10 Huddersfield
	(WBF Welterweight Title Defence)
01.05.04	Jason Williams W RSC 2 Bridgend
27.05.04	Moise Cherni W RSC 5 Huddersfield
12.11.04	David Barnes L RSC 6 Halifax
	(British Welterweight Title Challenge)
09.09.05	Sergey Starkov W PTS 6 Sheffield
14.10.05	Oscar Milkitas W RTD 5 Huddersfield
01.06.06	Ernie Smith W CO 5 Barnsley

Career: 36 contests, won 33, drew 1, lost 2.

Jimmy Harrington

Brigg. *Born* Doncaster, 5 August, 1977
Cruiserweight. Ht. 6'3"
Manager J. Rushton

03.03.06	Lee Nicholson DREW 4 Doncaster
21.04.06	Lee Nicholson W RTD 3 Doncaster

Career: 2 contests, won 1, drew 1..

Audley Harrison

Wembley. *Born* Park Royal, 26 October, 1971
Heavyweight. Former Undefeated WBF Heavyweight Champion. Ht. 6'4¾"
Manager Self

19.05.01	Michael Middleton W RSC 1 Wembley
22.09.01	Derek McCafferty W PTS 6 Newcastle
20.10.01	Piotr Jurczyk W RSC 2 Glasgow
20.04.02	Julius Long W CO 2 Wembley
21.05.02	Mark Krence W PTS 6 Custom House
10.07.02	Dominic Negus W PTS 6 Wembley
05.10.02	Wade Lewis W RSC 2 Liverpool
23.11.02	Shawn Robinson W RSC 1 Atlantic City, New Jersey, USA
08.02.03	Rob Calloway W RSC 5 Brentford
29.03.03	Ratko Draskovic W PTS 8 Wembley
31.05.03	Matthew Ellis W RSC 2 Bethnal Green
09.09.03	Quinn Navarre W RSC 3 Miami, Florida, USA
03.10.03	Lisandro Diaz W RSC 4 Las Vegas, Nevada, USA
12.12.03	Brian Nix W RSC 3 Laughlin, Nevada, USA
20.03.04	Richel Hersisia W CO 4 Wembley
	(WBF Heavyweight Title Challenge)
08.05.04	Julius Francis W PTS 12 Bristol
	(WBF Heavyweight Title Defence)
19.06.04	Tomasz Bonin W RSC 9 Muswell Hill
	(WBF Heavyweight Title Defence)
09.06.05	Robert Davis W RSC 7 Temecula, California, USA
18.08.05	Robert Wiggins W RTD 4 San Jose, California, USA
10.12.05	Danny Williams L PTS 12 Canning Town
	(Vacant Commonwealth Heavyweight Title)
14.04.06	Dominick Guinn L PTS 10 Rancho Mirage, California, USA
09.06.06	Andrew Greeley W CO 3 Atlantic City, New Jersey, USA

Career: 22 contests, won 20, lost 2.

Gary Harrison

Swadlincote. *Born* Burton, 26 May, 1969
Welterweight. Ht. 5'8"
Manager P. Newman

20.05.99	Chris Lyons W PTS 6 Barking
29.04.00	Mike Yikealo L PTS 4 Wembley
13.07.00	Costas Katsantonis L PTS 4 Bethnal Green
28.10.00	Kevin Bennett L RTD 2 Coventry
03.02.01	Casey Brooke W PTS 6 Brighton
05.05.01	Jason McElligott W PTS 6 Brighton
15.09.01	Michael Jennings L PTS 6 Manchester
23.11.01	Manzo Smith W PTS 4 Bethnal Green
10.05.02	Costas Katsantonis L PTS 10 Millwall
	(Southern Area L.Welterweight Title Challenge)
08.06.02	Ricky Burns L RSC 1 Renfrew
24.02.06	George Hillyard L RTD 4 Dagenham

Career: 11 contests, won 4, lost 7.

Jon Harrison

Plymouth. *Born* Scunthorpe, 18 March, 1977
L.Middleweight. Ht. 5'11½"
Manager Self

13.01.96	Mark Haslam L PTS 6 Manchester
13.02.96	Paul Samuels L CO 1 Cardiff
16.05.96	Dave Fallon W RSC 4 Dunstable
03.07.96	Allan Gray L PTS 6 Wembley
01.10.96	Cam Raeside L PTS 6 Birmingham
07.11.96	Nicky Bardle L PTS 6 Battersea
14.12.96	James Hare L PTS 4 Sheffield
19.04.97	Jason Williams W PTS 6 Plymouth
11.07.97	Pat Larner L PTS 6 Brighton
07.10.97	Paul Salmon L PTS 6 Plymouth
23.02.98	Alan Gilbert L PTS 6 Windsor
24.03.98	Brian Coleman DREW 6 Wolverhampton
14.07.98	Jason Williams L RTD 2 Reading
12.05.01	Ernie Smith W PTS 4 Plymouth
15.09.01	Darren Williams L PTS 6 Swansea
02.04.04	Nathan Wyatt W PTS 6 Plymouth
27.05.04	Ady Clegg W PTS 4 Huddersfield
17.09.04	Geraint Harvey W PTS 6 Plymouth
13.12.04	Simon Sherrington L RSC 5 Birmingham
04.02.05	Joe Mitchell W PTS 6 Plymouth
29.04.05	Neil Jarmolinski W PTS 6 Plymouth
10.02.06	Jamie Ambler W PTS 4 Plymouth

Career: 22 contests, won 9, drew 1, lost 12.

Scott Harrison

Glasgow. *Born* Bellshill, 19 August, 1977
WBO Featherweight Champion. Former Undefeated British, Commonwealth & IBO Inter-Continental Featherweight Champion. Ht. 5'7"
Manager Self

07.10.96	Eddie Sica W RSC 2 Lewisham
11.01.97	Pete Buckley W PTS 4 Bethnal Green
25.03.97	David Morris W PTS 4 Lewisham
04.10.97	Miguel Matthews L RSC 4 Muswell Hill
16.12.97	Stephane Fernandez DREW 6 Grand Synthe, France
31.01.98	Pete Buckley W PTS 4 Edmonton
09.06.98	Carl Allen W RSC 6 Hull
17.10.98	Rakhim Mingaleev W PTS 8 Manchester
06.03.99	John Matthews W RSC 4 Southwark
10.07.99	Smith Odoom W PTS 12 Southwark
	(IBO Inter-Continental Featherweight Title Challenge)
24.01.00	Patrick Mullings W PTS 12 Glasgow
	(Commonwealth Featherweight Title Challenge)

29.04.00 Tracy Harris Patterson W PTS 10 NYC, New York, USA
15.07.00 Tom Johnson W PTS 12 Millwall
(IBO Inter-Continental Featherweight Title Defence)
11.11.00 Eric Odumasi W RSC 12 Belfast
(Commonwealth Featherweight Title Defence)
24.03.01 Richie Wenton W RSC 4 Sheffield
(Vacant British Featherweight Title. Commonwealth Featherweight Title Defence)
15.09.01 Gary Thornhill W RSC 5 Manchester
(British & Commonwealth Featherweight Title Defences)
17.11.01 Steve Robinson W RSC 3 Glasgow
(British & Commonwealth Featherweight Title Defences)
11.03.02 Tony Wehbee W RSC 3 Glasgow
(Commonwealth Featherweight Title Defence)
08.06.02 Victor Santiago W RSC 6 Renfrew
(Vacant WBO Interim Featherweight Title)
19.10.02 Julio Pablo Chacon W PTS 12 Renfrew
(WBO Featherweight Title Challenge)
22.03.03 Wayne McCullough W PTS 12 Renfrew
(WBO Featherweight Title Defence)
12.07.03 Manuel Medina L PTS 12 Renfrew
(WBO Featherweight Title Defence)
29.11.03 Manuel Medina W RSC 11 Renfrew
(WBO Featherweight Title Challenge)
06.03.04 Walter Estrada W RSC 5 Renfrew
(WBO Featherweight Title Defence)
19.06.04 William Abelyan W RSC 3 Renfrew
(WBO Featherweight Title Defence)
29.10.04 Samuel Kebede W RSC 1 Renfrew
(WBO Featherweight Title Defence)
28.01.05 Victor Polo DREW 12 Renfrew
(WBO Featherweight Title Defence)
03.06.05 Michael Brodie W CO 4 Manchester
(WBO Featherweight Title Defence)
05.11.05 Nedal Hussein W PTS 12 Renfrew
(WBO Featherweight Title Defence)

Career: 29 contests, won 25, drew 2, lost 2.

Geraint Harvey

Mountain Ash. *Born* Pontypridd, 1 September, 1979
L.Middleweight. Ht. 5'9"
Manager Self

22.09.03 Steve Scott W PTS 6 Cleethorpes
29.10.03 Darren Covill W PTS 4 Leicester Square
21.12.03 Danny Moir L PTS 6 Bolton
14.02.04 Arek Malek L PTS 4 Nottingham
28.02.04 Jamie Coyle L PTS 4 Bridgend
15.04.04 Terry Adams L PTS 6 Dudley
24.04.04 Chas Symonds L PTS 4 Reading
08.07.04 Terry Adams L RSC 6 Birmingham
17.09.04 Jon Harrison L PTS 6 Plymouth
24.09.04 Gary Woolcombe L PTS 4 Bethnal Green
16.10.04 Danny Goode L PTS 4 Dagenham
23.10.04 Peter Dunn W PTS 6 Wakefield
21.11.04 Robert-Lloyd Taylor L PTS 4 Bracknell
03.12.04 Colin McNeil L PTS 6 Edinburgh
28.01.05 Chris Black L PTS 4 Renfrew
17.02.05 Young Muttley L PTS 6 Dudley
05.03.05 Duncan Cottier L PTS 4 Dagenham

29.04.05 Courtney Thomas L PTS 6 Plymouth
15.05.05 Stuart Brookes L PTS 6 Sheffield
01.06.05 Mark Franks L PTS 6 Leeds
16.06.05 George Hillyard L RSC 1 Dagenham
23.09.05 Mark Thompson L PTS 4 Manchester
07.10.05 Sam Webb L CO 1 Bethnal Green
19.11.05 Nathan Graham L PTS 4 Southwark
14.12.05 Brian Rose L PTS 6 Blackpool
20.03.06 Danny Reynolds L RTD 2 Leeds
06.05.06 John Rocco L PTS 6 Blackpool
21.05.06 Jamal Morrison L PTS 4 Bethnal Green
01.06.06 Kell Brook L RSC 3 Barnsley

Career: 29 contests. won 3, lost 26.

Lee Haskins

Bristol. *Born* Bristol, 29 November, 1983
Commonwealth Flyweight Champion.
Former Undefeated English Flyweight Champion. Ht. 5'5"
Manager C. Sanigar

06.03.03 Ankar Miah W RSC 1 Bristol
13.06.03 Chris Edwards W PTS 6 Bristol
09.10.03 Neil Read W PTS 4 Bristol
05.12.03 Jason Thomas W PTS 6 Bristol
13.02.04 Marty Kayes W PTS 6 Bristol
08.05.04 Colin Moffett W RSC 2 Bristol
03.07.04 Sergei Tasimov W RSC 5 Bristol
01.10.04 Junior Anderson W CO 3 Bristol
03.12.04 Delroy Spencer W RTD 3 Bristol
(Vacant English Flyweight Title)
18.02.05 Hugo Cardinale W CO 1 Torrevieja, Spain
08.04.05 Moses Kinyua W PTS 10 Bristol
29.04.05 Andrzej Ziora W RSC 1 Plymouth
16.09.05 Delroy Spencer W RTD 2 Plymouth
10.02.06 Anthony Mathias W RSC 2 Plymouth
(Vacant Commonwealth Flyweight Title)
07.04.06 Zolile Mbityi W PTS 12 Bristol
(Commonwealth Flyweight Title Defence)

Career: 15 contests, won 15.

Lee Haskins   Les Clark

Matthew Hatton

Manchester. *Born* Stockport, 15 May, 1981
L.Middleweight. Central Area Welterweight Champion. Former Undefeated Central Area L.Middleweight Champion. Ht. 5'8½"
Manager Self

23.09.00 David White W PTS 4 Bethnal Green
25.11.00 David White W PTS 4 Manchester
11.12.00 Danny Connelly W PTS 4 Widnes
15.01.01 Keith Jones W PTS 4 Manchester
10.02.01 Karl Taylor W PTS 4 Widnes
17.03.01 Assen Vassilev W RSC 5 Manchester
09.06.01 Brian Coleman W RTD 2 Bethnal Green
21.07.01 Ram Singh W RSC 2 Sheffield
15.09.01 Marcus Portman W RSC 3 Manchester
15.12.01 Dafydd Carlin W PTS 6 Wembley
09.02.02 Paul Denton W PTS 6 Manchester
04.05.02 Karl Taylor W PTS 6 Bethnal Green
20.07.02 Karl Taylor W RTD 2 Bethnal Green
28.09.02 David Kirk L PTS 6 Manchester
14.12.02 Paul Denton W PTS 6 Newcastle
15.02.03 David Keir L RSC 4 Wembley
08.05.03 Jay Mahoney W PTS 6 Widnes
17.07.03 Jay Mahoney W RSC 1 Dagenham
27.09.03 Taz Jones W PTS 6 Manchester
13.12.03 Franny Jones DREW 6 Manchester
26.02.04 Peter Dunn W PTS 6 Widnes
06.05.04 Robert Burton W PTS 10 Barnsley
(Central Area Welterweight Title Challenge)
12.06.04 Matt Scriven W RSC 4 Manchester
01.10.04 Lee Armstrong W PTS 8 Manchester
12.11.04 Robert Burton W PTS 10 Halifax
(Central Area L.Middleweight Title Challenge)
11.03.05 Franny Jones W RTD 6 Doncaster
03.06.05 Adnan Hadoui W PTS 8 Manchester
09.09.05 Dmitry Yanushevich W RSC 4 Sheffield
26.11.05 Sergey Starkov W PTS 10 Sheffield
18.03.06 Alexander Abramenko W RTD 6 Monte Carlo, Monaco
13.05.06 Jose Medina W PTS 8 Boston, Massachusetts, USA

Career: 31 contests, won 28, drew 1, lost 2.

Ricky Hatton

Manchester. *Born* Stockport, 6 October, 1978
WBA Welterweight Champion. Former Undefeated IBF & WBU L.Welterweight Champion. Former Undefeated British, WBO Inter-Continental & Central Area L.Welterweight Champion. Ht. 5'7½"
Manager Self

11.09.97 Kid McAuley W RTD 1 Widnes
19.12.97 Robert Alvarez W PTS 4 NYC, New York, USA
17.01.98 David Thompson W RSC 1 Bristol
27.03.98 Paul Salmon W RSC 1 Telford
18.04.98 Karl Taylor W RSC 1 Manchester
30.05.98 Mark Ramsey W PTS 6 Bristol
18.07.98 Anthony Campbell W PTS 6 Sheffield
19.09.98 Pascal Montulet W CO 2 Oberhausen, Germany
31.10.98 Kevin Carter W RSC 1 Atlantic City, New Jersey, USA
19.12.98 Paul Denton W RSC 6 Liverpool
27.02.99 Tommy Peacock W RSC 2 Oldham
(Vacant Central Area L. Welterweight Title)

03.04.99	Brian Coleman W CO 2 Kensington
29.05.99	Dillon Carew W RSC 5 Halifax
	(Vacant WBO Inter-Continental
	L. Welterweight Title)
17.07.99	Mark Ramsey W PTS 6 Doncaster
09.10.99	Bernard Paul W RTD 4 Manchester
	(WBO Inter-Continental
	L. Welterweight Title Defence)
11.12.99	Mark Winters W RSC 4 Liverpool
	(WBO Inter-Continental
	L. Welterweight Title Defence)
29.01.00	Leoncio Garces W RSC 3 Manchester
25.03.00	Pedro Teran W RSC 4 Liverpool
	(WBO Inter-Continental
	L. Welterweight Title Defence)
16.05.00	Ambioris Figuero W RSC 4 Warrington
	(WBO Inter-Continental
	L. Welterweight Title Defence)
10.06.00	Gilbert Quiros W CO 2 Detroit, Michigan, USA
	(WBO Inter-Continental
	L. Welterweight Title Defence)
23.09.00	Giuseppe Lauri W RSC 5 Bethnal Green
	(WBO Inter-Continental
	L.Welterweight Title Defence. WBA
	Inter-Continental L.Welterweight Title
	Challenge)
21.10.00	Jonathan Thaxton W PTS 12 Wembley
	(Vacant British L.Welterweight Title)
26.03.01	Tony Pep W CO 4 Wembley
	(Vacant WBU L. Welterweight Title)
07.07.01	Jason Rowland W CO 4 Manchester
	(WBU L.Welterweight Title Defence)
15.09.01	John Bailey W RSC 5 Manchester
	(WBU L.Welterweight Title Defence)
27.10.01	Fred Pendleton W CO 2 Manchester
	(WBU L.Welterweight Title Defence)
15.12.01	Justin Rowsell W RSC 2 Wembley
	(WBU L.Welterweight Title Defence)
09.02.02	Mikhail Krivolapov W RSC 9 Manchester
	(WBU L. Welterweight Title Defence)
01.06.02	Eamonn Magee W PTS 12 Manchester
28.09.02	Stephen Smith W DIS 2 Manchester
	(WBU L.Welterweight Title Defence)
14.12.02	Joe Hutchinson W CO 4 Newcastle
	(WBU L.Welterweight Title Defence)
05.04.03	Vince Phillips W PTS 12 Manchester
	(WBU L.Welterweight Title Defence)
27.09.03	Aldi Rios W RTD 9 Manchester
	(WBU L.Welterweight Title Defence)
13.12.03	Ben Tackie W PTS 12 Manchester
	(WBU L.Welterweight Title Defence)
03.04.04	Dennis Holbaek Pedersen W RSC 6 Manchester
	(WBU L.Welterweight Title Defence)
12.06.04	Wilfredo Carlos Vilches W PTS 12 Manchester
	(WBU L.Welterweight Title Defence)
01.10.04	Michael Stewart W RSC 5 Manchester
	(WBU L.Welterweight Title Defence.
	Final Elim. IBF L.Welterweight Title)
11.12.04	Ray Oliveira W CO 10 Canning Town
04.06.05	Kostya Tszyu W RSC 11 Manchester
	(IBF L.Welterweight Title Challenge)
26.11.05	Carlos Maussa W CO 9 Sheffield
	(IBF L.Welterweight Title Challenge.
	WBA L.Welterweight Title Defence)
13.05.06	Luis Collazo W PTS 12 Boston, Massachusetts, USA
	(WBA Welterweight Title Challenge)

Career: 41 contests, won 41.

Stephen Haughian

Lurgan Co. Armagh. *Born* Craigavon, 20 November, 1984
L.Welterweight. Ht. 5'10½"
Manager J. Breen/F. Warren

18.03.05	James Gorman W PTS 4 Belfast
14.10.05	Imad Khamis W RSC 4 Dublin
24.11.05	James Gorman W PTS 6 Lurgan
28.01.06	Duncan Cottier W PTS 4 Dublin
20.05.06	Pete Buckley W PTS 4 Belfast

Career: 5 contests, won 5.

David Haye

Bermondsey. *Born* London, 13 October, 1980
European Cruiserweight Champion. Former Undefeated English Cruiserweight Champion. Ht. 6'3"
Manager Self

08.12.02	Tony Booth W RTD 2 Bethnal Green
24.01.03	Saber Zairi W RSC 4 Sheffield
04.03.03	Roger Bowden W RSC 2 Miami, Florida, USA
18.03.03	Phill Day W RSC 2 Reading
15.07.03	Vance Wynn W RSC 1 Los Angeles, California, USA
01.08.03	Greg Scott-Briggs W CO 1 Bethnal Green
26.09.03	Lolenga Mock W RSC 4 Reading
14.11.03	Tony Dowling W RSC 1 Bethnal Green
	(Vacant English Cruiserweight Title)
20.03.04	Hastings Rasani W RSC 1 Wembley
12.05.04	Arthur Williams W RSC 3 Reading
10.09.04	Carl Thompson L RSC 5 Wembley
	(IBO Cruiserweight Title Challenge)
10.12.04	Valery Semishkur W RSC 1 Sheffield
21.01.05	Garry Delaney W RTD 3 Brentford
04.03.05	Glen Kelly W CO 2 Rotherham
14.10.05	Vincenzo Rossitto W RSC 2 Huddersfield
16.12.05	Alexander Gurov W CO 1 Bracknell
	(European Cruiserweight Title Challenge)
24.03.06	Lasse Johansen W RSC 8 Bethnal Green
	(European Cruiserweight Title Defence)

Career: 17 contests, won 16, lost 1.

David Haye   Les Clark

Peter Haymer

Enfield. *Born* London, 10 July, 1978
English L.Heavyweight. Champion.
Ht. 6'1¼"
Manager C. Hall

25.11.00	Adam Cale W RSC 1 Manchester
27.01.01	Darren Ashton W PTS 4 Bethnal Green
10.03.01	Daniel Ivanov W CO 2 Bethnal Green
26.03.01	Radcliffe Green W PTS 4 Wembley
05.05.01	Terry Morrill W PTS 4 Edmonton
22.09.01	Tony Booth W PTS 4 Bethnal Green
24.11.01	Nathan King L PTS 4 Bethnal Green
12.02.02	Nathan King L PTS 4 Bethnal Green
09.05.02	Mark Snipe W PTS 4 Leicester Square
15.06.02	Paul Bonson W PTS 4 Tottenham
30.10.02	Jimmy Steel W PTS 4 Leicester Square
18.03.03	Mark Brookes W PTS 6 Reading
18.09.03	Ovill McKenzie W PTS 4 Mayfair
10.12.03	Mark Brookes DREW 6 Sheffield
12.11.04	Steven Spartacus W PTS 10 Wembley
	(English L.Heavyweight Title Challenge)
10.12.04	Mark Brookes W RSC 10 Sheffield
	(English L.Heavyweight Title Defence)
24.04.05	Ryan Walls W PTS 6 Leicester Square
19.06.05	Tony Oakey W PTS 10 Bethnal Green
	(English L.Heavyweight Title Defence)
07.04.06	Leigh Alliss W RSC 9 Bristol
	(English L.Heavyweight Title Defence)
21.05.06	Varuzhan Davtyan W RSC 4 Bethnal Green

Career: 20 contests, won 17, drew 1, lost 2.

Scott Haywood

Derby. *Born* Derby, 5 June, 1981
Welterweight. Ht. 6'0"
Manager M. Shinfield

06.10.03	Pete Buckley W PTS 6 Barnsley
23.11.03	Arv Mittoo W PTS 6 Rotherham
16.02.04	Pete Buckley W PTS 6 Scunthorpe
26.04.04	Chris Brophy W RSC 5 Cleethorpes
27.09.04	Judex Meemea W PTS 6 Cleethorpes
16.12.04	Tony Montana L PTS 6 Cleethorpes
26.02.05	Jimmy Beech W PTS 6 Burton
24.04.05	Chris Long W PTS 6 Derby
02.09.05	Kristian Laight W PTS 6 Derby
08.12.05	Dave Hinds W RTD 3 Derby
28.01.06	Jus Wallie W PTS 4 Nottingham
25.03.06	Billy North W PTS 6 Burton
14.05.06	Surinder Sekhon W RSC 1 Derby

Career: 13 contests, won 12, lost 1.

Eugene Heagney

Huddersfield. *Born* Dublin, 4 April, 1983
Featherweight. Ht. 5'8"
Manager M. Marsden

29.06.06	Neil Marston W PTS 6 Dudley

Career: 1 contest, won 1.

Ciaran Healy

Belfast. *Born* Belfast, 25 December, 1974
S.Middleweight. Ht. 5'11"
Manager Self

05.04.03	Tomas da Silva W PTS 4 Belfast
18.09.03	Patrick Cito W PTS 4 Mayfair
04.10.03	Joel Ani W PTS 4 Belfast
22.11.03	Neil Addis W RSC 1 Belfast
26.06.04	Jason McKay L PTS 6 Belfast
25.04.05	Vince Baldassara L RSC 4 Glasgow

17.06.05 Chris Black DREW 4 Glasgow
18.02.06 Karoly Domokos W PTS 4 Dublin
21.04.06 George Hillyard L CO 6 Belfast
Career: 9 contests, won 5, drew 1, lost 3.

Jamie Hearn
Colnbrook. *Born* Taplow, 4 June, 1982
S.Middleweight. Ht. 5'11½"
Manager Self

27.09.02 Jimmy Steel W PTS 4 Bracknell
03.12.02 Mark Phillips W PTS 4 Bethnal Green
20.12.02 Danny Norton W PTS 4 Bracknell
18.03.03 Darren Stubbs L RSC 3 Reading
13.06.03 Liam Lathbury W RSC 4 Bristol
04.10.03 Jason McKay L PTS 8 Belfast
14.11.03 Harry Butler W PTS 4 Bethnal Green
30.03.04 Varuzhan Davtyan L PTS 4 Southampton
12.05.04 Hastings Rasani W RSC 4 Reading
10.09.04 Lee Woodruff W RSC 1 Wembley
21.11.04 Tom Cannon W PTS 6 Bracknell
21.01.05 Simeon Cover W PTS 4 Brentford
23.03.05 Simeon Cover L CO 7 Leicester Square
          (Vacant British Masters S.Middleweight Title)
18.09.05 Gareth Lawrence W RTD 3 Bethnal Green
25.10.05 Konni Konrad L PTS 10 Vienna, Austria
          (Vacant WBC Youth S.Middleweight Title)
16.12.05 Ryan Kerr DREW 10 Bracknell
          (English S.Middleweight Title Challenge)
04.03.06 Chad Dawson L RSC 3 Manchester
16.06.06 Tony Dodson L RSC 4 Liverpool
          (Vacant English S.Middleweight Title)
Career: 18 contests, won 10, drew 1, lost 7.

(Donvill) Jimi Hendricks
Birmingham. *Born* Birmingham, 2 April, 1973
Cruiserweight. Ht. 5'10"
Manager Self

21.02.03 Davey Jones L PTS 6 Doncaster
21.03.03 Kevin Phelan L RSC 6 Longford
09.05.03 Steve Scott W PTS 6 Doncaster
06.06.03 Steve Russell W PTS 6 Norwich
29.08.03 Carl Wall L PTS 6 Liverpool
18.09.03 Gokhan Kazaz L PTS 4 Dagenham
27.09.03 Jason Rushton L PTS 4 Manchester
10.10.03 Ricky Colquhoun W RSC 1 Darlington
29.10.03 Matthew Barr L RSC 4 Leicester Square
30.11.03 Mark Phillips L PTS 6 Swansea
03.09.05 Danny Smith L RSC 5 Norwich
16.10.05 Alex Carey L PTS 6 Peterborough
29.10.05 Tyan Booth L PTS 6 Aberdeen
08.11.05 Tyan Booth L PTS 6 Leeds
26.11.05 Amer Khan L PTS 4 Sheffield
08.12.05 Adie Whitmore L RSC 1 Derby
02.02.06 Simeon Cover L PTS 4 Holborn
23.02.06 Danny Wright L PTS 6 Leeds
05.03.06 Danny Grainger L PTS 6 Sheffield
31.03.06 Gordon Brennan L PTS 6 Inverurie
26.05.06 Ali Mateen L CO 2 Hull
Career: 21 contests, won 3, lost 18.

(Jack) Jak Hibbert
Sheffield. *Born* Sheffield, 21 September, 1985
L. Middleweight. Ht. 6'0"
Manager D. Hobson

12.12.04 Chris Black L RSC 2 Glasgow
04.03.05 Neil Jarmolinski W PTS 6 Rotherham
17.06.05 Vince Baldassara L RSC 1 Glasgow
24.02.06 Ryan Ashworth W PTS 6 Scarborough
22.06.06 Thomas Flynn W RSC 3 Sheffield
Career: 5 contests, won 3, lost 2.

Dean Hickman
West Bromwich. *Born* West Bromwich, 24 November, 1979
Midlands Area L.Welterweight Champion. Ht. 5'7"
Manager E. Johnson

17.02.02 Wayne Wheeler DREW 6 Wolverhampton
13.04.02 Wayne Wheeler W PTS 6 Wolverhampton
13.07.02 Dai Bando W RSC 1 Wolverhampton
02.11.02 Darren Goode W RSC 2 Wolverhampton
15.02.03 Gareth Wiltshaw W PTS 6 Wolverhampton
21.03.03 David Vaughan W PTS 6 West Bromwich
30.06.03 Dave Hinds W RSC 4 Shrewsbury
17.07.03 Lee McAllister W PTS 6 Walsall
30.10.03 John-Paul Ryan W PTS 6 Dudley
15.04.04 Tony Montana W PTS 6 Dudley
04.06.04 Adnan Amar W RSC 8 Dudley
          (Vacant Midlands Area L.Welterweight Title)
25.11.04 Ceri Hall W PTS 4 Birmingham
17.02.05 Gary Reid W PTS 10 Dudley
          (Midlands Area L.Welterweight Title Defence)
11.03.05 Nigel Wright L CO 7 Doncaster
          (Vacant English L.Welterweight Title)
16.02.06 Ernie Smith W PTS 4 Dudley
17.03.06 Barry Morrison L RSC 1 Kirkcaldy
          (Elim. British L.Welterweight Title)
29.06.06 Tom Hogan W RSC 2 Dudley
Career: 17 contests, won 14, drew 1, lost 2.

Graeme Higginson   Les Clark

Graeme Higginson
Blackburn. *Born* Blackburn, 31 July, 1982
Lightweight. Ht. 5'8¼"
Manager D. Coldwell

14.10.05 Darren Johnstone L PTS 6 Motherwell
03.11.05 Tom Hogan L PTS 6 Sunderland
19.11.05 Mark Alexander L PTS 4 Southwark
23.01.06 Paul Appleby L RTD 3 Glasgow
04.03.06 Dougie Walton DREW 6 Coventry
27.05.06 Omar Akram W RSC 2 Glasgow
01.06.06 Paul Appleby L RSC 2 Birmingham
Career: 7 contests, won 1, drew 1, lost 5.

Dwayne Hill
Sheffield. *Born* Sheffield, 31 January, 1986
L.Welterweight. Ht. 5'8"
Manager G. Rhodes

08.05.05 Anthony Christopher W PTS 6 Sheffield
24.07.05 Gary Coombes W RSC 3 Sheffield
30.10.05 Gavin Tait W PTS 6 Sheffield
12.11.05 Lance Verallo W PTS 6 Sheffield
17.02.06 Carl Allen W PTS 6 Sheffield
16.06.06 Daniel Thorpe W PTS 4 Liverpool
Career: 6 contests, won 6.

George Hillyard
Canning Town. *Born* Forest Gate, 19 November, 1984
L.Middleweight. Ht. 5'9¼"
Manager R. Callaghan

16.06.05 Geraint Harvey W RSC 1 Dagenham
30.09.05 James Gorman W RSC 1 Kirkcaldy
21.10.05 Ernie Smith L PTS 4 Bethnal Green
18.11.05 Richard Mazurek W PTS 6 Dagenham
24.02.06 Gary Harrison W RTD 4 Dagenham
21.04.06 Ciaran Healy W CO 6 Belfast
Career: 6 contests, won 5, lost 1.

George Hillyard   Les Clark

Dave Hinds
Birmingham. *Born* Leicester, 5 January, 1971
Welterweight. Ht. 5'5"
Manager Self

19.09.95 Martin Evans W RSC 5 Plymouth
08.11.95 Wayne Pardoe L CO 4 Walsall
04.04.96 Paul Salmon L RTD 5 Plymouth
06.10.97 Eddie Sica L RSC 1 Piccadilly
25.11.97 Graham McGrath W PTS 6 Wolverhampton
06.12.97 Adam Spelling W RSC 1 Wembley

27.01.98	Malcolm Thomas L PTS 6 Piccadilly
06.03.98	Jon Dodsworth W RSC 1 Hull
12.03.98	Jamie McKeever L PTS 4 Liverpool
20.03.98	John O'Johnson L PTS 6 Ilkeston
23.04.98	Roy Rutherford L RSC 5 Edgbaston
26.05.98	David Kehoe L RSC 5 Mayfair
07.10.98	Steve Saville L PTS 6 Stoke
26.10.98	Eddie Nevins L PTS 6 Manchester
26.11.98	Steve Saville L PTS 6 Edgbaston
07.12.98	Danny Bell L PTS 6 Nottingham
13.02.99	Michael Gomez L PTS 6 Newcastle
23.04.99	Mark Ramsey L PTS 6 Clydach
17.05.99	Jesse James Daniel L PTS 6 Cleethorpes
28.05.99	Jason Cook L RSC 1 Liverpool
17.07.99	Bradley Pryce L PTS 4 Doncaster
03.09.99	Young Muttley L RSC 4 West Bromwich
13.11.99	Humberto Soto L PTS 6 Hull
11.12.99	Gavin Rees L RSC 2 Liverpool
07.02.00	Liam Maltby L PTS 4 Peterborough
13.03.00	Danny Hunt L PTS 4 Bethnal Green
23.03.00	Marco Fattore L PTS 6 Bloomsbury
13.05.00	Alan Kershaw L PTS 4 Barnsley
22.05.00	Tony Conroy L PTS 4 Coventry
09.06.00	Elias Boswell W RSC 5 Blackpool
24.06.00	Brian Carr L PTS 4 Glasgow
01.07.00	Ricky Eccleston L PTS 4 Manchester
25.07.00	Kevin Lear L PTS 6 Southwark
09.09.00	Carl Greaves L PTS 6 Newark
16.09.00	Leo O'Reilly L RSC 2 Bethnal Green
27.11.00	Ricky Eccleston L PTS 4 Birmingham
04.12.00	Gavin Pearson L PTS 6 Bradford
11.12.00	Miguel Matthews W PTS 6 Birmingham
11.02.01	James Rooney L PTS 6 Hartlepool
26.03.01	Kevin Lear L CO 1 Wembley
03.06.01	Dafydd Carlin L PTS 4 Southwark
16.06.01	Carl Greaves L PTS 6 Derby
29.09.01	Scott Lawton L RSC 2 Southwark
15.12.01	Danny Hunt L PTS 4 Wembley
26.01.02	Chris McDonagh L PTS 4 Bethnal Green
03.03.02	Mally McIver L PTS 6 Shaw
11.03.02	Willie Limond L PTS 6 Glasgow
11.05.02	Craig Spacie L PTS 6 Chesterfield
15.06.02	Dave Stewart L PTS 6 Tottenham
23.06.02	Peter McDonagh L PTS 6 Southwark
13.07.02	Tony McPake L RSC 3 Coventry
22.03.03	Baz Carey L PTS 6 Coventry
29.03.03	Martin Power L PTS 4 Portsmouth
13.04.03	Nadeem Siddique L PTS 4 Bradford
06.06.03	Paul Rushton W PTS 6 Hull
20.06.03	Steve Mullin L PTS 4 Liverpool
30.06.03	Dean Hickman L RSC 4 Shrewsbury
05.09.03	Stefy Bull L PTS 6 Doncaster
13.09.03	Jamie Arthur L RTD 1 Newport
25.10.03	Colin Bain L PTS 4 Edinburgh
06.11.03	Andy Morris L PTS 4 Dagenham
18.11.03	Rob Jeffries L PTS 6 Bethnal Green
15.12.03	Matt Teague L PTS 6 Cleethorpes
27.03.04	Colin Bain L PTS 4 Edinburgh
23.04.04	Daniel Thorpe L PTS 4 Leicester
12.05.04	Nathan Ward L PTS 4 Reading
02.06.04	John O'Donnell L PTS 4 Nottingham
03.07.04	Isaac Ward L PTS 6 Blackpool
03.09.04	Barrie Jones L PTS 4 Newport
24.09.04	Nadeem Siddique L PTS 4 Nottingham
09.10.04	Jackson Williams L PTS 6 Norwich
20.11.04	Baz Carey L RSC 4 Coventry
15.04.05	Shaun Walton L PTS 6 Shrewsbury
28.04.05	Craig Morgan L PTS 4 Clydach
13.05.05	Tiger Matthews L CO 1 Liverpool

11.06.05	Stuart Green L PTS 6 Kirkcaldy
09.09.05	Kyle Simpson L PTS 4 Sheffield
16.09.05	Craig Bromley L PTS 4 Doncaster
06.10.05	Kyle Taylor L PTS 6 Dudley
16.10.05	Riaz Durgahed L PTS 6 Peterborough
12.11.05	Muhsen Nasser L PTS 6 Sheffield
25.11.05	Kyle Simpson L PTS 6 Hull
08.12.05	Scott Haywood L RTD 3 Derby
23.02.06	Gary Sykes L PTS 6 Leeds

Career: 84 contests, won 7, lost 77.

Mark Hobson

Huddersfield. *Born* Workington, 7 May, 1976

British & Commonwealth Cruiserweight Champion. Ht. 6'5"

Manager C. Aston

09.06.97	Michael Pinnock W PTS 6 Bradford
06.10.97	P. R. Mason W PTS 6 Bradford
13.11.97	P. R. Mason W PTS 6 Bradford
27.02.98	Colin Brown DREW 6 Irvine
21.05.98	Paul Bonson W PTS 6 Bradford
15.06.98	Martin Jolley L RSC 3 Bradford
25.10.98	Mark Snipe W RSC 3 Shaw
26.11.98	Danny Southam W RSC 5 Bradford
19.04.99	Mark Levy L PTS 8 Bradford
11.09.99	Paul Bonson W PTS 4 Sheffield
06.12.99	Brian Gascoigne W RSC 3 Bradford
11.03.00	Nikolai Ermenkov W RSC 3 Kensington
27.03.00	Luke Simpkin W PTS 4 Barnsley
13.05.00	Paul Bonson W PTS 4 Barnsley
25.09.00	Mark Dawson W CO 1 Barnsley
26.02.01	Billy Bessey W PTS 4 Nottingham
24.04.01	Sebastiaan Rothmann L RTD 9 Liverpool
	(WBU Cruiserweight Title Challenge)
08.10.01	Firat Arslan L RSC 7 Barnsley
10.12.01	Luke Simpkin W RTD 3 Liverpool
23.02.02	Valery Semishkur W PTS 6 Nottingham
27.04.02	Lee Swaby W PTS 10 Huddersfield
	(Final Elim. British Cruiserweight Title)
05.10.02	Varuzhan Davtyan W RSC 3 Huddersfield
25.01.03	Abdul Kaddu W RSC 4 Bridgend
	(Vacant Commonwealth Cruiserweight Title)
10.05.03	Muslim Biarslanov W RSC 2 Huddersfield
05.09.03	Robert Norton W PTS 12 Sheffield
	(Commonwealth Cruiserweight Title Defence. Vacant British Cruiserweight Title)
13.03.04	Tony Moran W RSC 3 Huddersfield
	(British & Commonwealth Cruiserweight Title Defences)
27.05.04	Lee Swaby W RSC 6 Huddersfield
	(British & Commonwealth Cruiserweight Title Defences)
17.12.04	Bruce Scott W PTS 12 Huddersfield
	(British & Commonwealth Cruiserweight Title Defences)
04.03.06	Enzo Maccarinelli L PTS 12 Manchester
	(WBU Cruiserweight Title Challenge)
01.06.06	John Keeton W RSC 4 Barnsley
	(British & Commonwealth Cruiserweight Title Defences)

Career: 30 contests, won 25, drew 1, lost 4.

Lee Hodgson

Hayes. *Born* Hammersmith, 28 June, 1973

Middleweight. Ht. 5'9½"

Manager D. Currivan

27.09.02	Kevin Phelan W RSC 1 Bracknell
03.12.02	Leigh Wicks W PTS 4 Bethnal Green
08.02.03	Dean Powell W PTS 4 Brentford
21.03.03	Elroy Edwards W RSC 3 Longford
29.03.03	Matthew Barr L RSC 1 Wembley
20.03.04	Rob MacDonald W RSC 3 Wembley
07.04.04	Conroy McIntosh L RSC 3 Leicester Square
25.09.05	Mark Phillips W PTS 6 Southampton
16.12.05	Steve Ede L PTS 4 Bracknell

Career: 9 contests, won 6, lost 3.

Tom Hogan

Carlisle. *Born* Wigan, 2 May, 1977

L.Welterweight. Ht. 5'9½"

Manager T. Conroy

09.11.04	Pete Buckley W PTS 6 Leeds
21.02.05	Mike Reid L PTS 6 Glasgow
06.10.05	Kristian Laight W PTS 6 Sunderland
03.11.05	Graeme Higginson W PTS 6 Sunderland
08.12.05	Adam Kelly W PTS 6 Sunderland
09.03.06	David Pinkney W PTS 6 Sunderland
31.03.06	Mike Reid W PTS 6 Inverurie
29.06.06	Dean Hickman L RSC 2 Dudley

Career: 8 contests, won 6, lost 2.

Gareth Hogg

Torquay. *Born* Newton Abbott, 21 October, 1977

Cruiserweight. Ht. 6'2"

Manager C. Sanigar

13.02.98	Harry Butler W RSC 3 Weston super Mare
09.05.99	Matthew Barney L PTS 4 Bracknell
07.08.99	Clive Johnson W PTS 4 Dagenham
27.02.00	Darren Covill W RSC 3 Plymouth
29.03.00	Simon Andrews W RSC 5 Piccadilly
12.05.01	Oddy Papantoniou W RSC 2 Plymouth
10.07.01	Kevin Rainey W RSC 1 Montreal, Canada
23.06.02	Mark Phillips W PTS 4 Southwark
08.01.03	Darren Ashton W RSC 2 Aberdare
13.02.04	Dale Nixon W RTD 4 Bristol
04.02.05	Radcliffe Green W PTS 4 Plymouth
10.02.06	Neil Simpson W PTS 6 Plymouth

Career: 12 contests, won 11, lost 1.

Paul Holborn

Sunderland. *Born* Sunderland, 1 March, 1984

L. Welterweight. Ht. 5'8½"

Manager Self

11.10.04	Stuart Green W PTS 6 Glasgow
15.12.04	Amir Ali L PTS 6 Sheffield
06.10.05	Daniel Thorpe W PTS 6 Sunderland
03.11.05	Haroon Din DREW 6 Sunderland
28.04.06	Billy Smith W PTS 4 Hartlepool
11.05.06	Kristian Laight W PTS 6 Sunderland

Career: 6 contests, won 4, drew 1, lost 1.

Jon Honney

Basingstoke. *Born* Basingstoke, 6 August, 1975

Lightweight. Ht. 5'7"

Manager Self

01.10.99	Peter Dunn W PTS 4 Bethnal Green
18.12.99	Marco Fattore W PTS 4 Southwark
21.02.00	Costas Katsantonis L RSC 1 Southwark
13.07.00	Mickey Yikealo L PTS 4 Bethnal Green
29.09.00	Manzo Smith L PTS 4 Bethnal Green
06.11.00	Jimmy Gould L PTS 6 Wolverhampton
16.03.01	Woody Greenaway W PTS 6 Portsmouth
07.09.01	Young Muttley L RSC 1 West Bromwich
20.10.01	Martin Watson L RSC 3 Glasgow
23.02.02	Darrell Grafton L RTD 1 Nottingham
28.11.02	Henry Jones W PTS 4 Finchley
20.12.02	Martin Hardcastle W PTS 4 Bracknell
05.03.03	Francis Barrett L PTS 10 Bethnal Green
	(Vacant Southern Area L.Welterweight Title)
27.05.03	Stephen Smith L PTS 8 Dagenham
26.07.03	Michael Ayers W PTS 6 Plymouth
11.10.03	Graham Earl L PTS 8 Portsmouth
07.04.04	Peter McDonagh L PTS 10 Leicester Square
	(Vacant Southern Area Lightweight Title)
12.05.04	John Alldis W PTS 6 Reading
22.05.04	Nigel Wright L RSC 2 Widnes
26.11.04	Rob Jeffries L PTS 8 Bethnal Green
25.02.05	Lee Beavis L PTS 6 Wembley
25.09.05	Daniel Thorpe L PTS 4 Southampton
04.11.05	Danny Hunt L PTS 8 Bethnal Green
27.01.06	Leo O'Reilly L PTS 6 Dagenham
11.02.06	Dean Phillips L RSC 2 Bethnal Green
26.05.06	Tontcho Tontchev L PTS 6 Bethnal Green

Career: 26 contests, won 7, lost 19.

Chris Hooper

Scarborough. *Born* Barking, 28 September, 1977
Featherweight. Ht. 5'9"
Manager Self

01.11.01	Jason Nesbitt W RSC 6 Hull
28.01.02	Greg Edwards W RSC 2 Barnsley
27.07.02	John Mackay L PTS 4 Nottingham
26.09.02	Sid Razak W PTS 6 Hull
21.11.02	Baz Carey W RTD 3 Hull
03.04.03	Buster Dennis W RSC 1 Hull
20.02.04	Buster Dennis L RSC 2 Bethnal Green
08.04.04	John Bothwell W CO 2 Peterborough
30.07.04	Steve Gethin W PTS 4 Bethnal Green
01.10.04	Andy Morris L RSC 3 Manchester
24.02.06	Gary Davis L RSC 1 Scarborough
	(Vacant Central Area S.Bantamweight Title. Vacant British Masters S.Bantamweight Title)
21.04.06	Martin Lindsay L RSC 1 Belfast

Career: 12 contests, won 7, lost 5.

Kerry Hope

Merthyr Tydfil. *Born* Merthyr Tydfil, 21 October, 1981
Middleweight. Ht. 5'10"
Manager F. Warren

21.01.05	Brian Coleman W PTS 4 Bridgend
08.04.05	Ernie Smith W PTS 4 Edinburgh
27.05.05	Lee Williamson W PTS 4 Spennymoor
10.09.05	John-Paul Temple W PTS 4 Cardiff
04.03.06	Matt Scriven W PTS 4 Manchester
01.06.06	Joe Mitchell W PTS 4 Barnsley

Career: 6 contests, won 6.

Richard Horton

Romford. *Born* Romford, 12 November, 1981
S.Middleweight. Ht. 6'0¾"
Manager D. Powell

25.02.06	Nick Okoth W CO 3 Canning Town
01.04.06	Ojay Abrahams W PTS 4 Bethnal Green
13.05.06	Mark Phillips W PTS 4 Bethnal Green

Career: 3 contests, won 3.

Matthew Hough

Walsall. *Born* Walsall, 5 January, 1977
S.Middleweight. Ht. 6'2"
Manager E. Johnson

17.02.05	Paddy Ryan W PTS 6 Dudley
21.04.05	Mark Phillips W PTS 4 Dudley
25.11.05	Robert Burton W PTS 4 Walsall
10.03.06	John Ruddock W PTS 4 Walsall
18.05.06	Dean Walker W PTS 6 Walsall

Career: 5 contests, won 5.

Ben Hudson

Cambridge. *Born* Cambridge, 29 March, 1973
Middleweight. Ht. 5'6"
Manager Self

23.08.02	Pete Buckley DREW 4 Bethnal Green
06.09.02	Scott Lawton L PTS 4 Bethnal Green
26.09.02	Jas Malik W CO 3 Fulham
27.10.02	Peter McDonagh W PTS 6 Southwark
08.12.02	Daffyd Carlin W PTS 6 Bethnal Green
18.02.03	Brian Coleman W PTS 6 Bethnal Green
08.04.03	Peter McDonagh L PTS 4 Bethnal Green
26.04.03	Robert Lloyd-Taylor W PTS 4 Brentford
27.05.03	Lenny Daws L RSC 2 Dagenham
25.09.03	Chas Symonds L PTS 6 Bethnal Green
09.07.05	John O'Donnell L RTD 3 Nottingham
30.09.05	Mike Reid L PTS 4 Kirkcaldy
07.10.05	Craig Watson L PTS 4 Bethnal Green
21.10.05	John O'Donnell L PTS 4 Bethnal Green
30.10.05	Wayne Goddard L PTS 4 Bethnal Green
12.11.05	Scott Lawton L PTS 6 Stoke
25.11.05	Stuart Elwell L PTS 4 Walsall
11.12.05	Surinder Sekhon L PTS 6 Chigwell
28.01.06	Adnan Amar L PTS 4 Nottingham
17.02.06	Lee Meager L PTS 4 Bethnal Green
03.03.06	Franny Jones L PTS 6 Hartlepool
24.03.06	Robert Lloyd-Taylor L PTS 6 Bethnal Green
06.04.06	Duncan Cottier L PTS 4 Piccadilly
14.04.06	Mark Lloyd L PTS 4 Telford
12.05.06	Allan Gray W PTS 4 Bethnal Green
03.06.06	Tom Glover L PTS 4 Chigwell
23.06.06	Jamie Coyle L PTS 6 Blackpool

Career: 27 contests, won 7, drew 1, lost 19.

Sean Hughes

Pontefract. *Born* Pontefract, 5 June, 1982
Central Area S. Bantamweight Champion.
Ht. 5'9"
Manager Self

02.03.02	Paddy Folan W PTS 6 Wakefield
25.06.02	John Paul Ryan W PTS 6 Rugby
05.10.02	Paddy Folan W PTS 4 Huddersfield

10.02.03	Neil Read W PTS 6 Sheffield
24.05.03	John-Paul Ryan W PTS 6 Sheffield
13.09.03	Daniel Thorpe W PTS 6 Wakefield
05.10.03	Paddy Folan W RSC 4 Bradford
	(Vacant Central Area S.Bantamweight Title)
07.12.03	Marty Kayes W PTS 6 Bradford
26.02.04	Steve Foster L RSC 6 Widnes
	(Vacant English Featherweight Title)
23.10.04	Kristian Laight W PTS 6 Wakefield
04.03.05	Michael Hunter L RSC 6 Hartlepool
	(British S.Bantamweight Title Challenge)
08.05.05	Billy Smith W PTS 6 Bradford
25.06.05	Pete Buckley DREW 6 Wakefield
14.10.05	Bernard Dunne L RSC 2 Dublin
	(Vacant IBC S.Bantamweight Title)
03.03.06	Marc Callaghan L PTS 10 Hartlepool
	(Vacant English S.Bantamweight Title)
28.05.06	Shaun Walton W PTS 6 Wakefield

Career: 16 contests, won 11, drew 1, lost 4.

John Humphrey

Newmarket. *Born* Kings Lynn, 24 July, 1980
Middleweight. Former Undefeated Southern Area & British Masters Middleweight Champion. Former Southern Area L.Middleweight Champion. Former Undefeated British Masters Welterweight Champion. Ht. 6'2"
Manager J. Bowers

20.05.99	Arv Mittoo W PTS 6 Barking
13.09.99	Les Frost W CO 1 Bethnal Green
05.10.99	David Kehoe W PTS 4 Bloomsbury
06.11.99	Emmanuel Marcos W PTS 4 Bethnal Green
25.02.00	Matthew Barr L RSC 1 Newmarket
18.05.00	Lee Molyneux W PTS 6 Bethnal Green
29.09.00	Chris Henry W RSC 4 Bethnal Green
15.02.01	Kevin McIntyre W RSC 4 Glasgow
09.03.01	Harry Butler W RSC 1 Millwall
20.04.01	Mark Ramsey W PTS 10 Millwall
	(Vacant British Masters Welterweight Title)
26.05.01	James Hare L RSC 7 Bethnal Green
	(Elim. British Welterweight Title)
28.09.01	Clive Johnson W PTS 6 Millwall
23.11.01	Matthew Barr W RSC 2 Bethnal Green
16.03.02	Ojay Abrahams W PTS 10 Bethnal Green
	(Vacant Southern Area L.Middleweight Title)
19.10.02	Robert Burton W RSC 4 Norwich
08.02.03	Delroy Leslie W RSC 2 Norwich
	(Southern Area L.Middleweight Title Defence)
27.05.03	David Walker L CO 2 Dagenham
	(Southern Area L.Middleweight Title Defence. Elim. British L. Middleweight Title)
05.03.05	Dean Powell W RSC 3 Dagenham
30.04.05	Michael Monaghan W PTS 6 Dagenham
18.09.05	Hussain Osman W PTS 10 Bethnal Green
	(Vacant Southern Area Middleweight Title)
30.10.05	Gokhan Kazaz W PTS 10 Bethnal Green
	(Vacant British Masters Middleweight Title)

Career: 21 contests, won 18, lost 3.

Danny Hunt

Southend. *Born* Rochford, 1 May, 1981
Lightweight. Former Undefeated English
Lightweight Champion. Ht. 5'7"
Manager F. Warren

29.11.99	Chris Lyons W PTS 4 Wembley
13.03.00	Dave Hinds W PTS 4 Bethnal Green
13.04.00	Steve Hanley W PTS 4 Holborn
13.07.00	Dave Travers W PTS 4 Bethnal Green
27.01.01	Lee Williamson L RSC 2 Bethnal Green
03.04.01	Lee Williamson W PTS 4 Bethnal Green
05.05.01	Pete Buckley W PTS 4 Edmonton
22.09.01	Dafydd Carlin W PTS 4 Bethnal Green
15.12.01	Dave Hinds W PTS 4 Wembley
02.03.02	Gary Flear W PTS 4 Bethnal Green
04.05.02	Jason Nesbitt W PTS 4 Bethnal Green
14.09.02	David Kehoe W RSC 3 Bethnal Green
15.02.03	Mark Bowen W RSC 1 Wembley
29.03.03	Daniel Thorpe W PTS 4 Portsmouth
02.10.03	Chill John W PTS 10 Liverpool
	(Vacant English Lightweight Title)
07.02.04	Anthony Maynard W PTS 10 Bethnal Green
	(English Lightweight Title Defence)
05.06.04	Chris McDonagh W CO 3 Bethnal Green
19.11.04	Lee Meager W PTS 10 Bethnal Green
	(English Lightweight Title Defence)
04.11.05	Jon Honney W PTS 8 Bethnal Green
13.05.06	Mounir Guebbas L RSC 3 Bethnal Green

Career: 20 contests, won 18, lost 2.

Rob Hunt

Stafford. *Born* Stafford, 9 November, 1985
L.Welterweight. Ht. 6'0"
Manager P. Dykes

18.05.06	Ian Clyde W RSC 1 Walsall
29.06.06	Pete Buckley W PTS 6 Dudley

Career: 2 contests, won 2.

Michael Hunter

Hartlepool. *Born* Hartlepool, 5 May, 1978
British, European & Commonwealth
S.Bantamweight Champion. Former
Undefeated WBF & Northern Area
S.Bantamweight Champion. Ht. 5'7½"
Manager D. Garside

23.07.00	Sean Grant W PTS 6 Hartlepool
01.10.00	Chris Emanuele W PTS 6 Hartlepool
24.11.00	Gary Groves W RSC 2 Darlington
09.12.00	Chris Jickells W PTS 4 Southwark
11.02.01	Paddy Folan W RSC 6 Hartlepool
06.05.01	Anthony Hanna W PTS 4 Hartlepool
04.06.01	Anthony Hanna W PTS 4 Hartlepool
09.09.01	John Barnes W RSC 8 Hartlepool
	(Vacant Northern Area S.Bantamweight Title)
29.11.01	Joel Viney W PTS 6 Hartlepool
26.01.02	Stevie Quinn W CO 2 Dagenham
18.03.02	Marc Callaghan DREW 6 Crawley
18.05.02	Mark Payne W PTS 8 Millwall
18.10.02	Frankie DeMilo W PTS 12 Hartlepool
	(Vacant WBF S. Bantamweight Title)
14.12.02	Anthony Hanna W PTS 8 Newcastle
07.06.03	Afrim Mustafa W RSC 5 Trieste, Italy
26.07.03	Rocky Dean W RSC 1 Plymouth
04.10.03	Nikolai Eremeev W PTS 6 Belfast
08.11.03	Gennadiy Delisandru W PTS 6 Bridgend
16.04.04	Mark Payne W RSC 7 Hartlepool
	(Vacant British S.Bantamweight Title)
02.06.04	Vladimir Borov W PTS 6 Hereford
19.11.04	Marc Callaghan W RSC 10 Hartlepool
	(British S.Bantamweight Title Defence)
04.03.05	Sean Hughes W RSC 6 Hartlepool
	(British S.Bantamweight Title Defence)
27.05.05	Kamel Guerfi W RSC 6 Spennymoor
28.10.05	Esham Pickering W PTS 12 Hartlepool
	(European & Commonwealth S.Bantamweight Title Challenges. British S.Bantamweight Title Defence)
03.03.06	Yersin Jailauov W RSC 2 Hartlepool
	(European S.Bantamweight Title Defence)
28.04.06	German Guartos W RTD 3 Hartlepool
	(European S.Bantamweight Title Defence)
23.06.06	Tuncay Kaya W CO 9 Blackpool
	(European S.Bantamweight Title Defence)

Career: 27 contests, won 26, drew 1.

Michael Hunter

Jamil Hussain

Bradford. *Born* Pakistan, 15 September, 1979
Bantamweight. Ht. 5'7"
Manager C. Aston

08.10.01	Andy Greenaway W RSC 3 Barnsley
28.01.02	Neil Read W CO 2 Barnsley
18.03.02	Darren Cleary DREW 4 Crawley
27.04.02	Darren Cleary DREW 4 Huddersfield
22.02.03	Danny Wallace L RSC 1 Huddersfield
30.03.06	Moses Kinyua W PTS 6 Peterborough

Career: 6 contests, won 3, drew 2, lost 1.

Khurram Hussain

Bradford. *Born* Bradford, 11 August, 1980
Welterweight. Ht. 5'10"
Manager J. Ingle

13.11.05	Peter Dunn W PTS 4 Leeds
03.12.05	Kyle Taylor W PTS 6 Coventry
23.02.06	Darren Gethin DREW 4 Leeds
04.03.06	Joe McCluskey W PTS 6 Coventry
28.05.06	Tye Williams W PTS 6 Wakefield

Career: 5 contests, won 4, drew 1.

Zahoor Hussain

Bradford. *Born* Bradford, 26 February, 1981
Middleweight. Ht. 5'11"
Manager C. Aston

11.05.06	Martin Sweeney W PTS 6 Sunderland

Career: 1 contest, won 1.

Johnny Hussey

Manchester. *Born* Manchester, 18 August, 1982
Welterweight. Ht. 6'0"
Manager J. Trickett

08.07.05	Joe Mitchell W PTS 4 Altrincham
01.10.05	Darren Gethin W PTS 6 Wigan
18.12.05	Karl Taylor W PTS 6 Bolton
12.02.06	Tye Williams W PTS 6 Manchester
18.06.06	Barry Downes W PTS 6 Manchester

Career: 5 contests, won 5.

Eddie Hyland

Wellingborough. *Born* Dublin, 24 April, 1981
S.Featherweight. Ht. 5'6½"
Manager J. Harding

26.11.04	Buster Dennis W PTS 4 Altrincham
04.06.05	Stefan Berza W RSC 1 Dublin
17.09.05	Peter Batora W RSC 1 Dublin
11.03.06	Tibor Rafael W RSC 2 Dublin
16.06.06	Steve Mullin L RTD 4 Liverpool

Career: 5 contests, won 4, lost 1.

Patrick Hyland

Wellingborough. *Born* Dublin, 16 September, 1983
Featherweight. Ht. 5'7¼"
Manager J. Harding

24.09.04	Dean Ward W PTS 4 Dublin
13.02.05	Steve Gethin W PTS 4 Brentwood
04.06.05	Pete Buckley W PTS 4 Dublin
17.09.05	Imrich Parlagi W PTS 4 Dublin
18.11.05	Craig Morgan W PTS 4 Dagenham
11.03.06	Tibor Besze W CO 1 Dublin

Career: 6 contests, won 6.

Paul Hyland

Wellingborough. *Born* Dublin, 19 November, 1984
Featherweight. Ht. 5'7"
Manager J. Harding

05.11.04	Janos Garai W RSC 2 Hereford
19.02.05	Vladimir Bukovy W RSC 3 Dublin
04.06.05	Ferenc Szabo W PTS 6 Dublin
17.09.05	Andrej Surina W RTD 4 Dublin
14.10.05	Peter Feher W PTS 4 Dublin
18.11.05	Rakhim Mingaleev W PTS 4 Dagenham
24.02.06	Dariusz Snarski W PTS 6 Dagenham
11.03.06	Sandor Paska W RSC 3 Dublin

Career: 8 contests, won 8.

Jon Ibbotson

Sheffield. *Born* Sheffield, 2 September, 1982
L.Heavyweight. Ht. 6'3½"
Manager D. Hobson

15.12.04	Paul Billington W PTS 4 Sheffield
20.02.05	Nick Okoth W PTS 6 Sheffield
22.04.05	Daniel Teasdale W RSC 1 Barnsley
18.06.05	Ojay Abrahams W PTS 4 Barnsley
05.03.06	Tony Booth W PTS 4 Sheffield
13.05.06	Magid Ben Driss W RSC 2 Sheffield
22.06.06	Robert Burton DREW 6 Sheffield

Career: 7 contests, won 6, drew 1.

David Ingleby

Lancaster. *Born* Lancaster, 14 June, 1980
Heavyweight. Ht. 6'3"
Manager Self

09.06.03	Costi Marin L RSC 1 Bradford
01.12.03	Paul Bonson L PTS 6 Leeds
28.02.04	Paul King L RSC 3 Manchester
01.05.04	Jason Callum L PTS 6 Coventry
10.07.04	Scott Lansdowne L RSC 4 Coventry
20.09.04	Dave Clarke W RTD 5 Glasgow
06.12.04	Paul Butlin L CO 5 Leicester
30.04.05	Paul Butlin W PTS 6 Coventry
02.06.05	Chris Burton L RSC 3 Yarm
12.12.05	Scott Lansdowne L RSC 1 Leicester
18.03.06	Paul Butlin L PTS 6 Coventry
06.04.06	Matt Paice L PTS 4 Piccadilly
13.05.06	Carl Baker L RSC 4 Sheffield

Career: 13 contests, won 2, lost 11.

David Ingleby   Les Clark

Hamed Jamali

Birmingham. *Born* Iran, 23 November,
1973
L.Heavyweight. Ht. 5'9"
Manager Self

| 09.12.02 | Dale Nixon W CO 1 Birmingham |

24.02.03	Harry Butler W PTS 6 Birmingham
06.10.03	Simeon Cover W PTS 6 Birmingham
08.12.03	Gary Ojuederie W PTS 6 Birmingham
08.03.04	Ojay Abrahams W PTS 8 Birmingham
10.05.04	Jason Collins W PTS 8 Birmingham
11.10.04	Hastings Rasani W PTS 8 Birmingham
13.12.04	Simeon Cover L PTS 10 Birmingham
	(Vacant British Masters
	S.Middleweight Title)
21.02.05	Michael Pinnock W PTS 8
	Birmingham
02.03.06	Lee Blundell L PTS 6 Blackpool
07.04.06	Dan Guthrie L RSC 3 Bristol

Career: 11 contests, won 8, lost 3.

Brett James (Eleftheriou)

St Pancras. *Born* London, 3 November,
1975
Welterweight. Former Southern Area
Welterweight Champion. Ht. 5'8"
Manager Self

20.01.00	Colin Vidler W PTS 6 Piccadilly
21.02.00	Julian Kacanolli W PTS 4 Southwark
04.07.00	Colin Vidler W PTS 4 Tooting
04.11.00	Matt Scriven W RTD 1 Bethnal Green
20.01.01	Jay Mahoney W PTS 4 Bethnal Green
07.04.01	Paul Denton W PTS 4 Wembley
16.06.01	Karl Taylor DREW 4 Wembley
14.07.01	Lee Williamson W PTS 6 Wembley
29.09.01	Ernie Smith W PTS 6 Southwark
12.02.02	Karl Taylor DREW 4 Bethnal Green
23.06.02	Lee Williamson W PTS 6 Southwark
23.08.02	Brian Coleman W PTS 6 Bethnal
	Green
25.10.02	David Walker L RSC 4 Bethnal Green
	(Southern Area Welterweight Title
	Challenge)
15.05.03	Keith Jones W PTS 4 Mayfair
01.08.03	Sammy Smith W PTS 10 Bethnal
	Green
	(Vacant Southern Area Welterweight
	Title)
18.11.03	Iain Eldridge W PTS 10 Bethnal Green
	(Southern Area Welterweight Title
	Defence)
20.02.04	Richard Inquieti W PTS 6
	Southampton
01.04.04	Michael Jennings L RTD 5 Bethnal
	Green
	(WBU International Welterweight Title
	Challenge)
25.06.04	Chas Symonds L RSC 4 Bethnal Green
	(Southern Area Welterweight Title
	Defence)
07.08.05	Leonard Bundu L PTS 6 Rimini, Italy
10.12.05	Ross Minter L RSC 4 Canning Town
	(Vacant English Welterweight Title)

Career: 21 contests, won 14, drew 2, lost 5.

Fred Janes

Cardiff. *Born* Cardiff, 17 December, 1984
Lightweight. Ht. 5'9"
Manager D. Gardiner

23.11.03	Paddy Folan W RSC 5 Rotherham
13.12.03	Steve Bell L PTS 4 Manchester
13.02.04	Michael Graydon DREW 6 Bristol
06.03.04	John Bothwell DREW 4 Renfrew
01.04.04	Martin Power L RSC 2 Bethnal Green
02.06.04	John Simpson L PTS 6 Hereford
10.09.04	Matthew Marsh L PTS 4 Bethnal Green
16.10.04	Warren Dunkley L PTS 6 Dagenham

06.12.04	Danny Wallace L RSC 2 Leeds
29.04.05	Paul Buckley L PTS 4 Southwark
30.09.05	Stuart Green L PTS 4 Kirkcaldy

Career: 11 contests, won 1, drew 2, lost 8.

Henry Janes

Cardiff. *Born* Cardiff, 24 May, 1983
Lightweight. Ht. 5'7"
Manager Self

24.05.03	Steve Foster L PTS 6 Bethnal Green
02.06.03	Matt Teague L PTS 6 Cleethorpes
20.06.03	Derry Matthews L RSC 1 Liverpool
07.09.03	Steve Gethin W PTS 4 Shrewsbury
30.10.03	Kevin O'Hara L PTS 6 Belfast
30.11.03	Ian Reid W PTS 6 Swansea
13.12.03	Andy Morris L PTS 4 Manchester
19.01.04	John Simpson L PTS 8 Glasgow
07.02.04	Lee Whyatt W PTS 4 Bethnal Green
06.03.04	Kevin O'Hara L PTS 6 Renfrew
13.03.04	Danny Wallace W PTS 4 Huddersfield
03.04.04	Derry Matthews L PTS 4 Manchester
22.04.04	Barry Hawthorne L PTS 6 Glasgow
19.06.04	Scott Flynn W RSC 4 Renfrew
16.10.04	John Mackay W PTS 4 Dagenham
04.11.04	Sam Rukundo L PTS 6 Piccadilly
19.11.04	Lee Beavis L PTS 4 Bethnal Green
11.12.04	Kevin Mitchell L PTS 4 Canning Town
11.02.05	Steve Bell L RTD 3 Manchester
02.07.05	Martin Lindsay L RSC 2 Dundalk
24.11.05	Paul McCloskey L RSC 3 Lurgan

Career: 21 contests, won 6, lost 15.

Ervis Jegeni

Wood Green. *Born* Tirana, Albania, 15
April, 1986
Heavyweight. Ht. 6'1"
Manager C. Hall

30.03.06	Tony Booth W RSC 1 Piccadilly
21.05.06	Istvan Kecskes W PTS 4 Bethnal
	Green

Career: 2 contests, won 2.

Michael Jennings

Chorley. *Born* Preston, 9 September, 1977
Welterweight. Former British Welterweight
Champion. Former Undefeated English
Welterweight Champion. Former
Undefeated WBU Inter-Continental
Welterweight Champion. Ht. 5'9½"
Manager F. Warren/B. Hughes

15.05.99	Tony Smith W RSC 1 Blackpool
11.12.99	Lee Molyneux W PTS 4 Liverpool
29.02.00	Lee Molyneux W PTS 6 Widnes
25.03.00	Brian Coleman W PTS 6 Liverpool
16.05.00	Brian Coleman W PTS 6 Warrington
29.05.00	William Webster W PTS 6 Manchester
08.07.00	Paul Denton W PTS 6 Widnes
04.09.00	Mark Ramsey W PTS 6 Manchester
25.11.00	Ernie Smith W PTS 4 Manchester
11.12.00	Paul Denton W PTS 4 Widnes
10.02.01	Mark Haslam W RSC 2 Widnes
07.07.01	David Kirk W PTS 6 Manchester
15.09.01	Gary Harrison W PTS 6 Manchester
09.02.02	James Paisley W RSC 3 Manchester
01.06.02	Lee Williamson W PTS 4 Manchester
28.09.02	Karl Taylor W RSC 4 Manchester
01.11.02	Richard Inquieti W RSC 2 Preston
18.01.03	Lee Williamson W RTD 4 Preston
08.05.03	Jimmy Gould W RTD 6 Widnes

(Vacant WBU Inter-Continental Welterweight Title)

27.09.03 Sammy Smith W RTD 4 Manchester
(WBU Inter-Continental Welterweight Title Defence)

13.12.03 Peter Dunn W PTS 6 Manchester

01.04.04 Brett James W RTD 5 Bethnal Green
(WBU Inter-Continental Welterweight Title Defence)

22.05.04 Rafal Jackiewicz W PTS 8 Widnes

01.10.04 Chris Saunders W RTD 5 Manchester
(English Welterweight Title Challenge)

11.02.05 Vasile Dragomir W CO 3 Manchester

03.06.05 Gavin Down W RSC 9 Manchester
(English Welterweight Title Defence)

16.07.05 Jimmy Vincent W CO 1 Bolton
(Vacant British Welterweight Title)

25.10.05 Bradley Pryce W PTS 12 Preston
(British Welterweight Title Defence)

28.01.06 Young Muttley L PTS 12 Nottingham
(British Welterweight Title Defence)

Career: 29 contests, won 28, lost 1.

Michael Jennings   Les Clark

Jav Jerome

Birmingham. *Born* Afghanistan, 1 June, 1982
Middleweight. Ht. 5'8"
Manager N. Nobbs

23.02.06 Gavin Smith L RSC 5 Leeds

20.05.06 Leon Owen L PTS 6 Bristol

Career: 2 contests, lost 2.

Carl Johanneson

Leeds. *Born* Leeds, 1 August, 1978
Central Area S.Featherweight Champion.
Former Undefeated WBF S.Featherweight Champion. Ht. 5'5"
Manager R. Manners

08.07.00 Calvin Sheppard W PTS 3 North Carolina, USA

15.09.00 Sean Thomassen W RSC 1 Paterson, New Jersey, USA

14.10.00 Hiep Bui W RSC 1 Scranton, Pennsylvania, USA

08.12.00 Walusimbi Kizito W PTS 4 Atlantic City, New Jersey, USA

12.04.01 Efrain Guzman W PTS 4 Melville, New York, USA

04.05.01 Calvin Sheppard W RSC 4 Atlantic City, New Jersey, USA

26.06.01 Joey Figueroa W PTS 6 NYC, New York, USA

26.10.01 Jose Ramon Disla W RSC 5 Atlantic City, New Jersey, USA

14.12.01 Angel Rios W PTS 6 Uncasville, Connecticut, USA

03.03.02 Kema Muse W PTS 6 Scranton, Pennsylvania, USA

02.07.02 James Baker W RSC 4 Washington DC, USA

16.01.03 Juan R. Llopis W RSC 5 Philadelphia, Pennsylvania, USA

05.06.03 Koba Gogoladze L PTS 8 Detroit, Michigan, USA

18.07.03 Reggie Sanders W PTS 6 Dover, Delaware, USA

21.08.03 Steve Trumble W RSC 2 Philadelphia, Pennsylvania, USA

30.01.04 Harold Grey W RSC 5 Philadelphia, Pennsylvania, USA

20.03.04 Carl Greaves W RTD 3 Wembley
(WBF S.Featherweight Title Challenge)

08.05.04 Andrew Ferrans W RSC 6 Bristol
(WBF S.Featherweight Title Defence)

19.06.04 Alexander Abramenko W RSC 5 Muswell Hill
(WBF S.Featherweight Title Defence)

02.12.04 Leva Kirakosyan L RSC 1 Crystal Palace

08.05.05 Jimmy Beech W CO 2 Bradford

09.07.05 Daniel Thorpe W RSC 3 Bristol

25.09.05 Peter Allen W RTD 9 Leeds
(Vacant Central Area S.Featherweight Title)

13.11.05 Carl Allen W RTD 2 Leeds

23.02.06 Andrew Ferrans W RSC 2 Leeds
(Final Elim. British S.Featherweight Title)

Career: 25 contests, won 23, lost 2.

Clint Johnson

Leeds. *Born* Leeds, 13 April, 1974
L.Heavyweight. Ht. 6'2"
Manager Self

11.11.97 Jon Penn W RSC 2 Leeds

04.12.97 John O'Byrne L PTS 6 Sunderland

17.02.98 Rob Galloway W PTS 6 Leeds

20.09.98 Rob Galloway W PTS 6 Sheffield

29.10.98 Mike White L PTS 6 Newcastle

06.11.98 Gerard Zdiarski W PTS 4 Mayfair

07.12.98 Carl Nicholson W PTS 6 Bradford

16.02.99 Danny Southam L RSC 5 Leeds

15.09.99 Steve Loftus W PTS 6 Harrogate

28.03.00 Martin Jolley W PTS 6 Hartlepool

17.04.00 Alex Mason L PTS 6 Birmingham

20.05.00 Jason Barker L RSC 1 Rotherham

23.10.00 Joe Gillon L CO 4 Glasgow

17.05.01 Paul Bonson L PTS 6 Leeds

18.06.01 Mark Brookes L PTS 6 Bradford

13.09.01 Darren Littlewood W PTS 6 Sheffield

03.11.01 Joe Gillon W CO 3 Glasgow

03.12.01 Jimmy Steel DREW 6 Leeds

15.12.01 Mark Brookes L PTS 4 Sheffield

18.02.02 Billy McClung L PTS 6 Glasgow

01.03.02 Billy McClung L PTS 6 Irvine

16.03.02 Clinton Woods L RSC 3 Bethnal Green

08.10.02 Allan Foster L PTS 6 Glasgow

02.12.02 Greg Scott-Briggs W PTS 6 Leeds
08.02.03 Andrew Lowe L PTS 6 Brentford
05.04.03 Darren Corbett L RSC 4 Belfast
12.10.03 Scott Lansdowne L PTS 4 Sheffield
01.12.03 Simeon Cover W PTS 6 Leeds
20.03.04 Courtney Fry L RSC 2 Wembley
28.02.06 Keiran O'Donnell L RSC 1 Leeds
21.04.06 Stewart Mitchell L PTS 4 Doncaster
Career: 31 contests, won 11, drew 1, lost 19.

Craig Johnson

Clay Cross. *Born* Chesterfield, 10
November, 1980
L.Welterweight. Ht. 5'7"
Manager J. Ashton/S. Calow

25.04.04 Peter Allen W PTS 6 Nottingham
18.09.04 David Bailey L PTS 6 Newark
22.10.04 Carl Allen W PTS 6 Mansfield
10.12.04 Pete Buckley W PTS 6 Mansfield
06.03.05 Ian Reid W PTS 6 Mansfield
11.09.05 Billy Smith W PTS 4 Kirkby in
          Ashfield
12.11.05 Jason Nesbitt W PTS 6 Sheffield

Career: 7 contests, won 6, lost 1.

Danny Johnston

Stoke. *Born* Stoke, 19 May, 1981
L.Middleweight. Ht. 5'10"
Manager M. Carney

26.09.04 Karl Taylor W PTS 6 Stoke
12.11.05 Manoocha Salari L RSC 5 Stoke
18.02.06 Terry Carruthers L PTS 6 Stoke
06.05.06 Derrick Grieve W RSC 3 Stoke

Career: 4 contests, won 2, lost 2.

Darren Johnstone

Larkhall. *Born* Motherwell, 30 March, 1982
British Masters S.Featherweight Champion.
Ht. 5'9"
Manager T. Gilmour

17.11.03 Jamie Hill W PTS 6 Glasgow
15.03.04 Ian Reid W PTS 6 Glasgow
07.06.04 Joel Viney W PTS 6 Glasgow
11.10.04 Pete Buckley W PTS 6 Glasgow
27.05.05 Gavin Tait W PTS 6 Motherwell
14.10.05 Graeme Higginson W PTS 6
          Motherwell
04.11.05 Jonathan Whiteman W RSC 3 Glasgow
21.11.05 Lance Verallo W PTS 6 Glasgow

24.04.06 Henry Jones W CO 4 Glasgow
          *(Vacant British Masters
          S.Featherweight Title)*
Career: 9 contests, won 9.

Alan Jones

Aberystwyth. *Born* Aberystwyth, 6
October, 1976
Middleweight. Ht. 6'1"
Manager T. Gilmour

15.09.01 Martyn Woodward W CO 3 Swansea
21.10.01 Kenny Griffith W RSC 4 Pentre
          Halkyn
17.02.02 Peter Jackson W PTS 6
          Wolverhampton
16.03.02 Allan Foster DREW 6 Northampton
07.10.02 Donovan Smillie W RSC 6
          Birmingham
23.02.03 Leigh Wicks W PTS 8 Aberystwyth
06.10.03 Jason Collins W PTS 8 Birmingham
30.10.03 Jim Rock W PTS 8 Belfast
02.06.04 Jason Collins W PTS 6 Hereford
05.11.04 Szabolcs Rimovszky W PTS 6
          Hereford
04.02.05 Scott Dann L CO 3 Plymouth
          (British Middleweight Title Challenge)
14.10.05 Jim Rock L PTS 12 Dublin
          (Vacant IBC Middleweight Title)
Career: 12 contests, won 9, drew 1, lost 2.

Barrie Jones

Rhondda. *Born* Tylorstown, 1 March, 1985
Welterweight. Ht. 5'11"
Manager D. Powell/F. Warren

03.07.04 Pete Buckley W PTS 4 Newport
03.09.04 Dave Hinds W PTS 4 Newport
21.01.05 Lea Handley W PTS 4 Bridgend
17.06.05 Marco Cittadini W RSC 2 Glasgow
10.09.05 Jas Malik W RSC 1 Cardiff
11.03.06 Terry Carruthers W RSC 1 Newport
29.04.06 David Kehoe W RTD 2 Edinburgh
Career: 7 contests, won 7.

Carl Johanneson   Les Clark

Barrie Jones   Les Clark

Davey Jones

Epworth. *Born* Grimsby, 30 May, 1977
Middleweight. Ht. 5'11"
Manager M. Shinfield

23.09.02	William Webster W PTS 6 Cleethorpes
08.11.02	William Webster W PTS 6 Doncaster
30.11.02	Matt Scriven W PTS 6 Newark
16.12.02	Gary Jones W PTS 6 Cleethorpes
21.02.03	Jimi Hendricks W PTS 6 Doncaster
09.05.03	Wayne Shepherd W PTS 6 Doncaster
22.09.03	Steve Brumant L PTS 6 Cleethorpes
26.02.04	Paul Smith L PTS 6 Widnes
06.03.04	Paul Buchanan L PTS 4 Renfrew
23.05.05	Ernie Smith DREW 6 Cleethorpes
15.12.05	Omar Gumati W PTS 6 Cleethorpes
16.02.06	Mark Lloyd L PTS 6 Dudley

Career: 12 contests, won 7, drew 1, lost 4.

Franny Jones

Darlington. *Born* Burnley, 7 February, 1981
L.Middleweight. Ht. 5'9½"
Manager M. Marsden

05.05.02	Surinder Sekhon W PTS 6 Hartlepool
28.09.02	Martin Scotland W PTS 6 Wakefield
18.10.02	Richard Inquieti W PTS 6 Hartlepool
27.02.03	Danny Moir DREW 6 Sunderland
17.03.03	Gary Porter W PTS 6 Glasgow
11.07.03	Gary Cummings W RSC 2 Darlington
10.10.03	Pedro Thompson W PTS 6 Darlington
13.12.03	Matthew Hatton DREW 6 Manchester
05.03.04	Danny Moir NC 3 Darlington
	(Vacant Northern Area L.Middleweight Title)
16.04.04	Brian Coleman W PTS 6 Hartlepool
19.11.04	Paul Lomax W RSC 2 Hartlepool
04.03.05	Ali Nuumbembe L PTS 6 Hartlepool
11.03.05	Matthew Hatton L RTD 6 Doncaster
02.06.05	Darren Gethin W PTS 8 Yarm
28.10.05	Ernie Smith W PTS 4 Hartlepool
03.03.06	Ben Hudson W PTS 6 Hartlepool
28.04.06	Richard Mazurek W PTS 6 Hartlepool
23.06.06	Stuart Elwell L RSC 1 Blackpool

Career: 18 contests, won 12, drew 2, lost 3, no contest 1.

Henry Jones

Pembroke. *Born* Haverfordwest, 23 December, 1975
Lightweight. Ht. 5'0"
Manager Self

17.06.95	Abdul Mannon W PTS 6 Cardiff
07.07.95	Harry Woods L PTS 4 Cardiff
07.10.95	Frankie Slane L PTS 4 Belfast
28.11.95	Jason Thomas L PTS 4 Cardiff
20.12.95	Brendan Bryce W PTS 6 Usk
20.03.96	Danny Lawson W CO 1 Cardiff
29.05.96	Ian Turner L PTS 6 Ebbw Vale
02.10.96	Jason Thomas W PTS 4 Cardiff
26.10.96	Danny Costello L RSC 3 Liverpool
29.04.97	Tommy Waite L PTS 4 Belfast
19.05.97	Francky Leroy L RSC 1 Coudekerque, France
02.12.97	Ian Turner L RSC 8 Swansea
	(Vacant Welsh Bantamweight Title)
30.10.98	Tiger Singh W CO 4 Peterborough
05.05.00	Jason Edwards L PTS 6 Pentre Halkyn

28.11.02	Jon Honney L PTS 4 Finchley
23.02.03	David Vaughan L PTS 6 Aberystwyth
10.04.03	Daleboy Rees L PTS 4 Clydach
07.05.03	Jason Nesbitt W PTS 6 Ellesmere Port
15.06.03	Dean Lambert L RSC 4 Bradford
20.04.04	Scott Lawton L PTS 6 Sheffield
19.06.04	Colin Bain L PTS 4 Renfrew
03.07.04	Michael Graydon DREW 6 Bristol
30.09.05	Jason Nesbitt W PTS 6 Carmarthen
24.04.06	Darren Johnstone L CO 4 Glasgow
	(Vacant British Masters S.Featherweight Title)
16.06.06	Furhan Rafiq W PTS 6 Carmarthen

Career: 25 contests, won 8, drew 1, lost 16.

Michael Jones Les Clark

Michael Jones

Liverpool. *Born* Liverpool, 14 November, 1974
L.Middleweight. Former British & Commonwealth L.Middleweight Champion. Ht. 6'0¼"
Manager Self

15.11.97	Harry Butler W PTS 4 Bristol
17.01.98	Martin Cavey W CO 1 Bristol
07.03.98	Darren McInulty W PTS 4 Reading
25.04.98	Koba Kulu W RSC 3 Cardiff
06.06.98	G. L. Booth W RSC 2 Liverpool
10.10.98	Takaloo W PTS 6 Bethnal Green
19.12.98	Ojay Abrahams W PTS 6 Liverpool
26.06.99	Paul King W PTS 6 Glasgow
11.03.00	Alan Gilbert W RTD 3 Kensington
02.06.00	Mohammed Boualleg W PTS 8 Ashford
03.02.01	Howard Clarke W PTS 4 Manchester
24.04.01	Judicael Bedel W PTS 6 Liverpool
06.10.01	Delroy Mellis W PTS 8 Manchester
10.12.01	Piotr Bartnicki W RSC 4 Liverpool
13.04.02	Mark Richards W RSC 1 Liverpool
28.05.02	Joshua Onyango W RSC 6 Liverpool
	(Commonwealth L. Middleweight Title Challenge)

08.02.03	Howard Clarke W PTS 6 Liverpool
19.04.03	Jamie Moore L PTS 12 Liverpool
	(Commonwealth L.Middleweight Title Defence. Vacant British L.Middleweight Title)
18.10.03	Ojay Abrahams W PTS 6 Manchester
13.03.04	Jason Williams W PTS 6 Huddersfield
10.04.04	Darren Rhodes W RSC 3 Manchester
	(Final Elim. British L.Middleweight Title)
26.11.04	Jamie Moore W DIS 3 Altrincham
	(British L.Middleweight Title Challenge)
08.07.05	Jamie Moore L RSC 6 Altrincham
	(British L.Middleweight Title Defence)
03.03.06	Ismael Kerzazi W RSC 6 Hartlepool
23.06.06	Sergey Starkov W PTS 6 Blackpool

Career: 25 contests, won 23, lost 2.

(Lee) Taz Jones

Abercynon. *Born* Aberdare, 24 August, 1982
Welterweight. Former Undefeated British Masters L.Middleweight Champion. Ht. 5'11"
Manager B. Coleman

15.09.02	David White DREW 4 Swansea
02.11.02	Gerard McAuley DREW 4 Belfast
21.12.02	Luke Rudd W RTD 1 Millwall
08.01.03	Elroy Edwards W PTS 6 Aberdare
27.09.03	Matthew Hatton L PTS 6 Manchester
06.12.03	Ernie Smith W PTS 4 Cardiff
21.02.04	Craig Lynch W PTS 4 Cardiff
17.04.04	Andy Gibson W PTS 6 Belfast
03.09.04	Karl Taylor W PTS 4 Newport
30.09.04	Craig Dickson DREW 6 Glasgow
08.12.04	Kevin Phelan W PTS 10 Longford
	(British Masters L.Middleweight Title Challenge)
18.03.05	Neil Sinclair W RSC 1 Belfast
23.07.05	Colin McNeil L PTS 10 Edinburgh
	(Vacant Celtic L.Middleweight Title)
10.09.05	Tony Doherty L PTS 10 Cardiff
	(Vacant Celtic Welterweight Title)
28.04.06	Graham Delehedy W CO 6 Hartlepool

Career: 15 contests, won 9, drew 3, lost 3.

Tommy Jones

Llanelli. *Born* Swansea, 6 July, 1983
L.Middleweight. Ht. 5'8"
Manager D. Davies

08.12.05	Simon Fleck L PTS 6 Derby
18.12.05	Alex Matvienko L PTS 6 Bolton
04.03.06	Richard Mazurek L PTS 6 Coventry
07.04.06	Danny Butler L PTS 4 Bristol
28.04.06	Prince Arron L PTS 6 Manchester
13.05.06	Mark Lloyd L PTS 6 Sutton in Ashfield
29.06.06	Mark Lloyd L PTS 6 Dudley

Career: 7 contests, lost 7.

Scott Jordan

Belfast. *Born* Dundonald, 22 April, 1984
Middleweight. Ht. 5'9¼"
Manager B. Hearn

21.04.06	Jamie Ambler W PTS 4 Belfast

Career: 1 contest, won 1.

K

Davis Kamara
Sheffield. *Born* Sierra Leone, 14 November, 1978
Welterweight. Ht. 5'10"
Manager W. Barker

06.09.03 Patrik Prokopecz W PTS 4 Berlin, Germany
18.12.03 Miro Dicky W PTS 4 Berlin, Germany
07.02.04 Roberto Jose Salas W PTS 4 Vigo, Spain
18.02.06 Gary Reid L PTS 6 Stoke
05.03.06 Nicki Smedley L PTS 6 Sheffield
28.04.06 Jason Nesbitt W PTS 6 Manchester
Career: 6 contests, won 4, lost 2.

George Katsimpas
Cheddar. *Born* Bristol, 8 June, 1980
S.Middleweight. Ht. 5'7¾"
Manager J. Evans

05.03.06 Leon Owen W RSC 2 Southampton
20.05.06 Tony Randell W RSC 1 Bristol
Career: 2 contests, won 2.

George Katsimpas   Les Clark

Gokhan Kazaz
Walthamstow. *Born* Turkey, 21 November, 1977
S.Middleweight. Ht. 5'9"
Manager J. Eames

17.07.03 Joel Ani W PTS 4 Dagenham
18.09.03 Jimi Hendricks W PTS 4 Dagenham
06.11.03 Tomas da Silva W PTS 4 Dagenham
07.02.04 Patrick Cito W PTS 4 Bethnal Green
13.05.04 Alan Gilbert W PTS 4 Bethnal Green
30.07.04 Dean Powell W RSC 2 Bethnal Green
10.09.04 Dmitry Donetskiy W RSC 4 Bethnal Green
11.12.04 Darren McDermott DREW 4 Canning Town
19.06.05 Alan Gilbert W PTS 6 Bethnal Green
30.10.05 John Humphrey L PTS 10 Bethnal Green

(Vacant British Masters Middleweight Title)
26.02.06 Manoocha Salari DREW 4 Dagenham
Career: 11 contests, won 8, drew 2, lost 1.

Gokhan Kazaz   Philip Sharkey

Istvan Kecskes
Wolverhampton. *Born* Nagykoros, Hungary, 26 January, 1980
Heavyweight. Ht. 6'1"
Manager E. Johnson

24.11.01 Piotr Scieszka L RSC 2 Lodz, Poland
29.12.01 Karol Nowinski L PTS 6 Konin, Poland
09.02.02 Karoly Farkas W RSC 2 Budapest, Hungary
01.04.02 Richel Hersisia L RSC 4 Gent, Belgium
20.05.02 Laszlo Virag DREW 4 Budapest, Hungary
01.06.02 Cengiz Koc L RSC 2 Nurnberg, Germany
24.11.02 Pavel Vanacek W PTS 4 Bad Honnef, Germany
21.12.02 Balu Sauer L RSC 4 Cottbus, Germany
14.03.03 Zoltan Petranyi L PTS 4 Budapest, Hungary
05.07.03 Rene Monse L RSC 2 Dessau, Germany
07.09.03 Aleh Dubiaha L RSC 4 Prague, Czech Republic
09.11.03 Josef Jakob L RSC 1 Bad Honnef, Germany
24.04.04 Volodia Lazebnik L RSC 3 Dabrowa Gornicza, Poland
03.03.06 Chris Burton L PTS 4 Hartlepool
11.03.06 Darren Morgan L PTS 4 Newport
25.03.06 Luke Simpkin L PTS 4 Burton
28.04.06 Chris Burton L PTS 4 Hartlepool
12.05.06 Sam Sexton L PTS 4 Bethnal Green
21.05.06 Ervis Jegeni L PTS 4 Bethnal Green
Career: 19 contests, won 2, drew 1, lost 16.

John Keeton
Sheffield. *Born* Sheffield, 19 May, 1972
Cruiserweight. Former Undefeated WBF & WBO Inter-Continental Cruiserweight Champion. Ht. 6'0"
Manager D. Ingle

11.08.93 Tony Colclough W RSC 1 Mansfield
15.09.93 Val Golding L PTS 6 Ashford
27.10.93 Darren McKenna W RSC 3 Stoke
01.12.93 Julius Francis L PTS 4 Bethnal Green
19.01.94 Dennis Bailey W RTD 2 Stoke
17.02.94 Dermot Gascoyne L RSC 1 Dagenham
09.04.94 Eddie Knight W RTD 5 Mansfield
11.05.94 John Rice W RSC 5 Sheffield
02.06.94 Devon Rhooms W RSC 2 Tooting
06.09.94 Mark Walker W RSC 5 Stoke
24.09.94 Dirk Wallyn L CO 3 Middlekerke, Belgium
26.10.94 Lee Archer W PTS 6 Stoke
09.12.94 Bruce Scott L CO 2 Bethnal Green
11.02.95 Rudiger May L PTS 6 Frankfurt, Germany
06.03.95 Simon McDougall W RSC 5 Mayfair
07.07.95 Nicky Piper L RTD 2 Cardiff
15.09.95 Steve Osborne W RSC 4 Mansfield
27.10.95 Nicky Wadman W RSC 1 Brighton
03.11.95 Monty Wright W RSC 4 Dudley
11.11.95 Denzil Browne W RSC 4 Halifax
30.01.96 Cesar Kazadi W RSC 3 Lille, France
11.05.96 Terry Dunstan L RSC 1 Bethnal Green
(British Cruiserweight Title Challenge)
14.09.96 John Pierre W PTS 4 Sheffield
14.12.96 Nigel Rafferty W RTD 3 Sheffield
12.04.97 Nigel Rafferty W RSC 6 Sheffield
11.10.97 Kelly Oliver L RSC 8 Sheffield
(Vacant WBO Inter-Continental Cruiserweight Title)
16.05.98 Jacob Mofokeng L RTD 4 Hammanskraal, South Africa
18.07.98 Kelly Oliver W RSC 2 Sheffield
23.01.99 Garry Delaney W PTS 12 Cheshunt
(Vacant WBO Inter-Continental Cruiserweight Title)
15.05.99 William Barima W RTD 3 Sheffield
29.02.00 Tony Booth W RSC 2 Widnes
16.12.00 Bruce Scott L CO 6 Sheffield
(Vacant British Cruiserweight Title)
21.07.01 Radcliffe Green W PTS 4 Sheffield
19.03.02 Butch Lesley W PTS 12 Slough
(Vacant WBF Cruiserweight Title)
16.04.04 Paul Bonson W PTS 4 Bradford
14.05.05 Paul Bonson W PTS 4 Aberdeen
11.06.05 Krzysztof Wlodarczyk L RTD 3 Gorzow Wielkopolski, Poland
(WBC Youth Cruiserweight Title Challenge)
10.09.05 Don Diego Poeder L CO 1 Rotterdam, Netherlands
01.06.06 Mark Hobson L RSC 4 Barnsley
(British & Commonwealth Cruiserweight Title Challenges)
Career: 39 contests, won 25, lost 14.

David Kehoe
Northampton. *Born* Northampton, 24 December, 1972
Welterweight. Ht. 5'10½"
Manager Self

06.02.96 Simon Frailing W CO 1 Basildon
20.04.96 Paul Salmon W PTS 6 Brentwood
12.11.96 Peter Nightingale L PTS 6 Dudley
28.04.97 Craig Kelley L DIS 3 Enfield
18.11.97 Peter Nightingale DREW 4 Mansfield
27.01.98 Paul Miles L PTS 4 Bethnal Green
11.03.98 Trevor Tacy W RTD 1 Bethnal Green
28.03.98 David Thompson W PTS 6 Crystal Palace
26.05.98 Dave Hinds W RSC 5 Mayfair

08.09.98	Marc Smith W PTS 6 Bethnal Green
12.01.99	Gary Flear L PTS 4 Bethnal Green
25.01.99	Roger Sampson L PTS 4 Glasgow
12.03.99	Jamie McKeever L RSC 2 Bethnal Green
02.07.99	Mark McGowan L RSC 3 Bristol (Vacant British Masters Lightweight Title)
13.09.99	Stephen Smith L DIS 2 Bethnal Green
05.10.99	John Humphrey L PTS 4 Bloomsbury
24.10.99	Young Muttley L RTD 1 Wolverhampton
02.12.99	Liam Maltby L PTS 4 Peterborough
19.02.00	Dariusz Snarski DREW 6 Prestwick
10.03.00	Ted Bami L PTS 4 Bethnal Green
17.04.00	Mark Hawthorne L PTS 4 Birmingham
25.07.00	P.J.Gallagher L PTS 6 Southwark
08.09.00	Dariusz Snarski W PTS 4 Hammersmith
27.11.00	Anthony Maynard L RSC 5 Birmingham
16.03.02	Wayne Wheeler DREW 6 Northampton
28.05.02	Ricky Eccleston L RSC 4 Liverpool
14.09.02	Danny Hunt L RSC 3 Bethnal Green
16.11.02	Gwyn Wale L PTS 4 Nottingham
01.02.03	Mark Winters L RSC 2 Belfast
29.10.03	Pete Buckley W PTS 6 Leicester Square
08.07.04	Rocky Muscus W PTS 6 The Strand
08.10.04	Graham Delehedy L RSC 2 Brentwood
18.03.05	Paul McCloskey L RSC 3 Belfast
24.04.05	Ashley Theophane L PTS 4 Leicester Square
26.06.05	Jay Morris L PTS 4 Southampton
24.07.05	Michael Grant L PTS 4 Leicester Square
30.09.05	Ceri Hall L PTS 6 Carmarthen
09.10.05	Ashley Theophane L PTS 4 Hammersmith
12.11.05	George Telfer L PTS 6 Glasgow
21.11.05	Craig Dickson L PTS 8 Glasgow
02.12.05	Stefy Bull L PTS 6 Doncaster
09.12.05	Grzegorz Proksa L RSC 3 Iver Heath
11.02.06	Lee Cook L RTD 2 Bethnal Green
13.03.06	Paul Burns L PTS 6 Glasgow
01.04.06	Dean Smith L PTS 4 Bethnal Green
13.04.06	Nadeem Siddique L PTS 6 Leeds
29.04.06	Barrie Jones L RTD 2 Edinburgh
30.05.06	Scott Woolford L PTS 4 Bethnal Green
16.06.06	Karl David L RSC 1 Carmarthen

Career: 49 contests, won 9, drew 3, lost 37.

Lee Kellett

Barrow. *Born* Barrow, 28 September, 1978
Cruiserweight. Ht. 6'2"
Manager M. Helliet

12.02.06	John Anthony L RSC 1 Manchester
23.06.06	Gary Thompson L PTS 4 Blackpool

Career: 2 contests, lost 2.

Adam Kelly

Sheffield. *Born* Sheffield, 8 August, 1987
Welterweight. Ht. 5'8"
Manager J. Ingle

08.12.05	Tom Hogan L PTS 6 Sunderland
05.03.06	Tye Williams W PTS 4 Sheffield
17.03.06	Stuart Green L PTS 4 Kirkcaldy
27.05.06	Mike Reid DREW 6 Aberdeen

Career: 4 contests, won 1, drew 1, lost 2.

Damaen Kelly

Belfast. *Born* Belfast, 3 April, 1973
Bantamweight. IBO S.Flyweight
Champion. Former Undefeated WBF &
IBO Flyweight Champion. Former
Undefeated European Flyweight Champion.
Former Undefeated WBC International
S.Flyweight Champion. Former British &
Commonwealth Flyweight Champion.
Ht. 5'5"
Manager Self

27.09.97	Chris Thomas W RSC 1 Belfast
22.11.97	Bojidar Ivanov W CO 1 Manchester
20.12.97	Anthony Hanna W PTS 4 Belfast
14.02.98	Hristo Lessov W RSC 2 Southwark
14.03.98	Mark Reynolds W RSC 4 Bethnal Green
02.05.98	Krasimir Tcholakov W RSC 3 Kensington
26.09.98	Mike Thomas W PTS 6 Uncasville, Connecticut, USA
12.12.98	Alfonso Zvenyika W PTS 12 Chester (Commonwealth Flyweight Title Challenge)
13.03.99	Anthony Hanna W PTS 12 Manchester (Vacant British Flyweight Title. Commonwealth Flyweight Title Defence)
22.05.99	Keith Knox L RTD 6 Belfast (British & Commonwealth Flyweight Title Defences)
16.10.99	Igor Gerasimov W RSC 4 Belfast (Vacant WBC International S. Flyweight Title)
12.02.00	Alexander Mahmutov W PTS 12 Sheffield (European Flyweight Title Challenge)
12.06.00	Jose Antonio Lopez Bueno W PTS 12 Belfast (European Flyweight Title Defence)
30.09.00	Zolile Mbitye W PTS 12 Peterborough (IBO Flyweight Title Challenge)
17.02.01	Paulino Villabos W PTS 12 Bethnal Green (IBO Flyweight Title Defence)
31.07.01	Sipho Mantyi W RSC 4 Bethnal Green
18.01.02	Simphewe Xabendini W RSC 1 Coventry
21.05.02	Celso Dangud W PTS 12 Custom House (Vacant WBF Flyweight Title)
05.10.02	Jovy Oracion W PTS 8 Liverpool
27.09.03	Irene Pacheco L RSC 7 Barranquilla, Colombia, (IBF Flyweight Title Challenge)
17.04.04	Andrei Kostin W RSC 1 Belfast
26.06.04	Delroy Spencer W RSC 4 Belfast
17.12.04	Jason Booth W PTS 12 Huddersfield (IBO S.Flyweight Title Challenge)
25.11.05	Ian Napa W PTS 10 Liverpool
21.04.06	Simone Maludrottu L PTS 12 Belfast (European Bantamweight Title Challenge)

Career: 25 contests, won 22, lost 3.

Michael Kelly

Dundalk. *Born* Dundalk, 28 April, 1975
Lightweight. Ht. 5'8"
Manager B. Hearn

28.02.04	Carl Allen W PTS 4 Bridgend
17.04.04	Baz Carey W PTS 4 Belfast
26.06.04	Simon Wilson W PTS 4 Belfast

02.07.05	Daniel Thorpe W PTS 4 Dundalk
17.09.05	Jozef Kubovsky W PTS 4 Dublin
21.04.06	Stuart Green W PTS 4 Belfast

Career: 6 contests, won 6.

Colin Kenna

Southampton. *Born* Dublin, 28 July, 1976
Heavyweight. Former Southern Area
Heavyweight Champion. Ht. 6'1"
Manager J. Bishop

25.02.01	Slick Miller W RSC 3 Streatham
22.04.01	Eamonn Glennon W PTS 4 Streatham
15.10.01	Tony Booth W PTS 6 Southampton
11.02.02	Dave Clarke W RSC 4 Southampton
08.04.02	James Gilbert W RSC 1 Southampton
12.07.02	Gary Williams W RSC 3 Southampton
01.11.02	Paul Buttery DREW 6 Preston
17.03.03	Derek McCafferty W PTS 6 Southampton
12.05.03	Paul Bonson W PTS 6 Southampton
01.08.03	Michael Sprott L RSC 1 Bethnal Green (Southern Area Heavyweight Title Challenge)
26.10.03	Darren Ashton W CO 1 Longford
20.02.04	Paul Bonson W PTS 6 Southampton
30.03.04	Chris Woollas W PTS 6 Southampton
12.05.04	Mark Krence L RTD 3 Reading
06.02.05	Oneal Murray W RTD 3 Southampton
19.02.05	Paul King DREW 6 Dublin
26.06.05	Julius Francis W PTS 4 Southampton
04.12.05	Wayne Llewelyn W CO 2 Portsmouth (Vacant Southern Area Heavyweight Title)
28.01.06	Luke Simpkin W PTS 8 Dublin
05.03.06	Micky Steeds L PTS 10 Southampton (Southern Area Heavyweight Title Defence)
22.04.06	Oleg Platov L RSC 5 Mannheim, Germany

Career: 21 contests, won 15, drew 2, lost 4.

Colin Kenna Les Clark

Ryan Kerr

Bannockburn. *Born* Falkirk, 19 March, 1982
S.Middleweight. Former Undefeated
English & Northern Area S.Middleweight
Champion. Ht. 5'9"
Manager Self

17.09.01	Pedro Thompson W RSC 1 Glasgow
04.10.01	Colin McCash W PTS 6 Sunderland
03.11.01	Tomas da Silva W PTS 4 Glasgow
21.02.02	Wayne Shepherd W PTS 6 Sunderland
03.10.02	Steve Timms W RSC 1 Sunderland
05.12.02	Martin Thompson W RSC 4 Sunderland
27.02.03	Surinder Sekhon W PTS 6 Sunderland
17.03.03	Lee Molloy W PTS 8 Glasgow
02.10.03	Eddie Haley W PTS 8 Sunderland
26.02.04	Eddie Haley W RSC 5 Sunderland
	(Vacant Northern Area S.Middleweight Title)
23.09.04	Gary Dixon W RSC 7 Gateshead
	(Northern Area S.Middleweight Title Defence)
24.02.05	Ryan Walls W PTS 10 Sunderland
	(Vacant English S.Middleweight Title)
03.11.05	Simeon Cover W PTS 10 Sunderland
	(English S.Middleweight Title Defence)
16.12.05	Jamie Hearn DREW 10 Bracknell
	(English S.Middleweight Title Defence)
09.03.06	Vince Baldassara DREW 6 Sunderland

Career: 15 contests, won 13, drew 2.

Ryan Kerr   Les Clark

Mo Khaled (Al Saroodi)

Sheffield. *Born* Doha, Qatar, 19 January, 1988
S.Bantamweight. Ht. 5'4"
Manager J. Ingle

26.05.06	Neil Marston L DIS 5 Hull

Career: 1 contest, lost 1.

Imad Khamis

Manchester. *Born* Egypt, 9 March, 1977
L. Welterweight. Ht. 5'11¼"
Manager W. Barker

13.05.05	Stephen Burke L RSC 3 Liverpool
17.06.05	Martin McDonagh L DIS 4 Glasgow
16.09.05	Michael Medor L PTS 4 Plymouth
14.10.05	Stephen Haughian L RSC 4 Dublin
26.11.05	Billy Dib L PTS 6 Sheffield
26.02.06	James Paisley W RSC 3 Dagenham
23.03.06	Silence Saheed L RSC 5 The Strand

Career: 7 contests, won 1, lost 6.

Amer Khan

Sheffield. *Born* Sheffield, 21 February, 1981
Central Area L.Heavyweight Champion.
Ht. 6'2"
Manager D. Ingle

06.06.03	Gary Jones W PTS 6 Hull
31.07.03	Michael Pinnock W PTS 6 Sheffield
05.09.03	Shpetim Hoti W RTD 4 Sheffield
04.12.03	Terry Morrill W PTS 6 Sunderland
06.02.04	Terry Morrill W PTS 6 Sheffield
03.04.04	Michael Pinnock W PTS 6 Sheffield
17.06.04	Hastings Rasani W PTS 6 Sheffield
24.10.04	Paulie Silva W PTS 6 Sheffield
04.03.05	Karl Wheeler W PTS 6 Rotherham
26.11.05	Jimi Hendricks W PTS 4 Sheffield
05.03.06	Paul Bonson W PTS 6 Sheffield
18.06.06	Darren Stubbs W PTS 10 Manchester
	(Vacant Central Area L.Heavyweight Title)

Career: 12 contests, won 12.

Amir Khan

Bolton. *Born* Bolton, 8 December, 1986
Lightweight. Ht. 5'10"
Manager F. Warren

16.07.05	David Bailey W RSC 1 Bolton
10.09.05	Baz Carey W PTS 4 Cardiff
05.11.05	Steve Gethin W RSC 3 Renfrew
10.12.05	Daniel Thorpe W RSC 2 Canning Town
28.01.06	Vitali Martynov W RSC 1 Nottingham
25.02.06	Jackson Williams W RSC 3 Canning Town
20.05.06	Laszlo Komjathi W PTS 6 Belfast

Career: 7 contests, won 7.

Amir Khan   Les Clark

Malik Khan

Blackburn. *Born* Blackburn, 3 March, 1981
L.Middleweight. Ht. 5'10"
Manager D. Coldwell

21.09.05	Mark Franks L RSC 1 Bradford
03.11.05	Martin Marshall L PTS 6 Sunderland
21.11.05	Paul Burns L RTD 2 Glasgow
17.02.06	Lee Edwards L RSC 6 Sheffield
18.05.06	Wayne Downing W RSC 3 Walsall

Career: 5 contests, won 1, lost 4.

Tasif Khan

Bradford. *Born* Bradford, 29 December, 1982
Featherweight. Ht. 5'7"
Manager C. Aston

20.11.05	Gary Ford DREW 6 Shaw
23.02.06	Neil Read W RSC 6 Leeds
28.05.06	Delroy Spencer W PTS 6 Wakefield

Career: 3 contests, won 2, drew 1.

(Maciej) Magic Kidem (Brzostek)

Birmingham. *Born* Poland,18 June, 1981
S.Middleweight. Ht. 5'10½"
Manager N. Nobbs

25.02.06	Danny Butler L PTS 6 Bristol
05.03.06	Stuart Brookes L RSC 1 Sheffield
24.04.06	Dave Pearson L PTS 6 Cleethorpes

Career: 3 contests, lost 3.

Nathan King

Mountain Ash. *Born* Aberdare, 19 March, 1981
S.Middleweight. Ht. 6'3"
Manager B. Coleman

27.01.01	Tony Oakey L PTS 6 Bethnal Green
28.04.01	Pinky Burton W PTS 4 Cardiff
09.06.01	Michael Pinnock W PTS 4 Bethnal Green
09.10.01	Darren Ashton W PTS 6 Cardiff
24.11.01	Peter Haymer W PTS 4 Bethnal Green
12.02.02	Peter Haymer W PTS 4 Bethnal Green
20.04.02	Radcliffe Green W PTS 6 Cardiff
17.08.02	Valery Odin L PTS 6 Cardiff
14.12.02	Paul Bonson L PTS 4 Newcastle
10.04.03	Ovill McKenzie L PTS 4 Clydach
28.06.03	Varuzhan Davtyan W PTS 4 Cardiff
21.02.04	Daniel Sackey L PTS 4 Cardiff
12.03.04	Elvis Michailenko L PTS 6 Millwall
03.07.04	Nick Okoth W PTS 4 Newport
22.10.04	Hastings Rasani W PTS 6 Edinburgh
24.11.04	Eric Teymour L PTS 12 Mayfair
	(Vacant WBU S.Middleweight Title)
13.02.05	Malik Dziarra W PTS 6 Brentwood
28.06.05	Malik Dziarra L PTS 8 Cuaxhaven, Germany
13.05.06	Tony Oakey L PTS 6 Bethnal Green

Career: 19 contests, won 10, lost 9.

Paul King

Sheffield. *Born* Sheffield, 9 August, 1974
Heavyweight. Ht. 6'3"
Manager G. Rhodes

10.02.04	Billy Wilson L PTS 6 Barnsley
28.02.04	David Ingleby W RSC 3 Manchester
12.03.04	Micky Steeds L PTS 6 Millwall
03.04.04	Carl Baker W PTS 6 Sheffield
10.04.04	Albert Sosnowski L PTS 4 Manchester
02.06.04	Scott Gammer L RSC 3 Hereford
18.09.04	Luke Simpkin W PTS 6 Newark
30.09.04	Chris Woollas W PTS 4 Glasgow

119

12.11.04	Leif Larsen L CO 1 Copenhagen, Denmark
06.02.05	Billy Bessey W PTS 6 Southampton
19.02.05	Colin Kenna DREW 6 Dublin
04.03.05	Carl Baker L RSC 2 Rotherham
30.04.05	Wayne Llewelyn L PTS 6 Dagenham
28.05.06	Tommy Eastwood L PTS 4 Longford

Career: 14 contests, won 5, drew 1, lost 8.

Moses Kinyua (Kinywa)

Bristol. *Born* Nairobi, Kenya, 29 October, 1976
Bantamweight. Ht. 5'1"
Manager C. Sanigar

28.04.99	Vusi Khumalo W PTS 4 Benoni, GT, South Africa
01.07.99	Hillary Olwenya W PTS 6 Nairobi, Kenya
30.07.99	Bernard Njorenge W PTS 6 Nairobi, Kenya
26.08.99	Bernard Balya W PTS 6 Dar Es Salaam, Tanzania
15.09.99	Teddy Adams W CO 6 Nairobi, Kenya
29.10.29	Jan Malekoa W RSC 3 Alberton, GT, South Africa
19.12.99	Sibongo Mchunu DREW 4 Umlazi, KZN, South Africa
02.02.00	Geoffrey Leteane W CO 2 Swaziland
28.05.00	Vincent Mogotsi L PTS 6 Maseru, Lesotho
29.07.00	Paul Malesela L TD 3 Nairobi, Kenya
29.10.00	Ali Mkande W CO 6 Nairobi, Kenya
28.07.01	Joseph Waweru W PTS 6 Nairobi, Kenya
08.06.02	James Wanene W CO 4 Nairobi, Kenya
27.07.02	Nicky Booth L RSC 7 Nottingham *(Commonwealth Bantamweight Title Challenge)*
29.03.03	Shaban Hamisi DREW 6 Nairobi, Kenya
27.05.04	Dale Robinson L PTS 6 Huddersfield
30.11.04	Bernard Inom L PTS 6 Berck, France
08.04.05	Lee Haskins L PTS 10 Bristol
16.10.05	Delroy Spencer W PTS 6 Peterborough
28.10.05	Dale Robinson DREW 6 Hartlepool
30.03.06	Jamil Hussain L PTS 6 Peterborough
01.06.06	Dale Robinson L PTS 6 Barnsley

Career: 22 contests, won 11, drew 3, lost 8.

David Kirk

Sutton in Ashfield. *Born* Mansfield, 5 October, 1974
Middleweight. Former Undefeated WBF European Welterweight Champion. Ht. 5'8"
Manager Self

01.11.96	Arv Mittoo W PTS 6 Mansfield
04.12.96	Stuart Rimmer W PTS 6 Stoke
20.02.97	Chris Price W PTS 6 Mansfield
16.03.97	Gary Hibbert L PTS 6 Shaw
25.03.97	Miguel Matthews W PTS 6 Wolverhampton
28.04.97	Mark Breslin L PTS 8 Glasgow
06.10.97	Christian Brady L PTS 6 Birmingham
30.10.97	Trevor Tacy L PTS 6 Newark
08.12.97	Nick Hall L PTS 6 Nottingham
12.01.98	Juha Temonen DREW 6 Helsinki, Finland
24.01.98	Jason Cook L RSC 3 Cardiff
24.02.98	Roy Rutherford L PTS 6 Edgbaston
11.03.98	Patrick Gallagher L PTS 6 Bethnal Green

27.04.98	Tommy Peacock L PTS 6 Manchester
08.05.98	Chris Barnett L PTS 6 Manchester
23.05.98	Graham Earl L PTS 4 Bethnal Green
04.06.98	Mark Richards L PTS 6 Dudley
21.09.98	Steve McLevy L PTS 8 Glasgow
12.10.98	Malcolm Melvin L PTS 10 Birmingham *(Midlands Area L. Welterweight Title Challenge)*
31.10.98	Bernard Paul L PTS 6 Southend
28.11.98	Glenn McClarnon L PTS 4 Belfast
11.12.98	Charlie Kane L PTS 8 Prestwick
20.02.99	Dennis Berry L PTS 10 Thornaby *(Vacant Continental European Welterweight Title)*
09.05.99	Sammy Smith L PTS 6 Bracknell
20.05.99	Steve Brumant W PTS 4 Kensington
05.06.99	Neil Sinclair L PTS 8 Cardiff
11.09.99	Glenn McClarnon L PTS 6 Sheffield
20.10.99	Dave Gibson W PTS 6 Stoke
18.11.99	Adrian Chase W PTS 10 Mayfair *(Vacant WBF European Welterweight Title)*
26.11.99	Gerard Murphy L RTD 3 Hull
25.03.00	Jacek Bielski L PTS 6 Liverpool
29.04.00	Eamonn Magee L RSC 8 Wembley
13.08.00	Ram Singh W PTS 6 Nottingham
09.09.00	Mally McIver L PTS 6 Newark
23.09.00	Steve Murray L PTS 4 Bethnal Green
09.10.00	Steve Saville W PTS 8 Birmingham
19.11.00	Gavin Down L PTS 10 Chesterfield *(Vacant British Masters L.Welterweight Title)*
01.12.00	Alan Bosworth DREW 8 Peterborough
04.02.01	Mark Winters L PTS 6 Queensferry
28.02.01	Ossie Duran L PTS 8 Kensington *(Vacant WBF European Welterweight Title)*
10.03.01	Junior Witter L RSC 2 Bethnal Green
10.04.01	Colin Lynes L PTS 6 Wembley
20.04.01	Mark Winters L PTS 6 Dublin
16.06.01	Oscar Hall L PTS 6 Derby
07.07.01	Michael Jennings L PTS 6 Manchester
28.07.01	Jonathan Thaxton L PTS 4 Wembley
13.09.01	David Walker DREW 8 Sheffield
17.11.01	Kevin McIntyre L PTS 4 Glasgow
24.11.01	Ivan Kirpa L PTS 4 Bethnal Green
08.12.01	Chris Saunders L CO 2 Chesterfield
26.01.02	Colin Lynes L PTS 6 Dagenham
09.02.02	David Barnes L RTD 1 Manchester
11.03.02	Matthew Macklin L PTS 4 Glasgow
25.05.02	Francis Barrett L PTS 6 Portsmouth
08.06.02	Kevin McIntyre L RTD 4 Renfrew
28.09.02	Matthew Hatton W PTS 6 Manchester
22.03.03	Kevin McIntyre L RSC 1 Renfrew
24.05.03	Nigel Wright L PTS 4 Bethnal Green
31.05.03	Sammy Smith L PTS 4 Bethnal Green
08.06.03	Adnan Amar L PTS 6 Nottingham
04.10.03	Francis Barrett L PTS 6 Muswell Hill
10.04.04	Albert Sosnowski L PTS 4 Manchester
07.05.04	Gary Woolcombe L PTS 4 Bethnal Green
19.06.04	Gary Young L PTS 4 Renfrew
03.07.04	Tony Doherty L PTS 4 Newport
19.11.04	Ross Minter L PTS 6 Bethnal Green
03.12.04	Martin Concepcion L PTS 4 Edinburgh
11.09.05	Gatis Skuja L PTS 6 Kirkby in Ashfield
12.11.05	Joe Mitchell W PTS 6 Sheffield
10.03.06	Stuart Elwell L PTS 10 Walsall *(Vacant Midlands Area Welterweight Title)*

Career: 70 contests, won 11, drew 3, lost 56.

Arial Krasnopolski

Nottingham. *Born* Warsaw, Poland, 8 May, 1987
L.Welterweight. Ht. 5'6"
Manager J. Gill/T. Harris

15.06.06	Jaz Virdee L PTS 6 Peterborough

Career: 1 contest, lost 1.

Mark Krence

Chesterfield. *Born* Chesterfield, 24 August, 1976
English Heavyweight Champion. Former Undefeated Midlands Area Heavyweight Champion. Ht. 6'5"
Manager D. Hobson

09.04.00	Slick Miller W PTS 6 Alfreton
21.10.00	Neil Kirkwood W PTS 6 Sheffield
11.12.00	Tony Booth W PTS 6 Sheffield
20.01.01	Nigel Rafferty W PTS 4 Bethnal Green
24.03.01	Mark Williams W PTS 4 Sheffield
27.07.01	Shane Woollas W PTS 4 Sheffield
13.09.01	Luke Simpkin W PTS 4 Sheffield
25.09.01	Darren Chubbs W PTS 4 Liverpool
15.12.01	Eamonn Glennon W RSC 2 Sheffield
16.03.02	Neil Kirkwood W RSC 4 Bethnal Green
11.05.02	Gary Williams W PTS 6 Chesterfield
21.05.02	Audley Harrison L PTS 6 Custom House
03.08.02	Tony Booth W PTS 4 Derby
05.10.02	Gary Williams W RSC 4 Chesterfield
24.01.03	Petr Horacek W RSC 4 Sheffield
18.03.03	Paul Bonson W PTS 4 Reading
10.06.03	Luke Simpkin W RTD 8 Sheffield *(Vacant Midlands Area Heavyweight Title)*
01.08.03	Derek McCafferty W PTS 4 Bethnal Green
05.09.03	Collice Mutizwa W CO 2 Sheffield
06.02.04	Mendauga Kulikauskas W PTS 8 Sheffield
12.05.04	Colin Kenna W RTD 3 Reading
10.09.04	Konstantin Prizyuk L RSC 6 Wembley
11.12.04	John McDermott W PTS 10 Canning Town *(Vacant English Heavyweight Title)*
15.05.05	Scott Gammer L RSC 8 Sheffield *(Elim. British Heavyweight Title Challenge)*
16.07.05	Matt Skelton L RTD 7 Bolton *(British Heavyweight Title Challenge)*
22.10.05	Ruslan Chagaev L CO 5 Halle, Germany
16.06.06	Scott Gammer L RSC 9 Carmarthen *(Vacant British Heavyweight Title)*

Career: 27 contests, won 21, lost 6.

Eder Kurti

Kennington. *Born* Albania, 29 August, 1984
S.Middleweight. Ht. 5'10³/₄"
Manager B. Baker

04.11.04	Cafu Santos W RSC 1 Piccadilly
02.12.04	Craig Lynch W DIS 4 Crystal Palace
27.01.05	Ojay Abrahams W PTS 6 Piccadilly
19.11.05	Gary Ojuederie L RSC 4 Southwark

Career: 4 contests, won 3, lost 1.

Kristian Laight

Nuneaton. *Born* Nuneaton, 15 June, 1980
L. Welterweight. Ht. 5'10"
Manager J. Gill

26.09.03	James Paisley L PTS 6 Millwall	
14.11.03	Matt Teague L PTS 6 Hull	
05.12.03	Justin Hicks L PTS 6 Bristol	
07.02.04	Kevin Mitchell L PTS 4 Bethnal Green	
30.03.04	Chris McDonagh L PTS 6 Southampton	
08.04.04	Jaz Virdee W PTS 6 Peterborough	
20.04.04	Femi Fehintola L PTS 6 Sheffield	
04.06.04	Gary Coombes DREW 6 Dudley	
19.06.04	Ryan Barrett L PTS 4 Muswell Hill	
23.10.04	Sean Hughes L PTS 6 Wakefield	
18.11.04	Martin Gethin L RSC 4 Shrewsbury	
17.12.04	Baz Carey L PTS 8 Coventry	
08.05.05	Nadeem Siddique L RSC 7 Bradford	
25.06.05	John-Paul Ryan DREW 6 Melton Mowbray	
09.07.05	Chris Long L PTS 6 Bristol	
02.09.05	Scott Haywood L PTS 6 Derby	
06.10.05	Tom Hogan L PTS 6 Sunderland	
24.10.05	Andrew Ferrans L PTS 8 Glasgow	
12.11.05	Danny Gwilym L PTS 6 Bristol	
20.11.05	Barry Downes DREW 6 Shaw	
02.12.05	Charlie Thompson DREW 6 Doncaster	
18.12.05	Gary O'Connor L PTS 6 Bolton	
16.02.06	Haider Ali L PTS 4 Dudley	
02.03.06	Jeff Thomas L PTS 6 Blackpool	
30.03.06	Jaz Virdee L PTS 6 Peterborough	
14.04.06	Tristan Davies L PTS 6 Telford	
21.04.06	Wez Miller W PTS 6 Doncaster	
11.05.06	Paul Holborn L PTS 6 Sunderland	
21.05.06	Chris Long L PTS 6 Bristol	
30.05.06	Akaash Bhatia L PTS 4 Bethnal Green	
15.06.06	Neal McQuade W PTS 6 Peterborough	

Career: 31 contests, won 3, drew 4, lost 24.

Scott Lansdowne

Leicester. *Born* Leicester, 11 August, 1972
Heavyweight. Former Undefeated Midlands Area Cruiserweight Champion. Former Undefeated WBF European S.Cruiserweight Champion. Ht. 5'10"
Manager Self

15.12.98	Gary Williams W PTS 6 Sheffield	
11.09.99	Luke Simpkin W PTS 4 Sheffield	
09.12.99	Geoff Hunter W PTS 6 Sheffield	
20.05.00	Gary Williams W RSC 1 Leicester	
	(Vacant WBF European S. Cruiserweight Title)	
21.10.00	Adam Cale W RSC 5 Sheffield	
29.01.01	Nigel Rafferty W PTS 4 Peterborough	
28.04.02	Tony Booth L RSC 4 Southwark	
23.06.02	Paul Bonson L PTS 4 Southwark	
30.11.02	Tony Dowling W RSC 2 Newark	
	(Vacant Midlands Area Cruiserweight Title)	
16.03.03	Michael Pinnock W PTS 6 Nottingham	
12.10.03	Clint Johnson W PTS 4 Sheffield	
11.12.03	Steven Spartacus L RSC 3 Bethnal Green	
	(Vacant English L.Heavyweight Title)	

10.07.04	David Ingleby W RSC 4 Coventry	
06.12.04	Jason Callum W CO 1 Leicester	
25.06.05	Carl Baker L RSC 8 Melton Mowbray	
	(Vacant British Masters Heavyweight Title)	
12.12.05	David Ingleby W RSC 1 Leicester	
21.05.06	Julius Francis W PTS 4 Bethnal Green	

Career: 17 contests, won 13, lost 4.

Gareth Lawrence

Sidcup. *Born* Barking, 21 August, 1980
L.Heavyweight. Ht. 6'2"
Manager Self

01.05.04	Paul Buchanan L PTS 4 Gravesend	
16.10.04	Dean Powell W PTS 4 Dagenham	
19.12.04	Tony Janes W PTS 4 Bethnal Green	
21.01.05	Matthew Barr L RSC 2 Brentford	
05.03.05	Leigh Wicks W PTS 4 Dagenham	
23.03.05	Howard Clarke W PTS 6 Leicester Square	
30.04.05	Michael Banbula W PTS 6 Dagenham	
26.05.05	Joey Vegas L PTS 4 Mayfair	
01.07.05	Michael Banbula W PTS 4 Fulham	
18.09.05	Jamie Hearn L RTD 3 Bethnal Green	
05.11.05	Lawrence Murphy L PTS 4 Renfrew	
24.11.05	Jason Samuels L PTS 6 Clydach	
19.12.05	Ryan Walls L RTD 6 Longford	
	(Vacant Southern Area S.Middleweight Title)	

Career: 13 contests, won 6, lost 7.

Gareth Lawrence   Philip Sharkey

Scott Lawton

Stoke. *Born* Stoke, 23 September, 1976
English Lightweight Champion. Former Undefeated Midlands Area Lightweight Champion. Ht. 5'10"
Manager M. Carney

29.09.01	Dave Hinds W RSC 2 Southwark	
08.12.01	Ilias Miah W PTS 4 Dagenham	
26.01.02	Pete Buckley W PTS 4 Bethnal Green	
26.04.02	Pete Buckley W PTS 4 Coventry	
06.09.02	Ben Hudson W PTS 4 Bethnal Green	
30.01.03	Dave Stewart L PTS 6 Piccadilly	
26.04.03	Chris McDonagh W RSC 2 Brentford	
13.06.03	Jason Nesbitt W PTS 6 Queensway	
14.11.03	Jimmy Beech W RSC 5 Bethnal Green	
20.04.04	Henry Jones W PTS 6 Sheffield	
17.06.04	Carl Allen W PTS 10 Sheffield	

	(Vacant Midlands Area Lightweight Title)	
17.09.04	Silence Saheed W PTS 6 Sheffield	
10.12.04	Roger Sampson W PTS 6 Sheffield	
04.03.05	Peter McDonagh W PTS 6 Rotherham	
15.05.05	Carl Allen W PTS 6 Sheffield	
24.07.05	Pete Buckley W PTS 6 Sheffield	
09.09.05	Alan Temple L PTS 6 Sheffield	
12.11.05	Ben Hudson W PTS 6 Stoke	
18.02.06	Surinder Sekhon DREW 8 Stoke	
06.05.06	Baz Carey W PTS 10 Stoke	
	(Midlands Area Lightweight Title Defence)	
09.06.06	Stefy Bull W RSC 8 Doncaster	
	(Vacant English Lightweight Title)	

Career: 21 contests, won 18, drew 1, lost 2.

Barrie Lee

Arbroath. *Born* Arbroath, 29 March, 1982
Scottish L. Middleweight Champion. Ht. 5'8"
Manager A. Morrison/K. Morrison

25.10.03	Dave Wakefield W PTS 4 Edinburgh	
29.11.03	Brian Coleman W PTS 4 Renfrew	
27.03.04	Arv Mittoo W PTS 4 Edinburgh	
23.04.04	William Webster W PTS 6 Glasgow	
28.05.04	Brian Coleman W PTS 6 Glasgow	
19.06.04	Craig Lynch W PTS 6 Renfrew	
08.10.04	Vince Baldassara DREW 6 Glasgow	
22.10.04	Craig Lynch W PTS 10 Edinburgh	
	(Vacant Scottish L.Middleweight Title)	
03.12.04	John-Paul Temple W PTS 4 Edinburgh	
08.04.05	Vince Baldassara W PTS 4 Edinburgh	
03.06.05	Thomas McDonagh L RSC 7 Manchester	
	(WBU Inter-Continental L.Middleweight Title Challenge)	
22.04.06	Chris Black W PTS 10 Glasgow	
	(Scottish L.Middleweight Title Defence)	
27.05.06	Kevin Phelan W PTS 6 Glasgow	

Career: 13 contests, won 11, drew 1, lost 1.

Willie Limond

Glasgow. *Born* Glasgow, 2 February, 1979
L.Welterweight. Former Undefeated Celtic & European Union S.Featherweight Champion. Ht. 5'7"
Manager F. Warren/A. Morrison

12.11.99	Lennie Hodgkins W RTD 1 Glasgow	
13.12.99	Steve Hanley W PTS 6 Glasgow	
24.02.00	Nigel Senior W RSC 6 Glasgow	
18.03.00	Phil Lashley W RSC 1 Glasgow	
07.04.00	Jimmy Beech W RSC 2 Glasgow	
26.05.00	Billy Smith W PTS 4 Glasgow	
24.06.00	Haroon Din W PTS 6 Glasgow	
10.11.00	Danny Connelly W PTS 6 Glasgow	
17.12.00	Billy Smith W PTS 6 Glasgow	
15.02.01	Marcus Portman W PTS 6 Glasgow	
03.04.01	Trevor Smith W PTS 4 Bethnal Green	
27.04.01	Choi Tseveenpurev W PTS 6 Glasgow	
07.09.01	Gary Reid W PTS 8 Glasgow	
03.11.01	Rakhim Mingaleev W PTS 6 Glasgow	
17.11.01	Keith Jones W PTS 4 Glasgow	
11.03.02	Dave Hinds W PTS 6 Glasgow	
06.09.02	Assen Vassilev W RSC 3 Glasgow	
22.03.03	Jimmy Beech W CO 4 Renfrew	
12.07.03	Alex Arthur L RSC 8 Renfrew	
	(British S.Featherweight Title Challenge)	
01.11.03	Dariusz Snarski W RSC 1 Glasgow	
29.11.03	Anthony Hanna W PTS 4 Renfrew	

06.03.04	Dafydd Carlin W RSC 1 Renfrew
19.06.04	Youssouf Djibaba W PTS 10 Renfrew
	(Vacant European Union
	S.Featherweight Title)
29.10.04	Frederic Bonifai W PTS 8 Glasgow
03.12.04	Alberto Lopez W PTS 10 Edinburgh
	(European Union S.Featherweight Title
	Defence)
20.05.05	John Mackay W RSC 5 Glasgow
17.06.05	Kevin O'Hara W PTS 10 Glasgow
	(Vacant Celtic S.Featherweight Title)
05.11.05	Jus Wallie W PTS 6 Renfrew

Career: 28 contests, won 27, lost 1.

Martin Lindsay

Belfast. *Born* Belfast, 10 May, 1982
Featherweight. Ht. 5'7"
Manager J. Rooney

02.12.04	Dai Davies W RSC 1 Crystal Palace
24.04.05	Rakhim Mingaleev W PTS 4 Leicester Squar
02.07.05	Henry Janes W RSC 2 Dundalk
17.09.05	Peter Feher W PTS 4 Dublin
21.04.06	Chris Hooper W RSC 1 Belfast

Career: 5 contests, won 5.

Neil Linford

Leicester. *Born* Leicester, 29 September, 1977
L.Heavyweight. Ht. 5'10¾"
Manager Self

30.10.98	Israel Khumalo W RSC 2 Peterborough
30.11.98	David Baptiste W PTS 4 Peterborough
15.12.98	Johannes Ngiba W CO 2 Durban, South Africa
16.01.99	Dean Powell W RSC 1 Bethnal Green
22.02.99	Leigh Wicks W PTS 4 Peterborough
24.04.99	Adrian Houldey W RSC 2 Peterborough
17.05.99	Jason Barker L RSC 3 Peterborough
15.07.99	Hussain Osman L RSC 5 Peterborough
07.02.00	Mark Dawson W PTS 4 Peterborough
04.03.00	Darren Ashton W PTS 6 Peterborough
25.05.00	Michael Pinnock W PTS 4 Peterborough
30.09.00	Matthew Barney W PTS 10 Peterborough
	(Elim. British S. Middleweight Title)
30.11.00	Darren Ashton W PTS 4 Peterborough
29.01.01	Brian Magee L PTS 12 Peterborough
	(Vacant IBO Inter-Continental
	S. Middleweight Title)
23.06.01	Jon Penn W RSC 3 Peterborough
29.09.01	David Starie L RSC 6 Southwark
	(British & Commonwealth
	S.Middleweight Title Challenges)
26.01.02	Ali Forbes W PTS 6 Bethnal Green
23.06.02	Tony Booth W RSC 5 Southwark
22.09.02	Paul Bonson W PTS 6 Southwark
27.10.02	Radcliffe Green DREW 10 Southwark
	(Vacant British Masters L.Heavyweight
	Title)
29.03.03	Tony Oakey L PTS 12 Portsmouth
	(WBU L. Heavyweight Title
	Challenge)
31.05.03	Andrew Lowe L PTS 10 Bethnal Green
	(Elim. British L. Heavyweight Title)
26.11.04	Brian Magee L RSC 7 Altrincham
24.09.05	Hastings Rasani L RSC 5 Coventry
23.03.06	Valery Odin W RSC 4 The Strand

Career: 25 contests, won 16, drew 1, lost 8.

Earl Ling

Norwich. *Born* Kings Lynn, 9 March, 1972
Cruiserweight. Ht. 5'10"
Manager Self

08.09.92	Eddie Collins W PTS 6 Norwich
11.05.93	Mark Hale L RSC 2 Norwich
12.12.94	Clinton Woods L RSC 5 Cleethorpes
04.12.95	Jeff Finlayson L PTS 6 Manchester
26.02.96	Peter Waudby L PTS 6 Hull
19.03.96	James Lowther L RSC 4 Leeds
16.05.98	Dean Ashton DREW 6 Chigwell
02.07.98	Dean Ashton L RSC 2 Ipswich
17.09.98	Jimmy Steel DREW 6 Brighton
19.01.99	Israel Khumalo L RSC 1 Ipswich
15.07.00	Mike Duffield W PTS 6 Norwich
04.11.00	Andrew Facey L PTS 6 Derby
16.06.01	Andrew Facey DREW 6 Derby
04.07.01	Calvin Stonestreet L PTS 4 Bloomsbury
13.04.02	Simeon Cover W CO 4 Norwich
25.04.02	Lee Whitehead W PTS 6 Hull
21.11.02	Michael Pinnock W PTS 6 Hull
12.04.03	Ryan Walls L RSC 4 Norwich
07.12.03	Nate Joseph DREW 6 Bradford
21.02.04	Hastings Rasani DREW 6 Norwich
09.10.04	Nate Joseph W PTS 6 Norwich
11.12.05	Oneal Murray L RSC 3 Norwich

Career: 22 contests, won 6, drew 5, lost 11.

Wayne Llewelyn

Beckenham. *Born* Greenwich, 20 April, 1970
Heavyweight. Ht. 6'3½"
Manager Self

18.01.92	Chris Coughlan W RSC 3 Kensington
30.03.92	Steve Stewart W RSC 4 Eltham
23.04.92	Gary Charlton W RSC 6 Eltham
10.12.92	Gary McCrory W RSC 2 Glasgow
23.05.93	Cordwell Hylton W PTS 6 Brockley
01.12.93	Manny Burgo W PTS 6 Bethnal Green
14.04.94	Vance Idiens W RSC 1 Battersea
22.05.94	Cordwell Hylton W CO 2 Crystal Palace
03.05.95	Mitch Rose W PTS 4 NYC, New York, USA
07.07.95	Vance Idiens W RSC 1 Cardiff
11.08.95	Carlos Monroe W RSC 3 New Orleans, Louisiana, USA
26.04.96	Steve Garber W CO 1 Cardiff
08.06.96	Dermot Gascoyne W RSC 4 Newcastle
22.03.97	Mike Sedillo W CO 2 Wythenshawe
20.09.97	Michael Murray W RTD 4 Aachen, Germany
21.03.98	Everton Davis W PTS 8 Bethnal Green
06.06.98	Pele Reid L CO 1 Liverpool
	(Elim. British Heavyweight Title)
18.02.99	Derek Williams W RSC 3 Bossier City, Louisiana, USA
03.06.99	Frankie Swindell L CO 2 Mount Pleasant, Michigan, USA
21.08.99	Terry Veners W RSC 3 Coachella, California, USA
28.11.99	Terry Veners W CO 2 Monterey, California, USA
10.03.00	William Barima W CO 1 Bethnal Green
19.03.00	Augustin Corpus L PTS 8 Tunica, Mississippi, USA
14.10.00	Michael Sprott W RSC 3 Wembley
08.12.00	Alex Vasiliev L RSC 1 Crystal Palace
01.04.01	Luke Simpkin W PTS 6 Southwark
19.01.02	Andreas Sidon W CO 1 Berlin, Germany

22.03.02	Ladislav Husarik W PTS 6 Berlin, Germany
25.08.02	Ergin Solmaz W RSC 3 Berlin, Germany
07.09.02	Vladislav Druso W PTS 6 Munich, Germany
11.10.03	Ervin Slonka W RSC 2 Velten, Germany
15.04.04	Jameel McCline L RSC 1 NYC, New York, USA
26.11.04	Roman Kaloczai W CO 1 Berlin, Germany
15.01.05	Vladislav Druso W RSC 1 Berlin, Germany
30.04.05	Paul King W PTS 6 Dagenham
04.12.05	Colin Kenna L CO 2 Portsmouth
	(Vacant Southern Area Heavyweight
	Title)

Career: 36 contests, won 30, lost 6.

Mark Lloyd

Telford. *Born* Walsall, 21 October, 1975
Middleweight. Ht. 5'10"
Manager E. Johnson

16.09.05	Dennis Corpe W PTS 6 Telford
04.12.05	Gatis Skuja W PTS 4 Telford
16.02.06	Davey Jones W PTS 6 Dudley
14.04.06	Ben Hudson W PTS 4 Telford
13.05.06	Tommy Jones W PTS 6 Sutton in Ashfield
29.06.06	Tommy Jones W PTS 6 Dudley

Career: 6 contests, won 6.

Robert Lloyd-Taylor (Lloyd)

Northolt. *Born* Perivale, 1 September, 1980
L.Middleweight. Ht. 5'11¼"
Manager Self

27.09.02	Wayne Wheeler W PTS 6 Bracknell
25.10.02	Nicky Leech L PTS 6 Cotgrave
20.12.02	Dean Larter W PTS 4 Bracknell
26.04.03	Ben Hudson L PTS 4 Brentford
31.05.03	Aidan Mooney W PTS 4 Bethnal Green
26.10.03	Arv Mittoo W PTS 6 Longford
14.11.03	Michael Lomax L PTS 6 Bethnal Green
07.04.04	Joe Mitchell W RSC 5 Leicester Square
07.05.04	Chas Symonds L RTD 5 Bethnal Green
08.07.04	Ivor Bonavic W PTS 4 The Strand
18.09.04	Matt Scriven W RTD 4 Newark
21.11.04	Geraint Harvey W PTS 4 Bracknell
21.01.05	Ivor Bonavic W CO 2 Brentford
16.06.05	Duncan Cottier W RSC 1 Mayfair
16.12.05	Karl David W PTS 4 Bracknell
24.03.06	Ben Hudson W PTS 6 Bethnal Green

Career: 16 contests, won 12, lost 4.

Gary Lockett

Cwmbran. *Born* Pontypool, 25 November, 1976
WBU Middleweight Champion. Former WBO Inter-Continental L.Middleweight Champion. Ht. 5'10"
Manager Self

06.09.96	Ernie Loveridge W PTS 4 Liverpool
26.10.96	Charlie Paine W RSC 4 Liverpool
24.10.98	Lee Bird W RSC 2 Liverpool
27.02.99	Carl Smith W RSC 2 Bethnal Green

15.05.99	Mike Whittaker W RSC 2 Blackpool
19.06.99	Kid Halls W CO 1 Dublin
09.03.00	Kevin Thompson W CO 2 Liverpool
04.11.00	David Baptiste W PTS 4 Bethnal Green
23.01.01	Abdul Mehdi W RSC 2 Crawley
03.03.01	Hussain Osman W CO 2 Wembley
07.04.01	Howard Clarke W RSC 2 Wembley
08.05.01	Mike Algoet W PTS 6 Barnsley
14.07.01	Howard Clarke W CO 1 Wembley
25.09.01	Denny Dalton W RSC 1 Liverpool
24.11.01	Chris Nembhard W RSC 2 Bethnal Green
09.02.02	Kevin Kelly W CO 4 Manchester *(Vacant WBO Inter-Continental L.Middleweight Title)*
20.04.02	Youri Tsarenko L PTS 12 Cardiff *(WBO Inter-Continental L.Middleweight Title Defence)*
23.11.02	Viktor Fesetchko W PTS 8 Derby
29.03.03	Jason Collins W CO 1 Portsmouth
08.05.03	Yuri Tsarenko W PTS 10 Widnes
28.06.03	Michael Monaghan W PTS 10 Cardiff
21.02.04	Kreshnik Qato W RSC 2 Cardiff
12.06.04	Matt Galer W RSC 4 Manchester
03.09.04	Michael Monaghan W RSC 3 Newport
10.09.05	Allan Gray W CO 2 Cardiff
26.11.05	Victor Kpadenue W PTS 8 Rome, Italy
11.03.06	Gilbert Eastman W RSC 1 Newport *(Vacant WBU Middleweight Title)*

Career: 27 contests, won 26, lost 1.

Michael Lomax

Chingford. *Born* London, 25 September, 1978
L.Middleweight. Ht. 6'0"
Manager Self

05.07.03	Ernie Smith W PTS 4 Brentwood
20.09.03	Peter Dunn W PTS 4 Nottingham
14.11.03	Robert Lloyd-Taylor W PTS 6 Bethnal Green
16.01.04	Craig Lynch W PTS 6 Bradford
31.01.04	Steve Brumant W PTS 6 Bethnal Green
08.05.04	David Keir W RTD 4 Dagenham
13.02.05	Terry Adams W RSC 1 Brentwood
16.06.05	Jamie Coyle W PTS 6 Dagenham
18.11.05	Kevin Phelan W PTS 8 Dagenham

Career: 9 contests, won 9.

Chris Long

Calne. *Born* Gloucester, 5 March, 1980
L.Welterweight. Ht. 5'9"
Manager Self

15.05.03	Darren Goode W RSC 1 Clevedon
21.09.03	Daniel Thorpe L PTS 6 Bristol
17.11.03	Stuart Green L PTS 6 Glasgow
13.02.04	Justin Hicks W RSC 4 Bristol
29.02.04	Gareth Perkins L PTS 6 Bristol
12.03.04	Ivor Bonavic W PTS 6 Millwall
01.05.04	Stuart Phillips W RSC 1 Bridgend
19.06.04	Ceri Hall L PTS 4 Muswell Hill
12.09.04	Ernie Smith DREW 6 Shrewsbury
24.09.04	John O'Donnell L RSC 4 Nottingham
02.12.04	Gavin Tait W PTS 6 Bristol
27.01.05	Sam Rukundo L PTS 4 Piccadilly
24.04.05	Scott Haywood L PTS 6 Derby
08.05.05	John Fewkes L PTS 8 Sheffield
09.07.05	Kristian Laight W PTS 6 Bristol
25.02.06	Muhsen Nasser L PTS 4 Bristol
05.03.06	Shane Watson L PTS 4 Southampton
25.03.06	Ryan Brawley L PTS 8 Irvine
21.05.06	Kristian Laight W PTS 6 Bristol

Career: 19 contests, won 7, drew 1, lost 11.

Gary Lockett   Les Clark

Andrew Lowe   Les Clark

Andrew Lowe

Hackney. *Born* Hackney, 23 June, 1974
Southern Area L. Heavyweight Champion.
Ht. 5'10"
Manager A. Sims

19.05.01	Rob Stevenson W PTS 4 Wembley
16.06.01	William Webster W RSC 2 Dagenham
20.10.01	Tom Cannon W PTS 4 Glasgow
24.11.01	Paul Wesley W PTS 4 Bethnal Green

15.12.01   Mark Snipe W PTS 4 Chigwell
12.02.02   Ali Forbes W PTS 4 Bethnal Green
04.05.02   Radcliffe Green W PTS 4 Bethnal Green
12.10.02   Paul Bonson W PTS 4 Bethnal Green
08.02.03   Clint Johnson W PTS 6 Brentford
29.03.03   Radcliffe Green W PTS 10 Wembley
          (Vacant Southern Area L.Heavyweight Title)
31.05.03   Neil Linford W PTS 10 Bethnal Green
          (Elim. British L. Heavyweight Title)
07.11.03   Radcliffe Green W PTS 6 Sheffield
20.03.04   Varuzhan Davtyan W PTS 6 Wembley
12.05.04   Peter Oboh L RTD 10 Reading
          (British & Commonwealth L.Heavyweight Title Challenges)
10.04.05   Varuzhan Davtyan W PTS 6 Brentwood
03.06.06   John Anthony W PTS 6 Chigwell
Career: 16 contests, won 15, lost 1.

Simone Lucas

Nottingham. *Born* Burundi, 6 August, 1978
Middleweight. Ht. 5'10"
Manager J. Gill/T. Harris

22.10.05   Simon Fleck L RSC 5 Mansfield
20.11.05   Rob MacDonald W RSC 4 Shaw
05.12.05   Mark Franks L RSC 6 Leeds
25.02.06   Matthew Crouch W PTS 6 Bristol
02.04.06   Marvyn Wallace L CO 4 Bethnal Green
26.05.06   Kreshnik Qato L PTS 4 Bethnal Green
Career: 6 contests, won 2, lost 4.

Freddie Luke

West Kingsdown. *Born* Dartford, 2 February, 1977
Welterweight. Ht. 5'7"
Manager M. Roe

01.05.04   Wayne Wheeler W RSC 1 Gravesend
16.10.04   Lea Handley W PTS 4 Dagenham
19.12.04   Peter Dunn W PTS 4 Bethnal Green
26.02.06   Chris Brophy W PTS 4 Dagenham
Career: 4 contests, won 4.

Craig Lynch

Edinburgh. *Born* Edinburgh, 22 July, 1974
Middleweight. Ht. 6'1"
Manager Self

13.05.95   James Clamp DREW 6 Glasgow
08.06.95   Gary Silvester W RSC 3 Glasgow
15.09.95   Adam Baldwin W PTS 6 Glasgow
25.11.95   Jim Rock L PTS 4 Dublin
02.03.96   Hughie Davey L PTS 4 Newcastle
08.06.96   Hughie Davey L PTS 4 Newcastle
24.10.96   Pat Wright L PTS 6 Wembley
21.02.02   Gary Firby W RSC 3 Sunderland
26.04.02   Kevin McIntyre L PTS 10 Glasgow
          (Vacant Scottish Welterweight Title)
25.10.02   Joel Ani W PTS 6 Millwall
23.11.02   Bradley Pryce L CO 4 Derby
16.01.04   Michael Lomax L PTS 6 Bradford
30.01.04   Gilbert Eastman L PTS 6 Dagenham
21.02.04   Taz Jones L PTS 4 Cardiff
03.04.04   Thomas McDonagh L PTS 6 Manchester
06.05.04   Matthew Hall L PTS 6 Barnsley
19.06.04   Barrie Lee L PTS 6 Renfrew
30.07.04   Neil Sinclair L PTS 6 Bethnal Green

22.10.04   Barrie Lee L PTS 10 Edinburgh
          (Vacant Scottish L.Middleweight Title)
02.12.04   Eder Kurti L DIS 4 Crystal Palace
25.02.05   Martin Concepcion L PTS 6 Wembley
03.06.05   Ryan Rhodes L RSC 3 Manchester
23.07.05   Robert Burton W PTS 4 Edinburgh
12.11.05   Vince Baldassara L PTS 10 Glasgow
          (Vacant Scottish Area Middleweight Title)
18.02.06   Ryan Rowlinson DREW 4 Edinburgh
29.04.06   Robert Burton W PTS 4 Edinburgh
Career: 26 contests, won 6, drew 2, lost 18.

Colin Lynes

Hornchurch. *Born* Whitechapel, 26 November, 1977
L.Welterweight. Former Undefeated IBO L.Welterweight Champion. Former IBO Inter-Continental L.Welterweight Champion. Ht. 5'7½"
Manager Self

04.06.98   Les Frost W CO 1 Barking
23.07.98   Ram Singh W CO 1 Barking
22.10.98   Brian Coleman W RSC 2 Barking
31.10.98   Marc Smith W PTS 4 Basingstoke
10.12.98   Trevor Smith W RSC 1 Barking
25.02.99   Dennis Griffin W PTS 6 Kentish Town
20.05.99   Mark Haslam W PTS 4 Barking
18.05.00   Jason Vlasman W RSC 2 Bethnal Green
16.09.00   Karl Taylor W PTS 6 Bethnal Green
14.10.00   Brian Coleman W PTS 6 Wembley

09.12.00   Jimmy Phelan W PTS 6 Southwark
17.02.01   Mark Ramsey W PTS 6 Bethnal Green
10.04.01   David Kirk W PTS 6 Wembley
10.11.01   Keith Jones W PTS 6 Wembley
01.12.01   Leonti Voronchuk W PTS 6 Bethnal Green
26.01.02   David Kirk W PTS 6 Dagenham
23.03.02   Peter Dunn W PTS 4 Southwark
18.05.02   Kevin Bennett W RSC 4 Millwall
29.06.02   Ian Smith W RSC 7 Brentwood
21.09.02   Abdelilah Touil W CO 7 Brentwood
07.12.02   Richard Kiley W RSC 9 Brentwood
          (Vacant IBO Inter-Continental L.Welterweight Title)
08.03.03   Samuel Malinga L RTD 8 Bethnal Green
          (IBO Inter-Continental L.Welterweight Title Defence)
18.10.03   Brian Coleman W PTS 4 Manchester
22.11.03   Fabrice Colombel W PTS 6 Belfast
31.01.04   Cesar Levia W RSC 8 Bethnal Green
08.05.04   Pablo Sarmiento W PTS 12 Dagenham
          (IBO L.Welterweight Title Challenge)
13.02.05   Juaquin Gallardo W PTS 12 Brentwood
          (IBO L.Welterweight Title Defence)
21.10.05   Junior Witter L PTS 12 Bethnal Green
          (British, Commonwealth & European L.Welterweight Title Challenges)
20.01.06   Lenny Daws L RTD 9 Bethnal Green
          (Elim. British L.Welterweight Title. Vacant Southern Area L.Welterweight Title)
Career: 29 contests, won 26, lost 3.

Freddy Luke (right) made it four out of four when outpointing Chris Brophy last February

Les Clark

Lee McAllister

Aberdeen. *Born* Aberdeen, 5 October, 1982
Scottish Lightweight Champion. Former
Undefeated British Masters L.Welterweight
Champion. Ht. 5'9"
Manager Self

19.10.02	Baz Carey W PTS 4 Renfrew	
17.11.02	Arv Mittoo W PTS 6 Bradford	
23.02.03	Lee Williamson W PTS 6 Shrewsbury	
13.04.03	Ernie Smith W PTS 4 Bradford	
12.05.03	Ernie Smith W PTS 6 Birmingham	
15.06.03	Brian Coleman W PTS 6 Bradford	
11.07.03	John-Paul Ryan W RTD 2 Darlington	
17.07.03	Dean Hickman L PTS 6 Walsall	
03.08.03	Brian Coleman W PTS 4 Stalybridge	
06.09.03	Jeff Thomas W PTS 10 Aberdeen *(Vacant British Masters L.Welterweight Title)*	
28.11.03	Ernie Smith W PTS 6 Hull	
30.01.04	Karl Taylor W PTS 4 Dagenham	
08.03.04	Lee Williamson W PTS 6 Birmingham	
15.05.04	Martin Hardcastle W PTS 8 Aberdeen	
13.02.05	Daniel Thorpe W PTS 4 Bradford	
26.04.05	Mark Wall W PTS 6 Leeds	
14.05.05	Karl Taylor W RTD 3 Aberdeen	
23.07.05	Billy Smith W PTS 4 Edinburgh	
29.10.05	Jackson Williams W RSC 5 Aberdeen	
18.02.06	Silence Saheed W PTS 4 Edinburgh	
29.04.06	Peter Dunn W PTS 6 Edinburgh	
12.05.06	Billy Smith W PTS 4 Bethnal Green	
27.05.06	Stuart Green W RSC 8 Aberdeen *(Vacant Scottish Area Lightweight Title)*	

Career: 23 contests, won 22, lost 1.

Gary McArthur

Clydebank. *Born* Glasgow, 27 July, 1982
L.Welterweight. Ht. 5'9"
Manager T. Gilmour

23.01.06	Lance Verallo W PTS 6 Glasgow	
13.03.06	Pete Buckley W PTS 6 Glasgow	
24.04.06	Darren Gethin W PTS 6 Glasgow	

Career: 3 contests, won 3.

Kevin McBride

Clones. *Born* Monaghan, 10 May, 1973
All-Ireland Heavyweight Champion. Ht. 6'5"
Manager Self

17.12.92	Gary Charlton DREW 6 Barking	
13.02.93	Gary Williams W PTS 4 Manchester	
15.09.93	Joey Paladino W CO 2 Bethnal Green	
13.10.93	Chris Coughlan W PTS 4 Bethnal Green	
01.12.93	John Harewood W RSC 3 Bethnal Green	
06.05.94	Edgar Turpin W RSC 1 Atlantic City, New Jersey, USA	
04.06.94	Roger Bryant W CO 1 Reno, Nevada, USA	
17.06.94	Stanley Wright W PTS 6 Atlantic City, New Jersey, USA	
26.08.94	James Truesdale W RSC 3 Upper Marlboro, Maryland, USA	

24.09.94	Graham Arnold W RSC 2 Wembley	
12.11.94	Dean Storey W RSC 3 Dublin	
10.12.94	John Lamphrey W RSC 1 Portland, Maine, USA	
07.02.95	Carl Gaffney W RSC 1 Ipswich	
03.03.95	Carl McGrew W RSC 5 Boston, Mass, USA	
22.04.95	Jimmy Harrison W RSC 1 Boston, Mass, USA	
13.05.95	Atelea Kalhea W CO 1 Sacramento, California, USA	
02.07.95	Steve Garber W RSC 7 Dublin	
06.11.96	Shane Woollas W RSC 2 Hull	
03.12.96	R.F. McKenzie W RSC 6 Liverpool	
21.01.97	Tui Toia W RSC 2 Kansas City, Missouri, USA	
07.02.97	Louis Monaco L RSC 5 Las Vegas, Nevada, USA	
28.04.97	Stoyan Stoyanov W RSC 1 Hull	
02.06.97	Paul Douglas W RSC 5 Belfast *(Vacant All-Ireland Heavyweight Title)*	
30.08.97	Axel Schulz L RSC 9 Berlin, Germany	
22.11.97	Yuri Yelistratov W RSC 1 Manchester	
11.04.98	Michael Murray L RSC 3 Southwark	
26.06.99	Domingo Monroe W CO 1 Boston, Mass, USA	
11.08.01	Willie Phillips W PTS 10 Little Rock, Arkansas, USA	
01.11.01	Rodney McSwain W PTS 10 Little Rock, Arkansas, USA	
18.01.02	Davarryl Williamson L RSC 5 Las Vegas, Nevada, USA	
27.05.02	Gary Winmon W RSC 2 Revere, Mass, USA	
26.07.02	Reynaldo Minus W RSC 3 Boston, Mass, USA	
26.10.02	Craig Tomlinson W RSC 3 Revere, Mass, USA	
17.03.03	Najee Shaheed W RSC 7 Brockton, Mass, USA	
09.08.03	Lenzie Morgan W CO 1 Brockton, Mass, USA	
04.12.03	Marcus Rhode W RSC 3 Boston, Mass, USA	
18.03.05	Kevin Montiy W RSC 5 Mashantucket, Connecticut, USA	
11.06.05	Mike Tyson W RSC 6 Washington DC, USA	
01.04.06	Byron Polley W RSC 4 Cleveland, Ohio, USA	

Career: 39 contests, won 34, drew 1, lost 4.

Enzo Maccarinelli

Swansea. *Born* Swansea, 20 August, 1980
WBU Cruiserweight Champion. Ht. 6'4"
Manager F. Warren/C. Pearson

02.10.99	Paul Bonson W PTS 4 Cardiff	
11.12.99	Mark Williams W PTS 4 Merthyr	
26.02.00	Nigel Rafferty W RSC 3 Swansea	
12.05.00	Lee Swaby L CO 3 Swansea	
11.12.00	Chris Woollas W PTS 4 Widnes	
28.04.01	Darren Ashton W CO 1 Cardiff	
09.10.01	Eamonn Glennon W RSC 2 Cardiff	
15.12.01	Kevin Barrett W RSC 2 Wembley	
12.02.02	James Gilbert W RSC 2 Bethnal Green	
20.04.02	Tony Booth W PTS 4 Cardiff	
17.08.02	Tony Booth W RTD 2 Cardiff	
12.10.02	Dave Clarke W RSC 2 Bethnal Green	
18.01.03	Paul Bonson W PTS 4 Preston	
29.03.03	Valery Shemishkur W RSC 1 Portsmouth	

28.06.03	Bruce Scott W RSC 4 Cardiff *(Vacant WBU Cruiserweight Title)*	
13.09.03	Andrei Kiarsten W CO 1 Newport *(WBU Cruiserweight Title Defence)*	
06.12.03	Earl Morais W RSC 1 Cardiff *(WBU Cruiserweight Title Defence)*	
21.02.04	Garry Delaney W RSC 8 Cardiff *(WBU Cruiserweight Title Defence)*	
03.07.04	Ismail Abdoul W PTS 12 Newport *(WBU Cruiserweight Title Defence)*	
03.09.04	Jesper Kristiansen W CO 3 Newport *(WBU Cruiserweight Title Defence)*	
21.01.05	Rich LaMontagne W RSC 4 Bridgend *(WBU Cruiserweight Title Defence)*	
04.06.05	Roman Bugaj W RSC 1 Manchester	
26.11.05	Marco Heinichen W RSC 1 Rome, Italy	
04.03.06	Mark Hobson W PTS 12 Manchester *(WBU Cruiserweight Title Defence)*	

Career: 24 contests, won 23, lost 1.

Glenn McClarnon

Lurgan. *Born* Carrickfergus, 1 July, 1974
Welterweight. Ht. 5'9"
Manager J. Breen/M. Callahan

20.12.97	Marc Smith W PTS 4 Belfast	
21.02.98	Andrew Reed W CO 1 Belfast	
28.04.98	Brian Robb W RSC 2 Belfast	
18.09.98	Mark Ramsey W PTS 4 Belfast	
28.11.98	David Kirk W PTS 4 Belfast	
12.01.99	Ram Singh W RSC 1 Bethnal Green	
25.01.99	Dean Nicholas W CO 1 Glasgow	
12.03.99	Mark Ramsey W PTS 6 Bethnal Green	
25.05.99	Steve Tuckett W PTS 6 Mayfair	
11.09.99	David Kirk W PTS 6 Sheffield	
27.11.99	Chris Barnett L PTS 12 Liverpool *(Vacant IBO International L.Welterweight Title)*	
01.04.00	Bernard Paul W RTD 5 Bethnal Green	
19.08.00	Brian Coleman W PTS 6 Brentwood	
13.10.00	Allan Vester L PTS 12 Aarhus, Denmark *(IBF Inter-Continental L.Welterweight Title Challenge)*	
02.12.00	John Ameline L PTS 4 Bethnal Green	
03.03.01	Peter Dunn W PTS 4 Wembley	
28.04.01	Jacek Bielski L PTS 12 Wroclaw, Poland *(Vacant IBO Inter-Continental Welterweight Title)*	
25.09.01	Gary Ryder L PTS 8 Liverpool	
10.11.01	Rosalin Nasibulin W PTS 6 Wembley	
26.01.02	Kevin Bennett W PTS 8 Dagenham	
16.11.02	Keith Jones W PTS 6 Nottingham	
22.02.03	Ossie Duran L RSC 2 Huddersfield	
30.10.03	Ronnie Nailen W RSC 1 Belfast	
03.04.04	David Barnes L PTS 12 Manchester *(British Welterweight Title Challenge)*	
31.01.05	Kevin Anderson L RSC 4 Glasgow *(Vacant Celtic Welterweight Title)*	
24.11.05	Mark Phillips W PTS 4 Lurgan	

Career: 26 contests, won 18, lost 8.

Paul McCloskey

Dungiven. *Born* Londonderry, 3 August, 1979
L. Welterweight. Ht. 5'8 1/2"
Manager J. Breen/F. Warren

18.03.05	David Kehoe W RSC 3 Belfast	
17.06.05	Oscar Milkitas W PTS 4 Glasgow	
05.11.05	Billy Smith W PTS 4 Renfrew	

24.11.05   Henry Janes W RSC 3 Lurgan
18.02.06   Duncan Cottier W PTS 6 Edinburgh
11.03.06   Surinder Sekhon W RSC 1 Newport
Career: 6 contests, won 6.

Paul McCloskey   Les Clark

Billy McClung

Kilmarnock. *Born* Irvine, 13 March, 1982
Cruiserweight. Ht. 6'3"
Manager T. Gilmour

19.11.01   Darren Ashton W PTS 6 Glasgow
18.02.02   Clint Johnson W PTS 6 Glasgow
01.03.02   Clint Johnson W PTS 6 Irvine
18.03.02   Shane White L RTD 4 Glasgow
25.02.05   Csaba Andras W PTS 6 Irvine
21.03.05   Henry Smith W PTS 6 Glasgow
06.05.06   Paul Bonson W PTS 6 Irvine
Career: 7 contests, won 6, lost 1.

Joe McCluskey

Coventry. *Born* Coventry, 26 November,
1977
Welterweight. Ht. 5'9"
Manager Self

01.05.04   John-Paul Ryan W RTD 2 Coventry
10.07.04   Declan English W RSC 4 Coventry
20.11.04   Judex Meemea DREW 6 Coventry
18.06.05   Carl Allen W PTS 6 Coventry
22.10.05   Darren Gethin DREW 6 Coventry
04.03.06   Khurram Hussain L PTS 6 Coventry
Career: 6 contests, won 3, drew 2, lost 1.

Peter McCormack

Erdington. *Born* Birmingham, 9 March,
1974
L.Heavyweight. Ht. 5'10"
Manager Self

07.10.96   Paul Webb DREW 6 Birmingham
21.11.96   Ozzy Orrock W RSC 2 Solihull
04.12.96   Lee Simpkin L PTS 6 Stoke
11.02.97   Mark Sawyers L RSC 2
           Wolverhampton
11.10.99   Andy Vickers L PTS 6 Birmingham
27.10.99   Paul Bonson L PTS 6 Birmingham

06.12.99   Andrew Facey L CO 2 Birmingham
28.03.00   William Webster W PTS 6
           Wolverhampton
11.10.04   Omid Bourzo W PTS 6 Birmingham
16.12.04   Dave Pearson L PTS 6 Cleethorpes
25.04.05   Dave Pearson L PTS 6 Cleethorpes
10.10.05   Mark Phillips L PTS 6 Birmingham
27.02.06   Paul David L RTD 2 Birmingham
22.05.06   Omid Bourzo L PTS 6 Birmingham
Career: 14 contests, won 3, drew 1, lost 10.

Darren McDermott

Dudley. *Born* Dudley, 17 July, 1978
Midlands Area Middleweight Champion.
Ht. 6'1"
Manager D. Powell

26.04.03   Leigh Wicks W PTS 4 Brentford
13.06.03   Gary Jones W RSC 1 Queensway
30.10.03   Harry Butler W PTS 4 Dudley
21.02.04   Freddie Yemofio W RSC 3 Cardiff
15.04.04   Mark Phillips W PTS 4 Dudley
03.07.04   Neil Addis W PTS 4 Newport
11.12.04   Gokhan Kazaz DREW 4 Canning
           Town
21.04.05   Howard Clarke W RTD 1 Dudley
06.10.05   Andy Halder W RTD 5 Dudley
           *(Midlands Area Middleweight Title
           Challenge)*
16.02.06   Michael Monaghan W RTD 9 Dudley
           *(Midlands Area Middleweight Title
           Defence)*
29.06.06   Andrzej Butowicz W RSC 3 Dudley
Career: 11 contests, won 10, drew 1.

Darren McDermott   Les Clark

John McDermott

Horndon. *Born* Basildon, 26 February,
1980
Heavyweight. Ht. 6'3"
Manager J. Branch

23.09.00   Slick Miller W RSC 1 Bethnal Green
21.10.00   Gary Williams W PTS 4 Wembley
13.11.00   Geoff Hunter W RSC 1 Bethnal Green
27.01.01   Eamonn Glennon W RSC 1 Bethnal
           Green
24.02.01   Alexei Osokin W PTS 4 Bethnal Green
26.03.01   Mal Rice W RSC 2 Wembley
09.06.01   Luke Simpkin W PTS 6 Bethnal Green

22.09.01   Gary Williams W RSC 4 Bethnal
           Green
24.11.01   Gordon Minors W RSC 3 Bethnal
           Green
19.01.02   Tony Booth W RSC 1 Bethnal Green
04.05.02   Martin Roothman W RSC 1 Bethnal
           Green
14.09.02   Alexander Mileiko W RSC 2 Bethnal
           Green
12.10.02   Mendauga Kulikauskas W PTS 6
           Bethnal Green
14.12.02   Jason Brewster W RSC 1 Newcastle
15.02.03   Derek McCafferty W PTS 4 Wembley
08.05.03   Konstantin Prizyuk W PTS 8 Widnes
18.09.03   Nicolai Popov L RSC 2 Dagenham
13.05.04   James Zikic W RSC 4 Bethnal Green
30.07.04   Suren Kalachyan W CO 7 Bethnal
           Green
11.12.04   Mark Krence L PTS 10 Canning Town
           (Vacant English Heavyweight Title)
08.04.05   Slick Miller W RSC 1 Edinburgh
10.12.05   Matt Skelton L RSC 1 Canning Town
           (British Heavyweight Title Challenge)
Career: 22 contests, won 19, lost 3.

Peter McDonagh

Bermondsey. *Born* Galway, 21 December,
1977
All-Ireland Lightweight Champion. Former
Southern Area Lightweight Champion.
Ht. 5'9"
Manager Self

28.04.02   Arv Mittoo W PTS 6 Southwark
23.06.02   Dave Hinds W PTS 6 Southwark
14.09.02   Pete Buckley W PTS 4 Bethnal Green
27.10.02   Ben Hudson L PTS 6 Southwark
18.02.03   Daffyd Carlin L PTS 4 Bethnal Green
08.04.03   Ben Hudson W PTS 4 Bethnal Green
08.11.03   Ceri Hall L PTS 4 Bridgend
22.11.03   James Gorman L PTS 4 Belfast
21.02.04   Chill John W RTD 2 Brighton
06.03.04   Barry Hughes L PTS 6 Renfrew
07.04.04   Jon Honney W PTS 10 Leicester
           Square
           *(Vacant Southern Area Lightweight
           Title)*
19.11.04   David Burke L PTS 8 Bethnal Green
21.01.05   Ryan Barrett L PTS 8 Brentford
04.03.05   Scott Lawton L PTS 6 Rotherham
30.04.05   Rob Jeffries L PTS 10 Dagenham
           *(Southern Area Lightweight Title
           Defence)*
14.05.05   Robbie Murray L PTS 10 Dublin
           (Vacant Irish L.Welterweight Title)
07.08.05   Brunet Zamora L PTS 6 Rimini, Italy
04.11.05   Anthony Christopher W PTS 4 Bethnal
           Green
28.01.06   Michael Gomez W RSC 5 Dublin
           (Vacant All-Ireland Lightweight Title)
Career: 19 contests, won 8, lost 11.

Thomas McDonagh

Manchester. *Born* Manchester, 8 December,
1980
L.Middleweight. Former Undefeated WBU
Inter-Continental L.Middleweight
Champion. Ht. 6'0"
Manager F. Warren/B. Hughes

09.10.99   Lee Molyneux W PTS 4 Manchester
06.11.99   Lee Molyneux W PTS 4 Widnes

11.12.99 Arv Mittoo W RSC 2 Liverpool
29.01.00 Emmanuel Marcos W PTS 4 Manchester
29.02.00 William Webster W RTD 2 Widnes
25.03.00 Lee Molyneux W PTS 6 Liverpool
16.05.00 Richie Murray W PTS 4 Warrington
29.05.00 David Baptiste W PTS 6 Manchester
04.09.00 Colin Vidler W PTS 6 Manchester
11.12.00 Richie Murray W PTS 6 Widnes
15.01.01 Kid Halls W RSC 4 Manchester
10.02.01 Harry Butler W PTS 6 Widnes
17.03.01 David Baptiste W PTS 4 Manchester
07.07.01 Paul Denton W PTS 6 Manchester
15.09.01 Howard Clarke W PTS 6 Manchester
27.10.01 Mark Richards DREW 4 Manchester
09.02.02 Tomas da Silva DREW 4 Manchester
01.06.02 Delroy Mellis W PTS 4 Manchester
28.09.02 Brian Coleman W RSC 1 Manchester
18.01.03 Tomas da Silva W PTS 4 Preston
05.04.03 Paul Wesley W PTS 6 Manchester
08.05.03 Marcus Portman W PTS 6 Widnes
27.09.03 Eugenio Monteiro W PTS 12 Manchester
        (Vacant WBU Inter-Continental L.Middleweight Title)
26.02.04 Bobby Banghar W CO 2 Widnes
        (WBU Inter-Continental L.Middleweight Title Defence)
03.04.04 Craig Lynch W PTS 6 Manchester
06.05.04 Bradley Pryce W PTS 12 Barnsley
        (WBU Inter-Continental L.Middleweight Title Defence)
12.11.04 Darren Rhodes W PTS 10 Halifax
        (Elim. British L.Middleweight Title)
03.06.05 Barrie Lee W RSC 7 Manchester
        (WBU Inter-Continental L.Middleweight Title Defence)
25.10.05 Dean Walker W PTS 6 Preston
04.03.06 Wayne Alexander L PTS 12 Manchester
        (WBU L.Middleweight Title Challenge)
Career: 30 contests, won 27, drew 2, lost 1.

(Stephen) Junior MacDonald

Lewisham. *Born* Lewisham, 9 August, 1979
Cruiserweight. Ht. 6'2½"
Manager F. Maloney

05.03.05 Tony Booth W PTS 4 Southwark
29.04.05 Gary Thompson W RSC 1 Southwark
19.06.05 Radcliffe Green W RTD 1 Bethnal Green
07.10.05 Paul Bonson W PTS 4 Bethnal Green
27.01.06 Sergey Voron W RSC 2 Dagenham
30.05.06 Julien Perriaux W RSC 5 Bethnal Green

Career: 6 contests, won 6.

Rob MacDonald

Droylsden. *Born* Manchester, 26 July, 1981
L. Middleweight. Ht. 6'0"
Manager Self

28.02.04 Vince Baldassara L PTS 6 Manchester
20.03.04 Lee Hodgson L RSC 3 Wembley
10.09.04 Martin Concepcion L RSC 2 Bethnal Green
06.03.05 Ali Mateen L PTS 6 Shaw
30.04.05 Mark Franks L RSC 6 Wigan
20.11.05 Simone Lucas L RSC 4 Shaw
Career: 6 contests, lost 6.

Jamie McDonnell

Doncaster. *Born* Doncaster, 3 March, 1986
Bantamweight. Ht. 5'8"
Manager J. Rushton

16.09.05 Neil Read W PTS 6 Doncaster
02.12.05 Delroy Spencer W PTS 6 Doncaster
03.03.06 Gary Sheil W PTS 6 Doncaster
21.04.06 Neil Marston W PTS 4 Doncaster
09.06.06 Dai Davies DREW 4 Doncaster
Career: 5 contests, won 4, drew 1.

Steve McGuire

Glenrothes. *Born* Kirkcaldy, 1 June, 1981
Cruiserweight. Ht. 6'2"
Manager Self

17.11.03 Shane White W CO 2 Glasgow
22.04.04 Paul Billington W RTD 3 Glasgow
15.10.04 Karl Wheeler W PTS 4 Glasgow
11.06.05 Varuzhan Davtyan W PTS 6 Kirkcaldy
30.09.05 Marcin Radola W RSC 1 Kirkcaldy
17.03.06 Paul David W PTS 6 Kirkcaldy
28.04.06 Valery Odin W PTS 6 Hartlepool
16.06.06 Simeon Cover W PTS 6 Liverpool
Career: 8 contests, won 8.

George McIlroy

Stevenston. *Born* Irvine, 12 March, 1984
L.Middleweight. Ht. 5'10"
Manager T. Gilmour

28.02.03 Paul McIlwaine W PTS 4 Irvine
14.04.03 Paul Rushton W RSC 1 Glasgow
20.10.03 Norman Dhalie W PTS 6 Glasgow
15.10.04 Ivor Bonavic DREW 4 Glasgow
31.01.05 Chris Brophy W RSC 6 Glasgow
06.05.06 Deniss Sirjatovs W RSC 2 Irvine
Career: 6 contests, won 5, drew 1.

Jamie McIlroy

Stevenston. *Born* Irvine, 14 September, 1985
L.Welterweight. Ht. 5'8"
Manager Self

25.02.05 John-Paul Ryan W PTS 6 Irvine
21.03.05 Rocky Flanagan W PTS 6 Glasgow
06.05.06 Sergei Rozhakmens W PTS 6 Irvine
Career: 3 contests, won 3.

Paul McInnes

Cannock. *Born* Lichfield, 11 January, 1978
Middleweight. Ht. 5'8½"
Manager Self

05.10.04 David Payne L RSC 1 Dudley
26.02.05 Richard Hackney W PTS 6 Burton
24.04.05 Sergey Haritonov W PTS 6 Derby
30.09.05 Peter Dunn W PTS 6 Burton
25.11.05 Manoocha Salari L PTS 6 Walsall
Career: 5 contests, won 3, lost 2.

Conroy McIntosh

Wolverhampton. *Born* Wolverhampton, 5 December, 1973
Middleweight. Ht. 5'7"
Manager Self

31.01.01 Ross Murray W CO 1 Piccadilly
23.06.01 Francie Doherty L PTS 4 Peterborough
22.09.01 Tomas da Silva L PTS 4 Canning Town
11.02.02 Ty Browne DREW 4 Southampton
03.03.02 Wayne Shepherd DREW 6 Shaw
21.05.02 Ty Browne DREW 4 Custom House
13.07.02 Darren Covill W PTS 4 Wolverhampton
17.11.02 Gary Dixon W RSC 2 Shaw
30.11.02 Andy Halder L PTS 4 Coventry
22.02.03 George Robshaw L PTS 4 Huddersfield
08.03.03 Andy Halder L PTS 4 Coventry
20.06.03 Michael Thomas W CO 2 Gatwick
07.09.03 Roddy Doran L PTS 10 Shrewsbury
        (Vacant Midlands Area Middleweight Title)
07.11.03 Patrick J. Maxwell L RSC 4 Sheffield
07.04.04 Lee Hodgson W RSC 3 Leicester Square
13.05.04 Ajay Abrahams W RSC 2 Bethnal Green
10.07.04 Andy Halder L PTS 10 Coventry
        (Vacant Midlands Area Middleweight Title)
10.12.04 Geard Ajetovic L PTS 6 Sheffield
24.07.05 Geard Ajetovic L PTS 6 Sheffield
21.09.05 Patrick J. Maxwell L RSC 2 Bradford
17.11.05 Joey Vegas L RSC 3 Piccadilly
10.02.06 Cello Renda L RSC 1 Plymouth
06.05.06 Lee Blundell L PTS 6 Blackpool
20.05.06 Jason McKay L PTS 6 Belfast
01.06.06 Paul Smith L PTS 8 Barnsley
Career: 25 contests, won 6, drew 3, lost 16.

Danny McIntosh

Norwich. *Born* Norwich, 1 March, 1980
L. Heavyweight. Ht. 6'2"
Manager J. Ingle

09.04.05 Omid Bourzo W PTS 6 Norwich
03.09.05 Howard Clarke W PTS 4 Norwich
06.10.05 Michael Banbula W PTS 6 Longford
Career: 3 contests, won 3.

Kevin McIntyre

Paisley. *Born* Paisley, 5 May, 1978
Scottish Welterweight Champion.
Ht. 5'10½"
Manager T. Gilmour

13.11.98 Ray Wood W RSC 4 Glasgow
18.02.99 Gareth Dooley W RSC 3 Glasgow
21.05.99 Mohamed Helel W PTS 6 Glasgow
26.06.99 Karim Bouali L RTD 1 Glasgow
18.03.00 Chris Hall W RSC 3 Glasgow
07.04.00 Dave Travers W RSC 4 Glasgow
26.05.00 Tommy Peacock W RSC 5 Glasgow
24.06.00 Lee Williamson W PTS 4 Glasgow
02.10.00 Paul Denton W PTS 6 Glasgow
10.11.00 Mark Ramsey W RSC 4 Glasgow
17.12.00 Ernie Smith W PTS 6 Glasgow
15.02.01 John Humphrey L RSC 4 Glasgow
27.04.01 Michael Smyth W PTS 6 Glasgow
17.11.01 David Kirk W PTS 4 Glasgow
16.12.01 Manzo Smith W PTS 6 Glasgow
11.03.02 Karl Taylor W PTS 4 Glasgow
26.04.02 Craig Lynch W PTS 10 Glasgow
        (Vacant Scottish Welterweight Title)
08.06.02 David Kirk W RTD 5 Renfrew
19.10.02 Nigel Wright W PTS 6 Renfrew
22.03.03 David Kirk W RSC 1 Renfrew
12.07.03 Paul Denton W PTS 4 Renfrew
25.10.03 Karim Hussine W PTS 6 Edinburgh
13.12.03 David Barnes L RTD 8 Manchester
        (British Welterweight Title Challenge)
02.06.04 Keith Jones W PTS 6 Hereford
17.12.04 Sergey Starkov W PTS 6 Huddersfield

05.11.05 Nigel Wright L RSC 1 Renfrew
(Final Elim. British L.Welterweight Title)
06.05.06 Gary Reid L RSC 6 Stoke
(Vacant British Masters L.Welterweight Title)
Career: 27 contests, won 22, lost 5.

Jason McKay

Banbridge. *Born* Craigavon, NI, 11 October, 1977
S. Middleweight. Ht. 6'1"
Manager F. Warren/J. Breen

18.02.02 Jimmy Steel W PTS 4 Glasgow
11.05.02 Harry Butler W PTS 4 Dagenham
27.07.02 Simon Andrews W RSC 3 Nottingham
08.10.02 Dean Cockburn W PTS 4 Glasgow
08.02.03 William Webster W RSC 1 Liverpool
12.04.03 Marcin Radola W RSC 1 Bethnal Green
17.05.03 Varuzhan Davtyan W PTS 6 Liverpool
04.10.03 Jamie Hearn W PTS 8 Belfast
22.11.03 Ojay Abrahams W PTS 4 Belfast
17.04.04 Alan Gilbert W PTS 6 Belfast
26.06.04 Ciaran Healy W PTS 6 Belfast
05.11.04 Paul Buchanan L PTS 6 Hereford
24.11.05 Ojay Abrahams W PTS 4 Lurgan
18.02.06 Dean Walker W RTD 1 Edinburgh
20.05.06 Conroy McIntosh W PTS 6 Belfast
Career: 15 contests, won 14, lost 1.

John Mackay (Mukaya)

Canning Town. *Born* Uganda, 20 October, 1981
Featherweight. Ht. 5'6"
Manager Self

15.06.01 Chris Emanuele L RSC 4 Millwall
22.09.01 Jason Nesbitt W PTS 4 Canning Town
16.11.01 Willie Valentine W RSC 4 Dublin
28.11.01 Jamie Yelland W RSC 6 Bethnal Green
18.01.02 Stephen Chinnock L PTS 4 Coventry
20.04.02 Dazzo Williams W PTS 6 Wembley
02.06.02 Choi Tseveenpurev L RSC 5 Shaw
27.07.02 Chris Hooper W PTS 4 Nottingham
23.11.02 Henry Castle W RTD 8 Derby
22.03.03 Brian Carr W PTS 8 Renfrew
16.01.04 Steve Molitor L PTS 8 Bradford
29.02.04 Choi Tseveenpurev L RSC 3 Shaw
01.05.04 Junior Anderson W CO 2 Gravesend
19.06.04 Mickey Bowden W PTS 8 Muswell Hill
16.10.04 Henry Janes L PTS 4 Dagenham
13.05.05 Derry Matthews L PTS 6 Liverpool
20.05.05 Willie Limond L RSC 5 Glasgow
30.09.05 Craig Docherty L RSC 7 Kirkcaldy
Career: 18 contests, won 9, lost 9.

Jamie McKeever

Birkenhead. *Born* Birkenhead, 7 July, 1979
Featherweight. Former British Featherweight Champion. Former Undefeated Central Area Featherweight Champion. Ht. 5'6½"
Manager Self

12.03.98 Dave Hinds W PTS 4 Liverpool
08.04.98 Kid McAuley W RTD 1 Liverpool
06.06.98 Brian Coleman W PTS 4 Liverpool
21.07.98 Stuart Rimmer W PTS 4 Widnes
31.10.98 John T. Kelly L PTS 6 Southend
22.01.99 Garry Burrell W RSC 2 Carlisle

12.03.99 David Kehoe W RSC 2 Bethnal Green
28.05.99 Arv Mittoo W PTS 6 Liverpool
02.10.99 Lee Armstrong DREW 6 Cardiff
27.11.99 Nigel Leake W RSC 2 Liverpool
01.07.00 Gary Flear L PTS 4 Manchester
09.10.00 Marc Callaghan W PTS 6 Liverpool
20.03.01 Craig Docherty L RSC 3 Glasgow
25.09.01 Sebastian Hart W PTS 4 Liverpool
10.12.01 Andrew Ferrans W PTS 6 Liverpool
09.03.02 James Rooney W PTS 6 Manchester
13.04.02 Barry Hawthorne W PTS 6 Liverpool
07.09.02 Tony Mulholland W PTS 10 Liverpool
(Vacant Central Area Featherweight Title)
08.02.03 Tony Mulholland W RSC 6 Liverpool
(Vacant British Featherweight Title)
17.05.03 Roy Rutherford L PTS 12 Liverpool
(British Featherweight Title Defence)
28.02.04 Dazzo Williams L PTS 12 Bridgend
(British Featherweight Title Challenge)
23.09.05 Jim Betts W RSC 4 Manchester
25.11.05 Dariusz Snarski W PTS 6 Liverpool
03.03.06 Riaz Durgahed W PTS 6 Hartlepool
16.06.06 Jackson Asiku L RSC 1 Liverpool
(Commonwealth Featherweight Title Challenge)
Career: 25 contests, won 18, drew 1, lost 6.

(Helen) Angel McKenzie (Hobbs)

Thornton Heath. *Born* Russia, 10 June, 1973
Lightweight. Ht. 5'7"
Manager D.V. Williams

26.02.06 Alena Kokavcova W PTS 4 Dagenham
Career: 1 contest, won 1.

Ovill McKenzie

Canning Town. *Born* Jamaica, 26 November, 1979
L. Heavyweight. Ht. 5'9"
Manager Self

06.03.03 Leigh Alliss W PTS 4 Bristol
10.04.03 Nathan King W PTS 4 Clydach
02.06.03 Pinky Burton L PTS 8 Glasgow
18.09.03 Peter Haymer L PTS 4 Mayfair
24.10.03 Courtney Fry L PTS 4 Bethnal Green
15.11.03 Edwin Cleary W PTS 4 Coventry
30.01.04 Steven Spartacus W PTS 6 Dagenham
12.03.04 Harry Butler W RSC 2 Millwall
03.04.04 Denis Inkin L PTS 8 Manchester
10.09.04 Tommy Eastwood L PTS 8 Wembley
04.12.04 Stipe Drews L PTS 8 Berlin, Germany
06.02.05 Paul Bonson W PTS 4 Southampton
13.02.05 Gyorgy Hidvegi W RSC 3 Brentwood
13.05.05 Courtney Fry W RSC 4 Liverpool
01.07.05 Hastings Rasani W PTS 6 Fulham
26.02.06 Tony Booth W PTS 4 Dagenham
23.03.06 Paul Bonson W PTS 6 The Strand
30.03.06 Paul Bonson W RSC 3 Bloomsbury
Career: 18 contests, won 12, lost 6.

Sean McKervey

Coventry. *Born* Coventry, 17 July, 1983
L.Middleweight. Ht. 5'8½"
Manager O. Delargy

04.03.06 Ernie Smith W PTS 6 Coventry
Career: 1 contest, won 1.

Matthew Macklin

Birmingham. *Born* Birmingham, 14 May, 1982
L.Middleweight. All-Ireland Middleweight Champion. Ht. 5'10"
Manager Self

17.11.01 Ram Singh W RSC 1 Glasgow
15.12.01 Christian Hodorogea W CO 1 Wembley
09.02.02 Dimitri Protkunas W RTD 3 Manchester
11.03.02 David Kirk W PTS 4 Glasgow
20.04.02 Illia Spassov W CO 3 Cardiff

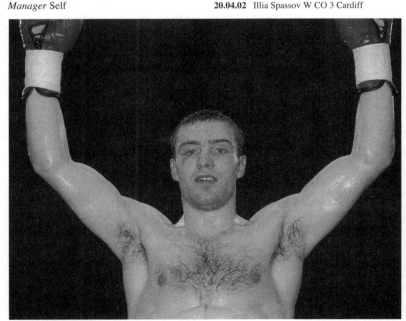

Matthew Macklin　　　　　　　　　　　　　　　Les Clark

01.06.02 Guy Alton W RSC 3 Manchester
28.09.02 Leonti Voronchuk W RSC 5 Manchester
15.02.03 Ruslan Yakupov W PTS 6 Wembley
24.05.03 Paul Denton W PTS 6 Bethnal Green
06.11.03 Andrew Facey L PTS 10 Dagenham
(Vacant English L.Middleweight Title)
21.02.04 Dean Walker W CO 1 Cardiff
24.04.04 Scott Dixon W RTD 5 Reading
12.06.04 Ojay Abrahams W PTS 4 Manchester
14.05.05 Michael Monaghan W CO 5 Dublin
(Vacant All-Ireland Middleweight Title)
04.08.05 Leo Laudat W RSC 3 Atlantic City, New Jersey, USA
28.10.05 Anthony Little W RSC 2 Philadelphia, Pennsylvania, USA
26.11.05 Alexey Chirkov W CO 1 Sheffield
01.06.06 Marcin Piatkowski W RSC 4 Birmingham
Career: 18 contests, won 17, lost 1.

Colin McNeil

Fauldhouse. *Born* Lanark, 21 December, 1972
Welterweight. Former Undefeated Celtic L.Middleweight Champion. Ht. 5'8"
Manager A. Morrison/F. Warren

06.03.04 Arv Mittoo W PTS 4 Renfrew
27.03.04 Lee Williamson W PTS 4 Edinburgh
19.06.04 Andrei Ivanov W RSC 2 Renfrew
22.10.04 Ivor Bonavic W PTS 4 Edinburgh
03.12.04 Geraint Harvey W PTS 6 Edinburgh
28.01.05 Matt Scriven W PTS 4 Renfrew
20.05.05 Duncan Cottier W PTS 6 Glasgow
23.07.05 Taz Jones W PTS 10 Edinburgh
(Vacant Celtic L.Middleweight Title)
23.09.05 Ossie Duran L PTS 12 Mayfair
(Commonwealth L.Middleweight Title Challenge)
29.04.06 Gary Young W CO 1 Edinburgh
(Elim.British Welterweight Title)
Career: 10 contests, won 9, lost 1.

Neal McQuade

Peterborough. *Born* London, 17 November, 1977
L.Welterweight. Ht. 5'4½"
Manager I. Pauly

15.06.06 Kristian Laight L PTS 6 Peterborough
Career: 1 contest, lost 1.

Brian Magee

Belfast. *Born* Lisburn, 9 June, 1975
S.Middleweight. Former IBO S.Middleweight Champion. Former Undefeated IBO Inter-Continental S.Middleweight Champion. Ht. 6'0"
Manager P. Magee

13.03.99 Dean Ashton W RSC 2 Manchester
22.05.99 Richard Glaysher W RSC 1 Belfast
22.06.99 Chris Howarth W RSC 1 Ipswich
13.09.99 Dennis Doyley W RSC 3 Bethnal Green
16.10.99 Michael Pinnock W RSC 3 Belfast
12.02.00 Terry Morrill W RTD 4 Sheffield
21.02.00 Rob Stevenson W RSC 5 Southwark
20.03.00 Darren Ashton W RTD 5 Mansfield
15.04.00 Pedro Carragher W CO 2 Bethnal Green

12.06.00 Jason Barker W PTS 8 Belfast
11.11.00 Teimouraz Kikelidze W RSC 4 Belfast
29.01.01 Neil Linford W PTS 12 Peterborough
(Vacant IBO Inter-Continental S. Middleweight Title)
31.07.01 Chris Nembhard W RSC 6 Bethnal Green
10.12.01 Ramon Britez W CO 1 Liverpool
(IBO S. Middleweight Title Challenge)
18.03.02 Vage Kocharyan W PTS 8 Crawley
15.06.02 Mpush Makambi W RSC 7 Leeds
(IBO S. Middleweight Title Defence)
09.11.02 Jose Spearman W PTS 12 Altrincham
(IBO S. Middleweight Title Defence)
22.02.03 Miguel Jimenez W PTS 12 Huddersfield
(IBO S.Middleweight Title Defence)
21.06.03 Andre Thysse W RSC 10 Manchester
(IBO S.Middleweight Title Defence)
04.10.03 Omar Eduardo Gonzalez W RSC 1 Belfast
(IBO S.Middleweight Title Defence)
22.11.03 Hacine Cherifi W RTD 8 Belfast
(IBO S.Middleweight Title Defence)
17.04.04 Jerry Elliott W PTS 12 Belfast
(IBO S.Middleweight Title Defence)
26.06.04 Robin Reid L PTS 12 Belfast
(IBO S.Middleweight Title Defence)
26.11.04 Neil Linford W RSC 7 Altrincham
16.07.05 Vitali Tsypko L PTS 12 Nürnberg, Germany
(Vacant European S.Middleweight Title)
14.10.05 Varuzhan Davtyan W RSC 2 Dublin
28.01.06 Daniil Prakapsou W RSC 2 Dublin
26.05.06 Carl Froch L RSC 11 Bethnal Green
(British & Commonwealth S.Middleweight Title Challenges)
Career: 28 contests, won 25, lost 3.

Eamonn Magee

Belfast. *Born* Belfast, 13 July, 1971
Welterweight. Former WBU Welterweight Champion. Former Undefeated Commonwealth L.Welterweight Champion. Ht. 5'9"
Manager Self

25.11.95 Pete Roberts W CO 4 Dublin
09.03.96 Steve McGovern W PTS 4 Millstreet
28.05.96 John Stovin W RSC 2 Belfast
03.09.96 Kevin McKillan W RTD 4 Belfast
05.11.96 Shaun Stokes W RSC 2 Belfast
28.01.97 Karl Taylor W PTS 6 Belfast
03.03.97 Troy Townsend W RSC 1 Austin, Texas, USA
28.03.97 Teddy Reid L PTS 6 Boston, Mass, USA
29.04.97 Peter Nightingale W RTD 2 Belfast
02.06.97 Kevin McKillan W RSC 3 Belfast
(Elim. All-Ireland L. Welterweight Title)
14.02.98 Dennis Griffin W RSC 2 Southwark
26.09.98 Allan Hall W RSC 7 York
30.11.98 Paul Burke L PTS 12 Manchester
(Vacant Commonwealth L. Welterweight Title)
22.05.99 Alan Temple W CO 3 Belfast
10.07.99 Karl Taylor W RTD 3 Southwark
13.09.99 Paul Burke W RSC 6 Bethnal Green
(Commonwealth L. Welterweight Title Challenge)
16.10.99 Radoslav Gaidev W RSC 1 Belfast

04.03.00 Joseph Miyumo W RSC 1 Peterborough
(Commonwealth L. Welterweight Title Defence)
29.04.00 David Kirk W RSC 8 Wembley
16.09.00 Pavel Melnikov W PTS 8 Bethnal Green
11.11.00 Shea Neary W PTS 12 Belfast
(Commonwealth L. Welterweight Title Defence)
13.03.01 Alan Bosworth W RSC 5 Plymouth
12.05.01 Harrison Methula W RSC 7 Plymouth
(Commonwealth L. Welterweight Title Defence)
27.10.01 Matthews Zulu W PTS 12 Manchester
(Commonwealth L.Welterweight Title Defence)
09.02.02 Jonathan Thaxton W RSC 6 Manchester
(Commonwealth L. Welterweight Title Defence)
01.06.02 Ricky Hatton L PTS 12 Manchester
(WBU L. Welterweight Title Challenge)
28.09.02 Alan Bosworth W RSC 5 Manchester
14.06.03 Otkay Urkal L PTS 12 Magdeburg, Germany
(European L.Welterweight Title Challenge)
06.12.03 Jimmy Vincent W PTS 12 Cardiff
(Vacant WBU Welterweight Title)
18.03.05 Allan Vester W RSC 3 Belfast
(WBU Welterweight Title Defence)
20.05.06 Takaloo L PTS 12 Belfast
(WBU Welterweight Title Defence)
Career: 31 contests, won 26, lost 5.

(Jasim) Jas Malik

Wandsworth. *Born* Cardiff, 4 April, 1973
Welterweight. Ht. 5'11½"
Manager Self

05.03.00 Steve Sharples W RSC 1 Shaw
04.07.00 Dave Travers W PTS 6 Tooting
30.11.00 Jimmy Phelan L RSC 4 Bloomsbury
29.03.01 Darren Melville L RSC 1 Hammersmith
26.09.02 Ben Hudson L CO 3 Fulham
01.08.03 Pete Buckley L PTS 4 Bethnal Green
24.10.03 Lance Hall L RSC 1 Bethnal Green
12.11.04 James Gorman L RTD 2 Belfast
10.09.05 Barrie Jones L RSC 1 Cardiff
Career: 9 contests, won 2, lost 7.

Dean Marcantonio (Springate)

Eltham. *Born* Isle of Sheppey, 8 August, 1976
L.Middleweight. Ht. 5'5"
Manager M. Roe

26.02.06 Dave Wakefield L RSC 3 Dagenham
Career: 1 contest, lost 1.

Matthew Marsh

West Ham. *Born* Sidcup, 1 August, 1982
Featherweight. Ht. 5'5¾"
Manager F. Warren/F. Maloney

10.09.04 Fred Janes W PTS 4 Bethnal Green
19.11.04 Dean Ward W PTS 4 Bethnal Green
11.12.04 Abdul Mougharbel W PTS 4 Canning Town
25.02.05 Dai Davies W PTS 4 Wembley
10.12.05 Darren Cleary W PTS 4 Canning Town
29.06.06 Frederic Gosset W PTS 6 Bethnal Green
Career: 6 contests, won 6.

Matthew Marsh   Philip Sharkey

John Marshall

Glossop. *Born* Australia, 28 May, 1975
L.Middleweight. Ht. 5'6"
Manager Self

07.09.01	Dave Stewart L PTS 6 Glasgow
23.12.01	Arv Mittoo W RSC 1 Salford
21.01.02	Gary Hamilton W PTS 4 Glasgow
17.02.02	Joel Viney W RSC 6 Salford
31.05.02	Tony Montana W PTS 6 Hull
21.07.02	Daniel Thorpe W RSC 1 Salford
02.11.02	Mark Winters L RSC 5 Belfast
28.04.03	Young Muttley L RSC 5 Nottingham
18.09.03	Ross Minter DREW 6 Dagenham
09.12.04	Tony Montana L PTS 4 Stockport
19.12.04	Martin Marshall W CO 5 Bolton
22.04.05	Robert Burton W RTD 4 Barnsley
12.05.05	Danny Moir W RSC 5 Sunderland
08.07.05	Zoltan Surman W RSC 3 Altrincham

Career: 14 contests, won 9, drew 1, lost 4.

Martin Marshall

Sunderland. *Born* Sunderland, 28 January, 1983
Middleweight. Ht. 6'1"
Manager T. Conroy

14.05.04	Richard Mazurek DREW 6 Sunderland
23.09.04	Richard Inquieti W PTS 6 Gateshead
28.10.04	Richard Inquieti W PTS 6 Sunderland
09.12.04	Gary Porter L PTS 6 Sunderland
19.12.04	John Marshall L CO 5 Bolton
12.05.05	Muhsen Nasser L PTS 6 Sunderland
27.05.05	Gary Porter L PTS 6 Motherwell
11.06.05	Keith Ellwood W PTS 6 Kirkcaldy
06.10.05	Alex Stoda W PTS 6 Sunderland
03.11.05	Malik Khan W PTS 6 Sunderland
08.12.05	Brendan Halford L RSC 5 Sunderland
09.03.06	Omar Gumati DREW 6 Sunderland

Career: 12 contests, won 5, drew 2, lost 5.

Neil Marston

Shrewsbury. *Born* Shrewsbury, 8 February, 1977
Featherweight. Ht. 5'7"
Manager E. Johnson

08.07.04	Dai Davies L PTS 6 Birmingham
12.09.04	Paddy Folan W PTS 6 Shrewsbury
18.11.04	Paddy Folan W PTS 6 Shrewsbury
06.12.04	Paddy Folan W PTS 6 Bradford
28.01.05	Scott Flynn L RSC 2 Renfrew
15.04.05	Craig Bromley L RSC 1 Shrewsbury
23.05.05	Wayne Bloy L PTS 6 Cleethorpes
19.09.05	Sandy Bartlett L PTS 6 Glasgow
13.11.05	Robert Nelson L PTS 6 Leeds
24.02.06	Shaun Doherty W PTS 6 Birmingham
04.03.06	Darren Cleary L PTS 4 Manchester
14.04.06	Neil Read W PTS 6 Telford
21.04.06	Jamie McDonnell L PTS 4 Doncaster
14.05.06	Pete Walkman W RSC 6 Derby
26.05.06	Mo Khaled W DIS 5 Hull
05.06.06	John Bothwell L PTS 6 Glasgow
29.06.06	Eugene Heagney L PTS 6 Dudley

Career: 17 contests, won 7, lost 10.

Shanee Martin

Colchester. *Born* Dagenham, 31 January, 1982
Bantamweight. Ht. 5'2"
Manager Self

16.10.04	Iliana Boneva W RSC 4 Dagenham
05.03.05	Svetla Taskova W PTS 6 Dagenham
18.09.05	Albena Atseva W RSC 3 Bethnal Green
19.11.05	Valerie Rangeard W PTS 6 Southwark
26.02.06	Maya Frenzel W RSC 5 Dagenham

Career: 5 contests, won 5.

Ali Mateen

Sheffield. *Born* Sheffield, 2 June, 1986
L.Middleweight. Ht. 5'11¹/₂"
Manager J. Ingle

15.11.04	Keith Ellwood W PTS 6 Glasgow
26.11.04	Glen Matsell L RTD 3 Hull
06.03.05	Rob MacDonald W PTS 6 Shaw
15.12.05	Richard Mazurek L PTS 6 Coventry
26.05.06	Jimi Hendricks W CO 2 Hull

Career: 5 contests, won 3, lost 2.

Derry Matthews

Liverpool. *Born* Liverpool, 23 September, 1983
English Featherweight Champion. Ht. 5'8¹/₂"
Manager F. Warren/S. Vaughan

18.01.03	Sergei Tasimov W CO 1 Preston
05.04.03	Jus Wallie W PTS 4 Manchester
08.05.03	Steve Gethin W RSC 3 Widnes
20.06.03	Henry Janes W RSC 1 Liverpool
29.08.03	Marty Kayes W RTD 2 Liverpool
02.10.03	Alexei Volchan W RSC 2 Liverpool
13.12.03	Pete Buckley W PTS 4 Manchester
26.02.04	Gareth Payne W RSC 4 Widnes
03.04.04	Henry Janes W PTS 4 Manchester
10.09.04	Buster Dennis W PTS 6 Liverpool
17.12.04	Dean Ward W RSC 1 Liverpool
13.05.05	John Mackay W PTS 6 Liverpool
16.07.05	Dai Davies W RSC 2 Bolton
25.10.05	Frederic Bonifai W PTS 6 Preston
28.01.06	Stephen Chinnock W RTD 6 Nottingham
	(Vacant English Featherweight Title)
01.06.06	Mickey Coveney W PTS 8 Barnsley

Career: 16 contests, won 16.

(Steven) Tiger Matthews

Liverpool. *Born* Liverpool, 1 April, 1981
Welterweight. Ht. 5'9¹/₂"
Manager S. Vaughan

10.09.04	Pete Buckley W PTS 4 Liverpool
13.05.05	Dave Hinds W CO 1 Liverpool
01.10.05	Dennis Corpe W PTS 4 Wigan

Career: 3 contests, won 3.

Alex Matvienko

Bolton. *Born* Bolton, 9 May, 1978
Middleweight. Ht. 5'11"
Manager S. Wood

18.12.05	Tommy Jones W PTS 6 Bolton
02.04.06	Tony Randell W PTS 6 Shaw

Career: 2 contests, won 2.

Patrick J. Maxwell

Sheffield. *Born* USA, 20 March, 1979
Middleweight. Ht. 5'8"
Manager Self

17.03.98	Danny Thornton W PTS 6 Sheffield
12.08.00	Matthew Ashmole W RSC 3 Wembley
26.03.01	Jason Collins L PTS 4 Wembley
27.10.01	Prince Kasi Kaihau W CO 4 Manchester
09.02.02	Leigh Wicks W PTS 4 Manchester
09.03.03	Surinder Sekhon W RSC 1 Shaw
10.06.03	Andy Halder W RSC 1 Sheffield
05.09.03	Isidro Gonzalez W RSC 8 Sheffield
07.11.03	Conroy McIntosh W RSC 4 Sheffield
17.06.04	Howard Clarke W RSC 1 Sheffield
21.09.05	Conroy McIntosh W RSC 2 Bradford

Career: 11 contests, won 10, lost 1.

Anthony Maynard

Birmingham. *Born* Birmingham, 12 January, 1972
L.Welterweight. Former Undefeated Midlands Area Lightweight Champion. Ht. 5'8"
Manager Self

17.10.94	Malcolm Thomas W PTS 6 Birmingham
02.11.94	Dean Phillips W PTS 6 Birmingham
25.01.95	Neil Smith L PTS 6 Stoke
07.02.95	Anthony Campbell W PTS 8 Wolverhampton
08.03.95	Scott Walker W PTS 6 Solihull
28.03.95	Kid McAuley W PTS 8 Wolverhampton
11.05.95	Gary Hiscox W RSC 4 Dudley
06.06.95	Richard Swallow L RSC 2 Leicester
02.10.95	Jay Mahoney W PTS 8 Birmingham
26.10.95	Ray Newby W PTS 8 Birmingham
17.01.96	Tom Welsh W RSC 8 Solihull
06.03.96	G. G. Goddard W RSC 3 Solihull
20.03.97	Richard Swallow W PTS 6 Solihull
24.10.97	Brian Coleman W CO 1 Birmingham
27.03.98	Gary Flear W RSC 9 Telford
	(Vacant Midlands Area Lightweight Title)
30.05.98	Michael Ayers W PTS 8 Bristol
21.11.98	Stephen Smith L PTS 10 Southwark
27.11.00	David Kehoe W RSC 5 Birmingham
07.04.01	Alfred Kotey L RTD 6 Wembley
	(Vacant WBF Inter-Continental Lightweight Title)
11.06.01	Woody Greenaway W PTS 4 Nottingham

08.10.01	Bobby Vanzie L RSC 1 Barnsley	

08.10.01 Bobby Vanzie L RSC 1 Barnsley
(British Lightweight Title Challenge)
09.03.02 David Burke L PTS 6 Manchester
09.11.02 Chris Barnett W PTS 6 Altrincham
08.02.03 Gary Hibbert DREW 6 Liverpool
18.10.03 Gary Hibbert L PTS 6 Manchester
07.02.04 Danny Hunt L PTS 10 Bethnal Green
(English Lightweight Title Challenge)
07.04.05 Tony Montana W PTS 4 Birmingham
23.06.06 Daniel Thorpe W PTS 4 Birmingham
Career: 28 contests, won 19, drew 1, lost 8.

Richard Mazurek

Leamington. *Born* Leamington, 20 January, 1977
Middleweight. Ht. 5'10"
Manager Self

15.11.03 Neil Addis W PTS 6 Coventry
21.02.04 Simon Hopkins W RSC 3 Brighton
01.05.04 Brian Coleman W PTS 6 Coventry
14.05.04 Martin Marshall DREW 6 Sunderland
10.07.04 Richard Inquieti W RSC 1 Coventry
20.11.04 David Payne W PTS 6 Coventry
18.06.05 Ernie Smith L PTS 6 Coventry
09.09.05 Jozsef Matolcsi L PTS 6 Sheffield
22.10.05 Robert Burton L PTS 6 Coventry
18.11.05 George Hillyard L PTS 6 Dagenham
15.12.05 Ali Mateen W PTS 6 Coventry
20.01.06 Darren Barker L PTS 8 Bethnal Green
04.03.06 Tommy Jones W PTS 6 Coventry
28.04.06 Franny Jones L PTS 6 Hartlepool
Career: 14 contests, won 7, drew 1, lost 6.

Lee Meager

Salford. *Born* Salford, 18 January, 1978
British Lightweight Champion. Ht. 5'8"
Manager Self

16.09.00 Pete Buckley W PTS 4 Bethnal Green
14.10.00 Chris Jickells W PTS 4 Wembley
18.11.00 Billy Smith W RSC 1 Dagenham
09.12.00 Jason Nesbitt W RSC 2 Southwark
05.02.01 Carl Allen DREW 6 Hull
13.03.01 Lennie Hodgkins W RSC 3 Plymouth
12.05.01 Jason White W PTS 4 Plymouth
31.07.01 Steve Hanley W PTS 6 Bethnal Green
13.09.01 Arv Mittoo W PTS 6 Sheffield
16.03.02 Jason Nesbitt W PTS 6 Bethnal Green
10.05.02 Pete Buckley W PTS 6 Bethnal Green
25.10.02 Iain Eldridge W RSC 5 Bethnal Green
21.12.02 Chill John W RSC 5 Dagenham
28.01.03 Carl Allen W PTS 8 Nottingham
28.11.03 Pete Buckley W PTS 4 Derby
11.12.03 Charles Shepherd W RTD 7 Bethnal Green
02.06.04 Michael Muya W PTS 8 Nottingham
19.11.04 Danny Hunt L PTS 10 Bethnal Green
(English Lightweight Title Challenge)
09.07.05 Martin Watson W PTS 10 Nottingham
02.12.05 Tony Montana W PTS 8 Nottingham
17.02.06 Ben Hudson W PTS 4 Bethnal Green
12.05.06 Dave Stewart W RSC 6 Bethnal Green
(Vacant British Lightweight Title)
Career: 22 contests, won 20, drew 1, lost 1.

Michael Medor

London. *Born* Mauritius, 23 May, 1982
L.Welterweight. Ht. 5'10¾"
Manager C. Sanigar

16.09.05 Imad Khamis W PTS 4 Plymouth

16.10.05 Jason Nesbitt W PTS 6 Peterborough
25.11.05 Martin Gethin L PTS 4 Walsall
Career: 3 contests, won 2, lost 1.

Judex Meemea

Walthamstow. *Born* Mauritius, 24 November, 1973
L.Welterweight. Ht. 5'10"
Manager C. Sanigar

21.02.04 Jay Morris DREW 4 Brighton
08.06.04 Tyrone McInerney DREW 6 Sheffield
27.09.04 Scott Haywood L PTS 6 Cleethorpes
20.11.04 Joe McCluskey DREW 6 Coventry
26.03.05 Ashley Theophane W PTS 6 Hackney
02.06.05 Andy Cosnett W PTS 6 Peterborough
18.06.05 Gwyn Wale L RSC 5 Barnsley
24.07.05 Bheki Moyo W PTS 4 Leicester Square
16.09.05 Michael Grant L RSC 3 Plymouth
21.10.05 Dave Stewart L PTS 6 Bethnal Green
12.05.05 Billy Smith W PTS 6 Peterborough
07.04.06 Garry Buckland L RSC 5 Bristol
15.06.06 Lea Handley W PTS 6 Peterborough
Career: 13 contests, won 5, drew 3, lost 5.

Delroy Mellis

Brixton. *Born* Jamaica, 7 January, 1971
L. Middleweight. Former Undefeated
Southern Area L. Middleweight Champion.
Ht. 5'8"
Manager B. Baker

27.02.98 Pat Larner L PTS 4 Brighton
16.04.98 Sonny Thind L RTD 5 Mayfair
09.06.98 Darren Christie L PTS 4 Hull
10.09.98 Paul Miles W RSC 3 Acton
03.10.98 Wayne Asker L PTS 6 Crawley
06.11.98 Darren Bruce L RTD 3 Mayfair
21.01.99 Darren Christie L PTS 6 Piccadilly
04.02.99 Sergei Dzindziruk L RSC 3 Lewisham
24.03.99 Martyn Thomas W RSC 3 Bayswater
20.05.99 Daniel James L PTS 4 Barking
02.07.99 Jason Williams L PTS 6 Bristol
30.09.99 Steve Brumant L PTS 6 Kensington
16.10.99 Jacek Bielski L PTS 4 Bethnal Green
18.11.99 Dennis Griffin W RSC 5 Mayfair
29.11.99 George Scott L PTS 6 Wembley
20.03.00 Lance Crosby L PTS 4 Mansfield
01.04.00 Paul Knights W PTS 4 Bethnal Green
15.05.00 Christian Brady W RSC 6 Birmingham
01.07.00 Cham Joof DREW 6 Southwark
22.07.00 Alan Gilbert W RSC 3 Watford
(Vacant Southern Area L.Middleweight Title)
22.10.00 Allan Gray W RSC 6 Streatham
(Southern Area L.Middleweight Title Defence)
23.01.01 Alan Gilbert W RSC 3 Crawley
(Southern Area L. Middleweight Title Defence)
20.04.01 Chris Nembhard W RSC 8 Millwall
(Southern Area L. Middleweight Title Defence)
07.09.01 Jason Collins L DIS 5 Bethnal Green
06.10.01 Michael Jones L PTS 8 Manchester
13.12.01 Ossie Duran L PTS 10 Leicester Square
(WBF European Welterweight Title Challenge)
01.06.02 Thomas McDonagh L PTS 4 Manchester
15.06.02 Chardan Ansoula L RTD 4 Tottenham
07.09.02 Jamie Moore L CO 6 Liverpool
06.12.03 Wayne Alexander W RSC 8 Cardiff

16.04.04 Gilbert Eastman L RSC 5 Bradford
(Southern Area L.Middleweight Title Challenge)
11.12.04 Wayne Alexander L PTS 10 Canning Town
23.03.05 Ernie Smith W PTS 6 Leicester Square
23.07.05 Takaloo L PTS 8 Edinburgh
07.10.05 Gary Woolcombe L RTD 8 Bethnal Green
(Vacant British Masters L.Middleweight Title)
Career: 35 contests, won 11, drew 1, lost 23.

Dale Miles

Alfreton. *Born* Mansfield, 19 November, 1984
Welterweight. Ht. 5'11"
Manager S. Calow

13.05.06 Karl Taylor W RSC 3 Sutton in Ashfield
Career: 1 contest, won 1.

Oscar Milkitas

Canning Town. *Born* Lithuania, 24 December, 1972
L.Middleweight. Ht. 5'8"
Manager M. Roe

07.06.00 Ciro Canales W PTS 4 Miami, Florida, USA
21.07.00 Andre Cody W CO 1 Miami, Florida, USA
16.08.00 Elvin Peluyera W PTS 4 Davie, Florida, USA
20.09.00 Hamilton Verano W PTS 4 Davie, Florida, USA
19.12.04 Gareth Couch L PTS 6 Bethnal Green
19.02.05 Francis Barrett L PTS 6 Dublin
14.05.05 Darren Melville L PTS 6 Dublin
17.06.05 Paul McCloskey L PTS 4 Glasgow
01.07.05 Arv Mittoo W PTS 6 Fulham
18.09.05 Ashley Theophane W PTS 4 Bethnal Green
14.10.05 James Hare L RTD 5 Huddersfield
10.12.05 Souleymane M'baye L RSC 6 Canning Town
18.02.06 Gary Young L PTS 8 Edinburgh
30.03.06 Peter Dunn W PTS 6 Bloomsbury
Career: 14 contests, won 7, lost 7.

Ian Millarvie

Hamilton. *Born* Bellshill, 7 April, 1980
Heavyweight. Ht. 6'5¾"
Manager T. Gilmour

31.01.05 Mal Rice W RTD 3 Glasgow
21.02.05 Luke Simpkin W PTS 6 Glasgow
27.05.05 Sergey Voron W RSC 1 Motherwell
17.03.06 Jason Callum W CO 3 Kirkcaldy
Career: 4 contests, won 4.

(Wesley) Wez Miller

Doncaster. *Born* Doncaster, 24 April, 1986
Lightweight. Ht. 5'8"
Manager J. Rushton

03.03.06 Gavin Deacon W PTS 4 Doncaster
21.04.06 Kristian Laight L PTS 6 Doncaster
09.06.06 Pete Buckley W PTS 6 Doncaster
Career: 3 contests, won 2, lost 1.

Ross Minter

Crawley. *Born* Crawley, 10 November, 1978
Welterweight. Former Undefeated Southern
Area & English Welterweight Champion.
Ht. 5'7¾"
Manager Self

26.03.01	Brian Coleman W PTS 4 Wembley
05.05.01	Trevor Smith W RTD 3 Edmonton
28.07.01	Lee Williamson W PTS 4 Wembley
24.11.01	Karl Taylor W PTS 4 Bethnal Green
15.12.01	Ernie Smith W RSC 2 Wembley
02.03.02	Paul Denton W PTS 6 Bethnal Green
25.05.02	Howard Clarke L RSC 2 Portsmouth
12.10.02	Dafydd Carlin W RSC 1 Bethnal Green
15.02.03	Karl Taylor W PTS 6 Wembley
29.03.03	Jay Mahoney W RSC 2 Portsmouth
24.05.03	Jay Mahoney W PTS 6 Bethnal Green
18.09.03	John Marshall DREW 6 Dagenham
19.11.04	David Kirk W PTS 6 Bethnal Green
25.02.05	Ernie Smith W PTS 4 Wembley
29.04.05	Chas Symonds W RSC 3 Southwark
	(Southern Area Welterweight Title Challenge)
23.09.05	Sammy Smith W RSC 3 Mayfair
	(Southern Area Welterweight Title Defence)
10.12.05	Brett James W RSC 4 Canning Town
	(Vacant English Welterweight Title. Southern Area Welterweight Title Defence)

Career: 17 contests, won 15, drew 1, lost 1.

Joe Mitchell

Birmingham. *Born* Birmingham, 8
February, 1971
Middleweight. Ht. 5'9"
Manager Self

20.02.04	Steve Scott W PTS 6 Doncaster
07.04.04	Robert Lloyd-Taylor L RSC 5 Leicester Square
08.07.04	Darren Gethin DREW 6 Birmingham
12.09.04	Darren Gethin L PTS 6 Shrewsbury
05.10.04	Mark Wall DREW 6 Dudley
22.10.04	Dennis Corpe W PTS 6 Mansfield
25.11.04	Ernie Smith L PTS 6 Birmingham
04.02.05	Jon Harrison L PTS 6 Plymouth
18.04.05	Darren Gethin L PTS 6 Bradford
18.06.05	Scott Conway W RSC 5 Barnsley
08.07.05	Johnny Hussey L PTS 4 Altrincham
16.09.05	Gary Round L PTS 6 Telford
10.10.05	Peter Dunn W PTS 6 Birmingham
30.10.05	Lee Edwards W RSC 2 Sheffield
12.11.05	David Kirk L PTS 6 Sheffield
02.12.05	Jason Rushton L PTS 6 Doncaster
24.02.06	Ernie Smith W PTS 6 Birmingham
23.04.06	Omar Gumati L PTS 4 Chester
01.06.06	Kerry Hope L PTS 4 Barnsley
23.06.06	Dave Wakefield L PTS 6 Birmingham

Career: 20 contests, won 6, drew 2, lost 12.

Kevin Mitchell

Dagenham. *Born* Dagenham, 29 October,
1984
IBF Inter-Continental S.Featherweight
Champion. Ht. 5'8"
Manager F. Warren

17.07.03	Stevie Quinn W CO 1 Dagenham
18.09.03	Csabi Ladanyi W RSC 1 Dagenham
06.11.03	Vlado Varhegyi W RSC 3 Dagenham
24.01.04	Jaz Virdee W RSC 1 Wembley

07.02.04	Kristian Laight W PTS 4 Bethnal Green
24.04.04	Eric Patrac W RSC 1 Reading
13.05.04	Slimane Kebaili W RSC 1 Bethnal Green
05.06.04	Jason Nesbitt W RSC 3 Bethnal Green
10.09.04	Arpad Toth W RSC 3 Bethnal Green
22.10.04	Mounir Guebbas W PTS 6 Edinburgh
19.11.04	Alain Rakow W CO 1 Bethnal Green
11.12.04	Henry Janes W PTS 4 Canning Town
08.04.05	Frederic Bonifai W PTS 6 Edinburgh
29.04.05	Karim Chakim W PTS 8 Southwark
23.09.05	Wladimir Borov W RSC 2 Mayfair
25.10.05	Daniel Thorpe W RSC 4 Preston
10.12.05	Mohammed Medjadji W RSC 6 Canning Town
	(Vacant IBF Inter-Continental S.Featherweight Title)
25.02.06	Youssef Djibaba W PTS 12 Canning Town
	(IBF Inter-Continental S.Featherweight Title Defence)
13.05.06	Kirkor Kirkorov W RTD 2 Bethnal Green
	(IBF Inter-Continental S.Featherweight Title Defence)

Career: 19 contests, won 19.

Kevin Mitchell   Les Clark

Stewart Mitchell

Doncaster. *Born* Forfar, 27 April, 1976
Cruiserweight. Ht. 6'0½"
Manager J. Rushton

03.03.06	Lee Mountford W PTS 4 Doncaster
21.04.06	Clint Johnson W PTS 4 Doncaster

Career: 2 contests, won 2.

(Arvill) Arv Mittoo

Birmingham. *Born* Birmingham, 8 July,
1971
Middleweight. Ht. 5'8"
Manager Self

31.01.96	Alan Bosworth L PTS 6 Stoke
13.02.96	Tommy Janes L PTS 6 Cardiff
21.02.96	Danny Lutaaya L PTS 6 Piccadilly
20.05.96	Terry Whittaker L CO 5 Cleethorpes
29.06.96	Craig Stanley L PTS 4 Erith
23.09.96	Thomas Bradley DREW 6 Cleethorpes
03.10.96	John T. Kelly L PTS 6 Sunderland

01.11.96	David Kirk L PTS 6 Mansfield
14.11.96	Thomas Bradley L RSC 4 Sheffield
22.05.97	Craig Stanley W RSC 3 Southwark
02.09.97	Trevor Tacy L PTS 6 Manchester
22.09.97	Steve Conway L PTS 6 Cleethorpes
09.10.97	Steve Conway L PTS 6 Leeds
23.10.97	Marco Fattore W PTS 6 Mayfair
11.11.97	Kevin McCarthy L PTS 6 Bethnal Green
03.12.97	Marc Smith W PTS 6 Stoke
31.01.98	Harry Andrews L PTS 4 Edmonton
06.03.98	Gavin McGill W PTS 6 Hull
18.03.98	Marc Smith W PTS 6 Stoke
26.03.98	Danny Lutaaya DREW 6 Piccadilly
11.04.98	Charlie Rumbol L PTS 4 Southwark
21.04.98	Adam Spelling W PTS 4 Edmonton
02.10.98	Sammy Smith L PTS 4 Cheshunt
16.10.98	Mark Haslam L PTS 6 Salford
25.11.98	Brian Coleman L PTS 6 Clydach
27.01.99	Ernie Smith DREW 6 Stoke
26.02.99	Mark Payne L PTS 4 Coventry
17.03.99	Marc Smith L PTS 6 Stoke
20.05.99	John Humphrey L PTS 6 Barking
28.05.99	Jamie McKeever L PTS 6 Liverpool
04.06.99	Oscar Hall L PTS 6 Hull
02.07.99	Wahid Fats L PTS 6 Manchester
21.07.99	Brian Gentry L RSC 4 Bloomsbury
20.10.99	Steve Saville L PTS 8 Stoke
31.10.99	Ross McCord L PTS 6 Raynes Park
15.11.99	Lee Sharp L PTS 6 Glasgow
22.11.99	Mohamed Helel L PTS 6 Piccadilly
29.11.99	Peter Swinney L PTS 4 Wembley
11.12.99	Thomas McDonagh L RSC 2 Liverpool
12.02.00	Mally McIver L PTS 4 Sheffield
10.03.00	Jason Hall W RSC 3 Bethnal Green
08.04.00	Junior Witter L PTS 4 Bethnal Green
17.04.00	Gavin Pearson L PTS 6 Glasgow
13.05.00	Chris Steele W RSC 3 Barnsley
21.05.00	Gavin Down L PTS 6 Derby
06.06.00	Casey Brooke W PTS 6 Brierley Hill
15.07.00	Steve Conway L PTS 6 Norwich
30.09.00	Mark Florian L PTS 4 Peterborough
07.10.00	Jesse James Daniel L PTS 4 Doncaster
16.11.00	Lance Crosby L RSC 3 Hull
28.01.01	Stuart Elwell L PTS 6 Wolverhampton
19.02.01	Lee Sharp L PTS 6 Glasgow
26.02.01	Gavin Wake L PTS 4 Nottingham
24.03.01	Richard Holden L PTS 6 Newark
01.04.01	Babatunde Ajayi L PTS 6 Southwark
20.04.01	Manzo Smith L PTS 4 Millwall
08.05.01	Robert Burton L PTS 4 Barnsley
04.06.01	Gary Porter L PTS 6 Glasgow
16.06.01	Gavin Down L PTS 6 Derby
14.07.01	Lee Byrne L PTS 4 Wembley
13.09.01	Lee Meager L PTS 6 Sheffield
23.09.01	Anthony Christopher DREW 6 Shaw
28.10.01	Peter Swinney L PTS 4 Southwark
16.11.01	Terry Ham L PTS 6 Preston
10.12.01	Lee Armstrong L PTS 6 Bradford
23.12.01	John Marshall L RSC 1 Salford
15.04.02	Chris Duggan L PTS 6 Shrewsbury
28.04.02	Peter McDonagh L PTS 6 Southwark
10.05.02	Oscar Hall L PTS 4 Bethnal Green
15.06.02	Chris Saunders L PTS 6 Norwich
23.06.02	Mark Stupple L PTS 6 Southwark
17.09.02	Gwyn Wale L PTS 6 Bethnal Green
05.10.02	Dean Lambert L PTS 4 Huddersfield
17.11.02	Lee McAllister L PTS 6 Bradford
30.11.02	Richard Swallow L PTS 4 Coventry
08.12.02	Elvis Mbwakongo L PTS 6 Bethnal Green
20.12.02	Nathan Ward L PTS 6 Bracknell
23.02.03	Adnan Amar L PTS 6 Shrewsbury

16.03.03	Jonathan Woollins L PTS 4 Nottingham	
08.04.03	Justin Hudson L PTS 4 Bethnal Green	
28.04.03	Barry Morrison L RSC 3 Nottingham	
03.06.03	Chas Symonds L PTS 6 Bethnal Green	
13.06.03	Gary Steadman L PTS 4 Queensway	
22.07.03	Gary Woolcombe L PTS 6 Bethnal Green	
01.08.03	Mark Alexander L PTS 4 Bethnal Green	
26.10.03	Robert Lloyd-Taylor L PTS 6 Longford	
23.11.03	Scott Haywood L PTS 6 Rotherham	
21.02.04	Steve Russell L PTS 6 Norwich	
06.03.04	Colin McNeil L PTS 4 Renfrew	
27.03.04	Barrie Lee L PTS 4 Edinburgh	
16.04.04	Nadeem Siddique L PTS 6 Bradford	
19.06.04	Ashley Theophane L PTS 4 Muswell Hill	
03.07.04	Tommy Marshall L PTS 6 Bristol	
29.10.04	Gary Connolly W RSC 5 Worksop	
08.12.04	Sammy Smith L PTS 6 Longford	
17.12.04	Jamie Coyle L RSC 5 Huddersfield	
26.02.05	Jonjo Finnegan L PTS 4 Burton	
01.07.05	Oscar Milkitas L PTS 6 Fulham	
09.07.05	Danny Gwilym L RSC 4 Bristol	
03.09.05	Steve Russell DREW 6 Norwich	

Career: 100 contests, won 10, drew 5, lost 85.

(Qais) Mo (Ariya)

Sheffield. *Born* Kabul, Afghanistan, 15 February, 1979
Middleweight. Ht. 5'9"
Manager Self

12.07.02	Danny Gwilym L PTS 6 Southampton	
27.09.02	Freddie Yemofio W PTS 4 Bracknell	
09.05.03	Freddie Yemofio W PTS 4 Longford	
12.10.03	Danny Gwilym W PTS 6 Sheffield	
10.02.04	Danny Thornton L PTS 6 Barnsley	
28.10.04	Eddie Haley DREW 6 Sunderland	
20.02.05	Dean Walker L PTS 6 Sheffield	
28.02.06	Ady Clegg L PTS 6 Leeds	

Career: 8 contests, won 3, drew 1, lost 4.

Colin Moffett

Belfast. *Born* Belfast, 15 April, 1975
Bantamweight. Ht. 5'6"
Manager Self

05.11.96	Shane Mallon W RSC 2 Belfast	
28.01.97	Anthony Hanna W PTS 4 Belfast	
29.04.97	Gary Hickman W PTS 4 Belfast	
02.06.97	Jason Thomas L RSC 3 Belfast	
20.12.97	Graham McGrath DREW 4 Belfast	
18.09.98	Anthony Hanna DREW 4 Belfast	
28.11.98	Shaun Norman W PTS 4 Belfast	
31.07.99	Waj Khan W CO 1 Carlisle	
16.10.99	Delroy Spencer L PTS 4 Bethnal Green	
31.03.00	Steffen Norskov L PTS 4 Esbjerg, Denmark	
05.06.00	Keith Knox L RSC 3 Glasgow	
02.12.00	Dale Robinson L PTS 4 Bethnal Green	
15.09.01	Chris Emanuele L RSC 4 Nottingham	
27.04.02	Levi Pattison L RSC 2 Huddersfield	
27.07.02	Jim Betts L RSC 3 Nottingham	
30.10.03	John Bothwell DREW 4 Belfast	
08.05.04	Lee Haskins L RSC 2 Bristol	
19.06.04	Michael Crossan DREW 4 Renfrew	
28.10.04	Chris Edwards W PTS 4 Belfast	
20.05.06	Delroy Spencer W PTS 4 Belfast	

Career: 20 contests, won 7, drew 4, lost 9.

Danny Moir

Gateshead. *Born* Gateshead, 21 January, 1972
L.Middleweight. Former British Masters L.Middleweight Champion. Ht. 5'11"
Manager Self

04.10.01	Richard Inquieti W PTS 6 Sunderland	
20.10.01	Lee Minter W RSC 1 Portsmouth	
06.12.01	Gary Jones W PTS 6 Sunderland	
08.02.02	Colin McCash W RSC 3 Preston	
08.03.02	Martyn Bailey L PTS 6 Ellesmere Port	
25.03.02	Gavin Pearson L PTS 6 Sunderland	
03.10.02	Andy Gibson L RTD 4 Sunderland	
22.12.02	Richard Inquieti W RTD 3 Salford	
20.01.03	Gary Porter W PTS 6 Glasgow	
27.02.03	Franny Jones DREW 6 Sunderland	
17.03.03	Ciaran Duffy L PTS 6 Glasgow	
29.05.03	Eugenio Monteiro L PTS 6 Sunderland	
09.06.03	Danny Parkinson L PTS 6 Bradford	
02.10.03	Omar Gumati W PTS 6 Sunderland	
20.10.03	Craig Dickson L RSC 3 Glasgow	
04.12.03	Wayne Shepherd W PTS 6 Sunderland	
21.12.03	Geraint Harvey W PTS 6 Bolton	
05.03.04	Franny Jones NC 3 Darlington *(Vacant Northern Area L.Middleweight Title)*	
12.03.04	Gary Porter DREW 6 Irvine	
25.03.04	Kevin Phelan W PTS 10 Longford *(Vacant British Masters L.Middleweight Title)*	
27.05.04	Kevin Anderson L RSC 1 Huddersfield	
23.09.04	Kevin Phelan L RTD 3 Gateshead *(British Masters L.Middleweight Title Defence)*	
12.11.04	David Walker L RSC 5 Wembley	
24.02.05	Gary Porter W PTS 6 Sunderland	
04.03.05	Kevin Bennett L RSC 3 Hartlepool	
12.05.05	John Marshall L RSC 5 Sunderland	
21.09.05	Peter Dunn W PTS 6 Bradford	
20.11.05	Mark Thompson L RSC 2 Shaw	
19.12.05	Kevin Phelan L CO 4 Longford	

Career: 29 contests, won 12, drew 2, lost 14, no contest 1.

Michael Monaghan

Lincoln. *Born* Nottingham, 31 May, 1976
Middleweight. Ht. 5'10¾"
Manager Self

23.09.96	Lee Simpkin W PTS 6 Cleethorpes	
24.10.96	Lee Bird W RSC 6 Lincoln	
09.12.96	Lee Simpkin W PTS 6 Chesterfield	
16.12.96	Carlton Williams W PTS 6 Cleethorpes	
20.03.97	Paul Miles W PTS 6 Newark	
26.04.97	Paul Ryan L RSC 2 Swadlincote	
05.07.97	Ali Khattab W PTS 4 Glasgow	
18.08.97	Trevor Meikle W PTS 6 Nottingham	
12.09.97	Willie Quinn L PTS 6 Glasgow	
19.09.97	Roy Chipperfield W PTS 6 Salford	
30.09.97	George Richards L PTS 6 Edgbaston	
10.03.98	Anthony van Niekirk L RTD 6 Hammanskraal, South Africa	
23.04.98	Darren Sweeney L PTS 10 Edgbaston *(Midlands Area Middleweight Title Challenge)*	
19.09.98	Jim Rock L PTS 12 Dublin *(Vacant WAA Inter-Continental S. Middleweight Title)*	
27.11.98	Mark Dawson W PTS 6 Nottingham	
07.12.98	Mike Whittaker L PTS 6 Manchester	
14.09.02	Paul Billington W RSC 4 Newark	
30.11.02	Gary Beardsley W PTS 6 Newark	

24.02.03	Jason Collins W PTS 8 Birmingham	
16.04.03	Carl Froch L RSC 3 Nottingham	
28.06.03	Gary Lockett L PTS 10 Cardiff	
13.09.03	Tomas da Silva W PTS 6 Newport	
25.04.04	Jason Collins W PTS 6 Nottingham	
05.06.04	Wayne Elcock L PTS 4 Bethnal Green	
03.09.04	Gary Lockett L RSC 3 Newport	
29.10.04	Lawrence Murphy L PTS 6 Renfrew	
20.02.05	Howard Clarke W PTS 6 Sheffield	
18.03.05	Jim Rock L PTS 8 Belfast	
27.03.05	Michal Bilak W PTS 6 Prague, Czech Republic	
30.04.05	John Humphrey L PTS 6 Dagenham	
14.05.05	Matthew Macklin L CO 5 Dublin *(Vacant All-Ireland Middleweight Title)*	
16.02.06	Darren McDermott L RTD 9 Dudley *(Midlands Area Middleweight Title Challenge)*	

Career: 32 contests, won 16, lost 16.

(Elton) Tony Montana (Gashi)

Sheffield. *Born* Yugoslavia, 5 August, 1982
L.Welterweight. Former Central Area L.Welterweight Champion. Ht. 5'8"
Manager Self

24.11.00	Dave Gibson W PTS 6 Hull	
03.12.00	Gary Greenwood DREW 6 Shaw	
31.01.01	Pete Buckley W PTS 6 Piccadilly	
13.02.01	Barrie Kelley L PTS 6 Brierley Hill	
06.03.01	Chris Price W PTS 6 Yarm	
18.03.01	Ray Wood DREW 6 Shaw	
26.03.01	Francis Barrett L PTS 4 Wembley	
24.05.01	Ajose Olusegun L RSC 1 Kensington	
07.09.01	Mark Hawthorne L CO 3 Bethnal Green	
16.11.01	Young Muttley L PTS 6 West Bromwich	
30.11.01	Brian Gifford W PTS 6 Hull	
17.12.01	Andrei Ivanov DREW 6 Cleethorpes	
31.01.02	James Paisley W PTS 6 Piccadilly	
11.02.02	Ernie Smith W PTS 6 Shrewsbury	
13.04.02	Nicky Leech L PTS 6 Wolverhampton	
11.05.02	Robbie Sivyer L PTS 6 Chesterfield	
31.05.02	John Marshall L PTS 6 Hull	
12.07.02	Chris McDonagh W PTS 4 Southampton	
08.09.02	Jimmy Gould W PTS 8 Wolverhampton	
21.09.02	Christophe de Busillet L PTS 6 Norwich	
02.11.02	Young Muttley L PTS 4 Wolverhampton	
22.12.02	Mark Haslam W PTS 6 Salford	
28.01.03	Gavin Down L PTS 4 Nottingham	
22.03.03	George Telfer W PTS 4 Renfrew	
17.07.03	Young Muttley L PTS 4 Walsall	
28.11.03	Lenny Daws L PTS 6 Derby	
06.02.04	Bobby Vanzie L PTS 6 Sheffield	
14.02.04	Gary Hibbert W PTS 6 Nottingham	
15.04.04	Dean Hickman L PTS 6 Dudley	
23.04.04	Lee Williamson W PTS 6 Leicester	
22.05.04	Wayne Rigby W PTS 10 Manchester *(Vacant Central Area L.Welterweight Title)*	
26.09.04	Gary Reid L PTS 10 Stoke *(Vacant British Masters L.Welterweight Title)*	
15.11.04	Craig Dickson L PTS 8 Glasgow	
26.11.04	Graham Delehedy L PTS 6 Altrincham	
09.12.04	John Marshall W PTS 4 Stockport	
16.12.04	Scott Haywood W PTS 6 Cleethorpes	

133

07.04.05 Anthony Maynard L PTS 4
Birmingham
25.04.05 Jamie Coyle L RSC 3 Glasgow
20.06.05 Sammy Smith L PTS 10 Longford
14.10.05 Barry Morrison L PTS 10 Motherwell
(British Masters L.Welterweight Title
Challenge)
30.10.05 John Fewkes L PTS 6 Sheffield
02.12.05 Lee Meager L PTS 8 Nottingham
17.02.06 John Fewkes L PTS 10 Sheffield
(Central Area L.Welterweight Title
Defence)
Career: 43 contests, won 15, drew 3, lost 25.

Eugenio Monteiro

Manchester. *Born* Capo Verde, Portugal, 16
August, 1970
L.Middleweight. Former Undefeated WBU
Middleweight Champion. Ht. 5'8"
Manager J. Gill

03.11.00 Gustavo Fernandez L RSC 1 Cordoba,
Spain
24.02.01 Spartak Chincharauli W PTS 4 Olhao,
Portugal
16.11.01 Jaroslaw Klimczuk W RSC 2 Vigo,
Spain
14.12.01 Rafael Perez L PTS 6 Barcelona, Spain
29.01.02 Miguel Angel Dominguez W PTS 6
Estoril, Portugal
15.02.02 Amadeo Pena Lloveras W RSC 4
Barcelona, Spain
22.03.02 Luca Mori W RSC 4 Toscolano
Maderno, Italy
06.04.02 Koren Gevor L PTS 6 Hamburg,
Germany
25.05.02 Ottavio Barone W RSC 5 Spoleto, Italy
05.07.02 Antonio Postigo Lagos W RSC 4
Algarve, Portugal
04.10.02 Ruben Varon Fernandez L PTS 8
Guadalajara, Spain
22.11.02 Lansana Diallo L PTS 8 Ixelles,
Belgium
14.12.02 Ruben Diaz W PTS 6 Zeanuri, Spain
07.02.03 Alvaro Moreno W RSC 6 Algarve,
Portugal
29.05.03 Danny Moir W PTS 6 Sunderland
27.09.03 Thomas McDonagh L PTS 12
Manchester
(Vacant WBU Inter-Continental
L.Middleweight Title)
28.11.03 Gilbert Eastman W PTS 8 Derby
24.01.04 Takaloo W PTS 8 Wembley
14.05.04 Albert Airapeitian L PTS 8
Torrelodones, Spain
12.06.04 Anthony Farnell W RSC 10
Manchester
(WBU Middleweight Title Challenge)
01.10.05 Jason Collins W PTS 6 Wigan
24.03.06 Gary Woolcombe L PTS 8 Bethnal
Green
08.06.06 Roman Dzuman L PTS 12 Lvov,
Ukraine
Career: 23 contests, won 14, lost 9.

Jamie Moore

Salford. *Born* Salford, 4 November, 1978
British L.Middleweight Champion. Former
Commonwealth L.Middleweight
Champion. Ht. 5'8"
Manager S. Wood

09.10.99 Clive Johnson W RSC 3 Manchester

13.11.99 Peter Nightingale W PTS 4 Hull
19.12.99 Paul King W PTS 6 Salford
29.02.00 David Baptiste W RSC 3 Manchester
20.03.00 Harry Butler W RSC 2 Mansfield
14.04.00 Jimmy Steel W PTS 6 Manchester
27.05.00 Koba Kulu W RTD 3 Southwark
07.10.00 Leigh Wicks W PTS 4 Doncaster
12.11.00 Prince Kasi Kaihau W RSC 2
Manchester
25.11.00 Wayne Shepherd W RSC 3 Manchester
17.03.01 Richie Murray W RSC 1 Manchester
27.05.01 Paul Denton W RSC 3 Manchester
07.07.01 Scott Dixon L CO 5 Manchester
(Vacant WBO Inter-Continental
L.Middleweight Title)
26.01.02 Harry Butler W RSC 3 Dagenham
09.03.02 Andrzej Butowicz W RSC 5
Manchester
07.09.02 Delroy Mellis W CO 6 Liverpool
08.02.03 Akhmed Oligov W PTS 6 Liverpool
19.04.03 Michael Jones W PTS 12 Liverpool
(Vacant British L. Middleweight Title.
Commonwealth L. Middleweight Title
Challenge)
18.10.03 Gary Logan W CO 5 Manchester
(British & Commonwealth
L.Middleweight Title Defences)
22.11.03 Andrew Facey W RSC 7 Belfast
(British & Commonwealth
L.Middleweight Title Defences)
10.04.04 Adam Katumwa W RSC 5 Manchester
(Vacant Commonwealth
L.Middleweight Title)
26.06.04 Ossie Duran L RSC 3 Belfast
(Commonwealth L.Middleweight Title
Defence)
26.11.04 Michael Jones L DIS 3 Altrincham
(British L.Middleweight Title Defence)
08.07.05 Michael Jones W RSC 6 Altrincham
(British L.Middleweight Title
Challenge)
23.09.05 David Walker W RSC 4 Manchester
(British L.Middleweight Title Defence)
27.01.06 Vladimir Borovski W RSC 3
Dagenham
Career: 26 contests, won 23, lost 3.

Thomas Moran

Edinburgh. *Born* Edinburgh, 5 June, 1985
L.Middleweight. Ht. 5'11¾"
Manager T. Gilmour

31.03.06 Lance Verallo W PTS 6 Inverurie
Career: 1 contest, won 1.

Tony Moran

Liverpool. *Born* Liverpool, 4 July, 1973
Cruiserweight. Ht. 6'6"
Manager Self

26.04.01 Shaun Bowes L PTS 6 Gateshead
13.11.01 Paul Bonson L PTS 6 Leeds
19.03.02 Graham Nolan W PTS 6 Slough
10.05.02 Eamonn Glennon W RTD 1 Preston
03.06.02 Dave Clarke W PTS 6 Glasgow
07.09.02 Adam Cale W PTS 4 Liverpool
05.10.02 Jason Brewster W PTS 4 Liverpool
29.11.02 Adam Cale W RSC 1 Liverpool
08.02.03 Michael Pinnock W PTS 4 Liverpool
17.02.03 Brian Gascoigne W RSC 1 Glasgow
19.04.03 Paul Bonson W PTS 4 Liverpool
17.05.03 Tony Booth W PTS 6 Liverpool
27.10.03 Matthew Ellis W RSC 4 Glasgow

13.03.04 Mark Hobson L RSC 3 Huddersfield
(British & Commonwealth
Cruiserweight Title Challenges)
30.04.05 Paul Bonson W PTS 6 Wigan
13.05.05 Lee Mountford W RSC 1 Liverpool
08.07.05 Neil Dawson L RSC 4 Altrincham
25.11.05 Csaba Andras W PTS 4 Liverpool
17.03.06 Gyorgy Hidvegi L RSC 5 Kirkcaldy
(Vacant WBF Cruiserweight Title)
Career: 19 contests, won 14, lost 5.

Craig Morgan

Llanharan. *Born* Church Village, 9 April,
1983
Lightweight. Ht. 5'7"
Manager P. Boyce

28.04.05 Dave Hinds W PTS 4 Clydach
30.09.05 Barrington Brown W PTS 6
Carmarthen
18.11.05 Patrick Hyland L PTS 4 Dagenham
Career: 3 contests, won 2, lost 1.

Darren Morgan

Swansea. *Born* Swansea, 26 October, 1976
Heavyweight. Ht. 6'1½"
Manager F. Warren

21.01.05 Ebrima Secka W RSC 1 Bridgend
04.06.05 Dave Clarke W RSC 1 Manchester
10.09.05 Tony Booth W PTS 4 Cardiff
25.02.06 Radcliffe Green W RSC 3 Canning
Town
11.03.06 Istvan Kecskes W PTS 4 Newport
20.05.06 Martin Rogan L PTS 4 Belfast
Career: 6 contests, won 5, lost 1.

Andy Morris

Wythenshawe. *Born* Manchester, 10 March,
1983
British Featherweight Champion. Former
Undefeated English Featherweight
Champion. Ht. 5'6½"
Manager F. Warren/F. Maloney

18.01.03 Jason Nesbitt W PTS 4 Preston
05.04.03 Haroon Din W RSC 1 Manchester
08.05.03 Daniel Thorpe W PTS 4 Widnes
06.11.03 Dave Hinds W PTS 4 Dagenham
13.12.03 Henry Janes W PTS 4 Manchester
26.02.04 Daniel Thorpe W RSC 3 Widnes
03.04.04 Carl Allen W PTS 4 Manchester
12.06.04 Jus Wallie W PTS 6 Manchester
01.10.04 Chris Hooper W RSC 3 Manchester
11.02.05 Buster Dennis W PTS 6 Manchester
20.05.05 Rocky Dean W PTS 10 Southwark
(Vacant English Featherweight Title)
23.09.05 Mickey Coveney W RSC 4 Mayfair
05.11.05 John Simpson W PTS 12 Renfrew
(Vacant British Featherweight Title)
29.04.06 Rendall Munroe W PTS 12 Edinburgh
(British Featherweight Title Defence)
Career: 14 contests, won 14.

Jay Morris

Newport, IoW. *Born* Newport, IoW, 8 May,
1978
L.Middleweight. Ht. 5'7"
Manager J. Bishop

21.02.04 Judex Meemea DREW 4 Brighton
30.03.04 Casey Brooke W RSC 1 Southampton

21.11.04 Chris Brophy W RSC 1 Bracknell
12.02.05 Pete Buckley W PTS 6 Portsmouth
26.06.05 David Kehoe W PTS 4 Southampton
25.09.05 Ivor Bonavic L PTS 6 Southampton
04.12.05 Ivor Bonavic W PTS 6 Portsmouth
05.03.06 Duncan Cottier L RSC 2 Southampton
Career: 8 contests, won 5, drew 1, lost 2.

Barry Morrison
Motherwell. *Born* Bellshill, 8 May, 1980
L.Welterweight. Former Undefeated
British Masters L.Welterweight Champion.
Ht. 5'7"
Manager T. Gilmour

12.04.03 Keith Jones W PTS 4 Bethnal Green
28.04.03 Arv Mittoo W RSC 3 Nottingham
05.07.03 Cristian Hodorogea W RSC 3
         Brentwood
06.09.03 Jay Mahoney W RSC 2 Huddersfield
04.10.03 Sergei Starkov W PTS 6 Belfast
01.11.03 Tarik Amrous W PTS 6 Nottingham
28.02.04 Zoltan Surman W RSC 3 Bridgend
22.04.04 Andrei Devyataykin W PTS 8 Glasgow
15.10.04 Adam Zadworny W RSC 2 Glasgow
27.05.05 Gary Reid W RTD 8 Motherwell
         (British Masters L.Welterweight Title
         Challenge)
14.10.05 Tony Montana W PTS 10 Motherwell
         (British Masters L.Welterweight Title
         Defence)
17.03.06 Dean Hickman W RSC 1 Kirkcaldy
         (Elim. British L.Welterweight Title)
21.04.06 Mihaita Mutu L PTS 8 Belfast
Career: 13 contests, won 12, lost 1.

Jamal Morrison
Kilburn. *Born* London, 17 February, 1981
L.Middleweight. Ht. 5'8¾"
Manager J. Tiftik

24.07.05 Casey Brooke W PTS 4 Leicester
         Square
30.03.06 Duncan Cottier DREW 4 Bloomsbury
21.05.06 Geraint Harvey W PTS 4 Bethnal
         Green
Career: 3 contests, won 2, drew 1.

Jamal Morrison   Les Clark

Abdul Mougharbel (Almgharbel)
Dewsbury. *Born* Syria, 10 November, 1975
S.Bantamweight. Ht. 5'4"
Manager C. Aston

15.03.04 Hussain Nasser W RTD 3 Bradford
19.04.04 Sandy Bartlett W PTS 6 Glasgow
11.10.04 Sandy Bartlett L PTS 6 Glasgow
22.10.04 Scott Flynn L PTS 4 Edinburgh
19.11.04 Isaac Ward L PTS 4 Hartlepool
11.12.04 Matthew Marsh L PTS 4 Canning
         Town
06.03.05 Andy Bell L PTS 4 Mansfield
18.04.05 Neil Read W PTS 6 Bradford
27.05.05 Kevin Townsley L PTS 6 Motherwell
06.06.05 Gary Ford W PTS 6 Glasgow
16.09.05 Shaun Walton DREW 6 Telford
28.10.05 Isaac Ward L PTS 6 Hartlepool
20.11.05 Shinny Bayaar L PTS 4 Shaw
04.12.05 Shaun Walton DREW 6 Telford
24.02.06 Wayne Bloy L PTS 6 Scarborough
Career: 15 contests, won 4, drew 2, lost 9.

Lee Mountford
Pudsey. *Born* Leeds, 1 September, 1972
Heavyweight. Ht. 6'2"
Manager Self

19.04.02 Gary Thompson DREW 4 Darlington
24.06.02 Eamonn Glennon L PTS 6 Bradford
20.11.02 Nate Joseph W PTS 6 Leeds
03.02.03 Eamonn Glennon DREW 6 Bradford
28.02.03 Gary Thompson W PTS 6 Irvine
13.05.03 Nate Joseph L PTS 6 Leeds
01.12.03 Dave Clarke W PTS 6 Bradford
15.03.04 Greg Scott-Briggs DREW 6 Bradford
09.04.04 Carl Wright L PTS 4 Rugby
20.04.04 Lee Swaby L RSC 1 Sheffield
26.09.04 Paul Butlin L PTS 6 Stoke
28.10.04 Martin Rogan L RSC 1 Belfast
13.02.05 Nate Joseph L PTS 6 Bradford
13.05.05 Tony Moran L RSC 1 Liverpool
18.06.05 John Anthony L RSC 5 Barnsley
25.09.05 Dave Clarke W PTS 4 Leeds
22.10.05 Tyrone Wright L CO 3 Mansfield
03.03.06 Stewart Mitchell L PTS 4 Doncaster
26.05.06 Tony Booth L PTS 6 Hull
Career: 19 contests, won 4, drew 3, lost 12.

Bheki Moyo
Earls Court. *Born* Pretoria, South Africa, 6
October, 1974
L.Welterweight. Ht. 5'7"
Manager J. Gill

24.07.05 Judex Meemea L PTS 4 Leicester
         Square
28.10.05 Damian Owen L PTS 6 Hartlepool
17.11.05 Garry Buckland L RSC 3 Bristol
21.05.06 Ali Wyatt L RSC 3 Bristol
29.06.06 Nathan Weise L PTS 4 Bethnal Green
Career: 5 contests, lost 5.

David Mulholland
Liverpool. *Born* Liverpool, 11 December,
1979
Featherweight. Ht. 5'9"
Manager J. Evans

13.05.06 Frederic Gosset W PTS 4 Sheffield
Career: 1 contest, won 1.

Steve Mullin
Liverpool. *Born* Liverpool, 7 July, 1983
L.Welterweight. Ht. 5'7"
Manager Self

19.04.03 Daniel Thorpe L RSC 1 Liverpool
20.06.03 Dave Hinds W PTS 4 Liverpool
29.08.03 Peter Allen W PTS 6 Liverpool
08.12.03 Sid Razak W PTS 6 Birmingham
08.03.04 Sid Razak W PTS 6 Birmingham
10.09.04 Peter Allen W PTS 4 Liverpool
17.12.04 Pete Buckley W PTS 4 Liverpool
25.11.05 Billy Smith W PTS 4 Liverpool
21.04.06 Damian Owen L RSC 6 Belfast
16.06.06 Eddie Hyland W RTD 4 Liverpool
Career: 10 contests, won 8, lost 2.

Rendall Munroe
Leicester. *Born* Leicester, 1 June, 1980
Featherweight. Ht. 5'7"
Manager M. Shinfield/D. Coldwell

20.09.03 Joel Viney W RTD 3 Nottingham
23.11.03 John-Paul Ryan W PTS 6 Rotherham
14.02.04 Neil Read W RSC 1 Nottingham
09.04.04 Anthony Hanna W PTS 6 Rugby
26.04.04 Baz Carey W PTS 6 Cleethorpes
27.09.04 David Bailey W PTS 6 Cleethorpes
08.10.04 David Killu W PTS 6 Brentwood
18.06.05 Darren Broomhall W RSC 3 Barnsley
02.09.05 Riaz Durgahed W PTS 6 Derby
28.01.06 Jonathan Whiteman W RSC 2
         Nottingham
29.04.06 Andy Morris L PTS 12 Edinburgh
         (British Featherweight Title Challenge)
Career: 11 contests, won 10, lost 1.

Brian Murphy
Cambuslang. *Born* Rutherglen, 16 August,
1987
Lightweight. Ht. 5'8½"
Manager T. Gilmour

25.03.06 Pete Buckley W PTS 6 Irvine
29.06.06 Ian Wilson L RTD 1 Bethnal Green
Career: 2 contests, won 1, lost 1.

Lawrence Murphy
Uddingston. *Born* Bellshill, 9 February,
1976
Middleweight. Former WBU Middleweight
Champion. Ht. 6'1"
Manager A. Morrison

15.05.98 Mark Owens W RSC 2 Edinburgh
17.09.98 Lee Bird W RSC 3 Glasgow
13.11.98 Ian Toby W PTS 6 Glasgow
18.02.99 Mike Duffield W RSC 2 Glasgow
26.06.99 Harry Butler W RSC 1 Glasgow
17.12.00 Michael Alexander W PTS 6 Glasgow
07.09.01 Chris Nembhard DREW 6 Glasgow
17.11.01 Leigh Wicks W PTS 4 Glasgow
16.12.01 Kreshnik Qato W PTS 6 Glasgow
11.03.02 Rob Stevenson W RSC 1 Glasgow
22.03.03 Leigh Wicks W PTS 4 Renfrew
12.07.03 Jason Collins W PTS 4 Renfrew
25.10.03 Howard Clarke W PTS 6 Edinburgh
29.11.03 Wayne Elcock W CO 6 Renfrew
         (WBU Middleweight Title Challenge)
06.03.04 Anthony Farnell L RSC 3 Renfrew
         (WBU Middleweight Title Defence)
29.10.04 Michael Monaghan W PTS 6 Renfrew
05.11.05 Gareth Lawrence W PTS 4 Renfrew

06.05.06 Wayne Elcock L RSC 5 Birmingham
(Elim. British Middleweight Title)
Career: 18 contests, won 15, drew 1, lost 2.

Andrew Murray

St Albans. *Born* Cavan, 10 September, 1982
Lightweight. Ht. 5'10"
Manager M. Helliet

18.03.05 Jonathan Jones W RSC 4 Belfast
09.10.05 Billy Smith W PTS 4 Hammersmith
17.11.05 Silence Saheed W PTS 4 Piccadilly
02.02.06 Ian Reid W RSC 4 Holborn
30.03.06 Frederic Gosset W PTS 6 Piccadilly
21.05.06 Carl Allen W PTS 4 Bethnal Green
03.06.06 Tony Jourda W RSC 3 Dublin
Career: 7 contests, won 7.

John Murray

Manchester. *Born* Manchester, 20
December, 1984
S. Featherweight. WBC Youth Lightweight
Champion. Ht. 5'8"
Manager S. Wood

06.09.03 Pete Buckley W PTS 4 Huddersfield
18.10.03 Matthew Burke W RSC 1 Manchester
21.12.03 Jason Nesbitt W PTS 6 Bolton
30.01.04 Norman Dhalie W CO 2 Dagenham
12.03.04 John-Paul Ryan W RSC 1 Nottingham
02.06.04 Anthony Hanna W PTS 4 Nottingham
24.09.04 Dariusz Snarski W RSC 2 Nottingham
31.10.04 Ernie Smith W PTS 4 Shaw
26.11.04 Daniel Thorpe W RSC 2 Altrincham
09.12.04 Harry Ramogoadi W RSC 4 Stockport
06.03.05 Karl Taylor W PTS 6 Shaw
08.07.05 Mounir Guebbas W PTS 8 Altrincham
06.08.05 Johnny Walker W PTS 6 Tampa,
Florida, USA
23.09.05 Azad Azizov W RSC 3 Manchester
29.10.05 Tyrone Wiggins W RSC 4 Gatineau,
Canada
02.12.05 Nacho Mendoza W TD 8 Nottingham
(Vacant WBC Youth Lightweight Title)
Career: 16 contests, won 16.

John Murray   Les Clark

Oneal Murray

Brixton. *Born* Jamaica, 8 March, 1973
Heavyweight. Ht. 6'0"
Manager B. Baker

29.03.01 Oddy Papantoniou L PTS 4
Hammersmith
04.10.01 Michael Pinnock W PTS 6 Finsbury
15.10.01 Joe Brame W RSC 2 Southampton
15.12.01 Steven Spartacus L RSC 4 Chigwell
27.01.02 Adam Cale W PTS 6 Streatham
23.02.03 Brodie Pearmaine L PTS 4 Streatham
13.04.03 Dave Clarke L PTS 4 Streatham
14.02.04 Tony Booth L PTS 8 Holborn
06.02.05 Colin Kenna L RTD 3 Southampton
28.06.05 Denis Boytsov L RSC 1 Cuaxhaven,
Germany
11.12.05 Earl Ling W RSC 3 Norwich
Career: 11 contests, won 4, lost 7.

Lee Murtagh

Leeds. *Born* Leeds, 30 September, 1973
Central Area L.Middleweight Champion.
Former Undefeated Central Area
Middleweight Champion. Former British
Masters Middleweight Champion. Former
British Masters L.Middleweight Champion.
Ht. 5'9¼"
Manager Self

12.06.95 Dave Curtis W PTS 6 Bradford
25.09.95 Roy Gbasai W PTS 6 Bradford
30.10.95 Cam Raeside L PTS 6 Bradford
11.12.95 Donovan Davey W PTS 6 Bradford
13.01.96 Peter Varnavas W PTS 6 Halifax
05.02.96 Shamus Casey W PTS 6 Bradford
20.05.96 Shaun O'Neill W PTS 6 Bradford
24.06.96 Michael Alexander W PTS 6 Bradford
28.10.96 Jimmy Vincent L RSC 2 Bradford
14.04.97 Lee Simpkin W PTS 6 Bradford
09.10.97 Brian Dunn W PTS 6 Leeds
05.03.98 Wayne Shepherd W PTS 6 Leeds
08.08.98 Alan Gilbert W PTS 4 Scarborough
13.03.99 Keith Palmer DREW 6 Manchester
27.09.99 Jawaid Khaliq L RSC 5 Leeds
*(Vacant WBF European
L. Middleweight Title)*
27.02.00 Gareth Lovell W PTS 6 Leeds
24.09.00 Jon Foster W PTS 6 Shaw
03.12.00 Michael Alexander W PTS 6 Shaw
17.05.01 Ojay Abrahams L RSC 2 Leeds
*(Vacant British Masters
L. Middleweight Title)*
03.03.02 Howard Clarke NC 2 Shaw
19.04.02 Neil Bonner W PTS 6 Darlington
21.06.02 Wayne Shepherd W PTS 10 Leeds
*(Vacant British Masters Middleweight
Title)*
02.12.02 Martyn Bailey L RSC 6 Leeds
*(British Masters Middleweight Title
Defence)*
10.05.03 Darren Rhodes L PTS 6 Huddersfield
15.09.03 Matt Scriven W DIS 9 Leeds
*(British Masters L.Middleweight Title
Challenge)*
01.12.03 Gary Beardsley L RSC 6 Leeds
*(British Masters L.Middleweight Title
Defence)*
08.06.04 Robert Burton L CO 3 Sheffield
*(Vacant Central Area L.Middleweight
Title)*
15.12.04 Dean Walker W PTS 10 Sheffield
*(Vacant Central Area Middleweight
Title)*
20.05.05 Jason Rushton W PTS 10 Doncaster
*(Central Area L.Middleweight Title
Challenge)*

27.01.06 Gary Woolcombe L RSC 4 Dagenham
Career: 30 contests, won 19, drew 1, lost 9, no
contest 1.

(Nikos) Rocky Muscus (Agrapidis Israel)

Chertsey. *Born* Athens, Greece, 5 August,
1983
Middleweight. Ht. 5'6½"
Manager Self

12.05.03 Danny Cooper L PTS 6 Southampton
18.09.03 Wayne Wheeler L PTS 6 Mayfair
27.10.03 Graham Delehedy L RSC 2 Glasgow
08.07.04 David Kehoe L PTS 6 The Strand
30.09.04 Richard Inquieti W PTS 4 Glasgow
23.10.04 Tye Williams L PTS 6 Wakefield
24.11.04 Ivor Bonavic L PTS 4 Mayfair
18.09.05 Danny Goode L PTS 4 Bethnal Green
25.09.05 Steve Ede L PTS 6 Southampton
Career: 9 contests, won 1, lost 8.

(Lee) Young Muttley (Woodley)

West Bromwich. *Born* West Bromwich, 17
May, 1976
Welterweight. Former British Welterweight
Champion. Former Undefeated WBF Inter-
Continental L.Welterweight Champion.
Former Undefeated English & Midlands
Area L.Welterweight Champion. Ht. 5'8½"
Manager Self

03.09.99 Dave Hinds W RSC 4 West Bromwich
24.10.99 David Kehoe W RTD 1 Wolverhampton
22.01.00 Wahid Fats L PTS 4 Birmingham
18.02.00 Stuart Rimmer W RSC 1 West
Bromwich
27.11.00 Peter Dunn W RSC 3 Birmingham
07.09.01 Jon Honney W RSC 1 West Bromwich
16.11.01 Tony Montana W PTS 6 West
Bromwich
26.11.01 Lee Byrne W RSC 1 Manchester
23.02.02 Brian Coleman W PTS 4 Nottingham
23.03.02 Adam Zadworny W RSC 3 Southwark
02.11.02 Tony Montana W PTS 4
Wolverhampton
21.03.03 Gary Reid W RSC 7 West Bromwich
*(Vacant Midlands Area L.Welterweight
Title)*
28.04.03 John Marshall W RSC 5 Nottingham
17.07.03 Tony Montana W PTS 4 Walsall
19.02.04 Peter Dunn W PTS 4 Dudley
08.05.04 Sammy Smith W RSC 1 Bristol
(Vacant English L.Welterweight Title)
05.10.04 Gavin Down W RSC 6 Dudley
*(English L.Welterweight Title Defence.
Vacant WBF Inter-Continental
L.Welterweight Title)*
17.02.05 Geraint Harvey W PTS 6 Dudley
21.04.05 Oscar Hall W PTS 10 Dudley
*(WBF Inter-Continental
L.Welterweight Title Defence)*
30.09.05 Surinder Sekhon W PTS 4 Burton
28.01.06 Michael Jennings W PTS 12
Nottingham
(British Welterweight Title Challenge)
01.06.06 Kevin Anderson L RSC 10
Birmingham
*(British Welterweight Title Defence.
Commonwealth Welterweight Title
Challenge)*
Career: 22 contests, won 20, lost 2.

Ian Napa

Hackney. *Born* Zimbabwe, 14 March, 1978
Bantamweight. Former Undefeated
Southern Area Flyweight Champion. Ht. 5'1"
Manager B. Lawrence

06.06.98	Nick Tooley W PTS 6 Liverpool	
14.07.98	Nicky Booth W PTS 6 Reading	
10.10.98	Sean Green W PTS 6 Bethnal Green	
30.01.99	Delroy Spencer W PTS 6 Bethnal Green	
15.11.99	Mark Reynolds W PTS 10 Bethnal Green	
	(Southern Area Flyweight Title Challenge)	
19.02.00	Anthony Hanna W PTS 6 Dagenham	
08.04.00	Delroy Spencer W PTS 8 Bethnal Green	
15.07.00	Jamie Evans W PTS 4 Millwall	
13.11.00	Jason Booth L PTS 12 Bethnal Green	
	(British & Commonwealth Flyweight Title Challenges)	
24.02.01	Oleg Kiryukhin W PTS 6 Bethnal Green	
09.06.01	Peter Culshaw L RSC 8 Bethnal Green	
	(WBU Flyweight Title Challenge)	
08.05.04	Danny Costello W PTS 4 Dagenham	
08.10.04	Steve Gethin W PTS 6 Brentwood	
13.02.05	Alexey Volchan W PTS 4 Brentwood	
16.06.05	Marc Callaghan L PTS 10 Dagenham	
	(Vacant Southern Area S.Bantamweight Title)	
04.11.05	Martin Power L PTS 12 Bethnal Green	
	(British Bantamweight Title Challenge)	
25.11.05	Damaen Kelly L PTS 10 Liverpool	

Career: 17 contests, won 12, lost 5.

Ian Napa   Les Clark

Muhsen Nasser

Sheffield. *Born* Yemen, 10 April, 1986
L.Middleweight. Ht. 5'11"
Manager J. Ingle

11.10.04	Andy Cosnett W PTS 6 Birmingham	

26.11.04	Rocky Flanagan W PTS 6 Hull	
27.01.05	Ernie Smith W PTS 6 Piccadilly	
12.05.05	Martin Marshall W PTS 6 Sunderland	
30.10.05	Lance Verallo W PTS 6 Sheffield	
12.11.05	Dave Hinds W PTS 6 Sheffield	
21.11.05	Peter Dunn W RSC 4 Glasgow	
25.02.06	Chris Long W PTS 4 Bristol	
05.03.06	Peter Dunn W PTS 4 Sheffield	

Career: 9 contests, won 9.

Johnny Nelson   Les Clark

Johnny Nelson

Sheffield. *Born* Sheffield, 4 January, 1967
WBO Cruiserweight Champion. Former
Undefeated British & European
Cruiserweight Champion. Former
Undefeated WBU Heavyweight Champion.
Former WBF Heavyweight Champion.
Former WBF Cruiserweight Champion.
Former Undefeated Central Area
Cruiserweight Champion. Ht. 6'2"
Manager D. Ingle

18.03.86	Peter Brown L PTS 6 Hull	
15.05.86	Tommy Taylor L PTS 6 Dudley	
03.10.86	Magne Havnaa L PTS 4 Copenhagen, Denmark	
20.11.86	Chris Little W PTS 6 Bredbury	
19.01.87	Gypsy Carman W PTS 6 Mayfair	
02.03.87	Doug Young W PTS 6 Huddersfield	
10.03.87	Sean Daly W RSC 1 Manchester	
28.04.87	Brian Schumacher L PTS 8 Halifax	
03.06.87	Byron Pullen W RSC 3 Southwark	
14.12.87	Jon McBean W RSC 6 Edgbaston	
01.02.88	Dennis Bailey L PTS 8 Northampton	
24.02.88	Cordwell Hylton W RSC 1 Sheffield	
25.04.88	Kenny Jones W CO 1 Liverpool	
04.05.88	Crawford Ashley W PTS 8 Solihull	
06.06.88	Lennie Howard W CO 2 Mayfair	
31.08.88	Andrew Gerrard W PTS 8 Stoke	
26.10.88	Danny Lawford W RSC 2 Sheffield	
	(Vacant Central Area Cruiserweight Title)	
04.04.89	Steve Mormino W RSC 2 Sheffield	
21.05.89	Andy Straughn W CO 8 Finsbury Park	
	(British Cruiserweight Title Challenge)	
02.10.89	Ian Bulloch W CO 2 Hanley	
	(British Cruiserweight Title Defence)	

27.01.90	Carlos de Leon DREW 12 Sheffield	
	(WBC Cruiserweight Title Challenge)	
14.02.90	Dino Homsey W RSC 7 Brentwood	
28.03.90	Lou Gent W CO 4 Bethnal Green	
	(British Cruiserweight Title Defence)	
27.06.90	Arthur Weathers W RSC 2 Kensington	
05.09.90	Andre Smith W PTS 8 Brighton	
14.12.90	Markus Bott W RSC 12 Karlsruhe, Germany	
	(Vacant European Cruiserweight Title)	
12.03.91	Yves Monsieur W RTD 8 Mansfield	
	(European Cruiserweight Title Defence)	
16.05.92	James Warring L PTS 12 Fredericksburg, USA	
	(IBF Cruiserweight Title Challenge)	
15.08.92	Norbert Ekassi L RSC 3 Ajaccio, France	
29.10.92	Corrie Sanders L PTS 10 Morula, South Africa	
30.04.93	Dave Russell W RSC 11 Melbourne, Australia	
	(WBF Cruiserweight Title Challenge)	
11.08.93	Tom Collins W RSC 1 Mansfield	
	(WBF Cruiserweight Title Defence)	
01.10.93	Francis Wanyama L DIS 10 Waregem, Belgium	
	(WBF Cruiserweight Title Defence)	
20.11.93	Jimmy Thunder W PTS 12 Auckland, New Zealand	
	(WBF Heavyweight Title Challenge)	
05.04.94	Henry Akinwande L PTS 10 Bethnal Green	
05.11.94	Nikolai Kulpin W PTS 12 Bangkok, Thailand	
	(WBF Heavyweight Title Defence)	
22.08.95	Adilson Rodrigues L PTS 12 Sao Paulo, Brazil	
	(WBF Heavyweight Title Defence)	
03.12.95	Adilson Rodrigues L PTS 12 Sao Paulo, Brazil	
	(WBF Heavyweight Title Challenge)	
20.01.96	Tony Booth W RSC 2 Mansfield	
14.12.96	Dennis Andries W RSC 7 Sheffield	
	(Vacant British Cruiserweight Title)	
22.02.97	Patrice Aouissi W RSC 7 Berck sur Mer, France	
	(Vacant European Cruiserweight Title)	
19.07.97	Michael Murray W PTS 4 Wembley	
11.10.97	Dirk Wallyn W RSC 1 Sheffield	
	(European Cruiserweight Title Defence)	
18.07.98	Peter Oboh W RTD 6 Sheffield	
27.03.99	Carl Thompson W RSC 5 Derby	
	(WBO Cruiserweight Title Challenge)	
15.05.99	Bruce Scott W PTS 12 Sheffield	
	(WBO Cruiserweight Title Defence)	
07.08.99	Willard Lewis W RTD 4 Dagenham	
	(WBO Cruiserweight Title Defence)	
18.09.99	Sione Asipeli W PTS 12 Las Vegas, Nevada, USA	
	(WBO Cruiserweight Title Defence)	
06.11.99	Christophe Girard W CO 4 Widnes	
	(WBO Cruiserweight Title Defence)	
08.04.00	Pietro Aurino W RTD 7 Bethnal Green	
	(WBO Cruiserweight Title Defence)	
07.10.00	Adam Watt W RSC 5 Doncaster	
	(WBO Cruiserweight Title Defence)	
27.01.01	George Arias W PTS 12 Bethnal Green	
	(WBO Cruiserweight Title Defence)	
21.07.01	Marcelo Dominguez W PTS 12 Sheffield	
	(WBO Cruiserweight Title Defence)	
24.11.01	Alex Vasiliev W PTS 12 Bethnal Green	
	(Vacant WBU Heavyweight Title)	
06.04.02	Ezra Sellers W CO 8 Copenhagen, Denmark	

(WBO Cruiserweight Title Defence)

23.11.02	Guillermo Jones DREW 12 Derby

(WBO Cruiserweight Title Defence)

15.11.03	Alexander Petkovic W PTS 12 Bayreuth, Germany

(WBO Cruiserweight Title Defence)

04.09.04	Rudiger May W RSC 7 Essen, Germany

(WBO Cruiserweight Title Defence)

26.11.05	Vincenzo Cantatore W PTS 12 Rome, Italy

(WBO Cruiserweight Title Defence)

Career: 59 contests, won 45, drew 2, lost 12.

Robert Nelson

Bradford. *Born* Bradford, 15 January, 1980
S.Bantamweight. Ht. 5'5"
Manager M. Marsden

27.05.05	Delroy Spencer W PTS 4 Spennymoor
25.06.05	Delroy Spencer W PTS 6 Wakefield
13.11.05	Neil Marston W PTS 6 Leeds
09.05.06	Delroy Spencer DREW 6 Leeds
28.05.06	Neil Read W PTS 6 Wakefield

Career: 5 contests, won 4, drew 1.

Jason Nesbitt

Nuneaton. *Born* Birmingham, 15 December, 1973
Lightweight. Ht. 5'9"
Manager Self

06.11.00	Stephen Chinnock L PTS 6 Wolverhampton
09.12.00	Lee Meager L RSC 2 Southwark
29.01.01	Henry Castle L RSC 6 Peterborough
27.03.01	Billy Smith W PTS 6 Brierley Hill
21.05.01	Sid Razak L PTS 6 Birmingham
04.06.01	Andrew Ferrans L RSC 2 Glasgow
07.07.01	Colin Toohey L PTS 4 Manchester
15.09.01	Colin Toohey L PTS 4 Manchester
22.09.01	John Mackay L PTS 4 Canning Town
01.11.01	Chris Hooper L RSC 6 Hull
16.03.02	Lee Meager L PTS 6 Bethnal Green
27.03.02	Greg Edwards W RSC 5 Mayfair
20.04.02	Henry Castle L PTS 4 Cardiff
04.05.02	Danny Hunt L PTS 4 Bethnal Green
15.06.02	Jesse James Daniel L PTS 4 Leeds
27.07.02	Craig Spacie L PTS 4 Nottingham
23.08.02	Billy Corcoran L PTS 4 Bethnal Green
25.10.02	Billy Corcoran L RSC 2 Bethnal Green
03.12.02	Mark Bowen L PTS 6 Shrewsbury
11.12.02	Matt Teague L PTS 6 Hull
20.12.02	Chris McDonagh L PTS 6 Bracknell
18.01.03	Andy Morris L PTS 4 Preston
09.02.03	Mally McIver L PTS 6 Bradford
09.03.03	Choi Tseveenpurev L PTS 6 Shaw
29.03.03	Kevin O'Hara L RSC 3 Portsmouth
07.05.03	Henry Jones L PTS 6 Ellesmere Port
02.06.03	Stefy Bull L PTS 6 Cleethorpes
13.06.03	Scott Lawton L PTS 6 Queensway
17.07.03	Haider Ali L PTS 4 Dagenham
29.08.03	Gary Thornhill L CO 1 Liverpool
05.10.03	Nadeem Siddique L PTS 6 Bradford
08.11.03	Harry Ramogoadi L PTS 6 Coventry
23.11.03	Amir Ali L PTS 6 Rotherham
10.12.03	Femi Fehintola L PTS 6 Sheffield
21.12.03	John Murray L PTS 6 Bolton
06.02.04	Femi Fehintola L PTS 6 Sheffield
23.02.04	Carl Greaves L PTS 6 Nottingham
05.03.04	Haroon Din L PTS 6 Darlington
12.03.04	Stuart Green L PTS 8 Irvine
03.04.04	Daniel Thorpe L PTS 6 Sheffield
16.04.04	John O'Donnell L PTS 4 Bradford

27.04.04	Jim Betts L PTS 6 Leeds
07.05.04	Jus Wallie L PTS 6 Bethnal Green
28.05.04	John Bothwell W RSC 3 Glasgow
05.06.04	Kevin Mitchell L RSC 3 Bethnal Green
30.07.04	Lee Beavis L PTS 4 Bethnal Green
20.09.04	Matt Teague L PTS 6 Cleethorpes
30.09.04	Eddie Nevins L PTS 6 Hull
18.11.04	Joel Viney W PTS 6 Blackpool
26.11.04	John Davidson W RSC 1 Altrincham
10.12.04	John Fewkes L PTS 6 Sheffield
17.12.04	Gwyn Wale L PTS 4 Huddersfield
13.02.05	Nadeem Siddique L PTS 6 Bradford
04.03.05	John Fewkes L PTS 6 Rotherham
01.04.05	Martin McDonagh L PTS 6 Glasgow
15.04.05	Martin Gethin L PTS 6 Shrewsbury
28.04.05	Ceri Hall L RTD 2 Clydach
02.06.05	Riaz Durgahed L PTS 6 Peterborough
24.07.05	Femi Fehintola L PTS 6 Sheffield
09.09.05	Nicki Smedley L PTS 4 Sheffield
30.09.05	Henry Jones L PTS 6 Carmarthen
16.10.05	Michael Medor L PTS 6 Peterborough
12.11.05	Craig Johnson L PTS 6 Sheffield
25.11.05	Nadeem Siddique L RSC 6 Hull
17.02.06	Dave Stewart L PTS 4 Bethnal Green
04.03.06	Tony Delaney L PTS 6 Manchester
01.04.06	Steve Bell L PTS 6 Bethnal Green
28.04.06	Davis Kamara L PTS 6 Manchester
06.05.06	Jimmy Doherty L PTS 6 Stoke
20.05.06	Anthony Christopher W RSC 4 Bristol
05.06.06	Mitch Prince L PTS 6 Glasgow

Career: 71 contests, won 6, lost 65.

Paul Newby

Keighley. *Born* Eastburn, 13 September, 1977
L.Welterweight. Ht. 5'6½"
Manager J. Ashton

13.11.05	Ian Reid W PTS 6 Leeds
13.04.06	Pete Buckley W PTS 4 Leeds
06.05.06	Steve Gethin W PTS 4 Birmingham

Career: 3 contests, won 3.

Lee Nicholson

Doncaster. *Born* Mexborough, 10 November, 1976
Cruiserweight. Ht. 5'11"
Manager Self

24.09.01	Jason Brewster L PTS 6 Cleethorpes
17.02.02	Jason Brewster L PTS 6 Wolverhampton
11.05.02	Fola Okesola L RSC 1 Dagenham
07.09.03	Stewart West L RSC 2 Shrewsbury
01.12.03	Mike Duffield W PTS 6 Barnsley
15.12.03	Simeon Cover L RSC 4 Cleethorpes
29.10.04	Dean Cockburn L RSC 2 Doncaster
13.12.04	Dean Cockburn L RSC 3 Cleethorpes
23.05.05	Slick Miller W PTS 6 Cleethorpes
03.03.06	Jimmy Harrington DREW 4 Doncaster
21.04.06	Jimmy Harrington L RTD 3 Doncaster

Career: 11 contests, won 2, drew 1, lost 8.

Robert Norton

Stourbridge. *Born* Dudley, 20 January, 1972
Cruiserweight. Former Undefeated British Masters Cruiserweight Champion. Former WBU Cruiserweight Champion. Ht. 6'2"
Manager J. Weaver

30.09.93	Stuart Fleet W CO 2 Walsall
27.10.93	Kent Davis W PTS 6 West Bromwich
02.12.93	Eddie Pyatt W RSC 2 Walsall
26.01.94	Lennie Howard W PTS 6 Birmingham

17.05.94	Steve Osborne W PTS 6 Kettering
05.10.94	Chris Woollas DREW 6 Wolverhampton
30.11.94	L. A. Williams W RSC 2 Wolverhampton
10.02.95	Newby Stevens W RSC 3 Birmingham
22.02.95	Steve Osborne W PTS 6 Telford
21.04.95	Cordwell Hylton W PTS 6 Dudley
25.10.95	Nigel Rafferty W RSC 6 Telford
31.01.96	Gary Williams W RSC 2 Birmingham
25.04.96	Steve Osborne W RSC 5 Mayfair
01.10.96	Andrew Benson W RSC 6 Birmingham
12.11.96	Nigel Rafferty W PTS 8 Dudley
11.02.97	Touami Benhamed W RSC 5 Bethnal Green
16.04.97	Tony Booth W RSC 4 Bethnal Green
20.12.97	Darren Corbett L PTS 12 Belfast

(Commonwealth Cruiserweight Title Challenge)

03.04.98	Adrian Nicolai W RSC 2 West Bromwich
03.10.98	Tim Brown W CO 3 West Bromwich
01.04.99	Jacob Mofokeng W PTS 12 Birmingham

(WBU Cruiserweight Title Challenge)

24.09.99	Sebastiaan Rothmann L RSC 8 Merthyr

(WBU Cruiserweight Title Defence)

30.09.00	Tony Booth W RSC 3 Peterborough
18.11.00	Darron Griffiths W PTS 10 Dagenham

(Elim. British Cruiserweight Title)

05.02.01	Lee Swaby W PTS 8 Hull
30.11.02	Paul Bonson W PTS 6 Coventry
05.09.03	Mark Hobson L PTS 12 Sheffield

(Commonwealth Cruiserweight Title Challenge. Vacant British Cruiserweight Title)

09.04.04	Greg Scott-Briggs W CO 1 Rugby
10.07.04	Chris Woollas W RSC 4 Coventry
06.12.04	Paul Bonson W CO 6 Leicester

(Vacant British Masters Cruiserweight Title)

22.10.05	Dmitry Adamovich W CO 2 Coventry

Career: 31 contests, won 27, drew 1, lost 3.

(Paulus) Ali Nuumbembe

Glossop. *Born* Oshakati, Namibia, 24 June, 1978
Welterweight. Ht. 5'8½"
Manager S. Wood

16.04.03	Dai Bando W PTS 4 Nottingham
15.06.03	Ernie Smith W PTS 4 Bradford
03.08.03	Lee Williamson W PTS 5 Stalybridge
29.08.03	Ernie Smith W PTS 6 Liverpool
05.10.03	Keith Jones W PTS 6 Bradford
07.12.03	Brian Coleman W RTD 2 Bradford
16.01.04	Wayne Wheeler W RSC 3 Bradford
29.02.04	William Webster W RSC 3 Shaw
10.04.04	Peter Dunn W PTS 6 Manchester
09.10.04	Bethuel Ushona L PTS 10 Windhoek, Namibia

(Vacant Namibian Welterweight Title)

09.12.04	Lee Armstrong W PTS 6 Stockport
04.03.05	Franny Jones W PTS 6 Hartlepool
22.04.05	David Barnes DREW 12 Barnsley

(Vacant WBO Inter-Continental Welterweight Title)

08.07.05	Dmitry Yanushevich W RSC 2 Altrincham
23.09.05	Gavin Down W RSC 3 Manchester
18.12.05	Ernie Smith W CO 4 Bolton
12.02.06	Sergey Starkov W PTS 8 Manchester
29.06.06	Ajose Olusegun L CO 6 Bethnal Green

Career: 18 contests, won 15, drew 1, lost 2.

Tony Oakey

Havant. *Born* Portsmouth, 2 January, 1976
L.Heavyweight. Former WBU
L.Heavyweight Champion. Former
Undefeated Commonwealth & Southern
Area L.Heavyweight Champion. Ht. 5'8"
Manager Self

12.09.98	Smokey Enison W RSC 2 Bethnal Green
21.11.98	Zak Chelli W RSC 1 Southwark
16.01.99	Jimmy Steel W PTS 4 Bethnal Green
06.03.99	Mark Dawson W PTS 4 Southwark
10.07.99	Jimmy Steel W PTS 4 Southwark
01.10.99	Michael Pinnock W PTS 4 Bethnal Green
21.02.00	Darren Ashton W PTS 4 Southwark
13.03.00	Martin Jolley W PTS 6 Bethnal Green
21.10.00	Darren Ashton W PTS 4 Wembley
27.01.01	Nathan King W PTS 6 Bethnal Green
26.03.01	Butch Lesley W PTS 10 Wembley *(Southern Area L. Heavyweight Title Challenge)*
08.05.01	Hastings Rasani W RSC 10 Barnsley *(Vacant Commonwealth L. Heavyweight Title)*
09.09.01	Konstantin Ochrej W RSC 4 Southwark
20.10.01	Chris Davies W PTS 12 Portsmouth *(Commonwealth L.Heavyweight Title Defence)*
02.03.02	Konstantin Shvets W PTS 12 Bethnal Green *(Vacant WBU L. Heavyweight Title)*
25.05.02	Neil Simpson W PTS 12 Portsmouth *(WBU L.Heavyweight Title Defence)*
12.10.02	Andrei Kaersten W PTS 12 Bethnal Green *(WBU L. Heavyweight Title Defence)*
29.03.03	Neil Linford W PTS 12 Portsmouth *(WBU L.Heavyweight Title Defence)*
11.10.03	Matthew Barney L PTS 12 Portsmouth *(WBU L.Heavyweight Title Defence)*
12.02.05	Varuzhan Davtyan W RTD 5 Portsmouth
19.06.05	Peter Haymer L PTS 10 Bethnal Green *(English L.Heavyweight Title Challenge)*
01.04.06	Radek Seman W PTS 8 Bethnal Green
13.05.06	Nathan King W PTS 6 Bethnal Green

Career: 23 contests, won 21, lost 2.

Gary O'Connor

Manchester, *Born* Manchester, 29 August, 1978
Welterweight. Ht. 5'10"
Manager Self

21.12.03	Chris Brophy W PTS 6 Bolton
29.02.04	Pete Buckley W PTS 6 Shaw
18.12.05	Kristian Laight W PTS 6 Bolton
12.02.06	Lance Verallo W RSC 4 Manchester
28.04.06	Pete Buckley W PTS 6 Manchester

Career: 5 contests, won 5.

Valery Odin

Canning Town. *Born* Guadeloupe, 23
December, 1974
Cruiserweight. Ht. 6'2½"
Manager P. McCausland

15.06.01	Tom Cannon W PTS 4 Millwall
22.09.01	Mark Brookes W PTS 4 Canning Town
09.10.01	Wayne Ellcock L PTS 4 Cardiff
10.11.01	Tony Dodson L RSC 4 Wembley
13.12.01	Calvin Stonestreet W RSC 2 Leicester Square
10.02.02	Radcliffe Green W PTS 6 Southwark
20.04.02	Toks Owoh W PTS 8 Wembley
21.05.01	Mark Smallwood L RSC 4 Custom House
17.08.02	Nathan King W PTS 6 Cardiff
17.09.02	Charden Ansoula L PTS 6 Bethnal Green
26.10.02	Chris Davies L PTS 6 Maesteg
28.01.03	Carl Froch L RSC 6 Nottingham
06.09.03	Kai Kurzawa L PTS 8 Efurt, Germany
19.06.04	Courtney Fry L PTS 8 Muswell Hill
11.10.04	Pinky Burton L PTS 6 Glasgow
05.11.04	Gyorgy Hidvegi L PTS 6 Hereford
03.12.04	Leigh Allis W RSC 5 Bristol
19.12.05	Hastings Rasani L PTS 4 Longford
23.03.06	Neil Linford L RSC 4 The Strand
28.04.06	Steve McGuire L PTS 6 Hartlepool

Career: 20 contests, won 7, lost 13.

John O'Donnell

Shepherds Bush. *Born* Croydon, 13
November, 1985
Welterweight. Ht. 5'11"
Manager R. McCracken

16.04.04	Jason Nesbitt W PTS 4 Bradford
02.06.04	Dave Hinds W PTS 4 Nottingham
24.09.04	Chris Long W RSC 4 Nottingham
12.11.04	Ernie Smith W PTS 5 Wembley
10.04.05	Duncan Cottier W PTS 4 Brentwood
09.07.05	Ben Hudson W RTD 3 Nottingham
21.10.05	Ben Hudson W PTS 4 Bethnal Green
20.01.06	Matt Scriven W RSC 4 Bethnal Green
28.01.06	Zaid Bediouri W PTS 6 Dublin
17.02.06	Karl Taylor W PTS 4 Bethnal Green
12.05.06	Duncan Cottier W RTD 3 Bethnal Green

Career: 11 contests, won 11.

Keiran O'Donnell

Leeds. *Born* Leeds, 10 December, 1974
Cruiserweight. Ht. 6'2"
Manager Self

11.11.03	Michael Pinnock W PTS 6 Leeds
28.02.06	Clint Johnson W RSC 1 Leeds

Career: 2 contests, won 2.

Kevin O'Hara

Belfast. *Born* Belfast, 21 September, 1981
Lightweight. Ht. 5'6"
Manager J.Breen/F.Warren

02.11.02	Mike Harrington W RSC 1 Belfast
01.02.03	Jus Wallie W RSC 2 Belfast
29.03.03	Jason Nesbitt W RSC 3 Portsmouth
14.06.03	Piotr Niesporek W PTS 4 Magdeburg, Germany
02.10.03	Vladimir Borov W PTS 6 Liverpool
30.10.03	Henry Janes W PTS 6 Belfast
29.11.03	Gareth Payne W PTS 4 Renfrew

06.03.04	Henry Janes W PTS 6 Renfrew
01.04.04	Buster Dennis W PTS 4 Bethnal Green
06.05.04	Choi Tsveenpurev L PTS 8 Barnsley
28.10.04	Jean-Marie Codet W PTS 8 Belfast
17.06.05	Willie Limond L PTS 10 Glasgow *(Vacant Celtic S.Featherweight Title)*
24.11.05	Damian Owen W PTS 6 Lurgan
20.05.06	Daniel Thorpe W PTS 6 Belfast

Career: 14 contests, won 12, lost 2.

Gary Ojuederie

Watford. *Born* Watford, 13 September, 1979
L.Heavyweight. Ht. 6'0"
Manager C. Sanigar

29.09.00	Chris Nembhard L RSC 1 Bethnal Green
08.12.03	Hamid Jamali L PTS 6 Birmingham
13.02.04	Jason Samuels L DIS 3 Bristol
28.02.04	Mike Allen W RSC 1 Bridgend
16.10.05	Karl Wheeler W RSC 4 Peterborough
19.11.05	Eder Kurti W RSC 4 Southwark
16.12.05	Sam Price W PTS 6 Bracknell
26.02.06	Simeon Cover W PTS 4 Dagenham

Career: 8 contests, won 4, drew 1, lost 3.

Nick Okoth

Battersea. *Born* Camden Town, 19 July, 1973
L. Heavyweight. Ht. 5'11"
Manager J. Evans

18.09.03	Mark Phillips W PTS 4 Mayfair
28.02.04	Paulie Silva L PTS 6 Manchester
08.04.04	Karl Wheeler L PTS 6 Peterborough
24.04.04	Daniel Sackey L RSC 2 Reading
03.07.04	Nathan King L PTS 4 Newport
31.10.04	Darren Stubbs L PTS 6 Shaw
25.11.04	Jonjo Finnegan DREW 6 Birmingham
03.12.04	Paul Henry W RSC 5 Bristol
21.01.05	Sam Price L PTS 6 Brentford
06.02.05	Mervyn Langdale DREW 6 Southampton
20.02.05	Jon Ibbotson L PTS 6 Sheffield
08.04.05	Dan Guthrie L RSC 2 Bristol
09.09.05	Steven Birch W PTS 4 Sheffield
28.01.06	Rod Anderton L PTS 4 Nottingham
25.02.06	Richard Horton L CO 3 Canning Town

Career: 15 contests, won 3, drew 2, lost 10.

Ajose Olusegun

Kentish Town. *Born* Nigeria, 6 December, 1979
Welterweight. Former Undefeated ABU
L.Welterweight Champion. Ht. 5'9"
Manager Self

24.05.01	Tony Montana W RSC 1 Kensington
21.06.01	Woody Greenaway W RSC 1 Earls Court
09.09.01	Sunni Ajayi W PTS 6 Lagos, Nigeria
04.10.01	Stuart Rimmer W RTD 2 Finsbury
13.03.02	Gary Flear W PTS 4 Mayfair
13.06.02	Keith Jones W PTS 6 Leicester Square
30.10.02	Martin Holgate W RSC 7 Leicester Square
27.11.02	Vladimir Kortovski W RSC 1 Tel Aviv, Israel
15.12.02	Adewale Adegbusi W RSC 6 Lagos, Nigeria
20.03.03	Cristian Hodorogea W PTS 4 Queensway
26.04.03	Keith Jones W PTS 6 Brentford

29.10.03	Karl Taylor W PTS 6 Leicester Square	
10.04.04	Victor Kpadenue W PTS 12 Carabas, Nigeria	
	(ABU L.Welterweight Title Challenge)	
03.09.04	Bradley Pryce W RSC 4 Newport	
26.03.05	Vasile Dragomir W PTS 8 Hackney	
26.05.06	Alexander Abramenko W RSC 2 Bethnal Green	
29.06.06	Ali Nuumbembe W CO 6 Bethnal Green	

Career: 17 contests, won 17.

Ajose Olusegun   Les Clark

Peter O'Neill

St Helens. *Born* Liverpool, 5 July, 1981
S.Featherweight. Ht. 5'5¼"
Manager J. Evans

18.09.05   Jed Syger L PTS 4 Bethnal Green
Career: 1 contest, lost 1.

Leo O'Reilly

Bexleyheath. *Born* Gravesend, 4 October, 1979
L.Middleweight. Ht. 5'6"
Manager F.Maloney

16.09.00	Dave Hinds W RSC 2 Bethnal Green
30.09.00	Stuart Rimmer W RSC 2 Peterborough
14.10.00	Marco Fattore W PTS 4 Wembley
18.11.00	Dave Travers W RSC 3 Dagenham
09.12.00	Pete Buckley W PTS 4 Southwark
05.02.01	Woody Greenaway W CO 1 Hull
13.03.01	Barrie Kelley W RSC 5 Plymouth
12.05.01	David White W PTS 4 Plymouth
13.09.01	Ernie Smith W PTS 6 Sheffield
16.03.02	Lance Crosby W PTS 8 Bethnal Green
10.05.02	Paul Denton W PTS 6 Bethnal Green
26.10.02	Alan Temple L RSC 4 Maesteg
08.03.03	Keith Jones W PTS 6 Bethnal Green
27.01.06	Jon Honney W PTS 6 Dagenham
02.04.06	Silence Saheed DREW 6 Bethnal Green
26.05.06	Gary Reid L RSC 2 Bethnal Green

Career: 16 contests, won 13, drew 1, lost 2.

Hussain Osman

Paddington. *Born* Syria, 25 July, 1973
S.Middleweight. Former IBO Inter-Continental & Southern Area S.Middleweight Champion. Former Undefeated WBO Inter-Continental Southern Area Middleweight Champion. Ht. 5'9½"
Manager J. Feld

09.05.99	Wayne Asker W PTS 4 Bracknell	
20.05.99	Karim Bouali W PTS 4 Barking	
15.07.99	Neil Linford W RSC 5 Peterborough	
05.10.99	Ojay Abrahams W PTS 4 Bloomsbury	
05.02.00	Joey Ainscough W PTS 4 Bethnal Green	
01.04.00	George Foreman W PTS 4 Bethnal Green	
22.05.00	Steve Timms W RSC 2 Coventry	
25.09.00	James Lowther L PTS 8 Barnsley	
03.03.01	Gary Lockett L CO 2 Wembley	
26.05.01	Lee Molloy W RSC 1 Bethnal Green	
04.06.01	Richard Williams L PTS 10 Hartlepool	
28.10.01	Gary Logan W PTS 10 Southwark	
	(Southern Area Middleweight Title Challenge)	
26.01.02	Matthew Barney W RTD 9 Dagenham	
	(Vacant IBO Inter-Continental S.Middleweight Title. Southern Area S.Middleweight Title Challenge)	
08.04.02	Matthew Barney L PTS 12 Southampton	
	(IBO Inter-Continental & Southern Area S. Middleweight Title Defences)	
21.05.02	Darren Rhodes W PTS 10 Custom House	
20.07.02	Gary Logan W PTS 12 Bethnal Green	
	(Vacant WBO Inter-Continental Middleweight Title)	
21.12.02	Howard Eastman L RTD 4 Dagenham	
31.05.03	Gary Beardsley W RSC 5 Bethnal Green	
09.10.03	Scott Dann L PTS 8 Bristol	
01.04.04	Eric Teymour L RSC 8 Bethnal Green	
18.09.05	John Humphrey L PTS 10 Bethnal Green	
	(Vacant Southern Area Middleweight Title)	
30.09.05	Jason Samuels L PTS 4 Carmarthen	
25.10.05	Ryan Rhodes L RTD 4 Preston	
11.03.06	Paul Smith L RSC 4 Newport	
01.06.06	Albert Rybacki L PTS 6 Birmingham	

Career: 25 contests, won 13, lost 12.

Lloyd Otte

West Ham. *Born* Australia, 26 June, 1981
S.Featherweight. Ht. 5'6½"
Manager Self

02.12.04	Riaz Durgahed W PTS 6 Crystal Palace
10.04.05	Peter Allen W PTS 6 Brentwood
18.11.05	Riaz Durgahed DREW 4 Dagenham
30.05.06	Barrington Brown L RSC 1 Bethnal Green

Career: 4 contests, won 2, drew 1, lost 1.

Damian Owen

Swansea. *Born* Swansea, 7 May, 1985
L.Welterweight. Ht. 5'7"
Manager T. Gilmour

01.10.04	Darren Payne W RSC 4 Bristol
05.11.04	Peter Allen W RSC 1 Hereford
08.04.05	Jus Wallie W PTS 4 Bristol
28.10.05	Bheki Moyo W PTS 6 Hartlepool
24.11.05	Kevin O'Hara L PTS 6 Lurgan
25.02.06	Carl Allen W PTS 6 Bristol
21.04.06	Steve Mullin W RSC 6 Belfast

Career: 7 contests, won 6, lost 1.

Leon Owen

Swansea. *Born* Mountain Ash, 7 October, 1983
S.Middleweight. Ht. 6'1"
Manager N. Hodges

26.02.06	Greg Barton W RSC 1 Dagenham
05.03.06	George Katsimpas L RSC 2 Southampton
20.05.06	Jav Jerome W PTS 6 Bristol

Career: 3 contests, won 2, lost 1.

Ricky Owen

Swansea. *Born* Swansea, 10 May, 1985
Featherweight. Ht. 5'6"
Manager B. Hearn

05.11.04	Sandy Bartlett W RSC 2 Hereford
16.06.05	Billy Smith W PTS 4 Dagenham
30.09.05	Rakhim Mingaleev W PTS 4 Carmarthen
03.03.06	Alexander Vladimirov W PTS 6 Hartlepool

Career: 4 contests, won 4.

Ricky Owen   Les Clark

(Tokunbo) Toks Owoh (Owomoyela)

Camden Town. *Born* Newham, 21 July, 1972
Cruiserweight. Ht. 5'10½"
Manager J. Tiftik

24.10.95	Marvin O'Brien W RSC 2 Southwark
08.11.95	Dave Fulton W RSC 1 Bethnal Green
29.11.95	Nicky Wadman W PTS 6 Southwark
19.01.96	Ernie Loveridge W PTS 4 Bracknell
27.03.97	James Branch W RSC 1 Norwich
02.08.97	Peter Vosper W RSC 1 Barnsley
29.11.97	Sven Hamer W PTS 8 Norwich
27.03.98	Darren Ashton W RSC 2 Telford
25.04.98	Omar Sheika L RSC 4 Cardiff
26.09.98	Tony Booth W PTS 6 Norwich
30.01.99	Israel Khumalo W RSC 2 Bethnal Green
03.04.99	Paul Wesley W CO 5 Kensington
26.06.99	Peter Mason W RSC 1 Millwall
23.10.99	Eddie Haley W RSC 3 Telford
29.02.00	Konstantin Okhrej W RTD 4 Widnes
19.06.00	Tony Booth W RSC 3 Burton
23.09.00	Glengoffe Johnson L RSC 6 Bethnal Green
	(Vacant IBF Inter-Continental S.Middleweight Title)
18.01.02	Mondli Mbonambi W PTS 8 Coventry
20.04.02	Valery Odin L PTS 8 Wembley
21.05.02	Erik Teymour L PTS 6 Custom House
08.05.04	Ryan Walls L PTS 6 Bristol
24.07.05	Paul Bonson W PTS 4 Leicester Square

Career: 22 contests, won 17, lost 5.

Chris Pacy

Bridlington. *Born* Doncaster, 17 May, 1983
Lightweight. Ht. 5'6"
Manager F. Maloney

30.05.06   Billy Smith W PTS 4 Bethnal Green
Career: 1 contest, won 1.

Matt Paice

Slough. *Born* Taplow, 19 June, 1983
Heavyweight. Ht. 6'6"
Manager T. Follett

16.12.05   Simon Goodwin W PTS 4 Bracknell
06.04.06   David Ingleby W PTS 4 Piccadilly
Career: 2 contests, won 2.

Matt Paice   Les Clark

James Paisley

Belfast. *Born* Ballymena, 4 January, 1980
Welterweight. Ht. 5'8"
Manager Self

09.09.01   Babatunde Ajayi L PTS 4 Southwark
28.10.01   Carl Walton W PTS 4 Southwark
15.12.01   David Barnes L RTD 2 Wembley
31.01.02   Tony Montana L PTS 6 Piccadilly
09.02.02   Michael Jennings L RSC 3 Manchester
11.03.02   Nigel Wright L PTS 4 Glasgow
23.06.02   Jason Gonzales W PTS 6 Southwark
17.09.02   Dave Stewart L RSC 5 Bethnal Green
20.10.02   Pete Buckley W PTS 4 Southwark
27.10.02   Elvis Mbwakongo L RSC 2 Southwark
22.02.03   Gwyn Wale L RSC 1 Huddersfield
26.09.03   Kristian Laight W PTS 6 Millwall
06.12.03   Tony Doherty L RSC 3 Cardiff
20.02.04   Justin Hudson W PTS 4 Bethnal Green
24.09.04   Nathan Ward L PTS 4 Bethnal Green
19.12.04   Ryan Barrett L DIS 5 Bethnal Green
19.06.05   Nathan Ward L RSC 4 Bethnal Green
           *(Vacant British Masters Welterweight
           Title)*
26.02.06   Imad Khamis L RSC 3 Dagenham
13.05.06   Alan Bosworth L PTS 4 Bethnal Green
Career: 19 contests, won 5, lost 14.

David Payne

Wellingborough. *Born* Kettering, 1 August,
1984
Middleweight. Ht. 5'8¹/₂"
Manager S. James

05.10.04   Paul McInnes W RSC 1 Dudley
20.11.04   Richard Mazurek L PTS 6 Coventry
02.12.04   Nathan Graham L RSC 3 Crystal Palace
10.02.06   Dan Guthrie L RSC 2 Plymouth
Career: 4 contests, won 1, lost 3.

Dave Pearson

Middlesbrough. *Born* Middlesbrough, 1
April, 1974
S. Middleweight. Ht. 6'2³/₄"
Manager M. Shinfield

15.04.02   Ian Thomas L CO 3 Shrewsbury
03.10.02   Gary Firby W CO 3 Sunderland
21.10.02   Gary Jones L RSC 3 Cleethorpes
05.12.02   Chris Steele W PTS 6 Sunderland
24.03.03   Reagan Denton L PTS 6 Barnsley
31.05.03   Gary Jones L RSC 2 Barnsley
11.07.03   Ben Coward L PTS 6 Darlington
16.02.04   Brian Coleman L PTS 6 Scunthorpe
26.02.04   Tony Quigley L RSC 1 Widnes
26.04.04   Mark Phillips L RSC 6 Cleethorpes
25.06.04   Gerard London L PTS 4 Bethnal Green
06.11.04   Brian Coleman W PTS 6 Coventry
16.12.04   Peter McCormack W PTS 6
           Cleethorpes
25.04.05   Peter McCormack W PTS 6
           Cleethorpes
02.09.05   Mark Phillips L PTS 6 Derby
15.12.05   Ryan Rowlinson L PTS 6 Cleethorpes
28.01.06   Jonjo Finnegan L PTS 4 Nottingham
25.03.06   Jonjo Finnegan L PTS 8 Burton
24.04.06   Magic Kidem W PTS 6 Cleethorpes
Career: 19 contests, won 6, lost 13.

Kevin Phelan

Slough. *Born* Slough, 11 June, 1977
L.Middleweight. Former British Masters
L.Middleweight Champion. Ht. 6'1"
Manager G. Carmen

27.09.02   Lee Hodgson L RSC 1 Bracknell
21.03.03   Jimi Hendricks W RSC 6 Longford
12.04.03   Steve Russell W PTS 4 Norwich
26.04.03   Dave Wakefield W PTS 4 Brentford
09.05.03   Leigh Wicks W PTS 6 Longford
26.10.03   Brian Coleman W PTS 6 Longford
27.11.03   Dave Wakefield W PTS 6 Longford
25.03.04   Danny Moir L PTS 10 Longford
           *(Vacant British Masters
           L.Middleweight Title)*
02.06.04   David Walker L PTS 6 Nottingham
23.09.04   Danny Moir W RTD 3 Gateshead
           *(British Masters L.Middleweight Title
           Challenge)*
08.12.04   Taz Jones L PTS 10 Longford
           *(British Masters L.Middleweight Title
           Defence)*
06.10.05   John-Paul Temple W PTS 6 Longford
18.11.05   Michael Lomax L PTS 8 Dagenham
19.12.05   Danny Moir W CO 4 Longford
07.04.06   Neil Bonner W RSC 2 Longford
27.05.06   Barrie Lee L PTS 6 Glasgow
03.06.06   Jim Rock L RTD 7 Dublin
           *(Vacant All-Ireland Middleweight
           Title)*
Career: 17 contests, won 10, lost 7.

Dean Phillips

Llanelli. *Born* Swansea, 1 February, 1976
Lightweight. Ht. 5'6"
Manager Self

10.03.94   Paul Richards L PTS 6 Bristol
23.03.94   Phil Janes W RSC 1 Cardiff
27.08.94   Craig Kelley W RSC 4 Cardiff
21.09.94   Steve Edwards W RTD 4 Cardiff
02.11.94   Anthony Maynard L PTS 6
           Birmingham
04.02.95   Greg Upton W PTS 6 Cardiff
04.03.95   Mike Deveney W PTS 8 Livingston
24.03.95   Bamana Dibateza W PTS 6 Swansea
16.06.95   Danny Luutaya W RSC 2 Southwark
22.07.95   Colin McMillan L PTS 8 Millwall
20.09.95   Mervyn Bennett W PTS 6 Ystrad
16.03.96   Mike Anthony Brown W RSC 6
           Glasgow
26.04.96   Bamana Dibateza W PTS 6 Cardiff
19.09.96   Peter Judson L RSC 10 Manchester
           *(Vacant IBF Inter-Continental
           S. Featherweight Title)*
24.01.98   Jimmy Phelan W PTS 6 Cardiff
25.04.98   Steve Conway L PTS 6 Cardiff
30.11.03   Nigel Senior W CO 1 Swansea
28.02.04   Gary Hibbert W RSC 5 Bridgend
01.05.04   Michael Muya W PTS 8 Bridgend
19.11.04   Kevin Bennett L PTS 12 Hartlepool
           *(Commonwealth Lightweight Title
           Challenge)*
11.02.06   Jon Honney W RSC 2 Bethnal Green
02.04.06   Tontcho Tontchev L RSC 1 Bethnal
           Green
Career: 22 contests, won 15, lost 7.

Mark Phillips

St Clare's. *Born* Carmarthen, 28 April,
1975
S.Middleweight. Ht. 6'0"
Manager Self

26.10.00   Shayne Webb W PTS 6 Clydach
12.12.00   Tommy Matthews W PTS 6 Clydach
13.03.01   William Webster W RTD 1 Plymouth
07.10.01   Danny Norton L PTS 6 Wolverhampton
12.12.01   Simon Andrews W PTS 6 Clydach
25.04.02   Mark Ellwood L PTS 6 Hull
10.05.02   Scott Dann L PTS 6 Bethnal Green
23.06.02   Gareth Hogg L PTS 4 Southwark
10.07.02   Scott Dann L PTS 4 Wembley
03.12.02   Jamie Hearn L PTS 4 Bethnal Green
20.12.02   Ryan Walls L PTS 4 Bracknell
06.03.03   Darren Dorrington L PTS 8 Bristol
21.03.03   Steve Timms L PTS 6 West Bromwich
05.04.03   Dale Nixon L PTS 6 Coventry
13.04.03   Donovan Smillie L PTS 6 Bradford
12.05.03   Leigh Alliss L PTS 6 Southampton
27.05.03   Steven Spartacus L RSC 2 Dagenham
30.06.03   Roddy Doran L PTS 6 Shrewsbury
06.09.03   Alan Page L PTS 6 Huddersfield
18.09.03   Nick Okoth L PTS 4 Mayfair
09.10.03   Leigh Alliss L PTS 4 Bristol
30.11.03   Jimi Hendricks W PTS 6 Swansea
16.01.04   Donovan Smillie L PTS 4 Bradford
07.04.04   Christian Imaga L PTS 6 Leicester
           Square
15.04.04   Darren McDermott L PTS 4 Dudley
26.04.04   Dave Pearson W RSC 6 Cleethorpes
04.06.04   Steve Timms L PTS 6 Dudley
03.12.04   Dan Guthrie L RSC 1 Bristol
26.02.05   Matt Galer L PTS 6 Burton
21.04.05   Matthew Hough L PTS 4 Dudley

141

09.07.05	Liam Stinchcombe L PTS 4 Bristol
02.09.05	Dave Pearson W PTS 6 Derby
25.09.05	Lee Hodgson L PTS 6 Southampton
10.10.05	Peter McCormack W PTS 6 Birmingham
04.11.05	Gary Woolcombe L PTS 4 Bethnal Green
24.11.05	Glenn McClarnon L PTS 4 Lurgan
04.03.06	James Davenport L PTS 4 Manchester
30.03.06	Danny Tombs L PTS 4 Bloomsbury
13.05.06	Richard Horton L PTS 4 Bethnal Green
01.06.06	Jonjo Finnegan L PTS 4 Birmingham
09.06.06	Jason Rushton L PTS 6 Doncaster

Career: 41 contests, won 8, lost 33.

Stuart Phillips

Port Talbot. *Born* Abergavenny, 24
January, 1981
Welterweight. Ht. 5'8"
Manager Self

08.11.03	Lance Hall W PTS 4 Bridgend
30.11.03	Wayne Wheeler W PTS 4 Swansea
01.05.04	Chris Long L RSC 1 Bridgend
17.02.05	Tristan Davies L PTS 6 Dudley
28.04.05	Duncan Cottier DREW 4 Clydach
17.11.05	Ali Wyatt W PTS 4 Bristol

Career: 6 contests, won 3, drew 1, lost 2.

Esham Pickering

Newark. *Born* Newark, 7 August, 1976
S.Bantamweight. Former Undefeated
British S.Bantamweight Champion. Former
European & Commonwealth
S.Bantamweight Champion. Former
Undefeated British Masters Bantamweight
Champion. Ht. 5'5"
Manager J. Ingle

23.09.96	Brendan Bryce W RSC 5 Cleethorpes
24.10.96	Kevin Sheil W PTS 6 Lincoln
22.11.96	Amjid Mahmood W RSC 2 Hull
09.12.96	Des Gargano W RTD 2 Chesterfield
16.12.96	Graham McGrath W PTS 6 Cleethorpes
20.03.97	Robert Braddock W RSC 6 Newark
12.04.97	Graham McGrath W PTS 4 Sheffield
26.04.97	Mike Deveney W PTS 4 Swadlincote
16.05.97	Chris Price W PTS 6 Hull
26.06.97	Graham McGrath W PTS 6 Salford
01.11.97	Mike Deveney W RSC 8 Glasgow
	(Elim. British Featherweight Title)
09.05.98	Jonjo Irwin L PTS 12 Sheffield
	(Vacant British Featherweight Title)
11.09.98	Louis Veitch W PTS 6 Newark
15.08.99	Chris Lyons W RSC 2 Derby
23.10.99	Ian Turner W PTS 6 Telford
20.11.99	Marc Smith W PTS 6 Grantham
19.02.00	Kevin Gerowski W PTS 10 Newark
	(Vacant British Masters Bantamweight Title. Elim. British Bantamweight Title)
13.08.00	Lee Williamson W PTS 6 Nottingham
16.12.00	Mauricio Martinez L RSC 1 Sheffield
	(WBO Bantamweight Title Challenge)
15.09.01	Carl Allen W PTS 6 Derby
08.12.01	Carl Allen W PTS 8 Chesterfield
20.04.02	Carl Allen W PTS 6 Derby
24.09.02	Alejandro Monzon L PTS 12 Gran Canaria, Spain
	(Vacant WBA Inter-Continental S.Featherweight Title)
02.12.02	Carl Allen W PTS 6 Leicester
08.02.03	Duncan Karanja W CO 5 Brentford

	(Vacant Commonwealth S.Bantamweight Title)
12.07.03	Brian Carr W RSC 4 Renfrew
	(Vacant British S.Bantamweight Title. Commonwealth S.Bantamweight Title Defence)
24.10.03	Alfred Tetteh W RSC 7 Bethnal Green
	(Commonwealth S.Bantamweight Title Defence)
16.01.04	Vincenzo Gigliotti W CO 10 Bradford
	(Vacant European S.Bantamweight Title)
12.05.04	Juan Garcia Martin W RSC 8 Reading
	(European S.Bantamweight Title Defence)
08.05.05	Noel Wilders W PTS 8 Bradford
09.06.05	Miguel Mallon W RSC 10 Alcobendas, Madrid, Spain
	(European S.Bantamweight Title Defence)
28.10.05	Michael Hunter L PTS 12 Hartlepool
	(European & Commonwealth S.Bantamweight Title Defences. British S.Bantamweight Title Challenge)
02.12.05	Frederic Bonifai W PTS 6 Nottingham

Career: 33 contests, won 29, lost 4.

Wayne Pinder

Manchester. *Born* Manchester, 15 April,
1978
S.Middleweight. Former WBF
Middleweight Champion. Ht. 6'0"
Manager Self

27.04.98	C. J. Jackson W PTS 6 Manchester
01.06.98	Carlton Williams W PTS 6 Manchester
26.10.98	Mark Owens DREW 6 Manchester
28.02.99	Lee Bird W RSC 5 Shaw
13.03.99	Paul O'Rourke W RSC 3 Manchester
02.05.99	Carl Smith W RSC 5 Shaw
02.07.99	Donovan Davey W PTS 6 Manchester
19.09.99	Paul King W PTS 6 Shaw
11.06.00	Colin Vidler W PTS 6 Salford
01.07.00	Gary Beardsley W PTS 4 Manchester
09.09.00	Ian Toby W PTS 4 Manchester
12.11.00	James Donoghue W PTS 6 Manchester
17.03.01	Leigh Wicks W PTS 4 Manchester
27.05.01	Dean Ashton W PTS 6 Manchester
07.07.01	Ian Toby W RTD 5 Manchester
26.11.01	Howard Clarke W PTS 6 Manchester
09.03.02	Jimmy Steel W PTS 4 Manchester
21.07.02	Darren Covill W CO 2 Salford
09.11.02	Darren Rhodes W RSC 4 Altrincham
28.01.03	Damon Hague W RSC 7 Nottingham
	(Vacant WBF Middleweight Title)
16.04.03	Damon Hague L RSC 2 Nottingham
	(WBF Middleweight Title Defence)
21.06.03	Howard Clarke W PTS 4 Manchester
12.03.04	Leigh Wicks W PTS 4 Nottingham
10.04.04	Howard Clarke W PTS 4 Manchester
23.09.05	Jason Collins W PTS 6 Manchester
25.11.05	Paul Buchanan DREW 6 Liverpool

Career: 26 contests, won 23, drew 2, lost 1.

David Pinkney

South Shields. *Born* South Shields, 14
August, 1975
Welterweight. Ht. 5'9"
Manager M. Gates

23.09.04	Sujad Elahi W PTS 6 Gateshead
09.03.06	Tom Hogan L PTS 6 Sunderland

Career: 2 contests, won 1, lost 1.

Michael Pinnock

Birmingham. *Born* Birmingham, 6 June,
1965
Cruiserweight. Ht. 6'0"
Manager Self

19.05.95	David Flowers L PTS 6 Leeds
13.06.95	Mark Snipe L PTS 6 Basildon
20.06.95	Darren Sweeney L PTS 8 Birmingham
06.09.95	Steve Loftus L PTS 6 Stoke
21.09.95	Luan Morena L PTS 4 Battersea
24.10.95	Graham Townsend L PTS 4 Southwark
17.11.95	Graham Townsend L PTS 4 Bethnal Green
03.12.95	Neville Smith L RSC 5 Southwark
23.01.96	Butch Lesley L PTS 4 Bethnal Green
05.03.96	Panayiotis Panayiotiou L PTS 4 Bethnal Green
16.03.96	Mark Hickey L PTS 6 Barnstaple
25.03.96	Lee Simpkin W PTS 6 Birmingham
03.04.96	Jason Hart L PTS 6 Bethnal Green
24.04.96	Gordon Behan L PTS 6 Solihull
03.05.96	David Larkin DREW 6 Sheffield
14.05.96	Mervyn Penniston L RSC 2 Dagenham
19.07.96	Chris Davies L PTS 6 Ystrad
29.07.96	Stuart Fleet L RSC 3 Skegness
04.10.96	Paul Bonson L PTS 6 Wakefield
28.10.96	Zak Goldman DREW 6 Leicester
14.11.96	Paul Bonson DREW 6 Sheffield
21.11.96	Darren Sweeney W RSC 5 Solihull
26.11.96	Mark Smallwood L PTS 6 Wolverhampton
03.02.97	Neil Simpson L PTS 6 Leicester
09.06.97	Mark Hobson L PTS 6 Bradford
05.07.97	Paschal Collins L PTS 6 Glasgow
02.09.97	Mike Gormley L PTS 6 Manchester
18.09.97	Martin Jolley DREW 6 Alfreton
04.10.97	Zoltan Sarossy L PTS 4 Muswell Hill
27.10.97	Johnny Hooks DREW 6 Nottingham
11.11.97	Graham Townsend L PTS 8 Bethnal Green
25.11.97	Barry Thorogood L PTS 8 Wolverhampton
15.12.97	Greg Scott-Briggs L PTS 6 Nottingham
02.02.98	Glenn Williams L CO 5 Bradford
30.04.98	Bobby Banghar L PTS 6 Purfleet
18.05.98	Jon O'Brien L PTS 6 Cleethorpes
22.10.98	Paul Carr L PTS 6 Barking
29.10.98	Paul Carr DREW 6 Bayswater
05.12.98	Dave Stenner W RSC 3 Bristol
03.04.99	Robert Zlotkowski L PTS 4 Carlisle
15.05.99	Damon Hague L PTS 4 Sheffield
05.06.99	Leif Keiski L PTS 6 Cardiff
02.07.99	Mike Gormley L RSC 6 Manchester
01.10.99	Tony Oakey L PTS 4 Bethnal Green
16.10.99	Brian Magee L RSC 3 Belfast
17.04.00	Gordon Behan L PTS 6 Birmingham
15.05.00	Tony Booth L PTS 6 Cleethorpes
25.05.00	Neil Linford L PTS 4 Peterborough
08.09.00	Steven Spartacus L PTS 4 Hammersmith
10.11.00	Tony Griffiths L PTS 4 Mayfair
01.12.00	Allan Foster L PTS 4 Peterborough
29.01.01	Ivan Botton W PTS 4 Peterborough
20.03.01	Joe Gillon L PTS 6 Glasgow
28.03.01	Darren Ashton DREW 6 Piccadilly
09.06.01	Nathan King L PTS 4 Bethnal Green
21.06.01	Paul Bonson L PTS 6 Sheffield
27.07.01	Mark Brookes L PTS 4 Sheffield
15.09.01	Tony Dowling L PTS 6 Derby
04.10.01	Oneal Murray L PTS 6 Finsbury
21.10.01	Peter Merrall DREW 6 Pentre Halkyn
28.10.01	Radcliffe Green L PTS 4 Southwark

24.11.01	Steven Spartacus L PTS 4 Bethnal Green
09.12.01	Andrew Facey L PTS 6 Shaw
16.12.01	Sam Price L PTS 4 Southwark
16.03.02	Carl Froch L RSC 4 Bethnal Green
21.11.02	Earl Ling L PTS 6 Hull
16.12.02	Eamonn Glennon DREW 6 Cleethorpes
08.02.03	Tony Moran L PTS 4 Liverpool
23.02.03	Ryan Walls L PTS 6 Streatham
16.03.03	Scott Lansdowne L PTS 6 Nottingham
24.03.03	Pinky Burton L PTS 4 Barnsley
10.06.03	Mark Brookes L PTS 6 Sheffield
31.07.03	Amer Khan L PTS 6 Sheffield
06.10.03	Reagan Denton L PTS 6 Barnsley
26.10.03	Ryan Walls L PTS 10 Longford
	(Vacant British Masters Cruiserweight Title)
11.11.03	Keiran O'Donnell L PTS 6 Leeds
03.04.04	Amer Khan L PTS 6 Sheffield
16.04.04	Nate Joseph L PTS 4 Bradford
08.05.04	Leigh Alliss L PTS 4 Bristol
07.06.04	Sandy Robb L PTS 6 Glasgow
19.12.04	Lee Blundell L PTS 6 Bolton
13.02.05	Donovan Smillie L PTS 6 Bradford
21.02.05	Hamed Jamali L PTS 8 Birmingham
22.04.05	Rod Anderton L PTS 6 Barnsley
13.05.05	Lee Blundell L PTS 4 Liverpool
08.07.05	Gyorgy Hidvegi L PTS 4 Altrincham
22.10.05	Nicki Taylor L PTS 6 Mansfield

Career: 87 contests, won 4, drew 9, lost 74.

(Patrick) Paddy Pollock

Wishaw. *Born* Bellshill, 10 October, 1985
Welterweight. Ht. 5'10½"
Manager A. Morrison

22.04.06	Duncan Cottier W PTS 6 Glasgow

Career: 1 contest, won 1.

Paul Porter

Luton. *Born* Luton, 4 October, 1978
L.Middleweight. Ht. 5'9¼"
Manager F. Maloney

11.02.06	Omar Gumati L RSC 3 Bethnal Green
02.04.06	Steve Anning DREW 4 Bethnal Green

Career: 2 contests, drew 1, lost 1.

Marcus Portman

West Bromwich. *Born* West Bromwich, 26
September, 1980
Middleweight. Former Undefeated British
Masters Welterweight Champion. Ht. 6'0"
Manager Self

18.02.00	Ray Wood W PTS 6 West Bromwich
28.03.00	Billy Smith W PTS 6 Wolverhampton
10.09.00	Alan Kershaw W RSC 2 Walsall
15.02.01	Willie Limond L PTS 6 Glasgow
01.04.01	Tony Smith W PTS 6 Wolverhampton
20.04.01	Darren Melville L RSC 3 Millwall
07.09.01	Tony Smith W PTS 6 West Bromwich
15.09.01	Matthew Hatton L RSC 3 Manchester
12.12.01	Ross McCord DREW 4 Clydach
18.01.02	Andy Egan W PTS 4 Coventry
25.02.02	Sammy Smith W PTS 6 Slough
27.04.02	Gavin Wake W PTS 4 Huddersfield
08.05.03	Thomas McDonagh L PTS 6 Widnes
17.05.03	Scott Dixon W PTS 6 Liverpool
30.06.03	Wayne Wheeler W RSC 3 Shrewsbury
07.09.03	Jason Williams W PTS 6 Shrewsbury
19.02.04	Richard Swallow W PTS 10 Dudley

	(British Masters Welterweight Title Challenge)
03.04.04	Chris Saunders L RSC 1 Sheffield
	(Vacant English Welterweight Title)
29.06.06	Peter Dunn W PTS 6 Dudley

Career: 19 contests, won 13, drew 1, lost 5.

Martin Power

St Pancras. *Born* London, 14 February,
1980
British Bantamweight Champion. Ht. 5'6"
Manager F. Maloney

09.06.01	Sean Grant W PTS 4 Bethnal Green
28.07.01	Andrew Greenaway W RSC 3 Wembley
22.09.01	Stevie Quinn W RSC 2 Bethnal Green
24.11.01	Anthony Hanna W PTS 4 Bethnal Green
19.01.02	Gareth Wiltshaw W PTS 4 Bethnal Green
08.07.02	Darren Cleary W PTS 4 Mayfair
12.10.02	Stevie Quinn W RSC 4 Bethnal Green
15.02.03	Stevie Quinn W RTD 1 Wembley
29.03.03	Dave Hinds W PTS 4 Portsmouth
17.07.03	Darren Cleary W PTS 6 Dagenham
06.11.03	Rocky Dean W PTS 6 Dagenham
24.01.04	Delroy Spencer W RTD 1 Wembley
01.04.04	Fred Janes W RSC 2 Bethnal Green
13.05.04	Jean-Marie Codet W PTS 8 Bethnal Green
30.07.04	Delroy Spencer W CO 2 Bethnal Green
11.12.04	Shinny Bayaar W PTS 10 Canning Town
20.05.05	Dale Robinson W PTS 12 Southwark
	(Vacant British Bantamweight Title)
04.11.05	Ian Napa W PTS 12 Bethnal Green
	(British Bantamweight Title Defence)
30.05.06	Isaac Ward W RSC 8 Bethnal Green
	(British Bantamweight Title Defence)
29.06.06	Tshifhiwa Munyai L RSC 9 Bethnal Green
	(Vacant Commonwealth Bantamweight Title)

Career: 20 contests, won 19, lost 1.

Martin Power Philip Sharkey

Sam Price

Reading. *Born* Hillingdon, 6 July, 1981
L. Heavyweight. Ht. 6'0¹/₂"
Manager G. Carman

16.12.01 Michael Pinnock W PTS 4 Southwark
10.02.02 Calvin Stonestreet W PTS 4 Southwark
19.03.02 Jimmy Steel W PTS 4 Slough
21.03.03 Harry Butler W PTS 4 Longford
25.03.04 Terry Morrill L RSC 3 Longford
28.10.04 Varuzhan Davtyan W PTS 6 Sunderland
08.12.04 Hastings Rasani W PTS 6 Longford
21.01.05 Nick Okoth W PTS 6 Brentford
10.04.05 Steven Spartacus L RSC 6 Brentwood
          *(British Masters L.Heavyweight Title
          Challenge)*
16.12.05 Gary Ojuederie L PTS 6 Bracknell

Career: 10 contests, won 7, lost 3.

Mitch Prince

Cumbernauld. *Born* Johannesburg, South
Africa, 15 March, 1984
Lightweight. Ht. 5'5¹/₂"
Manager T. Gilmour

05.06.06 Jason Nesbitt W PTS 6 Glasgow

Career: 1 contest, won 1.

Bradley Pryce (Price)

Newbridge. *Born* Newport, 15 March, 1981
Commonwealth L.Middleweight
Champion. Former Undefeated Welsh
Welterweight Champion. Former
Undefeated IBF Inter-Continental
L.Welterweight Champion. Former
Undefeated WBO Inter-Continental
Lightweight Champion. Ht. 5'11"
Manager Self

17.07.99 Dave Hinds W PTS 4 Doncaster
23.10.99 David Jeffrey W RSC 3 Telford
06.11.99 Eddie Nevins W RSC 2 Widnes
29.01.00 Pete Buckley W PTS 4 Manchester
29.02.00 Carl Allen W PTS 4 Widnes
16.05.00 Carl Allen W RSC 3 Warrington
15.07.00 Gary Flear W RSC 1 Millwall
07.10.00 Gary Reid W RSC 5 Doncaster
27.01.01 Joel Viney W RSC 3 Bethnal Green
17.03.01 Brian Coleman W PTS 4 Manchester
28.04.01 Jason Hall W PTS 12 Cardiff
          *(Vacant WBO Inter-Continental
          Lightweight Title)*
21.07.01 Stuart Patterson W RSC 5 Sheffield
09.10.01 Lucky Sambo W PTS 12 Cardiff
          *(WBO Inter-Continental Lightweight
          Title Defence)*
12.02.02 Gavin Down W RSC 9 Bethnal Green
          *(Vacant IBF Inter-Continental
          L.Welterweight Title)*
20.04.02 Dafydd Carlin W RSC 8 Cardiff
08.06.02 Pete Buckley W RSC 1 Renfrew
17.08.02 Ted Bami L RSC 6 Cardiff
23.11.02 Craig Lynch W CO 4 Derby
01.02.03 Neil Sinclair L RSC 8 Belfast
          (British Welterweight Title Challenge)
08.05.03 Ivan Kirpa W PTS 10 Widnes
21.02.04 Farai Musiiwa L PTS 6 Cardiff
06.05.04 Thomas McDonagh L PTS 12 Barnsley
          *(WBU International L.Middleweight
          Title Challenge)*
03.07.04 Keith Jones W RSC 8 Newport
          (Vacant Welsh Welterweight Title)
03.09.04 Ajose Olusegun L RSC 4 Newport

11.12.04 Sergey Styopkin W RSC 10 Canning
          Town
25.10.05 Michael Jennings L PTS 12 Preston
          (British Welterweight Title Challenge)
11.03.06 Ossie Duran W PTS 12 Newport
          *(Commonwealth L.Middleweight Title
          Challenge)*

Career: 27 contests, won 21, lost 6.

Kreshnik Qato

Wembley. *Born* Albania, 13 August, 1978
L.Heavyweight. Former Undefeated
Eastern European Boxing Association
S.Middleweight Champion. Ht. 5'9¹/₂"
Manager P. Fondu

28.09.01 Erik Teymour L PTS 6 Millwall
16.12.01 Lawrence Murphy L PTS 6 Glasgow
08.04.02 Ty Browne W PTS 4 Southampton
10.05.02 Paul Jones L PTS 6 Millwall
20.03.03 Jason Collins W PTS 4 Queensway
13.04.03 Mark Thornton W RSC 3 Streatham
13.05.03 Danny Thornton W PTS 6 Leeds
26.07.03 Scott Dann L RSC 2 Plymouth
26.09.03 Joel Ani W PTS 6 Millwall
14.11.03 Steven Bendall L PTS 8 Bethnal
          Green
21.02.04 Gary Lockett L RSC 2 Cardiff
16.10.04 Vladimir Zavgorodniy W PTS 10
          Yalta, Ukraine

*(Vacant Eastern European Boxing
Association S.Middleweight Title)*
05.03.05 Rizvan Magomedov W PTS 12 Durres,
          Albania
          *(Eastern European Boxing Association
          S.Middleweight Title Defence)*
12.06.05 Dmitry Donetskiy W RSC 6 Leicester
          Square
09.10.05 Daniil Prakapsou W PTS 8
          Hammersmith
02.04.06 Laurent Goury W PTS 6 Bethnal Green
26.05.06 Simone Lucas W PTS 4 Bethnal Green

Career: 17 contests, won 11, lost 6.

Tony Quigley

Liverpool. *Born* Liverpool, 1 October,
1984
L.Heavyweight. Ht. 5'10"
Manager F. Warren/D. Powell

26.02.04 Dave Pearson W RSC 1 Widnes
22.05.04 Patrick Cito W PTS 4 Widnes
01.10.04 Leigh Wicks W PTS 4 Manchester
11.02.05 Shpetim Hoti W CO 1 Manchester
03.06.05 Varuzhan Davtyan W PTS 4
          Manchester
04.03.06 Ojay Abrahams W PTS 4 Manchester
01.06.06 Simeon Cover W PTS 4 Barnsley

Career: 7 contests, won 7.

Bradley Pryce   Les Clark

Furhan Rafiq

Glasgow. *Born* Glasgow, 16 December, 1977
S.Featherweight. Ht. 5'8"
Manager T. Gilmour

19.04.04	Paddy Folan W PTS 6 Glasgow
15.11.04	Gary Davis L PTS 6 Glasgow
05.06.06	Shaun Walton W PTS 6 Glasgow
16.06.06	Henry Jones L PTS 6 Carmarthen

Career: 4 contests, won 2, lost 2.

Harry Ramogoadi

Coventry. *Born* South Africa, 21 March, 1976
Featherweight. Ht. 5'6"
Manager Self

20.11.98	Dan Ngweyna W PTS 4 Thembisa, South Africa
24.01.99	Zachariah Madau W PTS 4 Johannesburg, South Africa
26.03.99	Jan van Rooyen DREW 4 Witbank, South Africa
27.06.99	Kenneth Buhlalu W PTS 4 Durban, South Africa
23.07.99	Bethule Machedi W PTS 4 Johannesburg, South Africa
25.09.99	Malepa Levi W PTS 6 Nelspruit, South Africa
01.12.99	Mandla Mashiane L PTS 6 Johannesburg, South Africa
13.07.00	Martin Mnyandu L PTS 6 Johannesburg, South Africa
28.10.00	Trevor Gouws W PTS 6 Johannesburg, South Africa
18.02.01	Thomas Mashaba DREW 6 Johannesburg, South Africa
15.04.01	Malepa Levi W PTS 8 Johannesburg, South Africa
02.11.01	Malcolm Klaasen W PTS 6 Benoni, South Africa
08.02.02	Takalani Kwinda W PTS 8 Johannesburg, South Africa
09.10.02	Ariel Mathebula W PTS 6 Sandton, South Africa
24.10.03	Stephen Oates W PTS 6 Bethnal Green
08.11.03	Jason Nesbitt W PTS 6 Coventry
09.04.04	Nigel Senior W RSC 1 Rugby
10.07.04	Choi Tseveenpurev L RTD 6 Coventry *(British Masters Featherweight Title Challenge)*
09.12.04	John Murray L RSC 4 Stockport
06.03.05	Choi Tseveenpurev L RSC 5 Shaw *(British Masters Featherweight Title Challenge)*
01.06.05	Danny Wallace W PTS 6 Leeds
23.07.05	Jamie Arthur W RSC 5 Edinburgh

Career: 22 contests, won 15, drew 2, lost 5.

Tony Randell (Webster)

Birmingham. *Born* Peterborough, 11 April, 1982
Middleweight. Ht. 5'11½"
Manager Self

16.12.04	Scott Conway W PTS 6 Cleethorpes

13.02.05	Gavin Smith L PTS 6 Bradford
23.03.05	Danny Goode L PTS 6 Leicester Square
01.04.05	Chris Black L PTS 6 Glasgow
16.05.05	Sergey Haritonov W RSC 4 Birmingham
24.07.05	Stuart Brookes L PTS 6 Sheffield
09.09.05	Stuart Brookes L RSC 3 Sheffield
10.10.05	Simon Sherrington L PTS 6 Birmingham
30.10.05	Jake Guntert L PTS 4 Bethnal Green
18.12.05	Mark Thompson L RSC 2 Bolton
17.02.06	Reagan Denton L PTS 6 Sheffield
18.03.06	Sam Gorman W PTS 6 Coventry
02.04.06	Alex Matvienko L PTS 6 Shaw
13.04.06	Danny Wright L PTS 6 Leeds
20.05.06	George Katsimpas L RSC 1 Bristol

Career: 15 contests, won 3, lost 12.

Hastings Rasani

Birmingham. *Born* Zimbabwe, 16 April, 1974
Cruiserweight. Ht. 6'2"
Manager Self

21.12.97	Elias Chikwanda W RSC 4 Harare, Zimbabwe
28.02.98	Victor Ndebele W CO 1 Harare, Zimbabwe
04.04.98	William Mpoku W PTS 8 Harare, Zimbabwe
03.05.98	Nightshow Mafukidze W CO 3 Harare, Zimbabwe
30.05.98	Frank Mutiyaya W RSC 4 Harare, Zimbabwe
24.07.98	Ambrose Mlilo L RSC 9 Harare, Zimbabwe
13.01.99	Tobia Wede W RSC 4 Harare, Zimbabwe
27.02.99	Ambrose Mlilo L CO 9 Harare, Zimbabwe
17.04.99	Eric Sauti W RSC 2 Harare, Zimbabwe
05.06.99	Gibson Mapfumo W RSC 2 Harare, Zimbabwe
02.01.01	Neil Simpson L CO 4 Coventry *(Vacant Commonwealth L.Heavyweight Title)*
28.04.01	Arigoma Chiponda W DIS Harare, Zimbabwe
08.05.01	Tony Oakey L RSC 10 Barnsley *(Vacant Commonwealth L.Heavyweight Title)*
06.10.01	Sipho Moyo L CO 9 Harare, Zimbabwe
15.03.03	Elvis Michailenko L RSC 5 Millwall
24.05.03	Elvis Michailenko L RSC 4 Bethnal Green
31.07.03	Mark Brookes L PTS 6 Sheffield
05.09.03	Carl Thompson L RSC 1 Sheffield
04.10.03	Steven Spartacus L RSC 1 Muswell Hill
11.11.03	Denzil Browne L PTS 6 Leeds
13.02.04	Leigh Alliss L PTS 6 Bristol
21.02.04	Earl Ling DREW 6 Norwich
12.03.04	Simeon Cover W CO 6 Irvine
20.03.04	David Haye L RSC 1 Wembley
12.05.04	Jamie Hearn L RSC 4 Reading
17.06.04	Amer Khan L PTS 6 Sheffield
17.09.04	Mark Brookes L PTS 6 Sheffield
11.10.04	Hamed Jamali L PTS 8 Birmingham
22.10.04	Nathan King L PTS 6 Edinburgh
08.12.04	Sam Price L PTS 6 Longford
17.12.04	Neil Simpson L PTS 6 Coventry

21.02.05	Karl Wheeler L PTS 6 Peterborough
24.04.05	Nicki Taylor W RTD 4 Askern
08.05.05	Nate Joseph W RSC 4 Bradford
15.05.05	Danny Grainger W RSC 5 Sheffield
02.06.05	Karl Wheeler W RSC 5 Peterborough
01.07.05	Ovill McKenzie L PTS 6 Fulham
09.09.05	Lee Swaby L PTS 4 Sheffield
24.09.05	Neil Linford W RSC 5 Coventry
12.11.05	Dean Francis L RSC 6 Bristol
19.12.05	Valery Odin W PTS 4 Longford
11.03.06	Bruce Scott W PTS 8 Newport

Career: 42 contests, won 17, drew 1, lost 24.

Abdul Rashid

Manchester. *Born* Manchester, 17 February, 1975
Lightweight. Ht. 5'7"
Manager G. Hunter

18.06.06	Sergei Rozhakmens W PTS 6 Manchester

Career: 1 contest, won 1.

Neil Read

Bilston. *Born* Wolverhampton, 9 February, 1972
Featherweight. Ht. 5'4"
Manager P. Bowen

08.02.00	Gary Groves W PTS 6 Wolverhampton
10.09.00	Stephen Chinnock L RSC 5 Walsall
30.11.00	Paddy Folan L PTS 6 Blackpool
13.02.01	Sid Razak L PTS 6 Brierley Hill
08.03.01	John-Paul Ryan W PTS 6 Wolverhampton
26.08.01	Lee Holmes L PTS 6 Warrington
06.12.01	Chris Edwards L PTS 8 Stoke
28.01.02	Jamil Hussain L CO 2 Barnsley
13.04.02	Stephen Chinnock L CO 3 Wolverhampton *(Midlands Area Featherweight Title Challenge)*
29.06.02	Jamie Yelland L PTS 6 Brentwood
03.08.02	Isaac Ward L RSC 1 Blackpool
23.09.02	Andy Roberts L PTS 6 Cleethorpes
10.10.02	Chris Edwards L PTS 6 Stoke
08.11.02	Andy Roberts L PTS 6 Doncaster
02.12.02	Steve Gethin L RTD 3 Leicester
10.02.03	Sean Hughes L PTS 6 Sheffield
17.03.03	Junior Anderson W CO 2 Southampton
07.06.03	Gareth Payne L RSC 5 Coventry *(Vacant Midlands Area S.Bantamweight Title)*
05.09.03	Andy Roberts L PTS 6 Doncaster
09.10.03	Lee Haskins L PTS 4 Bristol
08.11.03	Gareth Payne L PTS 4 Coventry
14.02.04	Rendall Munroe L RSC 1 Nottingham
03.04.04	Mark Moran L RSC 2 Manchester
14.06.04	Wayne Bloy DREW 6 Cleethorpes
26.09.04	Chris Edwards L RSC 2 Stoke *(Vacant British Masters S.Bantamweight Title)*
31.10.04	Gary Ford L PTS 6 Shaw
18.04.05	Abdul Mougharbel L PTS 6 Bradford
24.07.05	Craig Bromley L PTS 4 Sheffield
16.09.05	Jamie McDonnell L PTS 6 Doncaster
12.11.05	Mick Abbott L PTS 6 Stoke
23.02.06	Tasif Khan L RSC 6 Leeds
14.04.06	Neil Marston L PTS 6 Telford
28.05.06	Robert Nelson L PTS 6 Wakefield

Career: 33 contests, won 3, drew 1, lost 29.

Gavin Rees

Newbridge. *Born* Newport, 10 May, 1980
L.Welterweight. Former Undefeated WBO
Inter-Continental Featherweight Champion.
Ht. 5'7"
Manager Self

05.09.98	John Farrell W PTS 4 Telford
05.12.98	Ernie Smith W PTS 4 Bristol
27.03.99	Graham McGrath W RSC 2 Derby
05.06.99	Wayne Jones W RSC 2 Cardiff
11.12.99	Dave Hinds W RSC 2 Liverpool
19.02.00	Pete Buckley W PTS 4 Dagenham
29.05.00	Willie Valentine W RSC 3 Manchester
23.09.00	Pete Buckley W PTS 4 Bethnal Green
13.11.00	Steve Hanley W RSC 1 Bethnal Green
15.01.01	Chris Jickells W RSC 2 Manchester
28.04.01	Vladimir Borov W RSC 4 Cardiff
	(Vacant WBO Inter-Continental Featherweight Title)
21.07.01	Nigel Senior W RSC 2 Sheffield
09.10.01	Nikolai Eremeev W PTS 12 Cardiff
	(WBO Inter-Continental Featherweight Title Defence)
12.02.02	Rakhim Mingaleev W PTS 6 Bethnal Green
20.04.02	Gary Flear W RTD 4 Cardiff
08.07.02	Ernie Smith W RSC 5 Mayfair
17.08.02	Sergei Andreychikov W RTD 1 Cardiff
14.12.02	Jimmy Beech W PTS 4 Newcastle
15.02.03	Andrei Devyataykin W PTS 6 Wembley
28.06.03	Daniel Thorpe W RSC 1 Cardiff
03.07.04	Michael Muya W RSC 2 Newport
03.09.04	Carl Allen W PTS 6 Newport
11.03.06	Daniel Thorpe W RSC 5 Newport

Career: 23 contests, won 23.

Duane Reid

Derby. *Born* Nottingham, 29 October, 1980
Cruiserweight. Ht. 6'2"
Manager C. Mitchell

25.03.06	Paul David L RSC 3 Burton
14.05.06	Nicki Taylor W RSC 2 Derby
22.05.06	Chris Rice W PTS 6 Birmingham

Career: 3 contests, won 2, lost 1.

Gary Reid

Stoke. *Born* Jamaica, 20 November, 1972
British Masters L.Welterweight Champion.
Ht. 5'5½"
Manager M. Carney

09.12.98	Carl Tilley W CO 1 Stoke
11.02.99	Ted Bami L RSC 2 Dudley
23.03.99	Lee Williamson W PTS 6 Wolverhampton
07.10.99	Stuart Rimmer W RSC 2 Mere
19.12.99	No No Junior L PTS 6 Salford
14.04.00	Lee Molyneux W PTS 6 Manchester
18.05.00	Sammy Smith W RSC 1 Bethnal Green
23.07.00	Kevin Bennett L RSC 4 Hartlepool
21.09.00	Karim Bouali L PTS 4 Bloomsbury
07.10.00	Bradley Pryce L RSC 5 Doncaster
07.09.01	Willie Limond L PTS 8 Glasgow
22.09.01	Francis Barrett L PTS 4 Bethnal Green
17.02.02	Richie Caparelli W PTS 6 Salford
02.03.02	Paul Halpin L RSC 3 Bethnal Green
26.04.02	Martin Watson L PTS 6 Glasgow
28.05.02	Gareth Jordan DREW 6 Liverpool

Ian Reid

Balham. *Born* Lambeth, 30 August, 1972
Lightweight. Ht. 5'2"
Manager Self

30.03.93	Russell Rees L PTS 6 Cardiff
31.08.93	Jason Hutson W RSC 6 Croydon
10.11.93	Marcus McCrae L PTS 6 Bethnal Green
09.12.94	Mark Bowers L PTS 6 Bethnal Green
17.05.95	Michael Brodie L RSC 3 Ipswich
30.11.03	Henry Janes L PTS 6 Swansea
07.12.03	John Bothwell L PTS 6 Glasgow
15.03.04	Darren Johnstone L PTS 6 Glasgow
31.10.04	Eddie Nevins L PTS 6 Shaw
12.11.04	Simon Wilson L PTS 6 Belfast
19.12.04	Warren Dunkley L PTS 4 Bethnal Green
18.02.05	Justin Murphy L PTS 6 Brighton
06.03.05	Craig Johnson L PTS 6 Mansfield
23.03.05	Gareth Couch L RSC 6 Leicester Square
30.04.05	Jed Syger L PTS 4 Dagenham
20.05.05	Lee Cook L PTS 4 Southwark
11.09.05	Jonathan Whiteman L PTS 4 Kirkby in Ashfield
07.10.05	Ian Wilson L PTS 4 Bethnal Green
13.11.05	Paul Newby L PTS 6 Leeds
10.12.05	Dean Smith L RSC 1 Canning Town
02.02.06	Andrew Murray L RSC 4 Holborn
17.03.06	Paul Appleby L RSC 3 Kirkcaldy

Career: 22 contests, won 1, lost 21.

Mike Reid

Aberdeen. *Born* Inverurie, 4 November, 1983
Welterweight. Ht. 5'8"
Manager T. Gilmour

15.11.04	Willie Valentine W PTS 6 Glasgow
21.02.05	Tom Hogan W PTS 6 Glasgow
11.06.05	Lance Verallo W PTS 6 Kirkcaldy
30.09.05	Ben Hudson W PTS 4 Kirkcaldy
24.10.05	Chris Brophy W RSC 2 Glasgow
31.03.06	Tom Hogan L PTS 6 Inverurie
27.05.06	Adam Kelly DREW 6 Aberdeen

Career: 7 contests, won 5, drew 1, lost 1.

13.07.02	Gary Greenwood L RSC 5 Coventry
05.10.02	Joel Viney W CO 2 Coventry
18.11.02	Martin Watson L RSC 4 Glasgow
21.03.03	Young Muttley L RSC 7 West Bromwich
	(Vacant Midlands Area L.Welterweight Title)
10.10.03	Oscar Hall W RSC 2 Darlington
26.09.04	Tony Montana W PTS 10 Stoke
	(Vacant British Masters L.Welterweight Title)
17.02.05	Dean Hickman L PTS 10 Dudley
	(Midlands Area L.Welterweight Title Challenge)
27.05.05	Barry Morrison L RTD 8 Motherwell
	(British Masters L.Welterweight Title Defence)
25.11.05	Jason Cook L DIS 2 Liverpool
18.02.06	Davis Kamara W PTS 6 Stoke
06.05.06	Kevin McIntyre W RSC 6 Stoke
	(Vacant British Masters L.Welterweight Title)
26.05.06	Leo O'Reilly W RSC 2 Bethnal Green

Career: 28 contests, won 12, drew 1, lost 15.

Robin Reid

Runcorn. Liverpool, 19 February, 1971
S.Middleweight. Former IBO
S.Middleweight Champion. Former
Undefeated WBF S.Middleweight
Champion. Former WBC S.Middleweight
Champion. Ht. 5'9"
Manager Self

27.02.93	Mark Dawson W RSC 1 Dagenham
06.03.93	Julian Eavis W RSC 2 Glasgow
10.04.93	Andrew Furlong W PTS 6 Swansea
10.09.93	Juan Garcia W PTS 6 San Antonio, Texas, USA
09.10.93	Ernie Loveridge W PTS 4 Manchester
18.12.93	Danny Juma DREW 6 Manchester
09.04.94	Kesem Clayton W RSC 1 Mansfield
04.06.94	Andrew Furlong W RSC 2 Cardiff
17.08.94	Andrew Jervis W RSC 1 Sheffield
19.11.94	Chris Richards W RSC 3 Cardiff
04.02.95	Bruno Westenberghs W RSC 1 Cardiff
04.03.95	Marvin O'Brien W RSC 6 Livingston
06.05.95	Steve Goodwin W CO 1 Shepton Mallet
10.06.95	Martin Jolley W CO 1 Manchester
22.07.95	John Duckworth W PTS 8 Millwall
15.09.95	Trevor Ambrose W CO 5 Mansfield
10.11.95	Danny Juma W PTS 8 Derby
26.01.96	Stinger Mason W RSC 2 Brighton
16.03.96	Andrew Flute W RSC 7 Glasgow
26.04.96	Hunter Clay W RSC 1 Cardiff
08.06.96	Mark Dawson W RSC 5 Newcastle
31.08.96	Don Pendleton W RTD 4 Dublin
12.10.96	Vincenzo Nardiello W CO 7 Milan, Italy
	(WBC S. Middleweight Title Challenge)
08.02.97	Giovanni Pretorius W RSC 7 Millwall
	(WBC S. Middleweight Title Defence)
03.05.97	Henry Wharton W PTS 12 Manchester
	(WBC S. Middleweight Title Defence)
11.09.97	Hassine Cherifi W PTS 12 Widnes
	(WBC S. Middleweight Title Defence)
19.12.97	Thulani Malinga L PTS 12 Millwall
	(WBC S. Middleweight Title Defence)
18.04.98	Graham Townsend W RSC 6 Manchester
13.02.99	Joe Calzaghe L PTS 12 Newcastle
	(WBO S. Middleweight Title Challenge)
24.06.00	Silvio Branco L PTS 12 Glasgow
	(WBU S. Middleweight Title Challenge)
08.12.00	Mike Gormley W RSC 1 Crystal Palace
	(Vacant WBF S. Middleweight Title)
19.05.01	Roman Babaev W RSC 3 Wembley
	(WBF S. Middleweight Title Defence)
14.07.01	Soon Botes W RSC 4 Liverpool
	(WBF S.Middleweight TitleDefence)
20.10.01	Jorge Sclarandi W CO 3 Glasgow
	(WBF S. Middleweight Title Defence)
19.12.01	Julio Cesar Vasquez W PTS 12 Coventry
	(WBF S. Middleweight Title Defence)
10.07.02	Francisco Mora W PTS 12 Wembley
	(WBF S. Middleweight Title Defence)
29.11.02	Mondili Mbonambi W RSC 2 Liverpool
05.04.03	Enrique Carlos Campos W RSC 8 Leipzig, Germany
04.10.03	Willard Lewis W RSC 6 Zwickau, Germany

24.10.03 Dmitri Adamovich W CO 4 Bethnal Green
13.12.03 Sven Ottke L PTS 12 Nuremberg, Germany
(WBA & IBF S.Middleweight Title Challenges)
26.06.04 Brian Magee W PTS 12 Belfast
(IBO S.Middleweight Title Challenge)
13.02.05 Ramdane Serdjane W PTS 6 Brentwood
06.08.05 Jeff Lacy L RTD 8 Tampa, Florida, USA
(IBF S.Middleweight Title Challenge. IBO S.Middleweight Title Defence)
Career: 44 contests, won 38, drew 1, lost 5.

(Marcello) Cello Renda
Peterborough. *Born* Peterborough, 4 June, 1985
Middleweight. Ht. 5'11"
Manager I. Pauly

30.09.04 Mark Ellwood W RSC 2 Hull
04.11.04 Joey Vegas L RSC 3 Piccadilly
12.12.04 Scott Forsyth W RSC 1 Glasgow
21.02.05 Tom Cannon W PTS 6 Peterborough
11.03.05 Ricardo Samms L PTS 4 Doncaster
02.06.05 Michael Banbula DREW 6 Peterborough
16.10.05 Howard Clarke W PTS 4 Peterborough
12.12.05 Robert Burton W CO 1 Peterborough
10.02.06 Conroy McIntosh W RSC 1 Plymouth
30.03.06 Terry Adams W PTS 4 Peterborough
15.06.06 Gatis Skuja W PTS 4 Peterborough
23.06.06 Howard Clarke W PTS 8 Birmingham
Career: 12 contests, won 9, drew 1, lost 2.

Danny Reynolds
Leeds. *Born* Leeds, 12 May, 1978
Middleweight. Ht. 5'8"
Manager K. Spratt

08.11.05 Karl Taylor W RSC 4 Leeds
28.02.06 Gary Coombes W CO 1 Leeds
20.03.06 Geraint Harvey W RTD 2 Leeds
09.05.06 Darren Gethin DREW 4 Leeds
28.05.06 Terry Adams W RSC 1 Wakefield
Career: 5 contests, won 4, drew 1.

Darren Rhodes
Leeds. *Born* Leeds, 16 September, 1975
Middleweight. Ht. 5'11"
Manager Self

18.07.98 Andy Kemp W RSC 1 Sheffield
10.10.98 Perry Ayres W CO 2 Bethnal Green
27.02.99 Gareth Lovell W PTS 4 Oldham
01.05.99 Carlton Williams W RSC 4 Crystal Palace
29.05.99 Sean Pritchard DREW 4 Halifax
09.10.99 Leigh Wicks W PTS 4 Manchester
11.12.99 Leigh Wicks W PTS 4 Liverpool
25.03.00 Leigh Wicks W PTS 4 Liverpool
29.05.00 Dean Ashton W RSC 3 Manchester
08.07.00 Jason Collins DREW 4 Widnes
04.09.00 Jason Collins L PTS 4 Manchester
11.12.00 Paul Wesley W PTS 4 Widnes
17.03.01 Andrew Facey W PTS 4 Manchester
07.07.01 Wayne Elcock L PTS 4 Manchester
24.11.01 Simeon Cover W RSC 5 Wakefield
02.03.02 Andrew Facey L RSC 6 Wakefield
(Vacant Central Area Middleweight Title)

21.05.02 Hussain Osman L PTS 10 Custom House
15.06.02 Harry Butler W PTS 4 Leeds
28.09.02 Martin Thompson W PTS 8 Wakefield
09.11.02 Wayne Pinder L RSC 4 Altrincham
12.04.03 Mihaly Kotai L PTS 10 Bethnal Green
10.05.03 Lee Murtagh W PTS 6 Huddersfield
05.07.03 Darren Bruce W RSC 3 Brentwood
06.09.03 Scott Dixon DREW 6 Huddersfield
04.12.03 Steve Roberts W CO 6 Huddersfield
10.04.04 Michael Jones L RSC 3 Manchester
(Final Elim. British L.Middleweight Title)
12.11.04 Thomas McDonagh L PTS 10 Halifax
(Elim. British L.Middleweight Title)
07.04.05 Wayne Elcock L CO 1 Birmingham
25.09.05 Howard Clarke W PTS 6 Leeds
13.11.05 Ernie Smith W PTS 6 Leeds
23.02.06 Peter Dunn W PTS 6 Leeds
Career: 31 contests, won 19, drew 3, lost 9.

Ryan Rhodes
Sheffield. *Born* Sheffield, 20 November, 1976
Middleweight. Former Undefeated WBO Inter-Continental Middleweight Champion. Former Undefeated British & IBF Inter-Continental L. Middleweight Champion. Ht. 5'8½"
Manager F. Warren/D. Coldwell

04.02.95 Lee Crocker W RSC 2 Cardiff
04.03.95 Shamus Casey W CO 1 Livingston
06.05.95 Chris Richards W PTS 6 Shepton Mallet
15.09.95 John Rice W RSC 2 Mansfield
10.11.95 Mark Dawson W PTS 6 Derby
20.01.96 John Duckworth W RSC 2 Mansfield
26.01.96 Martin Jolley W CO 3 Brighton
11.05.96 Martin Jolley W RSC 2 Bethnal Green
25.06.96 Roy Chipperfield W RSC 1 Mansfield
14.09.96 Del Bryan W PTS 6 Sheffield
14.12.96 Paul Jones W RSC 8 Sheffield
(Vacant British L. Middleweight Title)
25.02.97 Peter Waudby W CO 1 Sheffield
(British L. Middleweight Title Defence)
14.03.97 Del Bryan W RSC 7 Reading
(British L. Middleweight Title Defence)
12.04.97 Lindon Scarlett W RSC 1 Sheffield
(Vacant IBF Inter-Continental L. Middleweight Title)
02.08.97 Ed Griffin W RSC 2 Barnsley
(IBF Inter-Continental L. Middleweight Title Defence. Vacant WBO L. Middleweight Title)
11.10.97 Yuri Epifantsev W RSC 2 Sheffield
(Final Elim. WBO Middleweight Title)
13.12.97 Otis Grant L PTS 12 Sheffield
(Vacant WBO Middleweight Title)
18.07.98 Lorant Szabo W RSC 8 Sheffield
(WBO Inter-Continental Middleweight Title Challenge)
28.11.98 Fidel Avendano W RSC 1 Sheffield
(WBO Inter-Continental Middleweight Title Defence)
27.03.99 Peter Mason W RSC 1 Derby
17.07.99 Jason Matthews L CO 2 Doncaster
(Vacant WBO Middleweight Title)
15.01.00 Eddie Haley W RSC 5 Doncaster
16.05.00 Ojay Abrahams W PTS 6 Warrington
21.10.00 Michael Alexander W PTS 6 Wembley

16.12.00 Howard Clarke W PTS 6 Sheffield
21.07.01 Youri Tsarenko W PTS 6 Sheffield
27.10.01 Jason Collins W PTS 4 Manchester
16.03.02 Lee Blundell L RSC 3 Bethnal Green
(Vacant WBF Inter-Continental Middleweight Title)
16.04.03 Paul Wesley W CO 3 Nottingham
25.07.03 Alan Gilbert W RSC 5 Norwich
11.12.03 Peter Jackson W PTS 6 Bethnal Green
12.03.04 Scott Dixon W PTS 8 Nottingham
16.04.04 Tomas da Silva W RSC 4 Bradford
22.04.05 Peter Jackson W PTS 6 Barnsley
03.06.05 Craig Lynch W RSC 3 Manchester
16.07.05 Alan Gilbert W RSC 2 Bolton
25.10.05 Hussain Osman W RTD 4 Preston
01.06.06 Jevgenijs Andrejevs W PTS 8 Barnsley
Career: 38 contests, won 35, lost 3.

Chris Rice
Redditch. *Born* Birmingham, 2 December, 1977
Cruiserweight. Ht. 6'1½"
Manager P. Cowdell

22.05.06 Duane Reid L PTS 6 Birmingham
Career: 1 contest, lost 1.

Mal Rice
Flint. *Born* Mancot, 19 July, 1975
Heavyweight. Ht. 6'2"
Manager Self

26.11.97 Gary Cavey W CO 2 Stoke
29.01.98 Lennox Williams W PTS 6 Pentre Halkyn
30.03.98 Bruno Foster L PTS 6 Bradford
30.04.98 Lennox Williams W PTS 6 Pentre Halkyn
21.06.98 Shane Woollas L PTS 6 Liverpool
18.02.00 Gary Williams L PTS 6 Pentre Halkyn
13.03.00 Patrick Halberg W RSC 2 Bethnal Green
05.05.00 Gary Williams L PTS 4 Pentre Halkyn
27.05.00 Mark Potter L CO 1 Southwark
26.03.01 John McDermott L RSC 2 Wembley
28.07.01 Matt Legg L PTS 4 Wembley
13.09.01 Petr Horacek W RSC 1 Sheffield
04.10.01 Pele Reid L PTS 4 Finsbury
16.12.01 Greg Wedlake L RSC 3 Bristol
18.05.02 Danny Watts L RTD 3 Millwall
29.03.03 Terry Dixon L PTS 4 Wembley
31.01.05 Ian Millarvie L RTD 3 Glasgow
12.06.05 Micky Steeds L PTS 6 Leicester Square
25.06.05 Paul Butlin L PTS 4 Melton Mowbray
24.07.05 Terry Dixon L PTS 4 Leicester Square
Career: 20 contests, won 5, lost 15.

(Alexander) Sandy Robb
Nairn. *Born* Irvine, 5 April, 1981
Cruiserweight. Ht. 6'0"
Manager T. Gilmour

07.06.04 Michael Pinnock W PTS 6 Glasgow
20.09.04 Nicki Taylor W RSC 5 Glasgow
25.02.05 John Smith W RSC 5 Irvine
21.03.05 Shane White W RSC 4 Glasgow
19.09.05 Gary Thompson W PTS 6 Glasgow
04.11.05 John Anthony W PTS 6 Glasgow
06.05.06 Marcin Radola W RSC 4 Irvine
Career: 7 contests, won 7.

Dale Robinson

Huddersfield. *Born* Huddersfield, 9 April, 1980
Bantamweight. Former Undefeated Commonwealth Flyweight Champion. Former Undefeated Central Area Flyweight Champion. Ht. 5'4"
Manager Self

25.09.00	John Barnes W PTS 4 Barnsley	
28.10.00	Delroy Spencer W RSC 4 Coventry	
02.12.00	Colin Moffett W PTS 4 Bethnal Green	
26.02.01	Christophe Rodrigues W PTS 6 Nottingham	
07.04.01	Andrei Kostin W PTS 6 Wembley	
08.05.01	Terry Gaskin W RTD 3 Barnsley *(Central Area Flyweight Title Challenge)*	
27.04.02	Jason Thomas W RSC 4 Huddersfield	
18.05.02	Sergei Tasimov W RSC 3 Millwall	
15.06.02	Kakhar Sabitov W PTS 6 Leeds	
05.10.02	Alain Bonnel W PTS 8 Huddersfield	
30.11.02	Marc Dummett W RSC 3 Liverpool	
22.02.03	Spencer Matsangura W PTS 12 Huddersfield *(Vacant Commonwealth Flyweight Title)*	
10.05.03	Zolile Mbityi W PTS 12 Huddersfield *(Commonwealth Flyweight Title Defence)*	
09.10.03	Emil Stoica W RSC 3 Bristol	
04.12.03	Pavel Kubasov W CO 4 Huddersfield	
13.03.04	Jason Booth L PTS 12 Huddersfield *(IBO S.Flyweight Title Challenge)*	
27.05.04	Moses Kinyau W PTS 6 Huddersfield	
17.12.04	Lahcene Zemmouri W RSC 8 Huddersfield	
20.05.05	Martin Power L PTS 12 Southwark *(Vacant British Bantamweight Title)*	
28.10.05	Moses Kinyua DREW 6 Hartlepool	
04.03.06	Delroy Spencer W RSC 3 Manchester	
01.06.06	Moses Kinyua W PTS 6 Barnsley	

Career: 22 contests, won 19, drew 1, lost 2.

Dale Robinson   Les Clark

(Jonathan) John Rocco (Hussey)

Manchester. *Born* Manchester, 18 August, 1982
Welterweight. Ht. 6'0"
Manager J. Trickett

06.05.06	Geraint Harvey W PTS 6 Blackpool	

Career: 1 contest, won 1.

Jim Rock

Dublin. *Born* Dublin, 12 March, 1972
All-Ireland S.Middleweight & Middleweight Champion. IBC Middleweight Champion. Former Undefeated All-Ireland L.Middleweight Champion. Former Undefeated WAA Inter-Continental S.Middleweight Champion. Former Undefeated WBF European L.Middleweight Champion. Ht. 5'11"
Manager M. O'Callaghan

25.11.95	Craig Lynch W PTS 4 Dublin	
09.03.96	Peter Mitchell W PTS 6 Millstreet	
03.09.96	Rob Stevenson W PTS 6 Belfast	
05.11.96	Danny Quacoe W RSC 4 Belfast	
28.01.97	Roy Chipperfield W RTD 2 Belfast	
12.04.97	George Richards W PTS 6 Sheffield	
13.09.97	Robert Njie W CO 3 Millwall	
18.04.98	Ensley Bingham L RSC 7 Manchester	
19.09.98	Michael Monaghan W PTS 12 Dublin *(Vacant WAA Inter-Continental S. Middleweight Title)*	
14.12.98	Perry Ayres W RTD 3 Cleethorpes	
22.01.99	Jimmy Vincent W PTS 10 Dublin	
20.02.99	Pedro Carragher W RSC 3 Thornaby *(Vacant WBF European L. Middleweight Title)*	
17.04.99	Michael Alexander W RSC 1 Dublin *(Vacant All-Ireland S. Middleweight Title)*	
19.06.99	Kevin Thompson W PTS 4 Dublin	
15.04.00	Allan Gray W PTS 10 Bethnal Green *(Vacant All-Ireland L. Middleweight Title)*	
12.06.00	Alan Gilbert W PTS 6 Belfast	
20.10.00	Brooke Welby W RSC 3 Belfast	
11.11.00	David Baptiste W PTS 4 Belfast	
08.12.00	Tommy Attardo W PTS 8 Worcester, Mass, USA	
24.03.01	Hollister Elliott W CO 6 Worcester, Mass, USA	
20.04.01	Jason Collins W PTS 6 Dublin	
01.12.01	Ian Cooper L PTS 6 Bethnal Green	
24.04.02	Harry Butler W PTS 6 Dublin	
01.02.03	Takaloo L RSC 9 Belfast *(Vacant WBU L. Middleweight Title)*	
30.10.03	Alan Jones L PTS 8 Belfast	
24.09.04	Matt Galer W PTS 6 Dublin	
28.10.04	Sylvestre Marianini W PTS 6 Belfast	
19.02.05	Peter Jackson W CO 7 Dublin *(All-Ireland S.Middleweight Title Defence)*	
18.03.05	Michael Monaghan W PTS 8 Belfast	
14.10.05	Alan Jones W PTS 12 Dublin *(Vacant IBC Middleweight Title)*	
03.06.06	Kevin Phelan W RTD 7 Dublin *(Vacant All-Ireland Middleweight Title)*	

Career: 31 contests, won 27, lost 4.

Martin Rogan

Belfast. *Born* Belfast, 1 May, 1971
Heavyweight. Ht. 6'3"
Manager J. Breen/F. Warren

28.10.04	Lee Mountford W RSC 1 Belfast	
18.03.05	Billy Bessey W PTS 4 Belfast	
04.06.05	Tony Booth W RSC 2 Manchester	
20.05.06	Darren Morgan W PTS 4 Belfast	

Career: 4 contests, won 4.

Yuri Romanov

Hertford. *Born* Minsk, Belarus, 24 July, 1982
Lightweight. Former Undefeated WBO Inter-Continental & WBC Youth Lightweight Champion. Ht. 5'6"
Manager P. Fondu

11.04.02	Anton Serov W RSC 7 Molodechno, Belarus	
18.04.02	Ivan Dendik W PTS 8 Minsk, Belarus	
23.04.02	Valery Bondarenko W PTS 6 Moscow, Russia	
04.05.02	Krzysztof Bienias L PTS 10 Wroclaw, Poland *(Vacant IBF Youth L.Welterweight Title)*	
16.05.02	Igor Shkutnik W CO 7 Minsk, Belarus	
08.06.02	Dennis Makarov W RSC 4 Molodechno, Belarus	
28.06.02	Alexei Fefelov W RSC 6 Minsk, Belarus	
01.08.02	Valery Bondarenko W RSC 4 Minsk, Belarus	
31.08.02	Tigran Saribekyan W PTS 6 Moscow, Russia	
03.09.02	Andrey Burenko W CO 6 Molodechno, Belarus	
14.09.02	Steve Murray W RSC 10 Bethnal Green *(WBO Inter-Continental Lightweight Title Challenge)*	
21.12.02	Sergii Tertii W RSC 6 St Petersburg, Russia	
18.01.03	Bobby Vanzie W RSC 8 Preston *(WBO Inter-Continental Lightweight Title Defence)*	
22.02.03	Sergey Adreychikov W RSC 5 Kharkov, Ukraine	
19.04.03	Nigel Claasen W PTS 10 St Petersburg, Russia *(Vacant WBC Youth Lightweight Title)*	
06.11.03	Steve Conway W PTS 8 Dagenham	
16.06.04	Maxim Pougatchev W CO 1 Minsk, Belarus	
16.10.04	Sergey Starkov W PTS 10 Yalta, Ukraine	
27.01.06	Graham Earl L PTS 12 Dagenham	

Career: 19 contests, won 17, lost 2.

Brian Rose

Blackpool. *Born* Birmingham, 2 February, 1985
L.Middleweight. Ht. 6'0"
Manager W. Dixon/L. Veitch

14.12.05	Geraint Harvey W PTS 6 Blackpool	

Career: 1 contest, won 1.

Gary Round

Telford. *Born* Shrewsbury, 30 June, 1982
Middleweight. Ht. 5'11"
Manager E. Johnson/D. Bradley

16.09.05	Joe Mitchell W PTS 6 Telford	
18.12.05	Craig Bunn L PTS 6 Bolton	
14.04.06	Peter Dunn W PTS 4 Telford	

Career: 3 contests, won 2, lost 1.

Ryan Rowlinson

Rotherham. *Born* Mexborough, 4 June, 1979
Middleweight. Ht. 6'0"
Manager D. Coldwell

15.12.05	Dave Pearson W PTS 6 Cleethorpes
18.02.06	Craig Lynch DREW 4 Edinburgh
01.06.06	Robert Burton L PTS 4 Barnsley
18.06.06	Craig Bunn L PTS 6 Manchester

Career: 4 contests, won 1, drew 1, lost 2.

Sergei Rozhakmens

Sutton in Ashfield. *Born* Riga, Latvia, 6 May, 1979
Lightweight. Ht. 5'7"
Manager S. Nubley

13.11.02	Sergei Lazarenko W RSC 1 Tallin, Estonia
22.02.03	Leonti Voronchuk L RSC 3 Narva, Estonia
20.02.06	Jimmy Gilhaney L PTS 6 Glasgow
06.05.06	Jamie McIlroy L PTS 6 Irvine
18.06.06	Abdul Rashid L PTS 6 Manchester

Career: 5 contests, won 1, lost 4.

John Ruddock

Stoke. *Born* Coventry, 28 October, 1973
S.Middleweight. Ht. 5'10"
Manager O. Delargy

10.03.06	Matthew Hough L PTS 6 Walsall

Career: 1 contest, lost 1.

Sam Rukundo

Tottenham. *Born* Kampala Uganda, 18 May, 1980
British Masters Lightweight Champion. Ht. 5'7¼"
Manager M. Helliet

04.11.04	Henry Janes W PTS 6 Piccadilly
27.01.05	Chris Long W PTS 4 Piccadilly
23.03.05	Billy Smith W RSC 3 Leicester Square
26.05.05	John-Paul Ryan W RSC 4 Mayfair
14.10.05	Bela Sandor W PTS 6 Struer, Denmark
17.11.05	Haroon Din W RSC 3 Piccadilly
02.02.06	Silence Saheed W PTS 10 Holborn *(Vacant British Masters Lightweight Title)*

Career: 7 contests, won 7.

Sam Rukundo   Les Clark

Vinesh Rungea

Brentford. *Born* Mauritius, 25 December, 1980
S.Featherweight. Ht. 5'5¾"
Manager J. Rooney

26.03.05	Lee Whyatt W PTS 4 Hackney
09.10.05	Barrington Brown L PTS 6 Hammersmith
26.02.06	Rocky Dean L PTS 6 Dagenham

Career: 3 contests, won 1, lost 2.

Jason Rushton

Doncaster. *Born* Doncaster, 15 February, 1983
Middleweight. Former Central Area L.Middleweight Champion. Ht. 5'10"
Manager J. Rushton/F. Warren

27.10.01	Ram Singh W PTS 6 Manchester
09.02.02	Brian Gifford W RSC 1 Manchester
01.06.02	Tony Smith W PTS 4 Manchester
08.11.02	Gary Hadwin W CO 4 Doncaster
21.02.03	Wayne Shepherd W PTS 6 Doncaster
05.09.03	Harry Butler W PTS 4 Doncaster
27.09.03	Jimi Hendricks W PTS 4 Manchester
06.03.04	Peter Dunn W PTS 6 Renfrew
06.05.04	Peter Dunn W PTS 4 Barnsley
03.09.04	Ernie Smith W PTS 4 Doncaster
29.10.04	Brian Coleman W PTS 6 Doncaster
04.02.05	Howard Clarke W PTS 4 Doncaster
11.03.05	Lee Armstrong W PTS 10 Doncaster *(Vacant Central Area L.Middleweight Title)*
20.05.05	Lee Murtagh L PTS 10 Doncaster *(Central Area L.Middleweight Title Defence)*
02.12.05	Joe Mitchell W PTS 6 Doncaster
03.03.06	Darren Gethin L PTS 6 Doncaster
21.04.06	Peter Dunn W PTS 6 Doncaster
09.06.06	Mark Phillips W PTS 6 Doncaster

Career: 18 contests, won 16, lost 2.

Steve Russell

Norwich. *Born* Norwich, 1 September, 1979
Middleweight. Ht. 5'10"
Manager J. Ingle

12.04.03	Kevin Phelan L PTS 4 Norwich
06.06.03	Jimi Hendricks L PTS 6 Norwich
20.06.03	Carl Wall L PTS 4 Liverpool
21.02.04	Arv Mittoo W PTS 6 Norwich
30.03.04	Dmitry Donetskiy L PTS 6 Southampton
09.10.04	Peter Dunn L PTS 6 Norwich
03.09.05	Arv Mittoo DREW 6 Norwich

Career: 7 contests, won 1, drew 1, lost 5.

Roy Rutherford

Coventry. *Born* Coventry, 4 August, 1973
S.Featherweight. Former English S.Featherweight Champion. Former British Featherweight Champion. Ht. 5'6"
Manager Self

24.02.98	David Kirk W PTS 6 Edgbaston
26.03.98	Vic Broomhead W PTS 6 Solihull
23.04.98	Dave Hinds W RSC 5 Edgbaston
21.05.98	Carl Allen W PTS 6 Solihull
24.09.98	Dean Murdoch W RSC 3 Edgbaston
14.12.98	Keith Jones W PTS 6 Birmingham

08.03.99	Marc Smith W PTS 6 Birmingham
19.06.99	Marc Smith W RTD 2 Dublin
22.10.99	Woody Greenaway W PTS 4 Coventry
14.12.99	Keith Jones W PTS 4 Coventry
22.01.00	Chris Williams W PTS 8 Birmingham
22.05.00	Alexander Tiranov W PTS 6 Coventry
28.10.00	Richard Evatt L PTS 10 Coventry
07.04.01	Nikolai Eremeev DREW 4 Wembley
26.05.01	Marc Callaghan W RSC 3 Bethnal Green
10.12.01	Frederic Bonifai W RSC 4 Liverpool
12.04.03	Dariusz Snarski W RSC 4 Bethnal Green
17.05.03	Jamie McKeever W PTS 12 Liverpool *(British Featherweight Title Challenge)*
22.11.03	Dazzo Williams L PTS 12 Belfast *(British Featherweight Title Defence)*
14.02.04	Stephen Chinnock W RSC 4 Nottingham *(Vacant English S.Featherweight Title)*
02.06.04	Dazzo Williams L PTS 12 Hereford *(British Featherweight Title Challenge)*
21.10.05	Billy Corcoran L RTD 4 Bethnal Green *(English S.Featherweight Title Defence)*

Career: 22 contests, won 17, drew 1, lost 4.

John-Paul Ryan

Northampton. *Born* Enfield, 1 April, 1971
Welterweight. Ht. 5'5"
Manager Self

07.12.00	Paddy Folan W PTS 6 Stoke
08.03.01	Neil Read L PTS 6 Stoke
28.05.02	Paddy Folan W PTS 6 Leeds
25.06.02	Sean Hughes L PTS 6 Rugby
18.10.02	Isaac Ward L PTS 6 Hartlepool
20.01.03	John Simpson L PTS 6 Glasgow
16.02.03	Simon Chambers L RSC 2 Salford
22.03.03	Gareth Payne L PTS 4 Coventry
24.05.03	Sean Hughes L PTS 6 Sheffield
11.07.03	Lee McAllister L RTD 2 Darlington
13.09.03	Joel Viney L PTS 6 Coventry
26.09.03	Femi Fehintola L PTS 6 Reading
30.10.03	Dean Hickman L PTS 6 Dudley
23.11.03	Rendall Munroe L PTS 6 Rotherham
12.03.04	John Murray L RSC 1 Nottingham
01.05.04	Joe McCluskey L RTD 2 Coventry
24.10.04	Femi Fehintola L PTS 6 Sheffield
25.02.05	Jamie McIlroy L PTS 6 Irvine
26.05.05	Sam Rukundo L RSC 4 Mayfair
25.06.05	Kristian Laight DREW 6 Melton Mowbray
06.10.05	Martin Gethin L RSC 2 Dudley

Career: 21 contests, won 2, drew 1, lost 18.

(Patrick) Paddy Ryan

Nottingham. *Born* Nottingham, 30 November, 1974
L.Heavyweight. Ht. 6'4"
Manager J. Gill

24.09.04	Gerard London W PTS 4 Bethnal Green
26.11.04	Gerard London L PTS 4 Bethnal Green
17.02.05	Matthew Hough L PTS 6 Dudley
09.07.05	Shane White W RSC 6 Bristol

Career: 4 contests, won 2, lost 2.

(Saheed) Silence Saheed (Salawu)

Canning Town. *Born* Ibadan, Nigeria, 1 January, 1978
Welterweight. Ht. 5'6"
Manager Self

28.03.03	Martin Hardcastle W PTS 4 Millwall
10.04.03	Ceri Hall DREW 4 Clydach
27.05.03	Francis Barrett W RSC 1 Dagenham
11.10.03	Wayne Wheeler W RSC 1 Portsmouth
15.11.03	Gary Greenwood W RTD 1 Coventry
21.11.03	Jaz Virdee W RSC 2 Millwall
01.05.04	Alan Temple L DIS 8 Gravesend
	(Vacant British Masters Lightweight Title)
17.09.04	Scott Lawton L PTS 6 Sheffield
24.09.04	James Gorman W PTS 6 Millwall
09.10.04	Jonathan Thaxton L PTS 6 Norwich
22.10.04	Nigel Wright L PTS 8 Edinburgh
10.04.05	Lenny Daws L PTS 6 Brentwood
01.07.05	Gareth Couch L PTS 4 Fulham
30.09.05	Karl David W PTS 6 Carmarthen
21.10.05	Ted Bami L PTS 6 Bethnal Green
17.11.05	Andrew Murray L PTS 4 Piccadilly
24.11.05	Ceri Hall L PTS 6 Clydach
02.02.06	Sam Rukundo L PTS 10 Holborn
	(Vacant British Masters Lightweight Title)
18.02.06	Lee McAllister L PTS 4 Edinburgh
04.03.06	David Barnes L PTS 4 Manchester
23.03.06	Imad Khamis W RSC 5 The Strand
02.04.06	Leo O'Reilly DREW 6 Bethnal Green

Career: 22 contests, won 8, drew 2, lost 12.

Manoocha Salari

Worksop. *Born* Iran, 25 May, 1974
S.Middleweight. Ht. 5'9½"
Manager J. Ingle

12.11.05	Danny Johnston W RSC 5 Stoke
25.11.05	Paul McInnes W PTS 6 Walsall
12.12.05	Simon Sherrington DREW 6 Birmingham
28.01.06	Martin Concepcion W RSC 2 Nottingham
26.02.06	Gokhan Kazaz DREW 4 Dagenham
13.05.06	Geard Ajetovic L RSC 4 Sheffield

Career: 6 contests, won 3, drew 2, lost 1.

Ricardo Samms

Nottingham. *Born* Nottingham, 2 June, 1982
S.Middleweight. Ht. 6'1"
Manager D. Coldwell/F. Warren

11.03.05	Cello Renda W PTS 4 Doncaster
04.06.05	Ojay Abrahams W PTS 4 Manchester
25.10.05	Ojay Abrahams W PTS 4 Preston

Career: 3 contests, won 3.

Jason Samuels

Cardiff. *Born* Newport, 11 December, 1973
L.Heavyweight. Ht. 6'0"
Manager Self

02.07.99	Luke Clayfield W RSC 1 Bristol
10.10.00	Steve Brumant W PTS 6 Brierley Hill
23.09.02	Andy Gibson L PTS 4 Glasgow
25.01.03	Paul Astley W CO 1 Bridgend
17.05.03	Geard Ajetovic L PTS 4 Liverpool
13.02.04	Gary Ojuederie W DIS 3 Bristol
30.09.05	Hussain Osman W PTS 4 Carmarthen
24.11.05	Gareth Lawrence W PTS 6 Clydach

Career: 8 contests, won 6, lost 2.

Cafu Santos

Wellingborough. *Born* Kettering, 27 December, 1982
L.Heavyweight. Ht. 6'1½"
Manager S. James

22.10.04	Andiano Aubrey W PTS 6 Mansfield
04.11.04	Eder Kurti L RSC 1 Piccadilly
10.12.04	Karl Chiverton W RSC 4 Mansfield
21.02.05	Vince Baldassara L CO 2 Glasgow
30.04.05	Graham Delehedy L RSC 1 Wigan
12.12.05	Carl Wright L RSC 4 Leicester

Career: 6 contests, won 2, lost 4.

Bruce Scott

Hackney. *Born* Jamaica, 16 August, 1969
Cruiserweight. Former Undefeated British, Commonwealth & WBU Inter-Continental Cruiserweight Champion. Former Undefeated Southern Area Cruiserweight Champion. Ht. 5'9½"
Manager F. Warren

25.04.91	Mark Bowen L PTS 6 Mayfair
16.09.91	Randy B. Powell W RSC 5 Mayfair
21.11.91	Steve Osborne W PTS 6 Burton
27.04.92	John Kaighin W CO 2 Mayfair
07.09.92	Lee Prudden W PTS 6 Bethnal Green
03.12.92	Mark Pain W RSC 5 Lewisham
15.02.93	Paul McCarthy W PTS 6 Mayfair
22.04.93	Sean O'Phoenix W RSC 3 Mayfair
14.06.93	John Oxenham W RSC 1 Bayswater
04.10.93	Simon McDougall W PTS 6 Mayfair
16.12.93	Bobby Mack W RSC 4 Newport
05.04.94	Steve Osborne W RSC 5 Bethnal Green
17.10.94	Bobbi Joe Edwards W PTS 8 Mayfair
09.12.94	John Keeton W CO 2 Bethnal Green
19.04.95	Nigel Rafferty W RSC 2 Bethnal Green
19.05.95	Cordwell Hylton W RSC 1 Southwark
11.11.95	Tony Booth W RSC 3 Halifax
05.03.96	Nick Manners W RSC 5 Bethnal Green
13.07.96	Tony Booth W PTS 8 Bethnal Green
30.11.96	Nicky Piper L RSC 7 Tylorstown
	(Commonwealth L. Heavyweight Title Challenge)
15.05.97	Grant Briggs W RSC 2 Reading
04.10.97	Tony Booth L PTS 8 Muswell Hill
21.04.98	Dominic Negus W RSC 9 Edmonton
	(Southern Area Cruiserweight Title Challenge)
28.11.98	Darren Corbett W RSC 10 Belfast
	(Commonwealth Cruiserweight Title Challenge. Vacant British Cruiserweight Title)
15.05.99	Johnny Nelson L PTS 12 Sheffield
	(WBO Cruiserweight Title Challenge)
17.07.99	Juan Carlos Gomez L RSC 6 Dusseldorf, Germany
	(WBC Cruiserweight Title Challenge)
08.04.00	Chris Woollas W RSC 2 Bethnal Green
24.06.00	Adam Watt L RSC 4 Glasgow
	(Vacant Commonwealth Cruiserweight Title)
16.12.00	John Keeton W CO 6 Sheffield
	(Vacant British Cruiserweight Title)
10.03.01	Garry Delaney W RTD 3 Bethnal Green
	(British Cruiserweight Title Defence. Vacant Commonwealth Cruiserweight Title)
28.07.01	Rene Janvier W PTS 12 Wembley
	(Vacant WBU Inter-Continental Cruiserweight Title)
28.06.03	Enzo Maccarinelli L RSC 4 Cardiff
	(Vacant WBU Cruiserweight Title)
07.02.04	Radcliffe Green W PTS 6 Bethnal Green
17.12.04	Mark Hobson L PTS 12 Huddersfield
	(British & Commonwealth Cruiserweight Title Challenges)
10.12.05	Paul Bonson W PTS 4 Canning Town
11.03.06	Hastings Rasani L PTS 8 Newport

Career: 36 contests, won 27, lost 9.

Matt Scriven

Nottingham. *Born* Nottingham, 1 September, 1973
Middleweight. Former Undefeated Midlands Area L.Middleweight Champion. Former British Masters L.Middleweight Champion. Ht. 5'10"
Manager Self

26.11.97	Shamus Casey W PTS 6 Stoke
08.12.97	Shane Thomas W PTS 6 Bradford
20.03.98	C. J. Jackson L PTS 6 Ilkeston
15.05.98	Lee Bird W RSC 5 Nottingham
08.10.98	Stevie McCready L RTD 3 Sunderland
01.04.99	Adrian Houldey W PTS 6 Birmingham
25.04.99	Danny Thornton L RSC 4 Leeds
27.06.99	Shane Junior L RSC 2 Alfreton
11.09.99	David Arundel L RTD 1 Sheffield
20.03.00	James Docherty L PTS 8 Glasgow
27.03.00	Matt Mowatt L PTS 4 Barnsley
09.04.00	David Matthews W PTS 6 Alfreton
06.06.00	Jackie Townsley L RSC 3 Motherwell
04.11.00	Brett James L RTD 1 Bethnal Green
04.02.01	Mark Paxford L PTS 6 Queensferry
26.02.01	Pedro Thompson W RTD 1 Nottingham
12.03.01	Ernie Smith W PTS 6 Birmingham
20.03.01	James Docherty L RSC 1 Glasgow
21.05.01	Christian Brady L RSC 5 Birmingham
	(Vacant Midlands Area Welterweight Title)
21.10.01	Neil Bonner NC 1 Glasgow
04.03.02	Danny Parkinson L PTS 6 Bradford
22.04.02	Gary Porter L PTS 6 Glasgow
28.05.02	Peter Dunn W PTS 8 Leeds
14.09.02	Ernie Smith W PTS 6 Newark
29.09.02	James Lee L RTD 4 Shrewsbury
30.11.02	Davey Jones L PTS 6 Newark
16.03.03	Lee Williamson W PTS 10 Nottingham
	(Vacant Midlands Area & British Masters L. Middleweight Titles)
08.06.03	Wayne Shepherd W PTS 10 Nottingham
	(British Masters L.Middleweight Title Defence)
15.09.03	Lee Murtagh L DIS 9 Leeds
	(British Masters L.Middleweight Title Defence)
12.03.04	David Walker L RSC 3 Nottingham
12.06.04	Matthew Hatton L RSC 4 Manchester
18.09.04	Robert Lloyd-Taylor L RTD 4 Newark
28.01.05	Colin McNeil L PTS 4 Renfrew
06.03.05	Mark Wall W PTS 4 Mansfield

29.04.05   Gary Woolcombe L RSC 4 Southwark
04.06.05   Matthew Hall L RSC 2 Manchester
20.01.06   John O'Donnell L RSC 4 Bethnal
          Green
04.03.06   Kerry Hope L PTS 4 Manchester
Career: 38 contests, won 12, lost 25, no contest 1.

Surinder Sekhon

Barnsley. *Born* Birmingham, 4 October, 1979
L.Middleweight. Ht. 5'9"
Manager T. Schofield/D. Coldwell

05.05.02   Franny Jones L PTS 6 Hartlepool
28.09.02   Peter Dunn W PTS 6 Wakefield
27.02.03   Ryan Kerr L PTS 6 Sunderland
09.03.03   P.J.Maxwell L RSC 1 Shaw
09.09.05   Grzegorz Proksa L PTS 4 Sheffield
30.09.05   Young Muttley L PTS 4 Burton
14.10.05   Paul Burns L PTS 6 Motherwell
12.11.05   Jimmy Doherty L PTS 6 Stoke
11.12.05   Ben Hudson L PTS 6 Chigwell
18.02.06   Scott Lawton DREW 8 Stoke
11.03.06   Paul McCloskey L RSC 1 Newport
14.05.06   Scott Haywood L RSC 1 Derby
Career: 12 contests, won 1, drew 1, lost 10.

Sam Sexton

Norwich. *Born* Norwich, 18 July, 1984
Heavyweight. Ht. 6'2"
Manager G. Everett

03.09.05   Paul Bonson W PTS 6 Norwich
11.12.05   Jason Callum W PTS 6 Norwich
12.05.06   Istvan Kecskes W PTS 4 Bethnal Green
Career: 3 contests, won 3.

Gary Sheil

Chester. *Born* Chester, 29 June, 1983
Bantamweight. Ht. 5'2³/₄"
Manager S. Goodwin

03.03.06   Jamie McDonnell L PTS 6 Doncaster
23.04.06   Delroy Spencer L PTS 6 Chester
06.05.06   Chris Edwards L PTS 6 Stoke
Career: 3 contests, lost 3.

Simon Sherrington

Birmingham. *Born* Birmingham, 14 July, 1971
L. Middleweight. Ht. 5'9¹/₂"
Manager Self

09.10.00   Paddy Martin W RSC 5 Birmingham
28.11.00   Pedro Thompson W RSC 5 Brierley
          Hill
13.12.04   Jon Harrison W RSC 5 Birmingham
21.02.05   Lee Williamson DREW 6 Birmingham
16.05.05   Lee Williamson W PTS 8 Birmingham
10.10.05   Tony Randell W PTS 6 Birmingham
12.12.05   Manoocha Salari DREW 6
          Birmingham
27.02.06   Adnan Amar L RSC 6 Birmingham
          (Vacant British Masters
          L.Middleweight Title)
22.05.06   Gatis Skuja DREW 8 Birmingham
Career: 9 contests, won 5, drew 3, lost 1.

Nadeem Siddique

Bradford. *Born* Bradford, 28 October, 1977
L. Welterweight. Ht. 5'8"
Manager J. Ingle

17.11.02   Daniel Thorpe W PTS 4 Bradford
09.02.03   Norman Dhalie W PTS 4 Bradford
13.04.03   Dave Hinds W PTS 4 Bradford
15.06.03   Nigel Senior W PTS 6 Bradford
05.10.03   Jason Nesbitt W PTS 6 Bradford
27.10.03   Daniel Thorpe W PTS 6 Glasgow
07.12.03   Chris Duggan W RSC 2 Bradford
16.01.04   Pete Buckley W PTS 4 Bradford
16.04.04   Arv Mittoo W PTS 6 Bradford
15.05.04   Joel Viney W PTS 6 Aberdeen
24.09.04   Dave Hinds W PTS 4 Nottingham
13.02.05   Jason Nesbitt W PTS 6 Bradford
09.04.05   Pete Buckley W PTS 6 Norwich
08.05.05   Kristian Laight W RSC 7 Bradford
03.06.05   Daniel Thorpe W PTS 6 Hull
13.11.05   Billy Smith W PTS 6 Leeds
25.11.05   Jason Nesbitt W RSC 6 Hull
13.04.06   David Kehoe W PTS 6 Leeds
Career: 18 contests, won 18.

(Paulino) Paulie Silva

Droylsden. *Born* Almada, Portugal, 29 April, 1978
L. Heavyweight. Ht. 5'10"
Manager W. Barker

28.02.04   Nick Okoth W PTS 6 Manchester
02.04.04   Courtney Fry L PTS 4 Plymouth
24.10.04   Amer Khan L PTS 6 Sheffield
16.09.05   Dan Guthrie W RSC 2 Plymouth
Career: 4 contests, won 2, lost 2.

Luke Simpkin

Swadlincote. *Born* Derby, 5 May, 1979
Heavyweight. Ht. 6'2"
Manager Self

24.09.98   Simon Taylor W CO 3 Edgbaston
16.10.98   Chris P. Bacon L PTS 6 Salford
10.12.98   Jason Flisher W RSC 5 Barking
04.02.99   Danny Watts L CO 3 Lewisham
28.05.99   Tommy Bannister W RSC 4 Liverpool
07.08.99   Owen Beck L PTS 4 Dagenham
11.09.99   Scott Lansdowne L PTS 4 Sheffield
11.03.00   Albert Sosnowski L PTS 4 Kensington
27.03.00   Mark Hobson L PTS 4 Barnsley
29.04.00   Johan Thorbjoernsson L PTS 4
          Wembley
23.09.00   Mark Potter L PTS 6 Bethnal Green
30.09.00   Gordon Minors DREW 4
          Peterborough
18.11.00   Keith Long L RSC 3 Dagenham
03.02.01   Paul Buttery W RSC 1 Manchester
01.04.01   Wayne Llewelyn L PTS 6 Southwark
24.04.01   Darren Chubbs L PTS 4 Liverpool
06.05.01   Billy Bessey L PTS 6 Hartlepool
09.06.01   John McDermott L PTS 6 Bethnal
          Green
13.09.01   Mark Krence L PTS 4 Sheffield
10.12.01   Mark Hobson L RTD 3 Liverpool
27,.01.02   Pele Reid DREW 4 Streatham
15.03.02   Mike Holden L PTS 6 Millwall
13.04.02   Fola Okesola W PTS 4 Liverpool
10.05.02   Julius Francis DREW 6 Millwall
23.08.02   Mark Potter L PTS 6 Bethnal Green
10.06.03   Mark Krence L RTD 8 Sheffield
          (Vacant Midlands Area Heavyweight
          Title)
05.09.03   Roman Greenberg L RTD 4 Sheffield
25.04.04   Dave Clarke W RSC 2 Nottingham
18.09.04   Paul King L PTS 6 Newark
02.12.04   Micky Steeds L RSC 3 Crystal Palace
21.02.05   Ian Millarvie L PTS 6 Glasgow

26.04.05   Carl Baker W RSC 4 Leeds
09.07.05   Henry Smith W RSC 3 Bristol
11.09.05   Carl Baker L PTS 10 Kirkby in
          Ashfield
          (British Masters Heavyweight Title
          Challenge)
28.01.06   Colin Kenna L PTS 8 Dublin
25.03.06   Istvan Kecskes W PTS 4 Burton
Career: 36 contests, won 9, drew 3, lost 24.

John Simpson

Greenock. *Born* Greenock, 26 July, 1983
Featherweight. Ht. 5'7"
Manager F. Warren/A. Morrison

23.09.02   Simon Chambers W RSC 1 Glasgow
06.10.02   Lee Holmes L PTS 6 Rhyl
07.12.02   Matthew Burke W PTS 4 Brentwood
20.01.03   John-Paul Ryan W PTS 6 Glasgow
17.02.03   Joel Viney W RTD 1 Glasgow
14.04.03   Simon Chambers W PTS 6 Glasgow
20.10.03   Steve Gethin W PTS 8 Glasgow
01.11.03   Mark Alexander W PTS 6 Glasgow
19.01.04   Henry Janes W PTS 8 Glasgow
31.01.04   Gennadiy Delisandru W PTS 4 Bethnal
          Green
22.04.04   Jus Wallie W PTS 6 Glasgow
02.06.04   Fred Janes W PTS 6 Hereford
20.09.04   Marc Callaghan W PTS 8 Glasgow
05.11.04   Dazzo Williams L PTS 12 Hereford
          (British Featherweight Title
          Challenge)
06.06.05   Dariusz Snarski W RSC 3 Glasgow
05.11.05   Andy Morris L PTS 12 Renfrew
          (Vacant British Featherweight Title)
01.04.06   Steve Foster L PTS 12 Bethnal Green
          (WBU Featherweight Title Challenge)
Career: 17 contests, won 13, lost 4.

John Simpson   Les Clark

Kyle Simpson

Bridlington. *Born* Bradford, 2 January, 1986
S.Featherweight. Ht. 5'8"
Manager J. Ingle

03.06.05   Paddy Folan W RSC 3 Hull
09.09.05   Dave Hinds W PTS 4 Sheffield
25.11.05   Dave Hinds W PTS 6 Hull
Career: 3 contests, won 3.

Neil Simpson

Coventry. *Born* London, 5 July, 1970
Cruiserweight. Former Undefeated British
& Commonwealth L.Heavyweight
Champion. Former Midlands Area
L.Heavyweight Champion. Ht. 6'2"
Manager Self

04.10.94	Kenny Nevers W PTS 4 Mayfair	
20.10.94	Johnny Hooks W RSC 2 Walsall	
05.12.94	Chris Woollas L PTS 6 Cleethorpes	
15.12.94	Paul Murray W PTS 6 Walsall	
06.03.95	Greg Scott-Briggs W RTD 5 Leicester	
17.03.95	Thomas Hansvold L PTS 4 Copenhagen, Denmark	
26.04.95	Craig Joseph L PTS 6 Solihull	
11.05.95	Andy McVeigh L CO 2 Dudley	
24.06.95	Dave Owens W RSC 1 Cleethorpes	
25.09.95	Tony Booth L PTS 8 Cleethorpes	
11.10.95	Darren Ashton W RSC 3 Solihull	
29.11.95	Greg Scott-Briggs W DIS 7 Solihull *(Vacant Midlands Area L. Heavyweight Title)*	
19.02.96	Stephen Wilson L PTS 6 Glasgow	
27.03.96	Tony Booth W PTS 6 Whitwick	
26.04.96	Dean Francis L RSC 3 Cardiff	
02.10.96	Chris Davies W PTS 4 Cardiff	
28.10.96	Nigel Rafferty W PTS 8 Leicester	
03.12.96	Danny Peters L PTS 6 Liverpool	
03.02.97	Michael Pinnock W PTS 6 Leicester	
25.04.97	Stuart Fleet L PTS 10 Cleethorpes *(Midlands Area L. Heavyweight Title Defence)*	
20.10.97	Slick Miller W RTD 1 Leicester	
15.12.97	Chris Woollas L PTS 6 Cleethorpes	
11.05.98	Greg Scott-Briggs W PTS 6 Leicester	
30.11.98	Slick Miller W CO 3 Leicester	
26.02.99	Adam Cale W RSC 3 Coventry	
12.07.99	Tony Booth W PTS 10 Coventry *(Elim. British L. Heavyweight Title)*	
14.12.99	Darren Corbett L PTS 12 Coventry *(Vacant IBO Inter-Continental L. Heavyweight Title)*	
22.05.00	Mark Baker W PTS 12 Coventry *(Vacant British & Commonwealth L. Heavyweight Titles)*	
18.11.00	Mark Delaney W RSC 1 Dagenham *(British L. Heavyweight Title Defence)*	
02.01.01	Hastings Rasani W CO 4 Coventry *(Vacant Commonwealth L. Heavyweight Title)*	
06.04.01	Yawe Davis L RSC 3 Grosseto, Italy *(Vacant European L. Heavyweight Title)*	
25.05.02	Tony Oakey L PTS 12 Portsmouth *(WBU L. Heavyweight Title Challenge)*	
08.03.03	Peter Oboh L RSC 11 Coventry *(Commonwealth L.Heavyweight Title Challenge. Vacant British L.Heavyweight Title)*	
20.04.04	Mark Brookes L PTS 10 Sheffield *(Elim. British L.Heavyweight Title)*	
17.12.04	Hastings Rasani W PTS 6 Coventry	
18.06.05	Paul Bonson W PTS 6 Coventry	
16.09.05	Leigh Alliss L RSC 3 Plymouth	
10.02.06	Gareth Hogg L PTS 6 Plymouth	
18.03.06	Varuzhan Davtyan W RSC 1 Coventry	

Career: 39 contests, won 22, lost 17.

Deniss Sirjatovs

Sutton in Ashfield. *Born* Riga, Latvia, 14
November, 1984
L.Welterweight. Ht. 5'10¾"
Manager S. Nubley

06.05.06	George McIlroy L RSC 2 Irvine	

Career: 1 contest, lost 1.

Grant Skehill

Wanstead. *Born* London, 1 October, 1985
Welterweight. Ht. 5'11¼"
Manager F. Warren

13.05.06	Chris Brophy W PTS 4 Bethnal Green	

Career: 1 contest, won 1.

Matt Skelton

Bedford. *Born* Bedford, 23 January, 1968
Heavyweight. Former Commonwealth
Heavyweight Champion. Former
Undefeated British, WBU & English
Heavyweight Champion. Ht. 6'3"
Manager K. Sanders

22.09.02	Gifford Shillingford W RSC 2 Southwark	
27.10.02	Slick Miller W CO 1 Southwark	
08.12.02	Neil Kirkwood W RSC 1 Bethnal Green	
18.02.03	Jacklord Jacobs W RSC 4 Bethnal Green	
08.04.03	Alexei Varakin W CO 2 Bethnal Green	
15.05.03	Dave Clarke W RSC 1 Mayfair	
17.07.03	Antoine Palatis W RSC 4 Dagenham	
18.09.03	Mike Holden W RSC 6 Dagenham *(Vacant English Heavyweight Title)*	
11.10.03	Costi Marin W RSC 1 Portsmouth	
25.10.03	Ratko Draskovic W RSC 3 Edinburgh	
15.11.03	Patriche Costel W CO 1 Bayreuth, Germany	
07.02.04	Julius Francis W PTS 10 Bethnal Green *(English Heavyweight Title Defence)*	
24.04.04	Michael Sprott W CO 12 Reading *(British & Commonwealth Heavyweight Title Challenges)*	
05.06.04	Bob Mirovic W RTD 4 Bethnal Green *(Commonwealth Heavyweight Title Defence)*	
19.11.04	Keith Long W RSC 11 Bethnal Green *(British & Commonwealth Heavyweight Title Defences)*	
25.02.05	Fabio Eduardo Moli W RSC 6 Wembley *(Vacant WBU Heavyweight Title)*	
16.07.05	Mark Krence W RTD 7 Bolton *(British Heavyweight Title Defence)*	
10.12.05	John McDermott W RSC 1 Canning Town *(British Heavyweight Title Defence)*	
25.02.06	Danny Williams L PTS 12 Canning Town *(Commonwealth Heavyweight Title Challenge)*	
01.04.06	Suren Kalachyan W CO 4 Bethnal Green	

Career: 20 contests, won 19, lost 1.

Gatis Skuja

Bethnal Green. *Born* Latvia, 23 June, 1982
Welterweight. Ht. 5'9"
Manager C. Sanigar

26.03.05	Nathan Graham L RSC 1 Hackney	
11.09.05	David Kirk W PTS 6 Kirkby in Ashfield	
04.12.05	Mark Lloyd L PTS 4 Telford	
24.02.06	Terry Adams DREW 4 Birmingham	
24.03.06	Sam Webb L PTS 4 Bethnal Green	
22.05.06	Simon Sherrington DREW 8 Birmingham	
15.06.06	Cello Renda L PTS 4 Peterborough	

Career: 7 contests, won 1, drew 2, lost 4.

Gatis Skuja   Les Clark

Anthony Small

Deptford. *Born* London, 28 June, 1981
Middleweight. Ht. 5'9"
Manager A. Booth

12.05.04	Lance Hall W RSC 1 Reading	
10.09.04	Emmanuel Marcos W RSC 1 Wembley	
10.12.04	Howard Clarke W PTS 4 Sheffield	
21.01.05	Andrei Sherel W RSC 3 Brentford	
24.04.05	Dmitry Donetskiy W PTS 4 Leicester Square	
16.06.05	Howard Clarke W PTS 6 Mayfair	
20.07.05	David le Franc W RSC 1 Monte Carlo, Monaco	
14.10.05	Ismael Kerzazi W RSC 1 Huddersfield	
23.11.05	Ernie Smith W PTS 6 Mayfair	
24.03.06	Kai Kauramaki W CO 3 Bethnal Green	
30.05.06	Alexander Matviechuk W RSC 6 Bethnal Green	

Career: 11 contests, won 11.

Nicki Smedley   Les Clark

Nicki Smedley

Sheffield. *Born* Sheffield, 3 February, 1986
Welterweight. Ht. 5'10"
Manager D. Hobson

24.07.05	Lance Verallo	W PTS 6 Sheffield
09.09.05	Jason Nesbitt	W PTS 4 Sheffield
26.11.05	Rakhim Mingaleev	W PTS 4 Sheffield
05.03.06	Davis Kamara	W PTS 6 Sheffield
13.05.06	Artak Tsironyan	W PTS 4 Sheffield
22.06.06	Martin Sweeney	W RSC 3 Sheffield

Career: 6 contests, won 6.

Donovan Smillie

Bradford. *Born* Bradford, 9 August, 1975
S.Middleweight. Former English
Middleweight Champion. Former
Undefeated British Masters S.Middleweight
Champion. Ht. 5'10¹/₂"
Manager D. Ingle

10.04.99	Sean Pritchard	W RSC 1 Manchester
02.05.99	Mark Dawson	W PTS 6 Shaw
04.12.99	Mark Dawson	W PTS 4 Manchester
14.04.00	Dennis Doyley	W PTS 4 Manchester
25.11.00	Ojay Abrahams	L RSC 2 Manchester
30.11.01	Rob Stevenson	W PTS 6 Hull
17.12.01	Mark Chesters	W PTS 6 Cleethorpes
17.02.02	William Webster	W PTS 6 Salford
20.04.02	Mike Duffield	L PTS 4 Derby
15.06.02	Wayne Asker	DREW 6 Norwich
07.10.02	Alan Jones	L RSC 6 Birmingham
17.11.02	William Webster	W PTS 6 Bradford
09.02.03	Robert Burton	W PTS 6 Bradford
13.04.03	Mark Phillips	W PTS 6 Bradford
15.06.03	Mike Duffield	W RSC 3 Bradford
	(Vacant British Masters S.Middleweight Title)	
03.08.03	William Webster	W RSC 4 Stalybridge
05.10.03	Gary Jones	W CO 2 Bradford
07.12.03	Patrick Cito	W PTS 6 Bradford
16.01.04	Mark Phillips	W PTS 6 Bradford
16.04.04	Patrick Cito	W RSC 3 Bradford
18.11.04	Roddy Doran	W RSC 7 Shrewsbury
	(Vacant English Middleweight Title)	
13.02.05	Michael Pinnock	W PTS 6 Bradford
08.05.05	Ryan Walls	L PTS 6 Bradford
15.12.05	Steven Bendall	L RSC 5 Coventry
	(English Middleweight Title Defence)	
20.01.06	Matthew Thirlwall	L CO 9 Bethnal Green
	(Final Elim. English S.Middleweight Title)	
13.04.06	Robert Burton	DREW 6 Leeds

Career: 26 contests, won 18, drew 2, lost 6.

Billy Smith

Stourport. *Born* Kidderminster, 10 June, 1978
Welterweight. Ht. 5'7"
Manager Self

28.03.00	Marcus Portman	L PTS 6 Wolverhampton
07.04.00	Barry Hughes	L PTS 6 Glasgow
18.05.00	Manzo Smith	L PTS 4 Bethnal Green
26.05.00	Willie Limond	L PTS 4 Glasgow
07.07.00	Gareth Jordan	L PTS 6 Chigwell
15.07.00	David Walker	L RTD 2 Millwall
09.09.00	Ricky Eccleston	L PTS 4 Manchester
24.09.00	Choi Tsveenpurev	L RTD 2 Shaw
18.11.00	Lee Meager	L RSC 1 Dagenham
17.12.00	Willie Limond	L PTS 6 Glasgow

03.02.01	Scott Spencer	L PTS 6 Brighton
09.03.01	Darren Melville	L PTS 4 Millwall
27.03.01	Jason Nesbitt	L PTS 6 Brierley Hill
05.03.05	Lee Cook	L PTS 4 Southwark
23.03.05	Sam Rukundo	L RSC 3 Leicester Square
30.04.05	Baz Carey	L PTS 6 Coventry
08.05.05	Sean Hughes	L PTS 6 Bradford
20.05.05	Stefy Bull	L PTS 6 Doncaster
02.06.05	Isaac Ward	L PTS 8 Yarm
16.06.05	Ricky Owen	L PTS 4 Dagenham
25.06.05	John Fewkes	L PTS 6 Wakefield
16.07.05	Craig Watson	L PTS 4 Bolton
23.07.05	Lee McAllister	L PTS 4 Edinburgh
11.09.05	Craig Johnson	L PTS 4 Kirkby in Ashfield
24.09.05	Baz Carey	NC 5 Coventry
01.10.05	John Davidson	W PTS 6 Wigan
09.10.05	Andrew Murray	L PTS 4 Hammersmith
22.10.05	Jonathan Whiteman	L PTS 6 Mansfield
05.11.05	Paul McCloskey	L PTS 4 Renfrew
13.11.05	Nadeem Siddique	L PTS 6 Leeds
25.11.05	Steve Mullin	L PTS 4 Liverpool
03.12.05	Baz Carey	L PTS 6 Coventry
12.12.05	Judex Meemea	L PTS 6 Peterborough
11.02.06	Tom Glover	L PTS 4 Bethnal Green
24.02.06	Lance Hall	W PTS 4 Birmingham
25.03.06	Scott Haywood	L PTS 6 Burton
07.04.06	Michael Graydon	W PTS 4 Bristol
28.04.06	Paul Holborn	L PTS 4 Hartlepool
12.05.06	Lee McAllister	L PTS 4 Bethnal Green
21.05.06	Ashley Theophane	L PTS 4 Bethnal Green
30.05.06	Chris Pacy	L PTS 4 Bethnal Green
16.06.06	Ceri Hall	L PTS 4 Carmarthen
23.06.06	Paul Truscott	L PTS 4 Blackpool

Career: 43 contests, won 3, lost 39, no contest 1.

Clifford Smith

Woking. *Born* Guildford, 28 July, 1987
Featherweight. Ht. 5'6¹/₂"
Manager F. Maloney

30.05.06	Rakhim Mingaleev	W PTS 4 Bethnal Green
29.06.06	Kaloyan Stoyanov Dimov	W PTS 4 Bethnal Green

Career: 2 contests, won 2.

Danny Smith

Lowestoft. *Born* Great Yarmouth, 6 October, 1979
S.Middleweight. Ht. 6'0"
Manager Self

15.07.00	Gary Jones	W RSC 1 Norwich
04.11.00	Rob Stevenson	DREW 6 Derby
28.03.01	Simeon Cover	W PTS 6 Piccadilly
08.06.01	Rob Stevenson	W PTS 6 Hull
13.04.02	Freddie Yemofio	W PTS 6 Norwich
15.06.02	William Webster	W PTS 6 Norwich
21.09.02	Mike Duffield	W PTS 6 Norwich
12.04.03	Simeon Cover	W CO 5 Norwich
06.06.03	Gary Cummings	W PTS 6 Norwich
25.07.03	William Webster	W PTS 4 Norwich
21.02.04	Lee Williamson	W PTS 6 Norwich
09.10.04	Brian Coleman	W PTS 6 Norwich
09.04.05	Jason Collins	W PTS 6 Norwich
03.09.05	Jimi Hendricks	W RSC 5 Norwich

Career: 14 contests, won 13, drew 1.

Dean Smith

Dagenham. *Born* Romford, 11 May, 1985
Lightweight. Ht. 5'8³/₄"
Manager F. Warren

10.12.05	Ian Reid	W RSC 1 Canning Town
01.04.06	David Kehoe	W PTS 4 Bethnal Green
13.05.06	Daniel Thorpe	W PTS 4 Bethnal Green

Career: 3 contests, won 3.

Dean Smith   Les Clark

Ernie Smith

Stourport. *Born* Kidderminster, 10 June, 1978
Middleweight. Ht. 5'8"
Manager Self

24.11.98	Woody Greenaway	L PTS 6 Wolverhampton
05.12.98	Gavin Rees	L PTS 4 Bristol
27.01.99	Arv Mittoo	DREW 6 Stoke
11.02.99	Tony Smith	W PTS 6 Dudley
22.02.99	Liam Maltby	W PTS 4 Peterborough
08.03.99	Wayne Jones	W PTS 6 Birmingham
18.03.99	Carl Greaves	L PTS 6 Doncaster
25.03.99	Brian Coleman	L PTS 6 Edgbaston
27.05.99	Brian Coleman	W PTS 6 Edgbaston
14.06.99	Dave Gibson	W PTS 6 Birmingham
22.06.99	Koba Gogoladze	L RSC 1 Ipswich
03.10.99	Gavin Down	L RSC 1 Chesterfield
30.11.99	Brian Coleman	L PTS 8 Wolverhampton
13.12.99	Richie Murray	L RSC 5 Cleethorpes
24.02.00	Brian Coleman	L PTS 6 Edgbaston
02.03.00	Oscar Hall	L PTS 6 Birkenhead
10.03.00	John Tiftik	L PTS 4 Chigwell
18.03.00	Biagio Falcone	L PTS 4 Glasgow
07.04.00	Barry Connell	L PTS 6 Glasgow
14.04.00	Jose Luis Castro	L PTS 6 Madrid, Spain
06.05.00	Matthew Barr	L PTS 4 Southwark
15.05.00	Harry Butler	L PTS 6 Birmingham
26.05.00	Biagio Falcone	L PTS 4 Glasgow
06.06.00	Chris Henry	L PTS 8 Brierley Hill
08.07.00	Takaloo	L RSC 4 Widnes
13.08.00	Jawaid Khaliq	L RSC 4 Nottingham
	(Vacant Midlands Area Welterweight Title)	
24.09.00	Shaun Horsfall	L PTS 6 Shaw
09.10.00	Dave Gibson	W PTS 6 Birmingham
22.10.00	Matthew Barr	L PTS 4 Streatham
06.11.00	Stuart Elwell	L PTS 6 Wolverhampton
25.11.00	Michael Jennings	L PTS 4 Manchester
03.12.00	Shaun Horsfall	L PTS 6 Shaw

17.12.00 Kevin McIntyre L PTS 6 Glasgow
20.01.01 David Walker L RTD 1 Bethnal Green
12.03.01 Matt Scriven L PTS 6 Birmingham
24.03.01 Bobby Banghar L PTS 4 Chigwell
12.05.01 Jon Harrison L PTS 4 Plymouth
21.05.01 Brian Coleman W PTS 6 Birmingham
03.06.01 Babatunde Ajayi L PTS 4 Southwark
16.06.01 Bobby Banghar L PTS 4 Dagenham
26.07.01 Andy Abrol L PTS 6 Blackpool
13.09.01 Leo O'Reilly L PTS 6 Sheffield
29.09.01 Brett James L PTS 6 Southwark
01.11.01 Lance Crosby L PTS 6 Hull
17.11.01 Nigel Wright L PTS 4 Glasgow
15.12.01 Ross Minter L RSC 2 Wembley
11.02.02 Tony Montana L PTS 6 Shrewsbury
13.05.02 Martin Scotland W RTD 2 Birmingham
15.06.02 Gavin Wake L PTS 4 Leeds
08.07.02 Gavin Rees L RSC 5 Mayfair
06.09.02 Ricky Burns L PTS 6 Glasgow
14.09.02 Matt Scriven L PTS 6 Newark
29.09.02 Anthony Christopher L PTS 6
          Shrewsbury
18.11.02 Craig Dickson L PTS 6 Glasgow
03.12.02 Anthony Christopher W PTS 6
          Shrewsbury
23.02.03 Gary Greenwood L PTS 4 Shrewsbury
24.03.03 Darrell Grafton L PTS 6 Barnsley
13.04.03 Lee McAllister L PTS 4 Bradford
28.04.03 Adnan Amar L PTS 6 Cleethorpes
12.05.03 Lee McAllister L PTS 6 Birmingham
31.05.03 Robbie Sivyer L PTS 6 Barnsley
08.06.03 Jonathan Woollins W PTS 4
          Nottingham
15.06.03 Ali Nuumembe L PTS 4 Bradford
05.07.03 Michael Lomax L PTS 4 Brentwood
29.08.03 Ali Nuumembe L PTS 6 Liverpool
04.10.03 Lenny Daws L PTS 6 Muswell Hill
18.11.03 Chas Symonds L PTS 6 Bethnal Green
28.11.03 Lee McAllister L PTS 6 Hull
06.12.03 Taz Jones L PTS 4 Cardiff
07.02.04 Gary Woolcombe L PTS 4 Bethnal
          Green
09.04.04 Richard Swallow L PTS 4 Rugby
19.04.04 Craig Dickson L PTS 6 Glasgow
10.05.04 Adnan Amar L PTS 6 Birmingham
27.05.04 Graham Delehedy L RSC 3
          Huddersfield
08.07.04 Steve Brumant L PTS 8 Birmingham
30.07.04 Tony Doherty L PTS 6 Bethnal Green
03.09.04 Jason Rushton L PTS 4 Doncaster
12.09.04 Chris Long DREW 6 Shrewsbury
24.09.04 Lenny Daws L PTS 6 Nottingham
23.10.04 Steve Conway L PTS 6 Wakefield
31.10.04 John Murray L PTS 4 Shaw
12.11.04 John O'Donnell L PTS 6 Wembley
25.11.04 Joe Mitchell W PTS 6 Birmingham
03.12.04 George Telfer L PTS 4 Edinburgh
13.12.04 Luke Teague L PTS 6 Cleethorpes
27.01.05 Muhsen Nasser L PTS 6 Piccadilly
12.02.05 Nathan Ward L PTS 6 Portsmouth
25.02.05 Ross Minter L PTS 4 Wembley
05.03.05 Gary Woolcombe L PTS 6 Southwark
23.03.05 Delroy Mellis L PTS 6 Leicester Square
08.04.05 Kerry Hope L PTS 4 Edinburgh
21.04.05 Jimmy Gould L PTS 4 Dudley
30.04.05 Andy Egan DREW 6 Coventry
08.05.05 Danny Parkinson L PTS 6 Bradford
15.05.05 Kell Brook L PTS 6 Sheffield
23.05.05 Davey Jones DREW 6 Cleethorpes
03.06.05 Martin Concepcion L PTS 4
          Manchester
18.06.05 Richard Mazurek W PTS 6 Coventry
25.06.05 Adnan Amar L PTS 6 Melton
          Mowbray

09.07.05 Darren Barker L PTS 6 Nottingham
16.07.05 Tony Doherty NC 2 Bolton
23.07.05 Nathan Cleverly L PTS 4 Edinburgh
10.09.05 Kell Brook L PTS 4 Cardiff
25.09.05 Gavin Smith DREW 6 Leeds
06.10.05 Stuart Elwell L PTS 6 Dudley
21.10.05 George Hillyard W PTS 4 Bethnal
          Green
28.10.05 Franny Jones L PTS 4 Hartlepool
13.11.05 Darren Rhodes L PTS 6 Leeds
23.11.05 Anthony Small L PTS 6 Mayfair
02.12.05 Matthew Thirlwall L PTS 4
          Nottingham
18.12.05 Ali Nuumbembe L CO 4 Bolton
28.01.06 Tony Doherty L PTS 6 Nottingham
16.02.06 Dean Hickman L PTS 4 Dudley
24.02.06 Joe Mitchell L PTS 6 Birmingham
04.03.06 Sean McKervey L PTS 6 Coventry
02.04.06 Mark Thompson L PTS 6 Shaw
29.04.06 Kell Brook L PTS 6 Edinburgh
06.05.06 Terry Adams L PTS 6 Birmingham
13.05.06 Jonjo Finnegan L PTS 6 Sutton in
          Ashfield
01.06.06 James Hare L CO 5 Barnsley
Career: 120 contests, won 13, drew 5, lost 101,
          no contest 1.

Gavin Smith

Bradford. *Born* Bradford, 16 December,
1981
Middleweight. Ht. 5'7¾"
Manager Self

23.10.04 Mark Wall W PTS 6 Wakefield
10.12.04 Mark Wall W PTS 4 Sheffield
13.02.05 Tony Randell W PTS 6 Bradford
24.07.05 Terry Adams L PTS 6 Sheffield
25.09.05 Ernie Smith DREW 6 Leeds
23.02.06 Jav Jerome W RSC 5 Leeds
13.05.06 Aleksandr Zhuk W RSC 3 Sheffield
Career: 7 contests, won 5, drew 1, lost 1.

Henry Smith

Bristol. *Born* Bristol, 24 September, 1978
Heavyweight. Ht. 5'11½"
Manager Self

20.02.05 Radcliffe Green W PTS 6 Bristol
21.03.05 Billy McClung L PTS 6 Glasgow
09.07.05 Luke Simpkin L RSC 3 Bristol
Career: 3 contests, won 1, lost 2.

John Smith

Weston super Mare. *Born* Bristol, 2
February, 1980
Cruiserweight. Ht. 5'11"
Manager Self

25.02.05 Sandy Robb L RSC 5 Irvine
09.07.05 Gary Thompson W PTS 4 Bristol
Career: 2 contests, won 1, lost 1.

Paul Smith

Liverpool. *Born* Liverpool, 6 October,
1982
Middleweight. Ht. 5'11"
Manager F. Warren

05.04.03 Howard Clarke W PTS 4 Manchester
08.05.03 Andrei Ivanov W RSC 2 Widnes
20.06.03 Elroy Edwards W RSC 2 Liverpool
29.08.03 Patrick Cito W PTS 4 Liverpool
02.10.03 Mike Duffield W RSC 1 Liverpool

13.12.03 Joel Ani W PTS 4 Manchester
26.02.04 Davey Jones W PTS 4 Widnes
03.04.04 Howard Clarke W PTS 4 Manchester
12.06.04 Steve Timms W RSC 1 Manchester
10.09.04 Ojay Abrahams W PTS 4 Liverpool
01.10.04 Jason Collins W RSC 1 Manchester
17.12.04 Howard Clarke W CO 1 Liverpool
11.02.05 Robert Burton W CO 1 Manchester
03.06.05 Simeon Cover W PTS 6 Manchester
11.03.06 Hussain Osman W RSC 4 Newport
01.06.06 Conroy McIntosh W PTS 8 Barnsley
Career: 16 contests, won 16.

Paul Smith   Les Clark

Sammy Smith

Bracknell. *Born* Chichester, 12 May, 1978
Welterweight. Former Undefeated British
Masters L.Welterweight Champion.
Ht. 5'6"
Manager G. Carmen

26.03.98 Shaba Edwards W PTS 6 Acton
28.04.98 Les Frost W CO 2 Brentford
02.10.98 Arv Mittoo W PTS 4 Cheshunt
27.10.98 Rudy Valentino W PTS 6 Brentford
07.12.98 Ross McCord W RSC 5 Acton
25.02.99 Trevor Smith W RSC 2 Kentish Town
08.03.99 Brian Coleman L PTS 8 Birmingham
09.05.99 David Kirk W PTS 6 Bracknell
09.04.00 Gavin Down L PTS 6 Alfreton
18.05.00 Gary Reid L RSC 1 Bethnal Green
11.02.02 David Keir W PTS 6 Southampton
25.02.02 Marcus Portman L PTS 6 Slough
09.05.03 Brian Coleman W PTS 6 Longford
31.05.03 David Kirk W PTS 4 Bethnal Green
01.08.03 Brett James L PTS 10 Bethnal Green
          *(Vacant Southern Area Welterweight
          Title)*
27.09.03 Michael Jennings L RTD 4
          Manchester
          *(WBU Inter-Continental Welterweight
          Title Challenge)*
27.11.03 Keith Jones W PTS 10 Longford
          *(Vacant British Masters
          L.Welterweight Title)*
08.05.04 Young Muttley L RSC 1 Bristol
          (Vacant English L.Welterweight Title)
08.12.04 Arv Mittoo W PTS 6 Longford
20.06.05 Tony Montana W PTS 10 Longford
23.09.05 Ross Minter L RSC 3 Mayfair
          *(Southern Area Welterweight Title
          Challenge)*
Career: 21 contests, won 13, lost 8.

Paul Souter

West Ham. *Born* Forest Gate, 6 April, 1979
Heavyweight. Ht. 6'3¼"
Manager J. Eames/D. Powell

13.05.06 Tony Booth W PTS 4 Bethnal Green
Career: 1 contest, won 1.

Steven Spartacus (Smith)

Ipswich. *Born* Bury St Edmunds, 3
November, 1976
British Masters L.Heavyweight Champion
Former English L.Heavyweight Champion.
Ht. 5'10½"
Manager A. Sims

08.09.00 Michael Pinnock W PTS 4
Hammersmith
30.09.00 Martin Jolley W PTS 6 Chigwell
24.03.01 Calvin Stonestreet W PTS 4 Chigwell
16.06.01 Kevin Burton W RSC 1 Dagenham
07.09.01 Rob Stevenson W RSC 4 Bethnal
Green
27.10.01 Darren Ashton W PTS 4 Manchester
24.11.01 Michael Pinnock W PTS 4 Bethnal
Green
15.12.01 Oneal Murray W RSC 4 Chigwell
19.01.02 Darren Ashton W PTS 4 Bethnal Green
14.09.02 Calvin Stonestreet W RSC 3 Bethnal
Green
08.02.03 Paul Bonson W PTS 6 Norwich
27.05.03 Mark Phillips W RSC 2 Dagenham
25.07.03 Simeon Cover W CO 3 Norwich
*(Vacant British Masters L.Heavyweight
Title)*
04.10.03 Hastings Rasani W RSC 1 Muswell
Hill
11.12.03 Scott Lansdowne W RSC 3 Bethnal
Green
(Vacant English L.Heavyweight Title)
30.01.04 Ovill McKenzie L PTS 6 Dagenham
02.06.04 Varuzhan Davtyan W RSC 1
Nottingham
12.11.04 Peter Haymer L PTS 10 Wembley
(English L.Heavyweight Title Defence)
10.04.05 Sam Price W RSC 6 Brentwood
*(British Masters L.Heavyweight Title
Defence)*
11.12.05 Varuzhan Davtyan W RSC 1 Chigwell
17.02.06 Karim Bennama W PTS 6 Bethnal
Green
Career: 21 contests, won 19, lost 2.

Delroy Spencer

Walsall. *Born* Walsall, 25 July, 1968
Bantamweight. British Masters Flyweight
Champion. Ht. 5'4"
Manager Self

30.10.98 Gwyn Evans L PTS 4 Peterborough
21.11.98 Jamie Evans L PTS 4 Southwark
30.01.99 Ian Napa L PTS 6 Bethnal Green
26.02.99 Chris Edwards W PTS 6 West Bromwich
30.04.99 Nicky Booth L PTS 6 Scunthorpe
06.06.99 Nicky Booth L PTS 4 Nottingham
19.06.99 Willie Valentine L PTS 4 Dublin
16.10.99 Colin Moffett W PTS 4 Bethnal Green
31.10.99 Shane Mallon W PTS 6 Raynes Park
29.11.99 Lee Georgiou L PTS 4 Wembley
19.02.00 Steffen Norskov L PTS 4 Aalborg,
Denmark
08.04.00 Ian Napa L PTS 8 Bethnal Green
15.04.00 Lee Georgiou L PTS 4 Bethnal Green

04.07.00 Ankar Miah W RSC 3 Tooting
13.07.00 Darren Hayde W PTS 4 Bethnal Green
30.09.00 Paul Weir L PTS 8 Chigwell
28.10.00 Dale Robinson L RSC 4 Coventry
02.12.00 Keith Knox W PTS 6 Bethnal Green
08.05.01 Levi Pattison L PTS 4 Barnsley
22.05.01 Mimoun Chent L DIS 5 Telde, Gran
Canaria
16.06.01 Sunkanmi Ogunbiyi L PTS 4 Wembley
22.11.01 Darren Taylor W PTS 8 Paddington
(Vacant British Masters Flyweight Title)
09.12.01 Shinny Bayaar L PTS 4 Shaw
19.12.01 Gareth Payne L PTS 4 Coventry
18.01.02 Gareth Payne W PTS 4 Coventry
28.01.02 Levi Pattison L RSC 5 Barnsley
19.10.03 Shinny Bayaar L PTS 6 Shaw
13.12.03 Mark Moran L PTS 4 Manchester
24.01.04 Martin Power L RTD 1 Wembley
23.04.04 Chris Edwards DREW 6 Leicester
26.06.04 Damaen Kelly L RSC 4 Belfast
30.07.04 Martin Power L CO 2 Bethnal Green
31.10.04 Shinny Bayaar L PTS 6 Shaw
12.11.04 Stevie Quinn L PTS 6 Belfast
03.12.04 Lee Haskins L RTD 3 Bristol
(Vacant British Flyweight Title)
27.05.05 Robert Nelson L PTS 4 Spennymoor
25.06.05 Robert Nelson L PTS 6 Wakefield
16.09.05 Lee Haskins L RTD 2 Plymouth
16.10.05 Moses Kinyua L PTS 6 Peterborough
30.10.05 Lee Fortt L PTS 4 Bethnal Green
12.11.05 Chris Edwards L PTS 4 Stoke
02.12.05 Jamie McDonnell L PTS 6 Doncaster
11.02.06 John Armour L PTS 6 Bethnal Green
04.03.06 Dale Robinson L RSC 3 Manchester
02.04.06 Shinny Bayaar L PTS 6 Shaw
23.04.06 Gary Sheil W PTS 6 Chester
09.05.06 Robert Nelson DREW 6 Leeds
20.05.06 Colin Moffett L PTS 4 Belfast
28.05.06 Tasif Khan L PTS 6 Wakefield
Career: 49 contests, won 10, drew 2, lost 37.

Michael Sprott

Reading. *Born* Reading, 16 January, 1975
European Union Heavyweight Champion.
Former British & Commonwealth
Heavyweight Champion. Former
Undefeated Southern Area & WBF
European Heavyweight Champion. Ht. 6'0¾"
Manager D. Powell/F. Warren

20.11.96 Geoff Hunter W RSC 1 Wembley
19.02.97 Johnny Davison W CO 2 Acton
17.03.97 Slick Miller W CO 1 Mayfair
16.04.97 Tim Redman W CO 2 Bethnal Green
20.05.97 Waldeck Fransas W PTS 6 Edmonton
02.09.97 Gary Williams W PTS 6 Southwark
08.11.97 Darren Fearn W PTS 6 Southwark
06.12.97 Nick Howard W RSC 1 Wembley
10.01.98 Johnny Davison W RSC 2 Bethnal
Green
14.02.98 Ray Kane W RTD 1 Southwark
14.03.98 Michael Murray W PTS 6 Bethnal
Green
12.09.98 Harry Senior L RSC 6 Bethnal Green
*(Vacant Southern Area Heavyweight
Title)*
16.01.99 Gary Williams W PTS 6 Bethnal Green
10.07.99 Chris Woollas W RTD 4 Southwark
18.01.00 Tony Booth W PTS 6 Mansfield
14.10.00 Wayne Llewelyn L RSC 3 Wembley
17.02.01 Timo Hoffmann W PTS 8 Bethnal
Green
24.03.01 Timo Hoffmann L PTS 8 Magdeburg,
Germany

03.11.01 Corrie Sanders L RSC 1 Brakpan,
South Africa
20.12.01 Jermell Lamar Barnes W PTS 8
Rotterdam, Holland
12.02.02 Danny Williams L RTD 8 Bethnal
Green
*(British & Commonwealth
Heavyweight Title Challenges)*
09.05.02 Pele Reid W RSC 7 Leicester Square
*(Vacant WBF European Heavyweight
Title)*
10.07.02 Garing Lane W PTS 6 Wembley
17.09.02 Derek McCafferty W PTS 8 Bethnal
Green
12.12.02 Tamas Feheri W RSC 2 Leicester
Square
24.01.03 Mike Holden W RSC 4 Sheffield
18.03.03 Mark Potter W RSC 3 Reading
*(Southern Area Heavyweight Title
Challenge. Elim. British Heavyweight
Title)*
10.06.03 Petr Horacek W CO 1 Sheffield
01.08.03 Colin Kenna W RSC 1 Bethnal Green
*(Southern Area Heavyweight Title
Defence)*
26.09.03 Danny Williams L RSC 5 Reading
*(British & Commonwealth
Heavyweight Title Challenges)*
24.01.04 Danny Williams W PTS 12 Wembley
*(British & Commonwealth
Heavyweight Title Challenges)*
24.04.04 Matt Skelton L CO 12 Reading
*(British & Commonwealth
Heavyweight Title Defences)*
10.09.04 Robert Sulgan W RSC 1 Bethnal Green
23.04.05 Cengiz Koc W PTS 10 Dortmund,
Germany
*(Vacant European Union Heavyweight
Title)*
01.10.05 Paolo Vidoz L PTS 12 Oldenburg,
Germany
*(European Heavyweight Title
Challenge)*
13.12.05 Vladimir Virchis L PTS 12 Sölden,
Austria
*(WBO Inter-Continental Heavyweight
Title Challenge)*
18.02.06 Antoine Palatis W PTS 10 Edinburgh
*(Vacant European Union Heavyweight
Title)*
Career: 37 contests, won 28, lost 9.

Micky Steeds

Isle of Dogs. *Born* London, 14 September,
1983
Southern Area Heavyweight Champion.
Ht. 6'0"
Manager J. Rooney

18.09.03 Slick Miller W PTS 4 Mayfair
21.02.04 Brodie Pearmaine W RSC 1 Brighton
12.03.04 Paul King W PTS 6 Millwall
02.12.04 Luke Simpkin W RSC 3 Crystal Palace
18.02.05 Scott Gammer L PTS 6 Brighton
24.04.05 Julius Francis W PTS 8 Leicester
Square
12.06.05 Mal Rice W PTS 6 Leicester Square
24.07.05 Garry Delaney W PTS 6 Leicester
Square
05.03.06 Colin Kenna W PTS 10 Southampton
*(Southern Area Heavyweight Title
Challenge)*
Career: 9 contests, won 8, lost 1.

Dave Stewart

Ayr. *Born* Irvine, 5 September, 1975
Lightweight. Former Undefeated British
Masters Lightweight Champion. Ht. 6'0¼"
Manager Self

15.02.01 Danny Connelly W PTS 6 Glasgow
27.04.01 Woody Greenaway W PTS 6 Glasgow
07.09.01 John Marshall W PTS 6 Glasgow
15.06.02 Dave Hinds W PTS 6 Tottenham
06.09.02 Pete Buckley W PTS 6 Bethnal Green
17.09.02 James Paisley W RSC 5 Bethnal Green
30.01.03 Scott Lawton W PTS 6 Piccadilly
26.04.03 Nigel Senior W RSC 2 Brentford
(British Masters Lightweight Title Challenge)
27.05.03 Pete Buckley W PTS 4 Dagenham
01.08.03 Norman Dhalie W RTD 2 Bethnal Green
26.09.03 Jimmy Beech W RTD 2 Reading
14.11.03 Pete Buckley W PTS 4 Bethnal Green
16.04.04 Carl Allen W PTS 6 Bradford
10.09.04 Bobby Vanzie W PTS 4 Wembley
10.04.05 Daniel Thorpe W RSC 3 Brentwood
16.07.05 Anthony Mezaache W PTS 8 Chigwell
21.10.05 Judex Meemea W PTS 6 Bethnal Green
17.02.06 Jason Nesbitt W PTS 4 Bethnal Green
12.05.06 Lee Meager L RSC 6 Bethnal Green
(Vacant British Lightweight Title)
Career: 19 contests, won 18, lost 1.

Dave Stewart   Les Clark

Liam Stinchcombe

Bristol. *Born* Bristol, 25 July, 1983
Middleweight. Ht. 5'10"
Manager T. Woodward

09.07.05 Mark Phillips W PTS 4 Bristol
12.11.05 Jamie Ambler L RTD 3 Bristol
20.05.06 Lee Thomas W CO 2 Bristol
Career: 3 contests, won 2, lost 1.

(Alexei) Alex Stoda

Wisbech. *Born* Venemaa, Estonia, 21
February, 1978
Middleweight. Ht. 5'10"
Manager B. Lee

06.10.05 Martin Marshall L PTS 6 Sunderland
30.10.05 Anthony Young L PTS 6 Bethnal Green
30.05.06 Sam Webb W RSC 3 Bethnal Green

18.06.06 Mark Thompson L RSC 1 Manchester
Career: 4 contests, won 1, lost 3.

Darren Stubbs

Oldham. *Born* Manchester, 16 October, 1971
L.Heavyweight. Ht. 5'10"
Manager J. Doughty

02.06.02 Adam Cale W RSC 6 Shaw
21.06.02 Dean Cockburn L RSC 1 Leeds
17.11.02 Shpetim Hoti W RTD 2 Shaw
29.11.02 Jamie Wilson W PTS 6 Hull
09.03.03 Martin Thompson W RSC 3 Shaw
18.03.03 Jamie Hearn W RSC 3 Reading
08.06.03 Danny Grainger L RSC 2 Shaw
19.10.03 Paul Wesley W PTS 6 Shaw
29.02.04 Patrick Cito W PTS 6 Shaw
10.04.04 Alan Page L PTS 4 Manchester
20.04.04 Paul Owen W PTS 6 Sheffield
31.10.04 Nick Okoth W PTS 6 Shaw
20.11.05 Paul Bonson W PTS 6 Shaw
02.04.06 Howard Clarke W PTS 6 Shaw
18.06.06 Amer Khan L PTS 10 Manchester
(Vacant Central Area L.Heavyweight Title)
Career: 15 contests, won 11, lost 4.

Lee Swaby

Lincoln. *Born* Lincoln, 14 May, 1976
Cruiserweight. Former Undefeated British
Masters Cruiserweight Champion. Ht. 6'2"
Manager Self

29.04.97 Naveed Anwar W PTS 6 Manchester
19.06.97 Liam Richardson W RSC 4 Scunthorpe
30.10.97 Phil Ball W RSC 3 Newark
17.11.97 L. A. Williams W PTS 6 Manchester
02.02.98 Tim Redman L PTS 6 Manchester
27.02.98 John Wilson W CO 3 Glasgow
07.03.98 Phill Day L PTS 4 Reading
08.05.98 Chris P. Bacon L RSC 3 Manchester
17.07.98 Chris P. Bacon L PTS 6 Mere
19.09.98 Cathal O'Grady L RSC 1 Dublin
20.12.98 Mark Levy L RTD 5 Salford
23.06.99 Lee Archer W PTS 6 West Bromwich
04.09.99 Garry Delaney L PTS 8 Bethnal Green
03.10.99 Brian Gascoigne DREW 6 Chesterfield
11.12.99 Owen Beck L PTS 4 Liverpool
05.03.00 Kelly Oliver L PTS 10 Peterborough
(Vacant British Masters Cruiserweight Title)
15.04.00 Mark Levy W PTS 4 Bethnal Green
12.05.00 Enzo Maccarinelli W CO 3 Swansea
26.05.00 Steffen Nielsen L PTS 4 Holbaek, Denmark
09.09.00 Tony Dowling W RSC 9 Newark
(Vacant British Masters Cruiserweight Title)
05.02.01 Robert Norton L PTS 8 Hull
24.03.01 Crawford Ashley L PTS 8 Sheffield
30.04.01 Eamonn Glennon W PTS 6 Glasgow
02.06.01 Denzil Browne DREW 8 Wakefield
31.07.01 Stephane Allouane W PTS 4 Bethnal Green
13.09.01 Kevin Barrett W PTS 4 Sheffield
15.12.01 Chris Woollas W RSC 4 Sheffield
27.04.02 Mark Hobson L PTS 10 Huddersfield
(Final Elim. British Cruiserweight Title)
03.08.02 Greg Scott-Briggs W RSC 4 Derby
05.12.02 Eamonn Glennon W PTS 4 Sheffield
24.01.03 Tommy Eastwood W PTS 6 Sheffield

10.06.03 Paul Bonson W PTS 4 Sheffield
05.09.03 Brodie Pearmaine W RTD 4 Sheffield
20.04.04 Lee Mountford W RSC 1 Sheffield
27.05.04 Mark Hobson L RSC 6 Huddersfield
(British & Commonwealth Cruiserweight Title Challenges)
24.10.04 Denzil Browne W RSC 7 Sheffield
(Elim. British Cruiserweight Title)
09.09.05 Hastings Rasani W PTS 4 Sheffield
26.11.05 Vitaly Shkraba W RSC 3 Sheffield
04.03.06 Marco Huck L RTD 6 Oldenburg, Germany
Career: 39 contests, won 22, drew 2, lost 15.

Martin Sweeney

Darwen. *Born* Rochdale, 19 August, 1981
Middleweight. Ht. 5'7¾"
Manager T. Schofield

11.05.06 Zahoor Hussain L PTS 6 Sunderland
21.05.06 Danny Butler L PTS 6 Bristol
22.06.06 Nicki Smedley L RSC 3 Sheffield
Career: 3 contests, lost 3.

(Cevdet) Jed Syger (Saygi)

Mile End. *Born* Iskendurun, Turkey, 15 July, 1983
Lightweight. Ht. 5'8"
Manager Self

10.07.04 Frank Layz W PTS 4 Asbury Park, New Jersey, USA
11.09.04 Adam Allen W RSC 3 Philadelphia, Pennsylvania, USA
05.03.05 Jonathan Jones W PTS 4 Dagenham
30.04.05 Ian Reid W PTS 4 Dagenham
16.06.05 Junior Anderson W CO 2 Mayfair
18.09.05 Peter O'Neill W PTS 4 Bethnal Green
24.02.06 Rakhim Mingaleev W PTS 6 Dagenham
29.06.06 Dai Davies L PTS 6 Bethnal Green
Career: 8 contests, won 7, lost 1.

Jed Syger   Philip Sharkey

Gary Sykes

Dewsbury. *Born* Dewsbury, 13 February, 1984
S.Featherweight. Ht. 5'8"
Manager R. Manners/T. Schofield

23.02.06 Dave Hinds W PTS 6 Leeds
13.04.06 Dai Davies W CO 3 Leeds
Career: 2 contests, won 2.

Gavin Tait

Carmarthen. *Born* Carmarthen, 2 March, 1976
Welterweight. Ht. 5'7"
Manager Self

07.06.04	Stuart Green L PTS 6 Glasgow
03.07.04	Justin Hicks W RSC 5 Bristol
05.10.04	Tristan Davies L PTS 6 Dudley
24.11.04	David Pereira L PTS 6 Mayfair
02.12.04	Chris Long L PTS 6 Bristol
07.04.05	Gary Coombes W RSC 3 Birmingham
27.05.05	Darren Johnstone L PTS 6 Motherwell
30.10.05	Dwayne Hill L PTS 6 Sheffield
24.03.06	Tom Glover W PTS 4 Bethnal Green

Career: 9 contests, won 3, lost 6.

(Mehrdud) Takaloo (Takalobigashi)

Margate. *Born* Iran, 23 September, 1975
WBU Welterweight Champion. Former
Undefeated WBU L.Middleweight
Champion. Former Undefeated IBF Inter-
Continental L.Middleweight Champion.
Ht. 5'9"
Manager F. Warren

19.07.97	Harry Butler W RSC 1 Wembley
13.09.97	Michael Alexander W PTS 4 Millwall
15.11.97	Koba Kulu W RSC 3 Bristol
19.12.97	Mark Sawyers W PTS 4 Millwall
07.02.98	Jawaid Khaliq L RSC 4 Cheshunt
16.05.98	Anas Oweida W RSC 1 Bethnal Green
10.10.98	Michael Jones L PTS 6 Bethnal Green
30.01.99	Darren McInulty W RSC 5 Bethnal Green
03.04.99	Gareth Lovell W RSC 6 Kensington
26.06.99	Leigh Wicks W CO 3 Millwall
04.09.99	Carlton Williams W RSC 4 Bethnal Green
23.10.99	Prince Kasi Kaihau W RSC 3 Telford
29.01.00	Paul King W RSC 2 Manchester
08.04.00	Biagio Falcone W RTD 4 Bethnal Green
08.07.00	Ernie Smith W RSC 4 Widnes
12.08.00	Howard Clarke W PTS 12 Wembley *(Vacant IBF Inter-Continental L.Middleweight Title)*
13.11.00	Jason Collins W RSC 2 Bethnal Green
24.02.01	James Lowther W PTS 12 Bethnal Green *(IBF Inter-Continental L.Middleweight Title Defence)*
07.07.01	Anthony Farnell W RSC 1 Manchester *(Vacant WBU L.Middleweight Title)*
22.09.01	Scott Dixon W CO 1 Bethnal Green *(WBU L.Middleweight Title Defence)*
04.05.02	Gary Logan W RSC 10 Bethnal Green *(WBU L. Middleweight Title Defence)*
17.08.02	Daniel Santos L PTS 12 Cardiff *(WBO L.Middleweight Title Challenge. WBU L.Middleweight Title Defence)*
01.02.03	Jim Rock W RSC 9 Belfast *(Vacant WBU L. Middleweight Title)*
24.05.03	Jose Rosa W PTS 12 Bethnal Green *(WBU L.Middleweight Title Defence)*
13.09.03	Vladimir Borovski W CO 3 Newport
24.01.04	Eugenio Monteiro L PTS 8 Wembley
10.09.04	Wayne Alexander L RSC 2 Bethnal Green *(Vacant WBU L.Middleweight Title)*
23.07.05	Delroy Mellis W PTS 8 Edinburgh
25.02.06	Turgay Uzun W PTS 10 Canning Town
20.05.06	Eamonn Magee W PTS 12 Belfast *(WBU Welterweight Title Challenge)*

Career: 30 contests, won 25, lost 5.

Karl Taylor

Birmingham. *Born* Birmingham, 5 January, 1966
L.Middleweight. Former Undefeated
Midlands Area Lightweight Champion.
Ht. 5'5"
Manager Self

18.03.87	Steve Brown W PTS 6 Stoke
06.04.87	Paul Taylor L PTS 6 Southampton
12.06.87	Mark Begley W RSC 1 Leamington
18.11.87	Colin Lynch W RSC 4 Solihull
29.02.88	Peter Bradley L PTS 8 Birmingham
04.10.89	Mark Antony W CO 2 Stafford
30.10.89	Tony Feliciello L PTS 8 Birmingham
06.12.89	John Davison L PTS 8 Leicester
23.12.89	Regilio Tuur L RTD 1 Hoogvliet, Holland
22.02.90	Mark Ramsey L RSC 4 Hull
29.10.90	Steve Walker DREW 6 Birmingham
10.12.90	Elvis Parsley L PTS 6 Birmingham
16.01.91	Wayne Windle W PTS 8 Stoke
02.05.91	Billy Schwer L RSC 2 Northampton
25.07.91	Peter Till L RSC 4 Dudley *(Midlands Area Lightweight Title Challenge)*
24.02.92	Charlie Kane L PTS 8 Glasgow
28.04.92	Richard Woolgar W PTS 6 Wolverhampton
29.05.92	Alan McDowall L PTS 6 Glasgow
25.07.92	Michael Armstrong L RSC 3 Manchester
02.11.92	Hugh Forde L PTS 6 Wolverhampton
23.11.92	Dave McHale L PTS 8 Glasgow
22.12.92	Patrick Gallagher L RSC 3 Mayfair
13.02.93	Craig Dermody L RSC 5 Manchester
31.03.93	Craig Dermody W PTS 6 Barking
07.06.93	Mark Geraghty W PTS 8 Glasgow
13.08.93	Giorgio Campanella L CO 6 Arezzo, Italy
05.10.93	Paul Harvey W PTS 6 Mayfair
21.10.93	Charles Shepherd L RTD 5 Bayswater
21.12.93	Patrick Gallagher L PTS 6 Mayfair
09.02.94	Alan Levene W RSC 2 Brentwood
01.03.94	Shaun Cogan L PTS 6 Dudley
15.03.94	Patrick Gallagher L PTS 6 Mayfair
18.04.94	Peter Till W PTS 10 Walsall *(Midlands Area Lightweight Title Challenge)*
24.05.94	Michael Ayers DREW 8 Sunderland
12.11.94	P. J. Gallagher L PTS 6 Dublin
29.11.94	Dingaan Thobela W PTS 8 Cannock
31.03.95	Michael Ayers L RSC 8 Crystal Palace *(British Lightweight Title Challenge)*
06.05.95	Cham Joof W PTS 8 Shepton Mallet
23.06.95	Poli Diaz L PTS 8 Madrid, Spain
02.09.95	Paul Ryan L RSC 3 Wembley
04.11.95	Carl Wright L PTS 6 Liverpool
15.12.95	Peter Richardson L PTS 8 Bethnal Green
23.01.96	Paul Knights DREW 6 Bethnal Green
05.03.96	Andy Holligan L PTS 6 Barrow
20.03.96	Mervyn Bennett W PTS 8 Cardiff
21.05.96	Malcolm Melvin L PTS 10 Edgbaston *(Midlands Area L. Welterweight Title Challenge)*
07.10.96	Joshua Clottey L RSC 2 Lewisham
20.12.96	Anatoly Alexandrov L RSC 7 Bilbao, Spain
28.01.97	Eamonn Magee L PTS 6 Belfast
28.02.97	Mark Breslin L RSC 6 Kilmarnock
30.08.97	Gilbert Eastman L PTS 4 Cheshunt
25.10.97	Tontcho Tontchev L PTS 4 Queensferry
22.11.97	Bobby Vanzie L PTS 6 Manchester
18.04.98	Ricky Hatton L RSC 1 Manchester
18.07.98	James Hare L PTS 4 Sheffield
26.09.98	Oktay Urkal L PTS 8 Norwich
28.11.98	Junior Witter L PTS 4 Sheffield
06.03.99	George Scott L RSC 4 Southwark
15.05.99	Jon Thaxton L PTS 6 Sheffield
10.07.99	Eamonn Magee L RTD 3 Southwark
06.11.99	Alan Sebire W PTS 6 Widnes
15.11.99	Steve Murray L RSC 1 Bethnal Green
19.08.00	Iain Eldridge L PTS 4 Brentwood
04.09.00	Tomas Jansson L PTS 6 Manchester
16.09.00	Colin Lynes L PTS 6 Bethnal Green
09.12.00	David Walker L PTS 6 Southwark
10.02.01	Matthew Hatton L PTS 4 Widnes
10.03.01	Francis Barrett L RSC 3 Bethnal Green
10.04.01	Costas Katsantonis L PTS 4 Wembley
16.06.01	Brett James DREW 4 Wembley
15.09.01	David Barnes L PTS 4 Manchester
28.10.01	Babatunde Ajayi L PTS 4 Southwark
24.11.01	Ross Minter L PTS 4 Bethnal Green
15.12.01	Alexandra Vetoux L PTS 4 Wembley
12.02.02	Brett James DREW 4 Bethnal Green
11.03.02	Kevin McIntyre L PTS 4 Glasgow
04.05.02	Matthew Hatton L RSC 3 Bethnal Green
25.06.02	Rimell Taylor DREW 6 Rugby
20.07.02	Matthew Hatton L RTD 2 Bethnal Green
28.09.02	Michael Jennings L RSC 4 Manchester
16.11.02	Gavin Wake L PTS 4 Nottingham
30.11.02	Tony Conroy L PTS 4 Coventry
14.12.02	Alexander Vetoux L RTD 3 Newcastle
15.02.03	Ross Minter L PTS 6 Wembley
29.03.03	Alexander Vetoux L RSC 1 Portsmouth
08.05.03	Tony Doherty L PTS 4 Widnes
25.07.03	Lenny Daws L RTD 2 Norwich
06.10.03	Jonathan Woollins W PTS 6 Birmingham
29.10.03	Ajose Olusegun L PTS 6 Leicester Square
29.11.03	Gary Young L RSC 3 Renfrew
30.01.04	Lee McAllister L PTS 4 Dagenham
05.03.04	Oscar Hall L PTS 6 Darlington
27.03.04	Jamie Arthur L PTS 6 Edinburgh
06.05.04	Ashley Theophane L PTS 4 Barnsley
22.05.04	Tony Doherty L RTD 2 Widnes
03.09.04	Taz Jones L PTS 4 Newport
18.09.04	Karl Chiverton L PTS 6 Newark
26.09.04	Danny Johnston L PTS 5 Stoke
19.11.04	Tony Doherty L RSC 2 Bethnal Green
19.12.04	Kell Brook L PTS 6 Bolton
06.03.05	John Murray L PTS 6 Shaw
14.05.05	Lee McAllister L RTD 3 Aberdeen
26.06.05	Henry Castle L PTS 6 Southampton
24.07.05	John Fewkes L PTS 6 Sheffield
16.09.05	Tristan Davies L PTS 4 Telford
08.11.05	Danny Reynolds L RSC 4 Leeds
11.12.05	Paul Halpin L PTS 4 Chigwell
18.12.05	Johnny Hussey L PTS 6 Bolton
17.02.06	John O'Donnell L PTS 4 Bethnal Green
01.04.06	Ashley Theophane L PTS 4 Bethnal Green

24.04.06   Simon Fleck L PTS 6 Cleethorpes
13.05.06   Dale Miles L RSC 3 Sutton in Ashfield
18.06.06   Prince Arron L PTS 6 Manchester
Career: 113 contests, won 16, drew 6, lost 91.

Kyle Taylor
Birmingham. *Born* Birmingham, 13 May, 1987
Welterweight. Ht. 5'7"
Manager N. Nobbs

19.09.05   Lance Verallo W PTS 6 Glasgow
06.10.05   Dave Hinds W PTS 6 Dudley
23.11.05   Gareth Couch L PTS 6 Mayfair
03.12.05   Khurram Hussain L PTS 6 Coventry
Career: 4 contests, won 2, lost 2.

Kyle Taylor   Les Clark

Nicki Taylor
Askern. *Born* Doncaster, 6 July, 1979
L.Heavyweight. Ht. 5'11"
Manager M. Scriven

20.09.04   Sandy Robb L RSC 5 Glasgow
24.04.05   Hastings Rasani L RTD 4 Askern
18.06.05   Rod Anderton L RSC 4 Barnsley
22.10.05   Michael Pinnock W PTS 6 Mansfield
12.11.05   Danny Tombs DREW 4 Sheffield
12.12.05   Karl Wheeler L PTS 4 Peterborough
14.05.06   Duane Reid L RSC 2 Derby
Career: 7 contests, won 1, drew 1, lost 5.

Matt Teague
Grimsby. *Born* Grimsby, 14 July, 1980
Central Area & British Masters Featherweight Champion. Ht. 5'9"
Manager Self

21.11.02   Andy Robinson W RTD 3 Hull
11.12.02   Jason Nesbitt W PTS 6 Hull
17.04.03   Martin Hardcastle L PTS 6 Hull
02.06.03   Henry Janes W PTS 6 Cleethorpes
22.09.03   Tom Price W PTS 6 Cleethorpes
14.11.03   Kristian Laight W PTS 6 Hull
15.12.03   Dave Hinds W PTS 6 Cleethorpes
14.06.04   Dean Ward W PTS 6 Cleethorpes
20.09.04   Jason Nesbitt W PTS 6 Cleethorpes

13.12.04   Buster Dennis L PTS 6 Cleethorpes
05.12.05   Danny Wallace W PTS 10 Leeds
           (Vacant British Masters & Central Area Featherweight Titles)
Career: 11 contests, won 9, lost 2.

George Telfer
Hawick. *Born* Hawick, 26 May, 1979
Welterweight. Ht. 5'7"
Manager Self

14.03.03   Vince Baldassara W PTS 4 Glasgow
22.03.03   Tony Montana L PTS 4 Renfrew
12.07.03   Pete Buckley W PTS 4 Renfrew
25.10.03   James Gorman W PTS 4 Edinburgh
07.12.03   Dave Hill W RSC 4 Glasgow
06.03.04   Nigel Wright L RSC 3 Renfrew
29.10.04   Ivor Bonavic W PTS 4 Renfrew
03.12.04   Ernie Smith W PTS 4 Edinburgh
12.11.05   David Kehoe W PTS 6 Glasgow
Career: 9 contests, won 7, lost 2.

Alan Temple
Hartlepool. *Born* Hartlepool, 21 October, 1972
Welterweight. Former Undefeated British Masters Lightweight Champion. Ht. 5'8"
Manager Self

29.09.94   Stevie Bolt W CO 2 Bethnal Green
22.11.94   Phil Found W PTS 6 Bristol
07.02.95   Brian Coleman W PTS 6 Ipswich
27.04.95   Everald Williams L PTS 6 Bethnal Green
29.09.95   Kevin McKillan W PTS 6 Hartlepool
23.11.95   Rudy Valentino L RSC 3 Marton
02.03.96   Tony Foster W PTS 6 Newcastle
08.06.96   Micky Hall W RSC 2 Newcastle
20.09.96   Scott Dixon L PTS 4 Glasgow
24.10.96   Billy Schwer L PTS 8 Wembley
04.12.96   Harry Escott W PTS 8 Hartlepool
12.02.97   Tanveer Ahmed L RSC 8 Glasgow
           (Elim. British Lightweight Title)
13.02.98   Bobby Vanzie L CO 3 Seaham
           (Elim. British Lightweight Title)
21.03.98   Michael Ayers L RSC 2 Bethnal Green
31.10.98   Alan Bosworth W PTS 6 Basingstoke
20.02.99   Ivan Walker W PTS 4 Thornaby
05.03.99   David Burke L PTS 8 Liverpool
01.05.99   Jason Rowland L PTS 6 Crystal Palace
22.05.99   Eamonn Magee L CO 3 Belfast
26.06.99   Steve McLevy W RSC 6 Glasgow
11.09.99   Wayne Rigby W PTS 8 Sheffield
02.11.99   Souleymane M'Baye L RTD 7 Ciudad Real, Spain
12.08.00   Steve Murray L RSC 2 Wembley
           (IBF Inter-Continental Lightweight Title Challenge. Elim. British Lightweight Title)
26.03.01   Jonathan Thaxton L PTS 4 Wembley
04.06.01   Gary Hibbert W PTS 6 Hartlepool
21.07.01   Junior Witter L CO 5 Sheffield
10.11.01   Colin Dunne L RSC 7 Wembley
09.03.02   Gary Hibbert L RSC 1 Manchester
26.10.02   Leo O'Reilly W RSC 4 Maesteg
21.12.02   Darren Melville L PTS 8 Millwall
01.05.04   Silence Saheed W DIS 8 Gravesend
           (Vacant British Masters Lightweight Title)
17.12.04   David Burke L RSC 4 Liverpool
27.05.05   Pete Buckley W PTS 4 Spennymoor
23.07.05   Ricky Burns L PTS 4 Edinburgh
09.09.05   Scott Lawton W PTS 6 Sheffield

17.02.06   Jonathan Thaxton L RSC 5 Bethnal Green
Career: 36 contests, won 16, lost 20.

John-Paul Temple
Brighton. *Born* London, 30 May, 1973
L.Middleweight. Ht. 5'11"
Manager R. Davies

11.02.97   Mark O'Callaghan W PTS 6 Bethnal Green
17.03.97   Les Frost W CO 4 Mayfair
24.04.97   Chris Lyons W PTS 6 Mayfair
23.10.97   Chris Lyons W PTS 8 Mayfair
26.03.98   Trevor Smith L RSC 5 Piccadilly
28.04.98   Chris Price L PTS 6 Brentford
05.10.99   Jason Hall L PTS 6 Bloomsbury
25.02.00   Daniel James L PTS 10 Newmarket
           (Vacant Southern Area L.Welterweight Title)
21.11.04   Neil Jarmolinski DREW 4 Bracknell
03.12.04   Barrie Lee L PTS 4 Edinburgh
30.04.05   Danny Goode L PTS 4 Dagenham
26.06.05   Danny Goode L PTS 4 Southampton
10.09.05   Kerry Hope L PTS 4 Cardiff
06.10.05   Kevin Phelan L PTS 6 Longford
02.12.05   Darren Barker L RSC 6 Nottingham
Career: 15 contests, won 4, drew 1, lost 10.

Jonathan Thaxton   Les Clark

Jonathan Thaxton
Norwich. *Born* Norwich, 10 September, 1974
L.Welterweight. Former Undefeated WBF Lightweight Champion. Former Southern Area, IBF & WBO Inter-Continental L.Welterweight Champion. Ht. 5'6"
Manager Self

09.12.92   Scott Smith W PTS 6 Stoke
03.03.93   Dean Hiscox W PTS 6 Solihull
17.03.93   John O. Johnson W PTS 6 Stoke
23.06.93   Brian Coleman W PTS 8 Gorleston
22.09.93   John Smith W PTS 6 Wembley
07.12.93   Dean Hollington W RSC 3 Bethnal Green

10.03.94	B. F. Williams W RSC 4 Watford	
	(Vacant Southern Area L. Welterweight Title)	
18.11.94	Keith Marner L PTS 10 Bracknell	
	(Southern Area L. Welterweight Title Defence)	
26.05.95	David Thompson W RSC 6 Norwich	
23.06.95	Delroy Leslie W PTS 6 Bethnal Green	
12.08.95	Rene Prins L PTS 8 Zaandam, Holland	
08.12.95	Colin Dunne L RSC 5 Bethnal Green	
	(Vacant Southern Area Lightweight Title)	
20.01.96	John O. Johnson W RSC 4 Mansfield	
13.02.96	Paul Ryan W RSC 1 Bethnal Green	
25.06.96	Mark Elliot W CO 5 Mansfield	
	(Vacant IBF Inter-Continental L. Welterweight Title)	
14.09.96	Bernard Paul W PTS 12 Sheffield	
	(Vacant WBO Inter-Continental L. Welterweight Title)	
27.03.97	Paul Burke W RSC 9 Norwich	
	(IBF & WBO Inter-Continental L. Welterweight Title Defences)	
28.06.97	Gagik Chachatrian W RSC 2 Norwich	
	(IBF & WBO Inter-Continental L. Welterweight Title Defences)	
29.11.97	Rimvidas Billius W PTS 12 Norwich	
	(IBF & WBO Inter-Continental L. Welterweight Title Defences)	
26.09.98	Emanuel Burton L RSC 7 Norwich	
	(IBF & WBO Inter-Continental L. Welterweight Title Defences)	
15.05.99	Karl Taylor W PTS 6 Sheffield	
07.08.99	Brian Coleman W PTS 6 Dagenham	
15.11.99	Jason Rowland L RSC 5 Bethnal Green	

	(British L. Welterweight Title Challenge)	
15.07.00	Kimoun Kouassi W RSC 3 Norwich	
21.10.00	Ricky Hatton L PTS 12 Wembley	
	(Vacant British L.Welterweight Title)	
26.03.01	Alan Temple W PTS 4 Wembley	
28.07.01	David Kirk W PTS 4 Wembley	
09.02.02	Eamonn Magee L RSC 6 Manchester	
	(Commonwealth L.Welterweight Title Challenge)	
13.04.02	Chill John W RSC 2 Norwich	
15.06.02	Marc Waelkens W RSC 7 Norwich	
21.09.02	Viktor Baranov W RSC 1 Norwich	
09.10.04	Silence Saheed W PTS 6 Norwich	
13.12.04	Carl Allen W RSC 1 Birmingham	
09.04.05	Christophe de Busillet W CO 4 Norwich	
	(Vacant WBF Lightweight Title)	
03.09.05	Vasile Dragomir W CO 4 Norwich	
	(WBF Lightweight Title Defence)	
17.02.06	Alan Temple W RSC 5 Bethnal Green	
13.05.06	Jorge Daniel Miranda W PTS 10 Sheffield	

Career: 37 contests, won 30, lost 7.

Ashley Theophane
Kilburn. *Born* London, 20 August, 1980
Welterweight. Ht. 5'7"
Manager I. Akay/D. Coldwell

03.06.03	Lee Bedell W RSC 4 Bethnal Green	
22.07.03	Brian Coleman W PTS 6 Bethnal Green	
25.04.04	David Kirk W PTS 6 Nottingham	
06.05.04	Karl Taylor W PTS 4 Barnsley	
05.06.04	Chris Brophy W RSC 3 Bethnal Green	

19.06.04	Arv Mittoo W PTS 4 Muswell Hill	
02.12.04	Keith Jones W PTS 6 Crystal Palace	
26.03.05	Judex Meemea L PTS 6 Hackney	
24.04.05	David Kehoe W PTS 4 Leicester Square	
12.06.05	Jus Wallie W PTS 4 Leicester Square	
18.09.05	Oscar Milkitas L PTS 4 Bethnal Green	
09.10.05	David Kehoe W PTS 4 Hammersmith	
19.11.05	Duncan Cottier W PTS 6 Southwark	
25.02.06	Daniel Thorpe DREW 4 Canning Town	
17.03.06	Josef Holub W CO 3 Horka, Germany	
01.04.06	Karl Taylor W PTS 4 Bethnal Green	
21.05.06	Billy Smith W PTS 4 Bethnal Green	

Career: 17 contests, won 14, drew 1, lost 2.

Matthew Thirlwall
Bermondsey. *Born* Middlesbrough, 28 November, 1980
S.Middleweight. Ht. 5'9½"
Manager Self

16.03.02	William Webster W RSC 1 Bethnal Green	
10.05.02	Leigh Wicks W PTS 4 Bethnal Green	
23.08.02	Harry Butler W RSC 3 Bethnal Green	
25.10.02	Jason Collins W RSC 5 Bethnal Green	
21.12.02	Howard Clarke W PTS 6 Dagenham	
28.01.03	Gary Beardsley L PTS 6 Nottingham	
16.04.03	Gary Beardsley W PTS 6 Nottingham	
27.05.03	Leigh Wicks W PTS 6 Dagenham	
04.10.03	Dean Powell W RSC 2 Muswell Hill	
11.12.03	Harry Butler W PTS 6 Bethnal Green	
12.03.04	Patrick Cito W RSC 3 Nottingham	
24.09.04	Jason Collins L PTS 6 Nottingham	
02.12.05	Ernie Smith W PTS 4 Nottingham	
20.01.06	Donovan Smillie W CO 9 Bethnal Green	
	(Final Elim. English S.Middleweight Title)	
24.03.06	Moises Martinez W RSC 6 Hollywood, Florida, USA	

Career: 15 contests, won 13, lost 2.

Ashley Theophane (left) made it a double when outpointing Karl Taylor at York Hall on 1 April 2006
Les Clark

Matthew Thirlwall   Les Clark

Jeff Thomas

St Annes. *Born* Holland, 30 October, 1981
L.Welterweight. Ht. 5'10"
Manager Self

09.12.01	Peter Allen W PTS 6 Blackpool	
20.07.02	Pete Buckley W PTS 4 Bethnal Green	
03.08.02	Gareth Wiltshaw W DIS 2 Blackpool	
26.10.02	Dave Curran W RSC 6 Wigan	
28.04.03	Daniel Thorpe W PTS 6 Cleethorpes	
09.05.03	Carl Allen DREW 6 Doncaster	
08.06.03	Norman Dhalie W PTS 6 Shaw	
06.09.03	Lee McAllister L PTS 10 Aberdeen	

(*Vacant British Masters L.Welterweight Title*)

07.12.03 Martin Hardcastle L PTS 10 Bradford
(*Vacant British Masters S.Featherweight Title*)

03.07.04	Anthony Hanna W PTS 6 Blackpool
29.10.04	Ricky Burns L PTS 4 Renfrew
25.02.05	Steve Murray W RTD 3 Wembley
01.10.05	Anthony Christopher W PTS 6 Wigan
14.12.05	Baz Carey L PTS 6 Blackpool
02.03.06	Kristian Laight W PTS 6 Blackpool
03.06.06	Oisin Fagan L RSC 7 Dublin

(*Vacant All-Ireland L.Welterweight Title*)

Career: 16 contests, won 9, drew 1, lost 6.

Lee Thomas

Swansea. *Born* Swansea, 10 April, 1982
Middleweight. Ht. 5'10³/₄"
Manager N. Hodges

20.05.06 Liam Stinchcombe L CO 2 Bristol
Career: 1 contest, lost 1.

(Adrian) Carl Thompson

Manchester. *Born* Manchester, 26 May, 1964
Cruiserweight. Former Undefeated IBO Cruiserweight Champion. Former WBO Cruiserweight Champion. Former Undefeated European, British & WBC International Cruiserweight Champion. Ht. 6'0"
Manager Self

06.06.88	Darren McKenna W RSC 2 Manchester
11.10.88	Paul Sheldon W PTS 6 Wolverhampton
13.02.89	Steve Osborne W PTS 6 Manchester
07.03.89	Sean O'Phoenix W RSC 4 Manchester
04.04.89	Keith Halliwell W RSC 1 Manchester
04.05.89	Tenko Ernie W CO 4 Mayfair
12.06.89	Steve Osborne W PTS 8 Manchester
11.07.89	Peter Brown W RSC 5 Batley
31.10.89	Crawford Ashley L RSC 6 Manchester

(*Vacant Central Area L. Heavyweight Title*)

21.04.90 Francis Wanyama L PTS 6 St Amandsberg, Belgium
07.03.91 Terry Dixon W PTS 8 Basildon
01.04.91 Yawe Davis L RSC 2 Monaco, Monte Carlo
04.09.91 Nicky Piper W RSC 3 Bethnal Green
04.06.92 Steve Lewsam W RSC 8 Cleethorpes
(*Vacant British Cruiserweight Title*)
17.02.93 Arthur Weathers W CO 2 Bethnal Green
(*Vacant WBC International Cruiserweight Title*)
31.03.93 Steve Harvey W CO 1 Bethnal Green

25.07.93	Willie Jake W CO 3 Oldham
02.02.94	Massimiliano Duran W CO 8 Ferrara, Italy

(*European Cruiserweight Title Challenge*)

14.06.94 Akim Tafer W RSC 6 Epernay, France
(*European Cruiserweight Title Defence*)

10.09.94	Dionisio Lazario W RSC 1 Birmingham
13.10.94	Tim Knight W RSC 5 Paris, France
10.06.95	Ralf Rocchigiani L RSC 11 Manchester

(*Vacant WBO Cruiserweight Title*)

13.04.96	Albert Call W RTD 4 Wythenshawe
09.11.96	Jason Nicholson W PTS 8 Manchester
26.04.97	Keith McMurray W RSC 4 Zurich, Switzerland
04.10.97	Ralf Rocchigiani W PTS 12 Hannover, Germany

(*WBO Cruiserweight Title Challenge*)

18.04.98 Chris Eubank W PTS 12 Manchester
(*WBO Cruiserweight Title Defence*)

18.07.98 Chris Eubank W RSC 9 Sheffield
(*WBO Cruiserweight Title Defence*)

27.03.99 Johnny Nelson L RSC 5 Derby
(*WBO Cruiserweight Title Defence*)

03.12.99 Terry Dunstan W CO 12 Peterborough
(*Vacant British Cruiserweight Title*)

13.05.00 Alain Simon W RSC 6 Barnsley
(*Vacant European Cruiserweight Title*)

25.09.00 Alexei Illiin W RSC 2 Barnsley
(*European Cruiserweight Title Defence*)

03.02.01 Uriah Grant W RSC 5 Manchester
(*IBO Cruiserweight Title Challenge*)

26.11.01 Ezra Sellers L RSC 4 Manchester
(*IBO Cruiserweight Title Defence*)

10.06.03	Phill Day W CO 4 Sheffield
05.09.03	Hastings Rasani W RSC 1 Sheffield
07.11.03	Paul Bonson W PTS 6 Sheffield
06.02.04	Sebastiaan Rothmann W RSC 9 Sheffield

(*IBO Cruiserweight Title Challenge*)

10.09.04 David Haye W RSC 5 Wembley
(*IBO Cruiserweight Title Defence*)

26.11.05 Frederic Serrat W PTS 10 Sheffield
Career: 40 contests, won 34, lost 6.

Charlie Thompson

Doncaster. *Born* Doncaster, 18 September, 1985
Welterweight. Ht. 5'10"
Manager J. Rushton

02.12.05 Kristian Laight DREW 6 Doncaster
Career: 1 contest, drew 1.

Gary Thompson

Lancaster. *Born* Darwen, 22 June, 1981
Heavyweight. Ht. 5'9"
Manager D. Coldwell

22.09.01	Michael Thompson L RSC 3 Newcastle
16.11.01	Adam Cale W PTS 6 Preston
10.12.01	Rob Galloway W PTS 6 Bradford
23.12.01	Lee Whitehead L PTS 4 Salford
08.02.02	Shane White DREW 6 Preston
17.02.02	Lee Whitehead DREW 6 Salford
19.04.02	Lee Mountford DREW 4 Darlington
11.05.02	Tony Dowling L RSC 3 Newark
18.10.02	Michael Thompson L PTS 4 Hartlepool

26.10.02	Paul Richardson DREW 6 Wigan
02.12.02	Danny Thornton L PTS 6 Leeds
03.02.03	Nate Joseph L PTS 4 Bradford
28.02.03	Lee Mountford L PTS 6 Irvine
07.06.03	Carl Wright L RTD 2 Coventry
06.05.04	Simon Francis L PTS 4 Barnsley
15.05.04	Simeon Cover L PTS 6 Aberdeen
08.06.04	Simon Francis L RTD 2 Sheffield
04.11.04	Simeon Cover L PTS 6 Piccadilly
06.12.04	Nate Joseph W PTS 6 Bradford
20.02.05	Neil Dawson L PTS 6 Sheffield
11.03.05	Dean Cockburn L RSC 4 Doncaster
22.04.05	John Anthony L PTS 4 Barnsley
29.04.05	Junior MacDonald L RSC 1 Southwark
01.06.05	Danny Thornton L PTS 4 Leeds
09.07.05	John Smith L PTS 4 Bristol
11.09.05	Brian Gascoigne DREW 6 Kirkby in Ashfield
19.09.05	Sandy Robb L PTS 6 Glasgow
09.10.05	Paul Bowen L CO 1 Hammersmith
08.12.05	Rod Anderton L PTS 6 Derby
15.12.05	Tyrone Wright DREW 6 Cleethorpes
23.06.06	Lee Kellett W PTS 4 Blackpool

Career: 31 contests, won 4, drew 6, lost 21.

Mark Thompson

Heywood. *Born* Rochdale, 28 May, 1981
Middleweight. Ht. 5'11"
Manager S. Wood

23.09.05	Geraint Harvey W PTS 4 Manchester
20.11.05	Danny Moir W RSC 2 Shaw
18.12.05	Tony Randell W RSC 2 Bolton
12.02.06	Darren Gethin W PTS 4 Manchester
02.03.06	Simon Fleck W CO 3 Blackpool
02.04.06	Ernie Smith W PTS 6 Shaw
18.06.06	Alex Stoda W RSC 1 Manchester

Career: 7 contests, won 7.

Danny Thornton

Leeds. *Born* Leeds, 20 July, 1978
S.Middleweight. Former Undefeated Central Area Middleweight Champion. Ht. 5'10"
Manager Self

06.10.97	Pedro Carragher L PTS 6 Bradford
13.11.97	Shaun O'Neill DREW 6 Bradford
08.12.97	Shaun O'Neill DREW 6 Bradford
09.02.98	Roy Chipperfield W RSC 4 Bradford
17.03.98	Patrick J. Maxwell L PTS 6 Sheffield
30.03.98	Mark Owens W PTS 6 Bradford
15.05.98	Danny Bell W PTS 6 Nottingham
15.06.98	Jimmy Hawk W PTS 6 Bradford
12.10.98	Wayne Shepherd W PTS 6 Bradford
21.02.99	Shaun O'Neill W RSC 5 Bradford
25.04.99	Matt Scriven W RSC 4 Leeds
14.06.99	Martin Thompson W PTS 6 Bradford
18.10.99	Paul Henry W PTS 4 Bradford
14.11.99	Dean Ashton W PTS 4 Bradford
06.12.99	Lee Blundell L PTS 6 Bradford
05.02.00	Steve Roberts L PTS 6 Bethnal Green
25.03.00	Lee Molloy W RSC 2 Liverpool
06.06.00	Joe Townsley L RSC 7 Motherwell

(*IBO Inter-Continental L. Middleweight Title Challenge*)

30.11.00 Lee Blundell L RSC 8 Blackpool
(*Vacant Central Area L. Middleweight Title*)

20.03.01	Ian Toby W PTS 8 Leeds
13.11.01	Matt Galer L RSC 4 Leeds
02.12.02	Gary Thompson W PTS 6 Leeds

13.05.03	Kreshnik Qato L PTS 6 Leeds	
06.06.03	Jason Collins W PTS 10 Hull	
	(Vacant Central Area Middleweight Title)	
28.11.03	Jason Collins W PTS 10 Hull	
	(Central Area Middleweight Title Defence)	
10.02.04	Mo W PTS 6 Barnsley	
08.05.04	Scott Dann L RSC 3 Bristol	
	(Vacant English Middleweight Title)	
14.05.05	Simeon Cover DREW 6 Aberdeen	
01.06.05	Gary Thompson W PTS 4 Leeds	
25.09.05	Simeon Cover W PTS 6 Leeds	
29.10.05	Jozsef Nagy L PTS 12 Szentes, Hungary	
	(Vacant EBA S.Middleweight Title)	
23.02.06	Howard Clarke W PTS 6 Leeds	
20.03.06	Ojay Abrahams W PTS 6 Leeds	
12.05.06	Darren Barker L RSC 6 Bethnal Green	

Career: 34 contests, won 20, drew 3, lost 11.

Daniel Thorpe

Sheffield. *Born* Sheffield, 24 September, 1977
L.Welterweight. Former Central Area Lightweight Champion. Ht. 5'7¹/₂"
Manager D. Coldwell

07.09.01	Brian Gifford DREW 4 Bethnal Green
24.09.01	Ram Singh W RSC 4 Cleethorpes
17.11.01	Mally McIver L PTS 6 Dewsbury
10.12.01	Jason Gonzales W RSC 2 Birmingham
17.12.01	Joel Viney L RSC 2 Cleethorpes
11.02.02	Gareth Wiltshaw L PTS 6 Shrewsbury
04.03.02	Dave Travers W PTS 6 Birmingham
13.04.02	Jackson Williams L PTS 6 Norwich
11.05.02	Dean Scott W RSC 1 Chesterfield
21.05.02	Chris McDonagh L PTS 6 Custom House
08.06.02	Gary Young L RSC 1 Renfrew
12.07.02	Chill John L PTS 4 Southampton
21.07.02	John Marshall L RSC 1 Salford
22.09.02	Albi Hunt L PTS 6 Southwark
05.10.02	Gavin Down L RSC 2 Chesterfield
17.11.02	Nadeem Siddique L PTS 4 Bradford
29.11.02	Pete Buckley W PTS 6 Hull
21.12.02	Billy Corcoran L CO 2 Dagenham
16.02.03	Eddie Nevins L RSC 8 Salford
	(Vacant Central Area S.Featherweight Title)
22.03.03	Jamie Arthur L PTS 4 Renfrew
29.03.03	Danny Hunt L PTS 6 Portsmouth
12.04.03	Jackson Williams L PTS 6 Norwich
19.04.03	Steve Mullin W RSC 1 Liverpool
28.04.03	Jeff Thomas L PTS 6 Cleethorpes
08.05.03	Andy Morris L PTS 4 Widnes
08.06.03	Choi Tseveenpurev L PTS 8 Shaw
20.06.03	Colin Toohey L PTS 6 Liverpool
28.06.03	Gavin Rees L RSC 1 Cardiff
03.08.03	Joel Viney L PTS 6 Stalybridge
06.09.03	Joel Viney W PTS 6 Aberdeen
13.09.03	Sean Hughes L PTS 6 Wakefield
21.09.03	Chris Long W PTS 6 Bristol
12.10.03	Baz Carey DREW 6 Sheffield
19.10.03	Charles Shepherd L PTS 6 Shaw
27.10.03	Nadeem Siddique L PTS 6 Glasgow
06.11.03	Lee Beavis L PTS 4 Dagenham
07.12.03	Mally McIver W PTS 10 Bradford
	(Vacant Central Area Lightweight Title)
21.12.03	Pete Buckley W PTS 6 Bolton
26.02.04	Andy Morris L RSC 3 Widnes

03.04.04	Jason Nesbitt W PTS 6 Sheffield
23.04.04	Dave Hinds W PTS 6 Leicester
07.05.04	Stefy Bull L PTS 10 Doncaster
	(Central Area Lightweight Title Defence)
22.05.04	Gary Thornhill L RSC 4 Manchester
03.07.04	Joel Viney W RSC 1 Blackpool
10.09.04	Mickey Bowden W PTS 6 Wembley
18.09.04	Carl Greaves L PTS 6 Newark
01.10.04	Steve Bell L PTS 6 Manchester
08.10.04	Ricky Burns L PTS 6 Glasgow
16.10.04	Ryan Barrett L PTS 4 Dagenham
29.10.04	Adnan Amar L PTS 4 Worksop
06.11.04	Baz Carey W PTS 6 Coventry
26.11.04	John Murray L RSC 2 Altrincham
13.02.05	Lee McAllister L PTS 4 Bradford
04.03.05	Femi Fehintola L PTS 6 Rotherham
10.04.05	Dave Stewart L RSC 3 Brentwood
14.05.05	Tye Williams W RSC 3 Aberdeen
26.05.05	Baz Carey W PTS 6 Mayfair
03.06.05	Nadeem Siddique L PTS 6 Hull
24.06.05	James Gorman L PTS 6 Belfast
02.07.05	Michael Kelly L PTS 4 Dundalk
09.07.05	Carl Johanneson L RSC 3 Bristol
25.09.05	Jon Honney W PTS 4 Southampton
06.10.05	Paul Holborn L PTS 6 Sunderland
25.10.05	Kevin Mitchell L RSC 4 Preston
25.11.05	Haider Ali W RTD 4 Walsall
10.12.05	Amir Khan L RSC 2 Canning Town
27.01.06	Ian Wilson L PTS 4 Dagenham
25.02.06	Ashley Theophane DREW 4 Canning Town
11.03.06	Gavin Rees L RSC 5 Newport
13.05.06	Dean Smith L PTS 4 Bethnal Green
20.05.06	Kevin O'Hara L PTS 6 Belfast
28.05.06	Shane Watson L PTS 6 Longford
16.06.06	Dwayne Hill L PTS 4 Liverpool
23.06.06	Anthony Maynard L PTS 4 Birmingham

Career: 74 contests, won 19, drew 3, lost 52.

Neil Tidman

Bedworth. *Born* Nuneaton, 16 April, 1978
L.Heavyweight. Ht. 5'10"
Manager P. Carpenter

18.06.05	Lee Williamson W PTS 6 Coventry
22.10.05	Michael Banbula W PTS 6 Coventry
15.12.05	Omid Bourzo W RSC 3 Coventry

Career: 3 contests, won 3.

Danny Tombs

Sheffield. *Born* London, 26 May, 1986
L.Heavyweight. Ht. 5'10¹/₂"
Manager D. Hobson (senior)

12.11.05	Nicki Taylor DREW 4 Sheffield
19.11.05	Michael Banbula W RSC 2 Southwark
30.03.06	Mark Phillips W PTS 4 Bloomsbury

Career: 3 contests, won 2, drew 1.

Kevin Townsley

Cleland. *Born* Lanark, 21 September, 1982
Featherweight. Ht. 5'8"
Manager T. Gilmour

27.05.05	Abdul Mougharbel W PTS 6 Motherwell
20.02.06	Sandy Bartlett W PTS 4 Glasgow
24.04.06	Barrington Brown W PTS 6 Glasgow

Career: 3 contests, won 3.

Paul Truscott

Middlesbrough. *Born* Middlesbrough, 1 May, 1986
Featherweight. Ht. 5'9"
Manager M. Marsden

23.06.06	Billy Smith W PTS 4 Blackpool

Career: 1 contest, won 1.

Choi Tseveenpurev

Oldham. *Born* Mongolia, 6 October, 1971
WBF Featherweight Champion. Former Undefeated British Masters Featherweight Champion. Ht. 5'5³/₄"
Manager J. Doughty

22.11.96	Jeun-Tae Kim W CO 8 Seoul, South Korea
19.08.98	Veeraphol Sahaprom L PTS 10 Bangkok, Thailand
02.10.98	Surapol Sithnaruepol W CO 1 Bangkok, Thailand
07.01.99	Ekarat 13Reintower W CO 2 Krabi, Thailand
18.04.99	Bulan Bugiarso L PTS 12 Jakarta, Indonesia
01.05.99	Bulan Bugiarso L PTS 12 Kalimanton, Indonesia
12.08.99	Jiao Hasabayar W RSC 4 Ulan-Bator, Mongolia
22.08.99	Con Roksa W CO 3 Seinyeng, China
22.08.99	Thongdang Sorvoraphin W CO 4 Seinyeng, China
21.05.00	David Jeffrey W RSC 2 Shaw
24.09.00	Billy Smith W RTD 2 Shaw
03.12.00	Chris Williams W PTS 4 Shaw
27.04.01	Willie Limond W PTS 6 Glasgow
23.09.01	Steve Hanley W PTS 6 Shaw
06.10.01	Livinson Ruiz W PTS 4 Manchester
09.12.01	Kevin Gerowski W RSC 5 Shaw
	(Vacant British Masters Featherweight Title)
22.03.02	Chris Emanuele W PTS 4 Coventry
02.06.02	John Mackay W RSC 5 Shaw
17.11.02	Peter Allen W RSC 4 Shaw
09.03.03	Jason Nesbitt W PTS 8 Shaw
08.06.03	Daniel Thorpe W PTS 8 Shaw
29.02.04	John Mackay W RSC 3 Shaw
13.03.04	Lehlohonolo Ledwaba L PTS 8 Copenhagen, Denmark
06.05.04	Kevin O'Hara W PTS 8 Barnsley
10.07.04	Harry Ramogoadi W RTD 6 Coventry
	(British Masters Featherweight Title Defence)
06.03.05	Harry Ramogoadi W RSC 5 Shaw
	(British Masters Featherweight Title Defence)
20.11.05	Alexey Volchan W RSC 10 Shaw
02.04.06	David Kiilu W RSC 3 Shaw
	(Vacant WBF Featherweight Title)

Career: 28 contests, won 23, lost 5.

Richard Turba

Blackpool. *Born* Nitra, Slovakia, 21 February, 1985
S.Middleweight. Ht. 5'10"
Manager L. Veitch

14.12.05	Paul Billington W PTS 6 Blackpool
02.03.06	Csaba Andras W RSC 3 Blackpool
06.05.06	Tyan Booth L PTS 6 Blackpool
16.06.06	Mike Allen W RSC 2 Liverpool
23.06.06	Paul David L PTS 6 Blackpool

Career: 5 contests, won 3, lost 2.

UV

Vadim Usenko

Enfield. *Born* Donetsk, Ukraine, 18 August, 1986
Cruiserweight. Ht. 6'5½"
Manager P. Fondu

16.12.05 Czaba Andras W RSC 1 Bracknell
18.03.06 Nabil Haciani L RSC 6 Monte Carlo, Monaco
19.05.06 Olivier Bonvin W RSC 1 Grenoble, France
29.06.06 Tomas Mrazek W PTS 6 Carouge, Switzerland

Career: 4 contests, won 3, lost 1.

Joey Vegas (Lubega)

Tottenham. *Born* Namirembe Uganda, 1 January, 1982
British Masters S.Middleweight Champion. Ht. 5'8½"
Manager M. Helliet

04.11.04 Cello Renda W RSC 3 Piccadilly
27.01.05 Egbui Ikeagwo W PTS 4 Piccadilly
26.03.05 Egbui Ikeagwo W PTS 4 Hackney
26.05.05 Gareth Lawrence W PTS 4 Mayfair

17.11.05 Conroy McIntosh W RSC 3 Piccadilly
30.03.06 Simeon Cover W PTS 10 Piccadilly
(British Masters S.Middleweight Title Challenge)

Career: 6 contests, won 6.

Lance Verallo

Birmingham. *Born* Cardiff, 25 July, 1984
Welterweight. Ht. 5'11"
Manager Self

08.05.05 Sujad Elahi L PTS 6 Sheffield
11.06.05 Mike Reid L PTS 6 Kirkcaldy
19.06.05 Ian Wilson L PTS 4 Bethnal Green
24.07.05 Nicky Smedley L PTS 6 Sheffield
19.09.05 Kyle Taylor L PTS 6 Glasgow
30.09.05 Stephen Chinnock L PTS 4 Burton
14.10.05 Ryan Brawley L PTS 6 Motherwell
30.10.05 Muhsen Nasser L PTS 6 Sheffield
12.11.05 Dwayne Hill L PTS 6 Sheffield
21.11.05 Darren Johnstone L PTS 6 Glasgow
08.12.05 Scott Conway L PTS 6 Derby
23.01.06 Gary McArthur L PTS 6 Glasgow
12.02.06 Gary O'Connor L RSC 4 Manchester
31.03.06 Thomas Moran L PTS 6 Inverurie

Career: 14 contests, lost 14.

Jimmy Vincent

Birmingham. *Born* Barnet, 5 June, 1969
Welterweight. Former Undefeated British Masters L Middleweight Champion. Ht. 5'8"
Manager Self

19.10.87 Roy Williams W PTS 6 Birmingham
11.11.87 Mick Greenwood W PTS 6 Stafford
19.11.87 Darryl Pettit W RSC 6 Ilkeston
24.11.87 Roy Williams W PTS 6 Wolverhampton
14.02.88 Niel Leggett L PTS 6 Peterborough
29.02.88 Billy Cawley W CO 1 Birmingham
13.04.88 Dave Croft W PTS 6 Wolverhampton
16.05.88 Barry North W PTS 6 Wolverhampton
14.06.88 Dean Dickinson W PTS 6 Birmingham
20.09.88 Henry Armstrong L PTS 6 Stoke
10.10.88 Henry Armstrong L PTS 6 Manchester
17.10.88 Dean Dickinson W PTS 6 Birmingham
14.11.88 Peter Gabbitus L PTS 6 Stratford upon Avon
22.11.88 Barry North W RSC 4 Wolverhampton
12.12.88 Tony Feliciello L PTS 8 Birmingham
09.09.92 Mark Dawson L PTS 6 Stoke
23.09.92 Mark Epton W RSC 6 Leeds
17.12.92 Jason Rowland L PTS 6 Wembley
06.03.93 Mark Tibbs W PTS 6 Glasgow
27.08.96 Geoff McCreesh L RSC 1 Windsor
26.09.96 David Bain W RSC 3 Walsall
28.10.96 Lee Murtagh W RSC 2 Bradford
18.01.97 Tommy Quinn W RSC 1 Swadlincote
25.02.97 Kevin Adamson W PTS 6 Sheffield
25.03.97 Gary Jacobs L RSC 1 Lewisham
25.10.97 Ahmed Dottuev L PTS 6 Queensferry
29.01.98 Craig Winter L PTS 6 Pentre Halkyn
28.03.98 Zoltan Sarossy DREW 6 Hull
18.09.98 Danny Ryan L PTS 12 Belfast
(Vacant IBO Inter-Continental S. Middleweight Title)
24.10.98 Darren Dorrington DREW 6 Bristol
25.11.98 Cornelius Carr L PTS 6 Streatham
05.12.98 Wayne Alexander L RSC 3 Bristol
22.01.99 Jim Rock L PTS 10 Dublin
29.04.99 Anthony McFadden L PTS 6 Bethnal Green
11.12.00 Harry Butler W PTS 6 Birmingham
31.10.01 Jason Williams W PTS 10 Birmingham
(Vacant British Masters L.Middleweight Title)
10.12.01 Ojay Abrahams W PTS 10 Birmingham
(British Masters L.Middleweight Title Defence)
26.04.02 Darren McInulty W CO 6 Coventry
(British Masters L. Middleweight Title Defence)
21.12.02 David Walker W RSC 8 Dagenham
(Final Elim. British Welterweight Title)
17.07.03 David Barnes L PTS 12 Dagenham
(Vacant British Welterweight Title)
06.12.03 Eamonn Magee L PTS 12 Cardiff
(Vacant WBU Welterweight Title)
16.07.05 Michael Jennings L CO 1 Bolton
(Vacant British Welterweight Title)

Career: 42 contests, won 21, drew 2, lost 19.

(Jaspreet) Jaz Virdee

Peterborough. *Born* London, 26 March, 1979
L.Welterweight. Ht. 5'9"
Manager I. Pauly

22.07.03 Rob Jeffries L PTS 6 Bethnal Green
27.09.03 Steve Bell L RSC 1 Manchester
21.11.03 Silence Saheed L RSC 2 Millwall
24.01.04 Kevin Mitchell L RSC 1 Wembley
08.04.04 Kristian Laight L PTS 6 Peterborough
30.03.06 Kristian Laight W PTS 6 Peterborough
15.06.06 Arial Krasnopolski W PTS 6 Peterborough

Career: 7 contests, won 2, lost 5.

Joey Vegas   Les Clark

Dave Wakefield

Tooting. *Born* London, 8 January, 1979
L. Middleweight. Ht. 5'11"
Manager Self

12.12.02	Mark Thornton L PTS 4 Leicester Square
13.04.03	Jon Hilton W PTS 4 Streatham
26.04.03	Kevin Phelan L PTS 4 Brentford
03.06.03	Justin Hudson L PTS 4 Bethnal Green
13.06.03	William Webster DREW 6 Queensway
25.10.03	Barrie Lee L PTS 4 Edinburgh
27.11.03	Kevin Phelan L PTS 6 Longford
20.02.04	Chas Symonds L RSC 5 Bethnal Green
15.05.04	Alan Campbell DREW 6 Aberdeen
26.02.06	Dean Marcantonio W RSC 3 Dagenham
06.05.06	Lance Hall W PTS 6 Birmingham
23.06.06	Joe Mitchell W PTS 6 Birmingham

Career: 12 contests, won 4, drew 2, lost 6.

David Walker

Bermondsey. *Born* Bromley, 17 June, 1976
L.Middleweight. Former Undefeated
Southern Area L.Middleweight Champion.
Former Undefeated Southern Area
Welterweight Champion. Ht. 5'10"
Manager Self

29.04.00	Dave Fallon W RSC 1 Wembley
27.05.00	Stuart Rimmer W RSC 2 Southwark
15.07.00	Billy Smith W RTD 2 Millwall
16.09.00	Keith Jones W PTS 6 Bethnal Green
14.10.00	Jason Vlasman W RSC 1 Wembley
18.11.00	Gary Flear W PTS 4 Dagenham
09.12.00	Karl Taylor W PTS 6 Southwark
20.01.01	Ernie Smith W RTD 1 Bethnal Green
17.02.01	Paul Denton W PTS 4 Bethnal Green
19.05.01	Mark Ramsey W PTS 4 Wembley
14.07.01	David White W PTS 4 Liverpool
13.09.01	David Kirk DREW 8 Sheffield
16.03.02	Paul Dyer W RSC 6 Bethnal Green
	(*Vacant Southern Area Welterweight Title*)
10.05.02	Pedro Thompson W RSC 3 Bethnal Green
23.08.02	Robert Burton W RSC 2 Bethnal Green
25.10.02	Brett James W RSC 4 Bethnal Green
	(*Southern Area Welterweight Title Defence*)
21.12.02	Jimmy Vincent L RSC 8 Dagenham
	(*Final Elim. British Welterweight Title*)
05.03.03	Ojay Abrahams W PTS 6 Bethnal Green
16.04.03	Leigh Wicks W PTS 6 Nottingham
27.05.03	John Humphrey W CO 2 Dagenham
	(*Southern Area L.Middleweight Title Challenge. Elim. British L.Middleweight Title*)
25.07.03	Spencer Fearon W RSC 4 Norwich
	(*Southern Area L.Middleweight Title Defence*)
04.10.03	Roman Karmazin L RTD 3 Muswell Hill
	(*European L.Middleweight Title Challenge*)
12.03.04	Matt Scriven W RSC 3 Nottingham

02.06.04	Kevin Phelan W PTS 6 Nottingham
12.11.04	Danny Moir W RSC 5 Wembley
09.07.05	Howard Clarke W PTS 4 Nottingham
23.09.05	Jamie Moore L RSC 4 Manchester
	(*British L.Middleweight Title Challenge*)

Career: 27 contests, won 23, drew 1, lost 3.

Dean Walker

Sheffield. *Born* Sheffield, 25 April, 1979
L.Heavyweight. Ht. 5'11"
Manager D. Coldwell

21.10.00	Colin McCash DREW 6 Sheffield
11.12.00	James Lee L PTS 6 Sheffield
27.07.01	Chris Duggan W RSC 4 Sheffield
15.12.01	William Webster W PTS 6 Sheffield
03.03.02	Shaun Horsfall W PTS 6 Shaw
02.06.02	Wayne Shepherd W PTS 6 Shaw
03.08.02	Richard Inquieti W PTS 6 Derby
05.10.02	Martin Scotland W PTS 6 Chesterfield
24.05.03	Neil Bonner W PTS 6 Sheffield
12.10.03	Paul Lomax W PTS 6 Sheffield
10.02.04	Neil Addis W PTS 6 Barnsley
21.02.04	Matthew Macklin L CO 1 Cardiff
08.06.04	Andrei Ivanov W PTS 6 Sheffield
03.09.04	Dean Cockburn L PTS 10 Doncaster
	(*Vacant Central Area S.Middleweight Title*)
15.12.04	Lee Murtagh L PTS 10 Sheffield
	(*Vacant Central Central Area Middleweight Title*)
20.02.05	Mo W PTS 6 Sheffield
19.03.05	Jozsef Nagy L RTD 8 Tapolca, Hungary
	(*IBF Inter-Continental Middleweight Title Challenge*)
16.07.05	Darren Barker L PTS 6 Chigwell
25.10.05	Thomas McDonagh L PTS 6 Preston
18.02.06	Jason McKay L RTD 1 Edinburgh
18.05.06	Matthew Hough L PTS 6 Walsall

Career: 21 contests, won 11, drew 1, lost 9.

Pete Walkman

Derby. *Born* Burton, 22 November, 1977
S.Bantamweight. Ht. 5'7"
Manager M. Shinfield

| 14.05.06 | Neil Marston L RSC 6 Derby |

Career: 1 contest, lost 1.

Mark Wall   Les Clark

Mark Wall

Dudley. *Born* Sandwell, 1 September, 1978
S.Middleweight. Ht. 5'8"
Manager Self

09.04.04	Dean Lloyd W PTS 6 Rugby
27.04.04	Andrei Ivanov L CO 6 Leeds
25.06.04	Jake Guntert L CO 1 Bethnal Green
05.10.04	Joe Mitchell DREW 6 Dudley
23.10.04	Gavin Smith L PTS 6 Wakefield
10.12.04	Gavin Smith L PTS 4 Sheffield
06.03.05	Matt Scriven L PTS 4 Mansfield
26.04.05	Lee McAllister L PTS 6 Leeds
20.05.05	Vince Baldassara L PTS 6 Glasgow
26.06.05	Steve Ede L PTS 6 Southampton
13.05.06	Karl Chiverton L PTS 6 Sutton in Ashfield

Career: 11 contests, won 1, drew 1, lost 9.

Danny Wallace

Leeds. *Born* Leeds, 12 July, 1980
Featherweight. Ht. 5'7"
Manager R. Manners

24.08.01	Roger Glover W PTS 4 Atlantic City, USA
12.04.02	Michael Weaver DREW 4 Philadelphia, USA
22.02.03	Jamil Hussain W RSC 1 Huddersfield
12.04.03	Ian Turner W RSC 4 Bethnal Green
10.05.03	Marcel Kasimov L RSC 3 Huddersfield
06.09.03	Alexei Volchan W PTS 4 Huddersfield
31.01.04	Jamie Yelland W PTS 6 Bethnal Green
13.03.04	Henry Janes L PTS 4 Huddersfield
11.09.04	Joseph Barela W RSC 2 Philadelphia, Pennsylvania, USA
06.12.04	Fred Janes W RSC 2 Leeds
01.06.05	Harry Ramogoadi L PTS 6 Leeds
05.12.05	Matt Teague L PTS 10 Leeds
	(*Vacant British Masters & Central Area Featherweight Titles*)

Career: 12 contests, won 7, drew 1, lost 4.

Marvyn Wallace

Walworth. *Born* London, 15 April, 1979
Middleweight. Ht. 5'11½"
Manager A.A. Forbes

| 02.04.06 | Simone Lucas W CO 4 Bethnal Green |

Career: 1 contest, won 1.

(Walisundra) Jus Wallie (Mudiyanselage)

Balham. *Born* Sri Lanka, 14 May, 1976
Welterweight. Ht. 5'5"
Manager W. Fuller

01.02.03	Kevin O'Hara L RSC 2 Belfast
29.03.03	Henry Castle W RSC 2 Portsmouth
05.04.03	Derry Matthews L PTS 4 Manchester
08.05.03	Steve Bell DREW 4 Widnes
31.05.03	J.J.Moore W RSC 1 Bethnal Green
29.11.03	Haider Ali L PTS 4 Renfrew
06.12.03	Jamie Arthur L PTS 6 Cardiff
21.02.04	Samuel Kebede L PTS 8 Cardiff
22.04.04	John Simpson L PTS 6 Glasgow
07.05.04	Jason Nesbitt W PTS 6 Bethnal Green
12.06.04	Andy Morris L PTS 6 Manchester
19.06.04	Martin Watson L PTS 5 Renfrew
24.09.04	Lee Cook L RSC 2 Bethnal Green
08.04.05	Damian Owen L PTS 4 Bristol
12.06.05	Ashley Theophane L PTS 4 Leicester Square

19.06.05   Craig Watson L PTS 4 Bethnal Green
05.11.05   Willie Limond L PTS 6 Renfrew
28.01.06   Scott Haywood L PTS 4 Nottingham
25.02.06   Alan Bosworth L RSC 1 Canning
              Town

Career: 19 contests, won 3, drew 1, lost 15.

Ryan Walls

Slough. *Born* Reading, 29 January, 1979
Southern Area S.Middleweight Champion.
Former British Masters Cruiserweight
Champion. Ht. 6'0½"
Manager Self

20.12.02   Mark Phillips W PTS 4 Bracknell
23.02.03   Michael Pinnock W PTS 6 Streatham
21.03.03   Jimmy Steel W PTS 6 Longford
12.04.03   Earl Ling W RSC 4 Norwich
09.05.03   Darren Ashton W PTS 6 Longford
01.08.03   Darren Ashton W PTS 4 Bethnal Green
26.10.03   Michael Pinnock W PTS 10 Longford
              *(Vacant British Masters Cruiserweight
              Title)*
25.03.04   Pinky Burton L PTS 10 Longford
              *(British Masters Cruiserweight Title
              Defence)*
08.05.04   Toks Owoh W PTS 6 Bristol
08.12.04   Varuzhan Davtyan W PTS 4 Longford
24.02.05   Ryan Kerr L PTS 10 Sunderland
              (Vacant English S.Middleweight Title)
24.04.05   Peter Haymer L PTS 6 Leicester Square
08.05.05   Donovan Smillie W PTS 6 Bradford
20.06.05   Simeon Cover W RSC 8 Longford
19.12.05   Gareth Lawrence W RTD 6 Longford
              *(Vacant Southern Area S.Middleweight
              Title)*

Career: 15 contests, won 12, lost 3.

Ryan Walls   Les Clark

Dougie Walton

Coventry. *Born* Coventry, 9 August, 1981
S.Featherweight. Ht. 5'4"
Manager O. Delargy

04.03.06   Graeme Higginson DREW 6 Coventry
Career: 1 contest, drew 1.

Shaun Walton

Telford. *Born* West Bromwich, 2 January,
1975
S.Featherweight. Ht. 5'10"
Manager E. Johnson

15.04.05   Dave Hinds W PTS 6 Shrewsbury
16.09.05   Abdul Mougharbel DREW 6 Telford
14.10.05   Craig Bromley L PTS 4 Huddersfield
04.12.05   Abdul Mougharbel DREW 6 Telford
10.03.06   Andy Davis L PTS 6 Walsall
28.05.06   Sean Hughes L PTS 6 Wakefield
05.06.06   Furhan Rafiq L PTS 6 Glasgow

Career: 7 contests, won 1, drew 2, lost 4.

Isaac Ward

Darlington. *Born* Darlington, 7 April, 1977
Bantamweight. Ht. 5'5"
Manager M. Marsden

03.08.02   Neil Read W RSC 1 Blackpool
18.10.02   John-Paul Ryan W PTS 6 Hartlepool
14.12.02   Steve Gethin W PTS 4 Newcastle
11.07.03   Rocky Dean DREW 4 Darlington
13.09.03   Pete Buckley W PTS 6 Wakefield
10.10.03   Rocky Dean W PTS 6 Darlington
04.12.03   Jamie Yelland W PTS 6 Huddersfield
05.03.04   Steve Gethin W PTS 6 Darlington
16.04.04   Pete Buckley W PTS 6 Hartlepool
03.07.04   Dave Hinds W PTS 6 Blackpool
19.11.04   Abdul Mougharbel W PTS 4
              Hartlepool
04.03.05   Peter Allen DREW 6 Hartlepool
02.06.05   Billy Smith W PTS 8 Yarm
28.10.05   Abdul Mougharbel W PTS 6
              Hartlepool
28.04.06   Rakhim Mingaleev W PTS 4
              Hartlepool
30.05.06   Martin Power L RSC 8 Bethnal Green
              (British Bantamweight Title Challenge)

Career: 16 contests, won 13, drew 2, lost 1.

Craig Watson

Manchester. *Born* Oldham, 7 February,
1983
Welterweight. Ht. 5'10"
Manager F. Maloney

20.05.05   Willie Valentine W RTD 2 Southwark
19.06.05   Jus Wallie W PTS 4 Bethnal Green
16.07.05   Billy Smith W PTS 4 Bolton
07.10.05   Ben Hudson W PTS 4 Bethnal Green
04.11.05   Sergii Tertii W PTS 6 Bethnal Green

Career: 5 contests, won 5.

Martin Watson

Coatbridge. *Born* Bellshill, 12 May, 1981
Celtic Lightweight Champion. Former
Undefeated Scottish Lightweight
Champion. Ht. 5'8"
Manager R. Bannon/A. Morrison

24.05.01   Shaune Danskin W RSC 3 Glasgow
20.10.01   Jon Honney W RSC 3 Glasgow
16.12.01   Richie Caparelli W PTS 6 Glasgow
11.03.02   Pete Buckley W PTS 4 Glasgow
26.04.02   Gary Reid W PTS 6 Glasgow
08.06.02   Scott Miller W RSC 2 Renfrew
18.11.02   Gary Reid W PTS 6 Glasgow
22.03.03   Joel Viney W RSC 2 Renfrew
16.05.03   Barry Hughes W RTD 8 Glasgow
              (Vacant Scottish Lightweight Title)
30.10.03   Mark Winters DREW 8 Belfast

01.04.04   Steve Murray L PTS 10 Bethnal Green
19.06.04   Jus Wallie W PTS 6 Renfrew
29.10.04   Mark Winters W PTS 10 Renfrew
              (Vacant Celtic Lightweight Title)
28.01.05   Jimmy Beech W PTS 4 Renfrew
09.07.05   Lee Meager L PTS 10 Nottingham
01.04.06   Ryan Barrett W PTS 10 Bethnal Green
              (Elim. British Lightweight Title)
29.04.06   George Ashie W PTS 6 Edinburgh

Career: 17 contests, won 14, drew 1, lost 2.

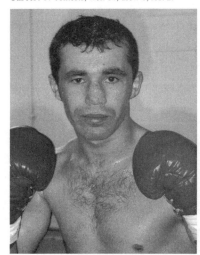

Martin Watson   Les Clark

Shane Watson

Ruislip. *Born* Hillingdon, 12 August, 1984
L.Welterweight. Ht. 5'9½"
Manager J. Evans

23.11.05   Pete Buckley W PTS 6 Mayfair
04.12.05   Duncan Cottier W PTS 4 Portsmouth
05.03.06   Chris Long W PTS 4 Southampton
07.04.06   Anthony Christopher W RSC 1
              Longford
28.05.06   Daniel Thorpe W PTS 6 Longford

Career: 5 contests, won 5.

Shane Watson   Les Clark

Sam Webb
Chislehurst. *Born* Sidcup, 11 April, 1981
L.Middleweight. Ht. 5'8³/₄"
Manager F. Maloney

07.10.05	Geraint Harvey W CO 1 Bethnal Green
04.11.05	Vadzim Astapuk W RSC 2 Bethnal Green
27.01.06	Aleksandr Zhuk W PTS 4 Dagenham
24.03.06	Gatis Skuja W PTS 4 Bethnal Green
30.05.06	Alex Stoda L RSC 3 Bethnal Green

Career: 5 contests, won 4, lost 1.

Sam Webb   Les Clark

Nathan Weise
Thameside. *Born* Bath, 7 July, 1984
L.Welterweight. Ht. 5'11¹/₂"
Manager F. Maloney

29.06.06 Bheki Moyo W PTS 4 Bethnal Green
Career: 1 contest, won 1.

Jason Welborn
Warley. *Born* Sandwell, 9 May, 1986
S.Middleweight. Ht. 5'10"
Manager O. Delargy

12.12.05 Jamie Ambler W RSC 1 Birmingham
27.02.06 Tyan Booth L CO 4 Birmingham
Career: 2 contests, won 1, lost 1.

Karl Wheeler
Peterborough. *Born* Peterborough, 30 May, 1982
Cruiserweight. Ht. 6'3"
Manager Self

07.05.03	Martin Thompson W PTS 6 Ellesmere Port
29.05.03	Paul Billington W PTS 6 Sunderland
14.02.04	Gary Jones W RSC 1 Holborn
08.04.04	Nick Okoth W PTS 6 Peterborough
03.07.04	Leigh Allis L PTS 4 Bristol
15.10.04	Steve McGuire L PTS 4 Glasgow
02.12.04	Shane White W PTS 6 Bristol
12.12.04	Tom Cannon L PTS 6 Glasgow
21.02.05	Hastings Rasani W PTS 6 Peterborough
04.03.05	Amer Khan L PTS 6 Rotherham
02.06.05	Hastings Rasani L RSC 5 Peterborough

16.10.05 Gary Ojuederie DREW 4 Peterborough
12.12.05 Nicki Taylor W PTS 4 Peterborough
Career: 13 contests, won 7, drew 1, lost 5.

Shane White
Wells. *Born* Bristol, 27 January, 1972
L. Heavyweight. Ht. 5'9"
Manager Self

08.02.02	Gary Thompson DREW 6 Preston
18.03.02	Billy McClung W RTD 4 Glasgow
21.09.03	Paul Billington DREW 6 Bristol
17.11.03	Steve McGuire L CO 2 Glasgow
21.12.03	Paul Billington W RSC 2 Bristol
29.02.04	Harry Butler W PTS 6 Bristol
01.10.04	Leigh Allis L RSC 2 Bristol
	(Vacant Western Area L.Heavyweight Title)
02.12.04	Karl Wheeler L PTS 6 Bristol
20.02.05	Sergey Haritonov W RSC 3 Bristol
21.03.05	Sandy Robb L PTS 4 Glasgow
09.07.05	Paddy Ryan L RSC 6 Bristol

Career: 11 contests, won 4, drew 2, lost 5.

Jonathan Whiteman
Mansfield. *Born* Sutton in Ashfield, 1 May, 1984
L.Welterweight. Ht. 5'11"
Manager M. Scriven

22.10.04	Pete Buckley W PTS 6 Mansfield
10.12.04	Joel Viney W RSC 4 Mansfield
06.03.05	Terry Carruthers DREW 6 Mansfield
24.04.05	Dave Curran L DIS 2 Askern
09.07.05	Kell Brook L RSC 2 Nottingham
11.09.05	Ian Reid W PTS 4 Kirkby in Ashfield
22.10.05	Billy Smith W PTS 6 Mansfield
04.11.05	Darren Johnstone L RSC 3 Glasgow
04.12.05	Tristan Davies L PTS 4 Telford
28.01.06	Rendall Munroe L RSC 2 Nottingham

Career: 10 contests, won 4, drew 1, lost 5.

Jonathan Whiteman   Les Clark

Adie Whitmore
Derby. *Born* Alfreton, 28 July, 1987
S.Middleweight. Ht. 6'2"
Manager M. Shinfield

08.12.05 Jimi Hendricks W RSC 1 Derby
14.05.06 Jon Foster W RSC 6 Derby
Career: 2 contests, won 2.

Noel Wilders
Castleford. *Born* Castleford, 4 January, 1975
Featherweight. Former European Bantamweight Champion. Former Undefeated IBO, British & Central Area Bantamweight Champion. Ht. 5'5"
Manager Self

16.03.96	Neil Parry W RTD 4 Sheffield
04.06.96	Graham McGrath W PTS 6 York
04.10.96	Tiger Singh W PTS 6 Wakefield
23.10.96	Jason Thomas W PTS 6 Halifax
12.03.97	John Matthews W PTS 6 Stoke
20.04.97	Shaun Anderson W PTS 6 Leeds
13.11.97	Anthony Hanna W PTS 6 Bradford
06.02.98	Marcus Duncan W RSC 6 Wakefield
	(Vacant Central Area Bantamweight Title)
21.05.98	Matthew Harris W PTS 6 Bradford
18.07.98	Sean Grant W RSC 4 Sheffield
23.10.98	Fondil Madani W DIS 7 Wakefield
28.11.98	Ross Cassidy W PTS 8 Sheffield
06.02.99	Jason Thomas W PTS 10 Halifax
	(Elim. British Bantamweight Title)
24.04.99	Anthony Hanna W PTS 6 Peterborough
22.06.99	Ady Lewis W RSC 6 Ipswich
	(Final Elim. British Bantamweight Title)
30.10.99	Francis Ampofo W PTS 12 Peterlee
	(Vacant British Bantamweight Title)
18.01.00	Steve Williams W RTD 11 Mansfield
	(British Bantamweight Title Defence)
20.03.00	Kamel Guerfi W PTS 12 Mansfield
	(Vacant IBO Bantamweight Title)
15.07.00	Paul Lloyd W PTS 12 Millwall
	(IBO Bantamweight Title Defence)
28.04.01	Stevie Quinn W RTD 6 Cardiff
21.07.01	Chris Emanuele W PTS 6 Sheffield
15.06.02	Sean Grant W RSC 3 Leeds
28.01.03	Fabien Guillerme W PTS 12 Nice, France
	(Vacant European Bantamweight Title)
18.03.03	Frederic Patrac DREW 4 Reading
	(European Bantamweight Title Defence)
10.06.03	David Guerault L RSC 7 Sheffield
	(European Bantamweight Title Defence)
06.02.04	Vladimir Borov W PTS 4 Sheffield
07.08.04	Silence Mabuza L CO 5 Temba, South Africa
	(IBO Bantamweight Title Challenge)
08.05.05	Esham Pickering L PTS 8 Bradford
28.01.06	Bernard Dunne L RSC 6 Dublin

Career: 29 contests, won 24, drew 1, lost 4.

Danny Williams
Brixton. *Born* London, 13 July, 1973
Commonwealth Heavyweight Champion. Former British Heavyweight Champion. Former Undefeated WBO & WBU Inter-Continental Heavyweight Champion. Ht. 6'3"
Manager F. Warren

21.10.95	Vance Idiens W CO 2 Bethnal Green
09.12.95	Joey Paladino W RSC 1 Bethnal Green
13.02.96	Slick Miller W RSC 1 Bethnal Green
09.03.96	James Wilder W PTS 4 Millstreet
13.07.96	John Pierre W PTS 4 Bethnal Green
31.08.96	Andy Lambert W RSC 2 Dublin
09.11.96	Michael Murray W CO 1 Manchester
08.02.97	Shane Woollas W RSC 2 Millwall

165

03.05.97	Albert Call W RSC 4 Manchester
19.07.97	R. F. McKenzie W RSC 2 Wembley
15.11.97	Bruce Douglas W RSC 2 Bristol
19.12.97	Derek Amos W RSC 4 NYC, New York, USA
21.02.98	Shane Woollas W RSC 2 Belfast
16.05.98	Antonio Diaz W CO 3 Bethnal Green
10.10.98	Antoine Palatis W PTS 12 Bethnal Green
	(Vacant WBO Inter-Continental Heavyweight Title)
03.04.99	Julius Francis L PTS 12 Kensington
	(British & Commonwealth Heavyweight Title Challenges)
02.10.99	Ferenc Deak W RTD 1 Namur, Belgium
18.12.99	Harry Senior W PTS 12 Southwark
	(Vacant Commonwealth Heavyweight Title)
19.02.00	Anton Nel W CO 5 Dagenham
06.05.00	Michael Murray W RSC 6 Frankfurt, Germany
24.06.00	Craig Bowen-Price W CO 1 Glasgow
23.09.00	Quinn Navarre W RSC 6 Bethnal Green
21.10.00	Mark Potter W RSC 6 Wembley
	(Commonwealth & WBO Inter-Continental Heavyweight Title Defences. Vacant British Heavyweight Title)
09.06.01	Kali Meehan W RSC 1 Bethnal Green
	(Commonwealth Heavyweight Title Defence)
28.07.01	Julius Francis W CO 4 Wembley
	(British & Commonwealth Heavyweight Title Defences)
15.12.01	Shawn Robinson W RSC 2 Mashantucket Connecticut, USA
12.02.02	Michael Sprott W RTD 7 Bethnal Green
	(British & Commonwealth Heavyweight Title Defences)
17.09.02	Keith Long W PTS 12 Bethnal Green
	(British & Commonwealth Heavyweight Title Defences)
08.02.03	Sinan Samil Sam L RSC 6 Berlin, Germany
	(European Heavyweight Title Challenge)
26.04.03	Bob Mirovic W RSC 4 Brentford
	(Commonwealth Heavyweight Title Defence)
26.09.03	Michael Sprott W RSC 5 Reading
	(British & Commonwealth Heavyweight Title Defences)
24.01.04	Michael Sprott L PTS 12 Wembley
	(British & Commonwealth Heavyweight Title Defences)
01.04.04	Ratko Draskovic W RSC 1 Bethnal Green
13.05.04	Augustin N'Gou W RTD 3 Bethnal Green
	(Vacant WBU Inter-Continental Heavyweight Title)
30.07.04	Mike Tyson W CO 4 Louisville, Kentucky, USA
11.12.04	Vitali Klitschko L RSC 8 Las Vegas, USA
	(WBC Heavyweight Title Challenge)
04.06.05	Zoltan Petranyi W RSC 3 Manchester
10.12.05	Audley Harrison W PTS 12 Canning Town
	(Vacant Commonwealth Heavyweight Title)

25.02.06	Matt Skelton W PTS 12 Canning Town
	(Commonwealth Heavyweight Title Defence)
20.05.06	Adnan Serin W RTD 3 Belfast

Career: 40 contests, won 36, lost 4.

Jackson Williams

Norwich. *Born* Norwich, 19 June, 1981
L.Welterweight. Ht. 5'6½"
Manager Self

13.04.02	Daniel Thorpe W PTS 6 Norwich
15.06.02	Jason Gonzales W PTS 6 Norwich
21.09.02	Baz Carey W PTS 6 Norwich
10.10.02	Jason Gonzales W PTS 4 Piccadilly
08.02.03	Joel Viney W PTS 4 Norwich
24.02.03	Anthony Hanna L PTS 6 Birmingham
12.04.03	Daniel Thorpe W PTS 6 Norwich
06.06.03	Nigel Senior W PTS 8 Norwich
25.07.03	Paul Rushton W PTS 4 Norwich
21.02.04	Nigel Senior W PTS 6 Norwich
14.05.04	Haroon Din L RSC 5 Sunderland
	(Vacant British Masters L.Welterweight Title)
09.10.04	Dave Hinds W PTS 6 Norwich
03.09.05	Pete Buckley W PTS 6 Norwich
29.10.05	Lee McAllister L RSC 5 Aberdeen
11.12.05	Tye Williams W PTS 6 Norwich
25.02.06	Amir Khan L RSC 3 Canning Town

Career: 16 contests, won 12, lost 4.

Richard Williams

Stockwell. *Born* London, 9 May, 1971
Middleweight. Former IBO
L.Middleweight Champion. Former
Undefeated Commonwealth & WBF
L.Middleweight Champion. Ht. 5'9½"
Manager Self

08.03.97	Marty Duke W RSC 3 Brentwood
30.06.97	Danny Quacoe W PTS 4 Bethnal Green
02.09.97	Michael Alexander L PTS 4 Southwark
16.10.99	Pedro Carragher W RSC 2 Bethnal Green
06.11.99	Lee Bird W RSC 4 Bethnal Green
20.12.99	Harry Butler W RSC 1 Bethnal Green
17.04.00	Kevin Thompson W CO 1 Birmingham
16.06.00	Piotr Bartnicki W RSC 3 Bloomsbury
08.09.00	Dean Ashton W RSC 1 Hammersmith
04.11.00	Howard Clarke W CO 4 Bethnal Green
02.12.00	Aziz Daari W RSC 2 Bethnal Green
23.01.01	Tony Badea W RSC 3 Crawley
	(Commonwealth L. Middleweight Title Challenge)
04.06.01	Hussain Osman W PTS 10 Hartlepool
25.09.01	Andrew Murray W RSC 3 Liverpool
	(Commonwealth L. Middleweight Title Defence)
20.10.01	Viktor Fesetchko W RSC 6 Portsmouth
01.12.01	Shannan Taylor W RSC 4 Bethnal Green
	(Commonwealth L. Middleweight Title Defence. Vacant IBO L. Middleweight Title)
29.06.02	Paul Samuels T DRAW 3 Brentwood
	(IBO L. Middleweight Title Defence)
07.12.02	Paul Samuels W RSC 10 Brentwood
	(IBO L. Middleweight Title Defence)
08.03.03	Andrei Pestriaev W PTS 12 Bethnal Green
	(IBO L. Middleweight Title Defence. WBF L. Middleweight Title Challenge)
21.06.03	Sergio Martinez L PTS 12 Manchester

	(IBO L.Middleweight Title Defence)
31.01.04	Ayittey Powers W RSC 7 Bethnal Green
	(Vacant Commonwealth L.Middleweight Title)
17.04.04	Sergio Martinez L RTD 9 Belfast
	(IBO L.Middleweight Title Challenge)
26.11.04	Szabolcs Rimovszky W RSC 3 Altrincham
24.02.06	Marcin Piatkowski W PTS 8 Dagenham

Career: 24 contests, won 20, drew 1, lost 3.

Tye Williams

Dewsbury. *Born* London, 9 June, 1976
L.Middleweight. Ht. 5'9"
Manager M. Marsden

23.10.04	Rocky Muscus W PTS 6 Wakefield
09.11.04	Lea Handley L RSC 1 Leeds
26.02.05	Darren Gethin DREW 4 Burton
14.05.05	Daniel Thorpe L RSC 3 Aberdeen
25.06.05	Gary Connolly W CO 4 Wakefield
11.12.05	Jackson Williams L PTS 6 Norwich
12.02.06	Johnny Hussey L PTS 6 Manchester
05.03.06	Adam Kelly L PTS 4 Sheffield
25.03.06	Scott Conway DREW 4 Burton
14.05.06	Scott Conway W RSC 5 Derby
28.05.06	Khurram Hussain L PTS 6 Wakefield

Career: 11 contests, won 3, drew 2, lost 6.

Lee Williamson

Worcester. *Born* Worcester, 3 February, 1974
L.Middleweight. Ht. 5'9"
Manager Self

26.10.98	Trevor Tacy L PTS 6 Manchester
26.11.98	David Smales W PTS 6 Bradford
16.01.99	Graham Earl L RSC 4 Bethnal Green
23.03.99	Gary Reid L PTS 6 Wolverhampton
22.04.99	Brian Gifford W PTS 6 Dudley
15.05.99	James Hare L RSC 2 Sheffield
11.09.99	Carl Allen W PTS 6 Birmingham
28.10.99	Mark Hargreaves L PTS 6 Burnley
30.11.99	Marc Smith W PTS 6 Wolverhampton
11.12.99	Brian Carr DREW 6 Liverpool
24.01.00	Craig Docherty L PTS 6 Glasgow
08.02.00	Carl Allen L PTS 8 Wolverhampton
19.02.00	Kevin Lear L PTS 4 Dagenham
04.03.00	Liam Maltby L PTS 6 Peterborough
28.03.00	Carl Allen L PTS 8 Wolverhampton
06.06.00	Dave Travers W PTS 6 Brierley Hill
24.06.00	Kevin McIntyre L PTS 4 Glasgow
08.07.00	Tony Mulholland L PTS 8 Widnes
13.08.00	Esham Pickering L PTS 6 Nottingham
29.09.00	Darren Melville L RSC 4 Bethnal Green
21.10.00	Graham Earl L RSC 3 Wembley
24.11.00	Pete Buckley W PTS 6 Hull
09.12.00	Terry Butwell L PTS 4 Southwark
27.01.01	Danny Hunt W RSC 2 Bethnal Green
10.02.01	Geir Inge Jorgensen L RSC 3 Widnes
20.03.01	James Rooney L PTS 4 Glasgow
26.03.01	Liam Maltby L PTS 6 Peterborough
03.04.01	Danny Hunt L PTS 4 Bethnal Green
06.05.01	James Rooney L PTS 6 Hartlepool
21.06.01	Gavin Wake L PTS 6 Sheffield
14.07.01	Brett James L PTS 6 Wembley
28.07.01	Ross Minter L PTS 4 Wembley
15.09.01	Gavin Down L PTS 6 Derby
10.12.01	David Keir DREW 4 Liverpool
04.03.02	Pedro Thompson W PTS 6 Bradford
13.04.02	David Keir L PTS 4 Liverpool

13.05.02	Chris Duggan W RSC 3 Birmingham
01.06.02	Michael Jennings L PTS 4 Manchester
23.06.02	Brett James L PTS 6 Southwark
28.09.02	Mickey Quinn L RSC 2 Manchester
16.11.02	Richard Swallow L PTS 4 Coventry
30.11.02	Mark Dillon W PTS 4 Liverpool
18.01.03	Michael Jennings L RTD 4 Preston
23.02.03	Lee McAllister L PTS 6 Shrewsbury
16.03.03	Matt Scriven L PTS 10 Nottingham
	(Vacant Midlands Area & British
	Masters L. Middleweight Titles)
07.06.03	Andy Egan L PTS 6 Coventry
12.07.03	Gary Young L PTS 4 Renfrew
03.08.03	Ali Nuumembe L PTS 6 Stalybridge
13.09.03	Andy Halder L PTS 6 Coventry
19.10.03	Mark Paxford L PTS 6 Shaw
08.11.03	Andy Halder L PTS 6 Coventry
21.11.03	Darren Covill W PTS 6 Millwall
01.12.03	Andrei Ivanov W RSC 4 Barnsley
14.02.04	Gary Woolcombe L PTS 6 Holborn
21.02.04	Danny Smith L PTS 6 Norwich
08.03.04	Lee McAllister L PTS 6 Birmingham
27.03.04	Colin McNeil W PTS 4 Edinburgh
23.04.04	Tony Montana L PTS 6 Leicester
07.05.04	Jake Guntert L PTS 6 Bethnal Green
04.06.04	Oscar Hall L PTS 6 Hull
09.11.04	Kell Brook L RSC 2 Leeds
13.02.05	Danny Parkinson L PTS 4 Bradford
21.02.05	Simon Sherrington DREW 6 Birmingham
05.03.05	Clint Smith L PTS 6 Southwark
26.03.05	Daniel Cadman L PTS 4 Hackney
16.05.05	Simon Sherrington L PTS 8 Birmingham
27.05.05	Kerry Hope L PTS 4 Spennymoor
18.06.05	Neil Tidman L PTS 6 Coventry
24.07.05	Lee Edwards L PTS 6 Sheffield
25.09.05	Steve Conway L PTS 6 Leeds

Career: 70 contests, won 12, drew 3, lost 55.

Ian Wilson

Camden. *Born* London, 9 June, 1981
S.Featherweight. Ht. 5'10½"
Manager F. Maloney

19.06.05	Lance Verallo W PTS 4 Bethnal Green
07.10.05	Ian Reid W PTS 4 Bethnal Green
27.01.06	Daniel Thorpe W PTS 4 Dagenham
24.03.06	Steve Gethin W PTS 4 Bethnal Green
29.06.06	Brian Murphy W RTD 1 Bethnal Green

Career: 5 contests, won 5.

Junior Witter

Bradford. *Born* Bradford, 10 March, 1974
L.Welterweight. Former Undefeated
British, Commonwealth & European
L.Welterweight Champion. Former
Undefeated European Union, WBU Inter-
Continental & WBF L.Welterweight
Champion. Ht. 5'7"
Manager J. Ingle

18.01.97	Cam Raeside DREW 6 Swadlincote
04.03.97	John Green W PTS 6 Yarm
20.03.97	Lee Molyneux W RSC 6 Salford
25.04.97	Trevor Meikle W PTS 6 Mere
15.05.97	Andreas Panayi W RSC 5 Reading
02.08.97	Brian Coleman W PTS 4 Barnsley
04.10.97	Michael Alexander W PTS 4 Hannover, Germany
07.02.98	Mark Ramsey DREW 6 Cheshunt
05.03.98	Brian Coleman W PTS 6 Leeds
18.04.98	Jan Bergman W PTS 6 Manchester
05.09.98	Mark Winters W PTS 8 Telford

28.11.98	Karl Taylor W PTS 4 Sheffield
13.02.99	Malcolm Melvin W RSC 2 Newcastle
	(Vacant WBF L. Welterweight Title)
17.07.99	Isaac Cruz W PTS 8 Doncaster
06.11.99	Harry Butler W PTS 6 Widnes
21.03.00	Mrhai Iourgh W RSC 1 Telde, Gran Canaria
08.04.00	Arv Mittoo W PTS 4 Bethnal Green
24.06.00	Zab Judah L PTS 12 Glasgow
	(IBF L. Welterweight Title Challenge)
20.10.00	Steve Conway W RTD 4 Belfast
25.11.00	Chris Henry W RSC 3 Manchester
10.03.01	David Kirk W RSC 2 Bethnal Green
22.05.01	Fabrice Faradji W RSC 1 Telde, Gran Canaria
21.07.01	Alan Temple W CO 5 Sheffield
27.10.01	Colin Mayisela W RSC 2 Manchester
	(Vacant WBU Inter-Continental L.Welterweight Title)
16.03.02	Alan Bosworth W RSC 3 Northampton
	(Vacant British L.Welterweight Title)
08.07.02	Laatekwi Hammond W RSC 2 Mayfair
	(Vacant Commonwealth L.Welterweight Title)
19.10.02	Lucky Samba W RSC 2 Renfrew
23.11.02	Giuseppe Lauri W RSC 2 Derby
	(Final Elim. WBO L. Welterweight Title)
05.04.03	Jurgen Haeck W RTD 4 Manchester
	(Vacant European Union L.Welterweight Title)
27.09.03	Fred Kinuthia W RSC 2 Manchester
	(Commonwealth L.Welterweight Title Defence)
16.04.04	Oscar Hall W RSC 3 Bradford
02.06.04	Salvatore Battaglia W RSC 2 Nottingham
	(Vacant European L.Welterweight Title)
12.11.04	Krzysztof Bienias W RSC 2 Wembley
	(European L.Welterweight Title Defence)
19.02.05	Lovemore N'Dou W PTS 12 Los Angeles, California, USA
	(Commonwealth L.Welterweight Title Defence)
09.07.05	Andreas Kotelnik W PTS 12 Nottingham
	(European L.Welterweight Title Defence)
21.10.05	Colin Lynes W PTS 12 Bethnal Green
	(British, Commonwealth & European L.Welterweight Title Defences)

Career: 36 contests, won 33, drew 2, lost 1.

Junior Witter   Les Clark

Clinton Woods

Sheffield. *Born* Sheffield, 1 May, 1972
IBF L.Heavyweight Champion. Former
Undefeated British, European, WBC
International & Commonwealth
L.Heavyweight Champion. Former
Commonwealth S.Middleweight
Champion. Former Undefeated Central
Area S.Middleweight Champion. Ht. 6'2"
Manager D. Hobson

17.11.94	Dave Proctor W PTS 6 Sheffield
12.12.94	Earl Ling W RSC 5 Cleethorpes
23.02.95	Paul Clarkson W RSC 1 Hull
06.04.95	Japhet Hans W RSC 3 Sheffield
16.05.95	Kevin Burton W PTS 6 Cleethorpes
14.06.95	Kevin Burton W RSC 6 Batley
21.09.95	Paul Murray W PTS 6 Sheffield
20.10.95	Phil Ball W RSC 4 Mansfield
22.11.95	Andy Ewen W RSC 3 Sheffield
05.02.96	Chris Walker W RSC 6 Bradford
16.03.96	John Duckworth W PTS 8 Sheffield
13.06.96	Ernie Loveridge W PTS 6 Sheffield
14.11.96	Craig Joseph W PTS 10 Sheffield
	(Vacant Central Area S. Middleweight Title)
20.02.97	Rocky Shelly W RSC 2 Mansfield
10.04.97	Darren Littlewood W RSC 6 Sheffield
	(Central Area S. Middleweight Title Defence)
26.06.97	Darren Ashton W PTS 6 Sheffield
25.10.97	Danny Juma W PTS 8 Queensferry
26.11.97	Jeff Finlayson W PTS 8 Sheffield
06.12.97	Mark Baker W PTS 12 Wembley
	(Vacant Commonwealth S.Middleweight Title)
28.03.98	David Starie L PTS 12 Hull
	(Commonwealth S. Middleweight Title Defence)
18.06.98	Peter Mason W RTD 4 Sheffield
30.11.98	Mark Smallwood W RSC 7 Manchester
13.03.99	Crawford Ashley W RSC 8 Manchester
	(British, Commonwealth & European L. Heavyweight Title Challenges)
10.07.99	Sam Leuii W RSC 6 Southwark
	(Commonwealth L. Heavyweight Title Defence)
11.09.99	Lenox Lewis W RSC 10 Sheffield
	(Commonwealth L. Heavyweight Title Defence)
10.12.99	Terry Ford W RTD 4 Warsaw, Poland
12.02.00	Juan Perez Nelongo W PTS 12 Sheffield
	(European L. Heavyweight Title Defence)
29.04.00	Ole Klemetsen W RSC 9 Wembley
	(European L. Heavyweight Title Defence)
15.07.00	Greg Scott-Briggs W RSC 3 Millwall
24.03.01	Ali Forbes W RTD 10 Sheffield
	(Vacant WBC International L. Heavyweight Title)
27.07.01	Paul Bonson W PTS 6 Sheffield
13.09.01	Yawe Davis W PTS 12 Sheffield
	(Final Elim.WBC L.Heavyweight Title)
16.03.02	Clint Johnson W RSC 3 Bethnal Green
07.09.02	Roy Jones L RSC 6 Portland, Oregon, USA
	(WBC, WBA & IBF L.Heavyweight Title Challenges)
24.01.03	Sergio Martin Beaz W RSC 3 Sheffield
18.03.03	Arturo Rivera W RSC 2 Reading
10.06.03	Demetrius Jenkins W RSC 7 Sheffield

07.11.03	Glengoffe Johnson DREW 12 Sheffield
	(Vacant IBF L.Heavyweight Title)
06.02.04	Glengoffe Johnson L PTS 12 Sheffield
	(Vacant IBF L.Heavyweight Title)
24.10.04	Jason DeLisle W RSC 12 Sheffield
	(Elim. IBF L.Heavyweight Title)
04.03.05	Rico Hoye W RSC 5 Rotherham
	(Vacant IBF L.Heavyweight Title)
09.09.05	Julio Gonzalez W PTS 12 Sheffield
	(IBF L.Heavyweight Title Defence)
13.05.06	Jason DeLisle W RSC 6 Sheffield
	(IBF L.Heavyweight Title Defence)

Career: 43 contests, won 39, drew 1, lost 3.

Clinton Woods   Les Clark

Gary Woolcombe
Welling. *Born* London, 4 August, 1982
Southern Area L.Middleweight Champion.
Former Undefeated British Masters
L.Middleweight Champion. Ht. 5'10¾"
Manager F. Maloney

15.05.03	Paul McIlwaine W RSC 2 Mayfair
22.07.03	Arv Mittoo W PTS 6 Bethnal Green
25.09.03	Pete Buckley W PTS 6 Bethnal Green
18.11.03	John Butler W PTS 4 Bethnal Green
07.02.04	Ernie Smith W PTS 4 Bethnal Green
14.02.04	Lee Williamson W PTS 4 Holborn
07.05.04	David Kirk W PTS 4 Bethnal Green
05.06.04	Ivor Bonavic W PTS 4 Bethnal Green
24.09.04	Geraint Harvey W PTS 4 Bethnal Green
19.11.04	Keith Jones W PTS 4 Bethnal Green
11.12.04	Peter Dunn W PTS 4 Canning Town
12.02.05	Howard Clarke W PTS 6 Portsmouth
05.03.05	Ernie Smith W PTS 6 Southwark
29.04.05	Matt Scriven W RSC 4 Southwark
20.05.05	Danny Parkinson W RSC 3 Southwark
19.06.05	Peter Dunn W RSC 6 Bethnal Green
07.10.05	Delroy Mellis W RTD 8 Bethnal Green
	(Vacant British Masters L.Middleweight Title)
04.11.05	Mark Phillips W PTS 4 Bethnal Green
27.01.06	Lee Murtagh W RSC 4 Dagenham

24.03.06	Eugenio Monteiro W PTS 8 Bethnal Green
26.05.06	Gilbert Eastman W RSC 7 Bethnal Green
	(Southern Area L.Middleweight Title Challenge)

Career: 21 contests, won 21.

Scott Woolford
Ramsgate. *Born* Rush Green, 6 September, 1983
Welterweight. Ht. 5'7"
Manager F. Maloney

30.05.06	David Kehoe W PTS 4 Bethnal Green

Career: 1 contest, won 1.

Carl Wright
Rugby. *Born* Rugby, 26 April, 1978
Midlands Area & British Masters
Cruiserweight Champion. Ht. 6'1¼"
Manager P. Carpenter

25.06.02	Dave Clarke W PTS 6 Rugby
05.10.02	Adam Cale W PTS 6 Coventry
16.11.02	Jimmy Steel W PTS 6 Coventry
08.03.03	Gary Williams W PTS 6 Coventry
16.03.03	Darren Ashton DREW 6 Nottingham
07.06.03	Gary Thompson W RTD 2 Coventry
13.09.03	Darren Ashton W PTS 4 Coventry
09.04.04	Lee Mountford W PTS 4 Rugby
01.05.04	Paul Bonson W PTS 6 Coventry
06.11.04	Chris Woollas W RSC 1 Coventry
17.12.04	Tony Dowling W PTS 10 Coventry
	(Vacant Midlands Area Cruiserweight Title)
18.06.05	Nate Joseph W CO 1 Coventry
	(Vacant British Masters Cruiserweight Title)
24.09.05	Tony Booth W PTS 4 Coventry
12.12.05	Cafu Santos W RSC 4 Leicester

Career: 14 contests, won 13, drew 1.

Danny Wright
York. *Born* York, 26 September, 1977
S.Middleweight. Ht. 5'10"
Manager R. Manners

23.02.06	Jimi Hendricks W PTS 6 Leeds
13.04.06	Tony Randell W PTS 6 Leeds

Career: 2 contests, won 2.

Nigel Wright
Crook. *Born* Bishop Auckland, 22 June, 1979
English L.Welterweight Champion. Ht. 5'9"
Manager G. Robinson

10.02.01	Keith Jones W PTS 4 Widnes
15.09.01	Tommy Peacock W RSC 1 Manchester
17.11.01	Ernie Smith W PTS 4 Glasgow
19.01.02	Woody Greenaway W CO 2 Bethnal Green
11.03.02	James Paisley W PTS 4 Glasgow
19.10.02	Kevin McIntyre L PTS 6 Renfrew
29.03.03	Darren Melville W PTS 6 Portsmouth
24.05.03	David Kirk W PTS 4 Bethnal Green
02.10.03	Nigel Senior W RSC 5 Liverpool
29.11.03	Jason Hall W PTS 6 Renfrew
06.03.04	George Telfer W RSC 3 Renfrew
22.05.04	Jon Honney W RSC 2 Widnes
22.10.04	Silence Saheed W PTS 8 Edinburgh

11.03.05	Dean Hickman W CO 7 Doncaster
	(Vacant English L.Welterweight Title)
27.05.05	Alan Bosworth W PTS 10 Spennymoor
	(English L.Welterweight Title Defence)
05.11.05	Kevin McIntyre W RSC 1 Renfrew
	(Final Elim. British L.Welterweight Title)
18.02.06	Valery Kharyanov W CO 4 Edinburgh
12.05.06	Lenny Daws L PTS 12 Bethnal Green
	(Vacant British L.Welterweight Title)

Career: 18 contests, won 16, lost 2.

Tyrone Wright
Nottingham. *Born* Nottingham, 7 September, 1978
Cruiserweight. Ht. 6'2"
Manager M. Shinfield

22.10.05	Lee Mountford W CO 3 Mansfield
15.12.05	Gary Thompson DREW 6 Cleethorpes
24.04.06	Csaba Andras W CO 2 Cleethorpes

Career: 3 contests, won 2, drew 1.

Ali Wyatt
Torquay. *Born* Iran, 15 May, 1977
Welterweight. Ht. 5'5¾"
Manager C. Sanigar

09.10.05	Michael Grant DREW 4 Hammersmith
17.11.05	Stuart Phillips L PTS 4 Bristol
21.05.06	Bheki Moyo W RSC 3 Bristol
03.06.06	Michael Grant L PTS 4 Chigwell
23.06.06	Lance Hall W RSC 5 Birmingham

Career: 5 contests, won 2, drew 1, lost 2.

Anthony Young
Crawley. *Born* Crawley, 10 April, 1984
Middleweight. Ht. 5'11¼"
Manager M. Alldis

30.10.05	Alex Stoda W PTS 6 Bethnal Green
05.03.06	Steve Ede L RSC 3 Southampton

Career: 2 contests, won 1, lost 1.

Gary Young
Edinburgh. *Born* Edinburgh, 23 May, 1983
Welterweight. Ht. 5'7"
Manager F. Maloney

11.03.02	Paul McIlwaine W CO 2 Glasgow
08.06.02	Daniel Thorpe W RSC 1 Renfrew
02.11.02	Keith Jones W PTS 4 Belfast
22.03.03	Dean Larter W RSC 2 Renfrew
12.07.03	Lee Williamson W PTS 4 Renfrew
25.10.03	Peter Dunn W PTS 6 Edinburgh
29.11.03	Karl Taylor W RSC 3 Renfrew
06.03.04	Anthony Christopher W CO 1 Renfrew
27.03.04	Keith Jones W PTS 6 Edinburgh
19.06.04	David Kirk W PTS 4 Renfrew
22.10.04	Lionel Saraille W RSC 3 Edinburgh
28.01.05	Thomas Hengstberger W RSC 3 Renfrew
08.04.05	Viktor Baranov W PTS 8 Edinburgh
05.11.05	Ivor Bonavic W RSC 8 Renfrew
18.02.06	Oscar Milkitas W PTS 8 Edinburgh
29.04.06	Colin McNeil L CO 1 Edinburgh
	(Elim. British Welterweight Title)

Career: 16 contests, won 15, lost 1.

British Area Title Bouts, 2005-2006

As from 1 September 2005, BBBoC Regulations stated that any Area champion who won English or Celtic championships would automatically relinquish their Area titles. A similar ruling was already in place as far as British, Commonwealth and European titles were concerned.

Central Area

Titleholders at 30 June 2006

Fly: *vacant*. **Bantam:** *vacant*. **S.Bantam:** Gary Davis. **Feather:** Matt Teague. **S.Feather:** Carl Johanneson. **Light:** Stefy Bull. **L.Welter:** John Fewkes. **Welter:** Matthew Hatton. **L.Middle:** Lee Murtagh. **Middle:** *vacant*. **S.Middle:** Dean Cockburn. **L.Heavy:** Amer Khan. **Cruiser:** *vacant*. **Heavy:** *vacant*.

Title Bouts Held Between 1 July 2005 and 30 June 2006

25 September	Carl Johanneson W RTD 9 Peter Allen, Leeds (Vacant S.Featherweight Title)
5 December	Matt Teague W PTS 10 Danny Wallace, Leeds (Vacant S.Bantamweight Title)
17 February	Tony Montana L PTS 10 John Fewkes, Sheffield (L.Welterweight Title Defence)
24 February	Gary Davis W RSC 1 Chris Hooper, Scarborough (Vacant S.Bantamweight Title)
18 June	Amer Khan W PTS 10 Darren Stubbs, Manchester (Vacant L.Heavyweight Title)

Between 1 July 2005 and 30 June 2006, Eddie Nevins (S.Feather) and Denzil Browne (Cruiser) retired, while Sean Hughes (S.Bantam) relinquished his title.

Midlands Area

Titleholders at 30 June 2006

Fly: *vacant*. **Bantam:** *vacant*. **S.Bantam:** Gareth Payne. **Feather:** Stephen Chinnock. **S.Feather:** *vacant*. **Light:** *vacant*. **L.Welter:** Dean Hickman. **Welter:** Stuart Elwell. **L.Middle:** Matt Galer. **Middle:** Darren McDermott. **S.Middle:** *vacant*. **L.Heavy:** *vacant*. **Cruiser:** Carl Wright. **Heavy:** *vacant*.

Title Bouts Held Between 1 July 2005 and 30 June 2006

30 September	Matt Galer W PTS 10 Terry Adams, Burton (Vacant L.Middleweight Title)
6 October	Andy Halder L RSC 5 Darren McDermott, Dudley (Middleweight Title Defence)
6 February	Darren McDermott W RTD 9 Michael Monaghan, Dudley (Middleweight Title Defence)
10 March	Stuart Elwell W PTS 10 David Kirk, Walsall (Vacant Welterweight Title)
6 May	Scott Lawton W PTS 10 Baz Carey, Stoke (Lightweight Title Defence)

Between 1 July 2005 and 30 June 2006, Scott Lawton (Light), Gavin Down (L.Middle) and Mark Krence (Heavy) relinquished their titles, while Peter Jackson (S.Middle) retired.

Northern Area

Titleholders at 30 June 2006

Fly: *vacant*. **Bantam:** *vacant*. **S.Bantam:** *vacant*. **Feather:** *vacant*. **S.Feather:** *vacant*. **Light:** *vacant*. **L.Welter:** *vacant*. **Welter:** Oscar Hall. **L.Middle:** *vacant*. **Middle:** Eddie Haley. **S.Middle:** *vacant*. **L.Heavy:** *vacant*. **Cruiser:** *vacant*. **Heavy:** *vacant*.

Title Bouts Held Between 1 July 2005 and 30 June 2006

None

Between 1 July 2005 and 30 June 2006, Ryan Kerr (S.Middle) relinquished his title.

Northern Ireland Area

Titleholders at 30 June 2006

Fly: *vacant*. **Bantam:** *vacant*. **S.Bantam:** *vacant*. **Feather:** *vacant*. **S.Feather:** *vacant*. **Light:** *vacant*. **L.Welter:** *vacant*. **Welter:** *vacant*. **L.Middle:** *vacant*. **Middle:** *vacant*. **S.Middle:** *vacant*. **L.Heavy:** *vacant*. **Cruiser:** *vacant*. **Heavy:** *vacant*.

Title Bouts Held Between 1 July 2005 and 30 June 2006

None

Between 1 July 2005 and 30 June 2006, Dafydd Carlin (Light) retired.

Scottish Area

Titleholders at 30 June 2006

Fly: *vacant*. **Bantam:** *vacant*. **S.Bantam:** *vacant*. **Feather:** *vacant*. **S.Feather:** *vacant*. **Light:** Lee McAllister. **L.Welter:** *vacant*. **Welter:** Kevin McIntyre. **L.Middle:** Barrie Lee. **Middle:** Vince Baldassara. **S.Middle:** Tom Cannon. **L.Heavy:** *vacant*. **Cruiser:** *vacant*. **Heavy:** *vacant*.

Title Bouts Held Between 1 July 2005 and 30 June 2006

12 November	Vince Baldassara W PTS 10 Craig Lynch, Glasgow (Vacant Middleweight Title)
22 April	Barrie Lee W PTS 10 Chris Black, Glasgow (L.Middleweight Title Defence)
27 May	Lee McAllister W RSC 8 Stuart Green, Aberdeen (Vacant Lightweight Title)

Between 1 July 2005 and 30 June 2006, Martin Watson (Light) relinquished his title.

Southern Area

Titleholders at 30 June 2006

Fly: *vacant*. **Bantam:** *vacant*. **S.Bantam:** *vacant*. **Feather:** Rocky Dean. **S.Feather:** *vacant*. **Light:** Rob Jeffries. **L.Welter:** *vacant*. **Welter:** *vacant*. **L.Middle:** Gary Woolcombe. **Middle:** *vacant*. **S.Middle:** Ryan Walls. **L.Heavy:** Andrew Lowe. **Cruiser:** *vacant*. **Heavy:** Micky Steeds.

Title Bouts Held Between 1 July 2005 and 30 June 2006

18 September	John Humphrey W PTS 10 Hussain Osman, Bethnal Green (Vacant Middleweight Title)
23 September	Ross Minter W RSC 3 Sammy Smith, Mayfair (Welterweight Title Defence)
4 December	Colin Kenna W CO 2 Wayne Llewelyn, Portsmouth (Vacant Heavyweight Title)
10 December	Ross Minter W RSC 4 Brett James, Canning Town (Welterweight Title Defence)
19 December	Ryan Walls W RTD 6 Gareth Lawrence, Longford (Vacant S.Middleweight Title)
20 January	Lenny Daws W RTD 9 Colin Lynes, Bethnal Green (Vacant L.Welterweight Title)
5 March	Colin Kenna L PTS 10 Micky Steeds, Southampton (Heavyweight Title Defence)
26 May	Gilbert Eastman L RSC 7 Gary Woolcombe, Bethnal Green (L.Middleweight Title Defence)

Between 1 July 2005 and 30 June 2006, Marc Callaghan (S.Bantam), Francis Barrett (L.Welter), Lenny Daws (L.Welter), Ross Minter (Welter) and John Humphrey (Middle) relinquished their titles.

Welsh Area

Titleholders at 30 June 2006

Fly: *vacant.* **Bantam:** *vacant.* **S.Bantam:** *vacant.* **Feather:** *vacant.* **S.Feather:** *vacant.* **Light:** *vacant.* **L.Welter:** *vacant.* **Welter:** *vacant.* **L.Middle:** *vacant.* **Middle:** *vacant.* **S.Middle:** *vacant.* **L.Heavy:** *vacant.* **Cruiser:** *vacant.* **Heavy:** *vacant.*

Title Bouts Held Between 1 July 2005 and 30 June 2006

None

Between 1 July 2005 and 30 June 2006, Bradley Pryce (Welter) relinquished his title.

Western Area

Titleholders at 30 June 2006

Fly: *vacant.* **Bantam:** *vacant.* **S.Bantam:** *vacant.* **Feather:** *vacant.* **S.Feather:** *vacant.* **Light:** *vacant.* **L.Welter:** *vacant.* **Welter:** *vacant.* **L.Middle:** *vacant.* **Middle:** *vacant.* **S.Middle:** *vacant.* **L.Heavy:** Leigh Alliss. **Cruiser:** *vacant.* **Heavy:** *vacant.*

Title Bouts Held Between 1 July 2005 and 30 June 2006

None

Micky Steeds (right) became the new Southern Area heavyweight champion on outpointing the holder, Colin Kenna, in Southampton last March

Les Clark

English and Celtic Title Bouts, 2005-2006

English Title Bouts

Due to the fact that was often a dearth of competition for certain weights at Area level, the BBBoC had long felt the need for an English championship competition and, having taken the necessary steps, Matt Skelton and Matt Holden were matched to contest the innaugural English title, at heavyweight, on 18 September, 2003.

Titleholders at 30 June 2006

Fly: *vacant*. **Bantam:** *vacant*. **S.Bantam:** Marc Callaghan. **Feather:** Derry Matthews. **S.Feather:** Billy Corcoran. **Light:** Scott Lawton. **L.Welter:** Nigel Wright. **Welter:** *vacant*. **L.Middle:** Andrew Facey. **Middle:** Steven Bendall. **S.Middle:** Tony Dodson. **L.Heavy:** Peter Haymer. **Cruiser:** Dean Francis. **Heavy:** Mark Krence.

Title Bouts Held Between 1 July 2005 and 30 June 2006

21 October	Roy Rutherford L RTD 4 Billy Corcoran, Bethnal Green (S.Featherweight Title Defence)
3 November	Ryan Kerr W PTS 10 Simeon Cover, Sunderland (S.Middleweight Title Defence)
10 December	Ross Minter W RSC 4 Brett James, Canning Town (Vacant Welterweight Title)
15 December	Donovan Smillie L RSC 5 Steven Bendall, Coventry (Middleweight Title Defence)
16 December	Ryan Kerr DREW 10 Jamie Hearn, Bracknell (S.Middleweight Title Defence)
28 January	Derry Matthews W RTD 6 Stephen Chinnock, Nottingham (Vacant Featherweight Title)
25 February	Dean Francis W PTS 10 Tommy Eastwood (Vacant Cruiserweight Title)
3 March	Marc Callaghan W PTS 10 Sean Hughes, Hartlepool (Vacant S.Bantamweight Title)
7 April	Peter Haymer W RSC 9 Leigh Alliss, Bristol (L.Heavyweight Title Defence)
9 June	Scott Lawton W RSC 8 Stefy Bull, Doncaster (Vacant Lightweight Title)
16 June	Tony Dodson W RSC 4 Jamie Hearn, Liverpool (Vacant S.Middleweight Title)

Between 1 July 2005 and 30 June 2006, Lee Haskins (Fly), Andy Morris (Feather), Danny Hunt (Light), Michael Jennings (Welter), Ross Minter (Welter) and Ryan Kerr (S.Middle) all relinquished their titles.

Celtic Title Bouts

Following the successful introduction of English titles, in August 2004 the BBBoC introduced the Celtic title to accommodate boxers from Ireland, Scotland and Wales, with the innaugural title bout being contested on 29 October 2004 by Martin Watson and Mark Winters at the lightweight limit.

Titleholders at 30 June 2006

Fly: *vacant*. **Bantam:** *vacant*. **S.Bantam:** *vacant*. **Feather:** *vacant*. **S.Feather:** *vacant*. **Light:** Martin Watson. **L.Welter:** *vacant*. **Welter:** Tony Doherty. **L.Middle:** *vacant*. **Middle:** *vacant*. **S.Middle:** *vacant*. **L.Heavy:** *vacant*. **Cruiser:** *vacant*. **Heavy:** *vacant*.

Title Bouts Held Between 1 July 2005 and 30 June 2006

23 July	Colin McNeil W PTS 10 Taz Jones, Edinburgh (Vacant L.Middleweight Title)
10 September	Tony Doherty W PTS 10 Taz Jones, Cardiff (Vacant Welterweight Title)

Between 1 July 2005 and 30 June 2006, Willie Limond (S.Feather) and Kevin Anderson (Welter) relinquished their titles, while Colin McNeil (L.Middle) forfeited his belt.

Tony Doherty, the current Celtic welterweight champion

Les Clark

PROFESSIONAL BOXING PROMOTERS' ASSOCIATION

PRESENTS

THE BRITISH MASTERS CHAMPIONS

UNDER BBB OF C RULES

HEAVY:	CARL BAKER
CRUISER:	CARL WRIGHT
LIGHT-HEAVY:	STEVEN SPARTACUS
SUPER-MIDDLE:	JOEY VEGAS
MIDDLE:	VACANT
LIGHT-MIDDLE:	ADNAN AMAR
WELTER:	NATHAN WARD
LIGHT-WELTER:	GARY REID
LIGHTWEIGHT:	SAM RUKUNDO
SUPER-FEATHER:	DARREN JOHNSTONE
FEATHER:	MATT TEAGUE
SUPER-BANTAM:	GARY DAVIS
BANTAM:	VACANT
FLYWEIGHT:	DELROY SPENCER

THE ONLY ALL-COMERS TITLE OPERATING IN BRITISH BOXING. OUR CHAMPIONS HAVE TO DEFEND WHEN A VALID CHALLENGE IS MADE WITH MORE THAN 30 DAYS NOTICE. TO CHALLENGE FOR OUR TITLE, PROMOTERS SHOULD APPLY TO:

THE PBPA
P O BOX 25188
LONDON
SW1V 3WL

TEL: 0207 592 0102
FAX: 0207 821 1831
EMAIL: bdbaker@tinyworld.co.uk

CHAIRMAN: Bruce Baker
GENERAL SECRETARY: Greg Steene
DIRECTORS: B. Baker, G. Steene, J. Gill, J. Evans

MEMBERSHIP IS BY INVITATION. INTERESTED PROMOTERS PLEASE APPLY

British Title Bouts, 2005-2006

All of last season's title bouts are shown in date order within their weight divisions and give the boxers' respective weights and the venues where the contests were held. As from 1 September it had been deemed by the BBBoC that in future all British title fights would be scored by three judges, with the referee being a non-scoring participant, and following that decision all officials and scorecards concerned are listed.

Flyweight
The title has been vacant since Jason Booth (England) handed back his belt in December 2003 after winning the IBO championship. Lee Haskins and Dale Robinson are due to contest the vacancy.

Bantamweight
4 November Martin Power 8.6 (England) W PTS 12 Ian Napa 8.5 (England), York Hall, Bethnal Green, London. Referee: Marcus McDonnell. Scorecards: Richie Davies 116-113, Ian John Lewis 116-113, John Keane 113-116.

30 May Martin Power 8.5 (England) W RSC 8 Isaac Ward 8.5$^{1}/_{2}$ (England), York Hall, Bethnal Green, London. Referee: Ian John-Lewis. Judges: Richie Davies, Mark Green, Victor Loughlin.

S.Bantamweight
28 October Michael Hunter 8.9$^{3}/_{4}$ (England) W PTS 12 Esham Pickering 8.9$^{3}/_{4}$ (England), Borough Hall, Hartlepool. Referee: John Keane. Scorecards: Richie Davies 115-112, Ian John-Lewis 114-113, Mark Green 113-113.

Featherweight
5 November Andy Morris 9.0 (England) W PTS 12 John Simpson 8.13$^{1}/_{2}$ (Scotland), Braehead Arena, Renfrew. Referee: Howard Foster. Scorecards: Victor Loughlin 118-111, Paul Thomas 118-111, Mickey Vann 118-110. Contested for the vacant title following Nicky Cook's decision to hand back his belt in September.

29 April Andy Morris 8.13$^{1}/_{2}$ (England) W PTS 12 Rendall Munroe 9.0 (England), Meadowbank Arena, Edinburgh. Paul Thomas. Scorecards: 117-112, Phil Edwards 116-113, Victor Loughlin 116-113.

S.Featherweight
18 February Alex Arthur 9.4 (Scotland) W PTS 12 Ricky Burns 9.2 (Scotland), Meadowbank Arena, Edinburgh. Referee: John Keane. Scorecards: Mickey Vann 118-110, Dave Parris 117-111, Paul Thomas 116-112. Arthur handed back his belt on 11 April to pursue his other championship ambitions and, on 12 July, Carl Johanneson stopped Billy Corcoran at York Hall, Bethnal Green, London to become the new champion.

Lightweight
12 May Lee Meager 9.8$^{3}/_{4}$ (England) W RSC 6 Dave Stewart 9.9 (Scotland), York Hall, Bethnal Green, London.

Referee: Marcus McDonnell. Judges: John Keane, Dave Parris, Mickey Vann. Contested for the vacant title after Graham Earl returned his belt in February to concentrate on going for the European championship.

L.Welterweight
21 October Junior Witter 9.13$^{3}/_{4}$ (England) W PTS 12 Colin Lynes 9.13$^{3}/_{4}$ (England), York Hall, Bethnal Green, London. Referee: Richie Davies. Scorecards: Mark Green 117-112, Mickey Vann 116-112, Terry O'Connor 115-114. Witter relinquished the title in January so that he could focus on a European defence and a prospective crack at the WBC version of the world championship.

12 May Nicky Daws 9.12 (England) W PTS 12 Nigel Wright 9.13$^{3}/_{4}$ (England), York Hall, Bethnal Green, London. Referee: John Keane. Scorecards: Marcus McDonnell 117-111, Dave Parris 117-111, Mickey Vann 117-111.

Welterweight
16 July Michael Jennings 10.6 (England) W CO 1 Jimmy Vincent 10.6 (England), The Arena, Bolton. Referee: Dave Parris. Contested for the vacant title after David Barnes had been stripped on 8 June, having received a 45 day suspension when due to defend against Vincent on the above date.

25 October Michael Jennings 10.6$^{1}/_{2}$ (England) W PTS 12 Bradley Pryce 10.5 (Wales), The Guildhall, Preston. Referee: Ian John-Lewis. Scorecards: Mark Green 116-111, John Keane 116-111, Marcus McDonnell 116-112.

28 January Michael Jennings 10.6 (England) L PTS 12 Young Muttley 10.5$^{1}/_{2}$ (England), The Ice Arena, Nottingham. Referee: Mark Green. Scorecards: John Keane 113-116, Terry O'Connor 113-116, Howard Foster 115-113.

1 June Young Muttley 10.6$^{1}/_{2}$ (England) L RSC 10 Kevin Anderson 10.6 (Scotland), Aston Villa Leisure Centre, Birmingham. Referee: Phil Edwards. Judges: Richie Davies, Marcus O'Donnell, Terry O'Connor.

L.Middleweight
8 July Michael Jones 11.0 (England) L RSC 6 Jamie Moore 11.0 (England), The Leisure Centre, Altrincham. Referee: Marcus McDonnell.

23 September Jamie Moore 11.0 (England) W RTD 4 David Walker 10.13$^{1}/_{2}$ (England), George Carnall Sports Centre, Manchester. Referee: Paul Thomas. Judges: Phil Edwards, Howard Foster, Terry O'Connor.

Middleweight

16 September   Scott Dann 11.5 (England) W PTS 12 Wayne Elcock 11.4 (England), The Pavilions, Plymouth. Referee: Mickey Vann. Scorecards: Richie Davies 118-111, Terry O'Connor 118-111, Mark Green 117-113.

S.Middleweight

9 July   Carl Froch 11.13½ (England) W PTS 12 Matthew Barney 12.0 (England), The Ice Arena, Nottingham. Referee: Phil Edwards 118-110.

26 May   Carl Froch 11.13¼ (England) W RSC 11 Brian Magee 11.13¾ (Northern Ireland), York Hall, Bethnal Green, London. Referee: Richie Davies. Judges: Ian John-Lewis, Terry O'Connor, Paul Thomas.

L.Heavyweight

Peter Oboh (England) failed to defend during the period, but is due to put his belt on the line against Gareth Hogg in October.

Cruiserweight

1 June   Mark Hobson 14.3½ (England) W RSC 4 John Keeton 14.3¾ (England), The Metrodome, Barnsley. Referee: Dave Parris. Judges: Mickey Vann, Howard Foster, Paul Thomas.

Heavyweight

16 July   Matt Skelton 18.2 (England) W RTD 7 Mark Krence 15.8¾ (England), The Arena, Bolton. Referee: Terry O'Connor.

10 December   Matt Skelton 18.3 (England) W RSC 1 John McDermott 17.12 (England), ExCel Arena, Canning Town, London. Referee: Terry O'Connor. Judges: Richie Davies, Mark Green, Ian John-Lewis. The title was declared vacant after Skelton lost his Commonwealth championship challenge to Danny Williams on 25 February.

16 June   Scott Gammer 16.9½ (Wales) W RSC 9 Mark Krence 15.11½ (England), The Showgrounds, Carmarthen. Referee: John Keane. Judges: Terry O'Connor, Paul Thomas, Richie Davies.

Coming back from the brink of defeat, Kevin Anderson (left), the Commonwealth champion, added the British welter title to his collection when stopping Young Muttley in the tenth round last June   Les Clark

Lord Lonsdale Challenge Belts: Outright Winners

Outright Winners of the National Sporting Club's Challenge Belt, 1909-1935 (21)

Under pressure from other promoters with bigger venues, and in an effort to sustain their monopoly – having controlled championship fights in Britain up until that point in time – the National Sporting Club launched the belt in 1909. They did so on the proviso that there should be eight weight divisions – fly, bantam, feather, light, welter, middle, light-heavy, and heavy – and that to win a belt outright a champion must score three title-match victories at the same weight, but not necessarily consecutively. Worth a substantial amount of money, and carrying a £1 a week pension from the age of 50, the President of the NSC, Lord Lonsdale, donated the first of 22 belts struck. Known as the Lonsdale Belt, despite the inscription reading: 'The National Sporting Club's Challenge Belt', the first man to put a notch on a belt was Freddie Welsh, who outpointed Johnny Summers for the lightweight title on 8 November 1909, while Jim Driscoll became the first man to win one outright. The record time for winning the belt is held by Jim Higgins (279 days).

FLYWEIGHT	Jimmy Wilde; Jackie Brown
BANTAMWEIGHT	Digger Stanley; Joe Fox; Jim Higgins; Johnny Brown; Dick Corbett; Johnny King
FEATHERWEIGHT	Jim Driscoll; Tancy Lee; Johnny Cuthbert; Nel Tarleton
LIGHTWEIGHT	Freddie Welsh
WELTERWEIGHT	Johnny Basham; Jack Hood
MIDDLEWEIGHT	Pat O'Keefe; Len Harvey; Jock McAvoy
L. HEAVYWEIGHT	Dick Smith
HEAVYWEIGHT	Bombardier Billy Wells; Jack Petersen

Note: Both Dick Corbett and Johnny King – with one notch apiece on the 'special' British Empire Lonsdale Belt that was struck in 1933 and later presented to the winner of the Tommy Farr v Joe Louis fight – were allowed to keep their Lonsdale Belts with just two notches secured; Freddie Welsh, also with two notches, was awarded a belt due to his inability to defend because of the First World War; the first bantam belt came back into circulation and was awarded to Johnny Brown; Al Foreman, with just one notch on the second lightweight belt, took it back to Canada with him without the consent of the BBBoC; while the second light-heavy belt was awarded to Jack Smith of Worcester for winning a novices heavyweight competition. Having emigrated to New Zealand, Smith later presented the visiting Her Majesty The Queen with the belt and it now hangs in the BBBoC's offices.

Outright Winners of the BBBoC Lord Lonsdale Challenge Belt, 1936-2006 (120)

Re-introduced by the British Boxing Board of Control as the Lord Lonsdale Challenge Belt, but of less intrinsic value, Benny Lynch's eight-round win over Pat Palmer (16 September 1936 at Shawfield Park, Glasgow) got the new version underway, while Eric Boon became the first man to win one outright, in 1939, following victories over Dave Crowley (2) and Arthur Danahar. Since those early days, six further weight divisions have been added and, following on from Henry Cooper's feat of winning three Lonsdale Belts outright, on 10 June 1981 the BBBoC's rules and regulations were amended to read that no boxer shall receive more than one belt as his own property, in any one weight division. A later amendment stated that from 1 September 1999, any boxer putting a notch on a Lonsdale Belt for the first time would require three more notches at the same weight before he could call the belt his own. However, men who already had a notch on the Lonsdale Belt prior to 1 September 1999 could contest it under the former ruling of three winning championship contests at the same weight. Incidentally, the fastest of the modern belt winners is Ryan Rhodes (90 days), while Chris and Kevin Finnegan are the only brothers to have each won a belt outright.

FLYWEIGHT	Jackie Paterson; Terry Allen; Walter McGowan; John McCluskey; Hugh Russell; Charlie Magri; Pat Clinton; Robbie Regan; Francis Ampofo; Ady Lewis
BANTAMWEIGHT	Johnny King; Peter Keenan (2); Freddie Gilroy; Alan Rudkin; Johnny Owen; Billy Hardy; Drew Docherty; Nicky Booth
S. BANTAMWEIGHT	Richie Wenton; Michael Brodie; Michael Alldis; Michael Hunter
FEATHERWEIGHT	Nel Tarleton; Ronnie Clayton (2); Charlie Hill; Howard Winstone (2); Evan Armstrong; Pat Cowdell; Robert Dickie; Paul Hodkinson; Colin McMillan; Sean Murphy; Jonjo Irwin; Dazzo Williams
S. FEATHERWEIGHT	Jimmy Anderson; John Doherty; Floyd Havard; Charles Shepherd; Michael Gomez; Alex Arthur

LIGHTWEIGHT	Eric Boon; Billy Thompson; Joe Lucy; Dave Charnley; Maurice Cullen; Ken Buchanan; Jim Watt; George Feeney; Tony Willis; Carl Crook; Billy Schwer; Michael Ayers; Bobby Vanzie; Graham Earl
L. WELTERWEIGHT	Joey Singleton; Colin Power; Clinton McKenzie; Lloyd Christie; Andy Holligan; Ross Hale; Junior Witter
WELTERWEIGHT	Ernie Roderick; Wally Thom; Brian Curvis (2); Ralph Charles; Colin Jones; Lloyd Honeyghan; Kirkland Laing; Del Bryan; Geoff McCreesh; Derek Roche; Neil Sinclair; David Barnes
L. MIDDLEWEIGHT	Maurice Hope; Jimmy Batten; Pat Thomas; Prince Rodney; Andy Till; Robert McCracken; Ryan Rhodes; Ensley Bingham; Jamie Moore
MIDDLEWEIGHT	Pat McAteer; Terry Downes; Johnny Pritchett; Bunny Sterling; Alan Minter; Kevin Finnegan; Roy Gumbs; Tony Sibson; Herol Graham; Neville Brown; Howard Eastman; Scott Dann
S. MIDDLEWEIGHT	Sammy Storey; David Starie
L. HEAVYWEIGHT	Randy Turpin; Chic Calderwood; Chris Finnegan; Bunny Johnson; Tom Collins; Dennis Andries; Tony Wilson; Crawford Ashley
CRUISERWEIGHT	Johnny Nelson; Terry Dunstan; Bruce Scott; Mark Hobson
HEAVYWEIGHT	Henry Cooper (3); Horace Notice; Lennox Lewis; Julius Francis; Danny Williams; Matt Skelton

Note: Walter McGowan, Charlie Magri and Junior Witter, with one notch apiece, kept their belts under the three years/no available challengers' ruling, while Johnny King, with two notches, was awarded the belt on the grounds that the Second World War stopped him from making further defences. Incidentally, King and Nel Tarleton are the only men to have won both the NSC and BBBoC belts outright.

The Pride of Hartlepool: Michael Hunter (left), who won the super-bantamweight Lonsdale Belt outright last October, is seen here with his manager, Dave Garside (centre), and trainer, Neil Fannan

British Champions Since Gloves, 1878-2006

The listings below show the tenure of all British champions at each weight since gloves (two ounces or more) were introduced to British rings under Queensberry Rules. Although Charley Davis (147 lbs) had beaten Ted Napper (140 lbs) with gloves in 1873, we start with Denny Harrington, who defeated George Rooke for both the English and world middleweight titles in London on 12 March 1878. We also make a point of ignoring competition winners, apart from Anthony Diamond who beat Dido Plumb for the middles title over 12 rounds, basically because full championship conditions or finish fights of three-minute rounds were not applied. Another point worth bearing in mind, is that prior to the 1880s there were only five weights – heavy, middle, light, feather and bantam. Anything above 154 lbs, the middleweight limit, was classified a heavyweight contest, whereas lightweight, feather and bantamweight poundages were much looser. Therefore, to put things into current perspective, in many cases we have had to ascertain the actual poundage of fighters concerned and relate them to the modern weight classes. Another point worth remembering is that men born outside Britain who won international titles in this country, are not recorded for fear of added confusion and, although many of the champions or claimants listed before 1909 were no more than English titleholders, having fought for the 'championship of England', for our purposes they carry the 'British' label.

Prior to 1909, the year that the Lord Lonsdale Challenge Belt was introduced and weight classes subsequently standardised, poundages within divisions could vary quite substantially, thus enabling men fighting at different weights to claim the same 'title' at the same time. A brief history of the weight fluctuations between 1891 and 1909, shows:

Bantamweight   With the coming of gloves, the division did not really take off until Nunc Wallace established himself at 112 lbs on beating (small) Bill Goode after nine rounds in London on 12 March 1889. Later, with Wallace fighting above the weight, Billy Plimmer was generally recognised as the country's leading eight stoner, following victories over Charles Mansford and Jem Stevens, and became accepted as world champion when George Dixon, the number one in America's eyes, gradually increased his weight. In 1895, Pedlar Palmer took the British title at 112 lbs, but by 1900 he had developed into a 114 pounder. Between 1902 and 1904, Joe Bowker defended regularly at 116 lbs and in 1909 the NSC standardised the weight at 118 lbs, even though the USA continued for a short while to accept only 116 lbs.

Featherweight   Between 1886 and 1895, one of the most prestigious championship belts in this country was fought for at 126 lbs and, although George Dixon was recognised in the USA as world featherweight champion – gradually moving from 114 to 122 lbs – no major international contests took place in Britain during the above period at his weight. It was only in 1895, when Fred Johnson took the British title at 120 lbs, losing it to Ben Jordan two years later, that we came into line with the USA. Ben Jordan became an outstanding champion who, between 1898 and 1899, was seen by the NSC as world champion at 120 lbs. However, first Harry Greenfield, then Jabez White and Will Curley, continued to claim the 126 lbs version of the British title and it was only in 1900, when Jack Roberts beat Curley, that the weight limit was finally standardised at nine stone.

Lightweight   Outstanding champions often carried their weights as they grew in size. A perfect example of this was Dick Burge, the British lightweight champion from 1891-1901, who gradually increased from 134 to 144 lbs, while still maintaining his right to the title. It was not until 1902 that Jabez White brought the division into line with the USA. Later, both White, and then Goldswain, carried their weight up to 140 lbs and it was left to Johnny Summers to set the current limit of 135 lbs.

Welterweight   The presence of Dick Burge fighting from 134 to 144 lbs plus up until 1900, explains quite adequately why the welterweight division, although very popular in the USA, did not take off in this country until 1902. The championship was contested between 142 and 146 lbs in those days and was not really supported by the NSC, but by 1909 with their backing it finally became established at 147 lbs.

On 8 September 1970, Bunny Sterling became the first immigrant to win a British title under the ten-year residential ruling, while earlier, on 28 June 1948, Dick Turpin won the British middleweight title and, in doing so, became the first coloured fighter to win the title, thus breaking down the so-called 'colour bar'.

Note that the Lonsdale Belt notches (title bout wins) relate to NSC, 1909-1935, and BBBoC, 1936-2006.

Champions in **bold** are accorded national recognition.

*Undefeated champions (Does not include men who forfeited titles).

Title Holder	Lonsdale Belt Notches	Tenure	Title Holder	Lonsdale Belt Notches	Tenure	Title Holder	Lonsdale Belt Notches	Tenure
Flyweight (112 lbs)			**Percy Jones**	1	1914	**Joe Symonds**	1	1915-1916
Sid Smith		1911	Joe Symonds		1914	**Jimmy Wilde***	3	1916-1923
Sid Smith	1	1911-1913	**Tancy Lee**	1	1914-1915	**Elky Clark***	2	1924-1927
Bill Ladbury		1913-1914	Jimmy Wilde		1914-1915	**Johnny Hill***	1	1927-1929

177

Title Holder	Lonsdale Belt Notches	Tenure
Jackie Brown		1929-1930
Bert Kirby	1	1930-1931
Jackie Brown	3	1931-1935
Benny Lynch*	2	1935-1938
Jackie Paterson	4	1939-1948
Rinty Monaghan*	1	1948-1950
Terry Allen	1	1951-1952
Teddy Gardner*	1	1952
Terry Allen*	2	1952-1954
Dai Dower*	1	1955-1957
Frankie Jones	2	1957-1960
Johnny Caldwell*	1	1960-1961
Jackie Brown	1	1962-1963
Walter McGowan*	1	1963-1966
John McCluskey*	3	1967-1977
Charlie Magri*	1	1977-1981
Kelvin Smart	1	1982-1984
Hugh Russell*	3	1984-1985
Duke McKenzie*	2	1985-1986
Dave Boy McAuley*	1	1986-1988
Pat Clinton*	3	1988-1991
Robbie Regan	1	1991
Francis Ampofo	1	1991
Robbie Regan*	2	1991-1992
Francis Ampofo	3	1992-1996
Mickey Cantwell*	1	1996-1997
Ady Lewis*	3	1997-1998
Damaen Kelly	1	1999
Keith Knox	1	1999
Jason Booth*	2	1999-2003

Bantamweight (118 lbs)

Title Holder	Lonsdale Belt Notches	Tenure
Nunc Wallace*		1889-1891
Billy Plimmer		1891-1895
Tom Gardner		1892
Willie Smith		1892-1896
Nunc Wallace		1893-1895
George Corfield		1893-1896
Pedlar Palmer		1895-1900
Billy Plimmer		1896-1898
Harry Ware		1899-1900
Harry Ware		1900-1902
Andrew Tokell		1901-1902
Jim Williams		1902
Andrew Tokell		1902
Harry Ware		1902
Joe Bowker		1902-1910
Owen Moran		1905-1907
Digger Stanley		1906-1910
Digger Stanley	2	1910-1913
Bill Beynon	1	1913
Digger Stanley	1	1913-1914
Curley Walker*	1	1914-1915
Joe Fox*	3	1915-1917
Tommy Noble	1	1918-1919
Walter Ross*	1	1919-1920
Jim Higgins	3	1920-1922
Tommy Harrison		1922-1923
Bugler Harry Lake	1	1923
Johnny Brown	3	1923-1928
Alf Pattenden	2	1928-1929
Johnny Brown		1928
Teddy Baldock		1928-1929
Teddy Baldock*	1	1929-1931
Dick Corbett	1	1931-1932
Johnny King	1	1932-1934

Title Holder	Lonsdale Belt Notches	Tenure
Dick Corbett*	1	1934
Johnny King	1+2	1935-1947
Jackie Paterson	2	1947-1949
Stan Rowan*	1	1949
Danny O'Sullivan	1	1949-1951
Peter Keenan	3	1951-1953
John Kelly	1	1953-1954
Peter Keenan	3	1954-1959
Freddie Gilroy*	4	1959-1963
Johnny Caldwell	1	1964-1965
Alan Rudkin	1	1965-1966
Walter McGowan	1	1966-1968
Alan Rudkin*	4	1968-1972
Johnny Clark*	1	1973-1974
Dave Needham	1	1974-1975
Paddy Maguire	1	1975-1977
Johnny Owen*	4	1977-1980
John Feeney	1	1981-1983
Hugh Russell	1	1983
Davy Larmour	1	1983
John Feeney	1	1983-1985
Ray Gilbody	2	1985-1987
Billy Hardy*	5	1987-1991
Joe Kelly	1	1992
Drew Docherty	4	1992-1997
Paul Lloyd	2	1997-1999
Noel Wilders*	2	1999-2000
Ady Lewis	1	2000
Tommy Waite	1	2000
Nicky Booth	5	2000-2004
Martin Power	3	2005-

S. Bantamweight (122 lbs)

Title Holder	Lonsdale Belt Notches	Tenure
Richie Wenton*	3	1994-1996
Michael Brodie*	3	1997-1999
Patrick Mullings	1	1999
Drew Docherty*	1	1999
Michael Alldis	3	1999-2001
Patrick Mullings	1	2001
Michael Alldis*	1	2002
Esham Pickering*	1	2003-2004
Michael Hunter	4	2004-

Featherweight (126 lbs)

Title Holder	Lonsdale Belt Notches	Tenure
Bill Baxter		1884-1891
Harry Overton		1890-1891
Billy Reader		1891-1892
Fred Johnson		1891-1895
Harry Spurden		1892-1895
Jack Fitzpatrick		1895-1897
Fred Johnson		1895-1897
Harry Greenfield		1896-1899
Ben Jordan*		1897-1900
Jabez White		1899-1900
Will Curley		1900-1901
Jack Roberts		1901-1902
Will Curley		1902-1903
Ben Jordan*		1902-1905
Joe Bowker		1905
Johnny Summers		1906
Joe Bowker		1905-1906
Jim Driscoll		1906-1907
Spike Robson		1906-1907
Jim Driscoll*	3	1907-1913
Spike Robson		1907-1910
Ted Kid Lewis*	1	1913-1914

Title Holder	Lonsdale Belt Notches	Tenure
Llew Edwards*	1	1915-1917
Charlie Hardcastle	1	1917
Tancy Lee*	3	1917-1919
Mike Honeyman	2	1920-1921
Joe Fox*	1	1921-1922
George McKenzie	2	1924-1925
Johnny Curley	2	1925-1927
Johnny Cuthbert	1	1927-1928
Harry Corbett	1	1928-1929
Johnny Cuthbert	2	1929-1931
Nel Tarleton	1	1931-1932
Seaman Tommy Watson	2	1932-1934
Nel Tarleton	2	1934-1936
Johnny McGrory	1	1936-1938
Jim Spider Kelly	1	1938-1939
Johnny Cusick	1	1939-1940
Nel Tarleton*	3	1940-1947
Ronnie Clayton	6	1947-1954
Sammy McCarthy	1	1954-1955
Billy Spider Kelly	1	1955-1956
Charlie Hill	3	1956-1959
Bobby Neill	1	1959-1960
Terry Spinks	2	1960-1961
Howard Winstone*	7	1961-1969
Jimmy Revie	2	1969-1971
Evan Armstrong	2	1971-1972
Tommy Glencross	1	1972-1973
Evan Armstrong*	2	1973-1975
Vernon Sollas	1	1975-1977
Alan Richardson	2	1977-1978
Dave Needham	2	1978-1979
Pat Cowdell*	3	1979-1982
Steve Sims*	1	1982-1983
Barry McGuigan*	2	1983-1986
Robert Dickie	3	1986-1988
Peter Harris	1	1988
Paul Hodkinson*	3	1988-1990
Sean Murphy	2	1990-1991
Gary de Roux	1	1991
Colin McMillan*	3	1991-1992
John Davison*	1	1992-1993
Sean Murphy	1	1993
Duke McKenzie*	1	1993-1994
Billy Hardy*	1	1994
Michael Deveney	1	1995
Jonjo Irwin	2	1995-1996
Colin McMillan	1	1996-1997
Paul Ingle*	3	1997-1998
Jonjo Irwin*	2	1998-1999
Gary Thornhill	1	2000
Scott Harrison*	3	2001-2002
Jamie McKeever	1	2003
Roy Rutherford	1	2003
Dazzo Williams	4	2003-2005
Nicky Cook*	1	2005
Andy Morris	2	2005-

S. Featherweight (130 lbs)

Title Holder	Lonsdale Belt Notches	Tenure
Jimmy Anderson*	3	1968-1970
John Doherty	1	1986
Pat Cowdell	1	1986
Najib Daho	1	1986-1987
Pat Cowdell	1	1987-1988
Floyd Havard	1	1988-1989
John Doherty	1	1989-1990
Joey Jacobs	1	1990

Title Holder	Lonsdale Belt Notches	Tenure
Hugh Forde	1	1990
Kevin Pritchard	1	1990-1991
Robert Dickie	1	1991
Sugar Gibiliru	1	1991
John Doherty	1	1991-1992
Michael Armstrong	1	1992
Neil Haddock	2	1992-1994
Floyd Havard*	3	1994-1995
P. J. Gallagher	2	1996-1997
Charles Shepherd	3	1997-1999
Michael Gomez*	5	1999-2002
Alex Arthur	3	2002-2003
Michael Gomez	1	2003-2004
Alex Arthur*	2	2005-2006

Lightweight (135 lbs)

Title Holder	Lonsdale Belt Notches	Tenure
Dick Burge		1891-1897
Harry Nickless		1891-1894
Tom Causer		1894-1897
Tom Causer		1897
Dick Burge*		1897-1901
Jabez White		1902-1906
Jack Goldswain		1906-1908
Johnny Summers		1908-1909
Freddie Welsh	1	1909-1911
Matt Wells	1	1911-1912
Freddie Welsh*	1	1912-1919
Bob Marriott*	1	1919-1920
Ernie Rice	1	1921-1922
Seaman Nobby Hall		1922-1923
Harry Mason		1923-1924
Ernie Izzard	2	1924-1925
Harry Mason		1924-1925
Harry Mason*	1	1925-1928
Sam Steward		1928-1929
Fred Webster		1929-1930
Al Foreman*	1	1930-1932
Johnny Cuthbert		1932-1934
Harry Mizler		1934
Jackie Kid Berg		1934-1936
Jimmy Walsh	1	1936-1938
Dave Crowley	1	1938
Eric Boon	3	1938-1944
Ronnie James*	1	1944-1947
Billy Thompson	3	1947-1951
Tommy McGovern	1	1951-1952
Frank Johnson	1	1952-1953
Joe Lucy	1	1953-1955
Frank Johnson	1	1955-1956
Joe Lucy	2	1956-1957
Dave Charnley*	3	1957-1965
Maurice Cullen	4	1965-1968
Ken Buchanan*	2	1968-1971
Willie Reilly*	1	1972
Jim Watt	1	1972-1973
Ken Buchanan*	1	1973-1974
Jim Watt*	2	1975-1977
Charlie Nash*	1	1978-1979
Ray Cattouse	2	1980-1982
George Feeney*	3	1982-1985
Tony Willis	3	1985-1987
Alex Dickson	1	1987-1988
Steve Boyle	2	1988-1990
Carl Crook	5	1990-1992
Billy Schwer	1	1992-1993
Paul Burke	1	1993
Billy Schwer*	2	1993-1995
Michael Ayers*	5	1995-1997
Wayne Rigby	2	1998
Bobby Vanzie	5	1998-2003
Graham Earl	1	2003-2004
Graham Earl*	3	2004-2006
Lee Meager	1	2006-

L. Welterweight (140 lbs)

Title Holder	Lonsdale Belt Notches	Tenure
Des Rea	1	1968-1969
Vic Andreetti*	2	1969-1970
Des Morrison	1	1973-1974
Pat McCormack	1	1974
Joey Singleton	3	1974-1976
Dave Boy Green*	1	1976-1977
Colin Power*	2	1977-1978
Clinton McKenzie	1	1978-1979
Colin Power	1	1979
Clinton McKenzie	5	1979-1984
Terry Marsh*	1	1984-1986
Tony Laing*	1	1986
Tony McKenzie	2	1986-1987
Lloyd Christie	3	1987-1989
Clinton McKenzie*	1	1989
Pat Barrett*	2	1989-1990
Tony Ekubia	1	1990-1991
Andy Holligan	3	1991-1994
Ross Hale	4	1994-1995
Paul Ryan	1	1995-1996
Andy Holligan*	1	1996-1997
Mark Winters	2	1997-1998
Jason Rowland*	2	1998-2000
Ricky Hatton*	1	2000-2001
Junior Witter*	2	2002-2006
Lenny Daws	1	2006-

Welterweight (147 lbs)

Title Holder	Lonsdale Belt Notches	Tenure
Charlie Allum		1903-1904
Charlie Knock		1904-1906
Curly Watson		1906-1910
Young Joseph		1908-1910
Young Joseph	1	1910-1911
Arthur Evernden		1911-1912
Johnny Summers		1912
Johnny Summers	2	1912-1914
Tom McCormick		1914
Matt Wells		1914
Johnny Basham	3	1914-1920
Matt Wells		1914-1919
Ted Kid Lewis		1920-1924
Tommy Milligan*		1924-1925
Hamilton Johnny Brown		1925
Harry Mason		1925-1926
Jack Hood*	3	1926-1934
Harry Mason		1934
Pat Butler*		1934-1936
Dave McCleave		1936
Jake Kilrain	1	1936-1939
Ernie Roderick	5	1939-1948
Henry Hall	1	1948-1949
Eddie Thomas	2	1949-1951
Wally Thom	1	1951-1952
Cliff Curvis*	1	1952-1953
Wally Thom	2	1953-1956
Peter Waterman*	2	1956-1958
Tommy Molloy	2	1958-1960
Wally Swift	1	1960
Brian Curvis*	7	1960-1966
Johnny Cooke	2	1967-1968
Ralph Charles*	3	1968-1972
Bobby Arthur	1	1972-1973
John H. Stracey*	1	1973-1975
Pat Thomas	2	1975-1976
Henry Rhiney	2	1976-1979
Kirkland Laing	1	1979-1980
Colin Jones*	3	1980-1982
Lloyd Honeyghan*	2	1983-1985
Kostas Petrou	1	1985
Sylvester Mittee	1	1985
Lloyd Honeyghan*	1	1985-1986
Kirkland Laing	4	1987-1991
Del Bryan	2	1991-1992
Gary Jacobs*	2	1992-1993
Del Bryan	4	1993-1995
Chris Saunders	1	1995-1996
Kevin Lueshing	1	1996-1997
Geoff McCreesh*	4	1997-1999
Derek Roche	3	1999-2000
Harry Dhami	3	2000-2001
Neil Sinclair*	4	2001-2003
David Barnes	4	2003-2005
Michael Jennings	2	2005-2006
Young Muttley	1	2006
Kevin Anderson	1	2006-

L. Middleweight (154 lbs)

Title Holder	Lonsdale Belt Notches	Tenure
Larry Paul	2	1973-1974
Maurice Hope*	3	1974-1977
Jimmy Batten	3	1977-1979
Pat Thomas	3	1979-1981
Herol Graham*	2	1981-1983
Prince Rodney*	1	1983-1984
Jimmy Cable	2	1984-1985
Prince Rodney	2	1985-1986
Chris Pyatt*	1	1986
Lloyd Hibbert*	1	1987
Gary Cooper	1	1988
Gary Stretch	2	1988-1990
Wally Swift Jnr	2	1991-1992
Andy Till	3	1992-1994
Robert McCracken*	3	1994-1995
Ensley Bingham*	2	1996
Ryan Rhodes*	3	1996-1997
Ensley Bingham	3	1997-1999
Wayne Alexander*	2	2000-2003
Jamie Moore	3	2003-2004
Michael Jones	1	2004-2005
Jamie Moore	2	2005-

Middleweight (160 lbs)

Title Holder	Lonsdale Belt Notches	Tenure
Denny Harrington		1878-1880
William Sheriff*		1880-1883
Bill Goode		1887-1890
Toff Wall*		1890
Ted Pritchard		1890-1895
Ted White		1893-1895
Ted White*		1895-1896
Anthony Diamond*		1898
Dick Burge*		1898-1900
Jack Palmer		1902-1903
Charlie Allum		1905-1906
Pat O'Keefe		1906

BRITISH CHAMPIONS SINCE GLOVES, 1878-2006

Title Holder	Lonsdale Belt Notches	Tenure
Tom Thomas	1	1906-1910
Jim Sullivan*	1	1910-1912
Jack Harrison*	1	1912-1913
Pat O'Keefe	2	1914-1916
Bandsman Jack Blake	1	1916-1918
Pat O'Keefe*	1	1918-1919
Ted Kid Lewis		1920-1921
Tom Gummer	1	1920-1921
Gus Platts		1921
Johnny Basham		1921
Ted Kid Lewis	2	1921-1923
Johnny Basham		1921
Roland Todd		1923-1925
Roland Todd		1925-1927
Tommy Milligan	1	1926-1928
Frank Moody		1927-1928
Alex Ireland		1928-1929
Len Harvey	5	1929-1933
Jock McAvoy	3+2	1933-1944
Ernie Roderick	1	1945-1946
Vince Hawkins	1	1946-1948
Dick Turpin	2	1948-1950
Albert Finch	1	1950
Randy Turpin*	1	1950-1954
Johnny Sullivan	1	1954-1955
Pat McAteer*	3	1955-1958
Terry Downes	1	1958-1959
John Cowboy McCormack	1	1959
Terry Downes	2	1959-1962
George Aldridge	1	1962-1963
Mick Leahy	1	1963-1964
Wally Swift	1	1964-1965
Johnny Pritchett*	4	1965-1969
Les McAteer	1	1969-1970
Mark Rowe	1	1970
Bunny Sterling	4	1970-1974
Kevin Finnegan*	1	1974
Bunny Sterling*	1	1975
Alan Minter	3	1975-1977
Kevin Finnegan	1	1977
Alan Minter*	1	1977-1978
Tony Sibson	1	1979
Kevin Finnegan*	1	1979-1980
Roy Gumbs	3	1981-1983
Mark Kaylor	1	1983-1984
Tony Sibson*	1	1984
Herol Graham*	1	1985-1986
Brian Anderson	1	1986-1987
Tony Sibson*	1	1987-1988
Herol Graham	4	1988-1992
Frank Grant	2	1992-1993
Neville Brown	6	1993-1998
Glenn Catley*	1	1998
Howard Eastman*	4	1998-2004
Scott Dann	4	2004-

S. Middleweight (168 lbs)

Title Holder	Lonsdale Belt Notches	Tenure
Sammy Storey	2	1989-1990
James Cook*	1	1990-1991
Fidel Castro	2	1991-1992
Henry Wharton*	1	1992-1993
James Cook	1	1993-1994
Cornelius Carr*	1	1994
Ali Forbes	1	1995
Sammy Storey*	1	1995
Joe Calzaghe*	2	1995-1997
David Starie	1	1997
Dean Francis*	2	1997-1998
David Starie*	5	1998-2003
Matthew Barney*	1	2003
Tony Dodson*	1	2003-2004
Carl Froch	3	2004-

L. Heavyweight (175lbs)

Title Holder	Lonsdale Belt Notches	Tenure
Dennis Haugh		1913-1914
Dick Smith	2	1914-1916
Harry Reeve*	1	1916-1917
Dick Smith*	1	1918-1919
Boy McCormick*	1	1919-1921
Jack Bloomfield*	1	1922-1924
Tom Berry	1	1925-1927
Gipsy Daniels*	1	1927
Frank Moody	1	1927-1929
Harry Crossley	1	1929-1932
Jack Petersen*	1	1932
Len Harvey*	1	1933-1934
Eddie Phillips		1935-1937
Jock McAvoy	1	1937-1938
Len Harvey	2	1938-1942
Freddie Mills*	1	1942-1950
Don Cockell	2	1950-1952
Randy Turpin*	1	1952
Dennis Powell	1	1953
Alex Buxton	2	1953-1955
Randy Turpin*	1	1955
Ron Barton*	1	1956
Randy Turpin*	2	1956-1958
Chic Calderwood	3	1960-1963
Chic Calderwood*	1	1964-1966
Young John McCormack	2	1967-1969
Eddie Avoth	2	1969-1971
Chris Finnegan	2	1971-1973
John Conteh*	2	1973-1974
Johnny Frankham	1	1975
Chris Finnegan*	1	1975-1976
Tim Wood	1	1976-1977
Bunny Johnson*	3	1977-1981
Tom Collins	3	1982-1984
Dennis Andries*	5	1984-1986
Tom Collins*	1	1987
Tony Wilson	3	1987-1989
Tom Collins*	1	1989-1990
Steve McCarthy	1	1990-1991
Crawford Ashley*	3	1991-1992
Maurice Core*	2	1992-1994
Crawford Ashley	3	1994-1999
Clinton Woods*	1	1999-2000
Neil Simpson*	2	2000-2002
Peter Oboh	2	2003-

Cruiserweight (200 lbs)

Title Holder	Lonsdale Belt Notches	Tenure
Sam Reeson*	1	1985-1986
Andy Straughn	1	1986-1987
Roy Smith	1	1987
Tee Jay	1	1987-1988
Glenn McCrory*	2	1988
Andy Straughn	1	1988-1989
Johnny Nelson*	3	1989-1991
Derek Angol*	2	1991-1992
Carl Thompson*	1	1992-1994
Dennis Andries	1	1995
Terry Dunstan*	3	1995-1996
Johnny Nelson*	1	1996-1998
Bruce Scott	1	1998-1999
Carl Thompson*	1	1999-2000
Bruce Scott	2	2000-2003
Mark Hobson	5	2003-

Heavyweight (200 lbs +)

Title Holder	Lonsdale Belt Notches	Tenure
Tom Allen*		1878-1882
Charlie Mitchell*		1882-1894
Jem Smith		1889-1891
Ted Pritchard		1891-1895
Jem Smith		1895-1896
George Chrisp		1901
Jack Scales		1901-1902
Jack Palmer		1903-1906
Gunner Moir		1906-1909
Iron Hague		1909-1910
P.O. Curran		1910-1911
Iron Hague		1910-1911
Bombardier Billy Wells	3	1911-1919
Joe Beckett		1919
Frank Goddard	1	1919
Joe Beckett*	1	1919-1923
Frank Goddard		1923-1926
Phil Scott*		1926-1931
Reggie Meen		1931-1932
Jack Petersen	3	1932-1933
Len Harvey		1933-1934
Jack Petersen		1934-1936
Ben Foord		1936-1937
Tommy Farr*	1	1937-1938
Len Harvey*	1	1938-1942
Jack London	1	1944-1945
Bruce Woodcock	2	1945-1950
Jack Gardner	1	1950-1952
Johnny Williams	1	1952-1953
Don Cockell*	1	1953-1956
Joe Erskine	2	1956-1958
Brian London	1	1958-1959
Henry Cooper*	9	1959-1969
Jack Bodell	1	1969-1970
Henry Cooper	1	1970-1971
Joe Bugner	1	1971
Jack Bodell	1	1971-1972
Danny McAlinden	1	1972-1975
Bunny Johnson	1	1975
Richard Dunn	2	1975-1976
Joe Bugner*	1	1976-1977
John L. Gardner*	2	1978-1980
Gordon Ferris	1	1981
Neville Meade	1	1981-1983
David Pearce*	1	1983-1985
Hughroy Currie	1	1985-1986
Horace Notice*	4	1986-1988
Gary Mason	2	1989-1991
Lennox Lewis*	3	1991-1993
Herbie Hide*	1	1993-1994
James Oyebola	1	1994-1995
Scott Welch*	1	1995-1996
Julius Francis	4	1997-2000
Mike Holden*	1	2000
Danny Williams	5	2000-2004
Michael Sprott	1	2004
Matt Skelton	4	2004-2006
Scott Gammer	1	2006-

Retired or Inactive Post-War British Champions: Career Summary

Includes all British champions, along with British boxers who have won major international titles since 1945, who had retired by July 2005 or have been inactive since that date. The section does not include champions still active (for their records see under Active British-Based Boxers), while undefeated champions are those who relinquished their titles, not forfeited them. *Current Champions.

George Aldridge British Middleweight Champion, 1962-1963. *Born* 01.02.36. *From* Market Harborough. *Pro Career* 1956-1963 (52 contests, won 36, drew 2, lost 14).

Michael Alldis British S. Bantamweight Champion, 1999-2001. Undefeated British and Commonwealth S. Bantamweight Champion, 2002. *Born* 25.05.68. *From* Crawley. *Pro Career* 1992-2002 (21 contests, won 24, lost 8).

Terry Allen British Flyweight Champion, 1951-1952. Undefeated British Flyweight Champion, 1952-1954. European and World Flyweight Champion, 1950. *Born* 18.06.24. *From* Islington. *Birthname* Edward Govier. *Deceased* 1987. *Pro Career* 1942-1954 (74 contests, won 60, drew 1, lost 13).

Francis Ampofo British Flyweight Champion, 1991. Undefeated British Flyweight Champion, 1992-1996. Undefeated Commonwealth Flyweight Champion, 1993. Commonwealth Flyweight Champion, 1994-1995. *Born* Ghana 05.06.67. *From* Bethnal Green. *Pro Career* 1990-2002 (28 contests, won 17, lost 11).

Brian Anderson British Middleweight Champion, 1986-1987. *Born* 09.07.61. *From* Sheffield. *Pro Career* 1980-1987 (39 contests, won 27, drew 3, lost 9).

Jimmy Anderson Undefeated British S. Featherweight Champion, 1968-1970. *Born* 01.10.42. *From* Waltham Cross. *Pro Career* 1964-1971 (37 contests, won 27, drew 1, lost 9).

Vic Andreetti Undefeated British L. Welterweight Champion, 1969-1970. *Born* 29.01.42. *From* Hoxton. *Pro Career* 1961-1969 (67 contests, won 51, drew 3, lost 13).

Dennis Andries Undefeated British L. Heavyweight Champion, 1984-86. World L. Heavyweight Champion (WBC version), 1986-1987, 1989, and 1990-1991. British Cruiserweight Champion, 1995. *Born* Guyana 05.11.53. *From* Hackney. *Pro Career* 1978-1996 (65 contests, won 49, drew 2, lost 14).

Derek Angol Undefeated British Cruiserweight Champion, 1991-1992. Undefeated Commonwealth Cruiserweight Champion, 1989-1993. *Born* 28.11.64. *From* Camberwell. *Pro Career* 1986-1996 (31 contests, won 28, lost 3).

Evan Armstrong British Featherweight Champion, 1971-1972. Undefeated British Featherweight Champion, 1973-1975. Commonwealth Featherweight Champion, 1974. *Born* 15.02.43. *From* Ayr. *Pro Career* 1963-1974 (54 contests, won 39, drew 1, lost 14).

Michael Armstrong British S. Featherweight Champion, 1992. *Born* 18.12.68. *From* Moston. *Birthname* Morris. *Pro Career* 1987-1994 (26 contests, won 18, drew 1, lost 7).

Bobby Arthur British Welterweight Champion, 1972-1973. *Born* 25.07.47. *From* Coventry. *Pro Career* 1967-1976 (41 contests, won 26, lost 15).

Crawford Ashley Undefeated British L. Heavyweight Champion, 1991-1992. British L. Heavyweight Champion, 1994-1999. European L. Heavyweight Champion, 1997 and 1998-1999. Commonwealth L. Heavyweight Champion, 1998-1999. *Born* 20.05.64. *From* Leeds. *Birthname* Gary Crawford. *Pro Career* 1987-2001 (44 contests, won 33, drew 1, lost 10).

Eddie Avoth British L. Heavyweight Champion, 1969-1971. Commonwealth L. Heavyweight Champion, 1970-1971. *Born* 02.05.45. *From* Cardiff. *Pro Career* 1963-1972 (53 contests, won 44, lost 9).

Michael Ayers Undefeated British Lightweight Champion, 1995-1997. *Born* 26.01.65. *From* Tooting. *Pro-Career* 1989-2003 (37 contests, won 31, drew 1, lost 5).

Pat Barrett Undefeated British L. Welterweight Champion, 1989-1990. European L. Welterweight Champion, 1990-1992. *Born* 22.07.67. *From* Manchester. *Pro Career* 1987-1994 (42 contests, won 37, drew 1, lost 4).

Ron Barton Undefeated British L. Heavyweight Champion, 1956. *Born* 25.02.33. *From* West Ham. *Pro Career* 1954-1961 (31 contests, won 26, lost 5).

Jimmy Batten British L. Middleweight Champion, 1977-1979. *Born* 07.11.55. *From* Millwall. *Pro Career* 1974-1983 (49 contests, won 40, lost 9).

Nigel Benn Commonwealth Middleweight Champion, 1988-1989. World Middleweight Champion (WBO version), 1990. World S. Middleweight Champion (WBC version), 1992-1996. *Born* 22.01.64. *From* Ilford. *Pro Career* 1987-1996 (48 contests, won 42, drew 1, lost 5).

Ensley Bingham Undefeated British L. Middleweight Champion, 1996. British L. Middleweight Champion, 1997-1999. *Born* 27.05.63. *From* Manchester. *Pro Career* 1986-1999 (28 contests, won 20, lost 8).

Jack Bodell British Heavyweight Champion, 1969-1970 and 1971-1972. Commonwealth Heavyweight Champion, 1971-1972. European Heavyweight Champion, 1971. *Born* 11.08.40. *From* Swadlincote. *Pro Career* 1962-1972 (71 contests, won 58, lost 13).

Jason Booth Undefeated British and Commonwealth Flyweight Champion, 1999-2003. *Born* 07.11.77. *From* Nottingham. *Pro Career* 1996-2004 (29 contests, won 25, lost 4).

Nicky Booth British Bantamweight Champion, 2000-2004. Commonwealth Bantamweight Champion, 2000-2002. *Born* 21.01.80. *From* Nottingham. *Pro Career* 1998-2003 (23 contersts, won 17, drew 1, lost 5).

Steve Boyle British Lightweight Champion, 1988-1990. *Born* 28.11.62. *From* Glasgow. *Pro Career* 1983-1993 (33 contests, won 25, drew 2, lost 6).

Cornelius Boza-Edwards Undefeated European S. Featherweight Champion, 1982. World S. Featherweight Champion, 1981 (WBC version). *Born* Uganda, 27.05.56. *From* London. *Pro Career* 1976-1987 (53 contests, won 45, drew 1, lost 7).

Jim Brady British Empire Bantamweight Championship Claimant, 1941-1945. *From* Dundee. *Deceased* 1980. *Pro Career* 1932-1947 (169 contests, won 104, drew 15, lost 50).

Jackie Brown British and British Empire Flyweight Champion, 1962-1963. *Born* 02.03.35. *From* Edinburgh. *Pro Career* 1958-1966 (44 contests, won 32, drew 1, lost 10, no contest 1).

Neville Brown British Middleweight Champion, 1993-1998. *Born* 26.02.66. *From* Burton. *Pro Career* 1989-2000 (40 contests, won 32, lost 8).

Frank Bruno Undefeated European Heavyweight Champion, 1985-1986. World Heavyweight Champion (WBC version), 1995-96. *Born* 16.11.61. *From* Wandsworth. *Pro Career* 1982-1996 (45 contests, won 40, lost 5).

Del Bryan British Welterweight Champion, 1991-1992 and 1993-1995. *Born* 16.04.1967. *From* Birmingham. *Pro Career* 1986-1998 (52 contests, won 32, drew 1, lost 19).

Ken Buchanan Undefeated British Lightweight Champion, 1968-1971, and 1973-1974. Undefeated European Lightweight Champion, 1974-1975. World Lightweight Champion, 1970-1971. World Lightweight Champion, (WBA version), 1971-1972. *Born* 28.06.45. *From* Edinburgh. *Pro Career* 1965-1982 (69 contests, won 61, lost 8).

Joe Bugner British, Commonwealth and European Heavyweight Champion, 1971. Undefeated European Heavyweight Champion, 1972-1975. European Heavyweight Champion, 1976-1977. Undefeated British and Commonwealth Heavyweight Champion, 1976-1977. *Born* Hungary, 13.03.50. *From* Bedford. *Pro Career* 1967-1999 (83 contests, won 69, drew 1, lost 13).

David Burke Undefeated Commonwealth Lightweight Champion, 2002. *Born* 03.02.75 *From* Liverpool. *Pro Career* 1997-2005 (28 contests, won 26, lost 2).

Paul Burke British and Commonwealth Lightweight Champion, 1993.

Commonwealth L. Welterweight Champion, 1997 and 1998-1999. *Born* 25.07.66. *From* Preston. *Pro Career* 1987-1999 (43 contests, won 28, drew 2, lost 13).

Alex Buxton British L. Heavyweight Champion, 1953-1955. *Born* 10.05.25. *From* Watford. *Pro Career* 1942-1963 (125 contests, won 78, drew 4, lost 43).

Jimmy Cable British L. Middleweight Champion, 1984-1985. European L. Middleweight Champion, 1984. *Born* 07.09.57. *From* Crawley. *Pro Career* 1980-1988 (41 contests, won 30, drew 2, lost 9).

Chic Calderwood British and British Empire L. Heavyweight Champion, 1960-1963. Undefeated British L. Heavyweight Champion, 1964-1966. *Born* 09.01.37. *From* Craigneuk. *Birthname* Charles Calderwood. *Deceased* 1966. *Pro Career* 1957-1966 (55 contests, won 44, drew 1, lost 9, no contest 1).

Johnny Caldwell Undefeated British Flyweight Champion, 1960-1961. British and British Empire Bantamweight Champion, 1964-1965. World Bantamweight Champion (EBU version), 1961-1962. *Born* 07.05.38. *From* Belfast. *Pro Career* 1958-1965 (35 contests, won 29, drew 1, lost 5).

Mickey Cantwell Undefeated British Flyweight Champion, 1996-1997. *Born* 23.11.64. *From* Eltham. *Pro Career* 1991-2001 (22 contests, won 14, drew 1, lost 7).

Brian Carr Commonwealth S.Bantamweight Champion, 2001-2002. *Born* 20.06.69. *From* Moodiesburn. *Pro Career* 1994-2003 (33 contests, won 25, drew 1, lost 7).

Cornelius Carr Undefeated British S. Middleweight Champion, 1994. *Born* 09.04.69. *From* Middlesbrough. *Pro Career* 1987-2001 (38 contests, won 34, lost 4).

Fidel Castro British S. Middleweight Champion, 1991-1992. *Born* 17.04.63. *From* Nottingham. *Birthname* Smith. *Pro Career* 1987-1995 (30 contests, won 22, lost 8).

Glenn Catley Undefeated British Middleweight Champion, 1998. World S. Middleweight Champion (WBC version), 2000. *Born* 15.03.72. *From* Bristol. *Pro Career* 1993-2003 (34 contests, won 27, lost 7).

Ray Cattouse British Lightweight Champion, 1980-1982. *Born* 24.07.52. *From* Balham. *Pro Career* 1975-1983 (31 contests, won 26, drew 3, lost 2).

Ralph Charles Undefeated British and British Empire/Commonwealth Welterweight Champion, 1968-1972. European Welterweight Champion, 1970-1971. *Born* 05.02.43. *From* West Ham. *Pro Career* 1963-1972 (43 contests, won 39, lost 4).

Dave Charnley Undefeated British Lightweight Champion, 1957-1965. British Empire Lightweight Champion, 1959-1962. European Lightweight Champion, 1960-1963. *Born* 10.10.35. *From* Dartford. *Pro Career* 1954-1964 (61 contests, won 48, drew 1, lost 12).

Lloyd Christie British L. Welterweight Champion, 1987-1989. *Born* 28.02.62. *From* Wolverhampton. *Pro Career* 1981-1989 (46 contests, won 24, drew 1, lost 21).

Johnny Clark Undefeated British and European Bantamweight Champion, 1973-1974. *Born* 10.09.47. *From* Walworth. *Pro Career* 1966-1974 (43 contests, won 39, drew 1, lost 3).

Ronnie Clayton British Featherweight Champion, 1947-1954. British Empire Featherweight Championship Claimant, 1947-1951. European Featherweight Champion, 1947-1948. *Born* 09.02.23. *From* Blackpool. *Deceased* 1999. *Pro Career* 1941-1954 (113 contests, won 79, drew 8, lost 26).

Pat Clinton Undefeated British Flyweight Champion, 1988-1991. Undefeated European Flyweight Champion, 1990-1991. World Flyweight Champion (WBO version), 1992-1993. *Born* 04.04.64. *From* Croy. *Pro Career* 1985-1991 (23 contests, won 20, lost 3).

Ray Close Undefeated European S. Middleweight Champion, 1993. *Born* 20.01.69. *From* Belfast. *Pro Career* 1988-1997 (29 contests, won 25, drew 1, lost 3).

Don Cockell British L. Heavyweight Champion, 1950-1952. Undefeated European L. Heavyweight Champion, 1951-1952. Undefeated British Heavyweight Champion, 1953-1956. British Empire Heavyweight Championship Claimant, 1953-1954. Undefeated British Empire Heavy-

weight Champion, 1954-1956. *Born* 22.09.28. *From* Battersea. *Deceased* 1983. *Pro Career* 1946-1956 (80 contests, won 65, drew 1, lost 14).

Steve Collins Undefeated World Middleweight Champion (WBO version), 1994-1995. Undefeated World S. Middleweight Champion (WBO version), 1995-1997. *Born* 21.07.64. *From* Dublin. *Pro Career* 1986-1997 (39 contests, won 36, lost 3).

Tom Collins British L. Heavyweight Champion, 1982-1984. Undefeated British L. Heavyweight Champion, 1987 and 1989-1990. European L. Heavyweight Champion, 1987-1988 and 1990-1991. *Born* Curacao, 01.07.55. *From* Leeds. *Pro Career* 1977-1993 (50 contests, won 26, drew 2, lost 22).

John Conteh Undefeated British, Commonwealth and European L. Heavyweight Champion, 1973-1974. World L. Heavyweight Champion (WBC version), 1974-1977. *Born* 27.05.51. *From* Liverpool. *Pro Career* 1971-1980 (39 contests, won 34, drew 1, lost 4).

James Cook Undefeated British S. Middleweight Champion, 1990-1991. British S. Middleweight Champion, 1993-1994. European S. Middleweight Champion, 1991-1992. *Born* Jamaica, 17.05.59. *From* Peckham. *Pro Career* 1982-1994 (35 contests, won 25, lost 10).

Johnny Cooke British and British Empire Welterweight Champion, 1967-1968. *Born* 17.12.34. *From* Bootle. *Pro Career* 1960-1971 (93 contests, won 52, drew 7, lost 34).

Gary Cooper British L. Middleweight Champion, 1988. *Born* 31.05.57. *From* Lymington. *Pro Career* 1978-1989 (27 contests, won 16, drew 2, lost 9).

Henry Cooper Undefeated British Heavyweight Champion, 1959-1969. British Heavyweight Champion, 1970-1971. British Empire/Commonwealth Heavyweight Champion, 1959-1971. Undefeated European Heavyweight Champion, 1964 and 1968-1969. European Heavyweight Champion, 1970-1971. *Born* 03.05.34. *From* Bellingham. *Pro Career* 1954-1971 (55 contests, won 40, drew 1, lost 14).

Darren Corbett Commonwealth Cruiserweight Champion, 1997-1998. *Born* 08.07.72. *From* Belfast. *Pro Career* 1994-2004 (31 contests, won 26, drew 1, lost 4).

Maurice Core Undefeated British L. Heavyweight Champion, 1992-1994. *Born* 22.06.65. *From* Manchester. *Birthname* Maurice Coore. *Pro Career* 1990-1996 (18 contests, won 15, drew 1, lost 2).

Pat Cowdell Undefeated British Featherweight Champion, 1979-1982. Undefeated European Featherweight Champion, 1982-1983. British S. Featherweight Champion, 1986 and 1987-1988. European S. Featherweight Champion, 1984-1985. *Born* 18.08.53. *From* Warley. *Pro Career* 1977-1988 (42 contests, won 36, lost 6).

Carl Crook British and Commonwealth Lightweight Champion, 1990-1992. *Born* 10.11.63. *From* Chorley. *Pro Career* 1985-1993 (31 contests, won 26, drew 1, lost 4).

Maurice Cullen British Lightweight Champion, 1965-1968. *Born* 30.12.37. *From* Shotton. *Deceased* 2001. *Pro Career* 1959-1970 (55 contests, won 45, drew 2, lost 8).

Peter Culshaw Commonwealth Flyweight Champion, 1996-1997. *Born* 15.05.73. *From* Liverpool. *Pro Career* (27 contests, won 24, drew 1, lost 2).

Hughroy Currie British Heavyweight Champion, 1985-1986. *Born* Jamaica, 09.02.59. *From* Catford. *Pro Career* 1981-1989 (29 contests, won 17, drew 1, lost 11).

Brian Curvis Undefeated British and British Empire Welterweight Champion, 1960-1966. *Born* 14.08.37. *From* Swansea. *Birthname* Brian Nancurvis. *Pro Career* 1959-1966 (41 contests, won 37, lost 4).

Cliff Curvis Undefeated British Welterweight Champion, 1952-1953. British Empire Welterweight Championship Claimant, 1952. *Born* 02.11.27. *From* Swansea. *Birthname* Cliff Nancurvis. *Pro Career* 1944-1953 (55 contests, won 42, drew 1, lost 12).

Najib Daho British S. Featherweight Champion, 1986-1987. Commonwealth Lightweight Champion, 1989-1990. *Born* Morocco, 13.01.59. *From* Manchester. *Deceased* 1993. *Pro Career* 1977-1991 (60 contests, won 34, drew 1, lost 25).

John Davison Undefeated British Featherweight Champion, 1992-1993.

Born 30.09.58. *From* Newcastle. *Pro Career* 1988-1993 (20 contests, won 15, lost 5).

Gary DeRoux British Featherweight Champion, 1991. *Born* 04.11.62. *From* Peterborough. *Pro Career* 1986-1993 (22 contests, won 13, drew 1, lost 8).

Mike Deveney British Featherweight Champion, 1995. *Born* 14.12.65. *From* Paisley. *Pro Career* 1991-1998 (42 contests, won 22, drew 1, lost 19).

Harry Dhami British Welterweight Champion, 2000-2001. *Born* 17.04.72. *From* Gravesend. *Pro Career* 1993-2003 (23 contests, won 17, drew 1, lost 5).

Robert Dickie British Featherweight Champion, 1986-1988. British S. Featherweight Champion, 1991. *Born* 23.06.64. *From* Swansea. *Pro Career* 1983-1993 (28 contests, won 22, drew 2, lost 4).

Alex Dickson British Lightweight Champion, 1987-1988. *Born* 01.10.62. *From* Larkhall. *Pro Career* 1985-1989 (22 contests, won 18, drew 1, lost 3).

Scott Dixon Undefeated Commonwealth Welterweight Champion, 2000. *Born* 28.09.76. *From* Hamilton. *Pro Career* 1995-2004 (40 contests, won 27, drew 3, lost 10).

Drew Docherty Undefeated British S. Bantamweight Champion, 1999. British Bantamweight Champion, 1992-1997. *Born* 29.11.65. *From* Condorrat. *Pro Career* 1989-2000 (24 contests, won 16, drew 1, lost 7).

John Doherty British S. Featherweight Champion, 1986, 1989-1990, and 1991-1992. *Born* 17.07.62. *From* Bradford. *Pro Career* 1982-1992 (39 contests, won 28, drew 3, lost 8).

Pat Doherty Commonwealth Lightweight Champion, 1989. *Born* 12.04.62. *From* Croydon. *Pro Career* 1981-1989 (32 contests, won 18, drew 3, lost 11).

Dai Dower Undefeated British Flyweight Champion, 1955-1957. Undefeated British Empire Flyweight Champion, 1954-1957. European Flyweight Champion, 1955. *Born* 26.06.33. *From* Abercynon. *Pro Career* 1953-1958 (37 contests, won 34, lost 3).

Terry Downes British Middleweight Champion, 1958-1959 and 1959-1962. World Middleweight Champion (NY/EBU version), 1961-1962. *Born* 09.05.36. *From* Paddington. *Pro Career* 1957-1964 (44 contests, won 35, lost 9).

Richard Dunn British and Commonwealth Heavyweight Champion, 1975-1976. European Heavyweight Champion, 1976. *Born* 19.01.45. *From* Bradford. *Pro Career* 1969-1977 (45 contests, won 33, lost 12).

Terry Dunstan Undefeated British Cruiserweight Champion, 1995-1996. Undefeated European Cruiserweight Champion, 1998. *Born* 21.10.68. *From* Vauxhall. *Pro Career* 1992-1999 (21 contests, won 19, lost 2).

Tony Ekubia British L. Welterweight Champion, 1990-1991. Commonwealth L. Welterweight Champion, 1989-1991. *Born* 06.03.60. *From* Manchester. *Pro Career* 1986-1993 (25 contests, won 21, lost 4).

Joe Erskine British Heavyweight Champion, 1956-1958. British Empire Heavyweight Champion, 1957-1958. *Born* 26.01.34. *From* Cardiff. *Deceased* 1990. *Pro Career* 1954-1964 (54 contests, won 45, drew 1, lost 8).

Chris Eubank Undefeated WBO Middleweight Champion, 1990-1991. WBO S. Middleweight Title, 1991-1995. *Born* 08.08.1966. *From* Brighton. *Pro Career* 1985-1998 (52 contests, won 45, drew 2, lost 5).

George Feeney Undefeated British Lightweight Champion, 1982-1985. *Born* 09.02.57. *From* West Hartlepool. *Pro Career* 1977-1984 (29 contests, won 19, lost 10).

John Feeney British Bantamweight Champion, 1981-1983 and 1983-1985. *Born* 15.05.58. *From* West Hartlepool. *Pro Career* 1977-1987 (48 contests, won 35, lost 13).

Gordon Ferris British Heavyweight Champion, 1981. *Born* 21.11.52. *From* Enniskillen. *Pro Career* 1977-1982 (26 contests, won 20, lost 6).

Darren Fifield Commonwealth Flyweight Champion, 1993-1994. *Born* 09.10.69. *From* Henley. *Pro Career* 1992-1996 (13 contests, won 7, drew 2, lost 4).

Albert Finch British Middleweight Champion, 1950. *Born* 16.05.26. *From* Croydon. *Deceased* 2003. *Pro Career* 1945-1958 (103 contests, won 72, drew 9, lost 21, no contest 1).

Chris Finnegan British L. Heavyweight Champion, 1971-1973. Undefeated British L. Heavyweight Champion, 1975-1976. Commonwealth L. Heavyweight Champion, 1971-1973. European L. Heavyweight Champion, 1972. *Born* 05.06.44. *From* Iver. *Pro Career* 1968-1975 (37 contests, won 29, drew 1, lost 7).

Kevin Finnegan British Middleweight Champion, 1977. Undefeated British Middleweight Champion, 1974 and 1979-1980. European Middleweight Champion, 1974-1975 and 1980. *Born* 18.04.48. *From* Iver. *Pro Career* 1970-1980 (47 contests, won 35, drew 1, lost 11).

Ali Forbes British S. Middleweight Champion, 1995. *Born* 07.03.61. *From* Sydenham. *Pro Career* 1989-2002 (25 contests, won 14, drew 1, lost 10).

Hugh Forde British S. Featherweight Champion, 1990. Commonwealth S. Featherweight Champion, 1991. *Born* 07.05.64. *From* Birmingham. *Pro Career* 1986-1995 (31 contests, won 24, lost 7).

Steve Foster Commonwealth L. Middleweight Champion, 1996-1997. *Born* 28.12.60. *From* Salford. *Pro Career* 1981-1999 (39 contests, won 20, drew 2, lost 17).

Johnny Frankham British L. Heavyweight Champion, 1975. *Born* 06.06.48. *From* Reading. *Pro Career* 1970-1976 (40 contests, won 28, drew 1, lost 11).

P.J. Gallagher British S. Featherweight Champion, 1996-1997. *Born* 14.02.73. *From* Wood Green. *Pro Career* 1993-2000 (20 contests, won 19, lost 1).

Jack Gardner British Heavyweight Champion, 1950-1952. British Empire Heavyweight Championship Claimant, 1950-1952. European Heavyweight Champion, 1951. *Born* 06.11.26. *From* Market Harborough. *Deceased* 1978. *Pro Career* 1948-1956 (34 contests, won 28, lost 6).

John L. Gardner Undefeated British Heavyweight Champion, 1978-1980. Undefeated Commonwealth Heavyweight Champion, 1978-1981. Undefeated European Heavyweight Champion, 1980-1981. *Born* 19.03.53. *From* Hackney. *Pro Career* 1973-1983 (39 contests, won 35, lost 4).

Teddy Gardner Undefeated British and European Flyweight Champion, 1952. British Empire Flyweight Championship Claimant, 1952. *Born* 27.01.22. *From* West Hartlepool. *Deceased* 1977. *Pro Career* 1938-1952 (66 contests, won 55, drew 3, lost 8).

Sugar Gibiliru British S. Featherweight Champion, 1991. *Born* 13.07.66. *From* Liverpool. *Pro Career* 1984-1995 (55 contests, won 16, drew 7, lost 32).

Ray Gilbody British Bantamweight Champion, 1985-1987. *Born* 21.03.60. *From* Warrington. *Pro Career* 1983-1987 (16 contests, won 11, drew 1, lost 4).

Freddie Gilroy Undefeated British and British Empire Bantamweight Champion, 1959-1963. European Bantamweight Champion, 1959-1960. *Born* 07.03.36. *From* Belfast. *Pro Career* 1957-1962 (31 contests, won 28, lost 3).

Tommy Glencross British Featherweight Champion, 1972-1973. *Born* 31.07.47. *From* Glasgow. *Pro Career* 1967-1978 (48 contests, won 31, drew 1, lost 16).

Herol Graham Undefeated British L. Middleweight Champion, 1981-1983. Undefeated Commonwealth L. Middleweight Champion, 1981-1984. Undefeated European L. Middleweight Champion, 1983-1984. Undefeated British Middleweight Champion, 1985-1986. British Middleweight Champion, 1988-1992. European Middleweight Champion, 1986-1987. *Born* 13.09.59. *From* Sheffield. *Pro Career* 1978-1998 (54 contests, won 48, lost 6).

Frank Grant British Middleweight Champion, 1992-1993. *Born* 22.05.65. *From* Bradford. *Pro Career* 1986-1993 (26 contests, won 22, lost 4).

Dave Boy Green Undefeated British and European L. Welterweight Champion, 1976-1977. European Welterweight Champion, 1979. *Born* 02.06.53. *From* Chatteris. *Pro Career* 1974-1981 (41 contests, won 37, lost 4).

Roy Gumbs British Middleweight Champion, 1981-1983. Commonwealth Middleweight Champion, 1983. *Born* St Kitts, 05.09.54. *From* Tottenham. *Pro Career* 1976-1985 (40 contests, won 26, drew 3, lost 11).

Neil Haddock British S. Featherweight Champion, 1992-1994. *Born*

22.06.64. *From* Llanelli. *Pro Career* 1987-1994 (26 contests, won 14, drew 1, lost 11).

Ross Hale British and Commonwealth L. Welterweight Champion, 1994-1995. *Born* 28.02.1967. *From* Bristol. *Pro Career* 1989-1998 (33 contests, won 29, lost 4).

Henry Hall British Welterweight Champion, 1948-1949. *Born* 06.09.22. *From* Sheffield. *Deceased* 1979. *Pro Career* 1945-1952 (66 contests, won 43, drew 3, lost 20).

Prince Naseem Hamed Undefeated European Bantamweight Champion, 1994-1995. Undefeated WBO Featherweight Champion, 1997-2000. Undefeated IBF Featherweight Champion, 1997. WBC Featherweight Champion, 1999-2000. *Born* 12.02.74. *From* Sheffield. *Pro Career* 1992-2002 (37 contests, won 36, lost 1).

Billy Hardy Undefeated British Bantamweight Champion, 1987-1991. Undefeated British Featherweight Champion, 1994. Undefeated Commonwealth Featherweight Champion, 1992-1996. European Featherweight Champion, 1995-1998. *Born* 05.09.1964. *From* Sunderland. *Pro Career* 1983-1998 (48 contests, won 37, drew 2, lost 9).

Peter Harris British Featherweight Champion, 1988. *Born* 23.08.62. *From* Swansea. *Pro Career* 1983-1996 (33 contests, won 16, drew 2, lost 15).

Paul Harvey Commonwealth S. Featherweight Champion, 1991-1992. *Born* 10.11.64. *From* Ilford. *Pro Career* 1989-1994 (22 contests, won 16, drew 1, lost 5).

Floyd Havard British S. Featherweight Champion, 1988-1989. Undefeated British S. Featherweight Champion, 1994-1995. *Born* 16.10.65. *From* Swansea. *Pro Career* 1985-1996 (36 contests, won 34, lost 2).

Vince Hawkins British Middleweight Champion, 1946-1948. *Born* 15.04.23. *From* Eastleigh. *Pro Career* 1940-1950 (86 contests, won 75, drew 1, lost 10).

Lloyd Hibbert Undefeated British L. Middleweight Champion, 1987. Commonwealth L. Middleweight Champion, 1987. *Born* 29.06.59. *From* Birmingham. *Pro Career* 1979-1987 (23 contests, won 19, lost 4).

Herbie Hide Undefeated British Heavyweight Champion, 1993-1994. World Heavyweight Champion (WBO version), 1997-1999. *Born* Nigeria 27.08.71. *From* Norwich. *Pro Career* 1989-2004 (39 contests, won 35, lost 4).

Charlie Hill British Featherweight Champion, 1956-1959. *Born* 20.06.30. *From* Cambuslang. *Pro Career* 1953-1959 (36 contests, won 31, lost 5).

Paul Hodkinson Undefeated British Featherweight Champion, 1988-1990. Undefeated European Featherweight Champion, 1989-1991. World Featherweight Champion, 1991-1993 (WBC version). *Born* 14.09.65. *From* Liverpool. *Pro Career* 1986-1994 (26 contests, won 22, drew 1, lost 3).

Mike Holden Undefeated British Heavyweight Champion, 2000. *Born* 13.03.68. *From* Manchester. *Pro Career* 1994-2003 (19 contests, won 10, lost 9).

Andy Holligan British and Commonwealth L. Welterweight Champion, 1991-1994 and 1996-1997. *Born* 06.06.67. *From* Liverpool. *Pro Career* 1987-1998 (30 contests, won 27, lost 3).

Lloyd Honeyghan Undefeated British Welterweight Champion, 1983-1985 and 1985-1986. Undefeated Commonwealth & European Champion, 1985-1986. World Welterweight Champion, 1986. World Welterweight Champion (WBC version), 1986-1987 and 1988-1989. World Welterweight Champion (IBF version), 1986-1987. Commonwealth L. Middleweight Champion, 1993-1994. *Born* 22.04.60, Jamaica. *From* Bermondsey. *Pro Career* 1980-1995 (48 contests, won 43, lost 5).

Maurice Hope Undefeated British L. Middleweight Champion, 1974-1977. Undefeated Commonwealth L. Middleweight Champion, 1976-1979. Undefeated European L. Middleweight Champion, 1976-1978. World L. Middleweight Champion (WBC version), 1979-1981. *Born* Antigua, 06.12.51. *From* Hackney. *Pro Career* 1973-1982 (35 contests, won 30, drew 1, lost 4).

Mickey Hughes Commonwealth L. Middleweight Champion, 1992-1993. *Born* 13.06.62. *From* St Pancras. *Pro Career* 1985-1993 (31 contests, won 24, lost 7).

Mo Hussein Commonwealth Lightweight Champion, 1987-1989. *Born*

17.11.62. *From* West Ham. *Pro Career* 1982-1989 (27 contests, won 23, lost 4).

Paul Ingle World Featherweight Champion (IBF Version), 1999-2000. Undefeated British Featherweight Champion, 1997-1998. Undefeated Commonwealth and European Champion, 1997-1999. *Born* 22.06.72. *From* Scarborough. *Pro Career* (25 contests, won 23, lost 2).

Jonjo Irwin British Featherweight Champion, 1995-1996. Undefeated British Featherweight Champion, 1998-1999. Commonwealth Featherweight Champion, 1996-1997. *Born* 31.05.69. *From* Doncaster. *Pro Career* 1992-1999 (24 contests, won 19, lost 5).

Gary Jacobs Undefeated British Welterweight Champion, 1992-1993. Commonwealth Welterweight Champion, 1988-1989. European Welterweight Champion, 1993-1994. *Born* 10.12.65. *From* Glasgow. *Pro Career* 1985-1997 (53 contests, won 45, lost 8).

Joey Jacobs British S. Featherweight Champion, 1990. *Born* 01.10.60. *From* Manchester. *Pro Career* 1986-1991 (15 contests, won 10, lost 5).

Ronnie James Undefeated British Lightweight Champion, 1944-1947. *Born* 08.10.17. *From* Swansea. *Deceased* 1977. *Pro Career* 1933-1947 (119 contests, won 98, drew 5, lost 16).

Tee Jay British Cruiserweight Champion, 1987-1988. *Born* Ghana, 21.01.62. *Birthname* Taju Akay. *From* Notting Hill. *Deceased* 2006. *Pro Career* 1985-1991 (19 contests, won 14, drew 1, lost 4).

Bunny Johnson British and Commonwealth Heavyweight Champion, 1975. Undefeated British L. Heavyweight Champion, 1977-1981. *Born* Jamaica, 10.05.47. *From* Birmingham. *Birthname* Fitzroy Johnson. *Pro Career* 1968-1981 (73 contests, won 55, drew 1, lost 17).

Frank Johnson British Lightweight Champion, 1952-1953 and 1955-1956. British Empire Lightweight Championship Claimant, 1953. *Born* 27.11.28. *From* Manchester. *Birthname* Frank Williamson. *Deceased* 1970. *Pro Career* 1946-1957 (58 contests, won 47, lost 11).

Barry Jones Undefeated WBO S. Featherweight Champion, 1997-1998. *Born* 03.05.74. *From* Cardiff. *Pro Career* 1992-2000 (20 contests, won 18, drew 1, lost 1).

Colin Jones Undefeated British Welterweight Champion, 1980-1982. Undefeated Commonwealth Welterweight Champion, 1981-1984. Undefeated European Welterweight Champion, 1982-1983. *Born* 21.03.59. *From* Gorseinon. *Pro Career* 1977-1985 (30 contests, won 26, drew 1, lost 3).

Frankie Jones British Flyweight Champion, 1957-1960. British Empire Flyweight Champion, 1957. *Born* 12.02.33. *From* Plean. *Deceased* 1991. *Pro Career* 1955-1960 (25 contests, won 17, lost 8).

Paul Jones Commonwealth Middleweight Champion, 1998-1999. *Born* 19.11.66. *From* Sheffield. *Pro Career* 1986-2002 (44 contests, won 31, drew 1, lost 12).

Peter Kane Undefeated World Flyweight Champion, 1938-1939. European Bantamweight Champion, 1947-1948. *Born* 28.04.18. *From* Golborne. *Birthname* Peter Cain. *Deceased* 1991. *Pro Career* 1934-1948 (102 contests, won 92, drew 2, lost 7, no contest 1).

Mark Kaylor British and Commonwealth Middleweight Champion, 1983-1984. *Born* 11.05.61. *From* West Ham. *Pro Career* 1980-1991 (48 contests, won 40, drew 1, lost 7).

Peter Keenan British Bantamweight Champion, 1951-1953 and 1954-1959. British Empire Bantamweight Champion, 1955-1959. European Bantamweight Champion, 1951-1952 and 1953. *Born* 08.08.28. *From* Glasgow. *Deceased* 2000. *Pro Career* 1948-1959 (66 contests, won 54, drew 1, lost 11).

Billy Spider Kelly British Featherweight Champion, 1955-1956. British Empire Featherweight Championship Claimant, 1954. British Empire Featherweight Champion, 1954-1955. *Born* 21.04.32. *From* Londonderry. *Pro Career* 1950-1962 (83 contests, won 56, drew 4, lost 23).

Joe Kelly British Bantamweight Champion, 1992. *Born* 18.05.64. *From* Glasgow. *Pro Career* 1985-1992 (27 contests, won 18, drew 2, lost 7).

John Kelly British and European Bantamweight Champion, 1953-1954. *Born* 17.01.32. *From* Belfast. *Pro Career* 1951-1957 (28 contests, won 24, lost 4).

Jawaid Khaliq Undefeated Commonwealth Welterweight Champion, 2000-2001. *Born* 30.07.70. *From* Nottingham. *Pro Career* 1997-2004 (25 contests, won 23, drew 1, lost 1).

Johnny King British Bantamweight Champion, 1932-1934 and 1935-1947. British Empire Bantamweight Championship Claimant, 1932-1934. *Born* 08.01.12. *From* Manchester. *Deceased* 1963. *Pro Career* 1926-1947 (222 contests, won 158, drew 15, lost 48, no contest 1).

Keith Knox British and Commonwealth Flyweight Champion, 1999. *Born* 20.06.67. *From* Bonnyrigg. *Pro Career* 1994-2001 (23 contests, won 13, drew 2, lost 8).

Kirkland Laing British Welterweight Champion, 1987-1991. European Welterweight Champion, 1990. *Born* 20.06.54, Jamaica. *From* Nottingham. *Pro Career* 1975-1994 (56 contests, won 43, drew 1, lost 12).

Tony Laing Undefeated British L. Welterweight Champion, 1986. Commonwealth L. Welterweight Champion, 1987-1988. *Born* 22.09.57. *From* Nottingham. *Pro Career* 1977-1988 (18 contests, won 13, drew 1, lost 4).

Davy Larmour British Bantamweight Champion, 1983. *Born* 02.04.52. *From* Belfast. *Pro Career* 1977-1983 (18 contests, won 11, lost 7).

Mick Leahy British Middleweight Champion, 1963-1964. *Born* Cork, 12.03.35. *From* Coventry. *Pro Career* 1956-1965 (72 contests, won 46, drew 7, lost 19).

Ady Lewis Undefeated British and Commonwealth Flyweight Champion, 1997-1998. British and Commonwealth Bantamweight Champion, 2000. *Born* 31.05.75. *From* Bury. *Pro Career* 1994-2001 (25 contests, won 19, drew 1, lost 5).

Lennox Lewis Undefeated British Heavyweight Champion, 1991-1993. Undefeated Commonwealth Heavyweight Champion, 1992-1993. Undefeated European Heavyweight Champion, 1990-1992. World Heavyweight Champion (WBC version), 1992-1994 and 1997-2001. Undefeated World Heavyweight Champion (IBF version), 2001-2002. Undefeated World Heavyweight Champion (WBA version), 1999-2000. Undefeated World Heavyweight Champion (WBC version), 2001-2004. *Born* 02.09.65. *From* London. *Pro Career* 1989-2004 (44 contests, won 41, drew 1, lost 2).

Stewart Lithgo Commonwealth Cruiserweight Champion, 1984. *Born* 02.06.57. *From* West Hartlepool. *Pro Career* 1977-1987 (30 contests, won 16, drew 2, lost 12).

Paul Lloyd British Bantamweight Champion, 1997-1999. Undefeated Commonwealth Bantamweight Champion, 1996-2000. Undefeated European Bantamweight Champion, 1998-1999. *Born* 07.12.68. *From* Ellesmere Port. *Pro Career* 1992-2000 (27 contests, won 20, lost 7).

Brian London British and British Empire Heavyweight Champion, 1958-1959. *Born* 19.06.34. *From* Blackpool. *Birthname* Brian Harper. *Pro Career* 1955-1970 (58 contests, won 37, drew 1, lost 20).

Jack London British Heavyweight Champion, 1944-1945. British Empire Heavyweight Championship Claimant, 1944-1945. *Born* 23.06.13. *From* West Hartlepool. *Birthname* Jack Harper. *Deceased* 1964. *Pro Career* 1931-1949 (141 contests, won 95, drew 5, lost 39, no contests 2).

Eamonn Loughran Undefeated Commonwealth Welterweight Champion, 1992-1993. WBO Welterweight Champion, 1993-1996. *Born* 05.06.70. *Fron* Ballymena. *Pro Career* 1987-1996 (30 contests, won 26, drew 1, lost 2, no contest 1).

Joe Lucy British Lightweight Champion, 1953-1955 and 1956-1957. *Born* 09.02.30. *From* Mile End. *Deceased* 1991. *Pro Career* 1950-1957 (37 contests, won 27, lost 10).

Kevin Lueshing British Welterweight Champion, 1996-1997. *Born* 17.04.1968. *From* Beckenham. *Pro Career* 1991-1999 (25 contests, won 21, lost 4).

Danny McAlinden British and Commonwealth Heavyweight Champion, 1972-1975. *Born* Newry, 01.06.47. *From* Coventry. *Pro Career* 1969-1981 (45 contests, won 31, drew 2, lost 12).

Les McAteer British and British Empire Middleweight Champion, 1969-1970. *Born* 19.08.45. *From* Birkenhead. *Pro Career* 1965-1979 (39 contests, won 27, drew 2, lost 10).

Pat McAteer Undefeated British Middleweight Champion, 1955-1958. British Empire Middleweight Champion, 1955-1958. *Born* 17.03.32. *From* Birkenhead. *Pro Career* 1952-1958 (57 contests, won 49, drew 2, lost 6).

Dave McAuley Undefeated British Flyweight Champion, 1986-1988. World Flyweight Champion (IBF version), 1989-1992. *Born* 15.06.61. *From* Larne. *Pro Career* 1983-1992 (23 contests, won 18, drew 2, lost 3).

Sammy McCarthy British Featherweight Champion, 1954-1955. *Born* 05.11.31. *From* Stepney. *Pro Career* 1951-1957 (53 contests, won 44, drew 1, lost 8).

Steve McCarthy British L. Heavyweight Champion, 1990-1991. *Born* 30.07.62. *From* Southampton. *Pro Career* 1987-1994 (17 contests, won 12, drew 1, lost 4).

John McCluskey Undefeated British Flyweight Champion, 1967-1977. Commonwealth Flyweight Champion, 1970-1971. *Born* 23.01.44. *From* Hamilton. *Pro Career* 1965-1975 (38 contests, won 23, lost 15).

John Cowboy McCormack British Middleweight Champion, 1959. European Middleweight Champion, 1961-1962. *Born* 09.01.35. *From* Maryhill. *Pro Career* 1957-1966 (45 contests, won 38, lost 7).

Young John McCormack British L. Heavyweight Champion, 1967-1969. *Born* Dublin, 11.12.44. *From* Brixton. *Pro Career* 1963-1970 (42 contests, won 33, drew 1, lost 8).

Pat McCormack British L. Welterweight Champion, 1974. *Born* Dublin, 28.04.46. *From* Brixton. *Pro Career* 1968-1975 (49 contests, won 30, drew 1, lost 18).

Robert McCracken Undefeated British L. Middleweight Champion, 1994-1995. Commonwealth Middleweight Champion, 1995-1997. *Born* 31.05.68. *From* Birmingham. *Pro Career* 1991-2001 (35 contests, won 33, lost 2).

Geoff McCreesh Undefeated British Welterweight Champion, 1997-1999. *Born* 12.06.70. *From* Bracknell. *Pro Career* 1994-2001 (30 contests, won 23, lost 7).

Glenn McCrory Undefeated British Cruiserweight Champion, 1988. Undefeated Commonwealth Cruiserweight Champion, 1987-1989. World Cruiserweight Champion (IBF version), 1989-1990. *Born* 23.09.64. *From* Annfield Plain. *Pro Career* 1984-1993 (39 contests, won 30, drew 1, lost 8).

Jim McDonnell Undefeated European Featherweight Champion, 1985-1987. *Born* 12.09.60. *From* Camden Town. *Pro Career* 1983-1998 (30 contests, won 26, lost 4).

Tommy McGovern British Lightweight Champion, 1951-1952. *Born* 05.02.24. *From* Bermondsey. *Deceased* 1989. *Pro Career* 1947-1953 (66 contests, won 45, drew 4, lost 17).

Walter McGowan Undefeated British Flyweight Champion, 1963-1966. Undefeated British Empire Flyweight Champion, 1963-1969. World Flyweight Champion (WBC version), 1966. British and British Empire Bantamweight Champion, 1966-1968. *Born* 13.10.42. *From* Hamilton. *Pro Career* 1961-1969 (40 contests, won 32, drew 1, lost 7).

Barry McGuigan Undefeated British Featherweight Champion, 1983-1986. Undefeated European Featherweight Champion, 1983-1985. World Featherweight Champion (WBA version), 1985-1986. *Born* 28.02.61. *From* Clones. *Pro Career* 1981-1989 (35 contests, won 32, lost 3).

Clinton McKenzie British L. Welterweight Champion, 1978-1979 and 1979-1984. Undefeated British L. Welterweight Champion, 1989. European L. Welterweight Champion, 1981-1982. *Born* 15.09.55. *From* Croydon. *Pro Career* 1976-1989 (50 contests, won 36, lost 14).

Duke McKenzie Undefeated British Flyweight Champion, 1985-1986. Undefeated European Flyweight Champion, 1986-1988. World Flyweight Champion (IBF version), 1988-1989. World Bantamweight Champion (WBO version), 1991-1992. World S. Bantamweight Champion (WBO version), 1992-1993. Undefeated British S. Featherweight Champion, 1993-1994. *Born* 05.05.63. *From* Croydon. *Pro Career* 1982-1998 (46 contests, won 39, lost 7).

Tony McKenzie British L. Welterweight Champion, 1986-1987. *Born* 04.03.63. *From* Leicester. *Pro Career* 1983-1993 (34 contests, won 26, drew 1, lost 7).

Ian McLeod Undefeated Commonwealth S. Featherweight Champion, 2000. *Born* 11.06.69. *From* Kilmarnock. *Pro Career* 1992-2000 (14 contests, won 11, drew 1, lost 2).

Colin McMillan Undefeated British Featherweight Champion, 1991-1992. British Featherweight Champion, 1996-1997. Undefeated Commonwealth Featherweight Champion, 1992. World Featherweight Champion (WBO version), 1992. *Born* 12.02.66. *From* Barking. *Pro Career* 1988-1997 (35 contests, won 31, lost 4).

Noel Magee Commonwealth L. Heavyweight Champion, 1995. *Born* 16.12.65. *From* Belfast. *Pro Career* 1985-1997 (37 contests, won 27, drew 2, lost 8).

Charlie Magri Undefeated British Flyweight Champion, 1977-1981. Undefeated European Flyweight Champion, 1979-1983 and 1984-1985. European Flyweight Champion, 1985-1986. World Flyweight Champion (WBC version), 1983. *Born* Tunisia, 20.07.56. *From* Stepney. *Pro Career* 1977-1986 (35 contests, won 30, lost 5).

Paddy Maguire British Bantamweight Champion, 1975-1977. *Born* 26.09.48. *From* Belfast. *Pro Career* 1969-1977 (35 contests, won 26, drew 1, lost 8).

Terry Marsh Undefeated British L. Welterweight Champion, 1984-1986. European L. Welterweight Champion, 1985-1986. Undefeated World L. Welterweight Champion (IBF version), 1987. *Born* 07.02.58. *From* Basildon. *Pro Career* 1981-1987 (27 contests, won 26, drew 1).

Gary Mason British Heavyweight Champion, 1989-1991. *Born* Jamaica, 15.12.62. *From* Wandsworth. *Pro Career* 1984-1991 (36 contests, won 35, lost 1).

Jason Matthews Undefeated Commonwealth Middleweight Champion, 1999. WBO Middleweight Champion, 1999. *Born* 20.07.70. *From* Hackney. *Pro Career* 1995-1999 (23 contests, won 21, lost 2).

Neville Meade British Heavyweight Champion, 1981-1983. *Born* Jamaica, 12.09.48. *From* Swansea. *Pro Career* 1974-1983 (34 contests, won 20, drew 1, lost 13).

Freddie Mills Undefeated British L. Heavyweight Champion, 1942-1950. British Empire L. Heavyweight Championship Claimant, 1942-1950. Undefeated European L. Heavyweight Champion, 1947-1950. World L. Heavyweight Champion (GB version), 1942-1946. World L. Heavyweight Champion, 1948-1950. *Born* 26.06.19. *From* Bournemouth. *Deceased* 1965. *Pro Career* 1936-1950 (101 contests, won 77, drew 6, lost 18).

Alan Minter British Middleweight Champion, 1975-1977. Undefeated British Middleweight Champion, 1977-1978. European Middleweight Champion, 1977. Undefeated European Middleweight Champion, 1978-1979. World Middleweight Champion, 1980. *Born* 17.08.51. *From* Crawley. *Pro Career* 1972-1981 (49 contests, won 39, lost 9, no contest 1).

Sylvester Mittee British Welterweight Champion, 1985. Commonwealth Welterweight Champion, 1984-1985. *Born* St Lucia, 29.10.56. *From* Bethnal Green. *Pro Career* 1977-1988 (33 contests, won 28, lost 5).

Tommy Molloy British Welterweight Champion, 1958-1960. *Born* 02.02.34. *From* Birkenhead. *Pro Career* 1955-1963 (43 contests, won 34, drew 2, lost 6, no contest 1).

Rinty Monaghan Undefeated British and World Flyweight Champion, 1948-1950. British Empire Flyweight Championship Claimant, 1948-1950. Undefeated European Flyweight Champion, 1949-1950. World Flyweight Champion (NBA version), 1947-1948. *Born* 21.08.20. *From* Belfast. *Birthname* John Monaghan. *Deceased* 1984. *Pro Career* 1934-1949 (66 contests, won 51, drew 6, lost 9).

Alex Moon Commonwealth S. Featherweight Champion, 2001-2002. *Born* 17.11.71. *From* Liverpool. *Pro Career* 1995-2003 (27 contests, won 19, drew 2, lost 6).

Des Morrison British L. Welterweight Champion, 1973-1974. *Born* Jamaica, 01.02.50. *From* Bedford. *Pro Career* 1970-1982 (50 contests, won 36, drew 2, lost 12).

Patrick Mullings British S. Bantamweight Champion, 1999 and 2001. Commonwealth Featherweight Champion, 1999-2000. *Born* 19.10.70. *From* Harlesden. *Pro Career* 1994-2001 (30 contests, won 24, lost 6).

Sean Murphy British Featherweight Champion, 1990-1991 and 1993. *Born* 01.12.64. *From* St Albans. *Pro Career* 1986-1994 (27 contests, won 22, lost 5).

Charlie Nash Undefeated British Lightweight Champion, 1978-1979.

Undefeated European Lightweight Champion, 1979-1980. European Lightweight Champion, 1980-1981. *Born* 10.05.51. *From* Derry. *Pro Career* 1975-1983 (30 contests, won 25, lost 5).

Dave Needham British Bantamweight Champion, 1974-1975. British Featherweight Champion, 1978-1979. *Born* 15.08.51. *From* Nottingham. *Pro Career* 1971-1980 (39 contests, won 30, drew 1, lost 8).

Bobby Neill British Featherweight Champion, 1959-1960. *Born* 10.10.33. *From* Edinburgh. *Pro Career* 1955-1960 (35 contests, won 28, lost 7).

Horace Notice Undefeated British and Commonwealth Heavyweight Champion, 1986-1988. *Born* 07.08.57. *From* Birmingham. *Pro Career* 1983-1988 (16 contests, won 16).

Peter Oboh* Undefeated British L.Heavyweight Champion, 2003-2005. Undefeated Commonwealth L.Heavyweight Champion, 2002-2005. *Born* Nigeria 06.09.68. *From* Brockley. *Pro Career* 1993-2004 (19 contests, won 14, lost 5).

John O'Brien British Empire Featherweight Champion, 1967. *Born* 20.02.37. *From* Glasgow. *Deceased* 1979. *Pro Career* 1956-1971 (47 contests, won 30, lost 17).

Chris Okoh Commonwealth Cruiserweight Champion, 1995-1997. *Born* 18.04.69. *From* Croydon. *Pro Career* 1993-1999 (16 contests, won 14, lost 2).

Spencer Oliver European S. Bantamweight Champion, 1997-1998. *Born* 27.03.75. *From* Barnet. *Pro Career* 1995-1998 (15 contests, won 14, lost 1).

Danny O'Sullivan British Bantamweight Champion, 1949-1951. *Born* 06.01.23. *From* Finsbury Park. *Deceased* 1990. *Pro Career* 1947-1951 (43 contests, won 33, drew 1, lost 10).

Johnny Owen Undefeated British Bantamweight Champion, 1977-1980. Undefeated Commonwealth Bantamweight Champion, 1978-1980. Undefeated European Bantamweight Champion, 1980. *Born* 07.01.56. *From* Merthyr. *Deceased* 1980. *Pro Career* 1976-1980 (28 contests, won 25, drew 1, lost 2).

James Oyebola British Heavyweight Champion, 1994-1995. *Born* Nigeria 10.06.61. *From* Paddington. *Pro Career* 1987-1996 (23 contests, won 18, drew 1, lost 4).

Jackie Paterson British Flyweight Champion, 1939-1948. British Empire Flyweight Champion, 1940-1948. World Flyweight Champion, 1943-1947. World Flyweight Champion (GB/NY version), 1947-1948. British Bantamweight Champion, 1947-1949. British Empire Bantamweight Championship Claimant, 1945-1949. European Bantamweight Champion, 1946. *Born* 05.09.20. *From* Springfield. *Deceased* 1966. *Pro Career* 1938-1950 (92 contests, won 64, drew 3, lost 25).

Bernard Paul Commonwealth L. Welterweight Champion, 1997-1999. *Born* 22.20.65. *From* Tottenham. *Pro Career* 1991-2000 (35 contests, won 21, drew 4, lost 10).

Larry Paul British L. Middleweight Champion, 1973-1974. *Born* 19.04.52. *From* Wolverhampton. *Pro Career* 1973-1978 (40 contests, won 30, drew 1, lost 9).

David Pearce Undefeated British Heavyweight Champion, 1983-1985. *Born* 08.05.59. *From* Newport. *Deceased* 2000. *Pro Career* 1978-1984 (21 contests, won 17, drew 1, lost 3).

Kostas Petrou British Welterweight Champion, 1985. *Born* 17.04.59. *From* Birmingham. *Pro Career* 1981-1988 (37 contests, won 30, lost 7).

Tiger Al Phillips European Featherweight Champion, 1947. British Empire Featherweight Championship Claimant, 1947. *Born* 25.01.20. *From* Aldgate. *Deceased* 1999. *Pro Career* 1938-1951 (89 contests, won 72, drew 3, lost 14).

Nicky Piper Undefeated Commonwealth L. Heavyweight Champion, 1995-1997. *Born* 05.05.66. *From* Cardiff. *Pro Career* 1989-1997 (33 contests, won 26, drew 2, lost 5).

Dean Pithie Commonwealth S. Featherweight Champion, 2002-2003. *Born* 18.01.74. *From* Coventry. *Pro Career* 1995-2003 (32 contests, won 25, drew 2, lost 5).

Dennis Powell British L. Heavyweight Champion, 1953. *Born* 12.12.24. *From* Four Crosses. *Deceased* 1993. *Pro Career* 1947-1954 (68 contests, won 42, drew 4, lost 22).

Colin Power Undefeated British L. Welterweight Champion, 1977-1978. British L. Welterweight Champion, 1979. European L. Welterweight Champion, 1978. *Born* 02.02.56. *From* Paddington. *Pro Career* 1975-1983 (34 contests, won 28, drew 1, lost 5).

Kevin Pritchard British S. Featherweight Champion, 1990-1991. *Born* 26.09.61. *From* Liverpool. *Pro Career* 1981-1991 (48 contests, won 23, drew 3, lost 22).

Johnny Pritchett Undefeated British Middleweight Champion, 1965-1969. Undefeated British Empire Middleweight Champion, 1967-1969. *Born* 15.02.43. *From* Bingham. *Pro Career* 1963-1969 (34 contests, won 32, drew 1, lost 1).

Chris Pyatt Undefeated British L. Middleweight Champion, 1986. European L. Middleweight Champion, 1986-1987. Undefeated Commonwealth L. Middleweight Champion, 1991-1992. Commonwealth L. Middleweight Champion, 1995-1996. World Middleweight Champion (WBO version), 1993-1994. *Born* 03.07.63. *From* Leicester. *Pro Career* 1983-1997 (51 contests, won 46, lost 5).

Des Rea British L. Welterweight Champion, 1968-1969. *Born* 09.01.44. *From* Belfast. *Pro Career* 1964-1974 (69 contests, won 28, drew 5, lost 36).

Mark Reefer Undefeated Commonwealth S. Featherweight Champion, 1989-1990. *Born* 16.03.64. *Birthname* Mark Thompson. *From* Dagenham. *Pro Career* 1983-1992 (32 contests, won 23, drew 1, lost 8).

Sam Reeson Undefeated British Cruiserweight Champion, 1985-1986. Undefeated European Cruiserweight Champion, 1987-1988. *Born* 05.01.63. *From* Battersea. *Pro Career* 1983-1989 (26 contests, won 24, lost 2).

Robbie Regan Undefeated World Bantamweight Champion (WBO version), 1996-1997. British Flyweight Champion, 1991. Undefeated British Flyweight Champion, 1991-1992. Undefeated European Flyweight Champion, 1992-1993 and 1994-1995. *Born* 30.08.68. *From* Cefn Forest. *Pro Career* 1989-1996 (22 contests, won 17, drew 3, lost 2).

Willie Reilly Undefeated British Lightweight Champion, 1972. *Born* 25.03.47. *From* Glasgow. *Pro Career* 1968-1972 (23 contests, won 13, drew 3, lost 7).

Jimmy Revie British Featherweight Champion, 1969-1971. *Born* 08.07.47. *From* Stockwell. *Pro Career* 1966-1976 (48 contests, won 38, drew 1, lost 9).

Henry Rhiney British Welterweight Champion, 1976-1979. European Welterweight Champion, 1978-1979. *Born* Jamaica, 28.11.51. *From* Luton. *Pro Career* 1973-1980 (57 contests, won 32, drew 6, lost 19).

Alan Richardson British Featherweight Champion, 1977-1978. *Born* 04.11.48. *From* Fitzwilliam. *Pro Career* 1971-1978 (27 contests, won 17, drew 1, lost 9).

Dick Richardson European Heavyweight Champion, 1960-1962. *Born* 01.06.34. *From* Newport. *Deceased* 1999. *Pro Career* 1954-1963 (47 contests, won 31, drew 2, lost 14).

Wayne Rigby British Lightweight Champion, 1998. *Born* 19.07.73. *From* Manchester. *Pro Career* 1992-2004 (31 contests, won 20, lost 11).

Steve Robinson European Featherweight Champion, 1999-2000. WBO Featherweight Champion, 1993-1995. *Born* 13.12.68. *From* Cardiff. *Pro Career* 1989-2002 (51 contests, won 32, drew 2, lost 17).

Derek Roche British Welterweight Champion, 1999-2000. *Born* 19.07.72. *From* Leeds. *Pro Career* 1994-2004 (34 contests, won 29, lost 5).

Ernie Roderick British Welterweight Champion, 1939-1948. European Welterweight Champion, 1946-1947. British Middleweight Champion, 1945-1946. *Born* 25.01.14. *From* Liverpool. *Deceased* 1986. *Pro Career* 1931-1950 (142 contests, won 114, drew 4, lost 24).

Prince Rodney Undefeated British L. Middleweight Champion, 1983-1984. British L. Middleweight Champion, 1985-1986. *Born* 31.10.58. *From* Huddersfield. *Pro Career* 1977-1990 (41 contests, won 31, drew 1, lost 9).

Stan Rowan Undefeated British Bantamweight Champion, 1949. British Empire Bantamweight Championship Claimant, 1949. *Born* 06.09.24. *From* Liverpool. *Deceased* 1997. *Pro Career* 1942-1953 (67 contests, won 46, drew 5, lost 16).

Mark Rowe British and Commonwealth Middleweight Champion, 1970.

Born 12.07.47. *Born* 12.07.47. *From* Camberwell. *Pro Career* 1966-1973 (47 contests, won 38, drew 1, lost 8).

Jason Rowland Undefeated British L. Welterweight Champion, 1998-2000. *Born* 06.08.70. *From* West Ham. *Pro Career* 1989-2003 (28 contests, won 26, lost 2).

Alan Rudkin British Bantamweight Champion, 1965-1966. Undefeated British Bantamweight Champion, 1968-1972. British Empire Bantamweight Champion, 1965-1966 and 1968-1969. European Bantamweight Champion, 1971. Undefeated Commonwealth Bantamweight Champion, 1970-1972. *Born* 18.11.41. *From* Liverpool. *Pro Career* 1962-1972 (50 contests, won 42, lost 8).

Hugh Russell Undefeated British Flyweight Champion, 1984-1985. British Bantamweight Champion, 1983. *Born* 15.12.59. *From* Belfast. *Pro Career* 1981-1985 (19 contests, won 17, lost 2).

Paul Ryan British and Commonwealth L. Welterweight Champion, 1995-1996. *Born* 02.02.65. *From* Hackney. *Pro Career* 1991-1997 (28 contests, won 25, lost 3).

Chris Saunders British Welterweight Champion, 1995-1996. *Born* 15.08.69. *From* Barnsley. *Pro Career* 1990-2004 (45 contests, won 22, drew 1, lost 22).

Billy Schwer British Lightweight Champion, 1992-1993. Undefeated British Lightweight Champion, 1993-1995. Commonwealth Lightweight Champion, 1992-1993 and 1993-1995. Undefeated European Lightweight Champion, 1997-1999. *Born* 12.04.69. *From* Luton. *Pro Career* 1990-2001 (45 contests, won 39, lost 6).

Charles Shepherd British S.Featherweight Champion, 1997-1999. Undefeated Commonwealth S.Featherweight Champion, 1999. *Born* 28.06.70. *From* Carlisle. *Pro Career* 1991-2004 (34 contests, won 21, drew 1, lost 12).

Tony Sibson British Middleweight Champion, 1979. Undefeated British Middleweight Champion, 1984 and 1987-1988. Undefeated Commonwealth Middleweight Champion, 1980-1983 and 1984-1988. Undefeated European Middleweight Champion, 1980-1982. European Middleweight Champion, 1984-1985. *Born* 09.04.58. *From* Leicester. *Pro Career* 1976-1988 (63 contests, won 55, drew 1, lost 7).

Steve Sims Undefeated British Featherweight Champion, 1982-1983. *Born* 10.10.58. *From* Newport. *Pro Career* 1977-1987 (29 contests, won 14, drew 1, lost 14).

Neil Sinclair Undefeated British Welterweight Champion, 2001-2003. *Born* 23.02.74. *From* Belfast. *Pro Career* 1995-2005 (32 contests, won 28, lost 4).

Joey Singleton British L. Welterweight Champion, 1974-1976. *Born* 06.06.51. *From* Kirkby. *Pro Career* 1973-1982 (40 contests, won 27, drew 2, lost 11).

Kelvin Smart British Flyweight Champion, 1982-1984. *Born* 18.12.60. *From* Caerphilly. *Pro Career* 1979-1987 (29 contests, won 17, drew 2, lost 10).

Roy Smith British Cruiserweight Champion, 1987. *Born* 31.08.61. *From* Nottingham. *Pro Career* 1985-1991 (26 contests, won 18, lost 8).

Vernon Sollas British Featherweight Champion, 1975-1977. *Born* 14.08.54. *From* Edinburgh. *Pro Career* 1973-1977 (33 contests, won 25, drew 1, lost 7).

Terry Spinks British Featherweight Champion, 1960-1961. *Born* 28.02.38. *From* Canning Town. *Pro Career* 1957-1962 (49 contests, won 41, drew 1, lost 7).

David Starie British S. Middleweight Champion, 1997. Undefeated British S. Middleweight Champion, 1998-2003. Commonwealth S. Middleweight Champion, 1998-2003. *Born* 11.06.74. *From* Bury St Edmunds. *Pro Career* 1994-2003 (35 contests, won 31, lost 4).

Bunny Sterling British Middleweight Champion, 1970-1974. Undefeated British Middleweight Champion, 1975. Commonwealth Middleweight Champion, 1970-1972. European Middleweight Champion, 1976. *Born* Jamaica, 04.04.48. *From* Finsbury Park. *Pro Career* 1966-1977 (57 contests, won 35, drew 4, lost 18).

Sammy Storey British S. Middleweight Champion, 1989-1990. Undefeated British S. Middleweight Champion, 1995. *Born* 09.08.63. *From* Belfast. *Pro Career* 1985-1997 (31 contests, won 25, lost 6).

John H. Stracey Undefeated British Welterweight Champion, 1973-1975.

Undefeated European Welterweight Champion, 1974-1975. World Welterweight Champion (WBC version), 1975-1976. *Born* 22.09.50. *From* Bethnal Green. *Pro Career* 1969-1978 (51 contests, won 45, drew 1, lost 5).

Andy Straughn British Cruiserweight Champion, 1986-1987 and 1988-1989. *Born* Barbados, 25.12.59. *From* Hitchin. *Pro Career* 1982-1990 (27 contests, won 18, drew 2, lost 7).

Gary Stretch British L. Middleweight Champion, 1988-1990. *Born* 04.11.65. *From* St Helens. *Pro Career* 1985-1993 (25 contests, won 23, lost 2).

Johnny Sullivan British Empire Middleweight Championship Claimant, 1954. British and British Empire Middleweight Champion, 1954-1955. *Born* 19.12.32. *From* Preston. *Deceased* 2003. *Birthname* John Hallmark. *Pro Career* 1948-1960 (97 contests, won 68, drew 3, lost 26).

Neil Swain Undefeated Commonwealth S. Bantamweight Champion, 1995 and 1996-1997. *Born* 04.09.71. *From* Gilfach Goch. *Pro Career* 1993-1997 (24 contests, won 17, lost 7).

Wally Swift British Welterweight Champion, 1960. British Middleweight Champion, 1964-1965. *Born* 10.08.36. *From* Nottingham. *Pro Career* 1957-1969 (88 contests, won 68, drew 3, lost 17).

Wally Swift Jnr British L. Middleweight Champion, 1991-1992. *Born* 17.02.66. *From* Birmingham. *Pro Career* 1985-1994 (38 contests, won 26, drew 1, lost 11).

Nel Tarleton British Featherweight Champion, 1931-1932 and 1934-1936. Undefeated British Featherweight Champion, 1940-1947. Undefeated British Empire Featherweight Championship Claimant, 1940-1947. *Born* 14.01.06. *From* Liverpool. *Deceased* 1956. *Pro Career* 1926-1945 (144 contests, won 116, drew 8, lost 20).

Wally Thom British Welterweight Champion, 1951-1952 and 1953-1956. British Empire Welterweight Championship Claimant, 1951-1952. European Welterweight Champion, 1954-1955. *Born* 14.06.26. *From* Birkenhead. *Deceased* 1980. *Pro Career* 1949-1956 (54 contests, won 42, drew 1, lost 11).

Eddie Thomas British Welterweight Champion, 1949-1951. European Welterweight Champion, 1951. British Empire Welterweight Championship Claimant, 1951. *Born* 27.07.26. *From* Merthyr. *Deceased* 1997. *Pro Career* 1946-1954 (48 contests, won 40, drew 2, lost 6).

Pat Thomas British Welterweight Champion, 1975-1976. British L. Middleweight Champion, 1979-1981. *Born* St Kitts, 05.05.50. *From* Cardiff. *Pro Career* 1970-1984 (57 contests, won 35, drew 3, lost 18, no contest 1).

Billy Thompson British Lightweight Champion, 1947-1951. European Lightweight Champion, 1948-1949. *Born* 20.12.25. *From* Hickleton Main. *Pro Career* 1945-1953 (63 contests, won 46, drew 4, lost 13).

Gary Thornhill British Featherweight Champion, 2000. *Born* 11.02.68. *From* Liverpool. *Pro Career* 1993-2004 (30 contests, won 24, drew 1, lost 5).

Andy Till British L. Middleweight Champion, 1992-1994. *Born* 22.08.63. *From* Northolt. *Pro Career* 1986-1995 (24 contests, won 19, lost 5).

Dick Turpin British Middleweight Champion, 1948-1950. British Empire Middleweight Championship Claimant, 1948-1949. *Born* 26.11.20. *From* Leamington Spa. *Deceased* 1990. *Pro Career* 1937-1950 (103 contests, won 76, drew 6, lost 20, no contest 1).

Randy Turpin Undefeated British Middleweight Champion, 1950-1954. British Empire Middleweight Championship Claimant, 1952-1954. European Middleweight Champion, 1951-1954. World Middleweight Champion, 1951. World Middleweight Champion (EBU version), 1953. Undefeated British L. Heavyweight Champion, 1952, 1955, and 1956-1958. British Empire L. Heavyweight Championship Claimant, 1952-1954. Undefeated British Empire L. Heavyweight Champion, 1954-1955. *Born* 07.06.28. *From* Leamington Spa. *Deceased* 1966. *Pro Career* 1946-1958 (73 contests, won 64, drew 1, lost 8).

Bobby Vanzie British Lightweight Champion, 1998-2003. Commonwealth Lightweight Champion, 1999-2001. *Born* 11.01.74. *From* Bradford. *Pro Career* 1995-2004 (32 contests, won 26, drew 1, lost 5).

Tommy Waite British and Commonwealth Bantamweight Champion, 2000. *Born* 11.03.72. *From* Belfast. *Pro Career* 1996-2001 (15 contests, won 11, lost 4).

Keith Wallace Undefeated Commonwealth Flyweight Champion, 1983-1984. *Born* 29.03.61. *From* Liverpool. *Deceased* 2000. *Pro Career* 1982-1990 (25 contests, won 20, lost 5).

Peter Waterman Undefeated British Welterweight Champion, 1956-1958. Undefeated European Welterweight Champion, 1958. *Born* 08.12.34. *From* Clapham. *Deceased* 1986. *Pro Career* 1952-1958 (46 contests, won 41, drew 2, lost 3).

Michael Watson Undefeated Commonwealth Middleweight Champion, 1989-1991. *Born* 15.03.65. *From* Islington. *Pro Career* 1984-1991 (30 contests, won 25, drew 1, lost 4).

Jim Watt British Lightweight Champion, 1972-1973. Undefeated British Lightweight Champion, 1975-1977. Undefeated European Lightweight Champion, 1977-1979. World Lightweight Champion (WBC version), 1979-1981. *Born* 18.07.48. *From* Glasgow. *Pro Career* 1968-1981 (46 contests, won 38, lost 8).

Paul Weir Undefeated WBO M. Flyweight Champion, 1993-1994. WBO L. Flyweight Champion, 1994-1995. *Born* 16.09.67. *From* Irvine. *Pro Career* 1992-2000 (20 contests, won 14, lost 6).

Scott Welch Undefeated British Heavyweight Champion, 1995-1996. Commonwealth Heavyweight Champion, 1995-1997. *Born* 21.04.1968. *From* Shoreham. *Pro Career* 1992-1999 (26 contests, won 22, lost 4).

Richie Wenton Undefeated British S. Bantamweight Champion, 1994-1996. *Born* 28.10.67. *From* Liverpool. *Pro Career* 1988-2001 (30 contests, won 24, lost 6).

Henry Wharton Undefeated British S. Middleweight Champion, 1992-1993. Undefeated Commonwealth Champion, 1991-1997. Undefeated European S. Middleweight Champion, 1995-1996. *Born* 23.11.1967. *From* York. *Pro Career* 1989-1998 (31 contests, won 27, drew 1, lost 3).

Dazzo Williams British Featherweight Champion, 2003-2005. *Born* 19.03.75. *From* Hereford. *Pro Career* 2001-2005 (15 contests, won 12, lost 3).

Derek Williams Commonwealth Heavyweight Champion, 1988-1992. European Heavyweight Champion, 1989-1992. *Born* 11.03.65. *From* Peckham. *Pro Career* 1984-1999 (35 contests, won 22, lost 13).

Johnny Williams British Heavyweight Champion, 1952-1953. British Empire Heavyweight Championship Claimant, 1952-1953. *Born* 25.12.26. *From* Rugby. *Pro Career* 1946-1956 (75 contests, won 60, drew 4, lost 11).

Tony Willis British Lightweight Champion, 1985-1987. *Born* 17.06.60. *From* Liverpool. *Pro Career* 1981-1989 (29 contests, won 25, lost 4).

Nick Wilshire Commonwealth L. Middleweight Champion, 1985-1987. *Born* 03.11.61. *From* Bristol. *Pro Career* 1981-1987 (40 contests, won 36, lost 4).

Tony Wilson British L. Heavyweight Champion, 1987-1989. *Born* 25.04.64. *From* Wolverhampton. *Pro Career* 1985-1993 (29 contests, won 20, drew 1, lost 8).

Howard Winstone Undefeated British Featherweight Champion, 1961-1969. European Featherweight Champion, 1963-1967. World Featherweight Champion (WBC version), 1968. *Born* 15.04.39. *From* Merthyr. *Deceased* 2000. *Pro Career* 1959-1968 (67 contests, won 61, lost 6).

Mark Winters British L. Welterweight Champion, 1997-1998. *Born* 29.12.71. *From* Antrim. *Pro Career* 1995-2004 (25 contests, won 18, drew 2, lost 5).

Tim Wood British L. Heavyweight Champion, 1976-1977. *Born* 10.08.51. *From* Leicester. *Pro Career* 1972-1979 (31 contests, won 19, drew 1, lost 11).

Bruce Woodcock British Heavyweight Champion, 1945-1950. British Empire Heavyweight Championship Claimant, 1945-1950. European Heavyweight Champion, 1946-1949. *Born* 18.01.21. *From* Doncaster. *Deceased* 1997. *Pro Career* 1942-1950 (39 contests, won 35, lost 4).

Richie Woodhall WBC S. Middleweight Champion, 1998-1999. Commonwealth Middleweight Champion, 1992-1995. Undefeated European Middleweight Champion, 1995-1996. *Born* 17.04.68. *From* Telford. *Pro Career* 1990-2000 (29 contests, won 26, lost 3).

Early Gloved Championship Boxing: A Selection of British Boxers' Records

by Harold Alderman

W PTS = Won Points. W RSF = Won Referee Stopped Fight. W RTD= Won Retired. W DISQ = Won Disqualified. W KO = Won by Knockout (Count Out). DREW = Contest Drawn. L PTS = Lost Points. L RSF = Lost Referee Stopped Fight. L RTD = Lost Retired. L DISQ = Lost Disqualified. L KO = Lost by Knockout (Count Out). EXH = Exhibition Bout.

Venues: Covent Garden = The National Sporting Club, 43 King Street
Whitechapel = 'Wonderland', Whitechapel Road

Charlie Allum

Born: 23 April 1876, Notting Hill. Died: 21 July 1918 - Killed in action in France with no known grave (Name on Memorial at Berks Cemetary at Ploegsteert, Belgium)

Served in Royal Fusiliers - Second Battalion - for three years in Boer War in South Africa 1899 (12 October) - 1902 (31 May). During 1914-18 First World War he won the Military Medal for bravery

Had a genuine claim to the English 10st 10lbs title on 27 February 1905, bout being of three-minute rounds. Also claimed the English 10st 4lbs title, but claim not valid as only over two-minute rounds. At that time the rules stated that a major title bout had to be held over three-minute rounds and of 12, 15, or 20 rounds, or more, duration. Began boxing as an amateur with Kensington ABC in 1896, finishing up as the captain of the club, and was always referred to to as 'The Amateur who boxed like a Pro'. Turned Pro: 23 February 1903. Height: 5'9"

1896

Joined Kensington Rugby Club Boxing Section and won the Kensington ABC Rugby 'Old Guards' Challenge Cup at catchweights, which meant any weight competition. However, no details traced

1897

Mr Edward Jones W RTD 1 Belsize BC, 'Eyre Arms', Wood Green. First series of open 10st competition
Mr Brown W PTS 3 Belsize BC, 'Eyre Arms', Wood Green. Semi-final Open 10st competition
Mr W.L.S. Arburthnott W PTS 6 Belsize BC, 'Eyre Arms', Wood Green. Final of open 10st competition

1898

December   Mr C.W. Humphries (Battersea BC) W PTS 3 'The Turnhalle', Kings Cross. First series German Gym Society 10st competition. Walked over in second series of above competition when Mr C.J.Clarke (Finchley BC) withdrew
December   Mr Albert Brewer (Polytechnic BC) W RSF 2 'The Turnhalle', Kings Cross. Final of German Gym Society 10st competition. According to the *Mirror of Life*, Brewer accused Allum 'of shaping like a professional'

1899

13 October   *Mirror of Life* – Allum was stated to have boxed on the opening show of season at Kensington BC, Wood Lane Drill Hall, Shepherds Bush, but no details were given. Joined Second Battalion Royal Fusiliers after the outbreak of the Boer War on 12 October

1900

10 January   *Mirror of Life* - Charlie Allum, the captain of Kensington ABC, who boxes like a disguised 'Professional', and who has now left for South Africa with his regiment - The Royal Fusiliers, is one of the best amateurs of his weight -10st
23 May   *Mirror of Life* - Charlie Allum, now at the front in South Africa with The Royal Fusiliers, had served with Captain Buller all through the siege of Ladysmith, 2 November 1899 to 28 February 1900. In a 10st competition at the 17th Middlesex Volunteers ABC club house, Allum had an accident when a needle of his opponents glove went into his eye (no details given)
22 August   Arrived back in England

1901

9 January   *Mirror of Life* - Charlie Allum is now back at the front in South Africa
25 November Mr H.J. Davis (Belsize ABC) EXH 3 'Eye Arms' Assembly Rooms, St John's Wood

1902

25 November   W. Peck (Bishops Stortford BC) W PTS 3 Polytechnic BC, Regent Street. Semi-final 11st 4lbs competition
25 November   Rube Warnes (Lynn BC) L PTS 3 Polytechnic BC, Regent Street. Final 11st 4lbs competition
November   R. Batchelor W KO 3 'The Turnhalle', Kings Cross. First series German Gym Societies 11st 4lbs competition
November   Rube Warnes (Lynn BC) L PTS 3 'The Turnhalle', Kings Cross. Final of German Gym Societies 11st 4lbs competition
3 December   R. Batchlor (Kensington BC) W RSF 3 Wood Lane Drill Hall, White City. Following the above contest, Allum announced that he was turning professional

1903

23 February   Ted Francis (Norwich) W RSF 2 (6) Covent Garden. This was Allum's 'pro' debut
12 March   J. Andrews (Bethnal Green) W PTS 3 Covent Garden. First series of 11st 'novices' competition
12 March   F. Blackwell (Drury Lane) W RSF 3 (3) Covent Garden. Second series of 11st 'novices' competition
23 March   Fred Robbins (Lambeth) W PTS 3 Covent Garden. Semi-final 11st 'novices' competition
23 March   Bill Curzon (Bloomsbury) L KO 2 (3) Covent Garden. Final of 11st 'novices' competition
28 March   Harry Sherring (Walthamstow) DREW 6 Whitechapel
6 April   Fred Blackwell (Drury Lane) W KO 1 (6) Covent Garden
18 Apr. Peter Brown (Woolwich) L PTS 6 Whitechapel
25 April   Alf Wicks (Stratford) Whitechapel. Bout was advertised for six rounds, but there were no reports on show, which was almost certainly cancelled
16 May   Harry Sherring (Walthamstow) DREW 6 Whitechapel
25 May   Harry Sherring (Walthamstow) DREW 6 Stamford Hill
6 June   Dick Jordan (Woolwich) DREW 6 Whitechapel
23 July   *Sporting Life* - Challenged 'All England' at 10st 6lbs limit
1 August   Dick Jordan (Woolwich) W PTS 6 Whitechapel
15 August   *Sporting Life* - Challenged 'All England' at 10st 8lbs limit
22 August   Bill Dooley W RTD 3 (6) Whitechapel
12 September   Charlie Knock (Stratford) L PTS 6 Whitechapel
26 October   Jack Clancy (Philadelphia & California, USA) EXH 3 Covent Garden
16 November   Charlie Knock (Stratford) W KO 9 (12) Whitechapel. Given billing as English 10st 6lbs title and £160, but only over two-minute rounds which thus disqualified it from title recognition. Weights: Allum 10st 6lbs, Knock 10st 4lbs
14 December   Mr J.W.H.T. Douglas EXH 3 Covent Garden. Douglas was the public schools middleweight champion and a famous cricketer whose initials, JWHT, because of his tactics, got him the nickname 'Johnny Won't Hit Today'

1904

1 February   Charlie Knock (Stratford) L PTS 12 Whitechapel. Originally billed as being for the English 10st 12lbs title, both men were over the

weight and the fight went on as a catchweight bout. This would have been disqualified from title recognition as only two-minute rounds (as was the custom at this venue) were contested. Also, a Mr Jones (The Green Gate, Barking) Silver Championship Cup was to have been at stake, plus £275. Weights were given in *Sporting Life* as Knock 10st 13½lbs, Allum 11st

2 March *Sporting Life* - Charlie Allum (Notting Hill), who has been getting billed as the English 10st 4lbs limit champion, challenges all England at the 11st limit, Peter Brown (Woolwich), Charlie Knock (Stratford), Jack Clancy (San Francisco), Arthur Cripps (Australia) or Dan Sinclair (Canada) preferred

18 April Pat O'Keefe (Canning Town) W PTS 6 Whitechapel. First series of an English 10st 4lbs championship competition

18 April Peter Brown (Woolwich) L PTS 6 Whitechapel. Semi-final of an English 10st 4lbs championship competition

4 June Jack Clancy (San Francisco, USA) L KO 3 (15) Newcastle. Although billed for the world 10st 6lbs title, £100 a side and £100 purse totalling £300, being over two-minute rounds disqualified it from full title recognition

16 November *Sporting Life* - Charlie Allum is the English 10st 10lbs limit champion

21 November Young Peter Jackson (Baltimore, USA) L KO 6 (15) Whitechapel. Made at catchweights, Jackson, the world 10st 8lbs limit champion - real name Sim Thompkins and a coloured man – was restricted to 10st 10lbs, while Allum could be any weight. Contested over 15 two-minute rounds for £100 a side and £100 purse, total £300. Allum was down three times in the fifth, being saved by the bell, and was down once in the sixth prior to being counted out. Weights: Jackson 10st 9½lbs, Allum 11st 9lbs

1905

11 January *Sporting Life* – Allum is challenged by Jack Kingsland (Paddington) for the English 10st 10lbs limit championship

18 January *Sporting Life* - Charlie Wilson is stated to have accepted purse offer for a bout against Allum on 21 January, but no such bout was reviewed, advertised or reported

23 January Charlie Wilson (Notting Hill) EXH 3 Harrow Road Drill Hall

27 February Jack Kingsland (Paddington) W RSF 10 (15) Covent Garden. Billed for the English 10st 10lbs limit title, £50 a side and £100 purse, total £200. Weights: Both men scaled 10st 9lbs

8 April *Sporting Life* – Challenged all England at 10st 10lbs up to 11st, £50 or £100 a side

21 June *Sporting Life* – Challenged Jack Palmer (Benwell, Newcastle) to a bout for the English 11st 4lbs limit title over 15 or 20 rounds

29 June Harry Smith (Birmingham) W KO 5 (15) Liverpool. In a catchweight bout contested over two-minute rounds for £25 purse, Smith was down in the first round

5 August *Sporting Life* – Challenged by Charlie Wilson (Notting Hill) over 20 rounds, £100 a side and an NSC purse, to decide the English 11st 4lbs middleweight title, now being claimed by both Allum and Jack Palmer (Benwell), with a 2pm weigh-in

8 August *Sporting Life* - Allum accepted the above challenge which Wilson repeated in 16 August issue of the *Sporting Life*

19 August *Sporting Life* – Allum stated that he would box Wilson at 11st 4lbs, but it must be a ringside weigh-in as he can easily do 10st 10lbs. He agreed to meet Wilson today in order to make the match

21 August *Sporting Life* – Charlie Wilson is surprised that Allum didn't turn up on 19 August and again repeated his challenge. This was repeated again in 11 September issue of *Sporting Life*

11 September *Sporting Life* – Challenged Charlie Wilson at 11st 4lbs ringside

4 November *Sporting Life* - Allum is being asked to call the 'Wonderland' promoter, Harry Jacobs, at once

6 November *Sporting Life* – Challenged all England 10st 10lbs up to 11st to decide the English 11st limit title, £200 up to £500 a side

7 November *Sporting Life* – Jack Kingsland (Paddington) accepted the above challenge

8 November *Sporting Life* – Allum is challenged by Harry Newmier (Stepney), recently returned from a tour of the USA, over ten or 15 rounds of three minutes each, £25 or £50 a side. In the same issue, Allum challenged Jack Kingsland (Paddington) over 15 or 20 rounds at 10st 10lbs, £100 a side upwards

18 November *Sporting Life* – Challenged Mike Crawley (Limehouse) and Charlie Knock (Stratford) at 11st over 15 or 20 rounds, £100 a side. Also in the same issue, he challenged Jack Kingsland (Paddington) to a bout for the English 10st 10lbs title, £100 a side, and an NSC purse

24 November Willie Burke W KO 3 Paris, France

16 December *Sporting Life* – Allum is challenged by Jack Kingsland (Paddington) to a bout for the English 10st 10lbs title over 15 or 20 rounds, £100 a side and best purse

18 December Pat O'Keefe (Canning Town) DREW 6 Covent Garden. Allum was a substitute for Private L.Casling, who was down to box O'Keefe over ten rounds, and the bout was cut to six rounds

1906

5 January *Sporting Life* – Allum is challenged by Pat O'Keefe (Canning Town) at 11st. Later that month Allum went to Stockholm Sweden to take up a position to teach boxing

3 February *Sporting Life* – Allum is now running a boxing school in Stockholm, Sweden and is hoping to bring a team of Swedish amateurs to London for a series of matches

7 February *Sporting Life* - Now in Paris, France, only a few days ago Allum was still in Stockholm

23 February Bill Higgins/Huggins W PTS 10 Civil Engineers School, Avenue 3, Athans, Paris, France. Although scheduled for 25 rounds, during the bout Allum suffered an injury and at the end of the tenth round the referee, Lovel Graham, stopped the bout and declared Allum to be the winner on points. With this win, Allum claimed the French 11st title, but neither man was French-born so therefore not eligible to box for the title. No weights were given

10 March *Sporting Life* – Challenged 'All England' at 10st 10lbs

13 March *Sporting Life* – Challenged Jack Kingsland (Paddington) to a bout for the English 10st 10lbs limit title, which Kingsland accepted on 15 March

21 April *Sporting Life* – Allum is challenged by Pat Daley (London-born, Ireland) at 11st, £50 or £100 a side. In the same issue, it stated that Charlie Allum boxes frequently on the continent and invariably wins

23 April Pat O'Keefe (Canning Town) L KO 6 (15) Covent Garden. Given English 11st 2lbs limit title billing, O'Keefe was on the weight, while Allum came in at 10st 10lbs

2 May *Sporting Life* – Challenged 'All England', 10st 10lbs up to 11st, and was accepted by Joe Platford (Tottenham) on 9 May

16 May *Mirror of Life* – Challenged 'All England', 10st 10lbs up to 11st

29 June *Sporting Life* – Challenged 'All England' at 10st 10lbs

17 July *Sporting Life* - Challenged the world at 150lbs, or the winner of the Pat Daley v Charlie Knock bout for the English 10st 10lbs title. Note: Allum had won this title on 27 February 1905 and had never lost it

1 August *Mirror of Life* - Charlie Allum shortly leaves for New Zealand

4 August *Sporting Life* - Repeated challenge of 17 July and stated that he had no intention of going to New Zealand

8 August *Sporting Life* – Challenged Pat Daley to a bout that will decide the English 10st 10 lbs title

8 September Frank Craig (Harlem, New York) L KO 5 (6) Whitechapel. The coloured man, Craig, who was famous as 'The Harlem Coffee Cooler', won when Allum was counted out after being floored by an uppercut to the jaw. Although a veteran, Craig was a one-time claimant to the world middleweight title

6 November *Sporting Life* – Challenged all England, 10st 10lbs up to 11st, £200 up to £500 a side, and the English title. The challenge was accepted a day later by Harry Newmier (Stepney)

1907

1 March Pat O'Keefe (Canning Town) L KO 7 (20) The Salle Wagram, Paris, France, Allum went over the ropes in the third then took a six count in the sixth. Articled for a £200 purse, £140 to winner £60 to loser, both men were invited to box at Baron Henri De Rothschild's House in Bordeaux on the Saturday, where Allum was disqualified in the fourth round of an unofficial bout against Adrian Hogan (France)

21 March *Sporting Life* - Charlie Allum, the English 10st 10lbs champion, challenges the world at 10st 10 lbs. He was to repeat his challenge throughout the year

6 April *Sporting Life* - Challenged Tom Lancaster (Spennymoor) at 10st 6lbs, £50 or £100 a side

26 April *Sporting Life* - Challenged Sam Langford (Boston, Mass, USA, born Nova Scotia, Canada) at 10st 10lbs. Note: The negro, Langford, was considered to be one of the greatest fighters of all time

27 July Mike Crawley (Limehouse) DREW 6 Whitechapel. Crawley was down twice in the sixth

31 August Mike Crawley (Limehouse) W RTD 2 (6) Whitechapel. Crawley, who was a substitute for Robert 'Curly' Watson (Chatham), was down four times in the first round and twice in the second before retiring from the contest

14 September Pat O'Keefe (Canning Town) L PTS 6 Whitechapel

16 September *Sporting Life* - Challenged ex-seaman Robert 'Curly' Watson (Chatham) at 10st 12lbs, £100 or £200 a side

2 October *Sporting Life* - Challenged Tom Lancaster (Spennymoor) at 11st

5 October Jack Scales (Bethnal Green) L PTS 6 Whitechapel. Scales, a one-time claimant to the English heavyweight title, was much bigger. Allum was down in the second

14 November James 'Tiger' Smith (Merthyr) L KO 1 (20) Welsh National AC, Merthyr. Made at 158lbs - no weights given – Smith, whose real name was Addis, was a southpaw

16 November Charlie Knock (Stratford) L PTS 10 Whitechapel. The contest was brought forward from Monday 18 November

27 November Withdrew from a bout against Charlie Knock (Stratford) on this date in Paris, France at the Salle Wagram and was substituted by Peter Brown (Woolwich). The original bout was put back to 4 December

1908

1 February *Sporting Life* - Charlie Allum, who has been on the retired list with an injured hand, is to have a benefit on Monday, 1 March at the Bletchynden Hall, Notting Hill. There was no further mention of this benefit show, with no further advertisement and no report carried

4 April *Sporting Life* - Charlie Allum is the English 10st 10lbs champion

10 April *Sporting Life* – The paper carried a list of English champions, with Allum listed as the 10st 10lbs champion

11 April *Mirror of Life* – Allum is called the English 10st 10lbs champion

11 April Jack Costello (Birmingham) L PTS 6 Whitechapel

27 April 'Jewey' Smith (Aldgate) L KO 2 (6) Whitechapel. Allum was a substitute for Tom Lancaster (Spenymoor). Despite being a novice, Smith was much heavier and just nine days previously, in Paris, had been stopped in five rounds by Tommy Burns in a bout for the world heavyweight title

13 June *Sporting Life* - Challenged 'All England' at 10st 10lbs, £100 a side, 'Bombardier' Davies, Sid Doyle (Islington), or ex-seaman Robert 'Curly' Watson preferred

19 June *Sporting Life* - Challenged 'All England' at 10st 10lbs, Joe White (Cardiff, late Canada) preferred

15 August Jack Williams (America) W PTS 6 Whitechapel. Williams, who was well over 6ft tall and almost 13st, claimed a long record but fought like a novice

26 November Mr A.W.Gleed EXH 3 'The Eyre Arms', St John's Wood. The 27th annual display by Belsize ABC, Charlie Allum being one of four professional instructors with them

1909

25 January Joe Smith (Canning Town) W PTS 8 Lime Grove Baths, Shepherds Bush

29 March Jack Kingsland (Paddington) DREW 20 Cromwell Hall, Putney. Kingsland was also the promoter of this show

26 June *Mirror of Life* - Challenged 'All England', 10st 10lbs up to 11st

3 July Jim Sullivan (Bermondsey) L PTS 6 Whitechapel

21 July W.Gent (Guernsey, late Manchester) W RSF 3 (15) St Julians Hall, Guernsey. Gent, the 'Channel Island champion', was put down in the third, but despite getting up he was in a dazed state and the bout was stopped by the referee, Mr O'Shea. Following the bout, Allum challenged 'All England' at 11st

10 September Bert Allum (Notting Hill) EXH 3 Rugby Victoria Works. Bert Allum was Charles' Brother

4 October Ted Nelson (Australia) L PTS 15 Covent Garden. Although Allum threw his man down in the second, a claim for foul was ignored. Allum took a 'seven' count in the eighth before again throwing his man in the ninth. Again it was ruled accidental. Allum then took two counts of 'eight' in the 11th

25 November Mr H.I.Davis EXH 3 'Eyre Arms', St John's Wood

13 December Mr G.Fidler (The Rugby BC) EXH 3 The Rugby BC, Clay Hall, Notting Hill

1910

21 April Gunner Rowles (Ireland) DREW 10 The Curragh Army Camp. Rowles was much the heavier of the two

12 September Frank Inglis (Birmingham, born St Lucia) W PTS 6 Hammersmith Palace

1 October Arthur Harman (Lambeth) L PTS 6 Whitechapel

1911

9 January Albert Jacobs (Mile End) W RSF 4 (6) The Empire, Holborn. In the fourth round, Allum's head came into contact with Jacobs' eye causing a cut. The bout was then stopped in Allum's favour

16 January Young Johnson (America) W PTS 6 The Empire, Holborn. Johnson looked the winner, but the decision of the judges went to Allum

12 April George Max (France) W KO 5 (10) 'Wonderland', Paris, France

21 October Karl Wonders (France) W DISQ 7 (10) 'Wonderland', Paris, France. This was the last bout traced for Charlie Allum, aged 35. Wonders, who boxed as Louis Verger, was put down in fifth, while Allum was wrestled down once before being disqualified when going low

Career: 54 contests, won 22, drew 7, lost 20, 5 exhibitions

Charlie Allum

Ike Bradley

Born: 11 February 1884, Liverpool. Died: 5 May 1951, Old Swan, Liverpool

Claimant: English 7st 12lbs to 8st championship, 1905-1906. English 7st 10lbs to 7st 12lbs championship, 1907. North of England 7st 12lbs to 8st championship, 1906-1907. North of England 8st 6lbs to 8st championship, 1910. He also boxed on the booths, hence a claim of over 400 bouts during his career. But claims like this, although common place, seldom had any substance. In fact, after retirement from boxing Bradley became the regular second at both Liverpool Stadiums. First, at the Pudsey Street venue and then at its replacement, adjoining the Exchange Station, up until his death. Married, he had nine children, six boys (two of whom were dead by June 1969) and three girls. Had an aggressive and persistent, all-out attacking style and never left his man alone. Was recognised as a top-class 'inside' fighter and body puncher, for which he was several times disqualified, and had a good punch in either hand. He was also good at slipping punches and making his man miss. Strong and durable, Bradley - who frequently gave away height, weight, and reach advantage to his opponents - preferred three-minute rounds and long distance 20-round bouts as it gave him more chance of catching up with his opponents. This, in many ways, is why certain opponents who faced him insisted on two-minute rounds. Although possessing unlimited stamina, he often had trouble with fast and clever boxers who could avoid his ceaseless attacks and counter him with a good left hand jab, etc

1902

3 March   Willie Gill (Seaforth) ND 5 Liverpool. This was a trial bout

27 March   Willie Smith (Liverpool) L RSF 9 Liverpool. Both the *Mirror of Life* and *Sporting Life* give this result, while the *Manchester Sporting Chronicle* differs and gives L KO 8

15 May   Willie Gill (Seaforth) EXH 3 Liverpool

24 July   Jack Mitchell (Liverpool) L PTS 6 Liverpool

14 August   'Young' Willie Dean (Liverpool) W RTD 2 Liverpool

11 September   Willie Gill (Seaforth) EXH 3 Liverpool

9 October   Frank Crewe EXH 3 Liverpool

23 October   'Owens Novice' (Liverpool) W PTS 4 Liverpool

13 November   Jack Mitchell W KO 2 Liverpool

20 November   Jack Mitchell W KO 5 Liverpool. Billy Halley/Haley (Bolton) W Liverpool. This fight has not been traced and is one of five claimed bouts given in 15 July 1903 *Mirror of Life*. Falling into the same category is Billy Murphy W Liverpool and Billy Edwards W Liverpool. On 26 November the *Mirror of Life* stated that Ike Bradley (Liverpool) has joined the Royal Navy. However, this statement appears to have been wrong as no further reference was ever made that Ike Bradley was in the Royal Navy. Maybe it stemmed from a jocular reference to his being tattooed all over like a sailor. Billy Stewart W Liverpool. Not traced, This is the fourth of five claimed but untraced bouts given in 15 July 1903 *Mirror of Life*

1903

5 February   Billy Cocker (Bury) W RTD 2 Liverpool

26 February   Jack Morris (Newcastle) W KO 3 Liverpool

2 March   Jack Owen (Liverpool) W PTS 6 Liverpool. This was Jack Owen's second bout on this bill, having W KO 1 earlier

9 March   Jack Turner (Birkenhead) W PTS 8 Liverpool

16 March   A. Murphy W KO 5 Liverpool

26 March   Jack Rose (Newcastle) W DISQ 10 Liverpool

2 April   Bill Lewis (Bethnal Green) L PTS 15 Liverpool

13 August   Fred Hickling (Birmingham) W PTS 6 Birmingham. Jack Tate (Newcastle) W. This is the last of five claimed but untraced bouts given in 15 July 1903 *Mirror of Life*

7 May   Tom Bond (Birmingham) W KO 4 Liverpool

28 May   Tom Edwards (Stockport) W KO 5 Liverpool

4 June   Martin Ford (Manchester) W KO 2 Liverpool

8 June   Fred Hickling (Birmingham) W KO 1 Liverpool

27 August   'Young' Frank Yates (Leeds) W RSF 5 Liverpool

10 September   'Young' Ward (Liverpool) W KO 4 Liverpool

26 September   Dai Jones (Ystalyera) ND 4 Swansea. This was a trial bout

3 October   Bill Phalin (Birmingham) W KO 4 Swansea

15 October   Willie Gill (Seaforth) L PTS 15 Liverpool. North of England 7st 10lbs to 7st 12lbs championship

29 October   Harry McLean (Manchester) EXH 3 Liverpool

5 December   'Young' James Southway (Pentre, Rhonda) W PTS 15 Swansea

10 December   'Young' Turner EXH 3 Liverpool

24 December   Billy 'Young Snowball' Jones W DISQ 4 Liverpool. Jones was coloured

1904

9 January   Johnny Emanuel Fenice (Cardiff) W PTS 15 Swansea. Fenice was a coloured fighter. The Ike Bradley report in the *Mirror of Life* credited him with 41 bouts, lost 1. Traced bouts, plus those claimed but untraced, exhibitions and no decision contests up to this time comes to 35, of which he lost 4

1 February   Tom Bond (Birmingham) ND 6 Liverpool

11 February   Tom Whelligan EXH 3 Liverpool

18 February   Jack Tate (Newcastle) EXH 3 Liverpool

29 February   Harry Brodigan (Manchester, born Sheffield) L DISQ 4 Manchester. Billed as for the North of England 7st 12lbs limit championship, but over two-minute rounds

1 March   Bill Phalin (Birmingham) W KO 3 Warrington

25 March   Jack Daly (London) W KO 3 Liverpool

4 April   Arthur Grimshaw (London) W KO 7 New Brighton

5 April   Arthur Grimshaw (London) W KO 3 Warrington

7 April   Arthur Grimshaw (London) EXH 3 Liverpool

14 April   'Tibby' Watson (Sydney, Australia) L PTS 15 Liverpool

21 April   Billy Johnson (Bolton) EXH 3 Liverpool

30 April   Arthur Wilkinson (Liverpool) W KO 7 Dublin. A win against Arthur Grimshaw (London) is one of six claimed but untraced bouts shown in 4 January 1905 *Mirror of Life* and *Sporting Life*. It was given as being the third win over Grimshaw (only two wins and an exhibition with Grimshaw have been traced). Four more were against 'Young' Percill/Pergival W, Joe Holden/Holding W, 'Topper' Brown W, Billy Taylor (Liverpool) W. The sixth untraced bout was supposedly against the famous George Dixon, known as 'Little Chocolate' because of his colour (Boston, MA, born Canada) W KO Dublin. Dixon, the ex-world bantam and featherweight champion issued a disclaimer in the 1 Feb 1905 *Mirror of Life*, stating "He had never fought Bradley, yet alone lose to him", but Bradley until his dying day always maintained bout did take place. However, he always emphasised the fact that Dixon was blind drunk at the time and was carried to the ring. All future pen pictures of Bradley published after 1 February 1905 carried a Dixon disclaimer

31 October   Willie Gill (Seaforth) W KO 1 New Brighton. Won North of England 7st 12lbs to 8st championship claim, although purse and side stakes only amounted to £35 and was of 15 rounds duration, not 20

24 November   Jack Daly (London) W KO 3 Liverpool

26 December   'Tibby' Watson (Sydney, Australia) DREW 15 Liverpool. On 4 January 1905 a pen picture in *Mirror of Life* credited Bradley with 62 bouts, lost 2, while traced records show 58 bouts, lost 5

1905

19 January   Ernie Godwin (Birmingham) DREW 12 Liverpool

23 January   'A Pupil' EXH 3 Liverpool

23 February   Jim Freeman (Wimbledon) W RSF 3 Liverpool

30 March   Willie Collins (Manchester) W KO 2 Liverpool

10 April   Jim Kenrick (Hackney) L PTS 15 Covent Garden. Billed for the English 7st 12lbs to 8st division title within the bantamweight class, although only of 15-round duration, not 20 which was the recognised distance for English title bouts

13 April   Johnny Hughes (Bloomsbury) W KO 9 Liverpool

4 May   Jim Kenrick (Hackney) DREW 20 Liverpool. Thought to be for the English 7st 12lbs to 8st division title within the bantamweight class, although there was no actual title billing in the majority of reports. Later gossip called it a title bout as it was made at the eight-stone limit. Kenrick was also billed in some quarters as Kendrick and Henrich

8 June   Harry Brodigan (Manchester, born Sheffield) L DISQ 11 Liverpool. Fight ended by a low blow

6 July   'Tibby' Watson (Sydney, Australia) W PTS 20 Liverpool

27 July   Jim Kenrick (Hackney) L PTS 20 Liverpool. Recognised as being for the English 7st 12lbs to 8st division title within the bantamweight class, as per their 4 May contest

21 September   Johnny Hughes (Bloomsbury) W PTS 20 Liverpool

19 October   Owen Moran (Birmingham) ND 6 Worcester. Seen as a trial bout

30 October   Harry Slough (West Hartlepool, born London) W DISQ 4 Newcastle. Was billed as being for the English 7st 12lbs to 8st division title in the bantamweight class, claimed by Slough. Although Slough was well and truly kayoed, his seconds entered the ring thus getting him disqualified and robbing Bradley of an official KO win. The *Sporting Life Record Book*, 1910 credits Bradley as a kayo winner

20 November   Harry Slough (West Hartlepool, born London) W KO 18 Newcastle. This win gave Bradley a clear claim to the English 7st 12lbs to 8st division title within the bantamweight class

14 December   Jack Guyon (Clerkenwell) W KO 7 Liverpool

1906

11 January   Willie Hook (Billingsgate) W KO 4 Liverpool

20 January   George 'Digger' Stanley (Fulham) L PTS 20 Newcastle. Billed for the world and English 7st 12lbs to 8st division title within the bantamweight class, claimed by both men

8 February   Harry Brodigan (Manchester, born Sheffield) W KO 1 Liverpool

10 March   Billy Hughes (Sunderland) W PTS 20 Sunderland. On 16 May, Bradley sailed for the USA with manager and trainer, George Harry, on the Cunard Liner, 'Campanla', for a contracted (by cable) world 8st limit division title fight within the bantamweight class with Jimmy Walsh (Boston, Mass), holder of 8st 2lbs to 8st 6lbs division title. Walsh had won this by beating 'Digger' Stanley at that weight. Arrived in Boston, Mass, USA on 20 May to finalise the match with Jimmy Walsh, but failed to agree terms

8 June   Tommy O'Toole (Philadelphia) ND 6 Philadelphia, Pennsylvannia, USA. O'Toole won the newspaper decision
13 July   Tommy Langdon ND 6 Philadelphia, Pennsylvannia, USA. Langdon won the newspaper decision
7 August   Al Delmont (Boston, Mass) L PTS 15 Providence, RI, USA
21 August   Freddy O'Brien (Chelsea, Mass) L PTS 6 Chelsea, Mass, USA. Bradley returned to England immediately following the above loss
20 September   Jack Fox (Birmingham) W KO 13 Liverpool
24 September   Tom Bond (Birmingham) W KO 3 Birkenhead
18 October   Bill King (Birmingham) W KO 6 Liverpool
1 November   Harry Brodigan (Manchester, born Sheffield) W KO 9 Liverpool. Was billed as being for the North of England 7st 12lbs to 8st division title within the bantamweight class
13 December   George 'Digger' Stanley (Fulham) L PTS 20 Liverpool. Billed for the world and English 7st 12lbs to 8st division title within the bantamweight class

1907

17 January   Bob Kendrick (Spitalfields) L PTS 20 Liverpool
21 February   Jack Ladbury (Poplar) W PTS 20 Liverpool
21 March   Johnny Hughes (Bloomsbury) W RTD 14 Liverpool. A losing bout against Darkie Haley (Leytonstone), which was given in 27 April 1907 Mirror of Life has yet to be traced
16 May   'Ginger' Osborne (Billed South Africa, born London) W KO 4 Liverpool. On 20 July in the Mirror of Life, Bradley claimed 190 bouts. That claim was thought to be highly unlikely as it would have meant that he had an average of 32 bouts a year
14 October   'Young' James Southway (Pentre, Rhonda) W KO 19 Merthyr. Billed for the English 7st 12lbs to 8st division title within the bantamweight class
28 October   Jack Fox (Birmingham) L PTS 20 Liverpool. Contested at catchweights, £25 a side and purse, Bradley was believed to be touring South Wales with a boxing booth for the rest of 1907 and the majority of 1908 and 1909

1908

14 March   Johnny 'Buck' Shine (Somers Town) W KO 7 Merthyr
21 March   Jack Guyon (Clerkenwell) W PTS 10 Merthyr
30 March   George 'Digger' Stanley (Fulham) L PTS 15 Mile End
6 April   Jim Kenrick/Kenrich (Hackney) L PTS 20 Merthyr
27 April   'Darkey' Haley (Leytonstone) L PTS 10 Mile End. Reported to be a return, Haley having won their first fight, this has yet to be verified
5 December   Jack Murphy (Merthyr) W KO 3 Merthyr

1909

8 February   'Young' Conroy (Birkenhead) L PTS 15 Birkenhead
8 April   'Young' Conroy (Birkenhead) DREW 8 Birkenhead
29 April   'Young' Conroy (Birkenhead) L PTS 20 Birkenhead
17 June   Fred Sydney (Boston, Mass, USA) EXH 3 Birkenhead. Sydney was a negro
1 July   Billy Jones (Birkenhead) L KO 5 Birkenhead
22 July   'Young Smokey' Bishop (Deptford) W KO 2 Birkenhead
28 September   Matt 'Kid' Saxby (Leeds) L DISQ 19 Manchester. Bradley was disqualified for holding
6 November   Jack Guyon (Clerkenwell) W KO 13 Merthyr. A fight against Bill Lewis (Bethnal Green) L KO 11 has not been traced, after being credited to Lewis in pen picture on him in 18 December 1909 Boxing. The claim was never contradicted by either Bradley or any one connected to him. In their only two traced bouts, Lewis won both on points, but although he carried respectable punch he wasn't known as a big puncher and a KO win over a renowned durable man such as Bradley would have been a big surprise
14 December   Sam Keller (Mile End) DREW 20 Manchester
27 December   Ralph Marshall (Glasgow) L PTS 20 Glasgow

1910

10 March   Sam Keller (Mile End) DREW 20 Liverpool. This one was not contested on Sunday, 13 March as reported in some quarters
5 May   Tom Cooper (Gateshead) W RSF 3 Liverpool. There was no national title billing and no weights given or stipulated for in this contest. It was also scheduled for 15 rounds, not 20. However, Cooper was billed as the North of England 8st 4lbs division champion within the bantamweight class and following his win Bradley was billed as such in future bouts
2 June   Eddie Carsey (California, late Canada) W KO 13 Liverpool

30 June   Eddie Carsey (California, late Canada) W RTD 6 Liverpool
4 July   Leslie Williams (Tonypandy) L PTS 20 Pontypridd
28 July   Sam Russell (Limehouse) L DISQ 2 Liverpool. The fight was ended by a low blow. Bradley's opponent was announced and reported as being 'Young' Cohen (Aldgate, London), who Russell substituted for. Unfortunately the change was not made public and even went into the 1910 Sporting Life Record Book under 'Young' Cohen
22 September   Billy Hughes (Sunderland) W KO 6 Liverpool
30 September   Paddy Carroll (Liverpool) EXH 3 Liverpool
3 November   Jim Dermody (Ystradgynlais) W RTD 6 Liverpool
24 November   'Young' Sullivan (Brierley Hill) W RTD 3 Liverpool
15 December   Jobey Jordan (Sheffield) W RTD 6 Liverpool
29 December   Harry Thomas (Birmingham) DREW 20 Liverpool

1911

26 January   Harry Thomas (Birmingham) L PTS 20 Liverpool
20 February   Bert Marsh (Philadelphia, USA) W KO 6 Blackpool. On 11 March, Bradley failed to pass the doctor for a bout on this date in Liverpool versus 'Young' Conroy (Birkenhead), due to a severely sprained left hand. Despite that, Bradley had still wanted to box. Please note that Bradley wasn't the 'Ike Bradley' who boxed in a six-round no-decision contest in New York, USA on 17 March against KO Smith
11 April   Jack Jaques (Liverpool) W KO 4 Liverpool. This was Bradley's first bout since his hand injury
18 April   'Young' Conroy (Birkenhead) W RTD 2 Liverpool
13 July   Johnny Hughes (Bloomsbury) W KO 2 Liverpool
22 July   Eddie Connelly (Philadelphia, USA) W KO 3 Fleetwood
14 September   George 'Digger' Stanley L PTS 10 Liverpool. Billed for the world and British 8st 6lbs bantamweight title
25 December   Arthur Hillier (Oxford) Christmas Day L DISQ 5 Liverpool. Bradley was disqualified following a low blow

1912

1 February   Eddie Morgan (Merthyr) L DISQ 8 Liverpool. A low blow saw Bradley turfed out of the ring
14 July   'Hookey' Green (Belfast) W KO 3 Birkenhead
5 August   Johnny Curran L DISQ 8 Dublin. Yet again it was a low blow which saw Bradley disqualified

1913

February   'Boyo' Bradley (Bristol) EXH 3 Birkenhead. There was no date reported in both 22 February Boxing and Mirror of Life, so it must have happened at least six days previous to that date
13 March   'Tibby' Watson (Sydney, Australia) W RTD 2 Warrington
24 July   Robert Dastillon (Aubervilliers) L PTS 15 Liverpool
28 August   Robert Dastillon (Aubervilliers) L RSF 11 Liverpool. Although the bout was made at 8st 6lbs, with Bradley scaling 8st 3lbs, Dastillon was well over 9st
9 October   Sid Smith (Bermondsey) L PTS 10 Liverpool

1914

26 January   Jim Lloyd (Liverpool, late Newcastle) L PTS 15 Birkenhead. Bradley was one stone lighter
6 March   Eddie Morgan (Merthyr) L PTS 15 Bolton
10 March   Marcel Lepreux (France) L PTS 15 Paris, France
28 May   Marcel Lepreux (France) L PTS 15 Liverpool. 4 August: Outbreak of World War I
30 November   'Young' Joe Fox (Leeds) L RTD 8 Southwark. Bradley had cut his left hand badly in the morning and should never have been allowed to box

1915

8 January   Joe Symonds (Plymouth) L PTS 15 Plymouth
4 February   Johnny Maguire (Belfast) L DISQ 4 Belfast. Bout was ended by a low blow
18 February   Fred Anderson (Lambeth) L PTS 10 Liverpool

1916

15 June   Johnny Bell W RSF 1 Liverpool. This is the final traced bout of Bradley's career

Career: 149 contests, won 79, drew 7, lost 43, no decision 6, 13 exhibitions, result unknown 1

Ike Bradley

Jim Kenrick (Kendrick also given)

From Hackney and Homerton. Born: 24 September 1880 at 54 Bromley Walk, Hackney, London. Real name: Thomas Joseph Grimwood. He took his ring name from the former English 10st championship claimant and winner of the English 10st 12lbs championship competition in 1887, 'Jim Kendrick' of Lambeth. Height 5'0"

English 7st 10lbs to 7st 12lbs limit title claimant, 1903. English 8st champion, 1905. Claimed that he made his boxing debut in a 12-round bout with a friend for a £5 a side, losing when he retired in the 11th round. Not traced were 12 straight losses he claimed at the start of his career

1898

5 February   Jack O'Connell L RSF 3 (10) Bethnal Green. O'Connell, who was one stone heavier and three inches taller, put Kenrick down five times in the third round before the bout was stopped
3 March   Bob Howard L PTS 8 Bermondsey
20 June   Bill Green L PTS 10 Bermondsey
12 September   Bob Howard DREW 11 (10) Bermondsey. An extra round was ordered and fought. A bare-knuckle prize fight against Jack Bartlett W 4 was claimed but not traced, as were fights against 'Kid' Lacey W 3, 'Wag' Collone W 3 and Jack Morgan W 7. The last three fights were claimed in a 31 August 1901 pen picture, but none have been traced

1899

8 February   Harry Ashley L KO 3 (6) Putney
7 March   Bill Ray L PTS 3 New Cross. First series of a 7st competition
29 March   Archie Wright W PTS 3 Pentonville. The first series of a 7st 6lbs competition, it was won on the referee's casting vote
29 March   George Dempsey L PTS 3 Pentonville. The semi-final of a 7st 6lbs competition
22 June   Jim Stroud L PTS 6 The Strand
9 September   Bill Easy W RSF 1 Woolwich. The first series of a 7st 2lbs competition
9 September   Bill Ray W PTS 3 Woolwich. The semi-final of a 7st 2lbs competition

9 September   Frank Morcombe L PTS 3 Woolwich. The final of a 7st 2lbs competition
5 October   Jim Stroud L PTS 3 The Strand. The first series of a 7st 6lbs competition
16 October   Herbert Rix W PTS 10 Covent Garden
28 October   Jim Exall L PTS 8 Woolwich. The opponent was also given as being Frank Exall
29 November   Jim Exall W PTS 10 Shoreditch
30 November   Jim Exall W PTS 10 Woolwich. This was their second bout in two days
4 December   Jim Exall ND 3 Covent Garden. Given as a trial bout
16 December   Charley Banks W PTS 3 Peckham. The first series of a 7st 2lbs competition
23 December   Tom Lamb W KO 2 (3) Peckham. The final of a 7st 2lbs competition

1900

10 January   Jim Weston W KO 2 (10) Shoreditch
15 January   Bob Woodley W RSF 3 (6) Covent Garden
25 January   George Dempsey L PTS 3 Drury Lane. The first series of an 8st competition
29 January   George Dunn W KO 2 (6) Covent Garden. The opponent's name was also given as Dunny/Denny
30 January   Jim Stroud L PTS 6 Oxford Street
7 February   Jack Guyon L KO 4 Shoreditch. While the *Mirror of Life* gave L KO 4, the *Sporting Life* gave L KO 3
8 February   Jim Richardson W PTS 6 The Strand
9 April   Jim Stroud L PTS 6 Covent Garden
7 May   Jack Guyon L PTS 6 Covent Garden
14 May   Jack Maloney W RTD 3 (6) Stamford Hill. The *Sporting Life* mispelt Kenrick (Kendrick) as Merrick
1 October   Jim Stroud W KO 2 (6) Covent Garden
2 November   Harry Ashley W PTS 6 Oxford Street
14 November   Jim Casey W KO 1 (3) Shoreditch. The first series of an 8st competition
14 November   W.Perry ND 3 Shoreditch. The semi-final of an 8st competition
14 November   Jack Guyon L RSF 4 (6) Shoreditch. The final of an 8st competition
15 November   Alf Rosser W PTS 6 Deptford
29 November   Joe Kenny W PTS 3 The Strand. The first series of an 8st competition
29 November   Alf Lloyd W RSF 2 (3) The Strand. The semi-final of an 8st competition
29 November   Dave Morbin L PTS 3 The Strand. The final of an 8st competition
3 December   'Toby' McKenzie W PTS 6 Covent Garden
5 December   Jim Murray W RSF 4 (6) Shoreditch
12 December   Charlie Exall W PTS 10 Shoreditch
19 December   'Toby' McKenzie W PTS 10 Shoreditch. While the *Mirror of Life* gave the same result, the *Sporting Life* gave W PTS 8

1901

31 January   'Toby' McKenzie W PTS 6 Whitechapel. On 16 March, through the auspices of the *Sporting Life*, Kenrick challenged 'All England' at 7st 12lbs, 2pm weigh-in, £25 a side and an NSC purse
1 April   Bill Pike W PTS 6 Stamford Hill
20 April   Ted Calder W RTD 2 Whitechapel. First series of 7st 10lbs local competition. Calder was initially given as Jack Calder, but was corrected in 26 April *Sporting Life*
20 April   Bill Field W PTS 6 (2) Whitechapel. The second series of a 7st 10lbs local championship competition
20 April   'Wag' Hampton L PTS 6 (2) Whitechapel. The third series of a 7st 10lbs local championship competition
29 April   Fred Herring W RTD 1 Whitechapel. The first series of an English 8st 4lbs championship belt competition
4 May   Tom Hands W PTS 6 (2) Whitechapel. The semi-final of an English 8st 4lbs championship belt competition
4 May   Bill Stonelake L KO 3 Whitechapel. The final of an English 8st 4lbs championship belt competition
25 May   George Collins W PTS 6 Whitechapel
22 June   Tom King DREW 6 Whitechapel
13 July   Charlie Smirke W PTS 6 Whitechapel
22 July   Tommy Urquart ND 3 Homerton. The first series of a 7st 6lbs competition

22 July   Jack Guyon EXH 3 Homerton. This was Kenrick's second bout on this private show promoted by Kenrick himself (Lew Kenrick also on bill)
3 August   'Wag' Hampton L PTS 6 Whitechapel
10 August   Jack Fitzpatrick W PTS 6 Whitechapel
21 August   Billy 'Kid' Veitch W KO 14 (20) Gateshead. Billed for the English 7st 10lbs title, for £90
28 September   Jack Christian W PTS 6 Woolwich
12 October   Jim Sweeney W RTD 5 (8) Woolwich
21 October   Jack Guyon W PTS 6 Covent Garden
24 October   Dave Morbin W PTS 6 The Strand
29 October   George Collins W PTS 8 Newmarket
2 November   Harry Smith W PTS 8 Woolwich
7 November   Jack Guyon L PTS 6 Tottenham Court Road
16 November   Bill Radley W PTS 4 (3) Whitechapel. The first series of an 8st competition, which saw an extra round contested
16 November   Tom King L PTS 3 Whitechapel. The semi-final of an 8st competition
23 November   Dave Morbin W PTS 6 Woolwich
7 December   Jack Guyon L PTS 6 Woolwich
18 December   George Collins W PTS 3 Lambeth. The first series of an 8st 4lbs competition
19 December   Jack Guyon W PTS 3 Lambeth. The semi-final of an 8st 4lbs competition
20 December   Dave Morbin W PTS 4 Lambeth. The final of an 8st 4lbs competition. The report stated: "prior to winning this competition, Kenrick had competed unsuccessfully in no less than six previous competitions". This traced record shows him winning one and proving unsuccessful in ten other competitions up to this date
21 December   Harry Churchill DREW 6 Woolwich

1902
18 January   Harold Root L PTS 6 Covent Garden
20 January   Harry Churchill DREW 6 Woolwich
27 January   George Collins NC 3 (6) West Croydon. The referee disqualified both for 'not trying' and declared a no contest
13 March   Johnny Somers W PTS 6 Woolwich
27 March   Mr Ernie Moody EXH 3 Tottenham Court Road
27 March   Bill Murray EXH 4 Kennington. This was the second of two exhibitions that Kenrick gave at two different venues on the same day
29 March   George 'Digger' Stanley L PTS 6 Whitechapel
26 April   Dave Job W PTS 10 Covent Garden. Made at 7st 9lbs, with no weights given and no title billing. On 5 May, it was reported that Jack Lamb (Lambeth), on a show at Woolwich on this date, had claimed to have recently 'run-up' to Jim Kenrick in the final of a 7st 6lbs competition at Lambeth. This contest has yet to be traced
12 May   Owen Moran L PTS 10 Covent Garden. Made at 7st 10lbs with no title billing, it was contested under the new safety rule brought in by the NSC that restricted all bouts to ten rounds. The rule only lasted for a short time. Kenrick was announced as being 7st 7lbs and Moran 7st 10lbs
2 June   Jack Guyon L PTS 10 Covent Garden. The *Sporting Life*, *Sportsman*, *Licensed Victualars Gazette* all give same result, but the *Mirror of Life* gave it as L KO 2
16 June   Dave Job W PTS 6 Whitechapel
19 July   Bill Bruce W PTS 6 Whitechapel
25 August   Dave Job W PTS 6 Whitechapel. On 26 August, Kenrick challenged 'All England' at 8st
6 September   'Tibby' Watson W PTS 6 Woolwich
8 September   Harry Churchill W DISQ 3 (6) Marylebone
27 September   Jack Fitzpatrick W PTS 6 Whitechapel
22 October   Jack Walker L PTS 15 Oxford Street. Billed for the English 7st 12lbs limit title, no weights were given but both men were announced as being inside. For a purse of £100, and refereed by Mr Ed Humphries, it had been postponed from 6 October. Kenrick was down twice in the 15th
15 November   Harry McDermott L PTS 15 Newcastle
27 December   Dave Morbin L PTS 6 Whitechapel

1903
17 January   Charlie Exall DREW 15 Newcastle. Billed for the world and English 7st 10lbs limit title and £100, the *Sporting Life* gave Kenrick as Jim McKendrick
21 February   Charlie Exall W PTS 20 Newcastle. Billed for the world and English 7st 10lbs limit title, but Kenrick was one pound overweight at 7st 11lbs, while Exall made 7st 7lbs. At that period, the ruling was if a man weighed in 'overweight' he faced forfeit and given no second chance to make the weight, it being considered that the time spent in training was the given time to make the contracted weight. Contested over the weight, with the win Kenrick claimed the English title at 7st 10lbs to 7st 12lbs. Refereed by William 'Billy' Bell
14 March   George 'Digger' Stanley L PTS 6 Whitechapel
25 March   George Smith EXH 3 Shepherds Bush. Kenrick was billed as the 7st 10lbs English champion. Having got married on 13 April, on 23 April he challenged the American 7st 10lbs champion, Jimmy Walsh (Boston, Mass), to a bout to decide the world 7st 10lbs title
15 June   'Tibby' Watson W PTS 6 Whitechapel
22 June   'Tibby' Watson EXH 3 Whitechapel. On 6 July, Kenrick opened out as a promoter at the Manor Theatre, Mare Street, Hackney. A month or so later, on 9 September, it was reported in the *Mirror of Life* that Kenrick claimed 200 bouts, of which he had won 150 and had started his career with 12 losses
14 September   'Young' Joseph L PTS 12 (2) Whitechapel. Made at 7st 10lbs for £30, there was no title involvement and was contested over two-minute rounds
26 October   Jack Walker DREW 6 Whitechapel
16 November   Bert Clark W PTS 10 Hackney
30 December   Johnny Thomas ND 3 Kensington. The second series of an 8st 6lbs competition

1904
25 January   Fred Herring W PTS 15 Covent Garden. Made at the 7st 12lbs limit, no weights were given and there was no title billing, possibly due to it being contested over only 15 rounds and the monetary return not being big enough
14 March   Jim Glover W KO 1 (10) Covent Garden. It was announced on 11 April that Kenrick's wife had given birth to a baby girl
30 May   Dave Job W RSF 12 (15) Covent Garden. No weights were given or stipulated and there was no title billing. On 4 June Kenrick challenged the world at 7st 10lbs, give or take 2lbs. This was followed on 2 July, when he stated that he had won the English 7st 10lbs title by beating Charlie Exall 18 months earlier
5 November   Jack Wren L PTS 6 Whitechapel
21 November   'Darkey' Haley DREW 6 Whitechapel. On 5 December, an advertised six-round bout against 'Darkey' Haley at 'Wonderland', Whitechapel was not carried in the show report, so it was either cancelled or went on late after the reporter had left

1905
8 February   Dick Golding EXH 3 Chelsea
27 February   Patrick 'Boyo' Driscoll W PTS 15 Covent Garden. Refereed by Bernard J. Angle, according to the *Mirror of Life* this was billed for the English 7st 12lbs to 8st limit title and carried a championship belt
10 April   Ike Bradley W PTS 15 Covent Garden. Billed for the English 7st 12lbs to 8st limit title, it was announced that both men made 7st 11lbs, although the *Mirror of Life* and *Sporting Life* gave Bradley as 7st 9lbs. Thus, it was the 7st 10lbs to 7st 12lbs limit title that was involved
4 May   Ike Bradley DREW 20 (2) Liverpool. No weights given or stipulated and contested over two-minute rounds
23 May   Dick Golding EXH 3 Homerton
25 May   Johnny Hughes W DISQ 10 Liverpool. No weights given or stipulated and contested over two-minute rounds. On 14 June in the *Mirror of Life*, Kenrick claimed the English 8st limit title
27 July   Ike Bradley W PTS 20 Liverpool. Made at the 8st limit, for £100, and refereed by Mr James, no weights were given. Although contested over three-minute rounds, the reports failed to mention any title billing, but it has to be seen as a defence of Kenrick's title claim at 8st
24 August   Owen Moran L KO 7 Liverpool. Made at 8st 2lbs, for £200, no weights were given and it failed to qualify as a title bout with two-minute rounds in place
12 October   Charlie Exall W KO 9 Liverpool. No weights were given or stipulated and contested ove two-minute rounds
19 October   Jack Fox L PTS 6 Worcester
23 October   Owen Moran EXH 3 Covent Garden
27 November   Jack Guyon W PTS 15 Covent Garden. Made at the 7st 12lbs limit, Kenrick scaled 7st 12lbs to Guyon's 7st 12lbs. Strangely, there was no title billing, but it had to be a defence of Kendrick's claim to 7st 12lbs limit, also claimed by Guyon. Referee Mr John H.Douglas

1906
1 February   Bob Kendrick L PTS 6 Whitechapel. On 19 February it was

reported that Kenrick, the English 7st 10lbs champion having never been beaten at the weight since winning the title from Charlie Exall in 1903, had challenged anyone in the world at 7st 10lbs for the world title at the weight, £100 a side

18 February   Johnny Hughes L PTS 6 Charing Cross

5 March   A.Dryden EXH 3 Cardiff

6 March   Patrick 'Boyo' Driscoll EXH 3 Cardiff. This was the last day of the world famous annual two-day Nazareth House Convent Fund show. On 6 March, Kenrick was challenged by Mark Verrall (Tottenham) to a bout for the English 7st 10lbs limit title claimed by Verrall

27 March   Fred Herring EXH 3 Homerton

2 April   Mark Verrall L DISQ 3 (15) Covent Garden. Decided by a low blow, the contest was stated to have involved the English 7st 10lbs title, but no weights were given or stipulated and no title billing shown in *Mirror of Life* report on 24 March. The *Sporting Life* stated that Kenrick was several pounds overweight and the bout went on over 15 rounds, not 20. Referee J.H.Douglas. On 27 April in the *Sporting Life*, Kenrick challenged the world at 7st 12lbs to 8st . Three days later, on 30 April, he was challenged by Johnny Hughes (Bloomsbury) at the 8st limit with a 2pm weigh-in

17 May   Jack Fox DREW 20 (2) Liverpool. This was a catchweights bout with no weights given. On 9 June in the *Sporting Life*, Kenrick was challenged again by Johnny Hughes (Bloomsbury), but this time at a limit of 7st 12lbs, 15 or 20 three-minute rounds, with a 2pm weigh-in. After several months out of the ring, Kenrick challenged 'All England' at 8st on 13 October

5 November   'Ginger' Osborne W PTS 10 Covent Garden. Made at 8st 2lbs, Osborne scaling 8st and Kenrick 8st 11lbs, there was no title billing as it was not contested over a recognised championship distance. Referee J.H.Douglas

27 December   Bill Lewis DREW 6 Lambeth

1907

7 January   Sam Keller DREW 10 Lambeth. Made at catchweights, no weights were given

17 January   Sam Keller L PTS 6 Whitechapel. On 24 January, Kenrick was challenged by Ralph Marshall (Scotland) at 7st 10lbs, give or take 2lbs, to a 7st 12lbs contest and a ringside weigh-in over 15 or 20 rounds. A day later, on 25 January, Kenrick challenged the world at 7st 12lbs up to 8st 2lbs, Ralph Marshall preferred, only to draw a challenge from 'Ginger' Owen over 15 or 20 rounds at 8st to 8st 2lbs the next day

26 January   Ted Moore L PTS 6 Woolwich. On 7 February, the *Sporting Life* reported Jim Kenrick as the English 7st 12lbs to 8st champion

21 February   Dave Morbin L PTS 6 Colchester

18 March   'Young' Smith W PTS 6 Camberwell. On 5 April, the *Sporting Life* repeated that Jim Kenrick was the 8st champion

15 April   Harry Churchill W PTS 6 Camberwell

19 April   Mr W.Nicholson EXH 3 Grays Inn Road

20 April   Mr E.Adams EXH 3 Grays Inn Road

22 June   Harry Slough W RTD 8 (15) West Hartlepool. No weights were given or stipulated. On 11 September in the *Sporting Life*, Kenrick challenged 'All England' at 8st and on 1 October he was called the English 7st 12lbs champion

5 October   Harry Smith W PTS 6 Lambeth. Made at 7st 12lbs

28 November   Johnny Hughes L PTS 6 Camberwell. Hughes won on the referee's casting vote after the judges had disagreed

9 December   Jack Guyon W PTS 10 Merthyr. Made at catchweights

14 December   'Young' Conroy W PTS 10 Merthyr. Made at catchweights

16 December   'Tibby' Watson DREW 10 Merthyr. Made at catchweights

21 December   Willie Hook W PTS 6 Merthyr. Made at catchweights

1908

16 January   Harry Brodigan W KO 7 (20) Liverpool. Made at catchweights

30 January   'Young' James Southway W PTS 15 (2) Merthyr. Made at catchweights and contested over two-minute rounds

22 February   Harry Norton W RTD 5 (10) Merthyr. Kenrick was billed as the English 8st champion

9 May   Jack Veitch W KO 4 (6) Whitechapel. Reported in one instance as W KO 3, W KO 4 was the correct result. On 13 May it was reported that Jim Kenrick was the English 8st champion

18 May   Frank McFoy W RTD 4 (6) Bermondsey

30 May   Albert Dabbs W KO 5 (6) Whitechapel. This was the pro debut of Dabbs, an ex amateur

13 June   Johnny 'Buck' Shine W KO 3 (6) Whitechapel. While the *Sporting Life* gave W KO 3, the *Mirror of Life* gave W KO 4

22 June   Matt 'Kid' Saxby W PTS 6 Birmingham. Although Kenrick was down in the first, he wasn't knocked out in the sixth as in some reports

1 July   Harry Ware W PTS 8 Birmingham

4 July   Charlie Dixon W PTS 6 Whitechapel

18 July   Bill Lewis L PTS 6 Whitechapel

25 July   Harry Ware DREW 6 Whitechapel

29 August   Johnny 'Buck' Shine W KO 4 (6) Cleethorpes. The venue was mistakenly given as being Grimsby because it was held at Blundell Park, the ground of the Grimsby Association Football Club, which was and still is situated in Cleethorpes

11 September   Johnny 'Buck' Shine W KO 4 (8) Hull. On 21 November, the *Mirror of Life* carried Kenrick's pen picture and a record (with no dates, years or venues) consisting of 128 bouts. Twenty seven of these claimed bouts have not been traced and several seem dubious. It could be a misprint of either the name of opponent or the original result, or just a previous bout repeated. Kenrick claimed about 200 bouts. Traced records up to this date shows 159 bouts, including exhibitions and no-decision bouts, but not the four untraced bouts carried in the *Mirror of Life* pen picture record of 31 August 1901; None of which, strangely enough, appeared in the 21 November 1908 pen picture record

30 November   Frank McFoy W PTS 6 Camberwell

19 December   Tom Smith W PTS 10 Birmingham

28 December   Frank McFoy L PTS 15 Walworth. This was a catchweights bout, refereed by 'Brummy' Meadows. On 1 January 1909, it was reported in the *Sporting Life* that Jim Kenrick was the English 8st champion. This was repeated in the 16 January issue, but the 18 January issue named Johnny Hughes (Bloomsbury) as the English 8st champion. On a monumental day for boxing in general, 11 February saw the National Sporting Club, Covent Garden, London, England announce the classification of eight named-weight divisions, along with the introduction of the Lord Lonsdale Championship Belts for English (now officially renamed British championship) winners. This statement effectively ended the championships at every two pounds era, although some fighters still struggled on for a few more years

1909

15 February   'Young' Smith L PTS 8 Bishopsgate

20 March   Harry Ware DREW 15 Merthyr

3 April   Harry Ware L PTS 15 Whitechapel. On 5 April, the *Sporting Life* reported that Kenrick, the English 8st champion, is to go to the USA to box for the world bantamweight 8st 6lbs title

10 April   'Boyo' Bradley W RTD 8 (15) Whitechapel. This was a catchweights bout

15 April   Sam Keller DREW 6 Hackney

19 April   'Young' Smith DREW 6 Hoxton. On 24 April, the *Mirror of Life* reported that 'Driver' Himphen, who started boxing in 1900, claimed that he had boxed a draw over six rounds with Jim Kenrick in a bout that was untraced in the latter's record

28 April   'Young' Smith DREW 6 London. This was a private show restricted to 40. The venue was not given. On 12 May, it was reported that Kenrick had sailed from Southampton on the 'Adriatic' for New York in the USA, where he will be managed by Tom O'Rourke and will make his debut against Johnny Coulon, the American 7st 7lbs paperweight champion. Bantamweight was also given

26 June   'Young' George Pierce ND 5 Philadelphia, Pennsylvania, USA. Pierce, who was coloured, was credited with the newspaper decision. On 29 June, the *Sporting Life* stated that the introduction of eight standard weights had dethroned all previous title claimants and those in the running for the newly introduced 8st flyweight class, a name previously unheard of, were Charlie Dew, Albert Cocksedge, Jim Kenrick and many others of high quality. Prior to that, paperweight and bantamweight had been the most commonly used names, other than the actual poundage title, there being a proliferation of boxers between 7st and 8st in Britain

2 July   Mike Malone ND 6 Philadelphia, Pennsylvania, USA. The newspaper decision was given as DREW 6, despite Kenrick being down three times in the second and once in the third. Although the date of the fight was given in the *Mirror of Life* as 2 July, the *Sporting Life* gave it as 3 July

July   Patsy Brannigan ND 6 La Trobe, Pennsylvania, USA. Kenrick was reported as being the English bantamweight champion, which he wasn't, and that this was his USA debut, according to the *Mirror of Life* on 7 August. The paper also stated that Kenrick really won every round, yet the newspaper decision went to Branigan. Following this, Kenrick challenged Monte Attell at 8st 3lbs

4 August   Johnny Daly ND 10 NYC, New York, USA

6 August   Patsy Brannigan ND 10 NYC, New York, USA. The 21 August

issue of the *Mirror of Life* gave 5 August as the date and stated that Brannigan was a good winner, who rightly got the newspaper decision. Kenrick was down in the eighth. On 13 October, Kenrick challenged Danny Webster (California) after he had outpointed Monte Attell over ten rounds on this date in Los Angeles in a bout billed as being for the world 8st 4lbs bantamweight title and championship belt. In a 6 December letter home, Kenrick stated he had signed up to meet Johnny Daly in New York on 12 December, but no report was found so it was possibly cancelled

1910

18 February   Johnny Coulon L PTS 10 New Orleans, Louisiana, USA. Made at 8st with no title billing, *Boxing's* report stated that Kenrick weakened himself in getting down to 8st, but floored Coulon in the second and slipped down himself in same round. Kenrick, who was then floored for 'nine' in the fourth, put up a terrific bout and asked for return, but over 20 rounds

6 March   Johnny Coulon L RTD 18 (20) New Orleans, Louisiana, USA. Made at 8st 3lbs with a ringside weigh-in, again there was no title billing in British press reports. The *Mirror of Life* American correspondent, G.D.Almy, stated that the bout showed the utter folly of a near champion like Coulon being allowed to meet a foreign fighter like Kenrick, who wrongly claimed to be the British bantamweight champion. Almy reported: "Kenrick was outclassed and showed only gameness. In the 19th he was put down by a blow to the midriff and fell on his head. Although he got up he fell partly through the ropes from weakness and was counted out without any protest". On 2 April, *Boxing* reported that Kenrick would now be undertaking a theatre engagement in New Orleans, with an offer of three more local bouts

2 April   Patsy Brannigan DREW 10 New Orleans, Louisiana, USA

24 April   Patsy Brannigan DREW 10 New Orleans, Louisiana, USA. Kenrick claimed that he won every round and that fans and press alike criticised the referee for his decision. However, this was not borne out by other reports. In mid June Kenrick returned to England, partly for a holiday and partly hoping to meet George 'Digger' Stanley for the British bantamweight title and Lonsdale Belt before returning to the USA in the fall

12 September   Johnny Condon L PTS 20 Whitechapel. Made at 8st 8lbs, Kenrick, who was ³/₄lb overweight at 8st 8³/₄lbs, floored Condon, 8st 7¹/₄lbs, for 'eight' in the second, breaking his right hand in the process. Kenrick also had his right eye closed tight from the sixth round on and was well beaten

27 October   Johnny Hughes W PTS 20 (2) Holborn. Made at 8st 4lbs, Kenrick scaling 8st 4lbs to Hughes' 8st 2lbs, this was stated to be their fifth meeting. The paper in question then went on to give the results of just two of their previous bouts. Only three previous bouts between them have been traced

5 December   Alf 'Spider' Stewart W RTD 7 (15) Covent Garden. Made at 8st 4lbs, Kenrick scaled 8st 2¹/₂lbs to Stewart's 8st 1lb

12 December   Bill King L PTS 20 Glasgow. Made at 8st 8lbs, King weighed 8st 7lbs and Kenrick 8st 5¹/₂lbs

1911

30 January   Johnny Hughes L PTS 20 Holborn

18 February   'Young' Jack Cohen L PTS 20 Whitechapel. Made at the 8st 6lbs limit and articled as being at 8st 4lbs, give or take 2lbs, what was unusual for this venue was the fact that they would be fighting over three-minute rounds. On 12 April Kenrick sailed for the USA on the 'Adriatic'

9 May   Young Wagner ND 10 NYC, New York, USA. Made at 8st 6lbs, Kenrick scaled 8st 3lbs while Wagner came in at 8st 13lbs, well over the weight. The newspaper decision went to Kenrick on points. According to *Boxing,* on 3 June, Kenrick insists that he can still make 8st and was still waiting to be chosen to contest the English flyweight title and Lonsdale Belt. The 17 June *Boxing* stated that Kenrick would most likely stay in the USA until March 1912, but would return at once if offered a bout with Sid Smith (Bermondsey) for the British flyweight title and Lonsdale Belt

14 July   Young Wagner ND 10 Brooklyn, NYC, New York, USA. The newspaper decision went against Kenrick after ten rounds of boxing

3 August   Patsy Brannigan L PTS 20 Springfield, Ohio, USA

30 August   Bobby Reynolds ND 6 Philadelphia, Pennsylvania, USA

29 September   Young Wagner ND 10 NYC, New York, USA. Kenrick, who was a short-notice substitute for Frankie Burns, was deemed to have lost the newspaper decision

11 October   'Young' Britt L KO 10 Baltimore, Maryland, USA

11 December   Jimmy Walsh ND 8 Boston, Mass, USA. Losing the newspaper decision, ten rounds also being given as the distance, Kenrick was down in both the second and fifth rounds

23 December   'Young' Reilly ND 10 NYC, New York, USA. Kenrick, who was falsely billed as the English 8st champion, lost the newspaper decision

1912

8 January   Monte Attell ND 6 Pittsburgh, Pennsylvania, USA. Attell won the newspaper decision

14 March   Frankie Burns L PTS 10 New Orleans, Louisiana, USA

20 August   Frankie Burns ND 10 Rockaway, New York, USA. Burns won the newspaper decision

18 September   Patsy Brannigan ND 10 NYC, New York, USA. Brannigan won the newspaper decision

5 October   Frankie Conley ND 6 Philadelphia, Pennsylvania, USA. Conley won the newspaper decision

14 December   Frankie Burns ND 6 Brooklyn, NYC, New York, USA. Burns won the newspaper decision

1913

10 March   'Young' Jabez White ND 10 Albany, New York, USA. Kenrick won the newspaper decision

14 March   'Young' Wagner ND 10 Manhattan, NYC, New York, USA. Kenrick won the newspaper decision

11 June   'Kid' Williams L RSF 6 Baltimore, Maryland, USA. *Boxing* of 21 June and *Mirror of Life* of 28 June both give the date as being 12 June

2 September   Jimmy Walsh ND 10 NYC, New York, USA. Walsh won the newspaper decision

14 October   'Young' Freddie Diggins ND 6 Philadelphia, Pennsylvania, USA. Kenrick won the newspaper decision according to the *Mirror of Life* of 1 November, while *Boxing*. On the same day, gave it to Diggins

1914

12 May   Steve 'Kid' Sullivan ND 10 Brooklyn, NYC, New York, USA. The newspaper decision was deemed to be a draw

7 July   Frankie Burns L KO 9 Rockaway, New York, USA. In what was the last traced bout for Kenrick at the age of 33, the *Ring Record Book* mistakenly gives this as taking place in 1913. Following the outbreak of World War One on 4 August, it was reported in *Sporting Life* on 21 October that Kenrick had recently returned to Britain from the USA

Career: 205 contests on traced records, including no-decision and exhibition contests, plus 31 contests that were claimed but untraced and two advertised but unreported bouts that were possibly cancelled

Jim Kenrick

Charlie 'Toff' Wall

Charlie 'Toff' Wall

From Hackney. Billed as the English 10st 4lbs champion in February 1885, 10st 8lbs champion in May 1886, 11st champion in August 1886 and 11st 4lbs champion from July 1885. Was the official English 11st 4lbs champion from 8 February 1890 to 19 October 1891. Championship recognition was withdrawn because of Wall's failure to go ahead with proposed bouts and he was so good that others refused to take him on in anything other than exhibition bouts. He claimed that he was never bested even when drunk, although it was alleged that the gentleman amateur, Robert 'Bob' Hare, had the best of their spar of 13 December 1886 when Wall was drunk

1884
28 January Jim Picton EXH 3 Hackney
15 February Jack Donoghue W PTS 3 Shoreditch. The first series of a 10st 4lbs, £5 competition
15 February Arthur Coooper W PTS 3 Shoreditch. The semi-final of a 10st 4lbs, £5 competition
15 February Tom Picton W PTS 3 Shoreditch. The final of a 10st 4lbs, £5 competition
20 February Jim Picton EXH 3 St Lukes
12 March Jim Picton EXH 3 Hackney
27 March Jim Picton EXH 3 Hackney
12 May Jim Picton EXH 3 Hackney
4 September Tommy Hill EXH 4 Shoreditch
22 September Jim Picton EXH 3 Hackney
26 September Charlie Parrish EXH 3 Hackney
6 October Jim Picton EXH 3 Kingsland
6 October Bill Cheese EXH 3 Kingsland. This was the second of two exhibitions on the same show
13 October Tom Symons EXH 3 Shoreditch
27 October H.Bussard EXH 3 Tottenham
18 November Mr Keightley EXH 3 Old Ford
25 November J.Thompson EXH 3 Oxford Street
23 December Bill Cheese EXH 3 Old Ford

1885
5 January Bill Cheese EXH 3 Shoreditch
13 January George 'Rough' Pearson EXH 3 Old Ford
26 January H.Boswell EXH 3 Tottenham
27 January George 'Rough' Pearson EXH 3 Old Ford
2 February Jim Picton EXH 3 Tottenham
2 February Bob Dunbar EXH 3 Shoreditch. This was the second of two exhibitions on the same day
14 February Bill Long EXH 3 Islington
24 February Manning Salmon EXH 3 Enfield Highway. Wall was billed as the English 10st 4lbs champion
16 March Bill Cheese EXH 3 Shoreditch
17 March Bill Cheese EXH 3 Shoreditch
20 April Bill Cheese EXH 3 Shoreditch
22 April Bob Preston EXH 3 Clapton Park
11 May J.'Yorkey' Cashley EXH 3 Shoreditch
14 July George 'Rough' Pearson W RTD 63 Epping Forest (start) and Chingford (finish). This was Wall's debut in a bare-knuckle prize fight under London Prize Ring Rules. The first 42 rounds, lasting 52 minutes, were fought at Epping Forest before being stopped by the police, so the fight moved on three miles to Chingford where 21 more rounds, lasting 30 minutes, were fought. Pearson was reported as being 5'10" and 11st 4lbs, with Wall 5'4½" and 10st 9lbs
22 September Mr McCarthy EXH 3 Tottenham
23 October 'An amateur' EXH 3 Shoreditch
26 October 'A pupil' EXH 3 Bethnal Green
2 November Mr Richardson EXH 3 Bethnal Green
3 November J.Thurgood EXH 3 Bethnal Green
17 November 'A pupil' EXH 3 Shoreditch
26 November 'A pupil' EXH 3 Shoreditch
30 November J.'Yorkey' Cashley EXH 3 Bethnal Green
7 December 'Ching Ghook' EXH 3 Shoreditch
8 December Bob Dunbar EXH 3 Bethnal Green
8 December Jack 'Baby' Partridge EXH 3 Hounsditch. This was the second of two exhibitions given on the same day

1895
5 February Mr George Jones EXH 3 Leytonstone
20 March William 'Cock Robin' Robinson EXH 3 Shoreditch
26 April Mr George Jones EXH 3 Canning Town. Wall's record between May 1885 and 5 February 1895 is currently being evaluated and will hopefully be available for inclusion in next year's book

1896
26 February Jem Smith EXH 3 Bethnal Green
12 March Mr George Jones EXH 3 Shoreditch
5 December Bill Day EXH 3 Shoreditch
14 December George Pearson EXH 3 Northampton
19 December 'Ginger' Osborne EXH 3 Shoreditch

1897
20 May Dido Plumb EXH 3 Tottenham
27 December Dido Plumb EXH 3 Islington
28 December Dido Plumb EXH 3 Islington
29 December Dido Plumb EXH 3 Islington
30 December Dido Plumb EXH 3 Islington
31 December Dido Plumb EXH 3 Islington

1898
1 January Dido Plumb EXH 3 Islington
26 October Dido Plumb EXH 3 Hounslow
12 December Dido Plumb EXH 3 West Brompton. There were no fights traced for Wall in 1899. On 24 March, 1900, in the *Mirror of Life,* it was stated that early in his career Dido Plumb had lost on points 'Toff' Wall. However, no such bout has ever been traced or even previously mentioned and Plumb was always stated to have been Wall's pupil

1900
21 June Dido Plumb EXH 3 Bermondsey

1901
28 March Dido Plumb EXH 3 Mildmay AC
1 April Mr William Ligo EXH 3 Stamford Hill

6 May   Dido Plumb EXH 3 Ponders End
17 July   'Leader of gang of toughs' W KO 6 Hackney. This was reported in *Mirror of Life*

1916
18 August   Bill 'Chesterfield' Goode EXH 3 Lambeth. This was the last traced ring appearance for Wall. Early in his career, Wall supposedly met Herr Kohl (Germany). Still untraced, the 8 December 1897 *Mirror of Life* stated that long ago 'Toff' Wall beat Coll (not Kohl) of Germany. Also a three-round exhibition bout against Jem Mace in Liverpool was reported as having taken place

Career: 227 contests, won 13, 214 exhibitions

Seaman Robert 'Curly' Watson
Born: 5 October 1883, Barrow in Furness, Lancashire. Died: 5 March 1910 – after being knocked out by Frank Inglis at 'Wonderland', Whitechapel, London

Although a championship claimant, Watson had no real title claim as all his billed English title bouts were contested over two-minute rounds, not the recognised three-minute round championship course. Was the winner of the 'Wonderland' English 10st 8lb championship belt competition on 18 April 1908, but this too was only over two-minute rounds

1901
G. Newman W PTS 6. This was stated to have been Watson's ring debut. Dicky Daws W PTS 6. Dicky Daws W PTS 8. Dicky Daws W PTS 10. 'Ginger' Morgan W PTS 10. 'Ginger' Dillon W PTS 8. Paddy Burke W RSF 3. Stoker Emery W RSF 3. Seaman Felton W KO 2. P/O Killman W KO 3. 'Nigger' Rollins W PTS 8. Seaman Mercer DREW 15. All of the above bouts took place in Malta

1902
9 January   Seaman Mercer L PTS 15. Seaman Arthur Hayes (Hoxton) L PTS 6. Both bouts took place in Malta. Private Smith W PTS 6. Billy Spree (Chatham) W PTS 6. Billy Spree (Chatham) W PTS 8. Manny Petts W PTS 6. Private Carter W PTS 6. Private Carter W KO 5. Jack Frost W KO 2. Jack Frost W PTS 6. Dick Hammerton W KO 5. Dick Hammerton W KO 2. The last ten bouts took place in Sheerness

1903
Bobby Law W PTS 3; First Series of Isle of Sheppey Silver Cup 10st 'Open' competition. Francis W PTS 3; Second Series. Seaman Driver W RSF; Third series. Dick Sivel W PTS 3; Semi-final. Barry Rogers W PTS 6; Final. Seaman Morgan W PTS 6; For 'Professor' Ball's Silver Medal. Seaman Dan Kirby W PTS 3. Seaman Dan Kirby W PTS 15. Seaman Dan Kirby W PTS 15. 10st championship of Sheerness Station. All of the above bouts took place in Sheerness

1904
6 January   Billy Spree (Chatham) DREW 6 Gillingham. Seaman Stone W KO 2 Sheerness. Gunner Cooper W PTS 6 Sheerness

1905
15 April   Gunner Hart W KO 2 (6) Whitechapel
15 April   Cpl Frampton W KO 2 (6) Whitechapel
12 August   Jack Meekins W PTS 6 Whitechapel
19 August   Jack Goldswain L RTD 5 (6) Whitechapel
5 September   Gunner Grainger W RSF 2 (3) Aldershot. First series Army & Navy middleweight championships
6 September   Sgt Rogers W KO 3 (3) Aldershot. Second series Army & Navy middleweight championships
6 September   Private Jim Warner W PTS 3 Aldershot. Semi-final Army & Navy middleweight championships
6 September   Private Salter W PTS 3 Aldershot. Final Army & Navy middleweight championships
9 September   Jack Meekins DREW 6 Whitechapel
16 September   Jack Goldswain L PTS 6 Whitechapel
25 November   Jack Goldswain W PTS 8 Whitechapel
4 December   Jack Meekins W PTS 10 Covent Garden
9 December   Arthur Warner W RSF 3 (6) Whitechapel. Fights with no dates which took place early in 1906 were: Bill Curzon W PTS 6, Bob

Wilson DREW 6, Seaman Len Chapple W RTD 11 and Tom Edmunds W PTS 6 New Brompton
21 April   Charlie Knock W PTS 6 Whitechapel
21 May   Charlie Knock L RSF 17 (20) Whitechapel. Billed as being for the English 10st 4lbs limit title, but being contested over two-minute rounds disqualified it as such. A contest against Stoker Williams (W KO 3) has no date or venue available
9 June   Charlie Knock W PTS 6 Whitechapel. A contest against Trooper Jim Warner W RSF 5 Covent Garden has no date
16 July   Gunner Hart W PTS 6 Chatham
16 July   P/O Pattenden ND 3 Chatham. Second series 9st 4lbs competition
30 July   Gunner Hart W PTS 10 Chatham
18 August   Steve Smith W PTS 6 Whitechapel
19 September   Jim Sullivan (St Georges) W PTS 6 Whitechapel
24 September   D.H.G.Smith W PTS 3 Aldershot. First series Army & Navy middleweight championship
25 September   P/O H.Dunston W PTS 3 Aldershot Second series Army & Navy middleweight championship
25 September   Private Salter W PTS 3 Aldershot. Third series Army & Navy middleweight championship
26 September   Bombardier W.S.Davies W PTS 3 Aldershot. Semi-final of Army & Navy middleweight championship
26 September   Private Jim Warner W PTS 3 Aldershot. Final of Army & Navy middleweight championship
6 October   Bob Russell DREW 6 Whitechapel
8 October   Harry Fowler W PTS 10 Gillingham
27 October   Bombardier W.S.Davies L RTD 6 Newcastle
7 November   Bill Curzon W RSF 4 Piccadilly
10 November   Charlie Knock W PTS 10 Whitechapel
19 November   Trooper Jim Warner W RSF 2 Covent Garden
24 November   Andrew Jeptha W PTS 10 Whitechapel
28 November   Private Jim Warner W PTS 10 Aldershot
12 December   Ted Hobart W KO 1 Maidstone
15 December   Charlie Knock W PTS 10 Whitechapel
December   Bombardier W.S.Davies W PTS 6 Aldershot. A claimed fight against Trooper Harper W RSF 5 Covent Garden has not been traced

1907
12 January   *Mirror of Life* - Watson has now left the RN
11 February   Andrew Jeptha W PTS 20 Whitechapel. Billed wrongly as being for the English 10st 4lbs limit welterweight title, as Jeptha was not eligible and it was contested over two-minute rounds
25 February   Bombardier W.S.Davies W KO 7 (10) Covent Garden
13 March   Cpl Bill Baker W PTS 6 Maidstone
25 March   Andrew Jeptha L KO 4 (20) Whitechapel. Although given publicity by 'Wonderland' as involving the English 10st 4lbs welterweight championship, Jeptha was not eligible and only two-minute rounds were contested. The sporting press all agreed that the English 10st 4lbs limit welterweight title was still vacant following the fight
11 April   Bombardier W.S.Davies W PTS 6 Aldershot
20 April   Cpl Bill Baker DREW 6 Whitechapel
29 April   Bill Cockayne W PTS 6 Whitechapel
6 May   Arthur Warner W PTS 10 Chatham
9 May   Bombardier W.S.Davies W PTS 8 Aldershot
1 June   Peter Brown W PTS 6 Whitechapel. No date or venue known for Bombardier W.S.Davies W KO 7
29 June   'Bermondsey' Jim Sullivan W PTS 6 Whitechapel
10 August   Charlie Knock W PTS 6 Whitechapel
14 September   Charlie Knock DREW 6 Whitechapel
28 September   'Plumstead' Jack Palmer W PTS 6 Lambeth. A supposed fight against Bill Cockayne W PTS 6 has not been traced
5 October   Seaman Wharton W RTD 4 Lambeth
21 October   Private Jack Killeen W PTS 15 Covent Garden
18 November   Andrew Jeptha W PTS 15 Covent Garden. Sometimes given in record books as being for the English welterweight title, for which Jeptha was not eligible. A claimed fight against Private Jack Killeen L PTS has not been traced
21 December   Arthur Warner L PTS 6 Whitechapel
28 December   Bombardier Morgan W PTS 6 Whitechapel

1908
4 January   Arthur Warner L PTS 6 Whitechapel
11 January   'Bermondsey' Jim Sullivan DREW 6 Whitechapel
18 January   Coeville W PTS 6 Paris, France

8 February   Arthur Warner L PTS 10 Whitechapel. A claimed fight against Cpl Bill Baker L PTS has not been traced
22 February   Dick Jordan L PTS 8 The Curragh
29 February   Frank Erne L PTS 10 Paris, France
20 March   Seaman F.Willis W RTD 10 Lambeth
30 March   Billy Edwards W PTS 6 Whitechapel. First series 'Wonderland' 10st 8lbs English championship belt competition
30 March   Seaman F.Willis W KO 1 Whitechapel. Semi-final of 'Wonderland' 10st 8lbs English championship belt competition
4 April   Willie Lewis L RTD 4 Paris, France
18 April   Charlie Knock W PTS 10 Whitechapel. Final of 'Wonderland' English 10st 8lbs championship belt competition
27 April   'Young' Joseph L PTS 10 Whitechapel
2 May   Charlie Knock W PTS 6 Whitechapel
12 May   Private Jim Warner W PTS 10 Aldershot
16 May   'Bermondsey' Jim Sullivan L PTS 8 Whitechapel
21 May   Joe White (Cardiff, born Canada) L PTS 20 Liverpool. Given in record books as being for the English welterweight title, but White was not eligible. Even if it had been given Imperial Empire title billing it would still have been disqualified due to it being contested over two-minute rounds
15 June   Seaman F.Willis W KO 5 Birmingham
20 June   Jack Meekins L PTS 6 Birmingham
6 July   Jack Meekins W KO 3 Birmingham
9 July   Jack Johnson EXH 2 Birmingham. Johnson, a negro, was to win the world heavyweight title on 26 December 1908
9 July   Bobby Dobbs W PTS 6 Birmingham
13 July   Bobby Dobbs W PTS 6 Birmingham
22 August   Cpl Bill Baker DREW 6 Whitechapel
29 August   Charlie Hickman W PTS 6 Whitechapel
12 September   Arthur Harman W PTS 6 Whitechapel
19 September   Charlie Hickman W PTS 6 Whitechapel
26 September   Charlie Knock DREW 6 Whitechapel
10 October   Arthur Harman W RTD 4 Whitechapel
24 October   Charlie Knock DREW 6 Whitechapel
7 November   'Bermondsey' Jim Sullivan DREW 6 Whitechapel. Not L PTS 10 as recorded in some record books
14 November   Seaman Brewer W PTS 6 Whitechapel
21 November   Charlie Hickman W PTS 6 Whitechapel
30 November   'Bermondsey' Jim Sullivan L PTS 10 Whitechapel
12 December   Stoker Charlie Griggs W RTD 6 Whitechapel
19 December   Arthur Harman DREW 6 Whitechapel

1909
9 January   Sid Davie W PTS 6 Whitechapel
23 January   Albert Jacobs L PTS 6 Whitechapel
30 January   Jack Goldswain W PTS 6 Whitechapel
6 February   L/Cpl Bill Baker DREW 6 Whitechapel
15 February   Albert Jacobs W PTS 10 Whitechapel
17 February   L/Cpl Bill Baker L PTS 10 Maidstone. A claimed fight against Albert Jacobs L PTS 10 has not been traced
27 February   Charlie Knock L PTS 6 Whitechapel
13 March   Jack Goldswain W PTS 6 Whitechapel
27 March   'Bermondsey' Jim Sullivan L KO 2 (6) Whitechapel. A claimed fight against Charlie Knock L PTS has not been traced
17 April   Fred Ward W PTS 6 Whitechapel
24 April   Willie Lewis L KO 8 Paris, France. Another claimed fight against Charlie Knock W PTS has not been traced
15 May   Bill Pearce W PTS 6 Whitechapel
22 May   Jack Goldswain L PTS 6 Whitechapel
29 May   Jack Meekins W KO 3 The Curragh
10 June   Billy 'Honey' Mellody L KO 5 Paris, France
12 June   Jack Goldswain W PTS 6 Whitechapel
10 July   'Blink' McCloskey W PTS 6 Charing Cross
31 July   Charlie Knock DREW 6 Whitechapel. A claimed fight against 'Blink' McCloskey W PTS 6 cannot be traced
21 August   Peter Brown L PTS 6 Whitechapel
18 September   Bob Scanlon W PTS 6 Whitechapel
2 October   'Bandsman' Dick Rice L PTS 6 Whitechapel
5 October   Pat Breslin W PTS 15 Manchester
11 October   Frank Inglis W PTS 10 Birmingham
16 October   Bombardier Morgan NC 2 The Curragh. Both men were thrown out for 'not trying', but Watson looked far from well
23 October   'Bandsman' Dick Rice W RTD 5 (8) Whitechapel. Rice injured his hand
30 October   Bob Scanlon L PTS 8 Whitechapel

6 November   Bill Curzon L RTD 2 (6) Whitechapel. Watson again looked far from well
15 November   Frank Inglis L RTD 18 (20) Glasgow. Sometime in December Watson fought an unknown opponent in Ireland and was forced to retire. Watson, looking far from well, should have been resting not boxing

1910
1 January   George Marchant L RTD 2 (6) Shoreditch. Yet again Watson looked far from well and should not have been boxing
13 January   Tom Stokes L KO 1 (15) Hull. Watson looked really ill
27 January   'Young' Joseph L PTS 6 Blackfriars. Watson was reported to be but a shadow of his former self
28 February   Albert Jacobs L PTS 6 Walworth
5 March   Frank Inglis L KO 10 Whitechapel. Having won the first nine rounds, Watson was put down in tenth. Although he got up he fell back to the floor, hitting head with a resounding thud and died while being counted out by the referee, Robert Watson (considered best of all referees, with over 40 years experience). Robert Watson nearly always refereed from inside the ring. Bout was with 6oz gloves, with the purse money being £7 to Watson, £9 to Inglis, plus £1 for training expenses. On 10 March the inquest verdict was death due to concussion of the brain following a diffusion of blood from a lacerated artery. There were also traces of old pleurisy discovered and both lungs and heart were found to be somewhat enlarged. However, the doctor, Bernard Wallace, stated that Watson was fit to box and it was the fact that his head and chin came into contact with the floor that would have caused his death. A verdict of accidental death was then brought in

Career: 175 contests, won 117, drew 15, lost 40, no decision 1, no contest 1, 1 exhibition

Seaman Robert 'Curly' Watson

Commonwealth Title Bouts, 2005-2006

All of last season's title bouts are shown in date order within their weight divisions and give the boxers' respective weights. As from 1 September it had been deemed by the BBBoC that in future all Commonwealth title fights held in Britain would be scored by three judges, with the referee being a non-scoring participant, and following that decision all officials and scorecards concerned are listed, along with the venues where applicable.

Flyweight

10 February   Lee Haskins 8.0 (England) W RSC 2 Anthony Mathias 7.13$\frac{1}{2}$ (Tanzania), The Pavilions, Plymouth, England. Referee: Mark Green. Judges: Paul Thomas, Howard Foster, Richie Davies. Contested for the vacant title after England's Dale Robinson forfeited in November 2004 for failing to defend within the requisite time.

7 April   Lee Haskins 8.0 (England) W PTS 12 Zolile Mbitye 8.0 (South Africa), Whitchurch Sports Centre, Bristol, England. Referee: Marcus McDonnell. Scorecards: Phil Edwards 117-112, Paul Thomas 119-110, Victor Loughlin 118-111.

Bantamweight

29 June   Tshifhiwa Munyai 8.6 (South Africa) W RSC 9 Martin Power 8.5$\frac{1}{2}$ (England), York Hall, Bethnal Green, London, England. Referee: Victor Loughlin. Judges: Phil Edwards, Mark Green, Ian John-Lewis. This bout came about after the Commonwealth Committee declared the title vacant on 29 April, due to the champion, Joseph Agbeko (Ghana), failing to defend within the time constraints.

S.Bantamweight

28 October   Esham Pickering 8.9$\frac{3}{4}$ (England) L PTS 12 Michael Hunter 8.9$\frac{3}{4}$ (England), Borough Hall, Hartlepool, England. Referee: John Keane. Scorecards: Ian John-Lewis 113-114, Richie Davies 112-115, Mark Green 113-113.

Featherweight

18 November   Jackson Asiku 8.12$\frac{3}{4}$ (Uganda) W RSC 1 Marc Callaghan 8.13$\frac{3}{4}$ (England), Goresbrook Leisure Centre, Dagenham, England. Referee: John Keane. Judges: Paul Thomas, Dave Parris, Mickey Vann. Given vacant title billing after Nicky Cook (England) handed back his belt on 15 November following an injury.

16 June   Jackson Asiku 9.0 (Uganda) W RSC 1 Jamie McKeever 8.12$\frac{3}{4}$ (England), Everton Park Sports Centre, Liverpool, England. Referee: Phil Edwards. Judges: Howard Foster, Marcus McDonnell, Mickey Vann.

S.Featherweight

18 February   Alex Arthur 9.4 (Scotland) W PTS 12 Ricky Burns 9.2 (Scotland), Meadowbank Arena, Edinburgh, Scotland. Referee: John Keane. Scorecards: Mickey Vann 118-110, Dave Parris 117-111, Paul Thomas 116-112.

Lightweight

Graham Earl (England) failed to defend during the period.

L.Welterweight

21 October   Junior Witter 9.13$\frac{3}{4}$ (England) W PTS 12 Colin Lynes 9.13$\frac{3}{4}$ (England), York Hall, Bethnal Green, London, England. Referee: Richie Davies. Scorecards: Mark Green 117-112, Mickey Vann 116-112, Terry O'Connor 115-114. Witter relinquished the title on 13 June to concentrate on his forthcoming WBC championship fight.

Welterweight

30 September   Joshua Okine 10.5 (Ghana) L PTS 12 Kevin Anderson 10.6$\frac{3}{4}$ (Scotland), Fife Ice Arena, Kirkcaldy, Scotland. Referee: Marcus McDonnell. Scorecards: Ian John-Lewis 113-116, John Keane 114-115, Phil Edwards 115-114.

17 March   Kevin Anderson 10.6$\frac{3}{4}$ (Scotland) W RSC 7 Craig Dickson 10.6 (Scotland), Fife Ice Arena, Kirkcaldy, Scotland. Referee: Victor Loughlin. Judges: Mark Green, Richie Davies, Ian John-Lewis.

1 June   Kevin Anderson 10.6 (Scotland) W RSC 10 Young Muttley 10.6$\frac{1}{2}$ (England), Aston Villa Events Centre, Birmingham, England. Referee: Phil Edwards. Judges: Richie Davies, Marcus McDonnell, Terry O'Connor.

L.Middleweight

23 September   Ossie Duran 10.11 (Ghana) W PTS 12 Colin McNeil 10.11 (Scotland), Hilton Hotel, Mayfair, London, England. Referee: Dave Parris. Scorecards: Mark Green 118-110, Ian John-Lewis 119-109, Marcus McDonnell 119-109.

11 March   Ossie Duran 10.11$\frac{1}{4}$ (Ghana) L PTS 12 Bradley Pryce 10.10$\frac{1}{2}$ (Wales), The Sports Centre, Newport, Wales. Referee: Ian John-Lewis. Scorecards: Mickey Vann 114-115, Dave Parris 113-116, 112-118.

Middleweight

10 February   Scott Dann 11.5$\frac{1}{2}$ (England) W CO 9 Larry Sharpe 11.5 (Canada), The Pavilions, Plymouth, England. Referee: Richie Davies. Judges: Howard Foster, Mark Green, Paul Thomas. Contested for the vacant title after James Obede Toney (Ghana) was stripped on 20 January, having stated that he was unable to make the weight for a defence against Dann.

S.Middleweight

9 July   Carl Froch 11.13$\frac{1}{2}$ (England) W PTS 12 Matthew Barney 12.0 (England), The Ice Arena, Nottingham, England. Referee: Phil Edwards. Scorecards: 118-110.

2 December   Carl Froch 11.12$\frac{3}{4}$ (England) W RSC 5 Ruben Groenewald 11.13$\frac{1}{4}$ (South Africa), The Ice Arena,

Nottingham, England. Referee: Howard Foster. Judges: John Keane, Terry O'Connor, Paul Thomas.

17 February   Carl Froch 11.13³/₄ (England) W RSC 9 Dale Westerman 11.13 (Australia), York Hall, Bethnal Green, London, England. Referee: John Keane. Judges: Ian John-Lewis, Marcus McDonnell, Terry O'Connor.

26 May   Carl Froch 11.13¹/₄ (England) W RSC 11 Brian Magee 11.13³/₄ (Northern Ireland), York Hall, Bethnal Green, London, England. Referee: Richie Davies. Judges: Ian John-Lewis, Terry O'Connor, Paul Thomas.

L.Heavyweight

Having made no defences since 12 May 2004, Peter Oboh (England, via Nigeria) handed the belt back on 26 April when in no position to put his title on the line.

Cruiserweight

1 June   Mark Hobson 14.3¹/₂ (England) W RSC 4 John Keeton 14.3³/₄ (England), The Metrodome, Barnsley, England. Referee: Dave Parris. Judges: Mickey Vann, Howard Foster, Paul Thomas.

Heavyweight

10 December   Danny Williams 19.6 (England) W PTS 12 Audley Harrison 18.1 (England), ExCel Arena, Canning Town, London, England. Referee: Dave Parris. Scorecards: Mark Green 114-113, Phil Edwards 116-113, Terry O'Connor 116-112. Contested for the vacant title following Matt Skelton's decision to hand in his belt after winning the WBU championship on 25 February 2005.

25 February   Danny Williams 19.0¹/₂ (England) W PTS 12 Matt Skelton 18.3¹/₂ (England), ExCel Arena, Canning Town, London, England. Referee: Terry O'Connor. Scorecards: Dave Parris 116-113, Richie Davies 115-114, Ian John-Lewis 114-115.

Despite setting Carl Froch (left) plenty of problems, Brian Magee eventually lost interest in proceedings when he was poleaxed by a cracking right uppercut to the jaw in the 11th round. Following the referee's decision to terminate the contest without taking up the count, Froch thus successfully defended his British & Commonwealth super-middleweight titles   Les Clark

Commonwealth Champions, 1887-2006

Since the 1997 edition, Harold Alderman's magnificent research into Imperial British Empire title fights has introduced many more claimants/champions than were shown previously. Prior to 12 October 1954, the date that the British Commonwealth and Empire Boxing Championships Committee was formed, there was no official body as such and the Australian and British promoters virtually ran the show, with other members of the British Empire mainly out in the cold. We have also listed Canadian representatives, despite championship boxing in that country being contested over ten or 12 rounds at most, but they are not accorded the same kind of recognition that their British and Australian counterparts are. On 8 September 1970, Bunny Sterling became the first immigrant to win a British title under the ten-year residential ruling and from that date on champions are recorded by domicile rather than by birthplace. Reconstituted as the British Commonwealth Boxing Championships Committee on 22 November 1972, and with a current membership that includes Australia, Bahamas, Barbados, Canada, Ghana, Guyana, Jamaica, Kenya, Namibia, New Zealand, Nigeria, South Africa, Tanzania, Trinidad & Tobago, Uganda and Zambia, in 1989 the 'British' tag was dropped.

COMMONWEALTH COUNTRY CODE

A = Australia; BAH = Bahamas; BAR = Barbados; BER = Bermuda; C = Canada; E = England; F = Fiji; GH = Ghana; GU = Guyana; I = Ireland; J = Jamaica; K = Kenya; N = Nigeria; NZ = New Zealand; NI = Northern Ireland; PNG = Papua New Guinea; SA = South Africa; SAM = Samoa; S = Scotland; T = Tonga; TR = Trinidad; U = Uganda; W = Wales; ZA = Zambia; ZI = Zimbabwe.

Champions in **bold** denote those recognised by the British Commonwealth and Empire Boxing Championships Committee (1954 to date) and, prior to that, those with the best claims

*Undefeated champions (Does not include men who forfeited titles)

Title Holder	Birthplace/Domicile	Tenure
Flyweight (112 lbs)		
Elky Clark*	S	1924-1927
Harry Hill	E	1929
Frenchy Belanger	C	1929
Vic White	A	1929-1930
Teddy Green	A	1930-1931
Jackie Paterson	S	1940-1948
Rinty Monaghan*	NI	1948-1950
Teddy Gardner	E	1952
Jake Tuli	SA	1952-1954
Dai Dower*	W	1954-1957
Frankie Jones	S	1957
Dennis Adams*	SA	1957-1962
Jackie Brown	S	1962-1963
Walter McGowan*	S	1963-1969
John McCluskey	S	1970-1971
Henry Nissen	A	1971-1974
Big Jim West*	A	1974-1975
Patrick Mambwe	ZA	1976-1979
Ray Amoo	N	1980
Steve Muchoki	K	1980-1983
Keith Wallace*	E	1983-1984
Richard Clarke	J	1986-1987
Nana Yaw Konadu*	GH	1987-1989
Alfred Kotey*	GH	1989-1993
Francis Ampofo*	E	1993
Daren Fifield	E	1993-1994
Francis Ampofo	E	1994-1995
Danny Ward	SA	1995-1996
Peter Culshaw	E	1996-1997
Ady Lewis*	E	1997-1998
Alfonso Zvenyika	ZI	1998
Damaen Kelly	NI	1998-1999
Keith Knox	S	1999
Jason Booth*	E	1999-2003
Dale Robinson	E	2003-2004

Title Holder	Birthplace/Domicile	Tenure
Lee Haskins	E	2006-
Bantamweight (118 lbs)		
Digger Stanley	E	1904-1905
Owen Moran	E	1905
Ted Green	A	1905-1911
Charlie Simpson*	A	1911-1912
Jim Higgins	S	1920-1922
Tommy Harrison	E	1922-1923
Bugler Harry Lake	E	1923
Johnny Brown	E	1923-1928
Billy McAllister	A	1928-1930
Teddy Baldock*	E	1928-1930
Johnny Peters	E	1930
Dick Corbett	E	1930-1932
Johnny King	E	1932-1934
Dick Corbett	E	1934
Frankie Martin	C	1935-1937
Baby Yack	C	1937
Johnny Gaudes	C	1937-1939
Lefty Gwynn	C	1939
Baby Yack	C	1939-1940
Jim Brady	S	1941-1945
Jackie Paterson	S	1945-1949
Stan Rowan	E	1949
Vic Toweel	SA	1949-1952
Jimmy Carruthers*	A	1952-1954
Peter Keenan	S	1955-1959
Freddie Gilroy*	NI	1959-1963
Johnny Caldwell	NI	1964-1965
Alan Rudkin	E	1965-1966
Walter McGowan	S	1966-1968
Alan Rudkin	E	1968-1969
Lionel Rose*	A	1969
Alan Rudkin*	E	1970-1972
Paul Ferreri	A	1972-1977

Title Holder	Birthplace/Domicile	Tenure
Sulley Shittu	GH	1977-1978
Johnny Owen*	W	1978-1980
Paul Ferreri	A	1981-1986
Ray Minus*	BAH	1986-1991
John Armour*	E	1992-1996
Paul Lloyd*	E	1996-2000
Ady Lewis	E	2000
Tommy Waite	NI	2000
Nicky Booth	E	2000-2002
Steve Molitor	C	2002-2004
Joseph Agbeko	GH	2004-2006
Tshifhiwa Munyai	SA	2006-
S. Bantamweight (122 lbs)		
Neil Swain	W	1995
Neil Swain	W	1996-1997
Michael Brodie	E	1997-1999
Nedal Hussein*	A	2000-2001
Brian Carr	S	2001-2002
Michael Alldis	E	2002
Esham Pickering	E	2003-2005
Michael Hunter	E	2005-
Featherweight (126 lbs)		
Jim Driscoll*	W	1908-1913
Llew Edwards	W	1915-1916
Charlie Simpson*	A	1916
Tommy Noble	E	1919-1921
Bert Spargo	A	1921-1922
Bert McCarthy	A	1922
Bert Spargo	A	1922-1923
Billy Grime	A	1923
Ernie Baxter	A	1923
Leo Kid Roy	C	1923
Bert Ristuccia	A	1923-1924
Barney Wilshur	C	1923

COMMONWEALTH CHAMPIONS, 1887-2006

Title Holder	Birthplace/ Domicile	Tenure	Title Holder	Birthplace/ Domicile	Tenure	Title Holder	Birthplace/ Domicile	Tenure
Benny Gould	C	1923-1924	Billy Spider Kelly	NI	1954-1955	Eddie Ndukwu	N	1977-1980
Billy Grime	A	1924	Hogan Kid Bassey*	N	1955-1957	Pat Ford*	GU	1980-1981
Leo Kid Roy	C	1924-1932	Percy Lewis	TR	1957-1960	Azumah Nelson*	GH	1981-1985
Johnny McGrory	S	1936-1938	Floyd Robertson	GH	1960-1967	Tyrone Downes	BAR	1986-1988
Jim Spider Kelly	NI	1938-1939	John O'Brien	S	1967	Thunder Aryeh	GH	1988-1989
Johnny Cusick	E	1939-1940	Johnny Famechon*	A	1967-1969	Oblitey Commey	GH	1989-1990
Nel Tarleton	E	1940-1947	Toro George	NZ	1970-1972	Modest Napunyi	K	1990-1991
Tiger Al Phillips	E	1947	Bobby Dunne	A	1972-1974	Barrington Francis*	C	1991
Ronnie Clayton	E	1947-1951	Evan Armstrong	S	1974	Colin McMillan*	E	1992
Roy Ankrah	GH	1951-1954	David Kotey*	GH	1974-1975	Billy Hardy*	E	1992-1996

Contesting the vacant Commonwealth bantam title against Tshifhiwa Munyai (left) at York Hall last June, Martin Power lost his unbeaten record when rescued by the referee in the ninth round

Les Clark

Title Holder	Birthplace/ Domicile	Tenure
Jonjo Irwin	E	1996-1997
Paul Ingle*	E	1997-1999
Patrick Mullings	E	1999-2000
Scott Harrison*	S	2000-2002
Nicky Cook*	E	2003-2005
Jackson Asiku	U	2005-

S. Featherweight (130 lbs)

Title Holder	Birthplace/ Domicile	Tenure
Billy Moeller	A	1975-1977
Johnny Aba*	PNG	1977-1982
Langton Tinago	ZI	1983-1984
John Sichula	ZA	1984
Lester Ellis*	A	1984-1985
John Sichula	ZA	1985-1986
Sam Akromah	GH	1986-1987
John Sichula	ZA	1987-1989
Mark Reefer*	E	1989-1990
Thunder Aryeh	GH	1990-1991
Hugh Forde	E	1991
Paul Harvey	E	1991-1992
Tony Pep	C	1992-1995
Justin Juuko*	U	1995-1998
Charles Shepherd*	E	1999
Mick O'Malley	A	1999-2000
Ian McLeod*	S	2000
James Armah*	GH	2000-2001
Alex Moon	E	2001-2002
Dean Pithie	E	2002-2003
Craig Docherty	S	2003-2004
Alex Arthur	S	2004-

Lightweight (135 lbs)

Title Holder	Birthplace/ Domicile	Tenure
Jim Burge	A	1890
George Dawson*	A	1890
Harry Nickless	E	1892-1894
Arthur Valentine	E	1894-1895
Dick Burge*	E	1894-1895
Jim Murphy*	NZ	1894-1897
Eddie Connolly*	C	1896-1897
Jack Goldswain	E	1906-1908
Jack McGowan	A	1909
Hughie Mehegan	A	1909-1910
Johnny Summers*	E	1910
Hughie Mehegan	A	1911
Freddie Welsh*	W	1912-1914
Ernie Izzard	E	1928
Tommy Fairhall	A	1928-1930
Al Foreman	E	1930-1933
Jimmy Kelso	A	1933
Al Foreman*	E	1933-1934
Laurie Stevens*	SA	1936-1937
Dave Crowley	E	1938
Eric Boon	E	1938-1944
Ronnie James*	W	1944-1947
Arthur King	C	1948-1951
Frank Johnson	E	1953
Pat Ford	A	1953-1954
Ivor Germain	BAR	1954
Pat Ford	A	1954-1955
Johnny van Rensburg	SA	1955-1956
Willie Toweel	SA	1956-1959
Dave Charnley	E	1959-1962
Bunny Grant	J	1962-1967

Title Holder	Birthplace/ Domicile	Tenure
Manny Santos*	NZ	1967
Love Allotey	GH	1967-1968
Percy Hayles	J	1968-1975
Jonathan Dele	N	1975-1977
Lennox Blackmore	GU	1977-1978
Hogan Jimoh	N	1978-1980
Langton Tinago	ZI	1980-1981
Barry Michael	A	1981-1982
Claude Noel	T	1982-1984
Graeme Brooke	A	1984-1985
Barry Michael*	A	1985-1986
Langton Tinago	ZI	1986-1987
Mo Hussein	E	1987-1989
Pat Doherty	E	1989
Najib Daho	E	1989-1990
Carl Crook	E	1990-1992
Billy Schwer	E	1992-1993
Paul Burke	E	1993
Billy Schwer	E	1993-1995
David Tetteh	GH	1995-1997
Billy Irwin	C	1997
David Tetteh	GH	1997-1999
Bobby Vanzie	E	1999-2001
James Armah*	GH	2001-2002
David Burke*	E	2002
Michael Muya	K	2003
Kevin Bennett	E	2003-2005
Graham Earl	E	2005-

L. Welterweight (140 lbs)

Title Holder	Birthplace/ Domicile	Tenure
Joe Tetteh	GH	1972-1973
Hector Thompson	A	1973-1977
Baby Cassius Austin	A	1977-1978
Jeff Malcolm	A	1978-1979
Obisia Nwankpa	N	1979-1983
Billy Famous	N	1983-1986
Tony Laing	E	1987-1988
Lester Ellis	A	1988-1989
Steve Larrimore	BAH	1989
Tony Ekubia	E	1989-1991
Andy Holligan	E	1991-1994
Ross Hale	E	1994-1995
Paul Ryan	E	1995-1996
Andy Holligan	E	1996-1997
Bernard Paul	E	1997-1999
Eamonn Magee	NI	1999-
Paul Burke	E	1997
Felix Bwalya*	ZA	1997
Paul Burke	E	1998-1999
Eamonn Magee*	NI	1999-2002
Junior Witter*	E	2002-2006

Welterweight (147 lbs)

Title Holder	Birthplace/ Domicile	Tenure
Tom Williams	A	1892-1895
Dick Burge	E	1895-1897
Eddie Connolly*	C	1903-1905
Joe White*	C	1907-1909
Johnny Summers	E	1912-1914
Tom McCormick	I	1914
Matt Wells	E	1914-1919
Fred Kay	A	1915
Tommy Uren	A	1915-1916

Title Holder	Birthplace/ Domicile	Tenure
Fritz Holland	A	1916
Tommy Uren	A	1916-1919
Fred Kay	A	1919-1920
Johnny Basham	W	1919-1920
Bermondsey Billy Wells	E	1922
Ted Kid Lewis	E	1920-1924
Tommy Milligan*	S	1924-1925
Jack Carroll	A	1928
Charlie Purdie	A	1928-1929
Wally Hancock	A	1929-1930
Tommy Fairhall*	A	1930
Jack Carroll	A	1934-1938
Eddie Thomas	W	1951
Wally Thom	E	1951-1952
Cliff Curvis	W	1952
Gerald Dreyer	SA	1952-1954
Barry Brown	NZ	1954
George Barnes	A	1954-1956
Darby Brown	A	1956
George Barnes	A	1956-1958
Johnny van Rensburg	SA	1958
George Barnes	A	1958-1960
Brian Curvis*	W	1960-1966
Johnny Cooke	E	1967-1968
Ralph Charles*	E	1968-1972
Clyde Gray	C	1973-1979
Chris Clarke	C	1979
Clyde Gray*	C	1979-1980
Colin Jones*	W	1981-1984
Sylvester Mittee	E	1984-1985
Lloyd Honeyghan*	E	1985-1986
Brian Janssen	A	1987
Wilf Gentzen	A	1987-1988
Gary Jacobs	S	1988-1989
Donovan Boucher	C	1989-1992
Eamonn Loughran*	NI	1992-1993
Andrew Murray*	GU	1993-1997
Kofi Jantuah*	GH	1997-2000
Scott Dixon*	S	2000
Jawaid Khaliq*	E	2000-2001
Julian Holland	A	2001-2002
James Hare*	E	2002-2003
Ossie Duran*	GH	2003-2004
Fatai Onikeke	NI	2004-2005
Joshua Okine	GH	2005
Kevin Anderson	S	2005-

L. Middleweight (154 lbs)

Title Holder	Birthplace/ Domicile	Tenure
Charkey Ramon*	A	1972-1975
Maurice Hope*	E	1976-1979
Kenny Bristol	GU	1979-1981
Herol Graham*	E	1981-1984
Ken Salisbury	A	1984-1985
Nick Wilshire	E	1985-1987
Lloyd Hibbert	E	1987
Troy Waters*	A	1987-1991
Chris Pyatt*	E	1991-1992
Mickey Hughes	E	1992-1993
Lloyd Honeyghan	E	1993-1994
Leo Young	A	1994-1995
Kevin Kelly	A	1995
Chris Pyatt	E	1995-1996
Steve Foster	E	1996-1997

COMMONWEALTH CHAMPIONS, 1887-2006

Title Holder	Birthplace/Domicile	Tenure
Kevin Kelly	A	1997-1999
Tony Badea	C	1999-2001
Richard Williams*	E	2001
Joshua Onyango	K	2002
Michael Jones	E	2002-2003
Jamie Moore*	E	2003-2004
Richard Williams*	E	2004
Jamie Moore	E	2004
Ossie Duran	GH	2004-2006
Bradley Pryce	W	2006-

Middleweight (160 lbs)

Title Holder	Birthplace/Domicile	Tenure
Chesterfield Goode	E	1887-1890
Toff Wall	E	1890-1891
Jim Hall	A	1892-1893
Bill Heffernan	NZ	1894-1896
Bill Doherty	A	1896-1897
Billy Edwards	A	1897-1898
Dido Plumb*	E	1898-1901
Tom Duggan	A	1901-1903
Jack Palmer*	E	1902-1904
Jewey Cooke	E	1903-1904
Tom Dingey	C	1904-1905
Jack Lalor	SA	1905
Ted Nelson	A	1905
Tom Dingey	C	1905
Sam Langford*	C	1907-1911
Ed Williams	A	1908-1910
Arthur Cripps	A	1910
Dave Smith	A	1910-1911
Jerry Jerome	A	1913
Arthur Evernden	E	1913-1914
Mick King	A	1914-1915
Les Darcy*	A	1915-1917
Ted Kid Lewis	E	1922-1923
Roland Todd	E	1923-1926
Len Johnson	E	1926-1928
Tommy Milligan	S	1926-1928
Alex Ireland	S	1928-1929
Len Harvey	E	1929-1933
Del Fontaine	C	1931
Ted Moore	E	1931
Jock McAvoy	E	1933-1939
Ron Richards*	A	1940
Ron Richards*	A	1941-1942
Bos Murphy	NZ	1948
Dick Turpin	E	1948-1949
Dave Sands*	A	1949-1952
Randy Turpin	E	1952-1954
Al Bourke	A	1952-1954
Johnny Sullivan	E	1954-1955
Pat McAteer	E	1955-1958
Dick Tiger	N	1958-1960
Wilf Greaves	C	1960
Dick Tiger*	N	1960-1962
Gomeo Brennan	BAH	1963-1964
Tuna Scanlon*	NZ	1964
Gomeo Brennan	BAH	1964-1966
Blair Richardson*	C	1966-1967
Milo Calhoun	J	1967
Johnny Pritchett*	E	1967-1969
Les McAteer	E	1969-1970
Mark Rowe	E	1970

Title Holder	Birthplace/Domicile	Tenure
Bunny Sterling	E	1970-1972
Tony Mundine*	A	1972-1975
Monty Betham	NZ	1975-1978
Al Korovou	A	1978
Ayub Kalule	U	1978-1980
Tony Sibson*	E	1980-1983
Roy Gumbs	E	1983
Mark Kaylor	E	1983-1984
Tony Sibson*	E	1984-1988
Nigel Benn	E	1988-1989
Michael Watson*	E	1989-1991
Richie Woodhall*	E	1992-1995
Robert McCracken	E	1995-1997
Johnson Tshuma	SA	1997-1998
Paul Jones	E	1998-1999
Jason Matthews*	E	1999
Alain Bonnamie*	C	1999-2000
Sam Soliman	A	2000
Howard Eastman*	E	2000-2004
James Obede Toney	GH	2004-2006
Scott Dann	E	2006-

S. Middleweight (168 lbs)

Title Holder	Birthplace/Domicile	Tenure
Rod Carr	A	1989-1990
Lou Cafaro	A	1990-1991
Henry Wharton*	E	1991-1997
Clinton Woods	E	1997-1998
David Starie	E	1998-2003
Andre Thysse	SA	2003
Charles Adamu	GH	2003-2004
Carl Froch	E	2004-

L. Heavyweight (175 lbs)

Title Holder	Birthplace/Domicile	Tenure
Dave Smith*	A	1911-1915
Jack Bloomfield*	E	1923-1924
Tom Berry	E	1927
Gipsy Daniels*	W	1927
Len Harvey	E	1939-1942
Freddie Mills*	E	1942-1950
Randy Turpin*	E	1952-1955
Gordon Wallace	C	1956-1957
Yvon Durelle*	C	1957-1959
Chic Calderwood	S	1960-1963
Bob Dunlop*	A	1968-1970
Eddie Avoth	W	1970-1971
Chris Finnegan	E	1971-1973
John Conteh*	E	1973-1974
Steve Aczel	A	1975
Tony Mundine	A	1975-1978
Gary Summerhays	C	1978-1979
Lottie Mwale	ZA	1979-1985
Leslie Stewart*	TR	1985-1987
Willie Featherstone	C	1987-1989
Guy Waters*	A	1989-1993
Brent Kosolofski	C	1993-1994
Garry Delaney	E	1994-1995
Noel Magee	I	1995
Nicky Piper*	W	1995-1997
Crawford Ashley	E	1998-1999
Clinton Woods*	E	1999-2000
Neil Simpson	E	2001
Tony Oakey*	E	2001-2002
Peter Oboh*	E	2002-2006

Cruiserweight (200 lbs)

Title Holder	Birthplace/Domicile	Tenure
Stewart Lithgo	E	1984
Chisanda Mutti	ZA	1984-1987
Glenn McCrory*	E	1987-1989
Apollo Sweet	A	1989
Derek Angol*	E	1989-1993
Francis Wanyama	U	1994-1995
Chris Okoh	E	1995-1997
Darren Corbett	NI	1997-1998
Bruce Scott	E	1998-1999
Adam Watt*	A	2000-2001
Bruce Scott*	E	2001-2003
Mark Hobson	E	2003-

Heavyweight (200 lbs +)

Title Holder	Birthplace/Domicile	Tenure
Peter Jackson*	A	1889-1901
Dan Creedon	NZ	1896-1903
Billy McColl	A	1902-1905
Tim Murphy	A	1905-1906
Bill Squires	A	1906-1909
Bill Lang	A	1909-1910
Tommy Burns*	C	1910-1911
P.O. Curran	I	1911
Dan Flynn	I	1911
Bombardier Billy Wells	E	1911-1919
Bill Lang	A	1911-1913
Dave Smith	A	1913-1917
Joe Beckett*	E	1919-1923
Phil Scott	E	1926-1931
Larry Gains	C	1931-1934
Len Harvey	E	1934
Jack Petersen	W	1934-1936
Ben Foord	SA	1936-1937
Tommy Farr	W	1937
Len Harvey*	E	1939-1942
Jack London	E	1944-1945
Bruce Woodcock	E	1945-1950
Jack Gardner	E	1950-1952
Johnny Williams	W	1952-1953
Don Cockell	E	1953-1956
Joe Bygraves	J	1956-1957
Joe Erskine	W	1957-1958
Brian London	E	1958-1959
Henry Cooper	E	1959-1971
Joe Bugner	E	1971
Jack Bodell	E	1971-1972
Danny McAlinden	NI	1972-1975
Bunny Johnson	E	1975
Richard Dunn	E	1975-1976
Joe Bugner*	E	1976-1977
John L. Gardner*	E	1978-1981
Trevor Berbick	C	1981-1986
Horace Notice*	E	1986-1988
Derek Williams	E	1988-1992
Lennox Lewis*	E	1992-1993
Henry Akinwande	E	1993-1995
Scott Welch	E	1995-1997
Julius Francis*	E	1997-1999
Danny Williams	E	1999-2004
Michael Sprott	E	2004
Matt Skelton*	E	2004-2005
Danny Williams	E	2005-

European Title Bouts, 2005-2006

All of last season's title bouts are shown in date order within their weight divisions and give the boxers' respective weights, along with scorecard if going to a decision. British officials and British venues are listed where applicable.

Flyweight

8 July   Ivan Pozo 7.13^1/$_4$ (Spain) W PTS 12 Andrea Sarritzu 7.12^1/$_2$ (Italy), Vigo, Spain. Referee: Ian John Lewis. Scorecards: 117-112, 117-112, 117-111. Contested for the vacant crown after Brahim Asloum (France) had relinquished the title on 13 June to concentrate on winning the WBA title.

16 September   Ivan Pozo 7.13^1/$_2$ (Spain) W RSC 3 Lahcene Zemmoun 8.0 (France), Vigo, Spain.

9 December   Ivan Pozo 7.13^3/$_4$ (Spain) W RSC 1 Robert Isaszegi 8.0 (Hungary), Alcobendas, Spain.

Bantamweight

12 November   Simone Maludrottu 8.5^1/$_4$ (Italy) W PTS 12 Carmello Ballone 8.5^3/$_4$ (Belgium), Olbia, Sardinia, Italy. Scorecards: 115-113, 116-113, 113-116.

21 April   Simone Maludrottu 8.5^1/$_2$ (Italy) W PTS 12 Damaen Kelly 8.5^1/$_4$ (Northern Ireland), Anderstown Leisure Centre, Belfast, Northern Ireland. Scorecards: 118-111, 116-113, 115-113.

S.Bantamweight

28 October   Esham Pickering 8.9^3/$_4$ (England) L PTS 12 Michael Hunter 8.9^3/$_4$ (England), Borough Hall, Hartlepool, England. Referee: John Keane. Scorecards: Richie Davies 112-115, Ian John-Lewis 113-114, Mark Green 113-113.

3 March   Michael Hunter 8.8^1/$_2$ (England) W RSC 2 Yersin Jailauov 8.10 (Kazakhstan), Borough Hall, Hartlepool, England.

28 April   Michael Hunter 8.9^3/$_4$ (England) W RTD 3 German Guartos 8.9^1/$_4$ (Spain), Borough Hall, Hartlepool, England.

23 June   Michael Hunter 8.9^3/$_4$ (England) W CO 9 Tuncay Kaya 8.9^1/$_4$ (France), Winter Gardens, Blackpool, England.

Featherweight

24 February   Nicky Cook 9.0 (England) W PTS 12 Yuri

Prior to relinquishing the European featherweight title last March, Englands Nicky Cook (left) overcame the tough Ukranian southpaw, Yuri Voronin, on points

Les Clark

Voronin 8.13½ (Ukraine), Goresbrook Leisure Centre, Dagenham, England. Scorecards: 116-110, 118-109, 115-111. Cook relinquished the title on 28 March to concentrate on a WBC championship eliminator.

20 May   Cyril Thomas 8.13¼ (France) W CO 2 Karim Ketoun 8.12 (France), St Quentin, France.

S.Featherweight

23 July   Boris Sinitsin 9.3 (Russia) L PTS 12 Alex Arthur 9.3 (Scotland), Meadowbank Arena, Edinburgh, Scotland. Scorecards: 108-119, 108-119, 109-118.

18 February   Alex Arthur 9.4 (Scotland) W PTS 12 Ricky Burns 9.2 (Scotland), Meadowbank Arena, Edinburgh, Scotland. Referee: John Keane. Scorecards: Mickey Vann 118-110, Dave Parris 117-111, Paul Thomas 116-112.

29 April   Alex Arthur 9.3¾ (Scotland) W TD 7 Sergey Gulyakevich 9.3½ (Belarus), Meadowbank Arena, Edinburgh, Scotland. Scorecards: 69-63, 68-63, 69-64.

Lightweight

4 November   Juan Carlos Diaz Melero 9.8¾ (Spain) W RSC 11 Stefano Zoff 9.8 (Italy), Leganes, Spain. Referee: Mark Green. Zoff, who had relinquished the title on 11 April in order to dispute the IBF crown, was making an effort to regain his former title, which was still vacant.

3 February   Juan Carlos Diaz Melero 9.8½ (Spain) W PTS 12 Mihaita Mutu 9.7¼ (Romania), Santa Cruz de Tenerife, Spain. Scorecards: John Keane 116-113, 117-111, 117-111.

L.Welterweight

9 July   Junior Witter 9.13½ (England) W PTS 12 Andreas Kotelnik 9.13½ (Germany), The Arena, Nottingham, England. 115-114, 115-114, 117-111.

21 October   Junior Witter 9.13¾ (England) W PTS Colin Lynes 9.13¾ (England), York Hall, Bethnal Green, London, England. Referee: Richie Davies. Scorecards: Mark Green 117-112, Mickey Vann 116-112, Terry O'Connor 115-114. Due to defend against Giuseppe Lauri (Italy), Witter was forced to relinquish the title on 20 June after being lined up for a vacant WBC championship fight against America's DeMarcus Corley.

Welterweight

3 September   Oktay Urkal 10.6½ (Germany) W PTS 12 Maxim Nesterenko 10.6½ (Russia), Berlin, Germany. Scorecards: 114-113, 116-111, 115-112. Urkal relinquished the title on 29 September after being promised a title shot at the WBA champion, Luis Collazo.

14 April   Frederic Klose 10.6½ (France) W PTS 12 Antonio Lauri 10.5½ (Italy), Reims, France. Referee: Ian John-Lewis. Scorecards: 117-111, 116-114, 114-112.

L.Middleweight

10 March   Michele Piccirillo 10.13½ (Italy) W PTS 12 Lukas Konecny 10.13 (Czech Republic), Bergamo, Italy. Scorecards: Richie Davies 117-110, 116-110, 115-112.

Contested for the vacant title after Sergei Dzindziruk (Ukraine) vacated on 21 November to prepare for a crack at the WBO crown held by Puerto Rica's Daniel Santos.

Middleweight

16 July   Morrade Hakkar 11.5½ (France) L PTS 12 Sebastian Sylvester 11.5½ (Germany), Nuremburg, Germany. Scorecards: 111-117, 113-115, 115-114.

12 November   Sebastian Sylvester 11.5¼ (Germany) W PTS 12 Lorenzo di Giacomo 11.4¼ (Italy), Alsterdorf, Germany. Scorecards: John Coyle 116-111, 115-112, 116-111.

22 April   Sebastian Sylvester 11.5½ (Germany) W RSC 3 Steven Bendall 11.5¾ (England), Manheim, Germany

3 June   Sebastian Sylvester 11.5½ (Germany) L RSC 8 Amin Asikainen 11.5½ (Finland), Hanover, Germany.

S.Middleweight

16 July   Vitali Tsypko 11.13¼ (Ukraine) W PTS 12 Brian Magee 11.13½ (Northern Ireland), Nuremburg, Germany. Scorecards: 115-113, 115-114, 114-115. The two men were matched for the vacant title after Rudy Markussen (Germany) handed in his belt to concentrate on winning the WBO title.

18 November   Vitali Tsypko 11.10¼ (Ukraine) L PTS 12 Jackson Chanet 11.13 (France), St Dizier, France. Scorecards: 113-115, 112-116, 112-116.

14 April   Jackson Chanet 11.9¼ (France) L CO 11 Mger Mkrtchian 11.13½ (Armenia), Reims, France. Referee: Ian John-Lewis.

L.Heavyweight

7 January   Stipe Drews 12.6½ (Croatia) W PTS 12 Antonio Brancalion 12.4 (Italy), Munchen, Germany. Scorecards: 117-109, 118-109, 119-108. With Thomas Ulrich (Germany) handing back his belt on 15 June in order concentrate on his world championship ambitions, this one involved the vacant title.

25 May   Stipe Drews 12.6½ (Croatia) W PTS 12 Kai Kurzawa 12.6¼ (Germany), Munchen, Germany. Scorecards: Mark Green 117-110, 119-118, 119-109.

Cruiserweight

16 December   Alexander Gurov 14.2½ (Croatia) L CO 1 David Haye 14.3 (England), The Leisure Centre, Bracknell, England.

24 March   David Haye 14.4 (England) W RSC 8 Lasse Johansen 14.2 (Denmark), York Hall, Bethnal Green, London, England.

Heavyweight

1 October   Paolo Vidoz 17.2½ (Italy) W PTS 12 Michael Sprott 16.6½ (England), Oldenburg, Germany. Scorecards: 117-112, 117-112, 117-113.

28 January   Paolo Vidoz 17.0¾ (Italy) W PTS 12 Cengiz Koc 15.8½ (Germany), Berlin, Germany. Scorecards: 117-112, 116-112, 117-112.

European Champions, 1909-2006

Prior to 1946, the championship was contested under the auspices of the International Boxing Union, re-named that year as the European Boxing Union (EBU). The IBU had come into being when Victor Breyer, a Paris-based journalist and boxing referee who later edited the Annuaire du Ring (first edition in 1910), warmed to the idea of an organisation that controlled boxing right across Europe, regarding rules and championship fights between the champions of the respective countries. He first came to London at the end of 1909 to discuss the subject with the NSC, but went away disappointed. However, at a meeting between officials from Switzerland and France in March 1912, the IBU was initially formed and, by June of that year, had published their first ratings. By April 1914, Belgium had also joined the organisation, although it would not be until the war was over that the IBU really took off. Many of the early champions shown on the listings were the result of promoters, especially the NSC, billing their own championship fights. Although the (French dominated) IBU recognised certain champions, prior to being re-formed in May 1920, they did not find their administrative 'feet' fully until other countries such as Italy (1922), Holland (1923), and Spain (1924), produced challengers for titles. Later in the 1920s, Germany (1926), Denmark (1928), Portugal (1929) and Romania (1929) also joined the fold. Unfortunately, for Britain, its representatives (Although the BBBoC, as we know it today, was formed in 1929, an earlier attempt to form a Board of Control had been initiated in April 1918 by the NSC and it was that body who were involved here) failed to reach agreement on the three judges' ruling, following several meetings with the IBU early in 1920 and, apart from Elky Clark (fly), Ernie Rice and Alf Howard (light), and Jack Hood (welter), who conformed to that stipulation, fighters from these shores would not be officially recognised as champions until the EBU was formed in 1946. This led to British fighters claiming the title after beating IBU titleholders, or their successors, under championship conditions in this country. The only men who did not come into this category were Kid Nicholson (bantam), and Ted Kid Lewis and Tommy Milligan (welter), who defeated men not recognised by the IBU. For the record, the first men recognised and authorised, respectively, as being champions of their weight classes by the IBU were: Sid Smith and Michel Montreuil (fly), Charles Ledoux (bantam), Jim Driscoll and Louis de Ponthieu (feather), Freddie Welsh and Georges Papin (light), Georges Carpentier and Albert Badoud (welter), Georges Carpentier and Ercole Balzac (middle), Georges Carpentier and Battling Siki (light-heavy and heavy).

EUROPEAN COUNTRY CODE
ARM = Armenia; AU = Austria; BEL = Belgium; BUL = Bulgaria; CRO = Croatia; CZ = Czechoslovakia; DEN = Denmark; E = England; FIN = Finland; FR = France; GER = Germany; GRE = Greece; HOL = Holland; HUN = Hungary; ITA = Italy; KAZ = Kazakhstan; LUX = Luxembourg; NI = Northern Ireland; NOR = Norway; POL = Poland; POR = Portugal; ROM = Romania; RUS = Russia; S = Scotland; SP = Spain; SWE = Sweden; SWI = Switzerland; TU = Turkey; UK = Ukraine; W = Wales; YUG = Yugoslavia.

Champions in **bold** denote those recognised by the IBU/EBU

*Undefeated champions (Does not include men who may have forfeited titles)

Title Holder	Birthplace/ Domicile	Tenure	Title Holder	Birthplace/ Domicile	Tenure	Title Holder	Birthplace/ Domicile	Tenure
Flyweight (112 lbs)			Dai Dower	W	1955	**Bantamweight (118 lbs)**		
Sid Smith	E	1913	Young Martin	SP	1955-1959	Joe Bowker	E	1910
Bill Ladbury	E	1913-1914	**Risto Luukkonen**	FIN	1959-1961	Digger Stanley	E	1910-1912
Percy Jones	W	1914	**Salvatore Burruni***	ITA	1961-1965	**Charles Ledoux**	FR	1912-1921
Joe Symonds	E	1914	**Rene Libeer**	FR	1965-1966	Bill Beynon	W	1913
Tancy Lee	S	1914-1916	**Fernando Atzori**	ITA	1967-1972	Tommy Harrison	E	1921-1922
Jimmy Wilde	W	1914-1915	**Fritz Chervet**	SWI	1972-1973	**Charles Ledoux**	FR	1922-1923
Jimmy Wilde*	W	1916-1923	**Fernando Atzori**	ITA	1973	Bugler Harry Lake	E	1923
Michel Montreuil	BEL	1923-1925	**Fritz Chervet***	SWI	1973-1974	Johnny Brown	E	1923-1928
Elky Clark*	S	1925-1927	**Franco Udella**	ITA	1974-1979	**Henry Scillie***	BEL	1925-1928
Victor Ferrand	SP	1927	**Charlie Magri***	E	1979-1983	Kid Nicholson	E	1928
Emile Pladner	FR	1928-1929	**Antoine Montero**	FR	1983-1984	Teddy Baldock	E	1928-1931
Johnny Hill	S	1928-1929	**Charlie Magri***	E	1984-1985	**Domenico Bernasconi**	ITA	1929
Eugene Huat	FR	1929	**Franco Cherchi**	ITA	1985	**Carlos Flix**	SP	1929-1931
Emile Degand	BEL	1929-1930	**Charlie Magri**	E	1985-1986	**Lucien Popescu**	ROM	1931-1932
Kid Oliva	FR	1930	**Duke McKenzie***	E	1986-1988	**Domenico Bernasconi**	ITA	1932
Lucien Popescu	ROM	1930-1931	**Eyup Can***	TU	1989-1990	**Nicholas Biquet**	BEL	1932-1935
Jackie Brown	E	1931-1935	**Pat Clinton***	S	1990-1991	**Maurice Dubois**	SWI	1935-1936
Praxile Gyde	FR	1932-1935	**Salvatore Fanni**	ITA	1991-1992	**Joseph Decico**	FR	1936
Benny Lynch	S	1935-1938	**Robbie Regan***	W	1992-1993	**Aurel Toma**	ROM	1936-1937
Kid David*	BEL	1935-1936	**Luigi Camputaro**	ITA	1993-1994	**Nicholas Biquet**	BEL	1937-1938
Ernst Weiss	AU	1936	**Robbie Regan***	W	1994-1995	**Aurel Toma**	ROM	1938-1939
Valentin Angelmann*	FR	1936-1938	**Luigi Camputaro***	ITA	1995-1996	**Ernst Weiss**	AU	1939
Enrico Urbinati*	ITA	1938-1943	**Jesper Jensen**	DEN	1996-1997	**Gino Cattaneo**	ITA	1939-1941
Raoul Degryse	BEL	1946-1947	**David Guerault***	FR	1997-1999	**Gino Bondavilli***	ITA	1941-1943
Maurice Sandeyron	FR	1947-1949	**Alexander Mahmutov**	RUS	1999-2000	**Jackie Paterson**	S	1946
Rinty Monaghan*	NI	1949-1950	**Damaen Kelly***	NI	2000	**Theo Medina**	FR	1946-1947
Terry Allen	E	1950	**Alexander Mahmutov**	RUS	2000-2002	**Peter Kane**	E	1947-1948
Jean Sneyers*	BEL	1950-1951	**Mimoun Chent**	FR	2002-2003	**Guido Ferracin**	ITA	1948-1949
Teddy Gardner*	E	1952	**Alexander Mahmutov***	RUS	2003	**Luis Romero**	SP	1949-1951
Louis Skena*	FR	1953-1954	**Brahim Asloum***	FR	2003-2005	**Peter Keenan**	S	1951-1952
Nazzareno Giannelli	ITA	1954-1955	**Ivan Pozo**	SP	2005-	**Jean Sneyers***	BEL	1952-1953

Title Holder	Birthplace/Domicile	Tenure
Peter Keenan	S	1953
John Kelly	NI	1953-1954
Robert Cohen*	FR	1954-1955
Mario D'Agata	ITA	1955-1958
Piero Rollo	ITA	1958-1959
Freddie Gilroy	NI	1959-1960
Pierre Cossemyns	BEL	1961-1962
Piero Rollo	ITA	1962
Alphonse Halimi	FR	1962
Piero Rollo	ITA	1962-1963
Mimoun Ben Ali	SP	1963
Risto Luukkonen	FIN	1963-1964
Mimoun Ben Ali	SP	1965
Tommaso Galli	ITA	1965-1966
Mimoun Ben Ali	SP	1966-1968
Salvatore Burruni*	ITA	1968-1969
Franco Zurlo	ITA	1969-1971
Alan Rudkin	E	1971
Agustin Senin*	SP	1971-1973
Johnny Clark*	E	1973-1974
Bob Allotey	SP	1974-1975
Daniel Trioulaire	FR	1975-1976
Salvatore Fabrizio	ITA	1976-1977
Franco Zurlo	ITA	1977-1978
Juan Francisco Rodriguez	SP	1978-1980
Johnny Owen*	W	1980
Valerio Nati	ITA	1980-1982
Giuseppe Fossati	ITA	1982-1983
Walter Giorgetti	ITA	1983-1984
Ciro de Leva*	ITA	1984-1986
Antoine Montero	FR	1986-1987
Louis Gomis*	FR	1987-1988
Fabrice Benichou	FR	1988
Vincenzo Belcastro*	ITA	1988-1990
Thierry Jacob*	FR	1990-1992
Johnny Bredahl*	DEN	1992
Vincenzo Belcastro	ITA	1993-1994
Prince Naseem Hamed*	E	1994-1995
John Armour*	E	1995-1996
Johnny Bredahl	DEN	1996-1998
Paul Lloyd*	E	1998-1999
Johnny Bredahl*	DEN	1999-2000
Luigi Castiglione	ITA	2000-2001
Fabien Guillerme	FR	2001
Alex Yagupov	RUS	2001
Spend Abazi	SWE	2001-2002
Noel Wilders	E	2003
David Guerault	FR	2003-2004
Frederic Patrac	FR	2004
Simone Maludrottu	ITA	2004-

S. Bantamweight (122 lbs)

Title Holder	Birthplace/Domicile	Tenure
Vincenzo Belcastro	ITA	1995-1996
Salim Medjkoune	FR	1996
Martin Krastev	BUL	1996-1997
Spencer Oliver	E	1997-1998
Sergei Devakov	UK	1998-1999
Michael Brodie	E	1999-2000
Vladislav Antonov	RUS	2000-2001
Salim Medjkoune*	FR	2001-2002
Mahyar Monshipour*	FR	2002-2003
Esham Pickering	E	2003-2005
Michael Hunter	E	2005-

Featherweight (126 lbs)

Title Holder	Birthplace/Domicile	Tenure
Young Joey Smith	E	1911
Jean Poesy	FR	1911-1912
Jim Driscoll*	W	1912-1913
Ted Kid Lewis*	E	1913-1914
Louis de Ponthieu*	FR	1919-1920
Arthur Wyns	BEL	1920-1922
Billy Matthews	E	1922
Eugene Criqui*	FR	1922-1923
Edouard Mascart	FR	1923-1924
Charles Ledoux	FR	1924
Henri Hebrans	BEL	1924-1925
Antonio Ruiz	SP	1925-1928
Luigi Quadrini	ITA	1928-1929
Knud Larsen	DEN	1929
Jose Girones	SP	1929-1934
Maurice Holtzer*	FR	1935-1938
Phil Dolhem	BEL	1938-1939
Lucien Popescu	ROM	1939-1941
Ernst Weiss	AU	1941
Gino Bondavilli	ITA	1941-1945
Ermanno Bonetti*	ITA	1945-1946
Tiger Al Phillips	E	1947
Ronnie Clayton	E	1947-1948
Ray Famechon	FR	1948-1953
Jean Sneyers	BEL	1953-1954
Ray Famechon	FR	1954-1955
Fred Galiana*	SP	1955-1956
Cherif Hamia	FR	1957-1958
Sergio Caprari	ITA	1958-1959
Gracieux Lamperti	FR	1959-1962
Alberto Serti	ITA	1962-1963
Howard Winstone	W	1963-1967
Jose Legra*	SP	1967-1968
Manuel Calvo	SP	1968-1969
Tommaso Galli	ITA	1969-1970
Jose Legra*	SP	1970-1972
Gitano Jiminez	SP	1973-1975
Elio Cotena	ITA	1975-1976
Nino Jimenez	SP	1976-1977
Manuel Masso	SP	1977
Roberto Castanon*	SP	1977-1981
Salvatore Melluzzo	ITA	1981-1982
Pat Cowdell*	E	1982-1983
Loris Stecca*	ITA	1983
Barry McGuigan*	NI	1983-1985
Jim McDonnell*	E	1985-1987
Valerio Nati*	ITA	1987
Jean-Marc Renard*	BEL	1988-1989
Paul Hodkinson*	E	1989-1991
Fabrice Benichou	FR	1991-1992
Maurizio Stecca	ITA	1992-1993
Herve Jacob	FR	1993
Maurizio Stecca	ITA	1993
Stephane Haccoun	FR	1993-1994
Stefano Zoff	ITA	1994
Medhi Labdouni	FR	1994-1995
Billy Hardy	E	1995-1998
Paul Ingle*	E	1998-1999
Steve Robinson	W	1999-2000
Istvan Kovacs*	HUN	2000-2001
Manuel Calvo*	SP	2001-2002
Cyril Thomas	FR	2002-2004
Nicky Cook*	E	2004-2006
Cyril Thomas	FR	2006-

S. Featherweight (130 lbs)

Title Holder	Birthplace/Domicile	Tenure
Tommaso Galli	ITA	1971-1972
Domenico Chiloiro	ITA	1972
Lothar Abend	GER	1972-1974
Sven-Erik Paulsen*	NOR	1974-1976
Roland Cazeaux	FR	1976
Natale Vezzoli	ITA	1976-1979
Carlos Hernandez	SP	1979
Rodolfo Sanchez	SP	1979
Carlos Hernandez	SP	1979-1982
Cornelius Boza-Edwards*	E	1982
Roberto Castanon	SP	1982-1983
Alfredo Raininger	ITA	1983-1984
Jean-Marc Renard	BEL	1984
Pat Cowdell	E	1984-1985
Jean-Marc Renard*	BEL	1986-1987
Salvatore Curcetti	ITA	1987-1988
Piero Morello	ITA	1988
Lars Lund Jensen	DEN	1988
Racheed Lawal	DEN	1988-1989
Daniel Londas*	FR	1989-1991
Jimmy Bredahl*	DEN	1992
Regilio Tuur	HOL	1992-1993
Jacobin Yoma	FR	1993-1995
Anatoly Alexandrov*	KAZ	1995-1996
Julian Lorcy*	FR	1996
Djamel Lifa	FR	1997-1998
Anatoly Alexandrov*	RUS	1998
Dennis Holbaek Pedersen	DEN	1999-2000
Boris Sinitsin	RUS	2000
Dennis Holbaek Pedersen*	DEN	2000
Tontcho Tontchev*	BUL	2001
Boris Sinitsin	RUS	2001-2002
Pedro Oscar Miranda	SP	2002
Affif Djelti	FR	2002-2003
Boris Sinitsin	RUS	2003-2005
Alex Arthur	S	2005-

Lightweight (135 lbs)

Title Holder	Birthplace/Domicile	Tenure
Freddie Welsh	W	1909-1911
Matt Wells	E	1911-1912
Freddie Welsh*	W	1912-1914
Georges Papin	FR	1920-1921
Ernie Rice	E	1921-1922
Seaman Nobby Hall	E	1922-1923
Harry Mason	E	1923-1926
Fred Bretonnel	FR	1924
Lucien Vinez	FR	1924-1927
Luis Rayo*	SP	1927-1928
Aime Raphael	FR	1928-1929
Francois Sybille	BEL	1929-1930
Alf Howard	E	1930
Harry Corbett	E	1930-1931
Francois Sybille	BEL	1930-1931
Bep van Klaveren	HOL	1931-1932
Cleto Locatelli	ITA	1932
Francois Sybille	BEL	1932-1933
Cleto Locatelli*	ITA	1933
Francois Sybille	BEL	1934
Carlo Orlandi*	ITA	1934-1935
Enrico Venturi*	ITA	1935-1936
Vittorio Tamagnini	ITA	1936-1937
Maurice Arnault	FR	1937
Gustave Humery	FR	1937-1938
Aldo Spoldi*	ITA	1938-1939
Karl Blaho	AU	1940-1941
Bruno Bisterzo	ITA	1941
Ascenzo Botta	ITA	1941
Bruno Bisterzo	ITA	1941-1942
Ascenzo Botta	ITA	1942
Roberto Proietti	ITA	1942-1943
Bruno Bisterzo	ITA	1943-1946
Roberto Proietti*	ITA	1946
Emile Dicristo	FR	1946-1947
Kid Dussart	BEL	1947
Roberto Proietti	ITA	1947-1948
Billy Thompson	E	1948-1949
Kid Dussart	BEL	1949
Roberto Proietti*	ITA	1949-1950
Pierre Montane	FR	1951
Elis Ask	FIN	1951-1952
Jorgen Johansen	DEN	1952-1954
Duilio Loi*	ITA	1954-1959
Mario Vecchiatto	ITA	1959-1960
Dave Charnley	E	1960-1963
Conny Rudhof*	GER	1963-1964
Willi Quatuor*	GER	1964-1965
Franco Brondi	ITA	1965
Maurice Tavant	FR	1965-1966
Borge Krogh	DEN	1966-1967
Pedro Carrasco*	SP	1967-1969
Miguel Velazquez	SP	1970-1971
Antonio Puddu	ITA	1971-1974
Ken Buchanan*	S	1974-1975
Fernand Roelandts	BEL	1976
Perico Fernandez*	SP	1976-1977
Jim Watt*	S	1977-1979
Charlie Nash*	NI	1979-1980
Francisco Leon	SP	1980

Title Holder	Birthplace/ Domicile	Tenure
Charlie Nash	NI	1980-1981
Joey Gibilisco	ITA	1981-1983
Lucio Cusma	ITA	1983-1984
Rene Weller	GER	1984-1986
Gert Bo Jacobsen	DEN	1986-1988
Rene Weller*	GER	1988
Policarpo Diaz*	SP	1988-1990
Antonio Renzo	ITA	1991-1992
Jean-Baptiste Mendy*	FR	1992-1994
Racheed Lawal	DEN	1994
Jean-Baptiste Mendy*	FR	1994-1995
Angel Mona	FR	1995-1997
Manuel Carlos Fernandes	FR	1997
Oscar Garcia Cano	SP	1997
Billy Schwer*	E	1997-1999
Oscar Garcia Cano	SP	1999-2000
Lucien Lorcy*	FR	2000-2001
Stefano Zoff*	ITA	2001-2002
Jason Cook	W	2002-2003
Stefano Zoff*	ITA	2003-2005
Juan Carlos Diaz Melero	SP	2005-

L. Welterweight (140 lbs)

Title Holder	Birthplace/ Domicile	Tenure
Olli Maki	FIN	1964-1965
Juan Sombrita-Albornoz	SP	1965
Willi Quatuor*	GER	1965-1966
Conny Rudhof	GER	1967
Johann Orsolics	AU	1967-1968
Bruno Arcari*	ITA	1968-1970
Rene Roque	FR	1970-1971
Pedro Carrasco*	SP	1971-1972
Roger Zami	FR	1972
Cemal Kamaci	TU	1972-1973
Toni Ortiz	SP	1973-1974
Perico Fernandez*	SP	1974
Jose Ramon Gomez-Fouz	SP	1975
Cemal Kamaci	TU	1975-1976
Dave Boy Green*	E	1976-1977
Primo Bandini	ITA	1977
Jean-Baptiste Piedvache	FR	1977-1978
Colin Power	E	1978
Fernando Sanchez	SP	1978-1979
Jose Luis Heredia	SP	1979
Jo Kimpuani	FR	1979-1980
Giuseppe Martinese	ITA	1980
Antonio Guinaldo	SP	1980-1981
Clinton McKenzie	E	1981-1982
Robert Gambini	FR	1982-1983
Patrizio Oliva*	ITA	1983-1985
Terry Marsh	E	1985-1986
Tusikoleta Nkalankete	FR	1987-1989
Efren Calamati	ITA	1989-1990
Pat Barrett	E	1990-1992
Valery Kayumba	ITA	1992-1993
Christian Merle	FR	1993-1994
Valery Kayumba	FR	1994
Khalid Rahilou*	FR	1994-1996
Soren Sondergaard*	DEN	1996-1998
Thomas Damgaard*	DEN	1998-2000
Oktay Urkal*	GER	2000-2001
Gianluca Branco*	ITA	2001-2002
Oktay Urkal*	GER	2002-2003
Junior Witter*	E	2004-2006

Welterweight (147 lbs)

Title Holder	Birthplace/ Domicile	Tenure
Young Joseph	E	1910-1911
Georges Carpentier*	FR	1911-1912
Albert Badoud*	SWI	1915-1921
Johnny Basham	W	1919-1920
Ted Kid Lewis	E	1920-1924
Piet Hobin	BEL	1921-1925
Billy Mack	E	1923
Tommy Milligan	S	1924-1925
Mario Bosisio*	ITA	1925-1928
Leo Darton	BEL	1928
Alf Genon	BEL	1928-1929

Title Holder	Birthplace/ Domicile	Tenure
Gustave Roth	BEL	1929-1932
Adrien Aneet	BEL	1932-1933
Jack Hood*	E	1933
Gustav Eder	GER	1934-1936
Felix Wouters	BEL	1936-1938
Saverio Turiello	ITA	1938-1939
Marcel Cerdan*	FR	1939-1942
Ernie Roderick	E	1946-1947
Robert Villemain*	FR	1947-1948
Livio Minelli	ITA	1949-1950
Michele Palermo	ITA	1950-1951
Eddie Thomas	W	1951
Charles Humez*	FR	1951-1952
Gilbert Lavoine	FR	1953-1954
Wally Thom	E	1954-1955
Idrissa Dione	FR	1955-1956
Emilio Marconi	ITA	1956-1958
Peter Waterman*	E	1958
Emilio Marconi	ITA	1958-1959
Duilio Loi*	ITA	1959-1963
Fortunato Manca*	ITA	1964-1965
Jean Josselin	FR	1966-1967
Carmelo Bossi	ITA	1967-1968
Fighting Mack	HOL	1968-1969
Silvano Bertini	ITA	1969
Jean Josselin	FR	1969
Johann Orsolics	AU	1969-1970
Ralph Charles	E	1970-1971
Roger Menetrey	FR	1971-1974
John H. Stracey*	E	1974-1975
Marco Scano	ITA	1976-1977
Jorgen Hansen	DEN	1977
Jorg Eipel	GER	1977
Alain Marion	FR	1977-1978
Jorgen Hansen	DEN	1978
Josef Pachler	AU	1978
Henry Rhiney	E	1978-1979
Dave Boy Green	E	1979
Jorgen Hansen*	DEN	1979-1981
Hans-Henrik Palm	DEN	1982
Colin Jones*	W	1982-1983
Gilles Elbilia	FR	1983-1984
Gianfranco Rosi	ITA	1984-1985
Lloyd Honeyghan*	E	1985-1986
Jose Varela	GER	1986-1987
Alfonso Redondo	SP	1987
Mauro Martelli*	SWI	1987-1988
Nino la Rocca	ITA	1989
Antoine Fernandez	FR	1989-1990
Kirkland Laing	E	1990
Patrizio Oliva*	ITA	1990-1992
Ludovic Proto	FR	1992-1993
Gary Jacobs*	S	1993-1994
Jose Luis Navarro	SP	1994-1995
Valery Kayumba	FR	1995
Patrick Charpentier*	FR	1995-1996
Andrei Pestriaev*	RUS	1997
Michele Piccirillo*	ITA	1997-1998
Maxim Nesterenko	RUS	1998-1999
Alessandro Duran	ITA	1999
Andrei Pestriaev	RUS	1999-2000
Alessandro Duran	ITA	2000
Thomas Damgaard	DEN	2000-2001
Alessandro Duran	ITA	2001-2002
Christian Bladt	DEN	2002
Michel Trabant*	GER	2002-2003
Frederic Klose	FR	2003-2005
Oktay Urkal*	GER	2005
Frederic Klose	FR	2006-

L. Middleweight (154 lbs)

Title Holder	Birthplace/ Domicile	Tenure
Bruno Visintin	ITA	1964-1966
Bo Hogberg	SWE	1966
Yolande Leveque	FR	1966
Sandro Mazzinghi*	ITA	1966-1968
Remo Golfarini	ITA	1968-1969

Title Holder	Birthplace/ Domicile	Tenure
Gerhard Piaskowy	GER	1969-1970
Jose Hernandez	SP	1970-1972
Juan Carlos Duran	ITA	1972-1973
Jacques Kechichian	FR	1973-1974
Jose Duran	SP	1974-1975
Eckhard Dagge	GER	1975-1976
Vito Antuofermo	ITA	1976
Maurice Hope*	E	1976-1978
Gilbert Cohen	FR	1978-1979
Marijan Benes	YUG	1979-1981
Louis Acaries	FR	1981
Luigi Minchillo*	ITA	1981-1983
Herol Graham*	E	1983-1984
Jimmy Cable	E	1984
Georg Steinherr	GER	1984-1985
Said Skouma*	FR	1985-1986
Chris Pyatt	E	1986-1987
Gianfranco Rosi*	ITA	1987
Rene Jacquot*	FR	1988-1989
Edip Secovic	AU	1989
Giuseppe Leto	ITA	1989
Gilbert Dele*	FR	1989-1990
Said Skouma	FR	1991
Mourad Louati	HOL	1991
Jean-Claude Fontana	FR	1991-1992
Laurent Boudouani	FR	1992-1993
Bernard Razzano	FR	1993-1994
Javier Castillejos	SP	1994-1995
Laurent Boudouani*	FR	1995-1996
Faouzi Hattab	FR	1996
Davide Ciarlante*	ITA	1996-1997
Javier Castillejo*	SP	1998
Mamadou Thiam*	FR	1998-2000
Roman Karmazin*	RUS	2000
Mamadou Thiam*	FR	2001
Wayne Alexander*	E	2002
Roman Karmazin*	RUS	2003-2004
Sergei Dzindziruk*	UK	2004-2005
Michele Piccirillo	ITA	2006-

Middleweight (160 lbs)

Title Holder	Birthplace/ Domicile	Tenure
Georges Carpentier*	FR	1912-1918
Ercole Balzac	FR	1920-1921
Gus Platts	E	1921
Willem Westbroek	HOL	1921
Johnny Basham	W	1921
Ted Kid Lewis	E	1921-1923
Roland Todd	E	1923-1924
Ted Kid Lewis	E	1924-1925
Bruno Frattini	ITA	1924-1925
Tommy Milligan	S	1925-1928
Rene Devos	BEL	1926-1927
Barthelemy Molina	FR	1928
Alex Ireland	S	1928-1929
Mario Bosisio	ITA	1928
Leone Jacovacci	ITA	1928-1929
Len Johnson	E	1928-1929
Marcel Thil	FR	1929-1930
Mario Bosisio	ITA	1930-1931
Poldi Steinbach	AU	1931
Hein Domgoergen	GER	1931-1932
Ignacio Ara	SP	1932-1933
Gustave Roth	BEL	1933-1934
Marcel Thil*	FR	1934-1938
Edouard Tenet	FR	1938
Bep van Klaveren	HOL	1938
Anton Christoforidis	GRE	1938-1939
Edouard Tenet	FR	1939
Josef Besselmann*	GER	1942-1943
Marcel Cerdan	FR	1947-1948
Cyrille Delannoit	BEL	1948
Marcel Cerdan*	FR	1948
Cyrille Delannoit	BEL	1948-1949
Tiberio Mitri*	ITA	1949-1950
Randy Turpin	E	1951-1954
Tiberio Mitri	ITA	1954

Title Holder	Birthplace/ Domicile	Tenure
Charles Humez	FR	1954-1958
Gustav Scholz*	GER	1958-1961
John Cowboy McCormack	S	1961-1962
Chris Christensen	DEN	1962
Laszlo Papp*	HUN	1962-1965
Nino Benvenuti*	ITA	1965-1967
Juan Carlos Duran	ITA	1967-1969
Tom Bogs	DEN	1969-1970
Juan Carlos Duran	ITA	1970-1971
Jean-Claude Bouttier	FR	1971-1972
Tom Bogs*	DEN	1973
Elio Calcabrini	ITA	1973-1974
Jean-Claude Bouttier	FR	1974
Kevin Finnegan	E	1974-1975
Gratien Tonna*	FR	1975
Bunny Sterling	E	1976
Angelo Jacopucci	ITA	1976
Germano Valsecchi	ITA	1976-1977
Alan Minter	E	1977
Gratien Tonna	FR	1977-1978
Alan Minter*	E	1978-1979
Kevin Finnegan	E	1980
Matteo Salvemini	ITA	1980
Tony Sibson*	E	1980-1982
Louis Acaries	FR	1982-1984
Tony Sibson	E	1984-1985
Ayub Kalule	DEN	1985-1986
Herol Graham	E	1986-1987
Sumbu Kalambay*	ITA	1987
Pierre Joly	FR	1987-1988
Christophe Tiozzo*	FR	1988-1989
Francesco dell' Aquila	ITA	1989-1990
Sumbu Kalambay*	ITA	1990-1993
Agostino Cardamone*	ITA	1993-1994
Richie Woodhall*	E	1995-1996
Alexandre Zaitsev	RUS	1996
Hassine Cherifi*	FR	1996-1998
Agostino Cardamone*	ITA	1998
Erland Betare*	FR	1999-2000
Howard Eastman*	E	2001
Christian Sanavia	ITA	2001-2002
Morrade Hakkar*	FR	2002
Howard Eastman*	E	2003-2004
Morrade Hakkar	FR	2005
Sebastian Sylvester	GER	2005-2006
Amin Asikainen	FIN	2006-

S. Middleweight (168 lbs)

Title Holder	Birthplace/ Domicile	Tenure
Mauro Galvano*	ITA	1990-1991
James Cook	E	1991-1992
Franck Nicotra*	FR	1992
Vincenzo Nardiello	ITA	1992-1993
Ray Close*	NI	1993
Vinzenzo Nardiello	ITA	1993-1994
Frederic Seillier*	FR	1994-1995
Henry Wharton*	E	1995-1996
Frederic Seillier*	FR	1996
Andrei Shkalikov*	RUS	1997
Dean Francis*	E	1997-1998
Bruno Girard*	FR	1999
Andrei Shkalikov	RUS	2000-2001
Danilo Haeussler	GER	2001-2003
Mads Larsen*	DEN	2003-2004
Rudy Markussen*	DEN	2004-2005
Vitali Tsypko	UK	2005
Jackson Chanet	FR	2005-2006
Mger Mkrtchian	ARM	2006-

L. Heavyweight (175 lbs)

Title Holder	Birthplace/ Domicile	Tenure
Georges Carpentier	FR	1913-1922
Battling Siki	FR	1922-1923
Emile Morelle	FR	1923
Raymond Bonnel	FR	1923-1924
Louis Clement	SWI	1924-1926
Herman van T'Hof	HOL	1926
Fernand Delarge	BEL	1926-1927
Max Schmeling*	GER	1927-1928
Michele Bonaglia*	ITA	1929-1930
Ernst Pistulla*	GER	1931-1932
Adolf Heuser	GER	1932
John Andersson	SWE	1933
Martinez de Alfara	SP	1934
Marcel Thil	FR	1934-1935
Merlo Preciso	ITA	1935
Hein Lazek	AU	1935-1936
Gustave Roth	BEL	1936-1938
Adolf Heuser*	GER	1938-1939
Luigi Musina*	ITA	1942-1943
Freddie Mills*	E	1947-1950
Albert Yvel	FR	1950-1951
Don Cockell*	E	1951-1952
Conny Rux*	GER	1952
Jacques Hairabedian	FR	1953-1954
Gerhard Hecht	GER	1954-1955
Willi Hoepner	GER	1955
Gerhard Hecht	GER	1955-1957
Artemio Calzavara	ITA	1957-1958
Willi Hoepner	GER	1958
Erich Schoeppner	GER	1958-1962
Giulio Rinaldi	ITA	1962-1964
Gustav Scholz*	GER	1964-1965
Giulio Rinaldi	ITA	1965-1966
Piero del Papa	ITA	1966-1967
Lothar Stengel	GER	1967-1968
Tom Bogs*	DEN	1968-1969
Yvan Prebeg	YUG	1969-1970
Piero del Papa	ITA	1970-1971
Conny Velensek	GER	1971-1972
Chris Finnegan	E	1972
Rudiger Schmidtke	GER	1972-1973
John Conteh*	E	1973-1974
Domenico Adinolfi	ITA	1974-1976
Mate Parlov*	YUG	1976-1977
Aldo Traversaro	ITA	1977-1979
Rudi Koopmans	HOL	1979-1984
Richard Caramonolis	FR	1984
Alex Blanchard	HOL	1984-1987
Tom Collins	E	1987-1988
Pedro van Raamsdonk	HOL	1988
Jan Lefeber	HOL	1988-1989
Eric Nicoletta	FR	1989-1990
Tom Collins	E	1990-1991
Graciano Rocchigiani*	GER	1991-1992
Eddie Smulders	HOL	1993-1994
Fabrice Tiozzo*	FR	1994-1995
Eddy Smulders	HOL	1995-1996
Crawford Ashley	E	1997
Ole Klemetsen*	NOR	1997-1998
Crawford Ashley	E	1998-1999
Clinton Woods*	E	1999-2000
Yawe Davis	ITA	2001-2002
Thomas Ulrich*	GER	2002-2003
Stipe Drews*	CRO	2003-2004
Thomas Ulrich*	GER	2004-2005
Stipe Drews	CRO	2006-

Cruiserweight (200 lbs)

Title Holder	Birthplace/ Domicile	Tenure
Sam Reeson*	E	1987-1988
Angelo Rottoli	ITA	1989
Anaclet Wamba*	FR	1989-1990
Johnny Nelson*	E	1990-1992
Akim Tafer*	FR	1992-1993
Massimiliano Duran	ITA	1993-1994
Carl Thompson	E	1994
Alexander Gurov	UK	1995
Patrice Aouissi	FR	1995
Alexander Gurov*	UK	1995-1996
Akim Tafer*	FR	1996-1997
Johnny Nelson	E	1997-1998
Terry Dunstan*	E	1998
Alexei Iliin	RUS	1999
Torsten May*	GER	1999-2000
Carl Thompson*	E	2000-2001
Alexander Gurov*	UK	2001-2002
Pietro Aurino*	ITA	2002-2003
Vincenzo Cantatore	ITA	2004
Alexander Gurov	UK	2004-2005
David Haye	E	2005-

Heavyweight (200 lbs +)

Title Holder	Birthplace/ Domicile	Tenure
Georges Carpentier	FR	1913-1922
Battling Siki	FR	1922-1923
Erminio Spalla	ITA	1923-1926
Paolino Uzcudun	SP	1926-1928
Harry Persson	SWE	1926
Phil Scott	E	1927
Pierre Charles	BEL	1929-1931
Hein Muller	GER	1931-1932
Pierre Charles	BEL	1932-1933
Paolino Uzcudun	SP	1933
Primo Carnera	ITA	1933-1935
Pierre Charles	BEL	1935-1937
Arno Kolblin	GER	1937-1938
Hein Lazek	AU	1938-1939
Adolf Heuser	GER	1939
Max Schmeling*	GER	1939-1941
Olle Tandberg	SWE	1943
Karel Sys*	BEL	1943-1946
Bruce Woodcock	E	1946-1949
Joe Weidin	AU	1950-1951
Jack Gardner	E	1951
Hein Ten Hoff	GER	1951-1952
Karel Sys	BEL	1952
Heinz Neuhaus	GER	1952-1955
Franco Cavicchi	ITA	1955-1956
Ingemar Johansson*	SWE	1956-1959
Dick Richardson	W	1960-1962
Ingemar Johansson*	SWE	1962-1963
Henry Cooper*	E	1964
Karl Mildenberger	GER	1964-1968
Henry Cooper*	E	1968-1969
Peter Weiland	GER	1969-1970
Jose Urtain	SP	1970
Henry Cooper	E	1970-1971
Joe Bugner	E	1971
Jack Bodell	E	1971
Jose Urtain	SP	1971-1972
Jurgen Blin	GER	1972
Joe Bugner*	E	1972-1975
Richard Dunn	E	1976
Joe Bugner	E	1976-1977
Jean-Pierre Coopman	BEL	1977
Lucien Rodriguez	FR	1977
Alfredo Evangelista	SP	1977-1979
Lorenzo Zanon*	SP	1979-1980
John L. Gardner*	E	1980-1981
Lucien Rodriguez	FR	1981-1984
Steffen Tangstad	NOR	1984-1985
Anders Eklund	SWE	1985
Frank Bruno*	E	1985-1986
Steffen Tangstad	NOR	1986
Alfredo Evangelista	SP	1987
Anders Eklund	SWE	1987
Francesco Damiani	ITA	1987-1989
Derek Williams	E	1989-1990
Jean Chanet	FR	1990
Lennox Lewis*	E	1990-1992
Henry Akinwande*	E	1993-1995
Zeljko Mavrovic*	CRO	1995-1998
Vitali Klitschko*	UK	1998-1999
Vladimir Klitschko*	UK	1999-2000
Vitali Klitschko*	UK	2000-2001
Luan Krasniqi	GER	2002
Przemyslaw Saleta	POL	2002
Sinan Samil Sam	TU	2002-2004
Luan Krasniqi	GER	2004-2005
Paolo Vidoz	ITA	2005-

A-Z of Current World Champions

by Eric Armit

Shows the record since 1 July 2005, plus career summary and pen portrait, of all men holding IBF, WBA, WBC and WBO titles as at 30 June 2006. The author has also produced the same data for those who first won titles between 1 July 2005 and 30 June 2006, but were no longer champions at the end of the period in question. Incidentally, the place name given is the respective boxer's domicile and may not necessarily be his birthplace, while all nicknames are shown where applicable in brackets. Not included are British fighters, Joe Calzaghe (WBO and IBF super-middleweight champion), Johnny Nelson (WBO cruiserweight champion), Ricky Hatton (WBA welterweight champion), Scott Harrison (WBO featherweight champion) and Clinton Woods (IBF light-heavyweight champion). Their full records can be found among the Active British-Based Boxers: Career Records' section.

Arthur Abraham

Yerevan, Armenia. *Born* 20 February, 1980
IBF Middleweight Champion

Major Amateur Honours: Competed in the 2000 European Olympic qualifiers
Turned Pro: August 2003
Significant Results: Christian Sanavia W CO 5, Nader Hamdan W RSC 12, Ian Gardner W PTS 12, Hector Velazco W CO 5
Type/Style: Is a tough, strong and aggressive fighter
Points of Interest: 5'10". Arthur's real name is Avetik Abrahamyan and he is based in Germany with the Sauerland Group, as is his brother Alex, who boxes as a pro at light-middleweight. Has 17 wins by stoppage or kayo after winning his first 14 bouts inside the distance

16.07.05	Howard Eastman W PTS 12 Nuremburg
01.10.05	Daniel Parada W RSC 5 Oldenberg
10.12.05	Kingsley Ikeke W RSC 5 Leipzig *(Vacant IBF Middleweight Title)*
04.03.06	Shannon Taylor W PTS 12 Oldenburg *(IBF Middleweight Title Defence)*
13.05.06	Kofi Jantuah W PTS 12 Zwickau *(IBF Middleweight Title Defence)*

Career: 21 contests, won 21.

Tomasz (Goral) Adamek

Bielsko Biala, Poland. *Born* 1 December, 1976
WBC L.Heavyweight Champion

Major Amateur Honours: Having won a bronze medal in the 1996 Copenhagen Cup and Acropolis Tournament, he competed in the 1997 World Championships before winning a bronze medal in the 1998 European Championships

Turned Pro: March 1999
Significant Results: Rudi Lupo W PTS 10, Zdravko Kostic W PTS 10, Sergei Karanevich W PTS 10, Roberto Coelho W PTS 8, Jabrail Jabrailov W CO 5, Ismail Abdoul W PTS 8, Paul Briggs W PTS 12
Type/Style: An upright, tough battler with a good jab and a hard right-hand punch
Points of Interest: 6'1" tall. Turned pro in Manchester and had his first two fights in England. He has 21 wins by stoppage or kayo and suffered a broken nose whilst preparing for the Paul Briggs fight for the vacant WBC title, but concealed it and then had it broken again during the fight. Has made just one defence

15.10.05	Thomas Ulrich W CO 6 Dusseldorf *(WBC L.Heavyweight Title Defence)*

Career: 30 contests, won 30.

Eric Aiken

Marysville, USA. *Born* 8 April, 1980
IBF Featherweight Champion

Major Amateur Honours: None known
Turned Pro: January 2001
Significant Results: Agnaldo Nunes W PTS 6, Al Seeger L PTS 8
Type/Style: Limited but heavy-handed, despite having a leaky defence he has a good chin
Points of Interest: Spent most of his career having only modest success on the small town circuit until beating a fading Tim Austin. He was pulled in as a late substitute at two weeks notice to fight Valdemir Pereira when Esham Pickering was injured. Has 12 wins inside the distance

01.10.05	Leo Martinez L PTS 6 Columbus
09.12.05	John Scalzi W RSC 1 Wheeling
20.01.06	Darby Smart W RSC 7 Columbus
18.03.06	Johnnie Edwards L PTS 6 Columbus
01.04.06	Tim Austin W RSC 6 Cleveland
13.05.06	Valdemir Pereira W DIS 8 Boston *(IBF Featherweight Title Challenge)*

Career: 20 contests, won 16, lost 4.

Carlos Baldomir

Santa Fe, Argentine. *Born* 30 April, 1971
WBC Welterweight Champion

Major Amateur Honours: Had a record of 46 wins, four losses and two draws, but only won provincial titles.
Turned Pro: February 1993
Significant Results: Soren Sondergard L PTS 12, Dingaan Thobela DREW 12, Joshua Clottey W DIS 11, Hassan Al Drew W PTS 12, Jose Luis Cruz DREW 12, Miguel Rodriguez W PTS 12
Type/Style: A tough battler, but not a puncher, he possesses a very good chin and is an awkward opponent
Points of Interest: 5'7" tall with a 67" reach. Having failed in three attempts to win the Argentinian welterweight title before winning a WBC eliminator in 2002, he then had to wait over three years for a title shot. He refused to pay the sanction fees to the IBF and WBA when challenging triple champion, Judah, so the contest was only for the WBC title. Carlos comes from the same city as Carlos Monzon and is also trained by Amilcar Brusa, who also trained Monzon. A true road warrior, he has fought in eight different countries and is unbeaten in 19 fights since 1998. Had only two fights in 2004 and 2005

07.01.06	Zab Judah W PTS 12 New York City
	(WBC Welterweight Title Challenge)

Career: 57 contests, won 42, drew 6, lost 9.

Cassius (Mr Shy Guy) Baloyi

Giyani, South Africa. *Born* 5 November, 1974
IBF S.Featherweight Champion

Major Amateur Honours: Was the South African champion in 1993 and competed in the World Championships the same year
Turned Pro: January 1994
Significant Results: Frankie Toledo W PTS 12, Anton Gilmore W PTS 12, Sergio Liendo W PTS 12, Brian Carr W RSC 10, Hector Lizarraga W CO 1, Steve Robinson W PTS 12, Phillip Ndou L PTS 12, Tiger Ari W RSC 6, Mbulelo Botile W RSC 11, Lehlohonolo Ledwaba W PTS 12 (twice)
Type/Style: Is a tall, stylish fighter
Points of Interest: 5'10" tall with a 75" reach. He was actually christened Cassuis by mistake as his father intended to name him Cassius after Cassius Clay, but he uses the right spelling. He is managed by the former WBA champion, Brian Mitchell, and has 17 wins inside the distance

31.08.05	Isaac Hlatshwayo L PTS 12 Brakpan
31.05.06	Manuel Medina W RSC 11 Airway Heights
	(Vacant IBF S.Featherweight Title)

Career: 34 contests, won 32, lost 2.

Marco Antonio (Baby Faced Assassin) Barrera

Mexico City, Mexico. *Born* 17 January, 1974
WBC S.Featherweight Champion. Former Undefeated IBF S.Featherweight Champion. Former Undefeated WBC Featherweight Champion. Former Undefeated WBO S.Bantamweight Champion. Former Undefeated Mexican S.Flyweight Champion

Major Amateur Honours: None known but claims only four losses in 60 fights
Turned Pro: November 1989
Significant Results: Carlos Salazar W PTS 10, Frankie Toledo W RSC 2, Kennedy McKinney W CO 12, Jesse Benavides W CO 3, Junior Jones L DIS 5 & L PTS 12, Richie Wenton W RTD 3, Paul Lloyd W RTD 1, Erik Morales L PTS 12 & W PTS 12 (twice), Jesus Salud W RSC 6, Prince Naseem Hamed W PTS 12, Enrique Sanchez W RSC 6, Johnny Tapia W PTS 12, Kevin Kelley W RSC 4, Manny Pacquiao L RSC 11, Paulie Ayala W CO 10, Mzonke Fana W RSC 2
Type/Style: Is a terrific box-fighter with a hard punch in both hands
Points of Interest: 5'7" tall. Attended University of Mexico. A natural southpaw who fights right-handed, despite losing a hotly disputed decision to Erik Morales in 2000, in a match for both the WBC and WBO super-bantamweight titles, the WBO reinstated him as champion. Moved up to lift the WBC featherweight title with a revenge win over Morales before bouncing back from a shock loss to Manny Pacquiao to beat Morales again for the WBC super-featherweight title. This put him 2-1 ahead in one of the great series in boxing history. Has taken part in 24 world title fights, with 42 wins inside the distance. The result of the Ricardo 'Rocky' Juarez fight was originally given as a draw, but the result was changed to a win for Barrera when an error was found in one of the judges' scorecards

17.09.05	Robert Peden W PTS 12 Las Vegas
	(WBC S.Featherweight Title Defence. IBF S.Featherweight Title Challenge)
20.05.06	Ricardo Juarez W PTS 12 Los Angeles
	(WBC S.Featherweight Title Defence)

Career: 67 contests, won 62, lost 4, no decision 1.

Marco Antonio Barrera

Jorge (La Hiena) Barrios

Tigre, Argentina. *Born* 1 August, 1976
WBO S.Featherweight Champion. Former Undefeated Argentinian S.Featherweight Champion

Major Amateur Honours: None known, but claims a record of 35 wins, ten losses and two draws
Turned Pro: August 1996
Significant Results: Cesar Domine L DIS 4 & W CO 2, Silvano Usini W RSC 8, Affif Djelti W PTS 12, Carlos Rios W TD 6, Orlando Soto W RSC 4, Acelino Freitas L RSC 12, Carlos Uribe W RSC 7, Mike Anchondo W RSC 4
Type/Style: Is rugged, rough and aggressive with a crude but effective style and a heavy punch
Points of Interest: 5'6" tall. Once trained by Amilcar Brusa, who also trained Carlos Monzon, he lost only one of his first 42 fights and that was on disqualification. Has 33 wins by stoppage or kayo and had Acelino Freitas on the floor in a challenge for the WBO title in August 2003. A reformed bad boy of Argentinian boxing, he won the WBO title when beating Mike Anchondo who had failed to make the weight for their bout in April 2005. Has made two defences

12.08.05	Victor Santiago W RSC 2 Cordoba
	(WBO S.Featherweight Title Defence)
16.12.05	Nazareno Ruiz W PTS 10 Buenos Aires
20.05.06	Janos Nagy W CO 1 Los Angeles
	(WBO S.Featherweight Title Defence)

Career: 50 contests, won 46, drew 1, lost 2, no decision 1.

O'Neil (Give 'em Hell) Bell

Atlanta, USA. *Born* Jamaica, 29 December, 1974
WBA & WBC Cruiserweight Champion. Former Undefeated IBF Cruiserweight Champion

Major Amateur Honours: None known
Turned Pro: February 1998
Significant Results: Mohamed Ben Guesmia L CO 4, Jason Robinson W PTS 10, Ka-Dy King W RSC 3, Ernest Mateen T DRAW 4, Arthur Williams W RSC 11 & W RSC 9, Kelvin Davis W RSC 11, Derrick Harmon W CO 8,

Ezra Sellers W CO 2, Dale Brown W PTS 12

Type/Style: A lanky, loose limbed boxer with an awkward leaning style and a big punch

Points of Interest: 6'2" tall with a 75" reach. He lost to Mohamed Ben Guesmia in only his second paid fight, but now has 24 wins inside the distance and in fact has only once won a fight on points. Has made two defences, including the win over Jean-Marc Mormeck, but was stripped of his IBF title for failing to defend when ordered to do so

26.08.05	Sebastian Rothmann W CO 11 Hollywood *(IBF Cruiserweight Title Defence)*
07.01.06	Jean-Marc Mormeck W RSC 10 New York City *(IBF Cruiserweight Title Defence. WBC & WBA Title Challenges)*

Career: 26 contests, won 24, drew 1, lost 1.

Markus (Boom Boom) Beyer

Eriabrunn, Germany. *Born* 28 April, 1971
WBC S.Middleweight Champion. Former German S.Middleweight Champion

Major Amateur Honours: A gold medallist in the 1988 European Junior Championships, he competed in the 1992 and 1996 Olympics and won a bronze medal in the 1995 World Championships, and a silver medal in the 1996 European Championships

Turned Pro: November 1996

Significant Results: Juan Carlos Viloria W PTS 12, Richie Woodhall W PTS 10, Leif Keiski W CO 7, Glenn Catley L RSC 12, Eric Lucas W PTS 12, Danny Green W DIS 5 & W PTS 12, Andre Thysse W PTS 12, Christian Sanavia L PTS 12 & W CO 6

Type/Style: Is a smart boxing southpaw and a real tactician, but not a puncher

Points of Interest: 5'9" tall. Won his European Junior gold medal at flyweight. Now in his third reign as WBC champion, having beaten Richie Woodhall for the title in October 1999 before losing it to Glenn Catley in his second defence in May 2000. Regained the title with a close points win over Eric Lucas in April 2003, only to lose it again to Christian Sanavia in June 200 before recapturing

it with a kayo over Sanavia in October 2004. Was on the floor twice and looked to be on the way to defeat until Danny Green was disqualified in their 2003 fight. With just 13 wins by stoppage or kayo, he has made ten title defences in his three reigns. The Bika fight was declared a technical draw when Beyer suffered a cut

03.09.05	Omar Sheika W PTS 12 Berlin *(WBC S.Middleweight Title Defence)*
28.01.06	Alberto Colajanni W RTD 12 Berlin *(WBC S.Middleweight Title Defence)*
13.05.06	Sakio Bika T DRAW 4 Zwickau *(WBC S.Middleweight Title Defence)*

Career: 36 contests, won 34, lost 2.

Ivan (Iron Boy) Calderon

Guaynabo, Puerto Rico. *Born* 7 January, 1975
WBO M.Flyweight Champion

Major Amateur Honours: A bronze medallist in the 1999 Pan-American Games, he also competed in the World Championships that year. Won a silver medal in 1999 Central American Games before competing in the 2000 Olympic Games. Claims 110 wins in 130 bouts

Turned Pro: February 2001

Significant Results: Jorge Romero W RTD 4, Alejandro Moreno W PTS 10, Eduardo Marquez W TD 9, Lorenzo Trejo W PTS 12, Alex Sanchez W PTS 12, Edgar Cardenas W CO 11, Roberto Leyva W PTS 12, Carlos

Markus Beyer   Les Clark

Fajardo W PTS 12, Noel Tunacao W RSC 8, Gerard Verde W PTS 12
Type/Style: Southpaw. Although an excellent boxer technically and good counter-puncher, he lacks power
Points of Interest: 5'0" tall. Won the WBO title with a technical verdict over Eduardo Marquez in May 2003 and has made nine defences. An extrovert who is tremendously popular in Puerto Rico, being voted 'Boxer of the Year' there in 2002, he has seven wins by stoppage or kayo

10.12.05	Daniel Reyes W PTS 12 San Juan *(WBO M.Flyweight Title Defence)*
18.02.06	Isaac Bustos W PTS 12 Las Vegas *(WBO M.Flyweight Title Defence)*
30.04.06	Miguel Tellez W RSC 9 Guaynabo *(WBO M.Flyweight Title Defence)*
Career: 26 contests, won 26.	

Martin (Gallo) Castillo

Mexico City. Mexico. *Born* 13 January, 1977
WBA S.Flyweight Champion

Major Amateur Honours: The Mexican Junior champion in 1993 and a silver medallist in the 1993 Pan-American Games, he also competed in the 1996 Olympics and the 1997 World Championships
Turned Pro: July 1998
Significant Results: Oscar Andrade W PTS 10, Gabriel Munoz W PTS 10, Francisco Tejedor W CO 1, Evangelista Perez W RSC 3, Ricardo Vargas W TD 6, Felix Machado L TD 6, Hideyasu Ishihara W RSC 11, Alexander Munoz W PTS 12, Eric Morel W PTS 12, Hideyasu Ishihara W PTS 12
Type/ Style: A compact, intelligent and patient boxer with a long, fast jab, he has excellent reflexes
Points of Interest: 5'6" tall with 67" reach. Beat both Floyd Mayweather and Eric Morel in the same month as an amateur. Was unsuccessful in a challenge for the IBF title when losing to Felix Machado in March 2002, but won the 'interim' WBA title on stopping Hideyasu Ishihara in May 2004 and the full title when beating Alexander Munoz in December 2004. Has made three defences and has 16 wins by kayo or stoppage

21.01.06	Alexander Munoz W PTS 12 Las Vegas *(WBA S.Flyweight Title Defence)*
Career: 31 contests, won 30, lost 1.	

Hugo (Fidel) Cazares

Los Mochis, Mexico. *Born* 24 March, 1978
WBO L.Flyweight Champion. Former Undefeated Mexican L.Flyweight Champion

Major Amateur Honours: None known
Turned Pro: February 1997
Significant Results: Sergio Perez L CO 1, Gerson Guerrero L RSC 5, Rafael Orozco W CO 6, Eric Jamili W CO 3, Valentin Leon W RSC 3, Juan Keb Baas W CO 9, Miguel del Valle W PTS 10, Nelson Dieppa W TD 10
Type/Style: Is a tough, aggressive switch-hitter
Points of Interest: 5'6" tall. Was already fighting over ten rounds by only his sixth fight. His record shows 17 wins by stoppage or kayo and he is unbeaten in his last 14 fights, with 11 of those ending inside the distance. Has made three defences since winning the title from Nelson Dieppa in April 2005

20.08.05	Alex Sanchez W RTD 7 Ponce *(WBO L.Flyweight Title Defence)*
29.10.05	Kaichon Sorvoraphin W CO 6 Tucson *(WBO L.Flyweight Title Defence)*
30.06.06	Domingo Guillen W RSC 1 Tucson *(WBO L.Flyweight Title Defence)*
Career: 27 contests, won 23, drew 1, lost 3.	

Jesus (El Matador) Chavez

Parral. Mexico. *Born* 12 November, 1972
IBF Lightweight Champion. Former WBC S.Featherweight Champion

Major Amateur Honours: None known
Turned Pro: August 1994
Significant Results: Carlos Gerena L PTS 8 & W RSC 6, Javier Jauregui W PTS 12, Julio Alvarez W PTS 12, Daryl Pinckney W RSC 6, Tom Johnson W RTD 7, Floyd Mayweather L RTD 9, Sirimongkol Singmanasak W PTS 12, Erik Morales L PTS 12, Carlos Hernandez W PTS 12
Type/Style: Is a tough pressure fighter who wears the opposition down and has a strong chin as well as good stamina
Points of Interest: 5'5" tall with a 65" reach. Jesus, whose father fought as a pro, served three and a half years in jail for assault and was deported from the USA twice as an illegal immigrant

before finally being allowed to re-enter the country. After being beaten in his fifth fight to Carlos Gerena he then won 31 in a row before losing to Floyd Mayweather in a challenge for the WBC super-featherweight title in November 2001. He then won the WBC title in his second attempt by beating Sirimongkol Singmanasak in August 2003, but lost the title in his first defence to Erik Morales in February 2004 when he suffered a torn rotator cuff. However, he still lasted the distance. Moved up to lightweight to win the IBF title, but sadly Leavander Johnson collapsed and died after their fight. Is trained by ex boxer, Ronnie Shields

17.09.05	Leavander Johnson W RSC 11 Las Vegas *(IBF Lightweight Title Challenge)*
Career: 45 contests, won 42, lost 3.	

Luis Collazo

Brooklyn, USA. *Born* 22 April, 1981
Former WBA Welterweight Champion

Major Amateur Honours: Was the New York Golden Gloves champion and Police Athletic League champion in 1998 prior to winning the New York Golden Gloves again in 2000. That year he also reached the quarter finals of the US Olympic trials
Turned Pro: May 2000
Significant Results: Luis Santiago W PTS 8, Edwin Cassiani L RSC 3, Felix Flores W PTS 10, Jose Antonio Rivera W PTS 12
Type/Style: Is a tough, strong, walk-in southpaw with an exciting and awkward style
Points of Interest: 5'9" tall with a 72" reach. He works as a barber. When he won the WBA welterweight title by beating Jose Antonio Rivera in April 2005, Zab Judah was 'super' champion, but Luis became full WBA champion when Carlos Baldomir refused to pay the WBA sanction fee when beating Judah in January

13.08.05	Miguel Angel Gonzalez W RTD 8 Chicago *(WBA Secondary Welterweight Title Defence)*
13.05.06	Ricky Hatton L PTS 12 Boston *(WBA Welterweight Title Defence)*
Career: 27 contests, won 25, lost 2.	

Diego (Chico) Corrales

Columbia, USA. *Born* 25 August, 1977
WBC Lightweight Champion. Former Undefeated WBO Lightweight Champion. Former Undefeated WBO S.Featherweight Champion. Former Undefeated IBF S.Featherweight Champion

Major Amateur Honours: Won silver medals in both the US Junior and Senior Championships 1994 and a bronze medal in the 1995 Pan-American Games
Turned Pro: March 1996
Significant Results: Steve Quinones W RSC 4, Rafael Meran W CO 2, Hector Arroyo W RSC 5, Gairy St Clair W PTS 12, Roberto Garcia W RSC 7, John Brown W PTS 12, Derrick Gainer W RSC 3, Justin Juuko W RSC 10, Angel Manfredy W RSC 3, Floyd Mayweather L RSC 10, Joel Casamayor L RSC 6 & W PTS 12, Acelino Freitas W RTD 10, Jose Luis Castillo W PTS 12
Type/Style: Although a strong, heavy hitter and a good combination puncher, his defence is not too sound

Points of Interest: 5'11" tall with a 73" reach. His Father was a pro and Diego started boxing at the age of 12.Won the IBF title in October 1999 by stopping Roberto Garcia and made four defences. When losing to Mayweather for the WBC title in January 2001 he was on the floor five times. Was jailed in 2001 for spousal assault and inactive for two years before returning to win the WBO super-featherweight title when beating Joel Casamayor in March 2004. Moved up to lightweight and won WBO title against Acelino Freitas in August 2004, before making a successful defence when beating Jose Luis Castillo, also winning the WBC title in what was a dramatic contest in May 2005. Castillo was overweight for their October fight so no title was at stake and was also overweight for their proposed third fight which was then cancelled. Has stopped or knocked out 33 opponents

08.10.05	Jose Luis Castillo L CO 4 Las Vegas
Career: 43 contests, won 40, lost 3.	

Diego Corrales   Les Clark

Miguel Angel Cotto

Caguas, Puerto Rico. *Born* 29 October, 1980
WBO L.Welterweight Champion

Major Amateur Honours: A bronze medallist in the 1997 Central American Games and a winner of silver medals in the 1997 and 1998 World Junior Championships, he went on to compete in the 1999 World Championships and the Pan-American Games. Won a gold medal in the 2002 Central American Games, having earlier competed in the 2000 Olympics where he lost to Muhamad Abdullaev
Turned Pro: February 2001
Significant Results: Justin Juuko W RSC 5, John Brown W PTS 10, Cesar Bazan W RSC 11, Joel Perez W CO 4, Demetrio Ceballos W RSC 7, Carlos Maussa W RSC 8, Victoriano Sosa W RSC 4, Lovemore Ndou W PTS 12, Kelson Pinto W RSC 6, Randall Bailey W RSC 6, DeMarcus Corley W RSC 5, Muhamad Abdullaev W RSC 9
Type/Style: Miguel is a classy, hard-hitting box puncher with an exciting style, but has been rocked a few times
Points of Interest: 5'8" tall with a 67" reach. His father, uncle and cousin all boxed and his brother, Jose Miguel Cotto, lost to Juan Diaz in a fight for the IBF lightweight title last April. Is trained by his uncle Evangelista and has 22 wins inside the distance. Has made six title defences since winning the WBO title by beating Kelson Pinto in September 2004

24.09.05	Ricardo Torres W CO 7 Atlantic City *(WBO L.Welterweight Title Defence)*
04.03.06	Gianluca Branco W RSC 8 Bayamon *(WBO L.Welterweight Title Defence)*
10.06.06	Paulie Malignaggi W PTS 12 New York City *(WBO L.Welterweight Title Defence)*
Career: 27 contests, won 27.	

Vic (Raging Bull) Darchinyan

Australia. *Born* Vanadvor, Armenia, 7 January, 1976
IBF Flyweight Champion. Former Undefeated Australian Flyweight Champion

Major Amateur Honours: Competed in

the 1997 World Championships before winning a bronze medal in the European Championships, the Goodwill Games and the World Cup, in 1998. He then competed in the 2000 European Championships and was a quarter-finalist in the 2000 Olympics
Turned Pro: November 2000
Significant Results: Raul Medina W TD 8, Wandee Chor Chareon W CO 4 & W CO 5, Alejandro Montiel W PTS 10, Irene Pacheco W RSC 11, Mzukisi Sikali W RSC 8
Type/Style: Is a strong, aggressive southpaw and a good boxer with a hard punch in both hands
Points of Interest: 5'5" tall. His real first name is Vakhtang, and he stayed and settled in Australia after representing Armenia in the Sydney Olympics. Trained by Jeff Fenech, he won the Australian title in only his seventh fight and the IBF title in December 2004 by stopping the previously unbeaten Irene Pacheco and has made four defences. Has stopped or kayoed 21 opponents

24.08.05	Jair Jimenez W RSC 5 Sydney *(IBF Flyweight Title Defence)*
03.03.06	Diosdado Gabi W RSC 8 Santa Ynez *(IBF Flyweight Title Defence)*
03.06.06	Luis Maldonado W RSC 8 Las Vegas *(IBF Flyweight Tile Defence)*
Career: 26 contests, won 26.	

Oscar (Golden Boy) De La Hoya

Montebello, USA. *Born* 4 February, 1973
WBC L.Middleweight Champion. Former Undefeated WBO Middleweight Champion. Former WBC & WBA L.Middleweight Champion. Former WBC Welterweight Champion. Former Undefeated WBC L.Welterweight Champion. Former Undefeated IBF & WBO Lightweight Champion. Former Undefeated WBO S.Featherweight Champion

Major Amateur Honours: Won the National Golden Gloves title in 1989 and was United States champion in both 1990 and 1991 before going on to win a gold medal in the 1992 Olympics.
Turned Pro: November 1992
Significant Results: Genaro Hernandez

W RSC 6, Jesse Leija W RSC 2, Julio Cesar Chavez W RSC 4 & W RTD 8, Miguel Gonzalez W PTS 12, Pernell Whitaker W PTS 12, Hector Camacho W PTS 12, Ike Quartey W PTS 12, Oba Carr W RSC 11, Felix Trinidad L PTS 12, Derrell Coley W RSC 7, Shane Mosley L PTS 12 (twice), Arturo Gatti W RSC 5, Javier Castillejo W RSC 12, Fernando Vargas W RSC 11, Yori Boy Campas W RSC 7, Felix Sturm W PTS 12
Type/Style: Is a smooth, classy boxer and a fast and accurate puncher
Points of Interest: 5'11" tall. Has been boxing since the age of six and has beaten 16 world or former world champions in winning seven versions of world titles in six divisions. Is now a leading promoter through his Golden Boys Promotions Company. Has 29 wins inside the distance

06.05.06	Ricardo Mayorga W RSC 6 Las Vegas *(WBC L.Middleweight Title Challenge)*
Career: 42 contests, won 38, lost 4.	

Juan (Baby Bull) Diaz

Houston, USA. *Born* 17 September, 1983
WBA Lightweight Champion

Major Amateur Honours: The Mexican Junior and Senior champion in 1999, he claims 105 wins in 110 fights, but was too young for the Sydney Olympics
Turned Pro: June 2002
Significant Results: John Bailey W RSC 7, Eleazar Contreras W PTS 10, Joel Perez W RSC 6, Martin O'Malley W CO 2, Lakva Sim W PTS 12, Julien Lorcy W PTS 12, Billy Irwin W RSC 9
Type/Style: Juan is a solid, busy fighter with great hand speed, but is not a big puncher
Points of Interest: 5'6" tall. Started boxing when he was eight years old, becoming the fourth youngest fighter to win a version of the lightweight title and was still a high school student at the time he beat Lakva Sim for the title in July 2004. He is now at College, taking Government studies. Trained by ex-pro Ronnie Shields and managed by Shelly Finkel, he has 15 wins by

Oscar de la Hoya

stoppage or kayo and has made three defences

| 16.07.05 | Arthur Cruz W RSC 5 Kinder |
| 08.04.06 | Jose Miguel Cotto W PTS 12 Las Vegas *(WBA Lightweight Title Defence)* |

Career: 29 contests, won 29.

Sergei Dzindziruk

Nozewska, Ukraine. *Born* 1 March, 1976
WBO L.Middleweight Champion. Former Undefeated European L.Middleweight Champion

Major Amateur Honours: After competing in both the 1993 European and 1994 World Junior Champion- ships, he went on to win a bronze medal in 1996 European Champion- ships and silver medals in the 1997 World Championships and 1998 European Championships
Turned Pro: February 1999
Significant Results: Ariel Chavez W RSC 7, Andrei Pestriaev W RSC 5, Mamadou Thiam W RTD 3, Hussein Bayram W CO 11, Jimmy Colas W PTS 12
Type/Style: A tall, lean southpaw, he is a good boxer with a hard right hook
Points of Interest: 6'0" tall. He is based in Germany but three of his first four pro fights were in Britain. However, his first fight in Poland was not sanctioned by the Polish

Juan Diaz Les Clark

Federation and so is not included on the record given below. He won the European title by beating Mamadou Thiam in July 2004 and made two defences. Has 22 wins inside the distance

| 03.12.05 | Daniel Santos W PTS 12 Magdeburg *(WBO L.Middleweight Title Challenge)* |
| 27.05.06 | Sebastien Lujan W PTS 12 Munich *(WBO L.Middleweight Title Defence)* |

Career: 32 contests, won 32.

Zsolt (Firebird) Erdei

Budapest, Hungary. *Born* 31 May, 1974
WBO L.Heavyweight Champion

Major Amateur Honours: The European Junior champion in 1992, he competed in the 1995 World Championships and 1996 Olympics and won a silver medal in the 1996 European Championships. He went on to win gold medals in the 1997 World Championship, 1998 and 2000 European Championships, and a bronze medal in the 2000 Olympics.
Turned Pro: December 2000
Significant Results: Jim Murray W CO 5, Juan Carlos Gimenez W RSC 8, Massimiliano Saiani W RSC 7, Julio Gonzalez W PTS 12, Hugo Garay W PTS 12 (twice), Alejandro Lakatus W PTS 12
Type/Style: Although an excellent, clever technical craftsman and quick combination puncher with a strong, accurate jab, he is not a puncher
Points of Interest: 5'10" tall with a 72" reach. Floored twice in early fights, he is based in Germany. On beating Julio Gonzalez in January 2004 he brought the WBO title back to his stable after fellow Universum fighter, Dariusz Michalczewski, had lost it to the same man. Has 15 wins inside the distance and has made five title defences

| 22.10.05 | Mehdi Sahnoune W RSC 12 Halle *(WBO L.Heavyweight Title Defence)* |
| 06.05.06 | Paul Murdoch W RSC 10 Dusseldorf *(WBO L.Heavyweight Title Defence)* |

Career: 24 contests, won 24.

Acelino Freitas   Les Clark

Acelino (Popo) Freitas
Salvador de Bahia, Brazil. *Born* 21 September, 1975
WBO Lightweight Champion. Former Undefeated WBO & WBA S.Featherweight Champion. Former Brazilian Lightweight Champion

Major Amateur Honours: he won a silver medal in the 1995 Pan-American Games and claims 72 wins in 74 fights.
Turned Pro: July 1995
Significant Results: Anatoly Alexandrov W CO 1, Claudio Martinet W CO 3, Barry Jones W RSC 8, Javier Jauregui W RSC 1, Lemuel Nelson W RSC 2, Carlos Rios W RSC 9, Orlando Soto W RSC 4, Alfred Kotey W PTS 10, Joel Casamayor W PTS 12, Daniel Attah W PTS 12, Juan Carlos Ramirez W RSC 4, Jorge Barrios W RSC 12, Artur Grigorian W PTS 12, Diego Corrales L RTD 10
Type/Style: A strong and aggressive fighter with fast hands, and a crushing punch, he sometimes gets careless and his heart has been questioned
Points of Interest: 5'7" tall. Following in the footsteps of his brother, Luiz Carlos, who was also a pro and double Brazilian champion, Acelino won his first 29 fights inside the distance, 22 within the first three rounds. After winning the WBO super-featherweight title from Anatoly Alexandrov he made ten defences of the title and won the WBA title in January 2002 by beating Joel Casamayor. He then made three defences of his combined title before moving up to lightweight where he won the WBO title by beating Artur Grigorian. Despite losing his title to Diego Corrales, he regained it following his win over Zahir Raheem

16.07.05	Fabian Salazar W CO 1 Salvador
29.04.06	Zahir Raheem W PTS 12 Mashantucket
	(Vacant WBO Lightweight Title)

Career: 39 contests, won 38, lost 1.

Jhonny Gonzalez
Mexico City, Mexico. *Born* 15 September, 1980
WBO Bantamweight Champion. Former Undefeated Mexican Bantamweight Champion

Major Amateur Honours: Won a bronze medal in the Pan-American Championships in 1997
Turned Pro: August 1999
Significant Results: Saul Briseno W RSC 8, Ablorh Sowah W RSC 10, Ricardo Vargas L PTS 10 & L TD 7, Francisco Mateos W RSC 1, Diego Andrade W RSC 1, Francisco Tejedor W RSC 1, Hugo Vargas W CO 3, Gabriel Elizondo W RSC 2, Adonis Rivas W PTS 12, Trini Mendoza W RSC 4
Type/Style: Although not a stylish boxer, he is a tough, rangy fighter and a very hard puncher
Points of Interest: 5'7" tall. The spelling of his Christian name is due to his father recording the name wrongly when obtaining the birth certificate. Having won the WBO bantamweight title, his first defence was supposed to be against Mark Johnson, but when the latter failed to make the weight their contest went on as a non-title fight. Lost his first two professional fights, but has 28 wins by kayo or stoppage and is trained by former pro, Miguel Angel 'Raton' Gonzalez

01.09.05	William Gonzalez W CO 3 Tucson
29.10.05	Ratanchai Sorvoraphin W RSC 7 Tucson
	(WBO Bantamweight Title Challenge)
25.02.06	Mark Johnson W CO 8 Las Vegas
27.05.06	Fernando Montiel W PTS 12 Carson
	(WBO Bantamweight Title Defence)

Career: 37 contests, won 33, lost 4.

Hozumi Hasegawa
Nishiwaki City. Japan. *Born* 16 December, 1980
WBC Bantamweight Champion

Major Amateur Honours: None known
Turned Pro: November 1999
Significant Results: Jess Maca W PTS 12, Gunao Uno W PTS 12, Alvin Felisilda W CO 10, Jun Toriumi W PTS 10, Veeraphol Sahaprom W PTS 12
Type/Style: He is a tall, fast and stylish southpaw
Points of Interest: 5'5" tall. With only seven wins inside the distance, he was once known as the 'Japanese Pernell Whittaker', due to his excellent boxing skills. Lost two of his first five fights, but is now unbeaten in 17 bouts, and Veeraphol Sahaprom had not tasted defeat in his last 45 fights before Hozumi beat him for the WBC title in April 2005. Has since made two defences

25.09.05	Gerardo Martinez W RSC 7 Yokohama
	(WBC Bantamweight Title Defence)
25.03.06	Veeraphol Sahaprom W RSC 9 Kobe
	(WBC Bantamweight Title Defence)

Career: 22 contests, won 20, lost 2.

Chris (The Dragon) John
Semarang, Indonesia. *Born* 4 September, 1981
WBA Featherweight Champion. Former Undefeated Indonesian Featherweight Champion

Major Amateur Honours: None as he had only a few bouts in local competitions
Turned Pro: June 1998
Significant Results: Ratanchai Sorvoraphin W PTS 10, Oscar Leon W PTS 10, Osamu Sato W PTS 12, Jose Rojas T DRAW 4, Derrick Gainer W PTS 12

Type/Style: He is a tall, switch-hitting, counter-puncher with good footwork
Points of Interest: 5'7½" tall with a 65" reach. Christened Johannes Christian John, his original nickname was 'Thin Man', which he took as a tribute to Alexis Arguello before eventually deciding that it was no longer suitable for his improved muscular build. His father was a former amateur boxer and Chris has been boxing since he was six, originally training in a garage before being based in a gym in Australia. He is also an international standard competitor at martial arts. Won the vacant 'interim' WBA featherweight title in September 2003 on beating Oscar Leon and made three defences until he was recognised as full champion when Juan Manuel Marquez was stripped of the title. He has 20 wins inside the distance

07.08.05	Tommy Browne W RTD 9 Sydney *(WBA Secondary Featherweight Title Defence)*
04.03.06	Juan Manuel Marquez W PTS 12 Tenggarong City *(WBA Featherweight Title Defence)*
Career: 38 contests, won 37, drew 1.	

Roman (Made In Hell) Karmazin

Kuztniesk, Russia. *Born* 7 March, 1973
IBF L.Middleweight Champion.
Former Undefeated European L.Middleweight Champion

Major Amateur Honours: None known
Turned Pro: August 1996
Significant Results: Robert Frazier W PTS 8, Hugo Sclarandi W PTS 8, Juan Italo Meza W PTS 8, Orhan Delibas W RSC 4, Sergey Tatevosyan W PTS 8, Javier Castillejo L PTS 12, Jorge Araujo W RSC 5, David Walker W RSC 3, Keith Holmes W PTS 12
Type/Style: Is a tall, long-armed box-puncher
Points of Interest: 5'11" tall. Roman, who started out in gymnastics before switching to boxing, first won the vacant European title by beating Orhan Delibas in June 2000. Failing to make a defence, he then won the vacant title again in February 2003 by beating Jorge Araujo and made two defences. Has 21 wins by stoppage or kayo

14.07.05	Kassim Ouma W PTS 12 Las Vegas *(IBF L.Middleweight Title Challenge)*
Career: 37 contests won 34, drew 1, lost 1, no decision 1.	

Mikkel (Viking Warrior) Kessler

Copenhagen, Denmark. *Born* 1 March, 1979
WBA S.Middleweight Champion

Major Amateur Honours: Was the European Junior champion in 1996 and the Danish Junior champion in 1996 and 1997
Turned Pro: March 1998
Significant Results: Elicier Julio W CO 3, Manny Sobral W RTD 5, Dingaan Thobela W PTS 12, Henry Porras W RSC 9, Julio Cesar Green W CO 1, Andre Thysse W PTS 12, Manny Siaca W RTD 7, Anthony Mundine W PTS 12
Type/Style: A tall, strong, quality box fighter with a good jab, he has been unfortunate to have had trouble with hand injuries in the past
Points of Interest: 6'1" tall with a 73" reach. Heavily tattooed, he came in against Manny Siaca in November 2004 for the title as a late substitute when Mads Larsen dropped out and made the most of his opportunity. Having made two defences, with 28 wins by stoppage or kayo on his record, he is managed by Team Palle and was voted the Danish Fighter of the Year for 2004

14.01.06	Eric Lucas W RTD 10 Copenhagen *(WBA S.Middleweight Title Defence)*
Career: 37 contests, won 37.	

Vladimir Klitschko

Kiev, Ukraine. *Born* 25 March, 1976
IBF Heavyweight Champion. Former WBO Heavyweight Champion.
Former Undefeated European Heavyweight Champion

Major Amateur Honours: Having won a gold medal in the 1993 European Junior Championships, a year later he took silver medals in the 1994 World Junior Championships and World Military Championships. He then went one better in the 1995 World Military Championship, winning the gold medal, and in 1996 he won a silver medal in the European Championships prior to picking up a gold medal in the Olympics
Turned Pro: November 1996
Significant Results: Ross Puritty L RSC 11, Axel Schulz W RSC 8, Chris Byrd W PTS 12, Frans Botha W RSC 8, Ray Mercer W RSC 6, Jameel McCline W RSC 10, Corrie Sanders L RSC 2, Lamon Brewster L RSC 5, DaVarryl Williamson W TD 5, Eliseo Castillo W RSC 4
Type/Style: Although he has a mechanical jab and cross approach, his reach and punching power makes him a difficult opponent. Despite being a champion, there are still some questions over his stamina and chin
Points of Interest: 6'6" tall. Despite losing his first amateur fight he was not deterred and has 41 wins inside the distance as a pro. After winning the European title by beating Axel Schulz in September 1999 he made only one defence before relinquishing it and going on to win the WBO title when outpointing Chris Byrd in October 2000. He made five defences before dropping the title in a shock stoppage loss to Corrie Sanders in March 2003. The younger brother of the former WBO and WBC champion, Vitali, he was then stopped by Lamon Brewster in a fight for the vacant WBO title in April 2004. He is now self managed

24.09.05	Samuel Peter W PTS 12 Atlantic City
22.04.06	Chris Byrd W RSC 7 Mannheim *(IBF Heavyweight Title Challenge)*
Career: 49 contests, won 46, lost 3.	

Takashi Koshimoto

Fukuoka, Japan. *Born* 5 January, 1971
WBC Featherweight Champion.
Former Undefeated Japanese Featherweight Champion

Major Amateur Honours: None known
Turned Pro: November 1992
Significant Results: Atushi Tamaki W RSC 8, Freddie Norwood L CO 9, Donny Suratin W PTS 12, Toshikage Kimura W PTS 12, Jaime Barcelona W PTS 10
Type/Style: Tall, rangy and a skilful southpaw counterpuncher, he is not a big puncher
Points of Interest: 5'9½" tall. Managed by his father, who also promotes his

fights and promoted his unsuccessful shot at the WBA title in 2000 when he lost to Freddie Norwood, Takashi then went on to win his next 16 fights. In winning the WBC title he became the oldest Japanese boxer to win a world title

29.01.06	In-Jin Chi W PTS 12 Fukuoka
	(WBC Featherweight Title Challenge)
Career: 42 contests, won 39, drew 1, lost 2.	

Eagle Kyowa

Pichit, Thailand. *Born* 4 December, 1978
WBC M.Flyweight Champion

Major Amateur Honours: None known
Turned Pro: January 2000
Significant Results: Nico Thomas W CO 3, Noel Tunacao W PTS 10, Elmer Gejon W PTS 8, Jose Antonio Aguirre W PTS 12, Satoshi Kogumazaka W TD 8, Isaac Bustos L RSC 4
Type/Style: Short, sturdy and orthodox, he is a good boxer who lacks a big punch
Points of Interest: 5'3½" tall. A Thai based in Japan, his real name is Den Junlaphan, but he has also boxed as Den Sorjaturong, Eagle Akakura and Eagle Okuda and is now boxing under the name of his new sponsor 'Kyowa' after falling out with his previous backer. He started as a pro in Thailand and was fighting over ten rounds by his third fight before moving his base to Japan after just five fights. Having won the WBC title by beating Jose Antonio Aguirre in January 2004, he then lost it to Isaac Bustos in his second defence in December 2004 after suffering an injury to his arm. Has won only five fights by stoppage or kayo and his wife is also a former boxer

06.08.05	Katsunari Takayama W PTS 12 Tokyo
	(WBC M.Flyweight Title Challenge)
09.01.06	Ken Nakajima W PRSC 7 Yokohama
	(WBC M.Flyweight Title Defence)
06.05.06	Rodel Mayol W PTS 12 Tokyo
	(WBC M. Flyweight Title Defence)
Career: 17 contests, won 16, lost 1.	

Sergei (White Wolf) Lyakhovich

Vitebsk, Belarus. *Born* 29 May, 1976
WBO Heavyweight Champion

Major Amateur Honours: After competing in the 1996 Olympics, he won a bronze medal in the 1997 World Championships before taking part in the 1998 European Championships, where he beat Audley Harrison. Claims 145 wins in 160 amateur fights
Turned Pro: December 1998
Significant Results: Maurice Harris L CO 9, Friday Ahunanya W PTS 10, Sione Asipeli W RSC 5, Dominic Guinn W PTS 10
Type/Style: Is a tall, solid fighter with a good jab and fast hands
Points of Interest: 6'4" tall with a 75" reach. Christened Sergei Petrovich, although he turned pro in Belarus he moved to the USA after just three fights and now lives in Arizona where he is trained by former pro, Kenny Weldon. He was only rated No 13 by the WBO and had been inactive for 16 months when he won the title from Lamon Brewster. Has 14 wins inside the distance

01.04.06	Lamon Brewster W PTS 12 Cleveland
	(WBO Heavyweight Title Challenge)
Career: 24 contests, won 23, lost 1.	

Antonio Margarito

Tijuana, Mexico. *Born* 18 March, 1978
WBO Welterweight Champion

Major Amateur Honours: None known
Turned Pro: January 1994
Significant Results: Larry Dixon L PTS 10, Rodney Jones L PTS 10, Alfred Ankamah W CO 4, Danny Perez W PTS 8 & W PTS 12, David Kamau W CO 2, Frankie Randall W RSC 4, Daniel Santos NC 1 & L TD 9, Antonio Diaz W RSC 10, Andrew Lewis W RSC 2, Hercules Kyvelos W RSC 2, Sebastien Lujan W RSC 10, Kermit Cintron W RSC 5
Type/Style: Is a tall, strong, aggressive banger. Although a bit one-paced, he has a good jab and a strong chin

Sergei Lyakhovich (right)   Les Clark

Points of Interest: 6'0" tall. Turned pro at the age of 15 and suffered three early defeats. His first fight with Daniel Santos for the WBO welterweight was stopped and declared a no contest due to Antonio suffering a bad cut, and when Santos handed in the belt he won the vacant title by beating Antonio Diaz in March 2002. His challenge against Santos for the WBO light-middleweight title also went to a technical decision due to a cut. Has made six defences and has 24 wins inside the distance

18.02.06	Manuel Gomez W RSC 1 Las Vegas *(WBO Welterweight Title Defence)*

Career: 38 contests, won 33, lost 4, no contest 1.

Rafael Marquez

Mexico City, Mexico. *Born* 25 March, 1975
IBF Bantamweight Champion

Major Amateur Honours: None known, but claims only one loss in 57 fights
Turned Pro: September 1995
Significant Results: Victor Rabanales L CO 8, Francisco Mateos L RSC 3, Tomas Rivera W CO 2, Genaro Garcia L RSC 2, Aquilies Guzman W RSC 7, Gerardo Espinoza W RSC 4, Mark Johnson W PTS 10 & W RSC 8, Tim Austin W RSC 8, Mauricio Pastrana W PTS 12 & W RSC 3, Peter Frissina W RSC 2, Heriberto Ruiz W CO 3, Ricardo Vargas W PTS 12
Type/Style: Compact and solid, he is a big puncher with the right hand. However, his defence is not too sound
Points of Interest: 5'5" tall. Lost his first pro fight against Victor Rabanales, who was a former WBC bantamweight champion with more than 50 fights to his name at the time. Rafael eventually won the IBF bantam title by stopping Tim Austin in February 2003, just two weeks after his brother, Juan Manuel, won the IBF featherweight title. Their father, also named Rafael, was a pro in the 1950s. With 31 wins by the short route and all of his losses also coming inside the distance, he is trained by the top Mexican trainer, Nacho Beristain. Has made five defences

05.11.05	Silence Mabuza W RSC 4 Stateline *(IBF Bantamweight Title Defence)*

Career: 38 contests, won 35, lost 3.

Ricardo (El Matador) Mayorga

Costa Rica. *Born* Granada, Nicaragua, 3 October, 1973
Former WBC L.Middleweight Champion. Former WBA & WBC Welterweight Champion. Former Undefeated Nicaraguan L.Welterweight Champion

Major Amateur Honours: None known
Turned Pro: August 1993
Significant Results: Roger Flores L PTS 10, Henry Castillo L PTS 10 & W RSC 7, Diosbelys Hurtado T DRAW 2, Elio Ortiz W CO 10, Andrew Lewis NC 2 & W RSC 5, Vernon Forrest W CO 3 & W PTS 12, Cory Spinks L PTS 12, Eric Mitchell W PTS 10, Felix Trinidad L RSC 8
Type/Style: Has a crude and wild style, but is very strong and a hard puncher
Points of Interest: 5'10" tall. Having lost his first professional fight on a stoppage, he went on to challenge Andrew Lewis for the WBA welterweight title in July 2001, only for the fight to be stopped and declared a no contest due to Lewis getting cut. In the return bout in March 2002 he halted Lewis to win the title and in March 2003 he kayoed Vernon Forrest to add the WBC title to his championship honours. He then beat Forrest in a defence but then lost WBA and WBC titles to Cory Spinks in December 2003, in a fight, which also involved the latter's IBF title. Now a Costa Rican citizen, he has 22 wins by stoppage or kayo

13.08.05	Michele Piccirillo W PTS 12 Chicago *(Vacant WBC L.Middleweight Title)*
06.05.06	Oscar de la Hoya L RSC 6 Las Vegas *(WBC L.Middleweight Title Defence)*

Career: 34 contests, won 27, drew 1, lost 5, no contest 1.

Floyd (Little Stone) Mayweather

Grand Rapids, USA. *Born* 24 February, 1977
IBF Welterweight Champion. Former Undefeated WBC L.Welterweight Champion. Former Undefeated WBC Lightweight Champion. Former Undefeated WBC S.Featherweight Champion

Major Amateur Honours: Was a national Golden Gloves champion in 1993, 1994 and 1996, and the US champion in 1995, with that first Golden Gloves title being at 106lbs. He competed in 1995 World Championships and won a bronze medal in the 1996 Olympics. Won 84 of 90 fights
Turned Pro: October 1996
Significant Results: Genaro Hernandez W RTD 8 & W PTS 12, Angel Manfredy W RSC 2, Carlos Rios W PTS 12, Justin Juuko W RSC 9, Carlos Gerena W RTD 7, Gregorio Vargas W PTS 12, Diego Corrales W RSC 10, Jesus Chavez W RTD 9, Jose Luis Castillo W PTS 12 (twice), Victoriano Sosa W PTS 12, Phillip Ndou W RSC 7, DeMarcus Corley W PTS 12, Henry Bruseles W RSC 8, Arturo Gatti W RSC 6
Type/Style: Is a talented, flashy fighter with fast hands, great reflexes and a hard punch
Points of Interest: 5'8" tall with a 72" reach. Floyd's father, also named Floyd, was a good professional and his uncle, Roger Mayweather, was WBA super-featherweight and WBC light-welterweight champion. Roger now trains Oscar de la Hoya, so boxing is well and truly in the blood. He won the WBC super-featherweight title in October 1998, beating Genaro Hernandez, and made eight defences before winning the WBC lightweight title when defeating Jose Luis Castillo in April 2002. Floyd then made two defences before moving up to win the light-welterweight title in June 2005 from Arturo Gatti. Not making a defence, he moved up again to beat Zab Judah for the IBF welter title, although he was lucky not to be disqualified when his trainer climbed into the ring during one of the rounds. Has 24 wins by stoppage or kayo

19.11.05	Sharmba Mitchell W RSC 6 Portland
08.04.06	Zab Judah W PTS 12 Las Vegas *(IBF Welterweight Title Challenge)*

Career: 36 contests, won 36.

223

Fernando Montiel

Fernando (Cochulito) Montiel

Los Mochis, Mexico. *Born* 1 March, 1979
WBO S. Flyweight Champion. Former Undefeated WBO Flyweight Champion

Major Amateur Honours: Claiming 33 wins in 36 fights, he was a local Golden Gloves champion.
Turned Pro: December 1996
Significant Results: Paulino Villalobos DREW 10 & W PTS 10, Sergio Millan W PTS 10, Cruz Carbajal W RSC 4, Isidro Garcia W RSC 7, Zoltan Lunka W RSC 7, Juan Domingo Cordoba W CO 1, Jose Lopez W PTS 12, Pedro Alcazar W RSC 6, Roy Doliguez W RSC 3, Mark Johnson L PTS 12, Reynaldo Hurtado W CO 7, Ivan Hernandez W RSC 7
Type/ Style: Clever and stylish, he has a good uppercut
Points of Interest: 5'4" tall. The youngest of a fighting family, his father and four brothers all being boxers, he won his first 11 bouts inside the distance. Jointly trained by his father, Manuel, and a Japanese trainer based in Mexico, Fernando has 24 wins by knockout or stoppage. He won the WBO title, stopping Isidro Garcia in December 2000, and made three defences before moving up to win the super-flyweight title by beating Pedro Alcazar in June 2002. Sadly, Alcazar collapsed and died after the fight. Having lost the title in his second

defence to Mark Johnson in August 2003, Fernando came back to regain it when stopping Ivan Hernandez in April 2005 and made two defences before an unsuccessful challenge to Jhonny Gonzales for the WBO bantamweight title

16.07.05	Evert Briceno W PTS 12 Las Vegas *(WBO S.Flyweight Title Defence)*
29.10.05	Pramuansak Phosuwan W PTS 12 Tucson *(WBO S.Flyweight Title Defence)*
27.05.06	Jhonny Gonzales L PTS 12 Carson *(WBO Bantamweight Title Challenge)*
Career: 35 contests, won 32, drew 1, lost 2.	

Vicente (El Loco) Mosquera

Puerto Caimito, Panama. *Born* 9 December, 1979
WBA S.Featherweight Champion

Major Amateur Honours: None known, but claimed 33 fights
Turned Pro: February 1998
Significant Results: Armando Cordova DREW 12 & L PTS 12, Ali Oubaali W PTS 10, Edgar Ilarraza W PTS 12, Victor Julio W RSC 3, Yodesnan Sornontachai W PTS 12
Type/ Style: A skilful boxer and good tactician who can fight on the inside and on the outside, he is a sharp but not hard puncher
Points of Interest: 5'8" tall. Starting boxing at the age of 16, in beating Yodesnan Sornontachai he became the first Panamanian to win a world title in Madison Square Garden since Roberto Duran in 1972. This followed a spell of inactivity between April 2000 and February 2003 when he was jailed for a crime for which he was subsequently proved to be innocent. Has only 12 wins inside the distance

10.12.05	Walter Estrada W RSC 8 Panama City
04.02.06	Carlos Saenz W RSC 6 Panama City
12.05.06	Jose Pablo Estrella W PTS 12 Cordoba *(WBA S.Featherweight Title Defence)*
Career: 24 contests, won 22, drew 1, lost 1.	

Omar (Huracan) Narvaez

Trelew, Argentina. *Born* 7 October, 1975
WBO Flyweight Champion

Major Amateur Honours: Won a

bronze medal in 1997 World Championships, a silver in the 1999 Championships, a gold medal in the 1999 Pan-American Games and competed in the 1996 Olympics, where he beat the future WBO super-bantamweight champion, Joan Guzman. He also competed in the 2000 Olympics
Turned Pro: December 2000
Significant Results: Carlos Montiveros DREW 4, Wellington Vicente W PTS 10, Marcos Obregon W PTS 10, Adonis Rivas W PTS 12, Luis Lazarate W DIS 10, Andrea Sarritzu W PTS 12 & DREW 12, Everardo Morales W RSC 5, Alexander Mahmutov W RSC 10
Type/ Style: A stocky and aggressive southpaw, he has fast hands
Points of Interest: 5'3" tall. Became the first of the 2000 Olympians to win a version of a world title when he beat Adonis Rivas in only his 12th paid fight in July 2002. Was originally trained by the Cuban, Sarbelio Fuentes, but now has a local trainer and has made seven defences. Has 15 wins inside the distance

05.12.05	Bernard Inom W RSC 11 Paris *(WBO Flyweight Title Defence)*
21.04.06	Dario Azuaga W RSC 6 Cordoba
Career: 23 contests, won 21, drew 2.	

Yutaka Niida

Kanagawa, Japan. *Born* 2 October, 1978
WBA M. Flyweight Champion. Former Undefeated Japanese M.Flyweight Champion

Major Amateur Honours: None known
Turned Pro: November 1996
Significant Results: Makoto Suzuki W RSC 9, Daisuke Iida DREW 10, Chana Porpaoin W PTS 12, Nohel Arambulet L PTS 12 & W PTS 12, Juan Landaeta W PTS 12, Jae-Won Kim W PTS 12
Type/Style: Aggressive, with good speed and a big right-hand punch, he has, however, a suspect chin
Points of Interest: 5'2" tall. Managed by Mitsunori Seki, who failed in five attempts to win versions of the world featherweight title, he climbed off the floor twice in the first round for his draw with Daisuke Iida. Although surprisingly retiring immediately after winning the WBA title on beating Chana Porpaoin in August 2001, he

returned to action in July 2003 and lost to Nohel Arambulet for the WBA title. In a return in July 2004, Arambulet failed to make the weight and Yutaka won the vacant title after outpointing the Venezuelan. Has made four defences

| 25.09.05 | Eriberto Gejon W TD 10 Yokohama *(WBA M.Flyweight Title Defence)* |
| 04.03.06 | Ronald Barrera W PTS 12 Tokyo *(WBA M.Flyweight Title Defence)* |

Career: 24 contests, won 20, drew 3, lost 1.

Lorenzo (Lencho) Parra

Machiques, Venezuela. *Born* 19 August, 1978
WBA Flyweight Champion

Major Amateur Honours: Competed in the 1996 World Junior Championships and claims 268 wins in 278 fights
Turned Pro: March 1999
Significant Results: Edicson Torres W RSC 12, Jose Lopez W CO 11, Edgar Velazquez W PTS 12, Eric Morel W PTS 12, Yo-Sam Choi W PTS 12, Masaki Nakanuma W PTS 12
Type/Style: A clever, stringy little fighter, he is recognised for his excellent movement and sharp punch
Points of Interest: 5'4¹/₂" tall with a 66" reach. Trained by Pedro Gamarro, who won a silver medal in the 1976 Olympics, he was fighting ten rounds in only his sixth bout. Won the WBA title by beating Eric Morel in December 2003 and has made five defences, all on the road. Has 17 wins by stoppage or kayo

| 19.09.05 | Takefumi Sakata W PTS 12 Tokyo *(WBA Flyweight Title Defence)* |
| 05.12.05 | Brahim Asloum W PTS 12 Paris *(WBA Flyweight Title Defence)* |

Career: 27 contests, won 27.

Valdemir (Sertao) Pereira

Cruz Das Almas, Brazil. *Born* 15 November, 1974
Former IBF Featherweight Champion

Major Amateur Honours: Was a three-time Brazilian champion and competed in the 2000 Olympics
Turned Pro: March 2001
Significant Results: Rogers Mtagwa W RSC 8, Emmanuel Lucero W PTS 10, Pastor Maurin W PTS 12, Whyber Garcia W PTS 12

Type/Style: A busy fighter with an excellent jab, he is also a good body puncher
Points of Interest: 5'5" tall. He works as an ice cream seller and is an unmarried father with three children. Trained by former pro, Servilio de Oliveira, he has 15 wins inside the distance, but threw his title away when he was disqualified for low blows against Eric Aiken

23.07.05	Victor Hugo Paz W PTS 10 Sao Paulo
20.01.06	Fahprakorb Rakkiatgym W PTS 12 Mashantucket *(Vacant IBF Featherweight Title)*
09.04.06	Yuri Romanovich W PTS 10 Sao Paulo
13.05.06	Eric Aiken L DIS 8 Boston *(IBF Featherweight Title Defence)*

Career: 25 contests, won 24, lost 1.

Luis (The Demolisher) Perez

Managua, Nicaragua. *Born* 6 April, 1978
IBF S.Flyweight Champion

Major Amateur Honours: None known
Turned Pro: November 1996
Significant Results: Leon Salazar W RSC 4, Justo Zuniga W CO 1, Vernie Torres L PTS 12, Moises Castro W PTS 10, Edicson Torres W PTS 12 (twice), Felix Machado W PTS 12 (twice), Luis Bolano W RSC 6
Type/Style: Is a skinny, skilful southpaw with a strong jab, but doesn't carry a big punch
Points of Interest: 5'5" tall with a 67" reach. Had only five days notice of the first fight with Felix Machado in January 2003 when he won the IBF title, but showed it was no fluke in the rematch. At one time he was managed by Anna Alvarez, the wife of the former WBA light-flyweight champion, Rosendo Alvarez, and has 15 wins inside the distance. Has made only three defences in over three years

| 06.05.06 | Dimitri Kirilov W PTS 12 Worcester *(IBF S.Flyweight Title Defence)* |

Career: 25 contests, won 24, lost 1.

Daniel Ponce De Leon

Cuauhtemoc, Mexico. *Born* 27 July, 1980
WBO S.Bantamweight Champion

Major Amateur Honours: Was Mexican amateur champion five times before winning a bronze medal in the Pan-American Games in 1999 and competing in the 2000 Olympics
Turned Pro: March 2001
Significant Results: Trinidad Mendoza W RSC 2, Francisco Tejedor W RSC 1, Jesus Perez W RSC 1, Cesar Figueroa W CO 6, Ivan Alvarez W RSC 5, Carlos Contreras W PTS 10, Emmanuel Lucero W RSC 3, Julio Gamboa W CO 4, Celestino Caballero L PTS 12, Ricardo Barajas W CO 2
Type/Style: Strong but crude, he is a southpaw with a big punch
Points of Interest: 5'5" tall. Started boxing at the age of 13 and was a member of the Mexican national squad at the age of 14. Initially signed up by a local promoter, he is now with Oscar de la Hoya's Golden Boy Promotions and has 27 wins inside the distance

| 29.10.05 | Sod Looknongyangtoy W PTS 12 Tucson *(Vacant WBO S.Bantamweight Title)* |
| 27.05.06 | Gerson Guerrero W CO 2 Carson *(WBO S.Bantamweight Title Defence)* |

Career: 29 contests, won 28, lost 1.

Muhammad (Rock Breaker) Rachman

Papua, Indonesia. *Born* 23 December, 1972
IBF M.Flyweight Champion. Former Undefeated Indonesian M.Flyweight Champion

Major Amateur Honours: None known
Turned Pro: January 1993
Significant Results: Jin-Ho Kim W PTS 10, Lindi Memani W PTS 12, Patrick Twala W PTS 10, Ernesto Rubillar W PTS 10, Jun Arlos W PTS 10, Noel Tunacao W RSC 2, Daniel Reyes W PTS 12, Fahlan Sakkreerin T DRAW 3
Type/Style: Is a busy southpaw, but not a puncher
Points of Interest: 5'3" tall with a 59" reach. Self-managed, his real name is Mohamed Rachman Sawaludin and he gained his nickname after beating a Filipino boxer known as 'The Rock'. He is unbeaten in his last 36 bouts, with 26 wins by stoppage or kayo, and has made two defences since winning

the IBF title by beating Daniel Reyes in September 2004. Has only fought outside Indonesia four times, and lost all four fights

06.05.06	Omar Soto W CO 6 Jakarta *(IBF M.Flyweight Title Defence)*
Career: 67 contests, won 56, drew 4, lost 7.	

Hasim (The Rock) Rahman

Baltimore, USA. *Born* 7 November, 1972
WBC Heavyweight Champion. Former WBC & IBF Heavyweight Champion

Major Amateur Honours: He competed in the 1994 United States Championships
Turned Pro: December 1994
Significant Results: Trevor Berbick W PTS 10; Jesse Ferguson W PTS 12, David Tua L RSC 10 & DREW 12, Oleg Maskaev L CO 8, Corrie Sanders W RSC 7, Lennox Lewis W CO 5 & L CO 4, Evander Holyfield L TD 8, John Ruiz L PTS 12, Alfred Cole W PTS 10, Kali Meehan W RSC 4
Type/Style: Is a solid fighter with limited skills, but has an an explosive right-hand punch
Points of Interest: Is 6'2" tall with an 82" reach. In a turbulent life he has had to overcome a career threatening spine injury, 500 stitches to head and face after a car accident, five bullets from a shooting still in his body, and being arrested about a dozen times. He won the WBC and IBF titles by kayoing Lennox Lewis in April 2001, but lost both titles in a return match seven months later. He then went on to lose to John Ruiz for the WBA 'interim' title in December 2003, before winning the WBC 'interim' title when beating Monte Barrett and then being recognised as the full champion when Vitali Klitschko retired. Has 33 wins inside the distance

13.08.05	Monte Barrett W PTS 12 Chicago *(Vacant WBC Interim Heavyweight Title)*
18.03.06	James Toney DREW 12 Atlantic City *(WBC Heavyweight Title Defence)*
Career: 48 contests, won 41, drew 2, lost 5.	

Jose Antonio (El Gallo) Rivera

Philadelphia, USA. *Born* 7 April, 1973
WBA L.Middleweight Champion

Major Amateur Honours: Competed in the 1991 National AAU Championships
Turned Pro: November 1992
Significant Results: Willie Wise L PTS 10, Teddy Reid W PTS 10, Pat Coleman L PTS 10, Robert Frazier L PTS 10, Frankie Randall W CO 10, Michel Trabant W PTS 12, Luis Collazo L PTS 12
Type/Style: Heavy handed with a good jab, but needs to tighten his defence
Points of Interest: 5'8" tall with a 70" reach. Having won his first 23 fights, 17 of them inside the distance, and collected the vacant 'secondary' WBA welterweight title by outpointing previously unbeaten Michael Trabant in Germany in September 2003, he lost the title in his first defence to Luis Collazo in April 2005. Had just two fights in over three years when he beat Alejandro Garcia and is now trained by former pro, John Scully

06.05.06	Alejandro Garcia W PTS 12 Worcester *(WBA L.Middleweight Title Challenge)*
Career: 43 contests, won 38, drew 1, lost 4.	

Wladimir Sidorenko

WBA Bantamweight Champion
Energodar, Ukraine. *Born* 23 September, 1975

Major Amateur Honours: Competed in the 1997 and 1999 World Championships and won a silver medal in the 2001 World Championships. Won a World Military Championship title three times and was a gold medallist in the 1998 European Championships before reaching the quarter-finals in the 2000 Olympics
Turned Pro: November 2001
Significant Results: Giovanni Andrade W RSC 3, Sergei Tasimov W PTS 8, Moises Castro W PTS 12, Joseph Agbeko W PTS 12, Silvio 'Leo' Gamez W PTS 12, Julio Zarate W PTS 12
Type/Style: Is a short, sturdy, busy counter-puncher with a tight guard
Points of Interest: 5'4" tall. Starting boxing in 1988, he comes from a boxing family, with his brother also being a pro, and had 310 amateur fights before punching for pay. He won the WBA title by decisioning

Julio Zarate in February 2005 and has made three defences. Not a puncher, he has only five wins inside the distance

26.11.05	Jose de Jesus Lopez W PTS 12 Leverkusen *(WBA Bantamweight Title Defence)*
11.03.06	Ricardo Cordoba DREW 12 Hamburg *(WBA Bantamweight Title Defence)*
Career: 18 contests, won 17, drew 1.	

Ulises (Archie) Solis

Guadalajara, Mexico. *Born* 28 August, 1981
IBF L. Flyweight Champion. Former Undefeated Mexican L.Flyweight Champion.

Major Amateur Honours: None known, but he claims only two losses in 38 fights
Turned Pro: April 2000
Significant Results: Omar Soto W PTS 10, Juan Keb Baas W RSC 9, Edger Sosa W PTS 12, Lee Sandoval W RTD 8, Gabriel Munoz W CO 3, Nelson Dieppa L PTS 12, Carlos Fajardo W RSC 8
Type/Style: Not a puncher, he is a stand-up boxer who uses a low guard
Points of Interest: 5'3" tall. Ulises is a member of a fighting family and his elder brother, Jorge, is a world-rated featherweight. Has 16 wins inside the distance, with his only defeat coming when he lost a majority verdict to Nelson Dieppa in a challenge for the WBO title in July 2004

07.01.06	Will Grigsby W PTS 12 New York City *(IBF L.Flyweight Title Challenge)*
25.03.06	Erick Ortiz W RSC 9 Guadalajara *(IBF L.Flyweight Title Defence)*
Career: 23 contests, won 21, drew 1, lost 1.	

Somsak Sithchatchawal

Lampang, Thailand. *Born* 17 July, 1977
WBA S. Bantamweight Champion

Major Amateur Honours: None known
Turned Pro: August 1995
Significant Results: Ratanchai Sorvoraphin L PTS 10, Edward Mpofu W RSC 12, Marcel Kasimov W CO 7, Dondon Lapuz W PTS 10, Vuysile Bebe W CO 5
Type/Style: An aggressive southpaw,

he has a dangerous left uppercut and a good chin

Points of Interest: 5'7" tall. Unbeaten in his last 37 fights stretching back to 1998, he also has 37 wins inside the distance. His win over Mahyar Monshipour was only his second fight outside Thailand

07.01.06	Will Grigsby W PTS 12 New York City
	(IBF L.Flyweight Title Challenge)
25.03.06	Erick Ortiz W RSC 9 Guadalajara
	(IBF L.Flyweight Title Defence)
Career: 23 contests, won 21, drew 1, lost 1.	

Jermain (Bad Intentions) Taylor

Little Rock, USA. *Born* 11 August, 1978
WBC, WBA & WBO Middleweight Champion. Former Undefeated IBF Middleweight Champion

Major Amateur Honours: A United States Junior champion in 1996, he went on to win two national Golden Gloves titles and collected bronze medals in the 1998 Goodwill Games and 2000 Olympics
Turned Pro: January 2001
Significant Results: Sam Hill W PTS 10, Alex Bunema W RSC 7, Raul Marquez W RTD 9, William Joppy W PTS 12, Daniel Edouard W RSC 3
Type/Style: Is a good, stylish boxer with an excellent jab
Points of Interest: 6'1" tall. His uncle boxed as an amateur and started Jermain in boxing at the age of 13, before he eventually progressed to a scholarship at the United States Olympic Centre, where he met and married an athlete. Although he won all four versions of the world title, he was forced to relinquish the IBF title when he elected to fight Bernard Hopkins in a return match

16.07.05	Bernard Hopkins W PTS 12 Las Vegas
	(WBA, WBC, WBO & IBF Middleweight Title Challenges)
03.12.05	Bernard Hopkins W PTS 12 Las Vegas
	(WBC, WBA & WBO Middleweight Title Defences)
17.06.06	Ronald Wright DREW 12 Memphis
	(WBC, WBA & WBO Middleweight Title Defences)
Career: 26 contests, won 25, drew 1.	

Fabrice Tiozzo

Saint Denis, France. *Born* 8 May, 1969
WBA L.Heavyweight Champion. Former WBA Cruiserweight Champion. Former Undefeated WBC L.Heavyweight Champion. Former Undefeated European & French L.Heavyweight Champion

Major Amateur Honours: In 1987 he won a silver medal in both the World Junior Championships and World Military Championships and was a French champion the following year
Turned Pro: November 1988
Significant Results: Virgil Hill L PTS 12 & L RSC 1, Mike McCallum W PTS 12, Eddy Smulders W RSC 7, Maurice Core W RSC 4, Nate Miller W PTS 12, Silvio Branco W PTS 12, Dariusz Michalczewski W RSC 6
Type/Style: Although he has an upright style, he is strong and skilful with a solid chin
Points of Interest: 6'1" tall. After successfully emulating his brother, Christophe, who was a WBA super-middleweight champion, Fabrice made only two defences of his WBC light-heavyweight title before weight problems forced him to move up to cruiserweight, where he won the WBA title by beating Nate Miller in 1997. Following that, he made four defences prior to losing his title to Virgil Hill in December 2000. Had only one fight in 27 months before returning as a light-heavyweight in March 2003 and won the WBA title when coming off the floor to decision Silvio Branco in March 2004. Has 31 wins inside the distance and when beating Dariusz Michalczewski he gained revenge for a loss suffered when they were amateurs. Was inactive during the period covered

Career: 49 contests, won 47, lost 2.

Masamori Tokuyama

North Korea.. *Born* Tokyo, Japan, 17 September, 1974
WBC S.Flyweight Champion

Major Amateur Honours: None. His record shows only 12 wins in 17 fights
Turned Pro: September 1994
Significant Results: Manny Melchor L

PTS 10, Nolito Cabato DREW 10 & L TD 7, Hiroki Ioka W RSC 5, Pone Saengmorakot W PTS 12, In-Joo Cho W PTS 12 & W CO 5, Akihiko Nago W PTS 12, Gerry Penalosa W PTS 12 (twice), Erik Lopez W RSC 6, Katsushiga Kawashima W PTS & L RSC 1, Dimitri Kirilov W PTS 12
Type/ Style: Is a tall, upright boxer with sharp jab and fast hand, but not a hard puncher
Points of Interest: 5'8" tall. His real name is Chang-Soo Hong and his father was a karate teacher. Masamori became the first North Korean to win a world title when he beat In-Joo Cho for the WBC super-flyweight title in August 2000, and his defence against Cho in May 2001 was the first time that a North Korean and a South Korean had fought each other for a world title in Korea. Was voted Japanese Boxer of the Year in 2002. Having previously beaten Katsuhige Kawashima in a championship defence he then lost his title to him on a shock first-round stoppage in June 2004, following eight successful defences. Taking just over a year out, revenge was sweet when Masamori regained the title from the man he had earlier lost it to

18.07.05	Katsushige Kawashima W PTS 12 Osaka
	(WBC S.Flyweight Title Challenge)
27.02.06	Jose Navarro W PTS 12 Osaka
	(WBC S.Flyweight Title Defence)
Career: 36 contests, won 32, drew 1, lost 3.	

Juan (Iron Twin) Urango

Jaraquielle, Colombia. *Born* 4 October, 1980
IBF L.Welterweight Champion

Major Amateur Honours: Competed in top amateur competitions, but lost twice to Miguel Cotto in qualifying bouts for the 2000 Olympics
Turned Pro: April 2002
Significant Results: Leva Kirakosayan W PTS 8, Mike Aranoutis DREW 12, Ubaldo Hernandez W CO 2, Francisco Campos W CO 5
Type/Style: Is a quick and smooth southpaw
Points of Interest: 5' 8" tall with a 71" reach. He gets his nickname from being one of twins, both of whom are

boxers, and he turned pro in Colombia before moving to Spain and eventually settling in Miami in 2004. Has 13 wins inside the distance, with all of his first ten fights finishing early

26.08.05	Andre Eason W RSC 7 Hollywood
30.06.06	Naoufel Ben Rabah W PTS 12 Hollywood
	(Vacant IBF L.Welterweight Title)
Career: 18 contests, won 17, drew 1.	

Nikolai (The Beast from the East) Valuev

St Petersburg, Russia. *Born* 21 August, 1973
WBA Heavyweight Champion

Major Amateur Honours: Had only 15 amateur fights, including participation in the 1994 Goodwill Games
Turned Pro: October 1993
Significant Results: Andreas Sidon W RSC 4, Taras Bidenko W PTS 12, Bob Mirovic W PTS 8, Dick Ryan W RSC 1, Marcelo Dominguez W PTS 8, Richard Bango W RSC 6, Paolo Vidoz W RSC 9, Gerald Nobles W DIS 4, Attila Levin W RSC 3, Cliff Etienne W CO 3
Type/Style: Is slow but very strong and uses his height and weight effectively
Points of Interest: At 7'2" tall he is the tallest fighter to win a version of the heavyweight title. Now based in Germany, he has scored 32 wins by stoppage or knockout

01.10.05	Larry Donald W PTS 12 Oldenburg
17.12.05	John Ruiz W PTS 12 Berlin
	(WBA Heavyweight Title Challenge)
03.06.06	Owen Beck W RSC 3 Hanover
	(WBA Heavyweight Title Defence)
Career: 44 contests, won 44.	

Israel (Magnifico) Vazquez

Mexico City, Mexico. *Born* 25 December, 1977
WBC S.Bantamweight Champion. Former Undefeated IBF S.Bantamweight Champion

Major Amateur Honours: None known, although he claims 58 wins
Turner Pro: March 1995
Significant Results: Marcos Licona L PTS 12, Eddy Saenz W CO 3, Ever Beleno W CO 2, Osvaldo Guerrero W PTS 10, Oscar Larios L CO 12, Jorge Julio W RSC 10, Trinidad Mendoza W

CO 7, Jose Luis Valbuena W RSC 12, Art Simonyan W RSC 5, Armando Guerrero W PTS 12
Type/Style: A quick, upright boxer with a high, tight guard, he is also a hard puncher
Points of Interest: 5'6" tall with a 66" reach. Having idolised Ruben Olivares, which inspired him to give up karate to concentrate on boxing, Israel lost to Oscar Larios for the vacant WBC 'interim' super-bantamweight title in May 2002. Regrouping, he then won the vacant IBF title in March 2004 by beating Jose Luis Valbuena, making two defences before winning the WBC title. He never got round to defending the IBF title, being stripped for failing to make a mandatory defence. Has 29 wins inside the distance

03.12.05	Oscar Larios W RSC 3 Las Vegas
	(IBF S.Bantamweight Title Defence. WBC S.Bantamweight Title Challenge)
10.06.06	Ivan Hernandez W RTD 4 Atlantic City
	(WBC S.Bantamweight Title Defence)
Career: 43 contests, won 40, lost 3.	

Brian (The Hawaiian Punch) Viloria

Waipahu, USA. *Born* 24 November, 1980
WBC L.Flyweight Champion

Major Amateur Honours: Won United States Junior titles in 1995 and 1996 at 100lbs. His senior career saw him win a gold medal in the 1999 World Championships, win the United States Championships and the national Golden Gloves and compete in the 2000 Olympics
Turned Pro: May 2001
Significant Results: Sandro Oviedo W CO 1, Alberto Rossel NC 3 & W PTS 12, Juan Javier Lagos W PTS 12, Valentin Leon W RSC 8, Luis Doria W RSC 1, Juan Alfonso Keb Baas W PTS 12, Gilberto Keb Baas W CO 11, Angel Priolo W CO 7
Type/Style: A stylish, sharp punching little fighter, who is a good body puncher, he sometimes makes hard work of what should be easy fights
Points of Interest: 5'4" tall. Although born in Hawaii, Brian is of Filipino parentage and was raised there before

winning a scholarship to the United States Olympic Education Centre. He moved down from flyweight to challenge for the WBC light-flyweight title and has 12 wins inside the distance

10.09.05	Erick Ortiz W CO 1 Los Angeles
	(WBC L.Flyweight Title Challenge)
18.02.06	Jose Antonio Aguirre W PTS 12 Las Vegas
	(WBC L.Flyweight Title Defence)
Career: 20 contests won 19, no contest 1.	

Pongsaklek Wonjongkam

Nakhorn Ratchasima, Thailand. *Born* 11 August, 1977
WBC Flyweight Champion

Major Amateur Honours: None
Turned Pro: December 1994
Significant Results: Jerry Pahayaha L PTS 8 & L CO 5, Randy Mangubat W CO 3 & W PTS 12 (twice), Mzukisi Sikali W RSC 1, Juanito Rubillar W PTS 10, Malcolm Tunacao W RSC 1, Daisuke Naito W CO 1, Jesus Martinez W PTS 12, Hidenobu Honda W PTS 12, Hussein Hussein W PTS 12, Masaki Nakanuma W PTS 12
Type/Style: A tough, aggressive, pressure fighter, he is also a southpaw with a wicked right hook
Points of Interest: 5'4". Christened Dongskorn Wonjongkan, Pongsaklek's last loss was in December 1995 and he is unbeaten in his last 52 bouts, having also boxed under the names of Nakornthong Parkview and Sithkanongsak. He first won the WBC title by halting Malcolm Tunacao in March 2001 and has made 15 defences. With 32 wins by stoppage or kayo his quickest victory came when he put Daisuke Naito away in just 34 seconds

29.07.05	Mark Sales W PTS 6 Bangkok
10.10.05	Daisuke Naito W TD 7 Tokyo
	(WBC Flyweight Title Defence)
23.12.05	Isidro Balabat W TD 5 Petchaboon
16.02.06	Gilberto Keb Baas W PTS 12 Chainart
	(WBC Flyweight Title Defence)
01.05 06	Daigo Nakahiro W PTS 12 Bangkok
	(WBC Flyweight Title Defence)
30.06.06	Everardo Morales W RSC 4 Bangkok
	(WBC Flyweight Title Defence)
Career: 64 contests, won 62, lost 2.	

World Title Bouts, 2005-2006

by Bob Yalen

All of last season's title bouts for the IBF, WBA, WBC and WBO are shown in date order within their weight division and give the boxers' respective weights as well as the scorecard if going to a decision. Because the IBO light-heavyweight belt was contested by the top men during the period, their results are shown for that division only. British officials, where applicable, are listed, along with the venue of contests taking place in Britain. Yet again there were no WORLD TITLE FIGHTS as such – even if you allow for Jermain Taylor (Middle), who holds three of the four major titles – just a proliferation of champions recognised by the above four commissions and spread over 17 weight divisions. Below the premier league, come other commissions such as the WBU, IBO, IBC and WBF, etc, etc, which would devalue the world championships even further if one recognised their champions as being the best in the world. Right now, the WBA have decided to continue recognising their champions who move on to claim other commissions' titles as super champions – despite vacating the title and creating a new champion, who, for our purposes, is classified as a 'secondary' champion – which if taken up in general could eventually lead to the best man at his weight being recognised universally as a world champion if the fights can be made.

M.Flyweight

6 August   Katsunari Takayama 7.7 (Japan) L PTS 12 Eagle Kyowa 7.6¾ (Thailand), Tokyo, Japan – WBC. Scorecards: 111-119, 113-117, 112-116.

25 September   Yutaka Niida 7.6¼ (Japan) W TD 10 Eriberto Gejon 7.6½ (Philippines), Yokohama, Japan – WBA. Scorecards: 96-95, 96-95, 93-97.

10 December   Ivan Calderon 7.6 (Puerto Rico) W PTS 12 Daniel Reyes 7.6½ (Colombia), San Juan, Puerto Rico – WBO. Scorecards: 120-108, 120-108, 119-109.

9 January   Eagle Kyowa 7.7 (Thailand) W RSC 7 Ken Nakajima 7.7 (Japan), Yokohama, Japan – WBC.

18 February   Ivan Calderon 7.6 (Puerto Rico) W PTS 12 Isaac Bustos 7.7 (Mexico), Las Vegas, Nevada, USA – WBO. Scorecards: 120-108, 119-109, 120-108.

4 March   Yutaka Niida 7.6¾ (Japan) W PTS 12 Ronald Barrera 7.7 (Colombia), Tokyo, Japan – WBA. Scorecards: 117-111, 116-112, 115-113.

29 April   Ivan Calderon 7.7 (Puerto Rico) W RSC 9 Miguel Tellez 7.7 (Nicaragua), Guaynabo, Puero Rico – WBO.

6 May   Eagle Kyowa 7.7 (Thailand) W PTS 12 Rodel Mayol 7.6¼ (Philippines), Tokyo, Japan – WBC.

6 May   Muhammad Rachman 7.7 (Indonesia) W CO 6 Omar Soto 7.6¼ (Mexico), Jakarta, Indonesia – IBF.

L.Flyweight

20 August   Hugo Cazares 7.10 (Mexico) W RTD 7 Alex Sanchez 7.9 (Puerto Rico), Ponce, Puerto Rico – WBO.

20 August   Roberto Vasquez 7.10 (Panama) W RSC 4 Jose Antonio Aguirre 7.9½ (Mexico), Panama City, Panama – WBA.

10 September   Erick Ortiz 7.10 (Mexico) L CO 1 Brian Viloria 7.10 (USA), Los Angeles, California, USA – WBC. On 8 October in Las Vegas, Nevada, Mexico's Jorge Arce halted Hussein Hussein (Australia) inside two rounds to retain his WBC 'interim' title before successfully defending it again, against Adonis Rivas (Nicaragua), by a tenth-round stoppage in Monterrey, Mexico on 16 December

and by a sixth-round retirement in Cancun, Mexico on 26 January 2006.

29 October   Hugo Cazares 7.10 (Mexico) W CO 6 Kaichon Sorvoraphin 7.9½ (Thailand), Tucson, Arizona, USA – WBO.

19 November   Roberto Vasquez 7.10 (Panama) W PTS 12 Nerys Espinoza 7.10 (Nicaragua), Panama City, Panama – WBA. Scorecards: 118-110, 117-110, 118-107.

7 January   Will Grigsby 7.9 (USA) L PTS 12 Ulises Solis 7.10 (Mexico), NYC, New York, USA – IBF. Scorecards: 110-118, 111-117, 112-116.

18 February   Brian Viloria 7.9 (USA) W PTS 12 Jose Antonio Aguirre 7.9½ (Mexico), Las Vegas, Nevada, USA – WBC. Scorecards: 116-112, 116-112, 117-111.

25 March   Ulises Solis 7.10 (Mexico) W RSC 9 Erick Ortiz 7.10 (Mexico), Guadalajara, Mexico – IBF.

20 May   Roberto Vasquez 7.9¾ (Panama) W PTS 12 Nohel Arambulet 7.9½ (Venezuela), Panama City, Panama – WBA. Scorecards: 120-107, 117-110, 119-108. Immediately following the fight, Vasquez relinquished the title in order to move up a weight division.

30 June   Hugo Cazares 7.10 (Mexico) W RSC 1 Domingo Guillen 7.10 (Dominican Republic), Tucson, Arizona, USA – WBO.

Flyweight

24 August   Vic Darchinyan 8.0 (Australia) W RSC 5 Jair Jimenez 7.13½ (Colombia), Sydney, Australia – IBF.

19 September   Lorenzo Parra 8.0 (Venezuela) W PTS 12 Takefumi Sakata 8.0 (Japan), Tokyo, Japan – WBA. Scorecards: 115-113, 114-113, 114-114.

10 October   Pongsaklek Wonjongkam 8.0 (Thailand) W TD 7 Daisuke Naito 8.0 (Japan), Tokyo, Japan – WBC. Scorecards: 68-64, 68-64, 68-64. Earlier, on 30 July, Jorge Arce (Mexico) won the vacant WBC 'interim' title following a third-round stoppage win over Angel Priola (Colombia) in Baja California, Mexico. Arce then put his 'interim' belt on the line 8 October, stopping Australia's Hussein Hussein in two rounds at Las Vegas, Nevada, USA, prior to making another successful defence when halting Nicaragua's Adonis Rivas in the tenth on 16 December, in Monterrey, Mexico.

5 December Lorenzo Parra 7.13½ (Venezuela) W PTS 12 Brahim Asloum 8.0 (France), Paris, France – WBA. Scorecards: 118-109, 120-107, 119-108.

5 December Omar Narvaez 8.13½ (Argentina) W RSC 11 Bernard Inom 8.12¾ (France), Paris, France – WBO. Judge: Paul Thomas.

16 February Pongsaklek Wonjongkam 8.0 (Thailand) W PTS 12 Gilberto Keb Baas 8.0 (Mexico), Chainart, Thailand – WBC. Scorecards: 119-110, 120-109, 120-109.

3 March Vic Darchinyan 8.0 (Armenia) W RSC 8 Diosdado Gabi 7.13 (South Africa), Santa Ynez, California, USA – IBF.

1 May Pongsaklek Wonjongkam 8.0 (Thailand) W PTS 12 Daigo Nakahiro 8.0 (Japan), Bangkok, Thailand – WBC. Scorecards: 120-107, 119-110, 120-107.

3 June Vic Darchinyan 8.0 (Armenia) W RSC 8 Luis Maldonado 8.0 (Mexico), Las Vegas, Nevada, USA – IBF.

30 June Pongsaklek Wonjongkam 8.0 (Thailand) W RSC 4 Everardo Morales 7.13½ (Mexico), Bangkok, Thailand – WBC.

S.Flyweight

16 July Fernando Montiel 8.3 (Mexico) W PTS 12 Evert Briceno 8.3 (Nicaragua), Las Vegas, Nevada, USA – WBO. Scorecards: 117-111, 118-110, 117-111.

18 July Katsushige Kawashima 8.2¾ (Japan) L PTS 12 Masamori Tokuyama 8.3 (Japan), Osaka, Japan – WBC. Referee: Ian John-Lewis. Scorecards: 109-118, 112-115, 110-117.

29 October Fernando Montiel 8.3 (Mexico) W PTS 12 Pramuansak Phosuwan 8.3 (Thailand), Tucson, Arizona, USA – WBO. Scorecards: 115-112, 114-112, 114-112.

21 January Martin Castillo 8.2½ (Mexico) W PTS 12 Alexander Munoz 8.3 (Venezuela), Las Vegas, Nevada, USA – WBA. Scorecards: 115-112, 116-111, 112-115.

27 February Masamori Tokuyama 8.3 (Japan) W PTS 12 Jose Navarro 8.2¾ (USA), Central Gymnasium, Osaka, Japan – WBC. Referee: Mark Green. Scorecards: 117-113, 116-113, John Keane 116-113.

6 May Luis Perez 8.2½ (Nicaragua) W PTS 12 Dimitri Kirilov 8.2½ (Russia), Worcester, Massachusetts, USA – IBF. Scorecards: 115-113, 114-113, 110-117.

Bantamweight

5 August Ratanchai Sowvoraphin 8.6 (Thailand) W PTS 12 Mauricio Martinez 8.6 (Panama), Phuket, Thailand – WBO. Scorecards: 116-112, 116-112, 114-114.

25 September Hozumi Hasegawa 8.5¼ (Japan) W RSC 7 Gerardo Martinez 8.5½ (Mexico), Yokohama, Japan – WBC.

29 October Ratanchai Sowvoraphin 8.6 (Thailand) L RSC 7 Jhonny Gonzalez 8.4¾ (Mexico), Tucson, Arizona, USA – WBO.

5 November Rafael Marquez 8.6 (Mexico) W RSC 4

Silence Mabuza 8.6 (South Africa), Stateline, Nevada, USA – IBF.

26 November Wladimir Sidorenko 8.5¾ (Ukraine) W PTS 12 Jose de Jesus Lopez 8.5¼ (Venezuela), Leverkusen, Germany – WBA. Scorecards: 118-111, 119-109, 119-109. On 31 August, in Bangkok, Thailand, Poonsawat Kratingdaenggym (Thailand) outpointed Ricardo Cordoba (Panama) to land the vacant WBA 'interim' title. He next defended the 'interim' title on 22 December in Bangkok and outscored Leo Gamez (Venezuela) over 12 rounds.

11 March Wladimir Sidorenko 8.5¾ (Ukraine) DREW 12 Ricardo Cordoba 8.5¾ (Panama), Hamburg, Germany – WBA. Scorecards: 118-111, 114-114, 114-114.

25 March Hozumi Hasegawa 8.6 (Japan) W RSC 9 Veeraphol Sahaprom 8.5¾ (Thailand), Kobe, Japan – WBC.

27 May Jhonny Gonzalez 8.5¾ (Mexico) W PTS 12 Fernando Montiel 8.5 (Mexico), Carson, California, USA – WBO. Scorecards: 116-112, 118-111, 113-115.

S.Bantamweight

16 July Oscar Larios 8.10 (Mexico) W RTD 10 Wayne McCullough 8.8 (Ireland), Las Vegas, Nevada, USA – WBC.

29 October Daniel Ponce de Leon 8.9 (Mexico) W PTS 12 Sod Looknongyangtoy 8.9 (Thailand), Tucson, Arizona, USA – WBO. Scorecards: 118-109, 115-112, 115-112. Contested for the vacant title after Joan Guzman (Dominican Republic) relinquished his hold on the belt in July to move up to featherweight.

3 December Oscar Larios 8.8½ (Mexico) L RSC 3 Israel Vazquez 8.9 (Mexico), Las Vegas, Nevada, USA – WBC/IBF. On winning Vazquez took over Larios' IBF belt. In Panama City, Celestino Caballero (Panama) retained his IBF 'interim' title when Roberto Bonilla (Nicaragua) retired at the end of the seventh round on 4 February, prior to Vazquez forfeiting the IBF belt in late March when failing to agree to a title defence.

18 March Mahyar Monshipour 8.9¼ (Iran) L RSC 10 Somsak Sithchatchawal 8.10 (Thailand), Paris, France – WBA. Referee: John Coyle. Judge: Paul Thomas. Earlier, on 19 November, in Panama City, Panama's Celestino Caballero outpointed Yober Ortega (Venezuela) to win the vacant WBA 'interim' title.

27 May Daniel Ponce de Leon 8.9½ (Mexico) W CO 2 Gerson Guerrero 8.7¼ (Mexico), Carson, California, USA – WBO.

10 June Israel Vazquez 8.10 (Mexico) W RTD 4 Ivan Hernandez 8.10 (Mexico), Atlantic City, New Jersey, USA – WBC.

Featherweight

5 November Scott Harrison 9.0 (Scotland) W PTS 12 Nedal Hussein 8.13½ (Australia), Braehead Arena, Renfrew, Scotland – WBO. Referee: Paul Thomas. Scorecards: Roy Francis 116-111, 116-111, 117-111.

20 January Valdemir Pereira 8.13 (Brazil) W PTS 12 Fahprakorb Rakkiatgym 8.13½ (Thailand), Mashantucket, Connecticut, USA – IBF. Scorecards: 118-108, 118-108, 118-108. Contested for the vacant title after Juan Manuel Marquez failed to go through with a defence against Rakkiatgym and was stripped by the IBF in August.

29 January In-Jin Chi 9.0 (South Korea) L PTS 12 Takashi Koshimoto 9.0 (Japan), Fukuoka City, Japan – WBC. Scorecards: 113-114, 112-115, 116-111. Having earlier outpointed America's Ricardo Juarez (in Rosemont, Illinois, USA on 20 August) to win the vacant WBC 'interim' title, on 17 February in Sinaloa, Mexico, Humberto Soto (Mexico) retained the title when stopping Colombia's Oscar Leon inside nine rounds.

4 March Chris John 8.13 (Indonesia) W PTS 12 Juan Manuel Marquez 8.13 (Mexico), Tenggarong City, Borneo, Indonesia – WBA. Scorecards: 116-110, 117-111, 116-112. John, the former 'secondary' champion had been given full championship status in January when it was accepted by the WBA that Marquez was no longer a multiple champion, having forfeited the IBF crown a short while before. Earlier, John had successfully defended the 'secondary' title when forcing Australia's Tommy Browne to retire after nine rounds on 7 August in Penrith, NSW, Australia.

13 May Valdemir Pereira 9.0 (Brazil) L DIS 8 Eric Aiken 8.13 (USA), Boston, Massachusetts, USA – IBF.

S.Featherweight

12 August Jorge Barrios 9.3¾ (Argentina) W RSC 2 Victor Santiago 9.3¾ (Puerto Rico), Cordoba, Argentina – WBO.

17 September Marco Antonio Barrera 9.4 (Mexico) W PTS 12 Robbie Peden 9.4 (Australia), Las Vegas, Nevada, USA – WBC/IBF. Scorecards: John Keane 118-109, 118-108, 118-108. By his victory, Barrera took over Peden's IBF title, but relinquished it in April on realising he couldn't meet that body's commitments along with those of the WBC.

12 May Vincente Mosquera 9.4 (Panama) W PTS 12 Jose Pablo Estrella 9.2¾ (Argentina), Cordoba, Argentina – WBA. Scorecards: 117-111, 116-112, 112-116.

20 May Marco Antonio Barrera 9.3 (Mexico) W PTS 12 Ricardo Juarez 9.3¾ (USA), Los Angeles, California, USA – WBC. Scorecards: 115-114, 115-113, 114-115.

20 May Jorge Barrios 9.3 (Argentina) W CO 1 Janos Nagy 9.3¾ (Hungary), Los Angeles, California, USA – WBO.

31 May Cassius Baloyi 9.4 (South Africa) W RSC 11 Manuel Medina 9.4 (Mexico), Airway Heights, Washington, USA – IBF.

Lightweight

17 September Leavander Johnson 9.9 L RSC 11 Jesus Chavez 9.9 (Mexico), Las Vegas, Nevada, USA – IBF. With Chavez, suffering a shoulder injury, unable to defend against his mandatory challenger, Ricky Quiles (USA), the latter took on Mexico's Julio Diaz in what was a battle for the 'interim' title. Contested in Hollywood, Florida, USA on 18 May, Diaz was returned the winner on points.

8 April Juan Diaz 9.9 (USA) W PTS 12 Jose Miguel Cotto 9.8 (Puerto Rico), Las Vegas, Nevada, USA – WBA. Scorecards: 116-112, 117-111, 118-110.

29 April Acelino Freitas 9.9 (Brazil) W PTS 12 Zahir Raheem 9.9 (USA), Mashantucket, Connecticut, USA – WBO. Although Diego Corrales continued to hold the WBC title, he forfeited the WBO version in February when he decided to go for a third fight against Jesus Chavez rather than honouring their mandatory requirements. Meanwhile, the WBC set up a vacant 'interim' title fight between Jose Armando Santa Cruz (Mexico) and Chikashi Inada (Japan), which was won by the former on a sixth-round stoppage in Los Angeles, California, USA on 20 May.

L.Welterweight

24 September Miguel Cotto 10.0 (Puerto Rico) W CO 7 Ricardo Torres 10.0 (Colombia), Atlantic City, New Jersey, USA – WBO.

26 November Ricky Hatton 9.13½ (England) W CO 9 Carlos Maussa 9.13¾ (Colombia), Hallam FM Arena, Sheffield, England – WBA/IBF. Referee: Mickey Vann. Judge: John Coyle. By his victory, Hatton took over Maussa's IBF title. Having given up his IBF belt in April when moving up a division to meet Luis Collazo for the WBA welter crown, Hatton then relinquished the WBA light-welter title in May when it became clear that he couldn't keep it.

4 March Miguel Cotto 10.0 (Puerto Rico) W RSC 8 Gianluca Branco 10.0 (Italy), Bayamon, Puerto Rico – WBO.

10 June Miguel Cotto 9.12½ (Puerto Rico) W PTS 12 Paul Malignaggi 9.12¼ (USA), NYC, New York, USA – WBO. Scorecards: 116-111, 115-112, 116-111.

30 June Juan Urango 9.12 (Colombia) W PTS 12 Naoufel Ben Rabah 9.12 (Tunisia), Hollywood, Florida, USA – IBF. Scorecards: 116-112, 115-113, 117-111.

Note: Coming into the 2005-2006 season Floyd Mayweather was the WBC champion, but was forced to relinquish the title in March on moving up a division to meet Zab Judah for the IBF crown.

Welterweight

7 January Zab Judah 10.6¾ (USA) L PTS 12 Carlos Baldomir 10.6¼ (Argentina), NYC, New York, USA – WBC. Scorecards: 113-115, 112-115, 113-114. On losing, Judah was stripped of his WBA crown, which passed to the 'secondary' champion, Luis Collazo (USA), but retained the IBF belt due to Baldomir failing to pay that body a sanction fee. Earlier, on 13 August, Collazo had made a successful defence of the 'secondary' title when forcing Miguel Angel Gonzalez to retire at the end of the eighth in Chicago, Illinois, USA.

18 February Antonio Margarito 10.6½ (Mexico) W RSC

Ronald 'Winky' Wright, who came close to lifting the WBA, WBC and WBO middleweight titles last June, is seen here at the International Boxing Hall of Fame in Canastota, New York

Les Clark

1 Manuel Gomez 10.7 (Mexico), Las Vegas, Nevada, USA – WBO.

8 April   Zab Judah 10.5$^1/_2$ (USA) L PTS 12 Floyd Mayweather 10.6 (USA), Las Vegas, Nevada, USA – IBF. Scorecards: 116-112, 117-111, 119-109.

13 May   Luis Collazo 10.7 (USA) L PTS 12 Ricky Hatton 10.7 (England), Boston, Massachusetts, USA – WBA. Scorecards: 112-115, 112-115, 113-114.

L.Middleweight

14 July   Kassim Ouma 11.0 (Uganda) L PTS 12 Roman Karmazin 10.13$^1/_2$ (Russia), Las Vegas, Nevada, USA – IBF. Scorecards: 108-118, 110-116, 109-117.

13 August   Ricardo Mayorga 11.0 (Nicaragua) W PTS 12 Michele Piccirillo 11.0 (Italy), Chicago, Illinois, USA – WBC. Scorecards: 117-108, 117-110, 120-105. Contested for the vacant title after Javier Castillejo (Spain) forfeited his belt in May 2005 for not meeting Mayorga.

13 August   Alejandro Garcia 11.0 (Mexico) W PTS 12 Luca Messi 10.10 (Italy), Chicago, Illinois, USA – WBA. Scorecards: 117-110, 119-108, 117-110.

3 December   Daniel Santos 11.0 (Puerto Rico) L PTS 12 Sergei Dzindziruk 11.0 (Ukraine), Magdeburg, Germany – WBO. Scorecards: Dave Parris 112-115, 112-115, 112-115.

6 May   Alejandro Garcia 10.12$^1/_2$ (Mexico) L PTS 12 Jose Antonio Rivera 10.12$^1/_2$ (USA), Worcester, Massachusetts, USA – WBA. Scorecards: 106-116, 106-116, 107-115.

6 May   Ricardo Mayorga 10.13$^1/_2$ (Nicaragua) L RSC 6 Oscar de la Hoya 10.13$^1/_2$ (USA), Las Vegas, Nevada, USA – WBC.

27 May   Sergei Dzindziruk 11.0 (Ukraine) W PTS 12 Sebastien Lujan 10.13$^3/_4$ (Argentina), Munich, Germany – WBO. Scorecards: 118-110, 117-110, 116-111.

Middleweight

16 July   Bernard Hopkins 11.6 (USA) L PTS 12 Jermaine Taylor 11.5 (USA), Las Vegas, Nevada, USA – IBF/WBO/WBA/WBC. Referee: Jay Nady. Scorecards: 113-115, 113-115, 116-112. After picking up all four belts on winning, Taylor relinquished the IBF title in November due to contractual problems.

3 December   Jermaine Taylor 11.5 (USA) W PTS 12 Bernard Hopkins 11.6 (USA), Las Vegas, Nevada, USA. Scorecards: 115-113,   115-113,   115-113.   WBO/ WBA/WBC. On 11 March in Hamburg, Germany, Germany's Felix Sturm outpointed Maselino Masoa over 12 rounds to take over the Western Samoan's WBA 'secondary' title.

10 December   Arthur Abraham 11.5 (Armenia) W RSC 5 Kingsley Ikeke 11.5 (Nigeria), Leipzig, Germany – IBF. Judge: Howard Foster.

4 March   Arthur Abraham 11.5$^3/_4$ (Armenia) W PTS 12 Shannan Taylor 11.5$^1/_2$ (Australia), Oldenburg, Germany – IBF. Scorecards: 120-107, 120-107, 120-106.

13 May   Arthur Abraham 11.6 (Armenia) W PTS 12 Kofi Jantuah 11.4$^3/_4$ (Ghana), Zwickau, Germany – IBF. Scorecards: Phil Edwards 115-112, 117-110, 116-111.

17 June   Jermain Taylor 11.6 (USA) DREW 12 Ronald Wright 11.5$^1/_2$ (USA), Memphis, Tennessee, USA – WBO/WBA/WBC. Scorecards: 115-113, 113-115, 114-114.

S.Middleweight

6 August   Jeff Lacy 11.13 (USA) W RTD 7 Robin Reid 11.13$^1/_2$ (England), Tampa, Florida, USA – IBF. Judge: Roy Francis.

3 September   Markus Beyer 11.13$^1/_4$ (Germany) W PTS 12 Omar Sheika 11.13$^1/_4$ (USA), Berlin, Germany – WBC. Scorecards: Mark Green 118-110, 116-112, 116-112.

10 September   Joe Calzaghe 11.13$^1/_2$ (Wales) W PTS 12 Evans Ashira 11.12 (Kenya), The International Arena, Cardiff, Wales – WBO. Scorecards: 120-107, 120-108, Paul Thomas 120-108.

5 November   Jeff Lacy 12.0 (USA) W CO 2 Scott Pemberton 12.0 (USA), Stateline, Nevada, USA – IBF.

14 January   Mikkel Kessler 12.0 (Denmark) W RTD 10 Eric Lucas 11.13 (Canada), Copenhagen, Denmark – WBA.

28 January   Markus Beyer 11.13 (Germany) W RTD 12 Alberto Colajanni 11.10 (Italy), Berlin, Germany – WBC. Referee: Larry O'Connell.

4 March   Joe Calzaghe 12.0 (Wales) W PTS 12 Jeff Lacy 11.13 (USA), MEN Arena, Manchester, England – WBO/IBF. Scorecards: 119-105, Roy Francis 119-107, 119-107. By his victory, Calzaghe took over Lacy's IBF crown.

13 May   Markus Beyer 11.13$^3/_4$ (Germany) T DRAW 4 Sakio Bika 12.0 (Cameroon), Zwickau, Germany – WBC. Judge: Ian John-Lewis.

L.Heavyweight

9 September   Clinton Woods 12.6$^3/_4$ (England) W PTS 12 Julio Gonzalez 12.7 (Mexico), Sheffield, England – IBF. Referee: Mickey Vann. Scorecards: Howard Foster 117-111, Roy Francis 118-112, 116-112.

1 October   Antonio Tarver 12.7 (USA) W PTS 12 Roy Jones 12.5 (USA), Tampa, Florida, USA – IBO. Scorecards: 116-112, 116-112, 117-111.

15 October   Tomasz Adamek 12.6$^3/_4$ (Poland) W CO 6 Thomas Ulrich 12.6$^3/_4$ (Germany), Dusseldorf, Germany – WBC. Referee: Ian John-Lewis.

22 October   Zsolt Erdei 12.6$^1/_4$ (Hungary) W RSC 12 Mehdi Sahnoune 12.7 (France), Halle, Germany – WBO.

6 May   Zsolt Erdei 12.4$^3/_4$ (Hungary) W RSC 10 Paul Murdoch 12.4$^1/_2$ (Australia), Dusseldorf, Germany – WBO.

13 May   Clinton Woods 12.6$^1/_2$ (England) W RSC 6 Jason DeLisle 12.4$^1/_2$ (Australia), Ponds Forge International Sports Centre, Sheffield, England – IBF. Referee: Dave Parris. Judge: Howard Foster.

10 June   Antonio Tarver 12.6 (USA) L PTS 12 Bernard Hopkins 12.6 (USA), Atlantic City, New Jersey, USA – IBO.

Note: The WBA champion, Fabrice Tiozzo (France), failed to make a single defence during the season due to an injury, but continued to hold on to his title.

Cruiserweight

26 August O'Neil Bell 14.4 (USA) W CO 11 Sebastiaan Rothmann 13.10 (South Africa), Hollywood, Florida, USA – IBF.

26 November Johnny Nelson 14.2$^1/_2$ (England) W PTS 12 Vincenzo Cantatore 14.3$^1/_4$ (Italy), Rome, Italy – WBO. Scorecards: 116-111, 115-112, 112-115.

7 January O'Neil Bell 14.3$^1/_2$ (USA) W RSC 10 Jean-Marc Mormeck 14.1$^3/_4$ (France), NYC, New York, USA – WBA/WBC/IBF. By his victory, Bell took over Mormeck's WBA and WBC titles. On 27 January in Las Vegas, Nevada, Virgil Hill (USA) won the vacant WBA 'secondary' title when outpointing Russia's Valery Brudov over 12 rounds. Meanwhile, in April, Bell forfeited the IBF title for not fulfilling his mandatory requirements.

Heavyweight

28 September Lamon Brewster 16.4 (USA) W RSC 9 Luan Krasniqi 16.0$^3/_4$ (Germany), Hamburg, Germany – WBO.

1 October Chris Byrd 15.3 (USA) W PTS 12 DaVarryl Williamson 16.1 (USA), Reno, Nevada, USA – IBF. Scorecards: 115-113, 116-112, 116-112.

17 December John Ruiz 16.13$^3/_4$ (Puerto Rico) L PTS 12 Nikolai Valuev 23.2$^1/_4$ (Russia), Berlin, Germany – WBA. Scorecards: 114-116, 113-116, 114-114.

18 March Hasim Rahman 17.0 (USA) DREW 12 James Toney 16.13 (USA), Atlantic City, New Jersey, USA – WBC. Scorecards: 117-111, 114-114, 114-114. On Vitali Klitschko (Ukraine) handing back the WBC belt in November, having decided to retire, the following month Hasim Rahman was announced as the new champion. Rahman had beaten Monte Barrett on points in Chicago, Illinois, USA on 13 August to win the vacant WBC 'interim' title.

1 April Lamon Brewster 16.8 (USA) L PTS 12 Sergei Lyakhovich 17.0$^1/_2$ (Belarus), Cleveland, Ohio, USA – WBO. Scorecards: 112-115, 113-115, 110-117.

22 April Chris Byrd 15.3$^1/_2$ (USA) L RSC 7 Vladimir Klitschko 17.3 (Ukraine), Mannheim, Germany – IBF. Judge: Roy Francis.

3 June Nikolai Valuev 22.12$^3/_4$ (Russia) W RSC 3 Owen Beck 17.4$^1/_2$ (Jamaica), Hanover, Germany – WBA.

In his first IBF light-heavyweight title defence of the new season, Clinton Woods (right) scored an emphatic points win over Mexico's Julio Gonzalez

Les Clark

World Champions Since Gloves, 1889-2006

Since I began to carry out extensive research into world championship boxing from the very beginnings of gloved action, I discovered much that needed to be amended regarding the historical listings as we know them, especially prior to the 1920s. Although yet to finalise my researches, despite making considerable changes, the listings are the most comprehensive ever published. Bearing all that in mind, and using a wide range of American newspapers, the aim has been to discover just who had claims, valid or otherwise. Studying the records of all the recognised champions, supplied by Professor Luckett Davis and his team, fights against all opposition have been analysed to produce the ultimate data. Because there were no boxing commissions as such in America prior to the 1920s, the yardstick used to determine valid claims were victories over the leading fighters of the day and recognition given within the newspapers. Only where that criteria has been met have I adjusted previous information.

Championship Status Code:

AU = Austria; AUST = Australia; CALIF = California; CAN = Canada; CLE = Cleveland Boxing Commission; EBU = European Boxing Union; FL = Florida; FR = France; GB = Great Britain; GEO = Georgia; H = Hawaii; IBF = International Boxing Federation; IBU = International Boxing Union; ILL = Illinois; LOUIS = Louisiana; MARY = Maryland; MASS = Massachusetts; MICH = Michigan; NBA = National Boxing Association; NC = North Carolina; NY = New York; PEN = Pennsylvania; SA = South Africa; TBC = Territorial Boxing Commission; USA = United States; WBA = World Boxing Association; WBC = World Boxing Council; WBO = World Boxing Organisation.

Champions in **bold** are accorded universal recognition.

*Undefeated champions (Only relates to universally recognised champions prior to 1962 and thereafter WBA/WBC/IBF/WBO champions. Does not include men who forfeited titles).

Title Holder	Birthplace	Tenure	Status
M. Flyweight (105 lbs)			
Kyung-Yung Lee*	S Korea	1987	IBF
Hiroki Ioka	Japan	1987-1988	WBC
Silvio Gamez*	Venezuela	1988-1989	WBA
Samuth Sithnaruepol	Thailand	1988-1989	IBF
Napa Kiatwanchai	Thailand	1988-1989	WBC
Bong-Jun Kim	S Korea	1989-1991	WBA
Nico Thomas	Indonesia	1989	IBF
Rafael Torres	Dom Republic	1989-1992	WBO
Eric Chavez	Philippines	1989-1990	IBF
Jum-Hwan Choi	S Korea	1989-1990	WBC
Hideyuki Ohashi	Japan	1990	WBC
Fahlan Lukmingkwan	Thailand	1990-1992	IBF
Ricardo Lopez*	Mexico	1990-1997	WBC
Hi-Yon Choi	S Korea	1991-1992	WBA
Manny Melchor	Philippines	1992	IBF
Hideyuki Ohashi	Japan	1992-1993	WBA
Ratanapol Sowvoraphin	Thailand	1992-1996	IBF
Chana Porpaoin	Thailand	1993-1995	WBA
Paul Weir*	Scotland	1993-1994	WBO
Alex Sanchez	Puerto Rico	1993-1997	WBO
Rosendo Alvarez	Nicaragua	1995-1998	WBA
Ratanapol Sowvoraphin	Thailand	1996-1997	IBF
Ricardo Lopez*	Mexico	1997-1998	WBC/WBO
Zolani Petelo*	S Africa	1997-2000	IBF
Ricardo Lopez*	Mexico	1998	WBC
Eric Jamili	Philippines	1998	WBO
Kermin Guardia*	Colombia	1998-2002	WBO
Ricardo Lopez*	Mexico	1998-1999	WBA/WBC
Wandee Chor Chareon	Thailand	1999-2000	WBC
Nohel Arambulet	Venezuela	1999-2000	WBA
Jose Antonio Aguirre	Mexico	2000-2004	WBC
Jomo Gamboa	Philippines	2000	WBA
Keitaro Hoshino	Japan	2000-2001	WBA
Chana Porpaoin	Thailand	2001	WBA
Roberto Levya	Mexico	2001-2003	IBF
Yutaka Niida*	Japan	2001	WBA
Keitaro Hoshino	Japan	2002	WBA
Jorge Mata	Spain	2002-2003	WBO
Nohel Arambulet	Venezuela	2002-2004	WBA
Miguel Barrera	Colombia	2002-2003	IBF
Eduardo Marquez	Nicaragua	2003	WBO
Ivan Calderon	Puerto Rico	2003-	WBO
Edgar Cardenas	Mexico	2003	IBF
Daniel Reyes	Colombia	2003-2004	IBF
Eagle Kyowa	Thailand	2004	WBC
Muhammad Rachman	Indonesia	2004-	IBF
Yutaka Niida	Japan	2004-	WBA
Isaac Bustos	Mexico	2004-2005	WBC
Katsunari Takayama	Japan	2005	WBC
Eagle Kyowa	Thailand	2005-	WBC
L. Flyweight (108 lbs)			
Franco Udella	Italy	1975	WBC
Jaime Rios	Panama	1975-1976	WBA
Luis Estaba	Venezuela	1975-1978	WBC
Juan Guzman	Dom Republic	1976	WBA
Yoko Gushiken	Japan	1976-1981	WBA
Freddie Castillo	Mexico	1978	WBC
Sor Vorasingh	Thailand	1978	WBC
Sun-Jun Kim	S Korea	1978-1980	WBC
Shigeo Nakajima	Japan	1980	WBC
Hilario Zapata	Panama	1980-1982	WBC
Pedro Flores	Mexico	1981	WBA
Hwan-Jin Kim	S Korea	1981	WBA
Katsuo Tokashiki	Japan	1981-1983	WBA
Amado Ursua	Mexico	1982	WBC
Tadashi Tomori	Japan	1982	WBC
Hilario Zapata	Panama	1982-1983	WBC
Jung-Koo Chang*	S Korea	1983-1988	WBC
Lupe Madera	Mexico	1983-1984	WBA
Dodie Penalosa	Philippines	1983-1986	IBF
Francisco Quiroz	Dom Republic	1984-1985	WBA
Joey Olivo	USA	1985	WBA
Myung-Woo Yuh	S Korea	1985-1991	WBA
Jum-Hwan Choi	S Korea	1986-1988	IBF
Tacy Macalos	Philippines	1988-1989	IBF
German Torres	Mexico	1988-1989	WBC
Yul-Woo Lee	S Korea	1989	WBC
Muangchai Kitikasem	Thailand	1989-1990	IBF
Jose de Jesus	Puerto Rico	1989-1992	WBO
Humberto Gonzalez	Mexico	1989-1990	WBC

Title Holder	Birthplace	Tenure	Status	Title Holder	Birthplace	Tenure	Status
Michael Carbajal*	USA	1990-1993	IBF	Small Montana	Philippines	1935-1937	NY/CALIF
Rolando Pascua	Philippines	1990-1991	WBC	Valentin Angelmann	France	1936-1938	IBU
Melchor Cob Castro	Mexico	1991	WBC	Peter Kane*	England	1938-1939	NBA/NY/GB/IBU
Humberto Gonzalez	Mexico	1991-1993	WBC	Little Dado	Philippines	1938-1939	CALIF
Hiroki Ioka	Japan	1991-1992	WBA	Little Dado	Philippines	1939-1943	NBA/CALIF
Josue Camacho	Puerto Rico	1992-1994	WBO	**Jackie Paterson**	Scotland	1943-1947	
Myung-Woo Yuh*	S Korea	1992-1993	WBA	Jackie Paterson	Scotland	1947-1948	GB/NY
Michael Carbajal	USA	1993-1994	IBF/WBC	Rinty Monaghan	Ireland	1947-1948	NBA
Silvio Gamez	Venezuela	1993-1995	WBA	**Rinty Monaghan***	Ireland	1948-1950	
Humberto Gonzalez	Mexico	1994-1995	WBC/IBF	**Terry Allen**	England	1950	
Michael Carbajal*	USA	1994	WBO	**Dado Marino**	Hawaii	1950-1952	
Paul Weir	Scotland	1994-1995	WBO	**Yoshio Shirai**	Japan	1952-1954	
Hi-Yong Choi	S Korea	1995-1996	WBA	**Pascual Perez**	Argentina	1954-1960	
Saman Sorjaturong*	Thailand	1995	WBC/IBF	**Pone Kingpetch**	Thailand	1960-1962	
Jacob Matlala*	South Africa	1995-1997	WBO	**Fighting Harada**	Japan	1962-1963	
Saman Sorjaturong	Thailand	1995-1999	WBC	**Pone Kingpetch**	Thailand	1963	
Carlos Murillo	Panama	1996	WBA	**Hiroyuki Ebihara**	Japan	1963-1964	
Michael Carbajal	USA	1996-1997	IBF	**Pone Kingpetch**	Thailand	1964-1965	
Keiji Yamaguchi	Japan	1996	WBA	**Salvatore Burruni**	Italy	1965	
Pichitnoi Chor Siriwat	Thailand	1996-2000	WBA	Salvatore Burruni	Italy	1965-1966	WBC
Mauricio Pastrana	Colombia	1997-1998	IBF	Horacio Accavallo*	Argentina	1966-1968	WBA
Jesus Chong	Mexico	1997	WBO	Walter McGowan	Scotland	1966	WBC
Melchor Cob Castro	Mexico	1997-1998	WBO	Chartchai Chionoi	Thailand	1966-1969	WBC
Mauricio Pastrana	Colombia	1997-1998	IBF	Efren Torres	Mexico	1969-1970	WBC
Juan Domingo Cordoba	Argentina	1998	WBO	Hiroyuki Ebihara	Japan	1969	WBA
Jorge Arce	Mexico	1998-1999	WBO	Bernabe Villacampo	Philippines	1969-1970	WBA
Will Grigsby	USA	1998-1999	IBF	Chartchai Chionoi	Thailand	1970	WBC
Michael Carbajal*	USA	1999-2000	WBO	Berkrerk Chartvanchai	Thailand	1970	WBA
Ricardo Lopez*	Mexico	1999-2002	IBF	Masao Ohba*	Japan	1970-1973	WBA
Yo-Sam Choi	S Korea	1999-2002	WBC	Erbito Salavarria	Philippines	1970-1971	WBC
Masibuleke Makepula*	S Africa	2000	WBO	Betulio Gonzalez	Venezuela	1971-1972	WBC
Will Grigsby	USA	2000	WBO	Venice Borkorsor*	Thailand	1972-1973	WBC
Beibis Mendoza	Colombia	2000-2001	WBA	Chartchai Chionoi	Thailand	1973-1974	WBA
Rosendo Alvarez	Nicaragua	2001-2004	WBA	Betulio Gonzalez	Venezuela	1973-1974	WBC
Nelson Dieppa	Puerto Rico	2001-2005	WBO	Shoji Oguma	Japan	1974-1975	WBC
Jorge Arce*	Mexico	2002-2005	WBC	Susumu Hanagata	Japan	1974-1975	WBA
Jose Victor Burgos	Mexico	2003-2004	IBF	Miguel Canto	Mexico	1975-1979	WBC
Erick Ortiz	Mexico	2005	WBC	Erbito Salavarria	Philippines	1975-1976	WBA
Roberto Vasquez*	Panama	2005	WBA	Alfonso Lopez	Panama	1976	WBA
Hugo Cazares	Mexico	2005-	WBO	Guty Espadas	Mexico	1976-1978	WBA
Will Grigsby	USA	2005-2006	IBF	Betulio Gonzalez	Venezuela	1978-1979	WBA
Brian Viloria	USA	2005-	WBC	Chan-Hee Park	S Korea	1979-1980	WBC
Ulises Solis	Mexico	2006-	IBF	Luis Ibarra	Panama	1979-1980	WBA
				Tae-Shik Kim	S Korea	1980	WBA
Flyweight (112 lbs)				Shoji Oguma	Japan	1980-1981	WBC
Johnny Coulon	Canada	1910	USA	Peter Mathebula	S Africa	1980-1981	WBA
Sid Smith	England	1911-1913	GB	Santos Laciar	Argentina	1981	WBA
Sid Smith	England	1913	GB/IBU	Antonio Avelar	Mexico	1981-1982	WBC
Bill Ladbury	England	1913-1914	GB/IBU	Luis Ibarra	Panama	1981	WBA
Percy Jones	Wales	1914	GB/IBU	Juan Herrera	Mexico	1981-1982	WBA
Tancy Lee	Scotland	1915	GB/IBU	Prudencio Cardona	Colombia	1982	WBC
Joe Symonds	England	1915-1916	GB/IBU	Santos Laciar*	Argentina	1982-1985	WBA
Jimmy Wilde	Wales	1916	GB/IBU	Freddie Castillo	Mexico	1982	WBC
Jimmy Wilde	Wales	1916-1923		Eleonicio Mercedes	Dom Republic	1982-1983	WBC
Pancho Villa*	Philippines	1923-1925		Charlie Magri	Tunisia	1983	WBC
Fidel la Barba	USA	1925-1927	NBA/CALIF	Frank Cedeno	Philippines	1983-1984	WBC
Fidel la Barba*	USA	1927		Soon-Chun Kwon	S Korea	1983-1985	IBF
Pinky Silverberg	USA	1927	NBA	Koji Kobayashi	Japan	1984	WBC
Johnny McCoy	USA	1927-1928	CALIF	Gabriel Bernal	Mexico	1984	WBC
Izzy Schwartz	USA	1927-1929	NY	Sot Chitalada	Thailand	1984-1988	WBC
Frenchy Belanger	Canada	1927-1928	NBA	Hilario Zapata	Panama	1985-1987	WBA
Newsboy Brown	Russia	1928	CALIF	Chong-Kwan Chung	S Korea	1985-1986	IBF
Johnny Hill	Scotland	1928-1929	GB	Bi-Won Chung	S Korea	1986	IBF
Frankie Genaro	USA	1928-1929	NBA	Hi-Sup Shin	S Korea	1986-1987	IBF
Emile Pladner	France	1929	NBA/IBU	Fidel Bassa	Colombia	1987-1989	WBA
Frankie Genaro	USA	1929-1931	NBA/IBU	Dodie Penalosa	Philippines	1987	IBF
Midget Wolgast	USA	1930-1935	NY	Chang-Ho Choi	S Korea	1987-1988	IBF
Young Perez	Tunisia	1931-1932	NBA/IBU	Rolando Bohol	Philippines	1988	IBF
Jackie Brown	England	1932-1935	NBA/IBU	Yong-Kang Kim	S Korea	1988-1989	WBC
Jackie Brown	England	1935	GB/NBA	Duke McKenzie	England	1988-1989	IBF
Benny Lynch	Scotland	1935-1937	GB/NBA	Elvis Alvarez*	Colombia	1989	WBO

Title Holder	Birthplace	Tenure	Status
Sot Chitalada	Thailand	1989-1991	WBC
Dave McAuley	Ireland	1989-1992	IBF
Jesus Rojas	Venezuela	1989-1900	WBA
Yukihito Tamakuma	Japan	1990-1991	WBA
Isidro Perez	Mexico	1990-1992	WBO
Yul-Woo Lee	S Korea	1990	WBA
Muangchai Kitikasem	Thailand	1991-1992	WBC
Elvis Alvarez	Colombia	1991	WBA
Yong-Kang Kim	S Korea	1991-1992	WBA
Pat Clinton	Scotland	1992-1993	WBO
Rodolfo Blanco	Colombia	1992	IBF
Yuri Arbachakov	Russia	1992-1997	WBC
Aquiles Guzman	Venezuela	1992	WBA
Pichit Sitbangprachan*	Thailand	1992-1994	IBF
David Griman	Venezuela	1992-1994	WBA
Jacob Matlala	S Africa	1993-1995	WBO
Saen Sorploenchit	Thailand	1994-1996	WBA
Alberto Jimenez	Mexico	1995-1996	WBO
Francisco Tejedor	Colombia	1995	IBF
Danny Romero*	USA	1995-1996	IBF
Mark Johnson*	USA	1996-1998	IBF
Jose Bonilla	Venezuela	1996-1998	WBA
Carlos Salazar	Argentina	1996-1998	WBO
Chatchai Sasakul	Thailand	1997-1998	WBC
Hugo Soto	Argentina	1998-1999	WBA
Ruben Sanchez	Mexico	1998-1999	WBO
Manny Pacquiao	Philippines	1998-1999	WBC
Silvio Gamez	Venezuela	1999	WBA
Irene Pacheco	Colombia	1999-2004	IBF
Jose Antonio Lopez	Spain	1999	WBO
Sornpichai Pisanurachan	Thailand	1999-2000	WBA
Medgoen Singsurat	Thailand	1999-2000	WBC
Isidro Garcia	Mexico	1999-2000	WBO
Malcolm Tunacao	Philippines	2000-2001	WBC
Eric Morel	USA	2000-2003	WBA
Fernando Montiel*	Mexico	2000-2002	WBO
Pongsaklek Wonjongkam	Thailand	2001-	WBC
Adonis Rivas	Nicaragua	2002	WBO
Omar Narvaez	Argentina	2002-	WBO
Lorenzo Parra	Venezuela	2003-	WBA
Vic Darchinyan	Armenia	2004-	IBF

S. Flyweight (115 lbs)

Title Holder	Birthplace	Tenure	Status
Rafael Orono	Venezuela	1980-1981	WBC
Chul-Ho Kim	S Korea	1981-1982	WBC
Gustavo Ballas	Argentina	1981	WBA
Rafael Pedroza	Panama	1981-1982	WBA
Jiro Watanabe	Japan	1982-1984	WBA
Rafael Orono	Venezuela	1982-1983	WBC
Payao Poontarat	Thailand	1983-1984	WBC
Joo-Do Chun	S Korea	1983-1985	IBF
Jiro Watanabe	Japan	1984-1986	WBC
Kaosai Galaxy*	Thailand	1984-1992	WBA
Elly Pical	Indonesia	1985-1986	IBF
Cesar Polanco	Dom Republic	1986	IBF
Gilberto Roman	Mexico	1986-1987	WBC
Elly Pical	Indonesia	1986-1987	IBF
Santos Laciar	Argentina	1987	WBC
Tae-Il Chang	S Korea	1987	IBF
Jesus Rojas	Colombia	1987-1988	WBC
Elly Pical	Indonesia	1987-1989	IBF
Gilberto Roman	Mexico	1988-1989	WBC
Jose Ruiz	Puerto Rico	1989-1992	WBO
Juan Polo Perez	Colombia	1989-1990	IBF
Nana Yaw Konadu	Ghana	1989-1990	WBC
Sung-Il Moon	S Korea	1990-1993	WBC
Robert Quiroga	USA	1990-1993	IBF
Jose Quirino	Mexico	1992	WBO
Katsuya Onizuka	Japan	1992-1994	WBA
Johnny Bredahl	Denmark	1992-1994	WBO
Julio Cesar Borboa	Mexico	1993-1994	IBF

Title Holder	Birthplace	Tenure	Status
Jose Luis Bueno	Mexico	1993-1994	WBC
Hiroshi Kawashima	Japan	1994-1997	WBC
Harold Grey	Colombia	1994-1995	IBF
Hyung-Chul Lee	S Korea	1994-1995	WBA
Johnny Tapia*	USA	1994-1997	WBO
Alimi Goitia	Venezuela	1995-1996	WBA
Carlos Salazar	Argentina	1995-1996	IBF
Harold Grey	Colombia	1996	IBF
Yokthai Sith-Oar	Thailand	1996-1997	WBA
Danny Romero	USA	1996-1997	IBF
Gerry Penalosa	Philippines	1997-1998	WBC
Johnny Tapia*	USA	1997-1998	IBF/WBO
Satoshi Iida	Japan	1997-1998	WBA
In-Joo Cho	S Korea	1998-2000	WBC
Victor Godoi	Argentina	1998-1999	WBO
Jesus Rojas	Venezuela	1998-1999	WBA
Mark Johnson	USA	1999-2000	IBF
Diego Morales	Mexico	1999	WBO
Hideki Todaka	Japan	1999-2000	WBA
Adonis Rivas	Nicaragua	1999-2001	WBO
Felix Machado	Venezuela	2000-2003	IBF
Masamori Tokuyama	Japan	2000-2004	WBC
Silvio Gamez	Venezuela	2000-2001	WBA
Celes Kobayashi	Japan	2001-2002	WBA
Pedro Alcazar	Panama	2001-2002	WBO
Alexander Munoz	Venezuela	2002-2004	WBA
Fernando Montiel	Mexico	2002-2003	WBO
Luis Perez	Nicaragua	2003-	IBF
Mark Johnson	USA	2003-2004	WBO
Katsushige Kawashima	Japan	2004-2005	WBC
Ivan Hernandez	Mexico	2004-2005	WBO
Martin Castillo	Mexico	2004-	WBA
Fernando Montiel	Mexico	2005-	WBO
Masamori Tokuyama	Japan	2005-	WBC

Bantamweight (118 lbs)

Title Holder	Birthplace	Tenure	Status
Tommy Kelly	USA	1889	
George Dixon	Canada	1889-1890	
Chappie Moran	England	1889-1890	
Tommy Kelly	USA	1890-1892	
Billy Plimmer	England	1892-1895	
Pedlar Palmer	England	1895-1899	
Terry McGovern	USA	1899	USA
Pedlar Palmer	England	1899-1900	GB
Terry McGovern*	USA	1899-1900	
Clarence Forbes	USA	1900	
Johnny Reagan	USA	1900-1902	
Harry Ware	England	1900-1902	GB
Harry Harris	USA	1901	
Harry Forbes	USA	1901-1902	
Kid McFadden	USA	1901	
Dan Dougherty	USA	1901	
Andrew Tokell	England	1902	GB
Harry Ware	England	1902	GB
Harry Forbes	USA	1902-1903	USA
Joe Bowker	England	1902-1904	GB
Frankie Neil	USA	1903-1904	USA
Joe Bowker*	England	1904-1905	
Frankie Neil	USA	1905	USA
Digger Stanley	England	1905-1907	
Owen Moran	England	1905-1907	
Jimmy Walsh	USA	1905-1908	USA
Owen Moran	England	1907	GB
Monte Attell	USA	1908-1910	
Jimmy Walsh	USA	1908-1911	
Digger Stanley	England	1909-1912	GB
Frankie Conley	Italy	1910-1911	
Johnny Coulon	Canada	1910-1911	
Monte Attell	USA	1910-1911	
Johnny Coulon	Canada	1911-1913	USA
Charles Ledoux	France	1912-1913	GB/IBU

WORLD CHAMPIONS SINCE GLOVES, 1889-2006

Title Holder	Birthplace	Tenure	Status	Title Holder	Birthplace	Tenure	Status
Eddie Campi	USA	1913-1914		**Lionel Rose**	Australia	1968-1969	
Johnny Coulon	Canada	1913-1914		**Ruben Olivares**	Mexico	1969-1970	
Kid Williams	Denmark	1913-1914		**Chuchu Castillo**	Mexico	1970-1971	
Kid Williams	Denmark	1914-1915		**Ruben Olivares**	Mexico	1971-1972	
Kid Williams	Denmark	1915-1917		**Rafael Herrera**	Mexico	1972	
Johnny Ertle	USA	1915-1918		**Enrique Pinder**	Panama	1972	
Pete Herman	USA	1917-1919		Enrique Pinder	Panama	1972-1973	WBC
Pal Moore	USA	1918-1919		Romeo Anaya	Mexico	1973	WBA
Pete Herman	USA	1919-1920		Rafael Herrera	Mexico	1973-1974	WBC
Joe Lynch	USA	1920-1921		Arnold Taylor	S Africa	1973-1974	WBA
Pete Herman	USA	1921		Soo-Hwan Hong	S Korea	1974-1975	WBA
Johnny Buff	USA	1921-1922		Rodolfo Martinez	Mexico	1974-1976	WBC
Joe Lynch	USA	1922-1923		Alfonso Zamora	Mexico	1975-1977	WBA
Joe Lynch	USA	1923-1924	NBA	Carlos Zarate	Mexico	1976-1979	WBC
Joe Burman	England	1923	NY	Jorge Lujan	Panama	1977-1980	WBA
Abe Goldstein	USA	1923-1924	NY	Lupe Pintor*	Mexico	1979-1983	WBC
Joe Lynch	USA	1924		Julian Solis	Puerto Rico	1980	WBA
Abe Goldstein	USA	1924		Jeff Chandler	USA	1980-1984	WBA
Eddie Martin	USA	1924-1925		Albert Davila	USA	1983-1985	WBC
Charley Rosenberg	USA	1925-1926		Richard Sandoval	USA	1984-1986	WBA
Charley Rosenberg	USA	1926-1927	NY	Satoshi Shingaki	Japan	1984-1985	IBF
Bud Taylor*	USA	1926-1928	NBA	Jeff Fenech*	Australia	1985-1987	IBF
Bushy Graham*	Italy	1928-1929	NY	Daniel Zaragoza	Mexico	1985	WBC
Al Brown	Panama	1929-1931		Miguel Lora	Colombia	1985-1988	WBC
Al Brown	Panama	1931	NY/IBU	Gaby Canizales	USA	1986	WBA
Pete Sanstol	Norway	1931	CAN	Bernardo Pinango*	Venezuela	1986-1987	WBA
Al Brown	Panama	1931-1933		Takuya Muguruma	Japan	1987	WBA
Al Brown	Panama	1933-1934	NY/NBA/IBU	Kelvin Seabrooks	USA	1987-1988	IBF
Speedy Dado	Philippines	1933	CALIF	Chang-Yung Park	S Korea	1987	WBA
Baby Casanova	Mexico	1933-1934	CALIF	Wilfredo Vasquez	Puerto Rico	1987-1988	WBA
Sixto Escobar	Puerto Rico	1934	CAN	Kaokor Galaxy	Thailand	1988	WBA
Sixto Escobar	Puerto Rico	1934-1935	NBA	Orlando Canizales*	USA	1988-1994	IBF
Al Brown	Panama	1934-1935	NY/IBU	Sung-Il Moon	S Korea	1988-1989	WBA
Lou Salica	USA	1935	CALIF	Raul Perez	Mexico	1988-1991	WBC
Baltazar Sangchilli	Spain	1935-1938	IBU	Israel Contrerras*	Venezuela	1989-1991	WBO
Lou Salica	USA	1935	NBA/NY	Kaokor Galaxy	Thailand	1989	WBA
Sixto Escobar	Puerto Rico	1935-1937	NBA/NY	Luisito Espinosa	Philippines	1989-1991	WBA
Harry Jeffra	USA	1937-1938	NY/NBA	Greg Richardson	USA	1991	WBC
Sixto Escobar	Puerto Rico	1938-1939	NY/NBA	Gaby Canizales	USA	1991	WBO
Al Brown	Panama	1938	IBU	Duke McKenzie	England	1991-1992	WBO
Sixto Escobar	Puerto Rico	1939		Joichiro Tatsuyushi*	Japan	1991-1992	WBC
George Pace	USA	1939-1940	NBA	Israel Contrerras	Venezuela	1991-1992	WBA
Lou Salica	USA	1939	CALIF	Eddie Cook	USA	1992	WBA
Tony Olivera	USA	1939-1940	CALIF	Victor Rabanales	Mexico	1992-1993	WBC
Little Dado	Philippines	1940	CALIF	Rafael del Valle	Puerto Rico	1992-1994	WBO
Lou Salica	USA	1940-1941		Jorge Elicier Julio	Colombia	1992-1993	WBA
Kenny Lindsay	Canada	1941	CAN	Il-Jung Byun	S Korea	1993	WBC
Lou Salica	USA	1942	NY	Junior Jones	USA	1993-1994	WBA
David Kui Kong Young	Hawaii	1941-1943	TBC	Yasuei Yakushiji	Japan	1993-1995	WBC
Lou Salica	USA	1941-1942	NY/NBA	John Michael Johnson	USA	1994	WBA
Manuel Ortiz	USA	1942-1943	NBA	Daorung Chuwatana	Thailand	1994-1995	WBA
Manuel Ortiz	USA	1943-1945	NY/NBA	Alfred Kotey	Ghana	1994-1995	WBO
David Kui Kong Young	Hawaii	1943	TBC	Harold Mestre	Colombia	1995	IBF
Rush Dalma	Philippines	1943-1945	TBC	Mbulelo Botile	S Africa	1995-1997	IBF
Manuel Ortiz	USA	1945-1947		Wayne McCullough	Ireland	1995-1997	WBC
Harold Dade	USA	1947		Veeraphol Sahaprom	Thailand	1995-1996	WBA
Manuel Ortiz	USA	1947-1950		Daniel Jimenez	Puerto Rico	1995-1996	WBO
Vic Toweel	S Africa	1950-1952		Nana Yaw Konadu	Ghana	1996	WBA
Jimmy Carruthers*	Australia	1952-1954		Robbie Regan*	Wales	1996-1998	WBO
Robert Cohen	Algeria	1954		Daorung Chuwatana	Thailand	1996-1997	WBA
Robert Cohen	Algeria	1954-1956	NY/EBU	Sirimongkol Singmanassak	Thailand	1997	WBC
Raton Macias	Mexico	1955-1957	NBA	Nana Yaw Konadu	Ghana	1997-1998	WBA
Mario D'Agata	Italy	1956-1957	NY/EBU	Tim Austin	USA	1997-2003	IBF
Alphonse Halimi	Algeria	1957	NY/EBU	Joichiro Tatsuyoshi	Japan	1997-1998	WBC
Alphonse Halimi	Algeria	1957-1959		Jorge Elicier Julio	Colombia	1998-2000	WBO
Joe Becerra*	Mexico	1959-1960		Johnny Tapia	USA	1998-1999	WBA
Alphonse Halimi	Algeria	1960-1961	EBU	Veeraphol Sahaprom	Thailand	1998-2005	WBC
Eder Jofre	Brazil	1960-1962	NBA	Paulie Ayala	USA	1999-2001	WBA
Johnny Caldwell	Ireland	1961-1962	EBU	Johnny Tapia*	USA	2000	WBO
Eder Jofre	Brazil	1962-1965		Mauricio Martinez	Panama	2000-2002	WBO
Fighting Harada	Japan	1965-1968		Eidy Moya	Venezuela	2001-2002	WBA

Title Holder	Birthplace	Tenure	Status
Cruz Carbajal	Mexico	2002-2004	WBO
Johnny Bredahl*	Denmark	2002-2004	WBA
Rafael Marquez	Mexico	2003-	IBF
Ratanchai Sowvoraphin	Thailand	2004-2005	WBO
Julio Zarate	Mexico	2004-2005	WBA
Wladimir Sidorenko	Ukraine	2005-	WBA
Hozumi Hasegawa	Japan	2005-	WBC
Jhonny Gonzalez	Mexico	2005-	WBO

S. Bantamweight (122 lbs)

Title Holder	Birthplace	Tenure	Status
Rigoberto Riasco	Panama	1976	WBC
Royal Kobayashi	Japan	1976	WBC
Dong-Kyun Yum	S Korea	1976-1977	WBC
Wilfredo Gomez*	Puerto Rico	1977-1983	WBC
Soo-Hwan Hong	S Korea	1977-1978	WBA
Ricardo Cardona	Colombia	1978-1980	WBA
Leo Randolph	USA	1980	WBA
Sergio Palma	Argentina	1980-1982	WBA
Leonardo Cruz	Dom Republic	1982-1984	WBA
Jaime Garza	USA	1983-1984	WBC
Bobby Berna	Philippines	1983-1984	IBF
Loris Stecca	Italy	1984	WBA
Seung-In Suh	S Korea	1984-1985	IBF
Victor Callejas	Puerto Rico	1984-1986	WBA
Juan Meza	Mexico	1984-1985	WBC
Ji-Won Kim*	S Korea	1985-1986	IBF
Lupe Pintor	Mexico	1985-1986	WBC
Samart Payakarun	Thailand	1986-1987	WBC
Louie Espinosa	USA	1987	WBA
Seung-Hoon Lee*	S Korea	1987-1988	IBF
Jeff Fenech*	Australia	1987-1988	WBC
Julio Gervacio	Dom Republic	1987-1988	WBA
Bernardo Pinango	Venezuela	1988	WBA
Daniel Zaragoza	Mexico	1988-1990	WBC
Jose Sanabria	Venezuela	1988-1989	IBF
Juan J. Estrada	Mexico	1988-1989	WBA
Fabrice Benichou	Spain	1989-1990	IBF
Kenny Mitchell	USA	1989	WBO
Valerio Nati	Italy	1989-1990	WBO
Jesus Salud	USA	1989-1990	WBA
Welcome Ncita	S Africa	1990-1992	IBF
Paul Banke	USA	1990	WBC
Orlando Fernandez	Puerto Rico	1990-1991	WBO
Luis Mendoza	Colombia	1990-1991	WBA
Pedro Decima	Argentina	1990-1991	WBC
Kiyoshi Hatanaka	Japan	1991	WBC
Jesse Benavides	USA	1991-1992	WBO
Daniel Zaragoza	Mexico	1991-1992	WBC
Raul Perez	Mexico	1991-1992	WBA
Thierry Jacob	France	1992	WBC
Wilfredo Vasquez	Puerto Rico	1992-1995	WBA
Tracy Harris Patterson	USA	1992-1994	WBC
Duke McKenzie	England	1992-1993	WBO
Kennedy McKinney	USA	1992-1994	IBF
Daniel Jimenez	Puerto Rico	1993-1995	WBO
Vuyani Bungu *	S Africa	1994-1999	IBF
Hector Acero-Sanchez	Dom Republic	1994-1995	WBC
Marco Antonio Barrera	Mexico	1995-1996	WBO
Antonio Cermeno *	Venezuela	1995-1997	WBA
Daniel Zaragoza	Mexico	1995-1997	WBC
Junior Jones	USA	1996-1997	WBO
Erik Morales*	Mexico	1997-2000	WBC
Kennedy McKinney*	USA	1997-1998	WBO
Enrique Sanchez	Mexico	1998	WBA
Marco Antonio Barrera	Mexico	1998-2000	WBO
Nestor Garza	Mexico	1998-2000	WBA
Lehlohonolo Ledwaba	S Africa	1999-2001	IBF
Erik Morales	Mexico	2000	WBC/WBO
Erik Morales*	Mexico	2000	WBC
Marco Antonio Barrera*	Mexico	2000-2001	WBO
Clarence Adams	USA	2000-2001	WBA

Title Holder	Birthplace	Tenure	Status
Willie Jorrin	USA	2000-2002	WBC
Manny Pacquiao*	Philippines	2001-2003	IBF
Agapito Sanchez*	Dom Republic	2001-2002	WBO
Yober Ortega	Venezuela	2001-2002	WBA
Yoddamrong Sithyodthong	Thailand	2002	WBA
Osamu Sato	Japan	2002	WBA
Joan Guzman*	Dom Republic	2002-2005	WBO
Salim Medjkoune	France	2002-2003	WBA
Oscar Larios	Mexico	2002-2005	WBC
Mahyar Monshipour	Iran	2003-2006	WBA
Israel Vazquez*	Mexico	2004-2005	IBF
Daniel Ponce de Leon	Mexico	2005-	WBO
Israel Vazquez	Mexico	2005-	IBF/WBC
Somsak Sithchatchawal	Thailand	2006-	WBA
Israel Vazquez	Mexico	2006-	WBC

Featherweight (126 lbs)

Title Holder	Birthplace	Tenure	Status
Ike Weir	Ireland	1889-1890	
Billy Murphy	New Zealand	1890-1893	
George Dixon	Canada	1890-1893	
Young Griffo	Australia	1890-1893	
Johnny Griffin	USA	1891-1893	
Solly Smith	USA	1893	
George Dixon	Canada	1893-1896	
Solly Smith	USA	1896-1898	
Frank Erne	USA	1896-1897	
George Dixon	Canada	1896-1900	
Harry Greenfield	England	1897-1899	
Ben Jordan	England	1897-1899	
Will Curley	England	1897-1899	
Dave Sullivan	Ireland	1898	
Ben Jordan	England	1899-1905	GB
Eddie Santry	USA	1899-1900	
Terry McGovern	USA	1900	
Terry McGovern	USA	1900-1901	USA
Young Corbett II	USA	1901-1903	USA
Eddie Hanlon	USA	1903	
Young Corbett II	USA	1903-1904	
Abe Attell	USA	1903-1904	
Abe Attell	USA	1904-1911	USA
Joe Bowker	England	1905-1907	GB
Jim Driscoll	Wales	1907-1912	GB
Abe Attell	USA	1911-1912	
Joe Coster	USA	1911	
Joe Rivers	Mexico	1911	
Johnny Kilbane	USA	1911-1912	
Jim Driscoll*	Wales	1912-1913	GB/IBU
Johnny Kilbane	USA	1912-1922	USA
Johnny Kilbane	USA	1922-1923	NBA
Johnny Dundee	Italy	1922-1923	NY
Eugene Criqui	France	1923	
Johnny Dundee*	Italy	1923-1924	
Kid Kaplan	Russia	1925	NY
Kid Kaplan*	Russia	1925-1926	
Honeyboy Finnegan	USA	1926-1927	MASS
Benny Bass	Russia	1927-1928	NBA
Tony Canzoneri	USA	1928	
Andre Routis	France	1928-1929	
Bat Battalino	USA	1929-1932	
Bat Battalino	USA	1932	NBA
Tommy Paul	USA	1932-1933	NBA
Kid Chocolate*	Cuba	1932-1934	NY
Baby Arizmendi	Mexico	1932-1933	CALIF
Freddie Miller	USA	1933-1936	NBA
Baby Arizmendi	Mexico	1934-1935	NY
Baby Arizmendi	Mexico	1935-1936	NY/MEX
Baby Arizmendi	Mexico	1936	MEX
Petey Sarron	USA	1936-1937	NBA
Henry Armstrong	USA	1936-1937	CALIF/MEX
Mike Belloise	USA	1936	NY
Maurice Holtzer	France	1937-1938	IBU

WORLD CHAMPIONS SINCE GLOVES, 1889-2006

Title Holder	Birthplace	Tenure	Status
Henry Armstrong*	USA	1937-1938	NBA/NY
Leo Rodak	USA	1938	MARY
Joey Archibald	USA	1938-1939	NY
Leo Rodak	USA	1938-1939	NBA
Joey Archibald	USA	1939-1940	
Joey Archibald	USA	1940	NY
Petey Scalzo	USA	1940-1941	NBA
Jimmy Perrin	USA	1940	LOUIS
Harry Jeffra	USA	1940-1941	NY/MARY
Joey Archibald	USA	1941	NY/MARY
Richie Lemos	USA	1941	NBA
Chalky Wright	Mexico	1941-1942	NY/MARY
Jackie Wilson	USA	1941-1943	NBA
Willie Pep	USA	1942-1946	NY
Jackie Callura	Canada	1943	NBA
Phil Terranova	USA	1943-1944	NBA
Sal Bartolo	USA	1944-1946	NBA
Willie Pep	USA	1946-1948	
Sandy Saddler	USA	1948-1949	
Willie Pep	USA	1949-1950	
Sandy Saddler*	USA	1950-1957	
Hogan Kid Bassey	Nigeria	1957-1959	
Davey Moore	USA	1959-1963	
Sugar Ramos	Cuba	1963-1964	
Vicente Saldivar*	Mexico	1964-1967	
Raul Rojas	USA	1967	CALIF
Howard Winstone	Wales	1968	WBC
Raul Rojas	USA	1968	WBA
Johnny Famechon	France	1968-1969	AUST
Jose Legra	Cuba	1968-1969	WBC
Shozo Saijyo	Japan	1968-1971	WBA
Johnny Famechon	France	1969-1970	WBC
Vicente Saldivar	Mexico	1970	WBC
Kuniaki Shibata	Japan	1970-1972	WBC
Antonio Gomez	Venezuela	1971-1972	WBA
Clemente Sanchez	Mexico	1972	WBC
Ernesto Marcel*	Panama	1972-1974	WBA
Jose Legra	Cuba	1972-1973	WBC
Eder Jofre	Brazil	1973-1974	WBC
Ruben Olivares	Mexico	1974	WBA
Bobby Chacon	USA	1974-1975	WBC
Alexis Arguello*	Nicaragua	1974-1977	WBA
Ruben Olivares	Mexico	1975	WBC
David Kotey	Ghana	1975-1976	WBC
Danny Lopez	USA	1976-1980	WBC
Rafael Ortega	Panama	1977	WBA
Cecilio Lastra	Spain	1977-1978	WBA
Eusebio Pedroza	Panama	1978-1985	WBA
Salvador Sanchez*	Mexico	1980-1982	WBC
Juan Laporte	Puerto Rico	1982-1984	WBC
Min-Keun Oh	S Korea	1984-1985	IBF
Wilfredo Gomez	Puerto Rico	1984	WBC
Azumah Nelson*	Ghana	1984-1988	WBC
Barry McGuigan	Ireland	1985-1986	WBA
Ki-Yung Chung	S Korea	1985-1986	IBF
Steve Cruz	USA	1986-1987	WBA
Antonio Rivera	Puerto Rico	1986-1988	IBF
Antonio Esparragoza	Venezuela	1987-1991	WBA
Calvin Grove	USA	1988	IBF
Jeff Fenech*	Australia	1988-1989	WBC
Jorge Paez*	Mexico	1988-1990	IBF
Maurizio Stecca	Italy	1989	WBO
Louie Espinosa	USA	1989-1990	WBO
Jorge Paez*	Mexico	1990-1991	IBF/WBO
Marcos Villasana	Mexico	1990-1991	WBC
Kyun-Yung Park	S Korea	1991-1993	WBA
Troy Dorsey	USA	1991	IBF
Maurizio Stecca	Italy	1991-1992	WBO
Manuel Medina	Mexico	1991-1993	IBF
Paul Hodkinson	England	1991-1993	WBC
Colin McMillan	England	1992	WBO

Title Holder	Birthplace	Tenure	Status
Ruben Palacio	Colombia	1992-1993	WBO
Tom Johnson	USA	1993-1997	IBF
Steve Robinson	Wales	1993-1995	WBO
Gregorio Vargas	Mexico	1993	WBC
Kevin Kelley	USA	1993-1995	WBC
Eloy Rojas	Venezuela	1993-1996	WBA
Alejandro Gonzalez	Mexico	1995	WBC
Manuel Medina	Mexico	1995	WBC
Prince Naseem Hamed*	England	1995-1997	WBO
Luisito Espinosa	Philippines	1995-1999	WBC
Wilfredo Vasquez	Puerto Rico	1996-1998	WBA
Prince Naseem Hamed *	England	1997	WBO/IBF
Prince Naseem Hamed*	England	1997-1999	WBO
Hector Lizarraga	Mexico	1997-1998	IBF
Freddie Norwood	USA	1998	WBA
Manuel Medina	Mexico	1998-1999	IBF
Antonio Cermeno	Venezuela	1998-1999	WBA
Cesar Soto	Mexico	1999	WBC
Freddie Norwood	USA	1999-2000	WBA
Prince Naseem Hamed	England	1999-2000	WBC/WBO
Paul Ingle	England	1999-2000	IBF
Prince Naseem Hamed*	England	2000	WBO
Gustavo Espadas	Mexico	2000-2001	WBC
Derrick Gainer	USA	2000-2003	WBA
Mbulelo Botile	S Africa	2000-2001	IBF
Istvan Kovacs	Hungary	2001	WBO
Erik Morales	Mexico	2001-2002	WBC
Frankie Toledo	USA	2001	IBF
Julio Pablo Chacon	Argentina	2001-2002	WBO
Manuel Medina	Mexico	2001-2002	IBF
Johnny Tapia	USA	2002	IBF
Marco Antonio Barrera*	Mexico	2002	WBC
Scott Harrison	Scotland	2002-	WBO
Erik Morales*	Mexico	2002-2003	WBC
Juan Manuel Marquez*	Mexico	2003	IBF
Juan Manuel Marquez	Mexico	2003-2005	IBF/WBA
In-Jin Chi	South Korea	2004-2006	WBC
Juan Manuel Marquez	Mexico	2005-2006	WBA
Valdemir Pereira	Brazil	2005-2006	IBF
Takashi Koshimoto	Japan	2006-	WBC
Chris John	Indonesia	2006-	WBA
Eric Aiken	USA	2006-	IBF

S. Featherweight (130 lbs)

Title Holder	Birthplace	Tenure	Status
Johnny Dundee	Italy	1921-1923	NY
Jack Bernstein	USA	1923	NY
Jack Bernstein	USA	1923	NBA/NY
Johnny Dundee	Italy	1923-1924	NBA/NY
Kid Sullivan	USA	1924-1925	NBA/NY
Mike Ballerino	USA	1925	NBA/NY
Tod Morgan	USA	1925-1929	NBA/NY
Benny Bass	Russia	1929-1930	NBA/NY
Benny Bass	Russia	1930-1931	NBA
Kid Chocolate	Cuba	1931-1933	NBA
Frankie Klick	USA	1933-1934	NBA
Sandy Saddler	USA	1949-1950	NBA
Sandy Saddler	USA	1950-1951	CLE
Harold Gomes	USA	1959-1960	NBA
Flash Elorde	Philippines	1960-1962	NBA
Flash Elorde	Philippines	1962-1967	WBA
Raul Rojas	USA	1967	CALIF
Yoshiaki Numata	Japan	1967	WBA
Hiroshi Kobayashi	Japan	1967-1971	WBA
Rene Barrientos	Philippines	1969-1970	WBC
Yoshiaki Numata	Japan	1970-1971	WBC
Alfredo Marcano	Venezuela	1971-1972	WBA
Ricardo Arredondo	Mexico	1971-1974	WBC
Ben Villaflor	Philippines	1972-1973	WBA
Kuniaki Shibata	Japan	1973	WBA
Ben Villaflor	Philippines	1973-1976	WBA
Kuniaki Shibata	Japan	1974-1975	WBC

240

Title Holder	Birthplace	Tenure	Status
Alfredo Escalera	Puerto Rico	1975-1978	WBC
Sam Serrano	Puerto Rico	1976-1980	WBA
Alexis Arguello*	Nicaragua	1978-1980	WBC
Yasutsune Uehara	Japan	1980-1981	WBA
Rafael Limon	Mexico	1980-1981	WBC
Cornelius Boza-Edwards	Uganda	1981	WBC
Sam Serrano	Puerto Rico	1981-1983	WBA
Rolando Navarrete	Philippines	1981-1982	WBC
Rafael Limon	Mexico	1982	WBC
Bobby Chacon	USA	1982-1983	WBC
Roger Mayweather	USA	1983-1984	WBA
Hector Camacho*	Puerto Rico	1983-1984	WBC
Rocky Lockridge	USA	1984-1985	WBA
Hwan-Kil Yuh	S Korea	1984-1985	IBF
Julio Cesar Chavez*	Mexico	1984-1987	WBC
Lester Ellis	England	1985	IBF
Wilfredo Gomez	Puerto Rico	1985-1986	WBA
Barry Michael	England	1985-1987	IBF
Alfredo Layne	Panama	1986	WBA
Brian Mitchell*	S Africa	1986-1991	WBA
Rocky Lockridge	USA	1987-1988	IBF
Azumah Nelson	Ghana	1988-1994	WBC
Tony Lopez	USA	1988-1989	IBF
Juan Molina*	Puerto Rico	1989	WBO
Juan Molina	Puerto Rico	1989-1990	IBF
Kamel Bou Ali	Tunisia	1989-1992	WBO
Tony Lopez	USA	1990-1991	IBF
Joey Gamache*	USA	1991	WBA
Brian Mitchell*	S Africa	1991-1992	IBF
Genaro Hernandez	USA	1991-1995	WBA
Juan Molina*	Puerto Rico	1992-1995	IBF
Daniel Londas	France	1992	WBO
Jimmy Bredahl	Denmark	1992-1994	WBO
Oscar de la Hoya*	USA	1994	WBO
James Leija	USA	1994	WBC
Gabriel Ruelas	USA	1994-1995	WBC
Regilio Tuur*	Surinam	1994-1997	WBO
Eddie Hopson	USA	1995	IBF
Tracy Harris Patterson	USA	1995	IBF
Yong-Soo Choi	S Korea	1995-1998	WBA
Arturo Gatti*	Canada	1995-1997	IBF
Azumah Nelson	Ghana	1996-1997	WBC
Genaro Hernandez	USA	1997-1998	WBC
Barry Jones*	Wales	1997-1998	WBO
Roberto Garcia	USA	1998-1999	IBF
Anatoly Alexandrov	Kazakhstan	1998-1999	WBO
Takenori Hatakeyama	Japan	1998-1999	WBA
Floyd Mayweather*	USA	1998-2002	WBC
Lakva Sim	Mongolia	1999	WBA
Acelino Freitas*	Brazil	1999-2002	WBO
Diego Corrales*	USA	1999-2000	IBF
Jong-Kwon Baek	S Korea	1999-2000	WBA
Joel Casamayor	Cuba	2000-2002	WBA
Steve Forbes	USA	2000-2002	IBF
Acelino Freitas*	Brazil	2002-2004	WBO/WBA
Sirimongkol Singmanassak	Thailand	2002-2003	WBC
Carlos Hernandez	El Salvador	2003-2004	IBF
Jesus Chavez	Mexico	2003-2004	WBC
Yodesnan Sornontachai	Thailand	2004-2005	WBA
Erik Morales	Mexico	2004	WBC
Diego Corrales*	USA	2004	WBO
Erik Morales	Mexico	2004	IBF
Mike Anchondo	USA	2004-2005	WBO
Marco Antonio Barrera*	Mexico	2004-2005	WBC
Robbie Peden	Australia	2005	IBF
Jorge Barrios	Argentina	2005-	WBO
Vincente Mosquera	Panama	2005-	WBA
Marco Antonio Barrera*	Mexico	2005-2006	WBC/IBF
Marco Antonio Barrera	Mexico	2006-	WBC
Cassius Baloyi	South Africa	2006-	IBF

Title Holder	Birthplace	Tenure	Status
Lightweight (135 lbs)			
Jack McAuliffe	Ireland	1889-1894	USA
Jem Carney	England	1889-1891	
Jimmy Carroll	England	1889-1891	
Dick Burge	England	1891-1896	GB
George Lavigne	USA	1894-1896	USA
George Lavigne	USA	1896	
George Lavigne	USA	1896-1897	
Eddie Connolly	Canada	1896-1897	
George Lavigne	USA	1897-1899	
Frank Erne	Switzerland	1899-1902	
Joe Gans	USA	1902	
Joe Gans	USA	1902-1906	
Jabez White	England	1902-1905	GB
Jimmy Britt	USA	1902-1905	
Battling Nelson	Denmark	1905-1907	
Joe Gans	USA	1906-1908	
Battling Nelson	Denmark	1908-1910	
Ad Wolgast	USA	1910-1912	
Willie Ritchie	USA	1912	
Freddie Welsh	Wales	1912-1914	GB
Willie Ritchie	USA	1912-1914	USA
Freddie Welsh	Wales	1914-1917	
Benny Leonard*	USA	1917-1925	
Jimmy Goodrich	USA	1925	NY
Rocky Kansas	USA	1925-1926	
Sammy Mandell	USA	1926-1930	
Al Singer	USA	1930	
Tony Canzoneri	USA	1930-1933	
Barney Ross*	USA	1933-1935	
Tony Canzoneri	USA	1935-1936	
Lou Ambers	USA	1936-1938	
Henry Armstrong	USA	1938-1939	
Lou Ambers	USA	1939-1940	
Sammy Angott	USA	1940-1941	NBA
Lew Jenkins	USA	1940-1941	NY
Sammy Angott*	USA	1941-1942	
Beau Jack	USA	1942-1943	NY
Slugger White	USA	1943	MARY
Bob Montgomery	USA	1943	NY
Sammy Angott	USA	1943-1944	NBA
Beau Jack	USA	1943-1944	NY
Bob Montgomery	USA	1944-1947	NY
Juan Zurita	Mexico	1944-1945	NBA
Ike Williams	USA	1945-1947	NBA
Ike Williams	USA	1947-1951	
Jimmy Carter	USA	1951-1952	
Lauro Salas	Mexico	1952	
Jimmy Carter	USA	1952-1954	
Paddy de Marco	USA	1954	
Jimmy Carter	USA	1954-1955	
Wallace Bud Smith	USA	1955-1956	
Joe Brown	USA	1956-1962	
Carlos Ortiz	Puerto Rico	1962-1963	
Carlos Ortiz*	Puerto Rico	1963-1964	WBA/WBC
Kenny Lane	USA	1963-1964	MICH
Carlos Ortiz	Puerto Rico	1964-1965	
Ismael Laguna	Panama	1965	
Carlos Ortiz	Puerto Rico	1965-1966	
Carlos Ortiz*	Puerto Rico	1966-1967	WBA
Carlos Ortiz	Puerto Rico	1967-1968	
Carlos Teo Cruz	Dom Republic	1968-1969	
Mando Ramos	USA	1969-1970	
Ismael Laguna	Panama	1970	
Ismael Laguna	Panama	1970	WBA
Ken Buchanan*	Scotland	1970-1971	WBA
Ken Buchanan	Scotland	1971	
Ken Buchanan	Scotland	1971-1972	WBA
Pedro Carrasco	Spain	1971-1972	WBC
Mando Ramos	USA	1972	WBC
Roberto Duran*	Panama	1972-1978	WBA

WORLD CHAMPIONS SINCE GLOVES, 1889-2006

Title Holder	Birthplace	Tenure	Status
Chango Carmona	Mexico	1972	WBC
Rodolfo Gonzalez	Mexico	1972-1974	WBC
Guts Ishimatsu	Japan	1974-1976	WBC
Esteban de Jesus	Puerto Rico	1976-1978	WBC
Roberto Duran*	Panama	1978-1979	
Jim Watt	Scotland	1979-1981	WBC
Ernesto Espana	Venezuela	1979-1980	WBA
Hilmer Kenty	USA	1980-1981	WBA
Sean O'Grady	USA	1981	WBA
Alexis Arguello*	Nicaragua	1981-1983	WBC
Claude Noel	Trinidad	1981	WBA
Arturo Frias	USA	1981-1982	WBA
Ray Mancini	USA	1982-1984	WBA
Edwin Rosario	Puerto Rico	1983-1984	WBC
Charlie Choo Choo Brown	USA	1984	IBF
Harry Arroyo	USA	1984-1985	IBF
Livingstone Bramble	USA	1984-1986	WBA
Jose Luis Ramirez	Mexico	1984-1985	WBC
Jimmy Paul	USA	1985-1986	IBF
Hector Camacho*	Puerto Rico	1985-1987	WBC
Edwin Rosario	Puerto Rico	1986-1987	WBA
Greg Haugen	USA	1986-1987	IBF
Vinny Pazienza	USA	1987-1988	IBF
Jose Luis Ramirez	Mexico	1987-1988	WBC
Julio Cesar Chavez*	Mexico	1987-1988	WBA
Greg Haugen	USA	1988-1989	IBF
Julio Cesar Chavez*	Mexico	1988-1989	WBA/WBC
Mauricio Aceves	Mexico	1989-1990	WBO
Pernell Whitaker*	USA	1989	IBF
Edwin Rosario	Puerto Rico	1989-1990	WBA
Pernell Whitaker*	USA	1989-1990	IBF/WBC
Juan Nazario	Puerto Rico	1990	WBA
Pernell Whitaker*	USA	1990-1992	IBF/WBC/WBA
Dingaan Thobela*	S Africa	1990-1992	WBO
Joey Gamache	USA	1992	WBA
Miguel Gonzalez*	Mexico	1992-1996	WBC
Giovanni Parisi*	Italy	1992-1994	WBO
Tony Lopez	USA	1992-1993	WBA
Fred Pendleton	USA	1993-1994	IBF
Dingaan Thobela	S Africa	1993	WBA
Orzubek Nazarov	Kyrghyzstan	1993-1998	WBA
Rafael Ruelas	USA	1994-1995	IBF
Oscar de la Hoya*	USA	1994-1995	WBO
Oscar de la Hoya*	USA	1995	WBO/IBF
Oscar de la Hoya*	USA	1995-1996	WBO
Phillip Holiday	S Africa	1995-1997	IBF
Jean-Baptiste Mendy	France	1996-1997	WBC
Artur Grigorian	Uzbekistan	1996-2004	WBO
Steve Johnston	USA	1997-1998	WBC
Shane Mosley*	USA	1997-1999	IBF
Jean-Baptiste Mendy	France	1998-1999	WBA
Cesar Bazan	Mexico	1998-1999	WBC
Steve Johnston	USA	1999-2000	WBC
Julien Lorcy	France	1999	WBA
Stefano Zoff	Italy	1999	WBA
Paul Spadafora*	USA	1999-2003	IBF
Gilberto Serrano	Venezuela	1999-2000	WBA
Takanori Hatakeyama	Japan	2000-2001	WBA
Jose Luis Castillo	Mexico	2000-2002	WBC
Julien Lorcy	France	2001	WBA
Raul Balbi	Argentina	2001-2002	WBA
Leonardo Dorin	Romania	2002-2003	WBA
Floyd Mayweather*	USA	2002-2004	WBC
Javier Jauregui	Mexico	2003-2004	IBF
Acelino Freitas	Brazil	2004	WBO
Lakva Sim	Mongolia	2004	WBA
Julio Diaz*	Mexico	2004-2005	IBF
Jose Luis Castillo	Mexico	2004-2005	WBC
Juan Diaz	USA	2004-	WBA
Diego Corrales*	USA	2004-2005	WBO
Diego Corrales	USA	2005-2006	WBC/WBO

Title Holder	Birthplace	Tenure	Status
Leavander Johnson	USA	2005	IBF
Jesus Chavez	Mexico	2005-	IBF
Diego Corrales	USA	2006-	WBC
Acelino Freitas	Brazil	2006-	WBO

L. Welterweight (140 lbs)

Title Holder	Birthplace	Tenure	Status
Pinkey Mitchell	USA	1922-1926	NBA
Mushy Callahan	USA	1926-1927	NBA
Mushy Callahan	USA	1927-1930	NBA/NY
Mushy Callahan	USA	1930	NBA
Jackie Kid Berg	England	1930-1931	NBA
Tony Canzoneri	USA	1931-1932	NBA
Johnny Jadick	USA	1932	NBA
Johnny Jadick	USA	1932-1933	PEN
Battling Shaw	Mexico	1933	LOUIS
Tony Canzoneri	USA	1933	LOUIS
Barney Ross*	USA	1933-1935	ILL
Maxie Berger	Canada	1939	CAN
Harry Weekly	USA	1941-1942	LOUIS
Tippy Larkin	USA	1946-1947	NY/NBA
Carlos Ortiz	Puerto Rico	1959-1960	NBA
Duilio Loi	Italy	1960-1962	NBA
Duilio Loi	Italy	1962	WBA
Eddie Perkins	USA	1962	WBA
Duilio Loi*	Italy	1962-1963	WBA
Roberto Cruz	Philippines	1963	WBA
Eddie Perkins	USA	1963-1965	WBA
Carlos Hernandez	Venezuela	1965-1966	WBA
Sandro Lopopolo	Italy	1966-1967	WBA
Paul Fujii	Hawaii	1967-1968	WBA
Nicolino Loche	Argentina	1968-1972	WBA
Pedro Adigue	Philippines	1968-1970	WBC
Bruno Arcari*	Italy	1970-1974	WBC
Alfonso Frazer	Panama	1972	WBA
Antonio Cervantes	Colombia	1972-1976	WBA
Perico Fernandez	Spain	1974-1975	WBC
Saensak Muangsurin	Thailand	1975-1976	WBC
Wilfred Benitez	USA	1976	WBA
Miguel Velasquez	Spain	1976	WBC
Saensak Muangsurin	Thailand	1976-1978	WBC
Antonio Cervantes	Colombia	1977-1980	WBA
Wilfred Benitez*	USA	1977-1978	NY
Sang-Hyun Kim	S Korea	1978-1980	WBC
Saoul Mamby	USA	1980-1982	WBC
Aaron Pryor*	USA	1980-1984	WBA
Leroy Haley	USA	1982-1983	WBC
Bruce Curry	USA	1983-1984	WBC
Johnny Bumphus	USA	1984	WBA
Bill Costello	USA	1984-1985	WBC
Gene Hatcher	USA	1984-1985	WBA
Aaron Pryor	USA	1984-1985	IBF
Ubaldo Sacco	Argentina	1985-1986	WBA
Lonnie Smith	USA	1985-1986	WBC
Patrizio Oliva	Italy	1986-1987	WBA
Gary Hinton	USA	1986	IBF
Rene Arredondo	Mexico	1986	WBC
Tsuyoshi Hamada	Japan	1986-1987	WBC
Joe Manley	USA	1986-1987	IBF
Terry Marsh*	England	1987	IBF
Juan M. Coggi	Argentina	1987-1990	WBA
Rene Arredondo	Mexico	1987	WBC
Roger Mayweather	USA	1987-1989	WBC
James McGirt	USA	1988	IBF
Meldrick Taylor	USA	1988-1990	IBF
Hector Camacho	Puerto Rico	1989-1991	WBO
Julio Cesar Chavez*	Mexico	1989-1990	WBC
Julio Cesar Chavez*	Mexico	1990-1991	IBF/WBC
Loreto Garza	USA	1990-1991	WBA
Greg Haugen	USA	1991	WBO
Hector Camacho	Puerto Rico	1991-1992	WBO
Edwin Rosario	Puerto Rico	1991-1992	WBA

Title Holder	Birthplace	Tenure	Status		Title Holder	Birthplace	Tenure	Status
Julio Cesar Chavez	Mexico	1991-1994	WBC		Jimmy Gardner	USA	1905	
Rafael Pineda	Colombia	1991-1992	IBF		Mike Twin Sullivan	USA	1905-1906	
Akinobu Hiranaka	Japan	1992	WBA		Joe Gans	USA	1906	
Carlos Gonzalez	Mexico	1992-1993	WBO		Joe Walcott	Barbados	1906	USA
Pernell Whitaker*	USA	1992-1993	IBF		Honey Mellody	USA	1906	USA
Morris East	Philippines	1992-1993	WBA		Honey Mellody	USA	1906-1907	
Juan M. Coggi	Argentina	1993-1994	WBA		Joe Thomas	USA	1906-1907	
Charles Murray	USA	1993-1994	IBF		Mike Twin Sullivan	USA	1907-1911	
Zack Padilla*	USA	1993-1994	WBO		Jimmy Gardner	USA	1907-1908	
Frankie Randall	USA	1994	WBC		Frank Mantell	USA	1907-1908	
Jake Rodriguez	USA	1994-1995	IBF		Harry Lewis	USA	1908-1910	
Julio Cesar Chavez	Mexico	1994-1996	WBC		Jack Blackburn	USA	1908	
Frankie Randall	USA	1994-1996	WBA		Jimmy Gardner	USA	1908-1909	
Konstantin Tszyu	Russia	1995-1997	IBF		Willie Lewis	USA	1909-1910	
Sammy Fuentes	Puerto Rico	1995-1996	WBO		Harry Lewis	USA	1910-1911	GB/FR
Juan M. Coggi	Argentina	1996	WBA		Jimmy Clabby	USA	1910-1911	
Giovanni Parisi	Italy	1996-1998	WBO		Dixie Kid	USA	1911-1912	GB/FR
Oscar de la Hoya*	USA	1996-1997	WBC		Ray Bronson	USA	1911-1914	
Frankie Randall	USA	1996-1997	WBA		Marcel Thomas	France	1912-1913	FR
Khalid Rahilou	France	1997-1998	WBA		Wildcat Ferns	USA	1912-1913	
Vince Phillips	USA	1997-1999	IBF		Spike Kelly	USA	1913-1914	
Carlos Gonzalez	Mexico	1998-1999	WBO		Mike Glover	USA	1913-1915	
Sharmba Mitchell	USA	1998-2001	WBA		Mike Gibbons	USA	1913-1914	
Terron Millett	USA	1999	IBF		Waldemar Holberg	Denmark	1914	
Randall Bailey	USA	1999-2000	WBO		Tom McCormick	Ireland	1914	
Kostya Tszyu*	Russia	1999-2001	WBC		Matt Wells	England	1914-1915	AUSTR
Zab Judah	USA	2000-2001	IBF		Kid Graves	USA	1914-1917	
Ener Julio	Colombia	2000-2001	WBO		Jack Britton	USA	1915	
Kostya Tszyu*	Russia	2001	WBA/WBC		Ted Kid Lewis	England	1915-1916	
DeMarcus Corley	USA	2001-2003	WBO		Jack Britton	USA	1916-1917	
Kostya Tszyu*	Russia	2001-2004	WBA/WBC/IBF		Ted Kid Lewis	England	1917	
Zab Judah*	USA	2003-2004	WBO		**Ted Kid Lewis**	England	1917-1919	
Kostya Tszyu	Russia	2004-2005	IBF		**Jack Britton**	USA	1919-1922	
Arturo Gatti	Canada	2004-2005	WBC		**Mickey Walker**	USA	1922-1923	
Vivien Harris	Guyana	2004-2005	WBA		Mickey Walker	USA	1923-1924	NBA
Miguel Cotto	Puerto Rico	2004-	WBO		Dave Shade	USA	1923	NY
Ricky Hatton*	England	2005	IBF		Jimmy Jones	USA	1923	NY/MASS
Carlos Maussa	Colombia	2005	WBA		**Mickey Walker**	USA	1924-1926	
Floyd Mayweather*	USA	2005-2006	WBC		**Pete Latzo**	USA	1926-1927	
Ricky Hatton*	England	2005-2006	IBF/WBA		**Joe Dundee**	Italy	1927-1928	
Juan Urango	Colombia	2006-	IBF		Joe Dundee	Italy	1928-1929	NY
					Jackie Fields	USA	1929	NBA
Welterweight (147 lbs)					**Jackie Fields**	USA	1929-1930	
Paddy Duffy	USA	1889-1890			**Young Jack Thompson**	USA	1930	
Tommy Ryan	USA	1891-1894			**Tommy Freeman**	USA	1930-1931	
Mysterious Billy Smith	USA	1892-1894			**Young Jack Thompson**	USA	1930	
Tommy Ryan	USA	1894-1897	USA		**Lou Brouillard**	Canada	1931-1932	
Tommy Ryan	USA	1897-1899			**Jackie Fields**	USA	1932-1933	
Dick Burge	GB	1897			**Young Corbett III**	Italy	1933	
George Green	USA	1897			**Jimmy McLarnin**	Ireland	1933-1934	
Tom Causer	GB	1897			**Barney Ross**	USA	1934	
Joe Walcott	Barbados	1897			**Jimmy McLarnin**	Ireland	1934-1935	
George Lavigne	USA	1897-1899			**Barney Ross**	USA	1935-1938	
Dick Burge	GB	1897-1898			Barney Ross	USA	1938	NY/NBA
Mysterious Billy Smith	USA	1898-1900			Felix Wouters	Belgium	1938	IBU
Bobby Dobbs	USA	1898-1902			**Henry Armstrong**	USA	1938-1940	
Rube Ferns	USA	1900			**Fritzie Zivic**	USA	1940	
Matty Matthews	USA	1900			Fritzie Zivic	USA	1940-1941	NY/NBA
Eddie Connolly	Canada	1900			Izzy Jannazzo	USA	1940-1942	MARY
Matty Matthews	USA	1900-1901			Red Cochrane	USA	1941-1942	NY/NBA
Rube Ferns	USA	1901			**Red Cochrane**	USA	1942-1946	
Joe Walcott	Barbados	1901-1906			**Marty Servo**	USA	1946	
Eddie Connolly	Canada	1902-1903	GB		**Sugar Ray Robinson***	USA	1946-1951	
Matty Matthews	USA	1902-1903			Johnny Bratton	USA	1951	NBA
Rube Ferns	USA	1903			Kid Gavilan	Cuba	1951-1952	NBA/NY
Martin Duffy	USA	1903-1904			**Kid Gavilan**	Cuba	1952-1954	
Honey Mellody	USA	1904			**Johnny Saxton**	USA	1954-1955	
Jack Clancy	USA	1904-1905	GB		**Tony de Marco**	USA	1955	
Dixie Kid	USA	1904-1905			**Carmen Basilio**	USA	1955-1956	
Buddy Ryan	USA	1904-1905			**Johnny Saxton**	USA	1956	
Sam Langford	Canada	1904-1905			**Carmen Basilio***	USA	1956-1957	
George Petersen	USA	1905			Virgil Akins	USA	1957-1958	MASS

Title Holder	Birthplace	Tenure	Status
Virgil Akins	USA	1958	
Don Jordan	Dom Republic	1958-1960	
Benny Kid Paret	Cuba	1960-1961	
Emile Griffith	Virgin Islands	1961	
Benny Kid Paret	Cuba	1961-1962	
Emile Griffith	Virgin Islands	1962-1963	
Luis Rodriguez	Cuba	1963	
Emile Griffith*	Virgin Islands	1963-1966	
Willie Ludick	S Africa	1966-1968	SA
Curtis Cokes*	USA	1966	WBA
Curtis Cokes*	USA	1966-1967	WBA/WBC
Charley Shipes	USA	1966-1967	CALIF
Curtis Cokes	USA	1968-1969	
Jose Napoles	Cuba	1969-1970	
Billy Backus	USA	1970-1971	
Jose Napoles	Cuba	1971-1972	
Jose Napoles*	Cuba	1972-1974	WBA/WBC
Hedgemon Lewis	USA	1972-1974	NY
Jose Napoles	Cuba	1974-1975	
Jose Napoles	Cuba	1975	WBC
Angel Espada	Puerto Rico	1975-1976	WBA
John H. Stracey	England	1975-1976	WBC
Carlos Palomino	Mexico	1976-1979	WBC
Pipino Cuevas	Mexico	1976-1980	WBA
Wilfred Benitez	USA	1979	WBC
Sugar Ray Leonard	USA	1979-1980	WBC
Roberto Duran	Panama	1980	WBC
Thomas Hearns	USA	1980-1981	WBA
Sugar Ray Leonard	USA	1980-1981	WBC
Sugar Ray Leonard*	USA	1981-1982	
Don Curry*	USA	1983-1984	WBA
Milton McCrory	USA	1983-1985	WBC
Don Curry*	USA	1984-1985	WBA/IBF
Don Curry	USA	1985-1986	
Lloyd Honeyghan	Jamaica	1986	
Lloyd Honeyghan	Jamaica	1986-1987	WBC/IBF
Mark Breland	USA	1987	WBA
Marlon Starling	USA	1987-1988	WBA
Jorge Vaca	Mexico	1987-1988	WBC
Lloyd Honeyghan	Jamaica	1988-1989	WBC
Simon Brown*	Jamaica	1988-1991	IBF
Tomas Molinares	Colombia	1988-1989	WBA
Mark Breland	USA	1989-1990	WBA
Marlon Starling	USA	1989-1990	WBC
Genaro Leon*	Mexico	1989	WBO
Manning Galloway	USA	1989-1993	WBO
Aaron Davis	USA	1990-1991	WBA
Maurice Blocker	USA	1990-1991	WBC
Meldrick Taylor	USA	1991-1992	WBA
Simon Brown*	Jamaica	1991	WBC/IBF
Simon Brown	Jamaica	1991	WBC
Maurice Blocker	USA	1991-1993	IBF
James McGirt	USA	1991-1993	WBC
Crisanto Espana	Venezuela	1992-1994	WBA
Gert Bo Jacobsen*	Denmark	1993	WBO
Pernell Whitaker	USA	1993-1997	WBC
Felix Trinidad*	Puerto Rico	1993-2000	IBF
Eamonn Loughran	Ireland	1993-1996	WBO
Ike Quartey	Ghana	1994-1998	WBA
Jose Luis Lopez	Mexico	1996-1997	WBO
Michael Loewe*	Romania	1997-1998	WBO
Oscar de la Hoya	USA	1997-1999	WBC
Ahmed Kotiev	Russia	1998-2000	WBO
James Page	USA	1998-2000	WBA
Oscar de la Hoya	USA	2000	WBC
Daniel Santos*	Puerto Rico	2000-2002	WBO
Shane Mosley	USA	2000-2002	WBC
Andrew Lewis	Guyana	2001-2002	WBA
Vernon Forrest	USA	2001	IBF
Vernon Forrest	USA	2002-2003	WBC
Antonio Margarito	Mexico	2002-	WBO
Ricardo Mayorga*	Nicaragua	2002-2003	WBA

Title Holder	Birthplace	Tenure	Status
Michele Piccirillo	Italy	2002-2003	IBF
Ricardo Mayorga	Nicaragua	2003	WBA/WBC
Cory Spinks*	USA	2003	IBF
Cory Spinks	USA	2003-2005	IBF/WBA/WBC
Zab Judah	USA	2005-2006	IBF/WBA/WBC
Carlos Baldomir	Argentina	2006-	WBC
Zab Judah	USA	2006	IBF
Luis Collazo	USA	2006	WBA
Floyd Mayweather	USA	2006-	IBF
Ricky Hatton	England	2006-	WBA

L. Middleweight (154 lbs)

Title Holder	Birthplace	Tenure	Status
Emile Griffith*	USA	1962-1963	AU
Denny Moyer	USA	1962-1963	WBA
Ralph Dupas	USA	1963	WBA
Sandro Mazzinghi	Italy	1963-1965	WBA
Nino Benvenuti	Italy	1965-1966	WBA
Ki-Soo Kim	S Korea	1966-1968	WBA
Sandro Mazzinghi	Italy	1968-1969	WBA
Freddie Little	USA	1969-1970	WBA
Carmelo Bossi	Italy	1970-1971	WBA
Koichi Wajima	Japan	1971-1974	WBA
Oscar Albarado	USA	1974-1975	WBA
Koichi Wajima	Japan	1975	WBA
Miguel de Oliveira	Brazil	1975	WBC
Jae-Do Yuh	S Korea	1975-1976	WBA
Elisha Obed	Bahamas	1975-1976	WBC
Koichi Wajima	Japan	1976	WBA
Jose Duran	Spain	1976	WBA
Eckhard Dagge	Germany	1976-1977	WBC
Miguel Castellini	Argentina	1976-1977	WBA
Eddie Gazo	Nicaragua	1977-1978	WBA
Rocky Mattioli	Italy	1977-1979	WBC
Masashi Kudo	Japan	1978-1979	WBA
Maurice Hope	Antigua	1979-1981	WBC
Ayub Kalule	Uganda	1979-1981	WBA
Wilfred Benitez	USA	1981-1982	WBC
Sugar Ray Leonard*	USA	1981	WBA
Tadashi Mihara	Japan	1981-1982	WBA
Davey Moore	USA	1982-1983	WBA
Thomas Hearns*	USA	1982-1986	WBC
Roberto Duran*	Panama	1983-1984	WBA
Mark Medal	USA	1984	IBF
Mike McCallum*	Jamaica	1984-1987	WBA
Carlos Santos	Puerto Rico	1984-1986	IBF
Buster Drayton	USA	1986-1987	IBF
Duane Thomas	USA	1986-1987	WBC
Matthew Hilton	Canada	1987-1988	IBF
Lupe Aquino	Mexico	1987	WBC
Gianfranco Rosi	Italy	1987-1988	WBC
Julian Jackson*	Virgin Islands	1987-1990	WBA
Don Curry	USA	1988-1989	WBC
Robert Hines	USA	1988-1989	IBF
John David Jackson*	USA	1988-1993	WBO
Darrin van Horn	USA	1989	IBF
Rene Jacqot	France	1989	WBC
John Mugabi	Uganda	1989-1990	WBC
Gianfranco Rosi	Italy	1989-1994	IBF
Terry Norris	USA	1990-1993	WBC
Gilbert Dele	France	1991	WBA
Vinny Pazienza*	USA	1991-1992	WBA
Julio Cesar Vasquez	Argentina	1992-1995	WBA
Verno Phillips	USA	1993-1995	WBO
Simon Brown	USA	1993-1994	WBC
Terry Norris	USA	1994	WBC
Vince Pettway	USA	1994-1995	IBF
Luis Santana	Dom Republic	1994-1995	WBC
Pernell Whitaker*	USA	1995	WBA
Gianfranco Rosi	Italy	1995	WBO
Carl Daniels	USA	1995	WBA
Verno Phillips	USA	1995	WBO
Paul Vaden	USA	1995	IBF

Title Holder	Birthplace	Tenure	Status	Title Holder	Birthplace	Tenure	Status
Terry Norris*	USA	1995	WBC	Eddie McGoorty	USA	1912-1913	
Paul Jones	England	1995-1996	WBO	Frank Klaus	USA	1913	IBU
Terry Norris	USA	1995-1997	IBF/WBC	Jimmy Clabby	USA	1913-1914	
Julio Cesar Vasquez	Argentina	1995-1996	WBA	George Chip	USA	1913-1914	
Bronco McKart	USA	1996	WBO	Joe Borrell	USA	1913-1914	
Ronald Wright	USA	1996-1998	WBO	Jeff Smith	USA	1913-1914	
Laurent Boudouani	France	1996-1999	WBA	Eddie McGoorty	USA	1914	AUSTR
Terry Norris	USA	1997	WBC	Jeff Smith	USA	1914	AUSTR
Raul Marquez	USA	1997	IBF	Al McCoy	USA	1914-1917	
Luis Campas	Mexico	1997-1998	IBF	Jimmy Clabby	USA	1914-1915	
Keith Mullings	USA	1997-1999	WBC	Mick King	Australia	1914	AUSTR
Harry Simon*	Namibia	1998-2001	WBO	Jeff Smith	USA	1914-1915	AUSTR
Fernando Vargas	USA	1998-2000	IBF	Young Ahearn	England	1915-1916	
Javier Castillejo	Spain	1999-2001	WBC	Les Darcy*	Australia	1915-1917	AUSTR
David Reid	USA	1999-2000	WBA	Mike Gibbons	USA	1916-1917	
Felix Trinidad*	Puerto Rico	2000	WBA	Mike O'Dowd	USA	1917-1920	
Felix Trinidad*	Puerto Rico	2000-2001	IBF/WBA	Johnny Wilson	USA	1920-1921	
Oscar de la Hoya*	USA	2001-2002	WBC	Johnny Wilson	USA	1921-1922	NBA/NY
Fernando Vargas	USA	2001-2002	WBA	Bryan Downey	USA	1921-1922	OHIO
Ronald Wright*	USA	2001-2004	IBF	Johnny Wilson	USA	1922-1923	NBA
Daniel Santos	Puerto Rico	2002-2005	WBO	Dave Rosenberg	USA	1922	NY
Oscar de la Hoya	USA	2002-2003	WBA/WBC	Jock Malone	USA	1922-1923	OHIO
Shane Mosley	USA	2003-2004	WBA/WBC	Mike O'Dowd	USA	1922-1923	NY
Ronald Wright	USA	2004	IBF/WBA/WBC	Johnny Wilson	USA	1923	
Ronald Wright	USA	2004-2005	WBA/WBC	Harry Greb	USA	1923-1926	
Verno Phillips	USA	2004	IBF	Tiger Flowers	USA	1926	
Kassim Ouma	Uganda	2004-2005	IBF	Mickey Walker	USA	1926-1931	
Ronald Wright*	USA	2005	WBC	Gorilla Jones	USA	1932	NBA
Travis Simms	USA	2005	WBA	Marcel Thil	France	1932-1933	NBA/IBU
Javier Castillejo	Spain	2005	WBC	Marcel Thil	France	1933-1937	IBU
Alejandro Garcia	Mexico	2005-2006	WBA	Ben Jeby	USA	1933	NY
Roman Karmazin	Russia	2005-	IBF	Lou Brouillard	Canada	1933	NY
Ricardo Mayorga	Nicaragua	2005-2006	WBC	Lou Brouillard	Canada	1933	NY/NBA
Sergei Dzindziruk	Ukraine	2005-	WBO	Vearl Whitehead	USA	1933	CALIF
Jose Antonio Rivera	USA	2006-	WBA	Teddy Yarosz	USA	1933-1934	PEN
Oscar de la Hoya	USA	2006-	WBC	Vince Dundee	USA	1933-1934	NY/NBA
				Teddy Yarosz	USA	1934-1935	NY/NBA

Middleweight (160 lbs)

Title Holder	Birthplace	Tenure	Status	Title Holder	Birthplace	Tenure	Status
Nonpareil Jack Dempsey	Ireland	1889-1891	USA	Babe Risko	USA	1935-1936	NY/NBA
Bob Fitzsimmons	England	1891-1893	USA	Freddie Steele	USA	1936-1938	NY/NBA
Jim Hall	Australia	1892-1893	GB	Fred Apostoli	USA	1937-1938	IBU
Bob Fitzsimmons	England	1893-1894		Edouard Tenet	France	1938	IBU
Bob Fitzsimmons	England	1894-1899		Young Corbett III	Italy	1938	CALIF
Frank Craig	USA	1894-1895	GB	Freddie Steele	USA	1938	NBA
Dan Creedon	New Zealand	1895-1897	GB	Al Hostak	USA	1938	NBA
Tommy Ryan	USA	1895-1896		Solly Krieger	USA	1938-1939	NBA
Kid McCoy	USA	1896-1898		Fred Apostoli	USA	1938-1939	NY
Tommy Ryan	USA	1898-1905		Al Hostak	USA	1939-1940	NBA
Charley McKeever	USA	1900-1902		Ceferino Garcia	Philippines	1939-1940	NY
George Gardner	USA	1901-1902		Ken Overlin	USA	1940-1941	NY
Jack O'Brien	USA	1901-1905		Tony Zale	USA	1940-1941	NBA
George Green	USA	1901-1902		Billy Soose	USA	1941	NY
Jack Palmer	England	1902-1903	GB	Tony Zale	USA	1941-1947	
Hugo Kelly	USA	1905-1908		Rocky Graziano	USA	1947-1948	
Jack Twin Sullivan	USA	1905-1908		Tony Zale	USA	1948	
Sam Langford	Canada	1907-1911		Marcel Cerdan	Algeria	1948-1949	
Billy Papke	USA	1908		Jake la Motta	USA	1949-1950	
Stanley Ketchel	USA	1908		Jake la Motta	USA	1950-1951	NY/NBA
Billy Papke	USA	1908		Sugar Ray Robinson	USA	1950-1951	PEN
Stanley Ketchel	USA	1908-1910		Sugar Ray Robinson	USA	1951	
Billy Papke	USA	1910-1913		Randy Turpin	England	1951	
Stanley Ketchel*	USA	1910		Sugar Ray Robinson*	USA	1951-1952	
Hugo Kelly	USA	1910-1912		Randy Turpin	England	1953	GB/EBU
Cyclone Johnny Thompson	USA	1911-1912		Carl Bobo Olson	Hawaii	1953-1955	
Harry Lewis	USA	1911		Sugar Ray Robinson	USA	1955-1957	
Leo Houck	USA	1911-1912		Gene Fullmer	USA	1957	
Georges Carpentier	France	1911-1912		Sugar Ray Robinson	USA	1957	
Jack Dillon	USA	1912		Carmen Basilio	USA	1957-1958	
Frank Mantell	USA	1912-1913		Sugar Ray Robinson	USA	1958-1959	
Frank Klaus	USA	1912-1913		Sugar Ray Robinson	USA	1959-1960	NY/EBU
Georges Carpentier	France	1912	IBU	Gene Fullmer	USA	1959-1962	NBA
Jack Dillon	USA	1912-1915		Paul Pender	USA	1960-1961	NY/EBU
				Terry Downes	England	1961-1962	NY/EBU

WORLD CHAMPIONS SINCE GLOVES, 1889-2006

Title Holder	Birthplace	Tenure	Status
Paul Pender	USA	1962	NY/EBU
Dick Tiger	Nigeria	1962-1963	NBA
Dick Tiger	Nigeria	1963	
Joey Giardello	USA	1963-1965	
Dick Tiger	Nigeria	1965-1966	
Emile Griffith	Virgin Islands	1966-1967	
Nino Benvenuti	Italy	1967	
Emile Griffith	Virgin Islands	1967-1968	
Nino Benvenuti	Italy	1968-1970	
Carlos Monzon	Argentina	1970-1974	
Carlos Monzon*	Argentina	1974-1976	WBA
Rodrigo Valdez	Colombia	1974-1976	WBC
Carlos Monzon*	Argentina	1976-1977	
Rodrigo Valdez	Colombia	1977-1978	
Hugo Corro	Argentina	1978-1979	
Vito Antuofermo	Italy	1979-1980	
Alan Minter	England	1980	
Marvin Hagler	USA	1980-1987	
Marvin Hagler	USA	1987	WBC/IBF
Sugar Ray Leonard	USA	1987	WBC
Frank Tate	USA	1987-1988	IBF
Sumbu Kalambay	Zaire	1987-1989	WBA
Thomas Hearns	USA	1987-1988	WBC
Iran Barkley	USA	1988-1989	WBC
Michael Nunn	USA	1988-1991	IBF
Roberto Duran	Panama	1989-1990	WBC
Doug de Witt	USA	1989-1990	WBO
Mike McCallum	Jamaica	1989-1991	WBA
Nigel Benn	England	1990	WBO
Chris Eubank*	England	1990-1991	WBO
Julian Jackson	Virgin Islands	1990-1993	WBC
James Toney*	USA	1991-1993	IBF
Gerald McClellan*	USA	1991-1993	WBO
Reggie Johnson	USA	1992-1993	WBA
Gerald McClellan*	USA	1993-1995	WBC
Chris Pyatt	England	1993-1994	WBO
Roy Jones*	USA	1993-1994	IBF
John David Jackson	USA	1993-1994	WBA
Steve Collins*	Ireland	1994-1995	WBO
Jorge Castro	Argentina	1994	WBA
Julian Jackson	Virgin Islands	1995	WBC
Bernard Hopkins*	USA	1995-2001	IBF
Lonnie Bradley*	USA	1995-1998	WBO
Quincy Taylor	USA	1995-1996	WBC
Shinji Takehara	Japan	1995-1996	WBA
Keith Holmes	USA	1996-1998	WBC
William Joppy	USA	1996-1997	WBA
Julio Cesar Green	Dom Republic	1997-1998	WBA
William Joppy	USA	1998-2001	WBA
Hassine Cherifi	France	1998-1999	WBC
Otis Grant*	Canada	1998	WBO
Bert Schenk	Germany	1999	WBO
Keith Holmes	USA	1999-2001	WBC
Jason Matthews	England	1999	WBO
Armand Krajnc	Slovenia	1999-2002	WBO
Bernard Hopkins*	USA	2001	WBC/IBF
Felix Trinidad	Puerto Rico	2001	WBA
Bernard Hopkins*	USA	2001-2004	WBC/WBA/IBF
Harry Simon	Namibia	2002-2003	WBO
Hector Javier Velazco	Argentina	2003	WBO
Felix Sturm	Germany	2003-2004	WBO
Oscar de la Hoya	USA	2004	WBO
Bernard Hopkins	USA	2004-2005	IBF/WBA/WBC/WBO
Jermain Taylor*	USA	2005	IBF/WBA/WBC/WBO
Jermain Taylor	USA	2005-	WBA/WBC/WBO
Arthur Abraham	Armenia	2005-	IBF

S. Middleweight (168 lbs)

Title Holder	Birthplace	Tenure	Status
Murray Sutherland	Scotland	1984	IBF
Chong-Pal Park*	S Korea	1984-1987	IBF
Chong-Pal Park	S Korea	1987-1988	WBA
Graciano Rocchigiani*	Germany	1988-1989	IBF
Fully Obelmejias	Venezuela	1988-1989	WBA
Sugar Ray Leonard*	USA	1988-1990	WBC
Thomas Hearns*	USA	1988-1991	WBO
In-Chul Baek	S Korea	1989-1990	WBA
Lindell Holmes	USA	1990-1991	IBF
Christophe Tiozzo	France	1990-1991	WBA
Mauro Galvano	Italy	1990-1992	WBC
Victor Cordoba	Panama	1991-1992	WBA
Darrin van Horn	USA	1991-1992	IBF
Chris Eubank	England	1991-1995	WBO
Iran Barkley	USA	1992-1993	IBF
Michael Nunn	USA	1992-1994	WBA
Nigel Benn	England	1992-1996	WBC
James Toney	USA	1993-1994	IBF
Steve Little	USA	1994	WBA
Frank Liles	USA	1994-1999	WBA
Roy Jones*	USA	1994-1997	IBF
Steve Collins*	Ireland	1995-1997	WBO
Thulani Malinga	S Africa	1996	WBC
Vincenzo Nardiello	Italy	1996	WBC
Robin Reid	England	1996-1997	WBC
Charles Brewer	USA	1997-1998	IBF
Joe Calzaghe*	Wales	1997-2006	WBO
Thulani Malinga	S Africa	1997-1998	WBC
Richie Woodhall	England	1998-1999	WBC
Sven Ottke*	Germany	1998-2003	IBF
Byron Mitchell	USA	1999-2000	WBA
Markus Beyer	Germany	1999-2000	WBC
Bruno Girard	France	2000-2001	WBA
Glenn Catley	England	2000	WBC
Dingaan Thobela	S Africa	2000	WBC
Dave Hilton	Canada	2000-2001	WBC
Byron Mitchell	USA	2001-2003	WBA
Eric Lucas	Canada	2001-2003	WBC
Sven Ottke*	Germany	2003-2004	IBF/WBA
Markus Beyer	Germany	2003-2004	WBC
Anthony Mundine	Australia	2004	WBA
Manny Sica	Puerto Rico	2004	WBA
Cristian Sanavia	Italy	2004	WBC
Jeff Lacy	USA	2004-2006	IBF
Markus Beyer	Germany	2004-	WBC
Mikkel Kessler	Denmark	2004-	WBA
Joe Calzaghe	Wales	2006-	WBO/IBF

L. Heavyweight (175 lbs)

Title Holder	Birthplace	Tenure	Status
Jack Root	Austria	1903	
George Gardner	Ireland	1903	
George Gardner	Ireland	1903	USA
Bob Fitzsimmons	England	1903-1905	USA
Jack O'Brien	USA	1905-1911	
Sam Langford	Canada	1911-1913	
Georges Carpentier	France	1913-1920	IBU
Jack Dillon	USA	1914-1916	USA
Battling Levinsky	USA	1916-1920	USA
Georges Carpentier	France	1920-1922	
Battling Siki	Senegal	1922-1923	
Mike McTigue	Ireland	1923-1925	
Paul Berlenbach	USA	1925-1926	
Jack Delaney*	Canada	1926-1927	
Jimmy Slattery	USA	1927	NBA
Tommy Loughran	USA	1927	NY
Tommy Loughran*	USA	1927-1929	
Jimmy Slattery	USA	1930	NY
Maxie Rosenbloom	USA	1930-1931	
Maxie Rosenbloom	USA	1931-1933	NY
George Nichols	USA	1932	NBA
Bob Godwin	USA	1933	NBA
Maxie Rosenbloom	USA	1933-1934	
Maxie Rosenbloom	USA	1934	NY
Joe Knight	USA	1934-1935	FL/NC/GEO

Title Holder	Birthplace	Tenure	Status
Bob Olin	USA	1934-1935	NY
Al McCoy	Canada	1935	CAN
Bob Olin	USA	1935	NY/NBA
John Henry Lewis	USA	1935-1938	NY/NBA
Gustav Roth	Belgium	1936-1938	IBU
Ad Heuser	Germany	1938	IBU
John Henry Lewis	USA	1938	
John Henry Lewis	USA	1938-1939	NBA
Melio Bettina	USA	1939	NY
Len Harvey	England	1939-1942	GB
Billy Conn	USA	1939-1940	NY/NBA
Anton Christoforidis	Greece	1941	NBA
Gus Lesnevich	USA	1941	NBA
Gus Lesnevich	USA	1941-1946	NY/NBA
Freddie Mills	England	1942-1946	GB
Gus Lesnevich	USA	1946-1948	
Freddie Mills	England	1948-1950	
Joey Maxim	USA	1950-1952	
Archie Moore	USA	1952-1960	
Archie Moore	USA	1960-1962	NY/EBU
Harold Johnson	USA	1961-1962	NBA
Harold Johnson	USA	1962-1963	
Willie Pastrano	USA	1963	
Willie Pastrano*	USA	1963-1964	WBA/WBC
Eddie Cotton	USA	1963-1964	MICH
Willie Pastrano	USA	1964-1965	
Jose Torres	Puerto Rico	1965-1966	
Dick Tiger	Nigeria	1966-1968	
Bob Foster	USA	1968-1970	
Bob Foster*	USA	1970-1972	WBC
Vicente Rondon	Venezuela	1971-1972	WBA
Bob Foster*	USA	1972-1974	
John Conteh	England	1974-1977	WBC
Victor Galindez	Argentina	1974-1978	WBA
Miguel Cuello	Argentina	1977-1978	WBC
Mate Parlov	Yugoslavia	1978	WBC
Mike Rossman	USA	1978-1979	WBA
Marvin Johnson	USA	1978-1979	WBC
Victor Galindez	Argentina	1979	WBA
Matt Saad Muhammad	USA	1979-1981	WBC
Marvin Johnson	USA	1979-1980	WBA
Mustafa Muhammad	USA	1980-1981	WBA
Michael Spinks*	USA	1981-1983	WBA
Dwight Muhammad Qawi	USA	1981-1983	WBC
Michael Spinks*	USA	1983-1985	
J. B. Williamson	USA	1985-1986	WBC
Slobodan Kacar	Yugoslavia	1985-1986	IBF
Marvin Johnson	USA	1986-1987	WBA
Dennis Andries	Guyana	1986-1987	WBC
Bobby Czyz	USA	1986-1987	IBF
Thomas Hearns*	USA	1987	WBC
Leslie Stewart	Trinidad	1987	WBA
Virgil Hill	USA	1987-1991	WBA
Charles Williams	USA	1987-1993	IBF
Don Lalonde	Canada	1987-1988	WBC
Sugar Ray Leonard*	USA	1988	WBC
Michael Moorer*	USA	1988-1991	WBO
Dennis Andries	Guyana	1989	WBC
Jeff Harding	Australia	1989-1990	WBC
Dennis Andries	Guyana	1990-1991	WBC
Leonzer Barber	USA	1991-1994	WBO
Thomas Hearns	USA	1991-1992	WBA
Jeff Harding	Australia	1991-1994	WBC
Iran Barkley	USA	1992	WBA
Virgil Hill*	USA	1992-1996	WBA
Henry Maske	Germany	1993-1996	IBF
Mike McCallum	Jamaica	1994-1995	WBC
Dariusz Michalczewski*	Poland	1994-1997	WBO
Fabrice Tiozzo	France	1995-1997	WBC
Virgil Hill	USA	1996-1997	IBF/WBA
Roy Jones	USA	1997	WBC
Montell Griffin	USA	1997	WBC

Title Holder	Birthplace	Tenure	Status
Dariusz Michalczewski*	Poland	1997	WBO/IBF/WBA
Dariusz Michalczewski	Poland	1997-2003	WBO
William Guthrie	USA	1997-1998	IBF
Roy Jones*	USA	1997-1998	WBC
Lou del Valle	USA	1997-1998	WBA
Reggie Johnson	USA	1998-1999	IBF
Roy Jones*	USA	1998-1999	WBC/WBA
Roy Jones*	USA	1999-2002	WBC/WBA/IBF
Roy Jones*	USA	2002-2003	WBA/WBC
Mehdi Sahnoune	France	2003	WBA
Antonio Tarver*	USA	2003	IBF/WBC
Silvio Branco	Italy	2003-2004	WBA
Julio Gonzalez	Mexico	2003-2004	WBO
Antonio Tarver*	USA	2003-2004	WBC
Zsolt Erdei	Hungary	2004-	WBO
Glengoffe Johnson*	Jamaica	2004	IBF
Fabrice Tiozzo	France	2004-	WBA
Clinton Woods	England	2005-	IBF
Tomasz Adamek	Poland	2005-	WBC

Cruiserweight (200 lbs)

Title Holder	Birthplace	Tenure	Status
Marvin Camel	USA	1979-1980	WBC
Carlos de Leon	Puerto Rico	1980-1982	WBC
Ossie Ocasio	Puerto Rico	1982-1984	WBA
S. T. Gordon	USA	1982-1983	WBC
Marvin Camel	USA	1983-1984	IBF
Carlos de Leon	Puerto Rico	1983-1985	WBC
Lee Roy Murphy	USA	1984-1986	IBF
Piet Crous	S Africa	1984-1985	WBA
Alfonso Ratliff	USA	1985	WBC
Dwight Muhammad Qawi	USA	1985-1986	WBA
Bernard Benton	USA	1985-1986	WBC
Carlos de Leon	Puerto Rico	1986-1988	WBC
Evander Holyfield*	USA	1986-1987	WBA
Rickey Parkey	USA	1986-1987	IBF
Evander Holyfield*	USA	1987-1988	WBA/IBF
Evander Holyfield*	USA	1988	
Taoufik Belbouli*	France	1989	WBA
Carlos de Leon	Puerto Rico	1989-1990	WBC
Glenn McCrory	England	1989-1990	IBF
Robert Daniels	USA	1989-1991	WBA
Boone Pultz	USA	1989-1990	WBO
Jeff Lampkin*	USA	1990-1991	IBF
Magne Havnaa*	Norway	1990-1992	WBO
Masimilliano Duran	Italy	1990-1991	WBC
Bobby Czyz	USA	1991-1993	WBA
Anaclet Wamba	Congo	1991-1995	WBC
James Warring	USA	1991-1992	IBF
Tyrone Booze	USA	1992-1993	WBO
Al Cole*	USA	1992-1996	IBF
Marcus Bott	Germany	1993	WBO
Nestor Giovannini	Argentina	1993-1994	WBO
Orlin Norris	USA	1993-1995	WBA
Dariusz Michalczewski*	Poland	1994-1995	WBO
Ralf Rocchigiani	Germany	1995-1997	WBO
Nate Miller	USA	1995-1997	WBA
Marcelo Dominguez	Argentina	1995-1998	WBC
Adolpho Washington	USA	1996-1997	IBF
Uriah Grant	USA	1997	IBF
Carl Thompson	England	1997-1999	WBO
Imamu Mayfield	USA	1997-1998	IBF
Fabrice Tiozzo	France	1997-2000	WBA
Juan Carlos Gomez*	Cuba	1998-2002	WBC
Arthur Williams	USA	1998-1999	IBF
Johnny Nelson	England	1999-	WBO
Vassily Jirov	Kazakhstan	1999-2003	IBF
Virgil Hill	USA	2000-2002	WBA
Jean-Marc Mormeck*	Guadeloupe	2002-2005	WBA
Wayne Braithwaite	Guyana	2002-2005	WBC
James Toney*	USA	2003-2004	IBF
Kelvin Davis	USA	2004-2005	IBF

Jean-Marc Mormeck	Guadaloupe	2005-2006	WBA/WBC
O'Neil Bell*	USA	2005-2006	IBF
O'Neil Bell	USA	2006	IBF/WBA/WBC
O'Neil Bell	USA	2006-	WBA/WBC

Heavyweight (200 lbs+)

John L. Sullivan	USA	1889-1892	USA
Peter Jackson	Australia	1889-1892	
Frank Slavin	Australia	1890-1892	GB/AUST
Peter Jackson	Australia	1892-1893	GB/AUST
James J. Corbett	USA	1892-1894	USA
James J. Corbett	USA	1894-1895	
James J. Corbett	USA	1895-1897	
Peter Maher	Ireland	1895-1896	
Bob Fitzsimmons	England	1896-1897	
Bob Fitzsimmons	England	1897-1899	
James J. Jeffries	USA	1899-1902	
James J. Jeffries	USA	1902-1905	
Denver Ed Martin	USA	1902-1903	
Jack Johnson	USA	1902-1908	
Bob Fitzsimmons	England	1905	
Marvin Hart	USA	1905-1906	
Jack O'Brien	USA	1905-1906	
Tommy Burns	Canada	1906-1908	
Jack Johnson	USA	1908-1909	
Jack Johnson	USA	1909-1915	
Sam Langford	USA	1909-1911	
Sam McVey	USA	1911-1912	
Sam Langford	USA	1912-1914	
Luther McCarty	USA	1913	
Arthur Pelkey	Canada	1913-1914	
Gunboat Smith	USA	1914	
Harry Wills	USA	1914	
Georges Carpentier	France	1914	
Sam Langford	USA	1914-1915	
Jess Willard	USA	1915-1919	
Joe Jeannette	USA	1915	
Sam McVey	USA	1915	
Harry Wills	USA	1915-1916	
Sam Langford	USA	1916-1917	
Bill Tate	USA	1917	
Sam Langford	USA	1917-1918	
Harry Wills	USA	1918-1926	
Jack Dempsey	USA	1919-1926	
Gene Tunney*	USA	1926-1928	
Max Schmeling	Germany	1930-1932	
Jack Sharkey	USA	1932-1933	
Primo Carnera	Italy	1933-1934	
Max Baer	USA	1934-1935	
James J. Braddock	USA	1935	
James J. Braddock	USA	1935-1936	NY/NBA
George Godfrey	USA	1935-1936	IBU
James J. Braddock	USA	1936-1937	
Joe Louis*	USA	1937-1949	
Ezzard Charles	USA	1949-1950	NBA
Lee Savold	USA	1950-1951	GB/EBU
Ezzard Charles	USA	1950-1951	NY/NBA
Joe Louis	USA	1951	GB/EBU
Jersey Joe Walcott	USA	1951	NY/NBA
Jersey Joe Walcott	USA	1951-1952	
Rocky Marciano*	USA	1952-1956	
Floyd Patterson	USA	1956-1959	
Ingemar Johansson	Sweden	1959-1960	
Floyd Patterson	USA	1960-1962	
Sonny Liston	USA	1962-1964	
Muhammad Ali	USA	1964	
Muhammad Ali*	USA	1964-1967	WBC
Ernie Terrell	USA	1965-1967	WBA
Muhammad Ali	USA	1967	
Muhammad Ali	USA	1967-1968	WBC
Joe Frazier*	USA	1968-1970	NY/MASS
Jimmy Ellis	USA	1968-1970	WBA
Joe Frazier	USA	1970-1973	
George Foreman	USA	1973-1974	
Muhammad Ali	USA	1974-1978	
Leon Spinks	USA	1978	
Leon Spinks	USA	1978	WBA
Larry Holmes*	USA	1978-1983	WBC
Muhammad Ali*	USA	1978-1979	WBA
John Tate	USA	1979-1980	WBA
Mike Weaver	USA	1980-1982	WBA
Michael Dokes	USA	1982-1983	WBA
Gerrie Coetzee	S Africa	1983-1984	WBA
Larry Holmes	USA	1983-1985	IBF
Tim Witherspoon	USA	1984	WBC
Pinklon Thomas	USA	1984-1986	WBC
Greg Page	USA	1984-1985	WBA
Tony Tubbs	USA	1985-1986	WBA
Michael Spinks	USA	1985-1987	IBF
Tim Witherspoon	USA	1986	WBA
Trevor Berbick	Jamaica	1986	WBC
Mike Tyson*	USA	1986-1987	WBC
James Smith	USA	1986-1987	WBA
Mike Tyson*	USA	1987	WBA/WBC
Tony Tucker	USA	1987	IBF
Mike Tyson	USA	1987-1989	
Mike Tyson	USA	1989-1990	IBF/WBA/WBC
Francesco Damiani	Italy	1989-1991	WBO
James Douglas	USA	1990	IBF/WBA/WBC
Evander Holyfield	USA	1990-1992	IBF/WBA/WBC
Ray Mercer	USA	1991-1992	WBO
Michael Moorer*	USA	1992-1993	WBO
Riddick Bowe	USA	1992	IBF/WBA/WBC
Riddick Bowe	USA	1992-1993	IBF/WBA
Lennox Lewis	England	1992-1994	WBC
Tommy Morrison	USA	1993	WBO
Michael Bentt	England	1993-1994	WBO
Evander Holyfield	USA	1993-1994	WBA/IBF
Herbie Hide	England	1994-1995	WBO
Michael Moorer	USA	1994	WBA/IBF
Oliver McCall	USA	1994-1995	WBC
George Foreman	USA	1994-1995	WBA/IBF
Riddick Bowe*	USA	1995-1996	WBO
George Foreman*	USA	1995	IBF
Bruce Seldon	USA	1995-1996	WBA
Frank Bruno	England	1995-1996	WBC
Frans Botha	S Africa	1995-1996	IBF
Mike Tyson	USA	1996	WBC
Michael Moorer	USA	1996-1997	IBF
Henry Akinwande*	England	1996-1997	WBO
Mike Tyson	USA	1996	WBA
Evander Holyfield*	USA	1996-1997	WBA
Lennox Lewis*	England	1997-1999	WBC
Herbie Hide	England	1997-1999	WBO
Evander Holyfield	USA	1997-1999	IBF/WBA
Vitali Klitschko	Ukraine	1999-2000	WBO
Lennox Lewis*	England	1999-2000	IBF/WBA/WBC
Chris Byrd	USA	2000	WBO
Lennox Lewis	England	2000-2001	IBF/WBC
Evander Holyfield	USA	2000-2001	WBA
Vladimir Klitschko	Ukraine	2000-2003	WBO
John Ruiz	USA	2001-2003	WBA
Hasim Rahman	USA	2001	WBC/IBF
Lennox Lewis*	England	2001-2002	WBC/IBF
Lennox Lewis*	England	2002-2004	WBC
Chris Byrd	USA	2002-2006	IBF
Roy Jones*	USA	2003	WBA
Corrie Sanders*	S Africa	2003	WBO
Lamon Brewster	USA	2004-2006	WBO
John Ruiz	Puerto Rico	2004-2005	WBA
Vitali Klitschko*	Ukraine	2004-2005	WBC
James Toney	USA	2005	WBA
John Ruiz	Puerto Rico	2005	WBA
Nikolai Valuev	Russia	2005-	WBA
Hasim Rahman	USA	2005-	WBC
Sergei Lyakhovich	Belarus	2006-	WBO
Vladimir Klitschko	Ukraine	2006-	IBF

Highlights from the 2005-2006 Amateur Season

by Chris Kempson

This was a season that truly confirmed the might and strength of amateur boxing at both domestic and international level throughout these islands. At all levels there was much success which augurs well for the coming season and well beyond for that matter.

The reform of the ABA of England Ltd's Board of Directors can only be for the good of our sport and is a welcome step. The departure of Richie Woodhall after only a few months in the post of England's High Performance Manager was disappointing, while the appointment of Paul King as the English ABA's new Chief Executive was welcome news. The innovative move to stage the English ABA finals in December to help pave the way for some of the boxers who were hoping to box in the Commonwealth Games could not be faulted; when viewed against the success achieved by England in Melbourne a few months later.

A special mention must go to the Kirkdale southpaw, Neil Perkins, who became only the third English boxer to win a medal at a World Senior Championship when taking bronze at welterweight. Womens' boxing also made good progress, with Ireland's Katie Taylor and England's Amanda Coulson continuing to be the main standard bearers, and we can expect further successes in the near future from our ladies.

So please join me now as we cruise through the season, taking a close look at all of the action and much more besides. As was the case in 2004-2005, the 2005-2006 season has also been one of the very best in recent years.

JULY

Great news greeted the arrival of the new season. First, the 2012 Olympic Games were awarded to London and second, amateur boxing was confirmed on the programme for those Games. What better incentive than that for aspiring Olympic hopefuls over the intervening years. For the first time since 1948 the Games are coming to these shores, a case for true celebration.

However, all was not sweetness and light on the domestic administrative front as the Directors of the ABA of England Ltd failed to remove themselves at the EGM held in London on 2 July. The 39 members of the ABA of England

Action from the James Fowl v Keith Spong ABA light-flyweight championship fight last season. Fowl (left), from Hoddesdon ABC, avenged a previous defeat when outscoring the Army's Spong to land the title

Les Clark

Ltd's Board of Directors had been asked to remove themselves and make way for a new streamlined Board.

England did the 'double' over Italy on 15 and 17 July respectively. First up in Bari the visitors triumphed 3-2, while in Sequals they got home by two bouts to one, with one draw. At the Liverpool Olympia, on 20 July, England defeated Canada 6-2 in a senior international.

Ireland's lone Athens Olympian, Andy Lee, the hugely talented Limerick southpaw, decided to turn professional. Andy, who will be missed by all those who follow amateur boxing in these Islands, has teamed up with America's legendary trainer and manager, Emanuel Steward, and looks set for a bright future in the paid ring.

The 11th Liverpool multi-nations tournament was staged at the Olympia venue on 25 and 27 July, with the finals taking place on 29 July. It focused on the Four Nations teams, together with boxers from Australia and Canada. Eight invited countries declined to send teams, which meant that just six countries were involved with this prestigious tournament. England netted a superb collection of six gold medals which went to in ascending order : Don Broadhurst (51kgs), Frankie Gavin (60kgs), Nathan Brough (64kgs), Neil Perkins (69kgs), Tony Jeffries (81kgs) and Danny Price (91kgs), who also collected the 'Boxer of the Tournament' award. Ireland's Darren Sutherland took gold at 75kgs. Two international female bouts between England and Italy, which started the action on finals night, ended with a victory to each country.

AUGUST

Shock news broke that former WBC super-middleweight champion, Richie Woodhall, had quit as England's High Performance Manager, having only been in the post since April 2005. Coaching issues appeared to be an important ingredient in Woodhall's decision. The amateur code can ill afford to lose the services of men like Woodhall, but it has and the 'dream job' for the well respected Midlander is over.

The European Junior (under-19) Championships took place in Tallinn, Estonia, from 29 July to 6 August and Irish lightweight (60kgs), Jonjo Joyce, was the only Four Nations boxer to get a medal, in his case a bronze. It is worth noting that in these championships no fewer than 88 bouts out of 175 (this represents 50.2%) ended on the outscored rule (20 points). This situation caused quite a stir among some nations and there were some who suggested that 'cheating' was being perpetrated by Eastern Bloc countries. In no way did these championships enhance the reputation of amateur boxing, either in Europe or beyond for that matter.

Glasgow's famous Kelvin Hall was the setting for the fourth Commonwealth Federation Championships from 15-20 August. The home countries did extremely well here, England capturing three golds and Wales one. England also secured two silvers and Scotland one. The gold standard for England was reached by Frankie Gavin (60kgs), James Degale (75kgs) and David Dolan (91kgs), while Mo Nasir at 48kgs was triumphant for Wales. England's

Fox's Anthony Crolla (left) celebrates his ABA lightweight title win last season with the loser, Chris Pacy (Army)   Les Clark

silvers went to Stephen Smith (57kgs) and Tony Jeffries (81kgs), with Scotland's Steve Simmons (91kgs) also gaining silver. Scotland captured five bronze medals, Northern Ireland three and England one, to complete the final medal tally.

On 27 August at an EGM the ABAE (32-2) voted to modernise itself, with five directors forming the boxing side of the Board and three directors coming from the business/commercial world. Jim Smart remained as chairman.

SEPTEMBER

In a magnificent effort, Ireland won four bronze and one silver medal at the European Schoolboy Championships in Tver, Russia from 30 August - 4 September. The silver went to Dungarvan's Darragh Power (52kgs), while bronzes were collected by Athy's David Joe Joyce (48kgs), his cousin David Joyce from Dealgan at 56kgs, Bernard Roe (Docklands') at 59kgs and Belfast's Thomas McCarthy (Oliver Plunkett) at 68kgs.

Ireland also excelled at the eighth Umakhanov multi-nations in Makhachkala, Russia from 6-12 September, picking up a gold and a silver medal. Silver was won by Neilstown's Kenneth Egan (81kgs), while his fellow Dubliner, St Saviour's Darren Sutherland (75kgs), brought back a superb gold strike.

Scottish heavyweight (91kgs) Steve Simmons secured gold at the Nationen Cup in Wiener Neustadt, Austria from 22-25 September. Scotland's welterweight (69kgs) Edward Finney lost in his semi-final, but then got a walkover against the other losing semi-finalist in a box-off for third and fourth place.

On 30 September, England made an impressive start to their international season with nine victories from 12 bouts against a combined Italy/Denmark team at the Crowtree Leisure Centre in Sunderland. Our women triumphed 3-0 (beating two Italians and a Dane), while our men 'bested' Italy 4-3 and Denmark 2-0. Also on 30 September, at the National Stadium in Dublin, Ireland came out on top against French and German opposition in a junior round-robin tournament, ultimately winning five gold, four silver and two bronze medals.

Liverpool's Paul King became the inspired choice as the English ABA's new Chief Executive.

OCTOBER

On 1 and 2 October the Welsh ABA, in conjunction with the Sports Council for Wales, held its first female squad training at the Sophia Gardens in Cardiff.

Once again Ireland were on the gold standard, this time in a multi-nations tournament in Tirana, Albania from 1-6 October. Four golds were the Emerald Isles's impressive medal tally, with Baldoyle's Conor Ahern (51kgs) and Eric Donovan, St Michael's, Athy (57kgs) and Dublin's Darren Sutherland (75kgs) and Kenneth Egan (81kgs), who had outpointed Scotland's Kenneth Anderson in their semi-final, all triumphant.

Team results saw Ireland go down 4-2 to a combined USA/Italy team in Cleveland, Ohio on 6 October, Scotland

'edge out' Wales 6-5 in a Cadet (Under-17) international at the Town Hall in Port Glasgow a day later and Ireland taking part in a mixed male/female squad to Canada from 12-17 October, where the hosts triumphed 6-4 over two encounters.

The city of Liverpool proudly hosted the World Cadets Championships, 10-18 October, and what a tremendously successful tournament it proved to be for the English representatives. This was the first time that a World Championship in amateur boxing had been held in England. The finals were staged at St George's Hall and England secured its first global Cadet gold medals via Birmingham City's Khalid Saeed (48kgs) and Lowestoft's Anthony Agogo (70kgs). A silver medal went to Headland's Michael Hadfield (46 kgs) and a bronze for Fisher's Obed Mbwakongo (80kgs). This was our best World Cadets medal tally so far and it promises many good things to come in the future for these fine young boxers. Saeed boxed three times for his golden triumph, with Agogo having four bouts to land his golden prize. Over 260 boxers from five continents took part in Liverpool and it is a championship which will remain long in the memory of amateur boxing fans in this country.

There were medals too in abundance at the annual Tammer multi-nations tournament in Tampere, Finland from 20-23 October. Welsh light-flyweight Mo Nasir (48kgs) from St Joseph's, Newport, Irish featherweight Eric Donovan (57kgs), and Scotland's Kenneth Anderson (81kgs) all struck gold. Silvers were brought back by Ireland's Conor Ahern (51kgs) and Roy Sheahan (69kgs), and the Scottish pair of Mark Hastie (64kgs) and Steve Simmons (91kgs). There were also two bronze medals for good measure, which went to Scotland's Gary McArthur (60 kgs) and Kevin Evans from Wales at 91kgs.

The Irish Under-21 Championships saw the finals take place at the National Stadium in Dublin on 28 October, earlier rounds having taken place on 21 and 22 October.

NOVEMBER

Kirkdale southpaw, Neil Perkins, became only the third English boxer to win a medal at a World Senior Championship when he took welterweight (69kgs) bronze in Mianyang City, Peoples Republic of China from 13-20 November. Perkins won three bouts, losing eventually in his semi-final to Nurudinov (Belarus) by 33-21. The Belarus boxer then lost in the final to Cuba's Erislandi Lara. Ireland and Wales returned home without a medal.

Ireland staged a multi-nations tournament at the Tintean Theatre in Ballybunion, County Kerry, from 22-25 November. Russia finished as the top nation, while Ireland - as hosts were allowed to field more than one boxer in some divisions - won three golds, two silver and seven bronze. Scotland won a gold and two bronze, while Wales won four silver and a similar number of bronze.

England won convincingly 10-5 over Ireland in their annual Schoolboy international, which was held at the Hotel Elizabeth in Ipswich on 25 November.

The annual England and USA duel took place on the Habad charity dinner show at London's Metropole Hilton

Hotel on 28 November and saw England triumph 4-2 to maintain a good run against the men from 'across the pond'.

DECEMBER

The Ulster senior finals were held at the Ulster Hall on 1 December.

On 2 December, the 117th ABA finals were boxed off at Wembley's Conference Centre. The annual Championships had been advanced this season to help pave the way for some of the boxers who were hoping to box in the Commonwealth Games that were due to be held in Australia from 15 -26 March 2006. Six of the 11 finals went to the North-West Counties, four to the West Lancs Division and two to the East. Winning their third ABA titles were Nick McDonald (54kgs) and Tony Bellew (91kgs), while Sunderland's Tony Jeffries (81kgs) and Finchley's Derek Chisora (91+kgs), both appearing in a final for the first time, came up trumps and Dale Youth's James Degale retained his middleweight crown (75kgs). The curtain raiser' to the finals saw two English women defeat their French counterparts in a pair of 3x2s.

England named their Commonwealth Games team on 7 December and what a successful squad it subsequently proved to be.

December is the traditional month when the NACYP finals are concluded and so it proved once again. The Class 'C' finals took place on 13 December at the Royal Lancaster Hotel in central London, the Class 'B' finals went to the Festival Hall at Kirkby in Ashfield, Nottinghamshire on 13 December, with the Class 'A' finals being hosted at the Adelphi Hotel in Liverpool on 16 December. Kettering School of Boxing's Michael Maguire, in notching-up his sixth national title, was the main feature.

In Dublin, the finals of the Irish Intermediate Championships took place on 16 December at the National Stadium, earlier rounds having been boxed-off on 2,3 and 9 December.

The finals of the national Golden Belt Championship for schoolboys with no more than ten bouts at the time of entry, took place at the Everton Park Sports Centre in Liverpool on 17 December.

JANUARY

In the New Year's Honours List there was an MBE for the legendary junior coach, George Bowers, who trained over 150 national junior champions in a long and distinguished training career with a number of clubs in the east-end of London. It is unlikely that Bowers' record will ever be equalled, let alone bettered. West Ham ABC's own legendary junior trainer, Mickey May, currently has over 100 national junior champions to his credit; although the Bowers' record still looks to be very safe.

Jamie Cox (right) of Walcot ABC showed his class when beating Stowe's Eddie Corcoran to take the ABA light-welter title in last season's championships

Les Clark

The first international of the New Year on 7 January saw Denmark defeat Scotland 5-4 at Bowhill, Fife.

It was determind by the ABAELtd's Board of Directors that the development of female boxing should rest in the hands of The Police and Community Boxing Association.

The Irish National Senior finals were staged at Dublin's National Stadium on 27 January, earlier rounds having been contested on 13,14, 20 and 21 January.

Scotland did especially well in the Norway Box Cup, held in Oslo from 27-29 January, landing five medals. Kenneth Anderson landed gold at 81kgs, while there were silvers for Craig McEwan (75kgs) and Kris Carslaw (69kgs) and bronze for Sam Scott (91+kgs) and Mark Hastie (64kgs). In the Womens' part of this tournament, Ireland's Katie Taylor (60kgs) from St Fergals BC, Bray won gold and was also recognised as the 'Best Female Boxer', while her team colleague, Eastwood's Alanna Murphy (63kgs) picked up a bronze. For Wales, Lynsey Holdaway (54kgs) also secured a bronze.

FEBRUARY

Ireland came out on top in the annual Four Nations Senior tournament, with no fewer than seven golds and three silver at the National Stadium in Dublin on 3 and 4 February. Wales bagged second place with two golds and three silvers, Scotland finished in third spot with one gold and three silvers and England were in last place with one gold and two silvers. England also landed five bronze, Scotland four and Wales one. This was a vintage display by the Irish boxers and augured well for the remainder of their year.

England engaged in two cadet/junior internationals against France, winning the first 6-2 at the Waveney Sports and Leisure Centre in Lowestoft on 15 February; before losing 4-3 at the Aldworth Science College in Basingstoke two days later.

At senior level, England performed very well at the Strandja multi-nations in Pleven, Bulgaria from 16-19 February. Darran Langley (48kgs) won gold, silvers went to Don Broadhurst (51kgs), Neil Perkins (69kgs) and Tony Jeffries (81kgs), while bronze medals were captured by Daniel Price (91kgs) and David Price (91+kgs). England finished a very creditable third (ranking on points) in the medal table of 12 nations, only being 'bested' by the home nation and the powerful Uzbekistan team.

Ireland won two silvers at the Stanislav Sorokin Memorial multi-nations junior tournament in Noginsk, Russia from 15-19 February. Steven Donnelly (All Saints, Belfast), at 48kgs, and Eamonn Corbett (Sacred Heart, Belfast), at 75kgs, took the honours for the Emerald Isle.

MARCH

In March, all roads led 'Down Under' to Melbourne in Australia and to the Exhibition Centre (17-25 March) for the Commonwealth Games and what a triumphant time it proved to be for England, with five gold, one silver and two bronze putting them top of the medal table. Scotland secured one gold medal, while Wales notched up one silver

and three bronze. Only Northern Ireland of the home nations - for the second time in a row - failed to win a medal. The English medal tally went like this: Don Broadhurst (51kgs) gold, Stephen Smith (57kgs) gold, Frankie Gavin (60kgs) gold, Jamie Cox (64kgs) gold and David Price (91+kgs) also gold; silver was claimed by Darran Langley (48kgs) and the two bronzes went to Neil Perkins (69kgs) and James Degale (75kgs). Scotland's Kenneth Anderson (81kgs) landed a gold medal, their first since Alex Arthur, at featherweight, in 1998. Anderson became the first Scot to land a Commonwealth gold at light-heavyweight. Wales too had a good 'Games' with a silver from Kevin Evans (91+kgs) and three bronzes via the fists of Mo Nasir (48kgs), Darren Edwards (57kgs) and Jamie Crees (64kgs).

Triple ABA heavyweight champion, Tony Bellew, secured silver at the eighth Jose Cheo Aponte multi-nations in Caguas, Puerto Rico from 22-26 March and was only deprived of gold when a hotly disputed decision in the final went in favour of Brazil's Rafael Lima 22-21.

The Scottish Senior Championships were held at the Ingliston Arena in Edinburgh on 24 March, while 'down south' the Golden Gloves finals took place at the Knottingley Leisure Centre in West Yorkshire on 25 and 26 March. Repton, the east-London based outfit from Bethnal Green, netted five champions, a record for this recently re-vamped national competition. Much credit here goes to Kelvin Wing (senior), Repton's junior team supremo.

On 25 and 26 March, the Scottish Cadets and Schoolboy Championships were staged. Although a couple of finals took place at Ingliston on 25 March, many semis and almost all the finals were held over for 24 hours and boxed off at the Edinburgh Gilmerton gymnasium.

APRIL

Ireland had a very fruitful time at the GeeBee multi-nations tournament in Helsinki, Finland from 6-10 April, claiming one gold, one silver and four bronze medals. The medallists were as follows: Kilkenny light-heavyweight Darren O'Neill (Paulstown BC) struck gold and also received the award for the 'Best Technical Boxer', while the Belfast flyweight, Carl Frampton (Midland White City BC), got silver and the Kildare quartet of David Oliver Joyce (bantam), his cousin Jonjo Joyce (light-welter), Eric Donovan (feather) and Roy Sheahan (welter), all from St Michael's BC in Athy, won bronze.

England entertained Ireland on 27 April in a senior international at the Brent Town Hall in north-west London, with the match ending in a 4-4 draw.

Irish light-heavyweight, Kenneth Egan (Neilstown BC) was in fine form when taking silver at the 'Chemiepokal' (Chemical Cup) in Halle, Germany from 26-30 April.

The Four Nations Schoolboys tournament, held at the Willow's High School in Cardiff on 28 and 29 April, saw the English team came out on top with six of the 14 gold medals. Ireland and Wales each picked up four golds, while Scotland took one silver.

MAY

The Welsh ABA Cadet and Youth finals were staged on 1 May at the Baglan Social Club, Port Talbot and on 3 May at the Electricity Club in Cardiff.

England undertook a second international with Ireland, which was staged at the Olympia (Liverpool) on 1 May with the host nation winning 5-3 on this occasion.

At the Ahmet Comert multi-nations tournament for women in Istanbul, Turkey from 2-7 May, Lynsey Holdaway from Wales took bronze at 52kgs.

The Junior ABA finals were boxed-off at the Barnsley Metrodome on 6 May.

There were two gold medals for England's women in the Maj Box Cup in Stockholm on 6 and 7 May. London's Laura Saperstein (60kgs) triumphed in the Senior Open Division, while Amanda Coulson (63kgs) came home as a winner in the Senior Open Division. Coulson shared the 'Best Senior Boxer' honour with Finland's Mariit Teuronen.

Ireland drew 4-4 in a senior international with Russia at the National Stadium in Dublin on 12 May, with Katie Taylor (60kgs) winning the sole womens' bout for the host country.

The Welsh ABA Senior Championships ended on 12 May with finals night at the Newport Leisure Centre.

In Scotland, the Four Nations Cadets tournament (15-16 year olds) was held at Greenock Sports Centre on 19 and 20 May. England triumphed in fine style when 'notching' up 16 gold medals, four silvers and four bronzes. Their nearest rivals were Ireland, who secured six gold medals.

England secured a fine bag of six medals at the junior multi-nations in Mostar, Bosnia-Herzegovina from 17-21 May. The very talented middleweight from Dale Youth, George Groves, won gold and also collected the 'Best Technical Boxer' award in the tournament, while the Earlsfield light-welterweight, Bradley Skeete, also won gold, as did Fisher's Obed Mbwakongo, at light-heavyweight. Headland flyweight, Michael Hadfield, won silver and there were bronze medals for Triple A's Anthony Agogo and Luke Campbell from St Pauls, Hull.

By beating Russia 7-3 at the York Hall in east London on 19 May and following it up with a 5-3 success at the Liverpool Olympia on 22 May, England performed a rare double over their rivals. Not wishing to take any of the 'cream' away from these two victories, it has to be said that many of the boxers from the Russian Federation teams were not their country's first choices.

At junior level, England's youngsters secured two medals at the European Union Championships in Pecs, Hungary from 22-28 May. Boarshaw bantamweight, Joe Murray, won silver, while Repton's Ryan Pickard took a bronze medal in the welterweight class.

Knottingley Leisure Centre was once again the venue for the National Novices finals, which were held on 27 May. On the same day, 'north of the border', the Scottish Womens' Championships and the Scottish Junior Championships were held at the Muggiemoss Club in Aberdeen.

On 27 May, the Irish Under-19 Championship finals took place at the National Stadium in Dublin, earlier rounds having been boxed-off on 12, 20 and 26 May.

JUNE

The Scottish Junior Championships were finally concluded at the Muggiemoss Club in Aberdeen on 3 June.

There was a fine medal tally for both England and Ireland in the European Union Junior (under-19) Championships in Rome from 6-11 June. Staged at the same time, but in Porto Torres, Italy, was the inaugural European Union Womens' Championships, where Amanda Coulson (Hartlepool Catholic Boxing & Community Police Club) won silver in the 63kgs division. Ireland's Alanna Murphy collected a bronze after falling victim to Coulson in the semi-finals.

In Rome, it was George Groves (Dale Youth) who was on the gold standard once more at middleweight. Further successes were achieved by Anthony Agogo (silver) at welterweight and Obed Mbwakongo with a bronze at light-heavyweight. Ireland got silver via Ryan Lindberg at bantamweight; while John Murray (featherweight) and Jonjo Joyce (lightweight) went home to the 'Emerald Isle' with bronze medals.

On 9 June, Wales saved the day, or rather the evening, for Scotland when the Bahamas pulled out at very short notice from their international match at Pettycut Bay, Kinghorn. The Scots triumphed 6-2, but all credit to the Welsh boys who helped to avoid a potentially embarrassing situation.

Tirana, Albania was the home for the European Cadet (under-17) Championships, held from 12-18 June, with only Ireland and Scotland sending teams from the four nations. Ireland's Jonjo Joyce came home with a bronze medal at 48kgs.

The ABAE Senior Women's Championships took place at the Hendon Police Training College on 17 June and the England representative from Leeds, Nicola Adams (Sharkey's), won her third title when outpointing Stevenage's Leah Flintham in the Class 'C' 54 kgs final.

Shortly before the end of the season, the Four Nations Junior tournament was held at Liverpool Olympia on 23 and 24 June. England topped the gold medal table with nine final victories, closely followed by Ireland on seven, excluding Joe Larmour the sole entrant at 91kgs in Class 'B'. Wales secured three golds, leaving Scotland as the only home nation not to get on the gold standard.

Well our journey through 2005-2006 is now over, but the new season will soon be upon us and will be one we can look forward to with real anticipation, expectation and hopefully much continued success from our many talented boxers. The European Senior Championships will have taken place by the time you pick up the Yearbook; but our ultimate goal must be, in time, to find a worthy successor to the likes of Audley Harrison and Amir Khan. It would be nice to secure several places at the Beijing Olympics of 2008 and this is the kind of objective our boxers must strive for. Here's hoping that next season will help to bring us a step closer to this aim.

ABA National Championships, 2005-2006

Note: Only men who fought at some stage of the competition are actually included.

Combined Services

RAF Camp, Uxbridge – 27 October

L.Fly: *final:* K.Spong (Army) wo. **Fly:** *final:* R.Burkinshaw (Army) wo. **Bantam:** *final:* A.Boyle (RN) w pts J.Bream (Army). **Feather:** *final:* A.Urrutia (RN) w pts J.Allen (Army). **Light:** *final:* C.Pacy (Army) wo. **L.Welter:** *semi-finals:* M.Stead (Army) wo, J.Brown (RN) w pts T.Carroll (RAF); *final:* M.Stead w rsc 2 J.Brown. **Welter:** *final:* B.Flournoy (Army) w pts A.Hunter (RN). **Middle:** *final:* S.Briggs (Army) w pts S.Tighe (RN). **L.Heavy:** *final:* S.McDonald (RN) w pts J.Whitfield (Army). **Heavy:** *final:* M.O'Connell (RN) w pts C.Dilks (Army). **S.Heavy:** *final:* S.Scott (RN) w pts J.Tuiauta (Army).

Eastern Counties

Semi-Finals & Finals   Hilton Hotel, Norwich – 14 October

L.Fly: no entries. **Fly:** *final:* R.Walsh (Kingfisher) wo. **Bantam:** *final:* L.Walsh (Kingfisher) wo. **Feather:** *final:* M.Poston (Harwich) w pts M.Romani (St Ives). **Light:** no entries. **L.Welter:** *final:* K.Allen (Eastgate) wo. **Welter:** *final:* P.McAleese (Haddenham) w rsc 2 M.Flowers (Ferry Street). **Middle:** *final:* W.Bayliss (New Astley) w pts J.Cullinane (Southend). **L.Heavy:** *semi-finals:* H.Seaman (Castle) wo, M.Redhead (Kingfisher) w pts P.Wright (Chatteris); *final:* M.Redhead w pts H.Seaman. **Heavy:** no entries. **S.Heavy:** no entries.

Home Counties v Midland Counties

Home Counties
The Club Gym, St Albans – 22 October

L.Fly: J.Fowl (Hoddesdon) wo. **Fly:** no entries. **Bantam:** no entries. **Feather:** *semi-finals:* I.Bailey (Slough) wo, C.Smith (Stevenage) w pts L.Lewis (Wolvercote); *final:* I.Bailey w pts C.Smith. **Light:** *semi-finals:* L.Shinkwin (Bushey) wo, D.Phillips (Luton Shamrock) w pts A.Lever (Bedford); *final:* L.Shinkwin w pts D.Phillips. **L.Welter:** *semi-finals:* M.McCullough (Chalfont) w pts B.Doherty (Hoddesdon), P.Steadman (Wolvercote) w pts B.Crotty (Cheshunt); *final:* M.McCullough w P.Steadman. **Welter:** *final:* P.Mullins (Wolvercote) w pts L.Hughes (Cheshunt). **Middle:** *final:* S.Mullins (Wolvercote) wo. **L.Heavy:** *final:* A.Dennis (Luton Shamrock) w pts L.Howkins (Pinewood Starr). **Heavy:** *final:* K.Earley (Cheshunt) wo. **S.Heavy:** *final:* C.Goldhawk (Cheshunt) wo.

Midland Counties
Northern Zone   The Liberal Club, Bedworth – 22 October, Standard Triumph Social Club, Coventry – 30 October & Newdigate Social Club, Bedworth – 5 November

L.Fly: no entries. **Fly:** *semi-finals:* J.Mulhern (Triumph) wo, U.Ahmed (Merlin Youth) w rsc 3 A.Pope (Wellingborough); *final:* U.Ahmed w pts J.Mulhern. **Bantam:** *final:* I.Ali (One Nation) w pts A.Brennan (Triumph). **Feather:** *final:* J.Spring (Tery Allen

Unique) wo. **Light:** no entries. **L.Welter:** *semi-finals:* J.Flinn (Triumph) wo, J.Spence (Kingsthorpe) w pts N.McQuade (Kettering SoB); *final:* J.Flinn w pts J.Spence. **Welter:** *semi-finals:* L.Morris (Phoenix) w pts S.McKervey (Bulkington), A.Lowe (Newark) w pts D.Watson (Boston); *final:* L.Morris w pts A.Lowe. **Middle:** *quarter-finals:* C.Johnson (Terry Allen Unique) wo, D.Davis (Trinity) wo, J.Easy (Huthwaite) w pts A.Blackett (Grimsby SoB), L.Anthony (Chadd) w pts J.Hockenhull (Belgrave); *semi-finals:* C.Johnson w pts D.Davis, L.Anthony wo J.Easy; *final:* C.Johnson w pts L.Anthony. **L.Heavy:** *semi-finals:* D.Ward (Belgrave) wo, V.Petkovic (One Nation) w pts E.Dube (Merlin Youth); *final:* V.Petkovic w pts D.Ward. **Heavy:** *final:* L.Robinson (Trinity) wo. **S.Heavy:** no entries.

Southern Zone   Lord Hill Hotel, Shrewsbury – 1 November

L.Fly: no entries. **Fly:** *final:* B.Lewis (Wolverhampton) wo. **Bantam:** no entries. **Feather:** no entries. **Light:** no entries. **L.Welter:** *final:* C.Truman (Aston) wo. **Welter:** *final:* L.Hawkins (Birmingham City) w pts J.Jeavons (Aston). **Middle:** *final:* S.Horton (Lions) w pts B.Murphy (Aston). **L.Heavy:** no entries. **Heavy:** *final:* E.Clayton (Donington) wo. **S.Heavy:** no entries.

Midland Counties Finals   Newdigate Social Club, Bedworth – 5 November

L.Fly: no entries. **Fly:** U.Ahmed (Merlin Youth) w rsc 3 B.Lewis (Wolverhampton). **Bantam:** I.Ali (One Nation) wo. **Feather:** J.Spring (Terry Allen Unique) wo. **Light:** no entries. **L.Welter:** J.Flinn (Triumph) w pts C.Truman (Aston). **Welter:** L.Morris (Phoenix) w rsc 4 L.Hawkins (Birmingham City). **Middle:** C.Johnson (Terry Allen Unique) w pts S.Horton (Lions). **L.Heavy:** V.Petkovic (One Nation) wo. **Heavy:** E.Clayton (Donington) w pts L.Robinson (Trinity). **S.Heavy:** no entries.

Home Counties v Midland Counties   Grundy Park Leisure Centre, Cheshunt – 11 November

L.Fly: J.Fowl (Hoddesdon) wo. **Fly:** U.Ahmed (Merlin Youth) wo. **Bantam:** I.Ali (One Nation) wo. **Feather:** I.Bailey (Slough) w pts J.Spring (Terry Allen Unique). **Light:** L.Shinkwin (Bushey) wo. **L.Welter:** J.Flinn (Triumph) w pts M.McCullough (Chalfont). **Welter:** L.Morris (Phoenix) w pts P.Mullins (Wolvercote). **Middleweight:** C.Johnson (Terry Allen Unique) w pts S.Mullins (Wolvercote). **L.Heavy:** A.Dennis (Luton Shamrock) w pts P.Petkovic (One Nation). **Heavy:** K.Earley (Cheshunt) w rsc 3 E.Clayton (Donnington). **S.Heavy:** C.Goldhawk (Cheshunt) wo.

London

North-East Division   York Hall, Bethnal Green – 27 October

L.Fly: no entries. **Bantam:** no entries. **Feather:** *final:* V.Mitchell (West Ham) w rsc 3 A.Nabizaden (Repton). **Light:** *final:* T.Mills (Repton) w pts B.Dodd (Hornchurch & Elm Park). **L.Welter:** *final:* N.Weise (West Ham) w pts M.Idress (Repton). **Welter:** *final:* L.Calvert (Dagenham) w pts D.Herdman (Repton). **Middle:** *semi-finals:* E.Matthews (Repton) w pts M.Wallace (Peacock), E.Monteith (West Ham) w pts J.Bishop (Dagenham); *final:* E.Matthews w rtd 2 E.Monteith. **L.Heavy:** *semi-finals:* D.Orwell (Dagenham) w pts M.Fante (Peacock), D.Lewis (Peacock) w pts M.Yousaf (Dagenham); *final:* D.Orwell w pts D.Lewis. **Heavy:** *final:* T.Conquest (Hornchurch & Elm Park) w pts O.Ossai (Repton). **S.Heavy:** *final:* R.McCallum (Broad Street) w rtd 4 R.Newland (Repton).

North-West Division   The Town Hall, Brent – 20 October
L.Fly: no entries. **Fly:** no entries. **Bantam:** *final:* J.Jaworski (Haringey Police) wo. **Feather:** *final:* F.Kamara (Haringey Police) wo. **Light:** *semi-finals:* B.Puddles (Dale Youth) wo, M.Sazish (Hanwell) w pts P.Liggins (Trojan); *final:* M.Sazish w pts B.Puddles. **L.Welter:** *final:* E.Corcoran (Stowe) w pts R.Ross (Haringey Police). **Welter:** *final:* O.Ekundayo (Camden Kronk) wo. **Middle:** *semi-finals:* S.O'Donnell (Dale Youth) wo, J.Degale (Dale Youth) w rsc 2 I.Malik (Hayes); *final:* J.Degale w pts S.O'Donnell. **L.Heavy:** *semi-finals:* J.Smyth (Finchley) wo, T.Salem (Camden Kronk) w pts D.Mohseni (All Stars); *final:* T.Salem w rsc 3 J.Smyth. **Heavy:** *final:* J.McDermott (Dale Youth) w pts N.Silkinas (All Stars). **S.Heavy:** *semi-finals:* E.Jegeni (Haringey Police) wo, D.Chisora (Finchley) w pts A.Al-Sady (All Stars); *final:* D.Chisora w pts E.Jegeni

South-East Division   National Sports Centre, Crystal Palace – 13 October
L.Fly: no entries. **Fly:** *final:* S.Langley (Hollington) w pts T.Ajagbe (Fitzroy Lodge). **Bantam:** *final:* M.Casey (Fisher) w rsc 4 C.Brahmbhatt (Bexley). **Feather:** *final:* A.Bhatia (Eltham) wo. **Light:** no entries. **L.Welter:** *semi-finals:* D.Davis (Fitzroy Lodge) wo, A.Ideh (Honor Oak) w pts D.Byrnes (Lynn); *final:* D.Davis w pts A.Ideh. **Welter:** *semi-finals:* J.Coyle (Fisher) wo, M.Welsh (Fitzroy Lodge) w pts G.Gardiner (New Addington); *final:* M.Welsh w pts J.Coyle. **Middle:** no entries. **L.Heavy:** *final:* I.Ssenyange (New Addington) wo. **Heavy:** *semi-finals:* J.Sawicki (St Peter's) wo, M.O.McDonagh (Hollington) w pts L.Williams (Fitzroy Lodge); *final:* M.O.McDonagh w rtd 3 J.Sawicki. **S.Heavy:** *final:* D.Akinlade (Fitzroy Lodge) wo.

South-West Division   The Town Hall, Brent – 20 October
L.Fly: no entries. **Fly:** no entries. **Bantam:** no entries. **Feather:** no entries. **Light:** no entries. **L.Welter:** no entries. **Welter:** *final:* L.McCain (Earlsfield) wo. **Middle:** *final:* S.Barr (Kingston) wo. **L.Heavy:** no entries. **Heavy:** *final:* A.Stables (Earlsfield) wo. **S.Heavy:** no entries.

London Semi-Finals & Finals   The Town Hall, Brent – 10 November
L.Fly: no entries. **Fly:** *final:* S.Langley (Hollington) wo. **Bantam:** *final:* M.Casey (Fisher) w pts J.Jaworski (Haringey Police). **Feather:** *semi-finals:* A.Bhatie (Eltham) wo, V.Mitchell (West Ham) w pts F.Kamara (Haringey Police); *final:* A.Bhatia w rsc 1 V.Mitchell. **Light:** *final:* T.Mills (Repton) w pts M.Sazish (Hanwell). **L.Welter:** *semi-finals:* E.Corcoran (Stowe) wo, N.Weise (West Ham) w pts D.Davis (Fitzroy Lodge); *final:* E.Corcoran w pts N.Weise. **Welter:** *semi-finals:* O.Ekundayo (Camden Kronk) wo, M.Welsh (Fitzroy Lodge) w pts L.McCain (Earlsfield); *final:* M.Welsh w pts O.Ekundayo. **Middle:** *semi-finals:* J.Degale (Dale Youth) wo, O.Matthews (Repton) w rsc 2 S.Barr (Kingston); *final:* J.Degale w pts E.Matthews. **L.Heavy:** *semi-finals:* D.Lewis (Peacock) wo, T.Salem (Camden Kronk) w pts I.Ssenyange (New Addington); *final:* T.Salem w pts D.Lewis. **Heavy:** *semi-finals:* J.McDermott (Dale Youth) w pts T.Conquest (Hornchurch & Elm Park), M.O.McDonagh (Hollington) w rsc 2 A.Stables (Earlsfield); *final:* J.McDermott w pts M.O.McDonagh. **S.Heavy:** *final:* D.Chisora (Finchley) w pts D.Akinlade (Fitzroy Lodge) – R.McCallum (Broad Street) withdrew.

North-West Counties v Western Counties
North-West Counties
East Lancs & Cheshire Division   Norbreck Castle Hotel – 21 October & The Guildhall, Preston – 31 October
L.Fly: no entries. **Fly:** no entries. **Bantam:** *final:* J.Murray (Boarshaw) wo. **Feather:** *final:* J.Kays (Arrow) wo. **Light:** *quarter-finals:* A.Winterbottom (Oldham Boys) wo, J.Cosgrove (Barton) wo, A.Crolla (Fox) w pts T.Bradford (Paramount); *semi-finals:* A.Winterbottom wo, A.Crolla w pts J.Cosgrove; *final:* A.Crolla w pts A.Winterbottom. **L.Welter:** *semi-finals:* D.Harding (Northside) w pts J.Baillie (Worthington Town), L.Graves (Chorley) w pts A.Horrocks (Middleton Select); *final:* D.Harding w pts L.Graves. **Welter:** *final:* D.Vassell (Fox) wo. **Middle:** *quarter-finals:* C.Bunn (Northside) wo, S.Brown (Kirkham) wo, K.Borucki (Manx) w pts K.Connolly (Collyhurst & Moston), B.Rose (Blackpool & Fylde) w pts M.King (Cleator Moor); *semi-finals:* C.Bunn w pts K.Borucki, B.Rose w pts S.Brown; *final:* B.Rose w pts C.Bunn. **L.Heavy:** *final:* R.Hough (Paramount) wo. **Heavy:** no entries. **S.Heavy:** no entries. Note: Following the last-minute withdrawal of his opponent at the lightweight semi-final stage, A.Winterbottom walked straight into the final where he would meet A.Crolla, who had already boxed twice.

West Lancs & Cheshire Division   Greenbank Academy, Aigburth, Liverpool – 16 October & Olympia, Liverpool – 28 October
L.Fly: no entries. **Fly:** *semi-finals:* A.Bridge (Golden Gloves) w pts G.Shields (Chester), P.Edwards (Salisbury) w pts C.Farrelly (Higherside); *final:* P.Edwards w pts A.Bridge. **Bantam:** *final:* N.McDonald (Vauxhall Motors) wo. **Feather:** *final:* S.Smith (Rotunda) w pts M.Robinson (Tower Hill). **Light:** *semi-finals:* S.Buckley (Chester) wo, S.Jennings (Tower Hill) w pts G.Duff (Stockbridge); *final:* S.Buckley w pts S.Jennings. **L.Welter:** *final:* M.Ungi (Golden Gloves) w pts D.Angus (Salisbury). **Welter:** *semi-finals:* A.Ismael (Salisbury) wo, S.Williams (Avalon) w pts L.Andrews (Croxteth); *final:* A.Ismael w disq 3 S.Williams. **Middle:** *semi-finals:* M.Phillips (Mersey) wo, J.McNally (Rotunda) w rsc 3 W.Pauline (Rotunda); *final:* J.McNally w rsc 3 M.Phillips. **L.Heavy:** *final:* J.Ainscough (Kirkdale) wo. **Heavy:** *final:* T.Bellew (Rotunda) wo. **S.Heavy:** no entries.

North-West Counties Finals   Everton Park Sports Centre, Liverpool – 5 November
L.Fly: no entries. **Fly:** P.Edwards (Salisbury) wo. **Bantam:** N.McDonald (Vauxhall Motors) w pts J.Murray (Boarshaw). **Feather:** S.Smith (Rotunda) w pts J.Kays (Arrow). **Light:** A.Crolla (Fox) w pts S.Buckley (Chester). **L.Welter:** M.Ungi (Golden Gloves) w pts D.Harding (Northside). **Welter:** D.Vassell (Fox) w rsc 4 A.Ismael (Salisbury). **Middle:** J.McNally (Rotunda) w pts B.Rose (Blackpool). **L.Heavy:** J.Ainscough (Kirkdale) w pts R.Hough (Paramount). **Heavy:** T.Bellew (Rotunda) wo. **S.Heavy:** no entries.

Western Counties
Northern Division   Lister Hall, Dursley – 8 October
L.Fly: no entries. **Fly:** *final:* D.Webb (Broad Plain) wo. **Bantam:** no entries. **Feather:** no entries. **Light:** *semi-finals:* D.Stewart (Broad Plain) wo, J.Jameson (Yeovil) w rtd 4 S.Main (Weston super Mare); *final:* D.Stewart w pts J.Jameson. **L.Welter:** *final:* J.Cox (Walcot Boys) wo. **Welter:** *semi-finals:* J.Gardiner (Broad Plain) wo, J.Hicks (Yeovil) w rsc 3 G.Reeves (Cleeve); *final:* J.Gardiner w pts J.Hicks. **Middle:** *final:* C.Woods (Malmesbury & Wolvercote) wo. **L.Heavy:** no entries. **Heavy:** *final:* G.Lee (Synwell) w co 1 S.Campbell (Cleeve). **S.Heavy:** no entries.

Southern Division   Carrick Street Leisure Centre, Exeter – 15 October
L.Fly: no entries. **Fly:** no entries. **Bantam:** no entries. **Feather:** *final:* R.Boyle (Pisces) wo. **Light:** *semi-finals:* B.Murray (Leonis) w co 1 P.Whiffen (Weymouth), B.Zacharkiw (Pilgrims) w pts J.Vannemmenis (Bideford); *final:* B.Murray w rsc 1 B.Zacharkiw. **L.Welter:** no entries. **Welter:** *semi-finals:* D.O'Connor (Devonport Police) w pts A.Coles (Camborne & Redruth), R.Fearnley (Pilgrims) w pts P.Young (Leonis); *final:* D.O'Connor w pts R.Fearnley. **Middle:** no entries. **L.Heavy:** no entries. **Heavy:** *final:* S.Haddon (Dorchester) w pts J.McKechnie (Leonis). **S.Heavy:** *final:* D.Lund (Leonis) wo.

Western Counties Finals   Broad Plain BC, Bristol – 29 October
L.Fly: no entries. **Fly:** D.Webb (Broad Plain) wo. **Bantam:** no entries. **Feather:** R.Boyle (Pisces) wo. **Light:** B.Murray (Leonis) w pts D.Stewart (Broad Plain). **L.Welter:** J.Cox (Walcott Boys) wo. **Welter:** D.O'Connor (Devonport Police) w co 4 J.Gardiner (Broad Plain). **Middle:** C.Woods (Malmesbury & Wolvercote) wo. **L.Heavy:** no entries. **Heavy:** G.Lee (Synwell) w co 4 S.Haddon (Dorchester). **S.Heavy:** D.Lund (Leonis) wo.

North-West Counties v Western Counties   Austin Rawlinson Sports Centre, Speke – 12 November
L.Fly: no entries. **Fly:** P.Edwards (Salisbury) w pts D.Webb (Broad Plain). **Bantam:** N.McDonald (Vauxhall Motors) wo. **Feather:** S.Smith (Rotunda) w pts R.Boyle (Pisces). **Light:** A.Crolla (Fox) w rsc 3 B.Murray (Leonis). **L.Welter:** J.Cox (Walcot Boys) w pts M.Ungi (Golden Gloves). **Welter:** D.Vassell (Fox) w rsc 3 D.O'Connor (Devonport Police). **Middle:** J.McNally (Rotunda) w pts C.Woods (Malmesbury & Wolvercote). **L.Heavy:** J.Ainscough (Kirkdale) wo. **Heavy:** A.Bellew (Rotunda) w rsc 3 G.Lee (Synwell). **S.Heavy:** D.Lund (Leonis) wo.

Southern Counties

Connaught Leisure Centre, Aldershot – 22 October & Effingham Park Hotel, Crawley – 4 November
L.Fly: no entries. **Fly:** no entries. **Bantam:** *final:* R.Smart (Southampton) w pts P.Barney (Lawrence). **Feather:** no entries. **Light:** *semi-finals:* R.Deakin (Crawley) w pts S.Tobias (Woking), B.Jones (Crawley) w pts B.Murphy (Hove); *final:* B.Jones w pts R.Deakin. **L.Welter:** *semi-finals:* A.Leigh (City of Portsmouth), S.Woolford (The Grange) w pts M.Tew (Southampton); *final:* S.Woolford w pts A.Leigh. **Welter:** *quarter-finals:* A.Watson (Crawley) wo, I.Hudson (St Mary's) w pts B.Madgwick (City of Portsmouth), L.Pritchard (St Mary's) w pts V.Woolford (The Grange), D.Smith (St Mary's) w pts D.Maka (Southampton); *semi-finals:* L.Pritchard w pts I.Hudson, A.Watson w pts D.Smith; *final:* L.Pritchard w pts A.Watson. **Middle:** *quarter-finals:* P.Morby (Bognor) wo, L.Kerr (Ryde) wo, T.Hill (Golden Ring) wo, N.Jenman (Adur) w rsc 2 M.Twyman (The Grange); *semi-finals:* P.Morby w pts L.Kerr, T.Hill w pts N.Jenman; *final:* T.Hill w pts P.Morby. **L.Heavy:** *semi-finals:* A.Gibbens (Bognor) w rsc 1 A.Hanover (Westhill), L.Jenman (Adur) w rsc 3 S.James (Crawley); *final:* A.Gibbens w pts L.Jenman. **Heavy:** *final:* D.Reid (City of Portsmouth) wo. **S.Heavy:** *final:* T.Dallas (St Mary's) w rtd 1 J.Swindles (Woking).

Tyne, Tees & Wear

Marton Country Club, Middlesbrough – 24 & 31 October
L.Fly: no entries. **Fly:** no entries. **Bantam:** *final:* S.Hall (Spennymoor) wo. **Feather:** *final:* P.Truscott (South Bank) w pts G.Reay (Spennymoor). **Light:** *final:* C.Dickson (Birtley) w pts A.Railton (Shildon). **L.Welter:** *semi-finals:* B.Saunders (South Durham) w pts R.Wainwright (Lambton Street), S.Kennedy (Sunderland) w pts P.Boyle (Halfpenny); *final:* B.Saunders w pts S.Kennedy. **Welter:** *final:* M.Clauzel (Grainger Park) w pts M.Hogarth (Bishop Auckland). **Middle:** *quarter-finals:* G.Barr (Birtley) wo, S.McCrone Spennymoor) wo, C.Denton (Headland) wo, I.Turnbull (Hylton Castle) w pts T.Grange (Phil Thomas SoB); *semi-finals:* G.Barr w co 2 I.Turnbull, S.McCrone w pts C.Denton; *final:* G.Barr w pts S.McCrone. **L.Heavy:** *final:* T.Jeffries (Sunderland) wo. **Heavy:** *final:* N.Thompson (Wellington) wo. **S.Heavy:** *final:* D.Ferguson (Newcastle East End) wo.

Yorkshire & Humberside

Birdwell Working Mens' Club, Barnsley – 4 November
L.Fly: no entries. **Fly:** *final:* A.Fadile (Unity) wo. **Bantam:** *final:* E.Heagney (Rawthorpe) wo. **Feather:** *final:* G.Sykes (Cleckheaton) wo. **Light:** *semi-finals:* A.Khan (Bateson's) w pts A.Cox (Unity), J.Dyer (Burmantofts) w pts L.Bennett (Parsons Cross); *final:* A.Khan w pts J.Dyer. **L.Welter:** *final:* C.Sebine (Burmantofts) w pts A.Anwar (Bateson's). **Welter:** *final:* T.Coward (Wombwell) w co 2 T.Broadbent (Bateson's). **Middle:** no entries. **L.Heavy:** *final:* P.Clarke (Sharkey's Gym) wo. **Heavy:** *final:* D.Slaney (Conisborough) wo. **S.Heavy:** no entries.

English ABA Quarter-Finals, Semi-Finals & Finals

Olympia, Liverpool – 17 & 18 November & The Conference Centre, Wembley – 2 December
L.Fly: *final:* J.Fowl (Hoddesdon) w pts K.Spong (Army). **Fly:** *quarter-finals:* R.Walsh (Kingfisher) wo, S.Langley (Hollington) wo, R.Burkinshaw (Army) w pts A.Fadile (Unity), P.Edwards (Salisbury) w pts U.Ahmed (Merlin Youth); *semi-finals:* S.Langley w pts R.Burkinshaw, P.Edwards w pts R.Walsh; *final:* P.Edwards w pts S.Langley. **Bantam:** *quarter-finals:* E.Heagney (Rawthorpe) w rsc 3 A.Boyle (RN), S.Hall (Spennymoor) w pts M.Casey (Fisher), R.Smart (Southampton) w pts L.Walsh (Kingfisher), N.McDonald (Vauxhall Motors) w rsc 3 I.Ali (One Nation); *semi-finals:* S.Hall w pts E.Heagney, N.McDonald w rsc 3 R.Smart; *final:* N.McDonald w pts S.Hall. **Feather:** *quarter-finals:* M.Poston (Harwich) wo, G.Sykes (Cleckheaton) w rsc 2 A.Urrutia (RN), A.Bhatia (Eltham) w pts P.Truscott (South Bank), S.Smith (Rotunda) w rsc 2 I.Bailey (Slough); *semi-finals:* A.Bhatia wo G.Sykes, S.Smith w pts M.Poston; *final:* S.Smith w pts A.Bhatia. **Light:** *quarter-finals:* B.Jones (Crawley) wo, C.Pacy (Army) w disq 3 A.Khan (Bateson's), T.Mills (Repton) w pts C.Dickson (Birtley), A.Crolla (Fox) w pts A.Shinkwin (Bushey); *semi-finals:* C.Pacy w pts T.Mills, A.Crolla w pts B.Jones; *final:* A.Crolla w pts C.Pacy. **L.Welter:** *quarter-finals:* M.Stead (Army) w pts C.Sebine (Burmantofts), E.Corcoran (Stowe) w pts B.Saunders (South Durham), S.Woolford (The Grange) w pts

K.Allen (Eastgate), J.Cox (Walcott Boys) w rsc 4 J.Flinn (Triumph); *semi-finals:* E.Corcoran w pts M.Stead, J.Cox w pts S.Woolford; *final:* J.Cox w pts E.Corcoran. **Welter:** *quarter-finals:* B.Flournoy (Army) w pts T.Coward (Wombwell), M.Clauzel (Grainger Park) w pts M.Welsh (Fitzroy Lodge), P.McAleese (Haddenham) w pts L.Pritchard (St Mary's), D.Vassell (Fox) w pts L.Morris (Phoenix); *semi-finals:* B.Flournoy w pts M.Clauzel, D.Vassell w pts P.McAleese; *final:* D.Vassell w pts B.Flournoy. **Middle:** *quarter-finals:* S.Tighe (RN) – replaced S.Briggs (Army) - wo, J.Degale (Dale Youth) w pts G.Barr (Birtley), T.Hill (Golden Ring) w pts W.Bayliss (New Astley), J.McNally (Rotunda) w pts C.Johnson (Terry Allen Unique), *semi-finals:* J.Degale w pts S.Tighe, J.McNally w pts T.Hill; *final:* J.Degale w pts J.McNally. **L.Heavy:** *quarter-finals:* S.McDonald (RN) w pts P.Clarke (Sharkey's Gym), T.Jeffries (Sunderland) w pts T.Salem (Camden Kronk), J.Ainscough (Kirkdale) w pts A.Dennis (Luton Shamrock), M.Redhead (Kingfisher) wo A.Gibbens (Bognor); *semi-finals:* T.Jeffries w rsc 1 S.McDonald, J.Ainscough w pts M.Redhead; *final:* T.Jeffries w rsc 3 J.Ainscough. **Heavy:** *quarter-finals:* D.Reid (City of Portsmouth) wo, M.O'Connell (RN) w pts D.Slaney (Conisborough), N.Thompson (Wellington) w pts M.O.McDonagh (Hollington) – replaced J.McDermott (Dale Youth), T.Bellew (Rotunda) w rsc 4 K.Earley (Cheshunt); *semi-finals:* T.Bellew w pts D.Reid, N.Thompson w pts M.O'Connell; *final:* T.Bellew w rsc 2 N.Thompson. **S.Heavy:** *quarter-finals:* S.Scott (RN) wo, T.Dallas (St Mary's) wo, M.O'Connell (RN) w pts D.Ferguson (Newcastle East End), C.Goldhawk (Cheshunt) w pts D.Lund (Leonis); *semi-finals:* D.Chisora w pts S.Scott, T.Dallas w pts C.Goldhawk; *final:* D.Chisora w pts T.Dallas.

Derek Chisora (left) of Finchley ABC takes evasive action prior to winning the ABA super-heavyweight title by a tight 16-14 points margin over St Mary's Tom Dallas

Les Clark

Irish Championships, 2005-2006

Senior Tournament

The National Stadium, Dublin – 13, 14, 20, 21 & 27 January
L.Fly: *semi-finals*: J. Moore (St. Francis, Limerick) wo, P. Barnes (Holy Family, Belfast) w pts G. McDonagh (Kilcullen, Kildare); *final*: J. Moore w pts P. Barnes. **Fly**: *quarter-finals*: C. Ahern (Baldoyle, Dublin) wo, C. Frampton (Midland White City, Belfast) wo, T.J. Doheny (Portlaoise, Laois) w pts S. Cox (Gorey, Wexford), J.P. Kinsella (Monkstown, Dublin) w pts M. Myers (Brosna, Westmeath), *semi-finals*: C. Ahern w pts J.P. Kinsella, T.J. Doheny w pts C. Frampton; *final*: C. Ahern w pts T.J. Doheny. **Bantam**: *semi-finals*: K. Fennessy (Clonmel, Tipperary) w pts F. Campbell (Edenderry, Offaly), D.O. Joyce (St. Michael's, Athy) w pts D. Thorpe (St. Aiden's, Ferns); *final*: D.O. Joyce w pts K. Fennessy. **Feather**: *quarter-finals*: E. Donovan (St. Michael's, Athy) wo, P. Duncliffe (Sunnyside, Cork) wo, R. Hickey (Grangecon, Kildare) wo, C. Bates (St. Mary's, Dublin) w co 1 J. Cooley (St. Joseph's, Derry); *semi-finals*: E. Donovan w pts P. Duncliffe, R. Hickey w pts C. Bates; *final*: E. Donovan w pts R. Hickey. **Light**: *quarter-finals*: J.P. Campbell (Edenderry, Offaly) wo, A. Sadlier (St. Saviour's OBA, Dublin) wo, J.J. Joyce (St. Michael's, Athy) wo, K. Doherty (Ring, Derry) w rsc 4 W. Delaney (Sacred Heart, Tolerton, Carlow); *semi-finals*: J.P. Campbell w pts A. Sadlier, J.J. Joyce w rsc 4 K. Doherty; *final*: J.J. Joyce w pts J.P. Campbell. **L.Welter**: *prelims*: D. Nevin (Cavan) wo, A. Carlyle (Golden Cobra, Dublin) wo, T. Dwyer (St. Aidan's, Ferns) wo, K. Boyle (St. Saviour's, Dublin) wo, J.J. McDonagh (Brosna, Westmeath) wo, N. Murray (Gorey, Wexford) wo, D. Hamill (All Saints, Ballymena) wo, D.A. Joyce (St. Michael's, Athy) w pts Z. Bugalisuas (Arklow, Wicklow); *quarter-finals*: D. Nevin w pts A. Carlyle, T. Dwyer w pts K. Boyle, J.J. McDonagh w pts N. Murray, D. Hamill w pts D.A. Joyce; *semi-finals*: D. Nevin w pts T. Dwyer, D. Hamill w pts J.J. McDonagh; *final*: D. Hamill w pts D. Nevin. **Welter**: *prelims*: D. Joyce (St. Michael's, Athy) wo, F. Redmond (Arklow, Wicklow) wo, T.J. Hamill (All Saints, Ballymena) wo, A. Fitzgerald (Corinthians, Dublin) wo, R. Sheahan (St. Michael's, Athy) wo, O. Kelly (Portlaoise, Laois) w pts P. Jennings (St. Matthew's, Dublin), T. O'Neill (Mount Tallant, Dublin) w pts F. Foley (St. Michael's, Athy), F. Turner (St. Ibar's/St. Joseph's, Wexford) w pts T. Duddy (Ring, Derry); *quarter-finals*: D. Joyce w pts F. Redmond, T.J. Hamill w pts A. Fitzgerald, R. Sheahan w pts O. Kelly, T. O'Neill w pts F. Turner; *semi-finals*: D. Joyce w pts T.J. Hamill, P. Sheahan w pts T. O'Neill; *final*: P. Sheahan w pts D. Joyce. **Middle**: *quarter-finals*: D. Sutherland (St. Saviour's, Dublin) wo, K. Whelan (St. Paul's, Waterford) wo, D. Gezim (St. Matthew's, Dublin) w rsc 2 C. Flynn (St. Mary's, Dublin), E. Healy (Portlaoise, Laois) w pts S. Shelvin (Dealgan, Louth); *semi-finals*: D. Sutherland w rsc 4 K. Whelan, E. Healy w pts D. Gezim; *final*: D. Sutherland w rsc 3 E. Healy. **L.Heavy**: *semi-finals*: K. Egan (Neilstown, Dublin) wo, D. O'Neill (Paulstown, Kilkenny) w pts T. Murray (Rylane, Cork); *final*: K. Egan w pts D. O'Neill.

Heavy: *quarter-finals*: I. Tims (St. Matthew's, Dublin) wo, S. Curran (Holy Trinity, Belfast) w pts M. Fouhy (St. Colman's, Cork), A. Reynolds (St. Joseph's, Sligo) w rsc 2 A. Hickey (K & K, Cavan), C. McMonagle (Holy Trinity, Belfast) w pts M. Oshun (Arklow, Wicklow); *semi-finals*: I. Tims w pts S. Curran, A. Reynolds w rsc 4 C. McMonagle; *final*: A. Reynolds w pts I. Tims. **S.Heavy**: *quarter-finals*: M. Sweeney (Drimnagh, Dublin) wo, C. Carmichael (Holy Trinity, Belfast) wo, A. Crampton (St. Broughan's, Offaly) w pts C. McClung (Holy Trinity, Belfast), M. McDonagh (Brosna, Westmeath) w disq 3 S. Belshaw (Eastside, Belfast); *semi-finals*: M. Sweeney w pts C. Carmichael, A. Crampton w pts M. McDonagh; *final*: A Crampton w pts M. Sweeney.

Intermediate Finals

The National Stadium Dublin – 16 December
L.Fly: S. Donnelly (All Saints, Belfast) w pts G. McDonagh (Kilcullen, Kildare). **Fly**: S. Cox (Gorey, Wexford) w pts G. Keating (St. Saviour's OBA, Dublin). **Bantam**: S. Kilroy (Holy Family, Drogheda) w pts C. Moynihan (St. Francis, Limerick). **Feather**: P. Duncliffe (Sunnyside, Cork) w pts J. Hand (Dunboyne, Meath). **Light**: J. Keenan (Glen, Cork) w pts T. Finnegan (Golden Cobra, Dublin). **L.Welter**: D. Barrett (Rylane, Cork) w pts P. Ward (Galway). **Welter**: F. Foley (St. Michael's, Athy) w pts T. McGrath (St. Colman's, Cork). **Middle**: S. Shelvin (Dealgan, Louth) w pts N. Higgins (Loughglynn, Roscommon). **L.Heavy**: M. Keenan (Glen, Cork) w pts M. Mullaney (Claremorris, Mayo). **Heavy**: M. Sweeney (All Stars, Ballinasloe) w pts P. Lee (Oughterard, Galway). **S.Heavy**: A. Crampton (St. Broughan's, Offaly) w pts S. Reilly (Drimnagh, Dublin).

Under-19 Finals

The National Stadium, Dublin – 27 May
L.Fly: J.J. Nevin (Cavan) w pts M. Kelly (Immaculata, Belfast). **Fly**: S. Cox (Gorey, Wexford) w pts S. Donnelly (All Saints, Ballymena). **Bantam**: R. Lindberg (Immaculata, Belfast) w pts E. Nesbitt (St. George's/St. Malachy's, Belfast). **Feather**: J. Murray (Gorey, Wexford) w pts J.J. Joyce (Brosna, Westmeath). **Light**: J.J. Joyce (St. Michael's, Athy) w pts A. Cacace (Oliver Plunkett's, Belfast). **L.Welter**: M. Carlyle (Crumlin, Dublin) w pts J. Keenan (Glen, Cork). **Welter**: F. Foley (St. Michael's, Athy) w pts M. Lynch (Illes Golden Gloves, Donegal). **Middle**: D. Nevin (Holy Family, Drogheda) w pts Martin Collins (Darndale, Dublin). **L.Heavy**: D. Joyce (Moate, Westmeath) w pts C. McCauley (Holy Family, Belfast). **Heavy**: C. Sheehan (Clonmel, Tipperary) w pts Michael Collins (Darndale, Dublin). **S.Heavy**: S. Gray (Kinsale, Cork) wo.

Scottish and Welsh Senior Championships, 2005-2006

Scotland ABA

Ingliston Showground Centre, Edinburgh – 4 & 24 March, Town Hall, Darvel – 17 March & Treetops Hotel, Aberdeen – 10 March

L.Fly: no entries. **Fly:** no entries. **Bantam:** *semi-finals*: D.Savage (Argo) w pts D.King (Madison), M.Steto (Kingdom) w rsc 2 G.Munro (Lochside); *final:* D.Savage w pts M.Steto. **Feather:** *semi-finals:* D.Traynor (Granite City) wo, M.Roberts (Forgewood) w pts G.Izzat (Clovenstone); *final:* D.Traynor w pts M.Roberts. **Light:** *quarter-finals:* S.Sharoudi (Forgewood) wo, R.Barclay (Noble Art) wo, S.Carroll (Granite City) wo, L.Phillips (Noble Art) w pts J.Thain (Leith Victoria); *semi-finals:* S.Sharoudi w pts R.Barclay, l.Phillips w pts S.Carroll; *final:* S.Sharoudi wo L.Phillips. **L.Welter:** *quarter-finals:* E.Doyle (Glenboig) wo, E.Finney (Kingdom) wo, R.Scott (Springhill) w pts A.Barlow (Kingdom), P.King (Forgewood) w pts J.Smith (Four Isles); *semi-finals:* E.Doyle w pts E.Finney, P.King wo R.Scott; *final:* P.King w pts E.Doyle. **Welter:** *semi-finals:* J.McLevy (Clydeview) w co 3 W.Bilan (Denbeath), S.Kynoch (Forgewood) w pts P.Deegan (Gilmerton); *final:* J.McLevy w rsc 3 S.Kynoch. **Middle:** *quarter-finals:* S.Weir (Wallace) wo, J.Lee (Madison) wo, G.Will (Kincorth) wo, D.Campbell (Denbeath) w pts K.Davidson (Cleland); *semi-finals:* D.Campbell w pts S.Weir, J.Lee w pts G.Will; *final:* D.Campbell w pts J.Lee. **L.Heavy:** *quarter-finals:* J.Quigley (Port Glasgow) wo, D.Anderson (Denbeath) wo, M.Kirwin (Dennistoun) w pts I.Bathgate (Clovenstone), J.Cunningham (Dennistoun) w pts M.Donald (Kincorth); *semi-finals:* J.Quigley w rsc 3 D.Anderson, M.Kerwin w pts J.Cunningham; *final:* M.Kerwin w pts J.Quigley. **Heavy:** no entries. **S.Heavy:** *quarter-finals:* S.Scott (Forgewood) wo, J.Perry (Larkhall) wo, S.Topin (Lochee Boys), A.Young (Inverness) w pts M.Warner (Springhill); *semi-finals:*S.Topin wo J.Perry, S.Scott w pts A.Young; *final:* S.Scott w pts S.Topin.

Wales ABA

East Street Sports Centre, Tylorstown – 8 & 22 April & The Leisure Centre, Newport – 12 May

L.Fly: *final:* G.Jones (Llay) w pts K.Spong (Army). **Fly:** *final:* C.Jenkins (Cwmgors) w pts A.Perry (Colcot). **Bantam:** no entries. **Feather:** *final:*L.Selby (Splott Adventure) w pts R.Bunford (Carmarthen). **Light:** *quarter-finals:* J.Evans (Army) wo, M.Evans (Red Dragon) wo, Z.Ummar (St Joseph's) wo, C.O'Sullivan (Merlin's Bridge) w pts D.Roberts (Premier); *semi-finals:* J.Evans w rsc 2 M.Evans, C.O'Sullivan w pts Z.Ummar; *final:* C.O'Sullivan w pts J.Evans. **L.Welter:** *quarter-finals:* S.Jama (Cardiff YMCA) wo, L.Champion (Victoria Park) wo, R.Evans (Dowlais) w rsc 3 A.Lamb (Barry East End), P.Ashton (Cwmavon Hornets) w pts J.Flinn (Triumph, Coventry); *semi-finals:* S.Jama w pts L.Champion, P.Ashton w pts R.Evans; *final:* P.Ashton w pts S.Jama. **Welter:** *prelims:* K.Nagle (Stable) wo, K.Scourfield (Palace) wo, P.Dowse (Aberystwyth) w pts J.Moss (Cwmbran), Y.Yusaf (Cardiff YMCA) w pts K.O'Sullivan (Fishguard), H.Evans (Carmarthen) w pts D.Baines (Welshpool), R.James (Merthyr Ex-Servicemen) w pts L.Trott (Towy), P.Chappell (Porthcawl & Pyle) w pts G.Connors (Splott Adventure), J.Way (Cwmcam) w pts T.Leigh (Palace), B.Phillips (Bonymaen) w pts K.Jodowski (Cardif YMCA). B.Phillips withdrew; *quarter-finals:* K.Nagle w pts K.Scourfield, P.Dowse w rsc 3 Y.Yusaf, R.James w rtd 2 H.Evans, J.Way w pts P.Chappell; *semi-finals:* P.Dowse w pts K.Nagle, R.James w pts J.Way; *final:* R.James w pts P.Dowse. **Middle:** *quarter-finals:* G.Jones (Army), L.Davies (Tiumph, Coventry) w pts L.Bannister (Dyffryn), D.Smith (Pontypool & Panteg) w rsc 2 V.Zangana (Cardiff YMCA), H.Miles (All Saints) w co 2 S.Irwin (Maesgeirchen); *semi-finals:* L.Davies w pts D.Smith, H.Miles w pts G.Jones; *final:* H.Miles w pts L.Davies. **L.Heavy:** *quarter-finals:* W.Lukins (Splott Adventure) w pts J.Evans (Pontypool & Panteg), W.Brooks (Ely Star) w co 1 I.Ivanov (Colcot), J.Hughes (St Joseph's) w pts S.Mattan (Ely Star), T.Webb (Bonnymaen) w pts S.Davies (Towy); *semi-finals:* W.Brooks w co 2 J.Hughes, T.Webb wo W.Lukins; *final:* W.Brooks wo T.Webb. **Heavy:** *semi-finals:* J.Bowland (Penarth) w pts J.Bunce (Merthyr Ex-Servicemen), C.Harman (Cardiff YMCA) w pts R.Davies (Trostre); *final:* V.Harman w pts J.Bowland. **S.Heavy:** *semi-finals:*A.Holloway (Rhoose) wo, A.Jones (Shotton) w rsc 3 O.Harries (Penyrheol); *final:* A.Jones w pts A.Holloway.

Four Nations Tournament, 2006

National Stadium, Dublin 3 & 4 February

L.Fly: *final:* M.Nasir (Wales) w pts J.Moore (Ireland). **Fly:** *semi-finals:* C.Jenkins (Wales) wo, C.Ahern (Ireland) w pts S.Langley (England); *final:* C.Ahern w rsc 3 C.Jenkins. **Bantam:** *semi-finals:* M.Edmonds (Wales) wo, D.O.Joyce (Ireland) w rsc 3 D.Savage (Scotland); *final:* D.O.Joyce w pts M.Edmonds. **Feather:** *semi-finals:* R.Hickey (Ireland) w pts J.Hastie (Scotland), S.Smith (England) w pts D.Edwards (Wales); *final:* S.Smith w pts R.Hickey. **Light:** *semi-finals:* J.J.Joyce (Ireland) w pts A.Crolla (England), M.Prince (Scotland) w pts R.Turley (Wales); *final:* J.J.Joyce w pts M.Prince. *Box-off:* A.Crolla w pts R.Turley. **L.Welter:** *semi-finals:* D.Nevin (Ireland) w pts M.Hastie (Scotland), J.Cox (England) w pts J.Crees (Wales); *final:* D.Nevin w pts J.Cox. **Welter:** *semi-finals:* R.Sheahan (Ireland) w pts K.Carslaw (Scotland), A.Thomas (Wales) w pts D.Vassell (England); *final:* R.Sheahan w pts A.Thomas. *Box-off:* K.Carslaw w pts D.Vassell. **Middle:** *semi-finals:* A.McKelvie (Scotland) wo, D.Sutherland (Ireland) w pts J.Degale (England); *final:* D.Sutherland w co 1 A.McKelvie. **L.Heavy:** *semi-finals:* K.Anderson (Scotland) wo, K.Egan (Ireland) w pts J.Ainscough (England); *final:* K.Egan w pts K.Anderson. **Heavy:** *final:* K.Evans (Wales) wo, S.Simmons (Scotland) w pts I.Timms (Ireland). **S.Heavy:** *semi-finals:* D.Chisora (England) w pts S.Scott (Scotland); *final:* K.Evans w pts D.Chisora.

James Degale (left), seen here outpointing Joe McNally to win the ABA middleweight title for the second year running, failed to get beyond the semi-final stage of the Four Nations Tournament

Les Clark

British Junior Championship Finals, 2005-2006

National Association of Clubs for Young People (NACYP)

The Adelphi Hotel, Liverpool – 16 December

Class A: 46kg: D.Lawler (Chelmsley Wood) w pts D.Perry (Norwich Lads). 48kg: B.Evans (Stevenage) w disq 2 P.Lovell (Chester). 50kg: M.Maguire (Kettering SoB) w rsc 2 J.Kelly (Earlsfield). 52kg: L.Browning (Exeter) w pts D.Walton (Chelmsley Wood). 54kg: B.Cunliffe (Bolton Lads) w rsc 2 R.Rose (St Mary's, Chatham). 57kg: D.O'Shaughnessy (West Ham) w rsc 2 J.Purvis (Sunderland). 60kg: T.Langford (Bideford) w pts L.Gent (Darlington). 63kg: C.Wallace (East Durham) w pts T.Humphreys (New Astley). 66kg: J.McGough (Triumph) w pts M.Innes (Cwmbran). 70kg: W Saunders (Cheshunt) w rsc 2 A.Cutts (Phoenix, Nottingham). 75kg: J.Gosling (Southend) w pts L.Holland (Jimmy Eagan's). 80kg: W.Welsh (Darlington) w pts L.Surin (Bromley & Downham). 86kg: O.Mbwakongo (Fisher) w rsc 3 T.Ward (Belgrave).

The Festival Hall, Kirkby in Ashfield – 13 December

Class B: 46kg: C.O'Brien (Northside) wo. 48kg: P.Butler (Vauxhall Motors) w pts B.Buckland (Repton). 50kg: L.Wood (Phoenix, Nottingham) wo. 52kg: K.Satchell (Everton Red Triangle) w pts D.Burrell (Samuel Montague). 54kg: M.Ward (Birtley) wo C.Williamson (Luton). 57kg: C.Kelly (St Theresa's) w pts R.Boylan (Earlsfield). 60kg: C.Greenwood (Kirkdale) w rsc 3 J.Horner (Rayleigh). 63kg: L.Smith (Rotunda) w pts R.Simmons (St Mary's, Chatham). 66kg: P.Roberts (Rotunda) w pts R.Taylor (Newham). 70kg: P.Nugent (West Ham) w pts K.Thompson (South Durham). 75kg: J.McCann (Kettering SoB) w pts J.Whiteside (National Smelting). 80kg: M.Shinkwin (Bushey) w rsc 2 C.Rowley (Queensbury).86kg: S.Jury (Thames Valley) w pts J.Franczek (Lion).

The Royal Lancaster Hotel, Bayswater – 13 December

Class C: 48kg: S.Smith (Kingsthorpe) w pts B.Fowl (Hoddesdon). 51kg: L.Lewis (ANA) w pts D.Keogan (Sefton). 54kg: S.Goff (St Mary's, Chatham) wo L.Campbell (St Paul's, Hull). 57kg: A.Dingsdale (Brompton) w pts D.Rogers (Kettering SoB). 60kg: T.Marcon (White Rose) w pts J.Radford (Newham). 64kg: B.Skeete (Earlsfield) w pts G.Foot (Marley Potts). 69kg: K.Kirkham (Blackpool & Fylde) w pts D.Butler (Broad Plain). 75kg: M.Palmer (Chorley) w pts I.Jenkins (Cwmgors). 81kg: J.Ingram (Aston) w rsc 2 S.Easton (Devonport). 91kg: C.Keane (Pleck) w pts M.Churcher (Thames Valley). 91+kg: D.Hughes (Hylton Castle) wo.

Golden Gloves (Schools)

The Leisure Centre, Knottingley – 25 & 26 March

Class 1: 30kg: C.Driscoll (West Ham) w pts L.Bunney (East Cleveland). 32kg: J.Grattan (Hall Green) w pts W.Tonne (Tommy's). 34kg: M.Cousins (West Ham) w pts T.Hallimond (Shildon). 36kg: Q.Ashfac (Bateson's) w pts J.Austin (Newham). 38kg: M.Morrison (Northside) wo J.McDonagh (Stowe). 40kg: B.Jackson (Spennymoor) w rsc 2 C.Delange (Blandford). 42kg: J.Hanrahan (Ruislip) w pts M.McDonnell (Northside). 44kg: D.Jones (Bateson's) w pts C.Doherty (Finchley). 46kg: Z.Smith (Tower Hill) w pts J.Murray (Five Star). 48kg: G.Walsh (Newham) w rtd 2 F.Bennett (Chelmsley Wood). 50kg: C.Robson (Bulkington) w pts W.Ingram (Gloucester). 52kg: S.Shane (Brompton) w pts O.Baig (Rawthorpe). 54kg: M.Rhone (Northolt) w pts J.Tight (Aycliffe). 57kg: L.Conely (Sporting Ring) w pts J.Wharton (Phoenix, Nottingham). 60kg: E.Frankham (Wisbech) w rsc 2 B.Danby (A One).

Class 2: 34kg: D.Painting (Bexley) w pts L.Wortley (Shepshed). 36kg: L.Bates (Earlsfield) w pts B.Sykes (South Normanton). 38kg: R.Walker (Redcar) w pts T.Price (Stevenage). 40kg: M.Hedges (West Ham) w pts J.Cocker (Karmand). 42kg: J.Langford (Bideford) w pts R.Fields (South Normanton SoB).

44kg: J.Dignam (Newham) w pts C.Winton (Hartlepool Catholic). 46kg: J.Ward (Repton) w pts B.Jenkinson (Bracebridge). 48kg: S.McNess (Repton) w pts J.Turner (Northside). 50kg: T.Ghent (Priory Park) w pts S.Wilson (Pilgrims). 52kg: D.Kelly (Kirkby) w pts T.Allen (Brompton). 54kg: A.Carolan (Doncaster Plant) w pts L.Adolphe (Earlsfield). 57kg: J.Kelly (Egan's Academy) w pts J.Docherty (Bushey). 60kg: G.McCorry (Aston) w pts M.Price (Foley). 63kg: M.Davies (Huyton) w pts T.Flynn (Walcot Boys). 66kg: N.Phillips (Shildon) w rsc 1 J.Oakley (Wallasey).

Class 3: 38kg: B.Truby (Bexley) w pts M.White (Birtley). 40kg: M.Ward (Repton) w pts J.Dickens (Golden Gloves). 42kg: C.Hoy (Cheshunt) w pts M.Heffron (Northside). 44kg: T.Baker (Repton) w pts M.Mongan (Arrow). 46kg: T.Holmes (Stevenage) w pts H.Khan (Bury). 48kg: J.Winson (Finchley) w pts A.Mahall (Northside). 50kg: G.Langley (Repton) w pts J.Saunders (South Durham). 52kg: J.Smith (West Hill) w pts S.Pealing (Transport). 54kg: N.Dale (Kingfisher) w pts A.Fowler (Golden Gloves). 57kg: J.Kerr (West Ham) w rsc 2 P.Longstaff (Newbiggin). 60kg: G.Carman (Bushey) w pts L.Taylor (Middleton Select). 63kg: R.Aston (Priory Park) w pts T.Goodjohn (Haddenham). 66kg: G.O'Neill (Horden Sports) w pts J.Cetaj (Walcot Boys). 70kg: D.Deevey (Braunstone) w pts F.Follows (Gloucester). 75kg: D.Benson (Nichols Police) w pts J.Avis (Dynamo).

ABA Youth

The Metrodome, Barnsley – 6 May

Class 4: 46kg: A.Seldon (Exeter) w pts N.French (Grimsby). 48kg: L.Pettitt (Nemesis) w pts B.Hinkler (Steel City). 50kg: W.Morgan (West Ham) w pts J.Barker (Northside). 52kg: A.Leake (Northside) w pts I.Weaver (Golden Ring). 54kg: M.McCarthy (Dagenham Police Community) w pts J.Sampson (Steel City). 57 kg: J.Hughes (Malmesbury) w pts D.Phillips (South Bank). 60kg: A.Price (Lions) w pts L.Dennard (Billericay). 63kg: D.Docherty (Bushey) w pts K.Spencer (Lions). 66kg: R.Phillips (Avalon) w pts J.Johnson (West Ham). 70kg: K.Garvey (Earlsfield) w pts L.Taylor (Steel City). 75kg: T.Quaddus (Phoenix, Peterborough) w pts J.Pollock (Phil Thomas SoB). 80kg: B.Heath (Queensberry) wo. S.Allen (Tom Lowe's) wo.

Class 5: D.Lawlor (Birmingham City Police) w pts C.Board (Exeter). 48kg: L.Ward (Bridgefoot) w pts D.Perry (Norwich Lads). 50kg: K.Saeed (Birmingham City Police) w pts J.Kelly (Earlsfield). 52kg: M.Maguire (Kettering SoB) w rsc 2 L.Browning (Exeter). 54kg: K.D'eath (Northside) w pts L.Gibbs (Nemesis). 57kg: T.Coyle (St Paul's, Hull) w pts R.Rose (St Mary's, Chatham). 60kg: W.Claydon (Guildford) w pts A.Vieyra (Olympic). 63kg: S.Henty (Eltham) w pts G.King (Meanwood). 66kg: S.Cardle (Kirkham) w rsc 1 P.Guest (Debden & Britannia). 70kg: W.Saunders (Cheshunt) w rsc 2 S.Aluko (Pool of Life). 75kg: J.Gosling (Southend) w pts S.Griffiths (Shrewsbury). 80kg: O.Mbwakongo (Fisher) wo R.Pearce (South Normanton SoB). 86kg: T.Ward (Belgrave) w pts A.Adele (Dagenham Police Community).

Class 6: 46kg: P.Douglas (Phil Thomas SoB) wo. 48kg: P.Butler (Vauxhall Motors) wo. 50kg: G.Smith (Royal Navy) w pts C.Varley (Burmantofts). 52kg: K.Satchell (Everton Red Triangle) wo. 54kg: S.Quigg (Bury) w pts J.Taylor (Lion). 57kg: M.Fagin (Vauxhall Motors) w pts J.Saeed (Samuel Montague). 60kg: D.Bharj (Walcot Boys) w pts C.Greenwood (Kirkdale). 63kg: L.Smith (Rotunda) w pts L.Gray (Stevenage). 66kg: J.Spencer (Rotunda) w pts C.Jefcoate (Eltham). 70kg: A.Agogo (Triple A) w rsc 1 P.Roberts (Rotunda). 75kg: T.Dickenson (Birtley Police) w rsc 1 G.Groves (Dale Youth). 80kg: J.McCann (Kettering SoB) w pts M.Shinkwin (Bushey). 86kg: J.Turner (Shildon) w rsc 3 J.Franczek (Lion).

ABA Champions, 1881-2006

Please note that despite the most recent champions being crowned in 2005, as the championships were held during the 2005-2006 season it is the latter year which is shown.

L. Flyweight
1971 M. Abrams
1972 M. Abrams
1973 M. Abrams
1974 C. Magri
1975 M. Lawless
1976 P. Fletcher
1977 P. Fletcher
1978 J. Dawson
1979 J. Dawson
1980 T. Barker
1981 J. Lyon
1982 J. Lyon
1983 J. Lyon
1984 J. Lyon
1985 M. Epton
1986 M. Epton
1987 M. Epton
1988 M. Cantwell
1989 M. Cantwell
1990 N. Tooley
1991 P. Culshaw
1992 D. Fifield
1993 M. Hughes
1994 G. Jones
1995 D. Fox
1996 R. Mercer
1997 I. Napa
1998 J. Evans
1999 G. Jones
2000 J. Mulherne
2001 C. Lyon
2002 D. Langley
2003 C. Lyon
2004 S. McDonald
2005 D. Langley
2006 J. Fowl

Flyweight
1920 H. Groves
1921 W. Cuthbertson
1922 E. Warwick
1923 L. Tarrant
1924 E. Warwick
1925 E. Warwick
1926 J. Hill
1927 J. Roland
1928 C. Taylor
1929 T. Pardoe
1930 T. Pardoe
1931 T. Pardoe
1932 T. Pardoe
1933 T. Pardoe
1934 P. Palmer
1935 G. Fayaud
1936 G. Fayaud
1937 P. O'Donaghue
1938 A. Russell
1939 D. McKay
1944 J. Clinton
1945 J. Bryce
1946 R. Gallacher
1947 J. Clinton
1948 H. Carpenter
1949 H. Riley
1950 A. Jones

1951 G. John
1952 D. Dower
1953 R. Currie
1954 R. Currie
1955 D. Lloyd
1956 T. Spinks
1957 R. Davies
1958 J. Brown
1959 M. Gushlow
1960 D. Lee
1961 W. McGowan
1962 M. Pye
1963 M. Laud
1964 J. McCluskey
1965 J. McCluskey
1966 P. Maguire
1967 S. Curtis
1968 J. McGonigle
1969 D. Needham
1970 D. Needham
1971 P. Wakefield
1972 M. O'Sullivan
1973 R. Hilton
1974 M. O'Sullivan
1975 C. Magri
1976 C. Magri
1977 C. Magri
1978 G. Nickels
1979 R. Gilbody
1980 K. Wallace
1981 K. Wallace
1982 J. Kelly
1983 S. Nolan
1984 P. Clinton
1985 P. Clinton
1986 J. Lyon
1987 J. Lyon
1988 J. Lyon
1989 J. Lyon
1990 J. Armour
1991 P. Ingle
1992 K. Knox
1993 P. Ingle
1994 D. Costello
1995 D. Costello
1996 D. Costello
1997 M. Hunter
1998 J. Hegney
1999 D. Robinson
2000 D. Robinson
2001 M. Marsh
2002 D. Barriball
2003 D. Broadhurst
2004 S. Langley
2005 S. Langley
2006 P. Edwards

Bantamweight
1884 A. Woodward
1885 A. Woodward
1886 T. Isley
1887 T. Isley
1888 H. Oakman
1889 H. Brown
1890 J. Rowe
1891 E. Moore

1892 F. Godbold
1893 E. Watson
1894 P. Jones
1895 P. Jones
1896 P. Jones
1897 C. Lamb
1898 F. Herring
1899 A. Avent
1900 J. Freeman
1901 W. Morgan
1902 A. Miner
1903 H. Perry
1904 H. Perry
1905 W. Webb
1906 T. Ringer
1907 E. Adams
1908 H. Thomas
1909 J. Condon
1910 W. Webb
1911 W. Allen
1912 W. Allen
1913 A. Wye
1914 W. Allen
1919 W. Allen
1920 G. McKenzie
1921 L. Tarrant
1922 W. Boulding
1923 A. Smith
1924 L. Tarrant
1925 A. Goom
1926 F. Webster
1927 E. Warwick
1928 J. Garland
1929 F. Bennett
1930 H. Mizler
1931 F. Bennett
1932 J. Treadaway
1933 G. Johnston
1934 A. Barnes
1935 L. Case
1936 A. Barnes
1937 A. Barnes
1938 J. Pottinger
1939 R. Watson
1944 R. Bissell
1945 P. Brander
1946 C. Squire
1947 D. O'Sullivan
1948 T. Proffitt
1949 T. Miller
1950 K. Lawrence
1951 T. Nicholls
1952 T. Nicholls
1953 J. Smillie
1954 J. Smillie
1955 G. Dormer
1956 O. Reilly
1957 J. Morrissey
1958 H. Winstone
1959 D. Weller
1960 F. Taylor
1961 P. Benneyworth
1962 P. Benneyworth
1963 B. Packer
1964 B. Packer
1965 R. Mallon

1966 J. Clark
1967 M. Carter
1968 M. Carter
1969 M. Piner
1970 A. Oxley
1971 G. Turpin
1972 G. Turpin
1973 P. Cowdell
1974 S. Ogilvie
1975 S. Ogilvie
1976 J. Bambrick
1977 J. Turner
1978 J. Turner
1979 R. Ashton
1980 R. Gilbody
1981 P. Jones
1982 R. Gilbody
1983 J. Hyland
1984 J. Hyland
1985 S. Murphy
1986 S. Murphy
1987 J. Sillitoe
1988 K. Howlett
1989 K. Howlett
1990 P. Lloyd
1991 D. Hardie
1992 P. Mullings
1993 R. Evatt
1994 S. Oliver
1995 N. Wilders
1996 L. Eedle
1997 S. Oates
1998 L. Pattison
1999 M. Hunter
2000 S. Foster
2001 S. Foster
2002 D. Matthews
2003 N. McDonald
2004 M. Marsh
2005 N. McDonald
2006 N.McDonald

Featherweight
1881 T. Hill
1882 T. Hill
1883 T. Hill
1884 E. Hutchings
1885 J. Pennell
1886 T. McNeil
1887 J. Pennell
1888 J. Taylor
1889 G. Belsey
1890 G. Belsey
1891 F. Curtis
1892 F. Curtis
1893 T. Davidson
1894 R. Gunn
1895 R. Gunn
1896 R. Gunn
1897 N. Smith
1898 P. Lunn
1899 J. Scholes
1900 R. Lee
1901 C. Clarke
1902 C. Clarke
1903 J. Godfrey

1904 C. Morris
1905 H. Holmes
1906 A. Miner
1907 C. Morris
1908 T. Ringer
1909 A. Lambert
1910 C. Houghton
1911 H. Bowers
1912 G. Baker
1913 G. Baker
1914 G. Baker
1919 G. Baker
1920 J. Fleming
1921 G. Baker
1922 E. Swash
1923 E. Swash
1924 A. Beavis
1925 A. Beavis
1926 R. Minshull
1927 F. Webster
1928 F. Meachem
1929 F. Meachem
1930 J. Duffield
1931 B. Caplan
1932 H. Mizler
1933 J. Walters
1934 J. Treadaway
1935 E. Ryan
1936 J. Treadaway
1937 A. Harper
1938 C. Gallie
1939 C. Gallie
1944 D. Sullivan
1945 J. Carter
1946 P. Brander
1947 S. Evans
1948 P. Brander
1949 H. Gilliland
1950 P. Brander
1951 J. Travers
1952 P. Lewis
1953 P. Lewis
1954 D. Charnley
1955 T. Nicholls
1956 T. Nicholls
1957 M. Collins
1958 M. Collins
1959 G. Judge
1960 P. Lundgren
1961 P. Cheevers
1962 B. Wilson
1963 A. Riley
1964 R. Smith
1965 K. Buchanan
1966 H. Baxter
1967 K. Cooper
1968 J. Cheshire
1969 A. Richardson
1970 D. Polak
1971 T. Wright
1972 K. Laing
1973 J. Lynch
1974 G. Gilbody
1975 R. Beaumont
1976 P. Cowdell
1977 P. Cowdell

Paul Edwards (left) outscored Hollington's Stewart Langley to win last season's ABA flyweight title   Les Clark

1978 M. O'Brien	1883 A. Diamond	1920 F. Grace	1957 J. Kidd	1990 P. Gallagher
1979 P. Hanlon	1884 A. Diamond	1921 G. Shorter	1958 R. McTaggart	1991 P. Ramsey
1980 M. Hanif	1885 A. Diamond	1922 G. Renouf	1959 P. Warwick	1992 D. Amory
1981 P. Hanlon	1886 G. Roberts	1923 G. Shorter	1960 R. McTaggart	1993 B. Welsh
1982 H. Henry	1887 J. Hair	1924 W. White	1961 P. Warwick	1994 A. Green
1983 P. Bradley	1888 A. Newton	1925 E. Viney	1962 B. Whelan	1995 R. Rutherford
1984 K. Taylor	1889 W. Neale	1926 T. Slater	1963 B. O'Sullivan	1996 K. Wing
1985 F. Havard	1890 A. Newton	1927 W. Hunt	1964 J. Dunne	1997 M. Hawthorne
1986 P. Hodkinson	1891 E. Dettmer	1928 F. Webster	1965 A. White	1998 A. McLean
1987 P. English	1892 E. Dettmer	1929 W. Hunt	1966 J. Head	1999 S. Burke
1988 D. Anderson	1893 W. Campbell	1930 J. Waples	1967 T. Waller	2000 A. McLean
1989 P. Richardson	1894 W. Campbell	1931 D. McCleave	1968 J. Watt	2001 S. Burke
1990 B. Carr	1895 A. Randall	1932 F. Meachem	1969 H. Hayes	2002 A. Morris
1991 J. Irwin	1896 A. Vanderhout	1933 H. Mizler	1970 N. Cole	2003 S. Burke
1992 A. Temple	1897 A. Vanderhout	1934 J. Rolland	1971 J. Singleton	2004 C. Pacy
1993 J. Cook	1898 H. Marks	1935 F. Frost	1972 N. Cole	2005 F. Gavin
1994 D. Pithie	1899 H. Brewer	1936 F. Simpson	1973 T. Dunn	2006 A. Crolla
1995 D. Burrows	1900 G. Humphries	1937 A. Danahar	1974 J. Lynch	
1996 T. Mulholland	1901 A. Warner	1938 T. McGrath	1975 P. Cowdell	**L. Welterweight**
1997 S. Bell	1902 A. Warner	1939 H. Groves	1976 S. Mittee	1951 W. Connor
1998 D. Williams	1903 H. Fergus	1944 W. Thompson	1977 G. Gilbody	1952 P. Waterman
1999 S. Miller	1904 M. Wells	1945 J. Williamson	1978 T. Marsh	1953 D. Hughes
2000 H. Castle	1905 M. Wells	1946 E. Thomas	1979 G. Gilbody	1954 G. Martin
2001 S. Bell	1906 M. Wells	1947 C. Morrissey	1980 G. Gilbody	1955 F. McQuillan
2002 D. Mulholland	1907 M. Wells	1948 R. Cooper	1981 G. Gilbody	1956 D. Stone
2003 K. Mitchell	1908 H. Holmes	1949 A. Smith	1982 J. McDonnell	1957 D. Stone
2004 D. Mulholland	1909 F. Grace	1950 R. Latham	1983 K. Willis	1958 R. Kane
2005 G. Sykes	1910 T. Tees	1951 R. Hinson	1984 A. Dickson	1959 R. Kane
2006 S. Smith	1911 A. Spenceley	1952 F. Reardon	1985 E. McAuley	1960 R. Day
	1912 R. Marriott	1953 D. Hinson	1986 J. Jacobs	1961 B. Brazier
Lightweight	1913 R. Grace	1954 G. Whelan	1987 M. Ayers	1962 B. Brazier
1881 F. Hobday	1914 R. Marriott	1955 S. Coffey	1988 C. Kane	1963 R. McTaggart
1882 A. Bettinson	1919 F. Grace	1956 R. McTaggart	1989 M. Ramsey	1964 R. Taylor

1965 R. McTaggart
1966 W. Hiatt
1967 B. Hudspeth
1968 E. Cole
1969 J. Stracey
1970 D. Davies
1971 M. Kingwell
1972 T. Waller
1973 N. Cole
1974 P. Kelly
1975 J. Zeraschi
1976 C. McKenzie
1977 J. Douglas
1978 D. Williams
1979 E. Copeland
1980 A. Willis
1981 A. Willis
1982 A. Adams
1983 D. Dent
1984 D. Griffiths
1985 I. Mustafa
1986 J. Alsop
1987 A. Holligan
1988 A. Hall
1989 A. Hall
1990 J. Pender
1991 J. Matthews
1992 D. McCarrick
1993 P. Richardson
1994 A. Temple
1995 A. Vaughan
1996 C. Wall
1997 R. Hatton
1998 N. Wright
1999 D. Happe
2000 N. Wright
2001 G. Smith
2002 L. Daws
2003 L. Beavis
2004 J. Watson
2005 M. Grant
2006 J. Cox

Welterweight
1920 F. Whitbread
1921 A. Ireland
1922 E. White
1923 P. Green
1924 P. O'Hanrahan
1925 P. O'Hanrahan
1926 B. Marshall
1927 H. Dunn
1928 H. Bone
1929 T. Wigmore
1930 F. Brooman
1931 J. Barry
1932 D. McCleave
1933 P. Peters
1934 D. McCleave
1935 D. Lynch
1936 W. Pack
1937 D. Lynch
1938 C. Webster
1939 R. Thomas
1944 H. Hall
1945 R. Turpin
1946 J. Ryan
1947 J. Ryan
1948 M. Shacklady
1949 A. Buxton
1950 T. Ratcliffe

1951 J. Maloney
1952 J. Maloney
1953 L. Morgan
1954 N. Gargano
1955 N. Gargano
1956 N. Gargano
1957 R. Warnes
1958 B. Nancurvis
1959 J. McGrail
1960 C. Humphries
1961 A. Lewis
1962 J. Pritchett
1963 J. Pritchett
1964 M. Varley
1965 P. Henderson
1966 P. Cragg
1967 D. Cranswick
1968 A. Tottoh
1969 T. Henderson
1970 T. Waller
1971 D. Davies
1972 T. Francis
1973 T. Waller
1974 T. Waller
1975 W. Bennett
1976 C. Jones
1977 C. Jones
1978 E. Byrne
1979 J. Frost
1980 T. Marsh
1981 T. Marsh
1982 C. Pyatt
1983 R. McKenley
1984 M. Hughes
1985 E. McDonald
1986 D. Dyer
1987 M. Elliot
1988 M. McCreath
1989 M. Elliot
1990 A. Carew
1991 J. Calzaghe
1992 M. Santini
1993 C. Bessey
1994 K. Short
1995 M. Hall
1996 J. Khaliq
1997 F. Barrett
1998 D. Walker
1999 A. Cesay
2000 F. Doherty
2001 M. Macklin
2002 M. Lomax
2003 D. Happe
2004 M. Murray
2005 B. Flournoy
2006 D. Vassell

L. Middleweight
1951 A. Lay
1952 B. Foster
1953 B. Wells
1954 B. Wells
1955 B. Foster
1956 J. McCormack
1957 J. Cunningham
1958 S. Pearson
1959 S. Pearson
1960 W. Fisher
1961 J. Gamble
1962 J. Lloyd
1963 A. Wyper

1964 W. Robinson
1965 P. Dwyer
1966 T. Imrie
1967 A. Edwards
1968 E. Blake
1969 T. Imrie
1970 D. Simmonds
1971 A. Edwards
1972 L. Paul
1973 R. Maxwell
1974 R. Maxwell
1975 A. Harrison
1976 W. Lauder
1977 C. Malarkey
1978 E. Henderson
1979 D. Brewster
1980 J. Price
1981 E. Christie
1982 D. Milligan
1983 R. Douglas
1984 R. Douglas
1985 R. Douglas
1986 T. Velinor
1987 N. Brown
1988 W. Ellis
1989 N. Brown
1990 T. Taylor
1991 T. Taylor
1992 J. Calzaghe
1993 D. Starie
1994 W. Alexander
1995 C. Bessey
1996 S. Dann
1997 C. Bessey
1998 C. Bessey
1999 C. Bessey
2000 C. Bessey
2001 M. Thirwall
2002 P. Smith

Middleweight
1881 T. Bellhouse
1882 A. H. Curnick
1883 A. J. Curnick
1884 W. Brown
1885 M. Salmon
1886 W. King
1887 R. Hair
1888 R. Hair
1889 G. Sykes
1890 J. Hoare
1891 J. Steers
1892 J. Steers
1893 J. Steers
1894 W. Sykes
1895 G. Townsend
1896 W. Ross
1897 W. Dees
1898 G. Townsend
1899 R. Warnes
1900 E. Mann
1901 R. Warnes
1902 E. Mann
1903 R. Warnes
1904 E. Mann
1905 J. Douglas
1906 A. Murdock
1907 R. Warnes
1908 W. Child
1909 W. Child
1910 R. Warnes

1911 W. Child
1912 E. Chandler
1913 W. Bradley
1914 H. Brown
1919 H. Mallin
1920 H. Mallin
1921 H. Mallin
1922 H. Mallin
1923 H. Mallin
1924 J. Elliot
1925 J. Elliot
1926 F. P. Crawley
1927 F. P. Crawley
1928 F. Mallin
1929 F. Mallin
1930 F. Mallin
1931 F. Mallin
1932 F. Mallin
1933 A. Shawyer
1934 J. Magill
1935 J. Magill
1936 A. Harrington
1937 M. Dennis
1938 H. Tiller
1939 H. Davies
1944 J. Hockley
1945 R. Parker
1946 R. Turpin
1947 R. Agland
1948 J. Wright
1949 S. Lewis
1950 P. Longo
1951 E. Ludlam
1952 T. Gooding
1953 R. Barton
1954 K. Phillips
1955 F. Hope
1956 R. Redrup
1957 P. Burke
1958 P. Hill
1959 F. Elderfield
1960 R. Addison
1961 J. Caiger
1962 A. Matthews
1963 A. Matthews
1964 W. Stack
1965 W. Robinson
1966 C. Finnegan
1967 A. Ball
1968 P. McCann
1969 D. Wallington
1970 J. Conteh
1971 A. Minter
1972 F. Lucas
1973 F. Lucas
1974 D. Odwell
1975 D. Odwell
1976 E. Burke
1977 R. Davies
1978 H. Graham
1979 N. Wilshire
1980 M. Kaylor
1981 B. Schumacher
1982 J. Price
1983 T. Forbes
1984 B. Schumacher
1985 D. Cronin
1986 N. Benn
1987 R. Douglas
1988 M. Edwards
1989 S. Johnson

1990 S. Wilson
1991 M. Edwards
1992 L. Woolcock
1993 J. Calzaghe
1994 D. Starie
1995 J. Matthews
1996 J. Pearce
1997 I. Cooper
1998 J. Pearce
1999 C. Froch
2000 S. Swales
2001 C. Froch
2002 N. Perkins
2003 N. Perkins
2004 D. Guthrie
2005 J. Degale
2006 J. Degale

L. Heavyweight
1920 H. Franks
1921 L. Collett
1922 H. Mitchell
1923 H. Mitchell
1924 H. Mitchell
1925 H. Mitchell
1926 D. McCorkindale
1927 A. Jackson
1928 A. Jackson
1929 J. Goyder
1930 J. Murphy
1931 J. Petersen
1932 J. Goyder
1933 G. Brennan
1934 G. Brennan
1935 R. Hearns
1936 J. Magill
1937 J. Wilby
1938 A. S. Brown
1939 B. Woodcock
1944 E. Shackleton
1945 A. Watson
1946 J. Taylor
1947 A. Watson
1948 D. Scott
1949 *Declared no contest*
1950 P. Messervy
1951 G. Walker
1952 H. Cooper
1953 H. Cooper
1954 A. Madigan
1955 D. Rent
1956 D. Mooney
1957 T. Green
1958 J. Leeming
1959 J. Ould
1960 J. Ould
1961 J. Bodell
1962 J. Hendrickson
1963 P. Murphy
1964 J. Fisher
1965 E. Whistler
1966 R. Tighe
1967 M. Smith
1968 R. Brittle
1969 J. Frankham
1970 J. Rafferty
1971 J. Conteh
1972 W. Knight
1973 W. Knight
1974 W. Knight
1975 M. Heath

1976 G. Evans	2002 J. Dolan	1919 H. Brown	1960 L. Hobbs	1997 B. Stevens
1977 C. Lawson		1920 R. Rawson	1961 W. Walker	1998 N. Hosking
1978 V. Smith	**Heavyweight**	1921 R. Rawson	1962 R. Dryden	1999 S. St John
1979 A. Straughn	1881 R. Frost-Smith	1922 T. Evans	1963 R. Sanders	2000 D. Dolan
1980 A. Straughn	1882 H. Dearsley	1923 E. Eagan	1964 C. Woodhouse	2001 D. Dolan
1981 A. Straughn	1883 H. Dearsley	1924 A. Clifton	1965 W. Wells	2002 D. Dolan
1982 G. Crawford	1884 H. Dearsley	1925 D. Lister	1966 A. Brogan	2003 M. O'Connell
1983 A. Wilson	1885 W. West	1926 T. Petersen	1967 P. Boddington	2004 T. Bellew
1984 A. Wilson	1886 A. Diamond	1927 C. Capper	1968 W. Wells	2005 T. Bellew
1985 J. Beckles	1887 E. White	1928 J. L. Driscoll	1969 A. Burton	2006 T. Bellew
1986 J. Moran	1888 W. King	1929 P. Floyd	1970 J. Gilmour	
1987 J. Beckles	1889 A. Bowman	1930 V. Stuart	1971 L. Stevens	**S. Heavyweight**
1988 H. Lawson	1890 J. Steers	1931 M. Flanagan	1972 T. Wood	1982 A. Elliott
1989 N. Piper	1891 V. Barker	1932 V. Stuart	1973 G. McEwan	1983 K. Ferdinand
1990 J. McCluskey	1892 J. Steers	1933 C. O'Grady	1974 N. Meade	1984 R. Wells
1991 A. Todd	1893 J. Steers	1934 P. Floyd	1975 G. McEwan	1985 G. Williamson
1992 K. Oliver	1894 H. King	1935 P. Floyd	1976 J. Rafferty	1986 J. Oyebola
1993 K. Oliver	1895 W. E. Johnstone	1936 V. Stuart	1977 G. Adair	1987 J. Oyebola
1994 K. Oliver	1896 W. E. Johnstone	1937 V. Stuart	1978 J. Awome	1988 K. McCormack
1995 K. Oliver	1897 G. Townsend	1938 G. Preston	1979 A. Palmer	1989 P. Passley
1996 C. Fry	1898 G. Townsend	1939 A. Porter	1980 F. Bruno	1990 K. McCormack
1997 P. Rogers	1899 F. Parks	1944 M. Hart	1981 A. Elliott	1991 K. McCormack
1998 C. Fry	1900 W. Dees	1945 D. Scott	1982 H. Hylton	1992 M. Hopper
1999 J. Ainscough	1901 F. Parks	1946 P. Floyd	1983 H. Notice	1993 M. McKenzie
2000 P. Haymer	1902 F. Parks	1947 G. Scriven	1984 D. Young	1994 D. Watts
2001 C. Fry	1903 F. Dickson	1948 J. Gardner	1985 H. Hylton	1995 R. Allen
2002 T. Marsden	1904 A. Horner	1949 A. Worrall	1986 E. Cardouza	1996 D. Watts
2003 J. Boyd	1905 F. Parks	1950 P. Toch	1987 J. Moran	1997 A. Harrison
2004 M. Abdusalem	1906 F. Parks	1951 A. Halsey	1988 H. Akinwande	1998 A. Harrison
2005 D. Pendleton	1907 H. Brewer	1952 E. Hearn	1989 H. Akinwande	1999 W. Bessey
2006 T. Jeffries	1908 S. Evans	1953 J. Erskine	1990 K. Inglis	2000 J. McDermott
	1909 C. Brown	1954 B. Harper	1991 P. Lawson	2001 M. Grainger
Cruiserweight	1910 F. Storbeck	1955 D. Rowe	1992 S. Welch	2002 M. Grainger
1998 T. Oakey	1911 W. Hazell	1956 D. Rent	1993 P. Lawson	2003 D. Price
1999 M. Krence	1912 R. Smith	1957 D. Thomas	1994 S. Burford	2004 J. Young
2000 J. Dolan	1913 R. Smith	1958 D. Thomas	1995 M. Ellis	2005 D. Price
2001 J. Dolan	1914 E. Chandler	1959 D. Thomas	1996 T. Oakey	2006 D. Chisora

Rotunda's Tony Bellew (left) made it three ABA cruiserweight title wins in succession when stopping Nathan Thompson (Wellington) inside two rounds last December

Les Clark

International Amateur Champions, 1904-2006

Shows all Olympic, World, European & Commonwealth champions since 1904. British silver and bronze medal winners are shown throughout, where applicable.

Country Code

ALG = Algeria; ARG = Argentina; ARM = Armenia; AUS = Australia; AUT = Austria; AZE = Azerbaijan; BE = Belarus; BEL = Belgium; BUL = Bulgaria; CAN = Canada; CEY = Ceylon (now Sri Lanka); CI = Channel Islands; CHI = China; CUB = Cuba; DEN = Denmark; DOM = Dominican Republic; ENG = England; ESP = Spain; EST = Estonia; FIJ = Fiji Islands; FIN = Finland; FRA = France; GBR = United Kingdom; GDR = German Democratic Republic; GEO = Georgia; GER = Germany (but West Germany only from 1968-1990); GHA = Ghana; GUY = Guyana; HOL = Netherlands; HUN = Hungary; IND = India; IRL = Ireland; ITA = Italy; JAM = Jamaica; JPN = Japan; KAZ = Kazakhstan; KEN = Kenya; LIT = Lithuania; MAS = Malaysia; MEX = Mexico; MRI = Mauritius; NAM = Nambia; NKO = North Korea; NIG = Nigeria; NIR = Northern Ireland; NOR = Norway; NZL = New Zealand; PAK = Pakistan; POL = Poland; PUR = Puerto Rico; ROM = Romania; RUS = Russia; SAF = South Africa; SCO = Scotland; SKO = South Korea; SR = Southern Rhodesia; STV = St Vincent; SWE = Sweden; TCH = Czechoslovakia; THA = Thailand; TUR = Turkey; UGA = Uganda; UKR = Ukraine; URS = USSR; USA = United States of America; UZB = Uzbekistan; VEN = Venezuela; WAL = Wales; YUG = Yugoslavia; ZAM = Zambia.

Olympic Champions, 1904-2004

St Louis, USA - 1904
Fly: G. Finnegan (USA). **Bantam:** O. Kirk (USA). **Feather:** O. Kirk (USA). **Light:** H. Spangler (USA). **Welter:** A. Young (USA). **Middle:** C. May (USA). **Heavy:** S. Berger (USA).

London, England - 1908
Bantam: H. Thomas (GBR). **Feather:** R. Gunn (GBR). **Light:** F. Grace (GBR). **Middle:** J.W.H.T. Douglas (GBR). **Heavy:** A. Oldman (GBR).
Silver medals: J. Condon (GBR), C. Morris (GBR), F. Spiller (GBR), S. Evans (GBR).
Bronze medals: W. Webb (GBR), H. Rodding (GBR), T. Ringer (GBR), H. Johnson (GBR), R. Warnes (GBR), W. Philo (GBR), F. Parks (GBR).

Antwerp, Belgium - 1920
Fly: F. Genaro (USA). **Bantam:** C. Walker (SAF). **Feather:** R. Fritsch (FRA). **Light:** S. Mossberg (USA). **Welter:** T. Schneider (CAN). **Middle:** H. Mallin (GBR). **L. Heavy:** E. Eagan (USA). **Heavy:** R. Rawson (GBR).
Silver medal: A. Ireland (GBR).
Bronze medals: W. Cuthbertson (GBR), G. McKenzie (GBR), H. Franks (GBR).

Paris, France - 1924
Fly: F. la Barba (USA). **Bantam:** W. Smith (SAF). **Feather:** J. Fields (USA). **Light:** H. Nielson (DEN). **Welter:** J. Delarge (BEL). **Middle:** H. Mallin (GBR). **L. Heavy:** H. Mitchell (GBR). **Heavy:** O. von Porat (NOR).
Silver medals: J. McKenzie (GBR), J. Elliot (GBR).

Amsterdam, Holland - 1928
Fly: A. Kocsis (HUN). **Bantam:** V. Tamagnini (ITA). **Feather:** B. van Klaveren (HOL). **Light:** C. Orlando (ITA). **Welter:** E. Morgan (NZL). **Middle:** P. Toscani (ITA). **L. Heavy:** V. Avendano (ARG). **Heavy:** A. Rodriguez Jurado (ARG).

Los Angeles, USA - 1932
Fly: I. Enekes (HUN). **Bantam:** H. Gwynne (CAN). **Feather:** C. Robledo (ARG). **Light:** L. Stevens (SAF). **Welter:** E. Flynn (USA). **Middle:** C. Barth (USA). **L. Heavy:** D. Carstens (SAF). **Heavy:** A. Lovell (ARG).

Berlin, West Germany - 1936
Fly: W. Kaiser (GER). **Bantam:** U. Sergo (ITA). **Feather:** O. Casanova (ARG). **Light:** I. Harangi (HUN). **Welter:** S. Suvio (FIN). **Middle:** J. Despeaux (FRA). **L. Heavy:** R. Michelot (FRA). **Heavy:** H. Runge (GER).

London, England - 1948
Fly: P. Perez (ARG). **Bantam:** T. Csik (HUN). **Feather:** E. Formenti (ITA). **Light:** G. Dreyer (SAF). **Welter:** J. Torma (TCH). **Middle:** L. Papp (HUN). **L. Heavy:** G. Hunter (SAF). **Heavy:** R. Iglesas (ARG).
Silver medals: J. Wright (GBR), D. Scott (GBR).

Helsinki, Finland - 1952
Fly: N. Brooks (USA). **Bantam:** P. Hamalainen (FIN). **Feather:** J. Zachara (TCH). **Light:** A. Bolognesi (ITA). **L. Welter:** C. Adkins (USA). **Welter:** Z. Chychla (POL). **L. Middle:** L. Papp (HUN). **Middle:** F. Patterson (USA). **L. Heavy:** N. Lee (USA). **Heavy:** E. Sanders (USA).
Silver medal: J. McNally (IRL).

Melbourne, Australia - 1956
Fly: T. Spinks (GBR). **Bantam:** W. Behrendt (GER). **Feather:** V. Safronov (URS). **Light:** R. McTaggart (GBR). **L. Welter:** V. Jengibarian (URS). **Welter:** N. Linca (ROM). **L. Middle:** L. Papp (HUN). **Middle:** G. Schatkov (URS). **L. Heavy:** J. Boyd (USA). **Heavy:** P. Rademacher (USA).

Silver medals: T. Nicholls (GBR), F. Tiedt (IRL).
Bronze medals: J. Caldwell (IRL), F. Gilroy (IRL), A. Bryne (IRL), N. Gargano (GBR), J. McCormack (GBR).

Rome, Italy - 1960
Fly: G. Torok (HUN). **Bantam:** O. Grigoryev (URS). **Feather:** F. Musso (ITA). **Light:** K. Pazdzior (POL). **L. Welter:** B. Nemecek (TCH). **Welter:** N. Benvenuti (ITA). **L. Middle:** W. McClure (USA). **Middle:** E. Crook (USA). **L. Heavy:** C. Clay (USA). **Heavy:** F. de Piccoli (ITA).
Bronze medals: R. McTaggart (GBR), J. Lloyd (GBR), W. Fisher (GBR).

Tokyo, Japan - 1964
Fly: F. Atzori (ITA). **Bantam:** T. Sakurai (JPN). **Feather:** S. Stepashkin (URS). **Light:** J. Grudzien (POL). **L. Welter:** J. Kulej (POL). **Welter:** M. Kasprzyk (POL). **L. Middle:** B. Lagutin (URS). **Middle:** V. Popenchenko (URS). **L. Heavy:** C. Pinto (ITA). **Heavy:** J. Frazier (USA).
Bronze medal: J. McCourt (IRL).

Mexico City, Mexico - 1968
L. Fly: F. Rodriguez (VEN). **Fly:** R. Delgado (MEX). **Bantam:** V. Sokolov (URS). **Feather:** A. Roldan (MEX). **Light:** R. Harris (USA). **L. Welter:** J. Kulej (POL). **Welter:** M. Wolke (GDR). **L. Middle:** B. Lagutin (URS). **Middle:** C. Finnegan (GBR). **L. Heavy:** D. Poznyak (URS). **Heavy:** G. Foreman (USA).

Munich, West Germany - 1972
L. Fly: G. Gedo (HUN). **Fly:** G. Kostadinov (BUL). **Bantam:** O. Martinez (CUB). **Feather:** B. Kusnetsov (URS). **Light:** J. Szczepanski (POL). **L. Welter:** R. Seales (USA). **Welter:** E. Correa (CUB). **L. Middle:** D. Kottysch (GER). **Middle:** V. Lemeschev (URS). **L. Heavy:** M. Parlov (YUG). **Heavy:** T. Stevenson (CUB).
Bronze medals: R. Evans (GBR), G. Turpin (GBR), A. Minter (GBR).

Montreal, Canada - 1976
L. Fly: J. Hernandez (CUB). **Fly:** L. Randolph (USA). **Bantam:** Y-J. Gu (NKO). **Feather:** A. Herrera (CUB). **Light:** H. Davis (USA). **L. Welter:** R. Leonard (USA). **Welter:** J. Bachfield (GDR). **L. Middle:** J. Rybicki (POL). **Middle:** M. Spinks (USA). **L. Heavy:** L. Spinks (USA). **Heavy:** T. Stevenson (CUB).
Bronze medal: P. Cowdell (GBR).

Moscow, USSR - 1980
L. Fly: S. Sabirov (URS). **Fly:** P. Lessov (BUL). **Bantam:** J. Hernandez (CUB). **Feather:** R. Fink (GDR). **Light:** A. Herrera (CUB). **L. Welter:** P. Oliva (ITA). **Welter:** A. Aldama (CUB). **L. Middle:** A. Martinez (CUB). **Middle:** J. Gomez (CUB). **L. Heavy:** S. Kacar (YUG). **Heavy:** T. Stevenson (CUB).
Bronze medals: H. Russell (IRL), A. Willis (GBR).

Los Angeles, USA - 1984
L. Fly: P. Gonzalez (USA). **Fly:** S. McCrory (USA). **Bantam:** M. Stecca (ITA). **Feather:** M. Taylor (USA). **Light:** P. Whitaker (USA). **L. Welter:** J. Page (USA). **Welter:** M. Breland (USA). **L. Middle:** F. Tate (USA). **Middle:** J-S. Shin (SKO). **L. Heavy:** A. Josipovic (YUG). **Heavy:** H. Tillman (USA). **S. Heavy:** T. Biggs (USA).
Bronze medal: B. Wells (GBR).

Seoul, South Korea - 1988
L. Fly: I. Mustafov (BUL). **Fly:** H-S. Kim (SKO). **Bantam:** K. McKinney (USA). **Feather:** G. Parisi (ITA). **Light:** A. Zuelow (GDR). **L. Welter:** V. Yanovsky (URS). **Welter:** R. Wangila (KEN). **L. Middle:** S-H. Park (SKO). **Middle:** H. Maske (GDR). **L. Heavy:** A. Maynard (USA). **Heavy:** R. Mercer (USA). **S. Heavy:** L. Lewis (CAN).
Bronze medal: R. Woodhall (GBR).

Barcelona, Spain - 1992

L. Fly: R. Marcelo (CUB). **Fly:** C-C. Su (NKO). **Bantam:** J. Casamayor (CUB). **Feather:** A. Tews (GER). **Light:** O. de la Hoya (USA). **L. Welter:** H. Vinent (CUB). **Welter:** M. Carruth (IRL). **L. Middle:** J. Lemus (CUB). **Middle:** A. Hernandez (CUB). **L. Heavy:** T. May (GER). **Heavy:** F. Savon (CUB). **S. Heavy:** R. Balado (CUB).
Silver medal: W. McCullough (IRL).
Bronze medal: R. Reid (GBR).

Atlanta, USA - 1996

L. Fly: D. Petrov (BUL). **Fly:** M. Romero (CUB). **Bantam:** I. Kovaks (HUN). **Feather:** S. Kamsing (THA). **Light:** H. Soltani (ALG). **L. Welter:** H. Vinent (CUB). **Welter:** O. Saitov (RUS). **L. Middle:** D. Reid (USA). **Middle:** A. Hernandez (CUB). **L. Heavy:** V. Jirov (KAZ). **Heavy:** F. Savon (CUB). **S. Heavy:** Vladimir Klitschko (UKR).

Sydney, Australia - 2000

L. Fly: B. Aslom (FRA). **Fly:** W. Ponlid (THA). **Bantam:** G. Rigondeaux (CUB). **Feather:** B. Sattarkhanov (KAZ). **Light:** M. Kindelan (CUB). **L. Welter:** M. Abdullaev (UZB). **Welter:** O. Saitov (RUS). **L. Middle:** Y. Ibraimov (KAZ). **Middle:** J. Gutierrez Espinosa (CUB). **L. Heavy:** A. Lebziak (RUS). **Heavy:** F. Savon (CUB). **S. Heavy:** A. Harrison (ENG).

Athens, Greece - 2004

L. Fly: Y. Bartelemi (CUB). **Fly:** Y. Gamboa (CUB). **Bantam:** G. Rigondeaux (CUB). **Feather:** A. Tichtchenko (RUS). **Light:** M. Kindelan (CUB). **L. Welter:** M. Boonjumnong (THA). **Welter:** B. Artayev (KAZ). **Middle:** G. Gaiderbekov (RUS). **L. Heavy:** A. Ward (USA). **Heavy:** O. Solis (CUB). **S. Heavy:** A. Povetkin (RUS).
Silver medal: A. Khan (ENG).

World Champions, 1974-2005

Havana, Cuba - 1974

L. Fly: J. Hernandez (CUB). **Fly:** D. Rodriguez (CUB). **Bantam:** W. Gomez (PUR). **Feather:** H. Davis (USA). **Light:** V. Solomin (URS). **L. Welter:** A. Kalule (UGA). **Welter:** E. Correa (CUB). **L. Middle:** R. Garbey (CUB). **Middle:** R. Riskiev (URS). **L. Heavy:** M. Parlov (YUG). **Heavy:** T. Stevenson (CUB).

Belgrade, Yugoslavia - 1978

L. Fly: S. Muchoki (KEN). **Fly:** H. Strednicki (POL). **Bantam:** A. Horta (CUB). **Feather:** A. Herrera (CUB). **Light:** D. Andeh (NIG). **L. Welter:** V. Lvov (URS). **Welter:** V. Rachkov (URS). **L. Middle:** V. Savchenko (URS). **Middle:** J. Gomez (CUB). **L. Heavy:** S. Soria (CUB). **Heavy:** T. Stevenson (CUB).

Munich, West Germany - 1982

L. Fly: I. Mustafov (BUL). **Fly:** Y. Alexandrov (URS). **Bantam:** F. Favors (USA). **Feather:** A. Horta (CUB). **Light:** A. Herrera (CUB). **L. Welter:** C. Garcia (CUB). **Welter:** M. Breland (USA). **L. Middle:** A. Koshkin (URS). **Middle:** B. Comas (CUB). **L. Heavy:** P. Romero (CUB). **Heavy:** A. Jagubkin (URS). **S. Heavy:** T. Biggs (USA).
Bronze medal: T. Corr (IRL).

Reno, USA - 1986

L. Fly: J. Odelin (CUB). **Fly:** P. Reyes (CUB). **Bantam:** S-I. Moon (SKO). **Feather:** K. Banks (USA). **Light:** A. Horta (CUB). **L. Welter:** V. Shishov (URS). **Welter:** K. Gould (USA). **L. Middle:** A. Espinosa (CUB). **Middle:** D. Allen (USA). **L. Heavy:** P. Romero (CUB). **Heavy:** F. Savon (CUB). **S. Heavy:** T. Stevenson (CUB).

Moscow, USSR - 1989

L. Fly: E. Griffin (USA). **Fly:** Y. Arbachakov (URS). **Bantam:** E. Carrion (CUB). **Feather:** A. Khamatov (URS). **Light:** J. Gonzalez (CUB). **L. Welter:** I. Ruzinkov (URS). **Welter:** F. Vastag (Rom). **L. Middle:** I. Akopokhian (URS). **Middle:** A. Kurniavka (URS). **L. Heavy:** H. Maske (GDR). **Heavy:** F. Savon (CUB). **S. Heavy:** R. Balado (CUB).
Bronze medal: M. Carruth (IRL).

Sydney, Australia - 1991

L. Fly: E. Griffin (USA). **Fly:** I. Kovacs (HUN). **Bantam:** S. Todorov (BUL). **Feather:** K. Kirkorov (BUL). **Light:** M. Rudolph (GER). **L. Welter:** K. Tszyu (URS). **Welter:** J. Hernandez (CUB). **L. Middle:** J. Lemus (CUB). **Middle:** T. Russo (ITA). **L. Heavy:** T. May (GER). **Heavy:** F. Savon (CUB). **S. Heavy:** R. Balado (CUB).

Tampere, Finland - 1993

L. Fly: N. Munchian (ARM). **Fly:** W. Font (CUB). **Bantam:** A. Christov (BUL). **Feather:** S. Todorov (BUL). **Light:** D. Austin (CUB). **L. Welter:** H. Vinent (CUB). **Welter:** J. Hernandez (CUB). **L. Middle:** F. Vastag (ROM). **Middle:** A. Hernandez (CUB). **L. Heavy:** R. Garbey (CUB). **Heavy:** F. Savon (CUB). **S. Heavy:** R. Balado (CUB).
Bronze medal: D. Kelly (IRL).

Berlin, Germany - 1995

L. Fly: D. Petrov (BUL). **Fly:** Z. Lunka (GER). **Bantam:** R. Malachbekov (RUS). **Feather:** S. Todorov (BUL). **Light:** L. Doroftei (ROM). **L. Welter:** H. Vinent (CUB). **Welter:** J. Hernandez (CUB). **L. Middle:** F. Vastag (ROM). **Middle:** A. Hernandez (CUB). **L. Heavy:** A. Tarver (USA). **Heavy:** F. Savon (CUB). **S. Heavy:** A. Lezin (RUS).

Budapest, Hungary - 1997

L. Fly: M. Romero (CUB). **Fly:** M. Mantilla (CUB). **Bantam:** R Malakhbekov (RUS). **Feather:** I. Kovacs (HUN). **Light:** A. Maletin (RUS). **L. Welter:** D. Simion (ROM). **Welter:** O. Saitov (RUS). **L. Middle:** A. Duvergel (CUB). **Middle:** Z. Erdei (HUN). **L. Heavy:** A. Lebsiak (RUS). **Heavy:** F. Savon (CUB). **S. Heavy:** G. Kandelaki (GEO).
Bronze medal: S. Kirk (IRL).

Houston, USA - 1999

L. Fly: B. Viloria (USA). **Fly:** B. Jumadilov (KAZ). **Bantam:** R. Crinu (ROM). **Feather:** R. Juarez (USA). **Light:** M. Kindelan (CUB). **L. Welter:** M. Abdullaev (UZB). **Welter:** J. Hernandez (CUB). **L. Middle:** M. Simion (ROM). **Middle:** U. Haydarov (UZB). **L. Heavy:** M. Simms (USA). **Heavy:** M. Bennett (USA). **S. Heavy:** S. Samilsan (TUR).
Bronze medal: K. Evans (WAL).

Belfast, Northern Ireland - 2001

L. Fly: Y. Bartelemi (CUB). **Fly:** J. Thomas (FRA). **Bantam:** G. Rigondeaux (CUB). **Feather:** R. Palyani (TUR). **Light:** M. Kindelan (CUB). **L. Welter:** D. Luna Martinez (CUB). **Welter:** L. Aragon (CUB). **L. Middle:** D. Austin (CUB). **Middle:** A. Gogolev (RUS). **L. Heavy:** Y. Makarenko (RUS). **Heavy:** O. Solis (CUB). **S. Heavy:** R. Chagaev (UZB).
Silver medal: D. Haye (ENG).
Bronze medals: J. Moore (IRL), C. Froch (ENG).

Bangkok, Thailand - 2003

L. Fly: S. Karazov (RUS). **Fly:** S. Jongjohor (THA). **Bantam:** A. Mamedov (AZE). **Feather:** G. Jafarov (KAZ). **Light:** M. Kindelan (CUB). **L. Welter:** W. Blain (FRA). **Welter:** L. Aragon (CUB). **Middle:** G. Golovkin (KAZ). **L. Heavy:** Y. Makarenko (RUS). **Heavy:** O. Solis (CUB). **S. Heavy:** A. Povetkin (RUS).

Mianyang City, China - 2005

L. Fly: S. Zou (CHI). **Fly:** O-S Lee (SKO). **Bantam:** G. Rigondeaux (CUB). **Feather:** A. Tischenko (RUS). **Light:** Y. Ugas (CUB). **L. Welter:** S. Sapiyev (KAZ). **Welter:** E. Lara (CUB). **Middle:** M. Korobev (RUS). **L. Heavy:** Y. Dzhanabergenov (KAZ). **Heavy:** A. Alexeev (RUS). **S. Heavy:** O. Solis (CUB).
Bronze medal: N. Perkins (ENG).

World Junior Champions, 1979-2004

Yokohama, Japan - 1979

L. Fly: R. Shannon (USA). **Fly:** P. Lessov (BUL). **Bantam:** P-K. Choi (SKO). **Feather:** Y. Gladychev (URS). **Light:** R. Blake (USA). **L. Welter:** I. Akopokhian (URS). **Welter:** M. McCrory (USA). **L. Middle:** A. Mayes (USA). **Middle:** A. Milov (URS). **L. Heavy:** A. Lebedev (URS). **Heavy:** M. Frazier (USA).
Silver medals: N. Wilshire (ENG), D. Cross (ENG).
Bronze medal: I. Scott (SCO).

Santo Domingo, Dominican Republic - 1983

L. Fly: M. Herrera (DOM). **Fly:** J. Gonzalez (CUB). **Bantam:** J. Molina (PUR). **Feather:** A. Miesses (DOM). **Light:** A. Beltre (DOM). **L. Welter:** A. Espinoza (CUB). **Welter:** M. Watkins (USA). **L. Middle:** U. Castillo (CUB). **Middle:** R. Batista (CUB). **L. Heavy:** O. Pought (USA). **Heavy:** A. Williams (USA). **S. Heavy:** L. Lewis (CAN).

Bucharest, Romania - 1985

L. Fly: R-S. Hwang (SKO). **Fly:** T. Marcelica (ROM). **Bantam:** R. Diaz (CUB). **Feather:** D. Maeran (ROM). **Light:** J. Teiche (GDR). **L. Welter:** W. Saeger (GDR). **Welter:** A. Stoianov (BUL). **L. Middle:** M. Franek (TCH). **Middle:** O. Zahalotskih (URS). **L. Heavy:** B. Riddick (USA). **Heavy:** F. Savon (CUB). **S. Heavy:** A. Prianichnikov (URS).

Havana, Cuba - 1987

L. Fly: E. Paisan (CUB). **Fly:** C. Daniels (USA). **Bantam:** A. Moya (CUB). **Feather:** G. Iliyasov (URS). **Light:** J. Hernandez (CUB). **L. Welter:** L. Mihai (ROM). **Welter:** F. Vastag (ROM). **L. Middle:** A. Lobsyak (URS). **Middle:** W. Martinez (CUB). **L. Heavy:** D. Yeliseyev (URS). **Heavy:** R. Balado (CUB). **S. Heavy:** L. Martinez (CUB).
Silver medal: E. Loughran (IRL).
Bronze medal: D. Galvin (IRL).

San Juan, Puerto Rico - 1989

L. Fly: D. Petrov (BUL). **Fly:** N. Monchai (FRA). **Bantam:** J. Casamayor (CUB). **Feather:** C. Febres (PUR). **Light:** A. Acevedo (PUR). **L. Welter:** E. Berger (GDR). **Welter:** A. Hernandez (CUB). **L. Middle:** L. Bedey (CUB). **Middle:** R. Garbey (CUB). **L. Heavy:** R. Alvarez (CUB). **Heavy:** K. Johnson (CAN). **S. Heavy:** A. Burdiantz (URS).
Silver medals: E. Magee (IRL), R. Reid (ENG), S. Wilson (SCO).

Lima, Peru - 1990
L. Fly: D. Alicea (PUR). **Fly:** K. Pielert (GDR). **Bantam:** K. Baravi (URS). **Feather:** A. Vaughan (ENG). **Light:** J. Mendez (CUB). **L. Welter:** H. Vinent (CUB). **Welter:** A. Hernandez (CUB). **L. Middle:** A. Kakauridze (URS). **Middle:** J. Gomez (CUB). **L. Heavy:** B. Torsten (GDR). **Heavy:** I. Andreev (URS). **S. Heavy:** J. Quesada (CUB).
Bronze medal: P. Ingle (ENG).

Montreal, Canada - 1992
L. Fly: W. Font (CUB). **Fly:** J. Oragon (CUB). **Bantam:** N. Machado (CUB). **Feather:** M. Stewart (CAN). **Light:** D. Austin (CUB). **L. Welter:** O. Saitov (RUS). **Welter:** L. Brors (GER). **L. Middle:** J. Acosta (CUB). **Middle:** I. Arsangaliev (RUS). **L. Heavy:** S. Samilsan (TUR). **Heavy:** G. Kandeliaki (GEO). **S. Heavy:** M. Porchnev (RUS).
Bronze medal: N. Sinclair (IRL).

Istanbul, Turkey - 1994
L. Fly: J. Turunen (FIN). **Fly:** A. Jimenez (CUB). **Bantam:** J. Despaigne (CUB). **Feather:** D. Simion (ROM). **Light:** L. Diogenes (CUB). **L. Welter:** V. Romero (CUB). **Welter:** E. Aslan (TUR). **L. Middle:** G. Ledsvanys (CUB). **Middle:** M. Genc (TUR). **L. Heavy:** P. Aurino (ITA). **Heavy:** M. Lopez (CUB). **S. Heavy:** P. Carrion (CUB).

Havana, Cuba - 1996
L. Fly: L. Hernandez (CUB). **Fly:** L. Cabrera (CUB). **Bantam:** P. Miradal (CUB). **Feather:** E. Rodriguez (CUB). **Light:** R. Vaillan (CUB). **L. Welter:** T. Mergadze (RUS). **Welter:** J. Brahmer (GER). **L. Middle:** L. Mezquia (CUB). **Middle:** V. Pletniov (RUS). **L. Heavy:** O. Simon (CUB). **Heavy:** A. Yatsenko (UKR). **S. Heavy:** S. Fabre (CUB).
Bronze medal: R. Hatton (ENG).

Buenos Aires, Argentina - 1998
L. Fly: S. Tanasie (ROM). **Fly:** S. Yeledov (KAZ). **Bantam:** S. Suleymanov (UKR). **Feather:** I. Perez (ARG). **Light:** A. Solopov (RUS). **L. Welter:** Y. Tomashov (UKR). **Welter:** K. Oustarkhanov (RUS). **L. Middle:** S. Kostenko (UKR). **Middle:** K. Kempe (GER). **L. Heavy:** H. Yohanson Martinez (CUB). **Heavy:** O. Solis Fonte (CUB). **S. Heavy:** B. Ohanyan (ARM).
Silver medal: H. Cunningham (IRL).
Bronze medal: D. Campbell (IRL).

Budapest, Hungary - 2000
L. Fly: Y. Leon Alarcon (CUB). **Fly:** O. Franco Vaszquez (CUB). **Bantam:** V. Tajbert (GER). **Feather:** G. Kate (HUN). **Light:** F. Adzsanalov (AZE). **L. Welter:** G. Galovkin (KAZ). **Welter:** S. Ustunel (TUR). **L. Middle:** D. Chernysh (RUS). **Middle:** F. Sullivan Barrera (CUB). **L. Heavy:** A. Shekmourov (RUS). **Heavy:** D. Medzhydov (UKR). **S. Heavy:** A. Dmitrienko (RUS).
Bronze medal: C. Barrett (IRL).

Santiago, Cuba - 2002
L. Fly: D. Acripitian (RUS). **Fly:** Y. Fabregas (CUB). **Bantam:** S. Bahodirijan (UZB). **Feather:** A. Tichtchenko (RUS). **Light:** S. Mendez (CUB). **L. Welter:** K. Iliyasov (KAZ). **Welter:** J. McPherson (USA). **L. Middle:** V. Diaz (CUB). **Middle:** A. Duarte (CUB). **L. Heavy:** R. Zavalnyuyk (UKR). **Heavy:** Y. P. Hernandez (CUB). **S. Heavy:** P. Portal (CUB).
Silver medal: A. Lee (IRL).
Bronze medal: N. Brough (ENG).

Jeju Island, South Korea - 2004
L. Fly: P. Bedak (Hun). **Fly:** I. Rahimov (UZB). **Bantam:** A. Abdimomunov (KAZ). **Feather:** E. Ambartsumyan (RUS). **Light:** A. Khan (ENG). **L. Welter:** C. Banteur (CUB). **Welter:** E. Rasulov (UZB). **Middle:** D. Tchudinov (RUS). **L. Heavy:** I. Perez (CUB). **Heavy:** E. Romanov (RUS). **S.Heavy:** D. Boytsov (RUS).
Bronze medal: D. Price (ENG).

European Champions, 1924-2006

Paris, France - 1924
Fly: J. McKenzie (GBR). **Bantam:** J. Ces (FRA). **Feather:** R. de Vergnie (BEL). **Light:** N. Nielsen (DEN). **Welter:** J. Delarge (BEL). **Middle:** H. Mallin (GBR). **L. Heavy:** H. Mitchell (GBR). **Heavy:** O. von Porat (NOR).

Stockholm, Sweden - 1925
Fly: E. Pladner (FRA). **Bantam:** A. Rule (GBR). **Feather:** P. Andren (SWE). **Light:** S. Johanssen (SWE). **Welter:** H. Nielsen (DEN). **Middle:** F. Crawley (GBR). **L. Heavy:** T. Petersen (DEN). **Heavy:** B. Persson (SWE).
Silver medals: J. James (GBR), E. Viney (GBR), D. Lister (GBR).

Berlin, Germany - 1927
Fly: L. Boman (SWE). **Bantam:** K. Dalchow (GER). **Feather:** F. Dubbers (GER). **Light:** H. Domgoergen (GER). **Welter:** R. Caneva (ITA). **Middle:** J. Christensen (NOR). **L. Heavy:** H. Muller (GER). **Heavy:** N. Ramm (SWE).

Amsterdam, Holland - 1928
Fly: A. Kocsis (HUN). **Bantam:** V. Tamagnini (ITA). **Feather:** B. van Klaveren (HOL). **Light:** C. Orlandi (ITA). **Welter:** R. Galataud (FRA). **Middle:** P. Toscani (ITA). **L. Heavy:** E. Pistulla (GER). **Heavy:** N. Ramm (SWE).

Budapest, Hungary - 1930
Fly: I. Enekes (HUN). **Bantam:** J. Szeles (HUN). **Feather:** G. Szabo (HUN). **Light:** M. Bianchini (ITA). **Welter:** J. Besselmann (GER). **Middle:** C. Meroni (ITA). **L. Heavy:** T. Petersen (DEN). **Heavy:** J. Michaelson (DEN).

Los Angeles, USA - 1932
Fly: I. Enekes (HUN). **Bantam:** H. Ziglarski (GER). **Feather:** J. Schleinkofer (GER). **Light:** T. Ahlqvist (SWE). **Welter:** E. Campe (GER). **Middle:** R. Michelot (FRA). **L. Heavy:** G. Rossi (ITA). **Heavy:** L. Rovati (ITA).

Budapest, Hungary - 1934
Fly: P. Palmer (GBR). **Bantam:** I. Enekes (HUN). **Feather:** O. Kaestner GER). **Light:** E. Facchini (ITA). **Welter:** D. McCleave (GBR). **Middle:** S. Szigetti (HUN). **L. Heavy:** P. Zehetmayer (AUT). **Heavy:** G. Baerlund (FIN).
Bronze medal: P. Floyd (GBR).

Milan, Italy - 1937
Fly: I. Enekes (HUN). **Bantam:** U. Sergo (ITA). **Feather:** A. Polus (POL). **Light:** H. Nuremberg (GER). **Welter:** M. Murach (GER). **Middle:** H. Chmielewski (POL). **L. Heavy:** S. Szigetti (HUN). **Heavy:** O. Tandberg (SWE).

Dublin, Eire - 1939
Fly: J. Ingle (IRL). **Bantam:** U. Sergo (ITA). **Feather:** P. Dowdall (IRL). **Light:** H. Nuremberg (GER). **Welter:** A. Kolczyski (POL). **Middle:** A. Raadik (EST). **L. Heavy:** L. Musina (ITA). **Heavy:** O. Tandberg (SWE).
Bronze medal: C. Evenden (IRL).

Dublin, Eire - 1947
Fly: L. Martinez (ESP). **Bantam:** L. Bogacs (HUN). **Feather:** K. Kreuger (SWE). **Light:** J. Vissers (BEL). **Welter:** J. Ryan (ENG). **Middle:** A. Escudie (FRA). **L. Heavy:** H. Quentemeyer (HOL). **Heavy:** G. O'Colmain (IRL).
Silver medals: J. Clinton (SCO), P. Maguire (IRL), W. Thom (ENG), G. Scriven (ENG).
Bronze medals: J. Dwyer (SCO), A. Sanderson (ENG), W. Frith (SCO), E. Cantwell (IRL), K. Wyatt (ENG).

Oslo, Norway - 1949
Fly: J. Kasperczak (POL). **Bantam:** G. Zuddas (ITA). **Feather:** J. Bataille (FRA). **Light:** M. McCullagh (IRL). **Welter:** J. Torma (TCH). **Middle:** L. Papp (HUN). **L. Heavy:** G. di Segni (ITA). **Heavy:** L. Bene (HUN).
Bronze medal: D. Connell (IRL).

Milan, Italy - 1951
Fly: A. Pozzali (ITA). **Bantam:** V. Dall'Osso (ITA). **Feather:** J. Ventaja (FRA). **Light:** B. Visintin (ITA). **L. Welter:** H. Schelling (GER). **Welter:** Z. Chychla (POL). **L. Middle:** L. Papp (HUN). **Middle:** S. Sjolin (SWE). **L. Heavy:** M. Limage (BEL). **Heavy:** G. di Segni (ITA).
Silver medal: J. Kelly (IRL).
Bronze medals: D. Connell (IRL), T. Milligan (IRL), A. Lay (ENG).

Warsaw, Poland - 1953
Fly: H. Kukier (POL). **Bantam:** Z. Stefaniuk (POL). **Feather:** J. Kruza (POL). **Light:** V. Jengibarian (URS). **L. Welter:** L. Drogosz (POL). **Welter:** Z. Chychla (POL). **L. Middle:** B. Wells (ENG). **Middle:** D. Wemhoner (GER). **L. Heavy:** U. Nietchke (GER). **Heavy:** A. Schotzikas (URS).
Silver medal: T. Milligan (IRL).
Bronze medals: J. McNally (IRL), R. Barton (ENG).

Berlin, West Germany - 1955
Fly: E. Basel (GER). **Bantam:** Z. Stefaniuk (POL). **Feather:** T. Nicholls (ENG). **Light:** H. Kurschat (GER). **L. Welter:** L. Drogosz (POL). **Welter:** N. Gargano (ENG). **L. Middle:** Z. Pietrzykowski (POL). **Middle:** G. Schatkov (URS). **L. Heavy:** E. Schoeppner (GER). **Heavy:** A. Schotzikas (URS).

Prague, Czechoslovakia - 1957
Fly: M. Homberg (GER). **Bantam:** O. Grigoryev (URS). **Feather:** D. Venilov (BUL). **Light:** K. Pazdzior (POL). **L. Welter:** V. Jengibarian (URS). **Welter:** M. Graus (GER). **L. Middle:** N. Benvenuti (ITA). **Middle:** Z. Pietrzykowski (POL). **L. Heavy:** G. Negrea (ROM). **Heavy:** A. Abramov (URS).
Bronze medals: R. Davies (WAL), J. Morrissey (SCO), J. Kidd (SCO), F. Teidt (IRL).

Lucerne, Switzerland - 1959
Fly: M. Homberg (GER). **Bantam:** H. Rascher (GER). **Feather:** J. Adamski (POL). **Light:** O. Maki (FIN). **L. Welter:** V. Jengibarian (URS). **Welter:** L. Drogosz (POL). **L. Middle:** N. Benvenuti (ITA). **Middle:** G. Schatkov (URS). **L. Heavy:** Z. Pietrzykowski (POL). **Heavy:** A. Abramov (URS).
Silver medal: D. Thomas (ENG).
Bronze medals: A. McClean (IRL), H. Perry (IRL), C. McCoy (IRL), H. Scott (ENG).

Belgrade, Yugoslavia - 1961
Fly: P. Vacca (ITA). **Bantam:** S. Sivko (URS). **Feather:** F. Taylor (ENG). **Light:** R. McTaggart (SCO). **L. Welter:** A. Tamulis (URS). **Welter:** R. Tamulis (URS). **L. Middle:** B. Lagutin (URS). **Middle:** T. Walasek (POL). **L. Heavy:** G.

269

Saraudi (ITA). **Heavy:** A. Abramov (URS).
Bronze medals: P. Warwick (ENG), I. McKenzie (SCO), J. Bodell (ENG).

Moscow, USSR - 1963
Fly: V. Bystrov (URS). **Bantam:** O. Grigoryev (URS). **Feather:** S. Stepashkin (URS). **Light:** J. Kajdi (HUN). **L. Welter:** J. Kulej (POL). **Welter:** R. Tamulis (URS). **L. Middle:** B. Lagutin (URS). **Middle:** V. Popenchenko (URS). **L. Heavy:** Z. Pietrzykowski (POL). **Heavy:** J. Nemec (TCH).
Silver medal: A. Wyper (SCO).

Berlin, East Germany - 1965
Fly: H. Freisdadt (GER). **Bantam:** O. Grigoryev (URS). **Feather:** S. Stepashkin (URS). **Light:** V. Barranikov (URS). **L. Welter:** J. Kulej (POL). **Welter:** R. Tamulis (URS). **L. Middle:** V. Ageyev (URS). **Middle:** V. Popenchenko (URS). **L. Heavy:** D. Poznyak (URS). **Heavy:** A. Isosimov (URS).
Silver medal: B. Robinson (ENG).
Bronze medals: J. McCluskey (SCO), K. Buchanan (SCO), J. McCourt (IRL).

Rome, Italy - 1967
Fly: H. Skrzyczak (POL). **Bantam:** N. Giju (ROM). **Feather:** R. Petek (POL). **Light:** J. Grudzien (POL). **L. Welter:** V. Frolov (URS). **Welter:** B. Nemecek (TCH). **L. Middle:** V. Ageyev (URS). **Middle:** M. Casati (ITA). **L. Heavy:** D. Poznyak (URS). **Heavy:** M. Baruzzi (ITA).
Silver medal: P. Boddington (ENG).

Bucharest, Romania - 1969
L. Fly: G. Gedo (HUN). **Fly:** C. Ciuca (ROM). **Bantam:** A. Dumitrescu (ROM). **Feather:** L. Orban (HUN). **Light:** S. Cutov (ROM). **L. Welter:** V. Frolov (URS). **Welter:** G. Meier (GER). **L. Middle:** V. Tregubov (URS). **Middle:** V. Tarasenkov (URS). **L. Heavy:** D. Poznyak (URS). **Heavy:** I. Alexe (ROM).
Bronze medals: M. Dowling (IRL), M. Piner (ENG), A. Richardson (ENG), T. Imrie (SCO).

Madrid, Spain - 1971
L. Fly: G. Gedo (HUN). **Fly:** J. Rodriguez (ESP). **Bantam:** T. Badar (HUN). **Feather:** R. Tomczyk (POL). **Light:** J. Szczepanski (POL). **L. Welter:** U. Beyer (GDR). **Welter:** J. Kajdi (HUN). **L. Middle:** V. Tregubov (URS). **Middle:** J. Juotsiavitchus (URS). **L. Heavy:** M. Parlov (YUG). **Heavy:** V. Tchernishev (URS).
Bronze medals: N. McLaughlin (IRL), M. Dowling (IRL), B. McCarthy (IRL), M. Kingwell (ENG), L. Stevens (ENG).

Belgrade, Yugoslavia - 1973
L. Fly: V. Zasypko (URS). **Fly:** C. Gruescu (ROM). **Bantam:** A. Cosentino (FRA). **Feather:** S. Forster (GDR). **Light:** S. Cutov (ROM). **L. Welter:** M. Benes (YUG). **Welter:** S. Csjef (HUN). **L. Middle:** A. Klimanov (URS). **Middle:** V. Lemechev (URS). **L. Heavy:** M. Parlov (YUG). **Heavy:** V. Ulyanich (URS).
Bronze medal: J. Bambrick (SCO).

Katowice, Poland - 1975
L. Fly: A. Tkachenko (URS). **Fly:** V. Zasypko (URS). **Bantam:** V. Rybakov (URS). **Feather:** T. Badari (HUN). **Light:** S. Cutov (ROM). **L. Welter:** V. Limasov (URS). **Welter:** K. Marjaama (FIN). **L. Middle:** W. Rudnowski (POL). **Middle:** V. Lemechev (URS). **L. Heavy:** A. Klimanov (URS). **Heavy:** A. Biegalski (POL).
Bronze medals: C. Magri (ENG), P. Cowdell (ENG), G. McEwan (ENG).

Halle, East Germany - 1977
L. Fly: H. Srednicki (POL). **Fly:** L. Blazynski (POL). **Bantam:** S. Forster (GDR). **Feather:** R. Nowakowski (GDR). **Light:** A. Rusevski (YUG). **L. Welter:** B. Gajda (POL). **Welter:** V. Limasov (URS). **L. Middle:** V. Saychenko (URS). **Middle:** I. Shaposhnikov (URS). **L. Heavy:** D. Kvachadze (URS). **Heavy:** E. Gorstkov (URS).
Bronze medal: P. Sutcliffe (IRL).

Cologne, West Germany - 1979
L. Fly: S. Sabirov (URS). **Fly:** H. Strednicki (POL). **Bantam:** N. Khrapzov (URS). **Feather:** V. Rybakov (URS). **Light.** V. Demianenko (URS). **L. Welter:** S. Konakbaev (URS). **Welter:** E. Muller (GER). **L. Middle:** M. Perunovic (YUG). **Middle:** V. Uusiverta (FIN). **L. Heavy:** A. Nikolyan (URS). **Heavy:** E. Gorstkov (URS). **S. Heavy:** P. Hussing (GER).
Bronze medal: P. Sutcliffe (IRL).

Tampere, Finland - 1981
L. Fly: I. Mustafov (BUL). **Fly:** P. Lessov (BUL). **Bantam:** V. Miroschnichenko (URS). **Feather:** R. Nowakowski (GDR). **Light:** V. Rybakov (URS). **L. Welter:** V. Shisov (URS). **Welter:** S. Konakvbaev (URS). **L. Middle:** A. Koshkin (URS). **Middle:** J. Torbek (URS). **L. Heavy:** A Krupin (URS). **Heavy:** A. Jagupkin (URS). **S. Heavy:** F. Damiani (ITA).
Bronze medal: G. Hawkins (IRL).

Varna, Bulgaria - 1983
L. Fly: I. Mustafov (BUL). **Fly:** P. Lessov (BUL). **Bantam:** Y. Alexandrov (URS). **Feather:** S. Nurkazov (URS). **Light:** E. Chuprenski (BUL). **L. Welter:** V. Shishov (URS). **Welter:** P. Galkin (URS). **L. Middle:** V. Laptev (URS). **Middle:**

V. Melnik (URS). **L. Heavy:** V. Kokhanovski (URS). **Heavy:** A. Jagubkin (URS). **S. Heavy:** F. Damiani (ITA).
Bronze medal: K. Joyce (IRL).

Budapest, Hungary - 1985
L. Fly: R. Breitbarth (GDR). **Fly:** D. Berg (GDR). **Bantam:** L. Simic (YUG). **Feather:** S. Khachatrian (URS). **Light:** E. Chuprenski (BUL) **L. Welter:** S. Mehnert (GDR). **Welter:** I. Akopokhian (URS). **L. Middle:** M. Timm (GDR). **Middle:** H. Maske (GDR). **L. Heavy:** N. Shanavasov (URS). **Heavy:** A. Jagubkin (URS). **S. Heavy:** F. Somodi (HUN).
Bronze medals: S. Casey (IRL), J. Beckles (ENG).

Turin, Italy - 1987
L. Fly: N. Munchyan (URS). **Fly:** A. Tews (GDR). **Bantam:** A. Hristov (BUL). **Feather:** M. Kazaryan (URS). **Light:** O. Nazarov (URS). **L. Welter:** B. Abadjier (BUL). **Welter:** V. Shishov (URS). **L. Middle:** E. Richter (GDR). **Middle:** H. Maske (GDR). **L. Heavy:** Y. Vaulin (URS). **Heavy:** A. Vanderlijde (HOL). **S. Heavy:** U. Kaden (GDR).
Bronze medal: N. Brown (ENG).

Athens, Greece - 1989
L. Fly: I.Mustafov (BUL). **Fly:** Y. Arbachakov (URS). **Bantam:** S. Todorov (BUL). **Feather:** K. Kirkorov (URS). **Light:** K. Tsziu (URS). **L. Welter:** I. Ruznikov (URS). **Welter:** S. Mehnert (GDR). **L. Middle:** I. Akopokhian (URS). **Middle:** H. Maske (GDR). **L. Heavy:** S. Lange (GDR). **Heavy:** A. Vanderlijde (HOL). **S. Heavy:** U. Kaden (GDR).
Bronze Medal: D. Anderson (SCO).

Gothenburg, Sweden - 1991
L. Fly: I. Marinov (BUL). **Fly:** I. Kovacs (HUN). **Bantam:** S. Todorov (BUL). **Feather:** P. Griffin (IRL). **Light:** V. Nistor (ROM). **L. Welter:** K. Tsziu (URS). **Welter:** N. Welin (SWE). **L. Middle:** I. Akopokhian (URS). **Middle:** S. Otke (GER). **L. Heavy:** D. Michalczewski (GER). **Heavy:** A. Vanderlijde (HOL). **S. Heavy:** E. Beloussov (URS).
Bronze medals: P. Weir (SCO), A. Vaughan (ENG).

Bursa, Turkey - 1993
L. Fly: D. Petrov (BUL). **Fly:** R. Husseinov (AZE). **Bantam:** R. Malakhbetov (RUS). **Feather:** S. Todorov (BUL). **Light:** J. Bielski (POL). **L. Welter:** N. Suleymanogiu (TUR). **Welter:** V. Karpaclauskas (LIT). **L. Welter:** F. Vastag (ROM). **Middle:** D. Eigenbrodt (GER). **L. Heavy:** I. Kshinin (RUS). **Heavy:** G. Kandelaki (GEO). **S. Heavy:** S. Rusinov (BUL).
Bronze medals: P. Griffin (IRL), D. Williams (ENG), K. McCormack (WAL).

Vejle, Denmark - 1996
L. Fly: D. Petrov (BUL). **Fly:** A. Pakeev (RUS). **Bantam:** I. Kovacs (HUN). **Feather:** R. Paliani (RUS). **Light:** L. Doroftei (ROM). **L. Welter:** O. Urkal (GER). **Welter:** H. Al (DEN). **L. Middle:** F. Vastag (ROM). **Middle:** S. Ottke (GER). **L. Heavy:** P. Aurino (ITA). **Heavy:** L. Krasniqi (GER). **S. Heavy:** A. Lezin (RUS).
Bronze medals: S. Harrison (SCO), D. Burke (ENG), D. Kelly (IRL).

Minsk, Belarus - 1998
L. Fly: S. Kazakov (RUS). **Fly:** V. Sidorenko (UKR). **Bantam:** S. Danilchenko (UKR). **Feather:** R. Paliani (TUR). **Light:** K. Huste (GER). **L. Welter:** D. Simion (ROM). **Welter:** O. Saitov (RUS). **L. Middle:** F. Esther (FRA). **Middle:** A. Lebsiak (RUS). **L. Heavy:** A. Lebsiak (RUS). **Heavy:** G. Fragomeni (ITA). **S. Heavy:** A. Lezin (RUS).
Silver Medals: B. Magee (IRL), C. Fry (ENG).
Bronze medal: C. Bessey (ENG).

Tampere, Finland - 2000
L. Fly: Valeri Sidorenko (UKR). **Fly:** Vladimir Sidorenko (UKR). **Bantam:** A. Agagueloglu (TUR). **Feather:** R. Paliani (TUR). **Light:** A. Maletin (RUS). **L. Welter:** A. Leonev (RUS). **Welter:** B. Ueluesoy (TUR). **L. Middle:** A. Catic (GER). **Middle:** Z. Erdei (HUN). **L. Heavy:** A. Lebsiak (RUS). **Heavy:** J. Chanet (FRA). **S. Heavy:** A. Lezin (RUS).

Perm, Russia - 2002
L. Fly: S. Kazakov (RUS). **Fly:** G. Balakshin (RUS). **Bantam:** K. Khatsygov (BE). **Feather:** R. Malakhbekov (RUS). **Light:** A. Maletin (RUS). **L. Welter:** D. Panayotov (BUL). **Welter:** T. Gaidalov (RUS). **L. Middle:** A. Mishin (RUS). **Middle:** O. Mashkin (URS). **L. Heavy:** M. Gala (RUS). **Heavy:** E. Makarenko (RUS). **S. Heavy:** A. Povetkin (RUS).

Pula, Croatia - 2004
L. Fly: S. Kazakov (RUS). **Fly:** G. Balakchine (RUS). **Bantam:** G. Kovalev (RUS). **Feather:** V. Tajbert (GER). **Light:** D. Stilianov (RUS). **L. Welter:** A. Maletin (RUS). **Welter:** O. Saitov (RUS). **Middle:** G. Gaiderbekov (RUS). **L. Heavy:** E. Makarenko (RUS). **Heavy:** A. Alekseev (RUS). **S. Heavy:** A. Povetkin (RUS).
Bronze medal: A. Lee (IRL).

Note: Gold medals were awarded to the Europeans who went the furthest in the Olympic Games of 1924, 1928 & 1932.

Plovdiv, Bulgaria - 2006
L. Fly: D. Ayrapetyan (RUS). Fly: G. Balakshin (RUS). Bantam: A. Aliev (RUS). Feather: A. Selimov (RUS). Light: A. Tishchenko (RUS). L. Welter: B. Georgiev (BUL). Welter: A. Balanov (RUS). Middle: M. Korobov (RUS). L. Heavy: A. Beterbiev (RUS). Heavy: D. Poyatsika (UKR). S. Heavy: I. Timurziev (RUS).
Bronze medals: S. Smith (ENG), F. Mhura (SCO), K. Egan (IRL).

European Junior Champions, 1970-2005

Miskolc, Hungary - 1970
L. Fly: Gluck (HUN). Fly: Z. Kismeneth (HUN). Bantam: A. Levitschev (URS). Feather: Andrianov (URS). Light: L. Juhasz (HUN). L. Welter: K. Nemec (HUN). Welter: Davidov (URS). L. Middle: A. Lemeschev (URS). Middle: N. Anfimov (URS). L. Heavy: O. Sasche (GDR). Heavy: J. Reder (HUN).
Bronze medals: D. Needham (ENG), R. Barlow (ENG), L. Stevens (ENG).

Bucharest, Romania - 1972
L. Fly: A. Turei (ROM). Fly: Condurat (ROM). Bantam: V. Solomin (URS). Feather: V. Lvov (URS). Light: S. Cutov (ROM). L. Welter: K. Pierwieniecki (POL). Welter: Zorov (URS). L. Middle: Babescu (ROM). Middle: V. Lemeschev (URS). L. Heavy: Mirounik (URS). Heavy: Subutin (URS).
Bronze medals: J. Gale (ENG), R. Maxwell (ENG), D. Odwell (ENG).

Kiev, Russia - 1974
L. Fly: A. Tkachenko (URS). Fly: V. Rybakov (URS). Bantam: C. Andreikovski (BUL). Feather: V. Sorokin (URS). Light: V. Limasov (URS). L. Welter: N. Sigov (URS). Welter: M. Bychkov (URS). L. Middle: V. Danshin (URS). Middle: D. Jende (GDR). L. Heavy: K. Dafinoiu (ROM). Heavy: K. Mashev (BUL).
Silver medal: C. Magri (ENG).
Bronze medals: G. Gilbody (ENG), K. Laing (ENG).

Izmir, Turkey - 1976
L. Fly: C. Seican (ROM). Fly: G. Khratsov (URS). Bantam: M. Navros (URS). Feather: V. Demoianeko (URS). Light: M. Puzovic (YUG). L. Welter: V. Zverev (URS). Welter: K. Ozoglouz (TUR). L. Middle: W. Lauder (SCO). Middle: H. Lenhart (GER). L. Heavy: I. Yantchauskas (URS). Heavy: B. Enjenyan (URS).
Silver medal: J. Decker (ENG).
Bronze medals: I. McLeod (SCO), N. Croombes (ENG).

Dublin, Ireland - 1978
L. Fly: R. Marx (GDR). Fly: D. Radu (ROM). Bantam: S. Khatchatrian (URS). Feather: H. Loukmanov (URS). Light: P. Oliva (ITA). L. Welter: V. Laptiev (URS). Welter: R. Filimanov (URS). L. Middle: A. Beliave (URS). Middle: G. Zinkovitch (URS). L. Heavy: I. Jolta (ROM). Heavy: P. Stoimenov (BUL).
Silver medals: M. Holmes (IRL), P. Hanlon (ENG), M. Courtney (ENG).
Bronze medals: T. Thompson (IRL), J. Turner (ENG), M. Bennett (WAL), J. McAllister (SCO), C. Devine (ENG).

Rimini, Italy - 1980
L. Fly: A. Mikoulin (URS). Fly: J. Varadi (HUN). Bantam: F. Rauschning (GDR). Feather: J. Gladychev (URS). Light: V. Shishov (URS). L. Welter: R. Lomski (BUL). Welter: T. Holonics (GDR). L. Middle: N. Wilshire (ENG). Middle: S. Laptiev (URS). L. Heavy: V. Dolgoun (URS). Heavy: V. Tioumentsev (URS). S. Heavy: S. Kormihtsine (URS).
Bronze medals: N. Potter (ENG), B. McGuigan (IRL), M. Brereton (IRL), D. Cross (ENG).

Schwerin, East Germany - 1982
L. Fly: R. Kabirov (URS). Fly: I. Filchev (BUL). Bantam: M. Stecca (ITA). Feather: B. Blagoev (BUL). Light: E. Chakimov (URS). L. Welter: S. Mehnert (GDR). Welter: T. Schmitz (GDR). L. Middle: B. Shararov (URS). Middle: E. Christie (ENG). L. Heavy: Y. Waulin (URS). Heavy: A. Popov (URS). S. Heavy: V. Aldoshin (URS).
Silver medal: D. Kenny (ENG).
Bronze medal: O. Jones (ENG).

Tampere, Finland - 1984
L. Fly: R. Breitbart (GDR). Fly: D. Berg (GDR). Bantam: K. Khdrian (URS). Feather: O. Nazarov (URS). Light: C. Furnikov (BUL). L. Welter: W. Schmidt (GDR). Welter: K. Doinov (BUL). L. Middle: O. Volkov (URS). Middle: R. Ryll (GDR). L. Heavy: G. Peskov (URS). Heavy: R. Draskovic (YUG). S. Heavy: L. Kamenov (BUL).
Bronze medals: J. Lowey (IRL), F. Harding (ENG), N. Moore (ENG).

Copenhagen, Denmark - 1986
L. Fly: S. Todorov (BUL). Fly: S. Galotian (URS). Bantam: D. Drumm (GDR). Feather: K. Tsziu (URS). Light: G. Akopkhian (URS). L. Welter: F. Vastag (ROM). Welter: S. Karavayev (URS). L. Middle: E. Elibaev (URS). Middle: A. Kurnabka (URS). L. Heavy: A. Schultz (GDR). Heavy: A. Golota (POL). S. Heavy: A. Prianichnikov (URS).

Gdansk, Poland - 1988
L. Fly: I. Kovacs (HUN). Fly: M. Beyer (GDR). Bantam: M. Aitzanov (URS). Feather: M. Rudolph (GDR). Light: M. Shaburov (URS). L. Welter: G. Campanella (ITA). Welter: D. Konsun (URS). L. Middle: K. Kiselev (URS). Middle: A. Rudenko (URS). L. Heavy: O. Velikanov (URS). Heavy: A. Ter-Okopian (URS). S. Heavy: E. Belusov (URS).
Bronze medals: P. Ramsey (ENG), M. Smyth (WAL).

Usti Nad Labem, Czechoslovakia - 1990
L. Fly: Z. Paliani (URS). Fly: K. Pielert (GDR). Bantam: K. Baravi (URS). Feather: P. Gvasalia (URS). Light: J. Hildenbrandt (GDR). L. Welter: N. Smanov (URS). Welter: A. Preda (ROM). L. Middle: A. Kakauridze (URS). Middle: J. Schwank (GDR). L. Heavy: Iljin (URS). Heavy: I. Andrejev (URS). S. Heavy: W. Fischer (GDR).
Silver medal: A. Todd (ENG).
Bronze medal: P. Craig (ENG).

Edinburgh, Scotland - 1992
L. Fly: M. Ismailov (URS). Fly: F. Brennfuhrer (GER). Bantam: S. Kuchler (GER). Feather: M. Silantiev (URS). Light: S. Shcherbakov (URS). L. Welter: O. Saitov (URS). Welter: H. Kurlumaz (TUR). L. Middle: Z. Erdie (HUN). Middle: V. Zhirov (URS). L. Heavy: D. Gorbachev (URS). Heavy: L. Achkasov (URS). S. Heavy: A. Mamedov (URS).
Silver medals: M. Hall (ENG), B. Jones (WAL).
Bronze medals: F. Slane (IRL), G. Stephens (IRL), C. Davies (WAL).

Salonika, Greece - 1993
L. Fly: O. Kiroukhine (UKR). Fly: R. Husseinov (AZE). Bantam: M. Kulbe (GER). Feather: E. Zakharov (RUS). Light: O. Sergeev (RUS). L. Welter: A. Selihanov (RUS). Welter: O. Kudinov (UKR). L. Middle: E. Makarenko (RUS). Middle: D. Droukovski (RUS). L. Heavy: A. Voida (RUS). Heavy: Vladimir Klitschko (UKR). S. Heavy: A. Moiseev (RUS).
Bronze medal: D. Costello (ENG).

Sifok, Hungary - 1995
L. Fly: D. Gaissine (RUS). Fly: A. Kotelnik (UKR). Bantam: A. Loutsenko (UKR). Feather: S. Harrison (SCO). Light: D. Simon (ROM). L. Welter: B. Ulusoy (TUR). Welter: O. Bouts (UKR). L. Middle: O. Bukalo (UKR). Middle: V. Plettnev (RUS). L. Heavy: A. Derevtsov (RUS). Heavy: C. O'Grady (IRL). S. Heavy: D. Savvine (RUS).
Silver medal: G. Murphy (SCO).
Bronze medal: N. Linford (ENG).

Birmingham, England - 1997
L. Fly: G. Balakshine (RUS). Fly: K. Dzhamaloudinov (RUS). Bantam: A. Shaiduline (RUS). Feather: D. Marciukaitis (LIT). Light: D. Baranov (RUS). L. Welter: A. Mishine (RUS). Welter: D. Yuldashev (UKR). L. Middle: A. Catic (GER). Middle: D. Lebedev (RUS). L. Heavy: V. Uzelkov (UKR). Heavy: S. Koeber (GER). S. Heavy: D. Pirozhenko (RUS).
Silver medal: S. Miller (ENG).
Bronze medals: S. Burke (ENG), M. Dean (ENG), P. Pierson (ENG), M. Lee (IRE).

Rijeka, Croatia - 1999
L. Fly: K. Kibalyuk (UKR). Fly: A. Bakhtin (RUS). Bantam: V. Simion (ROM). Feather: Kiutkhukow (BUL). Light: Pontilov (RUS). L. Welter: G. Ajetovic (YUG). Welter: S. Nouaouria (FRA). L. Middle: S. Kazantsev (RUS). Middle: D. Tsariouk (RUS). L. Heavy: Alexeev (RUS). Heavy: Alborov (RUS). S. Heavy: Soukhoverkov (RUS).
Bronze medal: S. Birch (ENG).

Sarejevo, Croatia - 2001
L. Fly: A. Taratokin (RUS). Fly: E. Abzalimov (RUS). Bantam: G. Kovaljov (RUS). Feather: M. Hratchev (RUS). Light: S. Aydin (TUR). L. Welter: D. Mikulin (RUS). Welter: O. Bokalo (UKR). L. Middle: M. Korobov (RUS). Middle: I. Bogdanov (UKR). L. Heavy: R. Kahkijev (RUS). Heavy: V. Zuyev (BE). S. Heavy: I. Timurziejev (RUS).
Bronze medal: K. Anderson (SCO).

Warsaw, Poland - 2003
L. Fly: P. Bedak (HUN). Fly: A. Ganev (RUS). Bantam: M. Tretiak (UKR). Feather: A. Alexandru (ROM). Light: A. Aleksiev (RUS). L. Welter: T. Tabotadze (UKR). Welter: Z. Baisangurov (RUS). Middle: J. Machoncev (RUS). L. Heavy: I. Michalkin (RUS). Heavy: Y. Romanov (RUS). S. Heavy: D. Arshba (RUS).
Bronze medal: S. Smith (E), F. Gavin (E), J. O'Donnell (E), T. Jeffries (E).

Tallinn, Estonia - 2005
L. Fly: S. Vodopyanov (RUS). Fly: S. Mamodov (AZE). Bantam: A. Akhba (RUS). Feather: M. Ignatev (RUS). Light: I. Iksanov (RUS). L. Welter: A.Zamkovoy (RUS). Welter: M. Koptyakov (RUS). Middle: S. Skiarov (RUS). L.Heavy: D. Chudinov (RUS). Heavy: S. Kalchugin (RUS). S. Heavy: A.Volkov (RUS).
Bronze Medal: J. Joyce (IRL).

Note: The age limit for the championships were reduced from 21 to 19 in 1976.

Commonwealth Champions, 1930-2006

Hamilton, Canada - 1930
Fly: W. Smith (SAF). **Bantam:** H. Mizler (ENG). **Feather:** F. Meacham (ENG). **Light:** J. Rolland (SCO). **Welter:** L. Hall (SAF). **Middle:** F. Mallin (ENG). **L. Heavy:** J. Goyder (ENG). **Heavy:** V. Stuart (ENG).
Silver medals: T. Pardoe (ENG), T. Holt (SCO).
Bronze medals: A. Lyons (SCO), A. Love (ENG), F. Breeman (ENG).

Wembley, England - 1934
Fly: P. Palmer (ENG). **Bantam:** F. Ryan (ENG). **Feather:** C. Cattarall (SAF). **Light:** L. Cook (AUS). **Welter:** D. McCleave (ENG). **Middle:** A. Shawyer (ENG). **L. Heavy:** G. Brennan (ENG). **Heavy:** P. Floyd (ENG).
Silver medals: A. Barnes (WAL), J. Jones (WAL), F. Taylor (WAL), J. Holton (SCO).
Bronze medals: J. Pottinger (WAL), T. Wells (SCO), H. Moy (ENG), W. Duncan (NIR), J. Magill (NIR), Lord D. Douglas-Hamilton (SCO).

Melbourne, Australia - 1938
Fly: J. Joubert (SAF). **Bantam:** W. Butler (ENG). **Feather:** A. Henricus (CEY). **Light:** H. Groves (ENG). **Welter:** W. Smith (AUS). **Middle:** D. Reardon (WAL). **L. Heavy:** N. Wolmarans (SAF). **Heavy:** T. Osborne (CAN).
Silver medals: J. Watson (SCO), M. Dennis (ENG).
Bronze medals: H. Cameron (SCO), J. Wilby (ENG).

Auckland, New Zealand - 1950
Fly: H. Riley (SCO). **Bantam:** J. van Rensburg (SAF). **Feather:** H. Gilliland (SCO). **Light:** R. Latham (ENG). **Welter:** T. Ratcliffe (ENG). **Middle:** T. van Schalkwyk (SAF). **L. Heavy:** D. Scott (ENG). **Heavy:** F. Creagh (NZL).
Bronze medal: P. Brander (ENG).

Vancouver, Canada - 1954
Fly: R. Currie (SCO). **Bantam:** J. Smillie (SCO). **Feather:** L. Leisching (SAF). **Light:** P. van Staden (SR). **L. Welter:** M. Bergin (CAN). **Welter:** N. Gargano (ENG). **L. Middle:** W. Greaves (CAN). **Middle:** J. van de Kolff (SAF). **L. Heavy:** P. van Vuuren (SAF). **Heavy:** B. Harper (ENG).
Silver medals: M. Collins (WAL), F. McQuillan (SCO).
Bronze medals: D. Charnley (ENG), B. Wells (ENG).

Cardiff, Wales - 1958
Fly: J. Brown (SCO). **Bantam:** H. Winstone (WAL). **Feather:** W. Taylor (AUS). **Light:** R. McTaggart (SCO). **L. Welter:** H. Loubscher (SAF). **Welter:** J. Greyling (SAF). **L. Middle:** G. Webster (SAF). **Middle:** T. Milligan (NIR). **L. Heavy:** A. Madigan (AUS). **Heavy:** D. Bekker (SAF).
Silver medals: T. Bache (ENG), M. Collins (WAL), J. Jordan (NIR), R. Kane (SCO), S. Pearson (ENG), A. Higgins (WAL), D. Thomas (ENG).
Bronze medals: P. Lavery (NIR), D. Braithwaite (WAL), R. Hanna (NIR), A. Owen (SCO), J. McClory (NIR), J. Cooke (ENG), J. Jacobs (ENG), B. Nancurvis (ENG), R. Scott (SCO), W. Brown (WAL), J. Caiger (ENG), W. Bannon (SCO), R. Pleace (WAL).

Perth, Australia - 1962
Fly: R. Mallon (SCO). **Bantam:** J. Dynevor (AUS). **Feather:** J. McDermott (SCO). **Light:** E. Blay (GHA). **L. Welter:** C. Quartey (GHA). **Welter:** W. Coe (NZL). **L. Middle:** H. Mann (CAN). **Middle:** M. Calhoun (JAM). **L. Heavy:** A. Madigan (AUS). **Heavy:** G. Oywello (UGA).
Silver medals: R. McTaggart (SCO), J. Pritchett (ENG).
Bronze medals: M. Pye (ENG), P. Benneyworth (ENG), B. Whelan (ENG), B. Brazier (ENG), C. Rice (NIR), T. Menzies (SCO), H. Christie (NIR), A. Turmel (CI).

Kingston, Jamaica - 1966
Fly: S. Shittu (GHA). **Bantam:** E. Ndukwu (NIG). **Feather:** P. Waruinge (KEN). **Light:** A. Andeh (NIG). **L. Welter:** J. McCourt (NIR). **Welter:** E. Blay (GHA). **L. Middle:** M. Rowe (ENG). **Middle:** J. Darkey (GHA). **L. Heavy:** R. Tighe (ENG). **Heavy:** W. Kini (NZL).
Silver medals: P. Maguire (NIR), R. Thurston (ENG), R. Arthur (ENG), T. Imrie (SCO).
Bronze medals: S. Lockhart (NIR), A. Peace (SCO), F. Young (NIR), J. Turpin (ENG), D. McAlinden (NIR).

Edinburgh, Scotland - 1970
L. Fly: J. Odwori (UGA). **Fly:** D. Needham (ENG). **Bantam:** S. Shittu (GHA). **Feather:** P. Waruinge (KEN). **Light:** A. Adeyemi (NIG). **L. Welter:** M. Muruli (UGA). **Welter:** E. Ankudey (GHA). **L. Middle:** T. Imrie (SCO). **Middle:** J. Conteh (ENG). **L. Heavy:** F. Ayinla (NIG). **Heavy:** B. Masanda (UGA).
Silver medals: T. Davies (WAL), J. Gillan (SCO), D. Davies (WAL), J. McKinty (NIR).
Bronze medals: M. Abrams (ENG), A. McHugh (SCO), D. Larmour (NIR), S. Oglivie (SCO), A. Richardson (ENG), T. Joyce (SCO), P. Doherty (NIR), J. Rafferty (SCO), L. Stevens (ENG).

Christchurch, New Zealand - 1974
L. Fly: S. Muchoki (KEN). **Fly:** D. Larmour (NIR). **Bantam:** P. Cowdell (ENG). **Feather:** E. Ndukwu (NIG). **Light:** A. Kalule (UGA). **L. Welter:** O. Nwankpa (NIG). **Welter:** M. Muruli (UGA). **L. Middle:** L. Mwale (ZAM). **Middle:** F.

Lucas (STV). **L. Heavy:** W. Knight (ENG). **Heavy:** N. Meade (ENG).
Silver medals: E. McKenzie (WAL), A. Harrison (SCO).
Bronze medals: J. Bambrick (SCO), J. Douglas (SCO), J. Rodgers (NIR), S. Cooney (SCO), R. Davies (ENG), C. Speare (ENG), G. Ferris (NIR).

Edmonton, Canada - 1978
L. Fly: S. Muchoki (KEN). **Fly:** M. Irungu (KEN). **Bantam:** B. McGuigan (NIR). **Feather:** A. Nelson (GHA). **Light:** G. Hamill (NIR). **L. Welter:** W. Braithwaite (GUY). **Welter:** M. McCallum (JAM). **L. Middle:** K. Perlette (CAN). **Middle:** P. McElwaine (AUS). **L. Heavy:** R. Fortin (CAN). **Heavy:** J. Awome (ENG).
Silver medals: J. Douglas (SCO), K. Beattie (NIR), D. Parkes (ENG), V. Smith (ENG).
Bronze medals: H. Russell (NIR), M. O'Brien (ENG), J. McAllister (SCO), T. Feal (WAL).

Brisbane, Australia - 1982
L. Fly: A. Wachire (KEN). **Fly:** M. Mutua (KEN). **Bantam:** J. Orewa (NIG). **Feather:** P. Konyegwachie (NIG). **Light:** H. Khalili (KEN). **L. Welter:** C. Ossai (NIG). **Welter:** C. Pyatt (ENG). **L. Middle:** S. O'Sullivan (CAN). **Middle:** J. Price (ENG). **L. Heavy:** F. Sani (FIJ). **Heavy:** W. de Wit (CAN).
Silver medals: J. Lyon (ENG), J. Kelly (SCO), R. Webb (NIR), P. Hanlon (ENG), J. McDonnell (ENG), N. Croombes (ENG), H. Hylton (ENG).
Bronze medals: R. Gilbody (ENG), C. McIntosh (ENG), R. Corr (NIR).

Edinburgh, Scotland - 1986
L. Fly: S. Olson (CAN). **Fly:** J. Lyon (ENG). **Bantam:** S. Murphy (ENG). **Feather:** B. Downey (CAN). **Light:** A. Dar (ENG). **L. Welter:** H. Grant (CAN). **Welter:** D. Dyer (ENG). **L. Middle:** D. Sherry (CAN). **Middle:** R. Douglas (ENG). **L. Heavy:** J. Moran (ENG). **Heavy:** J. Peau (NZL). **S. Heavy:** L. Lewis (CAN).
Silver medals: M. Epton (ENG), R. Nash (NIR), P. English (ENG), N. Haddock (WAL), J. McAlister (SCO), H. Lawson (SCO), D. Young (SCO), A. Evans (WAL).
Bronze medals: W. Docherty (SCO), J. Todd (NIR), K. Webber (WAL), G. Brooks (SCO), J. Wallace (SCO), C. Carleton (NIR), J. Jacobs (ENG), B. Lowe (NIR), D. Denny (NIR), G. Thomas (WAL), A. Mullen (SCO), G. Ferrie (NIR), P. Tinney (NIR), B. Pullen (WAL), E. Cardouza (ENG), J. Oyebola (ENG), J. Sillitoe (CI).

Auckland, New Zealand - 1990
L. Fly: J. Juuko (UGA). **Fly:** W. McCullough (NIR). **Bantam:** S. Mohammed (NIG). **Feather:** J. Irwin (ENG). **Light:** G. Nyakana (UGA). **L. Welter:** C. Kane (SCO). **Welter:** D. Defiagbon (NIG). **L. Middle:** R. Woodhall (ENG). **Middle:** C. Johnson (CAN). **L. Heavy:** J. Akhasamba (KEN). **Heavy:** G. Onyango (KEN). **S. Heavy:** M. Kenny (NZL).
Bronze medals: D. Anderson (SCO), M. Edwards (ENG), P. Douglas (NIR).

Victoria, Canada - 1994
L. Fly: H. Ramadhani (KEN). **Fly:** P. Shepherd (SCO). **Bantam:** R. Peden (AUS). **Feather:** C. Patton (CAN). **Light:** M. Strange (CAN). **L. Welter:** P. Richardson (ENG). **Welter:** N. Sinclair (NIR). **L. Middle:** J. Webb (ENG). **Middle:** R. Donaldson (CAN). **L. Heavy:** D. Brown (CAN). **Heavy:** O. Ahmed (KEN). **S. Heavy:** D. Dokiwari (NIG).
Silver medals: S. Oliver (ENG), J. Cook (WAL), M. Renaghan (NIR), M. Winters (NIR), J. Wilson (SCO).
Bronze medals: D. Costello (ENG), J. Townsley (SCO), D. Williams (ENG).

Kuala Lumpar, Malaysia - 1998
L. Fly: S. Biki (MAS). **Fly:** R. Sunee (MRI). **Bantam:** M. Yomba (TAN). **Feather:** A. Arthur (ENG). **Light:** R. Narh (GHA). **L. Welter:** M. Strange (CAN). **Welter:** J. Molitor (CAN). **L. Middle:** C. Bessey (ENG). **Middle:** J. Pearce (ENG). **L. Heavy:** C. Fry (ENG). **Heavy:** M. Simmons (CAN). **S. Heavy:** A. Harrison (ENG).
Silver medal: L. Cunningham (NIR).
Bronze medals: G. Jones (ENG), A. McLean (ENG), C. McNeil (SCO), J. Townsley (SCO), B. Magee (NIR), K. Evans (WAL).

Manchester, England - 2002
L. Fly: M. Ali Qamar (IND). **Fly:** K. Kanyanta (ZAM). **Bantam:** J. Kane (AUS). **Feather:** H. Ali (PAK). **Light:** J. Arthur (WAL). **L. Welter:** D. Barker (ENG). **Welter:** D. Geale (AUS). **L. Middle:** J. Pascal (CAN). **Middle:** P. Miller (AUS). **L. Heavy:** J. Albert (NIG). **Heavy:** J. Douglas (CAN). **S. Heavy:** D. Dolan (ENG).
Silver medals: D. Langley (ENG), P. Smith (ENG), S. Birch (ENG).
Bronze medals: M. Moran (ENG), A. Morris (ENG), C. McEwan (SCO), A. Young (SCO), K. Evans (WAL).

Melbourne, Australia - 2006
L. Fly: J. Utoni (NAM). **Fly:** D. Broadhurst (ENG). **Bantam:** G. Kumar (FIJ). **Feather:** S. Smith (ENG). **Light:** F. Gavin (ENG). **L. Welter:** J. Cox (ENG). **Welter:** B. Mwelase (SA). **Middle:** J. Fletcher (AUS). **L. Heavy:** K. Anderson (SCO). **Heavy:** B. Pitt (AUS). **S. Heavy:** D. Price (ENG).
Silver medals: D. Langley (ENG), K. Evans (WAL).
Bronze medals: M. Nasir (WAL), D. Edwards (WAL), J. Crees (WAL), N. Perkins (ENG), J. Degale (ENG).

The Triple Hitters' Boxing Quiz: Part 11

Compiled by Ralph Oates

QUESTIONS

1. On 16 October 1925, future world bantamweight champion, Panama Al Brown, outpointed Johnny Breslin. How many rounds were contested?
   A. Six.   B. Ten.   C. 12.

2. Max Schmeling met Max Diekmann in a contest staged over eight rounds in Berlin on 12 February 1926. What was the result?
   A. Points win for Diekmann.
   B. Points win for Schmeling.   C. A draw.

3. Tommy Loughran retained his world light-heavyweight championship on 12 December 1927 with a 15-round points decision over Jimmy Slattery. Who was the referee for this contest?
   A. Jack Denning.   B. Lou Magnolia.   C. Jed Gahan.

4. In which weight division was Marty Servo a world champion?
   A. Featherweight.   B. Lightweight.
   C. Welterweight.

5. On 10 January 1941, Steve Mamakos lost a ten-round points decision. Which boxer defeated him?
   A. Tony Zale.   B. Marcel Cerdan.   C. Jake LaMotta.

6. On 7 March 1951, Ezzard Charles retained his world heavyweight title when he outpointed Jersey Joe Walcott over 15 rounds. At this stage of his career, how many times had Walcott challenged for the title?
   A. Three.   B. Four.   C. Five.

7. On 27 January 1955, Henry Cooper stopped Colin Strauch. In which round?
   A. One.   B. Two.   C. Three.

8. Dai Dower challenged Pascual Perez in Argentina for the world flyweight title on 30 March 1957, but failed to win the crown when knocked out. In which round?
   A. One.   B. Two.   C. Three.

9. In what weight division was Alex Buxton a British champion?
   A. Middleweight.   B. Light-Heavyweight.
   C. Heavyweight.

10. Which British heavyweight was nicknamed 'The Blond Bomber'.
    A. Eddie Neilson.   B. Billy Walker.   C. Terry Daly.

11. On 12 October 1963, former British and Empire heavyweight champion, Joe Erskine, met Karl Mildenberger in a ten-round contest which took place in Germany. What was the result?
    A. Points win for Mildenberger.
    B. Points win for Erskine.   C. A draw.

12. In which round did Les McAteer knock out Sammy Robinson on 4 October 1965?
    A. One.   B. Two.   C. Three.

13. Which boxer did former British and Commonwealth champion, Evan Armstrong, not meet during his professional career?
    A. Jose Legra.   B. Howard Winstone.
    C. Arnold Taylor.

14. Which of these boxers did not box in the southpaw stance?
    A. Alan Minter.   B. Jim Watt.   C. Danny McAlinden.

15. During his professional career, in which country did the former British featherweight champion, Alan Richardson, not box?
    A. Belgium.   B. Denmark.   C. Nigeria.

16. On 6 April 1970, Ken Buchanan outpointed Chris Fernandez over ten rounds. Where did the contest take place?
    A. Glasgow.   B. Edinburgh.   C. Nottingham.

17. John McCluskey retained his British flyweight title on 14 October 1974 when he stopped Tony Davies in the opening round. At this stage of his professional career, how many opponents had McCluskey stopped in the first round?
    A. One.   B. Two.   C. Three.

18. On 15 February 1978, Alan Minter stopped Sandy Torres in round five. In which country did this contest take place?
    A. France.   B. Italy.   C. America.

19. Larry Holmes retained his WBC world heavyweight title against Randall (Tex) Cobb by way of a 15-round points decision, in a contest which took place on 26 November 1982. Who was the referee for this bout?
A. Steve Crosson.   B. Mills Lane.   C. Joey Curtis.

20. On 11 October 1989, Gary Stretch made the first defence of his British light-middleweight title when he stopped Derek Wormald. Which round did the stoppage occur?
A. One.   B. Two.   C. Three.

21. Tom Collins challenged Jeff Harding for the WBC world light-heavyweight title on 24 October 1989. However, Collins failed in his attempt when he was forced to retire in round two. In which country did this contest take place?
A. England.   B. France.   C. Australia.

22. In which weight division was Sugar Gibiliru (junior) a British champion?
A. Featherweight.   B. Super-Featherweight.
C. Lightweight.

23. On 7 April 1993, Brent Kosolofski won the vacant Commonwealth light-heavyweight title when he stopped Michael Gale in round nine. Who was the referee for this contest?
A. Mickey Vann.   B. Larry O'Connell.
C. John Coyle.

24. Former British and European welterweight champion, Kirkland Laing, failed to capture the vacant Southern Area light-middleweight title when he was stopped in round five by Kevin Lueshing on 23 June 1993. At this stage of his career, how many professional contests had Laing taken part in?
A. 50.   B. 51.   C. 52.

25. Over how many rounds did Howard Eastman outpoint Andy Peach on 14 March 1994?
S. Six.   B. Eight.   C. Ten.

26. On 5 November 1994, Johnny Nelson retained his WBF heavyweight title when he outpointed Nikolai Kulpin over 12 rounds. In which country did this contest take place?
A. Australia.   B. New Zealand.   C. Thailand.

27. Clinton Woods won the vacant Commonwealth super-middleweight title on 6 December 1997 when he outpointed Mark Baker over 12 rounds. Who held the crown prior to Woods?
A. Lou Cafaro.   B. Henry Wharton.   C. Rod Carr.

28. In defence of his WBC world heavyweight title, on 28 March 1998 Lennox Lewis stopped Shannon Briggs in round five. In which part of America did this contest take place?
A. New York.   B. Las Vegas.   C. Atlantic City.

29. In which weight division was Hassine Cherifi a WBC world title holder?
A. Welterweight.   B. Middleweight.
C. Super-Middleweight.

30. Joe Calzaghe retained his WBO world super-middleweight title against Juan Carlos Gimenez on 25 April 1998 by a retirement. Name the round the contest was concluded.
A. Nine.   B. Ten.   C. 11.

31. On 19 September 1998, Ricky Hatton knocked out Pascal Montulet in the second round. In which country did this contest take place?
A. America.   B. England.   C. Germany.

32. Who was the first opponent to defeat Cathy Brown in the professional ranks by way of a four-round points decision?
A. Marietta Ivanova.   B. Oksana Vasilieva.
C. Romona Gughie.

33. On 27 May 2001, Jamie Moore stopped Paul Denton in three rounds. At this stage of his career, Moore was undefeated in how many professional contests?
A. Ten.   B. 11.   C. 12.

34. On 20 April 2002, Audley Harrison knocked out Julius Long in the second round. At this stage of his career, Harrison was undefeated in how many professional contests?
A. Two.   B. Three.   C. Four.

35. On 14 December 2002, Joe Calzaghe retained his WBO world super-middleweight title when he stopped Tocker Pudwill. Which round did the stoppage occur?
A. One.   B. Two.   C. Three.

36. On 27 September 2003, Junior Witter retained his Commonwealth light-welterweight title when he stopped Fred Kinuthia in round two. Who was the referee for this contest?
A. Larry O'Connell.   B. Howard Foster.
C. Richie Davies.

37. On 13 December 2003, Michael Jennings outpointed Peter Dunn over six rounds. At this stage of his career,

Jennings was undefeated in how many professional bouts?

A. 19. B. 20. C. 21.

38. When Micky Steeds outpointed Paul King on 12 March 2004, how many rounds were contested?
A. Four. B. Six. C. Eight.

39. In which round did Nicky Cook knock out Cyril Thomas on 20 March 2004 to capture the European featherweight title?
A. Seven. B. Eight. C. Nine.

40. Scott Dann won the vacant English middleweight title on 8 May 2004, when he stopped Danny Thornton in the third round. Where did the contest take place?
A. Bristol. B. Plymouth. C. Nottingham.

41. David Haye stopped Arthur Williams in the third round on 12 May 2004. Which version of the world cruiserweight title did Williams formerly hold?
A. WBA. B. WBC. C. IBF.

42. On 13 May 2004, Kevin Mitchell stopped Slimane Kebaili in the first round. At this stage of his professional career how many contests had Mitchell won in the first round?
A. Three. B. Four. C. Five.

43. In which round did Scott Gammer stop Paul King on 2 June 2004?
A. Two. B. Three. C. Four.

44. On 13 February 2005, Colin Lynes retained his IBO world light-welterweight title when he outpointed Juaquin Gallardo over 12 rounds. Who was the referee for this contest?

A. Frank Santore. B. Jay Nady. C. Gino Rodriquez.

45. John Murray outpointed Johnny Walker in Florida, USA on 7 August 2005. Name the number of rounds that were contested?
A. Four. B. Six. C. Eight.

46. In a contest which took place on 7 August 2005 for the inaugural WBC womens' flyweight title, Cathy Brown failed in her attempt to win the championship when she was outpointed over ten rounds by Stefania Bianchini. In which country did this bout take place?
A. Spain. B. Denmark. C. Italy.

47. On 9 September 2005, Clinton Woods retained his IBF world light-heavyweight title when he outpointed Julio Gonzalez over 12 rounds. Which version of the light-heavyweight title did Gonzalez previously hold?
A. WBC. B. WBO. C. WBA.

48. Joe Calzaghe retained his WBO world super-middleweight crown on 10 September 2005 when he outpointed Evans Ashira over 12 rounds. At this stage of his career Calzaghe was undefeated in how many professional bouts?
A. 38. B. 39. C. 40.

49. On 10 September 2005, Amir Khan outpointed Baz Carey over four rounds. Who was the referee for this contest?
A. Wynford Jones. B. Lee Cook. C. Grant Wallis.

50. On 16 September 2005, Scott Dann retained his British middleweight title when he outpointed Wayne Elcock over 12 rounds. Who is Dann's manager?
A. Tania Follett. B. Chris Sanigar. C. Paul Boyce.

Directory of Ex-Boxers' Associations

by Ron Olver

BOURNEMOUTH Founded 1980. HQ: The Cricketers public house, Windham Road, off Ashley Road, Bournemouth. Dai Dower (P); Peter Fay (C); Dave Fry (VC); Percy Singer (T); Jack Streek (S), 38 St Leonard's Farm, Ringwood Road, Ferndown, Dorset BH22 0AG.

CORK Founded 1973. HQ: Glen Boxing Club, Blackpool, Cork. William O'Leary (P & C); Phil Murray (VC); John Martin (S); John Donovan (T).

CORNWALL Founded 1989. HQ: Fitzsimmons Arms, Coinage Hall Street, Helston. Salvo Nucciforo (C); Eric Bradshaw (S); Stan Cullis (P & PRO), Upper Tolcarne House, Burras Wendron, Nr. Helston TR13 0JD.

CROYDON Founded 1982. HQ: Ivy House Club, Campbell Road, West Croydon. Gilbert Allnutt (P); Derek O'Dell (T); Barry Penny (C); Paul Nihill MBE (S), 24 Walderslade Road, Chatham, Kent ME4 6NZ.

EASTERN AREA Founded 1973. HQ: Coach & Horses, Union Street, Norwich. Brian Fitzmaurice (P); Ron Springall (S & T); Clive Campling (C), 54 Robson Road, Norwich NR5 8NZ.

HOME COUNTIES Founded 2005. HQ: Golden Lion Public House, High Street, London Colney, Herts. Terry Downes (P); Bob Williams (C); Ann Ayles (T); Dave Ayles (S), 144 Trident Drive, Houghton Regis, Dunstable LU5 5QQ.

HULL & EAST YORKSHIRE Founded 1996. HQ: Tigers Lair, Anlaby Road, Hull. Don Harrison (C); Geoff Rymer (PRO & S); Bert Smith (T), 54 St Aidan Road, Bridlington, E. Yorks.

IPSWICH Founded 1970. HQ: Loco Club, Ipswich. Alby Kingham (P); Vic Thurlow (C & T); Michael Thurlow (S), 147 Clapgate Lane, Ipswich IP3 0RF.

IRISH Founded 1973. HQ: National Boxing Stadium, South Circular Road, Dublin. Val Harris (P); Martin Gannon (C); Tommy Butler (T); Paddy O'Reilly (VC); Willie Duggan (S), 175 Kimmage Road West, Dublin 6W.

KENT Founded 1997. HQ: RAFA Club, Dock Road, Chatham. Harry Doherty (P); Bill Quinton (C); Paul Nihill, MBE (S & T), 24 Walderslade Road, Chatham, Kent ME4 6NZ.

LEEDS Founded 1952. HQ: North Leeds WMC, Lincoln Green Road, Leeds 9. Alan Richardson (P); Kevin Cunningham (C); Peter Selby (S); Alan Alster (T); Frank Johnson (PRO), 82 Windmill Chase, Rothwell, Leeds LS 26 0XB

LEICESTER Founded 1972. HQ: The Jungle Club, Checketts Road, Leicester. Mick Greaves (P & C); Fred Roberts (T); Alan Parr (S), 22 Hewes Close, Glen Parva, Leicester LE2 9NU.

LONDON Founded 1971. HQ; The Queen Mary College, Bancroft Road, Mile End, London E1. Stephen Powell (P); Micky O'Sullivan (C); Charlie Wright (VC); Ron Olver (PRO); Ray Caulfield (T); Mrs Mary Powell (S), 36 St Peters Street, Islington, London N1 8JT.

Ron Olver, the man behind the EBAs   Pat Olver

MANCHESTER Founded 1968. HQ: Hat & Feathers Pub, Ancoats, Manchester. Tommy Proffitt (LP); Jack Edwards (P); Neville Tetlow (T); Jimmy Lewis (C); Eddie Copeland (S), 9 Lakeside, Hadfield, Glossop, Derby SK13 1HW.

MERSEYSIDE (Liverpool) Founded 1973. HQ: Arriva Club, Hockenhall Alley, Liverpool. Harry Scott (P); Terry Carson (C); Jim Boyd (VC); Jim Jenkinson (S & T), 13 Brooklands Avenue, Waterloo, Liverpool L22 3XY.
Website: www.lmu.livjm.ac.uk/inmylife/channels/sport/1116.htm

MIDLANDS EBA Founded 2002. HQ: The Portland Pavilions, Portland Road, Edgbaston, Birmingham. Bunny Johnson (P); Martin Florey (C); Paul Rowson (VC); Stephen Florey (T); Jerry Hjelter (S), 67 Abberley Avenue, Stourport on Severn, Warwicks DY13 0LY.

NORTHAMPTONSHIRE Founded 1981. HQ: Semilong Working Mens Club, 212 St Andrews Road, Northampton. Dick Rogers (P); Gil Wilson (C); George Ward (VC); Mrs Pam Ward (S & T), 6 Derwent Close, Kings Heath, Northampton NN5 7JS.

NORTHERN FEDERATION Founded 1974. Several member EBAs. Annual Gala. Jimmy Lewis (P); Terry Carson (C); John Redfern (PRO); Eddie Copeland (S & T), 9 Lakeside, Hadfield, Glossop, Derbyshire SK13 1HW.

NORTHERN IRELAND Founded 1970. HQ: Ulster Sports Club, High Street, Belfast. Gerry Hassett (P); Cecil Martin (C); S.Thompson (T); Terry Milligan (S), 32 Rockdale Street, Belfast BT12 7PA.

NORTH STAFFS & SOUTH CHESHIRE Founded 1969. HQ: The Saggar Makers Bottom Knocker, Market Place, Burslem, Stoke on Trent. Roy Simms (C); Larry Parkes (VC); Les Dean (S); John Greatbach (T); Billy Tudor (P & PRO), 133 Springbank Road, Chell Heath, Stoke on Trent, Staffs ST6 6HW.

NORWICH Founded 1990. HQ: West End Retreat, Brown Street, Norwich. Les King (P); John Pipe (C); Len Jarvis (T); Albert Howe (S), 15 Grange Close, Hoveton, Norwich NR2 8EA.

NOTTINGHAM Founded 1979. HQ: The Wheatsheaf, Sneinton Road, Nottingham. Len Chorley (P); Walter Spencer (C); Mick Smith (VC); Gary Rooksby (T); John Kinsella (PRO); Graham Rooksby (S), 42 Spinney Road, Keyworth, Notts NG12 5LN.

PLYMOUTH Founded 1982. HQ: Stoke Social Club, Devonport Road, Plymouth. Tom Pryce-Davies (P); Scott Dann (VP); Jimmy Ryan (C); Jimmy Bevel (VC); Arthur Willis (T); Pat Crago (S), 8 Hawkinge Gardens, Ernsettle, Plymouth PL5 2RJ.

PRESTON Founded 1973. HQ: Barney's Piano Bar, Church Street, Preston. John Allen (C & S); Eddie Monahan (P); Bobby Rhodes (T), 1 Norris Street, Preston PR1 7PX.

ST HELENS Founded 1983. HQ: Royal Naval Association, Volunteer Street, St Helens. Ray Britch (C); Tommy McNamara (T); Paul Britch (S), 16 Oxley Street, Sutton, St Helens WA9 3PE

SCOTTISH Founded 1997. HQ: Iron Horse Public House, Nile Street, Glasgow. Freddie Mack (P); Frank O'Donnell (LP); Al Hutcheon (C); Phil McIntyre (VC); Peter Baines (T); Liam McColgan (S), 25 Dalton Avenue, Linnvale, Clydebank G81 2SH.

SHEFFIELD Founded 1974. Reformed 2002. HQ: The Richmond Public House, Richmond Road, Sheffield. Billy Calvert (P & T); Harry Carnell (C); John Redfern (S & PRO), 33 Birch Avenue, Chapeltown, Sheffield S35 1RQ.

SQUARE RING (TORBAY) Founded 1978. HQ: Snooty Fox Hotel, St Marychurch. Ken Wittey (C); Johnny Mudge (S); Jim Banks (T); Paul King (P & VC), 8 Winchester Avenue, Torquay TQ2 8AR.

SUNDERLAND Founded 1959. HQ: River Wear Social Club, Sunderland. George Martin (P); Terry Lynn (C); Les Simm (T & S), 21 Orchard Street, Pallion, Sunderland SR4 6QL.

SUSSEX Founded 1974. Reformed 2003. HQ: British Legion Club, Shirley Street, Hove. Tommy Mellis (P); Mick Smith (VP & PRO); John McNeil (C); Ian Hargie (T); Karen Knight (S), 10 Viceroy Lodge, 143 Kingsway, Hove, BN3 4RA. Website: www.sussexexboxers.com

SWANSEA & SOUTH WEST WALES Founded 1983. HQ: The Conservative Club, Swansea. Cliff Curvis (P); Gordon Pape (C); Len Smith (S), 105 Cockett Road, Swansea SA2 0FG.

TYNESIDE Founded 1970. HQ: Pelaw Social Club, Heworth. Maxie Walsh (P & C); Dave McCormick (VC); Malcolm Dinning (VP & T); Maxie Walsh (Acting Secretary), c/o 9 Prendwick Court, Hebburn, Tyne & Wear NE31 2NQ.

WELSH Founded 1976. HQ: Rhydyfelin Labour Club, Pontypridd. Wynford Jones (P); Eddie Avoth (VP); John Floyd (C); Peter Rogers (VC); Mark Warner (T); Don James (S), 28 Woodfield Road, Talbot Green, Pontyclun, Mid-Glamorgan. Patron - Lord Brooks of Tremorfa.

WIRRAL Founded 1973. Reformed 2003. HQ: RNA Club, Thornberry Park Road East, Birkenhead. Frank Johnson (P); Pat McAteer (VP); Pat Garry (T); Terry Carson (C); Alan Crowther (S), 15 Scythia Close, New Ferry, Wirral, Merseyside CH62 1HH. Website: www.lmu.livjm.ac.uk/inmylife/channels/sport/1116.htm

The above information is set at the time of going to press and no responsibility can be taken for any changes in officers or addresses of HQs that may happen between then and publication or changes that have not been notified to me.

ABBREVIATIONS

P - President. HP - Honorary President. LP - Life President. AP - Acting President. C - Chairman. VC - Vice Chairman. T - Treasurer. S - Secretary. PRO - Public Relations Officer and/or Press Officer.

Paul King, once a rated British welterweight and currently the President of the Square Ring EBA

Obituaries

by Derek O'Dell

It is impossible to list everyone, but I have again done my best to include final tributes for as many of the well-known boxers and other familiar names within the sport who have passed away since the 2006 Yearbook was published. We honour them and remember them.

ADAMSON Bunty *From* Lisburn, Ireland. *Died* June 2006, aged 75. Robert Orr Anderson who used the name of Bunty Adamson during his boxing career, first donned the gloves as a professional in May 1950. Bunty was a welterweight and a good 'un, with a pedigree of 61 wins out of 65 amateur fights. His paid career started in style with a two-round stoppage over Jackie Hughes. He then went on for another 29 fights before stepping outside of Belfast and suffering his first defeat at the hands of red-hot prospect, Terry Ratcliffe. It was a big Jack Solomons promotion, with Randolph Turpin v George Angelo topping the bill. The trade paper reported that Adamson was "a joy to watch as he outboxed his man". Bunty put Ratcliffe down twice and was far ahead when one right-hand punch put him out for the count. He was Northern Ireland welterweight champion at the time, having won the title from Mickey O'Neill. In that year he'd beaten classy Dutchman, Giel de Roode, Harry Warner and Israel Boyle. With 17 of his wins coming inside the route, he showed ambition in putting that single defeat behind him when forcing former British champion, Eddie Thomas, to a draw in a British title eliminator before beating him in a return a year later. When Tim McLeary beat him in one round Bunty announced his retirement, but came back a year later only to lose to Charlie Curry and Santos Martins. He never fought again. Bunty had achieved much in reaching the top contender position in the ratings, but never having challenged for the British title remained a big disappointment in his life.

ANGELO George *From* Johannesburg, South Africa. *Died* 21 October 2005, aged 80. During his campaign in Britain, George was rated by his manager, Jim Wicks, as being the best man, in terms of boxing ability he'd handled and Wicks had a long history as a prominent boxers' manager. George was no puncher but made up for that deficit with a brand of sheer boxing artistry. He was also durable and never hit the deck in a seven-year career. Even Randolph Turpin, still a much feared puncher back in 1952, couldn't put George on the deck. This was Angelo's most important fight and he came out of it without a scratch, but never fought again. A detached retina, caused by an accident in the gym, forced him into retirement. The sad thing is that he still had so much to offer at top level. He came to Britain as holder of the South African middleweight title, with wins over former British champion, Vince Hawkins and Australia's Jackie Marr on his record, and by beating America's Mel Brown at London's Albert Hall George established himself as a man capable of mixing with the best men in Europe. Brown was an American who had been in with our best middles without tasting defeat, yet George conceded five pounds in weight and ran out a points winner. He was less fortunate in his next outing when Alex Buxton edged him out in another ten rounder, but he came back to build up a creditable record against British opposition. Les Allen, Eric McQuade and Jimmy Davis were all returned losers as were France's Georges Royer and the Americans, Baby Day and Burl Charity. The Turpin contest showed that George could compete at world level, but it was not to be. Because of the eye injury he never got the chance to prove himself.

Bunty Adamson

George Angelo

ARLT Ken *From* Portland, Oregon, USA. *Died* November 2005, aged 48. A durable American heavyweight, Ken never picked his opponents, while fighting from 1977 to 1984. In his ninth fight he lost on points to Pinklon Thomas, then went unbeaten for a year before being outscored by Pat Duncan. In four fights with Harvey Steichan (an early opponent of Frank Bruno) he won three and beat Mustafa Amin twice, and had good wins over Al Neuman, Mark Lee and Ron Gibbs. Others on his record include Scott LeDoux, Yaqui Lopez, Gordie Racette and Stan Ward.

BAILEY Tommy *From* Liverpool. *Died* June 2006, aged 81. In the years following the war, the British featherweight division was so strong that it was difficult to rate the top-ten performers. Tommy boxed during that time, 1947 to 1953 to be precise, and won the Central Area title in 1951 when those titles meant something. Tommy knocked out Bert Jackson of Fleetwood to annex the championship, and it was his only knockout win in a career of 78. Tommy was not a devastating puncher, but his clever boxing gave problems to the best fighters then active in British rings. His true name was Thomas Bayly and his father was also a good 'un in his day. There were seven children in the Bayly family, Tommy being one of three boys, the youngest of which, George, also fought professionally. As an amateur, Tommy did well, winning Northern Counties and Imperial Services' titles before reaching the ABA finals where that great boxer, Peter Brander, outscored him. It was time to punch for pay. Alas, in his first outing, an eye injury forced him to retire against Gerry Speers. There was a return a couple of months later and Tommy put the record straight by comprehensively outpointing his man. Before the year was out, he'd reached the ten-round class, following wins over Kid Tanner, Frankie Kelly, Ray Fitton and Ronnie Taylor of Horwich, with only a points loss to Jackie Turpin soiling his record. Turpin beat him again in 1948. Ray had to wait another couple of years before he got his revenge, but by that time he'd established himself as a contender for the Central Area title and was far too good for his old foe. Victory over Jim McCann was followed by stirring performances against Ben Duffy, Ray Fitton and Johnny Molloy, which gained him a rating of number-two featherweight behind Al Phillips. He got a fight with Phillips at Earls Court early in 1950, but the old Aldgate Tiger knew too much for him. Two other good men in Roy Ankrah and Luis de Santiago both outpointed him that year, but 1950 was, overall, a good one for Tommy. He'd lost only four of 15 outings and had established himself as a title contender. In 1951, he lost just one contest, beating Terry Riley, Fitton, Molloy (again), Dai Davies and Tommy Miller. He went on into 1952, beating Freddie King, before opting to go up a weight division. Fighting as a lightweight spoiled what had been an impressive record and of his last nine fights he won just one. All losses were to good men: Solly Cantor, Al Brown, Johnny Butterworth (with whom he boxed a draw), Tommy McGovern, European champion Jorgen Johansen, Charlie Tucker and Frank Johnson. He retired in

1953, having competed for the vacant Central Area lightweight title in his last fight. His overall record was 78 fights, 49 wins, 25 losses and four draws. He was never counted out and eye injuries accounted for many of his defeats.

BAIRD Roy *From* Sutton Coldfield. *Died* 3 November 2005, aged 78. Roy was a Belfast-born welterweight who moved to the midlands before he reached his teens. Being eligible to fight for Irish titles, he returned frequently to the province and won the Northern Ireland championship in 1956. He was never beaten for that title and retired as champion after being outpointed by Tommy Molloy, a man he'd previously beaten. Roy boxed from 1950 to 1956 and notched up 40 fights for 25 wins, a draw and 14 losses. He fought Peter Fallon, Laurie Buxton, Santos Martins, Peter Waterman, Terry Ratcliffe, Eric Davies, Gerry Hassett, Mickey O'Neill, Alf Danahar and Eddie Phillips, etc. In later years he became a victim of Alzheimers' which eventually claimed his life. He leaves a wife and two children.

Roy Baird

BARONE Nick *From* Syracuse, New York, USA. *Died* 11 March 2006, aged 79. Nick's physique often put him at a disadvantage with his adversaries. He was short for a light-heavyweight but broad and solid – a build that usually indicates that there is an abundance of inbuilt durability. Performing in London just once, it being his last fight, he took a lot of punishment from Don Cockell, who had world-title ambitions. A series of uppercuts sank Barone in the fifth round and convinced him that it was time to quit the fight game. He'd had ambition too in his earlier career when he faced Ezzard Charles for the top prize in boxing.

Charles was an underrated and skilful performer but found Barone tough. Nick took him into the 11th round. Nick was never as good after that even though he came back to beat Duilio Spagnola. Born Carmine Barrone, it was a victory over Chuck Hunter in 1948 that started him on the road to title contention. He beat Tommy Yarosz twice and lost to him once. Then came fine wins over Phil Muscato, Gino Buonvino, Dick Wagner and Jimmy Beau. He'd been in there with Bob Satterfield, Lee Oma, Reuben Jones and Dave Whitlock before facing Charles. In 57 contests, he won 44 and drew one and lost 12.

Nick Barone

BIONDI Gilberto *From* Melbourne, Australia. *Died* 14 October 2005, aged 71. Gilberto made his professional debut as a lightweight in his native Italy at the late age of 27, running up seven contests before emigrating to Australia in 1963. He made a bad start, losing to Graham Dicker and Terry Crimmins in his first two fights, but his fighting spirit saw him beat both men in return matches. A third fight with Dicker was for the Australian title, which he annexed with a 15-round points victory. A southpaw and a clever boxer, just after winning the title he was beaten on points by future world champion, Carlos Teo Cruz. It was only his 16th pro fight but he was successful the following year against another future world champion in Johnny Famechon. He beat the French-born Aussie over 12 rounds, but lost his form afterwards with successive defeats by Manny Santos, Kimpo Amarfio and Tony Barber. He was also unlucky against world-class American, Don Johnson, being stopped with bad cuts in six rounds.

Earlier that year he returned home for a brief stay, during which he won four out of five fights. Back in Melbourne he got his revenge over Amarfio, against whom he was to have five contests, with one loss, one draw and three good victories. Gilberto carried on boxing until he was 40, having never taken a bad beating, and in his final year he won the Australian junior-lightweight title by beating Andy Broome. He bowed out with a points win over Matt Ropis.

BRADY Jim *From* Belvedere, Illinois, USA. *Died* October 2005, aged 57. In boxing it isn't only the fighters who show courage, fearless journalist Jim being a prime example. He wrote without pulling punches and exposed much of which is corrupt with the sport's ruling bodies. I worked with him very briefly when the original editorial team of *Boxing Monthly* was formed. I remembered how much he impressed my colleague Fred Snelling with his professionalism. He could research a difficult subject and meet a deadline with punctilious reliability and he knew his boxing. His book *Boxing Confidential: Power, Corruption and the Richest Prize in Sport* probably added to his list of enemies, but that concerned Jim less than the necessity to speak out on which he considered was rotten in the game he loved. A heart attack killed him at an early age. He had so much more to offer us, but what he did for boxing is a monument to dedication, guts and integrity.

BUTLER Frank, OBE *From* London. *Died* 24 December 2005, aged 89. Frank and his father, James, covered boxing from early glove days up to the present. Between them they saw and reported on every leading fight in this country from 1896. James, whose boxing memories went back to the days of Pedlar Palmer, took Frank to see many of the big fights of the late 20s and early 30s, Frank seeing every world heavyweight champion in action from Primo Carnera. His favourite was Joe Louis. When in his teens he was phoning through his father's ringside reports to the *Daily Herald*. It was a solid grounding for a journalistic career and in 1933, aged 16, he joined the *Daily Express* as a junior sports' reporter, working at the fights with Trevor Wignall. Frank was covering boxing for his paper for two years before he got an assignment to report on the world-title fight between Ernie Roderick and Henry Armstrong. He was only 20, but his career was already established and it was then that he became Sports Editor of the *Sunday Express* – a position that often took him to America to cover the big fights. In 1949, he joined the *News of the World* and in a long career worked there until he retired. He became Chairman of the Boxing Writers' Club in 1950 and Honorary Secretary in 1982. Two years later he took up the position of Administrative Steward of the British Boxing Board of Control. In between these duties he wrote five books on boxing, one in conjunction with his father who, like Frank, enjoyed a long life. He was also President of the London Ex-Boxers' Association. One of his most prestigious awards was that of being Sports' Writer of the Year in 1970. His earliest boxing memories stem from watching fights at the old National Sporting Club in Covent Garden and later on at Premierland.

BUTTLE Mike *From* Johannesburg, South Africa. *Died* 19 August 2006, aged 58. Born in Bromley, England, Mike's family emigrated to Rhodesia when he was young and then settled in South Africa. He began boxing as an amateur before graduating to the pro ring, where he got his career underway with a first-round kayo over Des Brown in October 1967. Two fights later he was fighting ten rounders, drawing with the Welshman, Glyn Davies, and then beating Manchester's Tony Barlow, Battersea's Don Weller, Carmelo Massa and Ernie Baronet, prior to suffering his first defeat, at the hands of Scotland's John McCluskey. Winning the South African bantam title next time out when beating a shop-worn Dennis Adams, he went on to beat the same opponent twice more before being knocked out by the rising Arnold Taylor, who repeated the task a month later and relieved Mike of the title at the same time. Although he won two of his remaining four contests, with 11 wins from 19 outings he decided that he wasn't going anywhere and retired in February 1975.

CHALCRAFT Shaun *From* Redhill. *Died* 10 March 2006, aged 48. At a meeting of the Croydon Ex-Boxers' Association, colleague Simon Euan-Smith paid a tribute to crowd-pleasing Shaun, a former Southern Area light-heavyweight champion. Simon saw many of his fights and reminded us that in his match against Ken Jones at the Porchester Hall, nobbins were thrown in the ring. This is not a rare occurrence, but what made it so was that they were thrown in when the round was in progress. Southpaw Chalcraft was involved in many small-halls' great fights of the year. His bout with Carlton Benoit for the Southern Area title was one of them. He lost this title to Dennis Andries in another pulsating battle and had 27 fights, winning just over half of them. Considering the hard nature of most of them, he had much of which to feel proud.

CHAMI Bassam *From* Sydney, Australia. *Died* 20 March 2006, aged 26. A brief career, during which he was unbeaten in three contests as a middleweight, came to an end when he was shot dead in what appeared to have been a gang war.

COSTELLO Jack *From* Newark, New Jersey, USA. *Died* 19 July 2006, aged 85. Screen actor Jack Warden was born John H. Lebzelter in 1920. For the stage he took his father's middle name and took part in professional fights as Jack Costello. He did this while still at school, but his real identity was soon revealed to the education authorities who expelled him. This was in the 1930s when the establishment was not so liberal minded as it is in modern times. He claimed 13 fights at welterweight level before quitting to take a position of nightclub bouncer. After serving in the Navy he took acting lessons and quickly became famous as Jack Warden. He died in Manhattan from cardiac problems.

CULLEN Billy *From* Birmingham. *Died* 10 February 2006. A Midlands Area Council official, Billy died of asbestos related illness, having suffered from poor health during the past two years.

DAGGE Eckhard *From* Keil, Germany. *Died* April 2006, aged 58. Eckhard, who died of cancer, held three championships during his career – German, European and world. He gained the world (WBC) title with an unexpected stoppage win over Bahama's Elisha Obed and may have made an even bigger mark had it not been for his dislike of training and a continual struggle against alcoholism. Tough and a big puncher, after annexing the German middleweight championship, he fought Denny Moyer, Manny Gonzalez and Billy Backus, beating all three, and then challenged unsuccessfully for Jose Duran's European junior-middleweight crown. He got a return, which he won, and defended against Franz Csandl in Vienna before losing his title to Vito Antuofermo in 1976. Five months later he beat Obed for the WBC crown. Two defences followed, both of which the verdicts were hotly disputed, before Rocky Mattioli relieved him of the WBC belt and title. He'd been lucky in defences against Maurice Hope and Emile Griffith. A period of inactivity followed before a comeback in 1981, but when Britain's Brian Anderson beat him he chose the moment to announce his retirement from boxing.

Eric Davies

DAVIES Eric *From* Stourbridge. *Died* September 2005, aged 75. Vigilant historian Harold Alderman reported the death of this former welterweight who boxed professionally from 1950 to 1957. During that time he had 35 contests, winning 21 and drawing two, with 12 losses. Although he lived for most of his life in the midland's town of Stourbridge, Eric was born in Risca, Wales in 1929. As an amateur he won RAF, Imperial Services and NABC championships and was respected as being a hard puncher. His baptismal year saw him score wins over men such as Tommy Hinson, Eddie Cardew and that other very good Stourbridge fighter, Chris Jenkins. Jenkins had fought in an eliminator for the North-Midlands lightweight title but Eric beat him twice. He also knocked out Jackie Allpress and Joe Blytheway. Only one loss blotted his scoresheet and that was to the much underrated Peter Fallon, who was Central Area lightweight champion. Eddie Phillips from the George Middleton stable outpointed him at the start of 1951, but Eric came back with three knockout wins over Dennis Yearby, Les Garbutt and Eric Skidmore, and closed the year with a points win over his namesake from Spratton, Roy Davies. Others on his record are Santos Martins, Peter Smith, Phil Mellish, Eddie Ricketts, George Weston, Alf Danahar, Bernie Newcombe and Ron Price, whom he beat twice. Turning to rugby after retiring from the ring, for many years he played for the local team and was also an accomplished golfer, being named Midlands Sportsman of the Year in 1963. He leaves a wife, a daughter, a son and five grandchildren.

DAVIS Fate *From* Akron, Ohio, USA. *Died* 19 June 2005, aged 67. An American welterweight, Fate was a travelling fighter, fighting in England, Mexico, Canada, Puerto Rico, New Caledonia and New Zealand, as well as in his native country. He made one appearance in England when he drew with Mark Rowe. His was a long career, beginning in 1962 when he knocked out an innocuous foe in George White, and ending in 1977 with a stoppage victory over Frank Kolovart. Between those two fights there were another 53 spread over 15 years. Most of his early outings were against obscure opponents. It was mid-1965 before he started mixing with some name fighters. Fate was often thrown to the lions, being strictly of the 'opponent' category when he lost to Rubin Hurricane Carter and Stanley Hayward, but he was learning to take care of himself. Before drawing with Mark Rowe, he fought another draw with world-class Curtis Cokes. Having had five good wins in New Zealand and New Caledonia, this was followed by a loss to Jose Napoles. Another class fighter, Eugene Hart, beat him in 1971 and at this stage Fate took a three-year break before returning to stop Dave Wyatt. He fought just once more that year, losing to smooth-boxing Canadian, Clyde Gray. Fights were now few and far between, there being one in 1975, two in 1976 and his swan song in 1977. He was a man who did well against men of his class and proved to be a stubborn foe when opposed to those who were rated far above him.

DeLACY Barry *From* London. *Died* 3 February 2006, aged 63. M.C. Barry was stabbed to death in Leeds where he was a resident. He was treasurer of the Midlands' Ex-Boxers' Association and a founder-member.

DONAGHUE Roger *From* Yonkers, NYC, New York, USA. *Died* 20 August 2006, aged 75. Turning pro in 1948 as a promising young welterweight, Roger achieved more

fame from putting Marlon Brando through his paces in preparation for the film On the Waterfront and being credited with coining the immortal line 'I could have been a contender' uttered by Brando in the 1954 classic. That despite him going unbeaten in his first 20 fights and losing just four out of 32 before he called it quits in 1952. He is mainly remembered in boxing as being the last opponent of Georgie Flores, who died from his injuries after their bout in August 1951. Roger was never the same after that and three fights later he quit to become a beer salesman, the position he was holding down when hired by Elia Kazan to teach Brando the rudiments of boxing. He also coached James Dean for a film portraying his own life, but that never got off the ground following the actor's tragic death in 1955. A victim from complications of Alzheimer's disease, Roger never quite fulfilled his dreams.

DOYLE Kevin *From* Dublin, Ireland. *Died* April 2006, aged 83. One of Ireland's best-known amateur boxers of the 1940s, Kevin won the national senior title at middleweight in 1948 in the colours of Arbour Hill BC. Unfortunately, he was always in the shadows of the great Mick McKeon and would have won far more honours than he did if he had been in another weight division. Starting out as a featherweight he won the Irish junior lightweight title in 1942 and was in the 1944 senior final at welter. He also boxed for Ireland on several occasions after the war. Having settled in Australia in the 1950s and it was in Newcastle, New South Wales that he died just a week after celebrating his 83rd birthday.

DUKE Johnny *From* Hartford, Connecticut, USA. *Died* 4 March 2004, aged 81. Born Guilio Gallucci, Johnny was a boyhood pal of Willie Pep and it was a natural progression to do likewise when Willie first donned the gloves. Fighting as a welterweight from 1942 to 1946 as Julio Gallucci, like Pep he was a busy fighter. His first four recorded fights were all in December 1942 and he ran up a total of 30 in the following year. Johnny won a few and lost a few but when, in 1944, losses outnumbered wins he had obviously gone as far as he could. He carried on to 1946, then retired to become a very busy trainer, helping hundreds of aspiring local lads to further their boxing skills. Some of the men he met in his five-year career were Al Bummy Davis, Johnny Puig, Tony Vero, Joe Torrens and Tony Riccio.

DYKES Bobby *From* Miami, Florida, USA. *Died* June 2006, aged 77. A world-rated welterweight, Bobby fought from 1946 to 1957, during which he went to the well 146 times, losing only 23. Two of these came in his first few fights and they were to men who, like himself, were to make an impression against the cream of fighters active in the same era. Future champion Lauro Salas outpointed him, as did Fernando Sosa, but he would taste defeat only three times in his next 60 fights. A glance at his extensive record reveals how a well-managed fighter who learns his trade thoroughly can retire with his faculties unharmed and with his financial future secure. Bobby's life is one of boxing's success stories. Retiring on a winning note against Canada's Gordon Pouliot, he then ran a successful insurance agency and restaurant. He raised three children, retired from business, bought a yacht, and spent his leisure years contentedly. Taking those two great welterweight champions, Ray Robinson and Kid Gavilan, to split decisions and beating Gavilan in the return, his record contains the notable names of Lester Felton, Johnny Bratton, Willie Pastrano, Jean Walzach, Sonny Horne, Joey Giardello, Billy Kilgore, Joe Miceli, Ralph Zanelli, Pierre Langlois, Joey Giambra, Ralph Tiger Jones, Holly Mims, Ernie Durando, Gil Turner, Joe Rindone and Walter Cartier. Bobby beat most of them.

EVANS Johnny *From* Epsom and Ewell. *Died* September 2005. A top-class amateur welter and light-middle, who won four South-West London Divisional titles between 1967 and 1974, Johnny was good enough to captain England against Wales in 1974, defeating one S.Bateman. He never turned pro, despite beating Jimmy Batten and Alan Minter and meeting men such as Maurice Hope, Eckhard Dagge and Robbie Davies, preferring to enjoy a smoke and a drink along the way. Johnny died after suffering a fall in Ulverston, Cumbria.

FERNANDEZ Andres *From* Albuquerque, New Mexico, USA. *Died* 16 December 2005, aged 32. A couple of very hard fights late in his career must have contributed to the death of Andres. In 2001, he beat Jorge Reyes in a tough, uncompromising battle, following which he collapsed and went into a coma. He never retained his former well-being and after a four-year battle with his affliction he died peacefully. Andres had challenged Clarence Adams for the WBA super-bantamweight title in 2000, but was stopped with bad cuts after putting up stubborn resistance.

FINN Dave *From* Stepney. *Died* 10 November 2005, aged 90. Dave was born David Fineri and changed his name to Finn when he started boxing at the tender age of 15. It was September 1930 and once he'd got through to 1931, he became a very busy fighter. The nearest he got to a major title was when he annexed the Southern Area lightweight championship and such a title had a lot of meaning back in the 1930s. At best, he was a crowd-pleasing journeyman who excelled himself against good fighters. Some of those he beat were Dave Crowley, Charlie Jordan, Benny Thackeray, Stan Jehu, Johnny Peters, Dick Corbett, Tommy Hyams, Alby Day, Boyo Rees, Jack Carrick Robert Disch, Johnny Softley, Ronnie James, Freddie Simpson, Jackie Rankin, Hal Cartwright and Douglas Bygrave. He also drew with Mick Carney, Johnny McGrory, Maurice Holtzer, Bob Ramsey and Albert Lloyd. Dave was popular in London's east-end and being a nephew of Jack Solomons it is not surprising that he often boxed at the Devonshire Club. In 1941 he lost to a hard-punching protege of Jack Solomons, Eric Boy Boon, but the latter had to work hard to take the points. An American campaign in 1936-37 saw him returned winner of five fights for eight losses, but two of those defeats were against

world champions, Freddie Miller and Benny Bass. Dave fought Jimmy Vaughan, Cuthbert Taylor, Benny Caplan, Benny Sharkey, Jim Brady, Harry Mizler, Arthur Danahar, Tommy Hyams, Ronnie James, Harry Lazar, Tom Smith and Billy Thompson – an assortment of very good fighters. Losing to future British champion, Thompson, in 1946, prompted his retirement. Had it not been for sparse boxing activity during the war years, he would have almost certainly notched up 100 wins.

Dave Finn

FISKE Jack *From* NYC, New York, USA. *Died* 24 January 2006, aged 88. Veteran boxing scribe and Hall of Fame inductee, Jack, was a long-time boxing correspondent for the *San Francisco Chronicle* and *Boxing Update* newsletter. Born Jacob Finlestein, he was highly regarded by the sporting community and spoke out passionately about the marginalisation of boxing in the sporting media, incompetent referees, the 'alphabet' boxing organisations plus anything else that went against the grain. He was 100% honest and fearless. Over the years, Jack built up a fine reference library and collection of memorabilia. He knew his job inside out and his opinion was sought by many fighters when they were offered matches. He told them straight – no mincing of words. "The more tattoos a boxer wears, the more inept he is" said Jack in one of his columns and his columns were an example of excellence in journalism. He died from Parkinson's disease.

FONTILLIO Danny *From* Bermondsey. *Died* 29 May 2006, aged 56. Harold Alderman, who kindly supplied me with Danny's record, thinks that he might have gone a long way in the game had he been managed by one of the big names in the game. As it was, he was called on many times to substitute for incapacitated fighters and was also sent to continental Europe to meet men whose form was untested by our domestic fighters. Danny fought three times in France and once in Denmark and lost all four, but considering how hard a fight he gave Phil Martin and British light-heavyweight champions in Johnny Frankham and Tim Wood, it is obvious that his ten wins and 13 losses fail to do justice to his ability. As the late, lamented Vic Hardwicke often told me: "Never mind the win-loss ratio, have a look at the quality of the opposition". Danny, who came here from St Lucia, boxed from 1968 to 1977, with a two-year break in 1971-72. He was a Repton ABC member in his amateur days and got his professional start at the NSC, where he beat Wes Yapp. He also beat Vernon Shaw twice, but couldn't get past Eric Blake, to whom he twice lost. The second loss convinced him to have a rest and it was two years before he stepped in the ring again. The following two years were his best as far as winning verdicts was concerned. He stopped Frank Dolan and among those he outscored were Les Avoth, Peter Brisland and Bobby Barrett. After beating Mike Cottingham he never won another contest, but it was during those years that he put in some sterling performances, either against continental fighters or home-based rated men. After his ring days, he worked on the Channel Tunnel before returning to St Lucia, where he discovered a natural spring, the water of which he bottled. This became a thriving business which provided him with a good income and lifestyle. He kept fit by playing golf, but as is often the case with fit men, an unexpected heart attack cut him down in early middle age. He leaves a wife and three children.

FOWLER Len *From* New Barnet. *Died* 1 May 2006, aged 86. Len was a light-heavyweight who was active in the mid to late 1940s. He fought many of the rated men in his division and, as is so often the case, he ventured into the dreadnought division with varying results. He stopped Ted Kid Lewis's protege, Charles Henry of Croydon, early in his career, drew with Harold Anthony, outpointed Oxford's Sid Williams, but could never get the better of Ernie Woodman, who beat him three times. Having met Reg Andrews, Jock Taylor, Reg Spring and Len Bennett, his last fight was against the Canadian, Gene Fowler, whom he beat on points. After his ring days he started a business manufacturing sporting trophies and most trophies for big boxing occasions seem to have emanated from Len Fowler (Trophies) Ltd. Len suffered from a stroke 16 years ago, which partially disabled him, so he handed the reins to his wife who survives him, and son-in-law. Len had two daughters, grandchildren and great-grandchildren.

GALIANA Fred *From* Toledo, Spain. *Died* July 2005, aged 74. One hundred and 41 wins out of 175 fights, with 12 draws, is a record to be proud of at any period in gloved boxing history. Yet Fred, who was an unbeaten holder of the European featherweight championship, never got a world title shot and apart from a campaign in South America seldom fought outside of Europe. Moving up in weight, he relinquished his European title (won by stopping Ray Famechon in Paris) to compete in the lightweight division and all in all had 15 fights for Spanish titles. To pick some of the well-known names from his record, we have Fernand Nollet, Sauveur Chiocca, Hector Constance, Carmelo Bossi, Ebe Mensah, Jaime Gine, Bobby Ros, Rudi Langer, Victor Pepeder, Davey Moore, Luis Folledo, Luis Romero, Jean Matcherlink, Sammy Bonnici, Duillio Loi and Lucien Meraint. Fred's best wins were against Famechon, Juan Sombrita and Nollet, while his most disappointing showing came when he challenged world champion, Davey Moore, in a non-title affair. Fred retired after four rounds and the Spanish Federation suspended him indefinitely and stripped him of his Spanish title (subsequently he regained it). The Federation accused him of giving an unsatisfactory showing, but it was soon revealed that Fred had a severe arm injury and fought most of the four rounds with one arm out of action. Looking at a list of achievements, Galiana rates with Paolino Uzcudun, Luis Folledo, Baltazar Sangchilli and Luis Romero as being one of Spain's greatest fighters.

GARCIA Antonio Puppy *From* Havana, Cuba. *Died* 23 October 2005, aged 72. After turning pro at the age of 16 in 1949, Puppy was soon mixing in good company and in 1952 recorded two inside-the-distance wins over the highly-rated American, Pappy Gault. Although confining his career to his native Cuba, apart from three contests in Venezuela, he went on to meet some of the best featherweights around, recording wins over Charley Titone, Sonny Leon, Kid Anahuac, Luis Galvani, Frankie Sodano, Angel Robinson Garcia and Ernesto Parra. When one observes closely the eight defeats suffered in 50 recorded contests, only Tomas Valdez, Ciro Morasen (twice) and Lauro Salas escaped without losing in reply, and he went unbeaten in his last 12 fights before retiring in 1959.

GIBILIRU Sugar *From* Ghana. *Died* February 2006, aged 69. Sugar Gibiliru's professional career started in Ghana. His early career is skimpily recorded, the first details available being from 1955. He fought unsuccessfully for the Ghanaian featherweight title in 1956 and came to Britain in 1961, boxing here for a couple of years. Two names stand out on his Ghanaian record: Aryee Jackson, whom he knocked out early in his career, and Nigeria's Roy Jacobs, who outpointed him in 1956. Both these men were beaten by Percy Lewis in their British campaigns, but both did well subsequently. Gibiliru was a small-halls' fighter who performed just once at a major arena (Wembley Pool), where he drew with debutant scrapper, Jimmy Lloyd. He won and lost against Joe Somerville and stopped Terry Beeston. Other names on his record are Jackie Harwood, Tony Lewis, Billy Tarrant and Ian McKenzie. The father of the former British super-featherweight champion of the same name in 1991, his cause of death was not reported.

GIBSON Truman *From* Chicago, Illinois, USA. *Died* 23 December 2005, aged 93. One-time lawyer for Joe Louis, Truman Gibson, who fought racial discrimination all his adult life, became an influential and powerful figure in boxing during the days of the International Boxing Club. Truman Kella Gibson, who was born in Atlanta and left law-school with a degree to later become civilian advisor to the war department, was still practising law shortly before he died just before Christmas 2005. Following his tenure as President of the IBC, he was sentenced to a period of probation and a fine when the Supreme Court dissolved the Club for extortion and monopolistic practices. He was honoured in 2001 for his work in ending racial segregation in the armed forces.

GOMEZ Tommy *From* Port Tampa, Florida, USA. *Died* 28 April 2006, aged 86. In the early 1940s, Tommy was being groomed for a fight with Joe Louis, but wartime commitments scuppered his chances of fighting for boxing's biggest prize. Tommy joined the US army in 1942 and was wounded in Europe when fighting in the Battle of the Bulge in 1944, suffering multiple wounds which would have killed a lesser man. He survived and received a Purple Heart award. In civvy street again, he lost two back-to-back fights, against Jersey Joe Walcott and Joe Matisi, for the only time in his career. Having decided to retire from boxing, he changed his mind and made a successful return to the ring five months later. Tommy was an American of Spanish extraction and a formidable heavyweight. In 86 contests, of which he lost just nine, only 16 went the distance. With four of those distance fights being among his losses, the balance shows that he stopped 74 opponents and there are some big names amongst them: Teddy Yarosz, Art Sykes, Buddy Scott, Tommy Tucker, Tony Musto, Phil Muscato, Walter Hafer, Gunnar Barland, Natie Brown and Bill Petersen. On the debit side only top men beat him: Lee Oma, Walcott and, in his final fight, Bob Satterfield, who outpointed him in 1950. After turning his back on the ring, Tommy opened a restaurant and eventually worked for an insurance company. Married twice, losing his first wife in 1999, his second wife and four daughters survive him.

GOSSIP Stan *From* Hull. *Died* October 2005, aged 82. Stan will be remembered as a good journeyman fighter by fans fortunate enough to have been around during the boom period of the late 1940s. His record is typical of those days. Between 29 September and 8 November 1948 he fought six times, three of those fights coming within eight days. He got his career off to a good start by outpointing Woolwich featherweight Arthur Gould and one year later was in the opposite corner to Ronnie Clayton, who was two fights away from winning the British title. Stan took him the full ten rounds and it should be remembered that Clayton had already challenged for the European title. On the way to an eliminator for the British title, Stan fought Chris Kelly, Ray Fitton (three times) Black Bond Teddy Peckham, Eddie Dumazel, Allan Tanner, Jackie Lucraft, Jim McCann and Tommy Bailey. He beat Bert Jackson in 1949, but lost to him eight months later in the title eliminator. Defeats by Ron Cooper, Ray Fitton and Jim Kenny followed, but a good performance came against Teddy Peckham, whom he beat over eight rounders. Most of Stan's fights were either eight or ten rounders and he fought only twice over the six round distance. A boxer rather than a puncher, who stopped only one of his foes, he was also durable and was never counted out.

GRAHAM Bob, BEM *From* Newcastle. *Died* September 2005, aged 90. Long-serving BBBoC Inspector and Administrative Steward, and also Executive Director of the IBF, London-born Bob Graham's contribution to boxing was immense. His passing leaves a huge gap that will be very difficult to fill. In recent years, a stroke robbed him of his ability to speak, but such was his dedication that he carried on with his duties as far as he was able to. His interest in the game never flagged.

GRAVES Jackie *From* Austin, Minnesota, USA. *Died* 15 November 2005, aged 83. Boxing from 1944 to 1956, having been a Golden Gloves bantamweight champion in 1942, Jackie fought professionally in the featherweight division. One of his best performances came against Willie Pep, who was world title holder at the time, and Jackie gave him problems before succumbing in the eighth round. His record was unblemished against five other men who at one time held world titles, namely Jackie Callura, Jackie Wilson, Harry Jeffra, Manuel Ortiz and Harold Dade. Looking through his long record, I'm impressed that only 'name' fighters beat him and that a lot of those defeats were avenged. Graves beat Charley Riley, Charles Cabey Lewis, Lefty LaChance, Humberto Sierra, Pat Iocobucci, Miguel Acevedo, Teddy Davis, Luis Castillo, Diego Sosa, and two fighters from this side of the big pond in Wales' Eddie Dumazel and Finland's Elis Ask. He lost to Bernard Docusen, and to each of the Flanagan brothers, Del and Glen, the latter being his last fight, having won their first encounter in 1949. Sosa stopped him in Miami Beach but was clearly beaten in a return match, as was the aforementioned Acevedo. Graves was a heavy puncher, with many wins well within the scheduled distance, 27 of them within three rounds. He was also a generous man who devoted much of his money and time to charitable causes when the big purses were coming in. Alzheimer's Disease got him in the end and that was an opponent he fought a losing battle with for years. He was still popular in his hometown and remembered by the boxing fraternity.

GRAY Tommy *From* Fife. *Died* 20 August 2006, aged 56. Having won a Scottish youth title as an amateur, Tommy was deemed promising enough to be signed up by the former world middleweight champion, Terry Downes, prior to embarking on a pro career in October 1969. Domiciled in London, and boxing as a middleweight, he started well enough but failed to dedicate himself to the game and consequently he lost fights he should have won. Still, he beat Joe Sommerville, Dave Parris, Pat Vernie (twice), Freddie Wreden, Frank Isaacs (twice), Andy Peace, Fred

Powney, Ronnie Hough and Teddy Meho (twice), but was beaten by Ernest Musso, who handed him his first defeat, Phil Matthews (twice), Johnny Cooke, Lloyd Duncan, Tony Mundine, Tom Imrie, Billy May and Pat McCann. In five fights abroad, Tommy lost to Vincent Parra in France, Tom Jensen in Denmark, Jan Kies and Pierre Fourie in South Africa, and Tony Mundine in Australia. None of those men were easy and both Mundine and Fourie went on to challenge for world titles. Retiring after being badly cut up by McCann, Tommy eventually moved to Spain where he got married and had two sons. His brother George was also a pro and fought as a heavyweight between 1970 and 1978.

GREEN George *From* Warrington. *Died* 16 March 2006, aged 78. One of four fighting brothers, George fought from 1945 to 1952. He was a featherweight and although his career was much shorter than that of his brother, Jimmy, he mixed with some good fighters. His career kicked off with a second-round stoppage over Jim Malloy and he went on to have a further 23 fights. Two draws against Selwyn Evans and Peter Guichan are an indication of his status, both being good scrappers. There were wins over Harry Shaw, Pat Evans, Joe Carter of Mitcham, Zeke Brown and Ronnie Clayton's brother, Sid. George was unsuccessful against Bernard Pugh, Jim Kenny and Ronnie Gill and retired in 1950, only to come back two years later to lose on points to Steve Trainor.

GREEN Tony *From* Sheffield. *Died* January 2006, aged 64. A former A-class referee based in the Central Area from 1989, Tony operated until 2002.

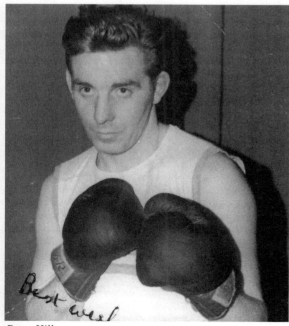

Peter Hill

HILL Peter *From* Walworth. *Died* September 2005, aged 74. Peter, a former ABA middleweight champion, was a brother of trainer, Freddie, whose obituary appeared in our 2004 edition. Both became trainers and both handled men of championship status. A good amateur middleweight in the 1950s, he was a Fitzroy Lodge member – a club that always brimmed with talented fighters. Peter brought honour to his club by winning the ABA title in 1958 and was a fearless fighter. I saw him knocked out by one punch against Jeff Beeston despite being well ahead at the time, but asked for a return which he clearly won. What impressed me was that he took the fight to his man rather than opting for the safety-first course. Peter trained Alan Rudkin when the Liverpudlian fought for the world title in Tokyo.

HOGBERG Bo *From* Sweden. *Died* 8 November 2005, aged 66. At the age of 18, Bo was Swedish Amateur middleweight champion, winning the championship again in 1961 and 1962 before turning professional. His paid career lasted until 1973, during which time he annexed the European light-middleweight by stopping Bruno Visintin in Copenhagen, only to lose it to Yolande Leveque a month later. Meantime, Sandro Mazzinghi had deposed of Leveque and would defend against Bo at the end of 1966. It turned out to be a heart-breaker for the Swede, who sustained a broken jaw and was stopped with just one round to go. Bo wouldn't quit – he was a hard man, dour and game to the core – so the referee was forced to intervene. He then went through a dozen fights before losing to that old warhorse, Harry Scott, who caught him cold and scored a first-round knockout. It was the only time that he was put down for the full count. Before that setback, Bo had stopped Holland's Toon Schuurmanns, Germany's Jupp Elze and Heini Freytag, America's Billy DePriest and the French-based Senegalese, Michel Diouf. He never lost to another Brit, Al Sharpe, Dennis Read, Johnny Cooke and Billy Tarrant all falling before the fists of this hard-punching Swede. There were bigger names too – Manuel Gonzalez, Bobby Cassidy, Gil Diaz and Fabio Bettini, etc. Retiring in 1968 after dropping a decision to Harold Richardson, he then made a brief and unsuccessful comeback in 1973 before calling it a day when losing to Jose Pacheco in Mallorca.

HOLMAN Jack *From* Canterbury. *Died* April 2006, aged 80. A coal miner by trade, Jack started his amateur career with the Prince of Wales ABC in Canterbury, prior to moving over to the Chislet Colliery ABC and winning the light-heavyweight title at the inaugural National Coal Board Championships on beating James Lamont (Wilson Town Colliery) at Wembley in 1948. Back at Wembley the following year, Jack won the same title when beating J.Gill (Washington Colliery, Durham), but lost in the Southern Zone finals to Albert Hoyle (1950) and Doug Bradbury (1951 and 1952) before retiring in 1952. Both Hoyle, the Welsh amateur champion in 1951, and Bradbury were highly rated, so losing to them was no disgrace. Another top man who Jack shared a ring with was Peter Messervy, the 1950 ABA champion. Married in 1950, when Chislet Colliery closed in 1959 he moved to Snowdown before taking early retirement in 1986 when the pit closed. A quiet and friendly man who didn't talk much about boxing away from the ring, it was some achievement for him to win two NCB titles when representing the smallest coalfield in Britain.

HOSTAK Al *From* Minneapolis, USA. *Died* 13 August 2006, aged 90. A former NBA middleweight champion, Al died of complications following a stroke in a Seattle nursing home. Tall for a middleweight, at 6ft, and a solid puncher, his early career, which began in 1934, is sketchy, but there are no losses recorded right up to the time he won the title from Freddie Steele in 1938. Solly Krieger inflicted the first blot on his record and took the title with it, but Al got it back seven months later by savagely stopping Krieger in four rounds. He then defended against Eric Seelig before losing it for the last time to Tony Zale. Zale had the Indian sign on Al, winning all three of their fights, with two of them being for the title. Former world champion, Ken Overlin, was another who beat Al, but these defeats are counterbalanced with wins over Harry Kid Matthews, Steve Belloise, Glen Lee, Anton Raadik and Paulie Perkins. Fighting on until 1949, he bowed out on his 33rd birthday with a knockout win over Jack Snapp in nine rounds.

Al Hostak

HUNTER Mike 'Bounty' *From* Los Angeles, California, USA. *Died* 8 February 2006, aged 45. Yet another shooting incident claimed the life of a fighter when this former rated American heavyweight was killed during a struggle with police who were investigating his alleged involvement with drugs. He was a former holder of the USBA title and had wins over Pinklon Thomas, Ossie Ocasio, Tyrell Biggs, Dwight Muhammad Quawi, Alexander Zolkin, Jimmy Thunder and Oliver McCall, despite drug problems affecting his career. A win over Buster Mathis (junior) was later changed to 'no contest' following a positive drugs test. Defeats began to sprinkle his record and he quit when Brian Neilsen of Denmark beat him. Later, Mike became a boxing instructor.

HYLAND Paddy *From* Kildare, Ireland. *Died* January 2006, estimated age 78. Paddy, a bantamweight, did all his fighting over here, which was why he was often billed from Grantham. He boxed from 1949 to 1951, starting in October with a points win over Doug Green. In 1950 he stopped Bob Birkenhead, outscored Jack Hodder, but lost in a return. Paddy was establishing himself as a useful fighter when he went through five fights without a loss. Later there were defeats to Mickey O'Sullivan, Jackie Fairclough, Peter Fay and Johnny Kent. In his final fighting year he beat Johnny Bartles, Sid Hiom, Billy Gibson and Robert Hecht on the way to notching up six wins in his last seven fights. Paddy learned his boxing while in the RAF, turning pro following demob, and joined George Gill's stable. An unusual feature in his record is a nine-round points loss to Eddie McCormick. McCormick had just fought a ten rounder and the rules stated that he was not allowed to fight two or more fights over that distance within so many days.

JAMES Percy *From* Southport. *Died* August 2006, aged 74. For a man who lost his first nine pro contests after starting out in 1949, Percy went quite a way in the game, beating Eddie McNally, Les Herbert, Alf Cottam (four times), Freddie Bancroft, Wally Barkess, Jack Skelly, Andy Monahan, Bernard Fairbanks, Nye Ankrah (twice), Sammy Cosgrove, Charles Odumasi, Pat McCarthy, Michael Feeney and two top men in Chic Brogan and Colin Barber. Some of the above also beat him but he never declined a challenge and met men of the calibre of Eddie Fitzsimmons, Glyn Evans, Mickey Roche (three times), Billy Ashcroft (twice), Steve Trainor (twice), Jackie Butler, Neville Tetlow, Bobby Gill (twice), Jim Fisher, Bobby Mason, Arthur Donnachie, Dave Croll (twice), Teddy Peckham, Roy Jacobs (twice) and Eddie Burns, all good featherweights. In 76 contests, Percy only boxed in London twice, losing on points to the future British featherweight champion, Bobby Neill, and drawing with Alf Drew, and became almost a fixture at the Blackpool Tower and Liverpool Stadium, where he delighted fans with his stoic displays. The other big name on his record was that of Dave Charnley, who would win British, Commonwealth and European lightweight honours and twice challenge for the world title. Percy called it a day in December 1957 after losing to Jacobs at Liverpool Stadium, having started his career there and fighting there on 42 occasions. He died in Australia, where he had lived for several years.

JAY Tee *From* Notting Hill. *Died* 19 May 2006, aged 44. It always surprised me that after so few professional fights, the Ghanaian-born Tee Jay was fighting at British championship level. He had a good amateur record when boxing for the All Stars ABC, twice winning NW London Divisional honours and putting up a magnificent fight with Evander Holyfield when representing Ghana in the 1984 Olympics. Even so, to be Southern Area cruiserweight champion after five fights and to challenge for the British title in the sixth is some achievement. Andy Straughan beat him for the national title, but was then deposed by Roy Smith. Jay then challenged Smith and stopped him in the first round. He'd won the British cruiserweight championship. Eventually, he lost his crown to Glenn McCrory in an exciting fight at the Latchmere Leisure Centre. I was impressed by the strong counter attacking of Jay and by the gracious manner in which he and his corner accepted the loss of his title. He challenged twice more for the title but was unsuccessful. In between those title fights he stopped Blaine Logsdon, Cordwell Hylton, Chris Jacobs and Alex Penarski. Jay, whose birthname was Taju Akay, was only 44 when he was cut down by a massive heart-attack. He was gifted with a superb physique and, in retirement, he spent hours in the gymnasium. He leaves three children.

JOHNSON Leavander *From* Atlantic City, New Jersey, USA. *Died* September 2005, aged 35. When fighting Jesus Chavez, Leavander lost not only his IBF lightweight title but also his life, having been one of those persistent fighters who never gave up. He lost in his first three attempts to win a world title, but got there in the end when he beat Stefano Zoff in Italy. Hard-punching Leavander stopped his man, a former WBA champion, in the seventh round for the vacant crown. He had 41 fights in total and lost five, but four of those were to men who were world title holders in Orzubek Nazarov, Javier Jauregui, Miguel Gonzalez, and in his last fight, Jesus Chavez. Although Leavander was on his feet when the referee stepped in, he collapsed in his dressing room and was taken to hospital, before undergoing an operation to remove a blood clot from his brain. It looked at one stage as if he would recover, but it was not to be. Despite being operated on within an hour of collapsing, then showing signs of improvement, he succumbed six days later.

KAKIZAWA Shinichi *From* Tokyo, Japan. *Died* 8 June 2006, aged 58. A former Oriental lightweight titleholder, 'Jaguar', as he was known, boxed as a pro from 1965 to 1971, winning 35 of 48 bouts. Despite lacking a big punch, his skill, speed and ringcraft accounted for good men such as Art Persley, Sebastiao Nascimento, Flash Elorde and Percy Hayles, while he was good enough to share a ring with likes of Johnny Jamito, Pedro Adigue, Guts Ishimatsu, Carlos Hernandez, Chango Carmona and Alfonso Frazer to

name but a few. After retiring from the ring he managed the Ashikaga JK Gym before succumbing to cancer.

KEEN Al *From* Newarhill. *Died* April 2006, aged 66. Based in London throughout his seven-year boxing career, Al was the brother of Sammy McSpadden. In his first year within the ropes, he stopped every opponent. A loss came in the following year just as he was beginning to establish himself in the game as a lightweight through victories over Tommy Tiger, Phil McGrath and Johnny McLaren. He dropped an eight-round points decision to Peter Cheevers, but scored good wins over Tommy Icke, Ricky Keirnan, Len Wilson and Manley Brown. Not surprisingly, he was outpointed by a rising Ken Buchanan in 1966. Having performed with credit, he seemed to realise that he'd gone as far as he could in his profession and had just one more fight, a points loss to Al White, before retiring to help Sammy with his coal delivery business. He died in Devon after some years of ill health, leaving a wife and five sons.

KERSHAW Lyndon *From* Bradford. *Died* December 2005, aged 32. A flyweight, cum bantamweight, Lyndon fought from 1992 to 1997, during which time he never had an easy fight, with his best win coming when he beat Mickey Cantwell. He was a clever boxer but lacked a finishing punch, with most of his wins coming via the full course. After losing on points to Brian Carr in a British title eliminator, he drifted away from the game. It was later revealed that he'd died of heroin poisoning.

Lyndon Kershaw   Les Clark

KIDD Johnny *From* Aberdeen. *Died* April 2006, aged 70. The winner of several amateur titles when representing the RAF, Johnny launched his professional career in 1957. He'd knocked out Dick McTaggart in the unpaid ranks and had annexed the ABA lightweight title in 1957 just before turning pro. He started his career in the paid ranks with an impressive stoppage of Don Flack and went unbeaten in nine fights before winning the Scottish lightweight title from Johnny McLaren by a ninth-round knockout. Although Johnny beat Bobby Neill, he found Terry Spinks too good when fighting in a British title eliminator, but he fought in top company with Vic Andreeti, Derry Treanor, Kenny Field, Roy Jacobs, Spike McCormick, Love Allotey, Tommy Tibbs and Sexton Mabena among his opponents. Of his 24 wins, 14 were scored inside the distance.

Johnny Kidd

LAVE Kitione *From* Tonga. *Died* June 2006, aged 72. It is difficult to trace Kitione's early record as he fought in the Fiji Islands and Tonga, both of whose boxing archives are limited. What his record during those years tells us is that he obviously carried a heavy dig. This was confirmed when he arrived on New Zealand soil and knocked out nine men in ten starts. He lost the tenth contest to Ken Brady, but knocked out Brady twice in return matches. The Tongan then tried his luck in Australia where he scored five wins and one draw in seven fights. At this stage he'd cleaned up most of the Antipodean heavies, with notable stoppage wins over Allen Williams, Steve Zoravich and Don Mullett. Only Brady had beaten him in his Australasian campaign and this blot had been emphatically erased in their final contest when the Englishman didn't get past round ten. In 1955, the time had come to campaign in England, but his handlers were far too ambitious in throwing him in with the British champion, Johnny Williams. For a change, it was Kitione who took the count and it happened after only two minutes of action. Back in action four weeks later with a stoppage win over the

Tyneside prospect, Manny Burgo, he then stopped Eddie Hearn, lost a close one to Joe Bygraves, and knocked out Fred Powell. He next lost another close one, this time to Jack Gardner, but it was this fight with the former British champion that showed just how powerful he was. Gardner had never been off his feet before and outweighed his foe by nearly two stone, but he was fortunate to survive the first round when he twice hit the deck before receiving a very unpopular points verdict. Four months later, the Tongan ended the career of Don Cockell with an emphatic second-round stoppage. A challenge for the Empire title failed, Joe Bygraves beating him on points, and later an up-and-coming Brian London survived some tough moments to do likewise. Kitione went back to Fiji and scored several knockout wins before surfacing in Bologna, where he was outpointed by Francesco Cavichi. Returning later, he outpointed Federico Friso before going on to Berlin where he was beaten by Ulli Nitzschke. He then tried his luck in the USA, but his form had gone and Tom McNeely stopped him in three rounds. His final years were spent in New Zealand, where he befriended former national dual champion, Johnny Hanks. It was Hanks who attended Kitione's funeral and who informed me of his death. "He was a likeable man and a mighty hitter", said Johnny. "He couldn't pull a punch either in the ring or in the gym, but in the street he was quiet, placid and friendly". His real name was Kitione Takitau Lavemai.

Kitione Lave

LEWIS Morton *From* Wallington, Surrey. *Died* 17 August 2006, aged 89. The boxing scene is duller following the death of Morton Lewis. He was a colourful character, sometimes argumentative, sometimes obdurate, but generous to a fault and a man who never refused to help the cause of boxing. He was the only son of the famous Ted Kid Lewis and it was he who wrote and financed the only book biography on his renowned father. Morton spent most of his childhood in America, where the Kid fought the bulk of his fights, and he proudly displayed belts, cups and trophies won by his father at an annual dinner of the Croydon Ex-Boxers' Association. It was a most impressive display and a tribute to one of our greatest ever fighters. He also financed the placing of a blue plaque on the wall of Nightingale House where his father spent his last years. Morton often made cash grants from his own pocket into EBA funds and never refused to help in any capacity asked of him. Morton worked in the film industry, with an office in Wardour Street, Soho and it afforded him a comfortable living and a host of friends. I recall an occasion when he invited a group of us to a dinner function at the Kensington Gardens Hotel. He was a marvellous host and genuinely pleased to treat us to an evening, with no expense too much for him. Morton was known throughout the boxing game and was, at one time, General Manager for Braitman and Ezra Promotions, for whom he also did the artwork and photography in their boxing programmes. With his passing, an era ends. He was often able to help me with queries on boxing from the 1920s, having seen the cream of boxers active on both sides of the big pond, and was a well of fistic information. He is survived by his wife, Sally, and generations of family going on to great-grandchildren by whom he was idolised. His famous father was once asked, when in his post-boxing days, how he was coping financially. The response was "I have a son who is very good to me". Morton always looked after his friends and family.

LEWIS Stan *From* Potters Bar. *Died* January 2006, aged 79. From a boxing family, Stan grew up in Potters Bar, Herts just yards away from his great friend and amateur rival, Johnny Wright, who would go on to win a silver medal at the 1948 Olympic Games. Both men were middleweights. A former ATC champion, Stan, boxing in the colours of Langham ABC, got to the middleweight final of the North-West London Championships in 1948, but was beaten by St Pancras' G.Leech. He came back strongly in 1949 to win the ABA title, beating men such as Wally Beckett, Jim Allsop and Ron Crookes, who he'd already beaten earlier in the year, on the way. Next came a points loss at the hands of Wright when representing the ABA against the Imperial Services, a decision which could have gone either way. Although Stan was first reserve for England in the 1949 European Championships he pulled out just prior to Wright also withdrawing and announcing his retirement. Stan then followed shortly after. A gifted all-round sportsman, Stan could have had a shot at pro soccer and played tennis, golf and bowls right into his 70s.

LOBO Rogerio *From* Sao Paulo, Brazil. *Died* 28 July 2006, aged 35. Yet another victim of a shooting, being killed by an armed gang intent on robbing his restaurant, he had knocked out Adilson Noli in the first round just two days earlier. A former Brazilian light-heavyweight and cruiserweight champion, Rogerio had turned pro in 1995 and mixed with the likes of Thomas Hansvoll, Vincenzo Cantatore, Owen Beck, Kelvin Davis, Michael Moorer and Kali Meehan. Although the majority of his 41 victims were relatively obscure outside South America, his 35 inside-the-distance wins show him to be a solid puncher. He leaves a wife and an 18-month-old son.

LOCCHE Nicolino *From* Mendoza, Argentina. *Died* September 2005, aged 66. A defensive master and superb boxing technician, Nicolino is remembered as one of the truly great South American fighters who, in 136 fights, lost only four. One of those defeats was against Antonio Cervantes in Maracay, when the latter's world junior lightweight title was at stake and bad cuts were the reason that the referee intervened. Cervantes is the only man to have stopped Nicolino, who announced his retirement from boxing soon afterwards. It took just 17 months for him to announce his intention to come back and he then went two years without losing another fight before calling it a day in August 1976. All of his final seven fights went the distance, which proved he was no puncher. He was a boxer in its true sense – a man difficult to hit and an accurate counter-puncher. Most of his fights took place in Buenos Aires or in his native Mendoza and the first time he boxed overseas was in 1968 after ten years of fighting for pay. It was also his first shot at a world championship and he brought the junior welterweight title home by stopping Paul Fujii in Tokyo. Nicolino successfully defended his title five times, against Carlos Hernandez, Joao Henrique, Adolph Pruitt, Domingo Berrara and Cervantes, before losing it in Panama City to local star, Alfonso Frazer. Nicolino was in poor health for the years just preceding his death, ultimately succumbing to a heart attack.

Nicolino Locche   Les Clark

McGUIRE Mickey *From* Byker. *Died* 24 July 2006, aged 93. Mickey, one of the best flyweights to emerge from north-eastern rings, was one of the last men to box at the 'Graveyard of Champions', the New St James' Hall. He came from a family of 12 children and was born Robert Drane. His brother, Paul, a middleweight, boxed as Paul McGuire, so when the younger Drane took up the game he adopted the 'McGuire' monniker and added 'Mickey' to it from a film character played by Mickey Rooney. Turning pro at 16, Mickey boxed a six-round draw with Roy Mills and went through another 40 fights with a solitary, later avenged, defeat, before climbing in the ring with British and European champion, Jackie Brown. He rose to the occasion and won 14 of the 15 rounds with a classic display of skills. Shrewdly, Brown had protected his titles by fighting at a weight limit of 8st 2lbs and insisting on two-minute rounds. This was 1932. Mickey was 19, but already a capable and experienced scrapper. In September he faced the Tunisian, Victor Young Perez. It looked a tough assignment as Perez was recognised by the NBA and IBU as being world champion, a distinction he'd gained by crushing Frankie Genaro. He'd also beaten Valentin Anglemann, Joe Mendida and Carlos Flix. McGuire, confident, cheeky and never overawed, sailed through round one and, in the second, threw the best punch of his career, a left hook which laid out the champion for the full count. This win put Mickey high in the world ratings, but he still wasn't champion. Perez, like Brown, had protected his title and refused to box a return under the championship weight limit. Beating champions at the wrong time was the story of Mickey's career. He held victories over Bert Kirby, Praxille Gyde, Valentin Anglemann and in 80 contests was to lose only 13, most losses coming at the end of his career. He was but a shadow of the man who beat Perez and Brown when he faced the great Benny Lynch, who stopped him in four rounds. There were only four fights left before he quit the ring, after losing to bantamweight, Teddy Rollins. After his ring career, he worked as an HGV driver during the Second World War and ended up in a factory that made tanks. He was married and had two children – a boy and girl, both of whom were to later give him grandchildren. Happy in his final years with a memory as sharp as ever, although wheelchair-bound and hard of hearing, Mickey died in his retirement home in Cramlington.

McNALLY Gerry *From* Liverpool. *Died* 27 December 2005, aged 73. After two years in the army, and a respected amateur, Gerry had his first pro fight. It was January 1953 and he took three rounds to knockout Harry Harvey at Watford. Gerry had a couple of early setbacks but they were against good 'uns in Eddie Wright and Ron Barton. This was a hiccup. He got through 1955 without a loss, beating Pat McAllister, Len Jarvis, Ron King and George Roe, before taking Jimmy Lynas to a six-round draw, then licking Charlie Lake and Ralph Scott. When Dick Tiger first came to these shores, Gerry was one of the men who beat him and he did the same to Alan Dean in an eight rounder at the old Liverpool Stadium. Yolande Pompey was another scrapper who saw McNally's arm raised, albeit via a disqualification. Gerry mixed with some of the best men in the country at middleweight and light-heavyweight: Alex Buxton whom he outpointed, Redvers Sangoe, Don Sainsbury, George Roe, Johnny Read, Freddie Cross, Jimmy Lynas, Stan Cullis and Ron Redrup, etc. He fought once in Germany but failed to get the decision against Rudi Nehring, but was more successful in South Africa where he lost to tough Gert Van Heerdan and beat Louis Thompson and Jan Scheepers. He leaves a widow, three children and three grandchildren.

MADERA Guadalupe 'Lupe' *From* Yucatan, Mexico. *Died* December 2005, aged 52. Lupe spent 11 years in the game trying to annex a world title, finally getting there in 1983 after a series of fights against the WBA junior flyweight champion, Katsuo Tokashiki. He lost in his first try, forced the Japanese to a draw in the return, then won on the third attempt. It was an indecisive way of getting to the top of the tree. Cuts forced the fight to be stopped after four rounds, the technical win going to the Mexican because of his being in front on the scorecards. He was man enough to grant Tokashiki a return, which he won. Both of these fights took place in Japan. Lupe held the title for a year before losing it to Francisco Quiroz of the Dominican Republic in 1984 and never fought again. In a career which stretched from 1972 to 1984, in 52 fights he'd won 37 and drew once, the sole draw coming against his arch-rival, Tokashiki.

MAHON John *From* Cork, Ireland. *Died* February 2006, aged 60. Honorary Vice-President of the Irish ABA, John died in a shooting incident outside his home. He acted in many capacities in Irish boxing and just prior to his shocking death had been voted as best referee by the Irish ABA. He leaves five children.

MAMAKOS Steve *From* Washington DC, USA. *Died* 26 July 2006, aged 88. Having started out as a pro in October 1937, and known as the 'Golden Greek', within a year Steve was mixing in top company and reversed an earlier defeat when taking a ten-round points decision from Georgie Abrams. Then, after victories over men such as Bobby Pacho, Andre Jessurun, Ralph Zannelli, Sammy Luftspring (twice) and Milt Aaron, he took on the NBA world middleweight champion, Tony Zale, in an overweight contest, losing on points over ten rounds. Such was his showing against Zale that it warranted a return with the title at stake in Chicago on 21 February 1941. In a sensational contest, Zale was floored heavily in the fifth and was behind on the cards going into the 13th round before rallying and knocking Steve out in the 14th. Although he beat Ernie Vigh next time out, there would be only sporadic successes over the next six years and Steve eventually hung up his gloves in 1947, having won 29 of 49 contests. An all-action fighter who never ducked anybody, big names on his record other than those already mentioned, included Tony Cisco, Cocoa Kid, Holman Williams, Izzy Jannazzo, Phil Furr, Tami Mauriello,

Johnny Colon, Ezzard Charles and Mose Brown. Retiring in the late 1970s following a bus accident, Steve had suffered from Alzheimer's disease for the past ten years. He leaves a wife of 65 years, a daughter and several grandchildren.

MARKS Don *From* Australia. *Died* 16 September 2005, aged 68. Don is remembered mainly for his prolific contribution to boxing journalism, but that was just one facet of interest in the fight game. He became a judge in 1968 and was also a timekeeper. Back in the 1960s, he was instrumental in forming the Australian Boxing Commission, of which he eventually became Treasurer and a Life-Member. His extensive knowledge of the Aussie boxing scene didn't stop him from becoming an authority on world boxing affairs. He is survived by his wife.

MITCHELL Ray *From* Sydney, Australia. *Died* 30 November 2005, aged 86. By participating in so many roles in the fight game, Ray will be remembered as a man who was perhaps the most experienced follower of Australian boxing of his day. He recorded the history of his country's boxing in the *Australian Ring Magazine* that he edited in the late 1950s and throughout the following decade. Most aspects of Australian boxing history were covered during the lifetime of his monthly journal and he also found time to produce four boxing books. It is a shame that he never undertook to produce a history of Australian boxing on the same lines as Chris Greyvenstein's *The Fighters*, which deals with South African boxing. Ray had the material and the knowledge to do so and I always suspected that he would have jumped at the opportunity if advancing years had not slowed him down. According to the blurb on the back cover of his books, Ray boxed as an amateur and a professional but Ray Wheatley of *World of Boxing* refutes this. What is certain is that he was a referee, promoter, boxing judge, trainer, broadcaster (radio and television), writer and agent. He edited six Australian *Boxing Record Books* during his stint with the monthly magazine and contributed to *The Ring* (American) and British *Boxing News*. He also belonged to most boxing collectors' clubs, which is how I first got to know him. It is strange that during the years that I spent in Sydney, our paths never crossed. We met for the first time in Watford, where he was living during a long stay away from home. Although his work-rate dropped during his later years, his interest in the game never stopped.

MURRAY Mick *From* Liverpool. *Died* 19 April 2006, aged 74. Mick first came to prominence when boxing for the famous Maple Leaf club and in 1957 he won the North-West Lancs light-middleweight title, beating Harry Scott along the way. Despite losing to Neil McAteer in the 1958 Divisional Championships, he received some consolation when being selected to box for England v Austria in January 1958, beating A.Exl on points. Felt by many good judges to be a cert to reach the top as an amateur, a mixture of bad luck, injuries and fighters avoiding him saw him leave the game without any major honours.

MWALE Lottie *From* Kitwe, Zambia. *Died* October 2005, aged 52. Big punching Lottie won the Commonwealth Games light-heavyweight championship in 1974 and was an experienced amateur by the time he turned professional three years later. He won a national title in his second fight and brushed away all local opposition inside the scheduled distance before throwing his hat into European rings. Lottie beat Bobby Lloyd in Oslo, then hopped across the North Sea to spectacularly knock out the previously unbeaten Tony Sibson in the first round. This win established him as a formidable fighter likely to make his presence felt at world level. He beat Marvin Johnson in Belgrade, then returned home to beat Lonnie Bennett and take the Commonwealth title from Gary Summerhayes. Now firmly established as a top-class boxer, he returned to Britain to beat Carlos Marks, Bunny Johnson, Jessie Burnett, Lee Royster and Vandell Woods before turning up in San Diego to challenge the WBC champion, Matt Saad Muhammad. The American inflicted the first loss on Lottie's record. Going into the fourth round, it was a close fight until a huge uppercut ended the challenger's dream. Lottie regrouped and won a series of fights inside the distance until the former WBA champion, Eddie Mustafa Muhammad, knocked him out in Las Vegas. From that point he was never quite as good again, but still retained enough ability to score creditable wins over Mustafa Wasajja and Chisanda Mutti (twice). When Leslie Stewart took his Commonwealth title in 1985, Lottie still had his African title, but he was to lose this in his next fight, which took place in Lagos. Stopped in eight rounds by Joe Lasisi, it was Lottie's first loss in 26 fights on African soil and Lasisi was never to reach the heights of the man he beat. Lottie, who was Zambia's greatest exponent of sock, boxed on until 1994.

NEEQUAYE Raymond Ben *From* Ghana. *Died* December 2005, aged 26. Aids claimed this Ghanaian lightweight at an age when he should have been in his physical prime. He came to Britain in May 2002 as West African champion and booked to fight at Portsmouth. A medical examination showed him to be HIV positive and his licence to box was refused. Raymond had won four out of six contests and was considered to be a prospect.

OSBORNE Buster *From* Bethnal Green. *Died* December 2005, aged 90. Buster was one of two fighting brothers, he and his brother, Len, both doing the bulk of their fighting in the welterweight division and often appearing on the same bill. Buster fought from 1931 to 1945, but the war years slowed down what had been a busy career. He had just one fight in 1939, when he beat Johnny Blake, and from then until 1945 just two, both wins over Frank Duffy and Ron Lindsey. When boxing activity picked up with gusto in 1945, he was ring-rusty and things just weren't like they were in the old days. After beating Jim Hockley on points, he packed it in. He was 30 and in the mid-'40s most welterweights were past their prime at that age. An unusual aspect of Buster's career occurred at the Holborn Stadium in 1934. Jack Powell scored a quick win over his brother Len and accepted an offer to take on Buster later on in the evening. Buster avenged Len's defeat when a cut eye forced Jack to quit in the tenth round. There was a return a couple of years later when Jack was rising up the fistic ladder. Jack turned the tables to make it one-all and received a *Boxing News Certificate of Merit* for that victory. The 1930s were good years for boxing and Buster got plenty of work and plenty of good wins over men like Jack Kid McCabe, Bill Hardy, George Rose, hard punching George Odwell, Jack McKnight, Jack Lewis, George Merritt and Dixie Dean, etc. He also forced Paddy Roche to a draw. Other names on his record that come to mind, despite them being losses, were Bob Simpkins, Harry Corbett, Harry Mason, George Davis and Billy Curran of Walton on Thames (twice). Buster fought in elite company. When the Ex-Boxers' movement was escalating, Buster regained his enthusiasm for the game and organised boxing shows for charity, getting many old timers to put on the gloves again to participate in non-serious, exhibition-style contests. I have a few of those programmes and the great names on them bring back so many precious memories.

O'TOOLE FX *From* Los Angeles, USA. *Died* July 2006, aged 76. Readers who've seen the film 'Million Dollar Baby' will recall that it was based on a story by FX O'Toole. The author's real name was Jerold Hayden Boyd and in a busy and varied life, he was regarded as an expert cut-man amongst other things such as matador, dock-worker and long-distance truck-driver. His fascination with boxing came in his mid-40s when he found himself hanging around gymnasiums, watching points and always learning. He became friends with Dub Huntley, an established trainer and cornerman and his time as a cuts man emanated from those days. His first book, *Rope Burns*, was published when he was 70. It was from a chapter in it that the 'Million Dollar Baby' film was based but, for me, the best chapter of all was the first one. The author's expertise as a cornerman is evident and only a man who understands his craft in depth could have penned such a gripping story. Another book – a novel – which was uncompleted when he died, is due to hit the book shops shortly.

OXLEY 'Nipper' Horace *From* South Elmsall. *Died* April 2006, aged 89. The coalmining areas have always produced good, tough and determined fighters. One such man was Horace. Like so many men of the 1930s, his fighting record is fragmentary and poorly chronicled. Local newspapers didn't always cover shows and that was particularly true in the north-east where Horace did most of his fighting as a lightweight, cum welter. Miles Templeton, via diligent research, has compiled a part record which begins in 1932 when Horace would have been 15. His daughter, Glenda, confirms that her father started at that age. Nearly all his defeats are shown as points losses, which indicates the durability and toughness of this man. There are draws with Boy Mallinson, Belfast's Al Pedlar and Wally Parkes, and wins over Jimmy Miller, Nipper Melgram, Alf Moran and Jim Roberts. He also lost to

Darkie Addinall and Freddie Warnock. Horace's win over Jimmy Miller came by a knockout. Miller was married earlier in the day and his wife, sitting ringside, fainted when the coup de grace was applied. A serious accident in the mine ended Horace's career, but he continued in the game as a trainer and kept active right up to his death. His wife pre-deceased him and he is survived by two children.

PASQUALITO Kid *From* Paraguay. *Died* 16 May 2006, aged 64. Western boxing record books give scant recognition to the exploits of this fighter. He won South American titles at bantamweight and featherweight and performed extensively in Mexico, where there were so many good men under nine stone in weight. A good puncher, he almost had Ruben Olivares out in 1971 and at that time Olivares had just one points loss on a record of over 70 fights. Valentin Galeano, fighting under the name Kid Pasqualito, had no luck against Alexis Arguello in 1973. Arguello was fighting in his home ring in Managua and was on his way to stardom, but Valentin didn't pick his opponents and was always in with a puncher's chance. Like most South American-based fighters, he was busy and in a career stretching from 1957 to 1976 he went to the well over 120 times.

PATRICK Vic *From* Sydney, Australia. *Died* August 2006, aged 86. When Vic beat fellow Australian, Tommy Burns, back in 1946, the referee, Joe Wallis, told him: "You are better than Les Darcy". Wallis, who was getting on in years and who'd seen all the greats since the early days of gloved boxing, in order not to upset the cognoscenti, later amended his tribute to refer to Patrick as the best since Darcy. There's no doubt that Vic had that touch of greatness and his achievements in the ring confirm this. Born Victor Patrick Lucca, with an Italian father and New Zealand mother, he had an awkward, southpaw style and could hit. Starting out in 1940, he rose up the ratings like a meteor before facing the former world junior-lightweight champion, Tod Morgan, who was a veteran at that stage. Patrick hammered him for round after round before being controversially disqualified for hitting his man while he was down. There was a return and Vic made sure of it this time, getting the decision and the Australian lightweight title with it. He beat Morgan twice more to prove that he was always Tod's master. After this, Vic had to fight bigger men to stay active, having cleaned up the lightweight division. In 1943 he knocked out Hockey Bennell to win the welterweight title, but lost a very narrow decision to middleweight, Bos Murphy, in New Zealand. The biggest fight of his career came in 1947 when he challenged the lightweight contender and all-time great of that division, the redoubtable Freddie Dawson. Dawson won it in the 12th round, but had to pull the fight out of the fire to do so. Vic well ahead on points, put Dawson down and nearly out in the 11th. Perhaps he wore himself out in trying to finish off the American and perhaps too many fights in which he gave away weight caught up with him. After losing to Dawson, he was never again the same fighter and following wins over Roy Treasure and a draw with Mickey Tollis he retired. Years later, he became a referee, usurping Joe Wallis as resident ref at Sydney Stadium. He was a truly great fighter, but he was also one of the best referees I've seen in over 60 years of watching boxing.

Vic Patrick

PATTERSON Floyd *From* Brooklyn, New York, USA. *Died* 11 May 2006, aged 71. When reviewing Floyd's tenure of the world heavyweight championship, it must be remembered that his manager, Cus D'Amato, was disenchanted with the IBC, which ran all the big matches in those days. As soon as Floyd annexed the title, via a five-round stoppage win over Archie Moore, D'Amato announced that the IBC would never promote a fight in which any of his fighters were involved. For Floyd, who at 21 was the youngest man ever to gain the top position in boxing, it meant a series of nondescript defences against the likes of Tommy Hurricane Jackson, Roy Harris, Brian London and Pete Rademcher, who was fresh out of the amateur ranks, albeit with credentials of Olympic champion. After disposing of all four challengers without being troubled, he underrated Sweden's Ingemar Johansson, who put him down seven times before the referee, Ruby Goldstein, called a halt. For a year, Floyd became a recluse and whipped himself into shape for the return match, in which he regained the title by knocking out the Swede with one of the hardest left hooks ever seen in a heavyweight championship fight. D'Amato still wanted to 'nurse' his charge, but Patterson had great pride and it was pride that kept him getting to his feet in the losing fight with Johansson. He wanted to defend his title against the much feared Sonny Liston. D'Amato was not happy with the idea but Floyd wanted to meet the best man around and that man was Liston. The fight was over inside a round as Liston brushed him away almost contemptuously and took only four seconds longer to win

the return. Floyd showed his mettle by fighting his way back into title contention with no soft touches. Both Eddie Machen and George Chuvalo were on the wrong end of points decisions and Sante Amonti, Charley Powell and Tod Herring all failed to go the scheduled distance. He then found himself facing Muhammad Ali, who had usurped Liston and who was making his second defence of the title. Plagued by back pains but gamely struggling on, Floyd lasted into the 12th round. He came back to knock out Henry Cooper with a left hook similar to that which chilled Johansson and found himself once more fighting in eliminating contests for the big prize, but a dubious points loss to Jerry Quarry, against whom he had previously boxed a draw, put a halt to his ambitions and he was also unsuccessful in a WBA challenge to Jimmy Ellis. Floyd's best days were gone, but he was good enough to go undefeated for another three years before he bowed out with another loss to Ali. He'd beaten Oscar Bonavena to get that match. A brilliant amateur, he was the Olympic middleweight gold-medal winner in 1952, turning professional the same year. In his first seven years of campaigning only Joey Maxim beat him and that decision created an uproar. Floyd fought his way out of reform school to become a model citizen, being of a shy and reticent nature and always polite. There was never any scandal in his private life. He served as chairman on the New York State Athletic Commission until failing memory forced him to resign his post. Floyd is survived by a wife and four children.

Floyd Patterson

PAYNE Kevin *From* Evansville, Indiana, USA. *Died* 20 March 2006, aged 34. An American source reports the death of Kevin being due to a brain haemorrhage. The previous day, Kevin had impressively beaten Ryan Maraldo, a victory that should have cemented a welterweight match with Julio Cesar Chavez (junior), but his subsequent collapse and tragic death means that his ambitions were never achieved. He leaves a wife and children. The boxing community is raising money to help the Payne family through a difficult time.

PEARL Davey *From* Nevada, USA. *Died* 12 March 2006, aged 88. A long-established referee, Davey was in the ring for some great fights and with some fighters. He is best remembered for his handling of the first match between Thomas Hearns and Sugar Ray Leonard, when he chose exactly the right moment to rescue Hearns in the penultimate round. Hearns had an unassailable points lead at the time. Davey was in charge for the first Ali v Leon Spinks clash and also in fights involving Evander Holyfield, Salvador Sanchez, Sonny Liston, Marvin Hagler and Julio Cesar Chavez. His twin brother died in 2004.

POOK George *From* Torquay. *Died* April 2006, aged 93. Old-timer George was just 15 when he outpointed Billy Ayson in 1928 to begin a fistic career that would take him through 97 fights in the next 23 years. He was always a little guy, but a little 'un with a fighting heart. Look at some of the men he fought: Jackie Paterson, Dave Crowley, Al Phillips, Nel Tarleton, Kid Tanner, Ronnie Clayton, Teddy Peckham and Johnny Molloy. Tanner was the only one in that list that George beat, but he managed a draw with the redoubtable Crowley and he gave Paterson a fright when dropping the Scot for a long count in the fifth round. Overall, George's record is a respectable one, in which he beat Jimmy Chinn, Stan Jehu, Len Pascoe, Syd Worgan, Percy Enoch, Mick Carney, Phineas John, and in an early career fight, Bob Squance of Plymouth. George could never get past Fleetwood's Bert Jackson, who came out on top in all their four fights. Other notables on his record are Joe Slark, Tucker Winch, Len Beynon, Tommy McGlinchey and Hal Bagwell. In his last fight, George annexed the South-Western Area featherweight championship by beating Billy Parsons of Highbridge, but he was very much a veteran by then. He was 37 and it was a good time to hang up the gloves.

POONTARAT Payao *From* Prachuap Khiri Khan, Thailand. *Died* 13 August 2006, aged 49. Payao became Thailand's first Olympic medal winner when he captured the light-flyweight bronze at the 1976 Games in Montreal. Turning pro in 1981, he won the WBC super-fly title in only his ninth fight when outpointing Rafael Orono on 27 November 1983. He then made a successful defence against Guty Espadas, via a tenth-round stoppage, before Jiro Watanabe relieved him of the belt when outpointing him on 5 July 1984. After an unsuccessful challenge and a defeat at the hands of Kongthoranee Payakaroon he retired after just 14 contests in 1985, having defeated good men such as Tito Abella, Soon-Chun Kwon, Kwon-Sok Lee and Julio Diaz. Payao later became a police officer before entering politics and being elected as a Democrat MP in 2001. Diagnosed with amyotrophic lateral sclerosis in 2002, he was in and out of hospital before eventually succumbing to what is commonly known as Lou Gehrig's disease.

PRIEST Frank *From* Northampton. *Died* December 2005, aged 74. Sid Green, Honorary Secretary of the Northampton and District Ex-Boxers' Association, reports on the death of Frank Priest. "I knew Frank well", says Sid. "I worked on the railways and Frank was in the fitting shop. The foreman knew the boxing game and entered Frank in the LMR (London and Midland Railways) championships at Crewe. Frank, a welterweight who eventually became a middleweight, won three by knockout and one on points. He turned pro under George Ingram in 1950 and knocked out Fred Archer, outpointed Johnny Hunt, drew with Ossie Wilson and then caused a big upset by knocking out Billy Ellaway in the first round. Mixed fortunes followed with knockout losses to Bobby Fish, Johnny Wright and Ellaway. I saw him stop Hugh Kirk of Wisbech at the Spalding Corn Exchange. This was an outside-broadcast bill covered by commentators Raymond Glendenning and W. Barrington-Dalby, both of whom thought highly of the victor. *Boxing News* described him as being a promising prospect. In 1952, Frank had only four fights, winning two and losing two, while the following year brought a loss at Preston prior to National Service. A return to the ring was not a success so Frank called it a day. He was a hard man. I mourn his passing".

PUTNAM Pat *From* USA. *Died* 27 November 2005, aged 75. A highly regarded boxing scribe, Pat wrote for the *Miami Herald* and *Sports Illustrated* and was a recipient of the prestigious Nat Fleischer award for excellent journalism. He died in New York.

QUARRY Mike *From* Orlando, Florida, USA. *Died* 11 June 2006, aged 55. Had Mike possessed a punch commensurate with his boxing ability, he may well have ruled the roost in the light-heavyweight division. Unfortunately, he will be remembered mainly for his chilling knockout loss to Bob Foster in a world-title challenge back in 1972. It was his first defeat and emphatic, in that he was unconscious for several minutes after sampling one of the hardest left hooks that Foster ever threw. In his early ring years he was a busy fighter, fighting three times in September 1969 and five times in October. A victory in California over the British champion, Eddie Avoth, in 1970, followed by wins over Enrique Villareal, Andy Kendall and Jimmy Dupree, brought him in line for the Foster fight. With his confidence dented, his form suffered. There were wins over Gary Summerhayes, Karl Zurheide, Eddie Owens, Tom Bethea and a prestigious points victory over Mike Rossman, but these were interspersed with losses to Chris Finnegan, Pierre Fourie,

Tom Bogs and old foe, Mike Rossman. From 1979 to 1982 he had only one fight per year and bowed out with consecutive losses to Bunny Johnson and Blufort Spencer. It would have been far better had he retired in 1975 after beating future champion, Mike Rossman, but boxing was his living. He went on too long and at an early age went in a nursing home where he eventually died.

REA Nick *From* Airdrie. *Died* September 2005. Nick did all his fighting at the Grove BC in Glasgow between 1941 and 1944. He was from a family of five fighting brothers, one of whom was the former light-heavyweight contender, Bert Gilroy. It is claimed that Nick had 15 fights, yet in those wartime years so many results never got into the trade papers. *Boxing News* reports just one fight and that took place on 8 January 1944. In a scheduled ten-rounder, Nick forced Birmingham's Jack Sibitter to retire in the eighth stanza. Should any record compiler have access to Glasgow daily papers for the years in question, I'd be grateful to be put in touch and can be contacted via the Editor.

ROONEY Phil *From* Wiltshire. *Died* August 2005, aged 66. Belfast-born Phil was a former boxing correspondent of the *Irish World* and his long-time friend, Chris Kempson, spoke highly of their association. Phil befriended Chris and introduced him to many boxing personalities. He was Damaen Kelly's uncle, a tireless worker for Salisbury City ABC, and an avid collector of boxing memorabilia.

ROQUE Rene *From* Lyons, France. *Died* July 2006, aged 64. When the Australian featherweight champion, Johnny Famechon, decided to visit the land of his birth, he accepted a match with Rene. Expecting a not-too-demanding workout, he came away with what was described to me as a sentimental draw. It looked as if Rene had won narrowly, but clearly, and the decision saved a lot of embarrassment. Rene was the French lightweight champion at the time and like most fighters, he was too proud to succumb to any man without putting up stern resistance. There were only four defeats on his record going into the Famechon fight. One was to another man destined to become world champion in Ken Buchanan and another two occurring just prior to the fight in question. He'd beaten Percy Hayles and had drawn with Aissa Hashas early in his career and that should have given out a warning that he was no pushover. He began boxing in 1962 and carried on until Baldassari Piccone beat him for the vacant French junior welterweight title in 1972, having won the European title at junior welterweight from Sandro Lopopolo in 1970 and defending it twice before being shorn of the belt by Pedro Carrasco. In between defending that title, he had an unsuccessful challenge for the WBC title, losing on a foul against Bruno Acari. Rene beat many good men, such as Olli Maki, Ernesto Miranda, Bruno Melissano, Roger Zami (from whom he won the French title), Joao dos Santos and Oscar Miranda to name a few. Then there were also drawn decisions with Fernand Ahumibe, Maurice Tavant, Cemal Kamaci and Borge

Krogh. He was badly injured in a shooting incident in 1972, which left him partially paralysed, and was looked after by staff in a clinic down in Nimes. His post-boxing life was therefore very difficult, but he made the most of it before a heart attack finished him.

ROSS Dr Oswald *From* Whetstone. *Died* 14 September 2005, aged 82. In a contact sport such as ours, a doctor's role is vitally important. Ossie served the Board of Control for over 40 years in a medical capacity and was elected Chairman of the Southern Area Council in 1987, before becoming a BBBofC Administrative Steward in 1993. Dr Ross, who was born in Belfast and into a boxing family, was connected to the game for most of his life and was appointed as Honorary Steward to the Board of Control six years ago. He is survived by two daughters.

SAINTSBURY Father George *Died* June 2006, aged 95. Father George Saintsbury was a man who dedicated his life to the furtherance of boxing in schools and fought hard to see it in every school's curriculum. He spoke up passionately against namby-pamby politicians, school governors, and medics who opposed the sport he loved dearly. Some years back, when he was in his late 80s, he asked me to write a few notes that he could use in a schools' boxing manual he was planning to produce. I've been informed that he was in the process of up-dating this before he died. Listening to George, on his soap box and haranguing members of parliament on the benefits of character-building fisticuffs, was inspiring. This grand old man was sharp and alert and a tireless worker. He was once a pupil of the late Andy Newton, who for countless years taught the art of taking knocks in his Marylebone Road gymnasium. George was a founder member of the Schools' ABA and never retired or slowed down from fighting for what he believed to be right. Boxing owes him a huge debt.

SANCHEZ Agapito *From* Dominican Republic. *Died* 15 November 2005, aged 35. Yet another shooting claimed the life of an active boxer, when this former WBO super-bantamweight champion died of gunshot wounds. He was a southpaw and a rated fighter who'd been in there with some of the best at his weight, with only the top men beating him. A measure of his ability can be assessed from his great battle with Marco Antonio Barrera. The WBO title was at stake and Barrera had to climb off the floor in the last round. Had the knockdown occurred earlier, the result may well have been different, but Barrera survived after having established a clear points lead. Agapito began his career in 1989 with a stoppage win over Jose Perez and boxed in the Dominican Republic or Panama until 1994. He'd lost just three of 19 fights before moving his base to the USA, having won Dominican titles at the super-fly and bantamweight limits, and added the USBA super-bantam crown to his collection in his first USA outing following a majority decision over Max Gomez. Losing his new title on a foul to Maui Diaz, he then picked up the WBC International featherweight title by beating Jose Pantalcon. There were four more title fights ahead when he was in the big-time, following his showing against Barrera. In 1998 he beat Javier Jauregui and stopped Oscar Larios in Acapulco, but was unlucky against Guty Espadas (junior), who got a majority points decision over him. There were wins over Nestor Lopez, Rafael de la Cruz, Javier Lucas and a knockout victory over Jorge Monsalvo to annex the vacant WBO super-bantamweight title, before defending same against the great Filipino fighter, Manny Pacquiao, who held the IBF title. Pacquiao was badly cut during a clash of heads and an unsatisfactory technical draw decision was given. Coming back from a two-year break after that, his eyes had developed cataracts and in his comeback outing he suffered his worst defeat when Joan Guzman scored a seventh-round stoppage. Agapito was always a trier and he got back on the winning trial, before losing to Carlos Navarro, but then won the USBA super-bantamweight title when stopping Artyom Simonyan. There was only one more fight – a win over Edinso Torres – before a bullet took his life two months later.

SAUNDERS Jackie *From* Dublin, Ireland. *Died* August 2005, aged 87. A legendary former amateur, Jackie will be remembered with affection in Dublin, being connected with boxing for most of his life. His career reached its apogee in the 1930s when he was still an amateur. He did eventually turn pro during World War Two, but tournaments were infrequent and his career was brief. In 1938 he fought in the Golden Gloves tournament in Chicago where, in a featherweight match, he upset the American champion, Bill Eddy, giving a performance that drew accolades from the sporting press. He was cheered and feted. Saunders won several Irish titles and represented his country in international matches held in five countries. He began as a flyweight and was boxing in the featherweight division when he retired, having been one of the best amateurs that Ireland ever produced.

SCHOEPPNER Erich *From* Witten (Ruhr), Germany. *Died* 9 September 2005, aged 73. British fans will remember Erich for his controversial wins over Albert Finch and Henry Cooper, both of which drew strong protests in the British press. He also beat Arthur Howard and Jack Whittaker. At European level, Erich could hold his own, being the European and German light-heavyweight champion from 1958 and also the German heavyweight champion in 1961. He knocked out Willi Hoepner for the European crown, defended against him in a return, then successfully put his title on line against Rocco Mazzola, Sante Amonte, Helmut Ball and Paul Roux. Stripped of the title due to failure to defend, he later lost to Giulio Rinaldi in Rome when attempting to regain his crown. This is the sole loss on his record. Erich was a vastly experienced amateur with 15 defeats in 276 contests and was holder of national and European titles. He was also an outstanding professional champion at European level and deserved his world rating, but was not so effective as a heavyweight. Some of the men he beat were Uwe Janssen, Eli Elandon, Ivano Fontana, Von Clay, Chuck Speiser, Peter Muller, Hans Kalbfell, Frankie Daniels, Jose Peyre

and Andre Wyns. He drew with America's Doug Jones, South Africa's Mike Holt, and France's Germinal Ballarin. After Rinaldi beat him, Erich remained inactive for three years before coming back to outpoint Wilhelm von Homburg. Then he retired for keeps.

Erich Schoeppner

SCOTT Don *From* Derby. *Died* February 2006, aged 77. In March 2005, a reception was held at Buckingham Palace to mark the centenary of the British Olympic Association. Among the boxers was Don, who'd gained a silver medal in 1948. I spoke to him afterwards by telephone and he was delighted to have been remembered. His voice was that of a man in his late years, but I did not expect to be informed of his death just under a year later. As can be expected of an Olympian, his amateur record was outstanding. He was beaten for the gold medal by South Africa's George Hunter, who won the Val Barker Cup as the best performer in the boxing section of the Games. It was a very narrow decision and Don was never again beaten as an amateur. Just before turning pro he won the Empire Games light-heavyweight title. What was ominous is that Don had been considering going into the heavyweight division. He didn't get an easy ride as a pro, but it was obvious that he had talent and a big punch. Although being beaten in his debut by Ray Widing, it was not before he'd had his man twice on the deck and had established a clear points lead. But running out of gas and a spell of bad nerves going into the fight did not help his cause. He soon showed the public what he could do when knocking out Harry Painter, Frank Walker, George Stern, Fred Powell (twice) and stopping Brian Anders and Ted Morgan. Only Wally Curtis and Terry O'Connor lasted the distance with him. It was disappointing to see him lose to the unbeaten Terry McDonald in two rounds at the end of 1951. After that he wisely concentrated on the light-heavyweight division and won the Midlands Area title a couple of months later before quitting the game. His career was a case of 'what might have been'. He had the talent to go a long way, but luck plays a big part in any sporting endeavour and had he had a few easier fights at the beginning, it may well have been a different story. What can't be taken away from him is that he was a competent boxer and that he could hit hard with both hands.

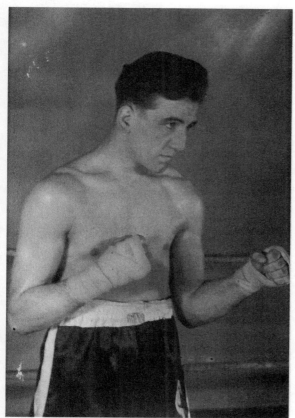

Don Scott

SERTI Alberto *From* La Spezia, Italy. *Died* 4 March 2005, aged 71. A former European and Italian featherweight champion, Alberto fought in this country against two of our champions, being outpointed by Bobby Neill in 1960 and losing his European title to Howard Winstone three years later. He fought from 1955 to 1964 and although not successful on these shores he lost only nine of 40 fights. His record shows that he beat Andre Valignat, Willi Quatuor and Letterio Petilli, en route to an Italian title fight with Raimondo Nobile. The contest was a draw. A couple of years previously, Nobile had put the first blot on Alberto's record, so progress was being made. It was 1962 before Alberto got the European championship belt around his waist. He'd come through an indifferent patch, losing to Olli Maki, Mario Sitri and Lino Mastellaro before turning in one of his best fights to lick Gracieux Lamperti in San Remo. His championship tenure was brief – just under a year. Having drawn with Primo Zamparini and beaten Michel Atlan, he then lost his crown to the brilliant Howard Winstone in Cardiff. He had a couple of more fights, then avenged a previous loss by beating Lino Mastellaro. With this victory came the Italian title, which he lost to Andrea Silanos in his first defence. This was to be his last fight. He'd fought some of Europe's best and had won two titles, but never had any pretensions to making a name at world level.

SHAW Tommy *From* Plymouth. *Died* 11 August 2006, aged 85. Having turned pro back in 1937, Tommy was just beginning to get into the swing of things when the war came and after being pressed into service there were very few recorded fights for him during the duration. Back in civvies, Tommy, whose real name was Joe Short, began to pick up some useful wins as a hard-hitting southpaw lightweight over men such as Jimmy Jury, Harry Legge (four times), Billy Barton, Vic Manini, Roy Coote, Hyman Williams, Ivor Thomas, Tommy Barnham and Vernon Ball, before taking a year out. He came back strongly, after signing up with Jack Bates in Manchester, with a shock victory over Bert Hornby in August 1950, and was looking to challenge the British champion, Billy Thompson. However, it was not to be and just four four fights later he retired after being stopped by Ivor Kid Germain at the Liverpool Stadium in November 1951. Not long before, the January edition of *Ring Magazine* even ran a piece on him, stating that of 113 pro contests he had lost just eight. The article also stated that he was currently a meter inspector and was studying to become a welfare officer. Tommy certainly didn't avoid an opponent and twice lost to Ric Sanders. He also met Bert Buxton, Bob Frost and Laurie Buxton, all recognised knockout punchers.

SHEPHERD Dennis *From* Johannesburg, South Africa. *Died* June 2006, aged 79. As the South African amateur featherweight champion in 1948, the Olympic Games beckoned and Dennis surprised many people by reaching the final where he was outpointed by Italy's Ernesto Formenti. Boxing out of a southpaw stance he advanced to the silver medal after outpointing Sydney Greve (Pakistan), Mohammed Ammi (France), Eddie Johnson (USA) and F.Nunez (Argentina). Dennis never did turn pro, once modestly saying: "I doubt I'd have been good enough".

SIKALI Mzukisi *From* Uitenhage, South Africa. *Died* September 2005, aged 34. A former holder of two WBU titles and one IBO (flyweight) title, Mzukisi was stabbed to death in the Port Elizabeth region by two assailants who robbed him of his mobile phone. The southpaw fought three times in London rings where he was too good for Anthony Hanna and Mark Reynolds, both of whom were summarily stopped inside the scheduled distance. He returned in 2001 to beat France's Cyril Bellanger. Mzukisi was never averse to boxing in an opponent's home ring, winning one title (WBU light-flyweight) against Thailand's Nungdiaw in Bangkok and journeying to Italy to win the WBU super-flyweight crown. He also fought unsuccessfully for the IBF flyweight title in Australia in March 2005. Of his 29 wins, 17 came via the short route.

SPAGNOLO Duilio *From* Milan, Italy. *Died* 15 April 2005, aged 82. An Italian heavyweight, Duilio was born in Vicenza and fought in Europe from 1944 to 1946 before making a name for himself in America. He'd arrived in the USA with the credentials of being the Italian champion, having picked up the title by licking Giovanni Martin after splitting a couple of decisions with Enrico Bertola. There were wins over Luigi Musina, Giorgio Milan and a draw with Gino Buonvino. With 11 fights under his belt, he was pitched in with seasoned Lee Savold in his American debut. Savold was a veteran of 124 fights and knew too much for the newcomer. Although losing by a stoppage, Spagnolo didn't disgrace himself and he went on to notch up ten fights before losing to Olle Tandberg. Georgie Kaplan got a split decision over him in 1949, but there were many good wins over men such as Bernie Reynolds, Pete Louthis, Johnny Kapovich and Charlie Norkus. Most of his losses were to big-name fighters, which included Roland LaStarza, Coley Wallace and Nick Barone, against whom he had his last contest in March 1951.

TAYLOR Ron *From* Cardiff. *Died* 20 July 2006, aged 95. With the death of Ron Taylor, the last link with boxing booths has been broken. Connected with fairground fighting all his life, his grandfather founded the Excelsior booth in 1861, which he passed on to Ron's father who, in turn, passed it on in 1936. Ron saw the heyday of booth fighting and kept the Excelsior going long after every other booth had closed for good, retiring four years ago at the ripe old age of 91. He loved the booth life and courageously carried on when his fighters no longer could rely on regular work. It was customary to plant another boxer midst the customers and I have a picture of my friend Harry Legge, who was one of Taylor's fighters, challenging from the crowd. Harry was an experienced booth fighter. It wasn't a soft job as the booths travelled with the fairgrounds and had to be assembled and taken down whatever the weather. Johnny Williams, Cliff Curvis, Randolph Turpin, Tommy Farr, Freddie Mills, Jim Driscoll, Joe Beckett and dozens of eight-round-class fighters were grateful for regular employment during the close season of the summer months. Men like Len Beynon, Hal Bagwell, Terry Ratcliffe, Peter Fay, Teddy Peckham, Len Johnson, Bob Hartley, Arnold Kid Sheppard, Reg Andrews, Billy Curran, Tiger Les Haycox, Hugh O'Donnell and Tommy Ryan, were always available when the booths were in town. Ron, who knew them all, still carried on when the number of professional fighters depleted as living standards rose. It pained him to resort to displaying wrestling and sometimes kick-boxing, but he struggled on. He was one of four brothers, Welsh by birth and a showman by choice. Rhys Rowland Taylor came into the world at the end of 1910 and was always destined to don the gloves, being reputed to have picked up some boxing titles in the army. He and his brothers all boxed on the Excelsior, but Ron didn't always have matters his own way and decided to devote his time to drumming up trade from the platform in front of the boxing tent, becoming a dab hand at drawing the attention of the public to his business. His booth has been handed to his two grandsons and they have a difficult task ahead to ensure the continuance of a tradition that is almost extinct. One can only hope that they have inherited much of Ron's courage and enthusiasm and the show will go on.

THOMAS John *From* Los Angeles, California, USA. *Died* 4 January 2006, aged 83. In the mid 1940s, John was a world-ranked lightweight with a superb record and in 61 recorded fights he beat Maxie Shapiro, Leo Rodak, Tony Chavez, Aldo Spoldi, Henry Armstrong, Baby Yucatan, Willie Joyce, Lupe Gonzales, Petey Scalzo, Jimmy Doyle and Lew Jenkins. There was one fight that the State of Maryland recognised as being for the world title and that was against Slugger White in 1943. It was a ten-round affair and brought about one of his only seven defeats as the slugger slugged too often against a rather subdued opponent and came away with the decision. Other men to beat him were Enrique Bolanos (twice), Californian Jackie Wilson and three men against whom he gained revenge, Henry Armstrong, Aldo Spoldi and Willie Joyce. There was just one occasion when he took the full count and that was in his last fight, against Bolanos. During the war, John was in the US army, but back in civvy street he licked Larry Cisneros in a terrific fight. He had a rapier-like straight left, was clever and elusive, and his death due to prostate cancer, further depletes the ranks of those men active in the war years.

THOMSEN Tue Bjorn *From* Copenhagen, Denmark. *Died* 22 April 2006, aged 33. The Dane, who was yet another boxer who met a violent death in the past 12 months, was recognised by the IBC as their super-cruiserweight champion and had won 22 out of 24 fights before retiring in 2002. A southpaw, he turned pro in 1997 and ran up 19 straight wins, beating men such as Damon Reed, Iran Barkley, Kimmuel Odum, Mike Sedillo and Nate Miller before falling foul of Jacob Mofokeng. Prior to that he'd won the Danish heavyweight title (1999) and the IBC super-cruiserweight crown on beating Miller. In his penultimate contest he beat Rob Calloway in defence of the IBC title.

TITE Jeff *From* Spratton. *Died* 24 March 2006, aged 80. When it comes to big punchers, Jeff's name is right up there with the likes of Stan Hawthorne, George Odwell, Bob Frost and Eric Boon. He never had an amateur fight and got into boxing after volunteering to spar with his friend, Roy Davies. Quickly developing a liking for the game, it was obvious that he was a powerful puncher but needed schooling in the fundamentals, so Davies' manager, George Biddles, saw that he got tuition in the gymnasium. At 19 he made his debut – a clean knockout over Teddy Black. It was mid-September 1947. Before the year was out, Biddles had sent him into battle another 13 times, all of them being wins with only one going the scheduled distance. Six were knockouts and six were won by the referee's intervention. It was three years before his name appeared in the British ratings, but wins over Jordan Tarone, Alf Danahar, Jesse Birtwhistle, Dick Shields, Bob Burniston and Piet van Staden indicated that he was learning his trade. He was still stopping some of the opposition, but in the higher echelons of the welterweight division the opposition was tougher and he had to go the full course to win. There were defeats but they were few. Alf Danahar beat him twice and so did that other power-puncher, Bob Frost of West Ham. Jeff beat Tommy Armour, Kay Kalio and Eddie Cardew, then stepped up too far in class and was stopped by the French champion and soon-to-be European champion, Charles Humez. Humez had been turned down by London-based fighters and Tite was thrown to the lions. It was a turning point in his career. Losses soon equalled the number of wins, yet he was good enough to beat Gwyn Williams, Bobby Blair and force a draw with future British champion, Henry Hall. In 61 wins, 36 were by knockout or by stoppages. Jeff, who had one of the hardest left hooks of his time, was left-handed but boxed from an orthodox stance.

Jeff Tite

WADHAM Billy *From* Tottenham. *Died* April 2006, aged 69. In his first year as a professional welterweight, Billy twice scored clean knockout wins over Joe Ceroni. Ceroni was a powerful puncher too, but did not have his opponent's solid grounding in the amateur ranks. It was a good start for Wadham and a draw with Dagenham's Paddy O'Callaghan was also a good result. Billy lost just one and that was a points loss to Ron Garnett, who was a middleweight. It looked as if he would be knocking on the championship door one day, but a title shot eluded him in a career that saw him beat Peter King, Ron Richardson, Roy Burke, Terry Banning, Peter Ratcliffe, Jimmy Daly and Harry Haydock. He was inactive in 1960 and the following year had just four fights, losing the last one to Billy Tarrant on points. It was a pity to see what could have been a good career fizzle out after only four years of activity.

WESTON Andrew *From* Florida, USA. *Died* April 2006, aged 25. With a clean record of five stoppage wins in as many fights, the future looked bright for London-born middleweight, Andy, but his lifestyle caught up with him and he was kidnapped and later shot dead. Having successfully applied for a British licence, he was planning to fight here when the tragedy struck.

WHITE Johnny *From* Mitcham. *Died* 5 April 2006. Johnny was a Surrey bantamweight champion in the late 1930s and like many contemporaries he was a very busy boxer, having taken an interest in the game from an early age. As soon as circumstances allowed, he joined the Devas ABC and progressed so well that, at the age of 18, he joined the professionals, getting off well by stopping Boy Gammack in two rounds. Gammack's name has faded into obscurity over the years, but many others on Johnny's record are known to boxing historians. Johnny fought Ron Kingston, Johnny Boom, Ronnie Burr, Harry Burnstone, Billy Tansey, Tommy McQueen, Mottee Kid Singh and Young Bullions, etc. Johnny claimed to have fought a young Gwyn Williams who was destined to fight at welterweight level against the best men in Europe. So far I haven't been able to trace this, but since it took place in Oxford where Williams had all his early fights I'm sure that it will be located as soon as I can get a few days to myself. Oxford shows for the 1930s were seldom reported in the trade press. Johnny was a hairdresser and taking his father's advice he retired from fighting just after the war. His hairdressing business flourished and he renewed his links with boxing through the ex-boxers' movement. He was Vice-President of Croydon EBA and a longtime member of London EBA and although he lived in Eastbourne the distance and encroaching years never prevented him from attending meetings.

WILLIAMS Frankie *From* Birkenhead. *Died* September 2005, aged 80. Starting as an amateur bantamweight, Frankie went into the featherweight ranks when he turned pro in 1944. Although he stopped Billy Barnes in his debut he wasn't happy with the professional game so he successfully applied to revert to the amateur ranks. He'd done well as a Simon Pure, annexing titles at bantam and featherweight limits. His pro career, phase two, kicked off in August 1945 and it was not long before he was mixing it in good company. Frankie won and lost to Cliff Curvis, knocked out Jim McCann, beat Kid Tanner and Johnny Cusick, before moving down to bantamweight where he seemed better suited. There was a good points win over Tommy Proffitt, but he couldn't beat Ben Duffy who seemed to have his number. He took the great French boxer, Ray Famechon, ten rounds before losing with honour and it may have been this contest that convinced him that a better future lay ahead as a bantamweight. Victories over Peter Fay, Gaetano Annaloro, Al Young, Theo Nolten, Ron Johnson and the future world champion, Hogan Kid Bassey, cemented him as a good-class man at European level. Although a dark horse, Manny Kid Francis halted his winning streak before he challenged for the British title in 1953. Unfortunately for Frankie, an outstanding champion in Peter Keenan was in the opposite corner. Keenan carried too many guns for Frankie, who then chose to bow out rather than slide down the fistic ladder to become a trial horse.

WILLIAMS Gwyn *From* Oxford. *Died* July 2006, aged 84. Born in Pontycymmer, Wales, this former Welsh Area welterweight champion was one of the many very good fighters active at his weight in the 1940s, having turned professional in 1938 after a long amateur career encompassing nearly 200 fights, most of which took place in the Oxford area. Oddly enough, he boxed only seven times in his native Wales, losing three of them. It was no disgrace as the men who beat him were fighters out of the top drawer: Cliff Curvis (who he'd previously knocked out), world-rated Frenchman, Charles Humez, and that great Swansea lightweight, Ronnie James. Another rated Frenchman, Robert Villemain, also beat him at the Albert Hall, but Gwyn put up a cracking fight. Gwyn definitely wasn't one of boxing's losers and, overall, his is a splendid record. In his first 38 outings he tasted defeat twice and he quickly avenged one of them. By 1946 he'd been in there with Jim Wellard, Laurie Buxton, Alf Edwards, Frankie Jackson, Bert Sanders, Lefty Satan Flynn, Henry Hall, Jimmy Brunt, Reg Hoblyn and Arthur Danahar. Of those, only Flynn and Danahar beat him and there was an outstanding victory in Stockholm when he outpointed the Finnish ace, Yrjoe Piitulainen. This win in Stockholm came soon after his demob from RAF service, in which he was a paratroop instructor. He'd enlisted in March 1940. Now out of service uniform, his boxing career rose a few notches and he was matched with Ernie Roderick in 1947. The British title was at stake, but the old veteran was too crafty and stole the points. Gwyn split a couple of decisions with Eddie Thomas, then had four more wins before going in with America's Tony Janiro, against whom he enhanced his reputation despite being on the losing end. There was a 'no-contest' with Eric Boon just after he'd won a title eliminator against Eddie Thomas, it being a clash of styles. By 1950 the clock was winding down. There were two fights that year and two in 1951, with a points loss to

power-punching Jeff Tite being his last contest. He won 57 fights out of 75 and got close to a British title five times. Gwyn went into a care-home after his wife died and is survived by a married daughter.

YAROSZ Tommy *From* Monaca, Pennsylvannia, USA. *Died* 27 March 2006, aged 84. When you have a brother, your elder by 12 years, who has won a world title, there's a lot to live up to when taking up boxing as a profession. Tommy didn't besmirch the family name, despite not winning a world title, because in his day the likes of Sugar Ray Robinson and Jake LaMotta ruled the middleweight division. He was a top contender in the 1940s and a classic-style boxer who never took a bad beating thanks to sound schooling in the defensive arts. The *Ring Record Book* credits him with 91 fights, of which he lost ten. Most of those came at the pinnacle of his career when he was mixing it with the best men around. Future world champions, Carl Olson and Randolph Turpin beat him and so did LaMotta, but many say that Jake was lucky to win. Tommy was too sharp for Dave Sands when the much-touted Aussie made his London debut and he also licked Chuck Hunter (twice), Dave Whitlock, Charley Anglee, Burl Charity and Sylvester Perkins. He stepped up a division to beat Nick Barone in 1949, but when Barone turned the tables four months later the signs were that the apogee of his career had then gone. A second defeat by Barone, which was his only stoppage loss, hastened the end. A young Turpin beat him on a disqualification and Tommy never fought again. He was behind on points at the time, but disillusioned by the verdict. Claims published in issue 90 of the *IBRO Journal* that Turpin had signed beforehand to fight Robinson, are incorrect as Turpin had just won the British title and was eyeing the European crown. Thoughts of challenging Robinson were months away. Tommy raised five children and was a respected family man, a class boxer, and always a credit to the game.

Tommy Yarosz

A Boxing Quiz with a Few Below the Belt: Part 11

Compiled by Les Clark

QUESTIONS

1. This former Southern Area bantamweight champion was a three times loser; Charlie Magri beat him in a vacant British flyweight title contest, Johnny Owen beat him in a challenge for the British and Commonwealth bantamweight titles, and John Feeney defeated him for the vacant British bantamweight title. Can you name him?

2. Who did Barry McGuigan face in a final eliminator before challenging for the British featherweight title?

3. Mike Barrett's first promotion was in December 1962, and his 150th promotion was at the Albert Hall. Do you know who topped the bill?

4. Cassius Clay was taken the distance in his first pro fight. How many more times was he taken the distance before winning the world title?

5. Chris Eubank was born in Dulwich, London. Can you name the amateur club he boxed for?

6. Do you know what the American Kevin Perry's claim to fame is?

7. Who was the first British boxer Jake Matlala fought?

8. How many major amateur titles did the former world champion, Konstantin Tszyu, win before joining the paid ranks?

9. Michael Watson took the Commonwealth middleweight title from Nigel Benn. Against whom did he make his first defence?

10. Alan Minter was involved in 12 championship fights, all at middleweight. How many were for vacant titles?

11. Two former world heavyweight champions fought each other on the undercard of the second Andrew Golota v Riddick Bowe fight in Atlantic City. Who were they?

12. Can you name the fighter who ended Miguel Angel Gonzalez's 41-fight unbeaten run?

13. Ingemar Johannson retired from the ring in 1963. Who was his last opponent?

14. Can you name a former British light-heavyweight champion who beat Baby Boy Rolle, Dennis Avoth and Boston Blackie, but lost to Les Stevens and Richard Dunn?

15. Can you name a British boxer who fought five times for the world flyweight title, with one win, one draw and three losses?

16. Where did the world title bout between Rocky Lockridge and Barry Michael take place?

17. In 1986 Terry Marsh defended his European light-welter title against Francesco Prezioso. Where did this take place?

18. How many British fighters fought Jose Legra for his European featherweight title?

19. Pete Rademacher's pro debut was a world title challenge against Floyd Patterson, who retained his title inside six rounds. How many times did Rademacher find himself on the canvas during this bout?

20. Can you name the ex-boxer who wrote *PENNY A PUNCH* and *A FEW PUNCHES MORE*?

21. What have former amateurs, Dave Stone, Bobby Kane, Brian Brazier, Tony Willis and Alan Hall got in common?

22. How many times did the legendary Jack Johnson fight Joe Jeannette for the coloured heavyweight title?

23. What did Casper Leon, Gene Fullmer and Abe Attell have in common?

24. Former world champion, Jawid Khaliq, won the 1996 ABA welterweight title. Who did he beat in the final?

25. Can you name the first two southpaw boxers to contest a British title?

26. Can you name a British fighter who lost a ten-round decision in a non-title bout against the WBA champion, Ray (Boom Boom) Mancini?

27. Who was the first man to beat Floyd Patterson in a pro ring?

28. Gerald (Ginger) John appeared in three ABA finals during the '50s. What were the results?

29. How many times did the former IBF super-featherweight champion, Barry Michael, fight in the UK?

30. Tyrone Booze stopped Derek Angol in seven rounds for the WBO cruiserweight title. Name the venue?

31. On how many occasions did Dennis Andries contest a world title?

32. Glenn McCrory contested the world cruiserweight title on three occasions. In which towns did they take place?

33. Chris Eubank won the WBO middleweight title from Michael Watson. Name his first challenger?

34. Against whom did Chris Pyatt defend his WBO middleweight title at the International Hall, Brentwood?

35. Julio Cesar Vasquez stopped Ahmet Dottuev for the WBA light-middleweight title. Do you know the name of the venue?

36. Name the two British champions who won outright an original Lonsdale Belt as well as the BBBoC version of the Lonsdale Belt?

37. Can you tell me the first British title fight that John Coyle refereed?

38. Wally Swift (senior) contested either British, British Empire or European titles on no less than nine occasions. How many did he win?

39. How many Swiss boxers have won professional titles?

40. Can you name the first Australian southpaw heavyweight champion?

41. Brian London's last fight was against Joe Bugner in 1970. Can you name the three Americans he fought and lost to in 1969?

42. When was the A.B.A. formed?

43. When Miguel Angel Gonzalez gave up his WBC lightweight title to move up a division, who was his first opponent at the higher weight?

44. Joe Erskine was the British heavyweight champion in 1957. Who was rated the number one challenger to him in the *Boxing News* annual ratings on 31st December?

45. What year did the last 20-round fight take place and who was involved?

46. Can you name the boxer who was unbeaten in 44 contests, winning 36 inside the distance, before being stopped in three rounds by Ruben Olivares? The boxer in question became a world champion at a later date.

47. Where would you find the following venues which, in the past, have been used for British title fights; Shawfield Park, Coney Beach Arena, Premierland, Caesar's Palace, The Pier Pavilion?

48. Joey Singleton took the British light-welterweight crown from Pat McCormack at The Stadium, Liverpool. At what venue did he make his first defence?

49. How many times did Dennis Andries contest the Southern Area light-heavyweight title?

50. Who was Nate Miller's opponent in his first world title challenge?

Leading BBBoC License Holders: Names and Addresses

Licensed Promoters

A Force Promotions
PO Box 577
Waltham Cross
Herts EN8 1AP
0199 262 3062

**Spencer Alton
(Contender Boxing Promotions)**
64 Glenmore Drive
Stenson Fields
Derby DE24 3HT
0133 223 2050

John Ashton
1 Charters Close
Kirkby in Ashfield
Notts NG17 8PF
0788 546 3676

Bruce Baker
The Garden Flat
38 Lupus Street
London
SW1V 3EB
0207 592 0102

Scott Bambrick
30 Easter Drylaw View
Edinburgh EH4 2QP
0131 476 0908

Mark Bateson
28 Scalebor Square
Burley in Wharfdale
Ilkley
Leeds LS29 7SP
0777 860 1427

Jack Bishop
76 Gordon Road
Fareham
Hants PO16 7SS
0132 928 4708

Paul Boyce
79 Church Street
Briton Ferry
Neath SA11 2JG
0163 981 3723

**Tony Burns
(TBS Promotions)**
67 Peel Place
Woodford Green
Essex IG5 0PT
0208 550 8911

Callahan & Breen Promotions
John Breen
Cedar Lodge
589 Antrim Road
Belfast
BT15 4DX
0289 077 0238

Scott Calow
18 Farnworth Grove
Huthwaite
Notts NG17 2NL
0787 664 1055

George Carman
5 Mansion Lane
Mobile Home Site
Iver
Bucks S10 9RQ
0175 365 3096

**Michael Carney
(Impact Boxing Promotions)**
Bradley Arms Farm
Alton Road
Cheadle
Staffs ST10 4RA
0797 049 5597

**Dave Coldwell
(Koncrete Promotions)**
5 Penwood Walk
Bramley
Rotherham
Yorks S66 3XS
0114 275 0303

**Annette Conroy
(North-East Sporting Club)**
144 High Street East
Sunderland
Tyne and Wear SR1 2BL
0191 567 6871

Jane Couch
Spaniorum Farm Gym
Berwick Lane
Bristol BS35 5RX
0772 504 5405

Coventry Sporting Club
Les Allen/Paul Carpenter
180 Longford Road
Longford, Coventry
0247 636 4237

Pat Cowdell
129a Moat Road
Oldbury, Warley
West Midlands
0121 552 8082

Dennis Cross
8 Tumbling Bank
Blackley
Manchester M9 6AU
0161 720 9371

David Currivan
15 Northolt Avenue
South Ruislip
Middlesex HA4 6SS
0208 841 9933

John Davies
14 Rectors Yard
Rectors Lane
Pentre
Deeside CH5 2DH
0124 453 8984

Wally Dixon
Littlemoss House
1 Wayne Close
Littlemoss
Droylesden
Manchester M43 7LQ
0161 301 5606

**Jack Doughty
(Tara Promotions)**
Lane End Cottage
Golden Street
Off Buckstone Road
Shaw
Oldham OL1 8LY
01706 845753

**Jim Evans
(Evans-Waterman Promotions)**
Abgah
88 Windsor Road
Bray
Berks SL6 2DJ
0162 862 3640

**Neil Featherby
(Sportslink Promotions)**
Unit 6
Drayton Business Park
Taversham
Drayton
Norwich NR8 6RL
0160 386 8606

**Jonathan Feld
(World Sports Organisation)**
c/o Angel Media Group
Ltd
The Office Islington
338 City Road
London EC1V 2PT
0207 284 2133

Joe Frater
The Cottage
Main Road
Grainthorpe
Louth,
Lincs
0147 234 3194

**Stephen Garber
(Premier SC)**
PO Box 704
Bradford
West Yorks BD3 7WU
0870 350 5525

Dave Garside
33 Lowthian Road
Hartlepool
Cleveland
TS26 8AL
0142 929 1611
07973 792588

**Jimmy Gill
(Prospect Promotions)**
Majestic Fitness
Academy
Prospect Place, Lenton
Notts
NG7 1HE
0115 913 6564

Christopher Gilmour
Holiday Inn
Glasgow City West
Bothwell Street
Glasgow G2 7EN
0773 041 5036

**Tommy Gilmour
(St Andrew's Sporting Club)**
Holiday Inn
Bothwell Street
Glasgow G2 7EN
0141 248 5461

Mike Goodall
Ringcraft
Unit 21
Briars Close Business
Park
Evesham
Worcestershire
WR11 4JT
0138 644 2118

Johnny Griffin
0116 262 9287
0798 921 5287

Jess Harding
c/o UK Industrial Pallets
Ltd
Travellers Lane
Industrial Estate
Travellers Lane
Welham Green
Hatfield
Herts
AL9 7HF
0170 727 0440

Tony Hay
Romilly House
201 First Avenue
Central Park
Petherton Road
Hengrove
Bristol
BS14 9BZ
0797 466 2968

**Barry Hearn
(Matchroom)**
'Mascalls'
Mascalls Lane
Great Warley
Essex
CM14 5LJ
0127 735 9900

Michael Helliet
Flat 1
102 Whitfield Street
London W1T 5EB
0207 388 5999
0784 363 6920

**Mick Hennessy
(Hennessy Sports)**
Ravensbourne
Westerham Road
Keston
Kent
BR2 6HE
0168 986 8080

Dennis Hobson
130 Handsworth Road
Sheffield
South Yorkshire
S9 4AE
0114 256 0555
07836 252429

**Dennis Hobson Snr
(DVSA Promotions)**
73 Darnall Road
Don Valley
Sheffield S9 5AH
0114 264 3067

**Jayson Hollier
(Shakespeare Promotions)**
61 Clifton Road
Rugby CV21 3QE
0178 833 6466

Lloyd Honeyghan
PO Box 17216
London SE17 1ZU
0795 640 5007

**Barry Hughes
(Braveheart Promotions)**
5 Royal Exchange
Square
Glasgow G1 3AH
0141 248 8882

**Hull & District
Sporting Club**
Mick Toomey
24 Schubert Close
Rutherglen Drive
Hull HU9 3PL
0148 282 4476

Alma Ingle
26 Newman Road
Wincobank
Sheffield S9 1LP
0114 281 1277

John Ingle
20 Rockmount Road
Wincobank
Sheffield S9 1NF
0114 261 7934

Erroll Johnson
(EJKO Promotions)
36 Newton Street
West Bromwich
B71 3RQ
0121 532 6118

Paul McCausland
1 Prospect Heights
Carrickfergus
Northern Ireland
BT38 8QY
0289 336 5942

Malcolm McKillop
14 Springfield Road
Mangotsfield
Bristol
0117 957 3567

Frank Maloney
(Maloney Promotions)
PO Box 79
Chislehurst
Kent BR7 5HR
0208 691 4165

Lee Maloney
4 St Pauls Cottages
Wenlock Court
Halewood
Liverpool
L26 0TA
0151 486 8050

Ricky Manners
Flat 5, Oakleah House
264 Lidgett Lane
Leeds LS17 6QE
0113 234 6017

Rebecca Margel
10 Bentcliffe Lane
Leeds LS17 6QF
0113 268 0681

John Merton
(John Merton
Promotions)
Merton Technologies Ltd
38 Delaune Street
London SE17 3UR
0207 582 5200

Alex Morrison
197 Swanston Street
Laird Business Park
Dalmarnock
Glasgow
G40 4HW
0141 554 7777

Katherine Morrison
197 Swanston Street
Laird Business Park
Dalmarnock
Glasgow
G40 4HW
0141 554 7777

Ian Pauly
1202 Lincoln Road
Peterborough
Cambs
PE4 6LA
0173 331 1266

Steve Pollard
899 Beverley High Road
Hull HU6 9NJ
0148 280 9455

Ken Purchase
Allscott Mill, Allscott
Telford TF6 5EE
0195 225 0950

Joe Pyle
36 Manship Road
Mitcham
Surrey CR4 2AZ
0208 646 2289
0208 646 7793

Glyn Rhodes
166 Oldfield Road
Stannington
Sheffield S6 6DY
0114 232 6513

Gus Robinson MBE
Stranton House
West View Road
Hartlepool
Cleveland TS24 0BB
0142 923 4221

Ian Robinson
7 Broomfield Lane
Hale
Cheshire WA15 9AP
0161 941 1599
0781 668 4749

Mark Roe
(AMPRO Promotions)
48 Westbrooke Road
Sidcup
Kent DA15 7PH
0208 309 9396

Paul Rowson
(PJ Promotions)
Roughstones
75 Catholic Lane
Sedgley
West Midlands DY3 3YE
0190 267 0007

Christine Rushton
20 Alverley Lane
Balby, Doncaster
Yorks DN4 9AS
0130 231 0919

John Rushton
20 Alverley Lane
Balby, Doncaster
Yorks DN4 9AS
0130 231 0919

Kevin Sanders
9 Moggswell Lane
Orton Longueville
Village, Peterborough
Cambs PE2 7DS
0173 337 1912

Chris Sanigar
Bristol Boxing Gym
40 Thomas Street
St Agnes, Bristol
Avon BS2 9LL
0117 949 6699

Jamie Sanigar
Bristol Boxing Gym
40 Thomas Street
St Agnes, Bristol
Avon BS2 9LL
0117 949 6699

Matt Scriven
(The Robin Hood
Executive Sporting Club)
The Old One, Two
Fitness & Boxing Studio
2a Thoresby Street
Mansfield
Notts NG18 1QF
0783 399 5770

Mike Shinfield
126 Birchwood Lane
Somercotes
Derbys DE55 4NF
0177 360 3124

Kevin Spratt
8 Springfield Road
Guisley
Leeds LS20 8AL
0194 387 6229

Keith Walker
(Walkers Boxing
Promotions)
Headlands House
Business Centre
Suite 21-35
Spawd Bone Lane
Knottingley
West Yorks WF11 0HY
0197 766 2616

Frank Warren
(Sports Network)
Centurion House
Bircherley Green
Hertford
Herts SG14 1AP
0199 250 5550

Derek V. Williams
65 Virginia Road
Thornton Heath
Surrey CR7 8EN
0208 765 0492

Geraldine Williams
Pendeen
Bodiniel Road
Bodmin
Cornwall PL31 2PE
0120 872 575

Stephen Wood
(VIP Promotions)
Edward Street
Cambridge Industrial
Area
Salford
Manchester M7 1RL
0161 834 9496

Licensed Managers

Isola Akay MBE
129 Portnall Road
Paddington
London W9 3BN
0208 968 5790

Michael Alldis
77 Buckswood Drive
Gossops Green
Crawley
West Sussex RH11 8HU
0773 435 1966

Spencer Alton
64 Glenmore Drive
Stenson Fields
Derby DE24 3HT
0133 223 2050

John Ashton
1 Charters Close
Kirkby in Ashfield
Notts NG17 8PF
0788 546 3676

Chris Aston
54/56 May Street
Crosland Moor
Huddersfield
West Yorks
HD4 5DG
0148 432 9112

Andy Ayling
Centurion House
Bircherley Green
Hertford
Herts
SG14 1AP
0199250 5550

Bruce Baker
Garden Flat
38 Lupus Street
Pimlico
London
SW1 U3EB
0207 592 0102

Robert Bannan
1c Thornton Street
Townhead, Coatbridge
North Lanarkshire
ML5 2NZ
0123 660 6736

Wayne Barker
34 Hampton Road
Failsworth
Manchester M35 9HT
0161 681 7088

Jack Bishop
76 Gordon Road
Fareham
Hants PO16 7SS
0132 928 4708

Adam Booth
57 Jackson Road
Bromley
Kent BR2 8NT
0779 382 5255

Gerald Boustead
46 Coombe Lane
St Marychurch
Torquay
Devon
TQ2 8DY
0180 332 5195

Peter Bowen
50 Newman Avenue
Lanesfield
Wolverhampton
West Midlands
WV4 6BZ
0190 282 8159

Jackie Bowers
36 Drew Road
Silvertown
London
E16
0796 188 3654

Paul Boyce
Winstones
Church Street
Briton Ferry, Neath
West Glamorgan
SA11 2GJ
0163 981 3723

David Bradley
The Dovecote
Aston Hall
Claverley WV5 7DZ
0174 671 0287

John Branch
44 Hill Way
Holly Lodge Estate
London NE6 4EP

John Breen
Cedar Lodge
589 Antrim Road
Belfast BT15
0289 077 0238

Steve Butler
107 Cambridge Street
Normanton
West Yorks
WF6 1ES
0192 489 1097

Roy Callaghan
49 Salisbury Walk
Upper Holloway
London N19 5DS
0793 994 7807

Scott Calow
18 Farnsworth Grove
Huthwaite
Notts
NG17 2NL
0787 664 1055

Enzo Calzaghe
51 Caerbryn
Pentwynmawr
Newbridge
Gwent
0149 524 8988

George Carman
5 Mansion Lane
Mobile Home Site
Iver
Bucks
S10 9RQ
0175 365 3096

Michael Carney
Bradley Elms Farm
Alton Road
Threapwood
Cheadle
Stoke on Trent
Staffs ST10 4RA
0797 049 5597

Paul Carpenter
42 The Willows
Woodlands Park
Bedworth
0788 654 9864

John Celebanski
5 Ling Park Avenue
Wilsden
Bradford
BD15 0NE
0127 482 4015

Nigel Christian
89 Oaklands Park
Polperro Road
Looe
Cornwall
PL13 2JS
0150 326 4176

Azumah Cofie
Suite 130
Dorset House
Duke Street
Chelmsford
Essex
CM1 1TB
0786 797 7406

David Coldwell
5 Penwood Park
Bramley
Rotherham
Yorks S66 3XS
0114 275 0303

Brian Coleman
31 Gwernifor Street
Mountain Ash
Mid Glamorgan
CF45 3NA
0144 347 4071

William Connelly
72 Clincart Road
Mount Florida
Glasgow G42
0141 632 5818

Tommy Conroy
144 High Street East
Sunderland
Tyne and Wear
0191 567 6871

Pat Cowdell
129a Moat Road
Oldbury
Warley
West Midlands
B68 8EE
0121 552 8082

John Cox
17a St Leonards Road
Far Cotton
Northants NN4 8DL
0781 499 2249

Dave Currivan
15 Northolt Avenue
South Ruislip
Middlesex
0208 841 9933

David Davies
10 Bryngelli
Carmel
Llanelli
Dyfed SA14 7TL
0126 984 3204

Glynne Davies
63 Parc Brynmawr
Felinfoel, Llanelli
Carmarthen SA15 4PG
0155 756 282

John Davies
Unit 14, Rectors Yard
Rectors Lane
Penre Sandycroft
Deeside
CH5 2DH
0124 453 8984

Ronnie Davies
3 Vallensdean Cottages
Hangleton Lane
Portslade
Sussex
0127 341 6497

Walter Dixon
Littlemoss House
1 Wayne Close
Littlemoss
Droylsden M43 7LQ
0793 170 0478

Jack Doughty
Lane End Cottage
Golden Street
Off Buckstones Road
Shaw
Oldham OL2 8LY
0170 684 5753

Mickey Duff
c/o Mrs E Allen
16 Herga Court
Harrow on the Hill
Middlesex HA1 3RS
0208 423 6763

Paul Dykes
Boxing Network
International
Suites 1, 2 & 3, Lord
Lonsdale Chambers
10 Furlong Passage
Burslem
Stoke on Trent
ST6 3AY
0783 177 7310

John Eames
83 Stokes Road
East Ham
London E6 3SF
0207 473 3173

Jim Evans
88 Windsor Road
Maidenhead
Berks SL6 2DJ
0162 862 3640

Graham Everett
7 Laud Close
Norwich NR7 0TN
0160 370 1484

Jonathan Feld
c/o Angel Media Group
Ltd
The Office Islington
338 City Road
London
EC1V 2PT
0207 284 2133

Chris Firth
14 Fisher Avenue
Whiston
Prescot
Merseyside L35 3PF
0151 289 3579

Stuart Fleet
Dairy Farm Cottage
Old Road
Great Coates
Grimsby
DN37 9NX
0147 231 3764

Tania Follett
123 Calfridus Way
Bracknell
Berks
RG12 3HD
07930 904303

Philippe Fondu
1b Nursery Gardens
Birch Cottage
Chislehurst
Kent
BR7 5BW
0208 295 3598

Ali Forbes
14 Overdown Road
Catford
London
SE6 3ER
0794 075 8091

Steve Foster
7 Howclough Close
Worsley
M28 3HX
0792 162 3870

Winston Fuller
271 Cavendish Road
Balham
London
SW12 0PH

Joseph Gallagher
0161 374 1683

Dai Gardiner
13 Hengoed Hall Drive
Cefn Hengoed
Mid Glamorgan
CF8 7JW
0144 381 2971

Dave Garside
33 Lowthian Road
Hartlepool
Cleveland
TS26 8AL
0142 929 1611

Malcolm Gates
78 Cedar Drive
Jarrow
Tyne & Wear
NE32 4BG
0191 537 2574

Jimmy Gill
13 Thompson Close
Chilwell
Notts
NG9 5GF
0115 913 5482

Tommy Gilmour
St Andrew's Sporting
Club
Holiday Inn
Bothwell Street
Glasgow
G2 7EN
0141 248 5461

Mike Goodall
Ringcraft
Unit 21
Briars Close Business
Park
Evesham
Worcs
WR11 4JT
0138 644 2118

Stephen Goodwin
Unit W1
Chester Enterprise Centre
Hoole Bridge
Chester
0124 434 2012

Alex Gower
22 Norwood Avenue
Rush Green
Romford
Essex RM7 0QH
0170 875 3474

Billy Graham
116 Stockport Road
Mossley
Ashton under Lyne
Manchester
0145 783 5100

Lee Graham
28 Smeaton Court
50 Rockingham Street
London SE1 6PF
0207 357 6648

Carl Gunns
14 Whiles Lane
Birstall
Leics LE4 4EE
0116 267 1494

Christopher Hall
38 Fairley Way
Cheshunt
Herts EN7 6LG
0783 813 2091

Jess Harding
c/o UK Industrial Pallets
Ltd
Travellers Lane
Industrial Estate
Travellers Lane
Welham Green
Hatfield
Herts AL9 7HF
0170 727 0440

Tony Harris
237 Stapleford Road
Trowell
Notts
NG9 3QE
0115 913 6564

Richard Hatton
25 Queens Drive
Gee Cross
Hyde
Cheshire SK14 5LQ
0161 366 8133

Pat Healy
1 Cranley Buildings
Brookes Market
Holborn
London EC1
0207 242 8121

Barry Hearn
'Mascalls'
Mascalls Lane
Great Warley
Brentwood
Essex
CM14 5LJ
0127 735 9900

Michael Helliet
Flat 1
Lower Ground Floor
102 Whitfield Street
London
W1T 5EB
0207 388 5999

Martin Herdman
24a Crown Road
St Margarets
Twickenham
Middlesex
TW1 3EE
0208 891 6040

Dennis Hobson
130 Handsworth Road
Sheffield
S9 4AE
0114 256 0555

Dennis Hobson Snr
73 Darnall Road
Sheffield
S9 5AH
0114 243 4700

Nicholas Hodges
Llys-y-Deryn
Cilcennin
Lampeter
Ceredigion
West Wales
SA48 8RR
0157 047 0452

Harry Holland
12 Kendall Close
Feltham
Middlesex
0208 867 0435

Gordon Holmes
15 Robert Andrew
Close
Morley St Botolph
Wymondham
Norfolk
NR18 9AA
0195 360 7887

Lloyd Honeyghan
PO Box 17216
London
SE17 1ZU
07956 405007

Barry Hughes
5 Royal Exchange Square
Glasgow G1 3AH
0141 248 8882

Brian Hughes MBE
41 Fold Green
Chadderton
Lancs OL9 9DX
0161 620 2916

Geoff Hunter
6 Hawkshead Way
Winsford
Cheshire CW7 2SZ
0160 686 2162

Dominic Ingle
5 Eccles Street
Sheffield S9 1LN
0114 281 1277

John Ingle
20 Rockmount Road
Wincobank
Sheffield S9
0114 261 7934

Steve James
55 Town Close
Little Harrowden
Wellingborough
Northants NN9 5BD
0193 322 2241

Errol Johnson
36 Newton Street
West Bromwich
West Midlands B71 3RQ
0121 532 6118

Thomas Jones
13 Planetree Road
Hale
Cheshire WA15 9JL
0161 980 2661

Brian Lawrence
218 Millfields Road
London E5 0AR
0208 561 6736

Buddy Lee
The Walnuts
Roman Bank
Leverington, Wisbech
Cambs PE13 5AR
0194 558 3266

Daniel Lutaaya
c/o Zaina Ainabukenya
41 Cresset House
Retreat Place
London E9 6RW
0795 162 7066

Pat Lynch
Gotherington
68 Kelsey Lane
Balsall Common
Near Coventry
CV7 7GL
0167 633374

Danny McAlinden
589 Antrim Road
Belfast BT15 4DX
0793 921 5235

Paul McCausland
1 Prospect Heights
Carrickfergus
Northern Ireland
BT38 8QY
0289 336 5942

Robert McCracken
Ravensbourne
Westerham Road
Keston
Kent BR2 6HE
0190 579 8976

Jim McDonnell
2 Meadway
Hillside Avenue
Woodford Green
Essex IG8 7RF
07860 770006

John McIntyre
123 Newton Avenue
Barrhead G78 2PS
0141 571 4393

Owen McMahon
3 Atlantic Avenue
Belfast BT15
0289 074 3535

Colin McMillan
60 Billet Road
Chadwell Heath
Romford
Essex RM6 5SU
0208 597 4464

Patrick Magee
35 Deramore Park South
Belfast BT9 5JY
0289 043 8743

Charlie Magri
Victoria Pub
110 Grove Road
London E3 5TH
0795 652 4060

Frank Maloney
PO Box 79
Chislehurst
Kent BR7 5HR
0208 468 1099

Rick Manners
Flat 5
264 Lidgett Lane
Leeds LS17 6QE
0113 243 6017

Michael Marsden
1 North View
Roydes Lane
Rothwell
Leeds
LS26 0BQ
0113 282 5565

Terry Marsh
60 Gaynesford
Basildon
Essex SS16 5SG
0207 0152207

Clifton Mitchell
42 Wiltshire Road
Derby DE21 6EX
01332 295380

Alex Morrison
197 Swanston Street
Laird Business Park
Dalmarnock
Glasgow G40 4HW
0141 554 7777

Katherine Morrison
197 Swanston Street
Laird Business Park
Dalmarnock
Glasgow
G40 4HW
0141 554 7777

Bert Myers
8 Thornhill Street
Burnley
Lancs
BB12 6LU
0781 696 6742

Trevor Nerwal
Wayside Cottage
64 Vicarage Lane
Water Orton
Birmingham
B46 1RU
0121 730 1546

Paul Newman
12 Edgehill Way
Portslade
Brighton
BN41 2PU
0127 341 9777

Norman Nobbs
364 Kings Road
Kingstanding
Birmingham
B44 0UG
0121 355 5341

Stewart Nubley
94 Richmond Road
Kirkby in Ashfield
Notts
NG17 7PW
0162 343 2357

Frankie O'Connor
15 Culloden Avenue
Mossend
Bellshill
0169 884 1813

James Oyebola
1 Mulgrave Road
London NW10 1BS
0208 930 9685
07931 370039

Terry O'Neill
48 Kirkfield View
Colton Village
Leeds
LS15 9DX
0113 225 6140

Ian Pauly
1202 Lincoln Road
Peterborough
PE4 6LA
0173 331 1266

Joseph Pennington
215 North Road
Clayton
Manchester
M11 4WQ
0161 223 4463

Steve Pollard
899 Beverley High Road
Hull
HU6 9NJ
0148 280 9455

Brian Powell
138 Laurel Road
Bassaleg
Newport
Gwent NP10 8PT
0163 389 2165

Dean Powell
Sports Network
Centurion House
Bircherley Green
Herts
07956 905741

Michael Quinn
64 Warren Road
Wanstead
London
E11 2NA
0208 989 0082

Paul Rees
11 Abbots Park
London Road
St Albans
Herts AL1 1TW
0172 776 3160

Michael Rennie
Homestead
Thanet Road
Westgate on Sea
Kent CT8 8PB
0184 383 6750

Glyn Rhodes
166 Oldfield Road
Stannington
Sheffield S6 6DY
0114 232 6513

Gus Robinson MBE
Stranton House
Westview Road
Hartlepool
TS24 0BB
0142 923 4221

Mark Roe
48 Westbrooke Road
Sidcup
Kent DA15 7PH
0208 309 9396

John Rooney
11 Cedar House
Erlanger Road
London
SE14 5TB
0788 407 7024

John Rushton
20 Alverley Lane
Balby
Doncaster
DN4 9AS
0130 231 0919

Kevin Sanders
9 Moggswell Lane
Orton Longueville
Village
Peterborough
Cambs
PE2 7DS
0173 337 1912

Chris Sanigar
Bristol Boxing Gym
40 Thomas Street
St Agnes
Bristol
BS2 9LL
0117 949 6699

Trevor Schofield
234 Doncaster Road
Barnsley
South Yorks
S70 1UQ
0122 629 7376

Matthew Scriven
The Old One, Two
Fitness & Boxing Studio
2a Thoresby Street
Mansfield
Notts NG18 1QF
0783 399 5770

Mark Seltzer
20 Grange Court
Upper Park
Loughton
Essex
IG10 4QY
0208 926 0647

Mike Shinfield
126 Birchwood Lane
Somercotes
Derbys
DE55 4NE
0177 360 3124

Gurcharan Sing
165 St Giles Road
Ash Green
Coventry
CV7 9HB
0777 576 7815

Tony Sims
67 Peel Place
Clayhall
Ilford
Essex IG5 0PT
0208 550 8911

Stephen Smith
80 Mast Drive
Victoria Dock
Hull
HU9 1ST
0148 258 7771

Les Southey
Oakhouse
Park Way
Hillingdon
Middlesex
0189 525 4719

Gerald Storey
41 Willowbank
Gardens
Belfast
BT15 5AJ
0771 821610

Glenroy Taylor
73 Aspen Lane
Northolt
Middlesex
U35 6XH
0795 645 3787

John Tiftik
2 Nuffield Lodge
Carlton Gate
Admiral Walk
London W9 3TP
0795 151 8117

Jack Trickett
Blossom Barn
Blossom Lane
Woodford
Cheshire SK7 1RE
0161 439 8943

Stephen Vaughan
c/o Lee Maloney
4 St Pauls Cottages
Wenlock Court
Halewood Village
Liverpool
L26 0TA

Louis Veitch
80 Sherborne Road
North Shore
Blackpool
FY1 2PQ
0125 362 8943

Keith Walker
Walkers Boxing
Promotions
Headland House
Suite 21-35
Spawd Bone Lane
Knottingley
West Yorks
WF11 0HY
0197 760 7888

Frank Warren
Centurion House
Bircherley Green
Hertford
Herts
SG14 1AP
0199 250 5550

Robert Watt
32 Dowanhill Street
Glasgow G11
0141 334 7465

Delroy Waul
35 Gair Road
Reddich
Stockport
SK5 7LH
07796 271968

Derek V. Williams
65 Virginia Road
Surrey
CR7 8EN
0208 765 0492

Derek Williams
Pendeen, Bodiniel Road
Bodmin
Cornwall
PL31 2PE
0777 633 0516

John Williams
3a Langham Road
Tottenham
London N15 3QX
0778 782 2245

Alan Wilton
The Bridge
42 Derryboy Road
Crossgar
BT30 9LH
0289 754 2195

Barry Winter
9 McNeill Avenue
Linnvale
Clydebank
G81 2TB
0141 952 9942

Stephen Wood
Viking Promotions
Edward Street
Cambridge Industrial
Area
Salford
Manchester
M7 1RL
0161 834 9496

Tex Woodward
Spaniorum Farm
Compton Greenfield
Bristol
BS12 3RX
0145 463 2448

Licensed Matchmakers

Neil Bowers
59 Carson Road
Canning Town
London E16 4BD
0207 473 5631

Nigel Christian
89 Oaklands Park
Polperro Road, Looe
Cornwall PL13 2JS
0150 326 4176

Jim Evans
88 Windsor Road
Bray
Maidenhead
Berks SL6 2DJ
0162 862 3640

John Gaynor
7 Westhorne Fold
Counthill Drive
Brooklands Road
Crumpsall
Manchester M8 4JN
0161 740 6993

Jimmy Gill
13 Thompson Close
Chilwell
Notts
NG9 5GF
0115 913 5482

Tommy Gilmour
St Andrew's SC
Holiday Inn
Bothwell Street
Glasgow
G2 7EN
0141 248 5461

Roy Hilder
2 Farrington Place
Chislehurst
Kent BR7 6BE
0208 325 6156

John Ingle
20 Rockmount Road
Wincobank
Sheffield S9 1LP
0114 261 7934

Stevie James
55 Town Close
Little Harrowden
Wellingborough
Northants
NN9 5BD
0193 322 2241

Ken Morton
3 St Quintin Mount
'Bradway'
Sheffield
S17 4PQ
0114 262 1829

Dean Powell
Sports Network
Centurion House
Bircherley Green
Herts
SG14 1AP
0199 250 5550

Richard Poxon
148 Cliffefield Road
Sheffield S8 9BS
0114 225 7856

John Rushton
20 Averley Lane
Balby, Doncaster
South Yorks
0130 231 0919

Chris Sanigar
Bristol Boxing Gym
40 Thomas Street
St Agnes
Bristol
BS2 9LL
0117 949 6699

Mark Seltzer
20 Grange Court
Upper Park
Loughton
Essex
IG10 4QY
0208 926 0647

Mike Shinfield
126 Birchwood Lane
Somercotes
Derbys
DE55 4NE
0177 360 3124

Tony Sims
67 Peel Place
Clayhall Avenue
Ilford
Essex
IG5 0PT
0773 961 7830

John Wilson
1 Shenley Hill
Radlett
Herts
WD7 3AS
0192 385 7874

Licensed BBBoC Referees, Timekeepers, Ringwhips and Inspectors

Licensed Referees

Class 'B'
Dean Bramhald	Midland Area
Kevin Durand	Central Area
Stephen Gray	Central Area
Christopher Kelly	Central Area
David Morgan	Welsh Area
Kenneth Pringle	Scottish Area
Sean Russell	Northern Ireland
Bob Williams	Southern Area
Gary Williams	Northern Area

Class 'A'
Terence Cole	Northern Area
Lee Cook	Southern Area
Mark Curry	Northern Area
Kenneth Curtis	Southern Area
Roddy Evans	Welsh Area
Keith Garner	Central Area
Paul Graham	Scottish Area
Michael Heatherwick	Welsh Area
Jeff Hinds	Southern Area
David Irving	Northern Ireland
Wynford Jones	Welsh Area
Shaun Messer	Midlands Area
Grant Wallis	Western Area
Andrew Wright	Northern Area

Class 'A' Star
Richie Davies	Southern Area
Phillip Edwards	Central Area
Howard Foster	Central Area
Mark Green	Southern Area
Ian John-Lewis	Southern Area
John Keane	Midlands Area
Victor Loughlin	Scottish Area
Marcus McDonnell	Southern Area
Terry O'Connor	Midlands Area
Dave Parris	Southern Area
Paul Thomas	Midlands Area
Mickey Vann	Central Area

Licensed Timekeepers
Arnold Bryson	Northern Area
Neil Burder	Welsh Area
Richard Clark	Southern Area
Anthony Dunkerley	Midlands Area
Andrew East	Central Area
Robert Edgeworth	Southern Area
Dale Elliott	Northern Ireland
Harry Foxall	Midlands Area
Eric Gilmour	Scottish Area
Gary Grennan	Central Area
Brian Heath	Midlands Area
Greg Hue	Southern Area
James Kirkwood	Scottish Area
Jon Lee	Western Area

Roddy McAllister	Scottish Area
Michael McCann	Southern Area
Peter McCann	Southern Area
Norman Maddox	Midlands Area
Barry Pinder	Central Area
Raymond Rice	Southern Area
Colin Roberts	Central Area
David Walters	Welsh Area
Nick White	Southern Area
Graeme Williams	Northern Area

Licensed Ringwhips
Michael Burke	Scottish Area
Steve Butler	Central Area
Ernie Draper	Southern Area
Simon Goodall	Midlands Area
Mark Currivan	Southern Area
Lee Gostolo	Central Area
Edward Higgins	Scottish Area
Stuart Lithgo	Northern Area
Tommy Miller (Jnr)	Central Area
Tommy Rice	Southern Area
Sandy Risley	Southern Area
Paul Rowson	Midlands Area
Stephen Sidebottom	Central Area
Gary Stanford	Southern Area

Inspectors
Herold Adams	Southern Area
Alan Alster	Central Area
William Ball	Southern Area
Richard Barber	Southern Area
Don Bartlett	Midlands Area
David Boulter	Midlands Area
Geoff Boulter	Central Area
Fred Breyer	Southern Area
Walter Campbell	Northern Ireland
Edward Cassidy	Northern Ireland
Michael Collier	Southern Area
Dai Corp	Welsh Area
Julian Courtney	Welsh Area
Maurice Cunningham	Northern Ireland
Robert Curry	Northern Area
Jaswinder Dhaliwal	Midlands Area
Christopher Dolman	Midlands Area
Gordon Foulds	Scottish Area
Kevin Fulthorpe	Welsh Area
Bob Galloway	Southern Area
James Gamble	Northern Ireland
Paul Gooding	Welsh Area
Michael Hills	Northern Area
Alan Honnibal	Western Area
Wayne Hutton	Northern Ireland
Philip Jones	Midlands Area
Francis Keenan	Northern Ireland
Nicholas Laidman	Southern Area

Kevin Leafe	Central Area
Denzil Lewis	Central Area
Eddie Lillis	Central Area
Fred Little	Western Area
Reginald Long	Northern Area
Bob Lonkhurst	Southern Area
Sam McAughtry	Northern Ireland
Dave McAuley	Northern Ireland
Liam McColgan	Scottish Area
Billy McCrory	Northern Ireland
Gerry McGinley	Scottish Area
Paul McKeown	Northern Ireland
Neil McLean	Scottish Area
Pat Magee	Northern Ireland
Paddy Maguire	Northern Ireland
Andy Morris	Central Area
Thomas Nichol	Northern Ireland
Phil O'Hare	Central Area
Ron Pavett	Welsh Area
Richard Peers	Central Area
Dave Porter	Southern Area
Fred Potter	Northern Area
Suzanne Potts	Midlands Area
Martin Quinn	Northern Ireland
Steve Ray	Central Area
Hugh Russell	Northern Ireland
Charlie Sexton	Scottish Area
Neil Sinclair	Southern Area
Bert Smith	Central Area
Glyn Thomas	Welsh Area
Nigel Underwood	Midlands Area
Richard Vaughan	Midlands Area
David Venn	Northern Area
Phil Waites	Midlands Area
Ron Warburton	Central Area
Mark Warner	Welsh Area
Danny Wells	Southern Area
Barney Wilson	Northern Ireland
Robert Wilson	Scottish Area
Fred Wright	Central Area

Bob Lonkhurst, Southern Area Inspector

MICHAEL HELLIET BOXING MANAGEMENT

BBBofC Licensed Promoter/Manager
Always happy to assist unattached pro's or good class amateurs.

Boxers available for 2006/7

Lightweight
Andrew Murray 7-0 (3 KO)
Sam 'Rocky' Rukundo 7-0 (3 KO)
British Masters Lightweight Champion
Barney Doherty No Bouts

Light-Middleweight
Sherman Alleyne No Bouts

Super-Middleweight
Joey Vegas 7-0 (2 KO)
British Masters Super-Middleweight Champion

Trainers
London: James Cook, Marvin Stone
St. Albans: Paul Rees, Andy Smith
Manchester: Gary Booth

Cruiserweights
Csaba Andras 0-5
Lee Kellett 0-2

Websites
www.mayfairsportingclub.com
www.hellietproductions.com

OFFICE: 0207 388 6999
MOB: 0784 3636 920
FAX: 0207 388 6053
EMAIL: mhelliet@mayfairsportingclub.com

Michael Helliet, Flat 1, Lower Ground Floor,
102 Whitfield Street, LONDON, W1T 5EB

CONTENDER

BOXING GYM

**Unit 1
Wombourne Enterprise Park
Bridgenorth Road
Wombourne
Wolverhampton
WV5 0AL
Telephone: 01902 893099
Fax: 01902 892943**

SUPPLIERS OF THE WORLDS BEST EQUIPMENT & CLOTHING SINCE 1974

INTRODUCING
TEAM
CONTENDER

TRAINER	MANAGER	PROMOTERS
ROBERT WRIGHT	**SPENCER ALTON**	**JULIE ALTON** **SPENCER ALTON**

BOXERS:

MARTIN GORDON	SAM HORTON	SIMON WOOD
WELTERWEIGHT	MIDDLEWEIGHT	CRUISERWEIGHT

UNATTACHED PRO'S WELCOME
AMATEURS WISHING TO TURN PRO
CALL
SPENCER ALTON
01902 893099

CONTENDER UK LTD REGISTERED IN ENGLAND & WALES 4518205
Director: SPENCER ALTON

Boxers' Record Index